35-

D0848430

# OXFORD ENGLISH DICTIONARY ADDITIONS SERIES

## VOLUME 1

# OXFORD ENGLISH DICTIONARY ADDITIONS SERIES

EDITED BY

JOHN SIMPSON AND EDMUND WEINER

VOLUME 1

CLARENDON PRESS · OXFORD

1993

Oxford University Press, Walton Street, Oxford OX2 6DP
Oxford New York Toronto
Delhi Bombay Calcutta Madras Karachi
Kuala Lumpur Singapore Hong Kong Tokyo
Nairobi Dar es Salaam Cape Town
Melbourne Auckland Madrid
and associated companies in
Berlin Ibadan

Oxford is a trade mark of Oxford University Press

Published in the United States
by Oxford University Press Inc., New York

British Library Cataloguing in Publication Data
Data available

Library of Congress Cataloging in Publication Data
Oxford English dictionary. Additions/edited by John A. Simpson and Edmund S. C. Weiner.
p. cm.   Includes index.
ISBN 0-19-861292-3 (v. 1): £25.00.—ISBN 0-19-861299-0 (v. 2): £25.00
1. English language—Dictionaries.   I. Simpson, John A.   II. Weiner, E. S. C.
III. Title: Oxford English dictionary
PE1625.O92   1993
423—dc20   92-47491

1 3 5 7 9 10 8 6 4 2

Typeset in Monotype Imprint by
Barbers Ltd., Wrotham, Kent
Printed in Great Britain
on acid-free paper by
Biddles Ltd., Guildford

# EDITORIAL STAFF

Working alongside the editorial staff of the Dictionary have been numerous freelance library researchers, concerned principally with tracing the
earliest uses of terms and with the verification of quotations cited in the
volume:

*Oxford:* Judy Bowdler (–1991), David Banks, Margaret Davies, Jane
Brownlow.

*Washington:* Adriana Orr (–1991), Daphne Gilbert-Carter, Nancy Balz
(–1992), Melissa Conway (1990–91), Jon Simon, Dorothy Hanks, Shari
Jacobson

*New York:* Rita Keckeissen.

*Boston:* Sally Hinkle.

*New Haven:* Lori Bronars.

*Kingston, Ontario:* Margery Fee.

*San Francisco:* Ken Feinstein.

Valuable additional assistance has been given by several others not on
the permanent staff of the Dictionary:

*Proof-reading:* Hazel Clark, Simon Hunt, Veronica Hurst.

*Proof administration:* Susan Vickers.

*Keyboarding:* Catherine Tennant, Susan Wilkin.

*Quotation-file sorting:* Alexandra Barratt, Juliet Field, Giles Goodland, Patricia Greene, Keith Jebb, Peter Jenkins, Lisa Johnston, Jonathan Jones, Barbara Levick, Brian McKenna, Paul Messerschmitt, Eric Peyton, Murray Pratt, Rob Pursey, Alastair Ricketts, Ian Sheils, Catherine Soanes, Andrew Strachan.

The following have contributed over 3,000 quotations to the reading programme since the publication of *OED2* (members of the North American reading programme unless otherwise indicated):

Pat Back (*UK*), Janet Begnoche, Chris Collier (*Austral.*), Sue Cowen, Emma Fontanella, Noel Marie Gaeta, Marybeth Geanious, Alesia Goginsky, Daria Goginsky, Tony Gordon (*UK*), Charlotte Graves Taylor (*UK*), Susan A. Hill, Joanne Hindman, Victoria Jansson, Daria Kelly-Uhlig, Anna Kirby, Andrew Lintern-Ball (*UK*), Andrea Nagy, Jennie Neary, Ruth Mateer (*UK*), Vivienne Painting (*UK*), Rebecca Pressman, Gillian Rathbone (*UK*), Stephen Redenbaugh, Vivien Redman (*UK*), Susan Rennie, David Rode, Allan Rostron (*UK*), Kathy Shock (*UK*), Trish Stableford (*UK*), Marcy Stamper, Sara G. Triggs, Peter Wexler (*UK*), Mary White (*UK*), Jelly Williams (*UK*), and Wayne Wunderlich.

A number of persons have been responsible for keying material collected by the reading programme. The following have keyed over 3,000 quotations (North American reading programme unless otherwise stated):

Charles Blackmore (*UK*), Sally Francisco, Noel Marie Gaeta, Marybeth Geanious, Phillip Gerrish (*UK*), Martin Green (*UK*), Susan A. Hill, Joanne Hindman, *Daria Kelly-Uhlig, Judi Lancashire (*UK*), Jessica Maybar, *Andrea Nagy, David Rode, Marcia Slater (*UK*), Marcy Stamper, *Sara G. Triggs, Helen Triggs, Wayne Wunderlich, *Alexandria Zander.

Lauren Busciglio and Sue Cowen have, along with those marked above with an asterisk, been responsible for processing over 3,000 quotations for the reading-programme database in Oxford.

The Editors are also indebted to the many others who have contributed information on particular entries in the Dictionary; also to the staff of the libraries, especially the Bodleian Library, the British Library, the Library of Congress, and the New York Public Library, who have unfailingly treated the Dictionary's requests for information and assistance with courtesy and dispatch; and to Bellcore at Morristown, NJ (particularly Dr Michael Lesk and Dr Donald Walker), which has generously provided resources assisting us in the development of the *OED*'s North American Reading Programme.

A number of people have been involved in other aspects of the preparation of this volume. The Editors are particularly indebted to the following, who between them shared the task of reading and commenting on ranges of proofs:

Robert Barnhart, Dr Robert Burchfield, Michael Grose, Dr Philip Hardie, Terry Hoad, Deborah Honoré, Dr Harry Logan, Hazel Wright. In addition to those listed on p. x of the first volume of the *Oxford English Dictionary*, valuable specialist comment on individual entries has been given by Dr P. Baker, Dr D. Barrett, Dr H. C. Bennet-Clark, Professor J. Black, Mr R. J. Bowater, Dr L. D. Carrington, Dr M. Clark, Dr S. V. Clube, Mr H. S. Colvin, Ms M.-H. Corréard, Mr A. Credland, Dr Q. C. B. Cronk, Dr J. H. C. S. Davidson, Dr M. Fee, Mr W. K. V. Gale, Dr W. J. Gould, Mrs J. Harrison, Dr T. S. Kemp, Dr A. M. Lackie, Mr R. P. W. Lewis, Dr T. W. A. Little, Dr I. W. F. MacLean, Dr D. W. Minter, Dr D. D. Murison, Dr H. Orsman, Professor A. Pawley, Mr G. Pointon, Ms J. Poke, Captain A. B. Sainsbury, Mr D. Shulman, Mrs P. Silva, Professor N. S. Sutherland, Dr S. S. Strickland, Lord Walton of Detchant, Mr K. Whyld, Professor J. D. A. Widdowson, Professor M. V. Wilkes, Mr T. Wilson, Professor J. C. Wright.

The Editors are sad to record the deaths during the preparation of the volume of four long-standing consultants: Professor J. Leech, Mr P. Kemp, Ms J. C. Swannell, and Professor T. G. Vallance.

# INTRODUCTION

THIS is the first of a series of volumes, planned to appear at roughly two-yearly intervals, containing new entries which have been prepared for the Third Edition of the *Oxford English Dictionary* (*OED*). Many of the entries represent entirely new headwords, others consist of new senses, collocations, phrases, etc. which supplement material already contained in the Second Edition of the Dictionary.

Even as the Second Edition of the *OED* was published in 1989, the editorial staff had in hand about two thousand new entries nearing the final stages of completion. Each year an equivalent number of additional new entries are edited. Our initial plan was to add these entries to the OED database during the course of revising the Dictionary for its third edition. A number of factors, however, led us to decide upon the present mode of publication; principally the quantity of unpublished entries, their utility to those interested in recent developments in the language, and the fact that it will be some years before the third edition of the Dictionary is ready to be published.

A second question had then to be addressed: should each volume confine itself to a particular alphabetical range, or should the volumes all contain entries throughout the alphabet? The principal advantage of the latter option was that any new entry could be included in any volume, rather than being forced to wait until the cycle of publication returned to the alphabetical range to which it belonged. A further advantage was that it would be possible to include in each volume entries which were related to, and to which reference was made by, another entry from which they were alphabetically separated. On this basis we decided to allow each volume the potential of a full alphabetical spread, even though different volumes would tend to contain concentrations of entries in particular parts of the alphabet. The second and subsequent volumes will contain a cumulative index of new entries, directing the user to the *Additions* volume in which they may be found.

The present volume includes many of those entries which were in process of preparation when the Second Edition of the *OED* was published. Some of these had originally been prepared with the needs of the forthcoming *New Shorter Oxford English Dictionary* in mind. The selection of others was influenced by the requirements of the *Concise Oxford Dictionary* (eighth edition) and other Oxford dictionaries, perhaps most notably the *Oxford Dictionary of New Words* (1991). Subsequent volumes of the *OED Additions* series will also attest to these same influences, as it is an integral part of the *OED*'s role today to provide fully researched and edited new material for the range of dictionaries produced by the Oxford University Press. However, the vast majority of new entries were the direct result of the systematic analysis of the *OED*'s quotation files, which are augmented each year by a further 200,000 citations of English usage collected by the Dictionary's international reading programme.

The *Additions* volumes should, therefore, be regarded as the result of work-in-progress on new entries for the *OED*. They are not intended individually to present a balanced picture of recent additions to the language; a fuller picture will establish itself as the series unfolds. It will in fact be noted that the majority of entries in each volume are not neologisms, but represent a heterogeneous collection of accessions to the language over the past few centuries. Some are surprising omissions from earlier editions of the Dictionary, others cover subjects which have recently gained in prominence, while yet others document the division into separate subsenses of meanings which were previously treated as a single sense.

The computerization of the *OED* has yielded substantial benefits to the editorial staff in the preparation of new entries. Quotations already included in the Dictionary for other words often provide earlier attestations of words and senses subsequently worked upon. In addition, it is possible to achieve a greater stylistic consistency through the comparison, by computer, of editorial styles used in entries similar to those currently under review, and the bibliographical standardization of short-titles is easier to achieve. These factors should also prove extremely useful in the full revision of the text of the Dictionary. It is our intention, however, that stylistic consistency should not prove a straitjacket when nuances of meaning or the convenience of the user require some slight deviation from it.

The editorial style and the format of entries in the *Additions* series follows in all essential details that of the Second Edition of the Dictionary. The procedure for adding new senses to existing entries follows that of the *Supplement to the OED* (1972–86), itself based on the former one-volume *Supplement* of 1933. Cross-references to entries which may be found within the *Additions* series are preceded by an asterisk, to distinguish them from entries cross-referring to material in the Second Edition of the *OED*. On occasion it has been necessary to upgrade to the status of main entry a word which previously was embedded in another entry (typically the root-word). Such alterations are signalled by the words 'Formerly at [the previous entry].' The traditional style adopted by the *OED* for many nested collocations and combinations has been modified: in the *Additions* series these are printed with the illustrative quotations immediately following the term whose history they document, and no longer as a list of lemmas followed by a paragraph of quotations in which the blocks illustrating each lemma are run on in alphabetical order. This new style has been adopted with the convenience of the user in mind. Introductory notes have been added to some entries detailing changes to the numbering of subsenses as a result of the insertion of new material within an existing sense-hierarchy.

Cross-references in the *Additions* volumes are made to the new sense numbers, in cases where a change has occurred. Other less significant innovations included the introducing of *n.* rather than *sb.* (= substantive) for the abbreviation of 'noun'; the placing of square brackets around sense numbers which already occur in the text of the Second Edition of the *OED,* so that entirely new subsenses can be identified at a glance; the use of capital initials for German nouns, principally in etymologies; and the ordering of homographs according to a regular sequence.

The entries included in this volume attest to the seemingly endless capacity of English to accept borrowings from other languages, and to the recognition by lexicographers of the many varieties of English throughout the world. The English of the Caribbean, whether spoken in its native countries, or transported abroad, brings fresh vocabulary to the lexicon of English, as does that of the Indian subcontinent or of Hispanic America. Many of the entries in this volume support the view that the majority of innovations in World English originate in the English of the United States of America. The present concern with 'political correctness' (a term itself to be treated in a subsequent volume) has generated new strains of vocabulary, some of which are here to stay, and some of which will in turn give way to new orthodoxies. The remarkable changes which the world has recently seen in eastern Europe have swept away terminology which had seemed established, and have opened the way for a new generation of terms to cover the new economic, political, and social structures. In its train comes a renewed interest on the part of the West in the cultures of hitherto little-known societies: their languages, customs, social organization, and everyday concerns. Sport, music, medicine, law, the environment, and computing have all contributed new terms: the word-hoard of English is changing every day.

The present volume is only the first in a series: the editors are aware that much remains to be done in the documenting of English throughout the world, both in terms of the language of today and of that of the past. One advantage of a regular series such as the *OED Additions* volumes is that readers can, we hope, feel that suggestions of new entries for inclusion in the Dictionary will be considered speedily: any suggestions of this kind are always welcome.

*Oxford, November* 1992                          J. A. S.   E. S. C. W.

# KEY TO THE PRONUNCIATION

THE pronunciations given are those in use in the educated speech of southern England (the so-called 'Received Standard'), and the keywords given are to be understood as pronounced in such speech.

## I. *Consonants*

b, d, f, k, l, m, n, p, t, v, z *have their usual English values*

g as in *g*o (gəʊ)
h ... *h*o! (həʊ)
r ... *r*un (rʌn), te*rr*ier ('tɛrɪə(r))
(r) ... he*r* (hɜː(r))
s ... *s*ee (siː), *s*ucce*ss* (sək'sɛs)
w ... *w*ear (wɛə(r))
hw ... *wh*en (hwɛn)
j ... *y*es (jɛs)
θ ... *th*in (θɪn), ba*th* (bɑːθ)
ð ... *th*en (ðɛn), ba*th*e (beɪð)
ʃ ... *sh*op (ʃɒp), di*sh* (dɪʃ)
tʃ ... *ch*op (tʃɒp), di*tch* (dɪtʃ)
ʒ ... vi*s*ion ('vɪʒən), dé*j*euner (deʒøne)
dʒ ... *j*u*dg*e (dʒʌdʒ)

ŋ as in si*ng*ing ('sɪŋɪŋ), thi*n*k (θɪŋk)
ŋg ... fi*ng*er ('fɪŋgə(r))

(FOREIGN AND NON-SOUTHERN)

ʎ as in It. serra*gli*o (ser'raʎo)
ɲ ... Fr. co*gn*ac (kɔɲak)
x ... Ger. a*ch* (ax), Sc. lo*ch* (lɒx), Sp. fri*j*oles (fri'xoles)
ç ... Ger. i*ch* (ıç). Sc. ni*ch*t (nıçt)
ɣ ... North Ger. sa*g*en ('zaːɣən)
c ... Afrikaans baardmanne*tj*ie ('baːrtmanəci)
ɥ ... Fr. c*u*isine (kɥizin)

Symbols in parentheses are used to denote elements that may be omitted either by individual speakers or in particular phonetic contexts: e.g. *bottle* ('bɒt(ə)l), *Mercian* ('mɜːʃ(ı)ən), *suit* (s(j)uːt), *impromptu* (ɪm'prɒm(p)tjuː), *father* ('fɑːðə(r)).

## II. *Vowels and Diphthongs*

SHORT

ɪ as in p*i*t (pɪt), -n*e*ss (-nɪs)
e ... p*e*t (pɛt), Fr. s*e*pt (sɛt)
æ ... p*a*t (pæt)
ʌ ... p*u*tt (pʌt)
ɒ ... p*o*t (pɒt)
ʊ ... p*u*t (pʊt)
ə ... *a*nother (ə'nʌðə(r))
(ə) ... beat*e*n ('biːt(ə)n)
i ... Fr. s*i* (si)
e ... Fr. béb*é* (bebe)
a ... Fr. m*a*ri (mari)
ɑ ... Fr. bâtiment (bɑtimɑ̃)
ɔ ... Fr. h*o*mme (ɔm)
o ... Fr. *eau* (o)
ø ... Fr. p*eu* (pø)
œ ... Fr. b*oeu*f (bœf) *coeur* (kœr)
u ... Fr. d*ou*ce (dus)
ʏ ... Ger. M*ü*ller ('mʏlər)
y ... Fr. d*u* (dy)

LONG

iː as in b*ea*n (biːn)
ɑː ... b*ar*n (bɑːn)
ɔː ... b*or*n (bɔːn)
uː ... b*oo*n (buːn)
ɜː ... b*ur*n (bɜːn)
eː ... Ger. Schn*ee* (ʃneː)
ɛː ... Ger. F*ä*hre ('fɜːrə)
aː ... Ger. T*a*g (taːk)
oː ... Ger. S*oh*n (zoːn)
øː ... Ger. G*oe*the ('gøːtə)
yː ... Ger. gr*ü*n (gryːn)

NASAL

ɛ̃, æ̃ as in Fr. f*in* (fɛ̃, fæ̃)
ɑ̃ ... Fr. fr*an*c (frɑ̃)
ɔ̃ ... Fr. b*on* (bɔ̃)
œ̃ ... Fr. *un* (œ̃)

DIPHTHONGS, etc.

eɪ as in bay (beɪ)

aɪ . . . buy (baɪ)

ɔɪ . . . boy (bɔɪ)

əʊ . . . no (nəʊ)

aʊ . . . now (naʊ)

ɪə as in peer (pɪə(r))

ɛə . . . pair (pɛə(r))

ʊə . . . tour (tʊə(r))

aɪə . . . fiery ('faɪərɪ)

aʊə. . . sour (saʊə(r))

The incidence of main stress is shown by a superior stress mark (') preceding the stressed syllable, and a secondary stress by an inferior stress mark (ˌ), e.g. *pronunciation* (prəˌnʌnsɪ'eɪʃ(ə)n).

For further explanation of the transcription used, see the 'General Explanations' in Volume I of the *Oxford English Dictionary*.

# PROPRIETARY NAMES

THIS Dictionary includes some words which are or are asserted to be proprietary names or trade marks. Their inclusion does not imply that they have acquired for legal purposes a non-proprietary or general significance nor any other judgement concerning their legal status. In cases where the editorial staff have established in the records of the Patent Offices of the United Kingdom and of the United States that a word is registered as a proprietary name or trade mark this is indicated, but no judgement concerning the legal status of such words is made or implied thereby.

# A

**A**. Add: [II.] **11.** *Biochem.* Designating a form taken by double-stranded DNA in conditions of low relative humidity, consisting of a right-handed double-helix in which the base pairs form an angle of about 70° with the helix axis. Cf. *B II. 2 b (vii).

**1953** FRANKLIN & GOSLING in *Nature* 25 Apr. 740/1 Sodium Thymonucleate fibres give two distinct types of X-ray diagram. The first corresponds to a crystalline form, structure *A*, obtained at about 75 per cent relative humidity... At higher humidities a different structure, structure *B*, showing a lower degree of order, appears and persists over a wide range of ambient humidity. The change from *A* to *B* is reversible. **1963** *Science* 31 May 946/2 A full account of *A* DNA will shortly be available. **1974** *Jrnl. Molecular Biol.* LXXXVIII. 524 We prepared specimens of *D*-DNA under the minimum retained salt conditions that would normally yield an *A*-DNA. **1988** P. W. KUCHEL et al. *Schaum's Outl. Theory & Probl. Biochem.* vii. 185 This is a result of a change to the A form, in which the base pairs are not perpendicular to the helix axis.

[III.] **A.O.B.**, any other business.

**1974** J. PAXTON *Everyman's Dict. Abbrev.* 28/1 *A.O.B.*,.. any other business. **1985** *Faith & Worship* Spring 13 It appeared as the last item before A.O.B.

**A.O.C.**, Appellation d'Origine Contrôlée.

**1957** L. W. MARRISON *Wines & Spirits* v. 97 Cognac and armagnac are also covered by *A.O.C.'s. **1965** A. SICHEL *Penguin Bk. Wines* III. 129 The A.O.C. is accorded to a region, such as Bordeaux, to a secondary area within that region, such as Médoc, or to a village within the secondary area, such as Saint-Julien. **1984** *Times* 4 Oct. 1/5 It is still too early to predict.. what the quality of the AOC wines will be like.

**AS** (also **A/S**) **level**, Advanced Supplementary level (of the General Certificate of Education).

**1984** *Times* 2 May 3/1 The advanced supplementary, or *AS level, will require two years of study, cover at least half the ground of an A level, and be worth half an A level to employers and.. admission tutors. **1986** *Times* 7 July 3/2 It is envisaged that students will take two A levels and two A/S levels, preferably in contrasting areas. **1990** *Guardian* 1 Aug. 3/2 Mr Dawson defended traditional A levels, dismissing both AS levels and the five-subject international baccalaureate.

**above**, *adv.* and *prep.* Add: [B.] **11.** In prep. phr. **above and beyond**. More than, in addition to, or beyond. Cf. OVER AND ABOVE *prep. (adv. and adj.) phr.*

**1876** J. R. LOWELL *Among My Bks.* 2nd Ser. 314 A bald egotism which is quite above and beyond selfishness. **1898** G. B. SHAW *You never can Tell* II. 261 Love! Nonsense: it's something far above and beyond that. It's life, it's faith. **1916** JOYCE *Portrait of Artist* (1969) iii. 110 Let us try.. to make this retreat in honour of saint Francis with our whole heart... But, above and beyond all, let this retreat be one to which you can look back in after years.

**abuse**, *n.* [6.] For def. read: Violation, defilement. In mod. use *esp.* sexual or other maltreatment, and freq. with qualifying word, as CHILD *abuse*, SELF-ABUSE *n.*, SEXUAL *abuse*, etc.

**1893** *Medico-Legal Jrnl.* (N.Y.) X. 377 Cruelty signifies abuse, and the law is to be construed in its application, to prevent the abuse of children. **1985** J. COSTA (*title*) Abuse of the elderly: a guide to resources and services.

**acceptable**, *a.* Add: **b.** Catch-phr. *the acceptable face of —*: that which represents or embodies the acceptable aspect of something usu. considered unpopular or unpalatable. (The converse of the earlier phr. *s.v.* UNACCEPTABLE *a.*)

**1981** Q. CRISP *How to become Virgin* vi. 83 Bit by bit.. I was becoming the almost acceptable face of homosexuality. **1986** *Times* 31 Oct. 21/1 Sheikh Yamani has long appeared as the acceptable face of Opec.

**access**, *n.* Add: V. **12.** Special Combs. **access charge**, a charge made for the use of computer or local telephone-network facilities.

**1977** *Washington Post* 8 Dec. D2/2 He said SP is willing to explore the concept of an '*access charge' to the national telephone system, if it can be demonstrated that such fees would insure adequate rural and residential services.

**access fee** = *access charge* above.

**1976** *U.S. News & World Rep.* 26 July 43/3 The client can.. request that the abstracts be fed directly into his computer. Mr. Monsen pays his sources license fees, *access fees and charges for computer time. **1985** *New Republic* 28 Jan. 20/2 Consumer groups now opposing access fees are being penny-wise and pound-foolish, because.. forcing down local monthly bills through political pressure will backfire.

**act**, *n.* Add: [7.] [d.] *a hard* (or *tough*) *act to follow*: an outstanding performance, one which is difficult to rival; hence, someone or something hard to equal. *colloq.* (orig. *U.S.*).

**1975** *Chemical Week* 12 Mar. 22/1 Tough acts to follow:.. companies in three other principal CPI segments are somewhat less sanguine about topping last year's results. **1975** *Business Week* 3 Nov. 24 (*heading*) A hard act to follow; after the third-quarter surge in GNP, growth is sure to be slower. **1981** P. F. BOLLER *Presidential Anecdotes* ii. 24 It was not easy being the second President of the United States; George Washington was a hard act to follow. **1983** *Listener* 29 Sept. 24/3 But Olivier, to say the least, was a hard act to follow. **1986** *Sunday Express Mag.* 6 Apr. 18/4, I was rash enough to remark that Wogan was a hard act to follow, and Jameson jumped down my throat.

**action**, *n.* Add: [16.] **Action Man**, a proprietary name for a type of male doll in combat dress; hence used *attrib.* to designate clothing, etc., characteristic of the doll or the soldier it represents; also applied allusively to a person (often *iron.*).

**1966** *Trade Marks Jrnl.* 3 Aug. 1130/2 *Palitoy *Action Man*... Dolls in the form of men, incorporating means of performing movements. **1976** *Oadby & Wigston* (Leics.) *Advertiser* 26 Nov. 7/1 (*caption*) Adventure clothes based on the Action Man theme, with knitted sweater, cotton drill trousers, maroon beret with badge, and belt with press stud pocket. **1982** BARR & YORK *Official Sloane Ranger Handbk.* 47/2 The Action Man sweater, the Army standard. Olive green—or navy—with cotton patches on shoulders and elbows. Going out—so many at

Milletts. **1988** *Sunday Mail Mag.* (Brisbane) 25 Sept. 4/2 Action man Michael .. became the Princess of Wales' driver.

‖**Action Directe** (aksjɔ̃ dirɛkt), *n. phr.* [Fr., lit. 'direct action'.] The name of an extreme left-wing terrorist group in France.

[**1980** *Times* 20 Mar. 7/1 A 'Direct Action Group' has claimed responsibility for a machine gun attack yesterday against the Ministry of Cooperation in Paris ... This is the eighth attack for which it has claimed responsibility since last May.] **1980** *Christian Science Monitor* 3 Apr. 3/4 They arrested two Frenchmen, alleged members of the Action Directe terrorist group, as they boarded a plane at Orly Airport March 27. **1982** *Times* 20 Aug. 5/4 Action Directe, a left-wing terrorist group banned by the French Government on Wednesday. **1986** *Times* 16 July 16/2 In May 1982 and January 1984 'joint strategy papers' were issued by the RAF [*sc.* Red Army Faction] and the French group Action Directe.

**addictive**, *a.* Add: **b.** *transf.* Characterized by or causing addiction to some object, activity, etc.; that promotes or exhibits habituation.

**1974** *Psychol. Rev.* LXXXI. 125 The duckling is exhibiting all criteria for addictive behavior. It is 'hooked' on the imprinting object. **1975** *Economist* 4 Jan. 60/4 Leisure surveys show television to be equally addictive to both sexes. **1983** *Washington Post* 3 Apr. LI/1 Just as eating chocolate tends to be addictive, so does working with it.

**admix** ('ædmɪks), *n.* [Back-formation f. ADMIXTURE *n.*, or directly f. the vb.] Something added as an ingredient, an admixture; also *loosely*, a mixture.

**1961** in WEBSTER. **1970** J. EARL *Tuners & Amplifiers* iii. 63, I am not at all happy with a.m./hi-fi admixes. I prefer an f.m.-only tuner as a separate unit. **1977** *Forbes* (N.Y.) 15 Dec. 98/1 He told us the other night on public television that boards are comprised of dotards, management lickspittles and a trendy admix of ghetto clerics and feminists. **1985** P. FERGUSON *Family Myths & Legends* xi. 80 Cissie and Jessie were smeared almost as thickly as the outhouse, with an admix of streaky soot between the colours.

**Adriamycin** (ˌeɪdrɪə'maɪsɪn), *n. Pharm.* Also **adriamycin.** [f. the name of the *Adria*(*tic* Sea + -MYCIN.] A proprietary name for (a preparation of) the cytotoxic antibiotic doxorubicin.

**1969** A. DI MARCO et al. in *Cancer Chemotherapy Rep.* Feb. 33/1 Adriamycin is a new antibiotic isolated from the cultures of a mutant of S[*treptomyces*] *Peucetius* called *S. Peucetius* var. *caesius*. **1969** *Brit. Med. Jrnl.* 30 Aug. 503/1 Adriamycin is a new antibiotic isolated in 1967 in the Farmitalia Research Laboratories. **1976** *Trade Marks Jrnl.* 22 Sept. 2000/2 Adriamycin .. Antibiotic preparations. **1980** *Jrnl. R. Soc. Med.* LXXIII. 207 We have now commenced a randomized trial of chemotherapy using 5-fluorouracil and adriamycin. **1984** *Official Gaz.* (U.S. Patent Office) 14 Feb. TM199/2 *Adriamycin* for cytotoxic antibiotic containing doxorubicin to be used in hospitals or in ambulatory patients under close medical supervision. **1988** *Guardian* 26 Mar. 2/8 Hundreds of patients in the UK are being treated with Adriamycin, the standard treatment for lung cancer, breast cancer and leukaemia.

**Advent**, *n.* Add: [**1.**] [**b.**] Special Combs. **Advent calendar**, a calendar celebrating the approach of Christmas, esp. one made with flaps or windows opened one each day to reveal a seasonal picture, gift, etc.

**1952** *Tablet* 14 Nov. 471/1 The firm of Hamish Hamilton has performed a good service in publishing here *Advent Calendars of the kind found .. in Germany and Austria. **1963** *Sunset* Dec. 110/1 A

child can start his private celebration of Christmas three weeks early with his own gift-laden Advent calendar. **1987** *N.Y. Times* 21 June X. 32/6 The fog kept clearing in patches, and suddenly a blue window would open like an Advent calendar.

**Advent candle**, a candle lit during Advent; *spec.* each candle in a ring of four, lit on successive Sundays in Advent to symbolize the coming of light into the world at Christmas (when a fifth central candle completes the group).

**1986** *N.Y. Times* 30 Nov. I. 1/1 He opened the Christmas season by lighting an *Advent candle in a stately town square.

**Advent ring**, a ring of four Advent candles. **1969** *Hymns & Songs* No. 88, On each Sunday in Advent, verses of this song may be sung while the candles for the day are lit on the *Advent Ring—recalling the witnesses to the coming of the True Light.

**advertising**, *vbl. n.* Add: [**2.**] Also *attrib.*, as *advertising agency, campaign*, etc.

**1951** *Oxf. Jun. Encycl.* VIII. 7/1 The agent who is asked to conduct an advertising campaign must first be told for what market .. the goods to be advertised are intended. **1984** D. E. SCHULTZ (*title*) Strategic advertising campaigns.

**aero-**, *comb. form.* Add: [**a.**] **aero'taxis** *Zool.* and *Bot.*, a taxis in which the stimulus is oxygen concentration.

**1895** *Jrnl. R. Microsc. Soc.* Oct. 515 Herr Curt Herbst .. discusses the *aero (oxygeno)-taxis of the segmentation cells in Arthropod ova. **1970** [see *aerotactic* adj. below]. **1981** *Sci. Amer.* Dec. 49/1 Magnetotaxis makes aerotaxis more efficient by reducing random excursions and promoting straight-line motility.

hence **aero'tactic** *a.*
**1940** *Chambers's Techn. Dict.* 15/2 *Aerotactic. **1970** *New Scientist* 26 Feb. 397/1 (*caption*) Aerotaxis. The bacteria under the coverslip at the left hand side are 'positively aerotactic', aggregating around the edges where the oxygen concentration is higher than in the centre. **1986** M. KOGUT tr. *Schlegel's Gen. Microbiol.* ii. 64 Some motile bacteria reveal their metabolic capacities relative to oxygen or air by their aerotactic movements.

**æthionema** (iːθɪəʊ'niːmə), *n. Bot.* [mod.L. (R. Brown, quot. 1812), f. Gr. αἴθειν light up, kindle + νῆμα thread, yarn.] Any plant of the cruciferous genus *Aethionema*, comprising mostly low-growing plants with showy racemes of pink, lilac, yellow, or white flowers, native to the Mediterranean but cultivated elsewhere as garden flowers; stone cress.

**1812** R. BROWN in W. T. Aiton *Hortus Kewensis* (ed. 2) IV. 80 Rock Æthionema, *Nat.* of the South of Europe ... One-seeded Æthionema, *Nat.* of Spain. **1934** F. STARK *Valleys of Assassins* iii. 209 A pink cruciform blossom, æthionema, which grew in tufts on the rocky ledges. **1963** *Times* 11 May 11/5 Among the worst hit among the rock garden plants have been the aethionemas.

**Afro-Asi'atic**, *a.* (and *n.*) [f. AFRO- + ASIATIC *a.*] Of or pertaining to a family of languages found in northern Africa and western Asia, of which Arabic is the most widespread. See HAMITO-SEMITIC *a.* and *n.* Also as *n.*

**1950** J. H. GREENBERG in *Southwestern Jrnl. Anthropol.* Spring 57 The term Hamito-Semitic is so well-entrenched that it will no doubt continue to be used. I rather hesitantly suggest the name Afroasiatic for this family as the only one found both in Africa and in Asia. In this way Hamitic could be entirely eliminated from use even as a linguistic term. **1961** WEBSTER, Afro-Asiatic languages. **1974** [see SEMITO-HAMITIC *a.* and *n.*]. **1984** *Trans. Philol. Soc.* 202 The

Agaw languages, spoken in widely distributed pockets in the northern half of Ethiopia, belong to the Cushitic family within the wider grouping of Hamito-Semitic (or Afroasiatic). **1985** G. T. NURSE et al. *Peoples Southern Afr.* xi. 283 The north-east Africans . . and the Ethiopians . . , all linguistically Afro-Asiatic, clearly distinguish themselves from the non-Caucasoid populations.

**Afro-Cari'bbean**, *a.* and *n.* (Formerly at AFRO- in Dict.) [f. AFRO- + CARIBBEAN *a.* and *n.*] **A.** *adj.* Of or pertaining to both Africa and the Caribbean; used to designate the culture, way of life, etc., or (esp.) the characteristic style of music of those people of Black African descent who are, or whose immediate forebears were, inhabitants of the Caribbean (esp. the West Indies).
**1958** *Oxf. Mail* 14 Feb. 9/6 Lessons in Afro-Caribbean dancing . . for members of the Oxford University Ballet Club. **1965** *Economist* 9 Jan. 98/1 Mr Pearson . . emerged . . as a convert to the Afro-Caribbean idea. **1976** *Daily Times* (Lagos) 26 Aug. 25/1 Among items to be performed are traditional African music, . . Afro-Latin-American music, Afro-Caribbean music and Australasian music. **1982** *Amer. Speech* LVII. 238 There is no logical connection between accepting an Irish source for consuetudinary *be* in vernacular black English and rejecting the Afro-Caribbean Creole hypothesis about the origin of the dialect. **1986** *Times* 28 Feb. 3/2 A black woman juror complained about the words 'coloured' and 'negroid' to describe the dead girl . . . The juror wanted the word . . 'negroid', used to describe her hair, altered to 'Afro-Caribbean'. **1987** *Daily Tel.* 24 Dec. 5/1 The fact that we wanted somebody who had an Afro-Caribbean background, preferably born in this country, rules out the majority of whites. **B.** *n.* A person of Afro-Caribbean origin or descent.
**1959** *Encounter* Dec. 53/1 In the bad old days, when . . the Afro-Caribbeans had little but humiliation. **1975** *Economist* 18 Oct. 33/1 A small survey on registration in seven constituencies, suggests that 30% of Afro-Caribbeans and Asians were not registered, compared with only 6% of whites. **1988** *Financial Times* 20 Aug. (Weekend Suppl.) p. xv/7 'My' people are the British-based black Africans and Afro-Caribbeans, and Jamaica-born Mr Dennis talks about them with knowledge and sympathy.

**age**, *n.* Add: [III.] **age gap**, a difference or disparity between the ages of persons; see GAP *n.*[1] 6 a and *generation gap* s.v. GENERATION *n.* 7.
**1963** A. HERON *Towards Quaker View of Sex* 60 The child finds himself to be . . isolated because of a large *age gap.* **1983** J. KELMAN *Not, not while Giro* 91 There was an age gap between them right enough.

**agnostic**, *n.* and *a.* Add: [B.] **2.** *Path.* = AGNOSIC *a.*
[**1935** *Bull. Johns Hopkins Hosp.* LVII. 332 It is significant that finger agnosia should be present without other autotopagnostic features.] **1941** J. M. NIELSEN *Clin. Neurol.* x. 274 Agnostic alexia is due to loss of power of visual recognition of the symbols of language. **1946** —— *Agnosia, Apraxia, Aphasia* (ed. 2) ii. 34 Agnostic alexia is the failure of recognition of letters, figures, syllables, and words. **1953** *Brain* LXXVI. 546 Our agnostic patient . . seemed to have an alexia. **1975** *Bull. N.Y. Acad. Med.* LI. 1161 The actions of naloxone were not agnostic, since the administration of either morphine or oxymorphone routinely reduced the amplitude of all reflexes tested.

**agro-**, *comb. form.* Add: [b.] **agro-'ecosystem**, an ecosystem on agricultural land.
**1968** J. S. KENNEDY in *Jrnl. Appl. Ecol.* V. 498 [Integrated pest control] is best suited, not to small-unit, complex *agro-ecosystems run by Farmer Giles,

but to the most advanced ones manned by specialists. **1972** *Science* 19 May 770/1 Management techniques directed toward the fullest utilization of natural insect mortality and other suppressive factors in any given agro-ecosystem. **1984** *McGraw-Hill Yearbk. Sci. & Technol. 1985* 75/1 Dairy farming and grazing systems are the only major two-trophic-level agroecosystems commonly left in developing countries.

‖**aimak** ('aɪmak, anglicized 'eɪmæk), *n.* Also **aymag.** Pl. unchanged or **aimaks.** [Mongolian *aimag* clan.] **a.** Now *Hist.* Among Mongol peoples, a tribe or clan; also, an area associated with such a tribe. **b.** In Mongolia, an administrative division roughly corresponding to such an area. Cf. *SOMON *n.*
**1839** *Penny Cycl.* XV. 330/2 The whole nation is divided into twenty-six tribes, called *aimak.* **1883** *Encycl. Brit.* XVI. 750/1 Another tribe separated from the rest of the Mongols is the so-called Hazára (the thousand), and the four Aimak (*i.e.,* tribes), who wander about as herdsmen in Afghanistan. **1949** *Britannica Bk. of Year* 429/2 The country [*sc.* the Mongolian People's Republic] was divided into 18 aimaks or provinces. **1974** *Encycl. Brit. Macropædia* XII. 368/1 The procurators of *aymags* and towns, appointed by the procurator of the republic, supervise the work of the courts. **1979** *Summary of World Broadcasts: Far East* (B.B.C.) c1/3 To make it incumbent upon aymag and city Party committees . . to adopt effective measures to utilize fully production capacities. **1985** *Nat. Geographic* Feb. 248/2 Each of Mongolia's 18 provinces (aimaks) is divided into somons.

**air**, *n.*[1] Add: [B.] [II.] **airhead** *slang* (chiefly *N. Amer.*), someone who is foolish, simple-minded, or stupid; a blockhead.
**1980** *Maclean's Mag.* 11 Aug. 54/3 One of the many *airheads who move torpidly through the $40-million mistake known as *Raise the Titanic* says in a throat-clutching voice: 'A ship that big down that deep!?!?' **1984** *Daily Tel.* 11 Feb. 16/4 One can imagine the media barons when they saw that these entertainment-world 'airheads' (the current preferred term) . . had concocted an irresponsibly tendentious account from these very Press reports.

**air-wave**, (*b*) usu. *pl.* as **airwaves**, with *the*: the medium of transmission of radio or television waves; also = AIRWAY *n.* 3.
**1942** BERREY & VAN DEN BARK *Amer. Thes. Slang* §618/4 'The air' (*the medium of transmission of radio waves*), . . airlanes, airline, air *or* ether waves. **1944** *Amer. Speech* XIX. 49 The New York agencies . . spread *fifth column* over the pages of every subscribing newspaper in the country and onto the air waves as well. **1967** *Economist* 28 Jan. 331/2 No platitude has been more abused than that of 'freedom of the airwaves'. **1977** *Daily Mail* 24 Sept. 15/1 Fab, groovy Radio 1 played its first record *Flowers in the Rain*, by 'The Move', on September 30, 1967, six weeks after the Marine Offences Act blew the pirate radio stations off the airwaves for good. **1982** *Listener* 16 Dec. 6/3 The pressure on states to honour their agreements and avoid chaos in the international airwaves will be very great.

[III.] [I.] **airside**, the side of an airport terminal building from which aircraft can be observed taking off and landing; hence, the area of an airport beyond passport and customs controls which gives immediate access to the aircraft, and in which only passengers and airline and airport officials are permitted: contrasted with *LAND-SIDE *n.* 2 b; hence *attrib.,* without art., and as *adv.*
**1955** *Daily Tel.* 28 Jan. 6/5 The waving base is on the '*airside' as distinct from the 'landside' of the building, and thus gives a clear view of the aircraft leaving the 'terminal apron'. **1956** J. CHANDOS

*London Airport* 19 (*caption*) The airside gallery. **1967** *Times Rev. Industry* Apr. 60/3 The British Airports Authority is to spend nearly £1m. on the first phase of expanding the passenger handling capacity of the Number 3 long-haul terminal by extending the airside arrival and departure lounges. **1984** *Times* 14 May 19/4 Decide now at what time you will yourself go through the controls which take you airside. **1986** *Daily Tel.* 18 Apr. 36/4 For several hours the terminal-building was plunged into chaos. 'Airside' was sealed off by armed police. **1987** *Pilot* Apr. 30/2 An airside bus operation, specifically for use by GA captains, passengers and baggage, has been provided by the Airport Authority free of charge.

**Albers-Schönberg** (ˌɑːlbəz ˈʃɜːnbɛəg), *n. Path.* Also -Schonberg. The name of H. E. *Albers-Schönberg* (1865-1921), German radiologist, used *attrib.* and in the possessive to designate osteopetrosis as it occurs in man (described by him in 1904), *esp.* the mild form.
  **1922**, etc. [see *marble bone* s.v. MARBLE *n.* 9]. **1937** *Amer. Jrnl. Dis. Children* LIV. 812 The right humerus appeared somewhat osteosclerotic... The increase in density approached that observed in cases of Albers-Schönberg's disease. **1986** *Oxf. Compan. Med.* II. 963/1 Osteopetrosis, also known as Albers-Schonberg or marble bone disease, is a rare genetically determined disorder of bone function.

**Albertan** (ælˈbɜːtən), *a. Geol.* [f. the name of *Alberta*, a province of western Canada + -AN.] Of, pertaining to, or designating the Middle Cambrian in (esp. western) North America. Also *absol.* (See quot. 1982 and cf. ACADIAN *a.* 2 a.)
  **1921** A. W. GRABAU *Textbk. Geol.* II. xxxii. 243 The best developed sections so far known are in the Cordilleran trough of western America, where, in Alberta, Canada, a thickness of 8300 feet has been measured. [*Note*] The name Albertan has been proposed by the author for the Middle Cambrian of the Pacific Province. **1940** —— *Rhythm of Ages* ix. 101 The best known section is that of Mount Bosworth, in British Columbia, where the Taconian .. is followed by 4,580 ft of Cambrian or Albertan. **1940** *Bull. Geol. Soc. Amer.* LI. 732 Important unsolved stratigraphic problems in the Waucobian and Albertan rocks of British Columbia. **1957** DUNBAR & RODGERS *Princ. Stratigr.* xvii. 297 In some systems the individual series have geographic or other distinctive names (e.g., Waucoban, Albertan, and Croixian Series of the Cambrian of North America; Lias, Dogger, and Malm Series of the Jurassic of western Europe). **1982** [see ACADIAN *a.* 2 a].

**albizzia** (ælˈbɪzɪə), *n. Bot.* Also albizia. [mod.L. *Albizia* (A. Durazzini 1772, in *Mag. Toscano* III. IV. 11), *Albizzia*, f. the name, *Albizzi*, of a family which introduced the silk-tree into Italy: see -IA¹.] Any plant of the genus *Albizia* (family Leguminosae), comprising flowering trees, shrubs, and lianas of tropical and subtropical regions, some of which are cultivated as ornamentals or for their timber.
  **1844** *London Jrnl. Bot.* III. 85 When the specimens are perfect *Albizzia* is easily distinguished from *Acacia.* **1868** [see *silk-tree* s.v. SILK *n.* and *a.* 10 b]. **1929** H. S. BANNER *Trop. Tapestry* 97 High overhead the giants of the forest [in Sumatra]—albizzia, waringin—intermesh their branches. **1957** M. WEST *Kundu* vi. 75 He saw the flash of brilliant scarlet as a Bird of Paradise made his mating dance on the branch of an albizzia tree. **1980** *Energy from Biomass* (Shell Internat. Petroleum Co.) 6 Trees in tropical forests are often fast growing—examples include the ipil ipil, Acacias, Albizias and Eucalyptus.

**algebraic**, *a.* Add: **2.** *Math.* **a.** Of, pertaining to, or designating an equation or formula in which a finite number of symbols are combined using only the operations of addition, subtraction, multiplication, division, and exponentiation with constant rational exponents. Cf. TRANSCENDENTAL *a.* 4.
  [**1728** CHAMBERS *Cycl.* I. 60/2 Algebraical curve, is a curve, wherein the relation of the abscisses to the semiordinates, may be defined by an algebraical equation... Algebraical curves stand contradistinguish'd to mechanical or transcendental ones.] **1738** *Ibid.* (ed. 2) I. opp. sig. 2 Hhh, Most authors, after Des Cartes, call algebraic curves, geometrical ones. **1871** TAIT & STEELE *Treat. Dynamics of Particle* (ed. 3) i. 26 When *e* = 1, the corrected integral .. is $2(x + a/4) = y^2/2a - a \log y/a$. This is the only case in which we do not obtain an algebraic curve. **1902** J. W. MELLOR *Higher Math.* i. 22 An algebraic function of *x* is an expression containing terms which involve only the operations of addition, subtraction, multiplication, division, evolution (root extraction) or involution. **1972** C. S. OGILVY *Tomorrow's Math* (ed. 2) viii. 153 The famous equation connecting $\pi$ and $e$, $e^{\pi i} = -1$, is not algebraic.
  **b.** Of a number: that can be expressed as a root of a polynomial with rational coefficients.
  [**1893** *Proc. London Math. Soc.* XXIV. 327 (*heading*) On the algebraical integers derived from an irreducible cubic equation.] **1937** A. A. ALBERT *Mod. Higher Algebra* xii. 288 Let us apply this to a field $\mathfrak{F} = \mathfrak{R}(\xi)$ which is algebraic of degree *n* over the field $\mathfrak{R}$ of all rational numbers. We call the quantities of $\mathfrak{F}$ algebraic numbers and say that $\mathfrak{F}$ is an algebraic number field. **1947** F. G. BROWN *Everyman's Math.* xxiii. 560 An algebraic number is any *x* that satisfies the equation $a_n x^n + a_{n-1} x^{n-1} + .. + a_1 x + a_0 = 0$ where all the coefficients are integers. **1972** M. KLINE *Math. Thought* xxv. 593 Any root, real or complex, of any algebraic (polynomial) equation with rational coefficients is called an algebraic number. **1982** *Sci. Amer.* Dec. 130/2 For example, $\sqrt{2}$, *i* (the imaginary square root of $-1$) and $(-1 + i\sqrt{3})/2$ are all algebraic integers because they are roots of the algebraic equations $x^2 - 2 = 0$, $x^2 + 1 = 0$ and $x^3 - 1 = 0$.

**alkalide** (ˈælkəlaɪd), *n. Chem.* [f. ALKALI *n.* + -IDE 1.] A binary ionic compound in which the anion is an alkali metal.
  **1979** J. L. DYE in *Angewandte Chemie* (Internat. ed.) XVIII. 590/1 Our search for salts of the alkali metal anions (which we refer to as 'alkalides') was .. based on thermodynamic predictions of their stabilities. **1983** *Jrnl. Amer. Chem. Soc.* CV. 6490/2 The optical spectrum of a thin film obtained by dissolving the crystals in methylamine and evaporating the solvent from a liquid film as with other alkalides and electrides is shown in Figure 1.

**All Black** (usu. ˈɔːl blæk, but stress somewhat variable), *n.* (and *a.*) [f. ALL *adv.* + BLACK *a.*, from the colour of the players' strip.] **1. a.** In *pl.*, usu. with *the.* The familiar nickname of the New Zealand international Rugby Union football team.
  The name was first applied to the team by British journalists at the beginning of the 1905 tour of Britain.
  **1905** *Daily Mail* 12 Oct. 7/7 The 'All Blacks', as the Colonials are dubbed. *Ibid.* 14 Oct. 5/7 The record of the 'All Blacks' now stands at 310 points against .. seven. **1935** *Times* 12 Oct. 6/4 Injuries are still adding to the All Blacks' difficulties. **1946** F. L. W. WOOD *This New Zealand* xv. 240 The year the All Blacks went home. **1976** *Economist* 3 Jan. 68/2 The final test in New Zealand, which the All Blacks had to win to square the series. **1986** *Guardian Weekly* 25 May 23/4 In South Africa the New Zealand Cavaliers—openly called All Blacks on match tickets—won the second 'test' at Durban 19-18 to level the series.
  **b.** *sing.* A member of the team.

**1905** *Daily Mail* 12 Oct. 7/7 Did Hartlepool expect an 'All Black' to pass, he did nothing of the kind. **1984** C. MEADS in Chester & McMillan *Centenary* 13/2, I waited for that unique moment when I ran out on to the field and began believing I was .. an All Black.
2. The sing. form used *attrib.* or as *adj.*
**1905** *Daily Mail* 1 Nov. 8/3 *(heading)* 'All Black' pet names. How the New Zealanders are known to each other. **1935** *Times* 7 Oct. 5/1 Their forwards nearly rushed the All Black defence off its legs. **1959** A. McLINTOCK *Descr. Atlas N.Z.* 73 There are few All Black teams .. without a leavening of Maori players. **1986** *Sunday Mail* (Brisbane) 24 Aug. 53/4 New Zealand squared the rugby union series against Australia with a 13-12 win .. in traditionally fierce All Black style.

**allelopathy** (æliːˈlɒpəθɪ), *n. Bot.* [ad. G. *Allelopathie* (H. Molisch *Der Einfluss einer Pflanze auf die andere—Allelopathie*, 1937), f. Gr. ἀλλήλ- one another: see -oˡ, -PATHY.] The deleterious process by which one organism influences others nearby through the escape or release of toxic or inhibitory substances into the environment: usu. restricted to such interaction between higher plants.
**1957** H. MARTIN *Chem. Aspects Ecol.* ii. 11 It would seem unnecessary to go to the extreme of Molisch .. who coined the word 'allelopathy' from the reciprocal influence of higher plants. **1961** *Symp. Soc. Exper. Biol.* XV. 242 There is .. a type of allelopathy which .. follows from the movement of metabolic products from one species into another. *Ibid.* 243 Perhaps the term 'allelopathy' should be extended to include the manifold mutual effects of metabolic products of both plants and animals. **1974** E. L. RICE *Allelopathy* i. 1, I feel that the current use of the term, allelopathy, should include any direct or indirect harmful effect by one plant (including microorganisms) on another through the production of chemical compounds that escape into the environment. **1982** J. B. HARBORNE *Introd. Ecol. Biochem.* (ed. 2) viii. 212 In this case of allelopathy, as in most others, the toxin is effective against many but by no means all competing plant species. **1988** *New Scientist* 7 July 54/1 The rhododendron also poisons the soil with short-chain aliphatic acids, deterring plant roots of other species—a phenomenon known as allelopathy.
Hence **a‚llelo'pathic** *a.*, pertaining to or of the nature of allelopathy; *esp.* designating a plant product having such toxic or inhibitory qualities.
**1960** *Bot. Rev.* XXVI. 414 The over-all growth of a plant undoubtedly is determined more by the proper balance of growth factors (space, light, water, mineral nutrients, etc.) than by allelopathic factors. **1984** E. J. KORMONDY *Concepts Ecol.* (ed. 3) iv. 139 This chemical results in the weaker filter feeder (*Epischura*) having an inhibiting, or allelopathic, impact on the stronger filter feeder (*Diaptomus*).

**alligator**, *n.*² Add: [4.] [a.] **alligator weed**, an orig. South American aquatic plant, *Alternanthera philoxeroides*, of the family Amaranthaceae, which has spread as a weed when introduced elsewhere.
**1942** *Geogr. Rev.* XXXII. 83 Alligator weed, commonly known as alligator grass, resembles water hyacinth in many ways. **1974** *Nature* 30 Aug. 704/1 Alligator weed (*Alternanthera philoxeroides*), a normally harmless aquatic weed, is spreading rapidly in the rivers and canals of eastern Australia. **1980** *Jrnl. Austral. Inst. Agric. Sci.* XLVI. 152/2 Floating mats of alligator weed are generally monocultures but occasionally other species occur.

**alloantibody** (æləʊˈæntɪbɒdɪ), *n. Immunol.* [f. ALLO- + ANTIBODY *n.*] = isoantibody s.v. ISO-.

**1964** [see ALLOANTIGEN *n.*]. **1977** *Lancet* 3 Sept. 465/1 These results suggest that positive B-lymphocyte crossmatches found in kidney transplantation do not detect alloantibodies. **1983** *Oxf. Textbk. Med.* II. XIX. 191 Production of allo-antibodies is seen most commonly in patients receiving long-term transfusion therapy. **1989** *Nature* 19 Jan. 220/3 In the commentary on Jean Dausset's discovery of human leukocyte alloantibodies .. there is no recognition of how the success of these analyses depended critically on the solution of at least three problems.

**Ally Pally** (ˌælɪ ˈpælɪ), *n. phr. colloq.* [Rhyming abbrev. of *Alexandra Palace* (see below): cf. PALLY *n.*] The familiar nickname of Alexandra Palace in Muswell Hill, N. London, the original headquarters of B.B.C. television.
**1949** PARTRIDGE *Dict. Slang* (ed. 3) Add. 978/2 *Ally Pally*, Alexandra Palace, London (the H.Q. of television): 1937+. Earlier is the sense 'Alexandra Park race-course'. **1967** *Observer* 21 May 24/4 The 14-hour 'Happening' at the Ally Pally. **1979** S. BRETT *Comedian Dies* iii. 39 Back in Ally Pally days, .. you were just a technical boffin with all the sound recording stuff. **1986** *N.Y. Times* 13 Nov. A31/4 The 'Hill' is Muswell Hill, where Alexandra Palace—'Ally Pally' to the British—is located.

**alpha**, *n.* Add: [3.] g. **alpha test**, a test of machinery, software, etc. in course of development, carried out in-house by the developer before the product is made available for beta testing (see *BETA *n.* 2 j); so **alpha testing**, etc.; **alpha-test** *v. trans.*, **alpha-tester**.
**1982** *Computerworld* 4 Jan. 33/2 He expects the word processing giant to have a voice/data PBX alpha test site by the end of next year. **1982** Alpha-tester [see BETA *n.* 2 j]. **1982** *Computerworld* 19 Apr. 47/1 Look currently is in alpha testing and is expected to complete beta testing and be available in the second quarter of 1982. **1983** *Byte* June 92/2 The proprietary operating system and applications software begin alpha tests at Gavilan in August and beta tests by selected outside users in September. **1986** *Computerworld* 13 Jan. 8/2 The network has been alpha tested at Carnegie-Mellon University in Pittsburgh. **1987** *Network World* 16 Mar. 39 Northern Telecom is currently alpha testing a network management system called the NM-1. **1989** *InfoWorld* 23 Oct. 110/4 Apple set Hypercard 2.0 into alpha test right before the quake, making a spring intro likely.

**alstonia** (ælˈstəʊnɪə), *n. Bot.* [mod.L. (R. Brown 1809, in *Mem. Wernerian Nat. Hist. Soc.* (1811) I. 75), f. the name of C. *Alston* (1683-1760), Scottish botanist and physician: see -IAˡ.] A plant of the genus *Alstonia* (family Apocynaceae), comprising trees and shrubs chiefly of S.E. Asia and the Pacific Islands, which have a milky sap and some of which yield a soft, light timber. Cf. *devil-tree* s.v. DEVIL *n.* 24.
**1852** G. W. JOHNSON *Cottage Gardeners' Dict.* 28/1 The leaves of alstonia are slightly astringent, and are used as tea. **1950** METCALFE & CHALK *Anat. of Dicotyledons* II. 916 It is, however, difficult to obtain long lengths of .. *Alstonia* free from the 'latex traces' described above. **1980** T. H. EVERETT *N.Y. Bot. Garden Illustr. Encycl. Hort.* I. 129 Alstonias are evergreen or deciduous and have milky sap and undivided leaves.

**amaranth**, *n.* Add: [3.] b. A moderately fast red azo dye used for dyeing textiles and as a biological stain and food colouring.
**1888** *Jrnl. Soc. Dyers & Colourists* IV. 46/2 An 'amaranth' is produced by several colour works from the residue of magenta. **1936** *Pharmaceutical Jrnl.* CXXXVI. 234 A search for an alternative colour led

us to examine amaranth, which gives a good clear red, described as 'raspberry' in the list. **1976** *Daily Colonist* (Victoria, B. C.) 20 Jan. 1/6 Schmidt's order will permit manufacturers to sell products that already contain the color additive, known generically as amaranth, but will prohibit them from using existing stocks. **1984** L. E. PARKER in J. Walford *Devel. in Food Colours* II. i. 8 Studies were being carried out in other parts of the world on amaranth, a colour to which an ADI had been assigned and which was on the EEC list of permitted colours. These studies resulted in the banning of amaranth in the USA, and a need to reconsider its status in the EEC.

**Amazon**, *n.* Sense 7 in Dict. becomes 8. Add: **7.** [f. the name of the River *Amazon*.] (Also with lower-case initial.) Any of numerous S. American parrots of the genus *Amazona*, often kept as cage-birds. Also *Amazon parrot*.
[**1836** P. L. SELBY in W. Jardine *Naturalist's Libr.: Ornith.* VI. 103 The true Amazons' Parrot has so frequently been confounded and mixed up with other nearly allied species, that a description of it may not be unacceptable to our readers.] **1878** C. E. DYSON *Bird-Keeping* 231 The common African Grey Parrot .. and the Amazon Green Parrot are, perhaps, the most common in this country. **1934** W. S. BERRIDGE *All about Birds* xxii. 242 The Amazon parrots are favourite cage-birds, the most familiar being the blue-fronted species. **1961** *Guardian* 4 Apr. 14/2, 10-year-old Polly Jolly, a green amazon, one of the birds stolen from a farm. **1985** PERRINS & MIDDLETON *Encycl. Birds* 227 In southeastern Brazil, for example, forest cover has been so reduced by felling that species such as the Glaucous macaw and the Red-tailed amazon are now seriously threatened.

**amber**, *n.*[1] and *a.* Add: [A.] [III.] **10.** *Biol.* [tr. G. *Bernstein*: app. named after Mrs. H. Bernstein, mother of a colleague of the scientists by whom the codon was isolated (see H. Bernstein in *Amer. Speech* (1983) LVIII. 86).] The nonsense codon UAG; also, a mutant fragment of genetic material containing this. Freq. *attrib.*, esp. as *amber mutant*. Cf. *OCHRE *n.* 4.
**1963** R. H. EPSTEIN et al. in *Cold Spring Harbor Symp. Quant. Biol.* XXVIII. 375/2 Recently, two types of conditional lethal mutants in bacteriophage T4D have been described and genetically characterized: temperature sensitive (*ts*) mutants .. and amber mutants (*am*) which form plaques on *Escherichia coli* CR63 but not on *E. coli* B. **1965** PEACOCKE & DRYSDALE *Molecular Basis Heredity* 169 Further support for the concept of a colinear relation between gene structure and protein structure has been obtained in studies of *amber* mutants which affect the head-protein of the bacteriophage T4D. **1976** *Nature* 26 Aug. 757/1 The three codons UAG (amber), UAA (ochre), and UGA (opal) serve as signals for polypeptide chain termination during messenger RNA translation in various prokaryotic and eukaryotic organisms. **1983** [see *OCHRE *n.* 4].

**Ames test** ('eɪmz ˌtest), *n. Med.* [Named after Bruce N. *Ames* (b. 1928), U.S. biochemist, who devised it.] A test for mutagenic activity in which the effect of a substance *in vitro* is observed on certain bacteria in which mutations are readily detected.
**1976** *New Scientist* 22 Jan. 168/1 Currently a number of test systems are being developed for detecting possible carcinogens, and one of them in particular—the so-called Ames test—seems just about ready for limited application at least. **1979** *Nature* 8 Nov. 134/1 The invaluable 'Ames test' (in reality a mini-battery of tests using bacteria as the test organisms) permits rapid bioassay of chemicals, or their reactive *in vitro* metabolites, for mutagenic activity. **1984** *McGraw-Hill Yearbk. Sci. & Technol.* *1985* 288/1 The Ames test has proved to be about

85% accurate in detecting certain classes of chemical carcinogens as mutagens and in predicting that a nonmutagenic compound is noncarcinogenic.

**Amex** ('æmeks), *n.*[1] (Entry in Dict. becomes AMEX *n.*[2]) *colloq.* (orig. and chiefly *U.S.*). [Blend f. the name of the *Am*erican Stock *Ex*change.] The American Stock Exchange in New York, the second largest U.S. securities exchange (the largest being the New York Stock Exchange).
**1961** *Newsweek* 24 July 56/3 Far from being .. defensive about the Amex record, they took the offensive from the start. *Ibid.*, [Both were] expelled from the Amex for stock manipulation. **1970** *Globe & Mail* (Toronto) 26 Sept. B1/3 The Amex price-change index gained 8 cents to $22.34. **1979** *Forbes* (N.Y.) 24 Dec. 80/3 What's true on the major exchange is equally true of the 25 biggest winners and the 25 biggest losers on the Amex and on the o-t-c market. **1987** *Financial World* 10 Mar. 82/1 Chieftain Development Co. Ltd. (AMEX, TSE: CID) had one of its best exploration years in 1986, the company reported.

**amphi-**, *comb. form.* Add: **amphi'pathic** *a. Chem.* [Gr. πάθος experience, state, property], having both a hydrophilic and a hydrophobic part; consisting of such molecules.
**1936** G. S. HARTLEY *Aqueous Solutions of Paraffin Chain Salts* vii. 44 It is .. because the paraffin-chain ion is *amphipathic that the paraffin-chain salts are good emulsifying, peptising, foaming and cleaning agents. **1972** *Sci. Amer.* Feb. 31/1 The lipids found in membranes are amphipathic. **1989** *Nature* 5 Jan. 94/2 This N-terminal layer is connected by a long loop to another layer which consists of two pairs of antiparallel amphipathic helices.
so **'amphipath**, an amphipathic molecule or substance.
**1971** *New Scientist* 14 Jan. 64/1 Liposomes, incorporating positively charged *amphipaths, .. are, to all intents and purposes, impermeable to monovalent cations like K⁺ or Na⁺, but permeable to anions. **1980** *Jrnl. Biol. Chem.* CCLV. 9331 (*heading*) The effect of cholesterol and other intercalated amphipaths on the contour and stability of the isolated red cell membrane.
**am'phipathy**, the quality of being amphipathic.
**1936** G. S. HARTLEY *Aqueous Solutions of Paraffin Chain Salts* vii. 44 The property is essentially the simultaneous presence of separately satisfiable sympathy and antipathy for water. I propose, therefore, to call this property '*amphipathy'—the possession of both feelings. **1979** D. CHAPMAN et al. in R. Perron *Physicochimie des Composés Amphiphiles* (Colloques Nationals du CNRS) 209/1 This property of amphipathy, this duality of properties within the same molecule, has great significance for all biology.

**ampulla**, *n.* Add: [**3.**] **b.** *ampulla of Lorenzini Ichthyol.* [named after Stefano *Lorenzini*, 17th-cent. It. physician, who described them], each of numerous sensory structures in the head of some fish, esp. elasmobranchs, consisting of small sacs sensitive to electric fields and connected to the surface by narrow tubes; usu. *pl.*
[**1868** *Archiv für Mikrosk. Anat.* IV. 375 (*heading*) Die Lorenzini'schen Ampullen der Selachier.] **1898** *Zool. Bull.* I. 167 At its inner end each ampullary tube from the surface opens into one of the so-called ampullae of Lorenzini. **1962** K. F. LAGLER et al. *Ichthyol.* xi. 388 The ampullae of Lorenzini .. are more or less sac-like structures in the head region of sharks and rays (Elasmobranchii) and also of *Plotosus*, a southeast Asian catfish. **1975** *Nature* 31 July 425/2 We have studied the sensory epithelium of the electroreceptor (ampulla of Lorenzini) of the skate. **1975** J. TAYLOR *Superminds* vii. 112 The elasmobranchs have electrical sense organs (exotically

called the ampullae of Lorenzini) seated in deep skin pores.

**anal**, *a*. Add: **3.** *Psychoanal.* Of, pertaining to, or designating the second stage of Freud's suggested process of libidinal development (lasting from about the age of eighteen months to three years), dominated by toilet training; displaying character traits such as obsessive orderliness, parsimony, or obstinacy that are thought to result from fixation at this stage.
**1930** W. HEALY et al. *Structure & Meaning of Psychoanal.* vi. 318 The 'anal character' was the first to be discovered and investigated … Freud's cardinal triad of anal characteristics comprises (a) orderliness ..(b) parsimony..(c) obstinacy. **1944** 'PALINURUS' *Unquiet Grave* III. 91 There is a Superego in our civilization which makes us all feel guilty, and a repressive and anal element in the bureaucratic tidiness, caution and frugality of the society which we have made. **1975** M. BRADBURY *Hist. Man* viii. 132, I think you've made a heavy, anal job of this, because you're a heavy, anal type. **1983** P. H. MILLER *Theories Developmental Psychol.* ii. 137 The child who survives the anal period relatively unscathed is ready to tackle the third stage, the phallic stage, when it arrives. **1990** *Premiere* May 22/3 As long as we're being anal about it, the guest that Monday was not Sammy Davis, Jr., but Flip Wilson.
**4.** Special collocations in *Psychoanal.* (see also sense 1 b): **anal retentive** *n.* and *a.*, (a person) displaying excessive orderliness and parsimony, interpreted by psychoanalysts as the result of fixation at the anal stage of development.
**1958** *Jrnl. Abnormal & Social Psychol.* LVII. 244/1 Individuals fixated at the late anal phase (the so-called *anal retentives) have a greater ability to recall verbal material than those fixated at the early anal phase (anal expulsives). **1960** *Jrnl. Clin. Psychol.* XVI. 219 They found that anal retentive females (as measured by the Blacky test) performed significantly better. **1977** C. McFADDEN *Serial* (1978) xii. 30/1 Her own father .. was practically a casebook example of an anal retentive. **1984** S. TOWNSEND *Growing Pains A. Mole* 27 'My mother said, 'You're an anal retentive, aren't you?' and my father said, 'You're tight-fisted, and you've always got your perfectly groomed head in a book.'
**anal sadism**, the aggressive and destructive tendencies associated with the anal stage of development.
**1945** O. FENICHEL *Psychoanalytic Theory of Neurosis* (1946) v. 66 The origin and character of the connection between anal and sadistic drives, hinted at in the term for the organization level (*anal sadism), is analogous to the discussed connection between orality and sadism. **1968** *Brit. Jrnl. Med. Psychol.* XLI. 311/1 Factor 5 also embraces .. fascination for height, .. phallic significance, and anal sadism. **1981** *Psychoanal. Rev.* LXVIII. 382 The significant impact of affects, particularly of those derived from oral and anal sadism, has been considered in relation to self and object representations.
**anal sadistic** *a.*, displaying anal sadism.
**1920** *Internat. Jrnl. Psychoanal.* I. 278 In Obsessional Neurosis there is a regression to the stage of *Anal-Sadistic organization. **1958** M. ARGYLE *Relig. Behaviour* xii. 167 From the theory that obsessionals regress to the anal-sadistic stage it would be expected that ritualists would engage in crimes of violence. **1973** T. PYNCHON *Gravity's Rainbow* (1975) I. 85 The sexual Other, whom he symbolizes on his map, most significantly, as a *star*, that anal-sadistic emblem of classroom success. **1983** *Rev. Eng. Stud.* May 210 It is a case of an anal-sadistic impulse 'piously denied or undone'.

**angel**, *n*. Add: [**B.**] [**2.**] **angel-shark**, any shark of the family Squatinidae, characterized by wing-like pectoral fins; *spec.* = MONK-FISH *n.* 1.

**1842** *United Service Mag.* May 3 The *Squalus squatina*, or *angel shark, *alias* monk-fish. **1883** [see MONK-FISH *n.* 1]. **1985** BANISTER & CAMPBELL *Encycl. Underwater Life* 136/2 The angelsharks are unusual, being very flat, and are considered to be more closely related to the skates and rays than to the more 'typical' sharks. They grow to more than 1.8m (6 ft) in length and there are about 10 species in the genus *Squatina*, found in all tropical to temperate seas.

**animal**, *n*. and *a*. Add: [**C.**] [**1.**] **animal-free** *a.*, (esp. of diet or foodstuffs) not containing or using animal products.
**1965** *Brit. Vegetarian* Mar.-Apr. 118 *Animal-free margarine and frying oil. **1970** *Ibid.* Nov.-Dec. 506 (*title*) Animal-free nutrition in man. **1986** *Green Cuisine* Sept.-Oct. 79/1 As a GP, I've certainly seen the beneficial effects of an animal-free diet.

**anthropometrics** (ˌænθrəpəʊˈmɛtrɪks), *n. pl.* (const. as *sing.*). [f. ANTHROPOMETRIC *a.*: see -IC 2.] Anthropometry, *esp.* as used in designing furniture and machinery; the use of anthropometric measurements in this way. In first quot., *spec.* = BERTILLONAGE *n.*
**1887** *Daily Tel.* 29 Sept. 5/3 The system formulated .. by this ingenious gentleman [*sc.* M. Bertillon] is termed anthropometrics, and is mainly based on the measurement and registration of certain bone dimensions in the human body. **1951** J. M. FRASER *Psychol.* ix. 89 A number of scientists, among whom was Sir Francis Galton, became interested in human measurements. They gave their studies the somewhat clumsy name of *anthropometrics*. **1966** *Jrnl. Indian Inst. Architects* Dec. 6/1 This study analyses various living activities performed in an average Indian household to outline their characteristics and formulate their groupings and space requirements in the light of anthropometrics and other guiding factors. **1970** *Homes & Gardens* June 159/1 The study of anthropometrics and the development of man-made frames and filling materials means that there is no excuse for even inexpensive upholstered furniture being uncomfortable. **1982** *Mini-Micro Syst.* Sept. 276/1 'Ergonomics' is generally defined as the science of making the work environment safer and more comfortable for workers … The term 'anthropometrics' is more discriminating, meaning the study of human body measurements, and may soon replace ergonomics as a buzzword.

**anticodon** (ˌæntɪˈkəʊdɒn), *n. Biochem.* [f. ANTI-¹ 2 + CODON *n.*] A triplet of nucleotides forming a unit of genetic code in transfer RNA, which binds to a complementary codon in messenger RNA, thereby determining the amino acid carried.
**1965** *Science* 19 Mar. 1464/3 There are several possible trinucleotide sequences that might represent the coding triplet or 'anticodon' for the transfer of alanine. **1971** J. Z. YOUNG *Introd. Study Man* iii. 57 An alanine transfer RNA molecule might have the anticodon CGA, which is the complement of GCU, one of the triplets that code for alanine. **1982** T. M. DEVLIN *Textbk. Biochem.* xix. 920 Anticodon sequences in tRNAs of known specificity have been used to confirm the genetic code. Conversely, tRNAs of unknown amino acid specificity have been identified by their anticodons. **1985** *Sci. Amer.* Oct. 56/1 At the opposite end of the tRNA molecule from the amino acid binding site there is a loop containing the 'anticodon', a nucleotide triplet that is complementary to a specific mRNA codon.
Hence ˌanticoˈdonic *a.*, of, pertaining to, or involving an anticodon.
**1975** *Bio Systems* VII. 32/2 These are of an anticodonic type. **1978** *Jrnl. Molecular Evol.* XI. 199 One can infer a general anticodonic relationship of properties of amino acids and nucleotides. **1980** *Biochem. & Biophys. Res. Communications* XCVI. 491 Further observations showed correlations of

properties of amino acids with those of their anticodonic nucleotides.

**antidiuretic** (ˌæntɪdaɪjʊ'rɛtɪk), *a.* and *n.* (Formerly at ANTI- 3 c in Dict.) *Med.* [ANTI-[1] 2.] **A.** *adj.* Inhibiting the production of urine; *antidiuretic hormone* = VASOPRESSIN *n.*
   **1926** *Proc. R. Soc.* B. XCIX. 511 Here we are concerned with the secretion by the pituitary body of an anti-diuretic and chloride-raising principle. **1951** A. GROLLMAN *Pharmacol. & Therapeutics* xxvi. 550 The antidiuretic effect of posterior pituitary extract is especially marked in cases of polyuria. **1961** *Lancet* 2 Sept. 522/2 Most cases of primary idiopathic diabetes insipidus respond to the antidiuretic hormone of the posterior pituitary. **1977** *Proc. R. Soc. Med.* LXX. 546/1 The low plasma osmolality with high urine osmolality suggested inappropriate antidiuretic hormone (ADH) secretion. **1984** J. F. LAMB et al. *Essent. Physiol.* (ed. 2) viii. 216 The distal convolution [of the kidney] is the site of action of the antidiuretic hormone which regulates water excretion.
   **B.** *n.* An antidiuretic agent.
   **1935** in Dorland & Miller *Med. Dict.* (ed. 17). **1964** W. G. SMITH *Allergy & Tissue Metabolism* vii. 77 Serotonin is a powerful bronchoconstrictor in most animals. It is an antidiuretic in the dog, rat and man.

**appraisal**, *n.* Add: **2.** A formal evaluation of the performance of an employee at work over a particular period; evaluation or assessment in this manner, intended to improve individual and organizational performance.
   **1955** *Personnel* Jan. 431/2 The two most frequently stated purposes of appraisal are: (a) to improve current performance; and (b) to build an adequate managerial reserve. **1962** JOHNSON & CASSELL *Appraising Personnel* i. 8 Other evidence .. would lead one to conclude that administrators, generally, view appraisals as an educational tool or as a supervisory tool. **1972** G. L. MORRISEY *Appraisal & Devel. through Objectives & Results* i. 6 Most managers are periodically required to evaluate the employees under their supervision for such things as salary determination, promotions, layoffs ... How convenient it is if we can cover all these bases with a single formal appraisal. **1986** *Professional Teacher* Summer 16/1 If teachers do not take appraisal seriously, and regulate their own profession, politicians will do it for them.

**appraise**, *v.* Add: [**2.**] **b.** To evaluate (an employee) formally in terms of progress, performance, etc.; to make an appraisal or assessment of. Also *absol.* Cf. *APPRAISAL *n.* 2.
   **1955** *Personnel* Jan. 434/2 How can the ability to appraise be increased? *Ibid.* Mar. 432/2 Often men find themselves being appraised for development by one method and for rewards by a second. **1959** *Appraisal of Job Performance: Stud. in Personnel Policy No. 121* (U.S. Nat. Industr. Conf. Board) 5/1 Here the slogan of one company is 'Appraise to improve'. **1962** JOHNSON & CASSELL *Appraising Personnel* i. 14 If the county agricultural agent is being appraised, the district agricultural supervisor .. may act in the capacity of chairman of a committee. **1976** *Harvard Business Rev.* May-June 159/1 There was a great uneasiness among management theorists and managers when employees were appraised .. on .. personality, potential, and ambition instead of on results. **1977** *Dun's Rev.* Jan. 71/2 Some people have wondered, however, about the independence or objectivity of a board member who is hired, promoted, appraised and rewarded by existing management. **1988** *Automotive News* 15 Aug. 10/3, I appraised people working under me and was appraised by management over me.

**apricot**, *n.* Add: [**3.**] **apricot plum**, (*a*) an old table variety of the domestic plum, large and pale yellow; (*b*) a Chinese tree, *Prunus simonii,*

of the plum family that is grown in parts of the U.S. and bears white flowers and an edible yellow fleshy stone-fruit; the fruit itself.
   **1707** J. MORTIMER *Husbandry* xix. 547 The Apricot Plum, a delicate Plum that parts clean from the Stone. **1731** P. MILLER *Gard. Dict.* s.v. *Prunus,* Prune d'Abricot, i.e. The Apricock Plum. This is a large round Fruit of a yellow Colour on the Out-side, powder'd over with a white Bloom; the Flesh is firm and dry, of a sweet Taste, and comes clean from the Stone. **1824** J. C. LOUDON *Encycl. Gardening* (ed. 2) III. 724 The table fruit in the Dalkeith garden are as under .. Blue gage, Blue perdrigron, Apricot plum, [etc.]. **1845** A. J. DOWNING *Fruit-Trees Amer.* xx. 272 Apricot Plum of Tours ... This is the true old Apricot plum of Duhamel. The Apricot Plum of Thomson is .. fit only for cooking. **1893** *Bull. Cornell Univ. Agric. Exper. Station* No. 51. 34 Simon or apricot plum.—Prunus simonii ... The flesh is yellow, hard, and clings .. to the somewhat apricot-like pit. **1957** *Encycl. Brit.* XVIII. 84/1 The Simon or apricot plum .. a native of China ... Varieties of *P. cerasifera* and *P. simoni* [sic] are noted for their ornamental foliage.

**arachno** (ə'ræknəʊ), *a. Chem.* Usu. italicized. [f. Gr. ἀράχν-η spider + -O[1].] Designating (the structure of) a boron compound in whose molecules boron atoms occupy all vertices but two of a notional triangulated polyhedron. Also (with hyphen) as a word-forming element.
   **1971** *Inorg. Chem.* X. 214/2 Of the many icosahedral fragment arachno structures which may be imagined the simple removal of a high-coordination vertex from the open face of the related nido structure empirically yields the correct or presumed to be correct structure in every case. **1984** GREENWOOD & EARNSHAW *Chem. of Elements* (1986) vi. 185 *Arachno*-boranes: $B_nH_{n+6}$, *n* corners of an (*n*+2) cornered polyhedron. **1988** *Jrnl. Chem. Soc.: Dalton Trans.* 1467/1 The factors that influence nuclear magnetic shielding in polyhedral boron compounds are not understood, and few reliable structure-shielding correlations that are useful in the general case have emerged. An exception to this generalization is in the $C_{2v}$ open ten-vertex cluster type .. in which a change from *nido* character, exemplified by $B_{10}H_{14}$, to *arachno* character, exemplified by $[B_{10}H_{14}]^{2-}$ is characterized by an inversion of the ordering of the [11]B resonance positions and an increase in the mean [11]B shielding of several p.p.m.

**area**, *n.* Add: [**1.**] **b.** With defining word, as DINING *area,* RECEPTION *area,* etc.: a part of a room, building, etc., set aside or used for a specific function.
   **1950** *Western Folklore* IX. 160 The following words and phrases were gathered from an employee of the atomic project [at Los Alamos, New Mexico] .. *Tech area.* The research area. **1968** *Globe & Mail* (Toronto) 17 Feb. 45 (Advt.), Kitchen has built-in appliances and eating area. **1979** N. HYND *False Flags* xv. 131 They entered a small cubicle converted into a work area. There was an old desk .. with a disorder of papers. **1986** C. PHILLIPS *State of Independence* 60 He .. looked off towards an open door, which Bertram knew led to a kitchen area.

**areal**, *a.* Add: **2.** *Linguistics.* Of, pertaining to, or relating to the comparative study of languages or dialects in terms of geographical distribution and contact rather than historical development: freq. as *areal linguistics, areal linguistic* adj.; hence less precisely (of distribution, etc.), geographical.
   **1944** [see NEO-LINGUIST *n.*]. **1945** *Word* I. 137 In many cases—perhaps in most—what Brugmann, Meillet, and all the other Indo-Europeanists of the older generation called *comparative method* or *comparison between languages* is nothing else than

*areal linguistics avant la lettre.* **1967** *Jrnl. Linguistics* III. 170 The absence of any discussion of the 'areal linguistic' position of the Neolinguists .. is indicative. **1968** *Language* XLIV. 170 The argument that areal phenomena deserve more serious consideration than they have received can scarcely be disputed. **1968** D. L. BOLINGER *Aspects of Lang.* 139 When [the linguist] speaks of dialectology, it is almost always in this sense, more specifically referred to as 'linguistic geography', 'areal linguistics', or 'dialect geography'. **1972** K. R. JANKOWSKY *Neogrammarians* 157 An illustration is seen in what happened to one of the most famous areal linguists, Georg Wenker. He set out to prove, with areal linguistic means, the existence of a definite linguistic boundary. **1980** A. R. THOMAS (*title*) Areal analysis of dialect data by computer: a Welsh example. **1985** *Canad. Jrnl. Linguistics* XXX. 199 Perhaps what similarities we see in putatively distantly related languages are areal rather than genetic.
Hence **'areally** *adv.*
**1960** [see TWANA *n.* 2].

**argentophil** (ɑːˈdʒɛntəfɪl), *a. Histol.* Also -phile (-faɪl). [f. ARGENTO- + -PHIL, -PHILE.] = *ARGYROPHIL *a.*
**1947** DAWSON & MOYER in *Anat. Rec.* XCVII. 328 These cells are demonstrable by the Bodian protargol method (even without reduction or gold toning) .. but are not chromaffin positive and are not impregnated by the Masson-Hamperl technique. Accordingly they are referred to as argentophine rather than argentaffin. **1952** G. H. BOURNE *Cytol. & Cell Physiol.* (ed. 2) vi. 253 Each piece of pre-substance gradually develops a double structure, with an argentophine and osmiophile cortex. **1954** H. W. DEANE in R. O. Greep *Histol.* xxi. 556 Argentophile cells .. contain granules that may be blackened with silver salts. These are related to the true argentaffin cells. **1983** *Acta Neuropath.* LIX. 79/1 Numerous inflated cells, intraneuronal argentophil Pick bodies and central chromolysis of neurons were found throughout the cerebral cortex.
Also **argento'philic** *a.*, in same sense.
**1959** W. ANDREW *Textbk. Compar. Histol.* i. 12 It is .. important to note the constancy with which we find this osmiophilic and argentophilic structure among the many types of cells in myriads of animal species. **1983** *Jrnl. Protozool.* XXX. 268/2 The intermeridional argentophilic band of granules .. is yet another example of the variety of cytological effects that can be achieved with the .. Chatton-Lwoff technique.

**argyrophil** ('ɑːdʒɪrəfɪl), *a. Histol.* Also -phile (-faɪl). [f. ARGYR-, ARGYRO- + -PHIL, -PHILE.] Pertaining to or possessing the property of being readily stained black by ammoniacal silver in the presence of a reducing agent.
**1928** *Proc. Soc. Exper. Biol. & Med.* XXV. 439 The fibrillae are argyrophile, *i.e.*, they are electively impregnated with silver. **1930** MAXIMOW & BLOOM *Text-bk. Histol.* iv. 95 Reticular or lattice fibers .. are electively impregnated with silver by modified Bielschowsky methods after which they appear as black, sharply drawn nets ... This gave them the name of argyrophil fibers. **1954** H. W. DEANE in R. O. Greep *Histol.* xxi. 574 Included among the epithelial cells are numerous slender, bipolar cells containing neurofibrils and silverable granules (argyrophile cells). **1969, 1976** [see ARGENTAFFIN *a.*]. **1978** G. G. BROWN *Introd. Histotechnol.* xv. 276 Argentaffin cell granules have the capability of reducing an ammoniacal silver nitrate solution to produce a visible black deposit of silver ... This capability differentiates them from the argyrophil cells that cannot reduce ammoniacal silver solutions directly, but require the use of a reducing agent such as hydroquinone. **1985** *Cancer* LV. 609/2 Argentaffin stain was negative, but argyrophil stain showed numerous positive neoplastic cells.

Hence **argyro'philia** *n.*, the property of being argyrophil; **argyro'philic** *a.* = *argyrophil* adj. above.
**1928** *Proc. Soc. Exper. Biol. & Med.* XXV. 440 Simultaneously the fibers in the thicker bundles lose their argyrophilia and become acidophilic. **1934** E. V. COWDRY *Textbk. Histol.* xxv. 370 The second stage was the differentiation of delicate fibrils within the collagen .. which began to exhibit an affinity for silver, in other words to become argyrophilic. **1954** H. W. DEANE in R. O. Greep *Histol.* v. 70 (*caption*) Kidney .. stained by Pap's ammoniacal-silver nitrate method, illustrating the argyrophilia of reticular fibers in basement membranes. **1959** W. ANDREW *Textbk. Compar. Histol.* viii. 338 The capillaries of all vertebrates are lined by endothelium and present a thin wall having delicate fibers of argyrophilic, reticular type. **1978** *Nature* 26 Oct. 746/2 We found most argyrophilic debris rostral to the graft. **1985** *Jrnl. Clin. Path.* XXXVIII. 52/1 The focal argyrophilia occasionally seen in otherwise unremarkable adenocarcinomas.

**Aridisol** (əˈrɪdɪsɒl), *n. Soil Sci.* [f. ARID *a.* + -I- + -SOL.] A soil of an order comprising usually saline and alkaline soils containing very little organic matter, characteristic of arid regions.
**1960** *Soil Classification: 7th Approximation* (U.S. Soil Conservation Service) 156/1 Included in Aridisols are most soils that have been called Desert Soils and Red Desert soils [etc.]. **1972** J. G. CRUICKSHANK *Soil Geogr.* iv. 142 Some Aridisols do have a clay-rich sub-surface horizon, but most are composed of larger size particles and stones. **1980** E. A. FITZPATRICK *Soils* v. 138 Some Aridisols occur in semiarid areas because the soils are slowly permeable and most of the water is lost by run-off.

**arithmetical**, *a.* (and *n.*) Add: [A.] (Later examples.) Cf. ARITHMETIC *a.*
**1949** D. R. HARTREE *Calculating Instruments & Machines* 55 Other machines .. use relays not only for control but for the storage and arithmetical units of the machines themselves ... The arithmetical operations may be carried out by a structurally distinct portion of the machine, which can then be regarded as a unit, the 'arithmetical unit'. **1980** J.-L. BAER *Computer Syst. Archit.* i. 4 The arithmetical-logical unit (ALU) performs arithmetic and logical operations.

**Armco** (ɑːmkəʊ), *n.* Also armco. [f. the initial letters of *A*merican *R*olling *M*ill *Co*mpany, former name of the manufacturing company.]
**1.** A proprietary name for a soft iron of high purity. Usu. *attrib.*
**1920** *Trade Marks Jrnl.* 11 Aug. 1471 Armco. Iron in bars, billets, ingots .. all being unwrought or partly wrought iron used in manufacture. **1920** *Official Gaz.* (U.S. Patent Office) 19 Oct. 515/2 Armco ... Bars, billets, castings, forgings, [etc.] ... Claims use since Aug. 1, 1910. **1925** *Jrnl. Iron & Steel Inst.* CXI. 571 The materials used in the investigation were Armco iron and mild steels. **1931** *Ann. Reg. 1930* 61 The specimens used were prepared by heating armco iron for twelve hours at 1,500°C. **1973** P. HANCOCK et al. in *Chem. Metall. Iron & Steel* 415/1 The oxide films formed on Armco iron and low-carbon steel have been shown to fail continually during isothermal growth at temperatures in the range 530°C–800°C.
**2.** A proprietary name for a crash barrier for a motorway or racing track.
**1961** *Official Gaz.* (U.S. Patent Office) 21 Nov. TM83 Armco ... For .. guard-rails, .. reinforcing bars [etc.]. **1962** *Trade Marks Jrnl.* 16 May 599/2 Armco ... Bridge decking, fences and guardrails. **1977** *Custom Car* Nov. 11/3 Paul took an involuntary nap at the wheel on the M4. An Armco barrier woke him up to the loss of one side of the car front suspension. **1986** *Motoring News* 27 Aug. 6/1 A car hit the barrier .. and instantly burst into flames,

finally coming to rest after skating along the armco for some 150 yards.

**aromatherapy** (ə,rəumə'θɛrəpɪ), n. Also **aromatotherapy** (ə,rəumətəu-). [ad. F. *aromathérapie* (R.-M. Gattefossé *Aromathérapie* (c 1937)), f. *arome* AROMA n. + *thérapie* THERAPY n.] The use of essential oils and other plant extracts to promote health and beauty.
**1949** 'A.R.I.C.' tr. *Gattefossé & Jonquières's Technique Beauty Products* p. vii, Our biological researches have been summarised in the following works .. *Cosmetology and Aromatherapy* (in the course of preparation). **1964** M. SAVILL tr. *Maury's Secret of Life & Youth* x. 161 We augment the aromatherapy treatment with homoeopathic remedies. **1973** *Times* 22 Feb. 11/2 The Princess has undergone .. cell implants .. silicone injections .. aromatotherapy. **1984** *New Yorker* 19 Nov. 155/1 'Aromatherapy' candles .. —the scent of one is said to relieve headaches, of another to help insomniacs, and of the third simply to promote euphoria. **1988** *Times* 16 Nov. 27/1 Visitors will be able to spend a sybaritic day—at £40 each—taking treatments ranging from aromatherapy to herbalism and osteopathy.
Hence **a,romathera'peutic** a., of or pertaining to aromatherapy; **a,roma'therapist** n., one who advocates or practises aromatherapy.
**1949** 'A.R.I.C.' tr. *Gattefossé & Jonquières's Technique Beauty Products* v. iii. 167 Aromatherapeutic advances. **1970** L. AVEDON *Beautiful People's Beauty Bk.* (1971) vi. 74 There are various aromatotherapists in London now. **1983** *Daily Tel.* 28 July 17/1 Harvey Nichols is to open an aromatherapeutic clinic in the hair and beauty salon. **1986-7** *Successful Slimming* Dec.-Jan. 24/1 A present-day aromatherapist might suggest ylang-ylang, rose, patchouli or sandalwood oil as a .. sure aid to seduction.

**aromatic**, a. and n. Add: [**B.**] **2.** *Chem.* An aromatic compound.
**1925** *Jrnl. Inst. Petroleum Technologists* XI. 5A β-Iso-amylnaphthalene forms some 10 per cent. of the total aromatics present in the crude oil. **1940** *Industr. & Engin. Chem.* Apr. 528/1 The problem of converting aliphatic hydrocarbons into aromatics is an old one. **1964** N. G. CLARK *Mod. Org. Chem.* xviii. 374 Aromatics have .. to be prepared from mineral oil by various high temperature reactions. **1973** *Daily Tel.* 25 Sept. 11/5 Abolishing five star could release up to 400,000 metric tons of aromatics and end the shortage of products such as styrene, polystyrene and phenol. **1986** *Oil & Gas Jrnl.* 25 Aug. 27 (*caption*) The 10 train plant will produce 300,000 tons/year of ethylene and 450,000 tons/year of aromatics.

**artemisinin** (ɑːtɪ'miːsɪnɪn), n. *Med.* and *Pharm.* Also -nine (-niːn). [Blend of ARTEMISIA n. and QUININE n.] = *QINGHAOSU n.
**1979** *Chem. Abstr.* 17 Dec. 684/1 Dihydro-artemisinine ethers, esters, and carbonates .. were prepared by reduction of artemisinine .. and subsequent etherification or esterification. **1980** *Trop. Dis. Bull.* LXXVII. 556 The active prinicple of qinghao, known as qinghaosu, is an endoperoxide of a sesquiterpene lactone ... This compound (which is also known as artemisinine, or arteannuin) has an entirely novel structure totally unlike that of any other known antimalarial. **1985** *Science* 31 May 1049 (*heading*) Qinghaosu (artemisinin): an antimalarial drug from China. *Ibid.* 1049/3 Because the material is a terpene, rather than an alkaloid or amine, which the 'ine' suffix suggests, the name 'artemisinin' .. is preferred by *Chemical Abstracts*. **1990** *WHO Techn. Rep. TRS 805*, 114 Artemisinin .. has marked activity against malaria parasites, including multidrug-resistant isolates of *P. falciparum*.

**assets**, n. pl. Add: [**5.**] **asset management** orig. *U.S.*, the active management of the financial and other assets of a company, etc., esp. in order to optimize the return on investment.
**1974** M. MAYER *Bankers* xiv. 376 This was '*asset management', the investment in highly liquid assets that could be cashed in at will. **1987** *Christian Science Monitor* 20 Feb. B2/3 One of the large mutual fund families .. offers not only a variety of funds but an asset management account that would give you a monthly record of all transactions, including reinvestment of dividends.
also **asset manager**, one employed professionally in this capacity.
**1975** *Business Week* 1 Sept. 42/3 There is already a scramble among professional pension managers, from places as far away as London, to take advantage of PBGC's expressed desire to hire three *asset managers and a custodial bank. **1985** *Investors Chron.* 1 Nov. 54/1 Guinness Peat's chief executive .. reckons that institutions in the post Big Bang City will take one of three forms—bankers, traders or asset managers.

**assisted**, ppl. a. Add: **b.** *assisted place U.K.*, in an independent school: a place which is subsidized or funded by the State, and is awarded to an able pupil who might otherwise be unable to attend (usu in pl.).
**1977** N. ST. JOHN-STEVAS *Better Schools for All* viii. 46 The direct grant will be replaced by an assisted places scheme, under which all the available money will be devoted to a partial or total remission of tuition fees in accordance with a generous income scale. **1980** *Education Act* c.80 §17(1) The Secretary of State shall .. operate a scheme whereby .. participating schools remit fees that would otherwise be chargeable in respect of pupils selected for assisted places. **1986** *Times Educ. Suppl.* 9 May 4/4 A Labour Government will introduce an ambitious programme .. designed to .. abolish the assisted places scheme.

**astrodome**, n. Restrict *Aeronaut.* to sense in Dict. and add: **2.** An enclosed stadium with a domed roof, *esp.* one in which sports events are held (first applied to the indoor stadium of the Houston Astros baseball team at Houston, Texas). orig. and chiefly *U.S.*
**1964** *N.Y. Times* 6 Dec. v. 2/3 The 'rain or shine stadium', also known as Houston's Big Bubble, but officially the Harris County Domed Stadium, will probably .. be called Astrodome Stadium. **1965** *Sports Illustr.* 12 Apr. 45 This week, on Friday evening, April 9, the Astrodome will open officially. **1968** *Surfer Mag.* Jan. 46/1 The world's biggest astrodome .. houses an indoor fun zone. **1977** *Sounds* 1 Jan. 21/1 Nugent, the fastest growing rock act in the States, has now graduated into the astrodome concert bracket. **1986** *Guardian* 5 Feb. 27/2 The designer, George Williamson, the Welshman who built the National Stadium at Cardiff Arms Park, has already put together astrodomes in Bahrain and places in the Far East.

**a'strologist**, n. Chiefly *N. Amer.* [f. ASTROLOG(Y n.[1] + -IST.] = ASTROLOGER n. 3 (though less frequent and not the preferred term amongst practitioners).
**1954** *Life* 5 Apr. 143/2 Carroll Righter is a Hollywood astrologer or, as he prefers to be called, an astrologian. He detests being called an astrologist. 'An astrologist is a quack,' he says. **1962** *N.Y. Times* 2 Feb. 4/8 Hindu holy men began a new series of prayers .. with the hope that their efforts will ward off the disaster predicted for the week-end by astrologists. **1978** *Economist* 4 Feb. 117/3 Records of his birth were destroyed in the San Francisco earthquake, but he is thought to have been the illegitimate son of an itinerant astrologist. **1985** *Washington Post* 20 Oct. D6/3, I side pretty steadily with history's eccentrics. 'I don't mean all the mad astrologists and mystics .. but simply the mundane eccentrics.'

**attack**, *n.* [2.] Delete 'a move directed to gain a point in *Chess*' and substitute: a move or series of moves directed to gain esp. material advantage in *Chess*. **1735** J. BERTIN *Noble Game of Chess* p. v, When you are well posted, either for attack or defence, you must not be tempted to take any of your adversary's men, which may divert you from the main design. **1745** P. STAMMA *Noble Game of Chess* 114 To form some Scheme for an attack. **1797** *Encycl. Brit.* IV. 641/2 As the queen, rook, and bishop, operate at a distance, it is not always necessary in the attack to have them near the adversary's king. **1932** [see NIMZOWITSCH *n.*]. **1964** *Illustr. London News* 24 Oct., The word 'attack' .. is really very vague. It indicates a certain keenness in the play, a concentration on definite, and early, objectives. **1984** *Byte* Mar. 289/1 Lazy players who make blunders and initiate half-baked attacks usually lose badly to a program.

**attack**, *v.* Add: **8.** *Chess.* **a.** *trans.* To mount or maintain an attack upon (an opponent's piece or pieces); to place or hold (a square, etc.) under attack. **1735** BERTIN *Noble Game of Chess* p. vi, Never attack, or defend the king, without a sufficient force. **1797** *Encycl. Brit.* IV. 640/1 To crowd the adversary's game, which may be done by attacking his pieces with the pawns. **1808** J. H. SARRATT *Treat. Chess* I. 151 If .. he should play his King's Pawn one step, attacking your Queen's Bishop, you must give him check with your Queen. **1861** *Chambers's Encycl.* II. 799/2 The king cannot castle .. when he passes over a square attacked or checked by an adverse piece. **1983** W. TEVIS *Queen's Gambit* viii. 129 She pushed her pawn up to rook three, attacking the bishop.
**b.** *absol.* or *intr.* **1745** P. STAMMA *Noble Game of Chess* 109 Your first View should be to open the Game so, as to make way for your Pieces to come out, that you may .. have them in Readiness, both to attack, and defend. **1796** C. JONES *Hoyle's Games Improved* 145 Be sure you bring out all your Pieces into Play before you begin to attack. **1808** J. H. SARRATT *Treat. Chess* I. 133 If he attacked heedlessly, his adversary might easily retrieve his game. **1861** *Chambers's Encycl.* II. 799/1 These sets of men are arrayed opposite to each other, and attack, defend, and capture, like hostile armies. **1983** W. TEVIS *Queen's Gambit* iv. 62 She began attacking on the eighth move.

**attention**, *n.* Add: [6.] **b.** Special Comb. **attention-seeking**, the action or process of deliberately seeking to draw attention to oneself; also as *adj.*, that seeks attention or notoriety. **1961** *Educ. of Children with Handicaps* (16th Yearbk. Ontario School Inspectors' Assoc.) 183 In summary, negativism may be mere *attention-seeking, or it may be a pathological symptom of serious proportion. **1965** M. MORSE *Unattached* v. 184 She began to develop more honest relationships and her attention-seeking behaviour began to ease up. **1986** *City Limits* 12 June 61 The complex relationship between predator and victim shows how rape is more than the cry of attention-seeking females.

**auto-de'struct**, *v.* (*adj. phr.* and *n.*) [f. AUTO-¹ + DESTRUCT *v.*, or as back-formation from

*AUTO-DESTRUCTIVE *a.*, etc.] **1.** *intr.* = SELF-DESTRUCT *v.* 1 (*lit.* and *fig.*). **1980** *Newsweek* 1 Sept. 18/3 Reagan penned in a few lines memorializing the war in Vietnam as 'a noble cause' ... The result .. encouraged his enemies to believe that he may yet auto-destruct. **1985** *Times* 4 Jan. 10/7 The city that perfected the dry Martini has yet to invent .. lavatory paper that does not auto-destruct on contact.
**2.** *attrib.* as *adj. phr.* = SELF-DESTRUCT *v.* 2. **1971** *New Scientist* 26 Aug. 452/1 The cell's 'auto-destruct' pack, the lysosome. **1980** *Aviation Week* 23 June 16/1 Engine D .. developed a combustion chamber pressure oscillation 4.4 sec. after ignition that led to the activation of the vehicle's auto-destruct mechanisms about 104 sec. later. **1983** *Listener* 16 June 4/1 Labour's leaders, Denis Healey in particular, became adept at pressing the auto-destruct button.
Also **auto-destruct** *n.*, = SELF-DESTRUCT *n.* **1977** *Economist* 31 Dec. 97/3 In this book he coarsens his darkly brilliant portrait of a close-knit group locked into auto-destruct by introducing the menace of commercial exploitation. **1978** *Ibid.* 25 Nov. 66/2 (*heading*) Auto-destruct... Rhodesia's transitional government appears so prone to discredit itself .. that such threats as the death list put out by Mr Mugabe's wing of the Patriotic Front seem quite unnecessary.

**auto-de'struction**, *n.* [f. AUTO-¹ + DESTRUCTION *n.*] Destruction brought about by an auto-destructive process rather than by any external agency; = SELF-DESTRUCTION *n.* **1970** *Guardian Weekly* 10 Jan. 20/3 Happenings, 'impossible art', auto-destruction art, multi-media events are alternative pursuits that can engage an artist's inventive powers. **1974** L. THOMAS *Lives of Cell* (1975) 9 It is autodestruction due to lytic mechanisms entirely under the governance of the smaller partner. **1986** B. BROPHY *Baroque-'n'-Roll* (1987) 6 Only in 1982 .. could I write the last of WAG's newsletters to its members and signal WAG's autodestruction.

**auto-de'structive**, *a.* [f. AUTO-¹ + DESTRUCTIVE *a.*] Having the property of bringing about its own destruction or annulment; *spec.* of or pertaining to an artistic movement founded by Gustav Metzger, in which the disintegration or decay of objects is elevated to an artistic process. Cf. SELF-DESTRUCTIVE *a.* **1959** *Daily Express* 12 Nov. 7/6 The ex-joiner [*sc.* Gustav Metzger] who has studied at art schools in Britain and the Continent asked whether I was interested in hearing his theory of 'auto-destructive art'. I said I had heard enough. **1966** *Listener* 22 Sept. 433/3 There was also a good moment when Mr. Pack explained to one of the young people involved that she had destroyed a piece of auto-destructive art. **1968** *Ibid.* 22 Feb. 252/2 Some of the far-out psychedelic or autodestructive groups justify their old-fashioned sub-Scriabin noises with a lordly take-it-or-leave-it, man. **1977** *Business Week* 12 Sept. 10/2 Some .. come through to me as real 'empire-builders' who .. grow out of proportion to their environment. Thus, they become autodestructive and disruptive.

**aymag** *n.*, var. *AIMAK *n.*

# B

**B**. Add: [**II.**] [**2.**] [**b.**] (vii) *Biochem.* Designating the most common form of double-stranded DNA, consisting of a right-handed double helix in which the base pairs are almost perpendicular to the helix axis.

**1953** [see *\*A* II. 11]. **1968** *Nature* 9 Nov. 563/2 RNA may not be able to adopt a structure like that of B-DNA with a C2-endo sugar conformation. **1983** *Sci. Amer.* Dec. 87/2 Fibers of DNA can exist in two forms: as *B* DNA under conditions of high humidity and as *A* DNA when the humidity is lower.

[**III.**] [**1.**] **B.A.L.P.A.** ('bælpə), British Air Line Pilots' Association.

**1937** *Aeroplane* LIII. 652/2 The *\*B.A.L.P.A.* was formed to present the pilots' cases in a way for which they reasonably contended there was no machinery then available. **1946** *Log* Dec. 215 This is an important month for B.A.L.P.A. **1970** D. FRANCIS *Rat Race* vii. 97 There's no B.A.L.P.A. to uphold your rights there.

**B and B, b and b,** bed and breakfast (see BED *n.* 1 g (a)); a guest-house, etc. offering bed-and-breakfast accommodation.

**1961** *People* 9 Apr. 11/5 The *\*B-and-B* raider. Police were yesterday searching for the bed-and-breakfast raider. After breaking into a factory .. he .. went to sleep in the managing director's chair. **1964** *Dalton's Weekly* 18 Dec. 16/2 (Advt.), Newquay, Cornwall.—Modn. bungalow. Excel. cuisine. B. & b., evening dinner. **1967** K. GILES *Death & Mr. Prettyman* vi. 121 Mr. S said I could stay here if I only charged ten bob for b and b, bought my own dinner and got back by nine-fifteen tomorrow. **1986** *Independent* 13 Dec. 10/6 My [Adelaide] hotel .. could have been any solid B & B in Eastbourne.

**BARB, Barb** (bɑːb), Broadcasters' Audience Research Board, an organization founded in 1981 to assess the size of the audience for individual television programmes.

**1982** *Daily Tel.* 9 Dec. 15/8 When broadcasting overseas the BBC is untroubled by the pedants of *\*Barb* .., and invariably speaks in well-rounded million[s]. **1982** *Listener* 16 Dec. 27/3 The homes on the BARB panel don't register time-shift use of video-recorders. **1986** *Stage* 7 Aug. 18/3 The weekly figures produced for BARB by AGB, show that the Royal Wedding dominated the week's viewing.

**B. Ed.,** Bachelor of Education.

**1941** J. M. CATTELL et al. *Leaders in Educ.* (ed. 2) 123/1 Brown, Dr. W(iley) G(len)... *\*B.* Ed. Nebraska State Normal School 08. **1963** *Higher Educ.: Rep. Comm. under Ld. Robbins 1961–3* 116 in *Parl. Papers 1962–3* (Cmnd. 2154) XI. 639 What should the degree awarded to Training College students be called? We think it should be distinctive and recommend that it should be called a B.Ed. The provisions we have envisaged should make certain that it is regarded as a degree equivalent in standard to the B.A. **1964** *New Statesman* 13 Mar. 390/2 The proposals .. would make the colleges university institutions, .. and entitled to prepare suitable students .. for a new degree, BEd. **1986** *Times Higher Educ. Suppl.* 13 June 7/4 Recruitment has completely altered since they introduced a four-year honours B Ed.

**bpi** *Computing*, bits per inch.

**1964** *IEEE Trans. Electronic Computers* XIII. 112/1 A recording technique was developed which achieves a packing density of 2500 bits per inch (\*bpi). **1985** *Computing Equipment* Sept. 13/1 The 8000 series are available .. storing up to 2.7 MBytes of formatted data on a DC 300 XL cartridge at 1600 bpi.

**bps** *Computing*, bits per second.

**1968** *New Acronyms & Initialisms* (Gale Research Co.) 32 *\*BPS*, Bits Per Second (Data processing). **1975** R. L. FREEMAN *Telecommunication Transmission Handbk.* viii. 389 Voice frequency carrier telegraph techniques handle data rates up to 1200 bps. **1983** *80 Microcomputing* Feb. 24/1 A modem can clock at 4800 or 9600 baud, but data will be transmitted at 1200 or 2400 BPS.

**Bq** = BECQUEREL *n.* 2.

**1975** *\*Bq* [see BECQUEREL *n.* 2]. **1986** *Nature* 31 July 393/1 Imports of foodstuffs from Eastern Europe would be prohibited while the content of radioactivity exceeded 600 Bq per kg.

**B.V.M.** [L. *Beata Virgo Maria*], The Blessed Virgin Mary.

[**1619** M. INCHOFER *Epistolae B. Virginis Mariæ ad Messanenses* 2 (*heading*) Epistolæ B.V.M. ad Messanenses.] **1838** *Catholic Directory* (verso title-page), Feasts observed in England and Scotland. .. 8 Sept. Nativity of *\*B.V.M.* **1884** *N. & Q.* 8 Nov. 377/1 This festival, more commonly known as the 'Assumption of the B.V.M.'.. is observed on August 15. **1952** C. S. LEWIS *Lett.* (1966) 243 A state .. where the B.V.M. is treated really as a divinity and even becomes the centre of the religion. **1957** *Oxf. Dict. Chr. Ch.* 868/1 Some cultus of the BVM is held to be a necessary element in the spiritual life of the Catholic. **1986** P. D. JAMES *Taste for Death* I. i. 17 'Don't you want 'em for the BVM?' 'We've got your uncle's roses for Our Lady.'

**BW, b/w, b & w** (*Cinematogr.* and *Television*), black and white, as opp. to colour.

**1960** O. SKILBECK *ABC of Film & T.V.* 22 *\*B/W*, Black and White film. It is usual to have B/W Rush Prints of colour film and to use them for the Cutting copy, to save expense. **1974** *New Acronyms & Initialisms* (Gale Research Co.) 11/2 *BW*, Black and White. **1985** *Music Week* 2 Feb. 42/5 Replacing the b/w with the original videotape colour recordings. **1986** *City Limits* 16 Oct. 57 A 25-page essay with b&w stills on some of the hidden history of films.

**Babylon,** *n.* Add: **2.** *Black* (chiefly *Jamaican*) *English.* A contemptuous or dismissive term for anything which to the Black (esp. Rastafarian) consciousness represents the degenerate or oppressive state of white culture; *spec.* the police, a policeman; (white) society or the Establishment.

**1943** in Cassidy & Le Page *Dict. Jamaican Eng.* (1967) 17/1 *Babylan*, police. **1952** in *Ibid.* 17/1 /bábilàn/ district constable, policeman. **1955** in *Ibid.* 17/1 *Babylon*, white man. **1960** M. G. SMITH et al. *Ras Tafari Movement in Kingston, Jamaica* 52 Since the Jamaican police are mainly black Ethiopians working for Babylon, their persecution of the brethren constitutes a 'tribal war' instigated by the white and brown oppressors. **1977** *Observer* 21 Aug. 11/1 'Babylon!'—a West Indian nickname for the police—yells a voice, and the blacks dart outwards .. as a police squad .. moves to the stranded Panda car. **1978** *Ibid.* 4 June 3/5 The police are simply the sharp and visible end of 'Babylon': white society and all its frustrations. 'There is nothing going on that is right,' said Derrick. 'Babylon don't really have nothing to offer I.' **1980** *Daily Mirror* 9 Apr. 16/4 Roots Boys—members of a West Indian youth cult. Their heady Caribbean-style street talk includes .. insulting names for the police, from 'Babylon' to 'The

Wicked'. **1986** G. SLOVO *Death by Analysis* v. 70 My father him a work as labourer for thirty years in Babylon.

**back**, *n.*[1] Add: [VI.] [23.] [g.] Also *in back*, in or at the back (*N. Amer. colloq.*); cf. *in (the) front* s.v. FRONT *n.* (and *a.*) 10 a.
   **1961** *Northwest Rev.* IV. 54 'In back, buddy,' the driver said to me. **1974** R. M. PIRSIG *Zen & Art of Motorcycle Maintenance* II. viii. 104 He's got to close a deal out in back on some Harley parts. I go with him out in a shed in back and see he is selling a whole Harley machine in used parts. **1987** *New Yorker* 5 Jan. 39/1 In front of the house was a small lawn.., and in back were another lawn, a small garden, and a garage.

**back**, *v.* Add: [VI.] [22.] e. *intr.* Of motor traffic: to form a stationary or slow-moving queue, as behind an obstruction. Also const. in perfect with *to be.* Also *fig. colloq.* (chiefly *U.S.*).
   **1964** *N.Y. Times* 24 June 24/8 Each time it [*sc.* a drawbridge] opens, traffic backs up on heavily traveled Bruckner Boulevard. **1977** *Washington Post* 9 Nov. B8/2 Another car, also with its hood up and facing the stalled car, was trying to give it a jump start... The transfusion wasn't working and traffic was backing up as far as the eye could see. **1979** *Ibid.* 1 Sept. C3/5 Traffic on the Capital Beltway was backed up for miles just before the rush to get away for the Labor Day weekend when a tractor-trailer truck collided head-on with another truck. **1983** J. M. COETZEE *Life & Times Michael K* I. 48 Backed up around the bend as far as K could see was the rest of the convoy. **1984** *New Yorker* 9 Apr. 72/2 Decisions backed up: the scheduler couldn't complete the campaign schedule until he had cleared it with the candidate; press releases waited for the candidate's approval. **1986** *Times* 25 Aug. 8/7 On the far side, traffic heading south is backed up for miles.

**back-board**, *n.* Add: [2.] b. *Basketball.* A board positioned immediately behind the basket, which forms part of the playing area and from which the ball may rebound into the basket to score.
   **1929** L. E. ANDERSON *Basketball for Women* viii. 74 The ball strikes the backboard at an angle and rebounds into the basket. **1935** *Encycl. Sports* 63/2 Free throws are given as penalties for fouls, and these are taken from a position behind the free-throw line, 9 ft. in front of the backboard. **1957** *Encycl. Brit.* III. 181/2 The backboard may be of two types: rectangular, 6 ft. horizontally and 4 ft. vertically, or fan-shaped, 54 in. wide with a 29-in. radius from centre base to top. It may be of any rigid material with flat front surface. **1960** J. UPDIKE *Rabbit, Run* 3 Boys are playing basketball around a telephone pole with a backboard bolted to it. **1986** *Basketball Monthly* Aug./Sept. 11/3 If you post up too low, you'll find your baseline moves put you behind the backboard.
   c. *Lawn Tennis.* A wall or other surface against which a player can practise shots. orig. *U.S.*
   **1935** H. I. DRIVER *Tennis for Teachers* xviii. 84 The backboard is the best opponent a player can have, because it always returns the ball. **1964** *World Tennis* June 30/2 You are now sufficiently advanced to play a game against the backboard. *Ibid.* 31/1 After several backboard sessions.. you can get further forehand practice by having someone play the ball to you. **1979** *United States 1980/81* (Penguin Travel Guides) 497 Facilities: 18 courts.. ball machines; practice alleys; backboard.
   d. *Ice-Hockey.* Any of the boards surrounding the area behind each goal. Usu. in *pl.*
   **1968** *Boston Globe* 3 Jan. 47/3 This is an important consideration in Madison Square Garden where there is a comparatively small area behind the nets and the

puck takes.. some bounces off the backboards. **1978** *Winnipeg Free Press* 25 Sept. 53/5 Hammarstrom slipped behind the Winnipeg defence to put away a rebound off the backboards.
   e. *Hockey.* A board placed at ground level across the back of the goal.
   **1987** *Guardian* 13 Apr. 27/2 A rare attacking sortie gave the patient Americans their chance and Donnelly's shot clattered the back board.

**back-up**, *n.* Add: [3.] b. An accumulation or tail-back of motor traffic, as behind an obstruction. Cf. *BACK *v.* 22 e. *N. Amer. colloq.*
   **1962** *Proc. Inst. Traffic Engineers* 117 Consideration will be increasingly given to 'graduated' traffic flow systems which avoid abrupt changes in the character of road facilities, thereby minimizing queuing, and backups. **1978** *Detroit Free Press* 16 Apr. 3A/2 Not knowing what's causing a traffic backup is frustrating to motorists. **1985** *City Cyclist* (Toronto) Summer 9/2 The expressway system.. has now succeeded in making suburbs themselves the very worst scenes of traffic jams and backups.

**bacon**, *n.* Add: [6.] *bacon sandwich* (also *sarnie*).
   **1931** 'G. ORWELL' *Coll. Ess.* (1968) I. 66 We started off for work, with *bacon sandwiches and a drum of cold tea. **1986** J. MILNE *Dead Birds* xv. 126 I've made bacon sandwiches for all of us. **1986** *Daily Express* 21 Aug. 25 You don't have to survive on *bacon sarnies and beans.

**bacteræmia**, *n.* Add: Hence **bacte'ræmic** *a.*, of, pertaining to, or caused by bacteræmia.
   **1951** WHITBY & HYNES *Med. Bacteriol.* (ed. 5) xi. 196 The mortality of this form of pneumonia is high, especially in bacteræmic cases. **1980** *Rec. Adv. Surg.* X. 24 The remaining cases died in the postoperative period as a result of bacteriaemic [*sic*] shock.

**BAFTA** ('bæftə), *n.* [Acronym f. the initial letters of *British Academy of Film and Television Arts.*] An organization founded in 1976 to promote British films and television. *BAFTA award*, any of a series of awards presented annually by the Academy for outstanding achievement in British films or television.
   **1976** *Vision* Mar. 2 (*heading*) What does BAFTA think the Government should do about the British Film Industry? **1978** *Ibid.* Apr. 3/1 (*heading*) The 1977 BAFTA awards. **1986** *Stage* 7 Aug. 18/1 Joanne Whalley, recently nominated for a BAFTA award for her performance.. is to take the leading role in a new BBC Screen 2 film. **1985-86** *Sight & Sound* Winter 26/3 The critics.. congregate around the BAFTA bar before smart magazine shows.

**bag**, *n.* Add: [V.] [22.] **bag lady** orig. *U.S.*, a homeless woman, often elderly, who carries her possessions in shopping bags; = *shopping-bag lady* s.v. SHOPPING *vbl. n.* 2.
   **1972** S. R. CURTIN *Nobody ever died of Old Age* vi. 85 Letty the *Bag Lady.. would pack all her valuables in two large shopping bags and carry them with her. **1977** *New Yorker* 17 Oct. 40/2 I did a bag-lady number on one of the platforms here in the bus station last year, and I almost got arrested. **1984** M. AMIS *Money* 105 They even had a couple of black-clad bagladies sitting silently on straight chairs by the door.

**bain't** (beɪnt), *v.* [See BE *v.* I. 1 e (b), h β, and AIN'T *v.*] Repr. dial. (chiefly Midlands and W. Country) form of the verb *to be* (present indicative, all persons) + *not*: 'am not' (also 'is not'), 'are not'.
   **1853** 'C. BEDE' *Adventures Verdant Green* viii. 73 'Bain't you well, sir?' repeated Mr. Filcher. **1857** C. M. YONGE *Dynevor Terr.* I. iii. 29 The candles baint

so good as they used, and I can't get no spectacles to suit me. **1876** —— *Three Brides* xxv. 368 He was born in one of they vans . . just like the gipsies, though he baint a gipsy neither. **1919** S. WEYMAN *Great House* xxx. 282 Well, I'm dommed! . . It be you, Squire, bain't it? **1939** JOYCE *Finnegans Wake* 285 Cat my dogs, if I baint dingbushed like everything! **1987** A. PUCKETT *Blood Stains* xvi. 169 'I want to speak to John Hill.' . . 'Bain't no such person yurr.'

**balanced**, *ppl. a.* Add: **7.** *Computing.* Of a binary tree: such that for each node the left and right subtrees are of equal or approximately equal size, as measured by the number of levels or the number of nodes in each.
**1962** *Symposium Symbolic Lang. Data Processing* 156 A Balanced Tree is accomplished by filling the levels of the tree to completion, i.e., no new levels are to be initiated as long as there are vacant catenae available in the preceding level. **1973** C. W. GEAR *Introd. Computer Sci.* vii. 285 A balanced tree leads to fewer operations on the average if any item is equally likely to be referenced. **1976** N. WIRTH *Algorithms plus Data Struct.* iv. 195 The rule is expressed as a recursive procedure as part of Program 4.3 which reads the input file and constructs the perfectly balanced tree. **1984** R. L. KRUSE *Data Struct. & Program Design* v. 221 The algorithm . . produces a binary search tree that is not always completely balanced.

**ball**, *n.*[1] Add: [V.] [**22.**] **balls-aching** *a.* coarse *slang*, that causes annoyance, revulsion, or boredom; extremely irritating or tedious.
?**1912** D. H. LAWRENCE in F. *Lawrence Mem. & Corr.* (1961) 189 *Balls-aching rot. **1973** M. AMIS *Rachel Papers* 157 Balls-aching drivel, unquestionably—and poor tactics, too. **1989** R. M. WILSON *Ripley Bogle* i. 8 I don't quite know why I bother with all this ballsaching fire and semi-satire.
   hence **balls-achingly** *adv.*
   **1972** J. METCALF *Going down Slow* iii. 48 'Oh, don't be so *ballsachingly adolescent!' snapped Garry.
   (as a back-formation) **balls-ache**, a state of annoyance or boredom.
   **1938** PARTRIDGE *Dict. Slang* Suppl. 1048/2 *You give me the *balls-ache! . . I disagree with your point of view; or, I disapprove of your behaviour.

**Balmer** ('bælmə(r)), *n.*[3] *Physics.* The name of Johann Jakob *Balmer* (1825–98), Swiss physicist, used *attrib.* and in the possessive with reference to a series of lines discovered by him in 1885 (*Ann. d. Physik u. Chemie* XXV. 80) in the visible and ultraviolet part of the spectrum of atomic hydrogen, with wave numbers represented by the formula $R(1/2^2 - 1/m^2)$ (where $R$ is the Rydberg constant and $m = 3,4, . .$).
[**1887** *Encycl. Brit.* XXII. 379/2 As a first approximation Balmer's expression gives a very good account of the hydrogen spectrum.] **1891** *Sci. Trans. R. Dublin Soc.* 2nd Ser. IV. 567 The discovery of Balmer's law has stimulated other inquirers to search for similar simple laws connecting the oscillation-frequencies. **1899** *Astrophysical Jrnl.* IX. 213 The value of the wave-length . . for hydrogen gas in vacuum tubes agrees with that deduced from Balmer's formula. **1901** *Proc. Amer. Acad. Arts & Sci.* XXXVII. 163, I have been unable to photograph the still weaker hydrogen lines of Balmer's series. **1922** [see LYMAN *n.*]. **1958** *New Scientist* 30 Jan. 17/3 The discharge showed Balmer lines for 20 microseconds. **1970** G. K. WOODGATE *Elem. Atomic Struct.* vi. 104 Equation (6.31) is obviously a modification of the Balmer formula for hydrogen. **1988** *Nature* 27 Oct. 802/2 Spectra that are dominated by Balmer line emission are seen in a number of supernova remnants (SNR).

**Bargello** (bɑːˈdʒɛləʊ), *n.* Also bargello. The name of the *Bargello* Palace in Florence, used *attrib.* and *absol.* to designate a kind of embroidery worked in flame stitch patterns on canvas, several examples of which could formerly be seen at the Palace. Cf. *FLORENTINE *a.* I c.
   **1942** D. G. LENT *Needle Point as Hobby* x. 139 The Florentine stitch you are going to learn now . . is also called Bargello embroidery. **1963** B. KING *Creative Canvas Embroidery* iii. 29 Florentine Stitch also called Flame or Bargello work . . originated in Florence. **1971** BARNES & BLAKE *Bargello & Related Stitchery* 11 The name Bargello appears to have become associated with a specific pattern, examples of which can be seen on a set of chairs presently in the Museo Nazionale in Florence . . . For several generations Bargello has been considered, and used, as the one all-inclusive name that best characterizes the various stitch arrangements. **1977** *Chicago Tribune* 2 Oct. XI. 12/3 The golden rule of Bargello stitching: Always begin your stitching in the middle of your canvas and your stitches (and design) will proceed equally in both directions. **1980** L. BIRNBACH et al. *Official Preppy Handbk.* 25/2 (caption) Needlepoint pillows . . . One is stitched in the bargello pattern.

**Barnardo** (bəˈnɑːdəʊ), *n.* Also *erron.* Barnado. The name of Thomas John *Barnardo* (1845–1905), British philanthropist, used *attrib.*, as *Barnardo child, orphan*, etc., and in the possessive to designate any of the destitute and homeless children brought up in the homes founded by Dr. Barnardo.
   **1904** KIPLING *Traffics & Discov.* 343 *All the time the beggar was a balmy Barnado Orphan! **1910** E. F. MURPHY *Janey Canuck in West* xxix. 210 Two Barnardo boys look on and enjoy the sport. **1914** KIPLING *Divers. Creatures* (1917) 49 They asked for a child from one o' those Lunnon societies—same as it might ha' been these Barnardo children—an' Mary was sent down to 'em, in a candle-box. **1968** 'P. HOBSON' *Titty's Dead* v. 57 She was a Barnardo baby. . . She was illegitimate. Her father was a grocer in Reading. He let her be brought up by Barnardo's. **1986** M. HARDWICK *Malice Domestic* xv. 211, I was a Barnardo's girl . . . They found me in a slum in Walsall.

**baro-** ('bærəʊ), *comb. form* of Gr. βάρος weight, used to form technical terms usu. with the sense 'pressure', as in BAROMETER *n.*, BARORECEPTOR *n.*

**baroclinic** (bærəˈklɪnɪk), *a. Meteorol.* [f. *BARO- + Gr. κλίν-ειν to bend, slope + -IC.] Characterized by or associated with an atmospheric condition in which surfaces of constant pressure intersect with those of constant density. Cf. *BAROTROPIC *a.*
   **1921** V. BJERKNES in *Geofysiske Publikationer* II. IV. 2 In all cases of well-defined curves of intersection and unit tubes, we shall call the field of mass baroclinic. In the case of degeneration we shall call it barotropic. **1934** D. BRUNT *Physical & Dynamical Meteorol.* viii. 166 In the baroclinic fluid pressure is not determined by density alone, and is in part determined by other factors such as temperature and water-vapour content. **1944** *Jrnl. Meteorol.* I. 18/2 A baroclinic westerly current is dynamically unstable for waves whose level of nondivergence is sufficiently low and tends to make these waves grow strong. **1968** *Sci. Jrnl.* Nov. 40/3 This instability, called baroclinic instability, . . was not discovered until the late 1940s. **1971** *Observatory* XCI. 54 The Earth's rotation . . constrains the convective flow to take the form of quasi-horizontal waves ('baroclinic waves' or 'sloping convection'). **1975** *Nature* 30 Oct. 778/2 As in the terrestrial and Martian systems, baroclinic instability again seems to be the primary energy conversion

process [in the atmosphere of Jupiter]. **1982** BARRY & CHORLEY *Atmosphere, Weather & Climate* (ed. 4) iii. 144 Eventually the flow becomes unstable in the Hadley mode, breaking down into a number of cyclonic and anticyclonic eddies. This phenomenon is referred to as baroclinic instability.

Hence **baro'clinically** *adv*., in a baroclinic manner; as regards baroclinicity; **barocli'nicity** *n*., the condition of being baroclinic; the extent to which a region is baroclinic; **baro'clinity** *n*. = *baroclinicity* n. above.

**1947** *Jrnl. Meteorol.* IV. 137/1 These phenomena.. are not explainable in terms of a barotropic atmosphere. They may, therefore, be attributed to the vertical shear of the zonal wind, i.e., to the baroclinicity of the atmosphere. **1950** *Tellus* II. 253/2 The baroclinically calculated height falls on the east side of the trough are more favorable. **1951** B. HAURWITZ in T. F. Malone *Compendium Meteorol.* 403/1 The significance of the distinction between barotropy and baroclinity for the variation of the circulation of a fluid. **1967** R. W. FAIRBRIDGE *Encycl. Atmospheric Sci.* 112/1 Since the baroclinity complicates the dynamic calculations, a barotropic condition is sometimes assumed. **1969** *Jrnl. Atmospheric Sci.* XXVI. 370/1 Major stabilization occurs for the short, baroclinically active waves. **1973** *Nature* 21 Sept. 133/1 It seems probable, but less certain, that the colder tropical troposphere was associated also with a reduced baroclinicity. **1978** *Ibid.* 10 Aug. 576/2 Studies so far on monsoon cyclogenesis have shown that the monsoon atmosphere is not baroclinically unstable.

**barotropic** (bærə'trɒpɪk, -'trəʊpɪk), *a. Meteorol.* [f. *BARO- + -TROPIC.] Characterized by or associated with an atmospheric condition in which surfaces of constant pressure coincide with those of constant density. Cf. *BAROCLINIC *a*.

**1921** [see *BAROCLINIC *a*.]. **1934** D. BRUNT *Physical & Dynamical Meteorol.* viii. 166 The fluid of 'classical' hydrodynamics, which is normally assumed to be homogeneous and incompressible, is obviously barotropic. **1949** *Jrnl. Meteorol.* VI. 106/1 A detailed study of the character of nondivergent horizontal wave motion in a barotropic atmosphere. **1976** *Sci. Amer.* Mar. 54/3 The atmosphere is said to be barotropic, as opposed to baroclinic, where the available energy is mainly gravitational and is associated with horizontal temperature gradients. **1986** *Icarus* LXVIII. 325/1 Another possibility is that the observed feature is produced by some form of barotropic instability. In addition to the conventional type of shallow barotropic instability appropriate to the Earth, there is the possibility of an alternative deep form for the outer planets.

Hence **baro'tropically** *adv*., in a barotropic manner; as regards barotropy; **ba'rotropy** *n*., the condition of being barotropic.

**1921** V. BJERKNES in *Geofysiske Publikationer* II. iv. 3 The case of barotropy appears, first when the equisubstantial surfaces coincide with the isobaric, i.e., when the specific volume, or the density, is a function of the pressure.. and secondly, in the case of complete homogeneity. **1950** *Tellus* II. 253/2 The correspondence is close and.. much better than the barotropically computed change. **1951** Barotropy [see *baroclinity* (s.v. *BAROCLINIC *a*.)]. **1959** S. L. HESS *Introd. Theoret. Meteorol.* xii. 193 Barotropy manifests itself on constant-level charts, in part, by parallelism of isobars and isotherms. **1978** *Nature* 10 Aug. 576/2 Shukla obtained barotropically unstable upper tropospheric modes.. but failed to get a preferred scale of maximum growth for lower tropospheric disturbances.

**Barr body** ('bɑː ˌbɒdɪ), *n. Genetics and Med.* [Named after M. L. *Barr* (b. 1908), Canadian anatomist, who first reported this with E. G. Bertram in *Nature* (1949) 30 Apr. 676-7.] A strongly heterochromatic body just inside the membrane of non-dividing cell nuclei in females, representing a condensed, inactive X chromosome and normally diagnostic of genetic femaleness.

**1961** *Amer. Jrnl. Med.* XXXI. 434/2 Anders and Prader studied a mentally retarded boy.. whose buccal smear nuclei contained double and triple Barr bodies. **1977** *Hongkong Standard* 14 Apr. 11/4 She said she is angry because she passed the Barr body test just two weeks ago.. and had forwarded the findings to the European tournament committees. **1983** J. R. S. FINCHAM *Genetics* xix. 570 The nuclei of XXX females have two inactivated X-chromosomes (seen as 'Barr bodies') instead of the normal one.

**barrel** *n*. Add: [I.] [2.] **b.** In fig. phr. *barrel of fun* (*laughs*, etc.): (the source of) a great deal of enjoyment or entertainment. *colloq.* (orig. *U.S.*).

**1915** *Dialect Notes* IV. 243, I had a barrel of fun when I went to Maccasin. **1939** L. BROWN *Beer Barrel Polka* 4 Roll out the barrel We'll have a barrel of fun. **1977** *Washington Post* 8 June B1 No one has ever accused Princess Anne of being a barrel of laughs. **1981** *Verbatim* Spring (Bk. Club Catal.) 3/3 (Advt.), A wonderful object to.. have a barrel of fun with. **1986** *Parents* Sept. 72/3 What they haven't bargained for is a wife who is so tired.. that she's even less of a barrel of laughs than she was while pregnant.

**base**, *n.*[1] Add: [III.] [15.] **e.** *Baseball. to load* (*fill*, etc.) *the bases*, to put a runner on all three bases; freq. *with the bases full* (*loaded*, etc., and conversely, *empty*); also as adj. phr. *bases-loaded* (also *-empty*).

**1894** *Spalding's Base Ball Guide* 58 To try for a homer over the heads of the out-fielders, is only admissible when the bases are full and a desperate chance has to be made. **1905** *Sporting Life* (U.S.) 2 Sept. 11/1 He helped materially to land the second game by bringing out a double with the bases filled. **1908** *Baseball Mag.* Dec. 35/2 With the bases all tenanted, 'Happy Jack' Melvin lacerated the firmament with a dollar and a quarter's worth of leather and filling. **1914** *Collier's* 1 Aug. 6/2 When the bases are loaded he stings 'em a mile. **1920** *Evening Star* (Washington, D.C.) 11 Oct. 21/1 On even rarer occasions is it that the colossus of swat connects for a round-trip swat with the bases loaded as did Smith. **1938** *Washington Star* 9 Oct. B10/8 With two out in the fourth innings and the bases empty, Bryant's spell was broken. **1944** *San Francisco Examiner* 5 July 21/4 Rube Fletcher.. walked three men to load the bases in the third frame. **1945** *Chicago Sun* 11 Oct. 19/6 This left the bases filled, and Richards quietly cleared them with a double. **1950** W. McCORMICK *Bases Loaded* xv. 171 Bases loaded, only one away, and Bronc Burnett to the plate. **1962** J. BROSNAN *Pennant Race* 124 He personally knocked Warren Spahn out of the box in the fifth, punching a bases-loaded single down the right field line. **1962** *Washington Post* 27 June 45/6 Bill White and Ken Boyer hit bases-empty round-trippers in the Cardinals' rout of the Cubs. **1965** *N.Y. Times* 4 July 3/3 With two out and the bases full, Frank Crosetti beat out a bunt. **1974** *State* (Columbia, S. Carolina) 26 Apr. 2-B/8 Jeff Grantz beat out a bunt to load the bases. **1976** *Billings* (Montana) *Gaz.* 5 July C1/4 Richard Farrell cracked a bases-empty homer in the second for the Giants. **1986** *N.Y. Post* 9 July 60/2 Wally Joyner hit a bases-loaded triple with one out to snap a scoreless tie and lift California into first place.

**baseband** ('beɪsbænd), *n. Telecommunications.* [f. BASE *n.*[1] + BAND *n.*[2]] **1.** A frequency band with a lower frequency limit close to zero; *spec.* such a band containing a signal before it is modulated on to a carrier wave; the frequency band occupied by an unmodulated signal or a signal used for modulation. Also, a baseband system.

**1960** *Times Rev. Industry* Oct. 65/2 The overall channel characteristics [are] . . fully up to agreed international standards even with basebands having as many as 2,700 channels. **1966** M. SCHWARTZ et al. *Communication Syst. & Techniques* iv. 173 The channel itself typically makes use of frequency ranges entirely different from those important in the baseband. **1972** *Sci. Amer.* Sept. 138/3 Coaxial cables can carry the bit stream directly at 'baseband', that is, without modulation of a carrier signal. **1983** E. TRUNDLE *Beginner's Guide Videocassette Recorders* ix. 184 The provision of input sockets for audio and video signals at baseband. **1983** *Austral. Microcomputer Mag.* Aug. 47/2 The alternatives provided between baseband and broadband provide a major division in local area network philosophies.

**2.** *attrib.*, *spec.* designating: (*a*) a signal used to modulate a carrier or transmitted without a carrier; (*b*) a telecommunication system in which signals are transmitted in this way.

**1961** E. J. BAGHDADY *Lect. Communication Syst. Theory* xix. 445 There are situations in which each of several different baseband signals (or messages) is first made to modulate the frequency of a . . sinusoidal carrier. **1975** D. G. FINK *Electronics Engineers' Handbk.* XXII. 57 The baseband repeater . . is the type usually employed for short-haul systems. . . The signal information is transferred within the repeater . . at baseband frequencies and transmitted on a radio-frequency channel. **1982** *Giant Bk. Electronics Projects* v. 201 The video and audio levels available from the baseband unit . . are entirely compatible with such modulators. **1983** *Austral. Microcomputer Mag.* Aug. 57/1 Time-division multiplexing permits baseband networks to carry multiple signals at baseband. **1987** T. HOUSLEY *Data Communications & Teleprocessing Syst.* (ed. 2) vii. 103 Over short distances and/or at low transmission speeds, we can send . . digital data signals straight down the line using a technique known as baseband signaling.

**basically**, *adv.* Add: **2.** In weakened, often parenthetical use and as a sentence-adverb: actually, in fact.

Freq. in speech; often condemned as more or less redundant.

**1929** *Collier's* 5 Jan. 41/1 It was basically a 'flop'. **1940** [see PEPSI-COLA *n.*]. **1969** [see INTO *prep.* 23]. **1969** L. MICHAELS *Going Places* 109, I know I'm attractive in a way, but basically I'm ugly. **1978** P. HOWARD *Weasel Words* v. 38 Basically has become a vogue as a conventional, almost meaningless rhetorical intensifier. **1984** *Washington Post* 14 Oct. K4/4 Basically, I solve your problem and show you that my company is a good company and stands behind its products—then you are a pigeon. **1987** *Daily Tel.* 4 Aug. 14/4 Mr. Titterington says: 'Basically, it was going to be a very Conservative show until I stuck my oar in.'

**Bastille**, *n.* Add: **5.** Special Comb. **Bastille Day** = QUATORZE JUILLET *n.*

**1900** *Outlook* (N.Y.) LXV. 909/1 The Spectator was in Paris on *Bastille Day. **1986** *Times* 16 July 17/3 By first invoking the ghost of President de Gaulle, . . and doing so moreover on Bastille Day—he has practically pinned the tricolor to his cause.

**batch**, *n.*[1] Add: **[6.]** **f.** *Computing.* A group of records processed together in a single operation using the same program.

**1956** *Jrnl. Assoc. Computing Machinery* III. 169 If this [address] function were known in advance for a particular batch of data and if it could be easily evaluated . . all items could be inserted initially in correct memory locations. **1964** T. W. MCRAE *Impact of Computers on Accounting* vi. 164 The

computer . . may run on to the end of the particular batch of data being processed. **1970** O. DOPPING *Computers & Data Processing* xvi. 252 The updating can be done in batches ('batch processing') or in real time. **1980** C. S. FRENCH *Computer Sci.* xvii. 92 At an early stage in processing, documents are arranged in batches, by being placed in a wallet or folder, or clipped together.

**[7.]** **b.** Special Combs.: **batch processing**, (*a*) in chemical engineering, the processing of raw materials in batches as opposed to continuously; (*b*) *Computing*, the processing of previously collected batches of data, computing jobs, etc., esp. without user intervention and usu. off-line, as a background process or at a time of low system activity.

**1948** C. TYLER *Chem. Engin. Econ.* (ed.3) v. 77 The trend in recent years has been toward the substitution of continuous for *batch processing. **1957** [see *chemical engineering* s.v. CHEMICAL *a.* 4b]. **1957** *IBM Jrnl. Res. & Devel.* I. 63/1 'Batch' processing techniques can be reserved for those applications, such as statistical analysis, that have an inherent batching requirement. **1979** J. E. ROWLEY *Mechanised In-House Information Syst.* I. 27 A data base can be designed for batch processing or real-time processing. **1980** C. S. FRENCH *Computer Sci.* xxxvi. 286 By its very nature a batch processing system will involve a degree of 'delay'.

hence (as a back-formation) **batch-process** *v. trans.*

**1964** *Datamation* May 39/1 The monitor would enable users to *batch process any mix of scientific, commercial, testing and production jobs. **1979** J. E. ROWLEY *Mechanised In-House Information Syst.* I. 65 Remote entry job processing. . . An on-line terminal is used to enter a job into the queue of jobs to be batch processed by the computer.

**Bayes** (beɪz), *n. Math.* The name of Thomas Bayes (1702–61), English mathematician, used *attrib.* and in the possessive to designate concepts relating to inverse probability, esp. **Bayes' theorem**, a theorem expressing the probability of one of a number of mutually exclusive events $H_i$, given some other event $E$, in terms of the probabilities of all the $H_i$ independently of $E$ and the probabilities of $E$ given each $H_i$.

**1865** I. TODHUNTER *Hist. Math. Theory Probability* xiv. 299 Lubbock and Drinkwater think that Bayes, or perhaps rather Price, confounded the probability given by Bayes's theorem with the probability given by the result just taken from Laplace. **1907** *Phil. Mag.* XIII. 366, I assume the truth of Bayes' theorem. **1922** R. A. FISHER in *Phil. Trans. R. Soc.* A. CCXXII. 324 The result, the datum, and the postulate implied by the scholium, have all been somewhat loosely spoken of as Bayes' Theorem. **1943** [see POSTERIOR *a.* 1 b]. **1967** CONDON & ODISHAW *Handbk. Physics* (ed. 2) I. xii. 164/2 Bayes' theorem is the cornerstone of inverse probability, a precise form of inductive inference that seeks to reason from observed events to the probabilities of the various hypotheses that may explain them. **1970** *Nature* 12 Sept. 1172/2 Empirical Bayes methods have been hailed as one of the major advances in modern statistics. **1985** *Brit. Med. Jrnl.* 9 Nov. 1354/1 Using Bayes' theorem . . more extensive information of this kind will enable us to make confident clinical diagnoses in sore throats. **1988** *Nature* 7 Apr. 496/2 A probabilistic argument based on the table leads to a likelihood ratio or Bayes factor of 100 in favour of the hypothesis H without even allowing for the elegance of the integers.

**Bayesian** ('beɪzɪən), *a.* and *n.* [f. *BAYES *n.* + -IAN.] **A.** *adj.* Of, pertaining to, or designating statistical methods based on Bayes' theorem.

**1956** R. A. FISHER *Statistical Methods & Sci. Inference* v. 111 (*heading*) Bayesian prediction. **1960**

Technometrics II. 341 (heading) Some remarks on the Bayesian solution of the single sample inspection scheme. **1965** Math. in Biol. & Med. (Med. Res. Council) III. 103 Various simple statistical procedures can be applied, using Bayesian or likelihood approaches, which depend on the assumptions that can be made about the prior probabilities of diseases and symptoms. **1972** A. W. F. EDWARDS Likelihood ii. 8 It [sc. the concept of likelihood] will .. be seen to supply precisely those elements which many hold to be essential in a scheme of inference, without any of the Bayesian features to which many object. **1976** Path. Ann. XI. 151 Three computer diagnostic methods were used in a group of psychiatric patients, a Bayesian method, discriminant function analysis, and a method using a logical decision tree. **1987** Jrnl. Pol. Econ. XCV. 658 Jovanovic's .. theory of firm growth in which firms uncover their true efficiency over time with a Bayesian learning process.
**B.** n. One who uses or advocates Bayesian methods.
**1962** M. S. BARTLETT in L. J. Savage et al. Found. Statistical Inference iii. 90 The Bayesian would not adopt a perfectly chosen and systematic design. **1973** Sci. Amer. May 83/1 Bayes's theorem has been widely exploited in recent years by statisticians who called themselves Bayesians, notably the late L. J. Savage.

**beam,** v. Add: [7.] **b.** Science Fiction. [Orig. from the U.S. television series Star Trek: see TREKKIE n. 2.] (a) intr. To travel through space as if along a beam of light or energy (esp. up to a spacecraft); (b) trans., to transport (someone or something) in this manner; freq. transf., esp. in catch-phr. **beam me up** (Scotty), i.e. out of an undesirable or dangerous situation.
The catch-phrase does not appear in this form in the original scripts (Mrs. M. B. Roddenberry).
**1966** RODDENBERRY & JOHNSON Man Trap in Star Trek (television script) 8 Sept., He beamed up to the ship with us—or something did. Ibid., Kirk speaking, three to beam up. Ibid., Captain, you can't just beam down here and bully us, and interfere with our work. **1967** Pop. Sci. Monthly Dec. 74/2 The 'Transporter' .. can convert matter into energy and 'beam' it to a fixed point, then reconvert it back into its original form. It is used for both crew and cargo. **1967-8** M. ARMEN Gamesters of Triskelion in Star Trek (television script), Kirk: Beam us up, Mr. Scott. **1984** Amer. Banker 31 July 52/1 'Beam me up Scotty, there's no prospect of finance down here.' Undoubtedly, that's what Star Trek's Captain Kirk, commander of the science-fiction Starship Enterprise, would say if he came here in search of bank loans to fund extraterrestrial activities. **1985** Melody Maker 22 June 6 Beam me up! Extra-terrestrial-being Grace Jones gets eyeball to eyeball with a passing stranger in order to practise her famed Vulcan neckgrip. **1987** Washington Post 21 Mar. F17 'Do you ever find yourself fantasizing about being "free"?' 'Beam me up, Scotty!'

**bear,** n.¹ Add: [III.] [10.] **bear market** Stock Exchange, a market characterized by the falling price of stock, etc. (see sense 8); opp. to bull market s.v. *BULL n.¹ 11.
**1903** H. I. SMITH Financial Dict. 63 *Bear market, a speculative term which signifies a declining market; in other words, that the tendency of prices is downward. **1926** H. J. WOLF Stud. Stock Speculation II. 25 If the above mentioned 'bear' will apply his remarks to a bear market, instead of a bull market, we are in agreement. **1971** H. D. BERMAN Stock Exchange (ed. 6) xiii. 127 It is the funds that are depressed, such as the capital trusts at the end of a bear market, which should be bought. **1986** What Investment July 15/3 Major bear markets of the past have always been caused by worldwide events.

**Beaujolais,** n. Add: **b. Beaujolais Nouveau** (nuː'vəʊ) [= new], a commercial name for young Beaujolais wine, sold during the first year of a vintage; **Beaujolais Primeur** (priː'mɜː(r)) [= early-season product], Beaujolais Nouveau, properly that sold during the first few months of a vintage.
**1972** Times 22 Nov. 16/4 Sir Charles Forte .. stopped at the counter set up to offer free tastings of the Beaujolais Nouveau in the foyer. The first sample he pronounced very green, acidic and tart. **1973** Times 15 Dec. 11/2 In the 1950s the restaurants of Lyons began to offer very young Beaujolais drawn from the cask within weeks of its vintaging. The vogue spread to Paris and, more recently, to export markets ... Some producers make a special type of wine ... 'Beaujolais Primeur' ... The 'Primeurs' of Beaujolais were .. released on .. November 15 ... They are known as 'Primeur' until the end of January, after which they are called 'Nouveau' until the next vintage. **1977** Washington Post 4 Aug. E1/4 Beaujolais became such a cult object that Beaujolais nouveau, the year's new wine, barely a month old, was flown across the Atlantic each November to make mouths pucker. **1979** Daily Tel. 3 Nov. 25/2 Prices for Beaujolais Nouveau or Primeur—there is no significance in the use of either name—should be around £2 to £2.25 per bottle. **1984** D. FRANCIS Proof vii. 76 A wine shipper telephoned that he'd reserved me fifty cases of Beaujolais Nouveau for November 15th ... I never waited for the Nouveau to be delivered but fetched it myself.

**beauty,** n. Senses II. 5-8 in Dict. become II. 6-9. Add: [I.] **5.** Particle Physics. [An arbitrary choice of name.] = BOTTOM n. 17.
**1977** [see BOTTOM n. 17]. **1978** Proc. Indian Nat. Sci. Acad. A. XLIV. 308 (heading) Beauty quark and new hadrons. **1979** [see TRUTH n. 8]. **1983** Sci. Amer. July 98/1 The first indication of the existence of quarks endowed with beauty came six years ago as the result of experiments in which a beam of high-energy protons was directed against a stationary target. **1985** Daily Tel. 7 May 18 Scientists have succeeded in proving that 'beauty' exists ... 'Beauty' lasts about one tenth of a millionth of a millionth of a second before decaying.

**beaver,** n.¹ Sense 1 e in Dict. becomes 1 f. Add: [1.] **e.** With capital initial. [tr. Chipewyan Tsa-ttiné, dwellers among beavers.] (a) (A member of) an Athapascan people of northern Alberta. Also attrib. or as adj.
**1801** A. MACKENZIE Voy. from Montreal ii. 17 The Slave and Beaver Indians .. would not be here till the time that the swans cast their feathers. **1881** [see DOGRIB n. (and a.) a]. **1916** P. E. GODDARD Beaver Indians (Anthropol. Papers Amer. Mus. Nat. Hist. X. VI.) 208 They often met Beaver from Vermilion and Fort St. John. **1946** J. J. HONIGMANN Ethnogr. & Acculturation Fort Nelson Slave (Yale Univ. Publ. Anthropol. No. 33) 133 The Cree interpreter .. who is part Beaver, was positive that the Beaver had a prophet in his grandfather's time. **1975** J. V. WRIGHT Prehist. Lake Athabasca iii. 143 The western portion of the lake was occupied by another group: possibly Athabascan-speaking Beavers.
(b) The Athapaskan language spoken by this people.
[**1862** R. G. LATHAM Elements Comparative Philol. lv. 391 The Beaver Indian is transitional to the Slave and the Chepewyan proper.] **1916** P. E. GODDARD Beaver Indians (Anthropol. Papers Amer. Mus. Nat. Hist. X. VI.) 209 As far as phonetics are concerned the Sarsi language is more nearly akin to Beaver than to any other east of the Rocky Mountains. **1933** [see DOGRIB n. (and a.) b]. **1946** J. J. HONIGMANN Ethnogr. & Acculturation Fort Nelson Slave (Yale Univ. Publ. Anthropol. No. 33) 130 The Cree, in interpersonal relations with the Slave, must speak either an Athapaskan dialect (generally Beaver or

Slave or a mixture of both) or must speak English. **1977** [see SARCEE *a.* and *n.*].

**bed**, *n.* Add: [V.] [19.] **bed-hopping** *a. colloq.*, habitually changing sexual partners; engaging in numerous casual sexual affairs, promiscuous; also as *n.*; hence (as back-formation) **bed-hop** *v. intr.*

**1943** S. LEWIS *Gideon Planish* xxx. 391, I might be able to use the lowdown on the virtuous shenanigans that Marduc and that *bed-hopping daughter of his may pull from now on. **1965** *New Republic* 4 Sept. 30/3 After all, there has been plenty of bed-hopping in religiously replete eras. **1979** J. COOPER *Class* ix. 162 The bedrooms have .. interlocking doors, so people can bedhop easily. **1986** *Observer* 19 Jan. 16/3, I would have had to read 'Goldilocks' under the bed-covers if they'd realised it was a story about 'A little girl who goes bed-hopping and gets her oats'.

**beefalo** ('biːfələʊ), *n.* Chiefly *U.S.* [Blend of BEEF *n.* and BUFFALO *n.*; cf. CATALO *n.*] A cross-bred livestock animal that is three-eighths bison and five-eighths domestic cow.

**1974** *National Observer* (U.S.) 17 Aug. 8/2 Basolo discusses cross breeding of buffalo and beef cattle to produce hybrid beefalo. **1974** *Daily Colonist* (Victoria, B.C.) 10 Dec. 17/4 D.C. (Buffalo Bill) Basolo believes his new king of the range—the beefalo—will soon be providing juicy steaks at low prices. **1976** *Sci. Amer.* Sept. 49/2 The objectives of the research should include .. the establishment through genetic techniques of new species of animals (such as the beefalo). **1981** *Animal Production* XXX. 215/1 It is not known how the Beefalo breeder overcame the fertility problem described .. as the limiting factor to the commercial development of Cattalo. **1986** *New Yorker* 8 Sept. 30/3, I was approached about having beefalo, but we wanted buffalo. Lots of people think it's an endangered species, but it's not.

**beer**, *n.*[1] Add: [II.] [4.] **beer belly** *slang*, (*a*) a protruding stomach or paunch caused by drinking large quantities of beer; (*b*) *transf.*, one who has such a stomach.

**1942** BERREY & VAN DEN BARK *Amer. Thes. Slang* §121/7 *Drunkard's paunch*, beer barrel, *-belly, -muscle or tumor. **1969** *Rolling Stone* 28 June 26/1 Woods pauses to tuck his shirt between a beer belly and a silver belt buckle. **1972** G. BEINE *Land of Coyote* 26 They described Pa as a beer-belly and said Ma was unfriendly. **1986** D. GETHIN *Dane's Testament* xviii. 120 He wore a ridiculously tight shirt that accentuated his beer belly.

**beer gut** *slang* = *beer belly (a).
**1976** *Sounds* 11 Dec. 12/1 A mouthful only as big as the man's beer-gut. **1983** *Listener* 6 Jan. 14/2 'The Teds are dated,' jeered an Ilford cat. 'They're all middle-aged with a beer gut and size 15 brothel-creepers.' **1986** *Los Angeles Times* 10 July III. 2/2 Fregosi took to wearing the jacket .. when he began to develop a beer gut while trying to play for the Mets.

**beggar**, *n.* Add: [6.] [b.] (Later examples.) Also euphemistically for BUGGER *n.*[1] 2 b (prob. from at least the early 20th cent.).
**1903** 'T. COLLINS' *Such is Life* (1944) i. 62 He came down on his hand, poor beggar; it's swelled like a boxing-glove. **1904** KIPLING *Traffics & Discov.* 343 'E said he was born at the back o' Vancouver Island, and *all* the time the beggar was a balmy Barnado Orphan! **1942** E. LANGLEY *Pea-Pickers* (1958) II. ii. 93 At last, the poor little beggars did their dialogue to a thunder of well-fed applause. **1978** *Fortune* 4 Dec. 100 The passenger's up there in the air flying at 500 miles an hour—his butt is on the plane for five hours. .. Then he comes down, and the plane starts taxiing in from the runway, and look: the beggars are already standing up, ready to jump off. **1980** F. WELDON *Puffball* 239 The surgeon found the head: used

forceps. He sweated. 'Little beggar,' he said. 'You seem to like it in there.'

**Belauan** *n.* and *a.*, var. *PALAUAN *n.* and *a.*

**bell**, *n.*[1] Add: [IV.] [12.] **bell curve**, a graph of a normal (Gaussian) distribution; also *fig.*
**1970** *Balance Sheet* Oct. 64/2 Research may be used to classify the effort into three basic methods: .. (2) through use of the normal distribution hypothesis (*bell curve) [etc.]. **1973** T. PYNCHON *Gravity's Rainbow* I. 51 Exit doors painted beige, but with edges smudged browner in bell-curves of farewell by the generation of hands. **1978** PASACHOFF & KUTNER *University Astron.* iv. 96 If the errors are purely random, then this plot will look like a Gaussian distribution (also called a normal or bell curve).

**bells and whistles** *colloq.* [as on a fairground organ], attractive additional features or trimmings, esp. in *Computing.*
**1977** *Byte* July 122/2 This simple circuit .. even has a few outputs that can be used to provide user defined functions, such as enabling external devices or turning on *bells and whistles. **1983** *Austral. Personal Computer* Dec. 82/3, 1-2-3 has a full complement of the usual bells and whistles ... Column widths can be varied, cells protected, screen split in two, models split, merged and printed. **1984** *Sunday Times* 26 Aug. 49/1 There are more than 600 microsystems on the market so it is hardly surprising that the manufacturers have taken to hanging a few bells and whistles on to their machines to get them noticed.

**Bell** (bɛl), *n.*[5] [The name of the N. Amer. *Bell* System or Telephone Company (from the surname of Alexander Graham Bell (1847-1922), Scots-born American inventor of the telephone), part of AT&T and before divestiture in 1984 the major U.S. telephone company; cf. AUNTIE *n.* b.] **Ma Bell**, a familiar name for the Bell System (see quot. 1947), orig. applied somewhat wryly by its employees; similarly **Mother Bell**; and hence **Baby Bell**, any of the subsidiary regional U.S. telephone companies after divestiture.
**1947** *Sat. Even. Post* 10 May 16/1 [Bell Telephone Laboratories] is apparently interested in their every waking and sleeping hour—a maternal solicitude which is largely responsible for the title of Ma Bell. **1948** *Bell Telephone Mag.* Winter 244/1 Mother Bell found that a lot of people wanted to work for her, even on a short-term basis. **1960** *Business Week* 8 Oct. 98/1 This year Mother Bell has really lived up to her name; she's given birth to a whole brood of new telephonic devices for the home. **1962** *Look* 29 Aug. 22/1 Sixty-four million [telephones] belong to the vast Bell System owned by the $24 billion American Telephone and Telegraph Company, known to its two million stockholders as AT&T, to its 781,000 employees as 'Ma Bell' and to at least one U.S. senator as 'the greatest monopoly in the history of the earth'. **1973** *Fortune* Feb. 130/3 As it has turned out, the quality of some phone lines is often below what Ma Bell promised. **1980** *Business Week* 26 May 110/2 The computer industry has already started to call the prospective AT & T subsidiary 'Baby Bell', anticipating that it will be a powerful clone of its mother. **1980** *Forbes* (N.Y.) 1 Sept. 6/3 Mother Bell is stepping up its efforts to keep foreign traffic humming without becoming a burden on the expense account. **1987** L. D. ESTLEMAN *Lady Yesterday* xvii. 123 You can still find it in the Yellow Pages ... Ma Bell knows.

**belt**, *n.*[1] Add: [6.] **beltway** *U.S.*, a highway circling all or part of a city or other metropolitan area, esp. that around Washington, D.C.; a ring road; also *transf.* (freq. *attrib.*) Washington, D.C., as the seat of the U.S. government.

**1952** *Sun* (Baltimore) 22 Jan. 7/2 Preliminary construction on the proposed *beltway circling the city through Baltimore county is expected to get under way. **1973** *Times* 13 Aug. 10/7 The beltway built round Washington to relieve traffic jams was jammed with traffic. **1986** *Observer* 14 Dec. 12/11 Two weeks ago Reagan was complaining that the whole affair was a 'Beltway' scandal, of interest only to people who live in the self-obsessed world inside Washington's ring road.

**benign,** *a.* Add: [**3.**] **b.** *benign neglect,* non-interference or neglect as a policy intended to benefit the subject more than continual attention; well-intentioned or beneficial neglect. orig. *U.S.*

**1970** D. P. MOYNIHAN in *N.Y. Times* 1 Mar. 69/4 The time may have come when the issue of race could benefit from a period of 'benign neglect'. **1971** *N.Y. Times* 27 June 11. 31/6 Black composers and women composers share a heritage of musical subjugation—of malign as well as benign neglect. **1977** *Harper's Mag.* Jan. 85/2 How we do, and at the same time, do not, think about our children's books, is best reflected by that infuriating form of benign neglect, the roundup review. **1985** *Daily Tel.* 19 Jan. 16/2 How difficult it is for modern governments—busy, garrulous, interfering bodies—to exercise 'benign neglect'.

**Benioff** ('bɛnɪɒf), *n. Geol.* [The name of (Victor) Hugo *Benioff* (1899-1968), U.S. seismologist.] **1.** Used *attrib.* and *absol.* with reference to a type of seismograph invented by Benioff (*Bull. Seismol. Soc. Amer.* 1935, XXV. 283-309), in which a horizontal rod, fixed at one end, carries an armature at its free end that is separated by a small gap from a fixed permanent magnet, so that movement of the rod induces a voltage in the armature.

**1936** N. H. HECK *Earthquakes* vi. 77 The Benioff seismometer differs..in that the principle of the horizontal pendulum is not used. **1938** *Bull. Seismol. Soc. Amer.* XXVIII. 217 The long-period Benioff record for a portion of an ordinary day. *Ibid.,* The general effect of the dying out of traffic on the short-period Benioff is illustrated. **1958** C. F. RICHTER *Elem. Seismol.* xv. 225 The Benioff seismometer adapts well to long-period recording. **1968** *Trans. Amer. Geophysical Union* XLIX. 499/1 The Benioff variable reluctance seismograph, developed in 1935, was selected for use in the worldwide standard seismograph network.

**2. Benioff zone:** an inclined zone of high seismicity situated beneath island-arc systems at the overlap of oceanic crust and a continental margin.

**1968** *Sci. News* 30 Mar. 301/2 What started the hypothesis was doctoral candidate George E. Rouse's observation that the deep quake zones around the planet—called Benioff zones—all seem to lie at surprisingly similar angles. **1971** I. G. GASS et al. *Understanding Earth* xix. 271/1 These inclined zones of seismicity characterize all active island-arc systems and are known as Benioff zones. **1972** *Sci. Amer.* May 57/3 Inclined earthquake zones, called Benioff zones, underlie active volcanic chains and have a variety of complex shapes. **1984** *Nature* 9 Feb. 505/1 The existence in deep Benioff zones of persistent planes of failure, or faults, has been an open question.

**best,** *a.* and *adv.* Add: [**A.**] [**I.**] [**1.**] **e.** *best boy* orig. and chiefly *U.S.,* the principal assistant to the chief electrician or 'gaffer' in a film crew.

**1937** J. ARNOLD in N. Naumburg *We make Movies* xi. 158 The gaffer's assistant..answers to the amusing title of *best boy!* **1954** *Western Folklore* XIII. 9 'Gaffer'..usually applies peculiarly to electrical foremen. The 'gaffer's' assistant is the 'best boy'. **1977** *Washington Post* 27 Feb. E13/2 There appears to

be a long tradition of providing detailed and exact information on cast and production personnel, down to such lower rungs of the status ladder as 'gaffer', 'key grip' and even, occasionally, 'best boy'. **1983** *Verbatim* Summer 8/1 I've known a few 'best boys', and most of them have been very close to the time of life for Social Security.

[**11.**] **c.** *Comb.* with prep. used *attrib.,* as *best before date,* the date marked on a food package, after which the contents may be expected to deteriorate. Cf. *sell-by date* s.v. SELL *v.* 15 b.

[**1980** *Food Labelling Regulations* (Statutory Instrument No. 1849) Reg. 20 (1), The minimum durability of a food shall be indicated by—(*a*) the words 'best before' followed by the date up to and including which the food can reasonably be expected to retain its specific properties if properly stored.] **1983** *Which?* Oct. 445/4 We'd prefer to see them labelled like other foods (some supermarkets already do label them in this way) with a 'sell-by' or 'best before' date. **1990** *Times* 28 Mar. 2/6 A particular concern has been the re-dating of food sold off cheap near to the expiry of the 'best before' date and then re-dated to appear on market stalls and the like.

**beta,** *n.* Add: [**2.**] **j.** *beta test,* a test of machinery, software, etc. in course of final development, carried out by a party or parties unconnected with the developer (freq. *attrib.*); so *beta testing, beta-test v. trans., beta-tester.* Cf. *alpha test* s.v. *ALPHA n.* 3 g.

**1978** *Aviation Week* 6 Feb. 243/3 A competition currently is under way to select a contractor to design and build a Beta testbed facility for evaluation during Fiscal 1980. **1981** *Electronics* 24 Feb. 250/2 Xidak has added a symbolic debugger that is now at the beta test-site stage. **1982** *Inc.* Jan. 68 The software is tested, usually by both an inhouse staff (called alpha-testers) and by outsiders (called beta-testers), and the manual is typeset and printed. **1982** *Electronics* 24 Feb. 174/3 Only now, following beta testing at about a dozen installations, is the system ready for customer deliveries. **1982** *Computerworld* 8 Mar. 63/3 The system is currently being beta tested and general customer deliveries are expected to begin this July. **1985** *Times* 21 Mar. 39/1 (Advt.), Problem solving together with alpha and beta testing of new products require a minimum of 2 years experience of IBM Assembler or Z80 programming. **1985** *Austral. Personal Computer* Nov. 77/1 The review software was a Beta-test version with a photocopied draft of the manual.

**4.** [Abbrev. *BETAMAX n.*] (With capital initial.) A name for one of the standard formats for videocassettes, orig. called *Betamax* (q.v.).

**1977** *Fortune* Sept. 180/2 There was a brief attempt by Sony back in 1975 to get Matsushita to adopt its Beta format, but by then the larger company was convinced it was perfecting a superior machine. **1984** *Listener* 19 July 34/2 There are around 10,000 rental outlets for tapes, many already reluctantly stocking the same titles in two, or even three formats (VHS, Beta and V2000). **1987** *Which?* June 286/2 Beta is gradually disappearing but you may find a few models in the shops.

**Betamax** ('bi:təmæks), *n.* [f. Jap. *beta*(-*beta* all over + -*max,* abbrev. of MAXIMUM *n.,* after the condensed format in which the signal is recorded. The formation was app. influenced by BETA *n.* (Jap. *beta*).] A proprietary name for the videocassette format also known as *Beta* (*BETA n.* 4).

**1975** *Pop. Photogr.* Aug. 208/3 But Sony..won't give up: its new Betamax ½ in. cassette system uses tape very sparingly. **1975** *Official Gaz.* (U.S. Patent Office) 2 Sept. TM21 Sony Corporation... Filed Oct. 29, 1974. *Betamax* for magnetic video recorders and/or reproducers and magnetic media therefor... First use Oct. 9, 1974. **1975** *Newsweek* 8 Dec. 57/2 Sony's Betamax video recorder unit will allow viewers to tape a show on one channel while watching another and, thanks to a digital timing device, to record programs while away from home. **1977** *Trade Marks Jrnl.* 19 Jan. 95/2 *Betamax* . . Electrical and electronic apparatus . . tapes for recording and reproducing visual and/or aural signals; and reels and cassettes . . . Sony Kabushiki Kaisha (Sony Corporation).

**bias**, *n.* Add: [7.] **b.** In recording on magnetic media, a high-frequency waveform on which the signal is superimposed in order to avoid distortion; also, the magnetic field generated by this waveform.
  **1949** FRAYNE & WOLFE *Elem. of Sound Recording* xxix. 588 The unmagnetized wire or tape is subjected in the recording magnet to a field compounded of the audio signal and a high-frequency component called the bias. **1961** G. A. BRIGGS *A to Z in Audio* 22 The strength of bias should be adjusted for optimum results with each type of tape. **1986** *Making Music* Apr. 35/1 Vesta recommend TDK SA-X or Maxell XLI15 cassettes (ie high bias types only, as usual).

**bibliometrics** (ˌbɪblɪəʊ'mɛtrɪks), *n. pl.* (const. as *sing.*). [f. BIBLIO- + -*metrics*, as in *econometrics*, etc.: see METRIC *a.*[1] 2.] The branch of library science concerned with the application of mathematical and statistical analysis to bibliography; the statistical analysis of books, articles, or other publications.
  **1969** A. PRITCHARD in *Jrnl. Documentation* XXV. 349 The present writer has never found the term *statistical bibliography* at all satisfactory. . . M. G. Kendall . . suggested that the name of the subject be changed. . . It is suggested that a better name . . is *bibliometrics*, i.e. the application of mathematics and statistical methods to books and other media of communication. An intensive search of the literature has failed to reveal any previous use of this term and an approach to the OED again failed to find that the term had been used before. **1972** *Jrnl. Amer. Soc. Information Sci.* XXIII. 313/1 *Bibliometrics* is quantitative analysis of gross bibliographical units such as books, journal articles, and the like . . . Brooks . . recommends one method of bibliometric analysis for use in 'reducing the quantitative untidiness of scientific documentation, information systems and library services'. **1978** NICHOLAS & RITCHIE (*title*) Literature and bibliometrics. **1988** *Daily Tel.* 5 July 19/6 'Bibliometrics' . . in plain English seems to be simply the weighing and measuring of the constant avalanche of papers, books, journals and other academic publications.
  Hence **biblio'metric** *a.*
  **1969** R. A. FAIRTHORNE in *Jrnl. Documentation* XXV. 319 (*heading*) Empirical hyperbolic distributions . . for bibliometric description and prediction. **1972** B. L. MAURSTAD (*Case Western Reserve Univ. thesis title*) Concerning the structural properties in the literature of the art historian—a bibliometric study. **1976** *Survey* Spring 73 Some works contain indicators computed in the USSR. Most of them could largely be described in terms of bibliometric aspects of library science. **1989** *Times* 26 Aug. 4/3 The use of 'bibliometric' methods to assess academics' performance—by measuring the number of times a person's work is cited by others—has caused much controversy in the United States.

**bicyclic** (baɪ'saɪklɪk, -'sɪk-), *a.*[2] [f. BI-[2] + CYCLIC *a.*] **1.** Consisting of or having two circles (see quots.). *rare*⁻⁰.
  **1889** *Cent. Dict.*, *Bicyclic*, consisting of or having two circles; specifically, in *bot.*, in two whorls, as the stamens of a flower. *Ibid.* s.v. *Chuck*⁴, *Bicyclic chuck*, a contrivance by which two rigidly connected points are forced to move on the circumference of two fixed circles.

**2.** *Chem.* (Composed of molecules) containing two usu. fused rings of atoms.
  **1907** *Chem. News* 30 Aug. 107/1 (*heading*) Methane 1,8-dicarboxylic acid. A new bicyclic ketone. **1923** *Chem. Abstr.* XVII. 749 (*heading*) Bicyclic and polycyclic compounds with bridging atoms. **1974** GILL & WILLIS *Pericyclic Reactions* vi. 157 The initial products have the expected stereochemistry and can be isomerized further to bicyclic molecules. **1977** J. L. HARPER *Population Biol. of Plants* 414 The plants contain small amounts of single bicyclic alkaloids in their inflorescences.

**big**, *a.* Add: [3.] **i.** In colloq. phr. *you're a big boy* (or *girl*) *now*, etc.: a usu. mock-serious reminder that the subject is no longer a child, and should act (or be treated) like an adult. orig. *U.S.*
  **1896** W. CATHER in *Home Monthly* Dec. 10 She is a big girl now, you know, and came out last winter. **1934** Z. N. HURSTON *Jonah's Gourd Vine* i. 25 Youse uh big boy now and you am gwine take offa 'im and swaller all his filth lak you been doin' here of late. **1938** M. ALLINGHAM *Fashion in Shrouds* xviii. 318 'I'm getting a big girl now,' she said. 'You can mention it in front of me.' **1961** 'B. WELLS' *Day Earth caught Fire* vii. 114 'I wouldn't say they were sex-mad, but they'd like to be . . .' Jeannie said with a gay smile: 'I'm a big girl now.' **1964** 'C. E. MAINE' *Never let Up* xv. 148 I'm a big boy now and I can put myself to bed. So why don't you do as I say. **1986** J. SAVARIN *Naja* ii. 39 Rhiannon's a big girl now and is quite capable of looking after herself.

**bijection** (baɪ'dʒɛkʃ(ə)n), *n. Math.* [f. BI-[2] after INJECTION *n.* 5.] A mapping that is both injective and surjective.
  **1963** D. G. BOURGIN *Mod. Algebraic Topol.* x. 215 If Ψ is both a monomorphism and an epimorphism, it is a bijection (so that a bijection is a sort of underprivileged bimorphism). **1968** E. T. COPSON *Metric Spaces* vii. 86 A mapping *f*: $E_1 \rightarrow E_2$ which is both an injection and a surjection is called a *bijection*. **1975** I. STEWART *Concepts Mod. Math.* ix. 128 Quite generally, two sets will have the same number of elements if and only if there is a bijection between them. **1982** W. S. HATCHER *Logical Found. Math.* viii. 249 The theory of cardinals is the study of properties of sets that are invariant under bijections.
  So **bi'jective** *a.*, of the nature of or pertaining to a bijection.
  **1962** J. T. MOORE *Elem. Abstr. Algebra* i. 8 A bijective mapping determines and is determined by a one-to-one correspondence between the elements of the two sets. **1982** W. S. HATCHER *Logical Found. Math.* iii. 82 It was Cantor (and also Dedekind) who defined the notion of cardinal similarity (i.e. sameness of number) of two sets as being the existence of a bijective (1-1 onto) correspondence between the two sets.

**bilayer** ('baɪleɪə(r)), *n. Biol.* and *Chem.* [f. BI-[2] II + LAYER *n.*] A layer or film two molecules thick; *esp.* one composed of lipids or phospholipids, as in cell membranes.
  **1962** *Nature* 9 June 979/1 This experimental structure . . is . . liquid in the plane of the bilayer. **1964** *Jrnl. Molec. Biol.* VIII. 149 Both faces of the bilayer are presumed to be covered with a molecular layer of protein. **1974** *Sci. Amer.* Mar. 27/2 The lipids in membranes . . form a bilayer, two layers back to back, so that their hydrophilic heads constitute the top and bottom surfaces of the membrane and their hydrophobic tails are buried in the membrane interior. **1976** *Nature* 19 Feb. 601/1 When immersed in an excess amount of water, bilayers of zwitterionic lecithin form a lamellar lattice. **1982** T. M. DEVLIN *Textbk. Biochem.* v. 230 This bilayer conformation is the basic lipid structure of all biological membranes.

**bi-level** ('baɪˌlɛvəl), *a.* and *n.* Also bilevel. [f. BI-[2] + LEVEL *n.*] **A.** *adj.* Having or functioning

on two levels, arranged on two planes; *spec.* (*N. Amer.*) designating a style of two-storey house in which the lower storey is partially sunk below ground level, and the main entrance is placed on an intermediate level between the two storeys. Cf. SPLIT-LEVEL *a.* 1 a.
**1929** *Jrnl. Gen. Physiol.* XII. 78 As curves of this shape are encountered very often in biochemical investigations (dissociation curves, titration curves, etc.) we have introduced the.. term 'bilevel' by which they may be designated. **1960** [see BRUNCH *n.* b]. **1968** *House & Garden Plans Guide* 124/1 This bi-level plan with a complete guest complex on the ground floor is perfect for the family that welcomes week-end visitors. **1977** R. WHITAKER *Fodor's Railways of World* 41 Amtrak-designed bi-level cars .. will provide coach seats, sleeping compartments and.. upstairs diners will enjoy a much smoother ride. **1983** L. WALKER *Amer. Shelter* 261 (*caption*) 1975 Plantation colonial style bi-level house. **1985** *News of World* 3 Mar. 13/2 (Advt.), Cab comforts include separate driver's seat with built-in head restraint, powerful heater and bi-level ventilation system.
**B.** *n.* A bi-level house. *N. Amer.*
**1965** *Best Homes* XXXVIII. 20/1 The clean contemporary lines of the exterior, in the styling so well-loved in California and other forward-looking states, distinguish this practical bi-level. **1972** *N.Y. Law Jrnl.* 31 Oct. 19/8 (Advt.), Kentwood Lake Estates.. Colonials—Ranches—BiLevels. **1983** L. WALKER *Amer. Shelter* 261 Once inside the bi-level, it functions as a simple two-story house. **1986** *N.Y. Times* 19 Oct. VIII. 9/1 Its properties.. range from single-family prewar colonials and expanded Cape Cods on small lots to large bilevels on quarter-acre plots.

**binary** *a.* and *n.* Add: [A.] **n.** *binary tree* (*Computing*): a tree in which each node has two or fewer subtrees or pointers, esp. a balanced tree of this kind; a configuration that can be represented in this way. Cf. *B-TREE *n.*
**1960** *Computer Jrnl.* III. 84/2 Any other point [than the root] is connected to one and only one point in the next lower level and up to *n* points in the next higher level. For a binary tree, *n* = 2 and we shall discuss only binary trees in what follows. **1968** D. E. KNUTH *Art of Computer Programming* I. ii. 315 General trees are usually represented in terms of some equivalent binary tree inside a computer. **1983** P. LINZ *Programming Concepts & Problem Solving* x. 255 Arithmetic expressions can also be represented by binary trees. **1984** *Sci. News* 16 June 380/2 Underpinning NON VON's architecture is a structural configuration known as a 'binary tree'. In it, a single, tiny processor is connected to two identical ones beneath it, each of which is in turn connected to two more below it, and so on.

**bind**, *v.* Add: [III.] [10.] **d.** *trans. Chem.* and *Biochem.* To combine chemically with; to form a chemical bond with.
**1928** *Jrnl. Gen. Physiol.* VIII. 271 The data appear to indicate that part of the metallic element is bound by casein in such a way as to produce a complex ion. **1930** *Jrnl. Biol. Chem.* LXXXVIII. 265 For 1 cc. of solution the glutamic acid will bind 0.07 mg. of iron. **1968** PASSMORE & ROBSON *Compan. Med. Stud.* I. xxix. 19/2 The possession by blood of carbonic anhydrase, and of buffers which bind H+, is the chief reason why blood is a better carrier of $CO_2$ than water. **1970** R. W. McGILVERY *Biochem.* vi. 116 The peptide chains of such enzymes have a third function. In addition to binding the substrate and providing groups required for catalysis, they also must be capable of binding the coenzyme. **1988** *New Scientist* 10 Dec. 17/2 The coral soil is basically composed of calcium carbonate which will bind strontium-90.
**e.** *intr. Chem.* and *Biochem.* To combine

chemically *with*; to become chemically bound *to*.
**1959** A. WHITE et al. *Princ. Biochem.* (ed. 2) xii. 208 Carbon monoxide competes with oxygen in binding with hemoglobin. **1965** *Biochim. & Biophys. Acta* CIII. 532 (*heading*) Failure of tetracycline to bind to *Escherichia coli* ribosomes. **1973** *Nature* 14 Sept. 64/2 'Paraquat' seems to have a particular affinity for lung tissue, where it probably binds to cell membranes. **1979** D. R. HOFSTADTER *Gödel, Escher, Bach* (1980) xvi. 516 Each base in one strand faces a complementary base in the other strand, and binds to it. **1982** *Sci. Amer.* June 50/3 Glutamate or aspartate .. supply negatively charged carboxylate (COO⁻) groups; it is primarily these groups that bind to the calcium ion.

**bio-**, *comb. form.* Add: ˌbioavaila'bility *Med.*, the proportion of a drug which reaches its site of pharmacological activity when introduced into the body; more loosely, that proportion of any substance so introduced which enters the circulation.
**1971** *Compton Yearbk.* 224/2 The FDA began to insist that any claims of *bioavailability equivalency made by the makers of generic drugs be true. **1979** *Daily Tel.* 5 Dec. 18 To avoid any problems associated with differing bio-availabilities, it does make sense, for some drugs, to prescribe by brand name to ensure the patient always receives the same quality of preparation. **1983** *Oxf. Textbk. Med.* I. VII. 5/2 By definition, the bioavailability of a drug after intravenous administration is 100 per cent. **1985** *Brit. Med. Jrnl.* 9 Nov. 1332/2 The bioavailability of iron in domestic water supplies is not known.
ˈbiohazard, a risk to mankind or the environment, *esp.* one arising out of biological or medical work, e.g. with micro-organisms; something that presents or constitutes such a risk.
**1965** *New Scientist* 30 Sept. 858/2 The control of *biohazards is a new kind of problem in cancer research. Only recently it has become apparent that viruses, which had been thought to be species-specific, can cross from one species to another and thus spread disease. **1975** *Nature* 5 June 442/1 This meeting was organised to review scientific progress in research on recombinant DNA molecules and to discuss appropriate ways to deal with the potential biohazards of this work. **1986** *Water, Air & Soil Pollution* XXVIII. 385 Exposure to $H_2S$ at the levels reported here may be less of a biohazard than previously supposed.
hence **bio'hazardous** *a.*, of, pertaining to, or constituting a biohazard.
**1975** *Sci. Amer.* July 32/1 The National Academy of Sciences had been urged to consider the 'possibility that potentially *biohazardous consequences might result from widespread and injudicious use' of these techniques. **1979** F. J. DYSON *Disturbing the Universe* xvi. 181 An ordinance was passed.. subjecting biohazardous research to municipal supervision. **1984** *Cancer Res.* XLIV. 478/1 Radioimmunoassays are both expensive and potentially biohazardous.
**biomass**, (*b*) (potential) fuel material derived immediately from living matter; living matter regarded as a source of fuel.
**1975** *Chem. & Engin. News* 2 June 19/2 Klass has computed the data for several proposed schemes for converting biomass into fuels. **1976** *Mech. Engin.* July 16/1 All these potential fuel sources, the organic matter produced through photosynthesis, are collectively called 'biomass'. **1986** *Forestry* LIX. 238 The potential of eucalypts for producing biomass and fuelwood has not been fully explored.

**biogas** (ˈbaɪəʊgæs), *n.* [f. BIO- + GAS *n.*[1]] Fuel gas (chiefly methane and carbon dioxide) obtained by the bacterial decomposition of animal and vegetable waste in the absence of

oxygen, often in a specially built digester or fermenter. Freq. *attrib.*
**1971** *Jrnl. Sci. of Food & Agric.* XXII. 164 (*heading*) Increased production of biogas from cowdung by adding other agricultural waste. **1978** *New Internationalist* May 13/1 If . . Hadji instead of burning cow-dung were to put it through a biogas digestor he would finish up with both methane to use as a fuel and with a solid residue which makes a valuable fertilizer. **1979** *Nature* 8 Mar. 117/1 In Szechwan province alone, 17 million people use biogas for cooking and lighting. **1985** B. W. ALDISS *Helliconia Winter* ix. 142 As the refuse rotted underground, it gave off biogas. **1986** *Illustr. Weekly India* 13 July 65/2 In order to reduce burden of fuel wood on the forests, 3,300 biogas plants were also installed during the period.

**biostatistics** (ˌbaɪəʊstəˈtɪstɪks), *n. pl.* (const. as *sing.*). [f. BIO- + STATISTICS *n. pl.*] The statistical study of biological data, esp. mortality and life expectancy (cf. *vital statistics* s.v. VITAL *a.* 4 d).
**1890** in WEBSTER. **1928** in Stedman *Med. Dict.* (ed. 10). **1953** *Postgrad. Med.* XIII. 334 (*heading*) Biostatistics—and why! **1960** *Jrnl. Med. Educ.* XXXV. 654/2 There is no longer any urgent reason why biostatistics should be identified with public health and preventive medicine. **1974** *Nature* 8 Nov. 178/2 While I hope that this modest analysis will be instructive and entertaining to students of biostatistics, I regret that astrologers may be disappointed. **1985** *Times* 20 May 25/6 (Advt.), Temporary lecturer in biostatistics.
Hence **biosta'tistical** *a.*; **biostati'stician** *n.*
**1953** *Postgrad. Med.* XIII. 334/1 To a good many clinicians, a biostatistician is a mechanism devoted mainly to asking embarrassing questions after it is too late to get an answer. **1961** WEBSTER, Biostatistical. **1963** *Poultry Sci.* XLII. 1282/1 (*heading*) Biostatistical study of growth in chickens. **1974** *Latin Amer. Econ. Rep.* 15 Mar. 42/2 A team of Pescaperú marine biologists and biostatisticians left for Panama to study anchovy resources and other species in Panamanian waters. **1981** *Brit. Med. Jrnl.* 3 Oct. 917/2 The dangers of biostatisticians taking over the design, conduct, and analysis of clinical trials. **1986** *N.Y. Times* 25 Aug. B7/4 The marriage of Alice J. Hausman . . to Jesse Aaron Berlin, an independent biostatistical consultant in Boston, took place yesterday.

**biostratigraphy** (ˌbaɪəʊstrəˈtɪgrəfɪ), *n.* [ad. F. *biostratigraphie* (L. Dollo 1904, in *Mém. de la Soc. Belge de Géol.* XVIII. 213): see BIO-, STRATIGRAPHY *n.*] Stratigraphy based on information provided by fossils; (see also quot. 1928).
**1928** *Jrnl. Paleont.* II. 158 Paleontology is more nearly related to zoölogy and botany, on the one hand, and to geology on the other. For these two major divisions of paleontology Dollo proposed the two terms 'Paleobiology' and 'Biostratigraphy'. **1945** M. F. GLAESSNER *Princ. Micropalaeont.* i. 6 Recent work on the morphogeny of foraminifera . . tends to bring micropalaeontology in line with the main trends of modern palaeontology, to which, among others, the names palaeobiology, palaeo-ecology, biostratigraphy have been applied. **1969** [see *lithostratigraphy* s.v. LITHO-]. **1975** *Nature* 18 Sept. 209/2 The Vendian and Yudomian are of similar age and the detailed biostratigraphy is uncertain, so that it is hard to say precisely which stock, calcareous or agglutinated, is the older. **1982** J. P. KENNETT *Marine Geol.* iii. 87 Quantification in geology requires a single numerical time scale resulting from the integration of stage stratotype information, biostratigraphy, paleomagnetic stratigraphy, and radiometric dating.
Hence **biostra'tigrapher** *n.*, an expert in or student of biostratigraphy; **biostrati'graphic**,

**biostrati'graphical** *adjs.*; **biostrati'graphically** *adv.*, in biostratigraphic terms, as regards biostratigraphy.
**1928** *Jrnl. Paleont.* II. 158 (*heading*) The biostratigraphic aspect of micropaleontology. **1950** Biostratigraphic [see *lithostratigraphic* s.v. LITHO-]. **1953** *Bull. Amer. Assoc. Petroleum Geologists* XXXVII. 2409 There are those cases in which the structural details involving thick, lithologically indivisible sequences can be unraveled only through detailed mapping of biostratigraphically defined units. **1958** *Bull. Geol. Soc. Amer.* LXIX. 99 (*heading*) Some biostratigraphical concepts. *Ibid.*, The biochronological standard, based for each period on biostratigraphically important groups of fossils, is known as the *orthochronologic* standard. *Ibid.* 112/2 Modern biostratigraphers. **1969** BENNISON & WRIGHT *Geol. Hist. Brit. Isles* ii. 25 The variation in the age of a diachronous deposit is presumed from its relation to a biostratigraphical time scale (a sequence of faunas). **1970** *Earth-Sci. Rev.* VI. 275 A biostratigraphic unit is a body of rocks which is delimited from the adjacent rock masses on the basis of unifying contemporaneous palaeontological characteristics (i.e., fossils deposited contemporaneously with the strata in which they occur). **1977** A. HALLAM *Planet Earth* 213 One of the main problems of Triassic biostratigraphers has been the lack of a marine rock succession in which there is unambiguous fossil evidence of an unbroken sequence of rocks from Permian through to Triassic. **1985** *Times* 22 Jan. 16/7 By 1948 White had established that the ostracoderms in the Welsh borderland could be used to correlate and age the rocks. This was the first time that such a biostratigraphic scheme had been achieved. **1988** *Nature* 4 Feb. 395/3 The Cenozoic is far better known biostratigraphically and palaeontologically than any other comparable interval since the opening of the Cambrian.

**biosystematics** (ˌbaɪəʊsɪstəˈmætɪks), *n. pl.* (const. as *sing.*). [f. BIO- + *systematics* s.v. SYSTEMATIC *n.* 2.] A branch of taxonomy based on the experimental study of the genetic and other properties of plant and animal populations. Orig. called biosy'stematy *n.* (now *rare*).
**1943** CAMP & GILLY in *Brittonia* IV. 324 It became evident that there is with us a new branch of the science of systematics—biosystematy—which we will later discuss. *Ibid.* 327 As here defined, Biosystematy seeks (1) to delimit the natural biotic units and (2) to apply to these units a system of nomenclature adequate to the task of conveying precise information regarding their defined limits, relationships, variability, and dynamic structure. **1950** *Madroño* X. 198 There has recently come into prominence a new term, namely, Biosystematics. **1951** *Brittonia* VII. 113 As was expected, the introduction of the term Biosystematy brought a series of protests. **1951** G. H. M. LAWRENCE *Taxon. Vascular Plants* viii. 172 It is significant that the findings of taxonomy (classical as well as modern) and of biosystematics are of mutual importance. **1963** E. MAYR *Animal Species & Evolution* xiv. 401 Some botanists have declared that the classification of specimens and the (experimental) study of natural populations were two independent branches of biology, . . orthodox taxonomy and . . 'genecology' or 'biosystematy'. **1971** *Language* XLVII. 867 The intuitive notions of taxonomy and taxonomic structure formalized here are similar to those of biosystematics. **1977** P. B. & J. S. MEDAWAR *Life Sci.* ii. 24 The purpose of biosystematics is to name animals and to arrange their names in some order and pattern.
Hence **biosyste'matic** *a.*; **biosy'stematist** *n.*, an expert in or student of biosystematics.
**1943** CAMP & GILLY in *Brittonia* IV. 333 The biosystematist must have species which are not only recognizable as such but which are organized about a

genetic system which is reasonably repetitive. *Ibid.* 374 It is certainly needful to note the presence of phenogenetic population segments in biosystematic analyses. **1951** G. H. M. LAWRENCE *Taxon. Vascular Plants* viii. 182 The species .. as conceived by the biosystematist, is a group of interbreeding or potentially interbreeding individuals reproductively isolated from other groups of individuals. **1963** *Watsonia* V. 304 The present work is based on a biosystematic study of these taxa with particular reference to variation in morphology, habit and cytology. **1970** *Nature* 11 July 124/2 Biosystematic work on the Middle East flora has developed rapidly during the past decade. **1984** *Oxf. Surveys Evol. Biol.* I. 69 This has significance for the bio-systematist because in western peninsular Florida what seems to be this same species has lost part of its flicker.

**bioturbation** (ˌbaɪəʊtɜːˈbeɪʃən), *n. Oceanogr.* [a. G. *Bioturbation* (R. Richter 1952, in *Notizblatt des Hess. Landesamtes f. Bodenforschung zu Wiesbaden* III. 68), f. L. *turbātio, -ōnem* disturbance: see BIO-.] The disturbance and mixing of sediment by the activity of living organisms; the disturbed state that results.
**1967** *Senckenbergiana Lethaea* XLVIII. 219 The sediment types, stratification fabrics, shells, and bioturbation fabrics are studied. **1976** *Nature* 17 June 576/2 Complete bioturbation extending over several centimetres has been noticed at three horizons. **1978** *Ibid.* 12 Jan. 124/1 Bioturbation of tephra layers mixes the tephra with other sediments and can reduce visible tephra layer thicknesses, dispersing tephra in the overlaying sediment. **1984** A. C. & A. DUXBURY *Introd. World's Oceans* xv. 487 Bottom photographs and cores show that the deep sediments are continually disturbed and reworked by sea cucumbers and worms in the process of extracting organic matter. This reworking of the sediment destroys layering and results in the uniform sediments that cover vast areas of the ocean floor. This process is called bioturbation.
Hence **'biotur,bated** *ppl. a.*, disturbed as a result of bioturbation; **,biotur'bational** *a.*, of or pertaining to bioturbation.
**1969** *Jrnl. Sedimentary Petrol.* XXXIX. 605/2 Almost all the muds are highly bioturbated. *Ibid.* 606/1 Bioturbational processes like .. closing of burrows by compaction and the bringing of sediment to the surface where it is effectively redeposited. **1973** *Nature* 30 Mar. 324/2 Even if deep sea meiobenthic communities are much sparser than their counterparts in shallower waters, their bioturbational effects .. may well assume a far greater significance. **1984** *Science* 25 May 873/1 *Chondrites* is a common trace fossil in .. bioturbated sequences.

**bis-,** *prefix*[1]. Add: **2.** *Chem.* Used in the names of compounds to signify two identical groups substituted in the same way.
**1931** *Jrnl. Chem. Soc.* I. 1616 The prefixes di-, tri-, tetra-, etc., will be used before simple expressions .. and the prefixes bis, tris, tetrakis, etc., before complex expressions. **1974** R. S. CAHN *Introd. Chem. Nomencl.* (ed. 4) iii. 42 Multiplicative prefixes bis-, tris-, tetrakis-, etc. are used in America for all complex expressions. **1975** R. F. BROWN *Org. Chem.* iv. 74 If complex substituents enclosed in parentheses are present more than once, we use the special multiplying prefixes of bis, tris, tetrakis, and so on, instead of di, tri, tetra, and so on. **1984** GREENWOOD & EARNSHAW *Chem. of Elements* (1986) viii. 374 Bis ($\eta^6$-arene) metal complexes have been made for many transition metals by the Al/AlCl₃ reduction method.

**Bislama** ('bɪsləmɑː), *n.* Also **Pislama.** [a. Bislama pidgin *Bislama, Bichelamar* (see BEACH-LA-MAR *n.*), alteration of Pg. *bicho do mar* BÊCHE-DE-MER *n.*] A form of Melanesian pidgin used as a lingua franca and contact

language in Vanuatu; New Hebrides pidgin. (Since 1980, the national language of Vanuatu.)
**1971** *Gud Nyus bilong Jisus Krais* (Bible Soc. in N.Z.) facing p. 1, The four Gospels in New Hebrides Bislama. **1974** *Times* 6 Mar. 13/8 A speaker .. welcomed the Queen .. to the New Hebrides on behalf of the chiefs of the islands. And the Queen—another 'chief'—replied through her 'speaker' .. who did an admirable job in English, French and the local lingua franca, Bislama. **1977** S. A. WURM in A. Valdman *Pidgin & Creole Linguistics* v. 334 Bichelamar (or Pislama), the pidgin language of the New Hebrides. **1979** *Guardian* 18 July 6/7 New Hebrideans .. talk a pidgin dialect called *Bislama* (from 'bêche de mer'). **1980** *English World-Wide* I. 7 Not only in the obvious cases of Bislama or Lallans can a contribution be doubly valuable, for content and form. **1984** *Ibid.* V. 107 The common history of Tok Pisin, Solomon Pijin and Bislama is first traced through jargonized varieties, plantation pidgins, and the spread of pidgins in the various recruiting areas.

**bite,** *n.* Add: [11.] **bite-size(d** *a.*, small enough to be eaten at one bite; also *fig.*
**1953** *U.S. Fish & Wildlife Service Special Sci. Rep.: Fisheries* CIV. 60 In 1948, the first pack of chunk style or *bite-size tuna was marketed. **1976** *S9* (N.Y.) Feb. 51/3 (Advt.), Read about the 'bite-size' lessons, self-pacing, and 'power-on' training. **1985** *Eating Out in London* 26/1 Aspects of nouvelle cuisine that we all hate (the bite-size portions .. the ubiquitous Kiwi fruit). **1962** L. DEIGHTON *Ipcress File* xx. 128 Small *bite-sized pieces of Hungarian ran like strands of a web across the clipped Harvard speech. **1969** *New Scientist* 29 May 469/1 Cheese sandwiches wrapped in bite-sized portions. **1984** K. HOM *Chinese Cookery* 53 Chinese food is always cut into bite-sized pieces.

**black,** *a.* Add: [19.] [a.] **black Irish** (see IRISH *n.* 1 a); **black lung (disease)** chiefly *U.S.* = ANTHRACOSIS *n.*
**1838** *Black lung [see ANTHRACOSIS n.].* **1892** J. T. ARLIDGE *Hygiene Dis. & Mortality of Occupations* v. 266 Dr. Totherick also describes .. an example of black lung which crumbled down between the fingers into a pultaceous mass. **1969** *Newsweek* 16 June 44/2 The dread black-lung disease .. annually disables thousands of miners. **1987** 'H. WAKEFIELD' *Price You Pay* vii. 128 He was telling her about his boyhood in South Yorkshire .. especially about his mother ... She'd been widowed when David was seven (his father had had black lung).
**black smoker** *Oceanogr.*, a sea-bed vent (see *SMOKER n.* 2 f) which ejects water rich in black particles, usu. sulphide minerals; cf. *white smoker* s.v. *WHITE a.* 11 e.
**1980** *Earth & Planetary Sci. Lett.* XLVIII. 2/2 The most vigorous hydrothermal activity occurs at the '*black smokers' ... Waters blackened by sulfide precipitates jet out at 1-5 m/s at temperatures of at least 350°C. **1987** JACKSON & MOORE *Life in Universe* ii. 66 Recent explorations of the sea bed have revealed the presence of unusual local conditions where hot vents (named *black smokers*) occur.
**black tar** *slang*, an exceptionally pure form of heroin originating in Mexico.
**1986** *N.Y. Times* 22 Jan. A15/6 Illegal aliens are used extensively by smugglers of a Mexican heroin known as '*black tar'. **1986** *Economist* 7 June 37/3 Black tar, also known as bugger, candy, dogfood, gumball, Mexican mud, peanut butter and tootsie roll .. started in Los Angeles and has since spread to 27 states ... What makes black tar heroin unique is that it has a single, foreign source—Mexico—and finds its way into Mexican-American distribution networks, often via illegal immigrants.

**Black Forest** (ˌblæk 'fɒrɪst), *n.* [The name of a mountainous wooded district in southern

Germany, tr. G. *Schwarzwald*, f. *schwarz* black + *Wald* wood, forest.] *Black Forest cake* (*gâteau*, etc.): a rich chocolate layer-cake with cherries and cream.

**1959** *Gourmet* Nov. 96/2 Black Forest Cake served at the Ridglea Country Club, Fort Worth, Texas, is superb. **1965** *Sunset* Feb. 134/1 Black Forest Cherry Cake.. is a dramatic multilayered dessert of yellow and chocolate cake layers, cherry butter cream, Kirsch-flavored whipped cream, and brandy-soaked cherries. **1974** S. BRITCHKY *Restaurants of N.Y.* 61 The customers come for pastry.. perhaps the Black Forest Cake. **1979** H. LAMBLEY *Home Bk. German Cookery* 232 Black Forest Gateau is popular in all areas of Germany and is reputed to taste its best when made with Black Forest morello cherries. **1982** S. TOWNSEND *Secret Diary A. Mole* 36 My father bought tins of salmon, crab and shrimps and a black forest cake. **1986** *Sunday Times* (Colour Suppl.) 23 Nov. 63/1 There was no prawn cocktail, no steak and no Black Forest gâteau on offer.

**blanket**, *n*. Add: [7.] [a.] *blanket man, prisoner, protest* (see *on the blanket*, sense 3 b above).

**1978** *Guardian* 22 Apr. 15/5 The condition of the '*blanket men*' has received little publicity. **1978** *New Statesman* 15 Dec. 813/3 Cases of four *blanket prisoners are already speeding through the .. procedures employed by the [European] Commission [of Human Rights]. **1982** U. O'CONNOR in B. Sands *Skylark sing your Lonely Song* 12 His description of his companions in the *blanket protest has a stark reality that no photograph could reproduce. **1986** Blanket protest [see H-block s.v. H 2].

**blast**, *n.*[1] Add: [10.] **blast-freezing**, freezing, esp. of foodstuffs, by means of a rapid current of chilled air; hence (as a back-formation) **blast-freeze** *v. trans.*; **blast freezer**, a machine for blast-freezing.

[**1943** TRESSLER & EVERS *Freezing Preservation of Foods* iii. 83 Air blast freezing at about −10°F was also used by a number of juice freezing companies.] **1948** W. A. GORTNER et al. *Princ. Food Freezing* xvi. 244 *Blast freezing, or freezing by the cold-air blast system, is the most rapid method of freezing in use in locker plants. A large blast freezer requires an extra room. **1965** *New Scientist* 18 Feb. 431/1 Trays of stabilised egg are 'blast-frozen' to -30°C. **1979** *Fortune* 29 Jan. 85 Fresh-caught whole salmon are being..transformed into..fillets which are immediately vacuum-packaged and blast-frozen. **1983** *Jrnl. Soc. Archivists* VII. 169 Many libraries.. are in the flood area... External preparation for flood requires rapid access to blast freezing. **1986** *Scotsman* 31 July 4 (Advt.), Smoked Salmon from fish which have not endured the confines of the rearing cage or the dessication [*sic*] of the blast freezer is rare indeed.

**bleomycin** (bliːəʊ'maɪsɪn), *n. Pharm.* [Arbitrary alteration of earlier *phleomycin*, name of a related antibiotic, f. *phleo-*, of unknown origin + -MYCIN.] An antineoplastic drug consisting of a glycopeptide or mixture of glycopeptides from the bacterium *Streptomyces verticillus*.

**1966** H. UMEZAWA in *Antimicrobial Agents & Chemotherapy 1965* 1080/2 An antibiotic complex produced by another strain of *Streptomyces* was more stable than phleomycin at acid and alkaline *p*H, but chelated with copper... This complex of the phleomycin group was named bleomycin. **1970** *Jrnl. Antibiotics* XXIII. 473 The bleomycins, water-soluble basic glycopeptide antibiotics, produced by *Streptomyces verticillus*, exhibit antitumour and antibacterial activity... There are more than 13 bleomycins. **1979** *Sci. Amer.* Aug. 33/3 The antitumor drug bleomycin..does its therapeutic work by damaging the DNA of tumor cells. **1981** M. C. GERALD *Pharmacol.* (ed. 2) xxx. 586 With the

exception of bleomycin, all other antitumor antibiotics..cause bone marrow depression. **1984** *Brit. Nat. Formulary* VIII. 269/1 Bleomycin is used to treat the lymphomas, certain solid tumours and.. malignant effusions.

**blepharo-**, *comb. form.* **blepharoplasty**: substitute for def.: plastic surgery on the eyelid; (examples); **blepharoplastic** *a.* (examples).

**1841** *Boston Med. & Surg. Jrnl.* 14 Apr. 149 (*heading*) Blepharoplastic operations for the restoration of the lower eyelid. **1842** T. D. MÜTTER *On Rec. Improvements in Surg.* 33 Adopting..the phraseology of Zeis, I include under the expression *plastic surgery*, all the specific terms employed in speaking of each particular modification of the principle; such as rhinoplasty when the nose is made, ..blepharoplasty when the eyelids, [etc.]. *Ibid.* 35 Dr. Post of New York has recently published a case of blepharoplastic operation. **1913** *Amer. Encycl. & Dict. Ophthalmol.* II. 1090 (*caption*) Richet's blepharoplastic method. **1964** S. DUKE-ELDER *Parsons' Dis. Eye* (ed. 14) xxxi. 499 More extensive cicatricial displacement requires some form of blepharoplasty, employing whole or split-skin grafts or flaps of skin taken from the upper lid. **1981** *Brit. Med. Jrnl.* 4 Apr. 1099/1 Breast enhancement, blepharoplasty, and facelifts seem, perhaps, to have a more positive basis with their aim of making the woman feel and appear more desirable.

**blepharoplast**, *n.* [b.] Substitute for def.: = KINETOSOME *n.*; also (*rare*), = KINETOPLAST *n.* a. (Further examples.)

**1907** D. NABARRO tr. *Laveran & Mesnil's Trypanosomes* iii. 52 In view of the meaning attributed to the word *blepharoplast* by Webber, who introduced it..the *Geisselwurzl* [of a flagellum] is a blepharoplast. **1912**, etc. [see PARABASAL *a.* (*n.*) 2]. **1925**, etc. [see KINETOPLAST *n.*]. **1940** L. H. HYMAN *Invertebrates* I. iii. 109 The basal granule is accompanied by another granule, variously called blepharoplast, kinetoplast, kinetonucleus, etc. **1961**, **1974** [see KINETOSOME *n.*]. **1986** M. KOGUT tr. *Schlegel's Gen. Microbiol.* v. 155 The flagella conform to the typical eukaryotic model; they originate from a blepharoplast in the cytoplasm.

**blood**, *n.* Add: [III.] [8.] b. *'new blood' post* U.K., a post created under a Government scheme for the recruitment of new entrants to university teaching at a time of generally low staff turn-over.

**1984** *Economist* 4 Feb. 36/2 In the universities, Sir Keith has been responsible for.. schemes to channel funds into.. 'new blood' posts (to make up for the worst effects on recruitment of three years of university cuts). **1986** *Times Higher Educ. Suppl.* 13 June 36/2 Much more would be needed if the Government.. wished to pursue particular initiatives like a second injection of 'new blood' posts.

**bloody**, *a.* and *adv.* Add: [A.] [4.] c. *Bloody Sunday*, the colloq. name for various Sundays on which blood was shed, esp. for political or industrial causes; *orig.* applied to 13 November 1887, when police violently broke up a socialist demonstration in Trafalgar Square against the British Government's Irish policy.

**1888** *Commonweal* 3 Mar. 68/1 The struggle for the elementary right of freedom of speech, of which the events of Bloody Sunday formed such a dramatic episode, is taking a new development. **1906** P. KROPOTKIN *Mem. Revolutionist* (ed. 2) Pref. p. xxvi, Five days after the 'bloody Vladimir Sunday' a mass-strike began at Warsaw and similar strikes soon spread all over Poland. **1907** T. ROTHSTEIN *Russ. Revolution* 8 The middle-classes.. had already before the 'bloody' Sunday of January 22nd begun to get restless. **1921** *Notes from Ireland* 1 Mar. 36/1 *Bloody Sunday*, November 21, 1920... On that day, fourteen British officers were murdered, some of them in their beds. **1936** *Zionist Rev.* July-Aug. 92/1 There were many deeds of Jewish valour and Arab kindness during the events at Jaffa on 'Bloody Sunday', April 19th. **1943** R. M. Fox *Irish Citizen Army* i. 7 They had the outstanding experience of 'Bloody Sunday' to teach them the wisdom of relying on their own strength... On Sunday, August 31, 1913.. it is calculated that there were at least 500 civilian casualties. **1972** *News Letter* (Belfast) 31 Jan. 7 (*heading*) Londonderry's Bloody Sunday. **1977** *Times Lit. Suppl.* 11 Mar. 279/5 The event that precipitated the 1905 revolution was the massacre by government officials of unarmed workers assembled in St Petersburg on January 9 (or January 22 in the New Style calendar), a day which became known as 'Bloody Sunday'. **1986** P. GILLIATT *Sunday Bloody Sunday* p. xviii, Didn't I know there was a famous Irish Bloody Sunday... Didn't I know about the Russian Bloody Sunday? Yes, I said. But it still wasn't the English bloody Sunday.

**blue**, *a.* Add: [III.] [13.] **blue line** [(*a*)] (example); (*b*) *Ice Hockey* (orig. *Canad.*), either of the two blue-coloured lines midway between the centre of the rink and each goal (freq. as one word).
**1887** *N.E.D.*, \*Blue line. **1925** *Gazette* (Montreal) 5 Jan. 14/3 He swung through the centre and crossing the blue line drove a terrific shot at the Hamilton goal. **1964** F. MAHOVLICH *Ice Hockey* i. 15 A defender may pass the puck from behind his own blueline to any team mate providing his team mate is NOT beyond the centre-ice red line. **1986** *New Yorker* 31 Mar. 21/2 Our goalie was subjected to.. slap shot after slap shot raining in from the blue line.
**blue shift**, a displacement of spectral lines, resonance peaks, etc., to shorter wavelengths (representing an approaching source in astronomical cases); = *violet shift* s.v. VIOLET *a.* 4.
**1961** *Jrnl. Chem. Physics* XXXV. 375/2 There is a \*blue shift of the peak which is quite independent of the compound involved. **1965** *N.Y. Times* 14 Nov. IV. 7/6 A search for objects with such a blue shift is being initiated in the vicinity of Centaurus. **1979** [see RED SHIFT *n.*]. **1985** *Sci. Amer.* Sept. 36/3 A decrease, or blue shift, in the wavelength of absorption lines from a particular part of the sun's disk means that region is moving toward the observer; an increase, or red shift, means it is receding.
hence **blue-shift** *v. trans.*, to displace in this way; **blue-shifted** *ppl. a.*
**1966** *Nature* 30 July 503/1 So far, no \*blue-shifted quasi-stellar radio sources have been observed while many have measured red-shifts. **1972** *New Scientist* 9 Nov. 318/2 The background radiation is a necessary feature of the universe. During the contracting phase of each cycle, starlight and other radiation is blueshifted to an ever-increasing degree, eventually being scrambled up in the fireball between cycles. **1973** *Nature* 21/28 Dec. 517/1 In general the absorbance spectra of the visual pigments of deep-water and pelagic marine animals are blueshifted compared to those of coastal and estuarine animals. **1978** PASACHOFF & KUTNER *University Astron.* xxiv. 600 If we were talking about light, this shift would be in the blue direction; even though we are discussing radio waves we say 'blueshifted' anyway.

**B'nai B'rith** (bəˈneɪ brɪθ), *n.* [ad. Heb. *bĕnē bĕrīt* sons of the covenant.] An international Jewish benevolent organization, founded in New York City in 1843.
**1862** *Jewish Chron.* 17 Oct. 6/3 The Order of B'Nai Berith has taken upon itself the task of uniting the Israelites of the United States in such a manner as to soonest further the development of the highest interests of Judaism among.. its professors. **1868** *N.Y. Times* 22 July 5/5 The Order of B'Nai B'Rith, a Jewish organization, founded to alleviate the wants of

the destitute, [etc.]. **1879** *Chicago Tribune* 13 May 6/1 (*heading*) B'nai B'rith. **1932** L. GOLDING *Magnolia St.* I. x. 181 He was.. a Freemason and a member of the Independent Order of B'nei Brith [*sic*]. **1948** *Daily Ardmoreite* (Ardmore, Okla.) 23 Apr. 10/1 He helped to organize the B'nai B'rith fraternal group here. **1957** *Encycl. Brit.* III. 761/1 *B'nai B'rith*.. is the oldest and largest Jewish service organization in the world, with men's lodges, women's chapters and youth chapters in about 35 countries by the latter 1950s. *Ibid.* XIII. 63D/1 The Anti-Defamation league of the B'nai B'rith (1913).. spoke for middle-class Jewry. **1968** *Guardian* 10 Sept. 9/2 The Democratic and Republican Presidential candidates happened to be in Washington laying down their proposed policies before a convention of B'Nai B'Rith. **1986** H. ENGEL *City called July* i. 6 He was a big wheel in the local chapter of B'nai Brith.

**board**, *n.* Add: [I.] [2.] **f.** *Cricket.* = *score-board* (b) s.v. SCORE *n.* 22; *esp.* in (so many runs) *on the board*, i.e. scored.
**1883** *Daily Tel.* 15 May 2/7 This hit caused three figures to appear on the board. **1932** *Times* 29 July 13/4 They had 84 on the board for eight wickets. **1951** *People* 3 June 8/7 George Lambert.. had Booth and Edrich out with only 40 on the board. **1977** J. LAKER *One-Day Cricket* 70 Ian Chappell.. had put West Indies in to bat and with only 12 runs on the board, Australia struck the first blow. **1985** *New Yorker* 5 Aug. 34/1 The Phillies.. put sixteen on the board in their first two turns at bat.
**g.** Any (usu. rectangular) flat piece of rigid material, or an assembly of several such pieces, to which are attached controls, switches, etc. Usu. preceded by a word denoting these fixtures or their purpose, as CONTROL *board*, SWITCHBOARD, etc. Cf. PANEL *n.*[1] 16.
**1940** *Chambers's Techn. Dict.* 99/2 Board (Elec. Eng.). See *control-board*, *distribution-board*. **1966** *Simulation* Jan. 56/1 The main control board on the right is in many respects a duplicate of our conventional boards with a combination bench and vertical panel design. **1972** *Gloss. Electrotechnical, Power Terms* (*B.S.I.*) II. vi. 9 Board, an assembly of panels, the principal function of which is indicated by the same prefix as is used for panels, e.g. switchboard, controlboard, etc. **1985** J. TRAPIDO *Internat. Dict. Theatre Lang.* 88 Board. 1. A general term for the central control device for the stage lighting circuitry. It normally implies direct control, as opposed to 'console', which denotes remote control apparatus, often computer assisted. The term is a shortened form of control board or, still older, switchboard.
**h.** *Electronics.* A printed circuit board together with its attached electronic components, esp. considered as an addition to existing circuitry in a computer, etc. Cf. \*DAUGHTERBOARD *n.*, \*MOTHERBOARD *n.*
**1979** *Personal Computer World* Nov. 56/1 They will also be demonstrating colour add-on boards for this machine. **1985** *Which Computer?* Apr. 66/1 Some of these applications require an internal board. **1988** *PC Mag.* Oct. 114/3 The board comes with a slim manual and a setup disc.

**boardsailing**, *n.* Add: 'boardsail *n.*, the art or practice of boardsailing (usu. *attrib.*); also as *v. intr.*, to participate in boardsailing; to travel by sailboard, to windsurf.
**1983** *E. Anglian Daily Times* 5 Nov. 3/3 Top speed for boardsail ace. **1984** *Sunday Tel.* (Colour Suppl.) 22 Jan. 22/4 Arnaud de Rosnay.. was being lionised after boardsailing across the Bering Strait. **1984** *Times* 25 Aug. 11/7, 160 British centres offer boardsail training. **1984** *Sunday Times* (Colour Suppl.) 28 Oct. 26/2 You can board sail in a variety of places from London Docks to reservoirs, estuaries and beaches.

**boatie** ('bəʊtɪ), *n. colloq.* (chiefly *Austral.* and *N.Z.*). [f. BOAT *n.* + -IE.] A person who sails a boat, esp. for pleasure; a boating enthusiast; *spec.* a member of the crew of a surf-boat. Usu. in *pl.* Cf. YACHTIE *n.*

**1962** *Austral. Women's Weekly* 24 Oct. (Suppl.) 3/1 *Boaties*, members of a surf club boat crew. **1963** J. POLLARD *Austral. Surfrider* 68 The routine jobs left to the boaties include patrolling against sharks. **1969** *Kings Cross Whisper* (Sydney) LXXVIII. 2/3 You turn on your television set and the screen is out of whack because some boatie is using a power drill. **1971** *N.Z. Listener* 25 Oct. 7/3 The 'elite' cutter group put themselves voluntarily 'on call' 24 hours a day for rescue work. Such dedication kept well before the boating public has undoubtedly allayed the fears of many would-be boaties. **1975** *Turangi* (N.Z.) *Chron.* 2 Apr. 1/1 The weed has only assumed importance with the increase in the number of boaties using the area. **1985** *South China Morning Post* (Hong Kong) 18 May 1 Yachties, boaties and junk owners will have to dig deeper into their pockets following the Government's increase in pleasure boat mooring charges. **1988** *Sydney Morning Herald* 5 Jan. 9/6 It is the boaties, those men who ride the big waves in the old wooden surf boats, who they say are the maddest.

**bobble**, *n.*[1] Add: **2.** A mistake or error, a failure, a bungle; *spec.* in *Sport*, an instance of fumbling or mishandling the ball. *U.S.*

**1887** J. C. HARRIS *Free Joe* 155 She jess reads right straight along from cover to cover without a bobble. **1906** *N. Lajoie's Official Baseball Guide* 33 Some days I may not feel just right and so be off my game, But let me make a bobble and I get it just the same. **1920** *Cosmopolitan* Aug. 101/2 The Committee on Arrangements had made it Impossible for the Dinner to be a Bobble. **1948** *Galveston* (Texas) *News* 14 June 7/2 Vidor got off to a shaky start, committing six bobbles. **1961** *Guardian* 13 Feb. 16/6 The first bad bobble of the Kennedy Administration has now occurred. **1974** *Cleveland* (Ohio) *Plain Dealer* 13 Oct. c3/1 Michigan took advantage of Michigan State fumbles..when Dan Jilek recovered a Spartan bobble in the end zone. **1985** *Dirt Bike* Mar. 8/2 He ..rode smartly, until he made a bobble and was forced to go for second gear to keep the little engine from bogging.

**bobble**, *v.* Add: **2.** *intr.* and *trans.* To make a mistake, to bungle or botch (something); *spec.* in *Sport*, to mishandle or fumble (the ball), esp. in taking a catch. Cf. *BOBBLE n.*[1] 2. *U.S.*

**1908** *Dialect Notes* III. 292 *Bobble*, v.i. to make a slight turn or twist from a direct or straight line, wabble; hence, to make a break or mistake. 'He can't plough a furrow without *bobbling* from one side of the row to the other.' **1942** BERREY & VAN DEN BARK *Amer. Thes. Slang* §644/17 *Make a bungling play*, blob, bobble, bonehead. **1959** F. ASTAIRE *Steps in Time* (1960) xviii. 192 We didn't fall but we bobbled on top of the table as we went over, causing an uncertainty to this finishing step which followed. **1971** L. KOPPETT *N.Y. Times Guide Spectator Sports* i. 31 He bobbles, drops or misses the ball. **1974** *Cleveland* (Ohio) *Plain Dealer* 13 Oct. c7/2 On the next series, Nebraska fullback Gary Higgs bobbled a pitchout. **1977** *New Yorker* 17 Oct. 178/2 The simplest plot points are bobbled, and when there's mayhem, it isn't clear who the participants are, or what the outcome is. **1984** *Miami Herald* 6 Apr. 3F/2 Got Dale Murphy to hit a one-hopper that Juan Samuel bobbled.

**body**, *n.* Add: [VI.] [30.] **body-bag**, (*b*) orig. *U.S.*, a strong bag in which a corpse is placed and transported (from the scene of an accident, etc.).

**1954** *Amer. Speech* XXIX. 273 *\*Body-bag*, a canvas bag for removing bodies of persons killed in fires. **1967** *N.Y. Times* 11 Oct. 35/3 The bodies were found beneath the approximate center of the dam... They were placed in 'body bags' and taken to Jackson, the state capital, for an autopsy. **1976** N. THORNBURG *Cutter & Bone* x. 245 Maybe I just scooped up too many guys and dumped them in body bags. **1984** J. DIDION *Democracy* IV. iii. 224 Before he zipped the body bag closed the Tamil doctor went through the pockets of Jack Lovett's seersucker jacket.

**body wave** *Hairdressing*, a soft, light wave designed to give the hair 'body' or substance; the curling process which imparts this.

**1966** J. S. COX *Illustr. Dict. Hairdressing* 22/2 *\*Body wave*, a curling process that is claimed to put 'body' into the hair and make it more suitable for bouffant styles. **1972** *Village Voice* (N.Y.) 1 June 12/2 (Advt.), Body waves—manicures. **1986** *City Limits* 12 June 78 Cuts are just £13.50 and bodywaves £9.95.

∥**Bokmål** ('boːkmɔːl), *n.* Also **bokmaal**. [Norw., f. *bok* book + *mål* language.] In Norway, a written language derived from Danish and now one of the two official languages (the other being NYNORSK *n.*); = *Dano-Norwegian* s.v. DANO-.

Formerly called *Riksmål* (q.v.). Bokmål was adopted as the official term in 1929.

**1931** *Statesman's Year-bk.* 1147 As to the written language, there exist two idioms ('bokmaal' and 'landsmaal') and both may be officially used. **1952** B. BERULFSEN in *Norseman* X. 187 In 1929 official action changed the names Landsmål to *Nynorsk* and Riksmål to *Bokmål*. **1966** [see NYNORSK *n.*]. **1974** *Florida FL Reporter* XIII. 24/2 Among native Norwegians the teaching of the standard language, *bokmal*, in the schools is accepted without question. **1989** *Encycl. Brit. Macropædia* XXIV. 1030/1 For more than 80 percent of the school children Bokmål is the main language in local schools.

**bomb**, *n.* Add: [2.] **g.** *Amer. Football.* A long, looping, forward pass.

[**1955** B. OATES *Los Angeles Rams* 51 That year Bob Waterfield and Elroy Hirsch had been the long-range bombers with, for example, a ninety-one yard touchdown in Chicago.] **1960** *Compl. Guide Prof. Football* 88 (*caption*) Ralph Gugliemi..threw four TD bombs in '59. **1970** *Globe & Mail* (Toronto) 28 Sept. 23/8 The bomb carried from the Packer end zone to the Atlanta 44. **1974** *Cleveland* (Ohio) *Plain Dealer* 13 Oct. c13/2 Shaw High quarterback Greg Shields stung Shaker Heights twice on long bombs to pace Shaw to its first Lake Erie League victory of the season, 14-7. **1984** J. LAWTON *All Amer. War Game* ix. 113 A big bomb of a pass can illuminate the murkiest of games.

[6.] **bomb factory** *colloq.*, a place where bombs are illegally manufactured or prepared, for use in terrorist activities.

**1975** *Facts on File* 20 Dec. 952/3 Police said that the arrest of the four had been instrumental in uncovering a London '\*bomb factory'. **1976** *Southern Even. Echo* (Southampton) 2 Nov. 3/4 Madden had said he heard from a stallholder in Kingsland market that a bomb factory had been found in Albion Towers. **1986** *Times* 21 June 3/2 He had no idea the four people in the room were turning it into a bomb factory.

**bomber**, *n.*, Add: [2.] [b.] **bomber jacket** *n.* [modelled on the flight jackets worn by U.S.A.F. air-crew], a fashionable style of (usu. leather) jacket, front-zippered and tightly gathered at the waist and cuffs.

**1973** *Daily News Record* 16 Nov. 13 (Advt.), Wool plaid *\*bomber jacket*.. with rugged zipper front. **1985** *Listener* 2 May 5/2 There was the Intourist taxi driver in his Western trainers and Western bomber jacket.

‖**Bon** (bɒn), *n.* Also O-Bon. [Jap.; also with honorific prefix *o-*.] A Japanese Buddhist festival held annually in August to honour the dead; the Festival of the Dead, or Lantern Festival.

[**1617** R. Cocks *Diary* 5 Aug. (1883) I. 292 This night began the feast of *bonbon*, or for the dead, with hanging out of candell light, and enviting the dead, etc.] **1899** L. Hearn *In Ghostly Japan* vi. 79 The time of the Bon—the great Festival of the Dead,—which begins upon the thirteenth day of the seventh month. **1965** W. Swaan *Jap. Lantern* xiv. 167 The most important festival in the lives of the people is that of *O-Bon*, the Buddhist equivalent of All Souls' Day or the Feast of the Dead. **1966** P. S. Buck *People of Japan* (1968) xii. 149 All Japan celebrates a reunion with the dead during the annual Bon Festival, a Buddhist festival often called the feast of lanterns. **1974** G. Wingate in *Folklore of Texan Cultures* (Texas Folklore Soc. Publ. No. 38) 332 There were harvest dances for the time on the moon calendar known as O-Bon, a three day period beginning August 13, when the spirits of the dead were said to come back to earth. **1985** Randle & Watanabe *Coping with Japan* 146 At special times in the year, particularly New Year and O Bon (when ancestors are remembered) people follow Japan's great traditional ceremonies.

**bond,** *v.* Add: [**1.**] **c.** To bind (contiguous surfaces or layers, esp. of different fabrics or clothing materials) *together* with an adhesive or by fusing; to cause (a surface or layer) to bind *with* or adhere *to* another surface or layer throughout its extent. Usu. in *pass.* Cf. BIND *v.* 10 a.

**1933** *Trans. Amer. Soc. Mech. Engin.* LV. WDI. 21/2 This moisture content will be that which obtained in the panel at the moment the various plies were bonded together. **1945** H. Barron *Mod. Plastics* xi. 250 The laminations are not so tightly bonded together as in the case of high pressure laminates. **1964** [see FIBRID *n.*]. **1965** *Sunday Mail* (Brisbane) 24 Oct. 24 The crepe, bonded to a slightly stiff, fine net-like fabric, is heavier and stiffer than normal crepe. **1983** J. S. Foster *Structure & Fabric* (rev. ed.) I. iv. 76/2 The wide stiff edge beam .. is bonded to the slab.

**d.** To endow with rigidity, stiffness, or structural stability by the addition of a solidifying or viscous matrix, esp. a resin; to set or fix in such a matrix. Freq. const. *with.*

**1955** *Times* 6 July 13/1 Structural plastics consist of a reinforcing agent, such as glass fibre, bonded with a synthetic resin. **1966** [see MONTMORILLONITE *n.*]. **1978** J. Miller *Body in Question* (1982) iii. 140 The substances from which a marble statue is made are stably bonded together, so that the object retains not only its shape but its original material.

[**6.**] **b.** *Chem.* To connect with a chemical bond (BOND *n.*[1] 13 e). Also *intr.* for *pass.*

**1923** [implied in *BONDING *ppl. a.*]. **1939** L. Pauling *Nature Chem. Bond* i. 32 Other factors .. provide a more serious limitation with respect to the number of atoms which can be bonded to a central atom. **1952** L. N. Ferguson *Electron Struct. Organic Molecules* ii. 14 Since an *s* orbital is spherical, it can overlap another orbital equally in all directions and the tendency to bond is equal in all directions. **1984** E. P. DeGarmo et al. *Materials & Processes in Manuf.* (ed. 6) iii. 64 Atoms .. are usually linked or bonded to other atoms in some manner as a result of interatomic forces.

**7.** *a. Anthropol.* To link (a person) *to* another person with an emotional or psychological bond; to bind (a group of people) *together* psychologically. Also *transf.* Cf. BIND *v.* 21, *BONDING *vbl. n.* 4.

**1965** [implied in *BONDING *vbl. n.* 4]. **1967** D. Morris *Naked Ape* 38 It meant that the females

remained bonded to their individual males and faithful to them while they were away on the hunt. **1984** E. Jong *Parachutes & Kisses* vii. 121 The animals bonded them; Josh and Isadora spoke a whole secret language about the dogs.

**b.** *intr.* for *pass.* To form an emotional or psychological bond *with* a person (esp. one's child) or social group.

**1976** *Time* 27 Sept. 81/2 You bonded with a team, and it became part of you. **1983** *Times* 26 Mar. 8/7, I .. saw a midwife get a prize for spouting out some stuff about being careful to watch whether mothers were 'bonding' with their children. **1985** A. Tyler *Accidental Tourist* xviii. 293 She and her husband need to bond with the baby. **1987** *Church Times* 27 Mar. 5/1 If a mother has the 'right' to procreate a child, hasn't she the 'right' to bond with it and call it hers?

**bonded,** *ppl. a.* Add: **3.** Of a material: strengthened by being bonded with a matrix (cf. *BOND *v.* 1 d). Of a fabric: that has been bonded to another layer of material; consisting of two or more layers of material bonded together (cf. *BOND *v.* 1 c). Freq. prefixed by a noun *attrib.* denoting the material constituting the matrix or the additional layer. Also applied to articles made from bonded materials.

**1938** *Trans. Amer. Soc. Mech. Engin.* LX. 63/2 Reinforced hot-pressed resin-bonded two-ply faces are also frequently used with crotch, burl, swirl, and stump veneers. **1940**, etc. [see *resin-bonded* adj. s.v. RESIN *n.* 4 a]. **1953** [see *chip-board* s.v. CHIP *n.*[1] 9 a]. **1963** A. J. Hall *Textile Sci.* iii. 156 A very convenient and satisfactory method for making bonded-fibre fabrics has been developed. **1965** *Sunday Mail* (Brisbane) 24 Oct. 24 California Miss has used bonded crepe to give the soft, gentle fabric a more substantial weight. **1986** *Horse & Rider* Sept. 6 (Advt.), Riding boot... Hard wearing, bonded lining.

Hence **'bondedness** *n.*

**1952** L. N. Ferguson *Electron Struct. Organic Molecules* ii. 43 Thus there is a decrease in the double-bondedness of the carbon-carbon bond that is common to the chelate and the aromatic rings. **1985** *Amer. N. & Q.* May/June 141/1 The anecdote .. illustrates only our need for bondedness to others.

**bonding,** *vbl. n.* Add: [**1.**] **d.** *Chem.* The formation of a chemical bond (BOND *n.*[1] 13 e); the linkage provided by such a bond.

**1940** Glasstone *Text-bk. Physical Chem.* v. 375 The atomic radii generally tabulated are those for univalent bonding and a co-ordination number of four, since these occur most frequently. **1947** E. B. Maxted *Mod. Adv. Inorg. Chem.* i. 72 It will be seen that the tetrahedral, $sp^3$, type of bonding leaves the *d* orbitals unaffected. **1969** R. F. Chapman *Insects* iii. 54 Bonding does not occur within the salivary gland because of the reducing conditions and dielectric effects produced by companion materials. **1973** [see PI *n.*[1] 3]. **1984** Greenwood & Earnshaw *Chem. of Elements* (1986) xxvii. 1346 The likelihood of $\pi$-bonding and attendant charge transfer makes a simple crystal-field treatment inappropriate.

**4.** *Anthropol.* The formation of an emotional bond between two individuals, or between an individual and a group; *spec.* the establishment of strong ties between a parent (esp. a mother) and a child, considered by some to result from physical contact immediately after birth. *male bonding*: see *MALE *n.*[2]; *pair-bonding*: see PAIR *n.*[1] 9.

**1965** [see *pair-bonding* vbl. n. s.v. PAIR *n.*[1] 9]. **1967** R. Fox *Kinship & Marriage* i. 38 Some writers have maintained that the lack of 'oestrus' .. in human females, leads to the setting up of nuclear families ... The argument .. probably both overestimates the human male and underestimates primate bonding tendencies. **1975** *Lancet* 16 Aug. 317/1 Intensive therapeutic work with families, in which child abuse had occurred, suggested that bonding failure related in part to the pregnancy, perinatal experience and early ill health of the abused proband and parents. **1977** J. & J. LENNANE *Hard Labour* vii. 118 There is a theory current at present that mother-baby 'bonding' will be defective if the mother does not touch, and preferably hold, the baby within minutes of the birth, their relationship possibly being thereby adversely affected for life. **1981** M. TUDOR *Child Devel.* 165/1 Bonding is beginning to replace the word attachment in the more current literature. **1985** G. T. NURSE et al. *Peoples of Southern Afr.* v. 113 One result of this type of bonding is that when a man changes bands, he takes with him not only his own family but his hunting partner and his family as well. **1986** *Times* 10 Sept. 11/1 Despite the vogue for 'new fatherhood', with its emphasis on birth and bonding and baby baths, few people would dare to stereotype a good father in the same way as they do a good mother.

**bonding** ('bɒndɪŋ), *ppl. a. Chem.* [f. BOND *v.* + -ING². ] That forms a bond or bonds (*BOND *v.* 6 b); *esp.* designating an orbital that may be hybridized to form a bond, or an electron occupying such an orbital.
    **1923** G. N. LEWIS *Valence* vi. 83 We may suppose that the normal state of the hydrogen molecule is one in which the electron pair is symmetrically placed between the two atoms. In sodium hydride, on the other hand, we may regard the bonding pair as lying nearer to the hydrogen than to the sodium, making the hydrogen negative. **1931** *Jrnl. Amer. Chem. Soc.* LIII. 1367 These rules provide information regarding the relative strengths of bonds formed by different atoms, .. the relation between the quantum numbers of bonding electrons and the number and spatial arrangement of the bonds, etc. **1965** PHILLIPS & WILLIAMS *Inorg. Chem.* I. iv. 104 A lone-pair of electrons appears to occupy a relatively larger volume than does a bonding-pair. **1974** GILL & WILLIS *Pericyclic Reactions* i. 23 The lowest orbital $\psi_1$ is clearly a bonding orbital since it has no nodes on the bond axis and its energy is less than $\alpha$. **1984** GREENWOOD & EARNSHAW *Chem. of Elements* (1986) iv. 112 There is one strongly bonding 4-centre orbital above each of the 4 faces.

**bonfire**, *n.* Add: [4.] **d.** Special Comb. **bonfire night**, a night on which bonfires are lit in celebration; *spec.* = *Guy Fawkes night* s.v. GUY *n.*² 1 b.
    **1936** N. SMITH *52 Yrs. at Labrador Fishery* 114 We opened the Club on *Bonfire Night, November 5th. **1968** *Listener* 26 Sept. 423/3, I have tried a sharp lemon icing with success on some 'special' occasions like bonfire night. **1976** *Sydney Morning Herald* 12 June 36 Police had warned against the misuse of firecrackers at traditional Queen's Birthday bonfire night celebrations tonight. **1985** *Financial Times* 26 Oct. p. xxi/3 In Birmingham, Hallowe'en and Bonfire night are a big event.

**boob**, *n.* Add: **5.** Special Comb. **boob tube** *colloq.*, (*a*) orig. and chiefly *N. Amer.* [in sense 3], a television set, television (see TUBE *n.* 2 k); (*b*) a woman's close-fitting strapless top, usu. made of knitted or elasticated fabric.
    **1966** *Current Slang* (Univ. S. Dakota) Fall 1 Let's catch the late show on the *boob tube. **1977** M. FRENCH *Women's Room* (1978) ii. 115, I sit and watch the stupid boob tube. **1978** *Daily Tel.* 25 Oct. 17/1 You wear strapless boob tubes of gold lamé, much-ruched, with your 1950s pirate pants. **1986** *My Weekly* 2 Aug. 16 Now the rush around to find .. a variety of tops from waterproofs to 'boob-tubes'.

**boogaloo** (buːgə'luː), *n.* orig. *U.S.* Also **bugaloo**. [Prob. alteration of BOOGIE *n.*² (or BOOGIE-WOOGIE *n.*), after *hullabaloo*, etc.] A modern dance to rock-and-roll music performed with swivelling and shuffling movements of the body, orig. popular in the 1960s.
    **1965** in *Dict. Amer. Regional Eng.* **1967** *Wall St. Jrnl.* 9 Feb. 1/4 After a person has outfitted himself at .. one of the 27 psychedelic shops .. he is ready to dance the Boog-a-loo at Cheetah, a New York nightspot. **1968** M. & J. STEARNS *Jazz Dance* 4 A second wave of dances crashed over American dance floors during and after the Twist: .. Hully-Gully, Jerk, Boogaloo, and so on. **1969** N. COHN *Pop from Beginning* ix. 84 In the absence of any dominant individuals, dance-crazes bossed pop right up until the Beatles broke. There was the Hully Gully .. the Monkey. A bit later, the .. Frug ... Right on into these last years and the Boogaloo, the Philly Skate, the Sanctification, the Beulah Wig. **1979** *Washington Post* 1 Apr. D13 They were trying to get some nice-looking women to teach them the boogaloo.
    Hence **'boogaloo** *v. intr.*, to dance the boogaloo.
    **1967** *Daily Tel.* 23 May 23/8 Some 3,000 girls—mostly in mini-skirts—and boys twisted and bugalooed to psychedelic sounds in this ecumenical effort to bring the Church to Washington's teenagers. **1971** B. MALAMUD *Tenants* 46 As they boogalooed in the center of the room .. Mary whispered to Lesser that she lived no more than two blocks away. **1975** FELTON & FOWLER *Best, Worst & most Unusual* 35 A chorus of go-go dancers boogalooed. **1979** *Washington Post* 2 Feb. C1/2 Nearly 2,000 people pressed in behind them to boogaloo along Pennsylvania Avenue. **1987** *Australian* 28 Apr. 18/6 Do I want to waltz, fox trot, rhumba or boogaloo? .. Sure!

**book**, *v.* Add: [2.] **e.** *Assoc. Football.* Of a referee: to record the name of (a player cautioned for a serious infringement of the rules); hence, to administer such a caution.
    **1959** *Daily Mirror* 29 Dec. 15/1 Two minutes later Hooper .. was booked for fouling goalkeeper Noel Dwyer. **1972** G. GREEN *Great Moments in Sport: Soccer* ix. 92 With 25 minutes left Hutchinson was booked. **1986** *Times* 19 June 46/1 The decision by .. the .. referee to book William Ayache, a defender, with a second yellow card—which puts him out of the quarter-final—was absurd.

**booking**, *vbl. n.* Add: [2.] **b.** *Assoc. Football.* An official caution given to a player for a serious infringement of the rules: see sense *2 e of the vb.
    **1969** *Daily Mirror* 30 Dec. 18/1 The last time he met Best .. was at Old Trafford earlier this season. It brought Mills a booking for fouling Best. **1976** *Daily Record* (Glasgow) 23 Nov. 26/5 Edwards trained yesterday despite being carried off at Ibrox on Saturday after a crunching tackle from Jim Steele which brought the Rangers player a booking. **1988** *Times* 2 Jan. 30/8 There was an element of frustration in the visitors' display which resulted in bookings for Reid and Sharp.

**bootleg**, *n.* Add: [1.] **b.** A gramophone record or tape prepared without authorization: see sense *2 b below.
    **1951** *Record Changer* Nov. 1 (*heading*) Victor presses bootlegs! **1971** *It* 2–16 June 18/1 This album of the Experience recorded at the Albert Hall in '69 is not a bootleg (although there's an inferior bootleg in mono selling at the same price), it's an official German release. **1979** *Sounds* 28 Apr. 52/2 I'd like to know where .. the customer .. stands. Can I get into trouble with the law for buying bootlegs? **1989** *Rolling Stone* 5 Oct. 16/2 Jon Bon Jovi .. left Moscow with caviar, watches, paintings, a Red Army coat, a bootleg of Elvis Presley hits and a new attitude.
    [2.] [b.] Also, *spec.* of gramophone records

and tapes prepared and distributed without authorization. (Further examples.)

**1951** *Record Changer* Nov. 1 He apparently has encountered no difficulty in persuading Victor to process and press.. four bootleg reissues of jazz classics. **1973** *Telegraph* (Brisbane) 27 Feb. 15/5 Bootleg records either can be re-pressed from legitimate records; taken from unauthorised recordings of live performances; or pressed from tapes stolen from recording studios. **1985** S. Booth *True Adventures Rolling Stones* xxiii. 238 How do bootleg records get around?

**Borsalino** (bɔːsəˈliːnəʊ), *n.* Also borsalino, *erron.* Borsolino. [f. the maker's name.] In full, *Borsalino hat.* A proprietary name for a hat made by the Italian company of Borsalino, *esp.* a type of man's wide-brimmed felt hat.

**1914** *Los Angeles Examiner* 23 Sept. I. 2/7 (Advt.), *Your Fall Hat* is here. It may be a Knox. It may be a Borsalino. It may be a Knapp-Felt. **1925** *Eaton's News Weekly* (T. Eaton & Co.) 26 Sept. 18/1 Borsalino hat with rolling, bound brim. **1930** H. Nicolson in *Listener* 3 Sept. 371/2, I explained to them that Alessandria was the home of hats. I should go out and buy a Borsalino immediately. **1940** R. Chandler *Farewell, my Lovely* i. 5 He wore a shaggy borsalino hat. **1952** J. L. Waten *Alien Son* 128 From under his new black borsalino hat he squinted sideways at Mr Smutkevitch. **1966** B. Glemser *Dear Hungarian Friend* xii. 203 He strode in.. carrying a narrow-brimmed Borsolino hat. **1971** *Official Gaz.* (U.S. Patent Office) 14 Dec. TM89/1 *Borsalino* ... For Hats and Articles in the Nature of Hats ... First use 1901; in commerce 1901. **1975** *Trade Marks Jrnl.* 14 May 983/1 Borsalino.. hats; headgear and ties, all for wear. **1978** J. Carroll *Mortal Friends* IV. vi. 454 Despite the heat he wore his Borsalino hat, and his black suit coat was buttoned twice.

**bossy**, *a.*² Move *colloq.* to precede etym. and add: **2.** Special collocation. **bossy-boots**, a domineering person (see BOOTS *n.*¹ 3).

**1983** *Observer* 24 July 7/3 Politics.. has caused these two amiable and bookish characters—neither of them a natural bossyboots—to fall out with each other. **1986** *Times* 31 May 8/6 She had not done so, she said, because everyone would have accused her of being a 'bossy-boots'.

**bottleneck**, *n.* Add: [1.] **b.** *Mus.* The neck of a bottle or similar device worn on the finger by an (esp. blues) guitarist to produce sliding effects on the strings over the fingerboard; the style of playing with a bottleneck, or a guitar so played. Cf. *slide-guitar* s.v. SLIDE- c.

**1965** *Melody Maker* 10 July 12/4 Bottlenecks are not manufactured yet, but most guitarists make them themselves. **1968** P. Oliver *Screening Blues* iii. 121 Muddy Waters's sliding, vibrating bottleneck on the strings gave a chilling, trembling excitement to the piece. **1976** *Rolling Stone* 22 Apr. 16/3 Slide guitars used to be referred to as bottlenecks. **1986** *Making Music* Apr. 28/3 His inability to master playing with a bottleneck.

[4.] **b.** In sense 1 b above, as *bottleneck playing, style.*

**1977** *Zigzag* Mar. 20/1 You feel that *bottleneck playing has been there all the time. **1989** *Q* Mar. 97/1 The latter's unorthodox style of bottleneck playing—derived from untutored attempts to mimic such legends as Robert Johnson, was ideally suited. **1978** *Gramophone* Feb. 1490/1 Clapton produces some fittingly earthy *bottleneck sounds. **1968** P. Oliver *Screening Blues* ii. 81 It is the blues guitarist who plays in '*bottleneck' style who often plays a similar accompaniment in both religious and blues recordings.

**bottleneck blues**, a style of blues played on a bottleneck guitar.

**1964** *Amer. Folk Music Occasional* 1. 19 Fred McDowell, a fine *bottle-neck blues player. **1985** *New Yorker* 10 June 36/1 It was a bottleneck-blues number—raucous, intense, galloping—that moved from conflict through struggle and on to resolution.

**bottleneck guitar**, a guitar played with a bottleneck; a style of music so produced.

**1968** *Blues Unlimited* Sept. 24 Mr Morganfield.. contributes some great *bottleneck guitar to make this the high spot of the record. **1985** *Music Week* 2 Feb. 28/1 Hall's piano and Peabody's exuberant bottleneck guitar obviously dominate.

**bought**, *ppl. a.* Add: **b.** *bought deal* (*Comm.*), an arrangement whereby a securities house buys a complete issue of shares and resells them at a price agreed with the issuer.

**1981** *Business Week* 2 Mar. 130/1 Another major concern is the 'bought deal'—the current method of marketing new issues overseas. **1986** *Economist* 6 Sept. 71/1 Many British companies will be tempted by bought deals: they are quicker to organise than rights issues and also cheaper. **1989** *Management & Leveraged Buy-Out Mag.* Summer 40/2 We can call on the vast resources of Lloyds Bank for the provision of the debt element in buy-outs which with our own underwriting capability enables us to finance major bought deals.

**bounce**, *n.*¹ Senses 5, 6 in Dict. become 6, 7. Add: **5.** *fig.* Energy, vitality; spirit, exuberance, verve.

**1909** P. Webling *Virginia Perfect* ix. 87, I don't consider that Connie is particularly clever ... She hasn't got enough bounce for the theatrical profession. She's too quiet and modest. **1914** G. B. Shaw *Fanny's First Play* 162 Bannal is obviously one of those unemployables of the business class who manage to pick up a living by a sort of courage which gives him cheerfulness, conviviality, and bounce. **1935** V. Sheean *Personal Hist.* ii. 42 The effect given was that of immense energy ... He moved with a combination of bounce and drive that brought one automatically to attention. **1948** *Wall St. Jrnl.* 6 Nov. 7/3 The market at almost no time during the day showed any particular 'bounce'. **1955** L. P. Hartley *Perfect Woman* xii. 118 All the glow and bounce and boyishness had gone out of him and he looked shrunken and peevish. **1985** *Times Lit. Suppl.* 5 Apr. 393/3 The optimistic humanism of Collins.. gives a bounce and freshness to these first encounters with such abiding questions in biblical criticism as historicity and canon.

**bound**, *n.*¹ Sense 5 in Dict. becomes 6. Add: **5.** Chiefly *Math.* Any number or magnitude such that either none of a specified set of numbers exceeds it, or none is less than it; an upper or lower limit to the magnitude something can have. Freq. as *upper, lower bound.* Cf. SUPREMUM *n.*, INFIMUM *n.*

**1917** G. H. Hardy in *Proc. Cambr. Philos. Soc.* XIX. 92 The upper bound. **1953** H. Eves *Introd. Hist. Math.* xi. 336 Rules for finding an upper bound to the roots of a polynomial. **1966** A. Battersby *Math. in Managem.* vi. 142 The figure 108, 417 belongs to a useful class of estimates called 'lower bounds'. We know that, whatever the final allocation may be, it cannot possibly give a lower 'cost' than this. **1977** *Sci. Amer.* Sept. 82/1 Heat generated by the vacuum tubes resulted in their having a relatively short operating life, which placed an upper bound on the size of computers. **1979** Page & Wilson *Introd. Computational Combinatorics* vi. 148 The quality of the bounds can also affect the amount of work in a calculation. **1986** *Nature* 23 Oct. 674/1 R. C. Vaughan has obtained substantial improvements to these bounds when *n* lies between 5 and 9.

**bouton**, *n.* Add: **3.** *Anat.* An enlarged part of a nerve fibre or cell, esp. an axon, where it forms a synapse with another nerve; ‖ *bouton terminal* (pl. *boutons terminaux*), a single bouton at the tip of a nerve fibre; ‖ *bouton de passage* (pl. *boutons de passage*), each of a series of boutons along the length of a nerve fibre.

[**1918** *Jrnl. Compar. Neurol.* XXX. 153, I could not find any place where the contact between the 'botones de traecto' and the cell surface takes place, as was described .. by Cajal.] **1932** *Proc. R. Soc.* B. CXI. 176 In preparations of new-born kittens it is impossible to observe any boutons on any of the cells in the cord. *Ibid.*, The *boutons terminaux* are small, oblong loops occurring at the end of nerve fibres and applied to cell-bodies and their dendrites. The *boutons de passage* are similar structures .. found along the length of the finest nerve fibres, on both cell- and dendrite-surfaces. **1937** A. KUNTZ *Text-bk. Neuro-Anat.* (ed. 2) v. 99 Fiber terminations consisting of delicate end-bulbs or end-loops (boutons). **1970** T. S. & C. R. LEESON *Histol.* (ed. 2) x. 196/2 (*caption*) Photomicrograph of an anterior horn cell to show boutons terminaux on the cell body and its dendrites. **1970** *Nature* 4 Apr. 21/1 Dense granular vesicles probably containing dopamine are present in the terminal boutons of striatal nerve endings. **1985** C. R. LEESON et al. *Textbk. Histol.* (ed. 5) vii. 207/1 In some cases, telodendria with their boutons are so numerous as to surround the neuron on which they terminate in a basket-like arrangement.

**bow**, *n.*[1] Add: [19.] **bow-hunter** chiefly *N. Amer.* and *N.Z.*, one who hunts deer, etc. with a bow as opp. to a gun (in *N.Z.*, as a target competition); also **bow-hunting** *vbl. n.* and (as a back-formation) **bow-hunt** *v. trans.*

**1939** P. H. GORDON *New Archery* II. v. 60 Another *bow hunter who has captured the fancy of the sport-minded world is Sasha Siemel, the 'tiger man' of Matto Grosso. **1947** *Collier's* 4 Jan. 46/2 *Bow hunting is something else. You must hunt even harder and more adroitly than the chap with the rifle because .. one chance is all the bow hunter gets. **1968** *Wanganui* (N.Z.) *Photo News* 6 July 23 The arrows were whistling in all directions at Upokongaru at Queen's Birthday weekend when the New Zealand bowhunters competitions were staged. **1971** *Outdoor Life* Mar. 211/1 Since then I have *bowhunted chucks at every opportunity. **1980** *Northeast Woods & Waters* Dec. 24/3 Bowhunting the whitetail deer played a major role in the Safari. **1984** L. MANTELL *Murder in Vain* iv. 54 Bowhunter's arrow. Don't go in for bowhunting myself. Mostly straight target shooting.

**box**, *n.*[2] Add: [1.] **e.** The female genitalia. *slang* (orig. and chiefly *N. Amer.*).

**1942** BERREY & VAN DEN BARK *Amer. Thes. Slang* §121/38 *Female pudendum*, .. hog-eye, hot box, jewelry. **1949** A. MARSHALL *How Beautiful are thy Feet* 150 'I believe Leila's running hot in the box,' said Sadie. **1963** 'J. PRESCOT' *Case for Hearing* vi. 96 And when you do take 'em out for an evening there's no holding 'em. As for putting one in the box, in my opinion most of 'em want it to happen. **1984** M. AMIS *Money* 164 Bum, box, belly, breasts—just incredibly prominent.

**boy**, *n.*[1] Add: [7.] **boy wonder** *colloq.*, an exceptionally talented young man or boy; cf. *wonder boy* s.v. WONDER *n.* 9 a.

**1925** *New Yorker* 5 Sept. 10/1 All sorts of names such as, 'infant phenomenon', and '*boy wonder', have been applied to Lacoste. **1951** *Sport* 30 Mar. 12/3 Seconds Out will be ridden by Lester Piggott, the boy wonder. **1986** *N.Y. Times* 31 Aug. VI. 25/2 All that might seem too downbeat for a man who still has the seductive charm and youthful vitality of an ageless boy wonder.

**braless** ('brɑːlɪs), *a.* Also **bra-less**. [f. BRA *n.*[1] +

-LESS.] *a.* Of a woman: without a brassière; not wearing a bra. Also *absol.*

**1964** *Women's Wear Daily* 27 Nov. 16/1 Now there's a bra-slip for the bra-less .. and watch the notion of double-duty fashion underlings grow. **1971** *Daily Colonist* (Victoria, B.C.) 19 Mar. 26/6 A report from Iowa State University indicated the majority of coeds there do not intend to go braless. **1979** *Daily Tel.* 25 Apr. 21/2 Trouble flared after the arrest of a bra-less woman. **1986** M. HOWARD *Expensive Habits* 168 Braless, breathless, her shirt stretched tight as though she is forever running against the wind.

**b.** Of the breasts: not supported or covered by a bra.

**1967** *Guardian* 5 Aug. 7/4 It was Poiret who first got women out of corsets, revealed bra-less bosoms. **1975** R. H. RIMMER *Premar Experiments* (1976) ii. 161 Wriggling her braless tits against me, she puppy-lapped me with wet sloppy kisses. **1985** 'J. ROSS' *Burial Deferred* xxxi. 161 A white T-shirt that stretched tautly over her bra-less breasts.

Hence **'bralessness** *n.*

**1973** *Black World* May 75/1 The low-cut tops, bralessness and brief skirts .. worn by many American girls .. are not appreciated by Africans. **1984** *National Law Jrnl.* 13 Aug. 47/3 Ms. BeSaw made repeated attempts to board the plane, even borrowing clothing from passengers to cover up her bralessness, says the lawyer, but they failed.

**brand**, *n.* Add: [9.] **brand leader**, the leading or best-selling product of its type.

**1967** *Times Rev. Industry* Feb. 30/1 The group's list of products .. contains not only a remarkably large number of household names .. but also many modern *brand leaders, such as Robinson's Barley Water, Windolene, Steradent, Harpic and Nulon. **1986** *Marketing Week* 29 Aug. 6/3 Chocolate countlines which include products such as Kit Kat (brand leader) and Wagon Wheels, represent two thirds of the advertising spend in the entire biscuit market.

hence **brand-leading** *a.*

**1985** *Financial Times* 1 May 27/1 The importance of flavour technology was demonstrated last week when Coca-Cola said it had changed the secret recipe for its *brand-leading drink.

**Brand X**, an unnamed brand contrasted unfavourably with a product of the same type which is being promoted; also *transf.*

**1934** J. RORTY *Our Master's Voice* xiii. 232 An Old Gold cigarette contains 6576 B.T.U.'s; whereas *Brand X contained 6688 B.T. U.'s, Brand Y 6731 B.T.U.'s and Brand Z 6732 B.T.U.'s. **1962** *Observer* 1 July 8/6 The evidence on which the [Pilkington] Committee bases its sweeping Brand X condemnation of the quality of the popular programmes on independent television is particularly thin. **1978** *N.Y. Times* 28 May IV. 7/2 Republican prospects of unity contrast with Brand X, which is likely to hold primaries for Comptroller and Attorney-General; even Governor Carey may face a primary contest. **1986** *Amer. Banker* 5 Nov. 8/4 The consumer really doesn't want Brand X. He doesn't want any old soft drink, or any old automobile, or any old bank.

**brass**, *n.* Add: [II.] [7.] **brass monkey weather** (see MONKEY *n.* 13 b).

**brat**, *n.*[2] Add: c. Special Comb. **brat pack** *slang* (orig. *U.S.*) [punningly after *rat pack* s.v. RAT *n.*[1] 7 e], a group of young Hollywood film stars of the mid 1980s popularly regarded as enjoying a rowdy, fun-loving lifestyle; hence, any precocious and aggressive clique; freq. *attrib.*

**1985** D. BLUM in *New York* 10 June 42/1 This is the Hollywood '*Brat Pack'. It is to the 1980s what the Rat Pack was to the 1960s—a roving band of famous young stars on the prowl for parties, women,

and a good time. **1986** *City Limits* 9 Oct. 29 Andie.. is torn between desire for rich kid Blane.. and contempt for his brat pack lifestyle. **1988** *Literary Rev.* Aug. 26/1 In the hands of a Brett Easton Ellis, McInerney's pace-maker within America's literary brat pack, a description of the situation would have sufficed. **1989** *Face* Jan. 3 Now 20, Molly Ringwald is finally shaking off the Brat Pack tag.
hence **brat packer**, a member of a brat pack. **1985** D. BLUM in *New York* 10 June 42/1 The *Brat Packers act together whenever possible. **1986** *Sunday Sun* (Brisbane) 22 June 22/5 Brat packer Judd Nelson is too big for his boots. He recently refused to be photographed. **1989** *Q* Mar. 119/4 *Young guns*. A new generation rediscovers an old genre: brat-packers Estevez, Sutherland, Sheen and Lou Diamond 'La Bamba' Phillips in a rollicking re-run of the Billy The Kid legend.

**breaker**, *n.*[1] Add: **8**. One who interrupts the conversation of others on a Citizens' Band radio channel, indicating that he or she wishes to transmit a message; hence, any CB radio user. *Citizens' Band Radio slang* (orig. *U.S.*).
**1963** *Time* 11 Jan. 39/2 *Sophie*: 10-4, Marcie... Oh-oh, here's a breaker; come in, breaker, and identify yourself. **1975** *Harper's Weekly* 6 Oct. 6/4 Break one-oh, break one-oh! Go ahead, breaker. Smokey in the Eastbound at exit three-two. **1981** *Times* 2 Nov. 2/3 Citizen's band radio, the new personal radio communication service, becomes legal in Britain today... CB enthusiasts, known as breakers, held a rally in London yesterday. **1985** *Truck & Driver* June 29/3 Brian's currently searching for a CB buff to set up shop in the cafe to repair broken sets and sell replacement ones to passing breakers.

**breast**, *n.* Add: [II.] [11.] **breast cancer**, cancer of a woman's breast.
**1915** *Surg., Gynecol. & Obstetr.* XX. 72/2 The surgery of *breast cancer.. can make sure advance only along the lines marked out by pathological research. **1985** *N.Y. Times* 14 Mar. A1/4 A major new study indicates that many women with breast cancer in its early stages can be treated just as well by small-scale surgery with little disfigurement.

**breath**, *n.* Add: [11.] **breath-test** *v. trans.* = BREATHALYSE *v.*
**1981** *Washington Post* 7 Mar. A12 His research team first studied drivers' drinking habits by stopping, interviewing and *breath-testing nearly 8,000 drivers at 2,000 accident-prone locations in Grand Rapids, Mich. **1986** *Independent* 26 Nov. 5/2 We will breath-test people when necessary.

**brecciate** ('brɛtʃıeıt), *v. Geol.* [Back-formation from BRECCIATED *a.*] *trans.* To reduce to breccia.
**1903** *Amer. Jrnl. Sci.* CLXVI. 111 Movements of that sort tend generally to brecciate rock along straight or open-curve lines. **1957** G. E. HUTCHINSON *Treat. Limnol.* I. i. 81 The main contribution of this process has been to brecciate, and so weaken, certain younger formations, and therefore to make them more easily excavated by ice. **1961** J. CHALLINOR *Dict. Geol.* 26/1 A sedimentary rock (usually a limestone) brecciated by some process involved in.. its consolidation.

**broad**, *a.* (*n., adv.*) Add: [D.] [2.] **broad-brush** *a.*, (as if) painted with a broad brush; wide-ranging but lacking in detail; general, sweeping.
**1967** *New Scientist* 28 Sept. 665/2 As a *broad brush' indication of the state of health of a project, the Confidence Profile may be used. **1985** *Austral. Business* 4 Sept. 141/2 A broad-brush picture of accountants who advertise divides firms into two categories.
**broad-leaf**, (*b*) any broad-leaved tree (see BROAD-LEAVED *a.* c); any of the dicotyledonous (hardwood) trees of the class Angiospermae, as contrasted with the conifers (softwoods) of the class Coniferae (and with monocotyledonous angiosperms such as palms); also *attrib.* or as *adj.*
**1909** *Forest Club Ann.* I. 23 The aspen is the most widely distributed and the most conspicuous broadleaf tree. **1939** F. H. LAMB *Bk. of Broadleaf Trees* 15 The Broadleafs are ubiquitous, varied, complex. **1985** *Nature* 8 Aug. 475/1 One-third of Britain's productive timberland.. is planted in broadleaves.

**Broad Left** *Pol.*, a loose coalition of socialist, communist, and other left-wing groups presenting a unified alternative to the candidates and policies of the right.
**1973** *Times Higher Educ. Suppl.* 30 Nov. 5/3 Left-wing groups from the *Broad Left to the 'ultra Left' were equally disillusioned after the overthrow of the .. Marxist government in Chile. **1986** *Courier-Mail* (Brisbane) 3 Sept. 5/1 The great danger for the Government, the Labor Party generally and what might loosely be called the Broad Left is that the New Right is starting to dictate the terms of the political agenda.
**broadscale** *a.*, on a broad scale; extensive; cf. *widescale* s.v. WIDE *a.* 12 c.
**1958** *Spectator* 30 May 703/2 The system simply does not work without modern *broadscale advertising. **1987** *Financial Times* 8 May (World Banking Suppl.) p. iii/4 Mr Coombes' last option was the broadscale alternative, sharing electronic systems with other banks, or buying in systems.

**Broederbond**, ('bruːdəbɒnd, ‖'brudərbɒnt), *n. S. Afr.* [a. Afrikaans, f. *broeder* BROTHER *n.* + *bond* league.] A largely secret society (founded in 1918) promoting the interests of and restricted in membership to male, Protestant Afrikaners.
**1935** *Times* 8 Nov. 13/3 The Afrikaner Broederbond, originally a laudable society interested in Afrikaans culture.. but now a secret society aiming for an independent Afrikaans form of government. **1945** *Round Table* No. 138. 184 General Smuts.. proposed to declare the Broederbond a political organization and ban its members from the public service. **1958** *Times* 1 July 9/3 Professor du Plessis is reputed to be a high official of the Broederbond, the society which is said to make and break Afrikaner leaders. **1963** A. DELIUS *Day Natal took Off* 47 He fell back upon the stock bogey of opposition politics, the Afrikaner Broederbond. **1986** *Christian Science Monitor* 28 Oct. 1/1 Recent splits in apartheid's other founding bodies—the ruling National Party and the semisecret cultural organization known as the Afrikaner Broeder-bond—suggest the change will be halting.

**bromocriptine** (brəʊməʊ'krıptiːn), *n. Pharm.* [f. BROMO- + alteration of ERGO)CRYPTINE *n.*] A synthetic analogue of the ergot alkaloids that stimulates the dopaminergic receptors of the brain, inhibiting the release of prolactin, and is used in the treatment of Parkinsonism, galactorrhoea, hypogonadism, and other conditions; 2-brom-α-ergocryptine, $C_{32}H_{40}$ $N_5O_5Br$.
**1974** *Brit. Med. Jrnl.* 25 May 419/1 Bromocriptine (2-brom-α-ergocryptine, CB 154) specifically reduces prolactin secretion by an action at the pituitary level. **1977** *Lancet* 19 Feb. 425/1 Wass et al. have reported six cases of peptic ulcer.. in patients treated with bromocriptine for acromegaly. **1987** *Oxf. Textbk. Med.* (ed. 2) I. x. 22/1 If functional hyper-prolactinaemia is associated with galactorrhoea or infertility, bromocriptine can be a most effective treatment.

**brotulid** ('brɒtjʊlıd), *n.* and *a.* [f. mod.L. *Brotula*, genus name, f. Amer. Sp. *brotula* lit.

'little bud', f. *brote* bud: see -ULE, -ID³.] **A**. *n*. Any of a numerous group of mostly deep-sea or cave-dwelling fishes placed either in the cusk-eel family, Ophidiidae, or separated as the Brotulidae.

**1895** GOODE & BEAN *Oceanic Ichthyol.* 316 Brotulids having the body elongate, covered with minute scales, and with lateral line interrupted over the vent. **1905** D. S. JORDAN *Guide Study of Fishes* II. xxix. 524 These blind Brotulids, called Pez Ciego in Cuba, are found in different caves in the county of San Antonio. **1931** J. R. NORMAN *Hist. Fishes* xii. 233 The two forms represent the only freshwater members of a large and varied family of fishes known as Brotulids (Brotulidae), the majority of which live at considerable depths in the oceans. **1975** *Sci. Amer.* Oct. 86/3 The brotulids (fishes distantly related to cods) remained almost motionless for hours, nibbling gently at the bait. **1986** *New Scientist* 8 May 47/1 *Lucifuga speleotes* is a brotulid, one of a group of stumpy, eel-like fish whose marine relatives inhabit the inside of reefs and crevices in undersea cliffs.

**B**. *adj*. Of, pertaining to, or designating a brotulid.

**1913** *Proc. Biol. Soc. Washington* XXVI. 75 (*heading*) The scales of . . brotulid . . fishes. **1926** *Zoologica* (N.Y.) VIII. 125 Brotulid eggs are somewhat if not entirely pelagic. **1961** E. S. HERALD *Living Fishes of World* 240/2 The only fish ever taken at a depth of more than four miles belonged to the brotulid genus *Bassogigas*. **1970** *Nature* 26 Dec. 1257/2 The brotulid fishes present a diversity surprising even to the ichthyologist.

**brown**, *a*. Add: [**7.**] **brown bag** chiefly *N. Amer.*, a plain brown paper-bag, *esp.* one in which a lunch is packed and carried to a work-place, meeting, etc.: freq. *attrib.*, esp. as *brown-bag lunch*.

**1947** *Brown bag [implied in *brown-bagger* below]. **1960** *N.Y. Times* 20 Nov. 2S/4 Wednesday and Thursday are what we call the 'brown bag' days. Since the players meet from 10 in the morning to 3.30 in the afternoon, they usually take lunches to practice. **1968** *U.S. News & World Rep.* 2 Sept. 88/3 Suburbanites are launching a 'brown bag' protest . . . Leaders of the drive are calling on the communities to take their lunch to work. **1976** *Daily Colonist* (Victoria, B.C.) 6 Mar. 19/5 Brown bag lunchers, backpackers, picnickers and no-frills airline travellers take heed. **1979** *Honolulu Advertiser* 8 Jan. A4/3 Senior Citizen Club . . Speakers, brown bag lunch, cards.

**brown-bag** *v. trans.* chiefly *N. Amer.*, to carry (one's lunch) in a brown paper-bag; also, to carry (alcoholic drink) concealed in such a bag (to conform to certain U.S. State laws), esp. to a restaurant; also *intr.* with *it*.

*a***1970** C. M. SHULZ in J. Dutton *Peanuts Lunch Bag Cook Bk.* 45/1 You had me take my lunch to school in a lunch box . . . All the other kids were *brown-bagging it! **1971** *Time* 8 Feb. 10/3 The mistrustful Russians brown-bagged their own caviar and vodka. **1977** C. MCCULLOUGH *Thorn Birds* xi. 249 Luke had brown-bagged two quart bottles of beer from the hotel. **1977** *Rolling Stone* 16 June 34/1 That other American, the devoted churchgoer who publicly votes against liquor but brown-bags it when he can. **1988** *Maclean's Mag.* 6 June 23/2 Dukakis's reputation as a penny pincher who brown-bags his lunches to the State House . . has become a . . joke.

**brown-bagger** chiefly *N. Amer.*, one who carries a brown bag, esp. containing food or drink; orig. *U.S. Services' slang*, a married man.

**1947** BERREY & VAN DEN BARK *Amer. Thes. Slang* Suppl. 13 *Brown bagger*, a married serviceman. **1958** *Oxf. Mail* 14 Aug. 6/6 Important are . . the graphic descriptions of 'brown-baggers'—married naval officers who regard the ship as an office. **1967** *News*

*& Observer* (Raleigh, N. Carolina) 9 Feb. 1/6 The 'brown-baggers' got in the first legislative lick . . on the explosive liquor issue. **1975** *Globe & Mail* (Toronto) 21 Apr. 27/8 The new kind of airline passengers have given birth to a brand new aviation term in the United States. They've been tagged 'brown baggers', in reference to their way of carrying their vittles in brown paper bags when they come aboard. **1986** *Los Angeles Times* 19 June VIII. 29/2 Brown-baggers should replace bags daily; never use a soiled or wet bag.

also **brown-bagging** *n*. and *a*.

**1966** *Economist* 26 Nov. 921/2 The officially tolerated subterfuge of '*brown-bagging'—buying the bottle at a state liquor shop and carrying it in a plain brown wrapper to restaurants. **1975** *Citizen* (Ottawa) 4 Oct. 73/3 The favorite bits for the audience, made up mostly of brown-bagging state employees . . was clearly the job description jargon. **1986** *Boston Globe* 28 May 45/1 Brown-bagging is given a new dimension with Eddie Bauer's lunch sacks.

**brown bomber** *Austral. slang* [introduced in 1946 as jobs were created for disabled war veterans; the brown uniforms were worn until 1975]: in New South Wales, an officer employed to enforce parking regulations (see quot. 1953); a traffic warden or 'parking cop'.

**1953** *Sydney Morning Herald* 3 Jan. 6/2 The year produced many slang words. Some of them were inherited from previous years but acquired wide usage in the past 12 months . . . '*Brown bombers', Sydney parking police, probably derived from the colour of their uniforms and influenced by the use of 'bomb' for an old car. **1968** D. IRELAND *Chantic Bird* vi. 61 Next day a brown bomber—a parking cop—gave me a fright. **1983** *Austral. Women's Weekly* Aug. 20/3 Parking inspectors in Victoria are Grey Ghosts, as they may be in NSW, though some people still call them Brown Bombers.

**brunch**, *n*. Add: Hence **brunch** *v. intr.*, to eat brunch.

**1938** *Time* 21 Nov. 12/1 He likes to sleep until 11 A.M., then brunches, sees visitors, plays squash. **1966** D. SKIRROW *It won't get you Anywhere* l. 249 We sat in the window and brunched. **1985** A. BLOND *Book Book* i. 14, I brunched with him over a smoked salmon omelette.

**brush**, *n.*² Add: [**I.**] [**1.**] **c**. In colloq. phr. as *daft* (*mad*, etc.) *as a brush*, quite daft or mad; crazy.

**1945** H. WILLIAMSON *Life in Devon Village* 12 'Mazed as a brish,' declared Mrs. 'Revvy' . . . 'I reckon he's not all there.' **1974** P. WRIGHT *Lang. Brit. Industry* xiv. 129 'As daft as a brush' (which flops, unable to stand upright). **1980** J. O'FAOLAIN *No Country for Young Men* vi. 136 She's as mad as a brush. Thinks she's privy to secrets of national importance.

**bruxism** ('brʌksɪz(ə)m), *n.* [f. Gr. βρυχ-ή grinding of teeth (f. βρύκειν, βρύχ- to eat greedily, to grind (teeth)) + -ISM.] Involuntary or unconscious grinding or clenching of the teeth, esp. during sleep.

**1932** *Psychoanal. Rev.* XIX. 299 A woman, aged forty-seven, was referred to me because of symptoms attributable to occlusal neurosis and bruxism. **1962** BLAKE & TROTT *Periodontology* iv. 47 Bruxism may be a reflection of the nervous condition of the patient. **1984** *Brit. Med. Jrnl.* 11 Feb. 436/1 Dentists see and treat most of these patients and usually attribute the disorder to both bruxism and malocclusion.

**B-tree** ('biː triː), *n. Computing.* [f. the letter *B*, repr. *balanced* or *binary*, + TREE *n*.] A tree in which all the terminal nodes are the same distance from the root and all the non-terminal nodes have between *n* and 2*n* subtrees or pointers, where *n* is an integer greater than or equal to one. (See also quot. 1968.)

**1968** D. E. KNUTH *Art of Computer Programming* I. ii. 315 Define a '*b*-tree' as a tree in which each node has exactly zero or two sons. **1972** *Acta Informatica* I. III. 174 The pages themselves are the nodes of a rather specialized tree, a so-called *B*-tree. **1976** N. WIRTH *Algorithms plus Data Struct.* iv. 250 Another positive quality of the B-tree organization is its suitability and economy in the case of purely sequential updating of the entire data bank. Every page is fetched into primary store exactly once. **1985** P. LAURIE *Databases* ii. 54 Advanced database managers now use a system called a 'B-tree' index.

**bubble**, *n.* Add: **6. bubble-gum**, (*b*) (in full, *bubble-gum music*), bland, repetitive pop music designed to appeal esp. to children and young teenagers (*dismissive*).

**1969** *Oz* Apr. 40/1 That group just couldn't get a tour .. in the States. America has enough of its own bubblegum music. **1971** *Melody Maker* 9 Oct. 11/7, I suppose one could say that bubblegum was outrageous, I mean there's nothing more outrageous than 'Chirpy Chirpy Cheep Cheep'. **1986** *N.Y. Times* 14 May C1/5 If old bubble gum music is on I sing at the top of my lungs, and if new funkadelic is on I bop in my seat.

**bubble memory** *Computing*, a type of memory which stores data as a pattern of magnetic bubbles (see MAGNETIC *a.* 5) in a thin layer of magnetic material.

**1971** *Jrnl. Appl. Physics* XLII. 2361 Recently proposed \*bubble-memory designs employing Permalloy rails are examined to determine an optimization of their geometries. **1984** *Austral. Micro Computerworld* Feb. 32/3 Some of the operating system is held on disk or bubble memory, and a bubble cartridge or disk drive is needed to boot the system. **1990** *Personal Computer World* Aug. 157/3 There have been some spectacular failures in the storage world (who remembers bubble memory?).

**buckle**, *v.* Add: [I.] [2.] **d.** *to buckle up*: to fasten one's seat-belt. *N. Amer.*

**1976** *Forbes* (N.Y.) 15 Oct. 40/1 As you gulp your martini and buckle up, a silver lining begins to girdle the clouds. **1986** *New Yorker* 7 Apr. 38/2 She settles in, buckles up, then leans forward and runs one finger over the dashboard. **1987** *Los Angeles Times* 27 Apr. v. 5/2 The Night Rider and another device, the Night Lighter, with lights that spin around the license plate, are displayed beneath a sign that reads 'Buckle Up and Light Up!'

**buddy**, *n.* Add: **2.** Special Comb. **buddy system** orig. *U.S.*, a co-operative arrangement whereby individuals are paired or teamed up, assuming responsibility for each other's safety and well-being, as while swimming or engaging in other hazardous activity; also *transf.*

**1931** *Swimming & Water Safety* (Boy Scouts of Amer.) (ed. 3) v. 102 With the \*Buddy system the victim of such an accident would be immediately missed and probably recovered in time for prompt restorative measures. **1950** A. V. MITCHELL *Camp Counseling* xv. 155 *The Buddy System.* Each camper chooses a companion of about his own ability, and the two stay constantly near each other, each being responsible for the other's safety. **1968** *Globe & Mail* (Toronto) 13 Jan. 41/7 This is a must for all safaris. If you take off into the wilderness carry a survival kit. .. Use the buddy system—two snowmobiles or more. **1971** *New Society* 1 July 22/3 Alcoholics Anonymous attribute much of their success to the 'buddy system'. **1989** *Combat & Survival Mag.* Oct. 58/2, I passed the time watching one of our four-man patrols working the buddy system as they dived in and out of the shadows.

**bug**, *v.*[3] Add: **2.** With *off*: to depart, go away. Freq. *imp.*

**1973** *Mad* Oct. 32/1 Bug off ye merry gentlemen, Our Christmas you won't mar—Without a woman giving birth You'd have no Super Star. **1974** *Guidelines to Volunteer Services* (N.Y. State Dept. Correctional Services) 38 *Bug off*, get away from me. **1982** M. PIERCY *Braided Lives* ii. 25 Freddie tried to get me to go upstairs with him. 'Bug off,' I said. **1983** J. WILCOX *Mod. Baptists* (1984) xxxiii. 227 I'm telling you to bug off. I'm tired of your advice, hear? **1989** M. ATWOOD *Cat's Eye* xvii. 97 Why don't you and your little friends bug off!

**builder**, *n.* Add: **3.** Special Comb. **builders' merchant**, a supplier of materials to the building trade.

**1870** *Post Office Directory of Building Trades* 144/2 \*Builders' Merchants, *See Building Material Dealers.* **1926** A. JAMES *Commerce Stage I* viii. 44 A builder's merchant will deal in timber, bricks and slates. **1977** *Whitaker's Almanack 1978*, 638/2 (*heading*) Builders Merchants (86). *Livery*, 180. **1990** *Practical Householder* Apr. 35/3 Your local builders' merchant may not carry many varieties.

**bulb**, *n.* Add: [2.] [a.] For last sentence of def. read: Sometimes popularly applied to a solid tuber of similar external shape and by metonymy, esp. in *Gardening*, to a plant which grows from a bulb.

**1727** *Bradley's Fam. Dict.* s.v. *Cyclamen*, The German Cyclamens are rather Turnep-rooted Plants than Bulbs. **1821** *Bot. Reg.* VII. App. 7 Other points of agreement with Crinum separate them [*sc.* the plants] still more widely from the occidental bulbs which I have heretofore called Amaryllis. **1901** W. ROBINSON *Eng. Flower Garden* (ed. 8) 162 A great number of our spring flowers and hardy bulbs mature their foliage and go to rest early in the year. **1988** *Gardening from 'Which?'* Aug. 245/1 Some autumn-flowering bulbs are suitable for partial shade.

**bull**, *n.*[1] Add: [IV.] [11.] **bull market** *Stock Exchange*, a market characterized by the rising price of stock, etc.

**1891** *Century Mag.* Jan. 426 No office of its size in the Street made so much money for its customers in a \*bull market. **1931** F. L. ALLEN *Only Yesterday* xii. 301 No aspect of the campaign was more interesting than the extent to which it reflected the obsession of the American people with bull-market prosperity. **1986** *What Investment* July 15/3 If historical precedent is followed, the present bull market will end by the next general election.

**bullet**, *n.*[1] Add: [8.] **bullet train**, a passenger train which travels at very high speeds; esp. the Japanese Shinkansen.

**1966** *Economist* 14 May 698/2 Before the 1964 Tokyo Olympics, the Japanese slapped the finishing touches on the world's longest monorail system and the world's fastest '\*bullet train'. **1988** *Nature* 11 Feb. 474/3 The train offers a smooth bump-free ride and can climb steeper inclines than a conventional bullet train.

**bullshit**, *n.* Add: '**bullshitter** *n.*, one who exaggerates or talks nonsense, esp. to bluff or impress.

**1941** BAKER *Dict. Austral. Slang* 15 *Bullsh*, nonsense, empty chatter, bragging. Whence 'bullsh-tter': one given to bragging or empty talk. **1942** BERREY & VAN DEN BARK *Amer. Thes. Slang* §422/3 '*Tall talker*', .. bull fighter, bull-shitter, bull shooter. **1950** C. MACINNES *To Victors the Spoils* I. 20 'Well .. I'll see what I can do,' he said, as we went out. 'A nice old bullshitter,' Walter told me. **1966** H. MARRIOTT *Cariboo Cowboy* i. 19, I had already had some experience with .. blowhards and bullshitters as they are called in the Cariboo. **1970** J. LENNON in J. Wenner *Lennon Remembers* (1972) 72 He is a bullshitter. But he made us credible with intellectuals. **1986** C. LASSALLE *Breaking Rules* 157 That bogus old bullshitter, Jung.

**bum**, *n.*[1] Add: **4. bumbag**, a small bag or pouch incorporated in a belt worn round the waist or across the shoulder (orig. designed for skiers and worn at the back); cf. *fanny pack* s.v. *FANNY n.*[4] 1 b.
    **1951** W. R. BRACKEN *Handbk. Ski-ing* i. 20 A Rucksack is not necessary .. but .. a '*Bumbag', worn round the waist on a belt, is very useful for carrying bits and pieces. **1987** *Motor Cycle News* 1 July 45/2 There's not much you can't get into Clovers new mega-sized enduro bum bag .. party packs of beer, a typewriter, cameras, or even tools if you're a serious enduro/beach racer.
    **bum-boy** *slang*, a young male homosexual, esp. a prostitute; a catamite.
    **1937** PARTRIDGE *Dict. Slang* 106/2 *Bum-boy. **1938** DYLAN THOMAS *Let.* 7 May (1985) 294 A ringed and dainty gesture copied from some famous cosmopolitan bumboy. **1959** M. SHADBOLT *New Zealanders* 50 'A job?' .. 'The job you people promised me. Now your bum boy out in the office tells me I can't have it. I want to know why.' **1984** M. AMIS *Money* 150 Jerome, the blue-jeaned bumboy with earring and dyed blonde hair, cruised over.

‖**bumiputra** (buːmɪˈpuːtrə), *n.* and *a.* [Malay *bumiput(ĕ)ra*, lit. 'sons of the soil', f. *bumi* (Skr. *bhūmi*) earth, soil + *putra* (also Skr.) son, child.] **A.** *n.* (*collect. sing* or in *pl.*). Malaysian citizens of indigenous Malay origin. **B.** *adj.* Of or pertaining to the bumiputra; indigenous Malay.
    **1966** *Economist* 22 Oct. 398/3 Malayan Banking .. as a Malay rather than Chinese concern, is particularly identified with the *bumiputras*, the Malayan sons of the soil. **1972** *Sunday Times* (Kuala Lumpur) 25 June 4/5 The Government was today urged to make it a policy of allocating 50 per cent of its supply contracts and those of its agencies to bumiputra firms. **1972** *Sunday Times* (Singapore) 24 Sept. 6/3 In the Faculty of Engineering, bumiputras now formed 7.3 per cent of the total enrolment. **1980** *Times Lit. Suppl.* 17 Oct. 1177/1 The Malays, now called the *bumiputra* or sons of the soil, .. impose the Malay language, or *bahasa Malaysia*, on a narrow minority of Chinese and Indians, and bask in a prosperity of tin, rubber and oil. **1980** *Times* 2 Sept. 15/5 Other plantation groups have moved to restructure their equity to raise Bumiputra shareholdings (i.e. those held by Malays and other native races). **1983** *Current Affairs Bull.* (Sydney) Nov. 27/1 The Government has established .. a national investment company to buy shares with public funds in trust for the *bumiputras* (Malay and other indigenous races).

**bummer** ('bʌmə(r)), *n.*[5] orig. and chiefly *U.S.* [f. BUM *a.* + -ER[1].] An unpleasant or depressing experience, *esp.* one induced by a hallucinatory drug (= *down trip* s.v. DOWN *a.* 1 e); a disappointment or failure. Freq. as complement to subj.: *to be a bummer*.
    **1967** J. DIDION in *Sat. Even. Post* 23 Sept. 26/3, I ask if he found a ride to New York. 'I hear New York's a bummer,' he says. **1968** *Electronic Music Rev.* Jan. 19 The declaimed lyric is an example of what heads would call a 'bummer'. **1968** T. LEARY *Politics of Ecstasy* viii. 166 The Western world has been on a bad trip, a 400-year bummer. **1970** *New Yorker* 3 Oct. 76/3 The newer kinds of movies don't satisfy *anybody* ... Almost all the films released this summer have been box-office bummers. **1974** *Daily Colonist* (Victoria, B.C.) 31 Dec. 15/1 Although a great many students are living together these days I still think the idea is a bummer. **1979** N. MAILER *Executioner's Song* (1980) I. xxi. 343 It was a bummer. Hitchhiking over to the nuthouse, the

whole day got lost. **1986** D. A. DYE *Platoon* (1987) v. 67, I ain't no sooner off the chopper than I get a letter from my wife sayin' she wants a fucking divorce. What a bummer, man! **1988** *Times Lit. Suppl.* 10 June 646/4 Twenty or so big fat poets on a tiny stage for the International Reading, which promises to be a bummer.

**bump**, *n.*[1] Add: [III.] **bump-start** *v. trans.* = *push-start* s.v. PUSH-; also *transf.*; also **bump-started** *ppl. a.*, **bump-starting** *vbl. n.*
    **1972** *Bike* Spring 26/3 Three or four tries usually got it going except in the extreme Welsh cold when *bumpstarting was the only solution to the motor's grumpiness. **1978** R. WESTALL *Devil on Road* xiii. 96, I kicked her over till my leg seized up. Tried bump-starting her. **1980** *Dirt Bike* Oct. 4/2 You park your bike on top of a hill, so you can bump-start it, instead of kickstarting. **1987** *Guardian* Feb. 12/3 Woe .. for Granny Weatherwax, all set with witchly role-conditioning and her bump-started broomstick!

**bun** *n.*[2] Add: [1.] **d.** *pl.* The buttocks; rarely *sing.*, the human posterior. *N. Amer. slang.*
    **1960** WENTWORTH & FLEXNER *Dict. Amer. Slang* 76/1 *Bun, n.,* the human posterior. **1968** J. T. STEWART in Jones & Neal *Black Fire* 202 For half a man I'd snuff twenty Armenians and tell their Episcopalian mothers to be on guard and find linoleum stratagems getting to your buns. **1973** *Playboy* Dec. 268/2 I'll grab Ron's or Alan's buns sometimes and they're firm and hard. **1983** *Gentlemen's Q.* Mar. 48/1 People still come up to me in airports or shopping malls and pinch my buns ... They think I'm one of their best friends. **1985** E. LEONARD *Glitz* xvii. 149 She saw .. a white band below his hips, sexy, really nice buns.

**bungarra** ('bʌŋərə), *n. W. Austral.* [ad. Aboriginal (Nhanta, Carnarvon region, Western Australia) *baṇarra*.] = *sand goanna* s.v. SAND *n.*[2] 10 b.
    **1897** A. HAYWARD *Along Road to Cue* 9 It grieves me sore To hear the batteries roar Where only roamed of yore The mild bungarra. **1924** LAWRENCE & SKINNER *Boy in Bush* vii. 95 In the spare time they would have little hunts of wallabies or bandicoots or bungarras, or boody-rats. **1961** D. STUART *Driven* iv. 35 The sight sometimes of a bungarra, the long sleek brown and buff big lizard, .. staring down with beady eyes in long reptilian head. **1970** *Southerly* XXX. 218 In some stage of the vast geological ages a brown snake, a bungarra, a dingo travelling, or a boobook owl sounding his double note across the lonely moonlit night.

**Burkitt** ('bɜːkɪt), *n. Path.* [The name of D. P. *Burkitt* (1911–93), British surgeon, who described the condition in 1958 (*Brit. Jrnl. Surg.* XLVI. 218).] *Burkitt's lymphoma, Burkitt tumour:* a malignant tumour of the lymphatic system occurring esp. on the jaw and viscera and affecting young children in parts of tropical Africa.
    **1963** *Lancet* 12 Jan. 109/2 Other tumours such as rhabdomyosarcoma or embryonal sarcoma of the orbit or jaw may mimic some of the features of the Burkitt tumour. **1963** *Brit. Jrnl. Cancer* XVII. 58 The cells in two biopsies of Burkitt's lymphoma have been studied in thin sections with the electron microscope. **1970** [see EPSTEIN–BARR VIRUS *n.*]. **1976** EDINGTON & GILLES *Path. in Tropics* (ed. 2) x. 501 The Burkitt tumour is the commonest tumour of childhood in Uganda and in Ibadan. **1984** TIGHE & DAVIES *Pathology* (ed. 4) x. 84 The best evidence for virus involvement is in Burkitt's lymphoma. **1987** *Oxf. Textbk. Med.* (ed. 2) II. XIX. 184/2 The Burkitt tumours are extremely sensitive to chemotherapy and long-term remissions sometimes result from a single dose of cytotoxic treatment. **1987** *Brit. Med. Jrnl.* 16 May 1247/2 In Burkitt's lymphoma there is a

translocation between chromosome 8 and the immunoglobulin genes on chromosomes 2, 14, or 22.

**burpee** ('bɜːpiː, bɜː'piː), *n.* Also Burpee, burpie. [The name of Dr. Royal H. *Burpee* (b. 1897), U.S. psychologist and service organization director.] A physical exercise consisting of a squat thrust performed from and completed in a standing position. Usu. in *pl.* Orig. in **Burpee test**, a test devised by Burpee to measure agility and muscular co-ordination, in which the subject executes a series of burpees in rapid succession.

**1939** C. H. McCloy *Tests & Measurements in Health & Physical Educ.* viii. 84 *The Burpee test* . . . Upon the command to begin, the subject flexes his hips to the squat-rest position [etc.]. **1957** Morgan & Adamson *Circuit Training* v. 58 *(caption) Burpee,* . . a continuous four-count movement as follows: (1) Stand (2) Crouch with hand support (3) Jump legs backward to front support (4) Jump legs forward to crouch position (1) Stand again. **1971** D. Rutherford *Rugby for Coach & Player* xiii. 161, 1 minute maximum burpees . . 1 minute burpee jumps. **1985** G. Keillor *Lake Wobegon Days* 186 Forty boys do pushups in unison, then stand up for the burpies. **1986** *Tennis* July 42/1 The Burpee strengthens arms, shoulders, chest, back, stomach and legs.

**bursectomy** (bɜː'sɛktəmɪ), *n. Med.* [f. burs(a *n.* + -ectomy.] Excision or destruction of a bird's bursa of Fabricius (the site where B lymphocytes are formed), usu. done in the egg or soon after hatching in research into immunity.

**1928** Riddle & Tange in *Amer. Jrnl. Physiol.* LXXXVI. 266 It was thought that observations on these processes in birds deprived of the bursa should supply further light on this problem. As a descriptive term for the process of extirpation of this bursa, we shall introduce and use the word 'bursectomy'. **1956** *Poultry Sci.* XXXV. 224/1 An experiment designed to study the effect of bursectomy. **1968** *Nature* 19 Oct. 294/1 Bursectomy was achieved either surgically on 1 day old chicks, or hormonally by injecting 6/7 day old incubated eggs with . . testosterone propionate. **1974** *Sci. Amer.* Nov. 60 A small portion of chicks subjected to this 'hormonal bursectomy' . . are tolerant of foreign skin.

Hence **bur'sectomize** *v. trans.*, to subject to bursectomy; **bur'sectomized** *ppl. a.*

**1928** Riddle & Tange in *Amer. Jrnl. Physiol.* LXXXVI. 271 The size of the ovaries of the bursectomized birds also falls within the normal range of variation of this organ. **1958** *Poultry Sci.* XXXVII. 1091/2 Ten birds were splenectomized at 2 weeks of age and bursectomized one week later. **1969** *Federation Proc.* XXVIII. 432/1, 3 out of 5 chicks bursectomized on the day of hatching failed to make detectable levels of antibody against BSA. **1970** *Nature* 11 Apr. 124/1 In hormonally bursectomized chickens tuberculin sensitivity could not be induced.

**bus**, *n.*² Add: [3.] **busway**, a road reserved exclusively for buses; *spec.* one constructed with grooves or tracks to guide the vehicle; cf. tramway *n.* 1.

**1961** *Wall St. Jrnl.* 27 Dec. 1/1 Baltimore would like to build three-lane '*busways*', for exclusive use by express buses. **1966** *Daily Tel.* 15 Aug. 16/3 Among the ideas for town travel now being assessed by Ministry scientific experts . . are high-speed mono-rails, guided buses to run along 'busways' only a few inches wider than the bus, [etc.]. **1976** P. R. White *Planning for Public Transport* iii. 68 The concept of providing bus priorities on existing roads, and building separate bus stations, may be extended to that of building entirely separate busways. **1984** *Buses* Feb. 69/3 The 600 metres of busway will give operating experience necessary for possible further extension to the [guided busway] system.

**bus**, *v.*² Add: [2.] **b.** [Back-formation from *busboy* s.v. bus *n.*² 3.] To clear (a table) of dirty dishes, etc., as in a restaurant or cafeteria; also, to carry or remove (dishes) from the table. *N. Amer.*

**1952** R. V. Williams *Hard Way* iii. 17 Laura and the guy with her . . sat a table across from us under a big sign that said *Bus your own trays*. **1958** *Fast Food* Jan. 40/3 Customers bus their own dishes to a window of the dishwashing room. **1979** *Washington Post* 4 Feb. G2/3 John, 12, helped out washing dishes; and Jimmy, 16, bussed tables. **1980** *News & Observer* (Raleigh, N. Carolina) 28 Oct. 4/4 Your message is clear: Blacks who agree with you may dine at your table; all others will please bus the dishes. **1988** *New Yorker* 1 Aug. 50/1 Chad Laughner, Chip's twelve-year-old son, buses tables at Castleton.

**bush**, *n.*¹ Add: [11.] **bush league** *Baseball*, a minor league, *esp.* one of mediocre quality; freq. *transf.* and *attrib.*

**1906** *Bush league* [implied in *bush leaguer* below]. **1908** *Baseball Mag.* July 79/2 Being from Chicago, that bush league town wasn't good enough to hold Hermaine's sandals. **1914** 'High Jinks, Jr.' *Choice Slang* 8 *Bush league trick,* a trick indulged in which is not in harmony with its surroundings. **1928** D. Parker in *New Yorker* 12 May 20/2 Well, well, well, to think of me having real Scotch; I'm out of the bush leagues at last. **1949** A. Hynd *We are Public Enemies* iv. 108 He was . . a bushleague Chicago gambler. **1955** *Sci. Amer.* Sept. 188/2 This is a first-class piece of ratiocination and scientific detection which makes the efforts of highly touted police and crime laboratories seem bush-league stuff. **1973** *Hockey Digest* Apr. 8/2 What does *Hockey Digest* think of the WHA and how long will it last? I think it is a bush league. **1986** *N.Y. Post* 9 July 57/3 This is an example of poor sportsmanship . . . It is international bush league.

hence **bush leaguer**, one who plays in a minor league; also *transf.*, small timer.

**1906** *Sporting Life* 10 Feb. 4/4 Consider the *bush leaguer* on the bench! He toils not neither does he spin; yet Solomon in all his glory was not arrayed like one of these. **1943** S. Lewis *G. Planish* xxv. 301 He peeped into every new organization to promote religion—and there were perhaps six new ones a week in New York City—because these bush-leaguers might have some new ideas. **1975** S. Bellow *Humboldt's Gift* (1976) 180, I don't care who she is and what she knows, compared to Polly she's a bush leaguer.

**business**, *n.* Add: [III.] [11.] **c.** In colloq. phr. *to be in the business of*, to be engaged or involved in, concerned with. Usu. in negative contexts.

**1977** *Times* 10 Aug. 16/3 Mr William Davis, editor of Punch, told the hearing that . . a humorous magazine was not in the business of being respectable. **1981** *Observer* 1 Mar. 13/6 Journalists are dealing with a more fragile commodity than ordinary manufacturers; and they are in the business, after all, of making a fuss. **1982** *Times Lit. Suppl.* 5 Feb. 146/2 Goldziher, as a scholar, was not in the business of either defending or attacking Islam.

[13.] **e.** *any other business*, matters not listed specifically on the agenda of a meeting, but raised after the main business has been discussed; abbrev. *A.O.B.* s.v. *A III.

**1935** G. K. Bucknall *Oldham's Guide to Company Secretarial Work* (ed. 7) xix. 152 Agenda . . 1. Minutes of last meeting . . 4. Overdue accounts . . 9. Any other business. 10. Next meeting. **1953** F. Shackleton *Chairman's Guide* ix. 74 The agenda for a general meeting other than the first would be as follows: . . (7) Any other business. **1968** Taylor & Mears *Right Way to conduct Meetings* (ed. 7) xiv. 94 No major matter should ever be put to the vote under 'Any other Business'. **1976** *Harvard Business*

*Rev.* Mar.–Apr. 50/2 Listing 'Any other business' on the agenda is an invitation to waste time.
[**24.**] **business studies** *n. pl.* (freq. const. *sing.*), the analysis of the structure and conduct of business as an academic discipline.
[**1914** C. B. THOMPSON *Scientific Management* (series title) Harvard Business Studies.] **1962** H. O. BEECHENO *Introd. Bus. Stud.* p. vii, With the introduction of the Ordinary and Higher National Certificates and the Higher National Diploma in *Business Studies many students will be studying the subject of the Structure of the Business World. **1986** *Economist* 18 Oct. 38/1 There are severe shortages of teachers of science, maths, technology, design and business studies.

**bustier** ('bʌstɪeɪ, 'bʊst-; ‖bystje), *n.* [a. Fr., f. *buste* BUST *n.*[1]] A short, close-fitting, often strapless bodice or top worn by women as a fashion garment.
**1979** *Evening News* 9 Aug. 25/4 A bustier is a tight, sculpted bodice with boning inserted in the side seams for extra shape and fit. **1982** *Christian Science Monitor* 10 Nov. 19/3 These can be worn with loose floating shirt-jackets or long blousons over bare-midriff suntops or *bustiers*. **1986** *Guardian* 10 Apr. 9/8 Other designers, too, have been producing denim lines—notably Katharine Hamnett, whose jeans, bustiers, shorts and jackets, trimmed with diamante, give nice well-off girls the chance to sleaze with the Rockers. **1989** *Times* 28 June 21/3 Young ladies were sunbathing topless or even naked in Hyde Park and wearing bustiers in Oxford Street.

**Butazolidin** (bjuːtə'zɒlɪdɪn), *n. Pharm.* Also -ine (-iːn) and with lower-case initial. [f. BUT(YL *n.* + AZO- + *pyra*)*zolidine* (f. PYRAZOLE *n.* + -IDINE).] A proprietary name for phenylbutazone.
**1951** *Trade Marks Jrnl.* 26 Sept. 896/1 *Butazolidin* .. Pharmaceutical preparations for human use and for veterinary use, sanitary substances, medical and surgical plasters, material .. for bandaging, disinfectants and antiseptics. **1952** *Times* 4 July 3/4 The new substance is called butazolidine and the discovery of its value as a pain reliever was almost accidental. **1963** [see PHENYLBUTAZONE *n.*]. **1974** R. M. KIRK et al. *Surgery* vi. 86 Acute gastric ulcers are increasingly recognised following major trauma, operations, and the administration of drugs such as .. butazolidine. **1978** G. A. SHEEHAN *Running & Being* x. 136 We begin to hear about Butazolidine and cortisone shots. **1987** *Brit. Nat. Formulary* (B.M.A.) (ed. 13) 315 Phenylbutazone (Butazolidin etc.) is another potent anti-inflammatory drug but because of occasional serious side-effects its use is limited to the hospital treatment of ankylosing spondylitis.

**button**, *n.* Add: [**5.**] **h.** *transf.* (*right*) *on the button*: on target, at exactly the right moment; exactly (right), precisely. *colloq.* (orig. *U.S.*).
**1928** HECHT & MACARTHUR *Front Page* I. 34 He takes a final drink from the flask, then throws it out the window. A scream of rage arises .. : *On the button!* **1937** *Printers' Ink Monthly* May 40/1 On the button, a program ending exactly on time. **1942** BERREY & VAN DEN BARK *Amer. Thes. Slang* §279/6 *Satisfactory*, .. (right) on the button, patsy, plenty good enough. **1949** *N.Y. Times Bk. Rev.* 25 Sept. 14 (*heading*) Right on the button. **1952** *New Yorker* 17 May 30/3, I .. then strolled jauntily over to Ricky's, at five o'clock on the button. **1962** J. GLENN in *Into Orbit* 142 All the factors of the flight .. would have to be right on the button or we would not get into a proper orbit. There was little tolerance for errors. **1985** W. SAFIRE in *N.Y. Times Mag.* 27 Oct. 14/5 Should you use a ring-a-ding word, smack on the button of your meaning, when your listener or reader is not likely to understand?

**butyrophenone** (ˌbjuːtɪrəʊfɪ'nəʊn, -'fɛnəʊn), *n. Chem.* and *Pharm.* [f. BUTYRO- + -*phenone* (f. PHEN(YL *n.* + KET)ONE *n.*).] *n*-Propyl phenyl

ketone, $C_6H_5 \cdot CO \cdot (CH_2)_2CH_3$, a liquid. Also, any compound whose structure contains this group.
**1908** *Chem. Abstr.* II. 1426 With $C_6H_6$ and $AlCl_3$ it forms the butyrophenone, $C_8H_8O_2$: $NCH_2CH_2 \cdot CH_2Bz$; flat, pointed needles, 132-3°. **1917** *Ibid.* XI. 3753/2 *Butyrophenone*, $CH_3CH_2CH_2COPh$. **1961** *Jrnl. Pharmaceutical Sci.* L. 350/1 On synthesizing a series of over 1,000 new substituted piperidines, it was found that the basic butyrophenones therein had powerful C.N.S.-depressant activity in various species. **1967** I. L. FINAR *Org. Chem.* (ed. 5) I. xxvii. 707 Willgerodt reaction ... The amido-group is always formed at the end of the chain whatever the size of the R group in $C_6H_5 \cdot CO \cdot R$; e.g., butyrophenone forms γ-phenyl-butyramide. .. $C_6H_5 \cdot CH_2 \cdot CH_2 \cdot CH_2 \cdot CONH \cdot_2$. **1968** *Brit. Med. Jrnl.* 27 Apr. 230/2 The butyrophenone derivatives are non-phenothiazine drugs which are useful in the treatment of psychotic patients, particularly those with manic overactivity. **1984** *Brit. Nat. Formularly* VIII. 139/2 Drugs of other chemical groups tend to resemble the phenothiazines ... They include the butyrophenones (benperidol, droperidol, haloperidol, and trifluperidol); [etc.].

**buy**, *v.* Add: **III. 17.** The vb.-stem in Comb. **buy-back** orig. *U.S.*, the buying-back or repurchase of goods, shares, etc., often by contractual agreement; *spec.* the repurchase by a company of its own stock, often as a defensive ploy against a takeover bid; freq. *attrib.*
**1954** *Wall St. Jrnl.* 7 May 1/4 This *buy-back* policy, which includes repurchase of Sheaffer goods involved in cut-price close-out sales, is aimed at protecting merchants who follow the company's 'fair trade' policies. **1963** *Ibid.* 25 Sept. 18/5 The AEC should be required .. to purchase the entire plutonium output of reactors ... 'Plutonium buy-back is one of the biggest subsidies Uncle Sam gives.' **1971** *Times* 22 Feb. (Canada Suppl.) p. ii/2, There is also a lobby .. which favours a buy-back policy from United States and other foreign interests in Canadian industry. **1985** *Observer* 6 Jan. 19/5 There were straightforward 'buybacks' of shares by companies which felt their shares were undervalued in a mostly flat market.

**buy-in**, (*a*) the purchase of shares on the stock exchange, esp. after the non-delivery of similar shares bought; (*b*) the buying-back of a company's own shares; also, the purchase of a controlling share in a company by an external party (esp. a management consortium): see BUY-OUT *n.*
**1968** *N.Y. Times* 3 Aug. 29/7 A *buy-in* occurs when a broker fails to receive from another broker securities he has purchased for a customer and he enters another order in the open market for the shares so that he can deliver them. **1982** *Sunday Times* 12 Dec. 46/8 (*heading*) Ins and outs of a buy-in. **1984** *Observer* 2 Dec. 29 Walt Disney Productions .. took further defensive action last week by announcing plans to purchase up to 3.5 million .. of its outstanding shares ... The Bass family .. will end up with 27.7 per cent of Disney's outstanding shares at the end of the buy-in.

**bypass**, *n.* Add: [**6.**] **b.** A permanent alternative pathway (usu. avoiding an obstruction or constriction) created surgically within the circulatory system (esp. in or near the heart or brain), alimentary canal, etc., incorporating a transplanted or synthetic vessel or chamber; also, an operation to create such an alternative route, or an artificial device incorporating one. Freq. *attrib.*, esp. as *bypass operation*, *surgery*.
**1964** H. LAUFMAN in L. Davis *Christopher's Textbk. Surg.* xxix. 1275/2 The saphenous vein is used for by-passing, replacing or patching the femoral and

popliteal arteries. When it is normal, its accessibility is a great advantage. However, it is not always available in sufficient length for by-pass surgery. **1970** *Sci. News Yearbk.* 84 The DeBakey bypass, a spherical plastic chamber the size of an apple, skirts the heart's left ventricle, through which blood is normally pumped, and offers a parallel route. **1972** P. F. Nora *Operative Surg.* xxxvii. 795 (*caption*) Bypass from subclavian to left carotid artery. **1984** A. Smith *Mind* iv. xiv. 275 Neurosurgeons are now performing bypass operations to rearrange certain blood vessels over the brain. **1986** *Daily News* (N.Y.) 23 May 65/3 A hospital spokeswoman said [he] .. was awake and in stable condition after his bypass operation.

# C

**C.** Add: [II.] **5.** *Biochem.* Designating a form of double-stranded DNA adopted in the presence of certain solvents, consisting of a right-handed double helix which is more tightly coiled than the more common A and B forms. Cf. *A II. 11, *B II. 2 b (vii).

**1958** D. A. MARVIN et al. in *Nature* 9 Aug. 387/2 We have observed a reversible transition between the *B* X-ray diffraction pattern of the lithium salt of deoxyribonucleic acid and a similar but distinct pattern we call *C*. **1961** *Jrnl. Molecular Biol.* III. 563 For *C* DNA, screw disorder is likely because the helix is non-integral. **1982** T. M. DEVLIN *Textbk. Biochem.* xvii. 807 Forms A and C differ from B in the pitch of the base pairs relative to the helix axis as well as in other geometric parameters of the double helix.

[III.] [3.] [a.] **c** (*Particle Physics*), charm, a quark flavour (CHARM *n.* 6); charmed.

**1975** *c* [see CHARM *n.* 6]. **1979** *Nature* 6 Sept. 18/1 Each generation of leptons and quarks (the first being e, $v_e$, u, d, the second $\mu$, $v_\mu$, c, s, the third $\tau$, $v_\tau$, t and b) can be fitted into the 16-dimensional representation of SU(5/1). **1983** *Sci. Amer.* July 106/2 The recent direct observations of $D^0$ mesons in B-meson decay demonstrates that the b quark does in fact decay to c at least some of the time.

**CAD,** computer-aided design.

**1965** *Mech. Engin.* May 41/2 The Computer-Aided Design (*CAD) project at M.I.T. is based on the absolute necessity of this type of rapport between man and machine. **1968** *New Scientist* 1 Feb. 245/2 For computer aided design (CAD) the input data would be in the form of overall requirements, with no limitations as to the types or manufacturers of components. **1979** *Arizona Daily Star* 5 Aug. (Advt. Section) 3 Establish and apply CAD/CAM in manufacturing engineering. **1984** *Ann. Rep. Racal Electronics PLC* 7/1 Several new products in the CAD/CAE area have been launched including powerful software for use on personal computers.

**cd** (*Physics*), candela.

**1950** *Cd [see CANDELA *n.*]. **1984** D. C. GIANCOLI *Gen. Physics* xxxvi. 704 We define the luminous intensity .. as the luminous flux per unit solid angle (steradian). Its unit is the candela (cd) where 1 cd = 1 lm/sr.

**CFC,** chlorofluorocarbon.

**1976** *New Scientist* 29 Apr. 213/1 (*heading*) The official view on *CFCs and the ozone layer. **1985** *Sci. Amer.* Aug. 5/1 The levels of these gases, most notably chlorofluorocarbon-11 (CFC-11), CFC-12, ozone methane and nitrous oxide, have increased dramatically. **1989** *Daily Tel.* 2 May 17/3 Shoppers are told that meat and eggs are packaged in CFC-free containers.

**C.M.G.,** Companion of the Order of St. Michael and St. George.

**1842** *Royal Kalendar* (verso of title-page), *Notes of Abbreviation* .. British *Orders of Knighthood* .. *C.M.G.*, Companion of St. Michael and St. George. **1861** *Foreign Office List* 132/2 Saunders, Sidney Smith, C.M.G. **1914** E. WALLACE *Bosambo of River* i. 21 'You'll become a colonial-made gentleman one of these days.' .. C.M.G.'s were not likely to come his way whilst Abdul Hazim was still at large. **1959** *Chambers's Encycl.* III. 513 The Most Distinguished Order of St Michael and St George was founded 27 Apr. 1818 by the prince regent .. to reward the services of the inhabitants of Malta and the Ionian islands .. and of other British subjects serving in

them ... In 1864 the order was extended so as to apply to service in all British colonies and by the statutes of 1868 its numbers were increased. **1986** *Independent* 31 Dec. 4/3 CMG is known by juniors as 'Call me God'.

**CMV,** cytomegalovirus.

**1969** *New Eng. Jrnl. Med.* 22 May 1145/2 Kääriäinen and his associates first recognized striking changes in the titer of cytomegalovirus (*CMV) antibody in association with these illnesses. **1980** *Jrnl. Clin. Invest.* LXV. 798/2 CMV is a member of the herpes group of viruses. **1987** *CDC AIDS Weekly* 28 Dec. 5 After testing those control proteins from CMV on the AIDS virus, we found that they also activated the promoter of the AIDS virus.

**CPM,** critical path method.

**1962** *CPM [see *network analysis* s.v. NETWORK *n.* 5]. **1973** C. W. GEAR *Introd. Computer Sci.* viii. 319 Complete programs that handle jobs, such as CPM, usually allow a very flexible input so that the user can describe his problem in easy-to-understand statements. **1983** *Chem. Engin.* 21 Feb. 53/1 Project information software, dubbed Pathfinder, is a CPM-based (*critical path method*) computer program for project scheduling.

**CP/M** [*control program/microcomputer*], a proprietary name for an operating system designed for single-user computers based on certain microprocessors.

**1976** *Dr. Dobb's Jrnl.* Apr. 5/1 We have the first tidbits of information on the floppy-disc operating system to which we have alluded in past issues. The system, called '*CP/M', runs on an 8080. **1978** *Official Gaz.* (U.S. Patent Office) 14 Nov. TM77/2 CP/M. For computer programs recorded on cards, tapes, disks, and diskettes. **1985** *Trade Marks Jrnl.* 29 May 1248/2 CP/M. Advertised before acceptance. ..Computer programmes recorded on cards, tapes and on discs. **1985** *Practical Computing* May 114/3 If you stick to a computer that runs one of the mainstream operating systems like CP/M or MS-DOS you will be on fairly safe ground.

**CW, cw,** continuous wave.

**1920** *Wireless World* Jan. 598/1 The relative advantages of separate heterodyne *versus* self-heterodyne for *C.W. reception. **1967** *Electronics* 6 Mar. 54/3 Other c-w gas lasers lose efficiency when operated at a single wavelength. **1982** *Giant Bk. Electronics Projects* iii. 124 The signal generator can be utilized with SSB/CW .. receivers.

**b.** *Chem.* In the symbols for various elements (see also *C* in sense 3 a): **Ca**, calcium.

**1830** *Phil. Mag.* VIII. 425 (*table*) Lime ... *Ca 3·5. **1982** T. M. DEVLIN *Textbk. Biochem.* i. 18 These two membrane systems in muscle actually control the cytosolic concentration of $Ca^{2+}$ by actively sequestering the cellular $Ca^{2+}$.

**Cd,** cadmium.

**1833** E. TURNER *Elements of Chem.* (ed. 4) II. 519 Cadmium .. oxide .. is regarded as a compound of one equivalent of each element ... Its formula is *Cd + O. **1982** *Nature* 15 July 260/2 Certain benthic foraminifera .. show a consistent relationship between the Cd/Ca of the bottom water and of their calcite shells.

**Ce,** cerium.

**1833** E. TURNER *Elements of Chem.* (ed. 4) 971 Cerium .. *Ce ... Chlorine .. Cl .. Chromium .. Cr .. Cobalt .. Co. **1985** *Chem. Abstr.* 18 Feb. 336/2 *S. mitis* .. aggregated when suspended in salt solns. contg. $Zn^{2+}$, $Al^{3+}$, $La^{3+}$, and $Ce^{3+}$.

**Cf**, californium.
**1950** S. G. THOMPSON et al. in *Physical Rev.* LXXVIII. 298/2 It is suggested that element 98 be given the name californium (symbol *Cf) after the university and state where the work was done. **1984** *IEEE Trans. Nuclear Sci.* XXXI. 1207/2 The experimental technique designed to study latch-up produced by fission particles from ²⁵²Cf was required to meet three objectives.

**Cl**, chlorine.
**1833** *Cl [see *Ce* above]. **1984** A. C. & A. DUXBURY *Introd. World's Oceans* v. 150 Anions .. are released during volcanic eruptions as gases (for example, hydrogen sulfide, sulfur, and chlorine), which are dissolved in rainwater or river water and are carried to the oceans as Cl⁻ (chloride) and SO²⁻₄ (sulfate).

**Co**, cobalt.
**1814** J. BERZELIUS in *Ann. Philos.* III. 52 *Co = cobaltum (cobalt). **1968** A. WHITE et al. *Princ. Biochem.* (ed. 4) xxiii. 534 Mucosal extracts also contain dipeptidases ... An example is glycylglycine dipeptidase, which requires Co⁺⁺ or Mn⁺⁺ for its action.

**Cr**, chromium.
**1833** *Cr [see *Ce* above]. **1967** A. H. COTTRELL *Princ. Metall.* xxv. 516 Medium carbon steels containing sufficient chromium for good stainless qualities (e.g. 15% Cr) can .. be quench hardened for cutlery use.

**Cs**, caesium.
**1861** *Chem. News* 26 Oct. 219/1 The hydrate of caesium, *CsO.HO + Aq, is deliquescent. **1982** *Nature* 11 Mar. 169/2 Substitution of K ions by Cs ions.

**Cu**, copper.
**1813** J. BERZELIUS in *Ann. Philos.* II. 359 In the class of combustibles which I call metalloids, I use only the initial letters. For example .. C = carbon, *Cu = copper (cuprum), [etc.]. **1987** K. A. RUBINSON *Chem. Anal.* xii. 389 In aqueous solution, the heavy metals such as Cu⁺⁺, Ni⁺⁺, and Cd⁺⁺ plate out whereas the alkali metals do not.

**cæcostomy** (si:'kɒstəmɪ), *n. Surg.* Also (*U.S.*) cec-. [f. CÆC(UM *n.* + -O¹ + -STOMY.] The operation of making an opening into the caecum through the abdominal wall through which the contents of the intestine may be removed.
[**1890** BILLINGS *Med. Dict.* I. 206/1 *Cæcostomie* (F.), formation of a permanent opening or artificial anus in the cæcum.] **1891** F. TREVES *Man. Operative Surg.* II. x. ix. 354 The ridiculous terms, cæcostomy and sigmoidostomy, have acquired no position in surgical literature. **1929** *Lancet* 20 July 119/2 The operation of cæcostomy is undertaken, more often than not, under the most adverse surgical circumstances. **1965** *Amer. Jrnl. Surg.* CX. 896/2 Problems previously encountered with a tube cecostomy have been obviated with the use of a large caliber tube and frequent postoperative irrigations. **1974** R. M. KIRK et al. *Surgery* vi. 124 Caecostomy. The caecum .. is sometimes opened on the surface to empty the right colon. **1982** *Jrnl. Nat. Med. Assoc.* LXXIV. 688/2 The present report highlights the use of complementary tube cecostomy in the management of strangulated Richter's inguinal hernia of the cecum.

**calanoid** ('kælənɔɪd), *a.* and *n. Zool.* [ad. mod.L. *Calanoida* (see below), f. *Calanus*, generic name (W. E. Leach 1819, in *Dict. des Sciences Naturelles* XIV. 539), after the L. name of an Indian philosopher of the 4th cent. B.C.: see -OID.] (Designating) a copepod of the order or suborder Calanoida, comprising free-living, filter-feeding, planktonic animals found in all parts of the oceans and important as food for fishes.
**1957** D. T. GAULD in *Nature* 9 Feb. 325/2 A similar membrane can easily be shown to surround the fæcal pellets of calanoid copepods. **1964** *Oceanogr. & Marine Biol.* II. 352 Among the calanoids, representatives of the following families have been found to be luminescent: Aetideidae, Lucicutiidae, [etc.]. **1966** *McGraw-Hill Encycl. Sci. & Technol.* II. 393/1 In biomass, the calanoids exceed all other copepod groups. **1979** *Nature* 13 Dec. 677/2 The herbivorous zooplankton of upwelling areas and of temperate waters are typically calanoid copepods.

**call**, *n.* Add: [6.] m. *Square-dancing.* A direction called to the dancers, announcing the next figure or set of steps. Cf. CALLER *n.* 1 e. orig. and chiefly *U.S.*
**1851** *Ball-Room Instructor* 13 The words in small capitals, in the beginning of the lines, are the names of the figures called by the leader of the orchestra ... To these calls all should pay particular attention. **1903** R. L. RICHARDSON *Colin of Ninth Concession* ix. 57, I shall here present a few 'calls', as I remember hearing them from Goarden's lips at the famous dance that Dooley gave. **1952** *Proc. Amer. Antiquarian Soc.* LXVII. 81 The prompter could and eventually did sing the calls, weaving rude rhymes, and filling out the calls with comments on the individuals present. **1989** *N.Y. Times* 6 Aug. (Westchester Weekly section) 10/6 On Friday at 8 p.m. swing your partner to the square-dance calls of Slim Sterling and a live country-western band.

**callistemon** (kælɪ'sti:mən), *n.* Also C-. [mod.L. (R. Brown: see below), f. Gr. κάλλος, καλλι-beauty + στήμων warp, thread (cf. STAMEN *n.*).] An evergreen shrub or small tree of the genus *Callistemon*, of the myrtle family, native to Australia and bearing spikes of red or yellow flowers resembling a bottle-brush.
[**1814** R. BROWN in M. Flinders *Voy. Terra Australis* II. 547 Callistemon, a genus formed of those species of Metrosideros that have inflorescence similar to that of Melaleuca, and distinct elongated filaments.] **1843** *Curtis's Bot. Mag.* LXIX. 3989 Pine-leaved callistemon. **1857** A. GRAY *First Lessons Bot.* ix. 69 The Callistemon or Bottle-brush Flower of our greenhouses. **1911** A. E. MACK *Bush Days* 51 A bend in the path had brought us face to face with the callistemons. **1975** *Advertiser* (Adelaide) 17 Oct. 13 Of all the colorful and free-flowering native Australian plants grown in home gardens, probably the most popular is the Callistemon or bottlebrush family of shrubs and small trees.

**cancericidal** (ˌkænsərɪ'saɪdəl), *a. Med.* [f. CANCER *n.* + -I- + -CIDE + -AL¹.] = *CANCEROCIDAL a.
**1957** in *Dorland's Med. Dict.* (ed. 23) 224/1. **1973** *Gynecol. Oncol.* I. 363 These [cell] aggregates are subjected to various cancericidal influences such as radiation therapy and various chemotherapeutic agents. **1980** *Jrnl. R. Soc. Med.* LXXIII. 734 A treatment of possible small metastatic remnants for which it was essential to give full cancericidal dose.

**cancerocidal** (ˌkænsərə'saɪdəl), *a. Med.* [f. CANCER *n.* + -O- + -CIDE + -AL¹.] Having a destructive effect on cancer cells. Cf. *CANCERICIDAL a.
**1938** in DORLAND & MILLER *Med. Dict.* (ed. 18) 261/1. **1961** *Lancet* 16 Sept. 615/1 In recent years considerable interest has centred on the cancerocidal drugs. **1974** *Cancer* XXXIV. 2034 A single dose of 3500 rad of an electron beam seems to be sufficient as a cancerocidal dose.

**canine**, *a.* (*n.*) Add: [A.] [3.] *canine parvovirus* (*Vet. Sci.*), a parvovirus that causes a frequently fatal disease in dogs, characterized by diarrhoea and vomiting; also, the disease itself.
**1972** ANDREWES & PEREIRA *Viruses Vertebr.* (ed. 3) xii. 286 Canine Parvovirus. A 'minute virus of

canines' was isolated from dog faeces by Binn et al. (1970). It was cultivable only in a line of dog cells. **1979** *Maclean's Mag.* 9 Apr. 49/1 Jim Henry is one of a handful of Canadian pathologists who have been working with canine parvovirus, the lethal disease that killed Kipp. **1984** G. SIEGL in K. I. Berns *Parvoviruses* ix. 373 During the original outbreaks of canine parvovirus disease in 1978 acute enteritis occurred in dogs of almost any age.

**cannabinoid** ('kænəbɪnɔɪd), *n. Chem.* [f. CANNABIN(OL *n.* + -OID.] Any of a group of closely related tricyclic compounds that includes cannabinol and cannabidiol.
   **1967** MECHOULAM & GAONI in *Fortschritte der Chemie Organischer Naturstoffe* XXV. 178 We propose the term *cannabinoids* for the group of $C_{21}$-compounds typical of and present in *C. sativa*, as well as for their analogs and transformation products. **1970** *Nature* 20 June 1171/2 A placebo was composed from an extract of marijuana with cannabinoids removed. **1974** M. C. GERALD *Pharmacol.* xviii. 339 *Cannabis* contains a group of closely related compounds that are collectively termed cannabinoids. .. These compounds do not contain a nitrogen atom and, therefore, are not alkaloids.

**Cantor** ('kæntɔː(r), ‖'kantor), *n.*² *Math.* The name of Georg *Cantor* (1845-1918), Russian-born German mathematician, used in the possessive and *attrib.* to designate various concepts relating to the theory of sets and infinite numbers arising out of his work, as **Cantor('s) (ternary) set**, the set of points left by removing from a line of unit length all points whose distance from one end is greater than $^1/_3$ and less than $^2/_3$, then removing similarly the middle third of the two segments so formed, and so on indefinitely.
   **1902** *Proc. London Math. Soc.* XXXIV. 286 H. J. S. Smith's ternary *derived* set is to all intents and purposes the same as Cantor's ternary set of numbers. *Ibid.*, The generalization of Cantor's set. *Ibid.* XXXV. 248 Cantor's Theorem. Every set of intervals on a straight line is countable, provided no two overlap. **1903** B. RUSSELL *Princ. Math.* xlii. 347 The thesis of the present chapter is, that Cantor's continuum is free from contradictions. *Ibid.* 527 There is a one-one relation of all ranges of propositions to some propositions, which is directly contradictory to Cantor's theorem. **1906** *Proc. London Math. Soc.* 2nd. Ser. IV. 272 We can prove .. that every ordinal number is a Cantor's ordinal number. **1940** *Amer. Math. Monthly* XLVII. 549 (*heading*) Distances between points of the Cantor set. **1953** A. A. FRAENKEL *Abstr. Set Theory* ii. 94 The highly comprehensive answer, often called Cantor's theorem, runs: .. To any set *S* there exist sets having larger cardinals than *S*; in particular, the set U*S*, whose elements are all the subsets of *S*, is of a larger cardinal than *S*. **1960** P. R. HALMOS *Naive Set Theory* xxv. 101 The contradiction, based on the assumption that there is such a set [of all cardinal numbers], is known as Cantor's paradox. **1975** I. STEWART *Concepts Mod. Math.* ix. 143 Prior to Cantor's theorem, mathematicians had become accustomed to thinking of transcendental numbers as being very rare, because they seldom seemed to use any. **1979** D. R. HOFSTADTER *Gödel, Escher, Bach* (1980) v. 142 When *a* is irrational, the bands shrink to points, of which there are infinitely many, very sparsely distributed in a so-called 'Cantor set'—another recursively defined entity which springs up in topology. **1987** *Nature* 24 Dec. 695/1 The resulting function resembles a mathematical function called a Cantor function or, more picturesquely, a 'devil's staircase'.
   Hence **Can'torian** *a.*, of or pertaining to Cantor or his work; having the attributes of a Cantor set; also **Can'torean** *a.*

**1912** WHITEHEAD & RUSSELL *Principia Mathematica* II. v. 614 A compact Dedekindian series is said to possess 'Dedekindian continuity'; such series have many important properties. They are a wider class than series possessing Cantorian continuity. **1946** *Mind* LV. 367 His theory made it impossible to prove the existence of the continuum and thus curtailed the Cantorean theory of sets. **1963** W. V. QUINE *Set Theory* 294 Classes that are not Cantorian behave unconventionally. **1982** W. S. HATCHER *Logical Found. Math.* vii. 225 A set *x* is 'Cantorian' if it is similar to its set of unit subsets.

**cap'n** ('kæp(ə)n), *n. colloq.* (chiefly *U.S.*). [Contraction of CAPTAIN *n.*] = CAPTAIN *n.*, esp. as a title or term of address.
   [**1679** *Rec. Colony of Rhode Island* (1858) III. 30 Voted, .. that Capt'n Samuel Gorton and Mr. Caleb Carr shall open the proxies.] **1829** *Yankee* Apr. 120/3 Cap'n Jessamine had got kicked out o' bed by his wife. **1866** 'F. KIRKLAND' *Pictorial Bk. Anecdotes* v. 408/2 I jerked my hat over my eyes and jogged along on the Cap'ns horse. **1904** J. C. LINCOLN *Cap'n Eri* xviii. 329 Cap'n Jonadab Wixon used to swear that his grandfather told him 'bout a gale that blew the hair all off a dog. **1936** H. PREECE in *Crisis* Dec. 374/1 The traditional 'Cap'n', will become the capitalist. **1949** *Sun* (Baltimore) 26 Aug. 10/3 Whenever travelers enter Baltimore from abroad by ship or air, they are given the onceover by Cap'n Jenks. **1972** G. S. HOLT in T. Kochman *Rappin' & Stylin' Out* 157 The ex-private was elevated to 'cap'n'.

**captain**, *n.* Add: [II.] [5.] **d.** The adult leader of a company of Girl Guides.
   Although formally replaced by *Guide Leader* in 1966, the term continued in use unofficially for some years.
   **1909** R. BADEN-POWELL *Girl Guides: Suggestion for Character Training* (Pamphlet A) 6 The unit for work or play is the 'Patrol' of eight girls, of whom one is 'Patrol Leader', another the 'Corporal'. Three or more Patrols form a Company under a 'Captain' and a 'Lieutenant'. **1926** R. KERR *Commissioner's Bk.* 196 Once a Ranger Company has been formed, the Captain should try and keep in touch with the Guide Companies that feed the Ranger. **1957** *Encycl. Brit.* X. 368/2 The Guides are organized in patrols of six or eight under a leader, two or more patrols forming a company under a captain. **1966** *Tomorrow's Guide* (Girl Guides Assoc.) iii. 21 Guide Leader [and] Assistant Guide Leader .. should be used instead of Captain and Lieutenant. We believe that the time has come to drop the terms Captain and Lieutenant which, when used in conjunction with each other, have a military sound. **1976** *Norwich Mercury* 10 Dec. 2/1 She is retiring from her post of Captain .. and handing over to Mrs. Dianne Perrott—who .. is her present lieutenant.

**capture**, *n.* Senses 1 b-e in Dict. become 1 c-f. Add: [1.] **b.** *Chess, Draughts*, etc. The act or process of taking an opposing piece.
   **1835** G. WALKER *Selection of Games at Chess* 79 Conway appears to disdain the inglorious capture of the Rook. **1850** *Bohn's Hand-bk. Games* 407 If several pieces, on forward diagonals, should be exposed by alternately having open squares behind them, they may all be taken at one capture. **1960** R. C. BELL *Board & Table Games* I. ii. 51 [Sixteen Soldiers] A capture is made by jumping over an enemy piece on to a vacant point beyond. **1984** *Byte* Mar. 294/1 An early stroll of its Queen leads to the capture of a poisoned pawn and then to the exchange of a pawn for a Knight.

**caput**, *n.* Add: **5.** *Obstetr.* Short for *CAPUT SUCCEDANEUM n.*
   **1871** A. MILNE *Princ. & Pract. Midwifery* xvi. 169 This caput indicates correctly the presenting part. **1924** S. J. CAMERON et al. *Glasgow Man. Obstetr.* xxi.

453 In face presentations the caput is formed on the soft tissues of the face. **1981** S. KITZINGER *Experience of Childbirth* (ed. 4) x. 252 The baby's head was born, the size of a pumpkin, not a grapefruit, as it had a caput.

|| **caput succedaneum** ('kæpʊt sʌksɪ'deɪnɪəm), *n.* *Obstetr.* [mod.L., = substitute head, f. L. CAPUT *n.* + *succēdāneum*, neut. sing. of *succēdāneus* substitute.] A temporary oedematous swelling on the presenting part (usu. the head) of a baby during birth.
**1839** DUNGLISON *Dict. Med. Sci.* (ed. 2) 104/2 *Caput succedaneum*, a term sometimes used for the tumefied scalp, which first presents in certain cases of labour. **1852** PAGE & MEIGS *Velpeau's Compl. Treat. Midwifery* (ed. 4) 624 The first variety of these tumors appears to me to be seated between the aponeurosis and cranial integuments... The *caput succedaneum* of certain German physicians .. very probably belongs to it. **1871** A. MILNE *Princ. & Pract. Midwifery* xvi. 169 The caput succedaneum is the tumour formed on the scalp by the pressure of the foetal head, first against the resisting circle of the os uteri, and then against that of the vaginal orifice. **1908** *Practioner* Apr. 467 The commonest injury of the head in the newly-born or young infant is haematoma; this must not be mistaken for the caput succedanum [*sic*], with which it is frequently associated, and which disappears shortly after birth. **1979** *Brit. Med. Jrnl.* 15 Dec. 1567/1 Cephalhaemotoma must be distinguished from caput succedaneum, which is a soft tissue swelling due to oedema of the part of the head presenting at the cervix and which is not limited by the [cranial] sutures.

**car**, *n.*[1] Add: [6.] **car wash** orig. *U.S.*, a building or other structure containing equipment for washing motor vehicles automatically; an establishment providing this, or the service itself.
[**1923** *Mod. Lang. Notes* XXXVIII. 188 Another series of new words [in California] .. has made use of the good old ending -ery of grocery, bakery, etc., thus: .. 'bootery', and 'car washery'.] **1948** *Pop. Sci.* Feb. 122/2 Even harried motorists often stay beyond their own three minute *car wash time to watch the spectacular blower-drier ... Made by Minit-Man Car Wash, of Detroit, Michigan. **1962** *Guardian* 9 Jan. 8/6 An automatic car-wash firm which advertises a five-minute service. **1965** R. HARDWICK *Plotters* (1966) xii. 109 Chris sold off his interest in a string of car washes. **1986** 'P. DUNANT' *Intensive Care* iii. 22 He did some shopping and called in at a carwash.

**caragana** (kærə'gɑːnə), *n.* Also C-. [mod.L. (A. van Royen *Floræ Leydensis Prodromus* (1740) 537), of Turkic origin; given current taxonomic status by P. C. Fabricius 1759, in *Enumeratio Meth. Plant. Horti Med. Helmstadiensis* 228.] Any of various shrubs and small trees of the leguminous genus *Caragana*, native to central Asia and Siberia and widely planted in N. America as a hardy hedge plant; *esp.* the Siberian pea-tree, *C. arborescens*.
**1866** *Treas. Bot.* 219 *Caragana*, the Siberian Pea Tree. **1885** G. NICHOLSON *Illustr. Dict. Gardening* I. 264/2 Caraganas are generally increased by grafting on *C. arborescens*. **1951** *Chambers's Jrnl.* Aug. 505/1 The yellow gorse-like blossoms of the caragana, or Siberian pea-tree, a hardy shrub used extensively for hedges [in Saskatchewan], are alive with bees during their short season of bloom. **1968** R. KROETSCH *Alberta* I. 16 When I last visited her she was out by the caragana hedge behind her ranch house. **1984** M. EPP tr. *Krüssman's Man. Cultivated Broad-Leaved Trees & Shrubs* I. 276/2 All the Caraganas need a location in full sun.

**carajura** (ˌkærə'dʒʊərə), *n.* Also -juru (-'dʒʊəru:). [ad. Pg. *carajuru*, f. Tupi *carajurú*.] **a.** = CHICA *n.*[1] **b.** The Brazilian vine *Arrabidaea chica*, of the bignonia family, from which chica can be obtained.
**1874** W. CROOKES *Pract. Handbk. Dyeing & Calico Printing* II. v. 388 (*heading*) Chica, crajura, or carajara. **1927** *Jrnl. Chem. Soc.* 3015 Carajura (Crajura, Chica red)..is a rare red pigment, prepared by the Indians of the Rio Meta and the Orinoco from *Bignonia Chica* for use as a flesh paint. **1966** MORS & RIZZINI *Useful Plants Brazil* vii. 56 *Carajuru*. This plant..is a small, bignoniaceous tree; its homeland covers the whole Amazon region, both of Brazil and the neighboring countries... Today it is a rare article and commercially unobtainable. Formerly it had a limited market under the name of 'chica red' or 'American vermillion'.

**carbamide**, *n.* Add: Hence also '**carbamyl** *n.* (-maɪl, -mɪl), the monovalent radical $NH_2CO-$, derived from carbamic acid; usu. *attrib.*
[**1906** TINGLE & ROBINSON in *Amer. Chem. Jrnl.* XXXVI. 230 The compound was designated .. as 'semicarbazine camphormeneaminecarboxylic acid'. .. The term 'carbamyl' designates satisfactorily the carbamide residue, $-NHCONH_2$, which is present.] **1907** *Chem. Abstr.* I. 2107 Carbamyl chloride does not react readily with phenols. **1954** S. DUKE-ELDER *Parsons' Dis. Eye* (ed. 12) v. 70 Two drugs are sometimes employed which combine the direct and indirect methods of stimulation [of the eye muscles]—doryl (carbachol) (carbamyl-choline chloride) (1.0 per cent.) and urecholine. **1970** R. W. McGILVERY *Biochem.* xx. 487 Uracil and thymine are metabolized by the same routes ... The two products are carbamyl derivatives of the corresponding β-amino acids ... The carbamyl group is removed by hydrolysis, releasing the free amino acids and ammonia and $CO_2$.

**carbonatite** (kɑː'bɒnətaɪt), *n.* *Petrogr.* [ad. G. *Karbonatit* (W. C. Brøgger 1921, in *Skrifter Vidensk.-Selsk. Kristiania* (*Mat.-natur. Kl.*) II. 350), f. *Karbonat* CARBONATE *n.*: see -ITE[1].] Any igneous rock composed chiefly of carbonates rather than silicates.
**1924** *Amer. Jrnl. Sci.* VIII. 2 The intrusion of carbonatite took place, in part at least, contemporaneously with that of ijolite. **1965** A. HOLMES *Princ. Physical Geol.* (ed. 2) xxix. 1077 We know nothing about the origin of the carbonatites that are so curiously involved in uplifts, rift valleys and alkaline rocks. **1977** A. HALLAM *Planet Earth* 164/3 Ancient carbonatite intrusions are composed of calcium, magnesium or iron carbonates; though at least one volcano .. has in recent times emitted ashes and flows of sodium carbonate. **1988** *Nature* 22 Sept. 295/2 Carbonatites, rare magmatic carbonate-rich rocks, are usually associated with silica-undersaturated rocks.

**carbonylation** (ˌkɑːbənɪ'leɪʃən), *n.* *Chem.* [f. CARBONYL *n.* + -ATION.] The introduction of a carbonyl group into a compound.
**1949** COPENHAVER & BIGELOW *Acetylene & Carbon Monoxide Chem.* vi. 247 Originally, the term 'carbonylation' was used by the Germans .. to denote reactions of carbon monoxide with an organic compound in the presence of a metal carbonyl. Although the term 'carbonylation' would seem to imply the introduction of a carbonyl group into the molecule, the reaction product in many carbonylation reactions was actually a carboxylic acid. **1961** *Times* 30 May (ICI Suppl.) p. xxii (Advt.), Commissars need carbonylation alcohols for making phthalates for p.v.c. compounding. **1984** J. PENNINGTON *Introd. Industr. Chem.* ix. 243 Halcon have now developed a process .. for the carbonylation of methyl acetate (or dimethyl ether) to acetic anhydride.

**carboxy-**, *comb. form.* Add:
**carboxy'dismutase**, an enzyme found in autotrophic plants which catalyses the addition of a molecule of carbon dioxide to one of ribulose bisphosphate; ribulose bisphosphate carboxylase.
**1956** M. CALVIN in *Proc. 3rd Internat. Congr. Biochem.* 218 Because the carboxylation reaction takes place at the expense of the oxidation of the $C_3$ of the ribulose to the carboxyl level, the name 'carboxydismutase' suggests itself as uniquely descriptive. **1976** BELL & COOMBE tr. *Strasburger's Textbk. Bot.* (rev. ed.) 250 A molecule of carbon dioxide becomes bound by a special enzyme, carboxydismutase (ribulose diphosphate carboxylase), to a molecule of the ribulose diphosphate. **1986** *Phil. Trans. R. Soc.* B. CCCXIII. 306 In the early 1970s carboxydismutase (or ribulose diphosphate carboxylase) as it was then called, was still an unresolved enigma.

**carboxylate** (kɑː'bɒksɪleɪt), *n. Chem.* [f. CARBOXYL *n.* + -ATE¹.] **a.** A salt or ester of a carboxylic acid. **b.** The ion −COO⁻ derived from the carboxyl group; an ion R·COO⁻ derived similarly from a carboxylic acid.
[**1881** *Jrnl. Chem. Soc.* XL. 266 Ammonium resocarboxylate forms concentric needles, very soluble in water.] **1884** ROSCOE & SCHORLEMMER *Treat. Chem.* III. ii. 627 Potassium Carboxylates. The normal salt, $C_{10}H_4O_{10}$, is red in colour and is obtained by the oxidation of the black potassium dihydrocarboxylate. **1913** *Jrnl. Soc. Dyers & Colourists* XXIX. 172/1 (*heading*) The application of β-naphthol carboxylates in dyeing and printing. **1951** C. R. NOLLER *Chem. Org. Compounds* x. 152 In the carboxylate ion the primary bonds between the carbon atom and the three groups to which it is attached are formed by the presence of two electrons in each of three σ-type orbitals. **1970** R. W. McGILVERY *Biochem.* xiv. 282 Carbon dioxide may be attached to a biotinyl group on an enzyme with a concomitant cleavage of ATP, followed by transfer of the resultant carboxylate group to another compound. **1983** NORMAN & WADDINGTON *Mod. Org. Chem.* (ed. 4) iv. 64 The carboxylate ion, $RCO_2^-$, in which the charge is delocalised, is relatively more stable.

**carboxylation** (kɑːˌbɒksɪ'leɪʃən), *n. Chem.* [f. CARBOXYL *n.* + -ATION.] Introduction of a carboxyl group or carbon dioxide into a molecule or compound to form a carboxylic acid or carboxylate.
**1921** *Chem. Abstr.* XV. 3211 The processes of sulfonation, .. carboxylation, [etc.]. **1951** *Sci. News* XXII. 78 Carbon dioxide is not directly reduced to formaldehyde by the photolytically produced hydrogen; it is incorporated into a carboxylation cycle and there reduced indirectly. **1962** S. G. WALEY in A. Pirie *Lens Metabolism Rel. Cataract* 357 Biotin is probably required here, as it is in the carboxylations in .. fatty acid synthesis. **1981** DUGAS & PENNEY *Bioorganic Chem.* vii. 460 The function of biotin is to mediate the coupling of ATP cleavage to carboxylation.

**carboxylic** (kɑː'bɒk'sɪlɪk), *a. Chem.* [f. CARBOXYL *n.* + -IC.] Of, pertaining to, or designating a carboxyl group; *spec.* designating organic acids containing one or more such groups.
[**1871** *Jrnl. Chem. Soc.* XXIV. 920 This may be unaltered naphthyl-carboxylic acid.] **1881** H. C. JONES *Text-bk. Pract. Org. Chem.* 61 It is only the carboxylic hydrogen that can be replaced by metals to form salts. **1883** *Jrnl. Chem. Soc.* XLIV. 802 (*heading*) Conversion of phenols into nitriles and carboxylic acids. **1959** *New Biol.* XXX. 99 The main part of the cuticle is composed of cutin; this is a polymer of high molecular weight formed from carboxylic acids. **1972** *Materials & Technol.* V. xiv.

482 Recently, carboxylated NBR has been introduced. .. The carboxylic groups enhance solvent resistance. **1987** TEDDER & NECHVATAL *Basic Org. Chem.* (ed. 2) xii. 152 The most important reaction of a cyanide is hydrolysis to yield first the amide and then the carboxylic acid.

**cardio-**, *comb. form.* Add: **,cardiomy'opathy** [MYO-], (a) disease of the heart muscle, *esp.* a chronic one of unknown or uncertain cause.
**1957** W. BRIGDEN in *Lancet* 14 Dec. 1179/1 The term *cardiomyopathy is used here to indicate isolated non-coronary myocardial disease. **1980** *Brit. Heart Jrnl.* XLIV. 672/1 Cardiomyopathies are heart muscle diseases of unknown cause. **1984** *Which?* Oct. 447/2 In addition, the heart muscle can be weakened by years of heavy drinking, this is called '[alcoholic] cardiomyopathy' and may result in heart failure. **1987** *Oxf. Textbk. Med.* (ed. 2) II. XIII. 209/1 When the cause of a cardiomyopathy is identified it becomes a specific heart muscle disorder and is known by this (e.g. sarcoid heart disease) even though the precise aetiology of the disorder may still be obscure.

**cardioid**, *n. and a.* Add: [A.] **2.** A cardioid microphone.
**1955** F. W. ALEXANDER in J. W. Godfrey *Studio Engin. for Sound Broadcasting* iii. 43 When broadcasting an orchestra from an empty concert-hall .. the wider acceptance angle of the cardioid is especially useful. **1961** [see UNIDIRECTIONAL *a.*]. **1983** A. NISBETT *Use of Microphones* (ed. 2) 42 The original way of producing a cardioid, by combining a moving coil and a ribbon in a single case, has fallen into disuse ... Most modern cardioids are even more complex.
**B.** *adj.* **1.** Having the characteristic shape of a cardioid.
**1922** R. KEEN *Direction & Position Finding by Wireless* ii. 38 The cardioid, heart-shape or apple diagram of reception. **1936** L. S. PALMER *Wireless Engin.* (ed. 2) xii. 493 This heart-shaped or cardioid figure represents the polar diagram of an aerial capable of determining 'sense' as well as direction. **1965** *Wireless World* Aug. 89 (Advt.), Grampian proudly present a microphone with a really good frequency response .. and a genuine cardioid pick-up pattern. **1977** *Rolling Stone* 13 Jan. 58/4 Many amateur recordists, in attempting to operate like the pros, choose directional or cardioid-pattern microphones.
**2.** Designating a type of microscope condenser for giving dark-ground illumination, in which the light is reflected first from the outside of a sphere and then from the inside of a surface whose cross-section is theoretically a cardioid.
**1932** L. C. MARTIN *Introd. Appl. Optics* II. iii. 124 Fig. 88 shows the course of the rays through a cardioid condenser as made by Zeiss. **1962** W. G. HARTLEY *Microscopy* vii. 126 Zeiss formerly produced a mount for the cardioid dark-ground illuminator.
**3.** Of a microphone: having a cardioid pattern of sensitivity, with a maximum in a single direction.
**1939** *Bell Lab. Rec.* XVII. 339/2 The cardioid microphone can be mounted either on a floor or on a desk. **1951** *Microphones* (B.B.C. Engin. Training Dept.) v. 65 In general, a cardioid microphone can .. be used at a distance from the sound source $\sqrt 3$ times as great as with an omni-directional microphone. **1975** G. J. KING *Audio Handbk.* ix. 205 Real cardioid microphones are costly and generally outside the pocket of the average enthusiast.

**career**, *n.* Add: [5.] [b.] **career structure**, a recognized pattern of career development and advancement within a job or profession.
**1965** *New Statesman* 7 May 707/2 Such a department .. would have to have a long-term career

structure. **1986** *Professional Teacher* Summer 4/3 The PAT paper..outlines the Association's standpoint on the five issues itemised in the panel's terms of reference: pay; career structure; career progression; conditions of service; and procedures for negotiation.

**cariogenic** (kærɪəʊ'dʒɛnɪk, kɛər-), *a.* [f. CARIES *n.* + -O[1] + -GENIC.] Promoting or causing tooth decay.
**1948** *Jrnl. Nutrition* XXXV. 372 Control animals were fed a dry ration known to be highly cariogenic. **1959** *Times* 11 Sept. 9/6 This fermentation produces the cariogenic agent which attacks the enamel. **1971** *Nature* 10 Dec. 330/1 Under cariogenic conditions, dissolution [of minerals] is greater than deposition. **1985** *Times* 3 May 13/7 Cheese, corn chips or peanuts—three foods which don't appear to be highly cariogenic.

**Carolina**, *n.* Add: Carolina duck = *summer duck* s.v. SUMMER *n.*[1] 6 b.
**1784** F. BOSCAWEN *Let.* in C. F. Aspinall-Oglander *Admiral's Widow* (1942) 115 Many winged families of most respectable size and beautiful feather, especially Carolina ducks, which I judged to be the Summer duck, so rare and beautiful. **1893** A. NEWTON *Dict. Birds* I. 1 *Acorn-duck*, a name given in some parts of North America to the Carolina or Wood-Duck. **1940** H. F. WITHERBY et al. *Handbk. Brit. Birds* III. 282 Wanderers from captivity or semi-captivity of..the Carolina or Wood-Duck,..and other species are frequently reported.

**carpet**, *n.* Add: [II.] [5.] [b.] *carpet layer*.
**1921** *Dict. Occup. Terms* (1927) §503 *\*Carpet layer* .., lays, stretches.., and fixes carpets. **1988** *Daily Tel.* (Colour Suppl.) 10 Sept. 30/1 The man who is painting the Queen's Head doubles as a carpet layer.
*-laying*.
**1946** *Carpet Rev.* Oct. 9/2 (*heading*) Better *\*carpet laying* methods overdue.

**carriage**, *n.* Add: [35.] carriage return, the operation of returning the carriage of a typewriter to its rightmost position, setting the type guide at the left margin (usu. in conjunction with a line-feed); hence, an analogous process on other equipment, esp. in *Computing*; freq. used *attrib.* of the device or mechanism that effects this, as *carriage-return key, lever*, etc.; cf. *\*RETURN *n.* 13 c.
**1904** *Official Gaz.* (U.S. Patent Office) 19 Jan. 572/2 (*heading*) *\*Carriage-return for type-writers. **1912** A. W. MATHYS *Brit. Pat.* 29,297 8 When carriage return magnet S[2] is energized, actuator rod 262 is pushed downwardly. **1929** *Encycl. Brit.* XXII. 645/1 Among its [*sc.* the Remington's] original features which remain standard in 1928 machines are the paper cylinder, with its line-spacing and carriage-return mechanism. **1962** *Which?* Dec. 353 (*caption*) Carriage locking lever..Carriage return lever.. Carriage release lever. **1981** *Osborne CP/M User Guide* ii. 45 Typing Control-M is exactly the same as pressing the Carriage Return key. **1982** *Papers Dict. Soc. N. Amer.* 1979 86 For more detail, I punch 'carriage return' and discover 8 titles.

**Carrion's disease** (kærɪ'ɒnz), *n. Med.* [tr. Sp. *enfermedad de Carrión* (E. Odriozola 1895, in *Monitor Méd.* (Lima) X. 309), f. the name of D. A. *Carrión* (1850–86), Peruvian physician, who died after inoculating himself with material from a verruga lesion.] A sometimes fatal bacterial disease that is endemic in Peru and is transmitted by sandflies; *esp.* the severe acute form of the disease (= OROYA FEVER *n.*), which may be followed by a mild chronic form, verruga peruana (see VERRUGA *n.*).
**1927** *Jrnl. Exper. Med.* XLV. 187 The inoculation ..of verruga peruana is capable of inducing in

susceptible individuals a severe febrile systemic infection, such as that to which Carrion succumbed. The designation 'Carrion's disease' is therefore appropriate one for both forms of the infection. **1949**, **1962** [see OROYA FEVER *n.*]. **1978** *Nature* 22 June 599/2 This was..achieved during intensive DDT spraying campaigns against *Lu. verrucarum*, which had been indicated as the vector of human bartonellosis (Carrion's disease). **1987** *Oxf. Textbk. Med.* (ed. 2) I. v. 373/2 Bartonellosis (Carrión's disease, verruga peruana, verruga fever, Oroya fever, Guaitará fever) is a non-contagious infectious disease, which is endemic in the Western Andes and Interandean valleys of Peru.

**carry-on**, *n.* Restrict labels in Dict. to sense 1. For etym. read: f. the vbl. phr. *to carry on*: see CARRY *v.* 52 (sense e in 1 below.) Add: **2.** *attrib.* Designating (an item of) luggage permitted to be carried on board an aircraft by a passenger and kept in the cabin during flight; also *ellipt.* orig. and chiefly *N. Amer.*
**1962** *Consumer Bull.* July 25/1, I have found the best set to be one large (26- or 29-inch) suitcase.. and a small carry-on canvas 21-inch suitcase. **1965** *Holiday* Dec. 136/2 *Carry-ons*, designed with the impatient American in mind, are deep and narrow double-compartmented bags made to hold everything .. for a brief trip. **1970** *Time* 19 Jan. 53/1 Coats and carry-on baggage are stowed in large overhead storage compartments. **1976** *Changing Times* July 42/1 A *club bag*..is more convenient than an overnight bag or a carry-on. **1984** A. LURIE *Foreign Affairs* (1985) i. 4 She outflanks a massed confusion of obvious rubes with carry-on bags labeled *Sun Tours*.

**cash**, *n.*[1] Add: [3.] [a.] cash cow *colloq.*, (a sector of) a business which provides a steady cash flow, *esp.* one considered as an attractive take-over target.
**1975** *Forbes* (N.Y.) 15 Feb. 55/1 For a while, the fire and casualty companies were great *\*cash cows* for their acquirers. **1986** *Economist* 13 Sept. 75/3 He had called Dairy Farm the company's 'cash cow' and its steady turnover had sustained the group's cash flow through Hong Kong's property slump from 1981 to 1983.

**Cassingle** (kə'sɪŋg(ə)l), *n. colloq.* Also cassingle. [Blend of CASSETTE *n.* and SINGLE *n.*] A proprietary name for an audio-cassette containing a single piece of (usu. popular) music on each side; *spec.* one adapted for repeated play without rewinding.
**1978** *Trade Marks Jrnl.* 29 Nov. 2633/2 *Cassingle*. .. Magnetic tapes contained in cassettes, adapted to play either of the two recordings on each side repeatedly without rewinding... 22 July, 1977. **1981** *N.Y. Times* 29 July C19/3 Now the idea of putting out singles on cassettes—they call them cassingles—seems to be catching on in Britain as well. **1982** *Washington Post* 31 Oct. L1 Singles.. recently introduced by CBS (which introduced the two-sided disc back in 1908); the cassingle, which lists for $2.98 and goes totally against the idea of convenience. **1983** *Official Gaz.* (U.S. Patent Office) 5 Apr. TM32/2 *Cassingle* ... For pre-recorded magnetic tape cassettes (U.S.Cl. 36). First use Jun. 22, 1982. **1987** *Independent* 20 Feb. 14/8 Single and LP records are on the way out. Within 10 years, we will all be buying 'cassingles', cassettes and compact discs. **1989** *Times* 14 Apr. 44/3 Until a few months ago the 'cassingle' was essentially a promotional device distributed free of charge to the radio stations.

**catecholamine** (kætɪ'kəʊləmiːn, -'kɒl-), *n. Biochem.* Also catechol amine. [f. CATECHOL *n.* + AMINE *n.*] Any amine derived from catechol, *esp.* one of the naturally-occurring compounds of this type, many of which act as neurotransmitters or hormones.

**1951** *Acta Physiol. Scand.* XXIV. Suppl. LXXXV. 9 The extract thus obtained.. could be used for chromatography and for colorimetric determinations of the catechol amines. **1956** *Lancet* 11 Aug. 283/1 A further step was necessary to separate the catecholamine fraction. **1968** PASSMORE & ROBSON *Compan. Med. Stud.* I. xxv. 29/1 Release of catecholamines from the medulla follows such stimuli as pain, emotional disturbances, hypotension, asphyxia, hypoglycaemia, exposure to severe cold and muscular exertion. **1973** *Times* 19 Mar. 3/2 Later studies revealed there was a mixture of two hormones. The second compound was noradrenalin, and the two substances were collectively named catecholamines. **1981** G. WINOKUR *Depression* ix. 89 The catecholamine hypothesis is concerned with the metabolism of.. tyrosine. **1987** *Economist* 13 June 101/1 Scientists guessed that depression was caused by a lack of catecholamines.

**cathedral**, *n.* Add: [1.] **c.** *transf.* Any important, large, or imposing church.

**1823** (*title*) History of the Cathedral, or, High Church of Glasgow. **1885** *Hist. Glasgow Cathedral* (ed. 17) 20 The Cathedral is the property of the Crown, in which is also vested the patronage of the living, the Crown thus coming in the place of the Bishop, Dean, and Chapter. **1933** *Christian Century* 3 Aug. 701/2 The 10,000 member Crystal Cathedral in Garden Grove, California, a highly atypical congregation of the Reformed Church in America. **1977** C. McWILLIAM in Binney & Burman *Change & Decay* I. 43/1 Kirkwall, Orkney; St. Magnus's Cathedral. A mediaeval cathedral which still bears this title although used for Church of Scotland worship.

**cecostomy**, *n.* U.S. var. \*CÆCOSTOMY *n.*

**cell**, *n.* Add: [II.] [9.] **d.** Each of a number of identical volumes into which space or a crystal is notionally divided; *spec.* = *unit cell* s.v. UNIT *n.* (and *a.*) 3 c, *primitive cell* s.v. PRIMITIVE *a.* 5 b.

**1903** H. HILTON *Math. Crystallogr.* xxiv. 241 We will now show how to fill up space with a series of cells each of which contains one point and one only of any equivalent system. **1910** A. E. H. TUTTON *Crystalline Struct. & Chem. Constitution* xvi. 198 We have learnt how to determine the relative dimensions of the unit of the crystal structure, the molecular cell. **1915** W. H. & W. L. BRAGG *X-Rays & Crystal Structure* v. 52 Space is divided into parellelepiped cells by three sets of parallel planes. *Ibid.* vii. 111 Whatever class of symmetry the crystal belongs to, this enables us to measure up an elementary cell of its structure. **1931** [see PRIMITIVE *a.* 5 b]. **1931** R. W. G. WYCKOFF *Struct. Crystals* (ed. 2) ix. 183 It is possible to choose as correct the simplest cell which accounts for all of the observed X-ray reflections and contains an integral number of chemical molecules. **1966** C. R. TOTTLE *Sci. Engin. Materials* iii. 50 Atoms in a simple cubic cell occupy 52% of the available space, those in the diamond structure 34%. **1987** *Jrnl. Appl. Crystallogr.* XX. 343/1 The method has been used successfully for crystals with cell dimensions greater than 300 Å.

**e.** A region of fluid that can be treated as a unit as regards its circulation; *esp.* = *convection cell* s.v. \*CONVECTION *n.* 1 b. [tr. F. *cellule* (H. Bénard 1900, in *Rev. gén. des Sci.* XI. 1266/1)].

**1916** *Phil. Mag.* XXXII. 529 The layer rapidly resolves itself into a number of cells, the motion being an ascension in the middle of a cell and a descension at the common boundary between a cell and its neighbours. **1940** *Proc. R. Soc.* A. CLXXVI. 313 A surface of symmetry between adjacent cells of a 'convection pattern'. **1955** *Sci. Amer.* Sept. 117/1 These cells in the classic model are supposed to be responsible for the tropical easterlies (trade winds),

the middle-latitude westerlies and the polar easterlies. **1968** *Nature* 9 Nov. 553/1 In simple thermal (Bénard) convection, in which a layer of viscous fluid is heated from below, material heated near the bottom of the layer rises up the centre of hexagonal cells and moves radially across the top of the cell while cooling and then sinks at the junctions of adjoining cells. **1980** D. CAMERON *Ballooning Handbk.* ii. 36 Such clouds often generate areas which are deceptively calm, but contain 'cells' of convection. **1984** A. C. & A. DUXBURY *Introd. World's Oceans* vii. 212 The vertical air movements in such a cell are caused by changes in the air's density.

**f.** Each of the locations in a statistical table or tabular display which may be occupied by a single datum, statistic, etc.; more generally, any location in a matrix-like diagram.

**1923** R. PEARL *Introd. Med. Biometry & Statistics* iv. 78 There are 8 x 12 = 96 elemental cells in this table. **1946** *Brit. Jrnl. Psychol.* Jan. 49 Figures were .. worked out to make a fourfold contingency table. .. The first cell of each table contained the number of cases in which the prayer.. was regarded as familiar. **1966** *Rep. Comm. Inquiry Univ. Oxf.* II. 416 Where cells in these and other breakdowns would contain only one individual, he has been transferred to the most closely comparable cell. **1972** *Sci. Amer.* May 115/1 It is easy to prove that nine kings, eight bishops or eight rooks are needed to attack all vacant cells on a standard chessboard. **1985** *Practical Computing* Dec. 81/2 You can write free text into any spreadsheet cell, and it will be displayed over existing columns unless they already have their own contents.

**g.** *Computing.* An identifiable or addressable unit of memory or data storage; *esp.* one with a capacity of one bit or one word.

**1951** *Proc. IRE* XXXIX. 272/1 *Binary cell*, an information-storing element which can have one or the other of two stable states. **1952** *Proc. Conf. Automatic Computing Machines, Sydney* 166 Recording positions or 'cells' on the tracks are defined by the intervals of the clock track and.. are ideally discrete... A '1' may be recorded in any cell by the application of a positive current pulse to the head at the appropriate instant. **1953** *Proc. IRE* XLI. 1438/1 The surface area of the drum is divided into cells, which are grouped into tracks and slots. A cell is the area assigned to a single bit of information. **1960** M. G. SAY et al. *Analogue & Digital Computers* viii. 215 The most important feature of a store in a digital computer is.. the mechanism by which a particular digit cell may be selected in order to record a new digit or to read the existing one. **1970** O. DOPPING *Computers & Data Processing* x. 133 A computer memory with addressable cells or positions is analogous to a mail sorter with pigeon-holes.

[IV.] [14.] **d.** A container specially made to hold a sample, usu. of fluid, while it is investigated or tested.

**1863** *Phil. Trans. R. Soc.* CLII. 607, I sometimes employ a small cell with parallel faces of quartz, sometimes a wedge-shaped vessel... The cell being filled with the solvent, a minute quantity of the substance is introduced, and the progress of the absorption is watched as the substance gradually dissolves. **1900** *Rep. Brit. Assoc. Adv. Sci.* 158 A 10 per cent. solution of carbamide in a cell 15 mm. in thickness transmits all rays to x 2140. **1935** *Jrnl. Optical Soc. Amer.* XXV. 355/1 We.. constructed a cell seventy feet in length from stainless steel tubing. **1973** WILLIAMS & FLEMING *Spectrosc. Methods Org. Chem.* (ed. 2) i. 2 A matched cell containing pure solvent is also prepared, and each cell is placed in the appropriate place in the spectrometer. **1987** *Nature* 3 Sept. 32/1 The expectation that flow in Hele–Shaw cells (two parallel glass plates with a small separation) exhibits the same properties as in real porous media is based on Darcy's law.

**Cellnet** ('sɛlnɛt), n. Telecommunications. Also cellnet. [f. CELL n.¹ or CELL(ULAR a. 4 + *-NET.] A proprietary name for a cellular radio service operating in the United Kingdom (and also of a similar service in the United States); also occas., a cellular telephone.

**1984** Financial Times 14 June 8/3 The BT–Securicor service, called Cellnet, has been used on trial in London as part of communications in the recent economic summit. **1985** Official Gaz. (U.S. Patent Office) 19 Feb. TM527/2 Cellnet.., for communications services—namely, providing a network for paging and mobile telephone services... First use Nov. 11, 1982; in commerce Nov. 11, 1982. **1986** Daily Tel. 18 Sept. 13/4 It was satisfying to find, while stuck at a railway signal for half an hour near St Mary Cray the other night, that a fellow traveller was carrying a cell-net telephone. **1987** Today 21 Oct. 36/2 'Darling can you keep next Friday free for our appointment at the amniocentisis [sic] clinic,' Nicola chirps to George down the Cellnet (Yuppiespeak for car phone). **1988** Truck Dec. 51/2 The spread of cellnet systems has been slow in Spain.

**cellphone** ('sɛlfəun), n. [f. CELL n.¹ or CELL(ULAR a. 4 + PHONE n².] A hand-held or mobile radio-telephone providing access to a cellular radio network; a cellular telephone.

**1984** Cellular Business Nov. 24/2 The Cellphone is available now with a suggested price of $1,995. **1985** Times 11 Apr. 12/6 If it's attached to the car—like a cellphone or CB radio—you find yourself being offered lifts by people who have never offered you lifts before. **1986** Sunday Tel. (Colour Suppl.) 7 Sept. 22 (Advt.), The new Excell Pocketphone. The smallest, lightest, most advanced cellphone in the world. **1988** Observer (Colour Suppl.) 19 June 1/4 Cellphones can now be used to transmit telexes or faxes. **1989** Satellite Times Feb. 105/2 There were only about half a dozen others.. taking trans-Atlantic phone calls on a cellphone.

**central**, a. Add: [4.] central bank, the principal regulatory bank of a country, which issues currency, holds the exchange reserves, and manages the volume of credit, dealing mainly with the government and commercial banks.

[**1866** A. CRUMP Banking ix. 203 Sir Robert Peel avowed his own predilection for a central bank of issue.] **1901** D. M. MASON in Jrnl. Inst. Bankers Apr. 152 It has been advocated by some bankers [in the U.S.] that what is required to give stability to the currency is a *central bank or institution similar to the Bank of England. **1930** J. M. KEYNES Treat. Money II. xxxii. 225 The first necessity of a Central Bank.. is to make sure that it has an unchallengeable control over the total volume of bank-money created by its Member Banks. **1965** J. L. HANSON Dict. Econ. 62/2 It is not thought advisable for a central bank to compete with the commercial banks and, therefore, it should not engage in ordinary banking business. **1986** Economist 14 June 63/2 Central bank money, one closely-watched measure of the money supply, has grown at an annual rate of 8.2% this year. hence central banker. **1963** Economist 28 Dec. 1318/1 These *central bankers.. have created, almost malgré eux, a code of practice. **1986** Times 12 May 17/6 There was a time when.. almost the only thing on which central bankers were agreed was the need to keep their intentions unclear.

**centre**, n. and a. Add: [I.] [6.] d. Usu. with capital initial. The place from which an espionage or terrorist network is co-ordinated, esp. (now Hist.) the headquarters of the Soviet Secret Service (usu. Moscow Centre); the controlling organization or group.

**1935** Internat. Press Correspondence 26 Jan. 107/1 The facts show that the so-called 'Moscow Centre' which consisted of the former leaders of the Zinoviev Anti-Soviet Group, knew of the terroristic sentiments of the members of this group. **1937** Southern Rev. (Baton Rouge) III. 60 Trotsky is alleged to have directed the organization in 1933 of a united Trotskyite-Zinovievite center in Leningrad, the agents of which encompassed the assassination of Kirov. **1955** Rep. R. Comm. Espionage (Australia) vii. 73 The Moscow Centre recruited for its work in Australia officials of other Departments who were being posted to the Embassy here by the Soviet Foreign Office. **1963** 'J. LE CARRÉ' Spy who came in from Cold xv. 140 She read the letter again. It was on Centre's writing paper, with the thick red print at the top and it began 'Dear Comrade'. **1974** —— Tinker, Tailor xxiii. 193 Moscow Centre was in pieces... There was a crop of defections among Centre officers. **1982** J. GARDNER Quiet Dogs (1984) ii. 15 Even with this new building, Moscow Centre—as it is known.. within Intelligence communities the world over—is now the Centre in name only. **1986** G. MARKSTEIN Soul Hunters lxi. 234 Leave nothing to chance. He was.. only implementing the Centre's philosophy.

**Centronics** (sɛn'trɒnɪks), n. Computing. Also centronics. A proprietary name for various printers and other computer peripherals, used attrib. and in comb. (as Centronics-type) with reference to a widely-used type of interface (the Centronics (parallel) interface) connecting a computer to a printer or other peripheral, through which data in the form of 8-bit characters may be transmitted along eight lines in parallel.

**1974** Official Gaz. (U.S. Patent Office) 16 July TM162/2 Centronics... For data terminals in the nature of high speed printers of the dot matrix type and components and sub-assemblies used therein... First use July 1968. **1979** Personal Computer World Nov. 52 (table) Centronics parallel interface board. **1984** Trade Marks Jrnl. 28 Mar. 785/1 Centronics. **1984** Personal Software Winter 54/2 An option is given for this translation to be output via the centronics interface to a printer for a permanent hard copy. **1984** Which Micro? Dec. 32/3 These are for Centronics-type printers. **1985** Personal Computer World Feb. 211/2 All Epson printers are supplied with a centronics interface.

**cervical**, a. Add: 3. Special collocations: cervical screening Gynæcol., the screening of women for early symptoms of cervical cancer.

**1967** Spectator 28 July 98/3 *Cervical screening therefore remains limited in value. **1987** Oxf. Textbk. Med. (ed. 2) I. IV. 124/2 Cervical screening, by taking a smear from the cervical mucosa and looking for atypical cells suggestive of a malignancy, was introduced soon after the second world war.

cervical smear Gynæcol., a smear of cells taken from the cervix of the womb, analysed for evidence of cervical cancer; cf. vaginal smear s.v. SMEAR n. 3 b.

**1944** J. E. AYRE in Canad. Med. Assoc. Jrnl. LI. 19/1 It is thought to be of advantage to take both smears, the vaginal and *cervical. **1947** Amer. Jrnl. Obstetr. & Gynecol. LIII. 610 In the ordinary vaginal or cervical smear the profuse purulent and sanguineous discharge.. frequently obscures the true .. cornification level associated with malignant disease. **1966** Lancet 24 Dec. 1423/1 There is a large variety of arrangements throughout Scotland for taking cervical smears. **1986** Nursing Times 3 Dec. 34/1 She had had a cervical smear which showed a positive malignancy and had been referred urgently to the gynaecology department of a local hospital.

**Cetti** ('tʃɛti), n. The name of Francesco Cetti (fl. 1776), Italian ornithologist, used in the possessive, as Cetti's warbler, to designate a chestnut-brown southern European warbler,

*Cettia cetti,* resident in Britain since the 1970s and noted for its strikingly loud and abrupt song.

**1875** L. H. L. IRBY *Ornithol. Straits Gibraltar* 93 Wherever there are thick bushes (generally bramble-brakes close to water) Cetti's Warbler is to be heard. **1904** *Bull. Brit. Ornithologists' Club* XIV. 84 Mr. M. J. Nicoll exhibited a specimen of Cetti's Warbler .. shot by a gardener-boy ... This was the first authentic occurrence [subsequently discredited] of Cetti's Warbler in Great Britain. **1972** *Brit. Birds* LXV. 496 At least one pair of Cetti's Warblers *Cettia cetti* bred successfully in southern England. **1983** D. TOMLINSON in Oddie & Tomlinson *Big Bird Race* 47 At 03.40 a burst of explosive song from a Cetti's Warbler was a welcome sound.

**chad** (tʃæd), *n.*[2] *Telegr.* and *Computing.* [Origin unknown.] (A piece of) the waste material removed from punched cards or tape during punching.

**1959** J. W. FREEBODY *Telegr.* xi. 460/2 The small hinged discs of paper, called 'chads', remain attached to the body of the tape. **1968** J. BLACKBURN *Nothing but Night* vii. 64 The machines .. spewed out the sixty-four-row punch cards ... At the base of each machine was a vacuum tube to remove the dust and the chads. **1982** *Computerworld* 9 Aug. 59 The reader head is mounted on the front of the unit next to the chad box.

Hence **'chadless** *a.*, not producing or accompanied by chads.

**1959** J. W. FREEBODY *Telegr.* xi. 460/2 In order .. that the printed characters are completely legible, the tape is perforated by the chadless method. **1971** *Gloss. Electrotechnical, Power Terms (B.S.I.)* III. iii. 19 Chadless perforation. **1984** *U.S. Patent* 4,425,394 1 Each tag has a chadless hole provided by a pattern of knife cuts.

**Chadic** ('tʃædɪk), *a.* [f. as CHADIAN *n.* and *a.* + -IC.] Of or pertaining to an Afro-Asiatic group of languages (of which the most prominent is Hausa) spoken in West and Central Africa.

**1977** C. F. & F. M. VOEGELIN *Classification & Index World's Lang.* 104 Most languages of the Chadic family are spoken in an area extending from the area of Lake Chad to the borderlands of Nigeria, Cameroon, and Central African Republic. **1983** *Word 1982* XXXIII. 233 In Guidar and Guiziga, and probably in other Chadic languages of North Cameroon, some ideophones .. may themselves be used as predicates without the corresponding verb. **1987** D. CRYSTAL *Cambr. Encycl. Lang.* lii. 316/2 Hausa .. is the only Chadic language to have a written form. **1989** *Encycl. Brit.* XXII. 740/1 Some linguists deny the genetic affinity of the Chadic languages with the other branches of Hamito-Semitic, while others .. accept it.

**chalk**, *n.* Add: [2.] **b.** *Geol.* A deposit or stratum composed mainly of chalk; freq. used to denote a particular stratum or system of such composition (usu. with capital initial).

**1811** T. WEBSTER *Let.* 7 June in H. C. Englefield *Descr. Isle of Wight* (1816) 149 On arriving at the pit, I found this was cut in the lower chalk, which was entirely without flints. **1814** *Trans. Geol. Soc.* II. 161 (*heading*) On the freshwater formations in the Isle of Wight, with some observations on the strata over the chalk in the south-east part of England. **1824** W. H. FITTON in *Ann. Philos.* VIII. 462 Proposed names of the strata. 1. Chalk .. Including chalk with and without flints—(the *craie blanche* of the French) and grey chalk—chalk marl of Mr. Webster. **1833** G. MANTELL *Geol. S. E. Eng.* v. 69 The Upper and Lower Chalk of Sussex. **1882** A. GEIKIE *Text-bk. Geol.* 820 The lower part of the Chalk has generally a somewhat greyish tint. *Ibid.* 821 A well-defined band between the Grey Chalk and the overlying lower subdivision of the White Chalk (Turonian). **1910**

*Bull. Geol. Survey W. Austral.* No. 36. 115 (*title*) The geological age and organic remains of the Gingin Chalk. **1930** F. J. NORTH *Limestones* xi. 250 'The Chalk', in the stratigraphical sense, includes some rocks that are hard and marly and others that are sandy. **1946** L. D. STAMP *Britain's Struct.* xii. 137 Permanent connection across the central ridge was probably not established till Lower Chalk times. **1969** BENNISON & WRIGHT *Geol. Hist. Brit. Isles* xiv. 323 In Yorkshire, north of the Humber only thin pre-chalk strata occur, the Red Chalk and Carstone. **1977** A. HALLAM *Planet Earth* 223/3 Also occurring in marine sediments, and best known from the chalks of Kansas .., are the last of the flying reptiles, the pterosaurs.

[6.] **c.** *chalk and talk*, a method of teaching consisting of lectures illustrated chiefly on the blackboard; also *chalk-and-talker* (*Austral.*), a school-teacher. *colloq.*

**1937** G. A. N. LOWNDES *Silent Social Revolution* ii. 36 The blackboard was replacing the reading cards or letter sheets hitherto almost universal. For the era of 'chalk and talk' had to intervene before the era of textbooks. **1941** BAKER *Dict. Austral. Slang* 17 *Chalk-and-talker*, a school-teacher. **1955** *School Sci. Rev.* June 394 All too frequently lessons become 'chalk and talk' illustrated with a few demonstration experiments. **1977** P. STREVENS *New Orientations Teaching Eng.* xiv. 166 Until some eight years ago, the teaching of foreign languages was a 'chalk and talk' profession. **1986** *Listener* 18 Sept. 5/2 What they want is a less didactic style in the classroom, less of what is called 'chalk and talk', the teacher lecturing and the children passively taking it in (or not).

**challenged**, *ppl. a.* Add: **b.** *euphem.* Of a person: disabled or handicapped, esp. physically. orig. and chiefly *N. Amer.*

**1985** *N.Y. Times* 20 Apr. 1. 26/3 The disabled skiers, whom Mr. Kennedy prefers to call 'physically challenged', achieve speeds on difficult runs that would be daunting to most competitors. **1986** *Publishers Weekly* 10 Jan. 4/1 (Advt.), This bestselling author [*sc.* R. Simmons] of *The Never Say Diet Book* creates a comprehensive fitness program for the physically challenged. **1987** *Los Angeles Times* 4 Oct. VII. 3/5 Dee Duncan has discovered the tremendous value of travel for what she fondly calls 'mentally challenged' individuals. **1989** *Computer Bull.* Mar. 10/1 Rank Xerox itself has provided office systems equipment .. which has been used to provide IT skills training .. to those who are physically challenged.

**chamber**, *n.* Add: [II.] [8.] **b.** An underground cavity, *esp.* one at least as large as a room; a cave.

**1744** *Phil. Trans. R. Soc.* XLI. 362 Most People that have gone into it, went by a Thread or Clue; .. which seems altogether unnecessary, there being no Windings or Chambers throughout any Extent. **1823** W. BUCKLAND *Reliquiæ Diluvianæ* 111 In the natural chambers there is not a single fragment of bone, except upon or below the floor. **1851** G. A. MANTELL *Petrifications & their Teachings* iv. 397 The entrance to this cave .. leads to a series of chambers from fifteen to twenty feet high, and several hundred feet in extent, terminating in a deep chasm. **1981** F. HOYLE *Ice* ii. 37 Although the cave is nearly 300 metres long, most of the paintings are in a chamber 18 by 9 metres, which has an average height of 2 metres.

**c.** *Mining.* A large ore deposit or lode with well-defined boundaries.

[**1884** J. A. PHILLIPS *Treat. Ore Deposits* i. 30 The regular unstratified metalliferous deposits comprehend true veins, segregated veins and gash veins; while the others, namely, impregnations, stockworks, fahlbands, contact and *chamber deposits*, are spoken of as irregular.] **1886** J. GEIKIE *Outl. Geol.* xvi. 207 *Chambers* or *pockets* is the name given to larger or smaller ore deposits filling up irregular cavities in calcareous rocks. **1935** STOČES & WHITE *Structural Geol.* 293 By the enlargement of certain parts of the vein, what are known as chamber lodes are formed. When the chambers are lenticular and frequent they are called lenticular veins. **1980** W. A. VISSER *Geol. Nomencl.* 299/1 Ore stock; ore chamber; ore pocket;—terms in common use to describe larger ore masses.

**chamosite** ('ʃæməzaɪt), *n.* (Formerly at CHAMOISITE *n.*) Also 9 chamoisite ('ʃæmwəzaɪt). [a. F. *chamosite* (P. Berthier 1820, in *Ann. des Mines* V. 393, as *chamoisite*), f. *Chamoson*, earlier *Chamoison*, the name of the village in the Valais, Switzerland, where first found: see -ITE¹. Berthier revised the spelling to *chamosite* in 1827 (*Ann. Chim. Phys.* XXXV. 258).] A hydrous silicate of iron often occurring in grains.
**1832** C. U. SHEPARD *Treat. Min.: Introd. Vol.* 123 Chamoisite appears to be an impure variety. **1868** J. D. DANA *Syst. Min.* (ed. 5) 511 Chamoisite. **1892** E. S. DANA *Dana's Syst. Min.* (ed. 6) 658 *Chamosite*, as originally described, occurs compact or oölitic. **1928** W. LINDGREN *Mineral Deposits* (ed. 3) xviii. 307 The common types of [Jurassic iron] ore are designated as 'chamositic mudstone' and 'chamositic, siderite mudstone:' a marine deposit composed of a matrix of fine-grained chamosite with oölites of same and rhombs and grains of siderite. **1951** *Proc. Yorks. Geol. Soc.* XXVIII. 61 'Chamoisite' slept peacefully in mineral collections for nearly 100 years. **1962** W. T. HUANG *Petrol.* vii. 294 Chamosite, an iron-rich chlorite, is an important constituent of some sedimentary iron ores. The Chamosite ironstones consist of a fine-grained aggregate of green, cryptocrystalline chamosite. **1983** B. SIMPSON *Rocks & Minerals* (rev. ed.) xix. 215 The presence of plant life . . ensures the formation of organic solutions and so of reducing environments under which siderite and chamosite are deposited.

**chamositic** (ʃæmə'sɪtɪk), *a. Geol.* [f. *CHAMOSITE *n.* + -IC.] Containing or composed of chamosite.
**1925** *Spec. Rep. Min. Resources Gt. Brit.* (Mem. Geol. Survey) XXIX. i. 7 Purely chamositic mudstones are rare, the best examples being certain beds in North Wales, among certain beds of the Lias clay. **1951** *Proc. Yorks. Geol. Soc.* XXVIII. 63 The secondary nature of the thuringite . . is plainly evident from the microstructure, in which the original chamositic constituents are replaced by fine, or even coarse, crystalline chlorite. **1971** I. G. GASS et al. *Understanding Earth* i. 32/2 Iron rich sediments such as the chamositic iron ores (rocks containing ooliths of the iron mineral chamosite, e.g. as in the bedded iron ores of the Midlands and Inner Hebrides).

**chanting**, *ppl. a.* Add: 3. Special collocations: **chanting falcon** = *chanting goshawk* below.
[**1799** F. LEVAILLANT *Hist. Nat. Oiseaux d'Afrique* I. 117 *(heading)* Le Faucon chanteur.] **1802** BINGLEY *Anim. Biog.* (1813) II. 60 The chaunting falcon. During the breeding season the male of this species is remarkable for its song. **1874** R. B. SHARPE *Catal. Birds. Brit. Mus.* I. 87 Melierax canorus . . . Chanting Falcon.

**chanting goshawk**, either of two African hawks, *Melierax metabates* and *M. canorus* (*M. poliopterus*), having a distinctive and melodious chanting call.
**1903** A. C. STARK *Birds S. Afr.* III. 362 The *Chanting Goshawk is essentially an inhabitant of the western and dryer half of South Africa. **1964** C. WILLOCK *Enormous Zoo* iii. 47 He almost certainly did not know a pale chanting goshawk from a pallid harrier. **1985** PERRINS & MIDDLETON *Encycl. Birds* 110/1 *(caption)* Gray chanting goshawk (*Melierax poliopterus*) calling on top of a termite mound.

†**chanting hawk** = *\*chanting goshawk* above (*obs.*).
**1868** *Ibis* IV. 145 *Chanting Hawk. **1903** *Westm. Gaz.* 28 Mar. 10/1 *(heading)* Chanting-hawks at the Zoo.

**charbroil** ('tʃɑːbrɔɪl), *v.* orig. and chiefly N. *Amer.* Also char-broil. [f. CHAR(COAL *n.* + BROIL *v.*¹] *trans.* To cook (meat) on a grill over charcoal. Hence **'charbroiled** *ppl. a.*, **'charbroiling** *vbl. n.*
The word is used by extension of meat grilled over (or under) ceramic briquettes.
**1959** *Fast Food* Feb. 45/1 Usually the char-broiled burger is somewhat larger than an ordinary hamburger . . . Hot dogs, chicken and chops are other meats frequently char-broiled. **1961** *Ibid.* Aug. 69 (Advt.), A Charco-Broiler? Like no other! . . It makes char-broiling any other way strictly old-fashioned! . . Gives meats truest char-broiled taste, aroma, and appearance! **1969** D. E. WESTLAKE *Up your Banners* vi. 44 Celibacy and Mum's home cooking were a lot better than Elizabeth Taylor and char-broiled steaks. **1971** *Sunday Times* (Colour Suppl.) 16 May 66/1 Since nobody charbroiled steak for us or handed round copies of *McCall's*, our diversions were few. **1978** *Detroit Free Press* 5 Mar. D19 (Advt.), Cold, dry champagne and sizzling charbroiled filet mignon served with a warm smile. **1986** *Country Life* 10 July 85/3 Those succulent Bresse chickens were not bred for charbroiling.

**'charbroiler**, *n.* *U.S.* [f. *CHARBROIL *v.* + -ER¹.] A grill or other apparatus on which meat is charbroiled.
**1982** *Restaurant Business* 1 Oct. 204/3 These units do not flare up and are properly called char-broilers. **1986** *Cambridge* (Mass.) *Chron.* 6 Mar. 2A (Advt.), Specializing in . . sausages on the charbroiler.

**charge**, *n.* Add: [I.] [5.] **b.** The process of charging a battery; *on charge*, in the state of undergoing this process.
**1887** P. B. ELWELL tr. *Planté's Storage Electr. Energy* ii. 46 Absorption of the gases during the charge of secondary cells. **1908** J. R. BARR *Princ. Direct-Current Electr. Engin.* v. 133 Variation of E.M.F. during charge and discharge. **1924** G. W. VINAL *Storage Batteries* vi. 233 The point at which gassing of a storage battery while on charge, begins is determined by the voltage. **1953** R. A. HARVEY *Battery Chargers & Charging* xii. 311 The miner passes through the lamp room on finishing his shift and . . puts the battery on charge himself. **1984** C. A. VINCENT et al. *Mod. Batteries* 240 The current is high at the beginning of the charge, and falls off as the charging proceeds.

**cheap**, *a.* and *adv.* Add: [A.] [1.] [a.] Also *cheap and cheerful* (*colloq.*), simple, cheap, and pleasant.
**1974** *Times* 12 Oct. 10/3 Cheap and cheerful chalets . . about 15 minutes' brisk trot from the centre of the village. **1988** *Daily Tel.* 25 Feb. 11/4 The parade of pleats spans all price levels from designer-label to cheap and cheerful.

**check-** *comb. form.* Add: **checksum, check sum** *Computing*, a sum calculated from the digits in a set of data and transmitted or stored with the data to provide a means of automatic checking for any subsequent corruption.
**1940** W. J. ECKERT *Punched Card Methods* iii. 27 *Check sums detect misplaced cards and errors of transposition. **1979** *Personal Computer World* Nov. 45/1 Rundle says that he was virtually forced to design a checksum cassette handling system because there was no other way of loading an 8K byte program. **1986** *ZX Computing Monthly* Oct. 52/3 The scope for errors when typing in the long lists of numbers is considerable, even with checksums.

**cheer**, _n._[1] Add: [8.] c. _pl._ In British English, = thank you, thanks. _colloq._
**1976** P. HOWARD in _Times_ 5 Aug. 12/1 By a remarkable transition from the pub to the sober world at large outside _cheers_ has become the colloquial synonym in British English for 'thanks'. **1978** in R. Buckle _U & Non-U Revisited_ 48 Do any small favour for a young Englishman these days and he will thank you by saying 'cheers'.

**cheese-paring**, (_vbl._) _n._ and _ppl._ _a._ Add: Hence (as a back-formation) '**cheesepare** _v._, (_a_) _intr._, to make cheese-paring economies (also _fig._); (_b_) _trans._, to save (money) in this way.
**1890** _Pall Mall Gaz._ 3 Feb. 2/2 But is it fair of Sir Hercules to throw all the blame on the Treasury? After all, it is the business of the Treasury to cheesepare. **1948** E. WAUGH _Ess., Articles & Rev._ (1986) 346 Don't cheat and don't cheese-pare: go where you are allowed and hope for better times. **1951** _Times_ 21 Sept. 3/1 By pointing to the decision of the Government 'to give away to the film industry a large part of the few millions they have cheese-pared out of people with bad teeth and weak eyesight'. **1984** _Times_ 12 Dec. 10/6 It is truly perverse that a Treasury which insists it is essential to cheesepare a few millions here and there from the science budget is so little interested. **1986** 'J. LE CARRÉ' _Perfect Spy_ xiii. 363 Why do I cheesepare and give him only two?

**chemical**, _a._ Add: [4.] [b.] _chemical weapon_, a weapon that depends for its effect on the release of a toxic or noxious substance; usu. in _pl._
**1920** E. S. FARROW _Gas Warfare_ viii. 100 The following types of chemical weapons have been approved for use by infantry: Incendiary grenades, gas grenades, smoke grenades, [etc.]. **1986** _Armed Forces_ Aug. 375/1 There was .. lack of progress for a chemical weapons convention.

**chemiosmotic** (ˌkɛmɪɒz'mɒtɪk), _a._ _Biochem._ [f. CHEMI(CAL _a._ + OSMOTIC _a._] Designating or in accordance with a theory (the _chemiosmotic hypothesis_ or _theory_) explaining the mechanism of oxidative phosphorylation by proposing that electron transport within the membranes of mitochondria and chloroplasts is associated with the 'pumping' of protons through the membranes into the cytoplasm via various chemical intermediates.
**1957** P. MITCHELL in E. M. Crook _Structure & Function Subcellular Components_ (1959) 90 (_heading_) Chemi-osmotic processes. _Ibid._ 91, I would venture to suggest that the function of the membranes of mitochondria and of the endoplasmic reticulum may be, like that of the plasma-membrane, to act as chemi-osmotic links between the media that they separate. **1969** _New Scientist_ 13 Nov. 327/3 The chemiosmotic theory, championed for several years by Peter Mitchell. **1971** _Nature_ 27 Aug. 606/2 In recent years the chemiosmotic scheme and chemical hypothesis .. have commanded the most attention. **1984** HOLTZMAN & NOVIKOFF _Cells & Organelles_ (ed. 3) II. vi. 189 Chemiosmotic mechanisms like the one suggested for mitochondria have provided convincing explanations for the functioning of other membrane systems with which mitochondria share some features. **1987** _New Scientist_ 10 Dec. 49/3 This may have been how the chemiosmotic production of ATP in virtually all modern organisms first evolved.

**chemo'therapist**, _n._ [f. CHEMOTHERAP(Y _n._ + -IST.] One who specializes in chemotherapy.
**1934** in WEBSTER. **1935** _Chambers's Encycl._ IV. 246/1 _Ehrlich_, Paul, a great bacteriologist and chemotherapist, was born of Jewish family at Strehelen, in Prussian Silesia, 14th March 1854. **1976** _Lancet_ 4 Dec. 1233/1 Head and neck cancers demand the multidisciplinary skills of 'head-and-neck

oncologists'—collaborating closely with plastic surgeons, maxillo-facial surgeons, radiotherapists, and chemotherapists. **1988** _Sci. Amer._ Aug. 50/2 The cancer chemotherapist attempts to interfere selectively with malignant cells.

**cherry**, _n._ Add: [I.] [1.] [b.] For def. read: In proverbial expressions. Esp. † _to make two bites at the cherry_, etc.: (usu. in negative contexts) to behave with affected nicety; to divide (a task, etc.) unnecessarily minutely; _to take two bites of a cherry_, etc.: to take or have a further opportunity to achieve something. Also, _a second bite at the cherry_, etc., a second chance.
**1666** G. TORRIANO _Piazza Universale di Proverbi Italiani_ II. 184/2 To play the Hypocrite, and be demure, are that will make two bits of one Chery, but in private can devour a pound and more. **1694** P. A. MOTTEUX tr. _Rabelais's Wks._ v. xxviii. 145 Nothing is to be got out of him but Monosyllables; by Jingo, I believe he would make three bits of a Cherry. **1819** _Farmer's Almanack 1820_ (Boston) XXVIII. 11 Never make two bites at a cherry. **1827** SCOTT _Two Drovers_ in _Chron. Canongate_ 1st. Ser. I. xiv. 315 Take it all, man—take it all—never make two bites of a cherry. **1861** C. READE _Cloister & Hearth_ II. xiv. 269 There were soldiers of a lower stamp, who would not make two bites of such a cherry. **1905** S. WEYMAN _Starvecrow Farm_ v. 41 I'll have no goings on with such in my house, and no making two bites of a cherry! **1966** [see SUPPLEMENTAL _a._ a]. **1968** 'A. GILBERT' _Night Encounter_ xi. 186 Never heard of taking two bites at a cherry? If he couldn't afford to let Mr. Crook go on breathing before, he's got twice as much reason to want to shut him up now. **1971** _Nature_ 1 Jan. 5/2 One of the chief purposes of the Open University is to provide a second bite at the higher education cherry for those students who .. have missed out on their first opportunity. **1986** _Sunday Tel._ 9 Nov. 11/8 In a second bite at the cherry last week the _Sunday Express_ clarified Dr Seale's position.
[II.] [10.] **cherry tomato** orig. _U.S._, any of several varieties of tomato plant, originating from South America but now also widely cultivated elsewhere, with fruit about the size of a cherry; the fruit itself.
**1859** G. THURBER _Darlington's Amer. Weeds & Useful Plants_ (rev. ed.) 251 The small round kind, known as '*Cherry Tomato', is probably _L. Cerasiforme_. **1887** [see SUPPLEMENTAL _n._ 2 a]. **1943** _Home Garden_ Aug. 75/1 Most people seem to think of the cherry tomato as a novelty or luxury. **1986** _New Yorker_ 3 Mar. 33/2 There are cherry tomatoes halved and stuffed with peaks of cheese.

**chicken**, _n._[1] Add: [8.] **chicken-breast**, (_b_) the breast of a chicken, esp. as an item of food.
**1941** G. A. ESCOFFIER _Cook Bk._ II. xvi. 525 *Chicken breasts with mushroom sauce. **1986** _Times_ 31 May 15/2 A chicken breast poached in a saffron sauce.

**chikungunya** (tʃɪkʊŋ'ɡʊnjə), _n._ [Bantu, prob. Makonde; cf. Yao _chi-_ noun prefix + _kunguna_ to bend, stoop. The word is said to mean 'that which folds up'.] A mosquito-borne viral disease of tropical Africa and southern Asia, marked by fever and joint pains of crippling intensity.
**1954** GILLETT & ROSS in _Ann. Rep. Virus Res. Inst. 1953_ (Entebbe) 13 Transmission experiment with Chikungunya A and B virus. **1960** A. J. HADDOW et al. in _Trans. R. Soc. Trop. Med. & Hygiene_ LIV. 517 The disease was probably Chikungunya fever, an East African virus infection. **1975** _Nature_ 31 July 355/1 _A. aegypti_ .. is the only proved natural vector of urban yellow fever; it is also a vector of dengue and chikungunya. **1987** _Oxf. Textbk. Med._ (ed. 2) I. v. 115/1 In India and Southeast Asia, chikungunya

virus has been implicated in outbreaks of haemorrhagic fever.

**child**, *n*. Add: [22.] **child allowance**, a tax allowance granted to parents of dependent children; also loosely, = *child benefit*.

**1954** *Hansard Commons* 9 Mar. 1922 Mr. Jay asked the Chancellor of the Exchequer whether . . he will give a high priority to a substantial increase in the Income Tax *child allowance. **1966** B. E. V. SABINE *Hist. Income Tax* ix. 148 Child allowances, still only granted for incomes not exceeding £500 . . doubled to £20 for each child. **1974** *Hansard Commons* 13 Nov. 418 The Government are committed to extend the family allowance to the first child under their child allowance scheme. **1985** J. WINTERSON *Oranges are not only Fruit* 25, I . . wrote on the back of a child allowance form.

**chill-**, *comb. form*. Add: [2.] **chill factor** *Meteorol.*, the perceived lowering of the air temperature caused by wind and other agencies; also, the effective temperature when this is taken into account; cf. *wind-chill factor* s.v. WIND *n.*[1] 32.

**1967** WEBSTER Add., *Chill factor. **1973** B. WRIGHT *Four Seasons North* 76 Cold in combination with wind produces the 'chill factor', which, more crucial than either temperature or wind velocity, can also be measured. **1977** *Daily Tel.* 19 Jan. 17/1 The 'chill factor'—the cold the body actually feels when wind conditions are taken into account—was minus 60 degrees in Chicago and about minus 30 in New York. **1984** A. MACLEAN *San Andreas* iii. 78 'Yes, Ferguson, I have heard of the chill factor.''For every knot of wind the temperature, as far as the skin is concerned, falls by one degree.'

**chilli**, *n*. Add: [2.] ‖**chiles rellenos** *n. pl.* orig. *U.S.* [Mexican Sp.: *relleno* = filled, stuffed], Mexican stuffed green peppers, esp. fried in batter; also in *sing.*; cf. *RELLENO *n.*

**1929** P. KLEEMANN *Ramona's Sp.-Mex. Cookery* 96 Stuffed Peppers a la Mexicana (Chiles Rellenos) No. 1. 6 large long chile peppers. 1 lb. diced white cream cheese. **1979** *Tucson Mag.* June 67/1 Papagayo Restaurant . . . Chef's specialty is the chile relleno, but every item tested was superior. **1984** L. DEIGHTON *Mexico Set* v. 68 He stopped at a stall to watch a man making *chiles rellenos*, putting meat fillings into large peppers.

**China**, *n.*[1] and *a*. Add: [I.] [2.] [b.] For 'in names . . products, etc.' read: Special combinations (esp. in the names of natural products, etc.) and add: **China syndrome**, an imaginary sequence of events following the meltdown of a nuclear reactor, in which so much heat is generated that the core melts through its containment structure and deep into the earth.

**1970** *Esquire* June 76/4 This 'fast-breeder reactor' required a large flow of coolant to keep control and prevent the '*China syndrome' — a constant worry to technicians, for once she starts melting, she'll melt her way all the way down to China. **1986** *Times* 12 May 1/5 Mr. Velikhov's announcement gave no clear indication just how close the Chernobyl disaster came to creating the so-called 'China Syndrome'.

**Chinese**, *a*. and *n*. Add: [A.] [2.] **Chinese leaf** = PE-TSAI *n.*, used esp. in salads; also in *pl.*, the leaves of this vegetable; cf. *Chinese cabbage* above.

**1976** *Good Housek. Cookery Bk.* (rev. ed.) 212 *Chinese leaves are a useful addition to the ranks of vegetables available mid-November until early June. **1978** J. GRIGSON *Vegetable Bk.* (1980) 221 Chinese leaf can be cooked like other, lustier cabbages, but remember to reduce the time. **1988** D. MACCARTHY *Prodfact 1988* 146 Similar but milder tasting than

cabbage, Chinese Leaf can be eaten raw or cooked. **1988** *Times* 15 Jan. 5/2 Chinese leaves 70p–95p a head and celery 40p–60p a head are the best salad buys.

**chip**, *n.*[1] Add: [9.] [a.] **chip card**, a card (CARD *n.*[1] 6 h) incorporating a microchip that stores information about transactions and provides security against misuse.

**1980** *Amer. Banker* 19 May 21/1 The important aspect of the chip in card technology is that the degree of security in a semiconductor chip card appears to be far superior to other card products in the marketplace. **1985** *Times* 21 Mar. 35/3 (Advt.), Technological developments in banking (e.g. EFTPOS, ATM reciprocity, chip cards, network linking . . ) are dependent upon standards being agreed amongst the many interested parties.

**chip**, *v.*[1] Add: 11. *Comb.* **chip-in** *Golf*, a chip shot which holes the ball.

**1977** *Washington Post* 5 Sept. D3/1 That made three birdies including the chip-in. **1986** *Golf Monthly* July 165/1 Clark won the Madrid Open with the aid of a chip-in.

**chiru** ('tʃɪruː), *n*. Also 9 chiro. [Of Tibeto-Burman origin; perh. a Bhutanese dialect word from northern Nepal. *Chiru* is not found in Tibetan, though it is likely that the final element represents the widespread Tibeto-Burman root *ru* horn.] The Tibetan antelope, *Pantholops hodgsoni*, with a thick, reddish-brown woolly coat, large nostrils, and (in the case of the male) very long straight horns.

**1825** *Phil. Mag.* LXV. 64 Its name is *chiro*; its colour bright bay, and its dwelling place the plains of B'hote. **1826** *Ibid.* LXVIII. 232 Mr. Hodgson's paper on the *chiru* concerned the animal which has been so often mentioned as the unicorn of the Himala. **1875** *Encycl. Brit.* II. 102/1 The chiru (*Pantholops Hodgsonii*), inhabiting Thibet and the mountainous slopes of the Himalayas, possesses elongated horns of an annulated character, and is besides distinguished by a soft glandular swelling above each nostril. **1893** R. LYDEKKER *Horns & Hoofs* 159 In order to withstand the intense cold of a Tibetan winter, the chiru is clothed with a thick and close woolly pile. **1965** D. MORRIS *Mammals* 420 The only close relative of the Saiga antelope is the immensely long-horned Tibetan Antelope, or Chiru (*Pantholops hodgsoni*) from the high plateaux of Tibet. **1973** *Times* 20 Feb. (India Suppl.) p. xi/3 The plateau of Ladakh in the high Himalayas harbours forms related to those in Tibet such as the wild yak, the kiang, and the chiru. **1990** *New Scientist* 26 May 48/2 Tibetan species of antelope (also known as chiru), gazelle, the rare argali sheep . . all make their home there.

**chlorolabe** ('klɔːrəʊleɪb), *n*. *Physiol*. [f. CHLORO-[1] + -*labe*, f. Gr. root λαβ- to take, seize.] A green-sensitive pigment present in the cones of the retina. Cf. *CYANOLABE *n.*, *ERYTHROLABE *n.*

**1958** W. A. H. RUSHTON in *Nature* 13 Sept. 691/1 This latter pigment may be named 'erythrolabe' (= red taking), the protanope pigment 'chlorolabe', [etc.]. **1959** [see ERYTHROLABE *n.*]. **1963** *Jrnl. Physiol.* CLXVIII. 358 The 'green pigment' of colour vision is not that which would look green if we could extract it, for in that case green rays would be transmitted unabsorbed and without effect. Quite the contrary, it is the pigment which catches green—chlorolabe. **1975** *Sci. Amer.* Mar. 71/3 D. E. Mitchell and I applied the same test to see whether or not the cone pigments chlorolabe or erythrolabe in the dichromat are the pigments of daylight vision in the protanope or the deuteranope.

**cholecalciferol** (ˌkəʊlɪkælˈsɪfərɒl), *n. Biochem.*
[f. CHOLE(STEROL *n.* + CALCIFEROL *n.*] = *vitamin D₃* s.v. VITAMIN *n.* 2.

**1952** *Chem. & Engin. News* 7 Jan. 104/2 A special subcommittee of the [International Union of Pure and Applied Chemistry] commission [on the nomenclature of biological chemistry] has been appointed on the nomenclature of vitamins ... The following names have been adopted:.. D₃ cholecalciferol. **1970** R. W. McGILVERY *Biochem.* xxiv. 604 Cholecalciferol is necessary for the mobilization of calcium from the bones. **1975** *Sci. Amer.* June 126/2 The relation of calcium absorption to vitamin D (cholecalciferol) and to sunlight is complicated. **1982** T. M. DEVLIN *Textbk. Biochem.* xv. 719 Vitamin D₃, or cholecalciferol, has been classified as a vitamin in human nutrition based on its low conversion from a precursor sterol under limiting (no sunlight) conditions.

**chromo-**, *comb. form.* Add: [2.] **chromodynamic** *a. Particle Physics,* of or pertaining to chromodynamics; usu. in *quantum(-)chromodynamic.*

**1979** *Physical Rev. Lett.* XLIII. 668 (*heading*) Higher-order quantum *chromodynamic corrections in *e* + *e* - annihilation. **1980** *Sci. News* 9 Feb. 85 How the charmonium states change into one another .. and differ from one another is extremely important for an understanding of the characteristic called charm and of the chromodynamic force that holds these structures together. **1985** *Physical Rev. D* XXXI. 917 (*heading*) Color confinement and the quantum-chromodynamic vacuum. **1987** *JETP Lett.* XLV. 515 The QCD structure of a finite hadronic state in deep inelastic scattering is discussed. Special attention is focused on the physics of the chromodynamic coherence.

**chromody'namics** *n. pl.* (const. as *sing.*) *Particle Physics* = *quantum chromodynamics* s.v. QUANTUM *n.* 7 a.

**1976** *Sci. News* 26 June 408/3 Theorists postulated intermediate particles that would carry the force between quarks. These intermediates are called gluons. The whole theory is called chromodynamics. **1985** *Physical Rev. D* XXXII. 223/1 This attempt to construct a quark model with chromodynamics for mesons has been reasonably successful.

**chuckawalla** *n.,* var. *CHUCKWALLA *n.*

**chuckwalla** (ˈtʃʌkwɒlə), *n.* Also chuckawalla, etc. [ad. Mexican Sp. *chacahuala,* f. Amer. Indian (Catuilla) name.] A large rock-dwelling iguanid lizard, *Sauromalus obesus,* common in the deserts of the south-western United States. Also *chuckwalla lizard.*

**1893** *N. Amer. Fauna* VII. 174 The 'chuck-walla', by which name this remarkable lizard is universally known to both Indians and whites .., inhabits many of the Lower Sonoran Desert ranges in the southern part of the Great Basin. **1914** E. A. BRININSTOOL *Trail Dust* 103 Let me see the chuckawalla and the Gila monster too. **1942** R. G. LILLARD *Desert Challenge* 248, I reckon my critics never .. lived on whang leather and Chuckawalla lizards. **1966** R. C. STEBBINS *Field Guide to Western Reptiles & Amphibians* 95 When disturbed, chuckwallas gulp air, distend their body, and wedge themselves in place. **1978** *Sci. Amer.* Aug. 88/3 Eugene C. Crawford and Billy J. Barber of the University of Kentucky found that the chuckwallah lizard exploits panting as a mechanism to lose heat if its skin temperature or deep-body temperature exceeds a certain level.

**cimetidine** (saɪˈmɛtɪdiːn), *n. Pharm.* [f. *ci-,* alteration of CY(ANO-, + MET(HYL *n.* + -IDINE.] An imidazole derivative, C₁₀H₁₆N₆S, with histamine H₂-receptor blocking properties, given (usu. in tablet form as the hydrochloride) in the treatment of peptic ulcers.

**1975** *Brit. Jrnl. Pharmacol.* LIII. 435 P/2 In male human volunteers cimetidine given intravenously has been shown to inhibit histamine- or pentagastrin-stimulated gastric secretion. **1977** *Lancet* 9 July 74/2 The third therapeutic approach involves antacids and drugs such as the H₂-receptor blockers metiamide and cimetidine which inhibit gastric secretion. **1986** C. W. THORNBER in C. A. Heaton *Chem. Industry* iv. 177 Cimetidine .. is currently the world's top selling drug. **1989** *Brit. Med. Jrnl.* 6 May 1266/1 H₂ receptor antagonists like cimetidine have reduced the need for hospital admission and for surgery in patients with uncomplicated duodenal ulcer.

**cinchocaine** (ˈsɪnkəʊkeɪn), *n. Pharm.* [f. CINCHO- + -*caine* after COCAINE *n.*] A powerful local anaesthetic, given as a spinal anaesthetic and externally (usu. as the hydrochloride) as a local surface anaesthetic; 2-butoxy-*N*-(2-diethylaminoethyl) quinoline-4-carboxamide, C₂₀H₂₉N₃O₂.

**1947** *Q. Jrnl. Pharmacy & Pharmacol.* XX. 383 Proprietary brands of amethocaine ('Anethaine') and cinchocaine ('Nupercaine') hydrochlorides. **1954** *Anæsthesia* IX. 277 Cinchocaine light injection began to decompose after the first hour. **1977** *Lancet* 29 Oct. 928/2 Cocaine, procaine, xylocaine, and cinchocaine ('Nupercaine') have all been reported to inhibit platelet aggregation when added in vitro.

**circlip** (ˈsɜːklɪp), *n.* [Blend of CIRCULAR *a.,* CIRCLE *n.,* etc., and CLIP *n.*¹] A metal ring that can be sprung into a slot or groove round a cylinder to hold something in place or to position it correctly.

**1903** *Lanchester Motor & Carriage Driving Man.* II. 190 Circlips. **1958** *Times Rev. Industry* May 32/3 An external circlip in the front end cap permits the easy replacement of gland packings **1970** K. BALL *Fiat 600, 600D Autobook* iv. 41/2 The larger diameter bearing .. is retained in position by the circlip. **1986** *Bicycle Action* June 16/2 The Mavic SSC rear mech disassembles .. by removing circlips, and allen key bolts.

**circus**, *n.* Add: [7.] **b.** *the Circus,* a nickname for the British Secret Service (see quot. 1982).

**1963** 'J. LE CARRÉ' *Spy who came in from Cold* vi. 51 Who's that man in the Labour Exchange—Pitt? Wasn't he in the Circus during the war? **1974** —— *Tinker, Tailor* iv. 36 In your day the Circus ran itself by regions ... Control sat in heaven and held the strings. **1979** H. McLEAVE *Borderline Case* i. 3 The Georgian house where his section of the Circus worked. **1982** *Verbatim* Spring 1/2 *Circus* is highly ambiguous jargon for 'London headquarters'; the word refers to the address at Cambridge Circus, but the expression *the Circus* also carries negative connotations of frivolity and confusion. **1984** B. REID *So much Love* xii. 235 He came to me .. only to get some information; to use my brain, which had been so invaluable to them when I was in what they called the Circus, in the Secret Service.

**cisoid** (ˈsɪsɔɪd), *a. Chem.* [f. CIS- + -OID; cf. TRANSOID *a.*] Designating a compound, group, or structure in which two like atoms or groups lie on the same side of a single bond or a line of bonds.

**1956** L. F. & M. FIESER *Org. Chem.* (ed. 3) xii. 302 Various combinations of chair and boat cyclohexane rings make possible a number of conformations, each of which retains its cisoid or transoid character. **1968** *Science* 23 Feb. 836/2 The *cisoid* conformation. **1972** DePUY & CHAPMAN *Molec. Reactions & Photochem.* iv. 59 1,3-Butadiene exists in solution as a rapidly equilibrating mixture of *transoid* and *cisoid* conformers, with the former predominating by nearly 20 : 1. **1984** GREENWOOD & EARNSHAW *Chem. of Elements* (1986) xv. 857 The S₄N₄ retains the same conformation and almost the same dimensions as in the free molecule, with 2 of the 4 planar N atoms acting as a *cisoid* bridge.

**clan**, *n.* Add: [3.] **b.** *Ecol.* A very localized group of plants most of which belong to a single species.
**1916** F. E. CLEMENTS in *Publ. Carnegie Inst.* No. 242. 134 A clan is composed of a secondary species. It is next below the society in rank, though it is not necessarily a subdivision of it. *Ibid.*, A clan differs from a society chiefly in being local or restricted to a few small and scattered areas. **1926** [see CONSOCIATION *n.* 5]. **1936** *Jrnl. Ecol.* XXIV. 278 Most clans are families developed in the climax matrix. **1960** N. POLUNIN *Introd. Plant Geogr.* xi. 334 Within societies etc., there may be . . clans. These represent the lowest climax unit, consisting each of a small aggregation of a single very locally but overwhelming dominant species.

**classist** ('klɑːsɪst), *a.* and *n.* [f. CLASS *n.* 2 + -IST.] **A.** *adj.* Of, pertaining to, or characterized by classism; discriminating on the grounds of social class. **B.** *n.* One who advocates or practises classism.
**1976** *National Observer* (U.S.) 12 June 14/5 Historically, the word was long used in the classist sense. A man of 'breeding' was a gentleman. **1981** *Daily Tel.* 19 June 18 Do not the classists cause as much trouble as the racists? **1986** *Spare Rib* May 6/2, I am not apologising for SM and believe that in itself it is neither racist, classist, disablist nor anti-semitic. **1988** *Amer. Speech* LXIII. 183 The user called another participant in the conversation 'a classist' for arguing that (particular) middle class values and behaviors were superior to those of working class values and behaviors.

**clear**, *a.*, *adv.*, and *n.* Add: [C.] [I.] Sense 6 in Dict. becomes **7. 6.** In Scientology, a person who has completed a course of dianetic therapy and is considered free of neuroses and other physical or mental ills. Cf. *PRECLEAR *n.*
**1950** L. R. HUBBARD *Dianetics* I. ii. 8 Dianetically, the optimum individual is called the *clear*. *Ibid.* Gloss. 437 *Clear*, the optimum individual; no longer possessed of any engrams. **1965** —— *Scientology Abridged Dict.*, *Clear*, . . a thetan who can be at cause knowingly and at will over mental matter, energy, space and time as regards the First Dynamic (survival for self). **1968** *Punch* 14 Aug. 230/3 The audit takes a considerable number of hours before the patient or 'preclear' becomes free or 'clear' of 'engrams', and, as each processing course costs money, becoming a 'clear' may cost hundreds or even thousands of pounds.

**climax**, *v.* Add: [2.] **c.** *intr.* To achieve sexual climax; = ORGASM *v.*
**1975** R. H. RIMMER *Premar Experiments* (1976) I. 24 I'd rather have seen the same movie a few weeks later for one dollar and discovered what it was like to climax with him doing it to me. **1982** S. CONRAN *Lace* IV. 228 After he climaxed, he kissed her gently on the lips. **1986** C. CLARKE *Rasputin Letter* i. 16 From the moment she opened her parachute, forty-five seconds later . . she climaxed two, three, even four times.

**cliometrics** (ˌklaɪəˈmɛtrɪks, ˌkliːəʊ-), *n. pl.* (const. as *sing.*). orig. *U.S.* [f. CLIO *n.* + -*metrics*, as in *biometrics*, *econometrics*, etc.] A technique for the interpretation of economic history, based on the statistical analysis of large-scale numerical data from population censuses, parish registers, and similar sources.
**1960** L. E. DAVIS et al. in *Jrnl. Econ. Hist.* XX. 540 The logical structure necessary to make historical reconstructions from the surviving debris of past economic life essentially involves ideas of history, economics and statistics. The offspring of such an act

of interdisciplinary miscegenation calls for a name worthy of it; at Purdue the resulting discipline has been labeled 'Cliometrics'. **1974** *Atlanta Jrnl. & Constitution* 9 June C-5 Fogel and Engerman obtained their conclusions through the use of cliometrics . . . They scoured a large chunk of the rural South for 10 years in pursuit of census-records, birth records, old plantation lists—anything which could shed light on how slaves lived and worked. **1979** *Eng. Hist. Rev.* XCIV. 683 Cliometrics and political science have yielded all too many articles that measure what is measurable rather than what is important. **1981** D. N. MCCLOSKEY *Enterprise & Trade in Victorian Brit.* i. 13 The *raison d'être* of cliometrics is avoiding the absurdities of economic history without economics. **1990** *Observer* 25 Mar. 67/1 Cliometrics, a word happily infrequent of late, announced itself as a school of rigorous quantitative history.
Hence **clio'metric** *a.*; **clio'metrically** *adv.*, by means of cliometrics; **cliome'trician** *n.*, an expert in or student of cliometrics.
**1966** *Explorations in Entrepreneurial Hist.* 2nd. Ser. IV. No. 1. Suppl. 66 The cleometrician [*sic*], on the other hand, is likely to respond with his traditional trilogy of criticism: inadequate specification, over-aggregation, and model simplistics. **1969** *N.Y. Times* 16 Dec. 57/1 Dr. Fogel . . has cliometrically calculated that railroads were not as crucial to industrial growth as the traditional wisdom has pictured them. **1972** *Computers & Humanities* VII. 69 In economic history, . . after a decade of susbstantial quantitative work, the field is clearly dominated by the self-styled cliometricians with their black boxes, magnetic tapes, punch cards, and canned programs. **1974** *Times* 10 Oct. 12/8 Hot after cliometric paradox, the authors do not always take this point. **1977** P. LASLETT *Family Life* 10 An econometrician, or cliometrician, as he is now being called. **1981** *Times Lit. Suppl.* 7 Aug. 897/3 A cliometric proposition . . once it is wrong tends to be wholly wrong.

**clioquinol** (ˌklaɪəʊˈkwiːnɒl, ˌkliːəʊ-), *n. Pharm.* [f. *Cl*, chemical symbol for chlorine (see *C III. 3 b) + 10(DINE *n.* + QUINOL(INE *n.*] A halogenated derivative of quinoline that has been used as an antiseptic to treat mild ear infections, intestinal amoebiasis, diarrhoea, and skin infections; 5-chloro-8-hydroxy-7-iodo-quinoline, $C_9H_5NOCII$.
**1967** *Martindale's Extra Pharmacopoeia* (ed. 25) 577/2 Clioquinol. **1970** *Which?* July 208/1 There are medicines advertised as helping you *avoid* diarrhoea. Almost all contain an antiseptic called clioquinol. **1977** *Lancet* 16 Apr. 859/2 There is no sound evidence for the medical use of clioquinol. **1983** [see ENTERO-VIOFORM *n.*]. **1989** *Nature* 16 Mar. 213/1 Clioquinol [is] . . a drug sold widely all over the world without manifesting toxicity like that seen in Japan.

**clip**, *v.*[2] Add: [1.] **e.** *Computing.* To process (a displayed image) so as to remove those parts that lie outside a specified area. Also *absol.*
**1968** [implied in *CLIPPING *vbl. n.*[2] 1 b]. **1973** NEWMAN & SPROULL *Princ. Interactive Computer Graphics* vii. 121 Ideally the information that is passed to the display should be clipped, i.e. restricted to just those parts that lie on the screen. **1982** [see VIEWPORT *n.* 2]. **1982** *Computerworld* 8 Nov. 87/2 An engineer can execute . . functions such as real zoom or scale, translate, clip, rotate, [etc.]. **1984** *Austral. Microcomputer Mag.* Jan. 69/4 The DM-40 also will clip, window, viewport and scale to six size.

**clipping**, *vbl. n.*[2] Add: [1.] **b.** *Computing.* The action of or facility for removing parts of a displayed image.
**1968** *AFIPS Conf. Proc.* XXXIII. 766/1 Windowing may . . be performed by clipping, the

process of discovering which portions of a drawing are within the window and computing appropriate scope coordinates for them. **1975** *Software Practice & Experience* V. 115 The windowing problem can be .. thought of as two processes: scaling and clipping. **1983** *Austral. Microcomputer Mag.* Dec. 104/1 To push back the limits of the world of microcomputer graphics means the programmer has to learn about clipping and viewports. **1986** *Computerworld* 7 Apr. 81/2 Reverse clipping with ZMD-Plot allows the user to blank out certain portions of the graphic image and overlay a second image.

**clo** (kləʊ), *n.*[2] orig. *U.S.* [Shortening of CLOTHING *vbl. n.*] A unit of thermal resistance used to express the insulating properties of clothing (see quots. 1941, 1986). Cf. TOG *n.*[1] 3.
    **1941** A. P. GAGGE et al. in *Science* 7 Nov. 429/1 The unit for thermal insulation of clothing is logically the amount of insulation necessary to maintain in comfort .. a sitting-resting subject in a normally ventilated room (air movement 20 ft/min or 10 cm/sec) at a temperature of 70°F (21°C) and a humidity of the air which is less than 50 per cent. This unit of insulation may be called 1 clo. **1951** *Canad. Mining Jrnl.* Aug. 65/3 It was not until the Second World War that .. a new unit called the 'clo' was coined in order to express .. the efficiency of a textile in retaining warmth. **1977** R. F. GOLDMAN in Hollies & Goldman *Clothing Comfort* i. 7 Proposed by Dr. Gagge and his colleagues .. some 30 years ago, one clo was characterized as the intrinsic insulation .. of the typical business suit worn in those days. **1980** *New Scientist* 14 Aug. 537 Wool fibre, several centimetres thick, down and the new 3M material have clo values of 0.9, 1 and 1.8 respectively. **1986** JERRARD & McNEILL *Dict. Sci. Units* (ed. 5) 29 A clo is defined in physical terms as the amount of insulation that will allow the passage of 1 calorie m$^{-2}$ h$^{-1}$ with a temperature gradient of 0.18°C between the two surfaces.

**clock,** *v.*[1] Add: **4.** To watch or observe; to look at, notice. *slang* (orig. *U.S.*).
    **1942** BERREY & VAN DEN BARK *Amer. Thes. Slang* §482/2 *Look at; see,* clock, decko, .. take a gander (at), [etc.]. **1943** *N.Y. Times* 9 May 11. 5/5 When Harry started to give out with the jive some alligators clocking the action started for the stage. **1960** *News Chron.* 16 Feb. 6/5 When she clocked the Fleet Street mob in the front of the gaff she said 'My God' and had it away double lively. **1962** F. NORMAN *Guntz* i. 5 They clocked me as I went past them, .. we just looked at each other and that's all. **1980** *Daily Mail* 19 July 11/6 We had to top them because they had clocked us. We had to shoot them. **1986** *Sunday Express Mag.* 3 Aug. 33/1 Our waiter .. was so busy clocking him that he spilt a bottle of precious appleade over the table cloth.

**closo** ('kləʊzəʊ), *a. Chem.* Usu. italicized. [Alteration (after *closed*) of *clovo* (J. R. van Wazer 1958, in *Phosphorus & its Compounds* I. iii. 89), f. Gr. κλωβός cage: see -o¹.] Designating (the structure of) a boron compound in whose molecules boron atoms occupy all the vertices of a notional triangulated polyhedron. Also (with hyphen) as a word-forming element.
    **1967** *Office of Naval Res. Techn. Rep.* (Aerojet-General Corp.) No. 15. 1 Until very recently, .. the only good method of synthesizing these *closo*-compounds was via the *nido*-carborane, $C_2B_4H_8$. **1968** *Inorganic Chem.* VII. 1947/2 Some members of the second class have structures very close to a closed structure. When it is desirable to indicate this situation in contrast to a known closo compound, the italic prefix *nido*- is used. *Ibid.*, The prefix *clovo*- derived from the Greek word for cage was changed to *closo*- at the request of the IUPAC Inorganic Nomenclature Commission. **1971, 1976**

[see \*NIDO *a.*]. **1984** GREENWOOD & EARNSHAW *Chem. of Elements* (1986) vi. 182 It is a general feature of *closo*-$B_nH_n^{2-}$ anions that there are no B-H-B or $BH_2$ groups.

**closure** *n.* Senses 10, 11 in Dict. become 11, 12. Add: [5.] **d.** *Surveying.* The act of closing a traverse by surveying a line back to the position from which the traverse was started. Esp. in phr. *error of closure* = MISCLOSURE *n.*; also *transf.*, any discrepancy between an initial and final estimate or measurement of a quantity.
    **1902** P. M. NUGENT *Plane Surveying* iii. 41 The ratio of the error of closure to the sum of the measured lengths of all the lines in the closed traverse is known as the 'ratio of closure'. **1981** *Sci. Amer.* Nov. 37/3 The difference between the precensus estimate and the actual count is known as the error of closure. It is the magnitude of the error of closure in the 1980 census that has most surprised demographers.
    **10.** *Math.* The property of being closed (CLOSED *ppl. a.* 2 a, b); also (const. *of*), the smallest closed set containing a given set. *point of closure*: a point which is such that any neighbourhood of it meets a given set (const. *of*).
    **1905** *Trans. Amer. Math. Soc.* VI. 165 (*heading*) Dedekind postulate of closure. **1910** E. H. MOORE in *New Haven Math. Colloq.* (Amer. Math. Soc.) 37 A class 𝔐 having the property $C_\mathfrak{M}$ of being closed to itself has the property $C$, and conversely. The notation $C$ and the designation *closure* are preferable to the $S$-$C$ and *self-closure* originally used. **1937** G. BIRKHOFF in *Ann. Math.* XXXVIII. 39 The 'closure' S̄ of any subset $S$ of ordinary space is composed of the limits of the convergent sequences of points of $S$. **1956** E. M. PATTERSON *Topology* ii. 29 The set of points of closure of $X$ is called the closure of $X$. **1974** G. REECE tr. *Hund's Hist. Quantum Theory* viii. 109 The periodic system is thus explained by the application of a closure law. **1977** *Nature* 8 Dec. 500/1 A black hole is the closure of the topologically smallest future set I$^+$ such that [etc.]. **1986** P. C. WEST *Introd. Supersymmetry & Supergravity* vi. 25 Closure confirms the choice of one auxiliary field, $D$ which is a pseudoscalar and requires $a = +1$.

**coax** ('kəʊæks), *n.*[2] [Abbrev. of COAX(IAL *a.*] Coaxial cable or line (see COAXIAL *a.* 2 c). Also *coax cable.*
    **1945** *Electronics Industries* Sept. 93 Coax dry load, a sand-carbon mixture in cable to act as dummy load. **1957** *Practical Wireless* XXXIII. 724/1 (*caption*) The simple coax-fed dipole. **1967** *Electronics* 6 Mar. 15/1 (Advt.), Microdot makes connectors, as a matter of fact, the best microminiature coax connectors in the industry. **1976** PERKOWSKI & STRAL *Joy of CB* x. 114 The most pleasing installations are those where the coax is entirely hidden from view. **1982** *Giant Bk. Electronics Projects* ii. 96 Connect your piece of coax cable to J2. **1987** *Ham Radio Today* Jan. 58/3 Power for the camera can be supplied by feeding it up the coax.

**cocktail,** *n.* and *a.* Add: [A.] [3.] **d.** *transf.* A mixture of chemical substances, esp. one which is dangerous. Hence *fig.*, any combination of ingredients, factors, or circumstances.
    **1971** *Daily Tel.* 16 Apr. 3 A clerk .. died after lying unconscious for a month as a result of drinking a 'cocktail' of drugs which included cannabis. **1978** *Nat. Westm. Bank Q. Rev.* 20 The Bank usually lends in several currencies and repayments are due in the currencies disbursed. But more recently it has introduced single currency loans, in addition to its cocktails of currencies. **1981** P. CAREY *Bliss* v. 230 There was no joy in their triumphs, only anger, revenge, nose-thumbing, name-calling, and .. Harry .. lent to this unpleasant cocktail a dominant flavour of fear. **1989** *New Scientist* 3 June 39/1 Scientists

describe a typical gas from a landfill site as a saturated cocktail of gases at 35°.

**e.** With qualifying word, as *atomic* (*lytic*, etc.) *cocktail*, a lethal concoction, or one which is humorously alleged to be so.

**1940** etc. [see *Molotov cocktail* s.v. MOLOTOV *n.*]. **1941** BAKER *Dict. Austral. Slang* 24 Domain cocktail, a lethal concoction of petrol and pepper which reputedly once had a vogue among deadbeat drinkers in the Sydney Domain. **1945** *Life* 27 Aug. 32/3 (*in photograph*) Atomic cocktail... The new era was met head on by a bartender in Columbus. **1949** *Lincoln Nebraska State Jrnl.* 7 Apr. 1/4 A.. girl drank her second 'atomic cocktail' Wednesday hoping to cure a rare glandular ailment... [She] drank a glass of radioactive phosphorus. **1954** *Time* 14 June 80/3 From its combined efforts came the 'lytic cocktail'. In this, chlorpromazine is combined with Phenergan and Dolosal to block the automatic nervous system.

**coco de mer** ('kəʊkəʊ də meə(r)), *n.* [a. Fr., lit., 'sea coco', in allusion to their being found floating in the Indian Ocean.] = *double coconut* s.v. COCO *n.* 5; also, the tall fan palm, *Lodoicea maldivica*, on which this nut grows.

**1827** W. J. HOOKER in *Curtis's Bot. Mag.* LIV. Plates 2734-8 f.5, A *Coco de Mer*, planted on M. de Quincy's estate, on the Isle Mahé, is thirteen feet and a half high.. and was planted forty years ago. **1864** *Gardeners' Chron.* 26 Mar. 294/3 Not many years can elapse before the Coco de Mer will become in reality as rare as was supposed by the voyagers who picked up the first-known specimens of the nuts floating on the sea. **1926** E. BLATTER *Palms Brit. India & Ceylon* ii. 245 (*caption*) A grave of *Lodoiceas* in the Coco-de-mer Valley of Praslin Island. **1934** *Discovery* Mar. 83/1 The Coco de Mer palm shoots up to a height of 130 feet, straight as a mast, and is covered with tufts of fan-like leaves. **1970** SIMON & HOWE *Dict. Gastron.* 130/2 Coco de mer is an extraordinary double-coconut, indigenous to the Seychelles and said to have been the fruit with which the Devil tempted Eve.

**code**, *n.*[1] Add: [**5.**] **code-breaker**, one who solves or breaks a code; also, a computer used for doing this; hence **code-breaking**.

**1932** *Pop. Mechanics* (Chicago) Apr. 639/1 The keenest *code breaker is said to have been an Oxford Greek professor. **1977** P. FITZGERALD *Knox Brothers* v. 136 Hall.. imperiously told the Treasury that he must have more money for more code-breakers. **1983** *Austral. Personal Computer* Aug. 106/3 Supposing that the original message, the plaintext, was '11', and the ciphertext was '2', the codebreaker has no way of working backwards from '2' to '11'.

**cœlurosaur** (sɪ'ljʊərəsɔː(r)), *n.* (and *a.*) [ad. mod.L. *Cœlurosauria*, f. Gr. κοῖλ-ος hollow + URO-[2] + Gr. σαῦρ-ος lizard + -IA[2].] Any of a group of small, slenderly built theropod dinosaurs with relatively long forelimbs. Also *attrib.* or as *adj.*

**1958** *Amer. Mus. Novitates* No. 1901. 1 (*heading*) Coelurosaur bone casts from the Connecticut Valley Triassic. *Ibid.* 3. *Ammosaurus*, commonly designated as a coelurosaur, is probably a prosauropod. **1962** E. H. COLBERT *Dinosaurs* iv. 76 The emphasis among coelurosaurs on lightness in weight, agility of movement, and adaptations for the pursuit of small animals enabled these little dinosaurs to continue through the Mesozoic era. **1970** *Nature* 11 Apr. 109/1 Theropods.. are usually divided into massive carnosaurs.. and smaller slenderly built coelurosaurs. *Deinonychus* has some carnosaur characters,.. some coelurosaur ones.. and some unique to itself. **1983** *Sci. Amer.* Jan. 73/2 Beside the nest was the fossilized skeleton of a predatory coelurosaur—a small bipedal carnivorous dinosaur.

Hence **cœ‚luro'saurian** *a.*

**1969** *Arnoldia* (Rhodesia) IV. XXVIII. 1 (*heading*) A new coelurosaurian dinosaur from the Forest Sandstone of Rhodesia. **1985** *Palaeontol.* XXVIII. 413 Most of these features were already present in the coelurosaurian dinosaur ancestors of birds.

**cognitive**, *a.* Add: **b.** Special collocations: *cognitive science*, the science of cognition or intelligence, the study of the cognitive processes involved in the acquisition and use of knowledge.

**1975** BOBROW & COLLINS (*title*) Representation and understanding: studies in *cognitive science. **1977** *Cognitive Sci.* I. 1 Recently there has begun to grow a community of people from different disciplines, who find themselves tackling a common set of problems in natural and artificial intelligence. The particular disciplines from which they come are.. cognitive and social psychology, artificial intelligence, computational linguistics, educational technology, and even epistemology... This discipline might have been called applied epistemology or intelligence theory, but someone on high declared it should be cognitive science. **1983** *Listener* 10 Feb. 29/1 Some hopes are pinned on a new kind of hybrid known as 'cognitive science'. **1985** H. GARDNER *Mind's New Sci.* i. 6, I define cognitive science as a contemporary, empirically based effort to answer long-standing epistemological questions—particularly those concerned with the nature of knowledge, its components, its sources, its development, and its deployment.

hence *cognitive scientist*.

**1980** *Cognitive Sci.* IV. 1 *Cognitive scientists as a whole ought to make more use of evidence from the neurosciences, from brain damage and mental illness, from cognitive sociology and anthropology, and from clinical studies of the human. **1985** H. GARDNER *Mind's New Sci.* iii. 39 Contemporary theoretical talk among 'card-carrying' cognitive scientists amounts, in a sense, to a discussion of the best ways of conceptualizing mental representations.

**cohabitation**, *n.* Add: **3.** *Pol.* Co-operation between members (esp. a President and Prime Minister) of opposing parties, orig. in France; an instance of this. (Sometimes pronounced as a Fr. word and printed in italics.)

**1978** *Washington Post 23 Mar.* A 23/1 Giscard said it was time to achieve 'a reasonable cohabitation' between the majority and the opposition in France. **1985** *Economist* 9 Feb. (Survey Suppl.: France) 20/1 Mr Barre rules out any talk of *cohabitation* with Mr Mitterand. **1986** *Economist* 5 Apr. 57/3 Like France, Portugal is adjusting to the 'cohabitation' of a Socialist president and a Conservative prime minister. **1987** *Times* 7 Apr. 15/3 There is evidence that *cohabitation* may, with time, erode France's considerable diplomatic influence.

**collaborative** (kə'læbərətɪv), *a.* [f. COLLABORATE *v.* + -IVE.] Characterized by, based upon, or produced in collaboration; co-operative.

**1927** *Observer* 27 Mar. 17/2 Mr. Amery's Dominion tour should give a real impetus to 'Imperialism' of the most practical kind—that which brings the collaborative thought of the Empire's centre and circumference to bear on common interests. **1957** J. D. SALINGER *Zooey* in *New Yorker* 4 May 33/3 The plot line.. is largely the result of a rather unholy collaborative effort. **1967** *Bull. World Health Organisation* XXXVII. 79 (*heading*) WHO collaborative study on the sero-epidemiology of Rubella. **1989** *Times* 31 Aug. 2/8 The result of this 'bibliometric' method of rating departments would [be] a shift by universities.. away from practical collaborative problem solving.

Hence **co'llaboratively** *adv.*

**1971** *Human World* Nov. 64 History's home is within this 'collaboratively created' world. **1989** *Newsday* 25 June 11. 17/1 Most of the 10 songs, written collaboratively by the four members, stick pretty much to the band's formula of mini-suites.

**college**, *n.* Add: [9.] [b.] **College of the Air** orig. *U.S.*, a college providing courses (esp. in technical and vocational subjects) based upon correspondence and radio and television broadcasts; cf. *University of the Air* s.v. UNIVERSITY *n.* 1 c.
**1977** (*title*) *College of the Air (prospectus issued by Montgomery College, Takoma Park, Maryland). **1986** *Times* 19 July 4/1 The Government proposed to create an open college, the College of the Air. The aim was to enlist the full contribution of radio and television to deliver open learning courses, in all areas of vocational competence.

**collider** (kə'laɪdə(r)), *n.* [f. COLLIDE *v.* + -ER¹.]
**1.** *Physical Chem.* A molecule or atom that collides with other molecules or atoms, esp. to an extent that needs to be allowed for in kinetics. Freq. with qualifying word, as *strong, weak collider.*
**1968** *Jrnl. Chem. Physics* XLVIII. 1285/2 In the second-order region the relative collisional activation efficiency depends simply on γᵧ, a relative measure of the transition probabilities of weak vs strong colliders. **1972** ROBINSON & HOLBROOK *Unimolecular Reactions* x. 324 It seems very reasonable to assume .. that these sufficiently large molecules behave effectively as strong colliders. **1977** *Chem. Physics Lett.* XLVIII. 207 The magnetic field effect is only observed in the presence of colliders. **1979** *Jrnl. Physical Chem.* LXXXIII. 93/2 Deviations from the behavior predicted .. are termed weak collider (WC) effects.
**2.** *Particle Physics.* An accelerator in which two beams of particles are accelerated independently and made to collide, so as to increase the effective energy of the collision.
**1979** *Nature* 29 Mar. 408/1 Another contender will be the p̄p collider planned at Fermilab using the superconducting magnet ring being installed to double the present accelerator's energy to 1,000 GeV; this may eventually allow 2,000 GeV to be reached in the collision. **1981** A. SALAM in J. H. Mulvey *Nature of Matter* v. 116 It is proposed to build the world's biggest electron-positron collider, called LEP. **1985** *Nat. Geographic* May 638/1 That relativity is .. the basis for Fermilab's collider.

**collision**, *n.* Sense 4 in Dict. becomes 5. Add:
**4.** *Computing.* **a.** The event of two or more records being assigned the same location in memory.
**1968** *Communications Assoc. Computing Machinery* XI. 39/1 Once some entries have been made into a scatter storage table, it becomes possible for the computed addresses of different keys to become the same, causing a collision between the storage locations allocated to each. **1975** C. J. DATE *Introd. Database Syst.* ii. 30 Another disadvantage of hash-addressing is the possibility of collisions—that is, two distant stored record occurrences whose keys hash to the same SRA. **1979** A. F. CARDENAS *Data Base Managem. Syst.* vi. 236 TOTAL accesses master records only by randomizing the value of the mandatory control key. Collisions do occur as in every known hashing method.
**b.** (An instance of) simultaneous transmission by more than one node of a network.
**1982** LONGLEY & SHAIN *Dict. Information Technol.* 62/2 In Ethernet, collision detection works in conjunction with carrier sense multiple access methods on a cable network. **1983** *Austral. Microcomputer Mag.* Aug. 56/2 A more critical problem is collision avoidance, or making sure that no more than one node is transmitting at any given time. **1985** *Which Computer?* Dec. 14/3 It's difficult to see where a collision has occurred, so terminals have to use a technique called 'collision detect' to

check the line is clear before sending a message. **1986** *Micro Decision* Oct. 25/3 The delays caused by collisions mean that networks using this protocol slow down in proportion to the amount of traffic on the network, rather than the number of nodes in the network.

**colloblast** ('kɒləblɑːst), *n.* *Zool.* [a. G. *Colloblast* (O. Hamann 1881, in *Jenaische Zeitschr. f. Naturwiss.* XV. 259), f. Gr. κόλλα glue: see -O¹ 3, -BLAST.] = *lasso-cell* s.v. LASSO *n.* 3.
**1900** *Mem. Boston Soc. Nat. Hist.* V. 202 The star-shaped cells remind one of osteoblasts... Hamann .. has called them *colloblasts.* **1907** *Zool. Jahrbücher: Abt. für Anat.* XXIV. 56 The secondary tentacles are covered with typical Ctenophoral adhesive cells (lassocells, colloblasts) that sometimes, when the tentacle is fully extended, appear to be arranged in groups or batteries. **1932** BORRADAILE & POTTS *Invertebrata* v. 172 The tentacles are armed with cells of a special type called 'lasso cells' or colloblasts, which take the place of nematocysts. **1978** *Bio Systems* X. 110/2 The former could have come from a radially symmetrical dinoflagellate with nematocysts and the latter from one having biradial symmetry and colloblast precursors.

**Coloradan** (kɒlə'rɑːdən), *a.* and *n.* [f. COLORAD(O *n.* + -AN.] **A.** *adj.* Of or pertaining to the State of Colorado. **B.** *n.* A native or inhabitant of Colorado.
**1879** B. F. TAYLOR *Summer-Savory* 33 There is yet another cough, which may be called the cough colloquial and Coloradan. **1931** *Amer. Speech* VI. 310 'Out-state' is a compound word .. frequently used by Nebraskans, Iowans, Coloradans, and Wyomingites. **1979** *Tucson Mag.* Feb. 30/3 Coloradans and Oregonians, accustomed to a much more ecologically active social environment, vigorously disagree. **1981** *Washington Post* 4 Oct. E2/5 An exhibit of Coloradan artists will be displayed at Seraph Gallery.., now through Oct. 9.
Also **Colo'radian** *n.* and *a.*, **Colo'radoan** *n.* and *a.*
**1863** N. H. WEBSTER *Jrnl.* 6 Nov. in *Montana Hist. Soc. Contrib.* (1900) III. 329 Drove to Rocky Point. There we met a train of Coloradians. **1869** S. BOWLES *Summer Vac. Colorado* 82 Long's Peak .. is the prominent north-eastern mountain of the Coloradian series,.. and is fourteen thousand feet high. **1876** H. T. WILLIAMS *Pacific Tourist* 79/1 Why, Coloradoans are the most disappointed people I ever saw. Two-thirds of them came here to die, and they *can't do it.* **1940** *Chambers's Techn. Dict.* 178/1 *Colora'doan Stage* (Geol.), synonymous with 'Lower Cretaceous' in the American sense.

**colorization**, *n.* Add: **b.** *Cinematogr.*, etc. The process or technique of adding colour to black-and-white films by means of a computer. (Proprietary in the U.S.).
**1983** *Financial Times* 12 Dec. 26/7 The art director in the colourisation process will choose colours and face tones appropriate to the place and season. **1986** *Times* 27 Sept. 18/8 The 'colorization' controversy thunders on. Now American studios have bagged the rights to two British classic black-and-white films .. and plan to colour them by computer and release them. **1986** *Courier-Mail* (Brisbane) 11 Oct. 8/7 Woody Allen, who still makes many of his movies in black and white .., is equally opposed to colorisation. **1987** *Byte* Mar. 164/1 A controversial process known as 'colorization', in which classic black-and-white films are being colored via computer and released for the home video market. **1987** *Official Gaz.* (U.S. Patent Office) 3 Nov. TM153 *Colorization*... For services consisting of computerized conversions of black and white films into color video tapes.

**colorize**, *v.* Restrict *rare* to sense in Dict. Add: **b.** *Cinematogr.*, etc. To add colour to (a black-and-white film) by means of a computer; to convert to a colour film in this way.

**1984** *What Video?* Aug. 41/2 It isn't the full extent of the camera's titling facilities, for it has the unique ability to colourise external titles. **1984** *Time* 5 Nov. 10/3 'Colorizing' great movies such as Casablanca.. is like spray-painting the Venus de Milo. **1986** *Publishers Weekly* 6 June 34/1 A number of publishers have.. begun colorizing movies to which they hold or have acquired exclusive rights. **1987** *Byte* Mar. 164/2 The Oscar-winning Laurel and Hardy film, *The Music Box*,.. was recently colorized.

Hence **'colorized** *ppl. a.*

**1986** *Video World* Festive Issue 4/4 We urge you to shun any 'colorized' tapes and stick with the original black and white. **1989** *Washington Post* 23 May C3/2 Segal.. ranks right up there with the inventors of phone sex, colorized movies and 900-numbers.

**colorizer**, *n.* Add: **b.** A computer process by which colour is added to black-and-white films (proprietary in N. Amer.); also, a person or organization that performs this.

**1984** *Trade Marks Jrnl.* (Ottawa) 4 July 51/1 *Colorizer*.. computer program for changing black and white film to coloured film for use in video machines. Used in Canada since at least.. January 1982. **1985** *Official Gaz.* (U.S. Patent Office) 18 June TM53/1 *Colorizer*,.. for computer program for changing black and white film to coloured [*sic*] film for use in video machines. **1985** *Washington Post* 4 May D3/2 Universal has retrieved.. some of the old introductions Hitchcock did for the shows and put them through the computer colorizer. **1986** *Los Angeles Times* 30 Nov. 103/2 The colorizers maintain that once a film leaves a director's hand.. they can do to it whatever they like.

**colugo** (kə'lu:gəʊ), *n.* Also 8 colago. [Native name in the Philippines, of uncertain origin.

Perh. related to Proto-Southern Philippine \**kulagu* monkey-eating eagle (Tagalog *kulagó* monkey eagle, Bikol *kulágo* hawk, Maranao *kolago*) and Proto-Philippine \**kuláRu* owl (Tagalog *kuwágo* night owl, Cebuano *kulágú* owl, *Tyto*), though the semantic shift required has not been satisfactorily explained.]

Either of two species of small arboreal mammal, *Cynocephalus volans* of the Philippines and *C. variegatus* of Indochina, which glide by stretching the membranes joining the limbs and tail; a flying lemur.

**1702** *Phil. Trans. R. Soc.* XXIII. 1065 Colago & Cagvang *Bysaiani*. Gigua *Pampangi & Tagali*. **1792** R. KERR *Linnæus's Animal Kingdom* 89 Colugo—.. *Lemur volans*.. has a membrane fitted for flying... Inhabits Guzurat, and the Philippine and Molucca islands. **1929** [see KUBONG *n.*] **1949** *Oxf. Jun. Encycl.* II. 243/2 The Colugos or Flying Lemurs are not now regarded as members of the Lemur family, but as a separate order, related to the *Insectivora*. **1965** D. MORRIS *Mammals* 89 The Flying Lemurs, or Colugos, have always presented zoologists with something of a problem, for these two closely related species.. have no other close relatives. **1971** *Country Life* 6 May 1098/1 The comments of Darwin.. are still the most quotable in respect.. of the colugos, mis-called flying lemurs, of South East Asia. **1987** *Jrnl. Human Evol.* XVI. 1 The Superorder Archonta (primates, tree shrews, bats, and colugos) is the only higher-level grouping including Euprimates that is based on uniquely derived morphological characters.

**comatic** (kəʊ'mætɪk), *a.* [f. L. *comāt-*, adj. stem f. *coma* COMA *n.*[2] + -IC.] **1.** *Optics.* Of, pertaining to, or exhibiting (a) coma: see COMA *n.*[2] 3; *comatic circle*, a circle produced in the focal plane by all rays from an off-axis point that pass through the same annular region of a lens, each such circle being a component of the coma associated with the image of the point.

**1906** H. D. TAYLOR *Syst. Appl. Optics* viii. 200

This circle we will call a comatic circle. **1923** *Trans. Optical Soc.* XXIV. 3 The comatic images cannot be examined properly with the objective in its normal position owing to the oblique passage of the light through the eyepiece. **1958** *Van Nostrand's Sci. Encycl.* (ed. 3) 380/1 Rays from an off-axis point through any zone of a lens meet the focal plane in a comatic circle. **1972** *IEEE Jrnl. Quantum Electronics* VIII. 724/1 An improved resonator configuration for CW dye lasers is described, permitting minimum circular waist areas and compensation for comatic as well as astigmatic aberration.

**2.** *Astron.* Of or pertaining to a cometary coma.

**1985** *Nature* 9 May 124/1 Rather significant variations in brightness were detected at solar distance 8 AU where no comatic activity is expected.

**combination**, *n.* Add: [**3.**] **c.** *Taxon.* A group of two or more Latin or modern Latin words conjoined to form the name of a species or lower taxon.

**1901** *Jrnl. Botany* XXXIX. 69 Mr. Jackson cites *Wedelia incarnata* (in italics) as from 'Linn. Syst. ed. X. 890'; this combination, however, is not given by Linnaeus. **1905** *Internat. Rules Zool. Nomencl.* 35 If it is desired to cite the author of the new combination, his name follows the parenthesis. **1910** *Opinions rendered by Internat. Commission Zool. Nomencl.* xii. 19 Montgomery, 1903, in adopting the combination *Stephanoceros fimbriatus* (Goldfuss, 1820) was, under the premises, justified, and this combination should be accepted. **1965** *Watsonia* 20 Oct. 128 Nevski.. decided that the two subgenera were better treated as distinct genera and adopted the generic name *Dactylorhiza*, making a new combination, *D. umbrosa* (Kar. & Kir.) Nevski. **1987** *Zool. Jrnl. Linn. Soc.* XC. 189 The morphology of the male terminalia and the forewings.. places these two species in *Mitrapsylla* and the following new combinations are proposed: *Mitrapsylla ceplaciensis* (White & Hodgson) comb. nov., *Mitrapsylla surinamensis* (Sulc) comb. nov.

**combinatorics** (ˌkɒmbɪnə'tɒrɪks), *n. pl.* (const. as *sing.*). *Math.* [f. COMBINATORIAL *a.*, after G. *Kombinatorik*: see -IC 2.] The branch of mathematics dealing with combinations of objects belonging to a finite set in accordance with certain constraints, such as those of graph theory; combinatorial analysis.

[**1902** *Science* 19 Sept. 469/2 In combinatorial analysis (combinatoric) the German school was contented with the deduction of rules for the writing down of all the combinations and permutations that are possible under given restrictions.] **1941** *Bull. Calcutta Math. Soc.* XXXII. 65 (*heading*) On a method of finite combinatorics which applies to the theory of infinite groups. **1953** *Ann. Math. Statistics* XXIV. 377 (*heading*) On some theorems in combinatorics relating to incomplete block designs. **1961** *Math. Gaz.* XLV. 199 (*heading*) Some problems in combinatorics. **1973** *Sci. Amer.* Apr. 113/1 As a little puzzle in combinatorics, can the reader determine the largest multiplicand one set of Napier's bones will form such that all smaller multiplicands can also be formed by the set? **1981** *Times* 5 Sept. 3/1 Solving the puzzle [*sc.* Rubik's cube] introduced three-dimensional geometry, general mathematical thought, group theory, combinatorics, and, if it was pulled apart, an introduction to a very clever piece of engineering.

**comfortable**, *a.* (*n.*) Add: [**7.**] **c.** *comfortable margin*, one great enough to rule out any challenge or doubt. Also *transf.* of a victory or the winner.

**1934** *Esquire* Feb. 96/2 This still leaves a comfortable margin of popular acclaim for the boys who couldn't read it but who.. knew how to *swing* it. **1964** *Observer* 28 June 8/5 The cost of carrying goods by liner trains will be so much less than by heavy lorries . . that he should be able to undercut the roads by a comfortable margin. **1978** *Dumfries Courier* 20 Oct. 5/1 Lochar Amateurs, with a comfortable 5-2 win over Abbey Vale, regained the top spot. **1980** *N.Y. Times* 12 Oct. 11. 21/2 He has enjoyed comfortable margins of victory in every race since 1964. **1986** *Lydney Observer* 12 Sept. 2/6 Sunday's game was a more lively affair, Berry Hill running out comfortable winners.

**comfortably**, *adv.* Add: **[5.] c.** Without excessive effort; with ease, easily.

**1932** S. GIBBONS *Cold Comfort Farm* xxiii. 304 The aeroplane . . was taxi-ing comfortably to a standstill. **1937** *Burlington Mag.* Oct. 195/1 Thus, such apparent mysteries as double crackle, . . the achievement of peach bloom . . are all comfortably disposed of. **1951** I. BROWN *I break my Word* 34 The common use of the adverb comfortably to mean easily can result in some surprising judgments . . . The doctor laid it down in giving his evidence that 'a human body could be cut up comfortably in about half an hour'. **1957** *Times* 6 Sept. 13/1 The English team coasted comfortably to a total of 246. **1971** *Farmers Weekly* 19 Mar. 83/3 One man with the buckrake comfortably kept pace with a double-chop harvester. **1977** *Daily Mirror* 15 Mar. 29/1 Very good effort to beat Isle of Man . . comfortably by three lengths at Sandown . . in January.

**command**, *n.* Add: **10. command-driven** *a.* (of a program or computer) operated by means of commands keyed in by the user or issued by another program or computer (opp. *menu-driven* adj. s.v. MENU *n.* 4).

**1983** *Your Computer* July 31/3 dBase is *command-driven; that is, it does not present the user with menus of possible actions but instead relies upon the user to type in 'English-like' sentences specifying what he wants done. **1986** S. P. HARTER *Online Information Retrieval* ii. 27 The major disadvantage of a command-driven system for online information retrieval is that the user must be quite familiar with the command language of the system to use it effectively.

**community**, *n.* Add: **[11.] [a.]** *community health.*

**1925** C. E. TURNER *Personal & Community Health* 5 Then follows a discussion of the development of the new science of disease prevention and its effect upon personal hygiene and upon public or *community health. **1970** *Times* 9 Nov. 38/2 Paramedic studies are wide-ranging—from community health to bacteriology and psychosomatic medicine.

**community architect**, an architect who works with a community in designing housing and other amenities, often as part of an urban improvement programme.

**1975** *Building Design* 11 July 8/1 His [*sc.* Dr. R. Hackney's] role as a *community architect came about . . when . . he started to look for a house with £1,000. **1986** *Daily Tel.* 13 Dec. 12/6 Once they have this help, the rest is up to them, under the guidance of their community architect, who is expected to live and work with people during the project.

hence **community architecture**.

**1977** *Architects' Jrnl.* 5 Oct. 630/2 There are still lessons to be learnt from his approach to *community architecture. **1984** PRINCE OF WALES in *Times* 31 May 16/2 It has been most encouraging to see the development of community architecture as a natural reaction to the policy of decamping people to new towns and overspill estates. **1986** *Daily Tel.* 9 Dec. 12/2 Community architecture involves local people in the design and building of their own projects as well as the maintenance of completed schemes.

**community charge** *temporary*, a tax or charge for local services levied on adult residents of a community (introduced as a flat-rate charge in

Scotland in 1989 and elsewhere in Great Britain in 1990 replacing household rates); commonly known as *poll tax.*

**1985** *Sunday Times* 22 Dec. 5/1 The government's green paper on rate reform . . is expected to recommend that an annual *community charge (the government's new term for a poll tax or residents' charge) of £50 on all adults over 18 should be introduced in 1990. **1987** *Daily Tel.* 1 May 11/3 Students would be deterred from going to Scottish universities because of having to pay 20 per cent of the community charge which is to replace rates. **1989** *Which?* July 355/1 Do you have any questions about how the poll tax (or 'community charge') works?

**community medicine**, a branch of medicine dealing with problems of health care affecting a whole community, rather than with the treatment of individual cases; public health medicine.

**1968** *Rep. R. Comm. Med. Educ.* iii. 66 in *Parl. Papers 1967-68* (Cmnd. 3569) XXV. 569 '*Community medicine' is . . concerned not with the treatment of individual patients but with the broad question of health and disease . . in the community at large. **1985** *Medical Woman* Spring 13, I joined the MWF . . . This was helpful in finding an interested and knowledgeable local person (a female specialist in community medicine) to educate me and to help set up a part-time scheme.

**community physician**, a specialist in community medicine; a public health physician.

**1974** *Daily Tel.* 1 Apr. 6/6 Regional health boards, executive health councils and local authority departments . . will disappear. So too will medical officers of health, some of whom will now become '*community physicians'. **1989** *Encycl. Brit.* XXIII. 917/2 Community physicians cooperate with such diverse groups as architects, builders, sanitary and heating and ventilating engineers, [etc.].

**community policeman**, a policeman employed in community policing.

**1982** *Economist* 22 May 40/1 Foot patrols based on specific areas, *community policemen, informal liaison groups were widely introduced. **1987** *Sunday Tel.* (Colour Suppl.) 10 May 47/1 Your neighbourhood 'community policeman' is not so much a crime preventer as a citizen soother.

**community policing**, a system of policing by officers who have personal knowledge of and involvement in the community they police.

**1975** *Economist* 22 Feb. 27/1 The loyalists . . fear it could be the first step towards *community policing in the light of Sinn Fein . . opposition to the Royal Ulster Constabulary. **1985** *Telegraph & Argus* (Bradford) 25 May 5/1 West Yorkshire's Chief Constable . . is assembling a 1,000-strong team of civilians to assist with his policy of community policing. **1989** *Listener* 4 May 28/1 The dear, departed days of Dixon of Dock Green, when 'community policing' would have seemed a tautologous concept, belong to a different age.

**community tax**, (a) local tax on members of a community; *spec.* = *community charge* above.

**1986** *Guardian* 29 Jan. 6/8 Some people, such as resident foreigners, would be liable for *community tax but not eligible to vote. **1987** *Church Times* 8 May 12/1 If the Tories get back in, they intend to abolish the rates (which we don't pay on our clergy houses) and introduce a community tax (based on mere existence).

**community worker**, a person employed by a local authority, voluntary agency, etc. to assist a community in promoting its own welfare.

**1975** *Economist* 10 May 34/3 Among those now appointed are the deputy director of Shelter, several *community workers and the founder of the Claimants and Unemployed Workers Union. **1987** *Church Times* 8 May 22/1 The Lambeth Methodist Mission require a full-time Church pastoral and community worker to work with the Superintendent Minister.

[**11.**] **b.** *attrib.* Designating persons whose job involves working in or with a local community (esp. in health care), often one making home visits rather than working in a hospital, as *community doctor, midwife, nurse,* etc.

**1966** *New Statesman* 29 Apr. 610/1 A population of 60,000 will be served by 30 'community doctors' who will work from a single health centre. **1982** M. T. TSUANG *Schizophrenia* viii. 65 [Patients] can be helped by .. home visits from .. a psychiatric community nurse. **1985** M. F. MYLES *Textbk. Midwives* (ed. 10) xliv. 724 The community midwife must keep controlled drugs such as pethidine in a locked receptacle.

**commutable,** *a.* Add: **2.** Of a place: that may be commuted from (*to* a city, place of work, etc.) or to (*from* elsewhere). Of a distance: able to be travelled by a commuter. orig. *U.S.*

**1976** *Washington Post* 19 Apr. c20/2 (Advt.), Convenient to 1–95 & commutable to Northern Virginia. **1981** *N.Y. Times* 11 Oct. v. 11/1 Close to an excellent school district ... Easily commutable to Philly. **1982** *Financial Times* 23 Sept. 30/5 Taiwan would be an additional market within commutable distance. **1986** J. MILNE *Dead Birds* vii. 47 Saffron Walden ... It's just about commutable from London.

**company,** *n.* Add: [**8.**] **c.** A local unit of the (Girl) Guide movement; equivalent to the Scouts' *troop.*

**1909** *Boy Scouts' Headquarters' Gaz.* Nov. 12/2 Girl Guides. Training and Organisation. Uniform.—Jersey of Company Colour .. Skirt, Knickers, Stockings dark blue. **1914** *Girl Guides' Gaz.* Feb. 3/1 We have done the work that scores of other Companies have done ... We remain at four Patrols of eight girls each. **1969** *Policy, Organisation & Rules of Girl Guides Assoc.* (ed. 33) 42 The Guide Guider and the Assistant Guide Guider are the adult leaders of the Company. **1983** *Guide Handbk.* 36 Some of the things you do will be done with your Guider and all the Guides in your Company.

**competence,** *n.* Senses 4 e, f in Dict. become 4 f, g. Add: [II.] [**4.**] **e.** *Med.* Ability (of a valve or sphincter) to function normally.

**1895** J. H. CLARKE *Dis. Heart & Arteries* ii. 22 The affection of the mitral valve was so far remedied that it has been restored to competence. **1902** *Amer. Jrnl. Physiol.* VI. 264 (*heading*) The competence of the ileocæcal valve. **1977** *Jrnl. Cardiovasc. Surg.* XVIII. 507/2 The method of assessment of insufficiency of canine aortic valves .. can be usefully employed for ascertaining the competence of the homograft valves, just before implantation. **1986** *Jrnl. Surg. Res.* XL. 567/1 This flow was maintained by the competence of the atrioventricular and pulmonary valves.

**competent,** *a.* Senses 5 d, e in Dict. become 5 e, f. Add: [**5.**] **d.** *Med.* Of a valve or sphincter: functioning normally; able to prevent reflux. Opp. INCOMPETENT *a.* 2 b.

**1881** G. STEELL *Physical Signs Cardiac Dis.* 16 Tricuspid incompetency may exist without this sign, if the venous valves remain competent. **1915** A. E. BARCLAY *Alimentary Tract* xii. 124 This [ileo-cæcal] valve was found to be perfectly competent at the operation. **1977** *Jrnl. Cardiovasc. Surg.* XVIII. 506/2 Only 4 out of ten pulmonary valves were competent at 20 mm of Hg pressure and all were incompetent at a mean pressure of 100 mm of Hg. **1982** *Brit. Heart Jrnl.* XLVII. 473 Relief of left ventricular outflow tract obstruction was achieved in a majority of cases and the valves were entirely competent.

**complete,** *v.* Add: [**1.**] **b.** *Law.* In conveyancing: to conclude (the sale or purchase of property) by the exchange of money for the property specified in the contract. Also *absol.*

**1794** F. W. SANDERS *J. T. Atkyns's Rep. Cases in Chancery* (ed. 3) I. 12/2 The purchase was to be completed on or before the 25th of *March,* 1793. **1805** E. B. SUGDEN *Law of Vendors & Purchasers of Estates* viii. 185 The purchaser was then out of town, and on his return .. , wrote, insisting that he would not complete. **1893** [see COMPLETION *n.* d]. **1957** *Encycl. Brit.* XIII. 804/1 This is executed by the vendor and delivered to his solicitor in escrow (*i.e.,* on condition that it is not to be effective unless the transaction is duly completed). **1971** *Reader's Digest Family Guide to Law* ix. 80/1 If the seller's solicitor suspects .. that the buyer is unlikely to complete unless he is forced to, he can serve a 'notice to complete' on the buyer. **1987** *Daily Tel.* 23 Sept. 16/6 Purchasers .. are bound to the extent of forfeiture of their deposit if they fail to complete.

**computational,** *a.* Add: Hence **compu'tationally** *adv.,* from the point of view of computation; in terms of computation.

**1957** *Ann. Math. Statistics* XXVIII. 50 Computationally, they are quite manageable. **1985** *Science* 26 Apr. 466/2 This proportionality has been demonstrated using Cm*, a 50-processor multiprocessor, for a number of computationally intensive jobs, including the checking of VLSI circuit designs.

**computer,** *n.* Add: [**3.**] **computer virus** = *VIRUS *n.* 2 d.

**1984** *Computer virus [see *VIRUS *n.* 2 d]. **1986** *Times* 12 Aug. 21/4 A computer virus attack might bring a major weapons system to a standstill, .. or wipe out computer-stored intelligence. **1989** *Daily Tel.* 14 Oct. 1/1 A computer virus triggered by the date Friday 13th struck computers at Britain's leading charity for the blind.

**comrade,** *n.* Add: **g.** *S. Afr.* Also with capital initial. A young, Black, left-wing political activist; hence, any more or less politically motivated township youth, *esp.* one involved in civil disorder. Usu. in *pl.*

**1979** E. JOUBERT in *Fair Lady* 9 May 120 The children who called themselves the Comrades .. forced the children out to the meetings. **1980** C. HERMER *Diary M. Tholo* 101 The comrades have stopped the children entering the schools even if there are no lessons. **1985** *Eastern Province Herald* (S. Afr.) 9 Oct. 2/3 Two African women, .. accused by youths who called themselves 'comrades' with having had relationships with black policemen, were burnt to death in an open lot. **1986** *Listener* 3 July 5/3 The vigilantes emerged .. because black township residents were sick and tired of the rule of the militant young 'Comrades'. **1987** *Sunday Tel.* 28 June 9/5 Comrades are the young blacks trying to drive 'collaborators' and 'informers' out of the townships which they wanted to turn into 'no-go' areas for police and soldiers.

**concave,** *a.* Add: [**2.**] **c.** *Math.* Of a plane figure, a solid, a set (of points), etc.: not convex (*CONVEX *a.* 1 c). Of a function: such that its negative is convex.

**1942** W. & R. C. JAMES *Math. Dict.* 41/1 An arc of a curve is concave toward a point (or line) if every segment of the arc cut off by a secant lies on the opposite side of the secant from the point (or line). **1974** ADBY & DEMPSTER *Introd. Optimization Methods* i. 10 The function *f* is concave if -*f* is convex. **1986** *Oxf. Econ. Papers* July 344 The production functions are concave and homogeneous of degree one.

**conceptus** (kən'sɛptəs), *n.* Pl. conceptuses. [a. L. *conceptus* conception, embryo, f. *conceptus* pa. pple. of *concipĕre* to CONCEIVE *v.*] The product of conception, i.e. the union of sperm and egg, esp. in the early stages of pregnancy; a fertilized egg before implantation; an embryo or foetus together with the placenta, amniotic fluid, and other products of conception. Also, an embryo, *esp.* a newly conceived one.

**1745** R. James *Medicinal Dict.* II, *Conceptus*, the very first Rudiments of the Fœtus in the Uterus after Conception. **1833** Dunglison *Dict. Med. Sci.* I. 221/2 *Conceptus*, the first rudiments of the fœtus, after conception. **1942** *Amer. Jrnl. Obstetr. & Gynecol.* XLIV. 979 Study of these two conceptuses indicates that contact with the endometrium may be established as early as the fifth or sixth postovulatory day. **1970** *Sci. Jrnl.* June 75/1 Each newly conceived embryo, or conceptus, is genetically different from the mother's tissues in which it grows. **1979** J. Macquarrie *Immaculate Conception* (Ecumenical Soc. B.V.M.) 3 We still argue over the question of when a human person comes into being—is it at conception . ., or is it only after the implanting of the conceptus in the wall of the womb? **1989** *New Scientist* 9 Dec. 39/2 To develop successfully, a conceptus (or pre-embryo) *must* acquire certain genes from its mother's chromosomes via the egg.

**concessional** (kən'sɛʃənəl), *a.* [f. concession *n.* + -al.] = concessionary *a.*

**1934** in Webster. **1936** *Discovery* Dec. 375/1 The concessional area of one million acres consisted almost entirely of virgin forest. **1953** *Times* 31 Oct. 7/8 Gifts of up to 22lb. can be sent at the forces concessional rates of postage. **1959** *Economist* 28 Feb. 804/2 The disposal of surplus wheat on concessional terms. **1975** *Petroleum Rev.* XXIX. 398/2 In the UK concessional waters we are witnessing a period of accelerated expansion. **1986** *Times* 11 Aug. 17/3 Many countries . . must receive substantially higher amounts of highly concessional aid.

**conduction**, *n.* Add: IV. 8. Special comb.: **conduction band** *Physics*, a partly-filled energy band in a solid, the electrons of which can move freely and so conduct current; cf. *valence band* s.v. valence *n.*² 5.

**1939** *Proc. R. Soc.* A. CLXXI. 282 To obtain a photo-electromotive force it is necessary to remove electrons from the full band to the empty *conduction band. **1975** H. M. Rosenberg *Solid State* ix. 143 The higher the temperature, the more electrons will be excited to the conduction band.

**conference**, *n.* Add: [4.] f. An association of sports teams or clubs in regular competition, esp. from one geographical area; (a division of) a league. Freq. *attrib.* Chiefly *N. Amer.* (orig. *U.S.*).

**1905** *Chicago Sunday Tribune* 19 Mar. II. 3/2 With Capt. Brietkreutz, holder of the conference half mile record, and L. Miller . . out of the meet, Michigan should not have great difficulty in winning. **1908** *Ibid.* 15 Mar. III. 3/3 Minnesota's basketball team fell an easy prey to the champion University of Chicago five in the concluding game of the conference season. **1916** *Outing* Jan. 411/1 In the Middle Western Conference Illinois and Minnesota played a tie game and defeated all other opponents. **1948** *Daily Ardmoreite* (Ardmore, Okla.) 15 Jan. 6/3 The Ardmore Douglass high school Dragon cagers will meet the Lawton Lions in their second conference game of the season. **1970** *Globe & Mail* (Toronto) 25 Sept. 32/4 Football Record . . Canadian League . . Eastern Conference . . Western Conference. **1986** *Vauxhall Bedford Mirror* 26 June 16/1 The two-year contract sees GM backing the Alliance League . . as the renamed GM Vauxhall Conference. The 'Conference' will comprise . . 22 clubs.

[9.] b. *attrib.* in *Teleph.* Pertaining to or designating a service or facility which enables three or more persons on separate lines to hold a joint conversation or conference by telephone, esp. as *conference call.*

**1934** *Electrical Communication* XII. 146/1 The British Post Office has introduced telephone (trunk) conference service . . . As many as six subscribers may be connected to these circuits at one time. **1939** *Sun* (Baltimore) 19 Jan. 11 Unite the members of your family by conference telephone service . . . Call 'conference operator'. **1940** *Chambers's Techn. Dict.* 189/2 *Conference system*, a telephone system used for conference between groups of persons at a distance; high-grade microphones and radiating receivers are employed. **1965** *Punch* 23 June 912/1 With a long-distance Conference Call you can talk to friends or relatives in as many as three or four cities at the same time. Just ask for Conference Operator. **1970** *N. Y. Times* 19 Nov. 47 Tuesday a bunch of us neighbors found ourselves being notified to stand by to come in for a conference call initiated by the White House. **1986** *Financial Times* 1 Dec. (World Telecom. Survey Suppl.) p. x/6 Modern digital PABXs provide advanced facilities such as 'follow-me' and conference calls to the users within a single site.

**conference**, *v.* Restrict *rare* to sense in Dict. Add: b. *spec.* To participate in a telephone conference call *with* others.

**1972** *N. Y. Law Jrnl.* 10 Oct. 2/5 (Advt.), With the flick of a switch, you and up to five key people can be conferencing with each other. **1976** *Aviation Week & Space Technol.* 10 May 49/3 There is a Norad telephone conferencing system that permits the SAC commander in chief to conference with National Command Authority.

Hence **'conferencing** *vbl. n.*

**1905** *Westm. Gaz.* 1 June 2/1 Delegates went home . . very much pleased with the social and official reception accorded to them, but sick of the conferencing. **1985** *Financial Times* 19 Apr. (Survey Suppl.) p. ii/6 Conferencing, both audio and visual, is another example of a value added services [*sic*] which can lessen the inconvenience of geographical separation. **1988** *Invision* Oct. 14/3 If IBC awakened you to the delights of conferencing by the sea, then Interactive '88 could provide the ideal excuse for yet another coastal jaunt.

**'congressperson**, *n.* *U.S.* Also C-. Pl. -s; also (by substitution) -people. [f. congressman *n.* or congresswoman *n.*, after *chairperson*, etc.: see person *n.* 2 f.] A member of the U.S. Congress (used as a common-gender form).

**1972** *Village Voice* (N.Y.) 1 June 4/3 Only if you have an Ed Koch or a Bella Abzug for a Congressperson . . then may be the District Attorney might be pressured into calling a grand jury. **1976** B. Bova *Multiple Man* x. 104 The people . . [will] lean on their Congresspersons to get the job done. **1980** *New Age* (U.S.) Oct. 4/3, I sent letters to many congresspeople. **1981** J. K. Galbraith *Life in Our Times* xxx. 485 Chairperson, Congressperson, Policeperson—have the jarring sound of any new construction. **1986** *Capital Times* (Madison, Wisconsin) 6 Mar. III. 25/4, I tell them to call their congresspersons.

**conjugate**, *a.* and *n.* Add: [A.] [II.] [6.] [a.] (*b*) Of a pair of arcs or angles: totalling 360°. Of two elements of a matrix: differing in position by having row and column numbers interchanged.

**1902** J. W. Mellor *Higher Math.* x. 411 When the two constituents of a determinant hold the same relative position with respect to the rows and columns, they are said to be conjugate. **1942** G. & R. C. James *Math. Dict.* 11/1 *Conjugate angles*, two angles whose sum is a perigon; two angles whose sum is 360°. *Ibid.* 46/1 *Conjugate arcs*, arcs whose sum is a complete circle.

[B.] [3.] Substitute for def.: *Chem.* and *Biochem.* A conjugated compound. (Examples.)

**1916** A. P. Mathews *Physiol. Chem.* xvii. 759 Hippuric acid is a glycine conjugate, but there are many others. **1924** T. B. ROBERTSON *Princ. Biochem.* (ed. 2) xxiii. 662 These substances are in themselves very toxic, but their conjugates with glucuronic acid are harmless. **1973** *Nature* 7 Dec. 350/2 The immunoglobin was .. conjugated with fluorescein... Twenty microlitres of cells .. was incubated with neat conjugate for 30 min at 20°C. **1988** *Sci. Amer.* Mar. 46/1 We synthesized such an analogue, coupled it to a carrier protein and immunized mice with the conjugate.

**conjugate**, *v.* Add: **4.** *trans.* *Chem.* and *Biochem.* To combine (one compound) with another, usu. of a different kind, to form a molecule in which the constituents retain their identity and from which they can be readily recovered.

**1863** [implied in \*CONJUGATED *ppl. a.* b]. **1900** J. A. MANDEL tr. *Hammarsten's Text-bk. Physiol. Chem.* (ed. 3) xv. 481 In birds .. the acid is conjugated to another substance, ornithin. **1913** J. WALKER *Org. Chem.* 302 Hæmoglobin .. consists of the protein globin conjugated with the pyrrole derivative hæmatin. **1924** T. B. ROBERTSON *Princ. Biochem.* (ed. 2) xxiii. 663 Lack of detoxication, of which the failure to conjugate phenols is an example. **1954** A. WHITE et al. *Princ. Biochem.* viii. 143 Lipoproteins .. are water-soluble proteins conjugated with lecithin, cholesterol, cephalin, etc. **1984** TIGHE & DAVIES *Pathology* (ed. 4) xvii. 167 The bilirubin becomes detached from the albumin and conjugated with glucuronic acid in the liver cell. **1987** *Nursing* Jan. 480/1 In newborn babies jaundice occurs .. because the enzyme, glucuronyl transferase, which is required to conjugate bilirubin so that it can be excreted through the gut, is lacking.

**conjugated**, *ppl. a.* [b.] Substitute for sub-entry: *Chem.* and *Biochem.* Of a compound: formed by conjugation of two simpler compounds. Of a constituent compound: that is conjugated with another; *conjugated protein*, a protein conjugated with a non-protein.

**1857** *Jrnl. Chem. Soc.* IX. 253 A similar increase of solubility is observed with the barium-salts of the series of conjugated acids. *Ibid.* 258 A conjugated sulpho-acid, containing an organic base in the place of hydrocarbons, alcohols, acids, &c., which are present in the usual sulpho-acids. **1863** WATTS *Dict. Chem.* VII. 7 Dumas and Piria .. designated them as 'conjugated acids'. **1863** tr. Gerhardt in *Ibid.* 8 Acetyl, $C^2H^3O$, may be regarded as a conjugated radicle composed of carbonyl, CO, and methyl, $CH^3$, because acetic acid and its derivatives are capable of splitting up into compounds containing carbonyl, and others containing methyl. **1895** A. H. ALLEN *Chem. Urine* 37 Glycuronic acid .. was first obtained in the conjugated form of campho-glycuronic acid. **1908** *Proc. Soc. Biol. Chemists* p. xlix in *Jrnl. Biol. Chem.* IV, *Conjugated proteins*, substances which contain the protein molecule united to some other molecule or molecules otherwise than as a salt. **1950** *Thorpe's Dict. Appl. Chem.* (ed. 4) X. 257/2 In a number of the conjugated proteins .. the union between protein and non-protein moiety may be presumed to be of a similar kind, even where .. reversible dissociation of the components has not been achieved. **1974** PASSMORE & ROBSON *Compan. Med. Stud.* III. xx. 8 In both syndromes, the main defect is in excretion of conjugated bilirubin which is regurgitated from the hepatocytes into the plasma. **1984** TIGHE & DAVIES *Pathology* (ed. 4) xvii. 167 The renal 'threshold' for albumin-bound bilirubin is much higher than for conjugated glucuronide.

**conjugation**, *n.* Add: [1.] **d.** *Chem.* and *Biochem.* Chemical combination, esp. of large or dissimilar molecules which retain their identity.

**1855** *Jrnl. Chem. Soc.* VII. 332 (*heading*) On the phenomenon of conjugation (Paarung), and the

formulæ by which they are represented. **1863** WATTS *Dict. Chem.* VII. 11 It would be well .. if the idea of conjugation, as denoting any peculiar mode of chemical combination, were altogether banished from the science. **1914** J. A. MANDEL tr. *Hammarsten & Hedin's Text-bk. Physiol. Chem.* (ed. 7) xiv. 777 By conjugation with sulphuric acid, the alcohols which are otherwise readily oxidizable may be protected against combustion. **1924** T. B. ROBERTSON *Princ. Biochem.* (ed. 2) xxiii. 663 The non-toxic phenols .. are excreted without undergoing conjugation. **1974** PASSMORE & ROBSON *Compan. Med. Stud.* III. xx. 7 The exact defect is unknown but may lie in the transport of unconjugated bilirubin into the liver cell and possibly in its conjugation. **1982** J. F. VAN PILSUM in T. J. Devlin *Textbk. Biochem.* xxi. 1033 A large number of compounds are detoxified by conjugation reactions in the liver.

**conjunction**, *n.* Add: **7.** Chiefly *Logic.* A complex proposition (typically of the form '*p* and *q*') which is true only when the component propositions are all true; the operation resulting in such a proposition.

**1903** B. RUSSELL *Princ. Math.* v. 57 We may call the first a numerical conjunction, since it gives rise to number, the second a propositional conjunction, since the proposition in which it occurs is equivalent to a conjunction of propositions. **1931** R. M. EATON *Gen. Logic* i. 29 The compound propositions in which *and*, *or*, and *if-then* figure as major logical relations are known respectively as conjunctions, disjunctions, and implications. **1941** O. HELMER tr. *Tarski's Introd. Logic* i. 20 The joining of two sentences (or more) by the word '*and*' results in their so-called conjunction or logical product. **1955** A. N. PRIOR *Formal Logic* i. 6 Medieval logicians described compounds of the form '*p* and *q*' as 'copulative' propositions; they are now generally called 'conjunctive' propositions or 'conjunctions'. **1980** C. S. FRENCH *Computer Sci.* xxii. 141 The AND operation may also be called the logical product, intersection or conjunction. **1982** W. S. HATCHER *Logical Found. Math.* i. 2 The truth table for the conjunction .. of two sentences is the following. *Ibid.*, Since conjunction is a binary operation, the number of possible cases of truth and falsity is greater than that of the negation operation.

**conjure**, *n.* Restrict †*Obs.* to senses in Dict. Add: **3.** *W. Indies* and *Southern U.S. Blacks'.* [f. the vb.] In folk-magic: a spell cast upon a person, = TRICK *n.* 5 c; the magic invoked by this. Chiefly *attrib.*, as *conjure doctor*, *man*, *woman* = WITCH-DOCTOR *n.* 1.

**1895** L. HERRON in A. Dundes *Mother Wit* (1973) 360/2 The conjure doctor's business was of two kinds; to conjure, or 'trick', a person, and to cure persons already 'conjured'. **1895** A. M. BACON in *Ibid.* 367/1 The doctor will make an effort to find the 'trick' or 'conjure' and to identify the miscreant who has caused the trouble. **1899** C. W. CHESNUTT *Conjure Woman* 146 En so w'en he did n' git no better, she .. went ter see ole Aun' Peggy, de cunjuh 'oman. **1909** *Sat. Even. Post* 29 May 16/1 His mammy used to scare him with tales of the potent 'conju-man' who came down in this very swamp and changed skins with the devil. **1933** E. CALDWELL *God's Little Acre* iii. 33, I don't take any stock in superstition and conjur and such things. **1941** *Alabama* (Federal Writers' Project) 380 There are 'conjure doctors', both white and black, who make their living by selling 'tricks' to the illiterate and superstitious. **1975** *New Yorker* 29 Dec. 20/3 An old Haitian 'conjure man' is selling dolls and amulets. **1982** *Amer. Speech* LVII. 55 The failure to make comparisons is least critical in the discussion of conjure .. for the obvious reason that conjure practice is largely unique to the black community.

**connect**, *v.* Add: II. The infin. used *attrib.*: **connect time**, the length of time that a terminal is actively connected or logged on to a computer system.

**1978** *Online* (U.S.) Apr. 57/2 We compared the advertised costs per hour of connect time . . and the calculated discounts. **1985** *Library Assoc. Rec.* Apr. 152/2 (Advt.), Connect time in excess of the 12 hours will be charged at the standard rate for the remainder of the year. **1987** *Stock & Land* (Melbourne) 2 July (CALM Suppl.) 4/1 Computer users pay connect time charges of $20 an hour.

**conquest**, *n.* Add: [I.] [2.] c. *Mountaineering.* The successful ascent of a mountain, esp. one previously unclimbed.

**1902** *Outing* May 207 (*heading*) The conquest of Assiniboine. **1913** B. BROWNE (*title*) Conquest of Mount McKinley: the story of three expeditions. **1964** A. L. KOPIT in *Mademoiselle* Nov. 159 (*title*) The conquest of Everest: a divertissement. **1980** *Christian Science Monitor* 17 Mar. B3/3 The story of Edward Whymper's conquest of this great mountain was known world wide. **1986** *Los Angeles Times* 15 May 1. 1/6 In the South Asian context . . far more than the conquest of a mountain occurred that day.

**continental**, *a.* (and *n.*) Add: [A.] [2.] **Continental day**, a school day extending from early morning to early afternoon, as is customary in many countries of mainland Europe.

[**1981** *Times Educ. Suppl.* 10 Apr. 3/1 A plan for a continental-style day in an East Sussex school, ending with lunch at 1.30 pm, has run into legal difficulties.] *Ibid.* 3 July 6 (*heading*) *Continental day dawns. **1984** *Education* 2 Mar. 184/1 The so-called Continental Day . . a gruelling Teutonic affair, starting 8 o'clock, breaking mid-morning for *würst*, and finishing at about 2 p.m. . . . I'm not aware of any English school which operates the Continental Day in its pure lunchless form. **1986** *Times* 13 June 13/1 Called variously the 'Continental', the compressed or the shortened day, the new schedule is being adopted by increasing numbers of schools. **Continental roast** *n.* and *a.*, (designating) dark-roasted coffee beans producing coffee with a Continental flavour, or the coffee itself.

**1958** *Catal. County Stores, Taunton* June 29 *Coffee* . . *Continental Roast—a lb. 7/6. **1962** L. DEIGHTON *Ipcress File* xxvii. 172 'You're up,' said Charlie, coming into the living-room with a big white coffeepot. 'Continental roast. O.K.?' **1985** S. REES *Devil's Looking-Glass* xvii. 138 Strong black coffee, continental-roast.

**contour**, *n.* Senses 1 d, e in Dict. become 1 e, f. Add: [1.] **d.** A contour line.

**1840** E. C. FROME *Outline Method Trig. Survey* v. 56 The system of tracing these horizontal lines at *fixed vertical intervals*, and drawing between the contours vertical strokes . . presents a far more easy method of expressing correctly the actual surface of the ground. **1861** A. W. DRAYSON *Pract. Milit. Surveying & Sketching* vi. 68 The contours were ten feet apart in vertical distance. **1923** J. JOHNSTONE *Introd. Oceanogr.* iii. 46 The contour passes as nearly as possible to *all* the points where depths of (say) 50 fathoms are marked. **1957** L. T. C. ROLT *Isambard Kingdom Brunel* viii. 132 Below, skirting the steeper contours, runs the later Bronze Age road. **1984** A. C. & A. DUXBURY *Introd. World's Oceans* viii. 260 The depth contours offshore tend to follow the shoreline pattern.

**contract**, *n.*[1] Add: [6.] b. In sense 1 h, *contract killer*.

**1980** *N.Y. Times* 28 July A20/1 Various harebrained schemes of eliminating Fidel Castro, . . one of which involved the use of *contract killers from the American underworld. **1986** *Times* 21 Nov. 5/7 Mr Ranuana's friend was a police informer and the two 'contract killers' were undercover detectives.

*contract killing.*

**1977** *Washington Post* 14 Jan. C2/3 The . . murder charge . . carries a maximum sentence of life, and involves the alleged '*contract' killing of a suspected drug dealer. **1987** *Daily Tel.* 17 Sept. 10/1 That unedifying period . . when gangsters ran Chicago, civic corruption was rife and a contract killing was only marginally more difficult to set up than a stiff drink.

**contract**, *v.* Add: [2.] f. To place under contract.

**1961** in WEBSTER. **1984** *Dictionaries* VI. 185 Oxford has contracted International Computaprint Corporation for the initial capture. **1988** A. LIVELY *Blue Fruit* 126 We've just contracted a bunch of black musicians.

**control**, *n.* Add: [4.] c. A member of an intelligence organization who personally directs the activities of a spy; a spymaster.

**1963** 'J. LE CARRÉ' *Spy who came in from Cold* ii. 19 Control went on: 'The ethic of our work . . is based on a single assumption . . . We are never going to be aggressors.' **1975** T. WILLIS *Left-Handed Sleeper* xiv. 215 'Aren't you forgetting the Rumborne woman?' . . 'She was the contact, not the control. No—it wasn't her'. **1986** B. FORBES *Endless Game* II. xxv. 250 He sat with his KGB control on the terrace of the Quaddan Hotel, listening with the respect he gave to few as the details of his new assignment were explained.

[5.] *control pod.*

**1972** L. M. HARRIS *Introd. Deepwater Floating Drilling Operations* xi. 121 The *control pod serves as a lower terminal for the hose bundle and houses the critical moving parts of the subsea hydraulic-control system. **1985** *Audio Visual* Feb. 56/1 The control 'pod' of the Galaxy 2 Arena includes channel control, two playbacks, memory, [etc.].

**control character** *Computing*, a character that does not represent a printable character but serves to initiate a particular action, e.g. in a peripheral device.

**1966** C. J. SIPPL *Computer Dict. & Handbk.* (1967) 74/1 *Control character. **1969** P. B. JORDAIN *Condensed Computer Encycl.* 127 The control character is embedded in the data stream. **1984** J. HILTON *Choosing & using Your Home Computer* VII. 202/1 The ASCII code uses one byte to represent the 94 printable characters, the 'space', and a number of control 'characters'.

**control code** *Computing*, a control character or group of control characters.

**1970** O. DOPPING *Computers & Data Processing* ii. 47 The codes are intended for several different uses. . . This is the reason for the great number of *control codes. **1985** *Personal Computer World* Feb. 212/1 To operate in the normal-density bit image mode, Epson printers must receive the control codes $1B, $4B.

**control key** *Computing*, a key which is held down while another key is depressed, altering the function of the latter.

**1978** *Pract. Computing* July-Aug. 43/3 Some of them [*sc.* keys] serve a dual function when certain *control keys are depressed first. **1984** *Which Micro?* Dec. 75/2 You can choose your own control keys if you wish.

**convection**, *n.* Add: [1.] [b.] **convection cell**, a relatively stable and self-contained region of convection (usu. one of a number) in which the upward motion of warmer fluid at the centre is balanced by the downward motion of cooler fluid at the periphery.

**1934** D. BRUNT *Physical & Dynamical Meteorol.* xii. 213 There is a type of eddy which can be produced and made visible in the laboratory, that has become known largely through the work of H. Bénard, for which the name of '*convection cell' is suggested as appropriate. **1983** *Geophysical Res. Lett.* X. 421/1 An uncompensated depression is consistent with the downgoing arm of a convection cell.

**convergence**, *n.* Add: [1.] d. *Oceanogr.* Any region where currents converge; *spec.* each of several named regions (esp. *Antarctic, Arctic convergence*) at the boundary between two converging currents, at which the denser body of water is subducted.
   **1933** G. E. R. DEACON in *Discovery Rep.* VII. 179 Along the Antarctic convergence . . Antarctic surface water sinks below sub-Antarctic water. **1942** H. U. SVERDRUP et al. *Oceans* iv. 139 The most conspicuous convergence is the Antarctic convergence, which can be traced all round the Antarctic Continent. **1963** G. L. PICKARD *Descriptive Physical Oceanogr.* vii. 114 The Subtropical Convergence is at about 40°S round most of the Antarctic. **1984** A. C. & A. DUXBURY *Introd. World's Oceans* vii. 231 There are three major zones of convergence: the tropical convergence at the equator, the subtropical convergences . . and the Arctic and Antarctic convergences.

**convert**, *v.* Add: [II.] [9.] [d.] Restrict †*Obs.* to sense (*b*). [(*a*)] (App. *Obs.* before 1700 and not recorded again until the mid-20th c.) (Later examples.)
   **1962** 'K. ORVIS' *Damned & Destroyed* xv. 106, I can't marry out of my religion. I can't . . and Helen won't convert. **1977** *Times Lit. Suppl.* 27 May 654/5 Some protest too should be raised against the extraordinary use of the verb 'convert'—he did not 'convert to Christianity', 'she had converted to the Christian faith'. **1979** C. FREEMAN *Portraits* lxviii. 614 So he marries a *goyishe maidel* who converts and becomes more Jewish than any of them. **1986** 'J. LE CARRÉ' *Perfect Spy* xiv. 371 He never even told us whether he converted . . . It took a jolly good talking to from Father D'Arcy before Harrison saw the light.

**convertible**, *a.* (*n.*) Add: [A.] [6.] b. Of bonds, loan stock, etc.: that can be converted into other shares (esp. ordinary shares) or another class of stock on a preferred basis, typically within or at a predetermined time.
   **1869** *Bradshaw's Railway Man.* XXI. 429 Of these convertible bonds $18,300 were paid off and never converted. **1908** F. LOWNHAUPT *Investment Bonds* xvii. 178 Exchange of bonds for new stock in reorganization . . is a mere accident, but as a privilege of contract in convertible bonds it has become a prominent feature in many large capital creations. **1946** J. H. PRIME *Investment Analysis* ii. 21 The implication in a convertible bond is that the investor has an opportunity to make profits while at the same time he is insured against loss. **1985** *Investors Chron.* 1-7 Nov. 29/1 It has lost out by being forbidden to hold convertible preference shares.
   [B.] 3. A convertible bond, etc.
   **1957** *N.Y. Post* 26 Mar. 18/3 A 'convertible' in Wall Street isn't an auto . . it's 'a bond, debenture or preferred share which may be exchanged by the owner for common stock or another security'. **1972** *N.Y. Law Jrnl.* 10 Oct. 3/4 Where both a convertible and the underlying security are being sold the amount of the underlying security for which the convertible being sold may be converted is aggregated with sales of the underlying security. **1985** *Investors Chron.* 1-7 Nov. 27/1 Gilt fund managers are thinking of convertibles, which allow capital growth as well as income.

**convex**, *a.* and *n.* Add: [A.] [1.] c. *Math.* Of a plane figure, a solid, a set (of points), etc.: containing the straight line segment joining any two points in the set. Of a function: having a graph which forms the lower boundary of a convex set. Of a linear combination of quantities: having coefficients which are non-negative and which total 1. Also applied to

other entities in analogous senses. Cf. *CONCAVE a.* 2 c.
   **1858** Q. *Jrnl. Pure & Appl. Math.* II. 340 Every number *n* answers to a *simple* polygon of *n* + 2 sides: that is, a polygon in which no side cuts another side. The simple polygon may be either convex, or with some angles re-entrant. [**1905** J. L. W. V. JENSEN in *Nyt Tidsskrift for Matematik* XVI B. 49 (*heading*) Om konvekse funktioner og uligheder imellem middelværdier.] **1915** *Proc. London Math. Soc.* XIV. 269 Log *M(r)* is a convex function of log *r*. **1930** *Proc. Nat. Acad. Sci.* XVI. 240 (*heading*) Combinatory topology of convex regions. **1951** E. W. BARANKIN in J. Neyman *Proc. 2nd Berkeley Symp. Math., Statistics & Probability* 167 (*heading*) Conditional expectation and convex functions. **1959** G. & R. C. JAMES *Math. Dict.* 234/2 A convex linear combination of quantities $x_i (i = 1, 2, \ldots, n)$ is an expression . . $\sum \lambda_i x_i$, where $\sum \lambda_i = 1$ and each $\lambda_i$ is a non-negative real number. **1965** *Ann. Math. Statistics* XXXVI. 703 (*heading*) Peakedness of distributions of convex combinations. **1974** ADBY & DEMPSTER *Introd. Optimization Methods* i. 10 More formally, a function of a single argument is convex if for all *x* and *y* and all numbers $\lambda$ between o and 1, $f(\lambda x + (1 - \lambda)y) \leqslant \lambda f(x) + (1 - \lambda)f(y)$. **1980** A. J. JONES *Game Theory* ii. 109 A continuous game is called convex if for each fixed *x*, $o \leqslant x \leqslant 1$, $P (x, y)$ is a convex function of *y*.
   3. Special collocations (in *Math.*): **convex envelope** = *convex hull.*
   **1964** A. P. & W. ROBERTSON *Topological Vector Spaces* i. 45 Each $x_i \in A$ is a convex set containing *A* called the *convex envelope of *A*.
   **convex hull**, the smallest convex set which contains a given set.
   **1951** E. W. BARANKIN in J. Neyman *Proc. 2nd Berkeley Symp. Math., Statistics & Probability* 168 The *convex hull of a set in $\varepsilon^k$ is the smallest convex set containing the given set. **1965** *Biometrika* LII. 331 (*heading*) The convex hull of a random set of points.
   **convex programming**, any of various procedures for finding the minimum value of a convex function subject to specified constraints.
   **1963** *Austral. Jrnl. Statistics* V. 14 (*heading*) An algorithm for *convex programming.

**cook**, *n.* Add: [3.] **cooktop** orig. *U.S.*, a cooking unit with hotplates or burners, *esp.* one built into or on top of a cabinet.
   **1959** *House Beautiful* Feb. 133/1 (*caption*) Other ready-to-heat foods have storage cupboard close to *cooktop. **1970** *Kitchen & Bath Guide* (House & Garden) 100/1 This model has glass ceramic electric cooktop. **1986** *House & Garden* July 20/1 (Advt.), The 2-plate electric hob . . and the 'pot-flat' glass-ceramic cooktop.

**Cooley's anæmia** ('kuːlɪz), *n. Path.* [Named after Thomas B. *Cooley* (1871-1945), U.S. paediatrician, who with P. Lee described the condition in 1925 (*Jrnl. Amer. Pediatric Soc.* XXXVII. 29).] = *thalassæmia major* s.v. THALASSÆMIA *n.*
   [**1936** WHIPPLE & BRADFORD in *Jrnl. Pediatrics* IX. 279 (*heading*) Mediterranean disease—thalassemia (erythroblastic anemia of Cooley).] **1937** R. L. CECIL *Textbk. Med.* 992 Certain diseases of childhood like erythroblastic anemia (Cooley's). **1959** *Listener* 26 Nov. 920/1 The widespread occurrence in certain parts of Italy of the disease known as Cooley's anaemia. **1979** *Nature* 26 July 275/2 Investigations of normal haemoglobin have paved the way for understanding the anatomy and physiology of the human genome and research into Cooley's anaemia has been well in the vanguard. **1983** E. C. MINKOFF *Evolutionary Biol.* xxvii. 537/2 Malaria resistance in Mediterranean latitudes . . is brought about largely by a totally different gene, responsible for the disease known as thalassemia (or Cooley's anemia).

**co-operative**, *a.* (*n.*) Add: co-,operativi'zation *n.*, the process or policy of organizing or restructuring agriculture, etc. on co-operative principles (esp. in Communist China); cf. COLLECTIVIZATION *n.*
   **1966** F. SCHURMANN *Ideol. & Organization in Communist China* 11 We continue, for the Communist period, with a discussion of the three stages of Chinese Communist village policy: land reform, cooperativization, and communization. *Ibid.* vii. 442 The term 'cooperativization' appears as a barbarism in English, yet it is an exact rendering of the term *hotsohua*, by which Chinese Communists designate the movement. **1972** *Times* 29 Dec. (Romania Suppl.) p. i/2, The outcome of the manysided development of the national economy in the conditions of industrialization and agricultural cooperativization, has been the continuous expansion of the country's resources. **1976** D. DAVIN *Woman-Work* (1978) iii. 101 Some people wrongly believed that the commonest reason for divorce after co-operativization . . was financial discontent. **1984** *Summary of World Broadcasts: Far East* (B.B.C.) 28 Feb. III. B/3 Cultural and ideological revolutions . . must be carried out in the rural areas after the completion of socialist cooperativization.

**co-opt**, *v.* Add: **2.** To absorb into a larger (esp. political) group; to take over or adopt (an idea, etc.). *U.S.*
   **1969** *Atlantic Monthly* Oct. 18/1 A Republican Party based in the 'Heartland' (Midwest), West, and South can and should co-opt the Wallace vote. **1970** *New Yorker* 16 May 34/3 All too often, mere approval of their social and political concern has, in the jargon, co-opted their causes and deadened them. **1982** *N.Y. Times* 22 Apr. A6/3 The argument has been, co-opt the left before it's too late. **1986** B. FUSSELL *I hear Amer. Cooking* IV. xvii. 315 As English as apple pie, colonists must have said before America co-opted the dish for its own.

**co-'optable**, *a.* [f. CO-OPT *v.* + -ABLE.] That may be co-opted; assimilable with a larger group or body.
   **1972** T. KOCHMAN *Rappin' & Stylin' Out* p. xv, Claude Brown's 'Language of Soul' . . makes the case for pronunciation ('Spoken Soul') as the essential element in black talk, all else being co-optable by the larger society. **1981** *N.Y. Times* 8 Nov. XI. 42/1 It is a mistake to see him purely as a graphic Weatherman co-optable by today's radicals.

**co-ordinate**, *a.* and *n.* Add: [A.] Sense 4 in Dict. becomes 5. **4.** Pertaining to or designating a college (esp. one for women) affiliated to but not fully integrated with a neighbouring college or university; also (formerly), designating or relating to a university having separate colleges or classes for men and women. *U.S.*
   **1912** *Richmond* (Va.) *Times-Dispatch* 12 Jan. 6/3 By Messrs. Early and Rison: A bill to establish a Coordinate State College for Women. **1929** T. WOODY *Hist. Women's Educ. in U.S.* II. vi. 316 In 1891, Brown University, through the Women's College, was open to women on the coördinate plan. **1938** *Radcliffe Q.* Nov. 10/1 The distinguishing virtue of the coördinate college is . . that it gives its students the advantages of the university while preserving for them some of the benefits of the separate college for women. **1970** E. W. FARELLO *Hist. Educ. of Women in U.S.* v. 193 Coeducation was truly of American origin but the idea of a coordinate college came from 'English practice' at Cambridge and Oxford Universities.
   [B.] **4.** A co-ordinate college. *U.S.*
   **1975** *Publishers Weekly* 28 July 66/1 Kirkland College in Clinton, N.Y., the women's coordinate of prestigious Hamilton College for men.

**cordia** ('kɔːdɪə), *n.* [mod.L., f. the name of Euricius *Cordus* (1486-1535) and Valerius his son (1515-44), German scholars + -IA¹.] Any plant of the tropical and subtropical genus *Cordia*, of the borage family, comprising evergreen and deciduous shrubs and trees grown as ornamentals for their showy flowers and in the tropics for timber.
   **1756** P. BROWNE *Civil & Nat. Hist. Jamaica* 202 The bushy *Cordia*, with large scarlet flowers. **1814** J. LUNAN *Hortus Jamaicensis* I. 198 Adorned with large bunches of fine scarlet flowers, (hence the name of *scarlet cordia*). **1905** *Chambers's Jrnl.* May 367/1 Probably the most beautiful and conspicuous trees [in the Bermudas] are . . the scarlet cordia, and others. **1939** *Florida* (Federal Writers' Project) III. 332 The rough-leaved cordia, or geiger tree. **1959** G. DRAYTON *Christopher* I. ii. 26 An orange moon was coming up over the cordia trees that lined the lawn. **1972** *Timber Trades Jrnl.* 13 May 40/2 The great virtue of cordia was its stability . . and it was in good supply, areas of Nigeria having some 400 cordia trees to a square mile.

**'corn dolly**, *n.* Also corn-dolly. [A popular corruption of *kirn-dolly* (s.v. KIRN-BABY *n.*), the first element taken as CORN *n.*¹; see CORN-BABY *n.*] = KIRN-BABY *n.*, a symbolic or decorative figure celebrating the harvest home.
   **1952** *Sunday Times* 21 Sept. 2 [Worcs.] His 'corn dollies' have attracted interest from museums and housewives looking for winter 'flower' decorations. **1967** V. PRITCHARD *Eng. Medieval Graffiti* 14 It is possible that the head was made of straw or basket-work, and interesting specimens of such work, called 'corn-dollies', can still be seen in some churches. **1976** M. HUNTER *Talent is not Enough* 41 The ancient rite of shaping the last sheaf into a corn dolly to perch high on the stacked straw. **1985** *Listener* 21 Mar. 20/2, I realise that this is not wine, but if the growers in the South of England can provide and sell teas and corn dollies, why not juices?

**corporate**, *a.* Add: [B.] [5.] [b.] corporate raider orig. *U.S.*, one who mounts an unwelcome takeover bid by buying up shares (usu. discreetly) on the stock market.
   **1967** *Congress. Rec.* 18 Jan. 858/1 The *corporate raider may thus act under a cloak of secrecy while obtaining the shares needed to put him on the road to a successful capture of the company. **1986** *Times* 19 Nov. 27/2 It rose 10p to 174p on speculation that one of the big Australian corporate raiders was trying to build a stake.

**corpse**, *v.* Add: [2.] **b.** *intr.* Of an actor: to forget one's lines; = DRY *v.* 2 d; to spoil one's performance by being confused or made to laugh by one's colleagues.
   **1874** HOTTEN *Slang Dict.*, *Corpse*, to stick fast in the dialogue. **1958** *News Chron.* 23 May 4/7 There's a new word, too, from drama school. When anyone forgot their lines in the past they had dried. Today, they have 'corpsed'. **1972** A. BENNETT *Getting On* I. 32 *Mrs Brodribb*: When Max—. *Geoff*: Max (*He corpses*). *Mrs Brodribb*: (*silencing him with a look*)—pauses by your doorstep he is not just relieving himself. He is leaving a message. **1987** *Observer* 8 Feb. 11/2 Gambon said his dying line ('Oh, I am slain') in the mode of a different theatrical grandee every night . . —a display of 'suicidal nerve', all to get his co-actor to corpse in the dark.

**correction**, *n.* Add: [9.] correction officer *U.S.* = *prison officer* s.v. PRISON *n.* 3 a.
   **1940** *Ann. Rep. N.Y. State Commission of Correction 1939* XIII. 141 The custodial staff consists of two Captains, three Acting Captains, and 97 *Correction Officers. **1986** *N.Y. Times* 13 Nov. B3/1 A car driven by an off-duty correction officer

slammed into the scene of an earlier, minor accident on a Queens highway.

**corset**, *n.* Add: [2.] **b.** A close-fitting support worn because of injury, weakness, or deformity, esp. of the thorax or spine.
**1833** DUNGLISON *Dict. Med. Sci.* 243/2 *Corset*, ... Different bandages, more or less complicated, which embrace the greater part of the trunk, are like wise so called. **1884** *Catal. Orthopaedical Apparatuses* (John Reynolds & Co.) 306 (*heading*) Sayre's Spinal Spring Corset. *Ibid.*, The corset is constantly making efforts to extend itself. **1907** A. THORNDIKE *Orthopedic Surg.* xx. 341 Corsets made of cloth re-inforced with steels .. have been used extensively. **1939** H. H. JORDAN *Orthopedic Appliances* v. 253 The illustrations .. show a leather-strip anklet .. combined with a metatarsal corset. **1951** F. J. & L. S. KNOCKE *Orthopaedic Nursing* vii. 155 A corset is a semirigid support, made of stout cloth reinforced with longitudinal supports. **1985** J. N. WALTON *Brain's Dis. Nervous Syst.* (ed. 9) xviii. 518 A light lumbar support or corset which is worn for three months or longer.

**countercurrent**, *a.* and *adv.* Add: Also **counter-current**. [A.] **2.** Involving currents flowing in opposite directions.
**1911** *Encycl. Brit.* XX. 48/2 In the case of cold extraction the seed is placed in a series of closed vessels, through which the solvent percolates by displacement, on the 'counter-current' system. **1940** *Rep. Progress Physics* VI. 59 In order to multiply the smaller differences in chemical properties it is necessary to make use of two-phase counter-current methods. **1970** S. HARLAND *Counter-Current Extraction* i. 1 This book considers .. the transfer of a single solute between two immiscible phases in counter-current flow. **1984** J. F. LAMB et al. *Essent. Physiol.* (ed. 2) viii. 202 This gradient is set up because the long loops of Henle of the juxtamedullary nephrons and the collecting ducts act with their associated blood vessels .. as a counter current system.
[B.] *adv.* = *countercurrently* adv. below.
**1922** *Jrnl. Industr. & Engin. Chem.* June 476/1 The capacity of a fractionating column is defined as a measure of the amount of vapor and liquid which can be passed countercurrent to each other in a column without causing the column to load or prime. **1939** *Biochem. Jrnl.* XXXIII. 1918 An extraction train in which water and chloroform flow counter-current at a controlled flow-ratio. **1972** *Materials & Technol.* V. x. 283 The weaker lyes .. are pumped from vessel to vessel, in such a manner that they pass counter-current to the soap.
Hence **counter'currently** *adv.*, in a countercurrent way; in or with opposite directions of flow.
**1930** *Industr. & Engin. Chem.* Mar. 221/2 Cooling is effected by the cold extract flowing countercurrently in its passage from the extract tank to the preheater. **1935** *Ibid.* Oct. 1213/1 Consider a series of *n* of these ideal exchangers working countercurrently. **1976** *Sci. Amer.* Dec. 31/2 (*caption*) Its height was needed so that process streams of organic and aqueous solutions could flow countercurrently by gravity through extraction columns.

**'counter,puncher**, *n.* Boxing (orig. *U.S.*). [COUNTER- 3.] A boxer whose style is characterized by countering after an opponent's punch is thrown. Cf. COUNTER *v.*[1] 5. Also *fig.*
**1932** E. HEMINGWAY *Death in Afternoon* xiii. 151 All those boxers who have lasted longest .. have been counter-punchers. **1962** *Courier-Jrnl.* (Louisville, Kentucky) 11 Nov. 11. 10/1 [Cassius Clay] is essentially a counter-puncher—a foe who waits for a foe to throw a punch and then counters. **1968** *Globe & Mail* (Toronto) 3 Feb. B4/4 The tobacco industry's best counter-puncher. **1972** 'H. PENTECOST' *Birthday, Deathday* I. i. 8 It's as if an attack has been

intended on him. I should like to go on record as saying that he is a pretty tough counterpuncher. **1986** *World Boxing* Sept. 48/2 Each is a superb counterpuncher, the type of fighter who would seem to excel against the free-swinging and sometimes careless Pazienza.
So **'counterpunch** *n.*[2], a return blow, *esp.* one that exploits a momentary lack of defence; also *fig.*; **'counterpunch** *v. intr.* and *trans.* = COUNTER *v.*[1] 5 a and b; **'counter,punching** *vbl. n.*
**1957** *Rocky Marciano's Bk. Boxing* ix. 103 The left jab .. can be a handicap, for some boxers leave themselves wide open when attempting to deliver it and can readily be hit by what are known as counterpunches. *Ibid.* (*heading*) Counterpunching. **1964** J. D. MACDONALD *Deep Blue Good-Bye* (1965) viii. 92, I counterpunched and knocked his mouth open with an overhand right. **1971** *Black Scholar* Jan. 43/2 He'd step inside their leads and counter punch them to death! **1974** *Spartanburg* (S. Carolina) *Herald-Jrnl.* 20 Apr. A7/4 The raid was a psychological counterpunch to the blow the Japanese had dealt Pearl Harbor. **1977** *Facts on File Yearbk.* 17 Dec. 970/3 Although Briscoe managed to bloody the Colombian's mouth in the 12th round, Valdes' superior counter-punching ability assured his victory. **1980** *Times* 13 May 8/2 Recent Soviet tactics have been confined to what was described as counterpunching. **1986** *World Boxing* Sept. 29/1 Will he patiently counterpunch, or foolishly attempt to initiate the action?

**,counter-'transference**, *n.* Psychoanalysis. [COUNTER- 9.] The transference by the analyst towards the patient of feelings and reactions similar to those aroused by significant figures (esp. parents) in the analyst's early life; more *loosely*, any emotion felt by the analyst towards the patient. Cf. DISPLACEMENT *n.* 2 f, TRANSFERENCE *n.* 1 b.
**1912** A. A. BRILL tr. *Freud's Selected Papers Hysteria* (ed. 2) 210 Our attention has been called to the 'counter-transference' which ensues in the unconscious feelings of the physician through the influence of the patient. **1920** *Internat. Jrnl. Psycho-Anal.* I. 292 The .. theme of the transference on the part of the analyst—the so-called counter-transference—is discussed. **1968** M. BALINT *Basic Fault* xviii. 115 The patient is always a 'worthwhile' person, someone who badly needs—and deserves—help—a clear diagnostic sign of positive counter-transference. **1979** A. STORR *Art of Psychotherapy* vii. 68 Part of counter-transference seems .. to be an irrational prejudice in favour of those whom, as a therapist, one comes to know intimately. **1981** M. I. LITTLE *Transference Neurosis & Transference Psychosis* vii. 129, I too think it very important that the term *countertransference* be reserved for the specific part of the analyst's total response to his patient's needs that has remained unconscious and under repression.

**coupler**, *n.* Senses 2 c, d, and e in Dict. become 2 d, f, and g. Add: [2.] **c.** = COUPLING *vbl. n.* 6 b.
**1879** *Car-Builder's Dict.* 48/1 *Coupler* ... In relation to cars the term usually designates the appliances for coupling or connecting cars together. **1897** KIPLING *Day's Work* (1898) 223 His brake-pump panting forty to the minute, his front coupler lying sideways on his cow-catcher, like a tired dog's tongue in his mouth. **1960** *Times* 7 Dec. 23/7 Automatic couplers and other items needed to give maximum control on fast and heavy trains. **1984** *Comprehensive Railroad Dict.* ('Railway Age') 44 A manual operation is necessary to uncouple two cars whose couplers are locked together.
**e.** A device that enables oscillatory energy to be transferred from one electric or

electromagnetic device to another, esp. other than by physical connection.

**1914** R. STANLEY *Text-bk. Wireless Telegr.* xi. 135 The jigger, or two-coil coupler, gives the sharpest tuning, and thus best avoids interference with, or by, other stations. **1924** *Harmsworth's Wireless Encycl.* I. 547/1 A disadvantage with the loose coupler method of tuning lies in the dead end effects of the wire not actually used in the tuning circuit, but still directly coupled to it. **1950** W. C. JOHNSON *Transmission Lines & Networks* vii. 188 A directional coupler is a device that couples a measuring instrument or an auxiliary line only to the wave traveling in one direction along the main line. **1982** *Giant Bk. Electronics Projects* vi. 279 If you use a coupler, detector and oscilloscope to tune up the rig, you may note a 15 to 20 MHz oscillation on the signal. **1987** *Flight Internat.* 10 Oct. 42/1 Connectorless inductive couplers, one per seat row, were used to pick up the transmission of information.

**culchie** ('kʌlʃɪ, 'kʌltʃɪ), *n.* (and *a.*) *Anglo-Ir. slang* (often mildly *derog.*). Also **culchee, culshie.** [App. alteration of *Kilti*magh, Ir. *Coillte Mach* (older *Mághach*), the name of a country town in Co. Mayo.] One who lives in or comes from a rural area; a (simple) countryman or -woman, a provincial, a rustic. (Chiefly in Dublin use, of people from any other part of Ireland.) Also *attrib.* or as *adj.*

**1958** B. BEHAN *Borstal Boy* III. 240 'That's it,' said I over my shoulder to him, 'you're coming on a very bright boy—for a Culchie.' **1975** *Irish Times* 9 May 1/4 He looked confused and puzzled for a moment, muttered, 'Bloody culchies,' and took off in the direction of Clontarf. **1978** *Times Lit. Suppl.* 20 Jan. 57/4 A tiny figure in black .. shouting 'Up de rebels'. The reader may be surprised to find Lady Gregory pronouncing English in this culchee way. **1982** M. BINCHY *Light Penny Candle* III. xiv. 309 Oh, nothing as bad as a culchie wedding I always say. **1982** P. McGINLEY *Goosefoot* ii. 22 'I'm .. new to the town, just up from the country.' 'Don't worry about that. I'm a culshie too.' **1986** B. GELDOF *Is that It?* iii. 26 We Dublin boys called the country pupils 'culchies', which they hated.

‖**culpa** ('kʌlpə), *n. Law.* [L. = fault, blame.] Neglect resulting in damage; negligence.

[**1723** G. MACKENZIE *Inst. Law Scotl.* (ed. 6) (Index), *Culpa lata, levis: ac levissima.* **1830** *U.S. Supreme Court Reports* 28 U.S. 230 Fraud must be a constituent of the act of barratry... The question seems to be between 'dolus' and 'culpa', which of these two words best conveys the sense of the law.] **1861** *Cases Court of Session, Scotl.* (Ser. 2) XXIII. 439 The peculiar circumstances which demand great care and caution raise the character of the *culpa*, which consists in the want of that care and caution. **1892** A. T. GLEGG *Reparation* i. 8 For delict, *culpa* must be proved. **1939** GLEGG & DUNCAN *Law Reparation Scotl.* (ed. 3) xv. 351 The *culpa* or negligence of the owner is the foundation on which the right of action against him rests. **1970** *Internat. & Compar. Law Q.* XIX. 125 The Italian and French members, familiar with *culpa* in their domestic law, preferred to continue the existing system of liability. **1985** *Times* 29 Jan. 4/8 Neither [passage] gave support to the contention that nuisance gave rise to liability even if culpa was not proved.

**culture**, *n.* Add: [5.] [d.] **culture-bound** *a.*, restricted in character, outlook, etc. by belonging to a particular culture; determined or limited by the presuppositions of one's culture (further examples).

**1951** R. FIRTH *Elem. Social Organiz.* iii. 109 He is culture-bound in his desires as well as his activities. **1963** J. LYONS *Structural Semantics* iv. 76 Let us here assume that the linguist has provisionally identified as

the same situational context (itself 'culture-bound') the events and activities which constitute making a purchase in a shop. **1980** *English World-Wide* I. 1. 4 Unmistakable culture-bound specimens like passages from an Onitsha Market novel, or Indian matrimonial advertisements.

**Cumberland**, *n.* Add: [1.] b. **Cumberland sausage**, a kind of coarse-cut pork sausage traditionally made in Cumberland and often sold in a continuous piece from which sections may be cut.

[**1949** F. GERRARD *Bk. of Meat Trade* I. xvi. 290 The coarse cut sausage of Cumberland .. compared with the finer cut sausage of London and the South of England generally.] **1966** *Meat Trades Jrnl.* 7 Apr. 3/1 'Mr S., Pork Butcher and Cumberland Sausage Maker, near the Co-Op, New Brighton, Wallasey, Cheshire' .. was the address on a letter delivered to Elston's .. last week. **1976** *Cumberland & Westmorland Herald* 4 Dec. 14/6 (Advt.), Cumberland sausage (loose) only 32p per lb. **1980** D. ST. J. THOMAS *Breakfast Bk.* v. 40 Georgette had one of the tastiest cheese omelettes of all time, along with a slice of my substantial Cumberland sausage.

**3.** Designating or characteristic of a catch-hold style of wrestling developed in the north of England. Also *Cumberland and Westmorland (style,* etc.).

**1823** W. LITT *Wrestliana* 32 We trust a due consideration will materially reduce the strength of the objections so warmly urged against our Cumberland mode of wrestling. *Ibid.* 34 If the trial be made, many of the Cumberland and Westmorland Wrestlers will find them sufficient work in their own way. **1889** W. ARMSTRONG in W. H. Pollock et al. *Fencing, Boxing & Wrestling* 204 The variation of falls, and of manœuvres leading up to them are even more endless than in the Cumberland and Westmoreland style. *Ibid.* 205 The hands are not obliged to remain locked, as in the Cumberland style. **1934** [see ALL-IN *a.* (*phr.*) 2 ]. **1968** G. KENT *Pict. Hist. Wrestling* v. 121 (*caption*) Dinnie's 'Scottish' style of wrestling was out of favour by the time he died in 1916, and Cumberland gained ground again. Here a Cumberland swing is performed in front of the Royal Enclosure .. Braemar .. (1955). **1983** P. BILLS *Wrestling* 14 In Cumberland and Westmorland, a wrestler is considered the loser if any part of his body except his feet touches the canvas.

**cumulation**, *n.* Add: [1.] b. *spec.* The process or result of cumulating lists of book titles or similar data; a cumulated list, index, catalogue, etc.

**1900** *Cumulated Index to Bks. 1898-99* 3 Before the publication of the *Index* of May 1898, which was a cumulation of sixteen months, the whole bibliography was thoroughly revised. **1918** (*title*) Cumulative book index. 18th-20th annual cumulation. **1950** (*title*) The music index 1949 annual cumulation. **1969** R. L. COLLISON *Indexes & Indexing* II. 128 If the periodicals index is .. printed for circulation at frequent intervals, the original slips should be retained to enable cumulated .. volumes to be compiled. They will of course require considerable editing for these cumulations. **1987** *Library Assoc. Rec.* Jan. 17/3 A number of title entries appear under 'A' or 'The' instead of the first significant word of the title, presumably because the cumulation is computer generated and some entries do not contain a skipcount.

**cumulative**, *a.* Add: [2.] [a.] Also, *cumulative effect.*

**1856** *Trans. Amer. Med. Assoc.* IX. 761 It was denied for years that strychnia could exhibit any cumulative effects on the animal system. **1914** A. S. BLUMGARTEN *Materia Medica for Nurses* v. 67 The effects produced by the amount of drug which accumulates in the body, are called cumulative effects. **1981** R. HAYMAN *Kafka* vii. 91 The cumulative effect of working six hours a day for six days a week.

**d.** *Math.* Designating a probability distribution which is the integral up to a particular value of a probability density function, and therefore represents the probability that this value is not exceeded by a random variable with this distribution.

**1950** W. FELLER *Introd. Probability Theory & its Applic.* I. vii. 133 The term *distribution function* is used in the mathematical literature for any never-decreasing function $F(x)$ which tends to 0 as $x \to -\infty$, and to 1 as $x \to \infty$. Statisticians currently prefer the term *cumulative distribution function*, but the adjective 'cumulative' is redundant. **1962** D. R. COX *Renewal Theory* i. 3 The distribution of $X$ is determined by the p.d.f., $f(x)$, but it is for some purposes convenient to work with other functions equivalent to $f(x)$. One such is the cumulative distribution function, $F(x)$, giving the probability that a component has failed by time $x$. **1976** *Biometrika* LXIII. 436 Let $G(\lambda)$ be the empirical cumulative distribution function of the numbers $\lambda_1, \ldots, \lambda_r$.

**cupful**, *n.* Add: **2.** *N. Amer. Cookery.* A measure of one half pint or eight fluid ounces.

**1896** F. M. FARMER *Boston Cooking-School Cook Bk.* ii. 28 A *cupful* is a measured level. To measure a cupful, put in the ingredient by spoonfuls or from a scoop, round slightly, and level with a case knife. **1965** R. CAVIN *Compl. Party Dinners for Novice Cook* 43 To make a spoonful or cupful level, smooth off the top with the straight edge of a knife.

‖**curandero** (kuran'dero), *n.* Fem. -era (-era). [Sp., f. *curar* to cure, f. L. *cūrāre.*] In Spain and Latin America: a healer who uses folk remedies, esp. in the treatment of poisonous bites and stings; a herb doctor.

**1943** V. SACKVILLE-WEST *Eagle & Dove* I. vi. 35 She was removed . . to the village of Becedas, where she was subjected to the excruciating mediaeval treatment of a *curandera* or medicine-woman. **1955** A. HUXLEY *Let.* 27 Aug. (1969) 761 Mr Wasson's *curandero* . . under mushroom trance . . in Mexico. **1963** J. R. PEAVEY *Echoes from Rio Grande* iv. 29 When a cure was effected it was not the medicine but the profound faith the patients had in the 'curandero' that accounted for their ultimate recovery. **1984** *Nat. Geographic* Feb. 233/1 Big Bend country, where Jewel Babb practiced the healing arts of the Mexican *curanderas.*

**curate** (kjʊəˈreɪt), *v.* orig. *U.S.* [Back-formation f. CURATOR *n.*; cf. *CURATING *vbl. n.*[3]] *trans.* To act as curator of (a museum, exhibits, etc.); to look after and preserve. So **cu'rated** *ppl. a.*

**1870** H. JAMES *Let.* 13 Feb. (1974) I. 205 Maddersfield Court—a most delightful old curated manor-house. **1934** WEBSTER, *Curate v.t.* **1969** *Daily Tel.* (Colour Suppl.) 6 June 43/4 All London Zoo's mammals were being curated with tremendous flair. **1972** *Nature* 20 Oct. p. xii (Advt.), Mineralogist to curate the meteorite collection which forms part of the National Collection of minerals, rocks, meteorites and ocean bottom deposits. **1978** *Amer. Poetry Rev.* Nov./Dec. 17/3 *A Nest of Hooks* reads like a sort of museum, a beautifully curated warehouse of strange and wonderful things. **1985** M. DIAMOND in S. Davies *By Gains of Industry* 5 We are . . conscious of the debt we owe to those who built what we are now privileged to curate.

**curating** (kjʊəˈreɪtɪŋ), *vbl. n.*[3] [f. *CURATE *v.* + -ING[1].] The supervision of a museum, gallery, or the like by a curator; the work of storing and preserving exhibits.

**1906** W. E. HOYLE in *Museums Jrnl.* July 6, I think it will be generally admitted that the business (or may I say 'profession') of museum 'curating' is one

which demands . . a special technical training. **1972** J. I. M. STEWART *Palace of Art* xxv. 230 You've been doing the curating, after all. **1986** *Sunday Express Mag.* 6 Apr. 90/3 Inheriting a family business such as this, you feel duty-bound to do your curating bit and carry on the history of it.

**curation**, *n.* Restrict †*Obs.* to sense 1 in Dict. and relabel sense 2 '*Obs.* exc. as in sense b.' Add: [2.] **b.** The supervision by a curator of a collection of preserved or exhibited items.

**1979** D. WORSLEY in M. G. Bassett *Curation Palaeontol. Collections* 145 It may be neither politically practical nor scientifically desirable to locate type collections in their country of origin, especially if that country cannot provide acceptable standards of curation. **1982** *Times* 21 Oct. 10/7 He continued his own research and also devoted himself to the curation of the university's important bird collection. **1986** *Times* 10 Nov. 17/4 Without a substantial increase . . in funds . ., this museum would have to . . reduce . . its curation of the national collections.

**current**, *n.* Add: [7.] **c.** *Particle Physics.* A transfer or exchange of a subatomic particle, esp. a particle that mediates an interaction between other particles; a particle so transferred.

**1958** *Physical Rev.* CIX. 196/1 Imagine that the interaction is due to some intermediate (electrically charged) vector meson of very high mass $M_0$. If this meson is coupled to the 'current' $(\bar{\psi}_p \gamma_\mu a \psi_n)$ and $(\bar{\psi}_\mu \gamma_\mu a \psi_\nu)$ by a coupling . ., then the interaction of the two 'currents' would result from the exchange of this 'meson' if $4\pi f^2 M_0^{-2} = (8)^{1/2}$ G. *Ibid.*, The current of pions. **1964** *Physics Lett.* XIII. 169/2 When we come to consider hadrons the absence of neutral leptonic currents interacting with heavy particles requires that we assume $X^0$ particles are at least as massive as $W^+$ or $W^-$. **1978** *Nature* 11 May 98/2 Here two charged leptonic currents interact, one of them turning a muon into a mu-neutrino, the other generating an electron and its antineutrino. **1980** J. TREFIL *From Atoms to Quarks* xiii. 203 The beta decay of the neutron . . . It proceeds by the exchange of a W boson which is called the charged current. A similar process in which a Z is exchanged would be said to proceed by the exchange of a neutral current. **1983** *McGraw-Hill Yearbk. Sci. & Technol. 1984* 142/2 Interest in beta decay stems from the predictions of modern gauge theories that the helicity of the weak leptonic current is not exact, being broken either by a small right-handed current admixture . . or by a nonzero neutrino mass.

**curricular**, *a.* Restrict *rare* to sense in Dict. and add: **2.** Of or pertaining to an educational curriculum. Cf. *extra-curricular* s.v. EXTRA- 1. orig. *U.S.*

**1909** in *Cent. Dict. Suppl.* **1915** *Jrnl. Proc. & Addresses National Educ. Assoc.* (U.S.) 738 In all strictly curricular activities the social aspects of education are sadly overlooked. **1924** C. F. ALLEN *Extra-Curricular Activities* 3 There must be a definitely planned program broader than is now generally provided in the curricular programs of secondary schools. **1975** *Language for Life* (Dept. Educ. & Sci.) xxvi. 547 Where a school has a curricular need for a particular audio-visual aid every effort should be made to provide it. **1985** *Chron. Higher Educ.* 27 Mar. 12/1 Many of the institutions that have pursued curricular reform have run into trouble because faculty members assigned the task have lacked the background . . to make broad changes.

‖**Cursillo** (kurˈsiʎo; kʊəˈsiːjəʊ, -ˈsiːljəʊ) *n.*, [Sp., lit. 'little course' (see quot. 1964).] A short, evangelizing course of intensive religious study and exercise, organized mainly by lay people and orig. developed in Spain in 1949 to counteract an apparent decline in popular religious commitment.

**1959** *Ultreya* 15 Aug. 9 The Cursillos can assume . . the role of being the most important social movement that Catholicism has produced in these latter days. **1961** *Lamp* Mar. 16/1 You'll never know what a *Cursillo* is until you've seen and lived one. **1964** *Ave Maria* Feb. 5/2 A Cursillo (from *Cursillos de Cristiandad*, Little Courses in Christianity) is a three-day program of intensive prayer, study, discussion and community living. **1973** *Episcopal Churchman Diocese of Dallas* Apr. 3/2 Cursillos are planned from May, July, September and October this year. **1986** *Oxf. Diocesan Mag.* Nov. 11/1 Cursillo, unlike a retreat, is not silent. **1987** *Washington Diocese* Feb.-Mar. 4/1 The Cursillo goal of Christianizing one's environment.

Hence **Cursi'llista** *n.* [Sp. *-ista* -IST], one who takes part in a *Cursillo.*

**1959** *Ultreya* 15 Aug. 2 We Cursillistas are bound together by the highest possible bond, supernatural charity. **1961** *Lamp* Mar. 17/2 This initial talk set up the *Cursillista* for his wholehearted acceptance of Christ as his ideal. **1978** *N.Y. Times* 9 Feb. 35 After the emotional reception, the new Cursillistas were escorted to parties throughout the area.

**cursus**, *n.* Add: **e. cursus honorum** (ɒ'nɔːrəm) [lit., 'course of honours'], an established hierarchy of positions through which a person may advance in a profession, career, etc., orig. in Anc. Rome leading to the consulship; hence, a succession of posts held on a course of advancement.

**1908** H. S. JONES *Roman Empire* vii. 270 The tribunate and ædileship were abolished, or at any rate ceased to form alternative steps in the *cursus honorum* of the senator. **1959** B. & R. NORTH tr. *Duverger's Pol. Parties* (ed. 2) I. iii. 160 To attain to the posts of real command, a slow *cursus honorum* must be completed; you have to be 'apprenticed' to the party. **1965** *Mod. Law Rev.* XXVIII. 517 By 1932 the *cursus honorum* had been established within the judiciary. **1970** *Times* 14 Mar. (Sat. Rev.) p. iv/7 Some might find it remarkable that such a *cursus honorum*—Dean of King's College London, Dean of Exeter, Dean of St. Paul's—should have fallen to so liberal a thinker.

**custodial**, *a.* Add: [2.] *custodial care* orig. *U.S.*, the supervision and care of mentally or physically infirm persons in an appropriate institution.

**1874** *Jrnl. Social Sci.* (N.Y.) July 61 An obligation rests upon the State to direct . . that the restraint should be properly and humanely exercised, and the *custodial care combined with . . remedial measures. **1914** H. H. GODDARD *Feeble-Mindedness* x. 578 These . . technically called *imbeciles*, also require more or less custodial care. **1949** A. DEUTSCH *Mentally Ill in Amer.* (ed. 2) xii. 233 Chronics, being for the most part beyond cure, require only custodial care and could be accommodated much more cheaply in asylums. **1986** *Guardian* 16 July 13/1 Any . . longstay institution with traditions of custodial care over patients who are particularly vulnerable.

**customize**, *v.* Add: **'customizer** *n.* (*esp.* one who customizes motor vehicles).

**1959** *N.Y. Times* 29 Nov. 83/1 Customizer, he found, was a youngster who delighted in changing the appearance of the family car. **1963** *Esquire* (U.K. ed.) Nov. 115/2 To Barris and the customizers there is no one great universe of form and design called Art. **1985** *Truck & Driver* June 46/1 The truck customisers themselves look set to become celebrities in their own right—even if their trucks do tend to take an unfair share of the glory.

**cutesy** ('kjuːtsɪ), *a. colloq.* (orig. and chiefly *N. Amer.*). Also **cutesie**. [f. CUTE *a.* + -SY.] Affectedly cute and clever, twee. Also with fanciful extension, **'cutesy-poo.**

**1968** *N.Y. Times Bk. Rev.* 25 Feb. 10 Start with the cutesie title. Pursue the mysteriously jumbled chronology. **1968** *Time* 7 June 4 The music that interrupts the cutesy dialogue is standard Mozart. **1973** *New York* 22 Oct. 104, I feel like a rotten old cynic saying anything narsty about so cutesy-poo an endeavor as *The Optimists*. **1976** *New Musical Express* 31 July 9/1 It works because it never gets cutesy. I'm proud of the music. **1976** *Daily Colonist* (Victoria, B.C.) 4 June 9/2 'It would look like a comic strip,' said Jamie, 'too cutesy.' **1979** R. JAFFE *Class Reunion* (1980) I. viii. 117 She had curly hair and a turned-up nose and looked so cutesy-poo that Chris wanted to smack her. **1987** *Washington Post* 19 Apr. E9/3 My ol' Daddy . . warned me never to eat at a place called Mom's . . and to stay away from restaurants with cutesy names like 'Ugly Mug'.

**cyanolabe** ('saɪənəʊˌleɪb), *n. Physiol.* [f. CYANO-1 + Gr. λαβ- to take, seize.] A blue-sensitive pigment present in the cones of the retina. Cf. *CHLOROLABE n.*, *ERYTHROLABE n.*

**1958** [see *ERYTHROLABE n.*] **1983** J. G. CREAGER *Human Anat. & Physiol.* xiv. 360/2 Cones that contain erytholabe are most sensitive to red light, those that contain chlorolabe are most sensitive to green light and those that contain cyanolabe are most sensitive to blue light.

**cyanophycin** (ˌsaɪənəʊ'faɪsɪn), *n. Biochem.* [a. It. *cianoficina* (A. Borzi 1886, in *Malpighia* I. 79): cf. CYANO-, PHYCIC *a.*, -IN¹.] A polypeptide present in the form of food storage granules in most cyanobacteria.

**1896** *Q. Jrnl. Microsc. Sci.* XXXVIII. 263 The granules he looks upon as crystals belonging to the regular system, and composed of a substance 'cyanophycin', which . . he regards as related to the chromatin and pyrenin of highly specialised vegetable cells. **1965** *Biol. Rev.* XL. 157 The characteristic storage product in blue-green algae is represented by large cyanophycin granules. **1983** S. HOLMES *Outl. Plant Classification* (1986) iv. 22 Food reserves include a special starch, cyanophycean or myxophycean starch, and a protein, cyanophycin.

**cyclic**, *a.* Add: [5.] **b.** *Algebra.* Of a group: having the property that each element of the group may be expressed as a power of a particular element, sometimes called the generator (see GENERATOR *n.* 4 b) of the group.

**1889** O. BOLZA in *Amer. Jrnl. Math.* XI. 205 The *cyclic group* of the order *n* can be generated by a single substitution *a*, satisfying the relation $a^n = 1$, and no other relation $a^{n'} = 1$ where $n' < n$. **1901** [see UNDER *prep.* 13 f]. **1940** [see GENERATOR *n.* 4 b]. **1983** R. B. J. T. ALLENBY *Rings, Fields & Groups* v. 213 In the case of infinite cyclic groups the prototype is the group $\mathbb{Z}, +$).

**cystinosis** (sɪstɪ'nəʊsɪs), *n. Path.* [f. CYSTINE *n.* + -OSIS.] An inborn error of metabolism resulting in the accumulation of cystine in the body.

**1949** *Adv. Pediatrics* IV. 265 The cystinuria in cystinosis . . is temporary and irregular in nature, and is never a particularly conspicuous feature of the disease. **1954** *Proc. R. Soc. Med.* XLVII. 882 This is a typical renal failure pattern, the presence of cystine being fully consistent with cystinosis. **1964** S. DUKE-ELDER *Parsons' Dis. Eye* (ed. 14) xvi. 219 Deposits of cystine may be associated with a generalized cystinosis, renal dwarfism and osteoporosis. **1973** *Nature* 3 Aug. 290/1 Hybridizing a fibroblast from a child with cystinosis with a non-cystinotic cell might elucidate the metabolism of cystine. **1983** *Oxf. Textbk. Med.* I. ix. 99/2 Cystinosis is not related to cystinuria; confusion has arisen in the past because the generalized amino aciduria, which is a component of the Fanconi syndrome induced by cystinosis, includes cystine and this amino acid was more easily detectable than most others before chromatographic methods became available.

Hence **cysti'notic** *a.*, containing excess cystine; exhibiting cystinosis.

**1961** *Lancet* 21 Oct. 909/2 The demonstration of almost total lack of succinic dehydrogenase activity in fresh necropsy samples of cystinotic liver. **1978** *Nature* 26 Oct. 696/1 Recently fibroblasts from a cystinotic patient were partially depleted of lysosomal cystine after exposure to liposome-entrapped cysteamine.

**cyto-**, *comb. form.* Add: ,**cytoarchitec'tonic** *a. Med.*, pertaining to the arrangement of cells in a tissue; *spec.* designating numbered areas of the cerebral cortex (associated with particular functions) which are characterized by the ways their cells are arranged in layers.

[**1911** M. LEYBOFF (*title*) Cyto-architektonische Studien über den Nucleus caudatus.] **1917** DORLAND *Med. Dict.* (ed. 9) 278/1 *Cytoarchitectonic. **1929** S. PARKER tr. *C. von Economo's Cytoarchitectonics Human Cerebral Cortex* ii. 24 Cytoarchitectonic pathology is .. still in its infancy. **1978** *Nature* 3 Aug. 423/2 Because no clear cytoarchitectonic differences are evident over large extents of the prestriate cortex, much of it (for example Brodmann's area 18) was considered, mistakenly as we now know, to be a single cortical 'area'. **1987** S. M. STAHL et al. *Cognitive Neurochem.* vii. 98 Each cytoarchitectonic subdivision cortex terminates in a specific region within the neostriatum.

,**cytoarchitec'tonics** *n. pl.* (const. as *sing.* or *pl.*) *Med.*, the cytoarchitectonic properties of a tissue or organ; the field of study concerned with these.

[**1909** G. MARINESCO in *Comptes Rendus Hebd. Soc. Biol.* (Paris) LXVI. 55 (*heading*) Note sur la cytoarchitectonie des circonvolutions Rolandiques. **1925** C. VON ECONOMO (*title*) Die Cytoarchitektonik der Hirnrinde des erwachsenen Menschen.] **1947** *Brain* LXX. 225 The assumption that the position of suppressor bands in man can be calculated from cortical *cytoarchitectonics is likely to be fallacious. **1978** *Nature* 3 Aug. 423/1 It was also based in part on the anatomical method of cytoarchitectonics, which analyses how cells in different parts of the cerebral cortex are grouped into layers. **1988** *Ibid.* 28 Jan. 348/1 At this age the cytoarchitectonics of area 17 are quite distinctive.

**cyto'architecture** *Med.* = *cytoarchitectonics* above.

**1933** *Arch. Neurol. & Psychiatry* (Chicago) XXX. 1205 (*heading*) Electrical excitability and *cytoarchitecture of the premotor cortex in monkeys. **1974** D. & M. WEBSTER *Compar. Vertebr. Morphol.* xii. 298 A close relationship is found between the anatomy of fiber projections, the physiology of responses, and the cytoarchitecture of the areas. **1987** SANETO & DE VELLIS in Turner & Bachelard *Neurochem.* ii. 27 The hierarchy of cytoarchitecture and network of cellular processes combined with isolation (blood-brain barrier) makes studies *in vivo* difficult to perform and interpret.

hence ,**cytoarchi'tectural** *a.*

**1936** *Jrnl. Compar. Neurol.* LXIII. 370 An attempt has been made to trace the efferent projection fibers of the *cytoarchitectural divisions of the frontal lobe. **1974** D. & M. WEBSTER *Compar. Vertebr. Morphol.* xii. 298 Cytoarchitectural studies on some other mammals .. have demonstrated similar cytoarchitectural areas in similar topographic areas.

,**cytoarchi'tecturally** *adv.*, as regards cytoarchitectonics, from a cytoarchitectonic point of view.

**1948** A. BRODAL *Neurol. Anat.* vi. 159 These sensory cortical areas differ *cytoarchitecturally from the surrounding areas. **1978** *Nature* 3 Aug. 423/1 Considered cytoarchitecturally, the entire

visual cortex of the rhesus monkey can be subdivided into two major zones.

'**cyto,centrifuge**, a centrifuge used for fixing cytological specimens (i.e. individual cells in fluid suspension) to microscope slides; freq. *attrib.*

**1967** in *Experientia* (1972) XXVIII. 775/2 (*title*) Shandon *Cyto-centrifuge SCA-0001, Shandon Scientific Co., Ltd., London, NW10, England; Operating Instructions. **1975** *Nature* 12 June 555/1 The cells were examined for rosette formation .. in a haemocytometer, and Giemsa stained cytocentrifuge preparations.

**cyto'cidal** *a.*, that kills cells.

**1929** DORLAND & MILLER *Med. Dict.* (ed. 15) 338/1 *Cytocidal. **1962** *Lancet* 22 Dec. 1312/2 He concludes that a continuing virus-cell relationship in which infectious virus is rarely released is characteristic of the tumour-producing infection, as opposed to the usual cytocidal infection. **1988** *Nature* 22 Sept. 369/1 Targeted toxins represent a new approach to specific cytocidal therapy.

hence **cyto'cidally** *adv.*

**1973** R. G. KRUEGER et al. *Introd. Microbiol.* xxi. 558/2 Cells .. *cytocidally or permissively infected with these agents .. yield 500-1000 progeny viruses per cell.

**cyto'megalic** *a. Med.*, characterized by enlarged cells; chiefly in **cytomegalic inclusion disease**, (a) disease caused by a cytomegalovirus.

**1950** J. P. WYATT et al. in *Jrnl. Pediatrics* XXXVI. 271 (*heading*) Generalized *cytomegalic inclusion disease. *Ibid.*, Cytomegalic is derived from the term 'cytomegalia' originally used by Goodpasture in 1921 to indicate the bizarre cytological alteration characteristic of the disease to be incorporated into its name. **1962** *Lancet* 15 Dec. 1267/2 Although as yet, only a few maternal diseases—such as syphilis, rubella .. and cytomegalic inclusion disease .. are definitely known to produce mental defect in the infant, these present distinct possibilities of prevention. **1976** EDINGTON & GILLES *Path. in Tropics* (ed. 2) iv. 262 Cytomegalic inclusion disease is a relatively common infection in the neonate and inclusion bodies were present in the submandibular salivary gland in 7 per cent of our necropsies performed on stillbirths and neonates. **1989** COLLIER & LONGMORE *Oxf. Handbk. Clin. Specialties* (ed. 2) ii. 98, 3/1000 live births are infected of whom 5% have cytomegalic inclusion disease.

'**cytophil, -phile** *a.* [a. G. *cytophil* (Ehrlich & Morgenroth 1901, in *Berliner klin. Wochenschr.* 27 May 571/1): see -PHIL, -PHILE], = *cytophilic* adj. below.

**1902** *Cytophil [see HAPTOPHOROUS *a.*]. **1906** C. BOLDUAN tr. *Ehrlich's Coll. Stud. Immunity* 581 The amboceptor has the affinity of its cytophile group increased.

**cyto'philic** *a.* [f. *cytophil* adj. above], having an affinity for cells; *spec.* designating an antibody which binds to cells other than at sites specific for it.

**1909** *Cent. Dict. Suppl.*, *Cytophilic. **1933** W. W. C. TOPLEY *Outl. Immunity* v. 81 The haptophore that attaches itself to the antigen-containing cell is the cytophilic group. **1977** *Lancet* 19 Mar. 637/2 Two further patients with systemic symptoms had immediate prick-test reactions to *A. fumigatus* and possessed IgE and IgG cytophilic antibody. **1981** GREENWOOD & WHITTLE *Immunol. of Med. in Tropics* ii. 35 Schistosomula can also be killed *in vitro* by macrophages armed with cytophilic IgE antibody.

hence **cyto'philically** *adv.*

**1970** HARRIS & SINKOVICS *Immunol. Malignant Dis.* i. 6 Antibody may have opsonized the antigen before it reaches the lymph node or may be *cytophilically attached to the phagocytic cell of the lymph node. **1978** *Clin. & Exper. Immunol.* XXXI. 226 The IgG is intrinsic to the cell and not cytophilically bound.

**cytopho'tometer**, a photometer for use in cytophotometry.

**1952** M. J. MOSES in *Exper. Cell Res. Suppl.* II. 75 Design and use of the *cytophotometer. **1978** *Nature* 24 Aug. 822/1 Proportional fluorometry of 1C, 2C and 4C mouse testis cells can be achieved by . . staining with ethidium bromide and mithramycin, and measurement in a pulse cytophotometer with a high numerical aperture for excitation and measurement.

**cytopho'tometry**, the investigation of the contents of cells by photometric measurement of the light they transmit after staining; hence ,**cytophoto'metric** *a.*; ,**cytophoto'metrically** *adv.*, by means of cytophotometry.

**1952** M. J. MOSES in *Exper. Cell Res. Suppl.* II. 82 Statistical variations within populations of typical *cytophotometric samples. **1973** *Nature* 12 Jan. 126/1 Cytophotometric measurements of Feulgen-stained erythrocyte nuclei show that the DNA content of *Latimeria* erythrocyte nuclei is 13.2 pg. **1970** *Nature* 21 Nov. 783/2 The density of the staining with azure B was measured *cytophotometrically at 545 nm. **1984** *Internat. Jrnl. Insect Morphol. & Embryol.* XIII. 21 The development of follicle cells encompassing the growing oocytes of the stick insect . . has been investigated cytologically and cytophotometrically. **1952** M. J. MOSES in *Exper. Cell. Res. Suppl.* II. 75 The same analytical spectrophotometric treatment that is applied to 'colored' solutions in tubes and cuvettes may also be applied to 'colored' cell structures imaged by the microscope . . . In the interest of clarification and simplification, the terms *cytophotometry* and *cytospectrophotometry* are proposed for the application of these methods in cytology. **1978** *Nature* 24 Aug. 821/2 We have been able to resolve the two classes of spermatids by pulse cytophotometry (that is, flow microfluorometry).

**'cytoskeleton**, a network of protein filaments and tubules in the cytoplasm of many eukaryotic cells that gives the cell shape and coherence; hence **cyto'skeletal** *a.*

**1949** R. A. PETERS in *Adv. Sci.* VI. 265/2 The '*cytoskeletal' hypothesis includes . . the assumption that there are fibres in cells maintaining the gel-like structure. **1981** *Sci. Amer.* Mar. 41/2 There are at least three chemically distinct cytoskeletal systems: the microtubules, the microfilaments and the intermediate filaments. **1984** HOLTZMAN & NOVIKOFF *Cells & Organelles* (ed. 3) ii. 287 In mammalian red blood cells, actin is linked to the protein spectrin, forming a cytoskeletal protein network that lies just below the cell surface. **1941** R. A. PETERS in G. Bourne *Cytol. & Cell Physiol.* (1942) p. v, Some years ago the writer of this foreword was forced to urge the need for . . co-operation [between cytologists and biochemists] . . about the nucleo-proteins, finding a possible solution of some difficulties about the living cell in a conception which has subsequently been called the '*cyto-skeleton'. **1987** *Nature* 26 Mar. 332/2 In fact it is not mitochondria, but the nucleus, endomembrane system and cytoskeleton that are the true hallmarks of the eukaryote cell.

**'cytosol** [SOL(UBLE *a.*], the aqueous part of cytoplasm, remaining as supernatant under centrifugation that precipitates the organelles.

**1965** H. A. LARDY in B. Chance et al. *Control of Energy Metabolism* 245 The term *cytosol* will be used to designate that portion of the cell which is found in the supernatant fraction after centrifuging the homogenate at 105,000 x g for 1 hour. It refers specifically to the cytoplasm minus mitochondria and endoplasmic reticulum components. **1972** *Science* 7 July 56/1 Although long-chain fatty acids are at best poorly soluble in aqueous media, a mechanism to account for the apparent facility with which they traverse the cytosol (aqueous cytoplasm) has not been identified. **1985** *Sci. Amer.* Aug. 32/3 At two junctures in the process of adrenaline synthesis crucial substances synthesized in the cytosol of the chromaffin cell must be transported into the chromaffin vesicles.

hence **cyto'solic** *a.*

**1971** *Biochem. & Biophys. Res. Communications* XLIV. 151 The extramitochondrial *cytosolic compartment of the liver cell. **1982** T. M. DEVLIN *Textbk. Biochem.* xxi. 1020 The mitochondria are impermeable to cytosolic oxalacetate.

**cytochalasin** (saɪtəʊkəˈleɪsɪn), *n. Biol.* [f. CYTO- + Gr. χαλάσις slackening, dislocation, f. χαλᾶν to relax: see -IN[1].] Any of several fungal metabolites (*cytochalasin A, B*, etc.) that are polycyclic macrolides used experimentally in cell research for their property of interfering with cellular processes; *esp.* cytochalasin B.

**1966** *New Scientist* 27 Oct. 170/1 An extraordinary group of organic compounds which have been isolated from mould culture filtrates by Dr. S. B. Carter and Dr. W. B. Turner . . have been called 'cytochalasins'. **1967** S. B. CARTER in *Nature* 21 Jan. 261/1 Several species of moulds have been found to produce a number of chemically related metabolites which show unusual biological activity. The name 'cytochalasin' . . is suggested for this new class of compounds. The name is . . a general description of the effects . . characteristic of these substances. *Ibid.* 261/2 Cytochalasin *B* . . has a novel macrolide structure in which the lactone ring is joined to a bicyclic lactam system. **1978** W. G. THILLY et al. in S. W. Tanenbaum *Cytochalasins* iii. 61 These studies may be summarized by concluding that cytochalasin A has been shown to be a bactericide and fungicide, cytochalasin D has been shown to be a fungicide but not a bactericide, while cytochalasin B has been shown to be without toxic effects for bacteria, fungi, algae, and protozoans. **1984** HOLTZMAN & NOVIKOFF *Cells & Organelles* (ed. 3) II. xi. 286 Probably the effects of cytochalasins and phalloidin on the filaments result in large part from their influencing actin assembly and interlinking.

**cytomegalovirus** (saɪtəʊˈmɛgələʊvaɪərəs), *n. Med.* [f. *cytomegalic* adj. s.v. *CYTO- + -O[1] + VIRUS n.*] Any of a group of herpesviruses which produce enlargement of infected cells and distinctive nuclear inclusion bodies, typically producing few or very mild symptoms but freq. leading to severe neurological symptoms in immunocompromised individuals and the new-born. Abbrev. *CMV* s.v. *C* III. 3.

**1960** T. H. WELLER et al. in *Virology* XII. 131 It is . . proposed that the so-called SGV-CID [*sc.* salivary gland virus-cytomegalic inclusion disease virus] viruses of man and animals be referred to as the 'cytomegalovirus' group. **1965** *Brit. Med. Jrnl.* 18 Sept. 663/2 Previously known as salivary-gland viruses, the cytomegaloviruses of man resemble the salivary-gland viruses of rodents. **1976** *Daily Colonist* (Victoria, B.C.) 17 Oct. 15/4 Some doctors suspect the malady may be caused by a virus of the cytomegalovirus family. Usually a cytomegalovirus causes such mild illness in adults they don't know they have it. **1976** *Path. Ann.* XI. 56 Cytomegalovirus (CMV) infection can be acquired in utero, or by persons in states of immune deficiency or suppression, and by immune competent infants shortly after birth. **1980** *Brit. Med. Jrnl.* 29 Mar. 892/2 Nineteen of the episodes had resulted from a viral hepatitis (caused by hepatitis B surface antigen in 18 cases and cytomegalovirus in one).

# D

**daily**, *a.* (*n.*) Add: [A.] [3.] **daily double** *Racing* (orig. and chiefly *U.S.*), a bet on the winners of two designated races (often the first and second) on one day of a meeting; also, the two races selected by the track for the bet; cf. \***DOUBLE** *n.* 3 s.

**1932** *N.Y. Times* 7 Sept. 15/2 The *daily double at Blue Bonnets today paid one man $3,489.50. **1964** A. WYKES *Gambling* viii. 193 You can put your money on a 'daily double', which is usually run on the first two races of the day. **1987** *Washington Post* 19 Sept. C3/5 Regular triple betting will be offered on the sixth and eighth races, and the daily double will be pushed back to the sixth and seventh races.

**dalapon** ('dæləpɒn), *n.* Also **Dalapon**. [Prob. f. initial and other letters of *di-alpha-propionic* (acid): see DI-².] A selective herbicide used against perennial grasses, usually as the water-soluble sodium salt; 2,2-dichloropropionic acid, $CH_3CCl_2COOH$.

**1953** *Farm Jrnl.* Sept. 17/1 A new chemical, called Dalapon, may be what we need to knock out some of the grassy weeds that 2,4-D won't touch. **1960** *Farmer & Stockbreeder* 8 Mar. 71/1 With the aid of dalapon, went on Dr. Hunter, we should be more able to change the botanical composition of hill swards. **1978** *Daily Tel.* 22 Apr. 11/8 But what about couch grass? There is weedkiller that deals specifically with this . . . This one is called Dalapon. **1988** *New Scientist* 17 Mar. 57/1 To prevent one variety of plant from dominating, you can burn or cut the vegetation or apply a herbicide such as dalapon.

**dangling**, *ppl. a.* Add: **b.** *Gram.* Not being part of a proper grammatical construction. Freq. as **dangling participle**, a participle in an absolute clause or phrase whose subject is omitted, resulting in ambiguity; an unattached participle. Also *dangling modifier, phrase*, etc.

**1909** WEBSTER, Dangling participle. **1935** A. G. KENNEDY *Current English* xii. 487 The so-called dangling participle has become one of the chief bugbears of the teacher of English composition. **1957** M. NICHOLSON *Dict. Amer.-Eng. Usage* 115/1 *Dangling participle.* Wrong: *Having just returned from a long cruise, the city seemed unbearably crowded to us both.* **1961** *Amer. Speech* XXXVI. 196 Let us examine, then, these dangling modifiers in 'Bartleby', looking at each of them in turn to see what . . aid it can give us in understanding the obscurities of the tale. **1972** R. D. WALSHE in G. W. Turner *Good Austral. Eng.* 256 Dangling phrases. In the sentence, 'Going into the bush, a snake bit me', the opening phrase 'dangles' because it is not followed by its proper subject. **1985** W. SAFIRE in *N.Y. Times Mag.* 12 May 14/2 Miss Shields, though perhaps guilty of a misplaced modifier, is surely innocent of a dangling modifier.

**darter**, *n.* Add: **6.** *Ent.* Any dragonfly whose flight behaviour is characterized by darting to and from a particular perch; *spec.* a member of the family Libellulidae. Also *darter dragonfly*.

[**1917** R. J. TILLYARD *Biol. Dragonflies* xvii. 322 Amongst the *Aeschnidae* in general, a 'darting' method of flight is very evident, the insect progressing by a series of jerks.] **1937** C. LONGFIELD *Dragonflies Brit. Isles* 38 Anisoptera. Hawker and darter dragon-flies. **1987** *Camera Weekly* 25 July 56/2

Powder blue or crimson darters repeatedly return to the same prominent twig.

**Dartford** ('dɑːtfəd), *n. Ornith.* [The name of a town in Kent near where the bird was first seen in England.] **Dartford warbler**, a small dark Old World warbler, *Sylvia undata*, of heaths and scrublands in southern Europe and parts of North Africa and southern England.

**1776** T. PENNANT *Brit. Zool.* (ed. 4) I. 329 Dartford warbler . . . A pair of these were shot on a common near Dartford, in April 1773, and communicated to me by Mr. Latham. **1831** J. RENNIE *Montagu's Ornith. Dict.* (ed. 2) 128 It is called the Dartford Warbler, from . . a pair having been killed on Bexley Heath, near Dartford, on the 10th of April, 1773. **1853** F. O. MORRIS *Hist. Brit. Birds* III. 256 The Dartford Warbler is exclusively confined to heaths and commons. **1930** J. S. HUXLEY *Bird-Watching* ii. 27, I saw my first dartford warbler, my first smew, Montagu's harrier, and so on. **1965** P. WAYRE *Wind in Reeds* ii. 19 The tiny Dartford warbler, the only warbler to brave the English winter. **1979** *Jrnl. R. Soc. Arts* CXXVII. 405/2 The heathland . . is the habitat . . of many insects and of the Dartford Warbler. **1989** *Times* 9 Feb. 18/3 Britain's small population of Dartford Warblers is now heavily concentrated in one area, the New Forest.

**Darwin**, *n.* Add: **2.** (Without cap. initial.) A proposed unit of rate of evolutionary change, equal to an increase or decrease in the size of some specified character by a factor of *e* per million years; one thousand millidarwins.

**1949** J. B. S. HALDANE in *Evolution* III. 55/2 It may be found desirable to coin some word, for example a *darwin*, for a unit of evolutionary rate, such as an increase or decrease of size by a factor of *e* per million years, or, what is practically equivalent, an increase or decrease of $1/1000$ per 1000 years. If so the horse rates would range round 40 millidarwins. **1970** *Nature* 17 Jan. 296/2 From *Homo erectus* at Choukoutien to *H. sapiens* the rate of decrease in both upper and lower canines was nearly 1 darwin. **1983** E. C. MINKOFF *Evolutionary Biol.* xix. 321/2 The evolutionist J. B. S. Haldane has proposed that a relative change by a factor of *e* (the base of natural logarithms) per million years be known as a *darwin*.

**dashing**, *ppl. a.* Add: [2.] **b.** *Dashing White Sergeant* [the title of a song composed *a* 1792 by General Burgoyne, and incorporated into the libretto of a popular operetta by Sir Henry Bishop], a lively Scottish country dance performed in sets of three (devised by David Anderson of Dundee *c* 1890 and set to Bishop's tune); also, †an English dance of the early 19th. cent.

[**1825** in C. E. Pearce *Madame Vestris* (1923) 116 The stamping sort of sauce-box air with which she marched away to the tune of the 'Dashing White Sergeant'.] **1929** G. D. TAYLOR *Some Trad. Scottish Dances* 76 (*heading*) The Dashing White Sergeant. **1956** J. C. MILLIGAN *101 Scottish Country Dances* 5 The dashing white sergeant . . is a circle reel-time dance. Dancers stand in a circle round the room in 3s. A man between 2 ladies faces a lady between 2 men. The man between 2 ladies moves clockwise and the other three counter-clockwise. **1977** *Time Out* 28 Jan.-3 Feb. 10/4 These societies gather and eat herrings and dance the Dashing White Sergeant (a

visionary Scottish country dance that involves two
people of one sex and one of the other).

**daughterboard** ('dɔːtəbɔːd), *n. Electronics.* Also
daughter board. [f. DAUGHTER *n.* + BOARD *n.*,
after \*MOTHERBOARD *n.*] A printed circuit board
on which are mounted some of the (esp.
optional or subsidiary) components of a
microcomputer or other electronic device, and
which may be connected to a motherboard.
**1971** *Electrical & Electronics Abstr.* LXXIV. 118/2
To allow each channel to have its own controls each
per channel circuitry is located on one daughterboard
mounted vertically on a computer size motherboard.
**1980** *Amer. Banker* 11 June 8/1 Eight 16K 'daughter
boards', each of which can be held in one's hand,
make up a complete memory board. **1986** *New
Scientist* 6 Feb. 34/1 The main memory of the M-780
..consists of one 'mother' board, with 32 'daughter'
boards mounted at right angles to it. **1987** *InfoWorld*
9 Nov. 33 Onboard with the Intel 80386 processor is
up to 8 megabytes of 32-bit dynamic RAM
shoehorned onto a daughterboard using 1-megabyte
chips.

**daunomycin** (,dɔːnəʊ'maisɪn), *n. Pharm.* [ad.
It. *daunomicina* (A. di Marco et al. 1963, in
*Tumori* (Milan) XLIX. 203), f. the name of
*Daun*(ia, a former region of Puglia (Apulia) in
S. Italy: see -o¹ and -MYCIN *n.*] =
\*DAUNORUBICIN *n.*
**1963** *Tumori* (Milan) XLIX. 203 Daunomycin is a
new antibiotic isolated from cultures of *Streptomyces
peucetius.* **1977** *Lancet* 14 May 1050/1 The patient..
went into early drug-resistant relapse with multiple
chloromas..7 months after the induction of a
complete remission following a course of cytarabine
and daunomycin. **1987** *Transplantation* XLIV. 770/1
We have used daunomycin..as the cytocidal
component of immunotoxin.

**daunorubicin** (,dɔːnəʊ'ruːbɪsɪn), *n. Pharm.* [f.
\*DAUNO(MYCIN *n.* + *rubi-* red (as in RUBICUND
*a.*, etc.) + MY)CIN *n.*] An anthracycline
antibiotic C₂₇H₂₉NO₁₀, with antineoplastic
activity, used against leukaemias, lymphomas,
and some other cancers.
**1969** *Lancet* 15 Feb. 333/1 Clinical interest in
daunorubicin..stemmed from the strong inhibitory
effects of this antibiotic on the in-vitro growth of
mammalian cells. **1977** *Ibid.* 18 June 1307/2 Six
adults (four with acute myeloblastic leukaemia and
two with promyelocytic leukaemia) were treated with
daunorubicin..associated with cytarabine. **1987**
*Analyst* CXII. 1303/1 The anthracycline antibiotic
daunorubicin is a widely used anticancer drug, owing
to its clinical efficacy against a wide range of
malignancies.

**day**, *n.* Add: [VI.] [24.] **day letter** *U.S.* (now
*Hist.*), a cheap-rate, low-priority telegram
delivered on the day it is sent; cf. NIGHT LETTER
*n.* a.
**1910** H. L. SELLERS in *Hearing Bill 19402* (U.S.
Congress. Senate Comm. on District of Columbia) 15
We naturally are very eager..to complete the line..
so that the..capital may have..a real night letter
that will mean something to them. It will be a \*day
letter as well as a night letter. **1960** NANASSY &
SELDEN *Business Dict.* 57 The day letter is not
handled so speedily as the full-rate message.

**dead lift**, *n.* Add: [3.] (Earlier and later
examples.) Also, a lift made without
mechanical or other assistance; *spec.* in
*Weightlifting*, the controlled raising of a weight
from the floor to hip-level and back again; an
instance of this.
**1828** in WEBSTER. *a*1865 SMYTH *Sailor's Word-bk.*
(1867) 236 *Dead-lift*, the moving of a very inert body.
**1910** W. S. CHURCHILL in R. S. Churchill *Winston S.*

Churchill (1969) II. Compan. II. xiii. 969 Even if by a
dead-lift effort we succeeded in carrying it..the
work would remain unfinished. **1942** *Life* 20 Apr.
92/2 *(caption)* Joe Frank..makes a new National
A.A.U. record in the one-hand dead lift. **1954** J.
MURRAY *Weight Lifting* ii. 43 The best clearly
authenticated dead lift on record is 725 pounds. **1986**
*Strength Athlete* June/July 33/4 The pulling speed
used in the deadlift..is slower because of the heavier
load.

**deafferent** (diː'æfərənt), *v. Biol.* and *Med.* [f.
DE- II. 2 + AFFERENT *a.*] *trans.* To interrupt or
destroy the afferent connections of (nerve cells);
to deprive (tissue, etc.) of afferent connection
with the central nervous system. Usu. as
**de'afferented** *ppl. a.*
**1909** C. S. SHERRINGTON in *Q. Jrnl. Exper. Physiol.*
II. 125 The reactions of the deafferented preparation
and of the other..were then compared. **1929** *Jrnl.
Compar. Neurol.* XLVIII. 412 The tonicity of the
crossed extensor reflex in the deafferented muscle
depends upon the level of decerebration. **1948** *Jrnl.
Neurophysiol.* XI. 236 Increased sensitivity of the
deafferented neurones did not develop to all the
tested agents simultaneously. **1984** *Science* 22 June
1354/2 Some regions of the target area that were
deafferented were never invaded by neuron X.

Hence **de,afferen'tation** *n.*, the action or result
of deafferenting; the state of having incomplete
afferent connection with the central nervous
system.
**1948** *Jrnl. Neurophysiol.* XI. 236 The effectiveness
of strychnine after deafferentation was found to
parallel that of all other tested stimulating agents.
**1971** *Nature* 24 Sept. 273/2 Jones and Thomas..
reported a decrease in the number and length of
dendrites after deafferentation. **1985** O. SACKS *Man
who mistook Wife for Hat* iii. 52 Her loss of
proprioception, her deafferentation, has deprived her
of her existential, her epistemic, basis.

**dean**, *n.*¹ Add: [8.] **d. dean's list** *N. Amer.*
(orig. *U.S.*), a list of students recognized for
academic achievement during a term by the
dean of the college they attend.
**1915** *Harvard Univ. Catal. 1914-15* 523 The
Dean's List. A student who records himself as
intending to become a candidate for a degree with
distinction in a subject or related subjects is entitled
to have his name placed upon a List at the beginning
of his Sophomore year. **1923** *Harvard Univ. Catal.
1923-24* 184 Any student who at the mid-year or
final examinations has attained an average of *B* in his
courses may be placed on the Dean's List for the
succeeding half-year. **1939** W. L. PHELPS *Autobiogr.
with Lett.* xiv. 98 All the students are trying to get on
the 'Dean's List' which means that if they are
sufficiently intelligent or industrious, they will not
have to attend classes regularly. **1974** *News &
Reporter* (Chester, S. Carolina) 22 Apr. 5-A/3 Miss
Swing..is a rising junior at the University of North
Carolina... She is majoring in Sociology and is a
dean's list student. **1986** *Cambridge* (Mass.) *Chron.* 6
Mar. 3/3 The following Cambridge residents have
recently been named to the dean's list at Newbury
College.

**dearly**, *adv.* Add: [2.] **b.** In weakened use with
verbs of estimation and desire: greatly, very
much.
**1843** DICKENS *Christmas Carol* ii. 69 And yet I
should have dearly liked, I own, to have touched her
lips. **1899** 'MARK TWAIN' in *Century Mag.* Nov. 77/1,
I dearly wanted to see the islands. **1952** B. PYM
*Excellent Women* ii. 17, I valued my independence
very dearly. **1976** A. PRICE *War Game* I. v. 90 He
would dearly have liked a pint now himself, but that
would have to wait.

**deathless**, *a*. Add: [2.] b. Freq. as *deathless prose* (*iron.*).
**1966** in *Random House Dict.* **1978** *Washington Post* 5 June A20/1 What reporter has not dreamed at some point in his career of being able to sue his editors for distorting his deathless prose on the copy desk? **1981** Q. CRISP *How to become Virgin* v. 62, I had imagined that my jumbled speech would be translated into deathless prose.

**deblur** (diː'bləː(r)), *v*. [DE- II. 1 + BLUR *v*.] *trans*. To make (a blurred image) sharper; to cancel the effect of blurring on (an image). So **de'blurred** *ppl. a*., **de'blurring** *vbl. n*.
**1968** *Physics Lett.* XXVII. A. 405 (*heading*) A new holographic method for a posteriori image-deblurring restoration of ordinary photographs using 'extended-source' lensless Fourier-transform holography compensation. *Ibid*., The new method . . makes direct use of $h(x, y)$, the 'blurred' image of a point in object space . . , to extract the de-blurred image. **1971** *New Scientist* 6 May 304/3 Any photograph which is out-of-focus or limited by an optical effect can be deblurred. **1973** *Daily Colonist* (Victoria, B.C.) 28 July 24/3 Three-dimensional holography . . has the ability to deblur optical images. **1981** *Sci. Amer.* Oct. 136/1 The techniques for deblurring images can be applied not only in scientific research and medicine but also in fields such as criminology and military intelligence.

**debt**, *n*. Add: [5.] **debt counsellor**, one who offers professional advice on methods of debt repayment to those who have fallen into debt.
**1982** *Christian Science Monitor* 17 Mar. 12/1 The Monitor interviewed several financial experts, including . . stock brokers, *debt counselors, and advisers from . . a . . financial service advising 25,000 women. **1985** *Financial Times* 18 May (Weekend Suppl.) p. vi/1, Agencies such as credit brokers, debt counsellors and debt collectors. **1987** *Money* Apr. 148/1 If you are earning $20,000 a year or less, debt counselors say your net income may leave only enough for essentials.

**debugger** (diː'bʌgə(r)), *n*. *Computing*. [f. DEBUG *v*. + -ER[1].] A program that facilitates debugging, e.g. by allowing the execution of programs to be examined by means of traces, break points, etc. Also *rarely*, a person who performs debugging.
**1969** W. H. JOSEPHS *On-Line Debugger for O/S 360 Assembly Lang. Programs* (RAND Rep. No. RM 6027 ARPA) 1 An on-line symbolic debugger can be invaluable. **1978** *Sci. Amer.* Feb. 29/2 (Advt.), Although most system designers and debuggers will declare the HP 1615 to be priceless, it can be purchased for $6800. **1983** *Pop. Computing* Nov. 70 A debugger allows you to . . set breakpoints in the program being tested where control returns to the debugger. These breakpoints are used to prevent system crashes or to test the operation of specific sections of your program. **1985** *Personal Computer World* Feb. 171/3 When you enter the debugger, a tracing finger follows program execution by moving to the line that Basic is currently executing.

**deca-**, *comb. form*. Add: [1.] **'decamer** *Chem*. and *Biochem*., a compound whose molecule is formed from ten monomers; also, a molecule of such a compound.
**1946** *Jrnl. Amer. Chem. Soc.* LXVIII. 359/1 A series of cyclic polymers increasing by units of $(CH_3)_2SiO$ have been isolated up to the *decamer. **1984** *Biophysical Jrnl*. XLV. 248a, *Octopus* hemocyanin exists *in vivo* as a 51S decamer of 11S subunits.
hence **deca'meric** *a*.
**1960** *Jrnl. Chem. Soc.* 3611 The *decameric phosphonitrilic fluoride . . boils only 1.2° below perfluorohexadecane. **1979** *Doklady Akademii Nauk*

*SSSR* CCXLIX. 8 (*heading*) Mass spectra and the structure of octa- and decameric organosylsesquioxanes.

**deca'metric** *a*. *Astrophysics*, consisting of or producing radio waves with a wavelength between 10m and 100m (i.e. a frequency between 3 and 30MHz).
**1960** *Science* 28 Oct. 1250/3 Since the spring of 1960 a strong positive correlation between Jupiter's *decametric emission and solar decametric continuum emission observed at Boulder has been evident. **1978** *Nature* 26 Jan. 313/1 This approach has been adopted by Melrose who suggests the same mechanism may explain the similar radiation from Jupiter in the decametric band. **1984** *Radio Sci.* XIX. 556/1 Jovian decametric radiation, or DAM, has been observed by ground-based radio astronomers at selected frequencies since the 1950s.

**deca'peptide** *Biochem*. [ad. G. *Decapeptid* (E. Fischer 1906, in *Ber. Deut. Chem. Ges.* XXXIX. 2904)], any peptide composed of ten amino-acid residues.
**1908** R. H. A. PLIMMER *Chem. Constitution of Proteins* II. 31 The compound bromisocapronyldiglycyl-glycyl chloride can be obtained, and by condensing it with the esters of amino acids and of polypeptides Fischer has prepared a hexa-, a hepta-, and a *deca-peptide. **1929** MITCHELL & HAMILTON *Biochem. of Amino Acids* i. 93 *Decapeptide*: leucyloctaglycyl-glycine. **1956** *Nature* 17 Mar. 527/2 Its amino-acid composition was consistent with a decapeptide structure. **1984** *Peptides* V. 865 The decapeptide form of human gastrin releasing peptide was isolated from acid extracts of liver tissue containing a metastatic human bronchial carcinoid tumor.

**decimetre** ('dɛsɪmiːtə(r)), *n*. (Formerly at DECI-1 in Dict.) Also (now *U.S.*) **decimeter**. [a. F. *décimètre* (1793): see DECI- and METRE *n*.[2]] 1. In the Metric system, a measure of length equal to $^1/_{10}$ of a metre.
**1797** *Jrnl. Nat. Philos.* Aug. 197 A vessel of a cubical form, having for its side one decimetre, . . has received the name of litre. **1809** *Naval Chron.* XXII. 363 It was about three decimetres in length. **1810** *Ibid*. XXIV. 301 Littre, Decimeter cube. **1883** *Daily News* 12 July 3/7 Cartridges of one decimetre in length each. **1964** *B.S.I. News* Mar. 6/1 The litre is to be a special name for the decimetre cube (dm³), a submultiple of the SI unit of volume. **1970** *Austral. Jrnl. Physics* XXIII. 197 (*heading*) Jovian decimetre radiation.
2. Special Comb.: **decimetre wave**, an electromagnetic wave of wavelength of the order of a decimetre.
**1934** *Proc. IRE* XXII. 634 This shows . . that . . in the rectification of *decimeter waves by the retarding-field tube, the cause is nothing other than the action of a nonlinear current. **1978** *Neurosci. & Behavioral Physiol.* VIII. 172 (*heading*) Selective action of decimetre waves on central brain structures.

**decimetric** (dɛsɪ'mɛtrɪk), *a*. [f. *DECIMETRE *n*. + -IC; cf. F. *décimétrique* (1836).] Of the order of a decimetre in length; of, pertaining to, or designating decimetre waves.
**1941** S. R. ROGET *Dict. Electr. Terms* (ed. 4) 86/1 *Decimetric waves*, electromagnetic waves of a wave length between one and 0.1 metre. **1947** R. C. NORRIS *Pract. Radio Ref. Bk.* 26/2 The use of metric, decimetric and centrimetric waves is being explored and yielding satisfactory results for signalling. **1961** *Austral. Jrnl. Physics* XIV. 403 Statistical studies of the day-to-day variation in radio emission from the whole Sun at various decimetric wavelengths. **1974** *Nature* 6 Sept. 20/1 We can use the theory of synchrotron radiation to extract the relativistic electron energy spectra of Earth based radiotelescope observations of the decimetric noise. **1976** *Astrophysics Lett.* XVII. 167 The non-Io-related

emission may originate in the trapped-particle radiation belts at larger values of $L$ than are observed at decimetric frequencies.

**deck**, *v.* Add: [III.] **7.** To knock (someone) to the ground, esp. with a punch; to floor. *slang* (orig. *U.S.*).
**1953** *Sat. Even. Post* 4 Apr. 118/4 They might wheel and deck me. **1968** *Tuscaloosa* (Alabama) *News* 18 Nov. 5/2 Starr gave way to Zeke Bratkowski early in the third quarter after being decked on an 11-yard scramble. **1970** *Toronto Daily Star* 24 Sept. 16/1 Before the . . flight in Toronto, Jimmy Ellis decked him. **1977** O. SCHELL *China* (1978) III. 267 After the robbery, I get decked by an incensed worker, who has been reborn in a whirlwind of anti-inflationist righteous wrath. **1985** G. V. HIGGINS *Penance for Jerry Kennedy* xxiv. 194 Janet got you riled enough so that you decided to deck Janet. Janet called the cops.

**declamatory**, *a.* (*n.*) Add: **de'clamatorily** *adv.*, in a declamatory manner; in the form of a declamation.
**1898** G. B. SHAW *You never can Tell* II. 241 Philip: . . My name is—Dolly: (completing his sentence for him declamatorily) 'Norval. On the Grampian hills'. **1971** P. SCOTT *Towers of Silence* III. iii. 192 A white horse with a dim uniformed figure declamatorily astride.

**declarative**, *a.* (*n.*) Add: [A.] [2.] **c.** *Computing.* Designating programming languages of the kind that specify properties rather than procedures.
**1977** A. B. TUCKER *Programming Languages* i. 2 High-level languages are not as close in many respects to the programmer's medium of discourse as [are] 'declarative' (or 'very high-level') languages that are found in data-base management systems, statistics packages, and so forth. **1983** *Economist* 28 May 97/2 Much effort is . . going into the development of new languages, called declarative languages . . . Such languages break down a complicated problem into a series of shorter, simpler ones—each of which can be worked on independently, and therefore simultaneously, by different processing chips in a computer. **1985** J. MARTIN *Fourth-Generation Languages* I. ii. 43 Declarative Language. A language that declares a set of facts and permits the statement of queries or problems that use those facts. It does not completely specify the sequence of steps (procedure) for handling the query or problem. A declarative language is thus a form of nonprocedural language.

**declive** (dɪˈklaɪv), *n. Anat.* [a. G. *Declive* (C. F. Burdach *Baue u. Leben des Gehirns* (1822) II. 59): cf. DECLIVE *a.*] A sloping part of the superior surface of the vermis of the cerebellum, posterior to the culmen and anterior to the folium.
**1889** in *Cent. Dict.* **1893** H. ST. J. BROOKS in H. Morris *Human Anat.* v. 754 The declive connects the posterior crescentic portions, and consists of about six or seven transverse folia. **1912** A. ROBINSON *Cunningham's Man. Pract. Anat.* (ed. 5) II. 530 Posterior to the central lobe is the *monticulus*, separable into two parts—an anterior elevated end, the *culmen*, and a posterior sloping ridge, the *declive*. **1975** *Developmental Med. & Child Neurol.* XVII. VI. Suppl. No. 35. 21 The six main lobes of the cerebellum (the nodule, uvula, pyramid, declive, culmen and central lobes). **1980** *Gray's Anat.* (ed. 36) VII. 912/2 The superior surface of the vermis is divided by short, deep fissures into the lingula, central lobule, culmen, declive and folium vermis in that anteroposterior order.

**decomplement** (diːˈkɒmplɪmɛnt), *v. Immunol.* [f. DE- II. 2 + COMPLEMENT *n.*] *trans.* To inactivate the complement in (blood serum of an animal).
**1942** [implied in DECOMPLEMENTED *ppl. a.* below]. **1959** *Proc. Soc. Exper. Biol. & Med.* CI. 505/1 Guinea pigs are difficult to decomplement by injection of antigen-antibody combinations. **1966** *Ann. N.Y. Acad. Sci.* CXXXV. 585 A normal human serum was decomplemented *in vitro* by an antigen-antibody precipitate. **1976** *Nature* 11 Mar. 140/1 After 4 weeks, immune serum was collected and decomplemented at 56°C for 30 min.
So **de'complemented** *ppl. a.* and **de'complementing** *vbl. n.* and *ppl. a.*
**1942** *Jrnl. Exper. Med.* LXXV. 291 Equivalent volume 'decomplemented' serum. **1955** *Internat. Arch. Allergy & Appl. Immunol.* VII. 8 The release of histamine by the decomplementing immune system might lead to a histamine depletion. *Ibid.*, The plasma of the decomplemented rats showed a reduction in their anaphylatoxin forming capacity. **1965** *Canad. Jrnl. Biochem.* XLIII. 756 The secondary aim of the study was to elucidate the effects of three decomplementing procedures on the electrophoretic patterns. **1977** *Lancet* 3 Dec. 1152/2 Decomplemented sera from myelofibrosis patients were as effective as whole sera in their ability to induce healthy leucocytes to phagocytose immune complexes.

**de,complemen'tation**, *n. Immunol.* [f. *DECOMPLEMENT v.* + -ATION.] The process or result of decomplementing; the removal of haemolytic activity from complement.
**1958** *Proc. Soc. Exper. Biol. & Med.* XCVIII. 270/1 Rats were chosen for these experiments because of low normal C' levels permitting decomplementation by means which might prove lethal in the guinea pigs. **1966** *Ann. N.Y. Acad. Sci.* CXXXV. 585 Reduction in the level of C' by decomplementation was accompanied by an increase in anti-complement activity. **1980** *Tropenmedizin und Parasitologie* XXXI. 103/1 Experimental decomplementation of mice and chickens.

**decondensation** (ˌdiːkɒndɛnˈseɪʃən), *n. Cytol.* [f. DE- II. 1 + CONDENSATION *n.*] A process in which chromatin becomes less dense and compact; the degree of looseness of texture that results.
**1900** *Zoologische Jahrbücher: Anat.* XIV. 303 These granules resulting from this gradual decondensation of the chromatin of the chromosomes vary considerably in volume. **1969** *Jrnl. Cell Sci.* IV. 583 It seems important to establish whether this decondensation of chromatin is impeded if DNA synthesis is inhibited. **1975** *Nature* 9 Oct. 503/2 Centric heterochromatin in *Drosophila* metaphase chromosomes is organised into large blocks which show various degrees of condensation in prometaphase and various degrees of decondensation when living cells are Hoechst treated.
Hence (as a back-formation) **decon'dense** *v. intr.* and *trans.*, to (cause to) undergo decondensation; **decon'densed** *ppl. a.*
**1965** Decondense [see INTERKINESIS *n.*]. **1969** *Jrnl. Cell Sci.* IV. 583 Evidence from several sources suggests that only chromatin in the decondensed form is active as a template for DNA synthesis. **1975** *Nature* 24 July 336/2 The heterochromatin of the X chromosome . . decondenses right from the first fixation times. **1989** B. ALBERTS et al. *Molecular Biol. Cell* (ed. 2) ix. 514 About 10% of the DNA in interphase vertebrate cells is in a relatively decondensed conformation that correlates well with DNA transcription in these regions. *Ibid.* x. 582 Some sequence-specific DNA-binding proteins may function solely to decondense the chromatin in a local chromosomal domain.

**deconvolution** (diːkɒnvə'l(j)uːʃən), *n. Math.* [f. DE- II. 1 + CONVOLUTION *n.*] The action or process of deconvolving.

**1967** *Physics Lett.* A. XXV. 89 (*title*) A posteriori image-correcting deconvolution by holographic Fourier-transform division. **1970** *Jrnl. Res. Nat. Bureau of Standards* (U.S.) LXXIV. A. 436/2 After change of variable, $F(\zeta)$ is inverted by a sequential deconvolution procedure. **1975** *Sci. Amer.* July 48/2 Digital techniques can be used for 'blind deconvolution', defined as the problem of unscrambling two signals that have become 'convolved' when both are unknown. **1980** *Nature* 29 May 313/1 At our resolution, deconvolution of this band and the 342 nm HONO band present in the reference spectrum is difficult, leading to distortion and masking of the HONO band.

**deconvolve** (diːkən'vɒlv), *v. Math.* [f. DE- II. 1 + CONVOLVE *v.*] *trans.* **a.** To resolve (a function) into the functions of which it is a convolution; also *transf.*, to resolve (any complex form) into its constituent elements.

**1971** *Physical Rev.* B. IV. 4192/2 We now face up to the possibility that the function we are given to deconvolve is actually a convolution product .. and not a true convolution square. **1972** *Nature* 3 Nov. 32/2 Theoretically, photographs from a single moving observation site such as an aircraft can be deconvolved by a computer to obtain neutral wind speed. **1975** *Sci. Amer.* July 48/3 A total of about three hours on a computer is needed to deconvolve an old-style recording and remove the unwanted contribution of the recording horn. **1988** *Nature* 21 Jan. 228 (*caption*) Six examples of HMC images .. that are filtered, calibrated and deconvolved by the point spread function.

**b.** To obtain (a constituent element) by deconvolution.

**1976** *Nature* 15 Jan. 99/1 Counting rates were then deconvolved from the detector response by considering the effects due to window thickness, crystal dead layer and K shell X-ray escape.

Hence **decon'volved** *ppl. a.*

**1974** *Nature* 26 Apr. 744/2 The deconvolved seismograms show that the shapes of the P and $\rho$P pulses .. are different.

**decouple**, *v.* Add: **3.** *intr. Physics* and *Astron.* To stop being coupled; to stop participating in interactions that maintain thermal equilibrium; *spec.* (of particles and fields) to become differentiated *from* or *into*, or into two or more kinds of entity.

**1966** *Physical Rev.* CXLVIII. 1348/1 The multichannel problem at the poles decouples into a series of single-channel problems. **1971** *Physics Bull.* Sept. 518/1 Some authors have even revived the possible connection of the pomeron and the f°, in particular noting that both decouple (to a good approximation) from the *s* channel helicity flip amplitude. **1977** M. ROWAN-ROBINSON *Cosmol.* v. 90, $T < 10^{12}$ K: muons annihilate; neutrinos and antineutrinos decouple from everything else. **1978** *Nature* 27 Apr. 787/3 Only muon neutrinos and antineutrinos decouple at $10^{12}$ K, whereas electron neutrinos and antineutrinos decouple at $10^{10}$ K. **1981** J. ELLIS in J. M. Mulvey *Nature of Matter* vi. 129 As the Universe expanded and cooled radiation and matter would eventually have decoupled. **1987** *Sci. Amer.* July 36/3 Matter began to decouple from radiation and the universe became transparent.

**4.** *trans.* More generally: to make separate or independent (*from*); to dissociate, disengage.

**1971** I. G. GASS et al. *Understanding Earth* xix. 270/1 The plates are of finite thickness and .. at some depth they become decoupled from what lies beneath. **1976** *Forbes* (N.Y.) 15 Jan. 53/3 He thinks lawmakers might simply 'decouple' benefits. That is, make future benefits depend upon wage increases or price increases, but not on both. **1979** *Dædalus*

Spring p. ix, Europeans have gradually decoupled their ideologies and values from those of the Third World. **1984** *Times* 6 Aug. 11/4 If we want to bring interest rates down we have to decouple the pound from the dollar. **1985** *N.Y. Times Mag.* 20 Jan. 11/1 There's not the slightest possibility that America would be decoupled from Europe by the pursuit of this vital initiative.

**dedicated**, *ppl. a.* Sense 2 in Dict. becomes 2 b. Add: [**2.**] **a.** *Forestry.* Of private woodland: managed for timber production according to an approved plan and with financial assistance from the forest authority.

**1943** *Post-War Forest Policy* (Forestry Comm.) 111 It is also assumed that the same ratio will apply in the case of dedicated plantations requiring replanting. **1948** *Forestry Comm. Booklet* No. 2. 6 The Forestry Commissioners are prepared to make available, to Owners of dedicated woodlands, loans to cover a substantial part of the costs of replanting. **1954** W. E. HILEY *Woodland Managem.* xxii. 385 Dedicated woods are not subject to Tree Preservation Orders. **1976** *Cumberland News* 3 Dec. 1/1 This part of my land is dedicated woodland so it had to be planted.

**c.** Of a ship or other vehicle carrying passengers or goods: allocated to a particular purpose or route. Also *transf.* of the route or service itself.

**1971** M. TAK *Truck Talk* 42 *Dedicated.* A tractor-trailer combination or a trailer is said to be dedicated to a particular terminal if it must return there directly after making a delivery in order to pick up another load. **1979** *Aviation Week* 26 Nov. 23/1 It hires an eight-truck dedicated convoy every day to transport the fuel to Chicago. **1980** *Business Week* 27 Oct. 66H/2 Many shippers believe that coal-fired ships would have to be put into service on such dedicated routes. **1983** *Railway Mag.* Nov. 464/1 At least one of the MkII coaches being allocated to the Victoria-Gatwick dedicated service .. already has been repainted. **1986** *Industry Week* 27 Oct. 66/2 Emery's fixed costs are high; unlike airfreight forwarders, it has its own dedicated fleet of planes and trucks to service the U.S. market.

**dedication**, *n.* Add: [**2.**] **b.** The quality of being dedicated in aims, vocation, etc. Cf. DEDICATED *ppl. a.* 1 b.

**1954** W. FAULKNER *Fable* 344 The Germans, the best soldiers on earth today .. the one people out of all the earth who have a passion and dedication not even for glory but for war. **1961** J. F. KENNEDY in *N.Y. Times* 10 Jan. 20/5 Were we truly men of dedication? **1979** P. MATTHIESSEN *Snow Leopard* iii. 216 But to renounce the world in this way requires the ultimate discipline ... My admiration is mingled with regret that, by comparison, my own dedication is halfhearted and too late. **1986** R. BARNARD *Political Suicide* xi. 117 He .. became convinced that the nurses .. had an unanswerable case ... He went around saying that the State had been capitalizing for years on their dedication.

**defence**, *n.* Sense 3 f in Dict. becomes 3 g. Add: [**II.**] [**3.**] [**c.**] (*b*) *Chess.* A move or series of moves played with the object of countering an opponent's attack; play of this nature; also, any opening or opening variation initiated by Black, many of which are distinguished by special names, as FRENCH (SICILIAN, etc.) *defence.*

**1614** A. SAUL *Chesse-Play* xix. sig. D3ᵛ (*heading*) The first way to make a defence for the hard play before mentioned. **1750** 'A. D. PHILIDOR' *Chess Analysed* 87 In the Defence, one is often forced to play against the general Rules. **1764** R. LAMBE *Hist. Chess* 120 The Queen's Gambit .. produces many different games ... This here is supposed to be its true defence. **1822** J. COCHRANE *Treat. Chess* 253 The principal error of the player of the defence consists in playing, at his fifth move, the queen's knight to king's fourth square. **1849** *Chess Player's Chron.* IX. 279 The Superlatively Close Defence. We have so named a defence which we find in Bilguer's Treatise. **1875** G. H. D. GOSSIP *Chess-Player's Manual* IV. xxx. 799 We are of opinion that the Sicilian defence is not so bad as it has been represented. **1935** *Chess* 14 Nov. 103/1 Nimzo-Indian Defence... White simply sought to *combat* and not to *refute* the Nimzo-Indian variation. **1983** W. TEVIS *Queen's Gambit* viii. 123 It started out as a routine Queen's Gambit Accepted... But as they got into the midgame it became more complex than usual, and she realized that he was playing a very sophisticated defense.

**f.** *Sport* (esp. *Boxing*). An attempt by a reigning champion to retain a title in competition. orig. *U.S.*

[**1935** *Ring* Feb. 4/2 [Baer] will smother any opposition he may be asked to face in defense of his crown this year.] **1940** *Detroit News* 4 Feb. (Sports section) 3/1 He'll probably defend next against Johnny Paychek..on April 5. The two other defenses will be June and September. **1953** *Ring* Feb. 5/2 In his second title defense of the year he was knocked out by Rocky Marciano. **1965** *Evening Star* (Washington, D.C.) 25 May 20/1 Clay will make his first defense against the elderly 'Bear'. **1976** *Facts on File* 12 June 424/3 Muhammad Ali, weighing in at 220 for a defense of his world heavyweight boxing title. **1987** *Los Angeles Times* 29 May III. 7/2 Mike Tyson will defend his heavyweight boxing title in Japan next year if he's successful in title defenses in the United States.

**defer**, *v.*[1] Add: [3.] **d.** To postpone the military call-up of (a person, esp. one in a protected occupation). Usu. in *pass. U.S.*

**1941** *Nation* (N.Y.) 17 May 596/1 The national draft board should promulgate a ruling to the effect that no worker deferred because of his employment in defense shall lose that deferment merely because he joins his fellow-workers in a strike. **1951** *Senior Scholastic* 25 Apr. 12/2 (*heading*) Should superior college students be deferred? **1969** M. PUZO *Godfather* I. i. 62 Paulie Gatto had been deferred from the draft himself because [he]..had received electrical shock treatments for a mental condition.

**deficit**, *n.* Add: **2.** Special Comb. **deficit financing**, the financing of (esp. government) expenditure in excess of revenue, with the difference made up by borrowing; cf. PUMP-PRIMING *vbl. n.*

**1943** J. M. KEYNES *Coll. Writings* (1980) XXVII. 353, I am sure that, if serious unemployment does develop, *deficit financing is absolutely certain to happen. **1964** GOULD & KOLB *Dict. Social Sci.* 561/2 Deficit financing might be relied upon to stimulate the economy so that it will move towards full employment. **1985** *Investors Chron.* 8 Nov. 30/1 The interest can be recovered immediately by development yields to avoid deficit-financing until the first rent-review.

**deficit spending**, expenditure (esp. governmental) which is in excess of revenue, and is financed by borrowing rather than by taxation.

**1941** H. H. VILLARD *Deficit Spending & National Income* xxvi. 369 To the extent that depressions result from financial panics..the role that can be played by *deficit spending is small. **1987** *Christian Science Monitor* 17 June 2/4 Heller advocated deficit spending to spur economic growth and supported federal revenue sharing with states.

**definitive**, *a.* and *n.* Add: [A.] [2.] **b.** *Philately.* Of a postage stamp: belonging to or forming part of the standard issue of a country. Cf. *PROVISIONAL *a.* 1 c.

**1929** K. B. STILES *Stamps* i. 8 Once more, provisionals appeared. These in turn were replaced by definitive stamps inscribed with the newly required values. **1961** K. F. CHAPMAN *Commonwealth Stamp Collecting* ii. 34 Both territories..have issued definitive stamps recognized by the Universal Postal Union for international use. **1977** *Globe & Mail* (Toronto) 23 Apr. 1/4 It is the first time the queen has not been on the definitive stamp. **1986** *Sunday Express* 21 Dec. 6/8 While 12p *Christmas* stamps were OK, 12p definitive stamps were not.

[B.] **3.** *Philately.* A definitive postage stamp.

**1929** K. B. STILES *Stamps* i. 7 Stamps which are called definitives..are of permanent character—for use *regularly* until such time as the government issuing them shall decide to replace them with stamps of another design. **1961** K. F. CHAPMAN *Commonwealth Stamp Collecting* ii. 34 The low value definitives with naye paise surcharges began to appear in 1960. **1986** *Stamp Mag.* Feb. 70/4 The initial issue will be of definitives (5, 30, 60 and 150 cents) and 'independence' commemoratives.

**degranulate** (diːˈgrænjʊleɪt), *v. Med.* [f. DE- II. 1 + GRANULATE *v.*] **a.** *trans.* To cause the degranulation of; to remove granules or granularity from.

**1952** [implied in *degranulated ppl. adj. below]. **1971** *Nature* 9 July 104/2 Carbon tetrachloride degranulates rough membranes only after activation by the hydroxylase system. **1977** *Lancet* 20 Aug. 389/1 Plasma or serum from this patient degranulated eosinophils from normal individuals, perhaps indicating an autoimmune mechanism.

**b.** *intr.* To undergo degranulation; to lose granules or granularity.

**1963** [implied in *degranulating ppl. adj. below]. **1978** *Nature* 22 June 619/1 In the presence of reaginic antibody and antigen, mast cells degranulate, releasing vasoactive substances which cause increased mucosal permeability. **1982** *Sci. Amer.* Aug. 85/1 The mast cell degranulates: the granules move to the surface of the cell and release their contents into the surrounding tissue. **1988** *Nature* 22 Sept. 292/1 The issue of whether basophils degranulate at infinite concentrations of IgE in a cyclic manner..is of great scientific and clinical interest.

So **de'granulated** *ppl. a.*, **de'granulating** *vbl. n.* and *ppl. a.*

**1952** *Proc. Soc. Exper. Biol. & Med.* LXXX. 678/1 In human patients the mast cells of dermal connective tissue decreased in number and became degranulated. **1963** *Jrnl. Amer. Med. Assoc.* 20 Apr. 174/1 Rabbits in good health are regularly satisfactory, but occasionally degranulating cells will be seen in the control. **1975** *Nature* 9 Oct. 511/1 Electron microscopic observations of haemostatic plugs in rabbits and dogs have shown that the platelets are mostly degranulated. **1989** *New Scientist* 15 July 49/1 The drug sodium cromoglycate is known to prevent mast cells from releasing their mediators (degranulating).

**degranulation** (ˌdiːgrænjʊˈleɪʃən), *n. Med.* [f. DE- II. 1 + GRANULATION *n.*] The loss or disappearance of (esp. intracellular) granules.

**1952** *Proc. Soc. Exper. Biol. & Med.* LXXX. 678/1 Administration of cortisone and ACTH is followed by more or less marked degranulation. **1961** *Nature* 9 Sept. 1057/1 Each of the five patients with a history of penicillin anaphylaxis showed significant degranulation of the basophils in the presence of penicillin *in vitro*. **1964** W. G. SMITH *Allergy & Tissue Metabolism* iii. 35 In tissues situated some distance from the site of injection, the mast cells were not destroyed but showed a sequence of swelling and degranulation followed by a recovery phase. **1974** *Nature* 6 Dec. 488/2 The estimation of changes inflicted on the endoplasmic reticulum..(such as the *in vitro* displacement of ribosomes (degranulation) of the liver endoplasmic reticulum by carcinogens). **1986** D. MALE *Immunol.* vi. 88 Degranulation occurs when mast cell granules fuse with the plasma membrane, releasing their contents to the exterior.

**dehydration** (ˌdiːhaɪˈdreɪʃən), n. (Formerly at DEHYDRATE v.) [f. DE- II. 1 + HYDR- + -ATION.]
**a.** The loss or removal of water, or the elements of water.
**1855** J. SCOFFERN in *Orr's Circ. Sci.: Chem.* 453 The result of difference between hydration and dehydration. **1876** HARLEY *Mat. Med.* (ed. 6) 159 The same complete dehydration is effected more slowly by mere exposure to the air. **1904** *Monogr. U.S. Geol. Survey* XLVII. 204 Dehydration is the subtraction of water from hydroxides... Anhydrous compounds are formed. **1921** C. V. EKROTH in A. Rogers *Industr. Chem.* (ed. 3) li. 1170 The dehydration of cow's milk, partial or complete, produces, in the former case, the condensed and evaporated milk so familiar to us. **1948** A. N. SACHANEN *Conversion of Petroleum* (ed. 2) iv. 315 This 'constitutional' water is an important part of active catalysts. The thermal treatment under more severe conditions causes total deactivation of catalysts and simultaneously dehydration. **1973** P. J. KING et al. in Hobson & Pohl *Mod. Petroleum Technol.* (ed. 4) vi. 186 The fluid obtained at the wellhead is submitted to degassing and dehydration operations. **1986** G. G. BIRCH et al. *Food Sci.* (ed. 3) viii. 94 The main methods of food preservation, are listed below: 1. Treatment with chemicals; 2. Freezing; 3. Dehydration; 4. Canning.
**b.** *spec.* A reduction in the amount of water in the body, esp. to an extent that is harmful to health.
**1912** *Jrnl. Hygiene* XII. 487 Great temporary dehydration may be very false economy; since while the depleted reserves are being restored, water may be run to waste in the form of unnecessary perspiration. **1934** *Lancet* 23 June 1331/1 Fluid may be given orally, subcutaneously, intraperitoneally, or intravenously in this order, until the dehydration is relieved. **1984** J. F. LAMB et al. *Essent. Physiol.* (ed. 2) vi. 174 The false thirst arising from a dry mouth after speaking etc. is satisfied by wetting the mouth, whereas real thirst due to dehydration is not.

**delaying**, *ppl. a.* Add: **b.** Special collocation. *delaying action*, a military engagement fought to delay the advance of the enemy; also *transf.*
**1913** R. S. WATERS *Simple Tactical Schemes* III. 172 It will always be possible to convert a '*delaying*' action into a 'passive' defence. **1951** *Jrnl. Dental Res.* XXX. 181 In cases of rampant caries, fluoridization of the teeth would simply provide a delaying action. **1987** *Economist* 9 May 6/3 Europe..must resign itself to rearguard delaying actions, to retard Finlandisation.

**delta**, n. Add: [4.] **delta cell** *Histol.*, a cell of the islets of Langerhans which produces the hormone somatostatin.
[**1931** W. BLOOM in *Anatomical Rec.* XLIX. 368, I have found three types of granular cells in the islets of Langerhans. One of these is the A type, [etc.]... In some of the D cells, the cytoplasm appears homogeneously blue.] **1942** T. B. THOMAS in *Anatomical Rec.* LXXXII. 334 The *delta cells contain bright blue granules and range in size from small wedge-shaped cells to large rounded ones similar to the beta cells. **1959** W. ANDREW *Textbk. Compar. Histol.* vii. 305 Birds have been shown to have two types of islets in the pancreas... The second is dark and consists of alpha and delta cells along with transitional forms. **1979** *Sci. Amer.* Nov. 57/3 The delta cells secrete the hormone somatostatin, which inhibits the secretion of both insulin and glucagon.

**demand**, n.[1] Add: [7.] **demand-led** a. *Econ.* = *demand-driven* adj.
**1981** *Economist* 7 Feb. (Amer. Real Estate Survey Suppl.) 11/3 A *demand-led inflation in rents in

several sunbelt cities. **1987** *New Statesman* 27 Nov. 14/2 There are not many ways of controlling the legal aid budget, because it is demand-led.

**Demerol** ('dɛmərɒl), n. *Pharm.* Also demerol. A proprietary term for pethidine (meperidine).
**1940** *Official Gaz.* (U.S. Patent Office) 2 July 17/2 *Demerol* for antispasmodic and analgesic preparation. **1941** *Jrnl. Pharmacol. & Exper. Therap.* LXXIII. 319 Ethyl ester of 1-methyl-4-phenyl-piperidine-4 carboxylic acid..is prepared for experimental and clinical uses in the form of the hydrochloride. This has been given the names Dolantin, Dolantol, D-140 and Demerol. **1942** *Trade Marks Jrnl.* 21 Oct. 431/2 *Demerol*..Pharmaceutical analgesic and antispasmodic preparations. **1947** *Times* 15 Nov. 5/7 These countries..are unanimous that demerol in its various forms should, like amidone, come under the appropriate international convention. **1956** 'R. MACDONALD' *Barbarous Coast* (1988) xxviii. 183 I'm not myself. I been full of demerol for the last three months. **1965** 'E. MCBAIN' *He who Hesitates* iii. 47 Heroin, cocaine, morphine, opium, codeine, demerol, benzedrine .. you name it. **1984** *N.Y. Times* 23 Nov. A26/3 According to an autopsy, [he]..died of 'combined drug intoxication' from cocaine, Demerol, a painkiller, and Mellaril, a tranquilizer.

**demodecic** a.: see *DEMODECTIC a.

**demodectic** (diːməʊˈdɛktɪk), a. [f. mod.L. *dēmodect-* stem of DEMODEX n. + -IC.] Of canine mange or scabies: caused by a parasitic mite of the genus *Demodex*. Also **demodecic** a. (-'diːsɪk).
**1892** G. FLEMING tr. *Neumann's Treat. Parasites & Parasitic Dis. Domesticated Animals* I. v. 217 (*caption*) A dog affected with advanced demodecic scabies. **1909** in *Cent. Dict.* Suppl. **1922** O. V. BRUMLEY *Dis. Small Domestic Animals* x. ii. 480 Demodectic scabies is produced by the parasite, Demodex folliculorum. **1932** RILEY & JOHANNSEN *Med. Entomol.* v. 63 In the dog the so-called demodecic mange is common. **1968** J. F. GORDON *Beagle Guide* xv. 211 Follicular Mange: this is sometimes known as demodectic mange, or red mange because of the raw, dark red patches. **1985** E. H. HART *German Shepherd Dog* xx. 276 Demodectic, or Red Mange..evidences itself through small, dry areas which are traumatized by scratching until they are red and raw.

**demodulate** (diːˈmɒdjʊleɪt), v. *Electr.* [Back-formation f. DEMODULATION n.] *trans.* **a.** To subject to demodulation; to separate a modulating signal from (a modulated wave or carrier). **b.** To recover (a modulating signal) from or *from* a modulated wave or carrier.
**1932** *Jrnl. Inst. Electr. Engin.* LXX. 351/1 Since the latter [*sc.* the Kerr cell] has an approximately bi-quadratic law, it would rectify and de-modulate a high-frequency signal. **1957** D. G. FINK *Television Engin. Handbk.* xvi. 150 The second method of separating the three signals is to detect the sound signal in one detector and to demodulate the luminance and chrominance signals in another detector. **1959** R. L. SHRADER *Electronic Communication* xvii. 532 A means of detecting, or demodulating, the modulation in the signal. **1970** J. EARL *Tuners & Amplifiers* ii. 47 The left and right audio signals are demodulated alternately from the two sides of the 'modulation envelope'. **1977** *Sci. Amer.* Feb. 63/2 The earth station amplifies and demodulates the television carrier. **1983** E. TRUNDLE *Beginner's Guide Videocassette Recorders* iv. 55 For luminance the basic idea is to modulate the signal on to an FM carrier for application to the recording head, and demodulate it to baseband during the replay process.
Hence **de'modulated, de'modulating** *ppl. adjs.*
**1933** *Proc. IRE* XXI. 210 A value of setting was found at which the modulations of the local oscillator just became intelligible..and below which they

appeared as . . a demodulated signal. **1948** A. L.
ALBERT *Radio Fund.* xi. 427 All other components
that exist in the demodulated signal either are
rejected or are of little consequence. **1971** D. M.
COSTIGAN *Fax* iv. 106 Fax terminal equipment
normally includes its own modulating and
demodulating circuitry. **1986** *Electronics* 2 June 25/1
Sampling for analog-to-digital conversion is
performed on the demodulated luminance and
chrominance signals.

**demonopolize**, *v.* Add: Hence
**‚demonopoli'zation** *n.*, the policy or process of
demonopolizing.
   **1973** M. FOOT *Aneurin Bevan* II. v. 231 The
Foreign Office doubtless believed they must act in
collaboration with the Americans who preferred a
policy of trust-breaking or 'demonopolization'. **1981**
*Daily Tel.* 26 Oct. 16 This I shall myself begin to
believe . . when Dr Owen welcomes measures of
industrial privatisation and demonopolisation.

**demonstrate**, *v.* Add: [3.] **b.** To display and
explain the operation or use of (a product), esp.
to a prospective buyer. orig. *U.S.*
   **1940** W. FAULKNER *Hamlet* I. iii. 58 He did not sell
sewing-machines for nothing; he had even learned to
operate one quite well from demonstrating them.
**1957** WODEHOUSE *Over Seventy* xvi. 153 There
appeared on the screen, demonstrating a mattress, a
well-upholstered young woman who was introduced
as Miss Foam Bedding of 1957. **1974** F. MUIR in
Muir & Norden *Upon my Word!* 25 A little bulky,
perhaps, . . when she is demonstrating an oven. **1985**
*Washington Post* 16 Jan. E6/1 We sell bastard
items—stuff that won't sell unless it's demonstrated.
Anything that's demonstrated has to be unique.

**demonstration**, *n.* Add: [5.] **b.** A practical
display of the operation or use of a product,
esp. to a prospective buyer. orig. *U.S.*
   **1934** *Amer. Year Bk. 1933* 697/2 The
demonstration of 'filamentless' tubes, not
commercially available as yet. **1941** R. WARNER
*Aerodrome* iii. 49 There would also be some
demonstrations of the latest type of machine guns.
**1966** G. N. LEECH *Eng. in Advertising* v. 39 The first
is a 45-second demonstration-type commercial. **1977**
*Washington Post* 6 Jan. (Virginia Weekly) 6/3 The
home party plan . . is an educational . . method of
selling direct to the consumer through
demonstrations by trained consultants. **1987** *Desktop
Publishing Today* July 16/2 Many people . . go to a
demonstration without having been able to formulate
their requirements.

**demonstrator**, *n.* Add: [2.] **b.** One who
demonstrates the operation or use of a product,
esp. to a prospective buyer.
   **1939** C. ISHERWOOD *Goodbye to Berlin* 243 In the
hardware department, an overalled woman
demonstrator was exhibiting the merits of a patent
coffee-strainer. **1987** *Desktop Publishing Today* July
16/2 The best demonstrator cannot possibly cater for
all possible circumstances.
   **5.** A motor vehicle in which a prospective
buyer may take a test drive; a demonstration
model. orig. *U.S.*
   **1930** *Amer. Speech* VI. 92 The following
expressions have to do with automobiles and their
accessories: . . demonstrator. **1934** J. O'HARA
*Appointment in Samarra* (1935) i. 23 It was a
demonstrator, and would be driven by Julian
English, the Cadillac distributor. **1968** *Globe & Mail*
(Toronto) 3 Feb. 46/2 (Advt.), Fairlane convertible,
low mileage demonstrator. **1976** *Milton Keynes
Express* 28 May 49/1 (Advt.), Peugeot 504 Diesel
Saloon . . . As new, our own demonstrator car would
cost new over £3,550. **1983** *Truckin' Life* Aug. 65/2
The truck . . had done 30,000 km as a demonstrator.

**den**, *n.*[1] Add: [3.] **d.** A local meeting-place for
Cub Scouts; hence (now the usual sense), a
small subdivision of a Cub Scout pack. *U.S.*
   **1930** *Survey* 15 Dec. 330/1 In each neighborhood is
a 'den' where the boys meet. **1946** *Parents' Mag.* Jan.
52/2 Our den elected to have refreshments at each
meeting. **1965** B. GRANT *Boy Scout Encycl.* 51/2 A
den is made up of from two to eight boys. **1985**
*Stockholm Stud. in Eng.* LXII. 26 It is common for
the mother of a Cub Scout to take charge of the
home-centred subdivision of the Cub Scout Pack, the
Den.
   [7.] **den mother** *N. Amer.* (orig. *U.S.*), the
woman leader of a den of Cub Scouts; also
*transf.*
   **1936** *National Republic* Feb. 4/2 The *Den Mother
is usually the kind of a mother whose yard . . is
usually full of boys anyway. **1961** M. BEADLE *These
Ruins are Inhabited* (1963) viii. 107, I put away my
damask tablecloths years ago, and so did most
American housewives, because we haven't time to
wash and iron them and still be Den Mothers. **1976**
*National Observer* (U.S.) 4 Dec. 22/1 *Linda's
Pictures*, for instance, is a collection of photographs
by Linda McCartney, den mother to the Beatles.
**1986** B. FREEMANTLE *Kremlin Kiss* xxxvii. 269 You'll
be here for years. You're going to become the den
mother of the diplomatic wives.

**denature**, *v.* Add: **3.** *intr.* Chiefly *Biochem.*
To become denatured, to undergo
denaturation.
   **1954** *Thorpe's Dict. Appl. Chem.* (ed. 4) XI. 173/2
Many proteins (e.g., egg albumin) tend to denature
irreversibly by adsorption at an air-water interface.
**1971** *Nature* 3 Sept. 12/1 Oxyhaemoglobin in such
dilute solution is prone to oxidize to the ferric form,
which then denatures, with irreversible formation of
monomeric chains. **1982** R. M. SCHULTZ in T. M.
Devlin *Textbk. Biochem.* i. 72 Addition of strong
base, acid, or organic solvent, or heating to
temperatures above 60°C are also common ways to
cause a protein to denature.

**dendroclimatic** (‚dɛndrəʊklaɪˈmætɪk), *a.* orig.
*U.S.* [f. DENDRO- + CLIMATIC *a.*] Of or
pertaining to past climates as revealed by the
growth rings in (ancient) timber.
   **1950** E. SCHULMAN in *Tree-Ring Bull.* July-Oct. 11
A new program . . of refinement and extension of
dendroclimatic indices in the Colorado River basin.
**1962** *Jrnl. Geophysical Res.* LXVII. 1419/1 The
earlywood width, latewood width, and year number
can be substituted . . , providing a dendroclimatic
estimate of the environmental parameters $x_8$ and
$x_8x_{39}$. **1972** *Geogr. Mag.* June 639/1 These trees . . are
important in dendro-climatic research—the study of
climatic change as revealed by tree-ring data. **1978**
*Nature* 23 Nov. 338/2 The future directions of
dendroclimatic research will undoubtedly be . .
influenced by the needs of the climatological research
community.

**dendroid**, *a.* and *n.* Add: [A.] **b.** *Palæont.*
Designating or pertaining to graptolites of the
order Dendroidea, which form many-branched
colonies.
   **1908** R. RUEDEMANN in *Mem. N.Y. State Mus.* XI.
59 All these graptolites are dendroid forms which
lived under the same conditions as the associated
benthonic forms. **1932** BORRADAILE & POTTS
*Invertebrata* v. 150 Certain forms, whose relationship
is not clear, occur very commonly in the Cambrian
and are grouped together as 'dendroid' graptolites.
**1979** D. L. DINELEY *Fossils* iii. 79 The late Cambrian
dendroid graptolites . . had three distinct kinds of
thecae.
   **B.** *n. Palæont.* A dendroid graptolite.
   **1912** F. F. HAHN in *Ann. N.Y. Acad. Sci.* XXII.
150 The sediments of those places on which the
dendroids actually flourished were not favorable for

preserving the delicate graptolites. **1958** G. A. KERKUT *Borradaile & Potts's Invertebrata* (ed. 3) xviii. 718 The dendroids show a branching pattern of uniserate stipes (thecae on one side of the stipe only). **1977** A. HALLAM *Planet Earth* 264/1 The earliest graptoloids are referred to a group known as the dendroids, which exhibit cups of differing shapes and developed into shrubby, lace-like colonies of moderate size.., in which the branches were commonly joined by transverse struts.

**densitometry** (dɛnsɪˈtɒmɪtrɪ), *n.* [f. DENSITOMETER *n.*: see -Y³.] The measurement of the darkness or opacity of a substance or specimen; analysis or investigation by means of this.

**1925** *Jrnl. Optical Soc. Amer.* X. 160 Gibson has used the photoelectric cell in transmissionometry, where the requirements are very similar to those of densitometry. **1942** C. E. K. MEES *Theory Photogr. Process* IV. xvii. 663 The barrier layer, self-generating, photoelectric cell introduced a new factor into physical densitometry. **1976** C. REYNOLDS *Photoguide to Filters* 191 Colour densitometry works by measuring the density (consecutively or simultaneously) through three primary filters. The balance between the three readings is a measure of the colour. **1978** *Nature* 16 Mar. 255/2 Microinjected N1 and N2 were found to be at least 120 times more concentrated in the nucleus than in the cytoplasm. (This was determined by densitometry of the gels.) **1989** *Brit. Med. Jrnl.* 3 June 1467/1 Identifying women most at risk is best achieved by bone densitometry.

So **densito'metric** *a.*

**1924** *Trans. Soc. Motion Picture Engineers* XVII. 154 The use of bar photometers for densitometric work. **1971** *Physics Bull.* Aug. 482/2 The resulting information is digitized in the form of 650 000 picture points; these are analysed by a special purpose computer which provides geometric and densitometric data describing the image. **1981** *Jrnl. Protozool.* XXVIII. 371/1 Densitometric estimation.

**density**, *n.* Add: [**2.**] **c.** *Computing.* = *packing density* s.v. PACKING *vbl. n.*¹ 3 c.

**1956** M. V. WILKES *Automatic Digital Computers* 178 A recording density of 100 digits per inch.. may be used with complete success on a drum about 10 in. in diameter. **1976** *Electronic Electro-Optic Infrared Countermeasures* June 33/2 (*caption*) Large-scale integration of MNOS transistors permits a memory density of 2048 bits on a 154-mil by 170-mil chip. **1980** C. S. FRENCH *Computer Sci.* iv. 15 The density of recording can vary between 200-6,250 characters to the inch. **1986** *ZX Computing Monthly* Oct. 78/3 Although eight inch drives are limited to single density, all other drives may be single, double or quad density.

**dent**, *n.*¹ Add: [**4.**] **b.** *fig.* A more or less significant impression made upon some situation or state of affairs, esp. by gradual, continued effort; a (detrimental) reducing effect or reduction. Freq. in phr. *to make* (also *put*) *a dent in. colloq.*

**1942** BERREY & VAN DEN BARK *Amer. Thes. Slang* §243/6 *Dent, nick, make a dent* or *nick in*, to make a showing or impression, make some progress. **1949** *Reader's Digest* Mar. 61/1 General Omar Bradley.. was unable to make a dent in the imperturbable bureaucracy of other divisions. **1965** MRS. L. B. JOHNSON *White House Diary* 10 June (1970) 286 We can work on domestic problems and make a dent—a rather wonderful dent—but the great world is more complex. **1985** *Times* 11 July 15/2 There is going to be a dent in our profits. But they will by no means be wiped out. **1986** *N.Y. Post* 9 July 56/4 It took the Statue of Liberty party to put a dent in the New York Bight bluefishing.

**dent**, *v.* Add: [**1.**] **b.** *fig.* To have an (esp. adverse) effect upon; to damage or weaken. *colloq.*

**1931** *Daily Express* 21 Sept. 3/7 Mr. Somerset Maugham's novel, 'The Painted Veil', made a deep impression on me. The play of the same name.. dented me but slightly. **1948** E. POUND *Pisan Cantos* (1949) lxxxii. 116 In that Fordie Never dented an idea for a phrase's sake. **1977** *Kuwait Times* 1 Nov. 7/3 West Germany's past economic success is now also denting her all-important export performance. **1986** *Daily Tel.* 8 Aug. 15/4 Dobbs' credibility in this respect.. is somewhat dented by the fact that he is himself a Saatchi man.

**Denticare** ('dɛntɪkɛə(r)), *n.* Chiefly *N. Amer.* Also d-. [f. DENTAL *a.*, after MEDICARE *n.*] (A scheme for providing) dental care; *spec.* in *Canad.*, a dental health-care scheme sponsored or provided by a provincial government.

A proprietary name in the U.S.

**1966** *New Society* 9 June 3/3 The essence of Denticare is this... If a dentist joins, it will cost him an initial participation fee... Dentists in the scheme can then offer their patients private treatment. **1967** *Maclean's Mag.* Jan. 1/3 There are no signs that denticare will stir up the militant professional opposition aroused by medicare. **1968** *Financial Post* (Toronto) 13 July 34/1 Establishment of pilot denticare programs in conjunction with government and municipal health departments has been suggested by the Canadian Medical Association. **1971** *Islander* (Victoria, B.C.) 18 Apr. 15/3 Ever-increasing demands by the public for more welfare, medicare, denticare, guaranteed incomes [etc.]. **1974** [see MEDICARE *n.*]. **1975** *Globe & Mail* (Toronto) 3 June 5/2 Introduction of a denticare program will be a part of the Liberal Party platform. **1981** *Official Gaz.* (U.S. Patent Office) 13 Jan. TM181/2 *Denticare*... For dentist services... First use Aug. 9, 1978.

**denturist** ('dɛntjʊərɪst), *n.* orig. and chiefly *N. Amer.* [f. DENTURE *n.*³ + -IST.] One who makes and supplies artificial dentures.

**1964** *Canada Month* Apr. 15/1 She had a petition she wanted to present him, asking permission for denturists (the technicians who make false teeth in Manitoba) to deal directly with the public. **1976** *Shreveport* (Louisiana) *Times* 21 Sept. 1/5 Rogers said he is a member of the National Denturists Association which was formed recently to spearhead the movement by denturists to sell their product directly to denture users. **1984** *Sunday Times* 18 Mar. 23/3 Denturists.. are, as you state, forbidden by law to intervene in a patient's mouth.

**depigmented** (diːˈpɪgmɛntɪd), *a.* [f. DE- II. 1 + PIGMENTED *a.*] Deficient in pigment.

**1902** *Buck's Handbk. Med. Sci.* (rev. ed.) V. 485/2 The lesions.. tend to become slightly elevated and to desquamate. Their centres become depigmented and anæsthetic. **1965** B. E. FREEMAN tr. *Vandel's Biospeleol.* ii. 20 The great majority of troglobia are partially or totally depigmented forms. **1984** *N.Y. Times* 25 July c8/4 Alternatives include.., in cases where most of the body has become depigmented, destroying the pigment in the remaining skin to create a more uniform color.

**deplore**, *v.* Add: [**1.**] **a.** Now usu., to regard as scandalous, to feel or express strong disapproval of. (Later examples.)

**1851** H. MELVILLE *Moby Dick* xxxv. 172 It is much to be deplored that the mast-heads of a southern whale ship are unprovided with.. *crow's-nests*. **1900** J. CONRAD *Lord Jim* xix. 213 This was the worst incident of all in his—his retreat. Nobody could deplore it more than myself. **1927** V. WOOLF *To Lighthouse* III. 265 There was Minta.. with a hole in her stocking... How William Bankes deplored it, without.. saying anything about it! **1945** W. STEVENS 'Transport to Summer' in *Voices* Spring 28 As one of the secretaries of the moon,.. you have deplored How she presides over imbeciles. **1979** D. MURPHY *Wheels within Wheels* iii. 47 Twice a week Mrs Mansfield called to drink tea with my mother and deplore the appalling inroads being made by democracy on good manners. **1984** G. SMITH *Eng. Compan.* (1985) 67 While they applaud her courage, her decision, and her skill, they deplore her inflexibility.

**deposit**, *n.* Add: [1.] **d.** *U.K. Pol.* A sum of money legally required to be deposited with the returning officer by a parliamentary candidate upon nomination, and forfeited by any candidate receiving less than a certain percentage of the votes cast.
[**1875** *Act 38 & 39 Vict.* c. 84 §3 (6) The balance (if any) of a deposit beyond the amount to which the returning officer is entitled in respect of any candidate shall be repaid to the person or persons by whom the deposit was made.] **1917** G. CAVE in *Parl. Deb.* (Commons) 22 May 2141 We .. propose that a candidate shall make a deposit, which will be returnable to him if he has not less than one-eighth of the votes. That is intended to prevent mere freak candidates. **1918** *Act 7 & 8 Geo. V* c. 64 §27 If a candidate who has made the required deposit is not elected, and the number of votes polled by him does not exceed .. one-eighth of the total number of votes polled .. the amount deposited shall be forfeited to His Majesty. **1955** *Times* 9 May 6/1 In 1951 no Liberals ran—they probably needed to convalesce after losing deposits. **1967** D. POTTER *Nigel Barton Plays* 124 Well it might even make you lose your deposit. And you have got to get elected somewhere. **1986** *Ann. Reg. 1985* 405 The *Representation of the People Act* .. increased to £500 the deposit at parliamentary elections while reducing the forfeiture threshold from one-eighth to one-twentieth of votes cast.

**deprecate**, *v.* Add: [3.] **b.** More generally, to express disapproval of (a person, quality, etc.); to disparage or belittle. (Sometimes confused with *depreciate*.) Cf. *self-deprecation*, etc. s.v. SELF-.
Widely regarded as incorrect, though found in the work of established writers.
**1897** *Daily News* 8 Jan. 6/3 It looks rather an attempt to deprecate distinguished commanders of the Commonwealth to please Restoration Royalists. **1927** V. WOOLF *To Lighthouse* 73 He was disposed to slur that comfort over, to deprecate it. **1960** C. S. LEWIS *Stud. in Words* i. 18 We tell our pupils that *deprecate* does not mean *depreciate* or that *immorality* does not mean simply *lechery* because these words are beginning to mean just those things. **1965** M. FRAYN *Tin Men* xv. 80 Trying to shrink into himself, as if to deprecate .. his authority and to become as other men.

**descramble** (diː'skræmb(ə)l), *v.* [f. DE- II. 1 + SCRAMBLE *v.*] *trans.* To convert or restore (a signal) to intelligible form by applying the reverse of the process used to scramble it; to recover an original signal from (a scrambled signal). Also, to counteract the effects of (a scrambling device). Cf. UNSCRAMBLE *v.* 2.
**1957** [implied in *descrambling* vbl. n. below]. **1970** *New Scientist* 4 June 470/1 Another scrambler .. was used by Churchill and Roosevelt .. and although more secure than the inverter it was successfully descrambled. **1983** *Listener* 29 Sept. 38/2 The receiver stays tuned to a single satellite frequency and is continually descrambling all 16 stereo channels. **1985** *Inmac Catal.* Spring/Summer 84/1 If the accessing device cannot exchange codes and descramble the data then your data link is safe. **1987** *New Scientist* 10 Dec. 29/1 The scrambled programmes will trigger a modified video recorder which has circuitry to descramble the programme.

So **de'scrambling** *vbl. n.*
**1957** D. DUNCAN *Occam's Razor* iii. 28 The message .. went through a descrambling process and emerged from the little loud speaker on his desk as a pleasant masculine voice. **1987** *Communications Daily* 21 July 4 Satellite TV descrambling problems have been solved.

**descrambler** (diː'skræmblə(r)), *n.* [f. *DESCRAMBLE v.* + -ER[1].] = UNSCRAMBLER *n.*
**1970** *New Scientist* 4 June 470/1 Industry .. may be willing to pay for devices that limit access to any communications link to those with the correct 'descrambler'. **1985** *Practical Computing* May 17/1 It is also possible to restrict access to certain parts of systems by giving users different levels of privilege according to the code of their descrambler. **1987** *New Scientist* 10 Dec. 29/1 Engineers are touring Britain with descramblers to check picture quality in the middle of the night.

**deseed** (diː'siːd), *v.* [f. DE- II. 2 + SEED *n.*] *trans.* To remove the seeds from (a plant, vegetable, etc.). Also **de'seeded** *ppl. a.*; **de'seeding** *vbl. n.*; **de'seeder** *n.*, a machine for deseeding.
**1931** *Melliand Textile Monthly* July 316/2 The Grant or Farmer's machine .. de-seeds the straw and decorticates it at the same time. Deseeding, threshing or rippling—each of which it is sometimes called—usually is a tedious hand operation. **1941** *Flax Cultivation* (Kenya Dept. Agric.) 4 The cost of deseeding machinery has induced many planters to evolve their own deseeding methods ... Rippling has a decided advantage over other methods of deseeding. **1943** T. L. McCLELLAND *Fiber-Flax Machinery* (U.S. Dept. Agric. Circular No. 667) 10 Deseeders of the type developed by the Department deseed approximately 15 tons of pulled flax per 8-hour day. **1958** *New Biol.* XXVII. 15 In most countries the deseeded flax straw is now retted in warm water in concrete tanks. **1970** J. TURNER *Sometimes into England* 1. i. 19 First of all the 'beets', as the bundles of flax straw are called, are put into a de-seeding machine. A pair of huge iron combs tears through the straw lengthwise and fetches off the seeds. **1985** L. BLUE *Kitchen Blues* 78, I add .. a minced deseeded green chili. **1986** *Wanganui* (N.Z.) *Chron.* 19 Feb. 8/8 Deseed the tomato and cut flesh finely.

**desireless**, *a.* Add: Hence **de'sirelessness** *n.*
**1940** *Illustr. London News* 6 Jan. 24/1 Mr. Propter is the first exponent of desirelessness to have left me cold. **1957** L. DURRELL *Justine* I. 84 As for me I was consumed by a terrible sort of desirelessness, a luxurious anguish of body and mind. **1970** R. D. TARING *Daughter of Tibet* xx. 272 Holy company brings desirelessness. **1980** *Church Times* 4 July 7/3 She traces her experience of the onset of desirelessness concerning this world's usual enjoyments.

**desk**, *n.* Add: [5.] **desk dictionary** chiefly *N. Amer.* (orig. *U.S.*), a one-volume dictionary of medium size, suited for use on a desk for general reference.
[**1915** J. C. FERNALD (*title*) The desk standard dictionary of the English language; designed to give the orthography, pronunciation, meaning, and etymology of about 80,000 words and phrases.] **1948** *New Republic* 2 Feb. 27/1 Almost all the *desk dictionaries have come to resemble one another. **1961** BAY & WENDELL in J. Barzun *Delights of Detection* 265 Four or five novels .. and .. a desk dictionary. **1982** *Papers Dict. Soc. N. Amer. 1977* 34 There are two other vowel distinctions that *are* made by W8 but not by other desk dictionaries.

**desmo-**, *comb. form.* Add: **'desmosome** *Cytology.* [ad. G. *Desmosom* (J. Schaffer *Vorlesungen über Histol. & Histogenese* (1920) III. 76)], a specialized area of a cell surface by which it is bound to another cell or structure; a pair of such areas, facing one another on adjacent cells and joined by filaments, with tonofilaments running into them on the intracellular side.

**1930** MAXIMOW & BLOOM *Textbk. Histol.* ii. 33 The intercellular bridges cross the clefts and each shows at its middle a small thickening, the bridge corpuscle or *desmosome. **1961** [see *tight junction* s.v. TIGHT *a.* 3]. **1982** ARMS & CAMP *Biol.* (ed. 2) iv. 59 In a desmosome, filamentous material is found in the space between the cells and in the cytoplasm of the cells on either side of the junction.

so **desmo'somal** *a.*
**1917** DORLAND *Med. Dict.* (ed. 9) 920/2 *Desmosomal. **1979** *Trans. R. Soc. Trop. Med. & Hygiene* LXXIII. 321/2 A clustering of particles is found at desmosomal sites.

**des res** (dɛz 'rɛz), *n.* Also **des. res.** [Shortened f. *desirable residence.*] A house or other dwelling-place presented as a highly desirable purchase (*Estate-agents' jargon*); freq. *pejorative* or *iron.* in wider use.
**1986** *Fulham Herald* 1 Feb. 1 This sort of estate is designed for people looking for a des res investment in town for weekdays, who already own weekend retreats in the country. **1986** *Sunday Times* 20 Apr. 40 (*heading*) Landlady of the scribes' des. res. **1987** *Punch* 15 Apr. 59/2 So the charmed grove was exchanged for a des res in Summertown, Oxford. **1990** *Times* 20 Apr. 2/3 The days of the 'des res' that clearly isn't are set to end for estate agents.

**destain** (di:'stem), *v. Biol.* and *Chem.* [f. DE- II. 2 + STAIN *n.*] *trans.* Selectively to remove stain from (a substrate, microscope specimen, etc.) after it has previously been stained. Also *absol.*
**1930** *Stain Technol.* V. 136 For paraffin sections of *Clarkia concinna* buds... Destain in a saturated aqueous solution of picric acid. **1940** D. A. JOHANSEN *Plant Microtechnique* xiii. 160 Destain and complete differentiation with absolute alcohol.. and mount in balsam. **1964** M. J. PURVIS et al. *Lab. Techniques in Bot.* iv. 119 As it is necessary that only the liquefied cell walls should be stained by the safranin, the sections are de-stained in acid alcohol. **1985** *Stain Technol.* LX. 176 (*caption*) Section destained and restained with PTA.

So **de'staining** *vbl. n.*
**1926** *Stain Technol.* I. 106 A lack of sufficient destaining may leave some vegetative cells red. **1933** *Jrnl. R. Hort. Soc.* LVIII. 357 Picric acid proved to be too slow a destaining agent. **1983** *Analytical Biochem.* CXXXI. 293/1 Because of variations in amounts of protein.. one has often to make a decision between incomplete and strong destaining.

**destroy**, *v.* Add: [4.] **b.** To put (a sick or unwanted animal) to death deliberately and humanely.
**1866** J. GAMGEE *Cattle Plague* I. 141 The only sure and certain way to annihilate this virus is to destroy the animals which by their sickness indicate its presence. **1911** *Coal Mines Act 1 & 2 Geo. V* c. 50 Sched. 3 §16 The owner, agent, or manager shall.. furnish a statement showing the number of horses.. during the year.. required to be destroyed in consequence of injury or disease. **1936** F. BULLOCK *Handbk. for Vet. Surgeons* (ed. 3) iv. 188 If it becomes necessary to destroy a horse below ground, the 'Exit' Humane Horse Killer.. must be used. **1958** M. BISHOP *It's Dog's Life* xi. 131 The dog can always be destroyed later if you feel he's not enjoying life. **1976** *New Yorker* 8 Mar. 105/2 When he could no longer get up in his stall.. he was destroyed. **1986** *Financial Times* 21 June 1/5 Mr Jopling said radiation levels were now falling and he did not anticipate any need for destroying animals.

**destroying**, *ppl. a.* Add: *destroying angel* (*b*), a highly poisonous mushroom of the genus *Amanita*, spec. *A. virosa.*
**1887** W. D. HAY *Elem. Text-bk. Brit. Fungi* x. 164 Agaricus vernus; Amanita verna; The Destroying Angel... Angelically beautiful and demoniacally poisonous. **1945** J. RAMSBOTTOM *Poisonous Fungi* 19 *Amanita virosus* [sic], destroying angel. *Amanita verna* and *Amanita virosa* are both closely allied to *Amanita phalloides* and are often regarded as varieties or sub-species. **1961** W. P. KELLER *Canada's Wild Glory* IV. 171 One variety quite similar to the meadow mushroom but less common and often found in the woods is the Destroying Angel. **1974** *Encycl. Brit. Micropædia* I. 289/2 *A*[*manita*] *verna* and *A. virosa*, the destroying angels, are the deadliest of all mushrooms. They develop a large white fruiting body and are found in forests during wet periods in summer and autumn. **1990** *Times* 13 Oct. 18/3 In Britain we have the Death Cap and the Destroying Angel, the world's two deadliest fungi.

**destructuration** (dɪˌstrʌktjʊ'reɪʃən), *n.* [f. DE- II. 1 + STRUCTURATION *n.*; cf. DESTRUCTURE *v.* and *restructuration* s.v. RE- 5 a.] The process of depriving of structure; the destruction or dismantling of structural organization.
**1970** B. BREWSTER tr. *Althusser & Balibar's Reading Capital* 322 The phase of transition itself.. is not a destructuration-restructuration, but a mode of production in its own right. **1982** *Spectator* 27 Mar. 18/3 The self-destructuration of worship. **1985** *Times Lit. Suppl.* 30 Aug. 948/3 The destruction of Veii by the Romans in 395 was the beginning of the long process of destructuration.

**detached**, *ppl. a.* Add: **2.** Special collocation: **detached retina** *Path.*, a retina which has become detached from the underlying layer of epithelium; also, = *retinal detachment* s.v. *RETINAL *a.* b.
**1863** W. BOWMAN in *Rep. R. Ophthalm. Hospital* IV. 134 When I first operated in cases of *detached retina, I only entertained faint hopes of arresting the spread of the disorganisation. **1966** *Brit. Jrnl. Ophthalm.* L. 268 Between November, 1961 and October, 1964, 182 cases of detached retina came to surgery.

**detect**, *v.* Add: [5.] **b.** *trans.* To discover or investigate as a detective. (Chiefly in the writings of D. L. Sayers.)
**1928** D. L. SAYERS *Unpleasantness at Bellona Club* xvi. 192 No wonder you detect things. I will *not* do your worming for you! **1935** —— *Gaudy Night* ii. 39 His hobbies of detecting crimes and collecting books. **1950** E. WELTY in *New Yorker* 1 Dec. 53/2 They'll open your case and see what there is to detect.

**de'tectional**, *a.* [f. DETECTION *n.* + -AL¹.] Of, pertaining to, or involving the detection of criminals.
**1930** *Punch* 23 Apr. 469/2 Sometimes I studied the works of the mighty And sometimes detectional stuff. **1968** *Ibid.* 2 Oct. 464/1 Detection with him is not like with the US Pres.,.. but more menial and less detectional, to my thinking, being a matter of clearing a path through TV crews and walking behind him on tarmac, etc. **1982** *Observer* 5 Dec. 32/4 Holmes's detectional methods depend on an acceptance of the physical world.

**de'tectival**, *a.* [f. DETECTIVE *a.* and *n.* + -AL¹.] Of or relating to detectives or detective work; pertaining to detective fiction.
**1919** B. CAPER *Skeleton Key* xix. 225 Sentiment could not be allowed to affect the detectival philosophy, or the Law became a dead letter. **1934** V. STARRETT in 'E. Queen' *Female of Species* (1943) 213 He had no objections to playing chauffeur to Sally Cardiff.. but her detectival activities set his

back up. **1986** *Daily Tel.* 7 Nov. 15/5 It is now just 50 years since Inspector Appleby..burst upon the detectival scene in 'Death at the President's Lodging'.

**deter**, *v.*[1] Add: [1.] **c.** To prevent or inhibit.
**1961** in WEBSTER. **1972** *Sci. Amer.* July 23/2 This tactic could deter torpedo attack..in just the same way that the strategic offensive force reliably deters a first strike. **1986** *Cambridge* (Mass.) *Chron.* 6 Mar. 1/3 Zoning regulations..deter the development of community residences.

**detour**, *v.* Add: **c.** To make a detour round; to bypass.
**1941** C. GRAVES *Life Line* 75 *Sylvia B.* picked up all the survivors instead of leaving them for the motor-launches to rescue. The other vessels astern just detoured her. **1946** J. HERSEY *Hiroshima* ii. 47 A station on a railroad line that detoured the city in a wide semi-circle. **1960** K. AMIS *Take Girl like You* v. 75 There was a long queue at the High Street traffic lights, mainly composed of westbound lorries detouring a more severe bottle-neck nearer London. **1986** *Aviation Week* 8 Dec. 93/1 The POM states, in part, that when a flight encounters thunderstorm conditions, 'detour the area' if possible.

**detritivorous** (dɛtrɪ'tɪvərəs), *a. Zool.* [ad. G. *Detritivor* (A. Handlirsch 1929, in C. Schröder *Handbuch d. Entomologie* II. 38), f. DETRIT(US *n.*: see -IVOROUS.] Feeding on detritus.
**1931** R. N. CHAPMAN *Animal Ecol.* vii. 160 Handlirsch..indicated 29 categories of food habits of insects:.. 13. Other animal waste, parts of integuments; scales, hair, feathers, wax, silk, etc. (Detritivorous.) **1967** *Oceanogr. & Marine Biol.* V. 542 The rapidly desiccating tidemark biocoenosis..is characterized by detritivorous amphipods, isopods, and insects of the genus *Bledius.* **1980** *Nature* 31 Jan. 429/1 Some fungi trap and consume detritivorous arthropods.
So **de'tritivore** *n.* [G. *Detritivore*], a detritivorous organism.
**1965** B. E. FREEMAN tr. *Vandel's Biospeleol.* xix. 328 Most cavernicoles are more or less polyphagous and their dietary categories cannot be distinguished... The term detritivore is the one which best suits the majority of them. **1978** *Nature* 4 May 24/1 Sustainable benthic biomass would increase by at least two orders of magnitude, and, with such a rich resource of detritivores and herbivores, the evolution of benthic predators would quickly follow. **1982** J. B. HARBORNE *Introd. Ecol. Biochem.* (ed. 2) i. 19 It appears that these sea creatures obtain their arsenic indirectly from the brown kelp via detritivores.

**deutan** ('djuːtæn), *n.* (and *a.*) *Ophthalm.* [f. *deut(er)an-* in *DEUTERANOMALY n.,* DEUTERANOPIA *n.,* etc.] A person with deuteranomaly or deuteranopia. Also as *adj.*
[**1944** D. FARNSWORTH in *Inter-Society Color Council News Let.* Nov. 8 Deutan, reduction of redpurple-green discrimination relative to intersecting axis.] **1948** *Jrnl. Optical Soc. Amer.* XXXVIII. 504 Deutans may be either deuteranomalous or deuteranopic. **1954** *Brit. Jrnl. Psychol.* May 119 The terms 'protan', for all protanopic subjects, and 'deutan' for all deuteranopic subjects, will be convenient. **1962**, etc. [see PROTAN *n.* (*a.*)]. **1974** *Ophthalmic Res.* VI. 285 Colour discrimination as tested with the Farnsworth Panel D-15 test indicated that he was a deutan. **1987** *Amer. Jrnl. Optometry & Physiol. Optics* LXIV. 2/1, 22 deutans and 78 normals were tested on a set of tasks which simulated critical tasks performed daily by air traffic controllers.

**deuteranomal** (ˌdjuːtərə'nɒməl), *n. Ophthalm.* [ad. G. *Deuteranomale* (W. A. Nagel 1907, in *Zeitschr. f. Psychol. und Physiol. d. Sinnesorgane: Abt. II* XLII. 67), f. Gr. δεύτερ-

DEUTERO- + G. *anomal* anomalous.] A person with deuteranomaly.
**1915** J. H. PARSONS *Introd. Study Colour Vision* ii. iii. 182 *Partial deuteranopes (deuteranomal,* Nagel). **1955** *Jrnl. Optical Soc. Amer.* XLV. 520/1 (*caption*) Distribution of anomalous quotients in an at random compiled material of 42 protanomals, 100 normals, and 170 deuteranomals. **1984** *Amer. Jrnl. Optometry & Physiol. Optics* LXI. 41/1 In the deuteranomal, the green response is similar to that of a normal but reduced in magnitude.

**deuteranomaly** (ˌdjuːtərə'nɒməlɪ), *n. Ophthalm.* [f. *DEUTERANOMAL n.* + -Y[3].] A form of anomalous trichromatism marked by a reduced sensitivity to green.
**1932** S. DUKE-ELDER *Text-bk. Ophthalm.* I. xxv. 975 There may be a relative failure in the appreciation of red or of green, the cases being respectively called partial protanopia (protanomaly or 'green-sightedness') and partial deuteranopia (deuteranomaly or 'red-sightedness'). **1946**, etc. [see PROTANOMALY *n.*]. **1956** *Brit. Jrnl. Ophthalm.* XL. 463 Weale's subject J. G. was a compound heterozygote for protanomaly and deuteranomaly. **1968** *Vision Res.* VIII. 469 (*heading*) A pedigree showing variability in deuteranomaly. **1984** *Ophthalmic Res.* XVI. 58/2 Deuteranomaly is explained by a dislocation of the medium wavelength absorbing cones from the normal 535 to 555 or 560 nm.., or by having two absorbing pigments from the 'erythrolabe cluster'.

**deutero-**, *comb. form.* Add: **'deuterostome** *Zool.*, a deuterostomatous animal; also as *adj.*
**1959** L. H. HYMAN *Invertebrates* V. xxi. 605 It may thus appear that *deuterostomes show a further development of characters beginning in an unclear way in lophophorates, and thus branch off from protostomes by way of the latter. **1967** E. J. W. BARRINGTON *Invertebr. Struct. & Function* xviii. 397 In echinoderms, where deuterostome characters are easiest to appreciate, there is no sign of spiral cleavage. **1988** R. S. K. BARNES et al. *Invertebrates* xv. 453/2 In deuterostomes the blastopore becomes the anus of the functional larva and often of the adult. The mouth will form as an ectodermal invagination.

**devein** (diː'veɪn), *v.* orig. *N. Amer.* [f. DE- II. 2 + VEIN *n.*] *trans.* To remove the vein or veins from; *esp.* in *Cookery*, to remove the dorsal 'vein' or intestinal tract from (a prawn).
**1952** H. WORTH *Shrimp Cookery* iii. 25 (*heading*) Deveining shrimp... If you live south of the Mason–Dixon line, you'll probably be consternated by all this talk of removing the vein. **1967** *Canad. Antiques Collector* Apr. 17/1 When hot add 14 ounces cooked, shelled, deveined shrimp. **1969** *Femina* (Bombay) 26 Dec. 57/3 Shell and devein prawns. Wash well. Smear with turmeric and salt and set aside. **1975** E. L. ORTIZ *Caribbean Cooking* (1977) 52 Shell and devein the prawns. **1981** T. MORRISON *Tar Baby* i. 38 She too took the pail of shrimp to shell and devein them.

**Devensian** (dɪ'vɛnzɪən), *a. Geol.* and *Archæol.* [f. L. *Dēvenses* people living by the Dee, f. L. *Dēva* Dee, a river on the Welsh border near which deposits from the period are particularly well represented: see -IAN 1.] Of, pertaining to, or designating the most recent Pleistocene glaciation in Britain (identified with the Weichsel of continental Europe); of or belonging to this glacial; *spec.* designating a stratigraphic stage of the Pleistocene thought to date from this period. Also *absol.*
**1968** *Geol. Soc. Lond. Recomm. Stratif. Classif.* 20 It is recommended that for the Pleistocene and Holocene of the British Isles the following ages/stages be adopted as a regional scale... Pleistocene:

Devensian [etc.]. **1975** J. G. EVANS *Environment Early Man Brit. Isles* ii. 34 The Devensian Glaciation is the latest major cold-climate episode to have affected the British Isles. **1978** *Nature* 2 Mar. 26/1 The extent of permafrost in Britain during the Devensian may be inferred from relict features. **1984** LOWE & WALKER *Reconstructing Quaternary Environments* II. 26 In Britain, the maximum extent of the last (Devensian) glaciation has traditionally been placed where a morphological distinction can be made.

**deviate** ('diːvɪət), *ppl. a.* Restrict *Obs. rare* to sense in Dict. and add: **2.** [f. the n.] = DEVIANT *ppl. a.*, esp. of social and sexual behaviour. Cf. DEVIATE *n.* 1.
   **1945** *Rep. Inter-Departmental Comm. on Deviate Children* (S. Afr.) I. viii. 157 If the reaction of the individual is in conflict with the generally accepted manner of reaction or differs from it in a striking way, such behaviour is deviate. **1961** R. DALVEN tr. *Cavafy's Compl. Poems* 71 Deviate erotic drunkenness Overcomes him. **1978** *Spectator* (New Canaan High School, Connecticut) 61 I'm taking a real neat course from her in deviate sex. **1981** *Jrnl. Clin. Psychiatry* XLII. 243/2 He took up religion in an attempt to control both his drinking and deviate thoughts.

**deviator**, *n.* Add: **3.** *Mech.* The non-isotropic component of a tensor, esp. a stress tensor. Freq. as *stress deviator*.
   **1937** *Jrnl. Appl. Physics* VIII. 207/2 The special tensor for this type of distortion [*sc.* plastic deformation] has sometimes been called a 'deviator'. **1951** PRAGER & HODGE *Theory perfectly Plastic Solids* iv. 117 The stress-strain law of Mises .. then shows that the radial and circumferential components of the stress deviator are equal in absolute value but opposite in sign, while the axial component $s_z$ vanishes. **1976** *Trans. Amer. Soc. Mech. Engin.* Ser. H. XCVIII. 282/1 The third invariant of stress deviator affects considerably the plastic deformation of the material.

**deviatoric** (ˌdiːvɪə'tɒrɪk), *a. Mech.* [f. DEVIATOR *n.* + -IC.] Of, associated with, or represented by a deviator (*DEVIATOR *n.* 3); not isotropic.
   **1944** *Q. Jrnl. Appl. Math.* II. 114 Define .. the deviatoric part of the stress tensor as $s_{ik} = \sigma_{ik} - \sigma\delta_{ik}$. **1951** PRAGER & HODGE *Theory perfectly Plastic Solids* i. 15 It is frequently convenient to decompose the stress tensor into a spherical part corresponding to the mean normal stress, and a deviatoric part. **1969** *Nature* 11 Jan. 165/2 It is necessary to suppose that the deviatoric stresses which are directly responsible for earthquakes must occur quite widely. **1984** *Jrnl. Glaciol.* XXX. 334 (*heading*) A glacier flow model incorporating longitudinal deviatoric stresses.

**devolatilize** (diːˈvɒlətɪlaɪz, -vəˈlæt-), *v.* (Formerly at DE- II. 1.) *Geol.* [f. DE- II. 1 + VOLATILIZE *v.* (or VOLATILE *n.* and *a.* + -IZE).] *trans.* To make less volatile; *esp.* to remove the volatile constituents of (a mineral).
   **1868** *Birm. Jrnl.* Sept. 12 The oil .. has been devolatilised, so that all danger of explosion is annihilated. **1913** *Bull. U.S. Bureau of Mines* No. 38. 104 The heat given off by the cooling matter of the dike is insufficient to raise the temperature of the contact rocks to the point of devolatilizing the coal. **1974** *Sci. Amer.* Mar. 22/3 The coal is devolatilized, or distilled, either in the gasifier or in a separate vessel.
   Hence **devolatilized** *ppl. a.*, **devolatilizing** *vbl. n.* (stresses variable), **deˌvolatiliˈzation** *n.* (also **devoˌlat-**), the process of losing volatile constituents.
   **1908** *Econ. Geol.* III. 314 The association of devolatilized fuels with jointing and highly developed cleavage is more than accidental. *Ibid.*, Local devolatilization, or coal metamorphism, is

occasionally observed in immediate proximity to a dyke. **1928** *Bull. Amer. Assoc. Petroleum Geologists* XII. 801 Apparently increase of depth of cover offers no difficulties to the escape of volatile constituents, thereby retarding the devolatilization of the coals. **1949** *Q. Jrnl. Geol. Soc.* CIV. 417 A stress- or shear-plane of such importance that its devolatilizing effect is registered by all seams throughout the main part of the coalfield. **1967** *Industr. & Engin. Chem.: Fund.* Feb. 20 (*heading*) Burning rates of devolatilized coal particles. **1982** *Nature* 28 Oct. 807/2 Substantial devolatilization and reduction is normal in the production of terrestrial tektites.

**Dewar**, *n.* Add: **b.** *Chem.* Used *attrib.* with reference to a possible structure (proposed by Dewar) for the benzene molecule in which one bond forms a bridge across the benzene ring; *Dewar benzene*, the isomer of benzene having a Dewar structure.
   **1913** J. B. COHEN *Org. Chem. Adv. Students* II. v. 387 That the parallel double linkage of the Dewar formula is responsible for luminescence .. is seen in certain hydropyridine carboxylic esters. **1949** G. W. WHELAND *Adv. Org. Chem.* (ed. 2) x. 420 Approximate calculations have .. led to the conclusion that the Dewar structures are of only small (although still far from insignificant) importance in the resonance. **1962** VAN TAMELEN & PAPPAS in *Jrnl. Amer. Chem. Soc.* LXXXIV. 3790/1 In this contribution we describe a hydrocarbon the properties of which lead us to propose that it is the first isolated member of the 'Dewar benzene' class. **1979** *Jrnl. Org. Chem. USSR* XV. 1401 (*heading*) Calculation of the reaction paths for 1,3-sigmatropic shifts of the C-S bond in allyl hydrosulfide and Dewar thiophene. **1987** *Jrnl. Amer. Chem. Soc.* CIX. 7888/1 The high aromatization temperature required for a short-bridged Dewar benzene has precedent.

**deworm** (diːˈwɜːm), *v.* [f. DE- II. 2 + WORM *n.*] *trans.* = WORM *v.* 4 b. Hence **deˈwormed** *ppl. a.*, **deˈworming** *vbl. n.*
   **1934** WEBSTER, Deworm. **1950** L. F. WHITNEY *Compl. Bk. Home Pet Care* xviii. 297 Friends .. will almost invariably insist that your dog, if he is out of sorts for any reason whatever, needs deworming—or 'worming', as they usually put it. **1961** A. CHRISTIE *Pale Horse* xxv. 254 Rhoda was busy doctoring dogs. This time, I think, it was deworming. **1969** *West Australian* 5 July 34/7 (Advt.), Pullets .., quality stock vac, dewormed, free delivery. **1981** *Washington Post* 30 July 13/1 Pet owners should make sure their pups and kittens are dewormed to avoid spreading disease to small children.

‖**dhania** ('daːnia), *n. Indian Cookery.* Also **dhaniya**. [Hindi *dhaniyā*, Punjabi *dhaniā*, f. Prakrit *dhānā-* in same sense.] Coriander; coriander-seed.
   **1925** J. G. BRUCE in E. F. Norton *Fight for Everest: 1924* 347 We brought from Darjeeling and put into the Base Camp .. chillies, dharria [*sic*], cloves and turmeric. **1952** S. SELVON *Brighter Sun* ix. 181 Urmilla knelt on the floor .. and crushed the *tumric* and *dhania* with the massala stone. **1958** *Catal. County Stores, Taunton* June 5 For curries .. Dhaniya (Coriander)—per oz. 4d. **1969** *Eve's Weekly* (Bombay) 20 Dec. 58/3 Mix in shredded cabbage, Teg's cheese, chillies, *dhania*, and salt. **1980** *Washington Post* 16 Oct. E1/6 Indians will travel miles to get some fresh *dhania*, .. and consider it an essential part of their cuisine.

**diagnostic**, *a.* and *n.* Sense B. 3 in Dict. becomes B. 4. Add: [**B.**] **3.** *Physics.* A method or technique used in plasma diagnostics; in *collect. pl.* = *plasma diagnostics* s.v. *PLASMA *n.* 8 a.
   **1962** *Jrnl. Appl. Physics* XXXIII. 2868 Errors in the microwave diagnostics of plasmas were

investigated with the use of dielectric and conducting models. **1965** R. H. HUDDLESTONE in Huddlestone & Leonard *Plasma Diagnostic Techniques* i. 6 Chapter 10, 'Optical Interferometry', treats space- and time-resolved interferometry and its applications to diagnostics of plasmas with electron concentrations greater than a few times $10^{14}$ electrons per $cm^3$. **1979** *Nature* 14 June 626/1 The ion temperature deduced by the magnitude of the neutron emission has been consistent with other PLT ion temperature diagnostic[s] such as charge exchange spectral observations. *Ibid.* 22 Nov. 366/1 It will now be possible to study this quiescence phase in detail with modern diagnostics and hence to assess the potential of the reversed field system.

**diaphthoresis** (ˌdaɪəfθəˈriːsɪs), *n. Petrol.* [f. Gr. διαφθείρειν to destroy utterly (f. as DIA- + φθείρειν to destroy), after Gr. nouns in -ησις: cf. G. *Diaphthorit* (F. Becke, 1909).] Retrograde metamorphism.
**1932** [see RETROGRADE *a.* 3 e]. **1948** *Mem. Geol. Soc. Amer.* XXX. 299 Retrogressive metamorphism, or diaphthoresis, is the mineralogical adjustment of relatively high-grade metamorphic rocks to temperatures lower than those of their initial metamorphism. **1957** *Encycl. Brit.* XV. 322/2 Reactions of adjustment to the conditions of lower temperature are . . by no means altogether absent. The process of retrograde metamorphism is known as diaphthoresis.

**diazomethane** (daɪˌæzəʊˈmiːθeɪn, daɪˌeɪzəʊ-), *n. Chem.* [ad. G. *Diazomethan* (H. von Pechmann 1894, in *Ber. d. Deut. Chem. Ges.* XXVII. 1888), f. DIAZO- + METHANE *n.*] An aliphatic diazo compound, $CH_2N_2$, a poisonous yellow gas used as a methylating agent.
**1894** *Jrnl. Chem. Soc.* LXVI. 1. 438 When nitrosomethylbenzamide, nitrosomethylurethane, and similar nitroso-derivatives of methylamine are treated with alkalis, a yellow gas is formed . . . This gas is diazomethane. **1935** *Ibid.* 1. 286 Further experience of the method of preparing diazomethane previously described . . revealed certain defects. **1968** I. L. FINAR *Org. Chem.* (ed. 4) II. vii. 242 More recent methods of methylation use sodium and methyl iodide in liquid ammonia, or diazomethane in the presence of moisture. **1980** M. ORCHIN et al. *Vocab. Org. Chem.* iv. 91 Alkanes in which two hydrogen atoms attached to the same carbon are replaced by the diazo group, $=N_2$. Examples. Diazomethane and diphenyldiazomethane.

**dichlorvos** (daɪˈklɔːvɒs), *n.* [f. DI-[2] + CHLOR-[2] + v(INYL + PH)OS(PHATE *n.*, elements in the systematic name (see def.).] A pale yellow liquid that is an organophosphorus insecticide used as a spray and impregnant against household and farm pests and as an anthelmintic for domestic animals; 2,2-dichlorovinyl dimethyl phosphate, $(CH_3O)_2 \cdot PO_2CHCCl_2$.
**1960** *Rev. Appl. Entomol.* A. XLVIII. 3 Dichlorvos . . Dimethyl 2,2-dichlorovinyl phosphate . . DDVP. **1972** *Nature* 15 Dec. 418/2 There have been several conflicting reports on the genetic effects of Dichlorvos . ., which is the active ingredient of Shell's pesticide, 'Vapona'. **1979** P. L. G. BATEMAN *Househ. Pests* II. 77 Impregnated strips of plastic giving off vapours of . . dichlorvos are also sold for domestic fly control. **1983** *Choice* (Marrickville, New South Wales) Nov. 11/3 Collars and medallions with dichlorvos release an insecticidal vapour that is dispersed via the animal's coat oils especially to places where fleas tend to hide.

**dicky**, *n.* Add: [III.] [7.] **b. dicky bow**, a bow-tie.
**1977** *Sounds* 9 July 34/4 He's even in a dickie bow and tuxedo, for Chrissakes! **1979** *Observer* 28 Jan. 9/2

The odds, however, would be completely revised if, as rumoured, Robin Day takes off his dickey-bow and leaps into the fray. **1987** *New Musical Express* 9 May 21/3 The other thing about bouncers is that, because they've got dickie bows and the suits . . you think they're even meaner.

**dictyosome** (ˈdɪktɪəʊsəʊm), *n. Biol.* [f. as DICTYOSPORE *n.* + -SOME[4].] One of the discrete bodies that constitute the Golgi apparatus in some cells, esp. in plants.
**1893** J. E. S. MOORE in *Q. Jrnl. Microsc. Sci.* XXXV. 263 At this period of the metamorphosis . . a number of most remarkable bodies make their appearance . . connected one to another and to the inner group of chromosomes by fine strands, which remain uncoloured by reagents; and, as their relation to these fine threads suggests the nodal points in a net, I have termed them dictyosomes. **1924** L. DONCASTER *Introd. Study Cytol.* (ed. 2) ii. 25 In some cells the Golgi elements may take the form of granules ('dictyosomes') which are recognisable by their staining reactions, and which multiply by division like the mitochondrial bodies. **1925** [see GOLGI *n.* d]. **1969** R. F. CHAPMAN *Insects* xv. 278 After the second meiotic division the dictyosomes . . fuse to a single body. **1984** HOLTZMAN & NOVIKOFF *Cells & Organelles* (ed. 3) II. v. 154 In many cells of higher plants, and in a very few animal cells, the Golgi apparatus appears to consist of many unconnected units, called dictyosomes.

**die**, *v.* Add: [II.] [8.] **c.** *transf.* Of an internal combustion engine: to cease to function, to stop running. Also with vehicle as subj.
**1927** C. A. LINDBERGH *We* viii. 134 At 5,000 feet the engine sputtered and died. **1970** G. F. NEWMAN *Sir, You Bastard* viii. 235 At ten past two Feast finally arrived home after running out of petrol; the gauge had indicated a quarter of a tank when it died. **1986** *Road Sport* Aug. 24/2 While queuing for the start the Manta died, but the marshals insisted that he start the stage on his due time.

**diegesis**, *n.* Add: **b.** [a. F. *diégèse*, introduced in this sense by E. Souriau 1953, *L'Univers Filmique* 7.] *spec.* The narrative presented by a cinematographic film or literary work; the fictional time, place, characters, and events which constitute the universe of the narrative.
**1973** D. MATIAS tr. C. Metz in *Screen* Spring/Summer 50 If the diegesis happens to contain some object which emits sound—a car starting up, . . etc—the sound should be audible on the sound track only if the image does not show the source of sound. **1974** M. TAYLOR tr. *Metz's Film Lang.* iv. 97 Diegesis . . designates . . the narration itself, but also the fictional space and time dimensions implied in and by the narrative, and . . the characters, the landscapes, the events, and other narrative elements, in so far as they are considered in their denoted aspect. **1984** P. DE MAN *Rhetoric of Romanticism* x. 275 The authentification of the diegesis can only proceed mimetically.
Hence **die'getic** *a.*, of or pertaining to diegesis.
**1973** D. MATIAS tr. C. Metz in *Screen* Spring/Summer 71 A distinction is made . . where the thing compared to and the thing compared both belong to the action . . ; and another for cases where only the thing compared belongs to the action . . . The term 'diegetic metaphor' is sometimes used for the first case. **1981** M. EATON in T. Bennett et al. *Pop. Television & Film* I. ii. 44 The first show 'introduced' the characters and situation and provided the diegetic explanation as to how they managed to be marooned in space. **1985** *Encounter* July-Aug. 27/2 Pip's diegetic report of his life includes mimesis of his own and other people's speech.

**dielectrophoresis** (daɪɪˌlɛktrəʊfəˈriːsɪs), *n.* *Chem.* [Blend of DIELECTRIC *n.* and ELECTROPHORESIS *n.*] The migration of particles of a dielectric, or other particles carrying no net charge, towards the position of maximum field strength in a non-uniform electric field.
**1951** H. A. POHL in *Jrnl. Appl. Physics* XXII. 869/1 The phenomenon seen in the relative motion of suspensoid and medium resulting from polarization forces produced by an inhomogeneous electric field is defined as 'dielectrophoresis'. **1972** *Science* 23 June 1336/1 Unlike electrophoresis, dielectrophoresis will occur in a-c as well as d-c fields provided that the frequency is low enough for the dipolar orientation to follow the field reversals. **1977** *Oil & Gas Jrnl.* 28 Mar. 73/1 This new system utilizes the principles of dielectrophoresis to remove fine solid particles from hydrocarbon streams. **1983** *Financial Times* 31 May 18/2 The a.c. field regiments the cells, lining them up 'shoulder-to-shoulder' between the electrodes. This is achieved with a frequency of 10,000 hertz-1 megahertz by a process called dielectrophoresis.

**diesel**, *n.* Add: [a.] Also *ellipt.*, fuel for diesel engines, diesel oil.
**1953** *Bus Transportation* (U.S.) July 56/3 Average miles per gallon of fuel for the test was 5.59 for diesel, 4.02 for gasoline, 3.36 for LPG. **1974** *Go West* Apr. 23/2 Many truck stops were *rationing diesel and gasoline* due to insufficient allocations. **1975** *University* (Princeton Univ.) Winter 8/1 The new discoveries which were exciting him suggested that the diesels could be improved to meet the more stringent standards and eliminate the problem of particulates. **1986** J. HIBBS *Country Bus* x. 127 Across the road, .. there was a yard with petrol and diesel storage.

**diestrum**, *n.*: see *DIŒSTRUS *n.*

**diestrus**, *n.*, var. *DIŒSTRUS *n.*

**diffractogram** (dɪˈfræktəɡræm), *n.* [f. DIFFRACT *v.* + -o¹ + -GRAM.] A diagram or photograph showing how the intensity of diffracted radiation varies with the angle of diffraction.
**1968** *Proc. Soil Sci. Soc. Amer.* XXXII. 342/1 Four aliquots of horizontally oriented Mg-clay were prepared . . . Diffractograms of each aliquot thus prepared were obtained with a Phillips Electronics Norelco Diffractometer. **1974** *Nature* 27 Sept. 305/2 A chart diffractogram with scan speed of 1° min⁻¹ in 2θ utilised graphite monochromatised CuKα radiation. **1976** *Minerals Sci. & Engin.* VIII. 117/2 With natural and synthetic specimens of monoclinic pyrrhotite, $Fe_7S_8$, the X-ray diffractograms usually show a characteristic splitting of the (102) reflexion into two peaks. **1989** *Nature* 11 May 129/2 After 24h some new peaks of low intensity appeared in the diffractogram.

**diffusion**, *n.* Add: Hence **di'ffusional** *a.*, of, characterized by, or involving diffusion.
**1950** *Jrnl. Chem. & Physics* XVIII. 2 Information of this kind can only be obtained from a solution of the diffusional boundary value problem involved. **1962** H. L. KERN et al. in A. Pirie *Lens Metabolism Rel. Cataract* 393 Diffusional exchange of the labelled atoms is minimal since they are diluted by the lenticular sodium on entry. **1985** *Canad. Jrnl. Linguistics* XXX. 199 These are in some way a universal tendency in languages whatever their genetic relationship or whatever their diffusional contacts.

**digest**, *n.* Add: 4. *Biol.* A substance obtained by digestion with heat, etc.
**1918** *Jrnl. Infectious Dis.* XXIII. 72 This blood digest . . is exceedingly cheap . . . We have used it as an equivalent substitute for other digests and found it to be excellent for the growth of delicate-growing organisms, like streptococci. **1930** C. L. EVANS

*Starling's Princ. Human Physiol.* (ed. 5) xxviii. 539 The stages in the action of saliva on boiled starch can be followed more easily when a very small amount of saliva is added to some starch solution at 37°, and portions of the digest are tested at intervals. **1983** J. R. S. FINCHAM *Genetics* xiv. 390 These workers isolated DNA from rabbit liver nuclei and digested it with each of six restriction endonucleases . . . Each of the digests was subjected to electrophoresis.

**digitalization** (ˌdɪdʒɪtəlaɪˈzeɪʃən), *n.²* [f. DIGITALIZE *v.²* + -ATION.] The action or process of digitizing; conversion into digital form.
**1965** *Simulation* V. 329/2 The purpose for this digitalization is to replace analog shaping networks by digital programs. **1970** O. DOPPING *Computers & Data Processing* i. 13 Digitalization can be effected by means of an apparatus resembling a TV camera or a telephoto transmitter. **1980** *Euronet DIANE News* Aug./Sept. 7/1 The cost of digitalization and teletransmission is falling.

**diner**, *n.* Add: [2.] c. See *kitchen-diner* s.v. KITCHEN *n.* 5 f.

**dinero**, *n.* Delete ‖ and for pronunc. read: (dɪˈnɛərəʊ, ‖diˈnero). Add: **2.** Money, cash. *slang* (orig. *U.S.*).
**1856** *Butte Record* (Oroville, Calif.) 29 Aug. 2/6 They pungled the dinero, and observed that, as it was cheap, they had a mind to play the 'balance of the day out'. **1906** 'O. HENRY' *Heart of West* (1907) vi. 84 'Here's a little bunch of the *dinero* that I drawed out of the bank this morning,' says he, and shows a roll of twenties and fifties. **1930** H. H. KNIBBS *Songs of Lost Frontier* 42 My friend is my little carbine, A trusty companion is she; My foe is the man in between His sack of *dinero* and me. **1959** C. MACINNES *Absolute Beginners* 90 So it's a touch? You need a bit dinero? Five pounds do? **1973** D. LANG *Freaks* 34 Annie and I had an extra day and night together, and I had ended with more dinero than I had expected.

**dingbat**, *n.* Add: [1.] (d) *Printing* (orig. *U.S.*). Any ornamental piece of type; *esp.* a typographical device other than a letter or numeral (e.g. a rule, asterisk), used for visual effect.
**1921** G. M. HYDE *Handbk. Newspaper Workers* xi. 173 *Dingbats*, heavy, wavy pieces of cut-off rule sometimes used beneath banner headlines. Also applies to any ornament. **1971** F. K. BASKETTE *Art of Editing* xvi. 360 A magazine page usually has . . a block of text, usually beginning with a typographical device that . . may be a dingbat such as a black square followed by a few words in all-capital letters. **1989** *PC World* 24 July 42/2 Like the [Zapf] Dingbats face, these symbols are scattered throughout the QWERTY keys.

**dingleberry** (ˈdɪŋɡ(ə)lˌbɛrɪ, -ˌb(ə)rɪ), *n.* orig. *U.S.* [f. *dingle*, of uncertain origin (perh. DINGLE *n.* or as in DINGBAT *n.*), + BERRY *n.*¹]
**1.** *U.S.* A cranberry, *Vaccinium erythrocarpum*, of the south-eastern U.S.
**1952** B. C. BLACKBURN *Trees & Shrubs Eastern N. Amer.* 334 Dingleberry, *Vaccinium erythrocarpum*. **1974** G. USHER *Dict. Plants used by Man* 594/2 *V. erythrocarpum* Michx. (Bear Berry, Dingleberry, Mountain Cranberry). S.E. N. America.
**2.** Transferred uses. a. *pl.* Dried faecal matter attached to the hair around the anus. Also *transf.* *slang* (orig. *U.S.*).
**1953** BERREY & VAN DEN BARK *Amer. Thes. Slang* (1954) §124/2 Dingbats, dingleberries, dried adherent dung. **1972** B. RODGERS *Queens' Vernacular* 19 *Dingle-berries* (late '50s-late '60s), dried globs of feces hanging to the anal hairs of an unfastidious person. *Ibid.* 25 *Ass* . . . Syn: *dingle-berry pie* (early '60s); *salad bowl* (late '50s). **1974** R. K. MUELLER

*Buzzwords* II. 67 Taken from the trade colloquialism referring to the splattered molten particles around a metallic weld on a pipe or vessel. His presentation 'left a lot of dingleberries' means he splattered thoughts and inferences all around the main task.
**b.** A fool, a stupid person. *slang.*
**1969** L. MICHAELS *Going Places* 158, I .. screeched, 'What a dingleberry.' **1990** *Righting Words* Spring 11/2 *Dingleberry*, a socially inept person. 'Tell that dingleberry I'm not here.'
**c.** *pl.* The female breasts. *slang.*
**1980** *Brit. Jrnl. Photogr.* 9 May 447/1 Daddy says tits. Daddy says knockers and jugs and bazooms and dingleberries and jujubes. And then he laughs and goes 'wuff! wuff!'

**dink** (dɪŋk), *n.⁵* Also Dink. *slang* (orig. *N. Amer.*). [f. as *DINKY *n.⁴] = *DINKY *n.⁴
**1987** *New York* 12 Jan. 16/1 When a friend referred to two young professionals as 'a couple of dinks', it was a bit surprising ... Double Income, No Kids. **1987** *Times on Sunday* (Sydney) 22 Feb. 32/3 The gurus of advertising are .. trying to find the real monied trendies who aren't wasting their time and income on children. These are DINKs, couples with Double Income No Kids. **1988** *N.Y. Times* 28 Apr. c11/1 Working people, whether single or dinks (dual income, no kids), are meeting other suburbanites. **1990** *Chicago Tribune* 26 Aug. (Travel Suppl.) 6/6 The DINKS .. and empty-nesters now have a greater potential to travel off-season.

**dinky** ('dɪŋkɪ), *n.⁴ slang* (orig. *N. Amer.*). Also dinkie and with cap. initial. Pl. dinkies, dinkys. [Acronym f. the initial letters of *d*ouble (also *d*ual) *i*ncome *n*o *k*ids + -Y⁶, -IE, on the model of *yuppie*. The final *y* is sometimes interpreted as 'yet'.] Either partner of a usu. professional working couple who have no children and are characterized (esp. in marketing) as affluent consumers with few domestic demands on their time and money. Freq. in *pl.*
**1986** *Sunday Tel.* 21 Dec. 2/1 Dinkies: Double Income No Kids couples are the latest upmarket target identified by financiers of Wall Street and Toronto for retailers of everything from unit trusts to after shave. *Ibid.*, British statistics released this weekend confirm that the Day of the Dinky has dawned here too. **1987** *Ibid.* 18 Jan. 3/1 A Swell Dinkie has her own Gold American Express card which her husband still aims for. **1987** *Observer* 21 June 59/3 People who will live in Docklands are empty nesters, dinkies, two incomes, two cars. **1987** *Los Angeles Times* 1 Nov. I. 7/2 A spokesman for the London Docklands Development Corp. .. describes the new resident as mainly DINKYS—standing for dual income, no kids yet. **1988** *Daily Tel.* 28 Mar. 24/8 Affluent dinkys (double income no kids yet) and married women with investment income and rich husbands will benefit from the end of aggregation.

**dioctahedral**, *a.* Restrict †*Obs.* to sense 1 and add: **2.** *Min.* Of a mineral or mineral structure: having two out of every three octahedrally co-ordinated sites in the crystal lattice occupied.
**1946** R. E. STEVENS in *Bull. U.S. Geol. Survey* No. 950. 103 The formulas of biotite .. and of talc. .. are trioctahedral .. whereas those of muscovite .. and pyrophyllite .. are dioctahedral, having one vacant octahedral position in the formula. **1953** [see ILLITE *n.*]. **1967** *Oceanogr. & Marine Biol.* V. 155 They did .. contain about 10% of dioctahedral montmorillonite together with traces of anhydrite, calcite, and quartz. **1984** GREENWOOD & EARNSHAW *Chem. of Elements* (1986) ix. 408 The gibbsite series is sometimes called dioctahedral .. in obvious reference to the number of octahedral sites occupied in the 'non-silicate' layer.

**diœstrus** (daɪˈiːstrəs), *n. Biol.* Also -um, (*U.S.*) diestrus (-ˈɛstrəs, -ˈiːstrəs), -um. [f. DI-³ + ŒSTRUS *n.*, ŒSTRUM *n.*] A relatively short period of

sexual quiescence between metoestrus and prooestrus.
**1900** W. HEAPE in *Q. Jrnl. Microsc. Sci.* XLIV. 8 Diœstrum, or the Diœstrous Period.—This is a brief period lasting only a few days ... It is followed at once by a new pro-œstrum, and the four periods, pro-œstrum, œstrus, metœstrum, and diœstrum, I have designated the diœstrous cycle. **1923** *Physiol. Rev.* III. 458 The interval of quietude following oestrus is called 'dioestrus' if it be only a relatively brief interlude between regularly recurrent oestrous periods, 'anoestrus' if it be so long as to cover a large part of the year between mating seasons. **1937** *Nature* 4 Dec. 949/2 The diœstrus is not simply a quiescent period, but is now known to be of the nature of an abbreviated pseudo-pregnancy. **1957** *Encycl. Brit.* XIX. 173/2 If coition does not take place at the first oestrus, or if for some other reason the ova discharged at ovulation are not fertilized, the animal, instead of experiencing a prolonged pseudopregnancy followed by an anoestrum (as with the bitch), undergoes a short period of apparent quiescence, called by Heape the dioestrum, then comes to heat again. **1966, 1973** [see METŒSTRUS *n.*].
Hence **di'œstrous** *a.*
**1900** [see *DIŒSTRUS *n.*]. **1956** [see METŒSTROUS *a.*]. **1974** D. & M. WEBSTER *Compar. Vertebr. Morphol.* xviii. 476 This is the diestrous period. It brings the estrous cycle fully around to where it can either be extended in a long asexual period .. or .. yield to a new proestrous period immediately.

**diogenite** (daɪˈɒdʒɪnaɪt), *n. Geol.* [ad. G. *Diogenit* (M. G. Tschermak 1883, in *Sitzungsber. K. Akad. Wissensch.* LXXXVIII. I. 366), f. Gr. Διογενής descended from Zeus: see -ITE¹.] Any of a group of calcium-poor achondrite meteorites that consist mainly of hypersthene or bronzite.
**1895** O. C. FARRINGTON *Handbk. & Catal. Meteorite Coll. Field Columbian Museum* (Publ. Field Columbian Mus. I. 1.) 24 The classification suggested by Tschermak for the äerolites is as follows .. II .. (c) Diogenite, composed of bronzite or hypersthene. (Ibbenbuhren, Shalka.) **1916** *Mineral. Mag.* XVIII. 36 The chladnites (diogenites), chassignites, amphoterites, and rodites have a ratio of MgO to FeO of 2 to 2½. **1971** [see HOWARDITE *n.* 2]. **1979** *Nature* 4 Oct. 361/2 We have found optical anisotropy in clear taenite from over 40 meteorites including .. chondrites, diogenites, iron meteorites, mesosiderites and pallasites.

**diol** ('daɪɒl), *n. Chem.* [f. the ending -*diol* (as in *œstradiol, pregnanediol, propanediol*, etc.), f. DI-² + -OL.] Any alcohol whose molecule contains two hydroxyl groups; a dihydric alcohol; = GLYCOL *n.* b.
**1920** *Chem. Abstr.* XIV. 2472 (*heading*) The positive influence of 1,3-diols on the conductivity of boric acid. **1967** MARGERISON & EAST *Introd. Polymer Chem.* iii. 122 The reaction between a diol and a diacid chloride rather than a diacid has the advantage of greater speed. **1980** *Nature* 8 May 99/1 Long chain 1,2- and 1,3-diols which are effective boundary lubricants chemisorb to the aluminium oxide surface more readily than the corresponding alcohols or acids.

**dip**, *n.¹* Senses 1 g, h in Dict. become 1 h, i. Add: [**1.**] **g.** A decline in the value or magnitude of share prices, profits, etc.; *esp.* a slight fall.
**1892** *Courier-Jrnl.* (Louisville, Kentucky) 1 Oct. 11/5 There was a disposition among a few houses to buy for a reaction after an early dip to-day. **1929** *Daily Express* 7 Nov. 1/4 Traders were ignorant in many instances of what the prevailing prices were, because of the rapid dips downward. **1958** *Economist* 6 Dec. 866/2 The white paper pins its hopes to the 'dip' years in the early sixties, when the present bulge

has passed, and before numbers begin to rise again. **1986** *Daily Tel.* 28 Feb. 19 (*heading*) Booming market unruffled by ICI £122m profit dip.

**dip**, *v.* Add: [II.] [12.] **b.** Of share prices, profits, etc.: to fall in value or size, esp. slightly.
**1956** *Time* 1 Oct. 78/2 Consumer prices dipped .02% last month. **1981** *Times* 4 Apr. 19/2 (*headline*) Sterling dips by 2½ cents. **1984** *Broadcast* 7 Dec. 31/1 This week's figures .. show .. its audience share dipping to just under 41%.

**diphenoxylate** (daɪfɛ'nɒksɪleɪt), *n. Pharm.* [f. DIPHEN(YL *n.* + *CARB)OXYLATE *n.*] A tetracyclic derivative, $C_{30}H_{32}N_2O_2$, of pethidine that reduces intestinal motility and is given orally as the hydrochloride in cases of diarrhoea and colitis.
**1960** *Amer. Jrnl. Gastroenterol.* XXXIV. 630 A new antidiarrheal agent, diphenoxylate hydrochloride, Lomotil (R-1132), was administered to 80 patients with diarrhea of various causes. **1976** *Brit. Med. Jrnl.* 20 Nov. 1240/2 Diphenoxylate with atropine (Lomotil) is popular nowadays. **1984** *Brit. Nat. Formulary* (B.M.A.) (ed. 8) 53/2 In chronic diarrhoeas .. loperamide may be preferable to the centrally acting opiates (morphine, codeine, and diphenoxylate) as it is unlikely to cause dependence.

**directory**, *n.* Add: [3.] **c.** *Computing.* (*a*) Any list of the locations of data items, files, subdirectories, sets of instructions, etc., usu. also containing other information such as the name and size of each file and the date of its most recent update; *spec.* a displayed version of such a list.
**1962** *Gloss. Terms Automatic Data Processing* (B.S.I.) 36 *Directory*, a list of addresses which are used as reference points in a program, for example, in relative coding. **1973** C. W. GEAR *Introd. Computer Sci.* vii. 268 To avoid this we must create an array that tells us where the I$^{th}$ member is located. Such an array is called an access table or directory. **1984** *QL User* Dec. 28 An advanced filing system permits data and program files to be split up into related groups or 'directories' on disk. **1986** *What Micro?* Nov. 51/2 Should a document become lost in a mess of directories on a hard disk, there is a search facility to locate it again.
(*b*) A data item describing the type and location of each field in a record.
**1964** *Gloss. Data Processing & Communications Terms* (Honeywell Inc.) 19/2 *Directory*, a file with the layout of each field of the record which it describes; thus a directory describes the layout of a record within a file.

**disabled**, *ppl. a.* Add: **b.** *absol.* as *n. pl.*: *the disabled*.
**1916** *19th Cent.* Oct. 823 The solution of the disablement problem is .. to train the disabled till they can earn a living wage. **1921** *Industrial Managem.* LXII. 345/1 France, Belgium, England, [etc.] .. saw the possibilities of salvaging the disabled and putting those disabled through war service back into their communities as re-built, re-trained men. **1961** *Hansard Commons* 20 Mar. 44 Houses for the old people, for the sick and the disabled. **1976** *Morecambe Guardian* 7 Dec. 19/2 'Never give up the fight to get four-wheeled cars for the disabled,' said the Mayor. **1985** *Sunday Tel.* 9 June 16/6 The union objects .. to the expression 'the disabled' as a collective label. The approved expression is 'people with disabilities'. **1990** *Social Work Today* 6 Sept. 12/1 It decided to rename the Minister for the Disabled .. Minister for Disabled People . . . [BASW] wants the Department to use the term 'people with disabilities'.

**disablist** (dɪs'eɪblɪst), *a.* [f. DISABL(ED *ppl. a.* + -IST, after *racist, sexist*, etc.] Discriminating or

prejudiced against disabled people; displaying discrimination on the basis of disability.
**1984** *Daily Tel.* 1 Nov. 18 The unfortunate employee wrote a report about the effect of abolition on the council's services, which was graphically described as 'crippling'. That, he was told, was 'disablist'. **1986** *Spare Rib* May 6/2, I am not apologising for SM and believe that in itself it is neither racist, classist, disablist nor anti-semitic. **1987** *Times* 29 June 12/3 In short, your company appears to be racist, sexist and disablist.

**disassemble**, *v.* Add: **2.** *intr.* To undergo disassembly; to disintegrate, separate into constituent elements.
**1961** in WEBSTER. **1970** G. R. TAYLOR *Doomsday Bk.* viii. 193 If you wish to refer to .. the whole plant exploding .. you say .. the plant 'will disassemble'. **1973** *Sci. Amer.* Nov. 54/3 If the calcium ion is removed by chelating agents, the subunits disassemble. **1976** *Laurel* (Montana) *Outlook* 30 June 14/3 The parade will .. follow First Ave. to Thomson Park, where the parade will disassemble. **1989** B. ALBERTS et al. *Molecular Biol. Cell* (ed. 2) viii. 425 When a nucleus disassembles in mitosis, its contents mix with those of the cytosol.
Hence **disa'ssemblage** *n.* = DISASSEMBLY *n.*
**1980** *Blair & Ketchum's Country Jrnl.* Oct. 127/2 He recommends .. complete disposal of hazardous wastes by means of disassemblage or direct destruction. **1986** *Los Angeles Times* 23 Nov. 4/1 The clothes I dance in have to allow me to make quick assemblages and disassemblages of imagery.

**disc**, *n.* Add: [8.] [f.] **disc emulator** *Computing*, a program that enables part of a memory to be used as if it were a disc.
**1982** *Interface Age* Nov. 102/1 With the Semidisk *disk emulator, Semidisk Systems .. incorporates the 64K-bit memory chip into a half-Mbyte memory board that is configured to look like a disk drive.
**disc file** *Computing*, a file consisting of or stored on a disc or discs.
**1961** *Instruments & Control Syst.* XXXIV. 2063/1 *Disc files are becoming increasingly popular for data storage where access to large amounts of data is required in milliseconds. **1984** *Which Micro?* Dec. 15 (Advt.), By creating special disc files .. you can link .. spreadsheets together.

**discount**, *v.*[1] Add: [3.] **c.** To reduce (a selling price) by means of a discount; hence, to sell (goods) at a discount.
**1955** *Business Week* 10 Sept. 54/2 Till now, a seller could discount his price to the buyer only by the amount that the buyer saved him in cost of distributing his product. **1975** *Ibid.* 16 June 24/3 The price of rock may even fall to less than $25 per metric ton . . . It is already being discounted to around $43 per metric ton. **1977** *Gramophone* June 4 (Advt.), Comet have been discounting Hi-Fi since 1968 and that makes us not only the biggest but one of the oldest-established discounters in the UK. **1981** *N.Y. Times* 18 Jan. III. 13/1 Stores such as Loehmann's and Barney's in New York .. have discounted brand-name merchandise for years.

**discourse**, *n.* Add: [3.] **e.** *Linguistics.* A connected series of utterances by which meaning is communicated, esp. forming a unit for analysis; spoken or written communication regarded as consisting of such utterances. Also *transf.* in *Semiotics.* Cf. *discourse analysis*, sense 8 below.
**1951** Z. S. HARRIS *Methods in Structural Linguistics* ii. 11 The universe of discourse for each statement in the descriptive analysis is a single whole utterance in the language in question. *Ibid.* iii. 28 For the incidence of formal features of this type only long discourses or conversations can serve as samples of the language. **1957** G. L. TRAGER in *Encycl. Brit.*

XIV. 162H/2 The syntax of any language can be arrived at in analogous ways. The phonologically determined parts of a discourse are found, and their constituent phrases separated out. **1976** T. EAGLETON *Crit. & Ideology* ii. 54 A dominant ideological formation is constituted by a relatively coherent set of 'discourses' of values, representations and beliefs. **1983** BROWN & YULE *Discourse Analysis* ii. 29 We can see little practical use, in the analysis of discourse, for the notion of logical presupposition.

**discover**, v. Add: [3.] **d.** *Theatr. pass.* or *pa. pple.* Of a person: to be disclosed on stage in a particular position or state as the curtain rises. (Usu. in stage directions.)
   [**1716**: see sense 3 a.] **1780** SHERIDAN *Sch. Scand.* I. i. 1 Lady Sneerwell and Snake discovered at a tea-table. *c***1852** D. BOUCICAULT *Corsican Brothers* I. i. 5 Marie discovered singing while she sits at her spinning wheel. ?**1884** W. S. GILBERT *Sorcerer* (new ed.) II. 18 All the peasantry are discovered asleep on the ground. **1920** E. O'NEILL *Beyond Horizon* III. i. 124 At the rise of the curtain Ruth is discovered sitting by the stove. **1973** A. AYCKBOURN *Time & Time Again* I. i. 1 When the Curtain rises, Leonard, a man in his late thirties, is discovered in the conservatory.

**disestablishment**, n. Add: Hence also **dise,stablishmen'tarianism** n., advocacy of disestablishment (usu. only as a factitious long word).
   **1897** N. & Q. 15 May 395/2, I once heard at a political meeting a speaker describe another as an advocate of 'disestablishmentarianism'. **1971** *Archivum Linguisticum* II. 47 The reader will recognize the composite nature not only of, say, familiar compounds like *armchair* or *milk jug* but also of *unfashionable* and *disestablishmentarianism*.

**dishonourable**, a. Add: [1.] **c.** *dishonourable discharge* U.S. Mil., dismissal with disgrace from military service by court martial.
   **1865** *Gen. Court Martial Orders* (U.S. War Dept.) 14 June No. 301, *Sentence.* 'Dishonorable discharge and imprisonment during the war.' **1919** *Forum* Oct. 448 These men have received harsh and unjustifiable sentences, imprisonment with dishonourable discharge, the death penalty, which .. I considered as beyond the scope of human justice. **1944** *Atlantic Monthly* June 51/2 A deserter who gave himself up after an absence of more than sixty days was liable to dishonorable discharge and confinement at hard labor for a year. **1989** K. GREEN *Night Angel* 279 While still in marine boot camp, he'd been given six months in the brig and a dishonorable discharge from the corps.

**disinhibit** (dɪsɪn'hɪbɪt), v. *Psychol.* [DIS- 6; cf. DISINHIBITION n.] *trans.* To cause the release of (a response that has been habituated, or one that has been learnt and then extinguished); also, to disable the inhibitory mechanism of. More generally, to release from (emotional) inhibitions, esp. temporarily; to make less inhibited. Also *absol.* or *intr.*
   **1927** G. V. ANREP tr. *Pavlov's Conditioned Reflexes* vi. 99 The extraneous stimulus acting on the positive phase of the reflex inhibits, and acting on the negative phase dis-inhibits. **1931** *Brit. Jrnl. Psychol.* July 38 The interference of generalization can be restored by the action of 'extra stimuli' in temporarily weakening (disinhibiting) the internal inhibition. **1935** *Psychol. Bull.* XXXII. 677 This procedure was continued until each rat had been disinhibited eight times. **1964** J. Z. YOUNG *Model of Brain* iv. 52 The effect of a particular demand would thus be to disinhibit the relevant enzyme system. **1974** K. CLARK *Another Part of Wood* iii. 100 As well

as dis-inhibiting me he educated me. **1977** *Lancet* 5 Feb. 313/1 The social obtruders (i.e. the incontinent, wandering, nocturnally disturbed, noisy, aggressive, or sexually disinhibited) are a subgroup of 'organic' patients on quite another social dimension. **1989** *Jrnl. Psychopharmacol.* III. 86 The factors which determine whether propranolol disinhibits non-rewarded responding or whether it has the opposite effect are obscure.

**disintermedi'ation**, n. *Econ.* (orig. *U.S.*). [DIS- 9.] A reduction in the use or role of banks and savings institutions as intermediaries between lenders and borrowers; the transfer of savings and borrowings away from the established banking system.
   **1968** *N.Y. Times* 2 May 67/1 The refinancing got high marks from Wall Street because of the Government's effort to lessen 'disintermediation'—heavy withdrawals from savings institutions for direct investment in the securities market. **1975** *Encounter* Feb. 46/1, I am told that economists have just discovered *disintermediation*, which they believe means the removal of money from savings banks. **1978** *U.K. Econ. Outlook* (National Westminster Bank) 3 July 1 The effect of the 'corset' will be to cause 'disintermediation', as public sector borrowers obtain funds direct from the markets rather than through the banking system. **1981** *Economist* 24 Jan. 28/1 The idea was to spare the thrifts from the recurrent flights of depositors anxious to get better returns on their money: the dread 'disintermediation'. **1986** *Times* 3 Jan. 13/8 Securitization is really just another word for disintermediation.

**dismissive**, a. Add: **dis'missiveness** n.
   **1980** *N.Y. Times* 16 Nov. VII. 26/3, I doubt that anybody who actually lays hands on this book will incline toward dismissiveness. **1982** K. ISHIGURO *Pale View of Hills* (1983) vii. 114, I was rather surprised at the dismissiveness of her tone.

**dispen'sationalism**, n. *Theol.* [f. DISPENSATIONAL a. + -ISM.] Belief in a system of historical progression, as revealed in the Bible, consisting of a series of (*spec.* seven) stages in God's self-revelation and plan of salvation. Cf. DISPENSATION n. 6.
   **1928** P. MAURO *Gospel of Kingdom* 8 Evangelical Christianity must purge itself of this leaven of *dispensationalism* ere it can display its former power. **1956** *Interpretation* X. 173 The principal feature of Dispensationalism and the one supplying its name is its teaching that seven Dispensations are to be discovered in Scripture, a dispensation being a span of time in which there is a revelation of God and a test of man's obedience. **1979** *Church Times* 23 Nov. 6/4 They find much truth in dispensationalism. Miraculous cures witness to unusual intrusions of the divine presence rather than to the normal ministry of the Church. **1986** *Observer* 26 Jan. 7/4 They all adhere to the doctrine of 'dispensationalism' which was first promulgated by the Plymouth Brethren in Britain in the 1830s ... These people believe that the Bible is an almanac, chronicling future events which will culminate in Armageddon.
   Hence **dispen'sationalist** n., an adherent of dispensationalism.
   **1948** L. G. CHAFER *Systematic Theol.* IV. i. 8 Antidispensationalists refer to the belief which dispensationalists hold—that Christ offered the Kingdom to Israel and that it was rejected. **1963** *Bibliotheca Sacra* CXX. 49 Dispensationalists believe there is a difference between Israel and the church, and that God has a literal kingdom future for Israel. **1983** RICHARDSON & BOWDEN *New Dict. Christian Theol.* 158/2 Dispensationalists trace their origins to the preaching and writings of John Nelson Darby of Dublin (1800-1882), one of the early leaders of the Plymouth Brethren.

**displacement**, *n.* Add: [**2.**] [**b.**] (ii) *Mech.* The volume swept by a reciprocating piston, as in a pump or engine.
**1897** K. P. DAHLSTROM tr. *Weisbach & Herrmann's Mech. Pumping Machinery* ii. 48 The volume below the piston then simply flows through it to the space above, and the amount delivered merely equals the displacement of the piston rod. **1922** GLAZEBROOK *Dict. Appl. Physics* I. 509/2 On the out stroke the delivery is equal to the difference between the volumes of the piston and plunger displacements. **1971** B. SCHARF *Engin. & its Lang.* xi. 193 Displacement may be measured in cubic inches (cubic centimetres) per stroke or per minute, or in gallons (litres) per minute.
**4.** Special Comb.: **displacement pump**, any pump in which liquid is moved out of the pump chamber by a moving surface or by the introduction of compressed air or gas.
**1924** N. SWINDIN *Mod. Theory & Pract. of Pumping* ix. 277 (*heading*) *Displacement pumps for inflammable liquids. **1976** I. J. KARASSIK et al. *Pump Handbk.* I. 4 Displacement pumps are essentially divided into reciprocating and rotary types.

**disposal**, *n.* Add: [**2.**] **b.** A domestic waste disposal unit. *U.S. colloq.*
**1953** *Wall St. Jrnl.* 14 Dec. 21/4 General Electric's Appliance Park development.. is already making kitchen ranges, automatic washers and dryers, dishwashers and disposals. **1967** MRS. L. B. JOHNSON *White House Diary* 25 June (1970) 539 Betty gave her the full treatment about the washer and dryer and disposal. **1973** *Washington Post* 13 Jan. E3/2 (Advt.), Each condominium comes equipped with an all electric kitchen, including dish-washer, frost-free refrigerator, range and disposal. **1986** *Cambridge* (Mass.) *Chron.* 6 Mar. 10 (Advt.), Wiring for elec. dryers, outlets, switches, ranges and disposals.

**dissensus** (dɪˈsɛnsəs), *n.* [Prob. blend of DISSENT *n.* and CONSENSUS *n.*; cf. L. *dissensus* dissension, disagreement.] Widespread dissent or disagreement in opinion; absence of collective unanimous opinion.
**1962** F. PINNER in N. Sandford *Amer. College* xxvii. 946 (*heading*) Dissensus and conventionality. **1968** *Economist* 17 Aug. 43/2 In the United States.. no single author can undertake a survey of this breadth..: there has to be a committee and a consensus or, as in this case, a dissensus. **1977** A. GIDDENS *Stud. in Social & Polit. Theory* x. 339 In any group which has a continued existence over time, those in power face problems of dissensus and the possibility of rebellion. **1983** J. BARZUN *Stroll with W. James* 246 Few spiritual facts receive universal assent. He might have instanced the permanent dissensus about art.

**dissertation**, *n.* Add: [**2.**] **b.** *spec.* An extended scholarly essay, usu. based upon original research, submitted for a degree or other academic qualification.
**1873** *Catal. Officers & Students 1873-74* (Columbia College, N.Y.) 114 Graduates of the School who pursue for one year a course of study prescribed by the Faculty, and present an acceptable dissertation embodying their results, receive the degree of Doctor of Philosophy. **1930** J. C. ALMACK *Research & Thesis Writing* i. 11 Like *thesis*, *dissertation* has come to connote research, but it is a more pedantic term, and usually is reserved strictly for the thesis for the doctorate. **1964** *Cal. Univ. Newcastle upon Tyne 1964-65* 327 The Final Honours Examination shall consist of nine papers, or eight papers and a dissertation. **1972** A. J. AYER *Russell* i. 14 Russell obtained his Fellowship at Trinity with a dissertation on the Foundations of Geometry. **1984** D. CUPITT *Sea of Faith* v. 142 Marx duly obtained his doctorate, moved to Bonn to work with Bauer, and began to write a qualifying dissertation.

**distal**, *a.* Add: **c.** *Geol.* Designating or characteristic of an area relatively far from a sedimentation zone, volcanic vent, or other region of geological activity, but close enough to have been influenced by it.
**1949** F. J. PETTIJOHN *Sedimentary Rocks* xiv. 444 The terms 'proximal', 'axial', or 'distal' may also be applied to the deposits according to their position in the trough of deposition. **1968** EMBLETON & KING *Glacial & Periglacial Geomorphol.* (1971) ix. 224 The features eroded by actively moving ice sheets are generally asymmetrical, having steeper proximal slopes than distal slopes. **1979** *Nature* 25 Jan. 290/1 The greywackes grade from a proximal, quartz-rich, conglomeratic facies at the base, to a distal, finegrained, apparently volcaniclastic facies towards the top. **1985** THORPE & BROWN *Field Descr. Igneous Rocks* v. 55 The distal zone (beyond *ca.* 5-15 km from the central vent, and extending beyond the volcano) is characterized by pyroclastic flow deposits.

**distantiate** (dɪˈstænʃɪeɪt), *v.* Restrict †*Obs.* to sense in Dict. and add: [**2.**] To set or keep at a distance, esp. mentally; to distance oneself from.
**1948** L. SPITZER *Linguistics & Lit. Hist.* iii. 111 The 'distantiating demonstrative'.. suggests a point of view from outside the situation; when we say, for example, *dans ce pays* 'in this country', instead of *dans notre pays* 'in our country', there is effected.. a disinterested comparison with other countries. **1972** M. MEAD *Blackberry Winter* (1973) 26 By putting the promptings of the senses and of the unconscious at a distance, she also distantiated humor. **1976** T. EAGLETON *Crit. & Ideology* iii. 70 [Jane] Austen's aesthetic forms.. so 'distantiate' ideology as to light up the shady frontiers where it abuts, by negation, onto real history.

**distantiation** (dɪstænʃɪˈeɪʃən), *n.* [f. DISTANTIATE *v.*: see -ATION.] The action or process of distantiating; putting or keeping at a distance.
**1948** L. SPITZER *Linguistics & Lit. Hist.* ii. 41 We find it [*sc.* perspectivism] in Cervantes' treatment of the plot.. as well as in his attitude of distantiation toward the reader. **1963** E. H. ERIKSON *Childhood & Society* (ed. 2) III. vii. 264 The counterpart of intimacy is distantiation. **1976** T. EAGLETON *Crit. & Ideology* iii. 74 It is this *distantiation* of history, this absence of any particular historical 'real', which confers on literature its air of freedom. **1986** *Brit. Jrnl. Aesthetics* Autumn 341 His reversal of the classic hermeneutic problem of distantiation.

**distort**, *v.* Add: [**2.**] **c.** *Electr.* To change the form of (a signal or waveform) during transmission, amplification, or the like in such a way as to misrepresent it.
**1887** *Electrician* 3 June 81/1 It is the mixing up of these tails that causes arbitrary waves to be distorted as they travel from beginning to end of the line. **1921** *Wireless Age* June 16/1 Side band frequencies which differ most from the frequency to which the antenna is tuned are noticeably suppressed, thereby distorting the modulated wave and impairing the reproduction at the receiving station. **1962** A. NISBETT *Technique Sound Studio* xi. 195 One of the simplest methods of distorting sound is restriction of the frequency range by means of filters. **1983** B. P. LATHI *Mod. Digital & Analog Communication Syst.* i. 4 The waveform is distorted because of different amounts of attenuation and phase shift suffered by different frequency components of the signal.

**distorted**, *ppl. a.* Add: **3.** *Electr.* Of a signal or waveform: affected by electrical distortion.
**1927** *Bell Syst. Techn. Jrnl.* VI. 445 It is this distorted wave which acts in the plate circuit, instead of the pure sine wave operating with constant $\mu$. **1935** *Wireless World* 19 Apr. 397/2 An analysis of the distorted wave.. shows that the predominant alien frequency is a second harmonic. **1962** *Newnes Conc.*

*Encycl. Electr. Engin.* 200/1 The distorted output wave form may contain the existing input components altered (1) in relative magnitude . . or (2) in relative phase. **1991** *IEEE Trans. Power Delivery* VII. 1161 Under distorted waveform conditions their readings can differ by several percent.

**distractor** (dɪ'stræktə(r)), *n. U.S.* [f. DISTRACT *v.* + -OR.] Any of the incorrect options in a multiple-choice question, *esp.* one which is beguilingly plausible.

**1951** R. L. EBEL in E. F. Lindquist *Educ. Measurement* vii. 195 The multiple-choice form consists of the item *stem* (an introductory question or incomplete statement) and two or more *responses* (the suggested answers to the questions, or completions of the statement). In this discussion the correct response or responses will be called the answer(s), and the incorrect responses, the distractors. **1966** GUTTMAN & SCHLESINGER *Devel. Diagnostic & Mech. Ability Tests* (Cooperative Research Project) 7 This method lends itself to the systematic construction of distractors differing in degree of attraction. **1976** *Woman's Day* (N.Y.) Nov. 60/3 The multiple-choice format usually provides one answer that the testers call a 'distractor' and kids call a trick because it's almost correct. **1984** B. DUVALL *Kindergarten Performance for Reading & Matching Four Styles of Handwriting* (ERIC Document 265 536) 3 Kindergarten children . . were asked to match typeset distractors to small letters *b*, *d*, *g*, *l*, *m*, [etc.] . . handwritten in four styles.

**distribution**, *n.* Add: [9.] **distribution function** *Math.*, (*a*) the number of distinct ways in which a given number of objects can be distributed according to a particular partition (PARTITION *n.* 6 b); (*b*) any non-decreasing function which takes non-negative values and tends to a maximum of 1, esp. when considered as the integral of a corresponding probability density function.

**1889** *Proc. London Math. Soc.* XIX. 223 The *Distribution Function of *n* objects into parcels (*p*, *q*, *r*, . .) is the expression [etc.]. **1924** *Astrophysical Jrnl.* LIX. 313 The distribution function for velocity has been established. **1935** *Trans. Amer. Math. Soc.* XXXVIII. 48 The proper method in dealing with distribution functions and their convolutions . . is the method of Fourier transforms. **1980** A. J. JONES *Game Theory* i. 49 A distribution function on [0, 1] is a non-decreasing real valued function $F$ such that $0 \leqslant F(x) \leqslant 1$ and $F(1) = 1$.

**district**, *n.* Add: [6.] **district auditor**, (*a*) one appointed by the Poor Law Commissioners to audit the accounts of a District Board of Guardians (now *Hist.*); hence (*b*) until 1983, a civil servant responsible for auditing the accounts of local authorities; subsequently, an auditor employed in this capacity by the Audit Commission, and (since 1990) also responsible for auditing the accounts of health authorities and other bodies within the National Health Service (no longer a statutory title).

[**1844** *Act 7 & 8 Vict.* c. 101 §49 The Poor Law Commissioners shall appoint some person . . who shall be the Auditor of such District, and shall be empowered and required to audit the Accounts of each District Board.] **1868** *Act 31 & 32 Vict.* c. 122 §24 So much of the Poor Law Amendment Act, 1844 . . as provides for the Election of *District Auditors, shall be repealed. **1879** *District Auditors Act 42 Vict.* c. 6 §2 All payments to district auditors out of any local rate shall cease, and the whole of the . . remuneration . . shall be paid out of moneys provided by Parliament. **1907** A. E. LAUDER *Municipal Manual* vi. 209 In all ordinary urban districts, in some half-dozen boroughs . . and in all boroughs as far as income and expenditure on education are concerned,

the accounts are audited by the district auditors of the Local Government Board. **1985** R. JONES *Local Govt. Audit Law* (ed. 2) i. 18 A by-product of the [1982 Local Government Finance] Act was that the historic title of 'district auditor' disappeared from the statute book . . . The district auditor still lives, however, the [Audit] Commission having . . retained the title in the appointment of its officers.

**ditto**, *n.* Add: [3.] **d.** With cap. initial. A proprietary name in the U.S. for a kind of duplicating machine that reproduces copies from a master.

**1919** *Official Gaz.* (U.S. Patent Office) 1 July 149/2 Duplicator Manufacturing Company, Chicago, Ill. . . *Ditto* . . . Claims use since Dec. 16, 1918. **1936** *Ibid.* 22 Dec. 781/2 Ditto, Incorporated, Chicago, Ill. . . *Ditto* . . . For electrically operated duplicating machines. **1967** KARCH & BUBER *Offset Processes* 536 *Ditto*, a small offset press; a duplicator. **1971** *Sci. Amer.* May 63/1 (Advt.), The typical office fairly bulges with typewriters, copiers, dictating machines, dittos—everything to record and circulate the printed word.

**e.** A ditto mark (sense *4 below).

**1933** [see *ditto mark*, sense *4 below].

[4.] **ditto mark**, a symbol („) representing the word 'ditto', placed under the word or number to be repeated.

**1879** *Harvard Lampoon* VIII. 134/1 One town clerk . . was unfortunate enough to show off his knowledge of the *ditto-mark („), which means, as our readers doubtless know, 'the same', when placed underneath a word or number. **1933** H. ALLEN *Anthony Adverse* I. II. xiv. 195 There now unrolled about a foot of paper with ditto marks under 'item' and a long line opposite each ditto.

**ditto** *v.*: (*c*) *N. Amer.*, to copy (a document) by means of a Ditto machine; '**dittoed** *ppl. a.*, reproduced by a Ditto machine.

**1955** *Biometrics* XI. 42 Tukey, J. W., 'The Problem of Multiple Comparisons', unpublished dittoed notes, Princeton University, 396 pp., 1953. **1969** *Canad. Jrnl. Linguistics* XV. 38 An extensive 'underground' literature—papers which are privately circulated in dittoed form and read and criticized before they appear in journals. **1980** *Maledicta* III. II. 252 Prewitt & Schaeffer dittoed a 9-page *Contalk, An Abridged Lexicon and Notes on Contemporary Prison Slang* (1962) and Tamony kindly provided me with all the card-file information in his dittoed version (1963).

**div** (dɪv), *n.*[2] *Math.* Also 9 with point. [Abbrev.] Divergence (of), chiefly in symbolic contexts: see DIVERGENCE *n.* 3 b.

**1883** O. HEAVISIDE in *Electrician* 14 Apr. 510/2 Let R denote the electrostatic force, and $\rho$ the volume density of electricity, then we may say $4\pi\rho = -\text{conv}$. R, or, $= \text{div}$. R, where we use conv. and div. as abbreviations. **1924** C. E. WEATHERBURN *Adv. Vector Analysis* i. 7 From a vector function F may be derived two other point-functions, the one a scalar . . called the *divergence* of F . . denoted by div F. **1953** E. R. PECK *Electr. & Magn.* xii. 425 The conservation of electric charge is stated in differential form by the equation of continuity . . div $\mathbf{J} + \partial\rho/\partial t = 0$. **1975** PARTON & OWEN *Appl. Electromagnetics* i. 18 The operations div and curl can be used to classify fields.

**divalent**, *a.* Add: Hence **di'valence** *n.*, **di'valency** *n.* = BIVALENCY *n.*

**1888** BEDSON & WILLIAMS tr. *Meyer's Mod. Theories Chem.* ix. 333 On account of the divalency of oxygen . . they [*sc.* compounds with oxygen] would at first sight appear to afford but an unsuitable and doubtful means of determining the valency. **1909** *Cent. Dict.* Suppl., Divalence. **1927** N. V. SIDGWICK *Electronic Theory of Valency* 270 These two effects can lead ultimately to the divalency of the elements of both subgroups. **1972** *Physical Rev. B* V. 2738 The divalence of both Cd and Hg in trivalent In suggests that solute electropositivity is a possible origin of the anomaly. **1979** *Nature* 13 Dec. 743/2 A new ultrastructural post-embedding staining technique, based on the divalency of IgG molecules. **1985** *Jrnl. Magnetism* XLVII–XLVIII. 594/1 Eu ions in the high temperature regions assume integral divalence in cerium.

**dive**, *n.* Add: [1.] **d.** In Boxing, Football, etc.: an intentional fall taken to deceive an opponent or official, *esp.* (in Boxing) a feigned knock-out. Freq. in phr. *to take a dive*. Also *transf.* and *fig. slang* (orig. *U.S.*).

   **1942** BERREY & VAN DEN BARK *Amer. Thes. Slang* §701/10 *Dive,.. take a dive, take it, throw a fight*, to allow an opponent to win by prearrangement. **1951** *N.Y. Times Mag.* 4 Mar. 58/3 Admittedly the sport still will come up occasionally with its 'dives'. (A dive is a phantom knockout in which a boxer 'swoons' or dives to the canvas under the impact of a light blow or, sometimes, no blow at all.) **1982** *Chicago Sun-Times* 21 June 5/1 'Freddy took a dive six times,' Time quoted one investigator as saying of Furino's performance on the polygraph.

**divergence**, *n.* Restrict *Math.* to senses 3 a, b in Dict. [3.] **[b.]** Substitute for def.: The scalar product (written div **F** or ∇·**F**) of the operator ∇ (see DEL *n.*) and some given vector **F**; it gives a measure of the quantity of flux emanating from any point of the vector field or the rate of loss of mass, heat, etc., from it. Abbrev. DIV *n.*[2] (Examples.)

   [**1871** J. C. MAXWELL in *Proc. London Math. Soc.* III. 231, I propose to call the scalar part the *Convergence* of σ. . . I think . . that the convergence of a vector function is a very good name for the effect of that vector function in carrying its subject inwards towards a point.] **1878** W. K. CLIFFORD *Elements of Dynamic* III. ii. 209 Prof. Clerk Maxwell calls the quantity −*E* the *convergence* of σ. We might perhaps therefore call *E* itself the divergence of σ. **1950** H. LASS *Vector & Tensor Analysis* ii. 46 The divergence of a curl is zero. **1973** J. YARWOOD *Electr. & Magnetism* 638 The divergence of a vector is concerned with the net outflow of some physical entity, such as heat or electric flux, through the surface area of a unit volume in a vector field.
   **c.** The horizontal movement of air or ocean currents away from a region, a process accompanied by a vertical movement into it; a mathematical measure of this, such as the divergence (sense 3 b) of the velocity vector.

   **1906** SHAW & LEMPFERT *Life Hist. Surface Air Currents* I. 18 A position of ascent is indicated by the trajectories where there is a convergence of the lines and a position of descent where there is divergence. . . These terms must be understood in a generalised or mathematical sense. **1919** N. SHAW *Man. Meteorol.* IV. 105 The mapping of a large area for air motion will generally disclose a series of lines or points of convergence or divergence of the instantaneous lines of flow with which must be associated instantaneous upward or downward flow. **1944** *Jrnl. Meteorol.* I. 3/1 In a qualitative sense we may visualize positive horizontal divergence as a horizontal spreading of air, and negative divergence (i.e. convergence) as a horizontal crowding of air. **1967** R. W. FAIRBRIDGE *Encycl. Atmospheric Sci.* 250/2 The large-scale motions of the atmosphere . . are characterized by very small values of the divergence (~10⁻⁶ sec⁻¹). **1984** A. C. & A. DUXBURY *Introd. World's Oceans* vii. 226 (*caption*) The major surface currents of the world's oceans, with principal zones of surface convergence and divergence shown.
   **d.** A region where there is a divergence of air or ocean currents.
   **1942** H. SVERDRUP *Oceanogr. for Meteorologists* v. 85 Ascending motion occurs in regions of diverging

currents (divergences). **1959** H. WEXLER in B. Bolin *Atmosphere & Sea in Motion* 113/2 It appears difficult to find a strictly internal explanation for such a sharp fixed line as the Antarctic Divergence. **1984** A. C. & A. DUXBURY *Introd. World's Oceans* vi. 186 Water from below is upwelled at a divergence.

**divide**, *v.* Add: [II.] [14.] **c.** Of a number or quantity: to admit of division.
   **1938** V. HOPPER *Medieval Number Symbolism* ii. 26 From its original meaning, 40 comes to be a 'fated' period, possibly as a result of the statement that after the flood man's days are to be 120 years, which divides exactly into 3 periods of 40 years each. **1985** *Nature* 31 Oct. 762/1, 12 can be divided by 2, 3, 4 and 6 while 10 divides by only 2 and 5. **1986** *Ibid.* 31 July 413/1 The scholarly reading population divides naturally into two types.

**dividend**, *n.* Add: [3.] **c.** A share in the payout from a football or other pool, received by a winner.
   **1929** *People* 13 Oct. 18/1 (Advt.), Our Pools pay the following dividends for Saturday, 5th October. **1937** E. JOHNSTONE *Profit from Football Pools* i. 1 The difference, between the support given to football and racing pools, shows that something, more than the chances of winning big dividends, adds to the attraction of this form of weekend competition. **1952** *Times* 16 May 7/5 The winning of dividends in the football pools follows exactly the pattern of random selection. **1986** *Financial Times* 1 May 1/1 A syndicate of 11 Wiltshire hospital staff shared a £1,017,890 football pool dividend, believed to be a record.

**divisionalization** (dɪˌvɪʒənəlaɪˈzeɪʃən), *n.* [f. DIVISIONAL *a.* + -IZATION.] The process or result of introducing a divisional structure into a company, organization, or the like, esp. along market or product lines, and with responsibility for the performance of a division held by its divisional or sectional manager. Cf. *departmentalization* n. s.v. DEPARTMENTAL *a.*
   **1967** *Times Rev. Industry* Apr. 81/3 As companies tend to group together into bigger units, so some degree of 'divisionalization' becomes essential if the career structure for the young man in industry is to be maintained. **1979** *Jrnl. R. Soc. Arts* CXXVII. 218/2 The very large enterprise nowadays has a problem of divisionalization. **1980** *Jrnl. Compar. Econ.* IV. 210 The divisionalization of large socialist enterprises in Yugoslavia. **1980** *Ann. Rep. Tunnel Holdings Ltd. 1979/80* 2/1 The corporate objective of broadening the industrial base involved divisionalisation on decentralized principles.

**divisionalize** (dɪˈvɪʒənəlaɪz), *v.* [Back-formation f. *DIVISIONALIZATION n.] *trans.* To organize (a company, etc.) on a divisional basis. Also *absol.*
   **1982** PETERS & WATERMAN *In Search of Excellence* viii. 272 We continuously divisionalize, and even set up new small buildings for the new units. **1984** *Austral. Transport* Mar. 21/2 Kwikasair Express has taken to the distribution tasks by designing and divisionalising resources.
   So **di'visionalized** *ppl. a.*
   **1976** *Harvard Business Rev.* Sept. 77/2 In a divisionalized, consumer goods manufacturer we know of, the first years of carrying on the planning process were viewed frankly as a learning experience. **1978** *Accountants Rec.* Dec. 20/1 Many large organizations have adopted a divisionalized organization structure. **1982** PETERS & WATERMAN *In Search of Excellence* xi. 309 This company represents an extreme of keeping the structure simple, divisionalized, and autonomous.

**divvy** ('dɪvɪ), *a.*[2] and *n.*[2] *dial.* and *slang* (*Midland* and *north.*). Also **divy.** [Of uncertain origin.] **A.** *adj.* Foolish, idiotic; half-witted, daft. Esp. of persons. **B.** *n.* A foolish or half-witted person.

**1975** P. O'SHAUGHNESSY in *Lore & Lang.* II. III. 25 [Boston] *Divvy*, . . daft. **1981** *Guardian* 1 Oct. 10/6 The instructor . . did rise to describing young Oxborrow's rather poor landing as 'divy-dancing down the runway'. The flight lieutenant must be from Liverpool, Divy is that city's word for moronic, or worse. **1987** *Ibid.* 23 Feb. 12/4 [Nottingham] I would be grateful for some enlightenment on another insult whose origins perplex me: the word 'divvy'—meaning 'thick as two short planks'—which seems to be in quite general use among schoolchildren. *Ibid.* 2 Mar. 12/7, I first started using the term 'divvy' some 20 years ago . . . When I was growing up in Liverpool in the 1960's it was commonly assumed to be derived from the word 'individual'. **1989** *Box* Autumn 30/1 It was an automatic which we shouldn't have used because you can't get the wheel spins and loads of the criminals around Liverpool were saying 'yah divvy ya shoulda used a turbo'.

**dizygous** (dar'zaɪgəs), *a. Biol.* [f. DI-² + Gr. ζυγ-όν + -OUS.] = DIZYGOTIC *a.*

**1940** *Jrnl. Heredity* XXXI. 277/1 The comparison of similarities in identical twins with similarities in fraternal or dizygous twins . . affords a clue to the rôle played by heredity in producing certain traits. **1950** RACE & SANGER *Blood Groups in Man* xx. 246 Distinction between monozygous and dizygous twins: blood groups are being used more and more for this purpose. **1973** B. J. WILLIAMS *Evolution & Human Origins* xiv. 245/2 Dizygous twins are genetically no more alike than siblings. **1983** *Oxf. Textbk. Med.* I. IV. 7 There is a multiplicity of twin types. The monozygous and dizygous forms are well known.

**DNA,** *n.* Substitute for entry: **DNA** (diːɛn'eɪ), *n. Biochem.* Also (*rare*) **D.N.A.** [Abbrev.] **1.** = DEOXYRIBONUCLEIC ACID *n.* Cf. RNA *n.*

**1944** *Jrnl. Biol. Chem.* CLVI. 691 The key rôle of the desoxyribose type of these substances in the reproduction of inheritable characteristics has been emphasized by the identification of desoxyribose nucleic acid (DNA) as a major component of chromosomal nucleoprotein. **1951** *Lancet* 16 June 1287/1 In normal animal and plant cells deoxyribonucleic acid (D.N.A.) is located entirely within the nucleus. **1955** *New Biol.* XIX. 9 DNA molecules are chains which can be broken down into nucleotides. Each nucleotide molecule can be broken down by hydrolysis into a molecule of phosphoric acid, one of desoxyribose (a five carbon sugar) and one of a purine (adenine or guanine) or of a pyrimidine (thymine, cytosine or 5-methyl cytosine, but in some phages thymine or 5-hydroxy-methyl-cytosine). **1955** *Sci. Amer.* Oct. 70/3 The chromosomes are made largely of DNA (desoxyribonucleic acid). DNA can exist in a great multitude of forms, all built of the same building blocks but with the units arranged in different sequences. The hereditary information carried by a DNA molecule is contained in the order of arrangement of these units. **1962** A. HUXLEY *Let.* 26 Dec. (1969) 945 He talked such nonsense . . about true intelligence residing only in the DNA molecule. **1970** *Nature* 5 Sept. 998/2 Demolition of the hallowed idea of the molecular biologist that RNA cannot synthesize DNA has prompted a reinvestigation of other ideas. **2.** Special Comb. **a. DNA fingerprinting** = *genetic fingerprinting* s.v. *GENETIC *a.* 1 g.

**1980** *Jrnl. Pediatrics* XCVII. 92/2 The technique used for viral *DNA fingerprinting has been described previously. **1989** *NERC News* VIII. 13 By applying DNA fingerprinting to whales it is possible to unravel some of the mysteries of their behaviour.

**b.** In names of enzymes acting on or catalysing the production of DNA, as *DNA ligase, methylase, polymerase,* etc.

**1962** *Federation Proc.* XXI. 456/2 DNA polymerase activity was measured in crude cell extracts according to Bollum. **1963** *Proc. Nat. Acad. Sci. L.* 906 The most serious difficulty is introduced by the DNA transcriptase. **1968** A. WHITE et al. *Princ. Biochem.* (ed. 4) xxviii. 654 The ends of the linear form were joined by using an enzyme called DNA ligase or joining enzyme to produce the double-stranded circular form. **1971** *Jrnl. Molecular Biol.* LVII. 486 As a necessary first step in the methylation process, DNA methylase must bind in some way to DNA. **1979** D. R. HOFSTADTER *Gödel, Escher, Bach* (1980) xvi. 530 The DNA polymerase is basically a copy-and-move enzyme. **1987** E. E. CONN et al. *Outl. Biochem.* (ed. 5) xix. 593 The DNA methylase in the bacterial restriction-modification system . . plays an important role in protecting the host DNA from destruction from restriction endonucleases.

**DNase** (diːɛ'neɪz), *n. Biochem.* Also **DNAase** (diːɛ'neɪeɪz). [f. DN(A *n.* + -ASE.] = DEOXYRIBONUCLEASE *n.* Cf. RNASE *n.*

**1949** ZAMENHOFF & CHARGAFF in *Jrnl. Biol. Chem.* CLXXX. 727 For the sake of brevity desoxypentose nucleic acid will be referred to as DNA, desoxypentose nuclease as DNase. **1971** J. Z. YOUNG *Introd. Study Man* xxii. 301 DNAase and DNA polymerase certainly exist in tissues that have a low mitotic activity. **1982** *Sci. Amer.* July 90/2 The breaking of the sugar-phosphate bond by DNase is favored energetically.

**do,** *n.*¹ Add: [**2.**] **d.** Also '**do.** An arrangement of hair; *spec.* = HAIR-DO *n.* *U.S. colloq.*

**1901** *Dialect Notes* II. 139 *Do,* n. In phrase, 'a great do', a child's word for a mass of woman's back hair. N.Y. **1966** J. S. COX *Illustr. Dict. Hairdressing* 48/1 *Do,* shortened form of Hairdo . . Slang. **1972** C. BUCHANAN *Maiden* iv. 44 Dinah Shore do's side by side with Afros. **1986** *Blactress* July 9/3 This smooth, short 'do that swerves over to one side in a series of short waves over the brow.

**e.** Excreta; excrement, esp. canine. *slang* (orig. *Children's*).

Remembered in use *c* 1920 (*private let.* to Ed.).

**1974** P. GZOWSKI *This Country* 12/2 About as naughty as I got on the air was to talk about 'doggy do'. **1977** *Sounds* 9 July 15/2 He . . adopts a facial expression when discussing punks of a man reluctantly handling doggy's do. **1985** *Time Out* 6 June 16/1 'Eat crap!' barked the [film] director. And suddenly Divi was up to his dentures in doggy doo.

**do,** *v.* Senses 11 g-l, m-q in Dict. become 11 h-m, o-s. Add: [**B.**] [**I.**] [**6.**] **h.** *to do it,* to urinate or defecate. *slang.*

**1922** JOYCE *Ulysses* 756 They ought to make chambers a natural size so that a woman could sit on it properly he kneels down to do it. **1956** H. GOLD *Man who was not with It* (1965) xxxiii. 222 It's so easy, boy, after you do it once. Before that it's hard. You sweat. You do it in your pants. **1963** M. McCARTHY *Group* xiv. 323 As soon as they took him off [the toilet-seat], he would do it in his crib.

**i.** In interrogative clauses introduced by an objective *what*: to carry on for a living; to follow as a profession.

**1925** F. SCOTT FITZGERALD *Great Gatsby* i. 12 'What you doing, Nick?' 'I'm a bond man.' 'Who with?' I told him. **1932** W. FAULKNER *Light in August* xiii. 277, I dont know who they is nor what they does. **1949** C. P. SNOW *Time of Hope* iii. 37 What will he do now—in the way of work, Mrs. Eliot? **1953** J. WAIN *Hurry on Down* i. 10 Robert . . had asked this candidate for the hand of the younger sister, what he intended to Do, and what his prospects were. **1974** J. BETJEMAN *Nip in Air* 27 You ask me what it is I do . . . I'm partly a liaison man and partly P.R.O. **1985** N. SHULMAN *Social Security* i. 13 Many people . . find themselves obliged to take up gainful employment out of sheer embarrassment at the inability to answer the question 'what do you do?' in less than eighty words.

**[10.] b.** To provide or offer (esp. meals) commercially. *colloq.*

**1966** *Observer* 13 Nov. 11/2 [Farmers'] wives are encouraged to take visitors and 'do teas'. **1970** W. J. BURLEY *To kill Cat* iii. 48 The Marina doesn't do meals other than breakfast.

**[11.] g.** To break into; to burgle or rob. *slang.*

**1774** *Sessions Papers: Proc. Old-Bailey* 7-13 Dec. (Wilkes Session) 16/1 *John Miller.* I and four or five more went to go to *do* a jew ladies; to break the house open. *Question.* What is that a cant term to break a house open? *Miller.* Yes. **1822** *Mem. Life & Trial James Mackcoull* 79 It was at first proposed to go to Aberdeen by sea and *do* either the Montrose or Dundee bank. **1865** *Leaves from Diary of Celebr. Burglar & Pickpocket* 27, I would go right there and 'do' that jeweler's 'crib'. **1930** 'INGRAM' & MACKENZIE *Hell's Kitchen* ii. 38 We had done two other houses in the neighbourhood that night... We therefore had little time left for our main objective. **1968** H. R. F. KEATING *Inspector Ghote hunts Peacock* xiv. 178 My Billy noticed the set in a shop-window... He did the place that very night.

**†n.** To take or consume (esp. alcoholic drink). Cf. sense r below. *Obs. slang.*

**1857** 'C. BEDE' *Mr. Verdant Green, Married & Done For* x. 78 To 'do bitters', as Mr. Bouncer phrased the act of drinking bitter beer. **1867** J. S. BORLASE *Night Fossikers* 116, I asked him to come to Poole's shanty and do a chop and a nobbler with me. **1888** *Civil & Mil. Gaz.* (Lahore) 8 May 2/1 Hulloo! Back again, old man?.. I think we might do a drink together in honour of the occasion. **1899** *Western Champion* (Barcaldine, Austral.) 21 Feb. 3/1 'Can you do a drink,' asked one out-of-work of another in like predicament.

**[II.] [18.] c.** Colloq. phr. *to do well out of:* to profit by or from.

**1919** J. M. KEYNES *Econ. Consequences of Peace* v. 133 They are a lot of hard-faced men.. who look as if they had done very well out of the war. **1951** J. B. PRIESTLEY *Festival at Farbridge* III. iii. 577 Seth.. had done very well out of the Festival. **1987** *Daily Tel.* (Weekend Suppl.) 31 Oct. p. vi/3 Russell is often portrayed as one of the greediest of the Tudor 'New Men' who did well out of the Dissolution of the Monasteries.

**[20.] [a.]** *that will do (that'll do),* for def. read: that is sufficient, often as exclam. phr. used (i) chiefly dismissively, *spec.* (*Naut.*) to dismiss the crew at the end of a voyage; (ii) repressively, esp. to children, = stop (doing) that! Cf. *have done!,* sense 17 above.

**1836** MARRYAT *Midsh. Easy* II. x. 287 A small pull of that weather main-top-gallant brace—that will do. **1856** DICKENS *Dorrit* I. xxxii. 287 Give me a back, Mr. Rugg—a little higher, sir—that'll do! **1863** M. E. BRADDON *Eleanor's Victory* III. vi. 89 'That will do, Jepcott,' said Miss Sarah, 'you may go now.' **1902** B. LUBBOCK *Round the Horn* x. 374 'That'll do, men!' were the magic words, and we quietly walked off to our various bunks. **1957** 'F. GAITE' *Far Traveller* i. 19 'But it is what one would do.. if one saw a pretty girl.'.. 'That will do, Franz,' said the Graf. **1968** L. MORTON *Long Wake* i. 37 Then the magic words which the sailors always wait for from the Mate at the end of a voyage: 'That will do, you men, pay off tomorrow at the Shipping Office.' **1987** REDMOND & ANGUS *Grange Hill Rebels* xiv. 59 'Er.. that'll do,' said the teacher, concerned by Wimbledon's violent tendencies.

**[24.] e.** In emphatic repetition of an assertion made in the preceding cl. *colloq.* and *dial.*

**1590** SHAKES. *Mids. N.* III. ii. 252 Helen, I love thee, by my life I doe. **1871** E. LEAR *Jumblies* in *Nonsense Songs* sig. 3/3 They went to sea in a sieve, they did. **1916** G. B. SHAW *Pygmalion* II. 123, I ain't dirty: I washed my face and hands afore I come, I did. **1967** P. BEER *Just like Resurrection* 44 He rang me up In a dream, My brother did.

**f.** Conveying assent to a suggestion, freq. with 'yes' or 'please'.

**1601** SHAKES. *All's Well* IV. iii. 153 *Int.* Shall I set downe your answer so? *Par.* Do, Ile take the Sacrament on't. **1693** CONGREVE *Old Batchelour* V. i. 47 Ay; do, do, Captain, if you think fit. **1799** *Sporting Mag.* XIII. 353/1 *Delville.*. I've a great mind to accept your offer, on purpose to make you pay for your presumption. *Gossamer.* Do: I'd take it as a favour, Ned. **1891** *Cassell's Family Mag.* May 375/1 'I'll give you instead a few recipes for the utilisation of your fragments.' 'Do, please.' **1916** JOYCE *Portrait of Artist* (1969) i. 53 I'd go straight up to the rector and tell him about it after dinner.—Yes do. Yes do, said Cecil Thunder. **1969** S. JAMESON *Journey from North* I. I. xvii. 85 'Don't feel that I want to push you aside.' 'Oh, but do!' I cried.

**[30.] e.** *let's don't* ( .. ): = 'let's not'. *U.S. colloq.*

**1939** D. PARKER *Here Lies* 33 Let's don't think about a lot of Chinese. **1986** *New Yorker* 24 Mar. 34/2 Let's don't go yet.

**[34.] d.** *to be doing.* In interrogative clauses introduced by an objective *what:* to have as an explanation or reason for being (in a place). Cf. the earlier *what make you here?* s.v. MAKE *v.* 58 a.

**1768** STERNE *Sentimental Journey* I. 154 Alas, poor Yorick! cried I, what art thou doing here? **1901** G. B. SHAW *Caesar & Cleopatra* I. 105 What are you doing here at this time of night? Do you live here? **1930** W. FAULKNER *As I lay Dying* 58 What are you doing here? Why didn't you answer when I called you? **1969** I. MURDOCH *Bruno's Dream* v. 45 She lay awake wondering what that huge paunchy sweating hairy body was doing in her bed. **1979** J. JOHNSTON *Old Jest* 153 The old man.. was looking the soldier up and down. 'Mary... What's that fellow doing here?'

**doc** (dɒk), *n.²* *colloq.* [Abbrev.: see DOCUMENTARY *a.* 4.] A documentary film. Freq. as *drama-doc:* see main entry.

**1978** *Broadcast* 29 May 3/1 The unit.. will be producing a variety of dramas, documentaries and drama docs. **1985** R. LOURIE *First Loyalty* xxii. 223 She.. did some documentaries with that famous woman producer.., then she went on to make a couple of docs on her own.

**docent,** *a.* and *n.* Add: [B.] **2.** One employed to instruct visitors about exhibits at a museum, art gallery, etc., esp. as a guide at historical homes and reconstructions. orig. and chiefly *U.S.*

**1906** *Bull. Mus. Fine Arts* (Boston) June 19/1 Through these *docents,* as it has been proposed to call them, the heads of departments could instruct many more persons than it would be possible for them to accompany through the galleries. **1914** L. CONNOLLY *Educ. Value of Museums* 29 When a docent tells you what you see, you do not wholly see, you partly hear. **1940** *Museum News* 1 May 11/1 Many kinds of jobs are being carried on.. by volunteers, including docent work with school children. **1978** J. WAMBAUGH *Black Marble* ii. 13 Active with Madeline in the Junior Philharmonic and the Huntington Library Docents. **1984** *N.Z. Herald* 17 Nov. 1. 6/1 There is nothing indecent about docent... One critic of the name—chosen for the guides at the Auckland City Art Gallery and at the Museum of Transport and Technology—says it is ugly, un-English, unfamiliar and harsh-sounding.

**dock,** *n.³* Add: **[5.] c.** Usu. in *sing.* A wharf or pier; a quay. orig. *U.S.*

**1817** *N.Y. Herald* 20 Aug. 2/2 He left town at 1 o'clock in the morning of the same day, in charge of a friend, who waked him up previous to the packet reaching the dock at Sing-sing. **1856** X. D. MACLEOD *Biogr. F. Wood* 193 Substantial stone or iron docks and piers should be constructed which would not only be durable, but in the result far more economical than those now in use. **1922** E. O'NEILL

*Anna Christie* III. 160 Guess I'll take a walk down to the end of the dock for a minute and see what's doing. I love to watch the ships passing. **1943** *N.Y. Times* 29 Sept. 20/4 With us a dock is what the British call a wharf. With them a dock is the body of water enclosed within wharves, the thing we call a basin. **1972** *Evening Telegram* (St. John's, Newfoundland) 27 June 3/7 The United States Coast Guard cutter Winnibago rammed into the dock bow first.

[**6.**] **b.** A raised platform from which lorries or railway trucks are loaded and unloaded. *N. Amer.*

**1918** S. V. NORTON *Motor Truck as Aid to Business Profits* viii. 127 It is adapted to packing the truck at all depths, and the shipper does not have to carry the material any further than to the edge of the dock. **1930** *Western Truck Owner* Oct. 28/2 The freight depot of the White Motor Express.. is a building 100 feet wide and 125 feet deep... On the first floor are the loading docks and a minor repair department. **1952** B. F. CONROY *Motor Freight Workshop* viii. 102 In a fork-lift-truck operation, the dock plates that are used to bridge the tailgate of the truck with the dock are most important. **1968** *Globe & Mail* (Toronto) 13 Feb. 31/9 (Advt.), *City ground floor* 9,000 sq. ft. can be divided... Truck level dock and grade level.

**dockominium** (ˌdɒkəˈmɪnɪəm), *n. U.S.* Also **dockaminium.** [f. DOCK *n.*³ + COND)OMINIUM *n.*] Any of a number of privately owned landing-stages at a marina, etc.; also, a waterfront condominium with a private mooring.

**1981** *Boating Industry* Jan. 105/2 When Marine Conversions, Inc. took over the prospering Skyline Nautical Yacht Basin in Dania, Fla., they renamed it Harbour Towne Marina at Dania, and instituted the 'dockominium' concept. **1984** *N.Y. Times* 6 May VIII. 14/1 A development such as Oyster River Landing, with its private slips just a few steps from the front door, can be a powerful inducement to live on the water year-round... Such projects, known informally as 'dockominiums', have become very popular in many waterfront communities throughout the metropolitan area. **1985** *New Yorker* 29 Apr. 75/1 The folks at Maximo Moorings would sell you a boat slip called a 'dockominium'. **1986** *Ibid.* 12 May 32/3 A large marina, the Newport City Yacht Club, and 'dockaminiums'.

**document**, *n.* Add: **5.** Special Comb. **document case**, a lightweight usu. flexible case for carrying papers.

**1936** C. DAY LEWIS *Friendly Tree* vii. 102 He deliberately chose the most expensive *document-case he could find. **1974** *Harrod's Christmas Catal.* 19 Under-arm document case £27.50.

**documentable** (ˈdɒkjuˌmɛntəb(ə)l, dɒkjuˈmɛntəb(ə)l), *a.* [f. DOCUMENT *v.* + -ABLE.] That may be documented; demonstrable or supportable by means of documentary evidence.

**1579** W. WILKINSON *Confut. Fam. Love* 39 We might.. stand single myndedly obedient vnto his documentable Sentences. **1962** *Economist* 22 Sept. 1082/1 The growing concentration.. is a documentable, statistical and social fact. **1984** *Word* XXXV. 52 All these problems can be empirically explored in real, documentable discourse events. Hence **documentably** *adv.*

**1984** *Nature* 12 Jan. 103/2 The amount of evolution covered in pre-college science books is documentably declining.

**documentarian** (ˌdɒkjʊmɛnˈtɛərɪən), *n.* [f. DOCUMENTARY *a.*: see -ARIAN.] **1. a.** A photographer who works in a documentary style.

**1951** KALISH & EDOM *Picture Editing* 11/1 (*caption*) A great photo documentarian. **1972** *Photogr. Communications* iv. 151 Two young documentarians,

William Albert Allard and Dallas Kenney then reveal their personal approaches. **b.** One who directs or produces documentary films; = DOCUMENTARIST *n.*

**1976** *National Observer* (U.S.) 6 Nov. 22/2 Controversial documentarian Frederick Wiseman.. presents his 10th film, an examination of the auctioning, fattening, slaughtering, packing, and selling in America of beef and lamb. **1979** *Daily Tel.* 7 Nov. 15/2 The director, Peter Morley, used no archive material to illustrate the story, as other documentarians have done. **1984** *New Yorker* 19 Mar. 33/2 What Flaherty.. distilled were the heroic beauty in simple everyday experience... (Like all great documentarians, he imparts his own spirit to his films.) **2.** One who is skilled in the analysis of documentary evidence.

**1963** *Listener* 21 Mar. 505/1 Such a devoted documentarian as George Paloczi-Horvath.. has this to say: '..no documentary evidence has been adduced to prove that the Soviet forces in Manchuria ever gave Japanese arms or other material aid to the Communists.' **1966** *Punch* 23 Mar. 437/2 Because Mr. Allen is more documentarian than social psychologist, he never examines that area of the German psyche which lusted after Nazism.

**documentative** (dɒkjʊˈmɛntətɪv), *a.* [f. DOCUMENT *n.* + -ATIVE.] Of the nature of a documentary; employing or providing documentation.

**1971** *Physics Bull.* Dec. 738/1 Taken together they make interesting contrasts of styles in presentation. To adopt the laconic address of film reviews they are (1) pedagogic, (2) technical, (3) documentative, (4) dialectical. **1980** *B.S.I. News* Apr. 5/4 This work.. is intended to assist terminologists, translators, [etc.].. to elaborate documentative languages such as thesauri. **1984** *N.Y. Times* 29 Jan. II. 14/1 This review, quoted in Hans M. Wingler's definitive documentative book, 'The Bauhaus', is descriptive of the 'Metal Dance' just presented under the sponsorship of The Kitchen and Goethe House.

**docutainment** (ˌdɒkjʊˈteɪnmənt), *n.* orig. and chiefly *N. Amer.* [f. DOCU(MENTARY *a.* + ENTER)TAINMENT *n.*; cf. *INFOTAINMENT *n.*] A film or other presentation which includes documentary materials, and seeks both to inform and entertain; entertainment provided by such presentations. Also in extended use.

**1978** *Globe & Mail* (Toronto) 5 May 15/5 Densham and Watson make what they call docutainments—documentary films whose first goal is to be entertaining. **1983** *Washington Post* 21 Dec. c8/5 'I call it "variety docutainment",' says the production's executive producer, Cindy Walker... 'We'll be using documentary inserts combined on stage with drama, song and dance.' **1985** *Los Angeles Times* 3 Mar. (Television Times) 3/1 This two-part production about the life and times of Douglas MacArthur is.. a documentary or, more precisely, five hours of 'docutainment', a fascinating.. biography based on William Manchester's book about America's most intriguing, epic soldier. **1989** *Wall St. Jrnl.* 18 Sept. 1/4 'Unsolved Mysteries' captured 16th place in the prime-time ratings with its special brand of 'docutainment'—re-enactments of puzzling crimes and other unexplained events.

**dodecahedrane** (ˌdəʊdɛkəˈhiːdreɪn, -ˌdɛk-), *n. Chem.* [f. DODECAHEDR(ON *n.* + -ANE 2 b.] A hydrocarbon, $(CH)_{20}$, in which the carbon atoms of each molecule lie at the vertices of a regular dodecahedron; also, any derivative or related compound with a similar molecular shape.

**1964** *Jrnl. Amer. Chem. Soc.* LXXXVI. 3163/1 A study of the capacity of triquinacene to form metal complexes would.. be of special interest, and its possible roles as a precursor of acepentylene .. and of dodecahedrane .. further make it an attractive object. **1974** *Nature* 15 Nov. 188/2 The non-appearance of the marvellous and unique dodecahedrane, which several groups have been rumoured to be close to synthesising. **1983** *Jrnl. Amer. Chem. Soc.* CV. 5449/1 The total synthesis of dodecahedrane has been achieved in 23 steps from cyclopentadienide anion. **1986** *Ibid.* CVIII. 1717/2 For the future, our intention is to broaden still further the scope of this useful dehydrocyclization reaction and to commence detailed chemical investigation of the resulting dodecahedranes.

**dodecamer** (dəʊ'dɛkəmə(r)), *n. Chem.* and *Biochem.* [f. DODECA- + -MER.] A compound whose molecule is formed from twelve monomers; also, a molecule of such a compound.

**1968** *Biochemistry* VII. 2150/1 Electron microscopic examination .. showed the presence of species of intermediate stages of disaggregation between intact dodecamer and monomer. **1971** *Nature* 25 June 495/1 At high resolution this dodecamer of six regulatory and six catalytic subunits will pose .. exciting problems on the mechanism of control. **1979** *Ibid.* 4 Oct. 342/1 For *Eurypelma* haemocyanin, three different types of subunit are needed for the formation of a 16S hexamer, five different for a 24S dodecamer, and all seven for a stable 37S aggregate or '24-mer' (which is the native form). **1983** *Sci. Amer.* Dec. 90 The longest DNA double helix that has yet been examined by single-crystal X-ray methods is the dodecamer *CGCGAATTCGCG*.

Hence ˌ**dodeca'meric** *a.*

**1968** *Biochemistry* VII. 2153/1 The glutamine synthetase isolated from *Escherichia coli* exists as a dodecameric aggregate of identical subunits. **1987** *Angewandte Chem.: Internat. Ed. in Eng.* XXVI. 587/1 (*heading*) Tetrameric and dodecameric *tert*-butylethynyllithium; a novel aggregation principle in organolithium compounds.

**dog**, *v.* Add: **9.** *intr.* With *it*. To act lazily or half-heartedly; to shirk or avoid responsibility, risk, etc.; to slack, idle. Also *trans. slang* (orig. and chiefly *U.S.*).

**1905** R. BEACH *Partners* (1912) i. 12, I expected to see the youngster dog it. **1928** R. J. TASKER *Grimhaven* xvi. 196 He hoped to goad me into action. 'Go ahead and use that shiv—don't dog it—come on and do something.' **1941** J. LILIENTHAL *Horse Crazy* 23 In Dellup's next race, Crump bet man-size money. .. But the horse dogged it, the same as it had done before. **1966** H. MARRIOTT *Cariboo Cowboy* xx. 189, I made up my mind I'd do little or nothing for quite a while ... So I just dogged it for several months. **1976** *Billings* (Montana) *Gaz.* 27 June 1-F/4 'I played aggressively for two or three holes, conservatively for 10 or 12 and the others I just dogged,' Dickson said. **1983** A. ALVAREZ *Biggest Game in Town* vii. 100 Most guys playing for that kind of money will dog it, but Doyle's got no fear.

**dogger**, *n.*[3] Add: [1.] **b.** Any large, more or less ovoid concretion, usu. of sandstone or limestone.

**1876** H. B. WOODWARD *Geol. Eng. & Wales* vii. 193 This formation .. is remarkable for the quantity of hard siliceous rock which is bedded with it, and sometimes occurs in enormous concretions or 'doggers'. **1894** —— *Jurassic Rocks Brit.* IV. i. 12

Concretionary masses of Sandstone or Doggers occur in the Midford and Northampton Sands. **1947** W. J. ARKELL *Geol. Oxf.* vii. 106 Hill's brickyard .. still shows a good section of .. the sands of the Pectinatus Zone, with enormous sandstone doggers. **1974** J. E. HEMINGWAY in Rayner & Hemingway *Geol. & Min. Resources Yorks.* vii. 167 In common with the Yorkshire Lias as a whole, the Lower Lias abounds with beds of both calcareous and sideritic concretions, both lithological types being locally known as 'doggers'.

**dog-watch**, *n.* Restrict *Naut.* to sense in Dict. and add: **2.** *transf.* A night shift, esp. in a newspaper office; any late or early period of duty; hence, the staff employed on this. *slang* (chiefly *U.S.*).

**1901** F. U. ADAMS *Kidnapped Millionaire* x. 135 The building shakes with the rumble of the presses; the 'dog watch', detailed to duty in the event of news demanding an extra, opens its game of poker. **1935** A. J. POLLOCK *Underworld Speaks* 32/1 Dog watch, employees of gambling house who begin work at midnight. **1939** C. BELTON *Outside Law in N.Z.* xv. 89, I congratulated myself I had not forgotten the morning 'dog watch' as we called it. This duty occurred about once in ten days. **1942** BERREY & VAN DEN BARK *Amer. Thes. Slang* §521/1 *Dogwatch, lobster trick*, the shift of newspapermen after the regular editions have gone to press. **1983** *Truckin' Life* Dec. 21/1 Alan and Sue are the hosts and Neville looks after the shop on the dogwatch shift.

**double**, *n.* Sense 3 s in Dict. becomes 3 t. Add: [3.] **s.** *Racing* (orig. *U.S.*). = *daily double* s.v. *DAILY *a.* 3.

**1931** *N.Y. Times* 15 Sept. 22/2 Only two men .. held tickets on the double, which is governed somewhat along the lines of a parley bet. **1951** [see ACCUMULATOR *n.* 4]. **1967** *Atlantic Monthly* Oct. 78, I hustled to the track, bet my 'doubles', and prepared to take my place in the sun. **1983** *Sporting Life* 8 Mar. 1/4 David Nicholson and Peter Scudamore .. brought off a 285-1 double on a day of shocks and spills at Windsor.

**drama**, *n.* Add: **4.** Dramatic quality or effect; colourfulness, excitement.

**1930** [see *time-traveller* s.v. TIME *n.* 60]. **1938** L. MACNEICE *I crossed Minch* I. v. 59 The hills to-day were monotonous, lacking in drama. **1941** D. C. PEATTIE *Road of Naturalist* v. 71 Californian trees are mostly evergreen, and thereby without seasonal drama. **1963** M. L. KING *Strength to Love* vii. 56 The fact that he died at this particular time adds verve and drama to the story. **1984** *Sears Catal. 1985* Spring-Summer 1144 Balloon Shades add drama to your windows.

**5.** Special Comb. **drama-documentary** *Broadcasting*, (the medium of) dramatized documentary; = DOCUDRAMA *n.*; freq. *attrib.*

**1970** N. GARNHAM in Bakewell & Garnham *New Priesthood* viii. 179 In the present climate .. the documentary film-maker .. is drawn towards the disputed territory of the *drama-documentary. **1984** K. AMIS *Stanley & Women* i. 21 One of those drama-documentaries about life in our hospitals today. **1989** *Movie* XXXIII. 35/2 It had .. a political attitude which I suppose can be described as left-wing. The people running the drama-documentary department .. thought it was unnecessary to the writing and a kind of conceit.

# E

‖ **El Niño** (εl 'niːɲo, anglicized εl 'niːnjəʊ), *n.* [a. Sp., shortened f. *El Niño de Navidad*, the Christmas Child; see quot. 1918. See also \*NIÑO *n.*] **a.** A warming of the water off the coast of northern Peru occurring annually between Christmas and March as a southward current of warm equatorial water displaces the northward Peru or Humboldt Current; the warm current itself. **b.** (Now the usual sense.) More fully, *El Niño-Southern Oscillation.* An extreme version of the same phenomenon, occurring at irregular intervals and extending westwards across the equatorial Pacific Ocean, which is associated with widespread changes in weather and severe ecological damage; all the climatic and ecological phenomena associated with this. Freq. *attrib.*

**1896** F. A. PEZET in *Rep. 6th Internat. Geogr. Congr.* 603 (*title*) The counter-current 'El Niño', on the coast of northern Peru. **1918** *Geogr. Rev.* V. 132 It is not uncommon for a current from the north—locally known as El Niño from its frequency during the Christmas season—to prevail in the region of Tumbes at 3½° S. **1942** H. U. SVERDRUP *Oceanogr.* ix. 191 In disturbed years .. the El Niño extends far south along the coast of Peru. **1963** G. L. PICKARD *Descriptive Physical Oceanogr.* vii. 165 At intervals of a few years the high temperatures extend 5 to 10 degrees farther south than usual, a condition known as 'El Niño'. **1980** *Christian Sci. Monitor* 22 Oct. 16/4 El Niño appears to be part of a large scale air-sea phenomenon that includes severe winters in North America. **1984** *Austral. Financial Rev.* 12 June 1/1 The El Nino effect .. has been largely blamed for the 1982 drought and .., in its decline, was responsible for the wet start to 1984. **1985** H. V. THURMAN *Introductory Oceanogr.* (ed. 4), When the oscillations are extreme—producing very widespread warm surface water conditions and minimal pressure differences across the tropical Pacific—they are called El Niño-Southern Oscillation. **1988** *New Scientist* 7 Jan. 40/1 The last five El Niños from 1965 until this year had coincided with a sharp increase in the number of earthquakes along the East Pacific Rise near Easter Island.

**erythrolabe** (ε'rɪθrəʊleɪb), *n. Physiol.* [f. ERYTHRO- + Gr. λαβ- to take, seize.] A red-sensitive pigment present in the cones of the retina. Cf. \*CHLOROLABE *n.*, \*CYANOLABE *n.*

**1958** W. A. H. RUSHTON in *Nature* 13 Sept. 691/1 Fig. 2 shows the results of partial photolysis of the normal fovea using red and green lights. This reveals two distinct pigments. One is the pigment of the protanope but in rather small amount; the other is a pigment which absorbs maximally at about 590 mμ and predominates. This latter pigment may be named 'erythrolabe' (= red taking), the protanope pigment 'chlorolabe', and the blue-sensitive pigment which does not here concern us, 'cyanolabe'. **1959** *Optica Acta* VI. 171 As the interaction between perceptual and physical processes is not likely to take place at a receptoral level, the terms chlorolabe and erythrolabe .. are here replaced by C.P.540 and C.P.600. **1973** *Nature* 18 May 168/2 Curve 2 is erythrolabe, present alone in the deuteranope.

**Euroconnector** ('jʊərəʊkə,nɛktə(r)), *n. Electronics.* [f. EURO- 1 + CONNECTOR *n.*] A SCART connector.

**1984** *Which?* Jan. 29/2 One particularly versatile audio/video socket is the new peritelevision, or SCART socket (called a Euroconnector by Pye and Philips) which is now fitted to a few TVs. **1985** *What Video?* Mar. 35/1 Input/output connections are via the new standard Euroconnector (the first machine I have reviewed with this), tape loading is automatic and the timer memory contains a day, month and year calendar. **1990** *CU Amiga* Apr. 27/1 (Advt.), *Monitors* .. SCART Euro-connector fitted as standard.

**eurytope** ('jʊərɪtəʊp), *n. Ecol.* [ad. G. *eurytop* adj. (F. Dahl 1896, in *Sitzungsber. d. k. Preuss. Akad. d. Wissensch.* 28), f. Gr. εὐρύ-ς wide + τόπ-ος place.] A eurytopic organism.

[**1896** *Jrnl. R. Microsc. Soc.* 617 Some animals are always associated with special conditions; others seem less sensitive and more independent; for these two sets the terms 'stenotop' and 'eurytop' are suggested.] **1938** J. R. CARPENTER *Ecol. Gloss.* s.v., Of/ organisms spending one or more stages in several habitats. **1977** *Zoologische Jahrbücher: Systematik, Ökologie und Geographie der Tiere* CIV. 433 Quantitative investigations showed significant preferences of vegetation-structures not only in stenotope but also in eurytope species. **1980** *S. Afr. Jrnl. Sci.* LXXVI. 79/2 One would expect lineages with relatively narrow species-specific adaptations (stenotopes) to be more prone to diversification than broadly adapted generalists (eurytopes). **1987** *Paleobiol.* XIII. 95/1 Low extinction rates coupled with low speciation rates are characteristic of wide-ranging eurytopes.

**eurytopic** (jʊərɪ'tɒpɪk), *a. Ecol.* [f. EURYTOP(E *n.* + -IC 1.] Of an organism: tolerant of a wide range of types of habitat and of ecological conditions. Opp. \*STENOTOPIC *a.*

**1937** [see STENOTOPIC *a.*]. **1974** *Amer. Naturalist* CVIII. 557 Eurytopic species are widely distributed and therefore achieve considerable evolutionary stability. **1987** *Nature* 10 Sept. 121/2 In graded mass extinctions, extinction rates are higher than background levels, but taxa disappear randomly throughout this interval, possibly along an ecological gradient from initially stenotopic to more eurytopic groups.

**expansion**, *n.* Add: [8.] **expansion slot** *Computing*, a socket in a piece of computing equipment to which an expansion board may be connected.

**1980** *Practical Computing* Aug. 82 (*caption*) The basic Tuscan board featuring the Z-80 CPU, 8k RAM, 8k ROM, on-board video and 1/0 section with five spare S-100 \*expansion slots. **1990** *Which?* Nov. 651/1 Many have expansion slots so that you can add extra memory, for example, but these are specific to each manufacturer, and your choice is limited.

**exploratorium** (εksplɒrə'tɔːrɪəm), *n.* orig. *U.S.* [Blend of EXPLORATORY *a.* or EXPLORATION *n.* and -ORIUM.] A museum or demonstration centre at which visitors have the opportunity to handle exhibits, perform pre-arranged experiments, etc. Cf. HANDS-ON *a.*1 2.

**1971** *Physics Today* June 62/1 A novel experiment in science education for the general public is under way in San Francisco. It is a museum of science and technology called the 'Exploratorium'. **1978** *Washington Post* 15 Nov. D3/4 Victor Cohn, science and medical reporter for The Washington Post, received the Exploratorium of San Francisco's second annual citation for newspaper science reporting. **1983** *New Scientist* 17 Nov. 485/2 Frank Oppenheimer's Exploratorium has thriving daughters in several American cities. **1987** *Sunday Times* 4 Oct. 12/6 Conran Roche proposes an 'exploratorium' where visitors make the exhibits work.

**exploratory** (ɛk'splɒrətərɪ), *n*. [f. EXPLORATORY *a*.] **1.** *ellipt*. An exploratory operation. *Med. colloq.*
**1942** BERREY & VAN DEN BARK *Amer. Thes. Slang* §534/5 *Exploratory*, exploratory laparotomy. **1984** A. F. LOEWENSTEIN *This Place* 90 Now that he knows the result of my exploratory I'm sure he'll be much easier to live with.
**2.** [By analogy with *observatory*; cf. *EXPLORATORIUM *n*.] Professor R. Gregory's term: = *EXPLORATORIUM *n*.; *spec*. the name of a science centre established in Bristol in 1984. Cf. *PLORE *n*.
**1982** *Times* 17 May 3/2 [Professor Gregory's] scheme proposes the establishment of an 'exploratory', a centre at which visitors would learn about science not by looking at exhibits but by actually performing experiments, operating computers and using information banks. *Ibid.* 3/3 Professor Gregory, professor of psychology at Bristol University, got the name exploratory by analogy with observatory. **1986** R. GREGORY *Hands-On Sci.* i. 11 As the usual museum terms, such as 'exhibit', are too passive for the Exploratory's 'hands-on' approach, we have coined the word 'plore', meaning a model, an experiment, or a problem to *explore*. **1988**

*Independent* 1 Aug. 6/4 Professor Gregory wants to transform the castle and the buildings on site into an Exploratory.

‖**ex proprio motu** (eks ˈprɒprɪəʊ ˈməʊt(j)uː), *adv. phr.* [late L., 'by his (its, etc.) own motion'; cf. *of one's motion* s.v. MOTION *n*. 9 c.] = MOTU PROPRIO *adv. phr.*; *spec*. in *Law*, of an action or decision taken by the court without any application by the parties involved. Cf. *PROPRIO MOTU *adv. phr.*
[*a***1680** T. GOODWIN *Works* (1703) V. I. II. iv. 83 The grace .. which super-adds to his love and mercy a freeness, as being extended to us upon, no Motives or Incentives in us, but *ex proprio suo motu*.] **1693** VISCT. STAIR *Inst. Law Scotl.* (ed. 2) IV. xlvi. 718 If the Lords by their Preliminaries find that there were other witnesses present called by neither Party, they may *ex proprio motu* call these (if there be any doubtfulness) before they determine. **1861** J. TRAYNER *Latin Maxims & Phr.* 95 The judge .. may order a more articulate statement, a more express answer ... Such orders are said to be pronounced *Ex proprio motu*. **1901** *Cases Adjudged U.S. Supreme Court* CLXXX. 91 If the state courts were utterly without jurisdiction, it was their duty to dismiss the proceedings *ex proprio motu*, and such is the jurisprudence of Louisiana. **1935** *Federal Reporter* (U.S.) (2nd Ser.) LXXVII. 731/2 Error is assigned to the refusal of the District Court to direct a verdict for the United States and to his action in directing a verdict for appellee *ex proprio motu*. **1982** *Ibid.* DCLXXIII. 789/1 The tape recording was excluded by the trial court almost *ex proprio motu*.

# F

**father**, *n.* Senses 11 and 12 in Dict. become 12 and 13. Add: **11.** *Computing.* A tape of data from which the current version has been generated, retained for security reasons. Cf. \*GRANDFATHER *n.* 1 c, \*SON *n.*[1] 9.

**1965** FRIEDMAN & RICE *Fund. Electronic Data Processing* ix. 405/2 This technique .. assures that .. today's updating does not deal with a 'father' or 'grandfather' tape, but uses the youngest 'son' of the series as input. **1967** R. W. LOTT *Basic Data Processing* viii. 125 A popular method is known as the grandfather cycle. In such a system, the father and grandfather of the current tape are always retained. As soon as the current tape has produced a son then the grandfather has become a great grandfather and can be converted to some other use. **1970** O. DOPPING *Computers & Data Processing* xvi. 265 The new master tape ('son') is retained till the next updating run in which it serves as the old master tape ('father'). **1980** C. S. FRENCH *Computer Sci.* xii. 65 There will be a definite policy with regard to how *many* generations [of tape] are kept; Grandfather—Father—Son should be adequate.

**filopodium** (faɪləʊˈpəʊdɪəm), *n. Zool.* Pl. -ia. [a. G. *Filopodium* (A. Lang, in *Lehrbuch der vergl. Anat. d. wirbellosen Thiere* (ed. 2, 1901) II. ix. 108), f. L. *fīlum* thread: see PODIUM *n.*] A thread-like pseudopodium.

**1926** G. N. CALKINS *Biol. Protozoa* iii. 143 Filopodia are .. formed of clear hyaline ectoplasm in typical cases... They are usually long and slender... They creep along the substratum where they serve mainly for food capture. **1973** *Nature* 13 July 93/2 On the growth cone, for example, there are numerous filopodia which extend for 10μm or more. **1987** P. R. GORDON-WEEKS in Turner & Bachelard *Neurochem.* i. 15 (*caption*) The inset shows a high power view of an individual growth cone bearing a filopodium.

Hence **filo'podial** *a.*

**1973** *Marine Biol.* XXI. 158/1 The filopodial baskets correspond in size to the substratum chips they embrace. **1988** R. S. K. BARNES et al. *Invertebrates* xv. 455 (*caption*) Gastrulation in a sea urchin ... (iv) Filopodial contacts by secondary mesenchyme.

**flimmer** (ˈflɪmə(r)), *n.*[2] *Biol.* Pl. flimmer. [a. G. *Flimmer* tinsel, in *Flimmergeissel* tinsel-like flagellum (Fischer 1894, in *Jahrb. f. wissensch. Bot.* XXVI. 191).] A mastigoneme, esp. a slender one.

**1945** H. P. BROWN in *Ohio Jrnl. Sci.* XLV. 249 He [*sc.* Fischer] termed these flagella Flimmergeisseln, or ciliated flagella. Since 'flimmer' appears to be a convenient word for the structures, and does not carry any obvious implications in the English language, I shall hereafter employ the term 'flimmer-flagellum' in reference to any flagellum bearing hair-like projections along one, two, or all sides. *Ibid.* 250 Regarding the arrangement of the flimmer, Fischer assumed that they must beat in unison, since, on any given flagellum, all the flimmer project in the same direction. **1947** [see \*MASTIGONEME *n.*]. **1965** BELL & COOMBE tr. *Strasburger's Textbk. Bot.* 417 (*caption*) The long 'tinsel-type' flagellum has two rows of fine flimmer hairs.

**Florentine**, *a.* and *n.* Senses A. a, b in Dict. become A. 1 a, 2. Add to etym.: [In senses A. 1 b and B. 3 b, ad. or influenced by F. *florentin*(*e*

in same sense.] [A.] [1.] **b.** Now usu. (ˈflɒrəntiːn). *Cookery.* Prepared in a style characteristic of Florence. Of eggs, fish, etc.: served on a bed of spinach; more generally, applied to other dishes involving spinach. Freq. postpositively, and as *à la Florentine*.

**1747** H. GLASSE *Art of Cookery* ix. 113 To make a Cheesecurd Florendine. Take two Pounds of Cheesecurd, break it all to pieces with .. some stewed Spinage cut small. **1911** M. A. FAIRCLOUGH *Ideal Cookery Bk.* 557 Oeufs à la Florentine ... Break the eggs upon the spinach, dust with salt and pepper, coat the eggs with Mornay sauce. **1950** E. DAVID *Bk. Mediterranean Food* 106 Cambacérès is one of the sign-posts, like parmentier (potatoes) or florentine (spinach). **1970** V. CANNING *Great Affair* ii. 14 There was a pair of fresh Torbay soles .. and some packets of frozen spinach, so .. I made the basis of a *sole Florentine*. **1985** D. SMITH *One is Fun!* VI. 145 Florentine eggs. This favourite classic egg dish is usually either baked in the oven or else the eggs are poached separately and served with a spinach and cheese sauce.

**c.** Of embroidery: worked using Florentine stitch.

**1909** *Embroidery* IV. 109/1 Florentine stitch .. is the stitch used in the well-known Florentine work. **1976** *Oxford Times* 3 Sept. 9/3, I promise my pupils they will be able to do Florentine embroidery by the end of the evening. **1980** *Pract. Needlework* 230/1 Shown here are a few of the most popular Florentine patterns—zigzag, ogee, flame.

**[2.] Florentine stitch**, an embroidery stitch creating a repeated zigzag or interlocking pattern by counting threads, either horizontally or diagonally, in contrasting or shaded colours; cf. BARGELLO *n.*

*c*1890 tr. *T. de Dillmont's Encycl. Needlework* 133 \*Florentine stitch is worked in slanting lines, the thread being carried, diagonally first over one and then over two double threads of the canvas. **1960** B. SNOOK *Eng. Hist. Embroidery* 86 The tiny things she made include two pincushions in cross stitch and Florentine stitch, needle and bodkin cases, [etc.].

**[B.] [3.] b.** Now usu. (ˈflɒrəntiːn). (*a*) [F. (*gâteau*) *florentin*.] A variety of almond cake. (*b*) A thin biscuit coated on one side with chocolate, and consisting chiefly of pieces of flaked nuts and preserved fruit.

**1948** A. R. DANIEL *Up-to-date Confectionery* (ed. 2) xxvi. 308 *Florentines*, this delicious Continental dainty is another almond cake that may be used for special occasions or for general café trade. **1959** T. E. THOMPSON *Fancies, Small Cakes & Chocolate Goods* xii. 187 Florentines ... Melt the butter, milk and sugar in a pan .. then stir in the almonds and fruit ... Leave the mixture to cool. **1968** *Guardian* 16 Dec. 7/5, 52 guineas buys the .. Luxury Hamper containing one bottle of champagne .. one tin of florentines .. [etc.]. **1981** *N.Y. Times* 30 Sept. C20/3 'Why do you call it a biscuit, rather than a cookie?' asked one woman as lacy Florentines were being made.

**fork**, *n.* Add: [III.] [16.] [a.] **forkball** *Baseball*, a pitch in which the ball is held tightly with the thumb, index, and middle fingers spread wide apart, in order to make it fall down sharply or behave in an otherwise unpredictable manner; cf. *split-fingered fastball* s.v. \*SPLIT *ppl. a.* 5 a.

**1923** *Spalding's Official Base Ball Guide* 191 Opponents scored 3.32 earned runs per game off 'Bullet Joe's' '*fork ball' delivery. **1962** J. BROSNAN *Pennant Race* 86 You oughta hurry that fork ball up, though. Any pitch that looks as much like a spitball as that has got to have a future. **1974** *Spartanburg* (S. Carolina) *Herald-Jrnl.* 21 Apr. B1 He was out to prove that what appears to be an illegal spitball pitch actually is a forkball. **1985** *Globe & Mail* (Toronto) 10 Oct. C3/4 Henke has added the forkball this year, but still does not have complete command of it.

**form**, *n.* Add: [III.] [**22.**] **form sheet** *Racing* (orig. *U.S.*), a (printed) record of the past performance of a racehorse or racehorses; a form book; also *transf.*, any past record, esp. of criminal convictions.
  **1911** G. ADE in *N.Y. Times Mag.* 17 Sept. 14/3 One day he was in a Pool Room working on the *Form Sheet with about 150 other Students. **1971** [see FLASHING *vbl. n.*[1] 5]. **1983** H. EVANS *Good Times, Bad Times* vi. 120 It was remarked that Thomson hardly had Murdoch's form sheet.

# G

**general**, *a.* and *n.* Add: [A.] [1.] [a.] **general paresis**: see *PARESIS *n.* 1 b.

**grandfather**, *n.* Add: [1.] c. *Computing.* A tape of data two versions earlier than the version currently being processed, retained for security reasons. Cf. *FATHER *n.* 11, *SON *n.*[1] 9.

   **1965** FRIEDMAN & RICE *Fund. Electronic Data Processing* ix. 405/2 On the chance that the new master tape may be lost, the old master is often saved until it is a 'grandfather'. This means that the records ..will have been updated twice... The second processing run uses the 'son' as input. It is updated and the old master's 'grandson' is produced. **1970** O. DOPPING *Computers & Data Processing* xvi. 265 After the run, the father goes to the tape library with the son and is kept there at least until it becomes 'grandfather' before it is again used as 'son' tape. **1980** C. S. FRENCH *Computer Sci.* xii. 65 There will be a definite policy with regard to how *many* generations are kept; Grandfather—Father—Son should be adequate.

**grandfather**, *v.* Restrict *rare* to senses in Dict. and add: **2.** *U.S.* [After *grandfather clause* s.v. GRANDFATHER *n.* 5.] To exempt from new legislation or regulations, usu. because of some prior condition of previously existing privilege. Freq. const. *in*, *out*, or with *advb. phr.* Also *transf.*

   **1953** *Kentucky Revised Statutes* 2190/2 All certificates or permits grandfathered shall be subject to the same limitations and restrictions. **1968** *N.Y. Times* 8 May 46/4 The committee 'grandfathered' out from effective coverage all existing distribution lines. **1980** *San Francisco Bay Guardian* 16–23 Oct. 5/1 Four of these planned buildings have already been exempted ('grandfathered' is the technical term) from the limits passed last March by the Supervisors. **1986** *Milwaukee* (Wisconsin) *Jrnl.* 6 Apr. (Accent Suppl.) 6/3 Under the impending federal law, after Oct. 1 those young drinkers could not be 'grandfathered' into a new 21 drinking-age statute. **1987** *Texas Monthly* Apr. 168/3 She already had privileges at the Metropolitan, and we hadn't heard anything upfront from the Nix, so we decided to grandfather her in.

# H

**hunt**, *n.*[2] Add: **6. hunt sab** *colloq.* = *\*hunt saboteur* below; also as *v. intr.*, to act as a hunt saboteur (*pres. pple.* in quot.); cf. *\*SAB *n.*[2]

**1981** *N.Y. Times* 11 Feb. C1/5 The '\*hunt sabs', as they call themselves, are mostly young, and many are vegetarians. **1986** *Peace News* 20 June 5/1 Sixty odd Hunt Sabs..talking and debating with the forty-strong hunt. **1986** G. F. NEWMAN *Set Thief* 8 In a village..where she had been hunt sabbing.., it [*sc.* the car] had been almost totally vandalized by hunt supporters.

**hunt saboteur**, a person whose intention is to disrupt a hunt.

**1964** *Western Times* (Exeter) 8 May 9/7 A broken jaw is said to be one of the relics \*hunt saboteurs took away with them from a meet of the Culmstock Otter Hunt at Colyford on Saturday. **1986** *Financial Times* 20 Oct. 1/1 Police are investigating clashes between hunt saboteurs and the North Surrey and Sussex Beagles at Lingfield.

**hunt saboteuse** *rare*, a female hunt saboteur.

**1977** 'E. CRISPIN' *Glimpses of Moon* xi. 215 'Polluters,' said the hunt saboteuse.

# I

**info-** ('ɪnfəʊ), *comb. form.* [Shortened f. INFORMATION *n.*] Prefixed to (esp. the latter part of) nouns to which it stands in attributive or appositive relation, forming chiefly portmanteau words in information technology or the media. **info'mania**, an excessive enthusiasm for the accumulation and dissemination of factual information (see also quot. 1984).

**1984** *PC* 16 Oct. 189/2 DELPHI has..a number of on-line special interest groups (SIGs) and an extensive member-publishing area called '*Infomania'. **1986** *Washington Post* 21 Aug. A19/2 Society's much bemoaned infomania, the need to stockpile contextless facts, is hard to distinguish from a good researcher's hunger for absolutely exhaustive background. **1989** *Independent* 30 Dec. 38/7 Infomania erodes our capacity for significance. With a mindset fixed on information, the attention span shortens.

**info'mercial:** see *INFORMERCIAL *n.*

**infopre'neur** [f. ENTRE)PRENEUR *n.* c], one who seeks to profit in business from the collection and dissemination of information (incorporated in a trademark in the U.S.).

**1985** *Official Gaz.* (U.S. Patent Off.) 6 Aug. TM174/1 *Infopreneur* (stylized). Weitzen, Harold F. .. Filed 2-1-1984. **1986** *Economist* 23 Aug. (High Technol. Suppl.) 15/2 American makers have used their knowhow to better commercial ends... Other countries—Britain and West Germany particularly —have been inexplicably making life as difficult as possible for their own infopreneurs.

**also infopre'neurial** *a.*

**1986** *Economist* 2 Aug. 16/1 To compete..in the *infopreneurial revolution, GEC and other European high-tech businesses will have to pick their partners with an eye for technological strengths to plug their most serious weaknesses.

**'infosphere** [-SPHERE], the sphere of human activity concerned with the collection and processing of information, esp. by computer; cf. *technosphere* s.v. TECHNO-.

**1971** *Time* 12 Apr. 96/2 In much the way that fish cannot conceptualize water or birds the air, man barely understands his *infosphere, that encircling layer of electronic and typographical smog composed of clichés from journalism, entertainment, advertising and government. **1980** A. TOFFLER *Third Wave* xiii. 181 A new info-sphere is emerging alongside the new techno-sphere. *Ibid.* xiv. 194 In all previous societies the info-sphere provided the means for communication between humans.

**'infotech** [TECH *n.*³] = *information technology* s.v. INFORMATION *n.* 8; freq. *attrib.*

**1981** *Times* 28 Aug. 19 (*heading*) Left behind in the '*infotech' race. *Ibid.* 19/5 The Government [is].. assigning specific responsibility for coordinating the country's 'infotech' efforts to the energetic Minister for Industry. **1985** *Sunday Times* 16 June 72/1 Silicon and the other basic building blocks of infotech. **1991** *Whole Earth Rev.* Summer 13/1 John Mayo's essay on infotech trends and the physical limits that constrain them, and Anne Branscomb's on

property rights in information, are two of the best overviews available.

**infotainment** (ɪnfəʊ'temmənt), *n.* orig. *U.S.* Also **info-tainment.** [f. *INFO- + ENTER)TAINMENT *n.*; cf. *DOCUTAINMENT *n.*] Broadcast material which seeks to inform and entertain simultaneously; information presented in an entertaining way.

**1980** R. A. EISENBERG in *Phone Call* Feb. 14/2 The telecommunications revolution is for real. The Age of Infotainment is upon us. The lives of all Americans are sure to be affected, if not dramatically changed. **1984** *Time* 16 Jan. 75/3 Henry and Thomas played cheery, gee-whiz hosts of an 'infotainment' show infatuated with swirling graphics and inane charts. **1987** *Daily Tel.* 4 Sept. 27/3 The Americans would call this 'infotainment' as Miller takes two singers through the last scene of *La traviata*. **1988** *Courier-Mail* (Brisbane) 1 June 24/3 Channel 9 has finally announced the starting date of its latest TV experiment—the info-tainment show called *Live at Five*. **1990** *Marxism Today* June 27 A much more widespread transformation of the 'infotainment' industries effected by the merger of what, within an earlier romantic ideology, were mutually opposed 'commercial' and 'cultural' values.

**iteroparous** ('ɪtərəʊ,pærəs), *a.* *Biol.* [f. *itero-* (f. stem of L. *iterum* again + -o) + -PAROUS.] Characterized by or designating the production of multiple sets of offspring; usu. applied to organisms or taxonomic groups in which the production of young occurs more than once during the life-cycle. Cf. *SEMELPAROUS *a.*

**1954** L. C. COLE in *Q. Rev. Biol.* XXIX. 118/1 Iteroparous species include some, such as small rodents, where only two or three litters of young are produced in a lifetime, and also various trees and tapeworms where a single individual may produce thousands of litters. **1970** *Amer. Naturalist* CIV. 8 Among the perennial organisms the two strikingly different kinds of life-history strategies are the repeated reproducers, or iteroparous organisms, and the big-bang reproducers, or semelparous organisms. **1979** *Nature* 7 June 554/1 For iteroparous plants it is often possible to show that reproduction has costs that are expressed in a reduced growth rate and/or an increased death rate. **1989** *Functional Ecol.* III. 646 For long-lived, iteroparous organisms fitness will always be extremely difficult to measure.

So **,itero'parity** *n.*, the state or condition of being iteroparous.

**1954** L. C. COLE in *Q. Rev. Biol.* XXIX. 118/1 The writer proposes to employ the term semelparity to describe the condition of multiplying only once in a lifetime... The contrasting condition will be referred to as iteroparity. **1975** E. O. WILSON *Sociobiol.* xvi. 338/2 Iteroparity is the rule in the vertebrates. **1987** *Amer. Naturalist* CXXIX. 498 Withholding energy investments may allow females to avoid energy depletion during egg laying and permit increased iteroparity.

# K

**kangaroo**, *n*. Sense 3 h in Dict. becomes 3 i.
Add: [3.] **h.** *pl.* (With capital initial.) A
nickname for the Australian international
†rugby union or rugby league team, esp. as a
touring party. Cf. WALLABY *n*. 1 b.

**1911** *Sydney Morning Herald* 4 Oct. 8/4 The side
over which the Kangaroos so convincingly triumphed
was a powerful one. **1930** J. BUCHAN *Castle Gay* i. 14
The Kangaroos had two halves possessed of
miraculous hands and a perfect knowledge of the
game. **1933** *Bulletin* (Sydney) 27 Sept. 24/4 The
Kangaroos continued their good run in the North of
England last week. **1945** BAKER *Austral. Lang.* ix. 178
Just as New Zealand football representatives acquired
the names *All Blacks*, *Fernleaves*, and *Kiwis*, so did
Australian representatives become known as
*Kangaroos*, *Wallabies* and *Waratahs*. **1964** *Rugby
League News* Oct. 4 Mr. W. G. Buckley . . presided at
the Kangaroos' Annual Re-Union . . on . . September
20. **1986** *Open Rugby* Sept. 16/1 The 'Australian
influence' of 1982 is now certainly taking effect, but
will it be in time for us to take on and beat the 1986
Kangaroos?

# L

**lamp-post**, *n*. Add: **b.** Colloq. phr. *between you and me and the lamp-post*: in strict confidence. Cf. GATE-POST *n*. b.

**1919** WODEHOUSE *Damsel in Distress* xxvi. 309 Between me and you and the lamp-post, you haven't an earthly! **1924** D. STONE *Yank Brown, Pitcher* i. 14 Even then, though, just between you and me and the lamp-post, when I wanted to eat a piece of pie, I ate it. **1940** J. L. BONNEY *Murder without Clues* vi. 94 Between you and me and the lamp-post I'm tickled you got here.

**land-side**, *n*. Add: [**2.**] **b.** *transf.* The side of an airport terminal building (hence, the area of an airport) to which the general public is allowed unrestricted access; contrasted with *airside* s.v. \*AIR *n*.[1] B. III. 1. Hence *attrib.*, without art., and as *adv.*

**1955** [see *airside* s.v. \*AIR *n*.[1] III. 1]. **1982** E. CONNOR *Working at Airport* 49/1 There are two main security functions at Gatwick. The first is to control access from landside to airside. **1984** *Times* 14 May 19/4 But if you want to eat at Gatwick there is more choice landside. **1986** A. M. WITTON *Buses Outer London* (ed. 3) 41 In 1981 the British Airports Authority re-awarded the contract for providing internal 'landside' transport at Heathrow Airport.

**legisign** ('lɛdʒɪsaɪn), *n*. *Philos.* and *Ling.* [f. L. *lēgi-*, *lex* law + SIGN *n*.] A term devised by C. S. Peirce (1839-1914) to designate a word or sign representing a category or universal ('type'), whose individual occurrences are sinsigns or tokens of the type. Cf. QUALISIGN *n*., \*SINSIGN *n*.

*a* **1914** C. S. PEIRCE *Coll. Papers* (1932) II. 142 A sign may be termed a *Qualisign*, a *Sinsign*, or a *Legisign* ... A *Legisign* is a law that is a Sign. *Ibid.* 148 The Interpretant of a Rhematic Indexical Legisign represents it as an Iconic Legisign. **1936** *Jrnl. Philos.* XXXIII. 701 C. S. Peirce .. called a word as a particular instance a 'token' or 'sinsign', and a word as a universal or kind a 'type' or 'legisign'. **1966** [see QUALISIGN *n*.]. **1973** *Screen* Spring/Summer 16 Certain of his [*sc.* Peirce's] distinctions have been completely absorbed into current usage, as for instance the *type* and *token* or *legisign* and *sinsign* distinctions.

**lexical**, *a*. Add: [**1.**] *lexical ambiguity*, ambiguity arising from homonymy rather than from grammatical structure (as between *brake* 'restrainer' and *brake* 'fence', or *well* noun and *well* adverb); contr. with *structural ambiguity* s.v. \*STRUCTURAL *a*. 5 b

[**1956** *Amer. Speech* XXXI. 102 The passage remains totally ambiguous; that is, its ambiguity is both structural and lexical.] **1970** F. BRENGELMAN *Eng. Lang.* vi. 71 For example, the structural and lexical ambiguity which we can tolerate in speech because we have a whole array of supplementary signalling devices—intonation, gestures, facial expressions, the physical context—cannot be tolerated in writing. **1980** M. S. SEIDENBERG et al. *Time-Course of Lexical Ambiguity Resolution in Context* (ERIC Doc. 184-092) (microfiche) 2 Lexical ambiguity is one of the most extensively researched topics in the study of language composition.

# M

**M**. Add: [III.] [6.] [a.] **ME**, myalgic encephalomyelitis (see *MYALGIC *a.* 2).
**1982** *Daily Tel.* 11 Dec. 14/3 The other day I mentioned the Richmond newspaper advertisement: *Jumble sale in aid of* *ME . . . There is, our medical correspondent confirms, one of those slow, destructive diseases called Myalgic Encephalomyelitis. **1990** *Health Now* July 15/1 It is widely taken throughout Brazil as an antidote to stress and is potentially a very valuable supplement for increasing energy levels of ME sufferers.

**male**, *a.* and *n.*² Add: [B.] [4.] **male bonding**, (the formation of) friendship and loyalty between males, esp. between a particular pair of male associates; cf. *BONDING *vbl. n.* 4.
**1969** L. TIGER *Men in Groups* ii. 18 In this chapter I want to try to indicate the importance of *male bonding in a number of animal communities. **1977** J. WEEKS *Coming Out* (1979) x. 116 His [*sc.* D. H. Lawrence's] ideas . . later became bitterly anti-homosexual, even while he extolled the virtues of male bonding. **1986** *N.Z. Listener* 15 Feb. 50/2 F F Coppola found a part for him in his beautifully filmed but simple-minded male-bonding advertisement *Rumble Fish*.

**mastigoneme** ('mæstɪgəʊ,niːm), *n.* Biol. [a. F. *mastigonème* (G. Deflandre 1934, in *Compt. Rend.* CXCVIII. 498), f. Gr. μάστιξ, μαστιγο-whip + νῆμα thread.] A hair-like structure attached to the surface of the flagellum in some unicellular eukaryotes, usually as one of a row. Cf. *FLIMMER *n.*²
**1935** *Biol. Abstr.* IX. 1150/1 The longitudinal flagellum of the Dinoflagellate, *Glenodinium uliginosum*, bears a long, slender, terminal filament, the transverse flagellum is provided with a row of mastigonemes. **1947** *Ann. Rev. Microbiol.* I. 8 Hair-like branches ('flimmer', 'mastigonemes') on one or both sides of flagella have been described. **1965** *New Scientist* 4 Mar. 568/3 The presence of lateral projections or 'mastigonemes' on the flagella of *Monas*. **1978** *Bio Systems* X. 75/1 Mastigonemes are absent from the prymnesiomonads.

**matrix**, *n.* Add: [3.] c. *Manuf.* A fine material used to bind together the coarser particles of a composite (usu. artificial) substance; *spec.* in *Building*, lime or fine cement.
**1838** [see PEBBLE-STONE *n.* a]. **1879** H. REID *Pract. Treat. Manuf. Concrete* (new ed.) i. 5 A concrete mass in the constructive sense means the binding together of variously selected aggregates by a cementatious matrix. **1910** *Encycl. Brit.* VI. 835/1 The matrix is the lime or cement, whose chemical action with the added water causes the concrete to solidify . . . The matrix most commonly used is Portland cement. **1947** J. C. RICH *Materials & Methods of Sculpture* xi. 323 White Portland cement is recommended as matrix for a colored concrete, because by its use a maximum coloring effect can be gained. **1984** E. P. DeGARMO et al. *Materials & Processes in Manuf.* (ed. 6) v. 123 The microstructure consists of three-dimensional graphite flakes dispersed in a matrix of ferrite.
[6.] [a.] Substitute for def.: A rectangular array of symbols or mathematical expressions arranged in rows and columns with one symbol or expression occupying each position on a rectangular grid, considered as a single entity and now usually written with enclosing round brackets. Also *transf.*, any similar arrangement or tabulation of words, data, etc. (Earlier and later examples.)
**1850** J. J. SYLVESTER in *Phil. Mag.* XXXVII. 369 We . . commence . . with an oblong arrangement of terms consisting, suppose, of *m* lines and *n* columns. This will not in itself represent a determinant, but is, as it were, a Matrix out of which we may form various systems of determinants by fixing upon a number *p*, and selecting at will *p* lines and *p* columns, the squares corresponding to which may be termed determinants of the *p*th order. **1945** E. T. BELL *Devel. Math.* (ed. 2) ix. 205 The elements of the theory of matrices are now included in the usual college course in algebra. *Ibid.*, The invention of matrices illustrates once more the power and suggestiveness of a well-devised notation. **1960** *IRE Trans. Med. Electronics* VII. 280/2 Let us start with a large matrix filled with 1's and 0's, depending upon whether a particular case does or does not have a particular symptom. **1964** GOULD & KOLB *Dict. Social Sci.* 452/2 The economy is divided into a number of sectors or industries, sometimes several hundred, and . . tables or matrices are constructed which show the goods-and-services inputs and outputs of each. **1990** *Accountancy* Mar. 45/2 The Bank of England has reviewed the matrix banks use to judge the adequacy of their provisions against exposure to countries experiencing debt repayment problems.
f. *spec.* in *Management.* An organizational structure in which two or more lines of command, responsibility, or communication may run through the same individual; *spec.* one in which project teams are formed of staff drawn from separate departments or functions within the organization. Usu. *attrib.*, esp. as *matrix management, organization*, by which a co-ordinated structure of this nature across a business, etc. supplements the traditional hierarchical model. Contr. with LINE *n.*² 19 d.
**1959** J. MARSCHAK in M. Haire *Mod. Organization Theory* xi. 308 (*caption*) A matrix of actions, observations, and internal communications. **1964** *Business Horizons* Summer 72/2 The concept of a matrix organization entails an organizational system designed to create a 'web of relationships' rather than a line and staff relationship of work performance. **1975** *Times Higher Educ. Suppl.* 26 Sept. 9/1 Matrix management is a relatively new approach to modifying and supplementing the conventional hierarchical type of industrial organization, which is based on a pyramid of superior-subordinate authority relationships. **1984** D. G. BEW in C. A. Heaton *Introd. Industr. Chem.* iii. 77 The development of some form of matrix organization is usual to ensure coverage of all the planned activities with minimum overlap.
g. *Computing.* A rectangular array of potential image points. Chiefly in *dot matrix* s.v. DOT *n.*¹ 8, *matrix printer* in sense 7 below.
**1958**, etc. [see *matrix printer*, sense 7 below]. **1985** *Which Computer?* Apr. 35/2 The screen matrix is 255 by 512 pixels.

**metroplex** ('mɛtrəʊplɛks), *n.* U.S. [f. METRO(POLITAN *a.* + *-PLEX².] A large, sprawling metropolitan area, esp. one consisting of two or more cities in an area of dense population.

**1969** *New Scientist* 7 Aug. 267/1 In parts of the US, notably in Los Angeles and in the metroplex of the eastern seaboard, the nitrogen oxides of car exhausts are activated by sunlight. **1972** *Globe & Mail* (Toronto) 9 Dec. 15/3 In Texas a new word has been born. Dallas and Fort Worth are now calling themselves *Metroplex*. **1980** *Times* 28 Nov. 8/2 The whole metroplex of Houston ranks as an enterprise zone, a city without planning. **1986** *Richmond* (Va.) *Times-Dispatch* 10 Feb. A10/6 The idea of the two-city 'metroplex', centered on an airport larger than Manhattan, has produced joint planning and much common sense.

**mobilism** ('məʊbɪlɪz(ə)m), *n.* Geol. [ad. F. *mobilisme* (E. Argand 1922, in *XIIIe. Congrès Géol. Internat.* (1924) I. 289): see MOBILE *a.*, -ISM.] The hypothesis that the physical character of the earth's crust is such as to sustain great lateral movements, whereby the configurations of continents and ocean basins are changed in time. Cf. *STABILISM *n.*

**1933** W. H. BUCHER *Deformation Earth's Crust* iv. 102 We have seen already that 'mobilism' grants continents that are capable of drifting also the capacity for stretching and deforming. **1969** tr. *Physics of Solid Earth* (Izvestiya Acad. Sci. U.S.S.R.) III. 139/2 Stille, who was no supporter of mobilism, estimated the overlapping of the ocean floor along . . deep-seated overthrusts to be 250 km or more for the Pliocene and Quaternary periods. **1985** *Nature* 25 July 303/1 The sudden and stunning success of 'mobilism' in the plate tectonics revolution of the 1960s.

Hence **'mobilist** *n.*, one who believes in mobilism or in its application in a particular case; also as *adj.*

**1972** *Jrnl. Geol.* LXXX. 36/2 The mobilist concept has been modified radically by the 1970–71 drilling results of JOIDES Leg 15. *Ibid.* 37/1 Both the mobilists and we agree on one point: the so-called Caribbean plate is moving eastward relative to the Atlantic, North America, and South America. **1975** E. UCHUPI in Nairn & Stehli *Ocean Basins & Margins* III. i. 50 Three origins have been proposed by the mobilists to explain the origin of the Caribbean. **1983** *Times Lit. Suppl.* 26 Aug. 903/3 Kuhn's idea of a sudden and total switch captured the *bouleversement* of the change from fixist to mobilist views of the continents.

**Montonero** (ˌmɒntəˈnɛərəʊ), *n.* Also montonero. [a. S. Amer.-Sp. *montonero* guerilla fighter, f. Sp. *montón* heap, mass, crowd + *-ero* -EER.]
**1.** In South America: a peasant rebel against imperial Spain. Usu. in *pl.* Now *Hist.*

**1825** R. PROCTOR *Narr. Journey across Cordillera* xxix. 215 The city, and even the Spanish camp, had been surrounded by bands of Guerrillas, called Montoneros, who cut off many of the supplies. **1852** *Househ. Words* 23 Oct. 128/1 The Sierra may be swarming with the bandit montoneros. **1868** H. C. ROSS JOHNSON *Long Vacation in Argentine Alps* xxi. 112 We were pretty well able to take care of ourselves against any nomadic party of Montanaros or cutthroats we were likely to come across.
**2.** A member of a left-wing Peronist guerilla organization in Argentina.

**1970** *N.Y. Times* 12 June 6/1 There was also a note, 'Communique No. 5', signed by 'the Montoneros', a terrorist group professing allegiance to former dictator Juan Domingo Perón. **1985** J. RATHBONE *Lying in State* xviii. 103 In Argentina he may be wanted as a Montonero. And that means death.

**montuno**, *n.* Add: **1.** A traditional costume worn by Panamanian men, consisting of short white cotton trousers and an embroidered shirt.

The equivalent costume for women, the *montuna* (-ˈtuːnə), consists of a flared skirt, embroidered bodice, and loose shawl.

**1941** D. G. SPICER *Latin Amer. Costumes* 62 The *montuno* costume, worn by the men, is of white cotton with short trousers and a handsome shirt of open work embroidery and cross-stitch. Originally the *montuno* was made by the men themselves. **1943** E. P. HANSON *New World Guides Latin Amer. Republics* I. (*Panama*) 38 The men wear montunas [ed. 2, 1945: montunos] with native woven hats and embroidered fringed blouses and trousers. **1946** I. SALEM tr. *M. & H. Larsen's Forests of Panama* vi. 70 In the country the *montuna* with its rustic colouring takes the place of the sumptuous and . . expensive *pollera* on gala occasions . . The *montuna* has . . the vivacity and gaiety of a wild flower.

**monument**, *n.* Add: [5.] **d.** A structure, edifice, or the like surviving from a past age; an 'ancient monument' (see ANCIENT *a.* 4 c).

**1880** [see ANCIENT *a.* 4 c]. **1932**, etc. [see HENGE *n.*²]. **1979** H. KISSINGER *White House Years* xxiv. 1066 A string of Presidential visits to the architectural and artistic monuments of China's past: the Great Wall, the Forbidden City, the Ming Tombs, [etc.]. **1988** *Daily Tel.* (Colour Suppl.) 6 Aug. p. ii/2 Its [*sc.* Rome's] monuments, sacred or profane, have always been built to accommodate, or to overawe, a multitude.
**e.** *transf.* Something that serves as a symbol of or witness *to* a way of life, characteristic attitude, etc.

**1937** *Maine* (Federal Writers' Project) 20A Visible monuments to the early struggles of the pioneers to establish themselves on the first frontiers of America are the old forts with their stockades and blockhouses. **1952** *Observer* 30 Nov. 5/4 The Pentagon, that immense monument to modern man's subservience to the desk. **1973** E. F. SCHUMACHER *Small is Beautiful* II. iv. 127 Disused nuclear power stations will stand as unsightly monuments to unquiet man's assumption that nothing but tranquillity, from now on, stretches before him. **1987** D. ROWE *Beyond Fear* v. 181 Psychiatric hospitals are monuments to the destruction of the human spirit.

**mooch**, *v.* Add: [3.] For 'to slouch *along*' read: to slouch *along* or *off*.

**1966** 'J. HACKSTON' *Father clears Out* 49 They both stood up, . . and mooched off down the back. **1977** *Belfast Tel.* 17 Jan. 6/7 So around about 11 pm . . I mooched off to bed.
**7.** *intr.* Western *U.S.* and *Canad.* To fish by mooching (sense 2); occas. *trans.*, to use (a small fish) as bait for a large fish.

**1947** C. HAURY in H. W. Howard *Salmon Fishing on Puget Sound* 86 To mooch in a given area successfully it is necessary to fish it often and do a lot of experimenting to find how deep it is. **1961** *Sun* (Vancouver) 17 Aug. 23/3 Most anglers troll, rather than mooch or strip-cast with light, sporty but riskier tackle. **1963** *Ibid.* 16 Feb. 17/1 Kelly started mooching a herring, caught himself a 10-pound chinook salmon. **1971** W. HILLEN *Blackwater River* iv. 36 Mooching between the big island and the west end . . I found several char holes with fish. **1980** D. NUTTALL *Mooching* i. 15 Those who have been mooching unsuccessfully frequently remove their leader and weights and put on a two-ounce sliding weight, [etc.].

**mooching** ('muːtʃɪŋ), *vbl. n.* [f. MOOCH *v.* + -ING¹.] **1.** Begging; sponging; scrounging. *slang* and *dial.*

**1899** 'J. FLYNT' *Tramping with Tramps* I. 145 Moochin' spiles workin' jes ez workin' spiles moochin'. **1979** L. DERWENT *Border Bairn* i. 17 The tramps were adepts at mooching, and never refused any cast-off. **1987** *Observer* (Colour Suppl.) 4 Oct. 63/1 The English talent for freeloading, which also goes by the names of sponging, leeching and the more American mooching.

**2.** *Western U.S.* and *Canad.* A method of angling from a stationary or slow-moving boat, using light tackle and a small fish as bait.

**1947** C. HAURY in H. W. Howard *Salmon Fishing on Puget Sound* 85 Mooching, a term applied to a combination of slow trolling with spinning gear is one of the most effective and popular ways of catching salmon. **1960** Duncan (B.C.) *Cowichan Leader* 28 Apr. 7/1 Mooching just consists of dropping a line over the side of a boat with a weight attached to take it to the required depth, and a herring strip attached to a hook for bait. **1963** *Sun* (Vancouver) 3 July 19/1 By 'mooching' I mean mostly drifting with light tackle for heavy fish. **1975** H. EVANS in H. White *Raincoast Chron.* (1976) 222/1 Mooring his boat .. he started casting with straight herring for bait ... So began what is currently known as mooching. **1980** D. NUTTALL *Mooching* i. 15 The two distinguishing features of mooching should be that there be no dodger or flasher and the tackle must be basically designed for still fishing or moving very slowly.

**moon,** *v.* Add: [**2.**] **c.** *intr.* To dream, to indulge in sentimental reverie *about*; to yearn sentimentally *over*, to gaze adoringly *at*; also without const. Also (*rare*), to pine or long *for*.

**1901** M. FRANKLIN *My Brilliant Career* vii. 51 It was daily dinned into my ears that the little things of life were the noblest, and that all the great people I mooned about said the same. **1929** E. O'NEILL *Dynamo* i. ii. 27 Mrs. Fife (Mooning at him with adoring eyes). **1929** D. H. LAWRENCE *Pansies* 151 It's no good mooning for sloppy ease When they're holding out the thunderbolt For you to take. **1949** *Richmond* (Va.) *Times-Dispatch* 19 May 11/8 There aren't any pictures of muscular pin-up boys to moon over. **1964** I. WALLACE *Man* (1965) vi. 442 When she had not been working, she was mooning and wanting to get back to George and marriage. **1968** T. ROETHKE *Coll. Poems* 24 Boys moon at girls with last year's fatuous faces. **1971** 'A. BURGESS' *MF* xvi. 177 She was merely kindly leaving an engaged couple to kiss and cuddle and moon about sunnier delights to come. **1988** R. CHRISTIANSEN *Romantic Affinities* i. 34 He .. mooned over his 'standard of female excellence' Mary Evans.

**moot,** *a.* Add: **b.** *U.S.* (chiefly *Law*). Of a case, issue, etc.: not (or no longer) having practical significance or relevance; abstract, academic.

**1899** *Atlantic Reporter* XLII. Jan.-Apr. 517/2 Because the plaintiff boarded the cars for the purpose of making a test case, this is a moot case, which the court will not entertain. **1946** *Univ. Pennsylvania Law Rev.* Jan. 126 A lawsuit which is, or has become, moot is neither a case nor a controversy in the constitutional sense and no federal court has the power to decide it. **1973** *N.Y. Law Jrnl.* 31 Aug. 18/4 Motion for an order dismissing this indictment for lack of prosecution is dismissed as moot. **1986** *New Yorker* 29 Sept. 112/3 By that point the judgment was more or less moot, since the commune was closing down.

**mopery** ('məʊpərɪ), *n. colloq.* [f. MOPE *v.* + -ERY.] Mopish behaviour; a fit of moping.

**1907** *McClure's Mag.* XXVIII. 380/1 Come along, children, before the boogie man sloughs you in the skookum for mopery! **1925** W. DE LA MARE *Broomsticks* 369 Tom's little moperies came very near at times to being a little mad. **1961** [see BOOK *n.* 10 d]. **1976** *New Musical Express* 12 Feb. 24/2 All that mopery and Ooooh, it's so hard and lonely at the top.

**morinite** ('mɒrɪnaɪt), *n. Min.* [a. F. *morinite* (A. Lacroix 1891, in *Bull. Soc. Min.* XIV. 189), f. the name of *Morineau*, director of the mine at Montebras, France, where it was first found.]

A hydrated basic fluophosphate of sodium, calcium, and aluminium, $NaCa_2Al_2(PO_4)_2$ $(OH)F_4.2H_2O$, occurring as colourless, white, or pale pinkish monoclinic crystals and red lamellar masses.

**1892** E. S. DANA *Dana's Syst. Min.* (ed. 6) 1042 Morinite ... A new species, announced but not fully described, occurring with the amblygonite at Montibras. **1935** *Amer. Mineralogist* XX. 196 A few small prismatic crystals of the morinite were obtained from cavities in the rock. **1958** *Ibid.* XLIII. 585 A somewhat wider zone consisting of faintly pinkish (nearly colorless) morinite crystals in masses of light greenish to light bluish apatite. The morinite is massive, coarsely crystalline. **1979** *Canad. Mineralogist* XVII. 93/2 Morinite, a rare hydrothermal hydrous fluorophosphate, is found in association with montebrasite, apatite, augelite and wardite in pegmatitic environments.

**mormoopid** (ˌmɔːməʊˈɒpɪd), *a.* (*n.*) *Zool.* [f. mod.L. *Mormoopidæ*, f. Gr. μορμώ MORMO *n.* + ὤψ face: see -ID[3].] Of or pertaining to the family Mormoopidae of small insectivorous bats of North and Central America, in which the nose-leaf is absent or rudimentary but the lips are elaborate and leaf-shaped. Also as *n.*, a bat of this family.

**1970** *Jrnl. Mammalogy* LI. 230 What are the major morphological adaptations of the mormoopid flight apparatus? *Ibid.* 232 Simplification of musculature is a clear trend in mormoopids. **1976** [see VESPERTILIONID *a.*]. **1984** J. E. HILL *Bats* xi. 202 Unlike the phyllostomids, mormoopids have only a rudimentary noseleaf which is little more than a bump on the nose .. and .. ornamentations give the mouth a distinct funnel-like shape when it is opened.

**Morningside** ('mɔːnɪŋsaɪd, *Sc.* mɔrnɪŋˈsaɪd), *n.* The name of a residential district of Edinburgh, used *attrib.* or *absol.* to designate the supposedly affected and refined accent of its residents. Cf. KELVINSIDE *n.*

**1953** W. TAYLOR *Scot Free* 89 The wrongly castigated Kelvinside or Morningside accents. **1973** *Lowland Scots* (Occas. Paper Assoc. Scottish Lit. Stud. No. 2) 10 The Scottish Augustans seem to have bequeathed us an inferiority complex and the Morningside accent. **1976** *Scotsman* 24 Dec. (Weekend Suppl.) 1/7 He talks awful tosted breed, if ye unnerstan' my Morningside accent. **1984** J. GIFFORD et al. *Edinburgh* 615 Morningside is a byword for Edinburgh gentility. **1986** *Sunday Tel.* 9 Nov. 14/2 The authors have a keen ear for accents, whether Somerset, Morningside or 'local'.

**morphallaxis,** *n.* Add: Hence **morpha'llactic** *a.*

**1937** *Biol. Bull.* LXXII. 115 A self-determined morphallactic process. **1952** A. E. NEEDHAM *Regeneration & Wound-Healing* i. 2 In the Amphibia portions of late blastula- and even gastrula-stages are able to regulate eventually by 'post-generation', again a morphallactic process. **1980** *Jrnl. Theoret. Biol.* LXXXII. 105 Animals with a morphallactic type of regeneration are assumed to possess a persistent signalling system similar to those believed to exist in embryos.

**morphologization** (mɔːˌfɒlədʒaɪˈzeɪʃən), *n. Linguistics.* [f. MORPHOLOGY *n.*: see -IZATION. Cf. earlier Fr. *morphologisé.*] The process whereby a phonetic feature or distinction becomes reinterpreted morphologically; an instance of this.

**1971** F. R. ADRADOS in *Archivum Linguisticum* II. 98 This means a progressive morphologization of *s.* **1974** J. B. HOOPER in *Parasession on Natural Phonol.* (Chicago Linguistic Soc.) 161, I will present one example of rule morphologization and demonstrate that the analysis required by NGG accounts correctly for linguistic data. **1977** *Language* LIII. 220

Telescoping, morphologization, and rule inversion are some of the mechanisms discussed in this light. **1985** *Canad. Jrnl. Linguistics* XXX. 65 The predominance of verbs in this list might suggest that it [*sc.* pretonic syllable prominence] is rather a morphologization of the syllable prominence.
Hence **mor'phologize** *v. trans.*, to subject (a feature or process) to morphologization; freq. in *pass.* Also **mor'phologized** *ppl. a.*
**1974** J. B. HOOPER in *Parasession on Natural Phonol.* (Chicago Linguistic Soc.) 161 The consequence of these constraints is that every rule of morpho-phonological grammar (i.e. both phonetically motivated rules and morphologically or grammatically conditioned rules, which I call morphophonemic or morphological rules) must represent [etc.]. *Ibid.* 165 We know that the tenseness distinction is morphologized. **1975** *Language* LI. 556 Obligatory natural rules cannot be simply dropped from the grammar; they can be morphologized and restricted, and eventually lost. **1981** *Canad. Jrnl. Linguistics* XXVI. 83 It has moved along the continuum from allophonic to automatic morphophonemic to morphologized and/or inverted to allomorph rules.

**morphopoiesis** (ˌmɔːfəʊpɔɪˈiːsɪs), *n. Biol.* Also (*rare*) -**poesis** (-pəʊˈiːsɪs). [f. Gr. μορφ-ή form + -o[1] + -POIESIS *n.*] The formation of an organic structure from a limited number of sub-units. Cf. MORPHOGENESIS *n.*
**1959** L. S. PENROSE in *New Biol.* XXVIII. 98, I had difficulty in finding a suitable name for the activated complexes produced in these experiments... In agreement with scientific terminology it could be a 'synapton' and its successful reproduction should, according to Mr N. W. Pirie, be called 'morphopoesis'. **1963** E. KELLENBERGER in M. Sela *New Perspectives in Biol.* VI. 242 To understand the mechanism of this morphopoiesis. **1966** —— in Wolstenholme & O'Connor *Princ. Biomolecular Organization* 192 Viruses and in particular bacteriophages provide very suitable experimental systems in which the morphopoiesis of the capsid or of tail components can be studied efficiently. **1977** *Jrnl. Protozool.* XXIV. 19/1 There are also specific articles concerning morphopoiesis.
Hence **morphopoi'etic** *a.*, assisting morphopoiesis; shape-determining.
**1963** E. KELLENBERGER in M. Sela *New Perspectives in Biol.* VI. 234 It may be foreseen .. that different mechanisms work in nature for the expression of this shape-determining—or morphopoietic—information. **1980** *Nature* 3 Jan. 34/1 Molecules of pC thus assembled into the core could further interact through their unique NH₂-terminal domains with other morphopoietic proteins such as pE, during the polymerisation of the capsid.

**mortise**, *v.*[1] Add: Hence '**mortiser** *n.*, a machine for cutting mortises.
**1886** *Carpentry & Building* VIII. 135/1 The improved power mortiser is shown in Fig. 1. **1942** H. J. MASSINGHAM *Field Fellowship* iv. 67 Clearing-irons, double-irons, scrapers, mortizers, beetles, tools enough to seat all the weary of the world. **1976** *S. Wales Echo* 23 Nov. 11/5 (Advt.), For Sale .. Mortiser. £150 ... Various other items for woodworking shop. **1990** *Practical Woodworking* Mar. 2 (Advt.), Ultimate accuracy of a mortiser plus a high precision drill press.

**Morton** ('mɔːtən), *n. Path.* The name of Thomas George Morton (1835–1903), U.S. surgeon, used in the possessive, esp. in *Morton's foot*, *metatarsalgia*, *toe*, to designate a condition of the foot described by him in 1876 (*Amer. Jrnl. Med. Sci.* LXXXI. 37), in which compression of a plantar nerve by a metatarsal bone causes pain in the metatarsal region and

sometimes a neuromatous swelling of the nerve concerned.
**1891** *Boston Med. & Surg. Jrnl.* 16 July 52/2 (*heading*) Metatarsal Neuralgia, or 'Morton's Affection of the Foot'. **1900** DORLAND *Med. Dict.* 397/2 Morton's foot. **1900** *Index-Cat. Libr. Surgeon-General's Office U.S. Army* 2nd Ser. V. 947/2 (*heading*) Morton's toe. **1925** J. J. NUTT *Dis. & Deformities of Foot* (ed. 2) x. 252 Morton's toe is a neuritis, caused by nerve pressure by the head of the fourth metatarsal. **1935** N. C. LAKE *Foot* xvii. 235 In 1876 Morton of Philadelphia described a painful affection of the forepart of the foot which has since that time gone by the name of 'Morton's metatarsalgia'. **1939** DICKSON & DIVELEY *Functional Disorders of Foot* ix. 186 (*heading*) Descent of the metatarsal arch and anterior metatarsalgia (Morton's toe). **1977** J. F. FIXX *Compl. Bk. Running* xxii. 252 Undoubtedly there was more than a little midnight oil burned as doctors the country over studied up on Morton's toe.

**Mossad** (mɒˈsæd, *U.S.* məʊˈsɑːd, ‖moˈsaːd), *n.* Also **Mosad**, **MOSSAD**. [ad. Heb. *mōsād* institution.] **a.** [Ellipt. for Heb. *Mōsād* (*lĕ-*) *'Aliyāh Bēt* Institution for the Second Immigration.] An underground organization formed in 1938 for the purpose of bringing Jews from Europe to Palestine.
**1954** J. & D. KIMCHE *Secret Roads* xvi. 219 The Mossad .. became the architect of the first mass migration to Zion. **1979** M. J. COHEN *Lett. & Papers C. Weizman* XX. 87 A clash between *Mosad* (organisation for illegal immigration into Palestine) and *Haganah*. **1982** —— *Palestine & Great Powers 1945–1948* x. 254 Yosi Har-el, senior representative on board of both the Hagana and the Mossad, thought the landing of the immigrants was a second priority.
**b.** [Ellipt. for Heb. *Mōsād 'Elyōn lĕ-Mōdī'īn u-Bitāhōn* Supreme Institution for Intelligence and Security.] The principal secret intelligence service of the state of Israel, established in 1951.
**1972** F. FORSYTH *Odessa File* xiii. 215 Three tiny fragments of information had come into the possession of the Mossad in the previous six days. **1973** *Times* 12 Apr. 8/4 Mossad, the group word given to the intelligence department, comes under the control of a powerful trio of politicians. **1975** M. H. ALBERT *Gargoyle Conspiracy* vi. 96 There was no message for him from Uri, so the Mossad agent still wasn't back in Rome. **1979** *Time* 7 May 40/3 The French had been stung many times before by MOSSAD, .. notably on Christmas morning 1969, when its agents piloted five embargoed gunboats from the port city of Cherbourg to Haifa. **1986** *Washington Post* 24 Apr. A20/5 The defendants claimed that they had used the Israeli intelligence service Mossad to check the backgrounds of some of the other conspirators.

**mother**, *n.* Senses 3 d–f in Dict. become 3 e–g. Add: **[I.] [3.] d.** A brothel-keeper. Chiefly as a title of courtesy.
**1785** GROSE *Dict. Vulgar Tongue*, *Mother*, or *the Mother*, a bawd. **1803** G. COLMAN *John Bull* III. ii. 36 *Mary.* The unfortunate must look up to such a lady, sure, as a mother. *Shuffleton.* She has acquired that appellation. *c*1810 W. HICKEY *Mem.* (1960) 56 The third brothel was kept by Mother Cocksedge, for all the Lady Abbesses were dignified with the respectable title of Mother. **1973** G. GREENE *Honorary Consul* I. iii. 96 It must be better than life at Mother Sanchez. **1980** E. JONG *Fanny* II. v. 207, I enter'd Mother Coxtart's House once more.
[**e.**] (Further examples.)
**1930** *Amer. Speech* V. 468 Theatrical rooming house—Diggings or diggs. *Mother* (*proprietress of same*)—Ma. **1953** J. G. MOORE in Cassidy & Le Page *Dict. Jamaican Eng.* (1967) 306/1 Mother = crowned shepherdess—the highest female office [in a Revival

religious group]. **1975** *Times* 27 Feb. 14/8 Believe it or not, there is [in the CIA] a Mother, whose office . . is guarded by young men in grey flannel suits. **1979** *Daily Mail* 8 Sept. 17/4 *Mother,* senior secretary. **1983** *Times* 17 Dec. 2/2 Miss Joanna Davies, mother of the NUJ chapel (chairman of the office branch).

**motherboard** ('mʌðəbɔːd), *n. Electronics.* Also mother-board, mother board. [f. MOTHER *n.*[1] + BOARD *n.*] A printed circuit board on which are mounted the principal components of a microcomputer or other electronic device, and to which other boards (daughterboards) may be connected.

**1971** [see *DAUGHTERBOARD *n.*]. **1978** *Gramophone* May 1960/1 All the signal processing electronics for recording and playback, plus the provision of erase and bias current and metering, are contained on five small printed circuit cards; these plug into sockets on a 'mother' board behind the control panel. **1984** *Which Micro?* Dec. 99 (Advt.), Microslot is a two-way mother-board . . to incorporate as many add-ons as you wish. **1986** [see MICROFLOPPY *n.*]. **1988** *PC Mag.* June 89/1 These four gate arrays integrate a large number of peripheral-control chips that would otherwise clutter up the motherboard.

**motive,** *n.* Add: [4.] c. *Law.* The purpose or end which motivates someone to commit an illegal, esp. criminal, act.

**1792** *U.S. Rep.* (Supreme Court Penn.) IV. 116 Neither the wildness of the boy's motive, for committing the crimes, nor his youth, can afford a satisfactory answer to the charge. **1842** *U.S. Rep.* (Supreme Court U.S.) XLI. 343 It has always been allowable . . to introduce evidence of other acts . . , in order to illustrate his intent or motive in the particular act directly in judgment. **1894** J. S. MACKENZIE in *Internat. Jrnl. Ethics* IV. 232 Why did this man commit a murder? He was carried away by passion . . . On the other hand . . why did Columbus cross the Atlantic? He hoped to discover land . . . Some writers would use the term motive in both . . cases . . . The motive is not the hope, but the object as hoped. **1906** *Corresp. respecting Attack on Brit. Officers at Denshawi* 13 in *Parl. Papers* 1906 (Cd. 3086) CXXXVII. 687 Two days ago three natives knocked a soldier off his donkey and kicked him in the stomach; his injuries are serious . . . Theft appears to have been the motive. **1936** A. CHRISTIE *ABC Murders* xxxiv. 238 When a man or woman is killed, what are the questions the police ask? Opportunity . . Motive. Who benefited by the deceased's death? **1987** A. BRIEN *Lenin* ii. 67, I attempted a crime. I exercise my right of defence only to explain my motives.

**moto** ('məʊtəʊ), *n.*[2] *Motor-cycling* and *Cycling.* [Shortened f. MOTO-CROSS *n.:* cf. ENDURO *n.*] Any of the heats in a moto-cross or BMX contest; a moto-cross or BMX race.

**1971** *Cycle Racing Ann.* 7/2 The motocross event consists of two or three heats (or 'motos') between 15 and 45 minutes long. **1974** G. BAILEY *How to win Motocross* 169 Between practice and the start of your first moto, you checked over your bike. **1975** J. THAWLEY *How to win Bicycle Motocross* 5/1 BMX races are short. Sometimes a race is called a moto. *Ibid.,* A two-lap moto is rare but even that would only last about a minute. **1980** *Dirt Bike* Oct. 37/1 Since the 465 has a tendency to suck up a lot of fuel, you need the tank to be near full when going into a long moto. **1985** *BMX Action Bike* Apr. 46 He was superfast in the motos but he couldn't break Ant Howells', Brad Smith's and Dale Holmes' grip on the first three places in the main.

**'motorized,** *ppl. a.* (Formerly at MOTORIZE *v.*) [f. MOTORIZE *v.* + -ED[1].] **1.** Equipped with or driven by a motor.

**1922** *Daily Mail* 24 Nov. 6 These machines have gone beyond the stage of motorised pedal cycles and

are in all respects real motorcycles. **1927** *Glasgow Herald* 5 Apr. 8 Serried ranks of tanks advancing against each other . . with motorised artillery bringing up the rear. **1958** *Edmonton* (Alberta) *Jrnl.* 24 June IV. 16/6 Motorized toboggans have made their appearance in the Mackenzie River delta. **1972** *Physics Bull.* July 402/2 The construction of a motorized drill table for physically handicapped operators. **1976** *Beano* 21 Feb. 8/2 I'll wait on the corner in my motorised bath-chair! **1983** *Which?* Sept. 388/3 On pricier cameras, the zoom action may be motorised.

**2.** Adapted to or accustomed to motor traffic.

**1933** ADE *Let.* 13 Nov. (1973) Now there ain't no income from the darn stuff [*sc.* farm lands]. I think it is entirely because of the fact that the world has become motorized but I am not proposing any remedies. **1972** *Daily Tel.* 1 Dec. 15/6 Why does Britain lag behind other highly motorised countries in giving pre-driver training to teenagers?

**3.** Provided or furnished with motor vehicles; *spec.* designating (a group of) members of the armed forces, police, etc., using motor vehicles for transport.

**1938** *Sun* (Baltimore) 31 Aug. 20/3 The regiment is motorized and will come over the Governor Nice Highway to the city. **1940** *Ann. Reg. 1939* 225 The Army of Moravia, consisting of 4 infantry and 2 motorised divisions. **1951** *Sun* (Baltimore) 30 Mar. 32/4 We were push-buttoned . . refrigerated, motorized and armed like marines. **1972** 'G. BLACK' *Bitter Tea* (1973) ii. 26 Angels mightn't be watching over them, but a good third of the motorized police in the State were. **1973** J. WAINWRIGHT *Devil you Don't* 31 The motorised cop was hard-nosed, and proud of it.

**mount,** *n.*[2] Add: [3.] [a.] (*d*) *Philately.* A piece of paper or card on which a stamp is mounted for display in an album, etc.; also, a stamp hinge.

**1882** *Stamp News* May 35/2 For mounting stamps I always use . . the best white gum arabic . . . This sort is much preferable to the yellow, and brown kinds, which are apt to dirty the stamps or the mount. **1885** E. B. EVANS *Philatelic Handbk.* 400 (Advt.), Prepared stamp mounts . . . Far superior to the old plan of gumming the stamps . . . They are to be used on the hinge system. **1912** *Gloss. Philatelic Terms* (Philatelic Congr. Gt. Brit.) 11 *Mount,* incorrectly used for the word 'Hinge'. **1948** J. BETJEMAN *Sel. Poems* 100 The stamp collection waits with mounts long dry. **1969** L. N. & M. WILLIAMS *Techniques Philately* iv. 20 Philatelists devised a method of showing up their finest specimens to better effect . . by affixing the stamp to a piece of black paper or card—a mount—slightly larger than the stamp itself, so as to provide a dark background. **1987** *Stamps* Feb. 62/2 If you use plastic mounts, make sure they are mounted straight and keep them trimmed as close as possible—heavy black borders are very off putting, while over-large mounts allow stamps to slip drunkenly around and look most untidy.

(*e*) *Photogr.* A fitting made to support a lens, *esp.* one on a camera with interchangeable lenses. Cf. *lens mount* s.v. LENS *n.* 4.

**1888** C. JONES *Introd. Sci. & Pract. Photogr.* 268 In almost every lens . . the mount is more or less in the way. It acts as a diaphragm towards the edges of the plate. **1901** E. MARRIAGE *Elementary Photogr.* ii. 19 Examples of negative lenses and suitable mounts for rectilinear and anastigmatic lenses are illustrated by figs. 2 to 10. **1963** R. KINGSLAKE *Lenses in Photogr.* (rev. ed.) viii. 161 In some cine lenses, especially those of short focal length, the deep mount provides an excellent hood automatically. **1986** *Photography* Nov. 8/1 The OM707 will accept any OM mount lens.

**mouse**, *n.* Add: [I.] [1.] c. *fig.* A timid or retiring person; one who is as quiet or insignificant 'as a mouse'. Cf. sense 2 and MOUSY *a.* 2.

**1935** *N. & Q.* 23 Nov. 366 *Mouse* .., a person who is timid—who plays best alone. **1952** M. ALLINGHAM *Tiger in Smoke* i. 31 That shady little mouse we just caught was frightened of somebody, wasn't he? **1975** D. CLARK *Premedicated Murder* vi. 92 Where he was an uncouth bully, she was a mouse, a nonentity. **1987** E. RHODE *Birth & Madness* iii. 86 Anna was no mouse. Even at the age of twenty-one, she had authority.

**mousse**, *n.* Sense 2 in Dict. becomes 3. Add:
2. A brown emulsion of sea water and oil produced by the weathering of oil spills and resistant to dispersal; also, a mass of this substance. Also *chocolate mousse*.
[**1967** *Guardian* 22 Apr. 3/3 No-one was able yesterday to give chapter and verse about which beaches have .. had their chocolate mousse of oil and sand cleared.] **1968** S. A. BERRIDGE et al. in *Jrnl. Inst. Petroleum* LIV. 334/1 'Chocolate mousse'. This term, which appears to have originated from the *Torrey Canyon* incident, is herein defined as [water-in-oil] emulsions of from 50 to 80 per cent water content, which have a solid or semi-solid grease-like consistency, maintain a rigid configuration that can only be changed by an applied force, and are not reverted to oil-in-water emulsions by agitation in sea water. *Ibid.* 337/1 Various methods of preparing 'mousse'-type emulsions were investigated. **1977** *Times* 28 Apr. 5/6 The water-in-oil emulsion known as 'chocolate mousse' persists in North Sea temperatures. **1978** *Marine Pollution Bull.* IX. 293/1 Rapid change-over from sheen oil to mousse formation. **1981** *Nature* 19 Mar. 235/1 The Ixtoc 1 well released oil for 9 months into the open ocean where winds and currents dispersed the floating mousse .. which had formed at the wellhead.

**mousseline**, *n.* Add: 3. *Cookery.* a. Chiefly *attrib.* or as *adj.* in *mousseline sauce* (also ‖*sauce mousseline*). A rich, frothy sauce consisting of hollandaise mixed with whipped cream (or egg whites).
**1906** *Mrs. Beeton's Bk. Househ. Managem.* 226 (*heading*) Green mousseline sauce. **1939** A. L. SIMON *Conc. Encycl. Gastron.* (1952) I. 39/1 Mousseline or mousseuse, Sauce. This is a Hollandaise .. to which is added an equal amount of stiffly-whipped cream. **1956** *Good Housek. Home Encycl.* (ed. 4) 562/1 *Mousseline sauce.* Hollandaise sauce to which beaten egg white or whipped cream has been added, giving a frothy effect. **1988** *N.Y. Times* 15 June C14/4 To accompany the first course, asparagus with sauce mousseline, he chose a 1986 Chinon.
b. A mousse with a soft or light texture.
**1907** G. A. ESCOFFIER *Guide Mod. Cookery* 469 *Mousses* are poached in a mould the contents of which are sufficient for a number of people, whereas *mousselines* are spoon-moulded quenelles, shaped like eggs. **1977** C. CONRAN tr. M. *Guérard's Cuisine Minceur* (1981) 134 Mousseline of frogs' legs with watercress. **1984** BARR & LEVY *Official Foodie Handbk.* IV. 133/2 Warm mousseline of white fish and salmon with a chive-flavoured beurre blanc.

**mousy**, *a.* Add: Hence 'mousily *adv.*, in a mouse-like manner; quietly, timidly.
**1910** 'H. H. RICHARDSON' *Getting of Wisdom* xxii. 229 She stole mousily in and out, avoiding the hours when Evelyn was there. **1987** *Nation* (N.Y.) 9 May 619/1 Bennett provides parallel scenes of Lahr's wife .. mousily typing and transcribing for him.

**mouth**, *n.* Add: [3.] r. Extravagant, insolent, or boastful talk, or a propensity for this (esp. *to be all mouth*); empty bragging, impudence. Cf. LIP *n.* 3 c. *slang* (orig. *U.S.*).

**1935** Z. N. HURSTON *Mules & Men* I. ii. 49 She got plenty hips, plenty mouf and no brains. **1942** BERREY & VAN DEN BARK *Amer. Thes. Slang* §351/2 *Impudent talk,* .. mouth. *a***1961** *Time* in WEBSTER s.v., He is not all mouth .. he gets results. **1970** G. F. NEWMAN *Sir, you Bastard* ii. 75 The youth .. for all his mouth and supposed cleverness was easily tricked. **1973** *Time Out* 2-8 Mar. 13/2 Even then, it was all mouth, to be truthful. **1986** *City Limits* 12 June 10 You're mouth man. All mouth.

**mouth**, *v.* Add: [1.] c. To articulate (a word, etc.) silently or whisperingly; to form on the lips without voicing. Freq. with direct speech as obj.
**1960** M. SPARK *Bachelors* ix. 134 He mouthed and breathed a message to her, contorting his face as if she were a lip-reader. **1968** M. WOODHOUSE *Rock Baby* xxiii. 227 'Security patrol,' she mouthed, and pulled my head down next to hers. **1981** M. GEE *Dying, in Other Words* 101 He still kept reading, bent over and frowning and sometimes mouthing a word. **1975** R. HILL *April Shroud* i. 11 'Good luck,' mouthed Dalziel at the passenger window. **1983** E. PIZZEY *Watershed* I. xv. 123 'Enjoying yourself?' Charles said. 'Lovely,' she mouthed back.

**move-in** ('muːvɪn), *n.* and *a.* [f. the vbl. phr. *to move in*: see MOVE *v.* 16 g.] A. *n.* The action or an instance of moving into or occupying a new place of residence, etc.
The influence of -IN[3] may perh. be felt in quot. 1969.
**1946** *College Topics* (Univ. Virginia, Charlottesville) 26 Nov. 1/5 Dormitory residents, having screamed objections since the proposed move-in was first announced last week, reached a crescendo with their protests last night. **1969** *Courier-Mail* (Brisbane) 25 Feb. 4/6 Uni. move-in ... About 50 unemployed Sardinians have moved in to live with student agitators in a Maoist 'Commune' set up in Rome University's law faculty.
B. *adj. move-in condition*: of a residence for sale or rent, suitable for moving into immediately. *N. Amer. Estate Agents' jargon.*
**1973** L. GILMORE *For Sale by Owner* iii. 84 Look over the headlines below that were selected from various residential classified ads throughout the country: .. Magnificent View .. Move-in Condition .. [etc.]. **1978** *Detroit Free Press* 5 Mar. C19/3 (*Advt.*), Brick Ranch with .. separate dining room, move-in condition thruout. **1985** *Globe & Mail* (Toronto) 9 Oct. E2/3 (*Advt.*), 3 bdrm., updated kitchen, fireplace, move-in condition.

**movement**, *n.* Add: [6.] e. With *the.* = *women's movement* (b) s.v. WOMAN *n.* 10.
**1971** *It* 9-23 Sept. 11/5, I spent ten years in 'the movement'. **1973** *Maclean's Mag.* Jan. 45/3 My editor in New York .. began writing 'Ms.' on her letters to me .. and the office was full of The Movement. **1977** C. MCFADDEN *Serial* (1978) x. 26/2 She had somehow reconciled shaving her legs with the Movement.

**mow**, *n.*[6] Substitute for etym.: [f. MOW *v.*[1]]
b. An act or instance of mowing something, esp. a lawn. *colloq.*
**1975** *Times* 10 Apr. 11/4 The inclement weather .. has enabled me to put off .. the first mow of the lawn. **1987** *S. Oxf. Courier* 16 Apr. 17/3 Never be tempted to cut off more than one third of the length of the grass in one mow as it weakens the growth. **1989** *Daily Tel.* 1 May 20/2 Giving the lawn its first mow of the season.

**mucho** ('mʌtʃəʊ, 'mʊtʃəʊ), *a.* (and *adv.*) *colloq.* and *jocular* (orig. *U.S.*). [a. Sp. *mucho* (pl. *muchos*) adj., much, many, *mucho* (adv.) very.] Much; many; 'a lot of' (something). Also as *adv.*, very, 'a lot'.

[**1886** J. G. Bourke *Apache Campaign* ii. 47 Sing heap; sleep mucho to-night.] **1942** Berrey & Van den Bark *Amer. Thes. Slang* §559/7 Large sum of money . . *mucho dinero*. **1973** *Houston Chron.* (Suppl.) 14 Oct. 5/1 There was mucho skinny dipping by some of the well known folks in town. **1977** *New Wave Mag.* No. 7. 7 This band will be a source of wonder and mucho enjoyment to you. **1978** *Tucson Mag.* Dec. 6/2 Your magazine is mucho enjoyable. **1986** *Making Music* Apr. 43/2 Warm valve distortion sound, plus mucho volume make this an amp worthy of its chart placing.

**mucicarmine** (mjuːsɪˈkɑːmaɪn), *n. Histol.* Also -min (-mɪn). [f. MUCI(N *n.* + CARMINE *n.*] A biological stain specific for mucin and consisting of a mixture of carmine, aluminium chloride, and water.
**1896** A. B. Lee *Microtomist's Vade-Mecum* (ed. 4) xxxiv. 463 Mucicarmine stains in sections or thin membranes *mucus only*. **1917** Dorland *Med. Dict.* (ed. 9) 617/1 Mucicarmin. **1946** H. J. Conn *Biol. Stains* (ed. 5) 196 A special formula containing aluminium chloride (known as muci-carmine) has been proposed by Mayer. **1959** W. Andrew *Textbk. Compar. Histol.* v. 146 When the reaction of the food vacuole changes from acid to alkaline, the staining properties change also, so that now instead of taking the light-green stain, it stains with mucicarmin. **1976** *Path. Ann.* XI. 303 A special stain (mucicarmine or methenamine silver) should also be employed when there is reason to suspect cryptococcosis. **1985** C. R. Leeson et al. *Textbk. Histol.* (ed. 5) ii. 94/1 Specific stains for mucoprotein, e.g. alcian blue, mucicarmine, and periodic acid-Schiff (PAS), demonstrate mucous acini well.

**muco-**, *comb. form.* Add: **muco'ciliary** *a. Anat.*, of, pertaining to, or designating a system of hairs and mucus-secreting glands in the lungs or nasal passages which serves to expel extraneous particles.
**1966** *Amer. Rev. Respiratory Dis.* XCIII. ii. 90/1 The measurement of mucous surface velocity in the intact living animal is a means of assessing the capabilities of the *mucociliary apparatus. **1987** *Brit. Jrnl. Dis. Chest* LXXXI. 362 Tracheobronchial mucociliary clearance was measured using a non-invasive radioaerosol technique.
'**mucocyst** *Microbiology*, a small sac-like organelle in some ciliate and flagellate protozoa which secretes mucus.
**1965** Tokuyasu & Scherbaum in *Jrnl. Cell Biol.* XXVII. 67/1 The structures containing the amorphous material are variously referred to as protrichocysts . ., mucoid trichocysts . ., mucigenic bodies . ., or secretory ampules . . . The latter four terms have apparently been used to describe similar or identical structures which we will refer to as '*mucocysts'. **1988** *Jrnl. Protozool.* XXXV. 46 It may be possible to purify a specific carbohydrate component of mucocysts which may be helpful in analyzing their function, biogenesis, and structural organization.

**muddie** ('mʌdɪ), *n. Austral. colloq.* (chiefly *Queensland*). Also muddy. [f. MUD *n.* + -IE, -Y⁶.] The mud-crab *Scylla serrata*, eaten as a delicacy.
**1953** Baker *Australia Speaks* viii. 183 *Muddy*, a mudcrab. **1969** *Telegraph* (Brisbane) 5 June 2/5 We've been getting 40 to 50 muddies a week-end—some of them old enough to vote. **1978** *Courier-Mail* (Brisbane) (Sat. Mag.) 25 Mar. 26/5 Queensland's renowned mud crab is down, of course, as 'muddie'. **1986** *Sunday Sun* (Brisbane) 21 Dec. 37/3 (*caption*) Confronted with snapping claws of big muddie he'd emptied out of bucket into kitchen sink, he yelled to son to grab cricket bat from shed.

**muddy** *n.*, var. of *MUDDIE *n.*

**muesli**, *n.* Add: **b. muesli belt** [see BELT *n.*¹ 5 a], (humorously) a region held to be densely populated by prosperous, middle-class, health-food faddists.
**1981** *Not The Church Times* 22 Sept. 6 Team vicar required. An attractive post in S.W. London 'Muesli belt'. **1986** *Times* 2 June 1/2 Many children are suffering from 'muesli-belt malnutrition', which could cause stunted growth and weight loss.

**muffin**, *n.* Add: [**1.**] [**b.**] For def. read: A flat, circular cake made from yeast dough cooked on an iron hotplate, and eaten toasted and buttered at breakfast or tea.
**1956** Spry & Hume *Cookery Bk.* 772, I had some good American books and found lots of recipes made with all manner of ingredients, nuts and fruit, eggs and sugar, but they were not at all what I wanted. I was after the muffin of the muffin-man, the floury, yeasty affair that has to be properly toasted and buttered before it is eaten. **1970** Simon & Howe *Dict. Gastron.* 270/1 Muffins are made with milk, butter, flour and yeast and are toasted, buttered and served hot.
**c.** *N. Amer.* (*a*) A small, spongy cake made with eggs and baking powder, cooked in a cup-shaped container; (*b*) **English muffin** = sense 1b above.
(*a*) **1835** A. B. Longstreet *Georgia Scenes* 36 Waffles were handed to Ned, and he took one: . . and so on of muffins, rolls and corn bread. **1887** *Century Mag.* Nov. 16/2 A procession of little darkies like an antique frieze was seen to pass and repass, supporting plates of hot batter-cakes, muffins, Sally Lunns, rice waffles. **1986** *Christian Science Monitor* 15 Jan. 27/2 Those first, delicious, baking powder muffins were only the beginning of my education about one of the most comforting of American foods.
(*b*) **1896** R. Baxter *Receipt Bk. for Bakers* 21 (*heading*) English muffins. *Ibid.* 22 These are the genuine English Muffins that were introduced into Chicago during the World's Fair. **1930** F. M. Farmer *Boston Cooking-School Cook Bk.* (rev. ed.) iv. 55 (*caption*) Serve toasted English Muffins very hot. **1972** *Guardian* 21 Jan. 9/4 The muffin . . had to take on the prefix 'English' to avoid getting mixed up with a quite different type of small hot bread also known in America as a muffin—also occasionally called a gem. **1984** J. Wilcox *Mod. Baptists* ix. 56 English muffins, his favorite, were on sale this week.

**mug**, *n.*⁵ Add: [**2.**] **b.** Freq. as *mug punter* (see PUNTER *n.*¹ 2).
**1922** E. Wallace *Flying Fifty-Five* xxxiii. 197 The mug punter was he who dreamed of long-priced winners and refused to bet on the six to four certainty. **1985** L. Griffiths *Arthur Daley's Guide to doing it Right* 98, I despise mug punters, the kind of people who bet on every race.

**muggee** (mʌˈgiː), *n.* [f. MUG *v.*³ 2 + -EE¹.] The victim of a violent attack or robbery; one who is 'mugged'. Usu. contrasted with MUGGER *n.*⁴ 2.
**1972** *Time* 27 Mar. 85/2 There is even a drawback to 'Super Sound', an ear-piercing air horn attached to an aerosol can and designed to summon help while startling attackers. It can damage the hearing of mugger and muggee alike. **1974** *Newsweek* 16 Sept. 53/2 It is no use saying a mugger is a symptom of social problems. For . . a muggee, the 'symptom' is the problem. **1976** *Maclean's Mag.* 22 Mar. 14/2 When attacked, the muggee should 'try not to make any ethnic slurs'. **1981** *Spectator* 28 Nov. 4/3 Have muggees, the majority of whom are white, no right to be protected against muggers? **1987** *Telegraph* (Brisbane) 9 Apr. 14/1 After proving four were tougher than one the muggers drove off and the muggee went home to bed.

**mulloway** ('mʌləweɪ), *n. Austral.* Also 9 mallowe, mullaway. [ad. Yaralde *malowe*.] A large edible sciaenid fish, *Argyrosomus hololepidotus*, occurring in Australian coastal waters.

**1846** H. E. A. MEYER *Manners & Customs Aborigines Encounter Bay* 6 They use the spear at the Murray in catching the large fish, *Mallowe*. **1871** *Austral. Town & Country Jrnl.* (Sydney) 22 Apr. 486/4 As much as three tons at a haul, consisting principally of mullaway, bream, [etc.]. **1906** D. G. STEAD *Fishes Australia* vi. 114 The Jewfish ... At the mouth of the Murray the fishermen call it 'Mulloway', or 'Butterfish'. **1969** *Man* (Austral.) Mar. 12/2 Over the season you get a variety of fish you'd be scratching to find anywhere else .. mulloway, trevally, [etc.]. **1988** *Courier-Mail* (Brisbane) 22 Apr. (Great Outdoors Suppl.) 10/4 The line came free and eventually John boated a 26-kilogram mulloway.

**Multics** ('mʌltɪks), *n. Computing.* [Acronym of *multiplexed information and computing service*.] A proprietary name for a multi-user operating system designed for use with mainframe computers. Cf. *UNIX *n.*

**1965** CORBATÓ & VYSSOTSKY in *AFIPS Conf. Proc.* XXVII. 1. 185/1 Multics .. is a comprehensive, general-purpose programming system which is being developed as a research project. The initial Multics system will be implemented on the GE645 computer. **1981** *Official Gaz.* (U.S. Patent Office) 2 June TM40/1 *MULTICS* for data processing systems, consisting of for example, central processors, peripherals, memories, controllers, front end processors and terminals; associated communications equipment. **1981** *Trade Marks Jrnl.* 2 Dec. 2576/2 *Multics* ... Computers for use in data processing; electronic apparatus and instruments, all for the input, output and processing of data; computer programmes; and parts and fittings. **1984** [see *UNIX *n.*].

**multiplexity** (mʌltɪ'plɛksɪtɪ), *n.* [f. MULTIPLEX *a.* + -ITY; cf. COMPLEXITY *n.*] The quality or condition of being multiplex (sense 2), or of having many aspects or interrelated features; multiplicity, complexity (esp. in terms of structure). Also an instance of this.

**1977** M. MACGRÉIL *Prejudice & Tolerance in Irel.* i. 12 Consistency in valence and multiplexity between the three components. **1979** *Internat. Jrnl. Sociol. of Law* Feb. 21 Gluckman contended that when such relationships .. were replaced in importance by myriad impersonal short-term 'ephemeral' contacts, the use of property as a symbol of multiplexity necessarily declined. **1980** *English World-Wide* I. 181 The primary nexus between the individual and the density and multiplexity of his network structure rather than between language and social class membership. **1988** *Time* 4 Jan. 75/2 For once, a virtue is made of multiplexity: the ten theaters are strung along an interior boulevard, each with its own distinct neon marquee.

**mumbo jumbo**, *n.* [2.] [b.] For def. read: Obscure or meaningless talk or writing; jargon intended to impress or mystify. Hence, nonsensical or ridiculous ritual, beliefs, etc.; = MUMMERY *n.* 2. Occas. *ellipt.* as mumbo. (Further examples.)

**1930** V. SACKVILLE-WEST *Edwardians* vii. 328 Sebastian .. swore loudly that nothing would induce him to take part in the mumbo-jumbo of the imminent Coronation. **1952** A. GRIMBLE *Pattern of Islands* viii. 165 The moon was above all constraint of sorcery's mumbo-jumbo. **1980** R. W. CLARK *Freud* (1982) ix. 165 The mumbo-jumbo of Fliess's numerology, which could make almost any date appear ominous.

**mump**, *v.²* In etym, for 'Sense 2' read: 'Senses 2 and 3'. Add: **3.** *intr.* Of the police: to accept small gifts or bribes: see *MUMPING *vbl. n.²* 2. *slang.*

**1970** P. LAURIE *Scotland Yard* x. 248 Many policemen mump to some extent.

**mumping**, *vbl. n.²* Add: **2.** The action or practice by the police of accepting small gifts or bribes, such as free meals, cheap goods, etc., from tradespeople. *slang.*

**1970** P. LAURIE *Scotland Yard* x. 248 'Mumping' is as old as policing. It has its pros and cons—one can look at it as a small tax. **1977** *New Society* 17 Feb. 328/2 Forms of corruption [of the police].. 'mumping' ('mooching' in the U.S.)—accepting free meals and drinks or goods and services at a discount. **1984** J. P. BEAN in *Police Rev.* 18 May 975/2 Nipping, demanding with menaces... One step above 'mumping'—begging without the threats.

**Munchkin** ('mʌntʃkɪn), *n.* Chiefly *N. Amer.* Also munchkin. In the children's fantasy *The Wizard of Oz*, by L. Frank Baum (1856-1919), U.S. writer: any of a race of small, child-like creatures who help Dorothy in her quest for the city of Oz; hence used allusively for a small, mischievous, gnome-like or elfish person (chiefly affectionately).

Public awareness of the Munchkins increased after the release of the film version of the story in 1939.

**1900** L. F. BAUM *Wonderful Wizard of Oz* ii. 21 You are welcome .. to the land of the Munchkins. *Ibid.* 26 Her tears seemed to grieve the kind-hearted Munchkins for they immediately took out their handkerchiefs and began to weep also. **1939** *St. Nicholas* Aug. 37/3 Nearly all the midgets in the United States, 116, were recruited and costumed and given gaily colored wigs and beards to play the Munchkins ... Few are taller than three feet. **1967** *Sunday Bull.* (Philadelphia) 9 July 1. 4/2 The Munchkins gathered yesterday on the eastern slope of one of Chester County's rolling hills, and ate fried honeybees and squealina. **1976** M. MACHLIN *Pipeline* xxviii. 325 The meeting consisted only of Marge, Sonia, Ernie Mason—the poetic munchkin—and Eli Hurwood. **1983** *Times* 10 Sept. 20 One of President Reagan's aides .. described a woman who left the President's employ as a 'Low-level munchkin'—a munchkin being a little creature in the Wizard of Oz.

**mundane**, *a.* (*n.*) Add: **[1.] d.** In weakened use: everyday, ordinary, commonplace; hence, banal, prosaic, dull; routine, trite.

**1898** *Westm. Gaz.* 28 July 2/3 To consider .. more mundane matters, such as the number and characters of transmigrating households. **1938** R. NARAYAN *Dark Room* iii. 29 The whole picture swept her mind clear of mundane debris. **1965** A. J. P. TAYLOR *Eng. Hist. 1914-1945* x. 322 There were also more mundane calculations. The Conservatives were confident they could win an election on the National cry. **1976** G. GORDON *100 Scenes from Married Life* 118 Inject a spot of excitement into our mundane and self-satisfied lives. **1986** P. READING *Essential Reading* 85 At least this would avoid your having to employ your pen on such mundane matters when it could be used to such good effect elsewhere!

**mundanity**, *n.* Add: **c.** The quality or condition of being 'mundane' (sense 1 d), commonplace, or uninteresting; an instance of this.

**1959** *Listener* 30 July 173/2 The outward mundanity of the master's life. **1963** *Movie* July-Aug. 20/2 The presentation of the torture sequences horrifies by its casual mundanity. **1972** *Daily Tel.* 27 Apr. 8/6 Nothing could be further removed from the mundanities of sausage and haddock than the subject of this book of circumferential recollections. **1974** *Nature* 17 May

199/2 It may mean the moral support that leads to a government grant, permission to work abroad for a spell or even such mundanities as the price of an airline ticket. **1982** *Times* 3 June 8/7 The rewritten military text-books may . . include a chapter or two on the mundanities and achievements of moving from a damp British spring to a frosty near-Antarctic winter. **1986** *Crafts* May/June 12/4 Compared to the majority of provincial galleries, full of aesthetically substandard mundanity, it is refreshing.

**muni** ('mjuːnɪ), *n.*[2] (and *a.*) *U.S.* [Colloq. abbrev. of *municipal* (*bond*).] = *municipal bond* s.v. \*MUNICIPAL *a.* 2 c and *n.* 4. Usu. in *pl.* Also *attrib.* or as *adj.*, esp. in *muni bond*.
**1973** *Newsweek* 13 Aug. 82 Paragon . . mounted an expensive advertising campaign aimed at peddling 'munis' to the masses and last year sold $750 million worth of securities. **1979** *Time* 2 Apr. 57/1 Bloch points out that munis are safe, and enormously liquid, and they can be bought in denominations as low as $1,000. **1983** *Fortune* 11 July 158/2 Investors can capitalize on Whoops worries by buying other munis at bargain prices. **1985** *Barron's* 11 Nov. 58/3 (*heading*) High yields and no taxes buoy muni bond funds. **1988** *Bond Buyer* 30 Aug. 4 (*heading*) A young muni analyst leaves Wall Street.

**municipal**, *a.* and *n.* Add: [A.] [2.] c. *municipal bond*, a security issued by a local authority or its agent, orig. to finance local projects, interest on which is generally exempt from federal income tax and other taxes in the state of issue. Chiefly *U.S.*
**1858** P. L. SIMMONDS *Dict. Trade Products* s.v. *Debenture*, the term has now got to be applied to . . municipal and other bonds or securities for money loaned. **1877** W. A. JOHNSON *Hist. Anderson County, Kansas* xvi. 160 People . . have adopted the system of aiding railway companies in the construction of their roads by voting and issuing municipal bonds of the county. **1915** *Municipal Obligations* (Baker, Watts, & Co.) i. 9 Municipal Bonds have come to be firmly demanded by the most advanced authorities and conservative investors. **1949** *Of People, by People* (J. Nuveen & Co.) ii. 5 While there are numerous technical differences between bonds issued by states and those issued by their underlying governmental units . . they are all generally known as 'Municipal Bonds'. **1983** *Fortune* 11 July 158/2 A bankruptcy . . that would trigger a chain reaction devastating the entire municipal bond market.
[B.] **4.** = *municipal bond* above. Usu. in *pl.* *U.S. colloq.*
**1916** *World's Work* Mar. 485/2 The cashier of his bank had argued convincingly that municipals were the only securities meeting such requirements. **1937** L. S. LEBENTHALL *ABC of Municipal Bonds* I. iv. 33 These insurance companies . . usually place a large percentage of their funds in municipals. **1949** *Of People, by People* (J. Nuveen & Co.) ii. 5 It is generally recognized that 'municipals' comprise one of the more important investment media available today. **1987** D. M. HOWELL *How to buy Tax Free Bonds* i. 9 The financial publications you read are full of articles about municipals.

**muninga** (mʊ'nɪŋɡə), *n.* *E. Afr.* [Of Bantu origin: cf. Sukuma, Swahili *mninga*.] = KIAAT *n.* Also *attrib.*, as *muninga wood*.
**1939** H. A. COX *Handbk. Empire Timbers* (DSIR Forest Products Res.) Muninga—*Pterocarpus angolensis* . . . Occurs scattered in the forests of Tanganyika Territory, Portuguese East Africa and parts of Rhodesia. **1956** [see KIAAT *n.*]. **1976** *Wymondham & Attleborough Express* 10 Dec. 16/1 Table lighters in many finishes: onyx marble, Wedgwood, Rosewood—even Muninga wood—as well as gold and silver plate. **1980** *Daily Tel.* 3 June 17/5 There is a six-seater, drop-leaf, circular dining table made in wild cherrywood, oak or muninga (an

East African timber of a distinctive reddish-brown colour).

**Munsterlander** ('mʌnstə-, 'mʊnstəlændə(r)), *n.* Also **munsterlander**. [a. Ger. *Münsterländer*, f. the name of *Münsterland*, a region of western Germany where the breed originated.] A breed of long-haired dog, originally bred for hunting, and occurring in two varieties, the larger black-and-white kind resembling a pointer or setter, the smaller more like a (usu. brown and white) spaniel; a dog of this breed.
[**1970** *Globe & Mail* (Toronto) 26 Sept. 40/7 The little German dog with the big name, the kleine Munsterlander Heidewachtel is known on this side of the water as a small Munsterland pointer.] **1970** *Dog World* 6 Nov. 1739/1 Munsterlander setters . . . This is a breed of gundog which looks very much like the English working Setter but is a little heavier in build. . . A long-haired dog, always black and white, who will point game and retrieve it . . . These dogs must not be confused with Munsterlander Spaniels, who are always brown and white and of Spaniel size. **1974** *Country Life* 21 Feb. 356/2 Pharaoh hounds, large munsterlanders and Hungarian pulis are well established. **1976** *Shooting Times & Country Mag.* 18–24 Nov., This Novice Stake was open to all breeds that hunt, point and retrieve and comprised five Weimaraners, six GSP's and one Large Munsterlander. **1988** *Courier-Mail* (Brisbane) 26 Apr. 2/5 Mrs Fergusson said she would have to wait until next year before she could get another munsterlander.

**muralist** ('mjʊərəlɪst), *n.* [f. MURAL *n.* + -IST.] A painter of murals; *spec.* a member of a Mexican school of mural painting that flourished in the first half of the 20th cent.
**1902** P. KING *Amer. Mural Painting* vii. 144 This . . will be the final impression, when Mr. Sargent has put his name to the last canvas . . —brilliant modern brother, as he is, of the muralists of old. **1933** *Nation* 24 May 596 None of the great muralists of the past seem to have known this rule. **1937** *Mexican Art Series* v. 1, Diego Rivera, the great Mexican muralist, painted the frescoes in the ancient Cortez Palace, in Cuernavaca, Marelos, in 1930. **1941** M. HELM *Modern Mexican Painters* 198 Even the muralists . . have not been coherently related by any really persuasive identity of object. **1957** *Encycl. Brit.* XV. 970/1 Among the foremost Greek muralists were Zeuxis (late 5th century B.C.), Polygnotus . . , and Apelles. **1960** A. M. REED *Mexican Muralists* 15/2 Another great stimulus for the incipient muralists was the open-air art schools founded by Alfredo Ramos Martinez . . in 1913. **1974** *Times* 8 Jan. 14/6 Siqueiros, the Mexican muralist, died on Sunday. **1979** L. EDEL *Bloomsbury* 249 Both found themselves presently in great demand beyond Bloomsbury as muralists and decorators. **1986** *N.Z. Herald* 7 Feb. IV.1/1 Muralist, glass artist, photographer, [etc.] . . . The choices of the art student have broadened from the traditional painting and sculpture to a wide range of occupations.

**myalgic** (maɪ'ældʒɪk), *a.* (Formerly at MYALGIA *n.*) [f. MYALGIA *n.* + -IC.] **1.** Of the nature of, characterized by, or affected with myalgia.
**1860** T. INMAN *On Myalgia* 187 Is the heart subject to myalgic affections? **1897** *Allbutt's Syst. Med.* III. 1 The word [Rheumatism] . . has now become a convenient term for embracing myalgic, neurotic and arthritic pain.
**2.** *myalgic encephalomyelitis*, a benign but debilitating form of encephalomyelitis, of unknown aetiology but usually occurring after a viral infection, and characterized by headaches, fever, and localized muscular pains and weakness; postviral syndrome. Abbrev. *ME* s.v. \*M III. 6 a.

**1956** *Lancet* 26 May 790/2 The term 'benign myalgic encephalomyelitis'.. does describe some of the striking features of a syndrome characterised by (1) symptoms and signs of damage to the brain and spinal cord .. (2) protracted muscle pain with paresis and cramp; (3) emotional disturbances in convalescence; (4) normal C.S.F... (7) a relatively benign outcome. **1978** *Brit. Med. Jrnl.* 3 June 1437/1 At a symposium held recently .. there was clear agreement that myalgic encephalomyelitis is a distinct nosological entity... From the patient's point of view the designation benign is .. misleading, since the illness may be devastating. **1987** *Oxf. Textbk. Med.* (ed. 2) I. v. 98/1 An increased prevalence of unusually high titres of antibody to group B coxsackieviruses has recently been found in sporadic and associated cases of 'myalgic encephalomyelitis', suggesting an aetiological relationship between this illness and enterovirus infections.

**mycosis**, *n.* Add: **2.** *mycosis fungoides* (fʌŋˈgɔɪdiːz), a malignant usu. protracted lymphoma affecting primarily the skin, ultimately producing dome-shaped tumours.
**1874** *Med. Times & Gaz.* II. 269/1 Alibert has described something similar under the name 'mycosis fungoides'. **1888** *Jrnl. Cutaneous & Genito-urinary Dis.* VI. 292 As to the etiology and exact nature of mycosis fungoides, I shall for the present .. forbear from expressing any positive opinion. **1965** *Jrnl. Nat. Cancer Inst.* XXXV. 175/1 Allergic reactions in patients with the lymphomatous disease mycosis fungoides have been observed to be associated with improvement of the disease. **1966** WRIGHT & SYMMERS *Systemic Path.* II. xxxix. 1602/1 Mycosis fungoides results from the progressive proliferation of the dermal cells of the lymphoreticular system. **1986** *Sci. Amer.* Dec. 83/3 Such a clinical picture has been called mycosis fungoides or Sézary T-cell leukemia. **1987** *Oxf. Textbk. Med.* (ed. 2) II. xx. 84/2 Mycosis fungoides is initially often no more than a non-specific dermatitis.

**mycotic** (maɪˈkɒtɪk), *a.* (Formerly at MYCOSIS *n.*) [f. as MYCOSIS *n.* + -OTIC.] Characterized by mycosis.

**1877** tr. *von Ziemssen's Cycl. Med.* XII. 573 Some cases [of meningitis] have been recognised to be of mycotic origin.

**myelinate** ('maɪəlɪneɪt), *v. Anat.* [f. MYELIN *n.*[1] + -ATE[3].] *intr.* To secrete myelin; to become myelinated. Cf. *MYELINATED *a.*
**1914** *Brain* XXXVI. 478 The globus pallidus and the ansa lenticularis myelinate earlier than the fibres of the rest of the striatum. **1930** *Arch. Neurol. & Psychiatry* XXIV. 852 The latter .. myelinates about the fifth or sixth month of fetal life, whereas the neostriatum myelinates later. **1977** *Lancet* 16 July 141/2 The human brain myelinates actively until the age of 16. **1987** *MS News* Autumn 35/1 When transplanted they [sc. Schwann cells] migrated into the central nervous system and started myelinating.
So **myeli'nation** *n.*, the process of becoming myelinated; the state of being myelinated. **1891** in *Syd. Soc. Lex.* **1899** *Allbutt's Syst. Med.* VII. 732 The changes in the cortex begin at a stage prior to the myelination of the pyramidal fibres. **1977** C. S. RAINE in P. Morell *Myelin* i. 9 Myelination in the CNS commences some days after its onset in the PNS. **1984** J. F. LAMB et al. *Essent. Physiol.* (ed. 2) ii. 32 Myelination confers two advantages on an axon compared to a bare axon of similar diameter.

**myelinated** ('maɪəlɪneɪtɪd), *a.* (Formerly at MYELIN *n.*[1]) *Anat.* [f. MYELIN *n.*[1] + -ATE[3] + -ED[1].] Of a nerve fibre: surrounded by a myelin sheath.
**1899** *Allbutt's Syst. Med.* VII. 75 An exceedingly small group of myelinated fibres. **1956** *Nature* 28 Jan. 164/2 His [sc. Kulchitsky's] name is continually recalled to neurologists by his modification of the Weigert method that made possible the better staining of myelinated fibres. **1974** D. & M. WEBSTER *Compar. Vertebr. Morphol.* ix. 185 Although protective cells enclose all nerve fibers, the myelin sheath is variable; thus there are heavily myelinated, lightly myelinated, and even unmyelinated fibers. **1987** *Nursing* Jan. 494/1 Unmyelinated fibres *can* convey pain impulse, albeit more slowly than myelinated fibres.

# N

**N.** Add: [**II.**] [**1.**] **NFL**, National Football League (*U.S.*).
**1946** *Encycl. Brit.* IX. 486c/1 Under Carr, the \*N.F.L. was developed from obscurity into a national enterprise. **1972** J. MOSEDALE *Football* i. 6 Jim Brown of the Cleveland Browns.. was the greatest groundgainer in NFL history. **1984** J. LAWTON *All Amer. War Game* p. viii, Gamblers.. wager more than $1 billion on college and NFL football each weekend.

**NIREX** ('naɪreks), Nuclear Industry Radioactive Waste Executive.
**1982** *Wastes Managem.* LXXII. 458/1 \*NIREX, which has been set up by British Nuclear Fuels Limited, the Central Electricity Generating Board, the South of Scotland Electricity Board and the United Kingdom Atomic Energy Authority, was welcomed by the Government. **1989** *New Scientist* 14 Jan. 30/1 Environmentalists are angry that NIREX has not considered as an option the long-term storage of nuclear waste above ground.

‖**naat** (nɑːt), *n. Diamond Industry.* [Afrikaans *naat* seam, suture, f. Du. *naad.*] An irregularity in the structure of a diamond, caused by a change of direction in the grain; a 'knot' or blemish. Also, a diamond having such a feature.
**1945** *Industrial Diamond Rev.* Sept. 205/2 *Knot, Naat* (Min.), irregularity of crystal structure in a single crystal diamond. Because the cleavage planes cannot easily be found, it is generally believed that such stones have a greater resistance to abrasion. **1962** S. TOLANSKY *Hist. & Use of Diamond* ix. 147 If changes in grain direction are encountered on a crystal (*naat* is the word for such a change), the impregnated wheel can readily cope. **1970** E. BRUTON *Diamonds* xi. 190 The sawyer.. has.. to watch for any changes of hardness through an area of different crystallization. These naats sometimes have rope formation or spider's web formation in a stone and will turn the blade and spoil the cut. **1984** G. DAVIES *Diamond* ix. 228 The blade.. will find it very difficult to make any progress if it comes up against a piece of the diamond which has a different crystallographic orientation. These mis-oriented pieces, the 'naats', are analogous to knots in a piece of wood.

**naches** ('nʌxəs), *n.* Also **nachas, nachus(s.** [a. Yiddish *nakhes,* ad. Heb. *naḥaṯ* contentment.] Among Jews, a sense of pleasure or pride at the achievements of one's children.
**1929** I. GOLLER *Five Bks. Mr. Moses* I. iii. 17 His daughter Rachel was once more the comfort and *nachas* of his life. **1932** L. GOLDING *Magnolia Street* III. iv. 522 You should have a great comfort, a *nachuss,* out of your son and your daughter-in-law that is to be. **1962** B. GLANVILLE *Diamond* I. v. 54, I only think of your poor father, the *nachus* he'd have had if he'd been here. **1965** C. BERMANT *Berl make Tea* vii. 57 'You know what real happiness is? *Naches.*' 'Naches? What's naches?'.. 'Naches is the happiness you get from doing well or seeing your children do well.' 'You mean the opposite of *tzores*?' 'Exactly.' **1969** B. RUBENS *Elected Member* (1980) xiii. 137 They're a kind of nachus too. **1970** L. M. FEINSILVER *Taste of Yiddish* 167 A New York Reform rabbi has established a 'Naches Fund' to supply camp scholarships, for which he encourages contributions to honor any naches-producing events such as the birth of a grandchild. **1976** C. BERMANT *Second Mrs Whitberg* i. 20 The house seemed to echo with.. the naches we had enjoyed. **1980** *Jewish Chron.* 30 May 13/1 Our imaginary folkorist would no doubt get extra *naches* from the fact that the part of Mistress Quickly is taken by a.. Jewish actress.

**nacho** ('nɑːtʃəʊ, 'nætʃəʊ), *n.* orig. *U.S.* [Prob. a. Mexican Sp. *Nacho,* abbrev. of the proper name *Ignacio.* A Mexican chef, Ignacio ('Nacho') Anaya, is often credited with creating the first nachos: see quot. 1970.] A Texas-Mexican snack or appetizer, consisting of a tortilla chip covered in melted cheese, peppers, spices, etc. Chiefly in *pl.*
**1949** J. TRAHEY *Taste of Texas* 27 Pedro left. Sometime later he returned carrying a large dish of *Nachos Especiales.* 'These *Nachos*,' said Pedro, 'will help *El Capitan*—soon he will forget his troubles for *nachos* make one romantic.' **1965** M. F. KOOCK *Texas Cookbk.* 219 Nachos show up at many cocktail parties in Texas. They are easy to make. **1970** *For Goodness Sake!* (Church of Redeemer, Eagle Pass, Texas) 89 Nacho Specials. This simple yet delicious snack originated some years ago in Old Victory Club in Piedras Negras, Mexico when a group of Eagle Pass women asked the chef, Nacho, to make something for them to eat with their cocktails. **1979** *United States 1980/81* (Penguin Travel Guides) 146 Our choice is the one on Maple Street, with.. excellent nachos and guacamole. **1983** *Fortune* 14 Nov. 126/1 The chain of Mexican fast-food restaurants is busily expanding its product line to include bigger tacos, lighter tacos.., a nacho side dish, and a salad. **1986** R. B. PARKER *Taming Sea-Horse* (1987) xviii. 109 The bars were serving nachos and potato skins.

**nail,** *v.* Add: [**1.**] [**d.**] Also, *to nail a lie* (*charge,* etc.): to expose or put out of circulation (a falsehood, allegation, etc.).
[**1624** J. GEE *Foot out of Snare* v. 33 Heere is a knocking and long-lasting lie, worthy to be nailed upon a post or pillory.] **1895** *Funk's Stand. Dict.* II. 1175/1 The phrase *to nail a lie* .. was suggested by the nailing of counterfeit coins to the counter by shopkeepers. **1915** E. POUND *Let.* 1 Dec. (1971) 66, I think however that the charge of my being jealous of Frost ought to be nailed, perhaps even at the disclosure of state secrets. **1987** *News on Sunday* 12 July 3/3 The caring family man.. has risked public ridicule in a bid to 'nail the lie' as he put it.

[**8.**] [**d.**] For def. read: To succeed in hitting, esp. with a punch or shot; to strike (a person, etc.) forcefully, put out of action. Freq. in *Boxing.* (Earlier and later examples.)
**1785** BURNS *Death & Dr. Hornbook* xxx, in *Poems & Songs* (1968) I. 84 I'll nail the self-conceited sot, As dead's a herrin. **1824** MACTAGGART *Gallovid. Encycl.* 356 We say when we see a hare shot, that she's nail'd. **1889** J. NICHOLSON *Folk-Speech E. Yorks.* 28 Jack Wilson lad brak oor windher wiv a cobble-steean, an Bob did nail him fo't. **1909** *Dialect Notes* III. 351 *Nail,* to strike, hit. 'I *nailed* him side o' the head.' **1942** BERREY & VAN DEN BARK *Amer. Thes. Slang* §342/6 *Shoot,* .. nail. **1950** J. DEMPSEY *Championship Fighting* 148 He.. is in a position to be nailed on the chin. **1978** *Detroit Free Press* 5 Mar. 24/3 Birkholm is careful to handle the snakes with his left hand... 'If I do get nailed, I want to save my good arm.' **1987** *Boxing News* 21 Aug. 15/3 Ayala rallied courageously in the third, putting punches together as he nailed Espinoza with left hooks and rights.

**e.** *Baseball.* Of a fielder: to put (a runner) out. Hence more generally in *Sport:* to beat (an opponent); *N. Amer. Football*, to tackle or bring down (an opponent). Chiefly *U.S.*

**1888** *N.Y. Press* 18 Apr. 4/1 He nailed every man who tried to steal a base. **1908** *N.Y. Even. Jrnl.* 20 Aug. 12/2 Donlin was pushed on home by McGraw, but it was too big an effort and he was nailed at the plate by a nose. **1959** F. ASTAIRE *Steps in Time* (1960) xxv. 286 This was a good horserace with . . a close finish with Trip coming from pretty far back to nail Louis B. Mayer's fine filly Honeymoon by a neck at the wire. **1974** *Cleveland* (Ohio) *Plain Dealer* 13 Oct. C. 6/2 Quarterback Tom Clements was nailed for no gain on a rollout. **1987** *Touchdown* Feb. 24/3 Banks led the club in tackles and has a knack of nailing the opposing runner in the backfield.

**f.** Usu. of a man: to have sexual intercourse with (freq. with implication of aggression); = SCREW *v.* 13 b. *U.S.*

**1960** J. UPDIKE *Rabbit, Run* 45 It seems a great loss that it hadn't been him about to nail her. Feel her open up in the cavity of the car, her seaweed hair sprawling. **1973** R. L. SIMON *Big Fix* (1974) i. 10 Everyone I knew wanted to nail her . . . She was something special. **1974** J. IRVING *158-Pound Marriage* v. 106 I've always wanted to nail you in your mother's bones. **1979** R. GROSSBACH *Never say Die* viii. 80 Who would you rather marry, then—the publishing cupcake in the Florsheims who nailed you on the couch and then fired you?

**nailable** ('neɪləb(ə)l), *a.* [f. NAIL *v.* + -ABLE.] That can be nailed; *spec.* of construction materials, etc.: admitting of being nailed into place.

**1954** *Archit. Rev.* CXV. 284/3 (*caption*) Walls. These are 1 m. wide, storey high, panels of timber framing impregnated against wet and dry rot, with a 'durable and nailable' cladding. **1966** *Car & Locomotive Cycl. Amer. Pract.* 47/1 Nailable Floor. A name given to a type of metal or metal and composition floors so designed that a wire nail driven into them will be held firmly. **1983** J. S. FOSTER *Structure & Fabric* (rev. ed.) I. vi. 150/1 So-called nailable sections can be formed which provide a grip to fixing nails. **1984** *Comprehensive Railroad Dict.* (Railway Age) 105 Nailable steel floor. Flooring for box, gondola, and flatcars made of specially formed steel channel sections. **1988** *ENR* 17 Mar. 80/2 This brochure lists detailed specifications for built-up roofing systems on nailable, non-nailable and insulated decks.

**naked**, *a.* and *n.*[1] Add: [A.] [II.] [7.] c. *Astron.* Designating a space-time singularity in the form of a collapsed material body which is not surrounded by an event horizon and is therefore visible to an external observer. Usu. as *naked singularity*.

**1969** R. PENROSE in *Rivista Nuovo Cimento* I. Numero Speciale. 273 (*caption*) A 'naked singularity' (Kerr-Newman solution with $m^2 < a^2 + e^2$). *Ibid.* 274 Have we any right to suggest that the *only* type of collapse which can occur is one in which the space-time singularities lie hidden, deep inside the protective shielding of an absolute event horizon? . . If in fact naked singularities do arise, then there is a whole new realm opened up for wild speculations! **1977** *N.Y. Rev. Bks.* 29 Sept. 23/1 If a spacetime singularity actually occurs and can be observed, it is called a 'naked singularity'. **1978** *Nature* 20 Apr. 740/2 Dr Wald pays more attention than most authors to the intriguing question of cosmic censorship—can gravitational collapse cause the occurrence of space-time singularities that are not hidden inside black holes, that is, are naked? **1981** P. DAVIES *Edge of Infinity* v. 92 A great deal of investigation has been undertaken to determine whether singularities can ever occur naked, or whether they will always be safely hidden inside black holes.

**nalbuphine** ('nælbjuːfiːn), *n. Pharm.* [f. NAL(OR)PHINE *n.* with inserted BU(TYL *n.*] A synthetic narcotic, $C_2H_{27}NO_4$, which is very similar to morphine in chemical structure and is given by injection (usually as the hydrochloride) as an analgesic.

**1969** *WHO Chron.* XXIII. 194 Nalbuphine. **1970** *Jrnl. Med.* I. 74 Nalbuphine . . is a potentially useful analgesic because of low toxicity, potent analgesic activity and moderate narcotic antagonist activity in animals. **1976** *Woman's Day* (N.Y.) Nov. 84/1 Dr. William T. Beaver . . and his research team are investigating a new drug, nalbuphine, which may be as effective as morphine but not so addictive. **1987** *Brit. Med. Jrnl.* 27 June 1685/2, I am assured that meptazinol for renal colic and nalbuphine for myocardial infarcts are in the British National Formulary and are adequate substitutes.

**naled** ('neɪlɛd), *n. Agric.* [Origin unknown.] A synthetic pesticide, $C_4H_7Br_2Cl_2O_4P$, of low toxicity to mammals and short lifetime; 1,2-dibromo-2,2-dichloroethyl dimethyl phosphate.

**1963** D. E. H. FREAR *Pesticide Index* (ed. 2) 171/1 Naled . . . Pure compound is a solid, mp. 26° C. Technical product is a liquid. **1978** *Mosquito News* XXXVIII. 488/1 New Jersey Airspray Program treated approximately 81,000 hectares . . with malathion and naled for the control of adult *Aedes sollicitans.* **1987** *Los Angeles Times* 17 July 11. 1/1 A combination of the sex lure methyl eugenol and pesticide naled will be sprayed on trees and telephone poles to kill the males.

**nalidixic** (nælɪ'dɪksɪk), *a. Pharm.* [f. parts of the systematic name of the acid rearranged.] *nalidixic acid*, an antiseptic, $C_{12}H_{12}N_2O_3$, which inhibits bacterial reproduction, and is given orally in the treatment of infections of the urinary tract; 1-ethyl-1,4-dihydro-7-methyl-4-oxo-1,8-naphthyridine-3-carboxylic acid.

**1962** *Jrnl. Med. & Pharmaceutical Chem.* V. 1064 The antibacterial activity of nalidixic acid has been demonstrated against a variety of microorganisms causing disease in man and animals. **1976** *Nature* 15 Apr. 643/1 Nalidixic acid (NAL) has been described as a specific inhibitor of bacterial DNA synthesis *in vivo* and *in vitro*, but its mechanism of action on susceptible bacteria remains obscure. **1977** *Lancet* 13 Aug. 343/1 Since the age of 3 she had been on continuous antibiotics which included co-trimoxazole, amoxycillin, nalidixic acid, [etc.]. **1988** *Med. Clin. N. Amer.* LXXII. 624 High level resistance of bacteria to nalidixic acid developed rapidly after the introduction of the drug in the early 1960s.

**Nalline** ('nælɪːn), *n. Pharm.* Also **nalline**. [f. N-*allyl*normorph*ine*: see NALORPHINE *n.*] A proprietary name in the U.S. for the drug nalorphine.

**1952** *Official Gaz.* (U.S. Patent Office) 28 Oct. 921/1 Nalline. For therapeutic substance useful in counteracting certain undesirable effects . . induced by natural and synthetic narcotic drugs. **1965** *New Scientist* 8 Apr. 124/3 A nalorphine (nalline) test is used on inmates after leave to detect relapse. **1968** *Brit. Jrnl. Addiction* LXIII. 227 The Nalline (nalorphine) Test is one of several anti-narcotic testing procedures used to detect surreptitious users of drugs. **1974** M. C. GERALD *Pharmacol.* xiii. 248 Nalorphine (Nalline), a chemical derivative of morphine . . , has many morphine-like effects.

**naltrexone** (næl'trɛksəʊn), *n. Pharm.* [f. as NALOXONE *n.* with arbitrary element -*tre*-.] A narcotic antagonist, $C_{20}H_{23}NO_4$, related to nalorphine and naloxone but usually given orally as the hydrochloride.

**1973** *Arch. Gen. Psychiatry* XXVIII. 785/2 Naltrexone is approximately 17 times more potent than nalorphine in precipitating abstinence in patients dependent on 60 mg of morphine a day. **1978** *Nature* 9 Mar. 167/1 This treatment is designed to diminish the efficacy of any self-administered opiate by 'blockading' the receptors with substances such as naloxone or naltrexone. **1988** *New Scientist* 9 June 83/3 A similar bait has been advocated in order to 'persuade' heroin addicts to submit to a course of naltrexone, or to encourage criminal alcoholics to take the very nasty Antabuse.

**name**, *n.* Add: [**15.**] **name-check**, (*a*) the public mention of a person's name, esp. in acknowledgement of his or her contribution to the matter in hand; (*b*) an official check on a person's credentials, esp. for purposes of security or criminal investigation.

**1972** *Daily Tel.* (Colour Suppl.) 10 Nov. 7/2 It would be an exercise hardly more valuable than.. reading out '*name-checks*' to gratify the vanity of listeners to record programmes. **1987** *Hi-Fi News* Jan. 125/2 The lyrics betray a hint of literacy, with namechecks for Mark Twain and J D Salinger. **1987** *Listener* 24 Sept. 38/3 Somebody, somewhere, probably knows whether.. Art Blakey and his sidemen have ever had a name-check for their help and encouragement to a British jazz band before. **1987** *N.Y. Times Mag.* 6 Dec. 30/3 A name check.. is run for some Federal agencies.. that require such criminal checks by statute.

**nandin** (næn'di:n), *n. Bot.* [a. Jap. *nandin*: see *NANDINA n.*] = *NANDINA n.*

**1936** N. TAYLOR *Garden Dict.* 519/1 The only species [of *Nandina*] is *N. domestica*, the nandin, sometimes called sacred bamboo, although it has nothing sacred to do with any bamboo. **1987** *Sat. Even. Post* Apr. 86/1 The winter landscape seems less stark here among the pines, witch hazels, viburnum, hawthorns, Pyracantha, and nandins aflame with yellow, orange, and red.

**nandina** (næn'di:nə), *n. Bot.* Pl. -a, -as. [f. mod.L. genus name *Nandina*, ad. Jap. *nandin*, *nanten*(*-chiku*), southern-sky (bamboo), f. *nan* south + *ten* sky.] The sacred bamboo, *Nandina domestica*, an evergreen shrub of the barberry family orig. of S. China, which is native to India and eastern Asia and is grown elsewhere as an ornamental for its cones of tiny white flowers and red (or purple) berries.

**1852** G. W. JOHNSON *Cottage Gardeners' Dict.* 628/1 (From *nandin*, the Japanese name)... Greenhouse shrub. **1881** P. HENDERSON *Handbk. Plants* 142/2 *Nandina*... It was introduced to cultivation in 1804. **1915** E. PHILPOTTS *My Shrubs* ix. 83 In prosperity this Nandina, of Japan, makes a very beautiful specimen. **1962** *Amat. Gardening* 13 Jan. 15 All through the summer the leaves of nandina change from beetroot to green to purple as they age. **1986** *New Yorker* 24 Mar. 33/1 The nandinas had grown tall. **1988** *Washington Post* 31 July F2/2 At the moment there is just the varied greenery of box and sweet olives, small hollies, barrenworts, nandina, azaleas, bugleweed and so on.

**naow** (næʊ), *adv.*[1] [Repr. colloq. or vulgar pronunc.] = NOW *adv.* Cf. NAH *adv.*[1]

**1897** KIPLING *Capt. Cour.* i. 16 Naow let's hear all abaout it. **1901** G. B. SHAW *Capt. Brassbound's Conversion* II. 250 Drinkwater (*in an agony of protest*) Naow, naow. Look eah—. **1963** N. MARSH *Dead Water* (1964) ii. 51 'Ah well, naow,' said the Mayor. **1982** *N.Y. Times* 7 Feb. II. 3/3 When his 'How now?' becomes 'Haow naow?', even Eliza Doolittle would disapprove. **1985** I. HANDL *Sioux* vii. 90 You, Ouisti,

y'all will got to hold it naow, Grand M'sieu he don't stop for nothing on the road.

**naow** (naʊ), *adv.*[2] [Repr. colloq. or vulgar pronunc.] = NO *adv.*[3] (also NO *a.*). Cf. NA *adv.*[2], NAH *adv.*[2]

**1901** G. B. SHAW *Capt. Brassbound's Conversion* I. 222 Ennywys, there ynt naow awm in ahr business. *Ibid.* II. 250 Na-a-a-a-ow. Aw cawnt, aw teol yer. Aw sy, look eah. Naow, naow, naow, naow, naow, NAOW!!! **1931** D. L. SAYERS *Five Red Herrings* viii. 92 'Did ye drive Mr. Gowan... In the two-seater?' 'Naow, in the saloon.' **1938** N. MARSH *Artists in Crime* iii. 31 'You don't usually start off like this, do you?' 'Naow, that's right, I don't, but I thought I'd give it a pop.' **1981** *Guardian Weekly* 8 Feb. 19/2 Does a sharp operator like Mr Murdoch want the Times in order to preserve it on the same sad course that loses it an annual fortune? Naow, cobber. **1987** A. PRICE *New Kind of War* II. 55 Under canvas?.. *Naow*, major, sir—we're snug enough.

**napkin**, *n.* Add: [**1.**] **d.** orig. and chiefly *N. Amer.* = *sanitary towel* s.v. SANITARY *a.* 3.

**1873** L. C. WARNER *Pop. Treat. Dis. Women* x. 91 In cool weather the lower part of the body should be dressed in flannel drawers, and the napkins employed should be dried and warmed before being used. **1895** *Montgomery Ward Catal.* Spring & Summer 88/3 The Faultless Serviette or Absorbent Health Napkin .., no washing, burned after using. **1900** DORLAND *Med. Dict.* 624/2 *Spotting*, a slight menstrual show upon a woman's napkin. **1956** *Sears, Roebuck Catal.* Fall & Winter 756/2 Nylon Sanitary panty... Inner napkin tabs. **1986** V. GOLDBERG *Margaret Bourke-White* xix. 221 'She just sent me out to get her some napkins.' 'Napkins?' 'I think you call it Kotex.'

**-napping** (-næpɪŋ), *suffix. colloq.* (orig. *U.S.*). [The final element of KID)NAPPING *vbl. n.*] Appended (with or without hyphenation) to nouns, and used to denote the action or process of stealing or carrying off (often for a ransom) a person, animal, etc., of the type specified by the first element, as DOGNAPPING *vbl. n.* '*petnapping*, '*ship-napping*, etc.

(Many of the words illustrated below or recorded in our files are humorous nonce-formations; typically those relating to the theft of small animals seem to be better established.)

**1967** *Compton Yearbk.* 111/1 In recent times petnapping has been a $50-million-a-year business. **1974** *New Yorker* 25 Feb. 122/3 Icarus, our hero, escapes from a novel being written by Hubert Lubert. .. Lubert, suspecting a character-napping by his rival Surget, hires the farcically inept detective Morcol. **1978** *Washington Post* 29 Dec. D1 The latest rash of art-nappings gives museums the jitters. **1984** *Observer* 5 Feb. 5/3 It is just a year since the most bizarre 'horsenapping' of all time took place. **1988** *New Republic* 24 Mar. 14/3 During the *Achille Lauro* ship-napping, the joke around Washington was that PLO stood for Push Leon (Klinghoffer) Over.

Also **-nap** (forming nouns and transitive vbs.), **-napped** (forming adjs.) and **-napper** (forming agent-nouns), as **art-nap** *n.*, **cat-nap** *v. trans.*, **horse-napper** *n.*, **petnapper** *n.*, etc.

**1966** *Sci. News* LXXXIX. 317/1 With the increasing number of animal care bills before Congress, medical researchers are worried that they might get hog-tied along with the petnappers. **1978** *Washington Post* 29 Dec. D2/6 What's happening here may be.. a whole rash of art-naps. **1983** D. FRANCIS *Danger* xii. 167 'Enough to put the horse-nappers off for life.' 'Would your firm work to free a horse?' she asked curiously. **1983** *Daily Tel.* 22 Sept. 19/6 Mr Smith said: 'I admit I shot a black and white cat but it was not his lordship's.'.. He suggested that Tilley may have been 'cat-napped'. **1989** *Oxford Star* 16 Mar. 1 (*heading*) Catnapped. Stolen cats are being killed for their fur.

**naproxen** (næ'prɒksɛn), *n. Pharm.* [f. NA(PHTHYL *n.* + PR(OPIONIC *a.* + OX(Y- + -*en*, after TAMOXIFEN *n.*, etc.] An anti-inflammatory analgesic substance, $C_{14}H_{14}O_3$, given orally (freq. as the sodium salt) as a pain-killer and in the treatment of some forms of arthritis; (+)-2-(6-methoxy-2-naphthyl)propionic acid.
**1971** *Jrnl. Pharmacol. & Exper. Therapeutics* CLXXIX. 121/1 Naproxen appears to act directly at inflamed tissue sites, probably in the same manner as other nonsteroidal agents like indomethacin and mefenamic acid act. **1980** *Nature* 20 Mar. 272/2 Pretreatment of rats with aspirin, indomethacin, naproxen and flurbiprofen always led to a potent inhibition of prostacyclin production *ex vivo*. **1988** *Jrnl. Internat. Med. Res.* XVI. 158/1 Recently, an oral instant suspension formulation of naproxen has become available.

**narcotize**, *v.* Add: [**2.**] **b.** *fig.* To render insensible or stupid, as with a narcotic.
**1942** *Sun* (Baltimore) 1 Apr. 10/1 It is not very difficult for a Goebbels to map out a program for narcotizing the German people. **1970** A. TOFFLER *Future Shock* (1971) xvi. 364 The family man who retreats into his evening . . allows televised fantasy to narcotize him. **1985** *Los Angeles Times* 20 Dec. v. 19/4 Has all this developed in us a trait of destructiveness, or narcotized what ought naturally to be an instinct for creativeness?

**Nardil** ('nɑːdɪl), *n. Pharm.* [f. NAR(CO- + -*dil*, of unknown origin.] A proprietary name for phenelzine.
[**1944** *Official Gaz.* (U.S. Patent Office) 7 Mar. 13/2 *Nardil* . . . For medicinal malt extract.] **1959** *Trade Marks Jrnl.* 18 Nov. 1196/1 *Nardil* . . . Anti-depressants. **1960** *Official Gaz.* (U.S. Patent Office) 5 Jan. TM10/1 *Nardil* . . . For psychic energizer. **1960** A. HUXLEY *Let.* 24 Jan. (1969) 885 Disasters in France . . the news of which . . keeps up her morale like a shot of adrenalin or a course of Nardil. **1965** [see PARNATE *n.*]. **1976** SMYTHIES & CORBETT *Psychiatry* x. 185 If anxiety symptoms of the phobic kind or depersonalization are present, a course of 'nardil' . . should be tried.

**narratee** (ˌnærə'tiː, ˌnæreɪ'tiː), *n.* Chiefly *Lit. Theory.* [f. NARRATE *v.* + -EE[1]; cf. Fr. *narrataire* (R. Barthes 1966, in *Communications* viii. 10).] One to whom a narrative is addressed: the counterpart of the *narrator*.
**1971** *Neophilologus* LV. 120 If narratives can be classified according to the receiver-directed signals they contain, they can also be classified by the kind of receivers—the 'narratees'—to whom they are supposedly addressed. **1974** *Southern Lit. Jrnl.* VI. 42 The two images of narrator and narratee. **1983** T. EAGLETON *Lit. Theory* iii. 106 The category of 'voice' . . concerns the act of narrating itself, what kind of narrator and narratee are implied.

**narrativity** (ˌnærə'tɪvɪtɪ), *n.* Chiefly *Lit. Theory.* [ad. Fr. *narrativité* (see quot. 1966): cf. NARRATIVE *n.* and -ITY.] The quality or condition of being or presenting a narrative; (the action or process of) story-telling.
[**1966** C. METZ in *Essais sur la Signification au Cinéma* (1968) viii. 185 (*title*) Le cinéma moderne et la narrativité.] **1973** G. PRINCE *Gram. of Stories* ii. 41 The ratio of narrative and non-narrative events in a given story is . . very important since it affects its degree of narrativity. **1974** M. TAYLOR tr. *Metz's Film Lang.* ii. 27 This does not imply that the *impression of narrativity*, the certainty of being confronted with a narrative . . is any more accessible to analysis. **1981** P. KERR in T. Bennett et al. *Popular TV & Film* I. v. 78 Narrativity and specific characeral voices remain privileged. **1982** *Times Lit. Suppl.* 5 Nov. 1207/1 Narrativity is the very essence of the Bible. **1987** *New Republic* 26 Oct. 28/3 In matters of literary theory the discourse is spankingly up to date. There is talk of narrativity, of canon-formation, canonicity.

**narratology** (ˌnærə'tɒlədʒɪ), *n. Lit. Theory.* [ad. Fr. *narratologie* (T. Todorov *Grammaire du Décaméron*, 1969, i. 10).] The study of the structure and function of narrative, esp. as analogous to linguistic structure; the examination and classification of the traditional themes, conventions, and symbols of the narrated story.
**1974** G. PRINCE in *Diacritics* IV. III. 2/2 The semiotic study of (verbal) narrative . . has increasingly refused to be called 'narrative semiology' . . . It has kept or acquired other names . . from the now banal 'structural analysis of narrative' and 'grammar of stories' to the newer, more elegant, and more fashionable 'narratology' and 'narrativics'. **1975** *Times Lit. Suppl.* 1 Aug. 879/3 Narratology, or the study of narrative, has so far been the victim of its own youthful exuberance. **1978** *Canad. Jrnl. Linguistics 1977* XXII. 219 The complete title of the book may be taken to include, or at least intersect, those fields commonly known as 'text linguistics', 'folkloristics' and 'narratology'. **1983** T. EAGLETON *Lit. Theory* iii. 103 It [*sc.* structuralism] created a whole new science—narratology. **1988** COHAN & SHIRES *Telling Stories* iii. 53 In breaking down narrative into story and narration, we are following a method of analysis called *narratology*. Narratology studies narrative as a general category of texts which can be classified according to *poetics*, the set of identifiable conventions that make a given text recognizable as a narrated story.
Hence **narrato'logical** *a.*; **narra'tologist** *n.*
**1974** *Diacritics* IV. III. 5/1 In *S/Z*, Barthes had relegated the activities of positivistic narratologists to the prehistory of semiotics. **1975** *Times Lit. Suppl.* 1 Aug. 879/3 Signor Segre traces the development of narratological speculation. **1984** *Ibid.* 3 Feb. 105/2 One of the best things that Greimas has done is partly to stabilize the terminology to which narratologists resort. **1987** R. ALTER in Alter & Kermode *Lit. Guide to Bible* 26 At the beginning of his narratological study of Deuteronomy.

**'narrowcasting**, *vbl. n.* orig. *U.S.* Also **narrow-casting.** [f. NARROW *a.* + CASTING *vbl. n.*, after BROADCASTING *vbl. n.*; cf. *narrow-cast* adv. s.v. NARROW *a.* 7.] The transmission of radio or television programmes to an audience defined either by special interest or geographical location; recently also applied *spec.* to the supplying of programmes to subscribers through cable television networks or other media.
**1932** H. ANGUS in *Broadcasting* 1 June 7/2 By 'narrow-casting' I mean any type of education or entertainment or information that isn't of interest to the general public. **1932** *Daily Progress* (Charlottesville, Va.) 23 Nov. 7/6 A searchlight beam flung the voices of men across the Adirondack foothills last night in the first recorded experiment in long distance 'narrowcasting'. **1948** *Sat. Rev. Lit.* (U.S.) 31 Jan. 30/1 Other broadcasters condemned it as being narrowcasting instead of broadcasting. **1974** *Listener* 19 Sept. 358/1 The two [cable] channels are booked with citizen-generated tapes about two-thirds of the time . . . But much of the material . . is dull and poorly produced . . . And it also tends to be highly specialised. This . . was supposed to be one of the advantages of 'narrowcasting'. **1976** *New Yorker* 15 Mar. 26/1 New York Cable television's first game show began live narrowcasting . . to eighty thousand apartments and houses . . on the southern half of Manhattan Island. **1985** *Listener* 16 May 39/3 The broadcast system supports, at this level, interests from club rugby to master bridge. That is broadcast narrowcasting, and quite right too.

Hence **'narrowcast** n. (a.) and v. trans. and intr.; also **'narrowcaster** n.; **'narrowcasting** ppl. a.
**1937** Nebraska State Jrnl. 26 Aug. 10/7 Truly, broadcasting is becoming less and less broadcast and more and more narrowcast. **1972** TV Guide 27 May 12/1 [Cable television's] chief advantage, he says, is its selectivity; candidates for lower-level offices need never again 'broadcast' their message prodigally to large masses of viewers who can't vote for them; instead they'll 'narrowcast' it cheaply only to those who can. **1977** Sunday Times 23 Jan. 52/3 Most narrowcasts tend to be a service of the BBC. **1978** Amer. Speech LIII. 215 The appearance of narrowcasting 'cable television transmission' as an entry in the 1978 edition of the World Book Dictionary is interesting. **1981** N.Y. Times 31 Aug. A16/1 That makes it possible for broadcasters to become 'narrowcasters', offering everything from programming in Chinese to soft-core porn to highbrow culture. **1986** Church Times 8 Aug. 9/4 The Cambridge Radio Course makes no bones about the need to be open: to broadcast, not to narrow cast. There is no point in Christians occupying the airwaves to speak only to themselves. **1987** Financial Rev. (Sydney) 10 Apr. 1/1 Powerplay .. also owns the satellite narrowcaster, Sportsplay Television Systems Pty Ltd. **1988** Creative Rev. Jan. 45/3 As the pirate stations have shown, narrowcast radio can work just as successfully as narrowcast magazines.

**Nasanov** n., var. *NASSANOFF n.

**Nassanoff** ('næsǝnɒf), n. Ent. Also **Nasanov**. The name of Nikolai Viktorovich Nasanov or in the Fr. transliteration Nassanoff (1855–1939), Russian entomologist, used attrib. and in the possessive with reference to his work on social insects, as **Nassanoff('s) gland**, a gland on the back of the honey bee, between the sixth and seventh segments of the abdomen, which secretes a pheromone that attracts workers; **Nassanoff pheromone**, the pheromone secreted by the Nassanoff gland.
[**1925** R. E. SNODGRASS Anat. & Physiol. Honeybee iv. 114 The abdominal scent glands, called also the glands of Nassonoff after their discoverer... The scent glands were first noted by Nassonoff, whose description and crude illustration were published by Zoubareff (1883).] **1953** Proc. R. Soc. B. CXL. 57 It seems likely that covering the Nasanov gland did not completely suppress the odour. **1959** Ann. Rev. Entomol. IV. 46 A hive-specific component was superimposed on the Nassanoff pheromone. **1969** R. F. CHAPMAN Insects xxxvi. 735 Honey bees have two important glands producing pheromones: the mandibular glands in the head and Nassanoff's gland in the abdomen. **1981** Sci. Amer. June 122/3 They arrive at the entrance of the cavity ahead of the mass of bees and release scent from the Nassanoff glands at the tip of their abdomen. **1981** Ann. Entomol. Soc. Amer. LXXIV. 67/1 Most swarms moved to the cage with the foreign queen and the artificial Nassanoff pheromone rather than to their own queen caged with paraffin oil.

**Nassonoff** n., var. *NASSANOFF n.

**nasty**, n.[1] Add: **3**. colloq. ellipt. for video nasty s.v. VIDEO-. Chiefly in pl.
**1982** Sunday Times 6 June 3/4 Three videos, part of the current crop of 'nasties' available in thousands of High Street rental shops, have been sent to the DPP. **1983** Observer 17 Apr. 3/1 The 'nasties'—the horror and terror films which have been one of the biggest high street money-spinners. **1985** Christian Science Monitor 3 May 30/1 With its tougher law on videocassettes, West Germany hopes to keep its youth away from the nasties. **1985** Financial Times 31 Aug. (Weekend Suppl.) p. viii/2 They pride themselves on being the Mr Cleans of the video

market—so if it's soft porn or nasties you are after, you should look elsewhere.

**natalid** ('nætǝlɪd), a. (n.) Zool. [f. mod.L. Natalus, generic name + -ID[3].] Of or pertaining to the family Natalidae of small long-legged insectivorous bats of North and Central America, characterized by large funnel-shaped ears and a nose tufted with hair but lacking a nose-leaf; natalid organ, an organ peculiar to natalids (see quot. 1959), of unknown function. Also as n., a bat of this family.
**1950** W. W. DALQUEST in Jrnl. Mammalogy XXXI. 437 Bats of the family Natalidae are of small size... Adult males possess a large, gland-like organ on the face or muzzle, which is here named the natalid organ. **1959** Amer. Mus. Novitates No. 1977. 4 The natalid organ is a thin, floating, glandular, bell-shaped disk covering the entire frontal region of the head, lying between the skin and the underlying muscles. It is peculiar to the genus Natalus. **1970** DALQUEST & WALTON in Slaughter & Walton About Bats ix. 173 Except a few cases of isolated individuals, natalid bats show a marked preference for caves and mine shafts. **1976** [see VESPERTILIONID a.]. **1984** J. E. HILL Bats xi. 209 Natalids are rather small, slim bats with a high, domed head.

**national**, a. and n. Add: [A.] [4.] c. Freq. with capital initial. Used in the names of various (esp. right-wing) political parties or groups to designate adherence to, support for, or identification with the supposed national interest, spec. as National Party; cf. National Front, Government, Republicans, Socialism, etc., below.
**1831** [see sense 5 below]. **1847** [see SUCCUMB v. 3 b]. **1876** N.Y. Tribune 18 May 1/1 Two National and five State Conventions were held yesterday, namely: Those of the National Greenback and Prohibition parties [etc.]. **1938** H. NICOLSON Diary 1 Oct. (1966) 373, I have to speak at a luncheon of the local National Labour Group. **1958** Economist 15 Nov. 612/1 The aim in most constituencies .. is to gain first place among 'national' (that is, non-communist) candidates. **1966** 'H. MacDIARMID' Company I've Kept viii. 185, I took an active part in the formation of the National Party of Scotland. **1973** W. LAQUEUR Dict. Politics 344 At the general election in Oct. 1931 the National Government (predominantly the Conservatives with National Labour and National Liberal) won over 60% of the vote, and the Labour Party won two million votes less than in 1929. **1987** Stock & Land (Melbourne) 12 Mar. 5/3 National Party MPs in Victoria and NSW will not permit their hands to be forced by the Queensland National Party and without their support the Coalition cannot be split on Tuesday.
[B.] Restrict † to sense 2 a. [2.] b. Usu. with capital initial. One who supports or represents a nationalist political group; spec. a member of a National Government or Party.
**1792** E. WYNNE Diary 3 Aug. (1952) ix. 122 They cryed, they cursed the Nationals. **1853** [see HARDSHELL n. 3]. **1939** G. B. SHAW Geneva I. 10 He got a clear majority over the Nationals and the Labor Party. **1940** J. REITH Diary 19 Jan. (1975) v. 238, I was standing as a National for a Liberal–National seat. **1965** J. P. TAYLOR Eng. Hist. 1914–1945 x. 326 The Conservatives .. and Liberal Nationals .. received slightly over 60 per cent. of the vote. **1987** Stock & Land (Melbourne) 12 Mar. 5/3 The 12 Queensland Nationals will vote one way and the 14 southern Nationals the other.
c. (Usu. without art.) ellipt. for National Party. N.Z.
**1938** Dominion (Wellington, N.Z.) 10 Oct. 8 (Advt.), Will she have to pay poll tax? Under Labour .. Yes! Boys and girls will have to pay ... Under National .. No! No boy or girl under 20 will pay Poll

Tax or Wage Tax... Vote National. **1958** *Political Sci.* (Wellington, N.Z.) X. 11. 23 The issue, as he defined it in each peroration, was simple: Socialism and restrictions and controls, or National and prosperity and a property-owning democracy. **1962** A. MITCHELL *Waitaki Votes* 9 The workers in the state and lower valuation housing areas..tend to support the Labour Party, while the business and professional people in the 'better' parts of town.. support National. **1977** *N.Z. Herald* 8 Jan. 1-6/4 In spite of all the pre-election talk about National's experience and expertise, New Zealand was in many respects in a worse position now than it was during Labour's period of office. **1983** M. GEE *Sole Survivor* iii. 22 His parents—'my old Mum and Dad'—had switched their vote to National before they died.

**nationalist**, *n.* and *a.* Add: **B.** *adj.* **1.** Of, pertaining to, or characterized by nationalism (esp. in sense 2); = NATIONALISTIC *a.*
**1907** G. B. SHAW *John Bull's Other Island* Pref. p. xxxv, Every judge is a partisan in the nationalist conflict; every speech is a dreary recapitulation of nationalist twaddle. **1922** JOYCE *Ulysses* 134 Great nationalist meeting in Borris—in—Ossory. **1933** J. J. BRONOWSKI in *Granta* 19 Apr. 358/1 This nationalist solidarity of teachers and lecturers has had a profound effect upon the generation which has grown up since the war. **1938** [see *bien pensant* s.v. BIEN *adv.*]. **1965** A. J. P. TAYLOR *Eng. Hist. 1914-1945* xv. 560 There had always been a suspicion that Churchill was only fighting a nationalist war against Germany, not an ideological war against 'fascism'. **1974** M. B. BROWN *Econ. of Imperialism* iv. 90 Schumpeter.. argued that German imperialism was accounted for precisely by the nationalist and militarist environment in which German capitalism emerged. **1984** V. S. NAIPAUL *Finding Centre* i. 95 The nationalist movement in the Ivory Coast had been simpler, a movement of farmers, *planteurs*, village people.
**2.** Usu. with capital initial. Used in the names of various political parties or groups to designate adherence to or support for national interests, chiefly as *Nationalist Party*; = *NATIONAL *a.* 4 c. Also, belonging to or supporting such a party or its policies.
**1884** *Sat. Rev.* 14 June 768/2 It is contended by the Government henchmen that there is..a strong Romanist and Nationalist..party in Ulster. **1885** [see PERSONATION *n.* 5]. **1901** [see MACHINE *n.* 8]. **1907** G. B. SHAW *John Bull's Other Island* Pref. p. xxxiv, It requires neither knowledge, character, conscience, diligence in public affairs, nor any virtue ..to thump the Nationalist or Orange tub. **1938** *Dominion* (Wellington, N.Z.) 4 Oct. 13/2 Parties are signified by the following abbreviations:—L., Labour; N., Nationalist; I., Independent. [etc.]. **1964** T. B. BOTTOMORE *Elites & Society* (1966) v. 99 Those who studied abroad created or helped to create the new nationalist parties. **1977** *Financial Times* 6 Apr. 7/2 The leader of the Nationalist Party, Mr. Sakiasi Butrodoka, who campaigned under the slogan 'Fiji for the Fijians' received enough support to put him into Parliament.

**native**, *a.* Sense 15 in Dict. becomes 16. Add:
[III.] **15.** *Computing.* Designed for or built into a given system; not enhanced by additional software or hardware; *spec.* designating the language (esp. machine code) associated with a given processor or computer, and programs written in it. Cf. *RESIDENT *a.* 2 c.
**1966** J. HORN *Computer & Data Processing Dict. & Guide* 87 *Native language*, the communication means between machine units which is peculiar to a class of equipment. **1983** *InfoWorld* 24 Jan. 9/4 Some of the new Milton Bradley expander games will work only with the expander system, and some will work with the native TI computer. **1984** *Austral. Personal Computer* Apr. 167 (Advt.), Compiling 6000 lines per minute directly into native machine code (not slow p-code). **1988** *Network World* 15 Aug. 1/5 Under the 3Com plan, IBM and Macintosh personal computers on the same local net will be able to..communicate with the server using the interface of their native operating systems.

**natty** ('nætɪ), *a.*[2] and *n.*[2] *Rastafarian slang.* [Repr. Black (Jamaican) pronunc. of KNOTTY *a.*, as in '(k)notty head': see DREADLOCKS *n. pl.*]
**A.** *adj.* Of the hair: knotty, matted, as in dreadlocks; hence of a person: wearing dreadlocks, Rastafarian, esp. as *natty dread*: see DREAD *n.* 4 b; also, characteristic or symbolic of Rastafarian culture. **B.** *n.* One who wears dreadlocks, a Rastafarian (see also quot. 1976).
**1974** COLE & ANDERSON (*song-title*) Natty dread. **1975** *Rolling Stone* 24 Apr. 52/1 Natty dreadlocks means hair with an attitude: kinky, jungle thick and matted into long tortuous antibraids. There's a tourist-tormenting gang of guerrilla hoodlums on the island of Domenica [*sic*] called the Natty Dreads. **1976** *Daily Mirror* 2 Apr. 20/2 Here's what some of the words heard in reggae lyrics mean: *dread*, tough, uncompromising, rebellious.. *dreadlocks*, long braided hair. *Jah*, God. *Natty*, black people, singular or plural. **1977** MCKNIGHT & TOBLER *Bob Marley* vii. 87 The origin of the terms 'natty dread' and 'dreadlocks' is considerably less devious and weighty than might be supposed. 'Natty dread' is derived from 'notty head', a term of abuse frequently hurled at 'Rasta ragamuffins' on many a street corner. **1977** *Transatlantic Rev.* LX. 186 Natty Hallelujah. **1984** *Washington Post* 7 Dec. (Weekend) 55/1 Big Youth is one of the legendary figures in Jamaica, a deejay rapper who also contributed the phrase 'natty dread' to the reggae vocabulary. **1985** B. ZEPHANIAH *Dread Affair* 19 Come natty dread youths get in there Give away what you have spare. *Ibid.* 94 Dread keep farm Dread sister know better Natty in sky Still natty grow pepper. **1987** *N.Y. Times* 17 Apr. C28/3 Jean-Michel Basquiat..sits doubled over as if trying to hide beneath his topknot of 'natty dreads'.

**natural**, *a.* and *adv.* Add: [A.] [19.] **b.** Of a decorative finish: that retains the colour and texture of the original material; also of wood, etc.: not painted or artificially coloured.
**1908** *Sears, Roebuck Catal.* 377/1 The frame is made of thoroughly seasoned hardwood, natural shellac finish. **1933** E. T. HAMILTON *Boy Builder* 48 These are known as 'natural' finishes, as they do not change the color of the wood. **1937** R. HOOPER *Woodcraft in Design & Pract.* ii. 8 Furniture of natural unpolished oak, oatmeal coloured walls, fabrics the same. **1954** L. HOCHMAN *How to refinish Furnit.* 55/1 (*caption*) The natural grain and wood colour of this walnut coffee table was enhanced with a natural finish. **1974** *Habitat Ann. Catal.* 40/2 Imagine a bedroom custom-built to your own specifications and finished in natural teak.
**B.** *adv.* or quasi-*adv.* In a natural manner; = NATURALLY *adv. colloq.* and *dial.*
**1793** J. WOODFORDE *Diary* 23 Feb. (1929) IV. 10 Hopes her Mother will..behave more natural to her than she ever yet did. **1869** 'MARK TWAIN' *Innoc. Abr.* xxvii. 290 The doctor asks the questions, generally, because he can keep his countenance... It comes natural to him. **1890** *Temple Bar* July 383 It comes quite natural to a poor woman to sit up the night with a sick neighbour. **1911** G. B. SHAW *Getting Married* 196 My wife had to break me into it. It came natural to her. **1942** Z. N. HURSTON in *S.E. Post* 5 Sept. 57/2 Natural, the future..looks something different from the past. **1952** E. O'NEILL *Moon for Misbegotten* I. 33 He'll keep acting natural enough, and you'd swear he wasn't bad at all. **1986** 'J. LE CARRÉ' *Perfect Spy* vii. 163 The most important thing to do is to look busy, act natural, keep everything normal.

**naturally,** *adv.* Add: [**I.**] [**3.**] [**II.**] [**5.**] [c.] Also in weakened use: = *of course* s.v. COURSE *n.* 37 c. Freq. as an emphatic affirmative reply.

**1888** H. JAMES in *Scribner's Mag.* Sept. 320/2 'Such a house as it is today!' 'Well, my dear, naturally.' **1934** G. B. SHAW *Too True to be Good* II. 76 And you mistook this great military genius for a half wit!!!.. Naturally. The symptoms are precisely the same. **1959** A. CHRISTIE *Cat among Pigeons* iii. 40 'If I ask you questions I shall expect answers.'.. 'Naturally.' **1970** M. ANGELOU in *Harper's Mag.* Feb. 91/2 In follow-the-leader, naturally he was the one who created the most daring and interesting things to do. **1973** I. MURDOCH *Black Prince* I. 24, I said, 'Naturally I won't mention this business to anyone.' **1983** J. KOSINSKI *Being There* vi. 95 When I took it upon myself to allude to Gardiner in my speech in Philadelphia, I naturally assumed that he was an established member of the Wall Street elite.

**Navier–Stokes** (ˌneɪvɪəˈstəʊks), *n. Physics.* The names of Claude-Louis-Marie *Navier* (1785-1836), French engineer, and Sir George Gabriel *Stokes* (1819-1903), Irish mathematician and physicist, used *attrib.* in **Navier–Stokes equation,** each of the one-dimensional equations of motion for a viscous fluid, derived by them in 1821 and 1845 respectively; also, the vector equation combining these, which may be written $dV/dt = -1/\rho \nabla p + F + \nu \nabla^2 V + \frac{1}{3}\nu \nabla(\nabla \cdot V)$ where $V$ is the fluid velocity, $\rho$ the density, $p$ the pressure, $F$ the total force per unit mass, and $\nu$ the kinematic viscosity.

**1949** H. F. P. PURDAY *Streamline Flow* xii. 173 (*heading*) Navier-Stokes equations. **1956** A. A. TOWNSEND *Struct. Turbulent Shear Flow* ii. 23 The problem of obtaining from the Navier–Stokes equations of motion complete solutions of any problem in turbulence appears impossibly difficult. **1957** *Encycl. Brit.* XIV. 191A/2 The Navier-Stokes equation together with the equation of continuity, $\nabla \cdot (\rho u) = -\partial \rho / \partial t$, describes the motion of viscous fluids. **1976** *Nature* 15 July 162/2 The atmosphere may be regarded as a compressible fluid, its behaviour being described by the Navier–Stokes equation and the thermodynamic equations concerned with sources, sinks and the transfers of energy. **1981** A. D. PIERCE *Acoustics* x. 536 We have no kinetic-energy term because we discarded the inertial term in the Navier-Stokes equation. **1987** *Nature* 19 Mar. 235/2 The Navier-Stokes equations have been called 'innocuous in appearance.. marked by insidious pitfalls', with more than 60 partial derivative terms when expressed in three dimensions.

‖**né** (ne), *a.* [Fr. masc. of pa. pple. of *naître* to be born; cf. the more frequent NÉE *a.*] Born, 'originally called': used after the name by which a man is currently known, to introduce his original or former name (see quots.). Also *transf.*

**1937** N. MARSH *Vintage Murder* xiv. 153 He's a very nasty little person, is Mr. St. John Ackroyd, *né* Albert Biggs, a thoroughly unpleasant piece of bluff and brass. **1972** *Times Lit. Suppl.* 27 Oct. 1271/1 Headlam-Morley (né Headlam) was born in 1863. **1977** *New Yorker* 10 Oct. 50/1 One of the few Western holders of the Lenin (né Stalin) Peace Prize. **1988** *Washington Post* 25 Sept. E6/1 L'Amiral de Grasse (né Francois Joseph Paul) played a brief but crucial role in the Revolutionary War.

**neato** ('niːtəʊ), *a. slang* (chiefly *N. Amer.*). Also **neat-o**(h. [f. NEAT *a.* + -O².] That is 'neat', excellent, or desirable; wonderful, 'fantastic'. See NEAT *a.* 11 b.

**1968** N. GIOVANNI in *Negro Digest* June 75/1, I have this really neato pink IBM—it was a gift. **1978** *Maledicta* II. 287 If such pearls as 'A woman without

a man is like a fish without a bicycle'.. get you down, you can pep up by looking at the photograph of the *neato* Indian actress Madhur Jaffrey. **1981** W. SAFIRE in *N.Y. Times Mag.* 15 Mar. 8/3 'Neat' and its intensified form, 'neat-o', have become.. universal forms of approbation in current slang. **1982** *Underground Grammarian* Jan. 1/2 We would probably never have heard of Peter Wagschal, or of his neato Ouija Board Studies Program, if it hadn't been for one Larry Zenke, a pretty neato guy himself. **1986** *More* (N.Z.) Feb. 49/1 Those were the days when Beaver used to.. have what she calls 'a neato free time'. **1986** *City Limits* 9 Oct. 38 Hum along with the neat-oh LA punk score.

**neb** (nɛb), *v.* (Formerly at NEB *n.*) [f. the *n.*] **a.** *intr.* To kiss or bill. **b.** *trans.* To adapt the point of (a pen) for writing. **c.** *intr.* To pry into the affairs of others; to behave in a 'nosy' or intrusive manner. Freq. const. *about, in,* etc. *dial.* (chiefly *north.* and *U.S.*).

**1609** ARMIN *Maids of More-Cl.* (1880) 90 Shall not busse knight, shall not neb? *a* **1819** in Hogg *Jacobite Relics* I. 241 These two drakes may neb, go hand in hand. **1880** GORDON *Chron. Keith* 69 (E.D.D.), Caught nebbing the pen on the desk, and not on the thumb. **1893-4** R. O. HESLOP *Northumb. Words* II. 494 He com nebbin up, as if he hed ony business wi'd. **1928** in H. Wentworth *Amer. Dial. Dict.* (1944) 408/2 She's always nebbin about. **1933** H. ALLEN *Anthony Adverse* III. IX. lxiii. 1088 Look at that smashed teakwood screen there. But come on; they don't like you nebbin' in just after a haul. **1948** MENCKEN *Amer. Lang.* Suppl. II. 204 *To neb,* to be inquisitive [is].. recorded for West Virginia. **1984** *Trans. Yorks. Dial. Soc.* LXXXIV. 53 The.. verb and noun *neb* and *nebbin* 'to gossip with the intention of being nosey' is commoner [than *neb,* the point of an object].

**necessarium** (nɛsɪˈsɛərɪəm), *n.* [a. med.L. *necessārium,* neut. sing. of *necessāri-us* necessary, used *absol.,* prob. for acc. (*locum*) *necessārium* necessary place.] A privy, esp. in a monastic building. Cf. NECESSARY *a.* 3 and *n.* 4.

**1848** *Archaeol. Jrnl.* V. 101 The other outlet from the pisalis.. leads to the necessarium, in the corner of which a light.. is kept burning. **1875** *Encycl. Brit.* I. 13/1 A passage at the other end leads to the 'necessarium' (1), a portion of the monastic buildings always planned with extreme care. **1967** *Listener* 21 Dec. 802/3 Viewers.. don't mind having a hundred variations, from 'The Necessarium' to 'The Thunder-Box' to choose from. **1984** *Maidenhead Advertiser* 10 Feb. 52/4 In the adjacent gardens the impressive remains of the Chapter House, Dormitory and Necessarium can still be visited.

**necrology,** *n.* Add: [1.] c. An account or listing of deaths, esp. of deaths due to a particular cause.

**1965** *New Statesman* 30 Apr. 684/2 The agonies one went through as a child listening to old people go over their necrology! **1975** *New Yorker* 26 May 117/1 One might begin with a necrology of famous women who died of complications attending pregnancy or childbirth. **1988** *Washington Post* 25 Sept. (Book World) 8/5 A necrology in which Ellison expresses his grief and bitterness at the recent deaths of numerous colleagues [etc.].

**nectarivore** (nɛkˈtærɪvɔː(r)), *n. Zool.* [f. NECTARIVOROUS *a.,* after CARNIVORE *n.,* etc.] A nectarivorous animal.

**1975** *Ecology* LVI. 851/1 Several species of bats not usually considered as nectarivores.. appear to rely heavily on nectar as a food source in the dry season. **1976** D. R. WELLS in Medway & Wells *Birds of Malay Peninsula* V. i. 9 Among nectarivores of Lowland forest, patterns of dispersion are poorly known. **1984** J. E. HILL *Bats* v. 67 The phyllostomid nectarivores may also include insects in their diets..

taken in accidentally just because they happen to be inside the flowers at the time of the bat's visit.

**née**, *a*. Add: **b.** Hence *transf.* (often humorously or for effect) after the current name by which a man, place, etc. is known, to introduce the former or original name. Cf. *NÉ *a*.
　　**1958** *Internat. Jrnl. Amer. Linguistics* XXIV. 273 (*heading*) On Tagmemes, née gramemes. *a***1961** P. H. LANG in *Webster* s.v., Sonata for flute, oboe, and basso continuo née sonata for violin and harpsichord. **1970** [see TRANSFER *n*. 2 c]. **1977** *Modern Railways* Dec. 459/2 The document..reiterates the GLC's determination to protect the alignment of Stage 2 of the Jubilee (née Fleet) Line. **1981** W. SAFIRE in *N.Y. Times Mag.* 12 Apr. 16/4 The flight attendant, née stewardess, singsongs over the loudspeaker. **1988** *Los Angeles Times* 1 Sept. III. 1/1 He once had a coach, the infamous Johnny Blood (nee McNally).

**need**, *n*. Add: [**10.**] [**c.**] Also in more general sense, freq. with *for* or *to* and infinitive.
　　**1914** G. B. SHAW *Misalliance* Pref. p. ci, The child's personal subjective need for a religion. *a***1930** D. H. LAWRENCE *New Eve & Old Adam* iii, in *Mod. Lover* (1934) 154 He was a rather fine-hearted young man, with a human need to live. **1945** E. WAUGH *Brideshead Revisited* I. v. 95 His year of anarchy had filled a deep, interior need of his, the escape from reality. **1959** J. BARZUN *House of Intellect* i. 26 What Intellect satisfies in us is the need for orderly and perspicuous expression. **1960** C. DAY LEWIS *Buried Day* i. 21 The need for my mother—a need of which I was never conscious—made me warmly reponsive to physical tenderness. **1981** A. HUTSCHNECKER *Hope* vii. 121 Thinkers, writers, painters, and other people feel an inner need to create goals for themselves. **1987** H. BAILEY *Vera Brittain* iii. 101 Her need to be needed tempted the others to exploit her.

**needle**, *n*. [**II.**] [**12.**] Senses 12 a, b in Dict. become 12 b, c. Add: **a.** The penis. *coarse slang* (now only *Hist.*).
　　**1638** NABBES *Covent Garden* I. vi. 14 Let my needle run in your Diall. **1707** *Misc. Wks. Rochester & Roscommon* I. 130 The Seamans Needle nimbly points the Pole But thine still turns to every craving Hole. **1720** T. D'URFEY *Wit & Mirth* VI. 92, I straightway whip my Needle out. **1980** E. JONG *Fanny* II. i. 165 'Won't ye have a Nestlecock?' cries the second Tart, '..a Needlewoman fer yer e'er-loving Needle?'
　　**c.** *to give* (*put in*, etc.) *the needle*: to provoke or annoy, esp. by criticism, teasing, or sarcasm.
　　**1962** *Listener* 20 Sept. 450/2 Spokesmen for the builders and the mortgage societies, who were given ..what I can only describe as a dose of the old needle. **1963** *Wall St. Jrnl.* 25 Jan., It's much easier to take the needle from this crowd. They're guys who like Scotch, American jazz and most of us. **1980** T. WOLFE *Right Stuff* (1981) vii. 147 Al..was not the type to let Glenn get away with it... Al kept putting the needle in.
　　**d.** *Sport.* Competitive spirit, antagonism provoked by rivalry. Also, a stimulus or spur to improve one's performance. Cf. *needle match* below.
　　**1923** *Daily Mail* 1 Aug. 8/2 It may be, of course, that there was too much 'needle' (to employ a boxing term which means bad spirit) about this contest. **1959** *Times* 8 June 3/1 Perhaps it was this very lack of needle, this air of unreality in the late evening of Saturday..that failed to see Davies home to a victory. **1970** *Times* 16 Mar. 8 Without the constant needle of improving competition, the men at the top will find it difficult to improve any further. **1983** J. HENNESSY *Torvill & Dean* 26 There was some friendly needle between the two couples because of their equality of performance in previous championships. **1987** *Squash Player Internat.* Mar.

6/1 That she was seeded 2 to Liz Irving's 1 was the sort of needle she needed.

**needle**, *v*. Add: [**1.**] **d.** *Surg.* To treat by the use of a needle or needles; *spec.* to use acupuncture on or cannulate.
　　**1936** [implied in *NEEDLING *vbl. n.* 2 d]. **1971** F. MANN *Acupuncture* (ed. 2) ii. 30 In one form of acupuncture the points spontaneously tender or those tender under pressure are needled. *Ibid.* iii. 43, I needled her once a month, halfway between the periods. **1982** *N.Y. Times Mag.* 28 Feb. 48 (*caption*) Emily Pinion was 'needled' in the womb to relieve fluid building up in the chest that had prevented her lungs from developing. **1987** A. CAMPBELL *Acupuncture* ii. 17 The acupuncture was fairly elementary, and for the most part consisted simply in needling the painful area.
　　[**2.**] **d.** To prick as with a needle; of driving rain, etc.: to cause a pricking sensation, esp. upon the skin. Also with *at, into*.
　　**1929** W. FAULKNER *Sound & Fury* 330 A moving wall of grey light..seemed to disintegrate into minute and venomous particles..that..needled laterally into her flesh. **1974** R. B. PARKER *God save Child* (1975) iii. 22 The rain..needled at my face as I ran. **1988** *Fitness* May 46/2 Helpful for getting cellular waste and other toxins on the move, as the jetting bubbles needle away at your body.

**needler**, *n*. Add: **2.** One who provokes or 'needles' (sense 1 b); *esp.* one who goads others to action or incites to anger.
　　**1947** F. WAKEMAN *Saxon Charm* iii. 41 The king roars at this remark by the world's champion needler of doctors. **1955** *Chem. & Engin. News* 30 May 2328/1 He describes himself as being..a 'needler' for inciting action where he sees the need. **1964** *Listener* 20 Feb. 299/2 When the needlers request the publication of attendance records.., many an indolent director begins to mend his ways. **1983** *Truck & Bus* Aug. 84/1 How to cope with the abrasive and the abusive and the needlers without building grudges.

**needling**, *vbl. n.* Add: [**2.**] **d.** Treatment with acupuncture needles; an instance of this.
　　**1936** K. C. WONG *Hist. Chinese Med.* (ed. 2) i. 3 'Needling' occupied a rather important position in ancient times. It developed into the art of acupuncture. **1971** F. MANN *Acupuncture* (ed. 2) xii. 201 At one moment on the second day I thought I was going to seize up as I've done before and I thought 'I must get to Dr. Mann for a needling.' **1979** *Sci. Amer.* July 70/2 Electrical rather than mechanical stimulation of the needles is also gaining ground, since it reduces the danger of contamination of the operation field by the acupuncturist and minimizes the tissue damage caused by needling. **1987** *Jrnl. Alternative Med.* Feb. 7/4 In the study, the needling was carried out by Dr. Jing Hua Chen.. with help from some British acupuncturists.

**needling** ('niːdlɪŋ), *ppl. a.* (Formerly at NEEDLING *vbl. n.*) [f. NEEDLE *v*. + -ING².] That needles, in various senses of the vb.; sharply piercing.
　　**1947** R. C. M. HOWARD in *Penguin New Writing* XXX. 124 We dreamed of the plunge and the rise and the endless wind and the rime Of the needling frost that ate its way into eyes and ears and brain. **1958** *Spectator* 10 Jan. 33/1 Their needling and often impertinent questions. **1962** *Listener* 7 June 999/1 When the next careful, needling letter arrived from Samuel, the black temper broke loose again. **1976** *Economist* 13 Nov. 139/1 This type of humour..is more needling and elusive than anything men can produce. **1984** S. NAIPAUL *Beyond Dragon's Mouth* 196 My nerves ripple in a radiation of fine, needling pain.

**negative**, *a.* Add: [I.] [2.] c. Of evidence, experimental results, etc.: providing no support for a particular hypothesis, esp. one concerning the presence or existence of something. Of a test or experiment, or the subject of one: producing a negative result. Opp. POSITIVE *a.* 8 f.

**1788** PRIESTLEY in *Phil. Trans.* LXXIX. 15 The positive evidence of actually finding a substance is always more conclusive than the negative one, of not finding it. **1889** *Cent. Dict.* s.v., Negative result of an experimental inquiry. **1890** *Lancet* 26 Apr. 896/1 The negative result with nitric acid seemed to prove conclusively the absence of albumen. **1926** R. A. KILDUFFE *Man. Clin. Lab. Procedure* vii. 203 In hereditary syphilis both parents may give a positive reaction or the father may be positive and the mother negative. **1943**, etc. [see *rhesus-negative* adj. s.v. RHESUS *n.* 2]. **1957** H. WILLIAMSON *Golden Virgin* I. xi. 172 The left lung showed symptoms of phthisis; a sputum test having proved negative, it was considered possibly to be due to chlorine gas inhalation. **1971** H. GUNTRIP *Psychoanalytic Theory* I. iii. 79 Physical tests had been made, all the findings were negative, and there was absolutely nothing wrong. **1974** CHAMBERLAIN & OGILVIE *Symptoms & Signs in Clin. Med.* (ed. 9) v. 166 A green colour indicates the presence of protein. If the tip remains yellow, the test is negative.
[II.] [5.] b. Of an attitude, response, etc.: that is the opposite of favourable or positive; hostile, critical, unfavourable.
**1921** G. B. SHAW *Back to Methuselah* Pref. p. lxxxii, Comedy, as a destructive, derisory, critical, negative art, kept the theatre open when sublime tragedy perished. **1930** E. BOWEN in *Broadsheet Press* May 1 Alban had few opinions on the subject of marriage; his attitude to women was negative—in particular he was not attracted to Miss Cuffe. **1971** D. FRANCIS *Bonecrack* iii. 34 His face was full of the negative attitude which erects a barrier against sympathy or understanding. **1978** S. BRILL *Teamsters* i. 22 Negative press coverage of the Teamsters had heightened. **1981** A. LURIE *Lang. of Clothes* v. 147 The wearing of outrageous clothes primarily in order to attract negative attention—to annoy and offend—may also be a claim for status. **1987** J. BERMAN *Talking Cure* i. 10 Transference is usually ambivalent .. consisting of positive (affectionate) and negative (hostile) feelings toward the analyst.
c. Pessimistic, defeatist.
**1930** H. CRANE *Let.* 22 May (1965) 351 The poem .. is .. an affirmation of experience, and to that extent is 'positive' rather than 'negative' in the sense that *The Waste Land* is negative. **1958** J. K. GALBRAITH *Affluent Society* i. 5 There are negative thoughts here, and they cannot but strike an uncouth note in the world of positive thinking. **1983** J. HENNESSY *Torvill & Dean* 72 There was no question of negative thinking and we had no intention of giving less than 101 per cent on the night. **1987** B. MOORE *Colour of Blood* vii. 51, I don't want to be negative, but I don't see how we could get away.
d. Of an emotion, experience, etc.: discouraging, unpleasant.
**1951** P. D. OUSPENSKY *Psychol. Man's Poss. Evol.* iv. 72 What would happen to all our life, without negative emotions? **1964** I. WALLACE *Man* (1965) ii. 50 Marriage was an affirmative act, and he had been shackled by countless negative fears. **1973** *Howard Jrnl.* XIII. 307 For many of their patients uniforms have associations with past negative experiences of authority. **1987** *Performance* Sept./Oct. 28/3 It is always 'negative' experiences such as fear that are wished upon that audience.
e. Designating an absolute lack of something; = NO *a.* 1 b. *colloq.* (?orig. *U.S. Services*').
[**1946** J. IRVING *Royal Navalese* 121 Orders for a Church Parade. 'Dress for Officers No. 3, negative swords'.] **1984** *Financial Times* 10 Dec. 10/6 Chief executives .. are guilty .. of the commercial sin of

non-communication. For which read *negative* communication and you begin to catch his drift. **1986** D. A. DYE *Platoon* (1987) ix. 228 Negative contact, lootenant. Can't raise Barnes or any of the squads. **1986** *Times* 28 Jan. 11/6 They were described as 'having negative vulnerability to water entry'.

**negative**, *v.* Add: [3.] c. To negate, cancel.
**1972** *Police Rev.* 10 Nov. 1463/1 Will the plate .. negative the need to undergo an examination for a ministry plate? **1982** *Financial Times* 15 June 11/7 In the present case, section 18 negatived the existence of any contract. **1986** *Oxf. Jrnl. Legal Stud.* VI. 401 We can conclude that the harm was a consequence of the use of the product ... Biological susceptibility .., even if abnormal, is said not to negative the connection.

**negativism**, *n.* Add: 3. The tendency to take an attitude which is 'negative' (sense 5 b); refusal to co-operate or agree; hostility, opposition.
**1970** *San Diego Union* 12 Sept. 1/5 Vice-President Spiro T. Agnew last night denounced the 'nattering nabobs of negativism,' the 'professional pessimists'. **1977** *Sci. Amer.* May 139/3 The third example showed 'adamant negativism' on the part of the U.S.S.R. in a matter of the verification of prohibited biological weapons. **1978** *Studies in Eng. Lit.: Eng. Number* (Tokyo) 176 This negativism took the form of an opposition towards the metropolis and its fashions. **1985** P. ZIEGLER *Mountbatten* III. xxix. 367 Nehru had presented him as a monster of negativism, a man who would agree to nothing because it might split his followers if he did. **1986** *N.Y. Times* 13 Nov. D27/1 The law was defeated partly because of voter negativism about other issues and races.

**neglect**, *n.* Add: [2.] e. Want of attention to a dependent person, esp. a child, so gross as to amount to maltreatment or cruelty.
**1722** DEFOE *Moll Flanders* 179 It touch'd my Heart so forcibly to think of Parting entirely with the Child, and for ought I knew, of having it murther'd, or starv'd by Neglect and Ill-usage. **1889** *Act 52 & 53 Vict.* c. 44 s. 1 (*note*) Punishment for ill-treatment and neglect of children. **1902** *Encycl. Brit.* XXVII. 7/1 Numberless cases of neglect and ill-treatment went unpunished. **1968** J. LOCK *Lady Policeman* xiv. 122 Some dealt frequently with pretty horrifying neglect cases. **1988** *Church Times* 28 Oct. 5/2 In Sunday schools and youth clubs there may be children who are experiencing neglect or abuse.

**neglect**, *v.* Add: [2.] [b.] *esp.* to fail to take proper and necessary care of (a child or other dependent person).
**1722** DEFOE *Moll Flanders* 179 To give them [*sc.* children] up to be Manag'd by those People, who have none of that needful Affection .. is to Neglect them in the highest Degree. **1889** *Act 52 & 53 Vict.* c. 44 s. 1 Any person .. [who] wilfully ill-treats, neglects, abandons, or exposes such child .. shall be guilty of a misdemeanor. **1955** L. G. HOUSDEN *Prevention of Cruelty to Children* II. iv. 221 Most of the 97,835 children helped by the Society's Inspectors in the twelve months ending February 1953 had been neglected. **1971** *Reader's Digest Family Guide to Law* 268/2 If a husband fails to give his wife a reasonable amount of housekeeping money, he can be shown to have wilfully neglected her and any children of the marriage. **1982** L. CODY *Bad Company* iv. 30 She has always neglected my daughter and now the results are plainly disastrous.

**negligence**, *n.* Add: [1.] d. *Law.* Omission to do something that a reasonable person would do; breach of a legally imposed duty of care, want of reasonable care. *contributory negligence*: see CONTRIBUTORY *a.* 2.
**1696** P. VENTRIS *Reports* I. 191 The Court inclined strongly for the Defendant, there being not the least

negligence in him. **1741** *Modern Reports* (Cases Court of King's Bench) (ed. 2) XII. 152 It is found to have been by his Negligence. **1823** W. P. TAUNTON *Rep. Cases Court of Common Pleas* VIII. 145 The only question in the cause was, whether the Defendants had conducted themselves with gross negligence. **1884** LD. ESHER in *Law Times Rep.* LXXIII. 616/2 (*note*), The deceased was also guilty of negligence or of want of reasonable care contributing to the accident. **1949** C. H. S. FIFOOT *Hist. & Sources Common Law* viii. 164 By the beginning of the eighteenth century the judges were familiar with the name and idea of negligence . . . It was, however, too early to speak boldly of an action of negligence. **1987** *Which?* Aug. 400/1 We drafted a letter for Mr Larsen to send to the other driver's insurance company saying that the accident was clearly caused by negligence on the part of their insured.

**negligent**, *a.* and *n.* Add: [A.] [1.] c. *Law.* Of a person: failing to show reasonable care.
**1882** *Encycl. Brit.* XIV. 174/1 The liability of the latter was not, before 1880, extended to make the master responsible in damages if the person injured and the negligent servant were both in his service. **1971** *Reader's Digest Family Guide to Law* 214/2 In deciding whether a minor has been 'negligent', the standard applied is that of a reasonably careful minor of that age. **1987** *Woman & Home* July 11/2 People who believe they have been damaged by drug side effects will no longer have to prove that a company was negligent—just that their drug caused the injury.
[2.] c. *Law.* Characterized by negligence (sense 1 d), careless; esp. (*U.S.*) *negligent driving.*
**1741** *Modern Reports* (Cases Court of King's Bench) (ed. 2) XII. 152 It was moved in Arrest of Judgment, that such an Action on the Case lies only for a negligent keeping his Fire in his House. **1861** *Rep. Supreme Court U.S.* XXIV. 124 The stable-keeper provided the driver through whose negligent driving an injury was done to the horse of a third person. **1917** *Northeastern Reporter* CXVI. 80/2 The accident was caused by the negligent driving of the servant. **1920** *Ibid.* CXXVI. 73/1 On the ground that the city was not liable for the negligent driving of the hose truck operated by a member of the city fire department while in the performance of his duties. **1973** *Daily Tel.* 21 Aug. 15 Joseph Kennedy, 21-year-old son of the late Senator Robert Kennedy, was fined $100 (£40) for negligent driving in Nantucket yesterday.

**negligently**, *adv.* Add: **b.** *Law.* In such a way as to fail to show a reasonable standard of care.
**1696** P. VENTRIS *Reports* I. 190 The plaintiff had caused to be laden on board her three trunks, [etc.] . . but he did so negligently keep them, that . . the same were totally lost out of the said ship. **1741** *Modern Reports* (Cases Court of King's Bench) (ed. 2) XII. 151 Case for negligently keeping his fire. **1814** E. H. EAST *Rep. Cases Court of King's Bench* XVI. 244 For improperly and negligently carrying a cask of brandy . . by which it was damaged and the greater part of the brandy lost. **1885** *Law Times Rep.* LIII. 325/2 The defendant . . negligently and unskilfully navigated and managed the said vessel. **1971** *Reader's Digest Family Guide to Law* 435/1 A professional man who gives advice negligently can face claims not only from his own client . . but also from others adversely affected.

**negligible**, *a.* Delete small-type note and add: also 'negligibleness *n.*, negligi'bility *n.*
**1906** *N.E.D.*, Negligibleness, Negligibility. **1957** L. Fox *Numerical Solution Two-Point Boundary Probl.* iii. 42 We have not yet given any precise meaning to the phrase 'negligibility of residuals'. Computational standards suggest that the residuals can be considered negligible when our approximate solution is correct.

**1988** *Los Angeles Times* 3 July 36B/2 This bee's stinger has atrophied into negligibility.

**negotiable**, *a.* Add: **4.** *fig.* Of an abstraction: having a commonly agreed basis for discussion.
**1938** J. C. RANSOM *World's Body* 339 Behind appreciation, which is private, and criticism, which is public and negotiable, and represents the last stage of English studies, is historical scholarship. **1961** J. DIDION in *Vogue* 1 Aug. 63/1 They display what was once called *character*, a quality which, although approved in the abstract, sometimes loses ground to other, more instantly negotiable virtues.
**5.** Usu. *pred.* To be decided or arranged by negotiation or mutual agreement. (Esp. of terms of employment.)
**1971** *Morning Star* 7 Dec. 1/3 Dublin Premier Jack Lynch . . said that the constitution of a future United Ireland was negotiable. **1987** *Shropshire Admag* (Telford ed.) 4 June 8/1 Part time bar staff required, hours negotiable. **1988** *Daily Tel.* 3 Nov. (Appointments Suppl.) p. xvi/2 We are offering an excellent salary negotiable according to experience.

**Negretti** (nɪ'grɛtɪ), *n.* Now *rare* exc. *Hist.* Also **Negret(t)e.** [ad. Sp. (*merino*) *negrete*, f. *negro* black, NEGRO *n.*] A strain of merino sheep, formerly widespread, having relatively short wool and a wrinkled fleece; a sheep of this type.
**1793** J. BANKS *Let.* 6 Aug. in H. B. Carter *His Majesty's Spanish Flock* (1964) v. 114 As soon as peace returns he means to avail himself of the Kings [*sic*] Gracious Permission to renew his attack upon the Negretti Flock. **1809** *Phil. Mag.* XXXIII. 247 (*table*) Negrete. **1837** W. YOUATT *Sheep* v. 156 The *Negretti* are the largest and strongest of all the Spanish travelling sheep. **1862** J. S. DOBIE *S. Afr. Jrnl.* (1945) 24 Two imported rams among them, a Negretti and a Sturgeon. **1887** J. COLEMAN *Cattle, Sheep & Pigs Gt. Brit.* II. xviii. 363 The Negrette merino is a native of Spain. **1891** R. WALLACE *Rural Econ. Austral. & N.Z.* xxvi. 357 The Negretti or German variety [of Merino] was at one time introduced in considerable numbers into New South Wales and Queensland. **1973** *Materials & Technol.* VI. iii. 240 The Negrette and Infando sheep were similar in being somewhat larger animals with folded skins and yielding a shorter fibre.

**neisseria** (naɪ'sɪərɪə), *n. Microbiology.* Pl. -æ. [a. mod.L. *Neisseria*, f. the name of Albert Ludwig Siegmund *Neisser* (1855–1916), German dermatologist and bacteriologist: see -IA[1].] Any bacterium of the genus *Neisseria* of aerobic, Gram-negative, parasitic or pathogenic diplococci found on mammalian mucous membranes.
**1950** C. J. WITTON *Microbiol.* xxvii. 377 All neisseriae are gram-negative paired cocci with flattened adjacent sides. **1962** *Lancet* 5 May 933/1 The effect could also be elicited by *Bacillus subtilis, Escherichia coli,* and a diphtheroid, but not by a commensal neisseria (one strain of each tested). **1976** B. M. MITRUKA *Methods Detection & Identification Bacteria* ii. 34/1 The neisseriae are Gram-negative diplococci, many species of which normally colonize the oropharynx and the gastrointestinal and genitourinary tracts of humans. **1982** K. KANO in Milgrom & Flanagan *Med. Microbiol.* xxvii. 362/2 The . . nonpathogenic neisseriae can grow in ordinary media such as nutrient agar at 22° C.

**nema** ('niːmə), *n.* [a. Gr. νῆμα thread.]
**1.** *Palæont.* [H. Lapworth 1897, in J. Walther *Zeitschr. d. deutsch. geol. Gesellsch.* XLIX. 250.] A thread-like tubular structure attached to the sicula in some graptolites.
**1901** ELLES & WOOD *Monogr. Brit. Graptolites* 6 (*caption*) Nema. **1923** H. H. SWINNERTON *Outl. Palæont.* iv. 35 The first polype of *Didymograptus* was enclosed in a . . sicula. The apex of this is sometimes

in the fossil .. drawn out into a long delicate tube, the nema. **1955** O. M. B. BULMAN *Treat. Invertebr. Paleont. Graptolithina* v6 Nema. Hollow threadlike prolongation of apex of prosicula by which rhabdosome was attached. **1970** R. M. BLACK *Elements Palaeont.* xiv. 211 The sicula .. is a conical structure about 1.5 mm in length. Its apex is extended as a thread-like tube, the nema. **1979** D. L. DINELEY *Fossils* iii. 78 The sicula also bears a thread (the nema).
   **2.** *Biol.* = NEMATODE *n.*
   **1917** *Jrnl. Agric. Res.* XI. 27 Our knowledge of nemas, especially those attacking the roots of plants, is relatively very meager. **1931** STEKHOVEN & ADAM (*title*) Freeliving marine nemas of the Belgian coast. **1946** *Nature* 26 Jan. 107/1 Many of the nema were [*sic*] found encysted within the host tissues as globular bodies. **1970** *Bitki Koruma Bülteni* (Ankara) X. 71 Besides studies of determining the species of plant parasitic nemas in the region, also tests were carried out to find out chemical control measures.

**-nema** ('niːmə), *suffix. Biol.* [f. Gr. νῆμα.] A word-forming element used in terms denoting thread-like structures, as in *PACHYNEMA *n.*, TREPONEMA *n.*, zygonema s.v. ZYGO-.

**nemacide** ('nɛməsaɪd), *n. Agric.* and *Bot.* [f. NEMA(TO- + -CIDE] = *nematocide* s.v. NEMATO-.
   **1933** F. D. HEALD *Man. Plant Dis.* (ed. 2) xxviii. 897 The methods of soil sterilization are: (1) the application of a nemacide or a chemical agent toxic to the nematodes: (2) drenching with boiling water; and (3) steaming. **1940** *Phytopathology* XXX. 334 (*heading*) Ethyl mercury iodide—an effective fungicide and nemacide. **1984** ROBERTS & BOOTHROYD *Fund. Plant Path.* (ed. 2) xiii. 181 Nematodes can be eradicated profitably by treating field soils with .. nemacides. **1987** *Stock & Land* (Melbourne) 12 Nov. 5/3 Trifluralin causing damage in wheat and poor emergence, particularly after interaction with seed dressings and nemacides.

**nemesis**, *n.* Add: [1.] **b.** Hence, a persistent tormentor; a long-standing (usu. unconquerable) rival or enemy. *N. Amer.*
   **1933** J. M. MITCHELL in *Calif. Hist. Soc. Q.* XII. 318 (*title*) Antonio Melendrez, nemesis of William Walker in Baja California. **1961** in WEBSTER s.v., The baseball team was defeated by the first-rate pitching of its old nemesis. **1975** *Business Week* 13 Jan. 78/3 Juan Pablo Perez Alfonzo .., long-time nemesis of the oil companies. **1988** *Fortune* 10 Oct. 11/3 Even IBM, Job's old nemesis, has had a tough time cracking Sun's stronghold.
   **3.** *Astron.* With capital initial. A hypothetical small dark star postulated in a model proposed to explain the supposed cyclical nature of terrestrial mass extinctions, according to which the star orbits the Sun in a highly eccentric orbit which causes it to disturb the Oort cloud approximately every 26 million years, sending a shower of comets into the inner solar system.
   **1984** M. DAVIS et al. in *Nature* 19 Apr. 717/2 If and when the companion is found, we suggest it be named Nemesis, after the Greek goddess ... We worry that if the companion is not found, this paper will be our nemesis. **1984** *N.Y. Times* 25 Dec. I. 36/1 If the Nemesis theory is right, and huge asteroids wipe out much of the life on Earth every 26 million years, where are the craters? **1985** *Nature* 7 Feb. 503/3 On present evidence, the Nemesis hypothesis is both contrived and unworkable. **1986** *Monthly Notes R. Astron. Soc.* CCXVIII. 19 In evolving from its original orbit to the present day, Nemesis should have undergone at least of order $10^3$ revolutions, which by its implication for the Oort Cloud and the cratering record seems to rule out the hypothesis. **1988** *New Scientist* 29 Sept. 65/3, I am sorry to say that almost all astronomers would today agree that Nemesis is dead.

**nemic** ('niːmɪk), *a. Biol.* [f. *NEM(A *n.* + -IC.] Of, pertaining to, or designating a nema or nemas; = NEMATODE *a.*
   **1925** *Official Rec.* (U.S. Dept. Agric.) 2 Sept. 5/1 (*heading*) The nemic parasites of grasshoppers. **1931** STEKHOVEN & ADAM *Freeliving Marine Nemas Belgian Coast* (Musée Royal d'Hist. Naturelle Belgique) 3 The marine nemic Fauna of the Belgian Coast was until now quite unknown. **1936** *Nature* 25 Apr. 709/2 It is found .. that, generally speaking, the richness in quantity of the nemic population depends on the amount of mud and detritus present in the habitat. **1940** B. G. CHITWOOD in B. G. & M. B. Chitwood *Introd. Nematol.* xiii. 193/1 Having brought forward the various theories to account for nemic origin we need examine them in the light of present knowledge. **1987** *Indian Jrnl. Nematol.* XVII. 122 (*heading*) Nemic associations of ginger and turmeric in Orissa. *Ibid.* 122/1 Not much is known about other nemic fauna associated with these crops.

**neo-con** (niːəʊ'kɒn), *a.* and *n. N. Amer.* (chiefly *U.S.*). Also **neocon**. [Abbrev. of *neo-conservative* adj. and n.] = *neo-conservative* adj. and n. s.v. NEO- 1 a.
   **1979** *Washington Post* 20 Feb. B4/2 The neocon movement has roots in the 18th-century concept of Edmund Burke. **1979** *Maclean's Mag.* 13 Aug. 50/3 This tends to make neocons very keen on liberty in the economic sense and a little less sensitive to it in manners and mores. **1985** *Village Voice* (N.Y.) 8 Jan. 10/2 Is this born-again font yet another sign of encroaching neocon hegemony? **1985** W. SAFIRE in *N.Y. Times Mag.* 18 Aug. 8/2 Suddenly most rightwingers started calling themselves *rightists* or *neocons*, short for *neo-conservatives*. **1988** *N.Y. Times* 18 Aug. A27/5 The neo-con intellectuals are privately dismayed at the choice of 'a Kemp without Kemp's baggage'.

**neolithic**, *a.* Add: **b.** In extended use, pejoratively: belonging to a former era; hopelessly outdated and unsophisticated. Cf. STONE AGE *n.* b.
   **1934** [implied in NEOLITHICALLY *adv.* below.] **1940** A. HUXLEY *Let.* 24 Apr. (1969) 452 All languages embody fossilized neolithic metaphysics. **1975** *Economist* 29 Nov. 15/1 A first-past-the-post system will be more likely to place the assembly in the sometimes more corrupt, often comatose and always neolithic hands of the Clydeside Labour party. **1977** *Business Week* 19 Dec. 6/3 Policies that were so Neolithic they created an antibusiness atmosphere as well as inflation and a recession.
   Hence **neo'lithically** *adv.*
   **1934** A. HUXLEY *Beyond Mexique Bay* 299 A baroque theme interpreted by neolithically minded craftsmen.

**neon**, *n.* Add: [3.] **c.** Passing into *adj.* Resembling a neon light in colour or brilliance; hence, bright, gaudy, glowing.
   **1961** in WEBSTER. **1977** *Blair & Ketchum's Country Jrnl.* May 5/3 We will always cherish our memories of .. hot nights around the pool under a neon sky. **1984** M. AMIS *Money* 93 Just then, a middle-aged, blow-dried villain .. urged a neon redhead past our table. **1986** *Good Housekeeping* Sept. 95/1 There are neon knits for bright sparks, cool classics for miniature purists—and plenty of sturdy knockabout pullovers.

**nepotism**, *n.* Add: [2.] **c.** *transf.* Unfair preferment of, or favouritism shown to, friends, protégés, or others within one's sphere of influence.
   **1952** A. BEVAN *In Place of Fear* v. 90 Entitlement to advancement on grounds of merit alone, free from any tinge of political nepotism, must be jealously guarded by any self-respecting profession. **1978** *Economist* 12 Aug. 74/3 A manager .. who actually

believes in management, not political nepotism upstream or down. **1985** *Maclean's Mag.* 23 Sept. 4/1 CPI has proven that corporate nepotism leaves the concertgoer in the last rows of the audience.

**neptunic** (nɛp'tjuːnɪk), *a. Geol.* [f. NEPTUNE *n.* + -IC 1.] = NEPTUNIAN *a.* 2 a; (see also quot. 1949).
   **1888** J. J. H. TEALL *Brit. Petrogr.* 424 Aqueous... This term embraces, or is synonymous with, the following: neptunic, hydatogenic, sedimentary, [etc.]. **1949** H. H. READ *Geology* iii. 93 For the writer, then, the terms igneous and metamorphic are useful only on restricted occasions; a classification of rocks into Neptunic or sedimentary, Volcanic, and Plutonic will be found, he believes, to suit the earth-machine as a whole much better than the customary classification. **1983** *Geology* XI. 455/3 A most puzzling feature of Alpine rocks is the origin of so-called neptunic dikes. *Ibid.*, Neptunic dikes consist of sedimentary materials that fill fissures in older sedimentary rocks.

**nerk** (nɜːk), *n. slang.* Also nurk. [Of uncertain origin: cf. NERD *n.* and JERK *n.*[1] 5.] A foolish, objectionable, or insignificant person. (*contemptuous.*)
   **1966** A. PRIOR *Operators* xv. 235 'Slow it down, you nerk, the girl has to get in,' he yelled. **1970** *Daily Tel.* (Colour Suppl.) 3 July 24/1 The total effect of this nifty trick is that you apparently shot the various paintings.. inside the gallery, without being confronted by a uniformed nurk and arrested on the spot. **1975** CLEMENT & LA FRENAIS *Porridge* 7 Charmless nurk. **1979** C. HAWKE *For Campaign Service* 193 The poor bloody squaddies carry the can, both from the nerks on the street and the nobbers in their own lot. **1980** J. WAINWRIGHT *Dominoes* vi. 143 Cooley turned.. and for the first time saw this latest nerk who wanted to blow holes in his hide. **1984** *Financial Times* 15 Sept. (Jobs Col. Suppl.) p. i/2 It dunmarrer if thas a nerk as longasatorks reet—an if tha dunt get rid o thi dialect wi goan ter collidge, thazzadit!
   Hence **'nerkish** *a.*
   **1975** CLEMENT & LA FRENAIS *Porridge* 60 You are a grotty, nurkish git.

**nerve**, *n.* Add: [8.] [d.] For 'nervousness' read: 'nervousness, esp. that suffered (by an actor, sportsman, etc.) before a performance'.
   **1960** J. BETJEMAN in *London Mag.* Nov. 13 Pre-prize day nerves? Or too much bitter beer? **1986** *Your Horse Mag.* 23/3 It's a complicated business analysing 'nerves'. **1987** *Even. Telegraph* (Grimsby) 7 Dec. 12 Just as nerves began to affect all four players Henry cleared the colours in the seventh frame.

**nervous**, *a.* Add: [9.] **b.** *transf.* Of money: invested cautiously at only short-term risk. Of trading on a stock market: characterized or dominated by apprehension over uncertainties in the market.
   [**1929** *Economist* 26 Oct. 777/1 Many brokers.. find that their correspondence nowadays consists very largely of nervous inquiries for adequate explanations of price-declines, followed.. by requests as to whether shares should be sold.] **1933** *Times* 13 Dec. 14/1 Mr. Douglas proceeds upon the assumptions.. that nervous capital would resume that long-term investment which will accelerate construction; [etc.]. **1955** *Times* 13 Aug. 10/2 Fresh nervous selling before Monday's Cabinet meeting kept stock markets dull yesterday. **1979** *Washington Post* 1 Apr. F17/6 Nervous buying helped push prices of scarce merchandise lower. **1983** *Economist* 24 Sept. 84/3 Markets were nervous ahead of the latest round of Sino-British talks on Hongkong's future.

**nervousness**, *n.* Add: **3.** *transf.* Apprehension caused by uncertainties on a stock market;

instability, 'jumpiness' (of a market or its investors).
   **1929** *Economist* 12 Oct. 674/2 Renewed selling of the shares of 'Red Triangle' cement group was productive of nervousness. **1975** *Forbes* (N.Y.) 15 Jan. 56/2 This all adds up to nervousness and low trading volume in the stock market this year. **1988** *Financial Times* 5 Dec. 29/5 Share prices in Taiwan plunged on Saturday.., amid renewed nervousness over a new capital gains tax on share trading.

**nest**, *n.* Add: [6.] **c.** *Computing.* A set of nested control structures, procedures, or subroutines; also (*Linguistics*), of syntactic units.
   **1963** *IBM Systems Jrnl.* II. 318 A complete DO nest is treated as an optimization unit, whereas the basic block was used in the non-DO case. **1964** *Communications Assoc. Computing Machinery* VII. 416/1 (*heading*) An automatic loader for subroutine nests. **1972** *Computer Jrnl.* XV. 199/1 When a stream is formed from a deep nest of stream functions, processing a single character can involve many function calls. **1985** *Word* XXXVI. 146 Recursion is also frequent on the phrase level where such nests occur as *the serious study of that two thirds of the surface of the earth.*

**net**, *n.*[1] Add: [4.] [c.] (*c*) *Computing*, a local area network.
   **1972** [see *PROTOCOL *n.* 5 d]. **1977** S. HOENER et al. in *Internat. Microcomputers/Minicomputers/Microprocessors '77* xiii. 99 Research has shown that in complex nets a data exchange by fixed data frames (packet switching) is to be aimed at. **1983** *Your Business Computer* Aug. 18/1 Diskless processor/ memory boxes which adapt a standard terminal to work on the net. **1985** *Today's Computers* Nov. 125/1 The net requires you to have intelligence at the terminals but the PCs don't have to be flash and you have to be careful the network will support them.

**-net** (nɛt), *suffix. Computing.* [Cf. *NET *n.*[1] 4 c (c).] Used in names of local area networks and other telecommunications networks, as in *Arpanet*, *CELLNET *n.*, *Euronet* s.v. EURO- 2 a, *Janet*.

**nettlesome**, *a.* Add: **2.** Irritating, vexatious, irksome; also, difficult, awkward, tricky. Chiefly *U.S.*
   *a* **1961** *Newsweek* in *Webster* s.v., Such nettlesome problems as traffic rules for orbiting spacecraft. **1969** *Time* 31 Jan. 52/3 The giants of electricity hope to get their arms around the nettlesome new technologies. **1976** *Times Lit. Suppl.* 18 June 161/5 Whenever what they deemed to be a nettlesome point of usage arose, they took a poll of their panel. **1982** *Times* 24 Nov. 6/7 There has been no movement in other, equally nettlesome problems, such as the current agricultural dispute with the EEC. **1984** S. LANDAU *Dictionaries* vi. 239 The difficulty of distinguishing between lexical units and items in a nomenclature is especially nettlesome in specialized dictionaries.

**network**, *n.* [2.] [c.] Substitute for def.: A net-like or complex system or collection of or of (*a*) topographical features; (*b*) lines of transportation; (*c*) telecommunications routes, esp. telephone lines. See also senses 2 e, f, j below. (Further examples.)
   **1889** [see SWITCHBOARD *a.*]. **1974** U. LE GUIN *Dispossessed* iv. 81 She intended that all communities be connected by communication and transportation networks, so that goods and ideas could get where they were wanted. **1986** *Fortune* 23 June 107/1 The company will concentrate on selling telephone networks and widely varied products, including computers, to plug into those networks.

i. *Math.* A graph, esp. a digraph, in which each edge has associated with it a non-negative number (its *capacity*).

**1962** FORD & FULKERSON *Flows in Networks* i. 2 A directed network or directed linear graph G = [N; *A*] consists of a collection *N* of elements *x*, *y*,.., together with a subset *A* of the ordered pairs (*x*, *y*) of elements taken from *N*. **1965** F. HARARY et al. *Structural Models* xiv. 363 A network consists of a relation on a finite set *V* of points, with its set of lines denoted as usual by *X*, but also including a 'value' assigned to each line. **1972** R. J. WILSON *Introd. Graph Theory* viii. 133 We may now define a network *N* to be a digraph to each arc *a* of which has been assigned a non-negative real number $\psi(a)$ called its capacity.

j. *Computing.* A system of interconnected computers; *spec. ellipt.* for *local area network* s.v. *LOCAL *a.* 2 d or *wide area network* s.v. *WIDE *a.* 12 c. Freq. *attrib.*

**1962** *Electr. Engin.* LXXXI. 376 (*heading*) Airline computer networks speed reservations. **1972** [see NODE *n.* 7 b]. **1977** S. HOENER et al. in *Internat. Microcomputers/Minicomputers/Microprocessors* '77 xiii. 99 Several computer networks already exist among large scale computers mainly,.. or a large scale computer is connected with a star-shaped net of minicomputers... But there are already pure networks made up of minicomputers only. **1984** *Which Micro?* Dec. 20/1 Extras:.. ECONET network interface. **1986** *Daily Tel.* 21 Nov. 4/4 One result of buying different types of equipment has been their lack of compatibility within a network.

**network**, *v.* Add: **2.** *intr.* To make use of one's membership of a 'network' (sense 2 h) to associate or communicate (*with* a person or group, esp. of business colleagues), usu. on an informal basis, and esp. for the exchange of information, etc., or for professional or other advantage. orig. *U.S.*

**1980** M. S. WELCH *Networking* 3 This book will show you how to network. **1982** *Working Woman* June 84 (*caption*) Recreational activities offer time to network with colleagues. **1983** *Washington Post* 20 Apr. B7/2 If you've networked with people when you were doing a film, you have a natural interest in seeing their reaction to the film. **1984** *South China Morning Post* (Business News Suppl.) 27 Jan. 8/7 Most female executives need to network with men more than women. **1988** *Times* 25 Mar. 21/1 She wanted publicity for her charity and seized the opportunity to network.

Also **'networker** *n.* one who uses a network (see esp. sense 2 of the vb.).

**1976** *Forbes* (N.Y.) 15 Feb. 65/1 What's in it for your adult participants, the networkers..? There's an ego gratification to sharing what you're good at with someone who really wants to lap it up. **1980** M. S. WELCH *Networking* i. 18 A good networker uses every resource available to her, and that includes men. **1983** *Internat. Managem.* Oct. 9/1 Many top managers are beginning to show signs of weariness from the demands placed on their time by 'networkers' who commonly seek advice and information and introductions leading to job opportunities. **1985** *Age* (Melbourne) 30 Nov. 13/1 The most successful networker of all time? *Has* to be fourth man Antony Blunt.

**'networking**, *vbl. n.* (Formerly at NETWORK *v.*) [f. NETWORK *v.* + -ING[1].] **1. a.** The action or process of broadcasting on a radio or television network.

**1940** PORTERFIELD & REYNOLDS *We present Television* iv. 149 Television, now that a practicable means of networking has been developed, has been supplied with the final implement necessary for the creation of what will eventually be a nation-wide service. **1956** *Newsweek* 7 May 59 The television networking business is a complicated and delicate

business. **1968** *Listener* 8 Aug. 187/1 The new companies.. operate within a networking system still dominated by Granada, ATV and Thames. **1970** *New Statesman* 4 Sept. 281/3 A small [television] company can rely on getting full networking for just about four programmes a year. **1971** *Writing for B.B.C.* 65 Plays intended for networking.. should not be so Scottish that they cannot be readily understood by listeners in the other parts of the British Isles. **1972** *Computers & Humanities* VII. 96 The potential contribution of computer networking to research and education. **1978** *New Scientist* 7 Sept. 669 Networking also means that particular jobs can be run on special machines rather than many machines handling all types of jobs which is inefficient. **1985** *Personal Computer World* Feb. 192/2 Local area networking involves the transmission of data.. between participating nodes on the network. **1985** *Acorn User* Feb. 21/3 Meadnet is a low-cost networking system which allows up to 16 BBC micros to share disc drives and printer.

**b.** The sharing and exchanging of information within a network of communication; also, in *Computing*, the action or process of linking a number of computers together, esp. within one establishment, in order to share and utilize their resources efficiently; the use of computer networks.

**1967** *Educom* Dec. 8/2 The immediate project involves the networking of medical information. **1972** *Datamation* Apr. 42/1 Unless the problems of [resource] sharing are properly managed, computer networking will fail. **1977** *Business Week* 19 Dec. 64 M/1 The idea of networking—linking work stations together so that they function separately but have access to the same information base—is being hotly debated. **1986** E. L. SCACE in T. C. Bartee *Digital Communications* iii. 130 User information is.. what networking is all about. **1988** COOPER & REDLINGER *Making Spies* vi. 300 These dangers can only be expected to increase as information management becomes more and more centralized and networking the order of the day.

**2.** The action or process of making use of a network (sense 2 h) for the exchange of information, etc., or for professional or other advantage (see sense 2 of the vb.).

**1976** C. L. ATTNEAVE in P. J. Guerin *Family Therapy* xii. 227 'Network' is a noun referring to entire social or family network as the unit of intervention... The techniques.. described by Speck and Attneave.. are those of *assembling* the social network, which they prefer to call a process of *retribalization* rather than 'networking'. **1979** *Working Woman* Oct. 4/2 The way networking works in real life for both men and women goes something like this: when you need help, someone you have known over a period of time, for whom you have done services and favors of friendship, takes your need as the opportunity to return then. **1984** M. PIERCY *Fly away Home* ix. 125 She had filled the house with books about being a successful woman executive, books about networking. **1985** *Toronto Life* Sept. 63/1 The success of a film festival depends on networking—to get the right films it helps to know the right people. **1987** *Catholic Leader* (Brisbane) 3 May 3/1 One of the major benefits from this kind of networking is mutual support by care-givers and the ease of exchange of ideas among people in overlapping fields of care.

**neural**, *a.* and *n.* Add: [A.] **4.** *neural net, network Computing* and *Math.*, any system of interconnections which resembles or is based on the arrangement of neurones in the brain and nervous system; a program, configuration of microprocessors, etc., designed to simulate this.

[**1943** MCCULLOCH & PITTS in *Bull. Math. Biophysics* V. 116 We have.. two explanations of inhibition based on the same general premises, differing only in the assumed nervous nets and, consequently, in the time required for inhibition.] **1950** A. RAPOPORT in *Ibid*. XII. 109 (*heading*) Contribution to the probabilistic theory of neural nets. **1951** J. VON NEUMANN in L. A. Jeffress *Cerebral Mechanisms in Behavior* 22 McCulloch and Pitts have used these units to build up complicated networks which may be called 'formal neural networks'. **1966** S. BEER *Decision & Control* xvii. 457 He has also been responsible for much of the pioneering work in the investigation, analysis and rigorous description of neural nets. **1988** *Times* 25 Feb. 14/6 As neural network computers have developed, so has the opportunity to compare their performance with that of the brain.

**B.** *n. Zool*. In chelonians, each of the row of eight or more bony plates lying along the dorsal line of the carapace between the nuchal and the pygal bones, and characterized by the attachment of the neural spine of an underlying vertebra to its inner surface.

**1896** R. LYDEKKER *R. Nat. Hist*. V. 45 In the middle line of the carapace we have a series of polygonal plates .. which are known as neurals. **1939** *Jrnl. Morphol*. LXV. 384 This seems to indicate that the neurals and the costals are not true dermal ossifications. **1967** P. C. H. PRITCHARD *Living Turtles of World* 10 Behind the proneural comes a midline row of eleven or fewer bones, called neurals. **1987** *Bull. Amer. Mus. Nat. Hist*. CLXXXVI. 20/2 The number of neurals appearing on the surface of the carapace in trionychids varies from 3 to 10.

**neuralgic**, *a*. Add: Hence **neu'ralgically** *adv*., in a neuralgic manner; (*fig*.) painfully.

**1898** G. B. SHAW *Let*. 4 Apr. (1972) II. 26 Fatigue of two days continuous talking & one day's riding struggling hysterically & somewhat neuralgically with effect of change of air. **1973** S. HEATH in *Screen* Spring/Summer 123 It is today that the reality of this break between film and text is beginning .. to be felt as radical experience of cinema; whether naively, .. neuralgically, without any real basis in a conscious theoretical practice. **1977** *Radio Times* 11 June 12/4 The Communist leaders in Prague are neuralgically sensitive about the dissidents' activities.

**neuropeptide** (njʊərəʊ'pɛptaɪd), *n. Biochem*. [f. NEURO- + PEPTIDE *n*.] Any short-chain protein in the nervous system which is capable of acting as a neurotransmitter.

**1975** *Nature* 13 Feb. 499/2 The idea that pituitary neuropeptides can influence behaviour by a direct action on the central nervous system is a recent one. **1980** [see RELEASABLE *a*.]. **1985** *Sci. Amer*. Aug. 36/1 Neuropeptides are short amino acid chains, some of which act both as neurotransmitters when released by neurons and as hormones when secreted by endocrine glands. **1987** *Economist* 26 Dec. 105/3 Neuropeptides, like other neurotransmitters, can be on/off switches; or they can act more subtly by amplifying or dampening a nerve signal.

**neurosis**, *n*. Add: [1.] In mod. use, any mental illness or disorder, not attributable to organic disease, in which contact with external reality is maintained but there is a disabling or distressing exaggeration of states such as anxiety, fear, or obsession. Cf. PSYCHOSIS *n*. 1. (Further examples.)

**1924** W. B. SELBIE *Psychol. Relig*. xv. 286 The inception of this method is due to Professor Sigmund Freud, of Vienna, whose study of neuroses led him to find underlying them certain unfulfilled desires, generally unknown to the patient, and based chiefly on repressed sexuality. **1957** *Encycl. Brit*. XVIII. 667/1 Every man has his breaking point, since neuroses are reactions of persons predisposed to respond in an individual manner to a particular quantity of a meaningful stress. **1970** T. LUPTON *Managem. & Social Sci*. (ed. 2) i. 14 Nor were they

due to neurosis, i.e. to failures in the mental capacity of individuals to adjust to reality. **1983** STAFFORD-CLARK & SMITH *Psychiatry for Students* (ed. 6) i. 16 Neuroses are those disorders of emotional and intellectual functioning which do not deprive a patient of contact with reality.

**3.** In extended use: any more or less specific anxiety or malaise experienced by an individual, group, nation, etc.

**1927** *New Republic* 21 Sept. 129/1 The emphasis has swung from thought to feeling, from bare information and skill to character and personality ... This began with the neuroses of the clinic, was transferred promptly to the neuroses of the family, then to the neuroses of all the large human enterprises, and the neuroses of nations. **1959** I. BERLIN *Four Ess. Liberty* (1969) IV. 198 The mass neurosis of our age is agoraphobia; men are terrified of disintegration and of too little direction. *a* **1967** J. R. ACKERLEY *My Father & Myself* (1971) xii. 106 One more neurosis, shared with my mother: I was worried about bad breath. **1984** V. S. NAIPAUL *Finding Centre* ii. 105 They could deal in an African way with African neuroses; they also knew about herbs and poisons.

**neuter**, *a*. and *n*. Add after NEUTER *v*.: **'neutered** *ppl. a*., castrated (esp. of cats); also *fig*.

**1963** B. VESEY-FITZGERALD *Cat Owner's Encycl*. 39 A neutered cat is much more likely to stay around the house. **1980** L. CODY *Dupe* (1981) xiv. 94 The cat woke Anna at eight, wailing outside her door like a neutered donkey. **1984** *Time* 19 Mar. 15/1 The establishment of a neutered 'civil religion' is offensive to many who believe deeply in their own faiths.

**neutralization**, *n*. Add: **4.** *euphem*. The action or process of rendering harmless; *spec*. killing, assassination. orig. *U.S*.

**1971** *N.Y. Times* 7 Apr. 87/2 His lawyer discussed 'precise neutralization' (the killing of a villager determined to be a Communist) and 'imprecise neutralization' (the killing of a villager not quite determined to be a Communist). **1976** L. JAWORSKI *Right & Power* iii. 32 On July 28, 1971, Hunt wrote a memorandum to Colson entitled 'Neutralization of Ellsburg' ... 'This basic tool is essential in determining how to destroy his public image and credibility.'

**neutralize**, *v*. Add: [3.] **d.** *euphem*. To render (someone) harmless; to put out of action; *spec*. to kill. orig. *U.S*.

**1970** J. G. LOWENSTEIN *Vietnam: December 1969* (U.S. Senate Comm. on Foreign Relations) 4 A coordinated intelligence and operational effort designed to route out Vietcong by killing them, capturing them, or converting them to the Government side; the term 'neutralized' is used for all these results. **1972** F. FITZGERALD *Fire in Lake* xvi. 412 In 1969 the United States set a goal for the Phoenix program to 'neutralize' twenty thousand NFL agents during the year. **1975** B. GARFIELD *Hopscotch* xviii. 172 It was .. possible they'd carry their innate nihilism to its logical extreme and neutralize the next one rather than risk another Kendig on the loose. **1983** 'J. LE CARRÉ' *Little Drummer Girl* II. xxiii. 366 'If you were me .. what would you do with him?' 'Neutralise him.' 'Shoot him?' 'That's your business.'

**nexin** ('nɛksɪn), *n. Biochem*. [f. L. *nex-us* bond + -IN[1].] The protein which constitutes the links between the outer microtubule doublets of the axonemes of eukaryotic cells.

**1970** R. E. STEPHENS in *Biol. Bull*. CXXXIX. 438 The protein represents about 2% of the total axonemal protein and hence less than 1% of the total flagellar protein. The molecular weight by SDS gel electrophoresis is 165,000 ± 10%. The term 'nexin' is proposed for this protein, derived from the Latin *nexus*, a tie binding together members of a group. **1973** *Jrnl. Cell Biol.* LVIII. 628/1 The outer doublet tubules of the axoneme tend to remain together in a cylinder long after digestion appears to have destroyed the nexin links. **1979** *Nature* 1 Mar. 70/2 Any or all of three morphological components of the axoneme might be implicated in either Ca²⁺-sensitive or Ca²⁺-insensitive aspects of the normal control of sliding: the dynein arms themselves; the spoke, central sheath complex; and the interdoublet (nexin) links. **1984** HOLTZMAN & NOVIKOFF *Cells & Organelles* (ed. 3) II. ii. 253 (*caption*) The fine links, made of the protein 'nexin', attaching adjacent doublets to one another, can be extensively stretched without breaking.

**next**, *a*. Add: [I.] [6.] **d.** *Black English* (chiefly *W. Indies*). With definite or indefinite art.: other (esp. designating the second of a pair of things). Freq. *a next* (...), another.
Prob. after African usage: see Holm & Shilling *Dict. Bahamian Eng.* 142.
*a* **1944** E. DUPUCH in Holm & Shilling *Dict. Bahamian Eng.* (1982) 142/1 A slice o' toast in one han' an' a cup o' cawfee in d'nex' han'. **1948** W. A. BUSTAMANTE in *Proc. Conf. Closer Assoc. Brit. W. Indian Colonies* (Colonial Office) 24 You have given us £6,000,000 for building houses to supply two-thirds of the houses. We require a next one-third. **1957** in Cassidy & Le Page *Dict. Jamaican Eng.* (1967) s.v., I use a nex brother name Carl . . I use to go to a nex school. **1961** F. G. CASSIDY *Jamaica Talk* vi. 125 The word *next* in standard English can be used after *the* but not after *a* . . . In Jamaica it has been generalised and is therefore used among the folk . . to mean 'other'; "Im gwine buy a nex' one'—another one. **1982** D. SUTCLIFFE *Brit. Black Eng.* 188 (Gloss.), *Nex'*, (can mean, as adjective) another, different. **1985** C. PHILLIPS *Final Passage* 29 It's only one aunt I has in Sandy Bay, or maybe you hear of a next one.

**nibble**, *n*. Add: **3.** A small quantity of food nibbled or consumed as a snack; (usu. in *pl.*) a morsel or titbit of food, *esp.* one eaten between meals or with a drink. *colloq.* (orig. *U.S.*).
**1909** in WEBSTER. **1968** *Better Homes & Gardens* Jan. 54/1 Appetizers, hors d'oeuvres, canapés, beverages, sweet nibbles, special dips and spreads—you'll find them all here and on the next few pages. **1973** *N.Y. Times Mag.* 2 Dec. 106 It is nice to have a nibble of food in the larder to bring out on occasions like this. **1975** *Times* 12 Apr. 11/2 Fine china and crystal, and fresh nibbles in the bar, are included in the bill. **1987** Z. TOMIN *Coast of Bohemia* iii. 78 We ate a huge plate of nibbles.
**4.** *Computing*. Also **nybble**. [Humorously, after BYTE *n*.] Half a byte; four bits.
**1970** H. A. RODGERS *Funk & Wagnalls Dict. Data Processing Terms* 67/2 *Nibble*, in programmer slang, a portion of a byte. **1977** A. MALVINO *Digital Computer Electronics* 359 We've replaced each 4-bit nibble by a 16-position rotary switch (a byte is 8 bits, a nibble is 4). **1980** B. A. ARTWICK *Microcomputer Interfacing* 331 *Nybble*, half a byte. **1983** *Softline* May-June 18/2 The top nibble of AUDCX contains the distortion parameter for the channel, and the bottom nibble contains the volume information. **1987** *Electronics & Wireless World* Jan. 44/1 A nibble selection input assigns the 4-bit a.d.p.c.m. sample to the first or second half of the 8-bit multiplexed time slot.

‖**Nibelung** ('niːbəluŋ), *n. Germanic Mythol.* Also *erron.* Niblung, Niebelung. Pl. Nibelungen, Nibelungs. [Ger.] **1.** A member of a race of subterranean dwarfs who guarded the hoard of gold and treasures sought and eventually taken by the hero Siegfried. Chiefly in *pl.*
**1814** H. WEBER *Illustr. Northern Antiquities* 25 The Song of the Nibelungen, and the Lament. **1831** CARLYLE in *Westm. Rev.* XV. 37 That night the wayworn Nibelungen are sumptuously lodged. **1867** J. A. SYMONDS *Let.* 1 June (1967) I. 717 The tale of the Niblungs, the story of Gudrun, survive in these churches. **1925** W. J. LOCKE *Great Pandolfo* v. 61 In this hot weather it's like the cave of the Nibelungs. **1959** M. CROSLAND tr. *Rovan's Germany* 168 The Dragon of the Niebelungen . . would one day . . turn Europe upside-down. **1983** *Classical Music* Nov. 21/1 At Covent Garden—gods all white, nibelungs black and everyone looking rather uncomfortable.
**2. a.** *attrib.* Of or pertaining to the Nibelungs. Also *fig*.
**1814** H. WEBER *Illustr. Northern Antiquities* 172 Gold . . from the mines of Nibelung-land. **1831** CARLYLE in *Westm. Rev.* XV. 29 Persuades her to send for the Nibelungen Hoard to Worms. **1898** *Folk-Lore* IX. 372 The Nibelung Treasure in English. References to the Nibelung story are not frequent in early English literature, and they are all old. **1960** T. HUGHES *Lupercal* 13 Nibelung wolves barbed like black pineforest.
**b. Nibelungenlied** (-liːt) [G. *Lied* song], a 13th-cent. Middle High German epic telling the story of Siegfried and the curse of the Nibelungs' treasure.
There have been many adaptations of the story, including Wagner's epic music drama *Der Ring des Nibelungen* (1852-74).
**1810** H. WEBER *Metrical Romances* I. p. lxx, The three principal romances . . are the *Nibelungen Leet, King Rother, and the Heldenbuch*. **1839** H. MARTINEAU *Jrnl.* 8 Sept. in *Autobiogr.* (1877) III. 190 Looked over frescoes from the Niebelungen Lied, in Penny Magazine. **1987** *Dict. Middle Ages* IX. 114/1 The stories told in the *Nibelungenlied* belong to an old and well-attested Germanic heroic style.

**nicad** ('naɪkæd), *n. Electr.* Also ni-cad and with cap. initial. [f. NI(CKEL *n.* + CAD(MIUM *n.*] A battery or cell with a nickel anode, a cadmium cathode, and an electrolyte of potassium hydroxide solution, having various useful properties such as rechargeability and the ability to deliver short bursts of high current. Freq. *attrib.* (Proprietary in U.S.)
**1955** G. W. VINAL *Storage Batteries* ii. 95 Progressive swelling of positive plates in American-made 'Nicad' batteries was corrected by the use of nickelic (black) hydroxide instead of the nickelous hydroxide (green) as the filling for the pockets. **1963** *Gas* Jan. 15/2 Ni-cad type batteries are supplying electrical energy to exotic space vehicles like Tel-Star and Mariner 2. **1979** *Elektor* June 6-04/3 Nicads are particularly suited to high discharge rates. **1985** *Pract. Computing* Oct. 60/1 A battery socket allows the Nicad batteries to be recharged: this takes five hours with the Liberator off, and eight hours with it on. **1986** *Cycletouring* Jan. 31/2 Ni-cads are better able to provide a sufficient current but, at 1.2 V instead of 1.5 V each, the effect is much the same.

**niche**, *n*. Add: [3.] **d.** *Comm.* A position from which an entrepreneur seeks to exploit a gap or opening in an economy, market, etc.; hence, a specialized but highly profitable corner of a commercial market. orig. *U.S.*
**1963** F. BARTH *Role of Entrepreneur* 9 The point at which an entrepreneur seeks to exploit an environment may be described as his *niche*: the position which he occupies in relation to resources, competitors and clients. **1972** *Network Anal. Stud. Human Interaction* 155 It was chiefly through violence and cunning . . that the successful modern entrepreneur could hope to exploit his niche. **1982** PETERS & WATERMAN *In Search of Excellence* vi. 182 Customer orientation is . . a way of finding a particular niche where you are better at something than anybody else. **1986** *Marketing Week* 29 Aug. 19/4 Even Boots . . is beginning to look for a new market niche and is testing concepts such as convenience-type foods and dairy products.

**[4.] b.** (In sense 3 d), *niche advertising, business, market(ing), player.*

**1979** *Business Week* 21 May 126 F/3 My guess is that they'll use it to buy into another smallish, niche market. **1986** *Times* 30 Jan. 17/2 Union would be able to find and occupy niche businesses in the securities industry. **1986** *Press & Jrnl.* (Aberdeen) 17 June 9/4 Some upland producers would survive through 'niche marketing'. **1986** *Times* 6 Sept. 19/2 The move completes the group's strategy of becoming a niche player in the new securities market after the big bang. **1988** *Creative Rev.* Jan. 15/4 Individualism can come in the form of small 'designer' shops, oblique niche advertising. **1988** *Daily Tel.* 30 Mar. 34/6 Pamela Bishop, director and promotions officer, .. defines her strategy as 'niche marketing'.

**nichemanship** ('nɪtʃmənʃɪp, 'niːʃmənʃɪp), *n.* *Comm.* [f. NICHE *n.* + -MANSHIP.] The strategy of (or skill in) identifying and exploiting a niche in the market: see *NICHE *n.* 3 d.

**1982** PETERS & WATERMAN *In Search of Excellence* vi. 183 Nichemanship is not always tidy. But it works. **1984** *Fortune* 19 Mar. 105/1 One strategy that has worked is nichemanship, as practiced by Jerry Sanders of Advanced Micro Devices. **1986** *Aslib Proc.* Apr. 127 Producers and vendors are extremely conscious of the need for perceived high quality services in an extremely volatile and competitive marketplace. 'Nichemanship' is the order of the day in the information industry. **1986** *Business Rev. Weekly* 29 Aug. 56/2 The only sensible strategy for non-bank financial institutions is nichemanship. **1988** *Financial Times* 5 Oct. (Survey Suppl.) p. vii/1 Dr D. R. Francis Narin .. is a successful practitioner of what James H. Kennedy .. of Consultants News, calls 'nichemanship'. Small consultants must find specialities to succeed as the number of consultants is growing faster than the appetite of clients.

‖ **Niçois** (niswa), *n.* and *a.* Also fem. **Niçoise** (niswaz); pl. **Niçois.** [Fr.] **A.** *n.* **1.** A native or inhabitant of the city of Nice in south-eastern France.

**1881** S. R. HOLE *Nice & her Neighbours* vi. 112 The Niçois is in his glory when he can afford to hire a carriage, drive .. to some fête in the neighbourhood, and eat the *lapin garanti.* **1935** LADY FORTESCUE *Perfume from Provence* 22 The Niçois, tired and furious, of course protested violently. **1959** *Chambers's Encycl.* X. 26/2 It [*sc.* the old town] contains the greater number of Italian-speaking Niçois. **1960** E. DAVID *French Provincial Cooking* 165 The Niçois have borrowed this sauce from their neighbours. **1964** E. AMBLER *Kind of Anger* vi. 205 A beautiful young Niçoise, Mademoiselle Lucia Bernardi. **1986** *Time* 17 Nov. 98/2 Museums, up to now, have not shown us much of Matisse the Niçois.

**2.** An object (in quot., a mantle) made in or characteristic of Nice. *rare.*

**1873** *Young Englishwoman* June 286/1 A Niçois of black Sicilienne forming a tight-fitting bodice at the back with a large basque.

**B.** *adj.* **a.** Of, belonging to, or characteristic of Nice, its inhabitants, or their speech.

**1881** S. R. HOLE *Nice & her Neighbours* viii. 147 There are three pictures by the great Niçois painter, Ludovico Bréa. **1897** *Private Life of Queen* ix. 80 She [*sc.* the Queen] bought the poor beaten donkey 'Jacko' from his cruel Niçois master. **1935** LADY FORTESCUE *Perfume from Provence* 18 The nasal Niçois twang. **1960** E. DAVID *French Provincial Cooking* 85 Basil .. figures in Provençal cookery, especially in the famous *Soupe au Pistou* of the Niçois country. **1964** E. AMBLER *Kind of Anger* iii. 73 Her French had a faint Niçois accent. **1981** *Times Lit. Suppl.* 9 Jan. 29/1 The Niçois dialect, and for that matter the Monegascan, is close to that of Genoa.

**b.** *spec.* in *Cookery.* Designating dishes or items of food, esp. garnished with tomatoes,

capers, anchovies, etc., characteristic of Nice or the surrounding region. Freq. used postpositively, as *ratatouille niçoise* s.v. RATATOUILLE *n.* b, SALADE NIÇOISE *n.* Also *absol.*

**1884** F. J. DÉLIÉE *Franco-Amer. Cookery Bk.* 261 (*heading*) Niçoise sauce. **1907** G. A. ESCOFFIER *Guide Mod. Cookery* 621 *Salade Niçoise*, take equal quantities of French beans, potato dice, and quartered tomatoes. Decorate with capers, small, stoned olives, and anchovy fillets. **1939** A. L. SIMON *Conc. Encycl. Gastron.* I. 41 *Niçoise*, (garniture pour poissons.) Tomatoes, garlic, capers and lemon. *Beurre d'Anchois.* **1960** E. DAVID *French Provincial Cooking* 165 A famous Niçois soup of which there are many versions.

**nido** ('naɪdəʊ), *a.* *Chem.* Usu. italicized. [f. L. *nīd-us* nest + -*o.*] Designating (the structure of) a boron compound in whose molecules boron atoms occupy all vertices but one of a notional triangulated polyhedron. Also (with hyphen) as a word-forming element.

**1967** *Office of Naval Res. Aerojet-General Corp. Techn. Rep.* No. 15. 1 Until very recently, .. the only good method of synthesizing these *closo*-compounds was via the *nido*-carborane, $C_2B_4H_8$. **1968** [see *CLOSO *a.*]. **1971** *Inorganic Chem.* X. 214/2 All these structures may also be derived from the parent polyhedral series by a similar repetition of the process by which the nido structures .. were generated from the closo structures. **1976** *Adv. Inorg. Chem. & Radiochem.* XVIII. 4 There are three main structural types, closo, nido and arachno. **1980** *Chem. in Brit.* Nov. 596/1 It is probable that open-cage, *ie* nido, species are involved in the growing of the BCl into the observed $B_nCl_n$ polymers. **1984** GREENWOOD & EARNSHAW *Chem. of Elements* (1986) vi. 185 Nido-boranes have the formula $B_nH_{n+4}$.

‖ **niente** (ni'ente), *n.* (and *adv.*) [It.] **1.** Nothing (more), not anything. Orig. in phr. DOLCE FAR NIENTE *n. phr.*

**1814**, etc. [see DOLCE FAR NIENTE *n. phr.*]. *a* 1930 D. H. LAWRENCE *Compl. Poems* (1964) II. 824 *Nullus, nullus,* nothing and nought *Nichts* and *niente, rien* and *nada.* **1948** E. POUND *Pisan Cantos* lxxiv. 12 Petty larceny In a regime based on grand larceny Might rank as conformity nient'altro With justice shall be redeemed. **1969** Y. CARTER *Mr. Campion's Farthing* xviii. 179 I'm not going to wear any more of it. *Niente.* **1983** *Fortune* 31 Oct. 31/2 Nothing is wrong. Nothing. *Rien. Nada. Niente.*

**2.** *Music.* (Esp. in the work of Ralph Vaughan Williams (1872-1958), British composer). A direction requiring that the sound or tone should fade away gradually to nothing; a fading ending in this style.

**1920** R. VAUGHAN WILLIAMS *London Symphony* (rev. ed.) II. 98 (*in score*) Niente. **1948** —— *Symphony in E Minor* IV. 158 (*in score*) Niente. **1959** D. COOKE *Lang. Mus.* V. 253 The slow finale, .. a hopeless wandering through a dead world ending literally in *niente* (Vaughan Williams's favourite word for a final fade-out of any kind)—nothingness. **1963** A. E. F. DICKINSON *Vaughan Williams* vii. 198 Rhapsody here reaches a new point of indeterminate finish, *niente,* and in a symphony.

‖ **niet** (ɲet), *adv.* and *n.* Also nyet. [Russ. *nyet* no.] **A.** *adv.* = NO *adv.*[3] Freq. denoting a blunt refusal, esp. on the part of Russia or (formerly) the Soviet state.

[**1925** FRASER & GIBBONS *Soldier & Sailor Words* 209 *Niet dobra,* no good. A Russian word used colloquially in the North Russia Expeditionary Force in the War, much as Nichevo .. and usually with an intermediary English expletive, *e.g.,* 'Niet blanky dobra'.] **1934** H. G. WELLS *Exper. Autobiogr.* II. ix. 807, I was all for the planetary rounding off of the revolutionary process. But Stalin .. shook his head and said 'Nyet' reflectively. **1957** *Time* 2 Sept. 16/2

'I sincerely hope,' said the President,.. 'that the Soviet Union will now join us in agreeing.' Preliminary Russian reaction: 'Nyet'. **1968** S. POTTER in H. Longhurst *Never on Weekdays* p. viii, Matchplay for ever! Stroke-play, *niet*. **1987** *Times* 2 Oct. 14/7 The Russians had come a long way from their original stance, which was basically *nyet* to Star Wars.

**B.** *n.* **1.** = NO *n.* 2; a blunt refusal. Also *attrib.*
**1957** *Time* 25 Feb. 31/1 (*heading*) The *Nyet* Man. *Ibid.* 31/2 Gromyko's televised image became a symbol of the cold war... As Russia's first U.N. representative, his *nyet*, uttered in the course of 26 Soviet vetoes, was a byword. **1969** S. HYLAND *Top Bloody Secret* ii. 162 Try the *Niet* stuff and keep them talking. **1972** *Guardian* 19 July 2/2 It is suspected that his [*sc.* Sadat's] Prime Minister.. was asking for offensive arms in Moscow.. and that he received a blunt 'niet'. **1988** *Independent* 26 Mar. 10 (*heading*) The people's *nyet* halts the Baikal pipeline.
**2. *Mr. Niet*,** a person (esp. a Soviet politician) noted for his negative or uncompromising attitude.
**1959** *Daily Mail* 19 May 2/6 Sir David has become Moscow's Mr. Niet. He has said 'No' to insistent demands for bigger credits for Russia. **1988** *Independent* 1 Oct. 5/5 Despite all the apparent hostility in the West to Mr Nyet—he gained his title by casting no less than 25 vetos at the United Nations Security Council in the 1950s—there was considerable respect for him [*sc.* A. Gromyko] as a negotiator.

**nigger,** *n.* (and *a.*) Add: [**1.**] **e.** A person of any colour considered to be despicable or inferior; one who is socially or economically disadvantaged. (*contemptuous* or *disparaging*.)
[**1837**, etc.: see *white nigger* s.v. WHITE *a.* 11 a.] **1922** C. T. CAMPION tr. *Schweitzer's On Edge of Primeval Forest* x. 164 Without this safeguard he [*sc.* the missionary] is soon in danger of becoming a nigger, as it is called here. **1978** *Maledicta* II. 164 The author was once warned by a black gang-leader that 'them Chinese niggers be the worst kind'. **1979** W. KENNEDY *Ironweed* v. 120 It was the church where the Italians went to preserve their souls in a city where Italians were the niggers and micks of a new day. *a***1986** R. DELLUMS in WEBSTER Add. s.v., It's time for somebody to lead all of America's niggers.. all the people who feel left out of the political process.
[**6.**] **d.** As *adj.* Supposedly used by, characteristic of, or suitable for Blacks (*dismissive* and *offensive*); contemptible, disreputable, or despicable; inferior. *U.S. slang.*
**1930** W. FAULKNER *As I lay Dying* 190 She would maybe buy a cheap comb or a bottle of nigger toilet water. **1953** *Sun* (Baltimore) 15 Aug. (B ed.) 10/6 John Kissel.. received a nigger offer from the Ottawa Rough Riders, and accepted it. **1965** 'MALCOLM X' *Autobiogr.* (1966) vi. 162 White gangsters had awakened to the fortunes being made in what they had previously considered 'nigger pennies'; and the numbers game was referred to by the white racketeers as 'nigger pool'. **1978** J. UPDIKE *Coup* (1979) vii. 258 In my student need across the seas I had held a variety of lowly jobs—'nigger work', in the friendly phrase of the lily-white elite of Franchise. **1978** *Maledicta* II. 165 *Nigger logic*, any inferior, erroneous, overly simplistic or absurdly convoluted form of reasoning.

**niggling,** *ppl. a.* Add: [**1.**] **c.** Causing one to experience slight but persistent anxiety or annoyance; troublesome or irritating in a petty way. Freq. as *niggling doubt, fear.*
**1945** J. CORBETT *Agent No. 5* vii. 71 Into seclusion where he could.. pour out the whole of his miserable thoughts and niggling suspicions. **1972** *Which?* Apr. 63/2 Not a high performance car, but quiet,

comfortable, touring saloon... A few niggling features like poor pedals and heavy steering. **1983** S. KITZINGER *Woman's Experience of Sex* i. 114 Perhaps there is the niggling fear that without sex we shall miss out on love and that nobody will want us. **1988** *N.Y. Times* 11 Mar. c22/4 There is a niggling doubt: Are these all actors?

**night,** *n.* Add: [**14.**] **night-terror:** for 'children' read: *esp.* children; usu. in *pl.*
**1892** J. ROYCE *Spirit Mod. Philos.* 241 *Night-terrors, of a known pathological type. **1937** *Discovery* Dec. 369/1 It would be easy to dismiss these stories as mere figments of the black man's night-terrors. **1986** *Sunday Times* 4 May 9/2 Night terrors are generally phenomena of the early night, arising during very deep, slow-wave sleep.

**Nikkei** ('nɪːkeɪ, nɪ'keɪ), *n.* (*attrib.*) [a. Jap., abbrev. of *Nihon Keizai Shimbun*, the Japanese Economic Journal, Japan's principal financial daily newspaper.] **Nikkei index, stock average,** etc., (an index of) the relative price of representative shares on the Tokyo Stock Exchange, calculated since 1974 by the newspaper. Formerly (now only unofficially) also **Nikkei Dow(-Jones) average,** etc. Cf. DOW-JONES *n.*
The index was originally calculated (from 1949) by the Tokyo Stock Exchange itself.
**1974** *Japan Econ. Jrnl.* 3 Dec. 1/5 The Nihon Keizai Shimbun has completed a composite daily index of most sensitive commodities, called the Nikkei Index of Commodity Prices, and begun printing it in its editions. **1975** *Bank of Japan Econ. Statistics Monthly* Apr. 111 (*table*) Principal Stock Price Indicators... Tokyo Stock Price Index.. (Base Period Jan. 4, 1968)... The Nikkei Dow Jones averages (T.S.E. 225 selected stocks).. (Base period .. May 16, 1949 (176.21)). **1977** *Economist* 8 Jan. 99/1 The Tokyo stock exchange.. reopened to break the Y5000 barrier on the Nikkei-Dow Jones industrial average for the first time since the summer of 1973. **1979** *Far Eastern Econ. Rev.* 18 May 104/1 The 225-stock Nikkei Dow Jones Average climbed to three consecutive all-time records. **1985** *Bank of Japan Econ. Statistics Monthly* June 109 (*table*) The Nikkei Stock Average (T.S.E. 225 selected stocks)... (Base period.. May 16, 1949 (176.21)). **1988** *Daily Tel.* 12 Jan. 16/4 (*table*) World market indices.. Japan *Nikkei Dow*. **1988** *Financial Times* 14 Oct. 19/1 The Nikkei index of leading shares is comfortably above its pre-crash high.

‖**ninja** ('nɪndʒa), *n.* Pl. **ninja.** [Jap., = practitioner of stealth, spy, f. *nin* stealth, invisibility + *ja* person.] A Japanese warrior trained in the art of *ninjutsu*. Also *transf.* and *attrib.*
**1964** I. FLEMING *You only live Twice* x. 126 The men.. are now learning to be *ninja* or 'stealers-in'. **1975** *Publishers Weekly* 31 Mar. 53/1 The medieval Japanese warrior clan called *ninja*. **1985** *Times* 27 Sept. 8/6 Two men dressed in Japanese ninja warrior clothes shot dead an elderly British couple. **1986** *Telegraph* (Brisbane) 9 July 5/2 An American burglar, reputed to have used the ancient arts of Ninja assassins during night prowls.. dubbed the 'Migrant Ninja' after the black-robed stealthy killers of old Japan.

‖**ninjutsu** (nɪn'dʒʊtsu), *n.* Also ninjitsu. [Jap., f. *nin* stealth, invisibility + *jutsu, jitsu* art, science.] The Japanese art of stealth or invisibility, developed in feudal times (esp. after the Azutsi-Momoyama Period) for military espionage, and subsequently used in the training of warriors and others.
**1964** I. FLEMING *You only live Twice* x. 126 My agents are trained in one of the arts most dreaded in Japan—*ninjutsu*, which is, literally, the art of stealth

or invisibility. **1970** WESTBROOK & RATTI *Aikido &* *Dynamic Sphere* 367 *Ninjutsu*, the technique of *ninja*, the Japanese 'commando' and super-spy. **1974** *Age* (Melbourne) 7 May 8/7 Ninjitsu, the fine art of espionage, was believed to have originated in China more than 2000 years ago. It took root in Japan many hundreds of years later. **1981** *Best of Karate '81* Spring 18/3 In order to keep tyranny from casting its ugly shadow upon that part of Japan for a long time to come, it became the duty of the young men, village farmers and tradesmen to study the art of ninjitsu. **1988** *Daily Tel.* 22 Nov. 3/2 He ran a club teaching Ninjutsu, which uses replicas of weapons wielded by the Ninja assassins hired by Japanese feudal war lords to eliminate their rivals.

‖**Niño** ('ni:ɲo, anglicized 'ni:njəʊ), *n.* [Shortening of \*EL NIÑO *n.*] = \*EL NIÑO *n.*
Since *El* = 'the', this is the more correct form with *the* or a plural.
**1932** *Geography* XVII. 94 The abnormal warm water of 25°-28°C. felt as warm current from the north . . is called the niño current by the Peruvian people. **1977** *Sci. Amer.* July 60/3 The Niño extended southward along the entire Peruvian coast and remained longer than ever before—more than a year and a half. **1986** *Ibid.* June 55H/3 Such relatively intense Niños were observed . . most recently . . in 1982-83, when the sea surface off Peru warmed by more than seven degrees Celsius. **1986** *Independent* 29 Dec. 2 Normally dry areas, such as the western coast of Peru, have heavy rains during an extreme Niño.

**nipple** *n.* Add: 'nippled (*ppl.*) *a.*, furnished with or possessing a nipple or nipples; also *fig.*
**1971** *Daily Tel.* (Colour Suppl.) 19 Feb. 28/1 An enormous pinkish castle, proudly nippled with a pair of towers. **1978** M. PUZO *Fools Die* xxxvii. 425 At the sight of the nippled breasts Janelle felt a surge of sexual lust.

**niridazole** (‚naɪ'rɪdəzəʊl), *n.* *Pharm.* [f. NI(T)R(O- + IM)IDAZOLE *n.*] An anthelminthic drug which has been used in the treatment of schistosomiasis and is usually given orally; 1-(5-nitrothiazol-2-yl) imidazolidin-2-one, $C_6H_6$-$N_4O_3S$.
**1966** *Brit. Med. Jrnl.* 19 Nov. 1261/2 A male child aged 17 months weighing 23 lb. 14 oz. (11 kg.) recently died in the Mwanza General Hospital following Ambilhar (niridazole) therapy. **1968** *Sci. Jrnl.* Oct. 7/1 It is only some two years ago that CIBA scientists achieved the breakthrough that made niridazole, better known as Ambilhar, available as an alternative to the harsh antimony drugs. **1978** *Nature* 22 June 628/1 The development of niridazole has provided an important new therapy for schistosomiasis due to *Schistosoma haematobium.* **1985** *Ann. Rev. Pharmacol. & Toxicol.* XXV. 499 Factors other than the need for multiple dosing and the occurrence of occasional severe CNS side effects, which militate against the clinical acceptability of niridazole, are immunosuppression . . , mutagenicity, and carcinogenicity.

**nitrene** ('naɪtri:n), *n.* *Chem.* [f. NITR(O- + -ENE.] Any organic compound whose molecule contains a nitrogen atom bearing two lone pairs of electrons.
**1960** G. SMOLINSKY in *Jrnl. Amer. Chem. Soc.* LXXXII. 4717/2 It appeared likely that in a suitably constituted molecule such as 2,4,6-trimethyl-2'-azidobiphenyl . . it might prove possible to observe an insertion of the 'nitrene', -N:, into a C–H bond. **1966** *Jrnl. Org. Chem.* XXXI. 3883/2 It seems clear . . that nitrenes are frequently involved as intermediates in the triethyl phosphite deoxygenation of aromatic nitro compounds. **1979** *Nature* 30 Aug. 841/1 Nitrenes generated from aryl azides have been used to distinguish intrinsic from extrinsic membrane proteins. **1987** *Tetrahedron Lett.* XXVIII.

5497 The azo/azide substrate . . was chosen for its seemingly favorable prerequisites: Slow photo-$N_2$-elimination, fixation of the potential nitrene function in close proximity to the $\pi$-plane of the N=N double bond.

**nobbler**, *n.*[1] Add: [1.] **b.** One who secures the support of jurors, etc. by bribery or intimidation.
**1982** *Times* 2 Oct. 3/2 Judge Peter Slot ordered a 48-strong police guard on the jury . . to deter would-be 'nobblers' because of recent approaches to jurors in other cases. **1987** *Independent* 2 July 3/5 Nobblers were paid to intimidate jury members or witnesses in major court cases involving organised crime gangs.

**noddy**, *n.*[3] Add: **3.** *slang.* Usu. with capital initial. **a. Noddy bike**, a lightweight motorcycle used by police officers on patrol duty before the introduction of panda cars.
**1964** in Hamblett & Deverson *Generation X* 162 We got down the road and a Lawman came up on a Noddy bike (Vesper [*sic*]). **1984** P. BEALE *Partridge's Dict. Slang* (ed. 8) 800/1 Noddy-bike, the L. E. Velocette light motorcycle used by the police for general use before the introduction of 'panda cars'. **1988** P. HOWARD *Winged Words* 42 *Community policing*, the contradiction in terms which tries to square riot shields and baton rounds with memories of the golden age of Noddy bikes, Panda cars, and bobbies on the beat.
**b.** = \**Noddy bike* above; hence, a police officer who rides such a motorcycle.
**1970** P. LAURIE *Scotland Yard* 292 *Noddy*, the lightweight silent motorcycle issued to beat men in the suburbs, so called because their riders cannot safely salute. When they were new, a legendary old sergeant, aggrieved at this lack of respect, growled: 'Well then boy, when you see me, nod your head.' **1972** *Police Rev.* 10 Nov. 1465/1 Making its debut appearance yesterday was the probable successor to the Noddy. **1980** *Amer. Speech 1976* LI. 288 Motorcycle policeman . . noddy.

**Noddy** ('nɒdɪ), *n.*[5] *colloq.* Also **noddy.** [The name of a small, elf-like boy, the central character in a series of stories for young children set in Toyland: f. NOD *v.* (or *n.*[1]) and perh. influenced by NODDY *n.*[1]] *attrib.* Characteristic of or resembling the simple-minded Noddy, his possessions, etc. (esp. dismissively or humorously); of things: toy-like or inconsequential compared with their real counterparts. Esp. as *Noddy car, house.*
**1973** *Times* 16 Feb. 25/3 Ignorance further encourages governments, newspapers and public itself to laugh off hairdressing as a noddyland where the teazy-weazies wave and blow. **1974** *New Society* 11 Apr. 83/1 The family garage built its first ice cream van . . for friends. Those 1955 prototypes have a distinctly Noddy-car air; the front ends were pure cartoon-faces. **1982** *Economist* 6 Mar. 85/1 Architects worry about the British retreating to energy-efficient Noddy houses: bricky dwellings with dormer windows and fancy roofs. **1982** *Christian Science Monitor* 28 Dec. 17/1 The canals are a world of their own, mirroring the English class system. 'There are the noddy, or Tupperware, boats,' the upper-class owner of a luxury narrow-boat observed one morning. **1986** *Daily Express* 20 Aug. 21 A few look like . . plastic noddy cars.

'**noddy**, *n.*[6] *Cinematogr.* and *Television slang.* Also **noddie.** [f. NOD *v.* or *n.*[1]; cf. NODDY *n.*[3]] A brief shot in which the interviewer (or interviewee) is filmed listening or nodding in agreement, usu. recorded after the main interview and edited to form part of it; also, the action captured by such a shot. Usu. in *pl.* Also *attrib.*, as *noddy-shot.*

**1982** *Observer* 12 Dec. 26/1 Those shots of the interviewer agreeing with the interviewee (which as everyone knows are filmed after the interview) are called 'noddies'. **1985** *Listener* 16 May 31/2 This form of TV has the basic features of actuality coverage:.. the voice-over confident of its terms and values, the articulate subject with a point of view, the besuited interviewer performing 'noddies'. **1985** D. MAY in D. J. Enright *Fair of Speech* 132 These [shots] are known as 'noddies', a word delightful both for its nursery air and for its sharp observation of the sage nods that participants in television discussions are inclined to give if they think the cameras are on them. **1986** *Financial Times* 5 Dec. 25/8 Talk of establishing shots, eye-lines and noddy-shots touched tantalisingly on the graft (beside the craft) of television.

**node**, *n.* Add: [**7.**] **c.** *spec.* in *Linguistics.* Any point of a tree diagram (representing sentence structure, etc.) at which branching occurs; also, the end-point of a branch, and as *node point.*

**1957** N. CHOMSKY *Syntactic Structures* vii. 68 The phrase structure of a terminal string is determined from its derivation, by tracing segments back to node points. **1964** J. J. KATZ in Fodor & Katz *Struct. of Lang.* 526 The amalgam is assigned to the set of paths associated with the node (i.e., the point at which an *n*-ary branching occurs) that immediately dominates the sets of paths from which the paths amalgamated were drawn. The amalgam provides one of the meanings for the sequence of lexical items that the node dominates. **1972** R. A. PALMATIER *Gloss. for Eng. Transformational Gram.* 103 In the diagram.. the S labels the sentence node, the NP labels the noun phrase node, and the VP labels the verb phrase node. **1975** *Language* LI. 388 The use of the empty node in the derivation of truncated passives is not motivated empirically, but rather is a way of retaining a transformational analysis of passives. **1976** J. S. GRUBER *Lexical Struct. Syntax & Semantics* I. iv. 96 This is interpreted as a rule which says that a node characterized by v can be lexicalized as *verb.* **1986** *Canad. Jrnl. Linguistics* XXXI. 165 Any grammatical rule which operates to build a constituent and attach it to some node is assumed to have correctly operated.

**d.** *Computing* and *Telecommunications.* A junction in a local or wide area network or any similar system of components interconnected by telecommunications lines; a device occupying such a position.

**1964** *IEEE Trans. Communication Syst.* XII. 5/1 A key attribute of the new media is that it permits cheap formation of *new routes*, yet allows transmission on the order of a million or so bits per second, high enough to be economic yet low enough to be inexpensively processed with existing digital computer techniques at the relay station nodes. **1972** *Sci. Amer.* June 52/3 By last month the network.. included 24 computer centers ('nodes' in the terminology of the system), ranging from Massachusetts to California. **1981** B. KAMDOUM in L. Csaba et al. *Networks from User's Point of View* 471 The network manager.. must design an algorithm which at each node of the network determines the link on which a packet or a message should be routed if it is not already at its destination. **1985** *Personal Computer World* Feb. 195/2 Designs published to date have concentrated on putting the intelligence in the node controller which then allows operation of the system through an ordinary VDU. **1987** *Electronics & Wireless World* Jan. 34/4 Because Infotrac has 65 nodes strategically sited throughout the UK, it almost doubles the number of travel agents who can access Horizon's viewdata booking system.

‖**nomenklatura** (naˌmjɛnklaˈtura, anglicized nəˌmɛnkləˈtjuːrə), *n. Pol.* [Russ., f. L. *nōmenclātūra* NOMENCLATURE *n.*] In the former Soviet Union and other Communist countries: a list of influential posts in government and industry that were filled by Party appointees; *collect.*, the holders of these posts, who enjoyed a number of social and economic privileges. Hence, the powerful élite or 'priviligentsia'.

The influence of the *nomenklatura* waned as a result of perestroika, and the term may be now considered more or less *Hist.*

[**1959** A. AVTORKHANOV *Stalin & Soviet Communist Party* 55 The so-called 'nomenclature officials' of district committees, oblast committees, and the Central Party Committee.] **1963** M. FAINSOD *How Russia is Ruled* (ed. 2) xv. 518 Key functionaries at every supervisory level of the trade-union apparatus are on the nomenklatura of the corresponding or superior Party committee. **1975** *Economist* 12 Apr. 66/1 Russia publishes no Who's Who, and the *nomenklatura* or name list of top office-holders is classified. **1975** G. V. DANIELS tr. *Sakharov's My Country* i. 25 As early as the 1920's and 30's—and definitively in the postwar years—a special Party-bureaucratic stratum was formed... This is the *nomenklatura*, as its members call themselves; or the 'new class', as Milovan Djilas has named them... The *nomenklatura* has.. an inalienable status, and has recently become hereditary. **1986** W. GARNER *Zones of Silence* v. 32 'Stolichnaya'. He poured out a generous measure of vodka. 'The best. Only the *nomenklatura* can buy it in the Soviet workers' paradise.' **1990** *Times* 25 Jan. 13/1 The Mongolian People's Revolutionary Party, 'guiding force' of the world's second-oldest Communist state, this week renounced many of the *nomenklatura's* special privileges.

**nominally**, *adv.* Add: [**3.**] Also in weakened sense: ostensibly, apparently, supposedly; theoretically.

**1926** J. BUCHAN *Dancing Floor* ii. 37, I went to Oxford occasionally, nominally to visit Charles; but.. it generally ended by my spending my time with Vernon. **1963** L. MACNEICE *Varieties of Parable* (1965) iii. 75 Certain very adult things could best be said in books which, nominally at least, were meant for children. **1985** C. RYCROFT *Psychoanalysis & Beyond* xx. 204, I was nominally doing research, though nothing worth publishing ever emerged.

**nonamer** ('nəʊnəmə(r)), *n. Chem.* and *Biochem.* [f. NONA- b + -MER.] A compound whose molecule is formed from nine monomers; also, a molecule of such a compound.

**1946** [see *heptamer* s.v. HEPTA-]. **1987** *Jrnl. Chem. Physics* LXXXVI. 3667 The solvent effect on the structure and dynamics of a polymer is determined by solving the generalized Langevin equation.. for a nonamer in a solvent.

Hence **nona'meric** *a.*

**1960** *Jrnl. Chem. Soc.* 3612 This [flexibility] is even more marked in the nonameric fluoride.

**nootropic** (nəʊəˈtrɒpɪk), *a.* and *n. Pharm.* [f. F. *nootrope* (C. Giurgea 1972, in *Actualités Pharmacologiques* XXV. 150), f. Gr. νόο-ς mind + τροπ-ή turning: see -IC 1.] **A.** *adj.* Designating or characteristic of a group of drugs considered to improve cognitive functioning, esp. to enhance memory, and used to treat some cases of dementia.

**1972** *Arzneimittel-Forschung* XXII. 975/1 Piracetam may be regarded as a precursor of an entirely new category of drugs, for which the designation of 'nootropic agents' has been suggested. **1980** *Psychopharmacol.* LXVIII. 235/1 Nootropic drugs have been shown to facilitate learning and memory and to improve interhemispheric communication in the absence of any analeptic

effects. **1988** *Arch. Internat. de Pharmacodynamie et de Thérapie* CCXCII. 32 The findings presented in this paper give evidence that WEB 1881 FU combines cytoprotective, nootropic and cholinomimetic actions.
**B.** *n.* A nootropic drug.
**1976** C. GIURGEA in *Current Devel. Psychopharmacol.* III. 264 Since piracetam interferes directly with higher brain integrative mechanisms we have suggested for this new class of psychotropic drugs the term, *nootropics*... New 'nootropics' should be made available. **1980** *Times* 22 Aug. 2/8 The preparation is not similar to other drugs, such as ..nootropics.. whose presence is disclosed by the standard tests at athletics meetings. **1982** *Ciba-Geigy Jrnl.* I. 13/3 People suffering from Alzheimer's disease are typical of the patients whom we hope to help by developing new medicines known as nootropics. **1986** *Fortune* 20 Jan. 51/1 Warner-Lambert has been particularly successful, synthesizing a piracetam-based memory-enhancing drug, pramiracetam, and an unrelated nootropic called CI-911.

**noov** (nuːv), *n. slang.* Also noove, noovo. [Repr. abbrev. of NOUV(EAU RICHE *n.*, with (u) lengthened and loosely anglicized to -*oo*- (uː), as in *too, moon*, etc.] A member of the *nouveaux riches*; = *NOUVEAU *n.*
**1984** BARR & LEVY *Official Foodie Handbk.* I. 24/2 *Harpers & Queen* christened the equivalent type the Noovos or Noovs, from nouveaux riches. **1985** S. MOODY *Penny Post* iii. 31 A neighbour of ours... A real noove, pretending to be a farmer. **1986** *Observer* 23 Nov. 57 Noovs could feel gentrified behind a walnut dash. **1986** *Times* 7 Oct. 14/6 The pupils: 45 per cent sons of Old Etonians... Also largish element of noovs to keep up academic standards and/or provide useful business contacts.

**nopaline** ('nəʊpəliːn), *n. Biochem.* [a. F. *nopaline* (A. Goldman et al. 1969, in *Compt. Rend.* CCLXVIII. D. 852), f. *nopal* NOPAL *n.*: see -INE⁵.] An opine, $C_{11}H_{20}N_4O_4$, synthesized by plant cells infected by some tumour-inducing plasmids present in the crown gall pathogen *Agrobacterium tumefaciens.* Cf. OCTOPINE *n.*
**1972** *Plant Physiol.* XLIX. 135/1 Nopaline-producing tumors induced by strain T-37 responded to lysopine and valine as well as to nopaline. **1977** *Nature* 10 Feb. 561/1 Nopaline is not commercially available and this restricts its use. **1983** *Sci. Amer.* June 36/3 One [finding] was that whether a tumor synthesizes octopine or nopaline depends not on the species of the host plant but on the strain of the bacterium that induces the tumor. **1988** *Plant cell Physiol.* XXIX. 777/2 In the present study, we tried to correlate the in vitro *ent*-kaurene synthesizing capacity to the endogenous GA [*sc.* gibberellin] levels of shoot forming, nopaline-type tobacco crown galls.

**Norian** ('nɔːriən), *a. Geol.* [f. NOR(ITE *n.* + -IAN 1.] Of, pertaining to, or designating the second of the three stages constituting the Upper Triassic in Europe. Also *absol.*
**1872** C. H. HITCHCOCK in *Amer. Jrnl. Sci.* III. 44 Recently Dr. T. Sterry Hunt has briefly described the various localities where these rocks occur, and proposed for them the designation of *Norian*, after Norite (from Norway), a name early used for a labradorite rock in Norway. **1888** [see LABRADORIAN *n.* and *a.*]. **1987** *N.Z. Jrnl. Geol. & Geophysics* XXX. 389/1 The bivalves include *Halobia lilliei* Marwick of Oretian age (Late Triassic; Late Karnian-Early Norian). **1985** *Sci. Amer.* Aug. 66/3 The occurrence of the phytosaur genera *Belodon* and *Mystriosuchus* in the Huai Hin Lat formation shows that it must be roughly contemporaneous with formations in Germany that contain the same genera; the latter

formations are assigned to a particular part of the late Triassic, the part called the Norian stage.

**normative**, *a.* Add: '**normativism** *n.*, a normative approach or attitude.
**1970** R. W. FRIEDRICHS *Sociol. of Sociol.* x. 254 Bidney, a sharp critic of the relativizing motifs that have dominated anthropology since the turn of the century, is equally unhappy with the reductive normativism of F. S. C. Northrop. **1979** *Internat. Jrnl. Sociol. of Law* VII. 357 This search for a new professional identity, together with other economic and political factors, made 'normativism', of Kelsenian origin, into the dominant legal theory in legal education. **1984** *Dictionaries* VI. 279 Geeraerts and Janssens conclude by again considering the question of normativism or prescriptivism.

‖**norteamericano** (ˌnɔːrteameriˈkaːno), *n.* and *a.* Also as two words; fem. **norteamericana**. [Sp. and Pg., f. *norte* north + *americano* American.]
**A.** *n.* In Latin America: a citizen or inhabitant of North America, esp. the United States; = NORTH AMERICAN *n.* **B.** *adj.* Of or pertaining to North America (esp. the United States) or its inhabitants, culture, way of life, etc.; = NORTH AMERICAN *a.*
**1910** N. O. WINTER *Brazil & her People of Today* i. 1 'Norte-Americano,' politely suggested a Brazilian to me.. and I accepted the correction. 'We also are Americanos', he continued... 'Ingles' or 'Norte-Americano' would sometimes be asked, although most of the Brazilians can spot the 'Yanqui'. **1947** M. LOWRY *Under Volcano* xii. 372 'Norteamericano, eh,' said the Chief... 'What the hell you think you do around here?' **1956** E. BIRNEY *Sel. Poems* (1966) II. 41 The starchy guitarist will cast His one good eye's black glitter on this *Norteamericano's* by-then-bloodshot face. **1966** E. McGIRR *Funeral was in Spain* 84 'And.. the strongarm boy?' '*Norte americano.* Twenty-four. Around for two years.' **1977** *Time* 28 Mar. 61/1 To begin with, there is Charlotte's education as a *norteamericana.* **1985** J. A. MICHENER *Texas* v. 300 Maria.. was satisfied.. that her norteamericano husband was a good man.

**northing**, *vbl. n.* Add: **3.** *Cartogr.* and *Surveying.* Distance north of a point of origin; hence, a unit of measurement used in calculating this (usu. *pl.*), and expressed as the second co-ordinate of a grid-reference, etc.; also, the co-ordinate or reference itself.
**1767** [see *SOUTHING vbl. n.* 3]. **1820** J. GUMMERE *Treat. Surveying* (ed. 3) II. 115 In a true survey the sum of the northings and southings will be equal, and also those of the eastings and westings. **1902** J. WHITELAW *Surveying* ii. 93 The most accurate method of plotting is.. to calculate the latitudes and departures, or northings, southings, eastings, westings, as they are also called, of each of the lines. **1938** *Final Rep. Departmental Comm. Ordnance Survey* (Min. Agric. & Fisheries) 4 In the case of Farnham Castle keep (562,685 E. 126,897 N.) with a grid interval of 250 metres the 'Eastings' would be 185 units east of grid line 562,500, and the 'Northings' would be 147 units north of grid line 126,750. **1949** T. W. BIRCH *Maps* xv. 112 Location of the point in North London shown in Fig. 63 may be described by saying it is 538,932 metres east of the point of origin, and 177,061 metres north of the point of origin.. as Eastings are always written before Northings, the reference may be written 538932 177061. **1963** P. DRACKETT *Motor Rallying* iii. 40 Let's take a six-figure reference... The first three figures are the 'eastings', and the last three the 'northings'. **1975** J. B. HARLEY *Ordnance Survey Maps* ii. 24 To avoid inconvenience 400 km are added to all easting co-ordinates and 100 km subtracted from all northing co-ordinates. **1985** *Defence Electronics* Oct. 92/1 The MAPS-equipped howitzer will be initialized at a survey station where

universal transverse mercator easting and northing
and altitude co-ordinates are known.

**nortriptyline** (nɔː'trɪptɪliːn), n. Pharm. [f. NOR-
+ TRI- + HE)PTYL n. + -INE⁵: cf. AMITRIPTYLINE
n., PROTRIPTYLINE n.] A tricyclic antidepressant
drug, $C_{19}H_{21}N$, given orally (frequently as the
hydrochloride).
    **1962** Jrnl. Nerv. & Mental Dis. CXXXIV. 564/1
Nortriptyline . . is          5-(gamma-methylaminopro-
pylidene)              dibenzo[a,d]cyclohepta[1,4]diene
hydrochloride. **1965** J. POLLITT Depression &
its Treatment iv. 57 The imipramine group of
drugs   includes   imipramine   (Tofranil),   amitriptyline (Tryptizol, Saroten, Laroxyl), and nortriptyline (Allegron, Aventyl). **1978** [see PROTRIPTYLINE
n.]. **1986** Approved Names (Brit. Pharmacopœia
Comm.)   83   Nortriptyline,   3-(10,11-dihydro-5H-
dibenzo[a,d]cyclohepten-5-ylidene)-propyl(methyl)-
amine.   **1988** Chromatography   CDXXXIX.   359
A   chromatogram   illustrating   the   separation   of
amitriptyline   and   nortriptyline,   with   complete
recovery, from blood plasma is shown in Fig. 3.

**nostalgia**, n. Add: [2.] **b.** Cause for nostalgia
(sense 2 a above); freq. as a collective term for
objects   which   evoke   a   former   era,   esp.
remembered past. Cf. MEMORABILIA n. pl.
    **1976** P. DE VRIES I hear Amer. Swinging ii. 28 Her
potato bread was sheer mouth-watering nostalgia.
**1978** F. WELDON Praxis xxiv. 261 The diet was
nostalgia enough—a daily reminder . . of Willy and
her distracted youth. **1979** United States 1980/81
(Penguin Travel Guides) 320 Pizazz . . sell amusing
nostalgia   and   contemporary   adaptations.   **1988**
Independent 20 Oct. 17/1 It was a curious mixture of
early Seventies nostalgia and third-world embroidery
worn by pale, languid models with decorated feet.

**nostalgist** (nɒ'stældʒɪst), n. [f. NOSTALG(IA n. +
-IST.] A professedly or habitually nostalgic
person;   one   who   attempts   to   recreate   or
sentimentally recollects the past.
    **1962** Economist 1 Sept. 743/1 The railways are
attracting nostalgists whom speed cannot compensate
for the lack of steam. **1977** N.Y. Times Mag. 16 Oct.
130/4 This is the Algonquin [Hotel] of history, of
legend,   of   the   Round   Table,   and   for   die-hard
nostalgists thus it shall ever remain. **1979** Washington
Post 10 Dec. B12/3 Notwithstanding his recent
statement that he doesn't cater to nostalgists, Herman
presented a program that resurrected the past as well
as reflected current popular taste. **1987** N. RANKIN
Dead Man's Chest xv. 143 A fake trappers' annual
rendezvous when nostalgists dress in buckskins.

**notarization** (ˌnəʊtəraɪ'zeɪʃən), n. orig. and
chiefly U.S. [f. NOTARIZE v. + -ATION.] The act
or process of notarizing a document; a record of
this, as stamped and signed by a notary directly
on a document, or in the form of a certificate.
    **1932** North Western Reporter CCXLI. 246/2
Without in any way approving of the notarization of
a statement before an interested attorney acting as
notary, we find there is no impropriety in reading a
statement to the jury provided the notarization or
acknowledgment is omitted. **1977** Transatlantic Rev.
LX. 12 The lawyer had to have the money for
photocopies and notarizations. **1983** Sci. Amer. Mar.
11/1 Eventually one of the three record books turned
up: the slim volume containing the letters from
Cardinal Bellarmine and Galileo's notarization of the
testimony, all illustrated in my article.

**notional**, a. Sense 1 c in Dict. becomes 1 d.
Add: [1.] **c.** Of a period of time (esp. during a
working week): equivalent for the purposes of
calculation to the period stated.
    **1949** Brit. Med. Jrnl. 19 Mar. (Suppl.) 150/1 The
object is to express this aggregate number of hours

per week as a number of notional 'half-days' per
week. **1961** Times 5 Oct. 3/1 The appointment is for
one notional half-day a week. **1976** B. ARMSTRONG
Gloss. TV Terms 65 Notional weekend, the 'floating'
Saturday and Sunday break which production crew,
who are required to work during a normal weekend,
sometimes enjoy on Tuesdays and Wednesdays, thus
suffering two Mondays in a week.

‖**nouveau** (nuvo, nuː'vəʊ), a. and n. Pl.
nouveaux; anglicized -s. [Fr., = new; in sense
A. 1 after NOUVEAU RICHE n. (cf. NEW a. 8 d).]
    **A.** adj. **1. a.** Of persons: possessing recently
acquired   wealth   or   position   (usu.   with
connotation of ostentation or vulgar show);
nouveau riche. Also of wealth so acquired.
    **1955** Holiday Jan. 76/3 The Hollywood rich were
flamboyantly nouveau in the 1920s. **1966** Guardian
12 Jan. 7/6 The nouveau middle classes who just
pulled themselves out of the two up and two down.
**1971** Rolling Stone 24 June 15/2 He walks around the
swimming pool behind his nouveau-money home.
**1987** Observer (Colour Suppl.) 4 Oct. 65/1 Brits seem
to believe that New Yorkers can spiritually launder
their nouveau wealth by spending it on civilised
English folk.
    **b.** nouveau poor, partial tr. of NOUVEAU
PAUVRE n.
    **1975** Sat. Rev. (U.S.) 22 Mar. 43/1 'We are the
nouveau poor,' wails a suburban matron viewing the
shrunken dollar. **1976** Abingdon Herald 25 Nov. 23/5
The Nouveau Poor . . are the sort of people who a
mere decade ago were probably causing equal social
distress by being Nouveau Rich. **1986** Los Angeles
Times (Valley ed.) 21 Dec. II. 14/1 'E. J.'s Gems goes
out on the street and seeks out what I call "A, the
nouveau poor" and "B, the misfits",' Peaker said.
    **2.** Characteristic of the modern style, up-to-
date; new. Cf. NOUVELLE CUISINE n., etc.
    **1974** H. L. FOSTER Ribbin' vi. 287 Still others may
be the children of the noveau [sic] liberated or
'swinger' parents who have not taught them how to
control or withdraw their sensory sexual impulses.
**1982** Face May 4/1 King of nouveau smooch Vic
Godard. **1985** S. LOWRY Young Fogey Handbk. v. 50
One college in particular has accrued fame (or
infamy) as the hotbed of Nouveau Rightism. **1986**
Sunday Express Mag. 2 Nov. 12/3 Regine wants to
shock, revolutionise and woo London to her £2
million nouveau niterie, housed in the old Empress
Club in Berkeley Street.
    **B.** absol. as n. = NOUVEAU RICHE n. (usu. in
pl.).
    **1977** Time 13 June 80/3 Almost all the nouveaux
share a drive to accumulate assets beyond any
expectation of liquidating the lucre. **1980** Washington
Post 20 Jan. E9/5 In fact, the Nouveaux could be
heard muttering enviously that 'the families are as
antique as the antiques'. **1981** C. Ross Scaffold 21
His wife . . was not the jumped-up nouveau that he
had anticipated. **1988** Financial Times 3 Sept. II. p.
xx/6 We are a nice cosy bunch. We don't want any
frightful nouveaus jostling in and shouting, revving
their Volvos, frightening the horses.

‖**nouvelle** (nuvɛl, nuː'vɛl), a. [F. nouvelle, fem.
of nouveau new.] **1.** = NOVEL a. 2 a. Cf.
*NOUVEAU a. 2. Now rare or Obs.
    **1781** in T. Wilkinson Wandering Patentee (1795) II.
106 Mr Wilkinson . . submits to the public, if he
could bring forward detached acts from Shakespear,
Massinger, and others . . it would be affording a
nouvelle and instructive amusement for one night's
performance. **1812** P. EGAN Boxiana 347 His nouvelle
rapid style of execution baffled all his competitors.
**1818** [see FLY n.² 3 b]. **1823** 'J. BEE' Slang 210
Nouvelle—style, and 'quite nouvelle manner of
flooring, his man, the John Bull boxer, &c.' The
word means new; but the impropriety, the silliness of
introducing this and a thousand such French words,
to explain transactions that are purely English, must

strike every one (except '*the historian*') that 'tis a bul[l] confessed.

**2.** *Gastron.* Of, pertaining to, or making use of *nouvelle cuisine*; *spec.* designating a restaurant specializing in this style of cooking, or food prepared in this way. Also *Comb.* as *nouvelle-style*.

**1975** *Newsweek* 11 Aug. 53/1 Loup de Mer en Croûte . . was not exactly light, but Bocuse justifies its *nouvelle* standing by cooking the fish for a mere two minutes under very high heat. **1977** *Bon Appétit* May 24/1 Flour, butter and cream were cut back even below the *nouvelle* minimum. **1981** *Cuisine* Jan.–Feb. 18/2 But few of [the recipes] . . are for elaborate restaurant masterpieces buried under lavish decorations, nor are they the most ostentatiously *nouvelle* of the *nouvelle*. **1983** *N.Y. Times* 27 Feb. x36/6 The food at the Mariposa matches that found in some of New York's best nouvelle restaurants. **1985** *Eating Out in London* (Time Out) 12/3 They do an amazing value set lunch at £8, which is good; light, nouvelle-style food. **1986** *Guardian* 28 Feb. 12/8 The cooking is modern without being nouvelle. **1988** *N.Y. Times* 30 Sept. c21/3 As SoHo rents soared, TriBeCa became a mecca, first for painters and performance artists, then nightclubs and nouvelle bistros, and finally real-estate agents cashing in on the area's new-found cachet.

# O

‖**Obaku** (obaku), *n*. Also (in early use) Oobate. [Jap. *Ōbaku*, f. the name of the monastery near Kyoto at which Ingen (see def.) was superior, named after the monastery to which he belonged in mainland China (in turn named after a master (Chinese *Huang Po*, d. *c*850) of the pre-Rinzai school.] One of the three principal branches of Zen Buddhism, founded in Japan by the Chinese monk Ingen *c*1661. Cf. \*Rɪɴᴢᴀɪ *n*., Soᴛo *n*.

**1833** *Chinese Repository* Nov. (1834) II. 323 There are now in Japan the following sects.. 1. Zen; of which there are three subdivisions, viz. Rinzai, Syootoo, and Oobate, named after Chinese monks. **1894** *Trans. Asiatic Soc. Japan* XXII. 430 The Zen sects.. are divided.. into three divisions. The Rinzai .. from 1168 A.D., the *Sōtō* from 1223 A.D. and the Obaku from 1650 A.D. **1949** [see Soᴛo *n*.]. **1957** *Encycl. Brit.* XII. 955/1 The Zen sect (with its three branches Rinzai, Soto and Obaku) won great favour with the samurai or warrior knights of Japan.

**ochre**, *n*. Sense 4 in Dict. becomes 5. Add: **4.** *Biol.* [After \*ᴀᴍʙᴇʀ *n*.[1] 10.] The nonsense codon UAA; also, a mutant fragment of genetic material containing this. Freq. *attrib.*

**1965** S. Bʀᴇɴɴᴇʀ et al. in *Nature* 5 June 994 We show that the triplets of the *amber* and *ochre* mutants are UAG and UAA, respectively. We suggest that the 'nonsense' codons should be more properly considered to be the codons for chain termination. **1973** R. G. Kʀᴜᴇɢᴇʀ et al. *Introd. Microbiol.* xii. 363/2 Like the amber mutants ochre mutants were capable of growth on some strains of E[*scherichia*] *coli* but not others. **1976** [see \*ᴀᴍʙᴇʀ *n*.[1] 10.] **1983** J. R. S. Fɪɴᴄʜᴀᴍ *Genetics* xiii. 367 We have already.. reviewed the evidence that the amber and ochre codons are UAG and UAA, respectively.

**old**, *a.* (*adv.*, *n*.[1]) Senses 12 c–g in Dict. become 12 d–h. Add: **[B.]** **[I.]** **[1.]** **[c.]** Also *old boot*, a woman or wife.

**1958** F. Nᴏʀᴍᴀɴ *Bang to Rights* III. 129 What about the ironing said Sopey? Well what about it said the old boot. **1974** *Canad. Forces Sentinel* (Ottawa) X. II. 9/2 Talk turns to 'seeing the old boot and sprogs' again. Especially among the younger crew.

**[4.]** **c.** With nouns not usu. considered as marking the passage of time (as '*x* yards old'). *colloq.*

**1967** N. Lᴜᴄᴀs *C.I.D.* vi. 70 Their getaway was only two hundred yards old when their luck changed. **1977** *Observer* 30 Jan. 23/8 The innings was no more than three overs old when Bedi came on. **1984** *Nutshell* (Gainesville ed.) Spring 33 (Advt.), Even after a Maxell recording is 500 plays old, you'll swear it's not a play over five. **1984** *N.Y. Times* 28 May 32/2 The race was 58 laps old when Bedard struck the inside wall between the first and second turns. **1988** *Los Angeles Times* 15 Oct. III. 12/1 Parker made an error before the game was an inning old.

**[III.]** **[12.]** **c.** Designating the oldest district or historic centre of a city, region, etc. Cf. ᴏʟᴅ ᴛᴏᴡɴ *n*. and *vieux port* s.v. ᴠɪᴇᴜx *a*.

**1752**, etc. [see ᴏʟᴅ ᴛᴏᴡɴ *n*.]. **1885** *Weekly New Mexican Rev.* 9 Apr. 3/3 Albuquerque.. has an old town like nearly all of the New Mexico cities. **1933** F. Dᴇ L. Lᴇᴇᴛᴇ *Palestine* vii. 75 The old city [of Jerusalem], as enclosed by Suleiman the Magnificent in 1542, covers little more than two hundred acres of ground. **1952** 'W. Cᴏᴏᴘᴇʀ' *Struggles of Albert Woods*

II. v. 115 Albert met Margaret Dibdin.. at about ten o'clock in the old port. **1970** N. Mᴀʀsʜ *When in Rome* (1972) ii. 24 He stayed at a small hotel.. in Old Rome.

**old lag**, *n. slang*. [f. ᴏʟᴅ *a*. + ʟᴀɢ *n*.[5]] **1.** A former convict or 'lag', *esp.* one previously transported or sentenced to penal servitude. *Austral.*

**1812** J. H. Vᴀᴜx *Vocab. Flash Lang.* in *Mem.* (1819) II. 193 *Old lag*, a man or woman who has been transported, is so called on returning home, by those who are acquainted with the secret. **1853** A. Kɪɴʟᴏᴄʜ *Murray River* 19 They were probably *ci devant* convicts, or, as they are here termed, 'old lags'. **1935** H. McCʀᴀᴇ *My Father* 73 Ulladulla.. was a convict settlement, populated by timbergetters, old lags, bullock-drivers. **1977** B. Sᴄᴏᴛᴛ *My Uncle Arch* 48 Another old lag.. used to make dud two-bobs for a sideline.

**2.** A hardened or habitual prisoner; a recidivist.

**1929** *Times* 6 July 15/2 Sir Henry Dickens.. fully agrees that the 'old lag' is irreclaimable. **1949** A. Wɪʟsᴏɴ *Wrong Set* 131 God knows what sort of awful snobbery the presence of a 'public schoolman' arouses among the old lags, or the warders too for that matter. **1971** Aᴜᴅᴇɴ *Academic Graffiti* No. 51 He would hire old lags To carry his bags. **1986** A. Pᴏᴡᴇʟʟ *Fisher King* xxiv. 150 One is always reading of the overcrowding in prisons, how young offenders are confined with old lags.

**old maid**, *n*. Add: **[1.]** **b.** *fig.* A prim, fussy, or nervous person supposedly reminiscent of an old maid.

**1851** T. Pᴀʀᴋᴇʀ in J. Weiss *Life T. Parker* (1863) II. xix. 105, I am only an *old maid in life*, after all my bettying about in literature and philanthropy. **1911** G. B. Sʜᴀᴡ *Getting Married* 201 I'm a regular old maid. I'm very particular about my belongings. **1989** *Chicago Tribune* 13 Jan. 1. 24/3 He seems to be enjoying himself a little too much and seems more prissy old maid than confirmed old bachelor.

**Olds** (əuldz, əulz), *n*. N. Amer. colloq. [Abbrev. of *Oldsmobile*, the brand name of a type of motor car first built by Ransom Eli *Olds* at the Olds Motor Works in Michigan in 1896 and subsequently by General Motors Corporation.] An Oldsmobile car, *esp.* a large family saloon model.

**1932** *Amer. Motorist* Feb. 4/3 An oil-tempered regulator, automatic choke and thermostatic manifold heat control are refinements destined to play a part in Olds popularity for 1932. **1942** Bᴇʀʀᴇʏ & Vᴀɴ ᴅᴇɴ Bᴀʀᴋ *Amer. Thes. Slang* §81/7 Makes of automobiles.. Olds. **1959** C. Wɪʟʟɪᴀᴍs *Man in Motion* vii. 83, I saw the blue Olds coming. It slid to a stop at the curb. **1976** L. Sᴀɴᴅᴇʀs *Hamlet Warning* iv. 34 Loomis backed his Olds Regency from the *palacio* garage. **1987** A. M. Kᴀʙᴀʟ *Bad Money* II. vi. 161 'I assume you hired some monster.' 'I got an Olds,' Caro admitted.

**olefin**, *n*. Add: **b.** A man-made fibre made from or consisting of a polyolefin, as polyethylene or polypropylene.

**1960** *Mod. Textiles Mag.* Sept. 58 *Olefin*, a manufactured fiber in which the fiber-forming substance is any long chain synthetic polymer composed of at least 85% by weight of ethylene, propylene, or other olefin units. **1975** C. CALASIBETTA et al. *Fairchild's Dict. Fashion* 368/1 *Olefin*, generic term for a man-made fiber made from petroleum by-products, used for women's knitted underwear and hosiery. **1985** *Cincinnati Enquirer* 18 Oct. A10/2 Choose from Queen Anne style and swivel rockers in shrimp, blue or beige.. olefin velvet. **1987** *N.Y. Times* 2 July A10 (Advt.), Heavy olefin pile in natural colors in a chic Berber.

**oleoresinous** (ˌəuliːəuˈrɛzinəs), *a.* (Formerly at OLEORESIN *n.*) Also oleo-resinous. [f. OLEORESIN *n.* + -OUS.] Of the nature of an oleoresin; consisting of or containing oleoresins; *spec.* designating a resin-based varnish which has been mixed with a drying oil in order to increase its drying rate.
**1861** BENTLEY *Man. Bot.* 474 Trees, which abound in an oleo-resinous juice. **1883** HALDANE *Workshop Receipts* II. 289/1 Dissolving any oleo-resinous deposit in.. rectified spirit. **1910** *Chem. Abstr.* IV. 1109 (*heading*) Recent progress in the manufacture of oleo-resinous varnishes without previous fusion. **1935** C. ELLIS *Chem. Synthetic Resins* II. lxx. 1377 The durability was high although oleoresinous varnishes had poor durability if the oil content was low. **1954** H. F. PAYNE *Org. Coating Technol.* I. iv. 191 The oleoresinous varnishes are mixtures of drying oils and varnish resins, usually combined by a heating or 'cooking' process and then thinned or 'reduced' to normal viscosity with a volatile solvent. **1967** LEE & NEVILLE *Handbk. Epoxy Resins* xvii. 29 Oleoresinous enamel was the earliest here enamel introduced. **1979** J. HELLER *Good as Gold* 350 The other vocational opportunities opening up on all sides that he oozed into naturally like an oleoresinous jelly.

**oligarchy**, *n.* Add: **2.** *transf.* Any organization in which power and authority is confined to a small group; the controlling faction in such an organization.
**1933** *Encycl. Social Sci.* XI. 462/2 Oligarchy .. is capable of wide application both to governments and to such extragovernmental groups as parties, churches and business corporations. **1953** *Amer. Political Sci. Rev.* XLVII. 779 The definition of the concept of oligarchy to be adopted is the following: An·oligarchy is an organization characterized by the fact that part of the activities of which it consists, viz., the activities having the highest degree of authority (which have been called 'leadership' or 'executive' activities), are free from control by any of the remainder of the organizational activities. *a*1961 *Sat. Rev.* (U.S.) in *Webster* s.v., High schools are oligarchies .. or whatever you like, but not democracies. **1975** *Economist* 18 Oct. 14/2 New town corporations have a reputation for behaving like marauding giants towards their reluctant host authorities. Labour councillors in particular rail against these undemocratic oligarchies. **1977** LD. ARMSTRONG in *Observer* 8 May 10/1 The Civil Service is a self-perpetuating oligarchy, and what better system is there? **1988** *N.Y. Times* 27 Nov. VII. 23/1 Speech is.. subtly suppressed and homogenized by burgeoning media oligarchies and the tyranny of commerce in the West.

‖**olim** (oˈlim), *n. pl.* [Heb., pl. of *'ōleh* one who ascends.] Jewish immigrants who settle in their spiritual home of Israel.
[**1958** *New Outlook* Jan. 50/1 Nahum Manelson is the teacher of a group of 'Noar Oleh' (immigrant youth), in one of the kibbutzim. **1961** A. A. WEINBERG *Migration & Belonging* 309 Were you ever in a temporary reception camp, Beit Olim, Ulpan or Maabarah before you found your permanent place of abode?] **1962** A. RAMATI *Israel Today* ix. 90 The Jewish Agency.. had spent £340 million on bringing in olim. **1966** *New Yorker* 27 Aug. 54/3 The *olim* who came to Israel are, in Zionist terminology, to be considered as seekers after social and spiritual integration as Jews in the land of the Bible, the home of Jewish history. Hence the *'aliya'* or 'ascent'. **1973** *Jewish Chron.* 19 Jan. 7/4 (Advt.), Pilot tour for intending olim. **1980** *N.Y. Times Mag.* 7 Dec. VI. 100/2 Those who immigrate to the Jewish state have fulfilled the ultimate Zionist injunction and are called olim ('those who go up').

‖**olim** ('əulim), *adv.* [L.] At one time, formerly.
Chiefly introducing an earlier name or style and placed parenthetically after that currently in use.
**1645** S. LUKE *Let.* 23 June in H. Ellis *Orig. Lett. Eng. Hist.* (1846) 3rd Ser. IV. 262 These two men Hobson and Beaumont (olim Capt'.) should come countenanced with your authority to preach the working of miracles. **1901** *N.E.D.* s.v. *Jordan*[1] 1, *Sloane MS.* 73 lf. 133 b (olim 138 b). **1975** *Times Lit. Suppl.* 28 Nov. 1423/1 The former colonial archive at Jakarta (*olim* Batavia).

**olive**, *n.*[1] Add: [7.] **d.** A metal ring or fitting which is tightened under a threaded nut to form a seal, as on a compression joint.
**1919** *Gloss. Aeronaut. Terms* (R. Aeronaut. Soc.) 62 Olive joint. **1946** *Jrnl. R. Aeronaut. Soc.* L. 136/2 These tubes are fitted 5 rows wide and 12 deep into header tanks, by means of gland nuts and olives. **1972** H. KING *Install your own Central Heating* ix. 57 A body sealing cone or 'olive' which slides over the pipe, and a threaded nut, which is tightened on the olive, compressing this on to the pipe to provide a water-tight joint. **1987** *Which?* Sept. 409/2 Remove the old olive from the flow pipe by cutting it off with a hacksaw, taking care not to damage the pipe.

**-olol** (əlɒl), *suffix. Pharm.* [Shortened form of PROPRANOLOL *n.*] Used in the names of beta-adrenoceptor blocking drugs derived from propranolol or having a similar molecular structure.
**1973** *Approved Names* (Brit. Pharmacopœia Comm.) 83 If the following syllables are used, they should be restricted to the groups indicated.. -olol for beta adrenergic receptor blocking agents derived from 1-oxy-3-aminopropan-2-ol.

**Olympian**, *a.* and *n.* Sense A. 1 b in Dict. becomes B. 1 b. Add: [A.] [1.] For def. read: Of, belonging to, or characteristic of Olympus or its inhabitants, the greater gods of ancient Greek mythology; heavenly, celestial; god-like, majestic; also, aloof or superior in manner. (Later examples.)
**1903** G. B. SHAW *Man & Superman* I. 8 The Olympian majesty with which a mane.. of hazel colored hair is thrown back from an imposing brow, suggest[s] Jupiter rather than Apollo. **1944** J. S. HUXLEY *On Living in Revolution* 116 In Olympian detachment from popular feeling. **1975** *Business Week* 17 Feb. 11/1 They [*sc.* the Irish] concocted Olympian heroes from the wars they fought, for themselves and for others. **1988** A. STORR *School of Genius* p. xii, To impose order upon the turmoil and confusion of so long a period of history required an Olympian perspective.
[B.] **3.** *transf.* or *allusively.* One who resembles the gods of Olympus in power, majesty, or detachment; a person of app. superhuman ability or attainment. Cf. TITAN *n.*[1] 2 b.
**1870** [see TITAN *n.*[1] 2 b]. **1933** *Canadian Forum* May 319/3 Obviously there could be no conversation with an Olympian. **1952** C. M. FUESS *Independent Schoolmaster* xii. 189 Side by side with these Olympians the less conspicuous who are glad for modest honors. **1976** BOTHAM & DONNELLY *Valentino* xvii. 120 The Olympians of the dream-making industry were exposed as mere mortals with very basic weaknesses of the flesh.
**O'lympianism** *n.*: also *transf.*, an Olympian sense of power, detachment, etc.

**1982** *Times Lit. Suppl.* 17 Aug. 915/4 Emerson's heirs..edited the Journal according to their own literary notions and their sense of family privacy and Emersonian Olympianism.

**Olympism** (əʊ'lɪmpɪz(ə)m, ə'lɪmp-), *n.* Chiefly *U.S.* [ad. F. *olympisme* (P. de Coubertin 1894, in *L'Idée Olympique* (1966) 5): cf. OLYMPIC *a.*, -ISM.] The spirit, principles, and ideals of the Olympic Games; commitment to or promotion of these values.

**1967** J. G. DIXON tr. *P. de Coubertin's Olympic Idea* 6 In the evening electricity transmitted everywhere the news that hellenic Olympism had re-entered the world after an eclipse of several centuries. **1967** *Internat. Olympic Comm. Newslet.* (1968) X. 349 The IOC has asked what Olympism means to me as a former champion and prize-winner. **1976** R. D. MANDELL *First Mod. Olympics* iv. 89 The members.. were to represent the principles of modern Olympism to their home countries. **1980** *Times* 16 July 19/8 He received a bronze medal for 'assiduously covering the Olympic Games, and the tenth Olympic Congress and IOC sessions and communicating, through his writing, his enthusiasm for Olympism and his faith in the movement'. **1988** *Financial Times* 17 Sept. (Weekend Suppl.) p. xxiv/1 All week, South Korean politicians and Olympic officials have struggled to best each other with rhapsodies on the grand theme of 'Olympism'—arguing that the Seoul Games will be looked back upon as Games of peace, friendship and reconciliation.

**ombro-**, *comb. form.* Add: **ombro'trophic** *a.* *Ecol.* [ad. G. *ombrotroph* (G. E. du Rietz 1954, in *Vegetatio* V.–VI. 572)], chiefly or entirely dependent on precipitation for all nutrients; usu. applied to bogs or mires and their vegetation.

**1964** D. A. RATCLIFFE in J. H. Burnett *Vegetation of Scotl.* x. 428 Some peatland ecologists prefer a simpler initial separation into minerotrophic types.. depending on a terrestrial and therefore nutrient-enriched water supply, and *ombrotrophic types (raised and blanket bogs) depending solely on nutrient-deficient atmospheric moisture and wind-borne particles. **1983** *Jrnl. Bryol.* XII. 335 The ombrotrophic vegetation in Ireland (and especially in western parts) includes several species which are restricted to minerotrophic vegetation in Fennoscandia.

**omertá**, *n.* Add: **2.** *transf.* An oath or code of silence, by which one seeks to protect one's associates or those to whom one feels a sense of obligation.

**1978** *Washington Post* 27 Apr. A22/2 They [*sc.* extreme leftists] cover the terrorists... They even serve as couriers for them... There is a certain *omerta* surrounding terrorism. **1987** *Sunday Tel.* 19 July 20/4 Corruption remains a grave problem in the Met, as does a deeper form of corruption, the *omertà* which seals all lips. **1987** *Independent* 17 Oct. 11/4 Public school delinquency, with its traditions of *omertà*.

**omomyid** (ˌəʊməʊ'maɪɪd), *n.* and *a.* *Palæont.* [f. mod.L. *Omomyidæ*, f. the generic name *Omomys*: see -ID³.] **A.** *n.* An extinct tarsiiform primate belonging to the family Omomyidae, known from Palaeogene fossil remains found in North America and Europe. **B.** *adj.* Of, pertaining to, or resembling an animal of this kind.

**1958** *Smithsonian Misc. Coll.* CXXXVI. I. 31 The lower molars of *Adapis* combine still other characters seen in omomyids, such as the *Omomys*-like talonid and *Washakius*-like metastylid, but with great reduction of the paraconid. *Ibid.* 48 The omomyid lower molars generally show a primitive tricuspid arrangement on the trigonid, although the paraconid

in some forms may be reduced or obscure. **1970** *Nature* 25 July 355/1 Omomyid, anaptomorphid and other predominantly early Tertiary primates of Europe and North America. **1987** *Jrnl. Human Evolution* XVI. 465 Among roughly contemporaneous and older omomyids, *Jemezius* possesses the most detailed similarities with *Steinius* and *Anemorhysis*.

**omphalo-**, *comb. form.* Add: **ˌomphalo'skepsis** [Gr. σκέψις inquiry] = *omphaloscopy* above. **1925** A. HUXLEY *Those Barren Leaves* v. iv. 366 The flesh dies... And there's an end of your *omphaloskepsis. **1983** *Verbatim* Summer 23/1 Presumably, one arrives at game theory through omphaloskepsis.

hence **ˌomphalo'skeptic**, one who engages in omphaloskepsis.

*c***1915** A. HUXLEY *Let.* (1969) 78 You must admit that no *omphaloskeptic, nay, not Plotinus, could have so utterly realized the Infinite as at moments one did to night.

**ˌomphalo'skeptical** *a.* **1978** *Maledicta 1977* I. 268 Please continue your piperitious, planiloquent polemics against those *omphaloskeptical, onychophagic, uxoravalent, philalethic..acritochromatic, and tragomaschaliac pseudoacademicians. **1988** *National Rev.* (U.S.) 30 Sept. 56/3 Everyone from Borromini to Wright..has had his convoluted theosophical and omphalo-skeptical theories and convictions.

**on**, *adv.* (*a.*, *n.*¹) Add: [**A.**] [**13.**] [**f.**] For 'In negative' read 'Freq. in negative', and add further examples.

**1958** *Listener* 30 Oct. 709/2 East might think that Six would be on, but he could reflect that he had shown both his features. **1987** C. LLOYD *Year at Great Dixter* 51, I have never really succeeded with tulips..in a meadow setting... And yet I still feel that, given the right tulip..it should be on.

**i.** Performing or functioning well; *ellipt.* for *on form.*

**1968** *Blues Unlimited* Dec. 10 He was so good and 'on' that he pulled an impromptu encore. **1969** *Listener* 8 May 651/2 Form is elusive. If a footballer is 'on', and the ball is running for him, there is the anxiety that this may not last. **1976** in *Webster's Sports Dict.* 289/1 He was *on* and couldn't miss a shot.

**on**, *prep.* Senses 20 a–f in Dict. become 20 b–g. Add: [**I.**] [**1.**] [**b.**] (*b*) Said in reference to the level or storey of a building, as *on the first floor,* etc. (i.e. located at or within; occupying all or part of).

**1751** JOHNSON *Rambler* No. 161 ¶5 The lodgers on the first floor had stipulated that [etc.]. **1837** [see BAGATELLE *n.* 2 b]. **1891** HARDY *Group of Noble Dames* I. i. 3 Eastward, one window on the upper floor was open. **1916** G. B. SHAW *Pygmalion* II. 117 It is a room on the first floor. **1939** W. S. MAUGHAM *Christmas Holiday* iii. 70 We heard that he'd been taken to a cell on the fourth floor of the prison. **1962** I. MURDOCH *Unofficial Rose* II. vii. 69 The room, which was on the ground floor, had windows on both sides. **1980** V. S. PRITCHETT *Edge of Cliff* 112 Their flat was on the ground floor.

[**g.**] (*e*) In receipt of a wage, salary, etc. of (a specific amount).

**1972** *Daily Tel.* (Colour Suppl.) 4 Feb. 19 (Advt.), Think about the pay (by 20, as aircrew, you could be on £2110 a year). **1987** *World Soccer* Mar. 18/2 While he was with Sampdoria, he was 'on' some £300,000 a year, tax free, plus free accommodation and travel and car.

[**2.**] **b.** Above or against a background of (a contrasting colour). Freq. in *Heraldry.* Also *transf.*

**1572** J. BOSSEWELL *Armorie* II. f. 34ᵛ, The fourth beareth Azure, on a Bende Argent..a Lyon Sable.

**1751** CHAMBERS *Cycl.*, *Ermines* is used by some English writers for the reverse of ermine, i.e. for white spots on a black field. **1858** HAWTHORNE *Passages from Fr. & It. Note-bks.* (1871) I. 160 A statelier dome . . shining on the background of the night of Time. **1929** E. BOWEN *Last Sept.* I. viii. 88 On the bright sky, opposite, Mr. Montmorency's pale face hung like an apparition's. **1936** G. B. SHAW *Millionairess* II. 159 A design of dull purple wreaths on a dark yellow background. **1973** 'E. McBAIN' *Let's hear It* vi. 75 The headline is 'Red On Red' . . . The idea is to get this big *red* feeling.

**c.** Indicating possession of a characteristic feature, esp. of appearance.

**1869** 'MARK TWAIN' *Innoc. Abr.* 434 One brute . . had a neck on him like a bowsprit. **1939** I. BAIRD *Waste Heritage* xxiii. 324 The Hindu had the most perfect body Matt had ever seen on a man. **1985** 'J. HIGGINS' *Confessional* (1986) 9 The white devil's face on him beneath the brim of the old felt hat.

**d.** Carried on or about one's person.

**1932** D. L. SAYERS *Have his Carcase* xxvi. 352 Do you happen to have a railway time-table on you? **1968** E. BOWEN *Eva Trout* (1969) I. vii. 87 She . . drew out what remained in the bank in cash and brought it to Broadstairs on her person. **1976** *S. Wales Echo* 27 Nov. 3/5 She couldn't have gone far, she only had about £1 on her.

**[3.] b.** *Sport.* Expressing the relationship between opposing players in attacking or defensive situations: in opposition to, against, as in *one-(two-,* etc.)*on-one, man-on-man.* Also *transf.* in gen. contexts. Chiefly *N. Amer.*

**1939** *Scholastic Coach* Oct. 34/3 Other basic defensive drills include the one-on-one, where an offensive man receives the ball and tries to outmaneuver a guard. **1948** A. F. RUPP *Championship Basketball* xix. 172 This brings us to our next situation which is the 3 on 2. **1955** K. LOEFFLER *On Basketball* vi. 121 Its front three can break quickly going from defense to offense with three on two. **1973** J. BUKATA *One-on-One* 8 He would often spend 12 to 14 hours a day . . participating in one-on-one, two-on-two or three-on-three games. **1989** *New Yorker* 2 Jan. 38/3 As he [*sc.* Reagan] had done in Sacramento, he decided against having one-on-one meetings with aides and officials. He wanted other people . . in the room.

**[10.] d.** Indicating position in serial order: up to, at (a specific point). *colloq.*

**1971** P. PURSER *Holy Father's Navy* iv. 22 We were already on the second of the two bottles we'd bought at the duty-free shop. **1988** A. LURIE *Truth about Lorin Jones* ii. 28 He was now on his third wife, Polly's mother having been the first.

**[11.] c.** According to; in the style of, on the model of, after; = UPON *prep.* 11 b.

**1805** WORDSWORTH *Ode to Duty*, This ode is on the model of Gray's Ode to Adversity. **1820** SCOTT *Let.* in J. G. Lockhart *Mem. Life W. Scott* (1837) IV. xi. 371 She ran a set of variations on 'Kenmure's on and awa'. **1886** *Pall Mall Gaz.* 10 Dec. 12/1 Percival's new model of the præpostorial system, carried out on Dr. Arnold's lines. **1942** E. BOWEN *Bowen's Court* i. 16 The inner frame of the front door and the mantelpiece are on the Roman pattern. **1967** A. CARTER *Magic Toyshop* i. 3 She performed a number of variations on the basic bread-pudding recipe. **1977** B. F. CHAMBERLIN in Bond & McLeod *Newslett. to Newspapers* IV. 252 A spoof on a pirated letter written by Williams.

**[II.] [20.] a.** Indicating that which forms the means of sustenance. Also *fig.* Cf. UPON *prep.* 11 e.

*c*1000 *Leechd. Early Eng.* (1865) II. 62 Eft genim swines scearn þær þe on dun lande and wyrtum libbe. **1486** *Bk. St. Albans* sig. C viij, She fedith on all maner of flesh. **1591** SHAKES. *Two Gent.* I. ii. 106 Injurious Waspes, to feede on such sweet hony, And kill the Bees that yeelde it, with your stings. **1661** PEPYS *Diary* 10 Mar. (1970) II. 52 Dined at home on

a poor Lenten dinner of Coleworts and bacon. **1733** POPE *Ess. Man* III. 61 All feed on one vain patron. **1871** E. LEAR *Owl & Pussy-Cat* in *Nonsense Songs*, They dined on mince and slices of quince, Which they ate with a runcible spoon. **1950** G. B. SHAW *Farfetched Fables* VI. 126 They found they could live on air, and that eating and drinking caused diseases of which their bodies died. **1954** D. ABSE *Ash on Young Man's Sleeve* 62 Then he'd feed us on ice cream. **1975** G. LYALL *Judas Country* xxiv. 179 A TWA crew . . was breakfasting on turkey sandwiches at the next table.

**on-,** *prefix*[1]. Add: [4.] [b.] **on-chip**, designating or pertaining to circuitry included in a single integrated circuit or in the same integrated circuit as a given device.

**1976** *Aviation Week* 20 Sept. 65/2 Funded industry study to determine how best to use new 'computer-on-a-chip' microcircuit technology to achieve on-chip fault-detection circuitry . . is planned by Air Force Avionics Laboratory. **1983** *Sci. Amer.* Apr. 46/1 The smallest accelerometer fabricated up to now is an oxide-cantilever device with an on-chip amplifier. **1988** *Computer Weekly* 1 Dec. 26/5 Browne observes that the huge transistor count could be used to add all kinds of on-chip functionality, like several Mbytes of on-chip memory, local area network interfaces and maybe more than one cpu.

**on-coming,** *a.* Add: [1.] **b.** *spec.* of traffic, a motor vehicle, etc.: facing, travelling towards, or in the opposite direction to another road-user.

**1931** *Draft of Highway Code* (Min. of Transport) 4 It is the usual practice when leading an animal to keep to the right so as to face oncoming traffic. **1944** 'A. A. FAIR' *Give 'em Ax* xiv. 159 Then you turned abruptly in front of oncoming traffic. **1963** 'J. LE CARRÉ' *Spy who came in from Cold* xxiv. 208 He had his headlights on full . . and didn't bother to dip for oncoming traffic on the other lane. **1976** M. HINXMAN *End of Good Woman* i. 5 The headlights of the on-coming cars. **1987** J. UGLOW *George Eliot* vi. 107 The young girl . . about to be rudely awoken by the crash of the oncoming barge.

**one,** *numeral a., pron.,* etc. Add: [B.] [V.] [21.] **b.** Denoting the speaker, esp. in direct or indirect speech, with a hint or suggestion of social superiority or affectation.

**1844** *Punch* VI. 52/2, I mean not to include the real ills, but to speak of the numberless trifles that irritate and annoy one. **1905** H. A. VACHELL *Hill* v. 92 The Caterpillar . . murmured—'One doesn't pretend to be a Christian, but as a gentleman one accepts a bit of bad luck without gnashing one's teeth.' **1942** E. WAUGH *Put out More Flags* i. 24 Lady Seal . . had told Anderson it [*sc.* the bombardment] was probably only a practice. That was what one told servants. **1956** R. HENRIQUES *Red over Green* iii. 60 He meant nothing . . . One can't even remember his face. **1959** E. H. CLEMENTS *High Tension* ii. 19 'Do you often have your fan-mail in person?' . . 'Not often. One isn't in the telephone book.' **1982** F. JOHNSON *Out of Order* 9 How to persuade the *Telegraph* that . . one was a man of immense culture? (Saying 'one' when you mean 'I' would do for a start, I decided.)

**onlend** (ɒn'lɛnd), *v. Comm.* Also **on-lend.** [f. ON-[1] + LEND *v.*[2]] *trans.* To lend (borrowed money) to a third party. Also *absol.*

**1972** *Times* 6 June 2/2 Except for on-lending to local and public authorities, nearly all capital expenditure of the Stormont Government has . . been met from revenue. **1973** *Times* 12 Dec. 21/7 The clearers on-lent a net £523m to other banks. **1979** *Economist* 14 July 93/1 They can also on-lend as much as they can raise on current account. **1981** *Daily Tel.* 28 July 15/2 With interest rates reaching record levels during the year, the Bank was able to make a handsome return by investing this money or

onlending it to customers. **1988** *Euromoney* Feb. 93/1 When manufacturing subsidiaries find themselves short of cash they call the co-ordination centre which uses any excess liquidity to onlend.
Hence **on'lending** *vbl. n.*
**1976** *N.Z. Financial Times* 10 Dec. 27/2 Several loans were by way of direct onlending of overseas borrowings. **1987** *Amer. Banker* 15 Apr. 2/3 Onlending is a technique in which a bank lends money to the central bank, which is immediately returned to the lending bank and then 'onlent' to one of the bank's clients in the country.

**onomastician** (ˌɒnəmæ'stɪʃən), *n.* [f. ONOMASTIC *a.* and *n.* + -IAN: see -ICIAN.] One who studies the origins and formation of proper names; a student of onomastics.
**1975** *Verbatim* II. 7/2 Many a serious onomastician has begun by collecting odd names for fun. **1978** McDAVID & O'CAIN in *Names* Mar. 112 Such research can only be carried out where intrepid and dedicated onomasticians like Claude Neuffer have first laid the foundation. **1984** *Word Ways* XVII. 1. 25 Onomasticians and name aficionados are invited . . to join the recently-formed Illinois Names Society. **1987** I. A. FRASER in A. Small *Picts* 68 The subject of place-names, especially those of Pictland, has always proved to be a minefield strewn with the casualties of would-be onomasticians.

**on-screen** (ɒn'skriːn), *adv.* (*phr.*) and *a.* Also **onscreen,** (as *adv. phr.*) **on screen.** [f. ON *prep.* + SCREEN *n.*: cf. OFF SCREEN *adv.* (*phr.*) and *a.*]
**A.** *adv.* (*phr.*) On a cinema, television, or VDU screen; in a film or television programme.
**1955** *Film Daily* 20 Jan. 1/2 (*heading*) Garbo back on screen—in Metro Camille. **1961** E. GOODMAN *Fifty-Year Decline & Fall of Hollywood* vii. 257 Bogart looked his role on screen and off. **1963** G. JENNINGS *Movie Bk.* iv. 58 Miss Novak began getting actual parts onscreen, the first in *Pushover* with Fred MacMurray. **1972** *New Yorker* 2 Dec. 159/2 A white man being ridiculed the way black men onscreen used to be. **1984** *Times* 3 Dec. 2/6 Management is keen to introduce subbing on-screen. **1985** *Times* 21 Mar. 40/3 (Advt.), We provide worldwide financial news services delivered to customers on-screen through a variety of systems, and by teleprinter.
**B.** *adj.* Shown or appearing on a cinema, television, or VDU screen; making use of or performed with the aid of a VDU screen.
**1963** G. JENNINGS *Movie Bk.* iii. 37 Warner's Vitaphone process, though a historical milestone, did not last long. The disc records were difficult to synchronize with the onscreen action. **1976** *Listener* 23 Sept. 366/3 Let me thank . . the TV Times for revealing what 'today's on-screen faces'—a new and horrible expression—were doing 21 years ago. **1978** *Time* 3 July 45/1 Buck Henry got the job, as well as the on-screen role of Mr. Jordan's celestial assistant. **1983** *Austral. Personal Computer* Sept. 103/2 Some of the six function keys . . were used to select word processing modes from on-screen menus. **1984** *Which Micro?* Dec. 73 (Advt.), Full on-screen editing is available. **1986** *Keyboard Player* Apr. 3/3 The . . edit facilities allow . . musical forms to be . . perfected with the aid of on-screen menus.

**onsell** (ɒn'sɛl), *v. Comm.* Also **on-sell.** [f. ON-¹ + SELL *v.*] *trans.* To sell (an asset, esp. one recently acquired) to a third party, usu. for a profit. Also *absol.*
**1979** 'D. MEIRING' *Foreign Body* x. 100 The four Aramoco partners—can onsell the Arab Light they get. **1981** *Courier-Mail* (Brisbane) 13 Oct. (Business Mail) 6/4 BABs arise when the company gives a security acceptable to a bank in exchange for cash. The bank can then onsell this bill, which has a fixed maturity date, to other organisations with money to invest. **1986** *Euromoney* Jan. (Suppl.) 79/1 The Euro CP dealers, in bidding for paper, will most likely

remain exposed to interest rate movements overnight, since they cannot onsell it until the following morning. **1987** *Business Rev. Weekly* 11 Sept. 107 Leighton is also a property developer, but has traditionally chosen to build and then onsell.

**onyx,** *n.* (and *a.*) Sense 4 in Dict. becomes 4 a. Add: [**4.**] **b.** *attrib.* passing into *adj.* Possessing or characterized by the translucent, striated quality of onyx.
**1890** KIPLING in *Macm. Mag.* Apr. 467/1 His big onyx eyes. **1912** W. B. YEATS in *Poetry* (Chicago) Dec. 67 All wisdom shut into his onyx eyes. Our Father Rosicross sleeps in his tomb. **1976** *Star* (Sheffield) 26 Nov. (Advt.), 1973 Cortina GXL 2000 c.c., onyx green: £950.

**ookinete** (ˌəʊəkɪ'niːt, -'kaɪniːt), *n. Biol.* [ad. G. *Ookinet* (F. Schaudinn 1899, in *Sitzungs-Ber. Gesellsch. naturforsch. Freunde zu Berlin* 176): cf. OO-, KINETIC *a.*] A zygote capable of autonomous movement, *esp.* as a stage in the life cycle of some parasitic protozoa.
**1902** *Proc. R. Soc.* LXX. 74 'Sporozoites', 'blasts', 'ookinetes', 'schizonts', 'amphionts', and 'sporonts' —terms which have their place in schemes dealing with the general morphology and life-history of the group Sporozoa, but are not, as experience shows, well suited for immediate use in describing and referring to the stages of the malaria parasite. **1968** *Trans. R. Soc. Trop. Med. & Hygiene* LXII. 462 The tapering anterior end is truncated, not pointed, and is surmounted by a prominent dense ring, staining red. This is present in all vermicular ookinetes. **1977** T. I. STORER et al. *Elem. Zool.* (ed. 4) xv. 262/2 This becomes a worm-like ookinete that penetrates the gut wall. **1988** *Jrnl. Parasitol.* LXXIV. 433/1 Ookinetes in refractory and susceptible mosquitoes were morphologically similar to those observed in previous studies of this and other malaria species.

**oomycete** (ˌəʊə'maɪsiːt), *n. Biol.* Also **Oo-.** [Anglicized sing. of mod.L. *Oomycetes*, f. Gr. ᾠό-ν egg + MYCETES *n. pl.*] A fungus belonging to the class *Oomycetes* of mainly aquatic saprobic and parasitic fungi, characterized by having a zoospore with two flagella. Usu. *attrib.*
**1901** *Ann. Bot.* XV. 306 This view gives us a provisional explanation of the periplasm . . whilst limiting our speculations to the Oomycetes themselves. **1930** A. T. HENRICI *Molds, Yeasts, & Actinomycetes* i. 18 The common water molds of the genus *Saprolegnia* may be considered to illustrate the life history of an Oomycete. **1967** G. STEVENSON *Biol. Fungi, Bacteria & Viruses* vii. 138 Some Oomycete thalli are self-fertile, others require cross-fertilization between two morphologically similar but compatible strains which are sometimes called plus and minus. **1973** R. G. KRUEGER et al. *Introd. Microbiol.* iii. 75/1 The structural material of the oomycete wall is cellulose, whereas in the chytrids it is usually chitin. **1982** *Developmental Biol.* XCI. 274/2 *Achyla ambisexualis*, an oomycete, grows vegetatively as a multinucleate mycelium on relatively simple media.

**opal,** *n.* Senses 3, 4 in Dict. become 4, 5. Add: **3.** *Biol.* The nonsense codon (NONSENSE *n.* 6 c) UGA; also, a mutant fragment of genetic material containing this. Freq. *attrib.* Cf. *AMBER *n.*¹ 10, *OCHRE *n.* 4.
**1971** *Biochimie* LIII. 503/1 (*table*) Opal. **1976** *Nature* 26 Aug. 757/1 The three codons UAG (amber), UAA (ochre), and UGA (opal) serve as signals for polypeptide chain termination during messenger RNA translation in various prokaryotic and eukaryotic organisms. **1979** [see *AMBER *n.*¹ 10]. **1988** *Proc. Nat. Acad. Sci.* LXXXV. 7064 By using a sensitive opal codon reversion assay, single-base

substitution errors were readily detected in the replication products.

**open**, *a.* (*adv.*) Add: [**I.**] [**5.**] **f.** *U.S. Sport.* Of a player: unmarked or unguarded by a member of the opposing team; *esp.* in phr. *to find* (*hit*, etc.) *the open man*, to pass the ball to the player in a position to receive it.

**1937** F. C. ALLEN *Better Basketball* xxi. 321 This player is now in [a] favorable position to pass to an open man. **1947** D. X. BIBLE *Championship Football* v. 53 (*heading*) Getting Open. Before catching a pass, the receiver must get..away from the defenders. **1964** ANDERSON & ALBECK *Coaching Better Basketball* vii. 118 He will pass to the open cutter as his first duty. **1974** *State* (Columbia, S. Carolina) 15 Feb. 2-B/4 We're passing the ball better, hitting the open man now. **1986** *New Yorker* 24 Mar. 61/3 What sets Bird apart..is his..bent for..finding the open man.

[**7.**] **c.** *Sport.* Of a game or style of play: characterized by action which is spread out over the field; *opp.* TIGHT *a.* 11 a.

**1934** D. JACK *Soccer* 135 Where there is speed and goal-scoring power in the middle and down the wings every effort should be made to exploit them to the full by keeping the game as open as possible. **1954** F. C. AVIS *Soccer Ref. Dict.* 86 Open game, that in which the ball is moved long distances at a time, because the players are well spaced out. **1976** *Morecambe Guardian* 7 Dec. 8/7 Both sides played fast, open rugby to produce a high scoring game. **1981** *Old Etonian Assoc. Rep. 1980* 9 The ground was firm, owing to an overnight frost, and so an open game could be played.

[**22.**] [**c.**] **open date**, (*a*) *U.S. Sport*, a future date for which no fixture has yet been arranged; a date that is free or available. (*b*) an unspecified future date, *esp.* one left undetermined when a travel ticket is bought; (*c*) on pre-packed perishable goods: a date marked to indicate clearly either the date of packing or the latest recommended date for sale; also as *v. trans.*, to mark (a package) with an open date.

**1949** *Richmond* (Va.) *Times-Dispatch* 10 Oct. 13/5 There will be no meeting of the teams to determine which is the better, although each has an *open date on November 12. **1967** B. NORMAN *Matter of Mandrake* i. 9 I'll have a return ticket with an open date. **1971** D. MACKENZIE *Sleep is for Rich* vi. 189 The aeroplane tickets..had been issued in Hamburg, two first class singles from Paris to Sao Paulo, Brazil, with an open date. **1973** *Britannica Bk. of Year* (U.S.) 306 Comprehensive proposals were made [in the U.K.] for a system of open-date marking of prepacked foods. **1977** *N.Y. Times* 1 Sept. A20/4, I congratulate those manufacturers who have been willing to open-date their products. **1979** *Tucson* (Arizona) *Citizen* 20 Sept. 3D/2 The Toros had an open date for an exhibition game against the Rangers. Texas, with an open date available on the way to Anaheim, backed away.

**open-dated** *a.*, (of a ticket) valid for an unspecified period.

**1971** P. DRISCOLL *White Lie Assignment* i. 9 From Munich I had an *open-dated return air ticket.

**open dating** *vbl. n.*, the marking of packaged goods with an open date.

**1970** *Wall St. Jrnl.* 27 July 4/4 The companies generally oppose any *open dating of their products. They argue that their code dates are meant primarily as a management tool to assure that older items are sold first. **1976** *NBR Marketplace* (Wellington, N.Z.) III. 35/3 Unit pricing and open dating are inevitable with the multiplicity of products available and the consumer's growing and real desire for more information on which to base his/her selection of products.

**open goal** *Assoc. Football*, an undefended goal(-mouth); a goal scored into this; also *fig.*

**1934** D. JACK *Soccer* 36, I always endeavoured to draw him near enough to me to indulge in a feint or a dribble past him to an *open goal. **1972** G. GREEN *Great Moments in Sport: Soccer* xv. 134 Sadler..gave Henrique..the chance to save an open goal with his feet after Best had mesmerised and opened the defence with a dazzling dribble. **1986** *Marxism Today* Sept. 17/1 Some of the very important debates like those on Cheltenham, which was an open goal for the trade union movement, were just buried without trace because of all these constant to-ings and fro-ings.

**open interest** *Comm.* (orig. *U.S.*), the number of contracts or commitments outstanding on a commodity market at any given time.

**1959** E. E. NEMMERS *Dict. Econ. & Business* 206 *Open interest, in trading, the amount of a commodity required to satisfy unliquidated futures contracts at any given time. **1967** L. W. BELVEAL *Commodity Speculation* iii. 40 This 10,000 bushels of July wheat..accounted for 80,000 bushels of trading volume and 10,000 bushels of 'open interest' throughout the life of the contract. **1981** G. CHAMBERLAIN *Trading in Options* ii. 15 A broker will be able to provide up-to-date information regarding the open-interest position (i.e. the number of listed option contracts outstanding (open) at any particular time).

**open outcry** *Comm.* (orig. *U.S.*), a system of trading on an organized market or stock exchange in which the dealers call their bids and contracts aloud.

**1968** *Commodity Trading Man.* (Chicago Board of Trade) ix. 43/2 All offerings and bids must be made by *open outcry. **1981** G. CHAMBERLAIN *Trading in Options* viii. 119 Dealing in traded options is by 'open outcry'. **1989** *Independent* 28 Mar. 22 The London International Financial Futures Exchange has also sought to replicate open-outcry trading with its Automated Pit Trading technology.

**open plan**: after 'freq. *attrib.*' read: 'also *transf.* and *fig.*'

**1977** 'A. T. ELLIS' *Sin Eater* 62 The forced bonhomie of open-plan living. **1984** *Spectator* 20 Oct. 29/2 Heaven, I imagine, is open-plan, so we can all be present at the reunification of the Linklaters and their relations.

**Open Tech** [see TECH *n.*[1]], a technical college modelled on the Open University, and providing distance-learning courses of training in technical subjects.

**1980** *Times* 29 Jan. 4/3 The establishment of an 'Open Tech', using the distance-learning techniques of the Open University, to provide part-time courses for adults at technician level was suggested yesterday by Mr James Prior, Secretary of State for Employment. **1986** *Financial Times* 8 Jan. (Survey Suppl.) p. viii/8 An Open Tech has now been founded to use similar distance-learning methods to offer retraining for adults at technician level in industry.

**open**, *v.* Add: [**I.**] [**4.**] **d.** To cut open (the leaves of a book).

**1815** JANE AUSTEN *Let.* 23 Nov. (1952) 432 We have heard much of Scott's account of Paris... Would you favour us with it, supposing you have any set already opened? **1989** *Daily Tel.* (Weekend Suppl.) 25 Feb. p. xiii/7, I..watched him open the uncut pages of a handsome volume with his spectacles..which..left the edge of each page in tatters.

**e.** To cut or polish part of (a rough gem) in order to examine its interior. Occas. with *up*.

**1916** F. B. WADE *Diamonds* iv. 105 When in the rough, the cutter can 'open up' the stone; that is, polish a tiny spot on the surface through which to study the interior. **1961** G. F. LEECHMAN *Opal Bk.* vi. 165 Before our find can be made into a jewel it must be cleaned off and 'opened' here and there to see just where the colour lies. **1965** J. Y. DICKINSON *Bk. Diamonds* viii. 215 *Opening a diamond*, a trade term among diamond cutters for the polishing of a facet on a heavily coated or rough surface diamond in order to secure a 'window' into the interior of the diamond. **1970** E. BRUTON *Diamonds* xvii. 295 It is normally a highly speculative financial operation to buy a coated crystal which has not been opened.

**opener**, *n.* Senses 1 c–f in Dict. become 1 d–g. Add: [**1.**] **c.** *Cards.* One who commences the betting or bidding. Cf. sense 3 below.
   [**1880** W. B. DICK *Amer. Hoyle* (ed. 13) 203 The opener of the pot makes the first bet.] **1892** *Ibid.* (ed. 15) 184 If the delinquent opener discovers and announces his error previous to the draw, any one of the remaining players holding opening cards may . . break the pot. **1932** *Daily Tel.* 8 Oct. 15/5 If the responder makes a minimum bid of One No-Trump or Two of a minor suit over the opener's One of a major suit, the first message it conveys is that he has not got normal support in the opener's suit. **1964** N. SQUIRE *Bidding at Bridge* iii. 29 The opener must have a minimum of 12 points. **1980** A. J. JONES *Game Theory* 258 Working clockwise from the player on the dealer's left, each player has an opportunity to make the opening bet. The player to do so, known as the opener, must hold at least a pair of jacks.

**opening**, *vbl. n.* Senses 1 b–c in Dict. become 1 c–d. Add: [**1.**] **b.** *spec.* in Quaker use, a divine disclosure or revelation; an intuitive insight (into the nature of God, etc.).
   *c* **1675** G. FOX *Jrnl.* (1952) i. 11 After I had received one opening from the Lord that to be bred at Oxford or Cambridge was not sufficient to fit a man to be a Minister of Christ, I regarded the priests less, and looked more after the dissenting people. **1786** J. SCOTT *Jrnl.* (1798) 130 The Lord my gracious Preserver . . is learning me to depend on and attend to his *shuttings* as well as his *openings*. **1855** *Friends' Intelligencer* (Philadelphia) XII. 113/2 It was as though it had been spoken to me, 'If I restore thee, go to Pennsylvania'. To which, the answer of my soul was,—Wherever thou pleasest. This opening appeared strange to me at that time. **1947** *Friends' Q.* Jan. 9 The Puritans . . distrusted the 'openings' and the 'experiences' by which the Quaker claimed to receive revelation. **1975** R. HETHERINGTON *Sense of Glory* vi. 64 The Society of Friends has never had a priesthood. Instead, they have put the 'openings' of individuals within the context of the group.

**operate**, *v.* Add: III. **9.** The infin. used *attrib.*, in the sense 'operating', to designate that which causes or enables something to operate, or a period during which a thing is operative.
   **1954** *Brit. Jrnl. Psychol.* XLV. 219 For cycling, the operate key is set in the upward position. **1969** *Rev. Electr. Communication Lab.* (Tokyo) XVII. 809/2 The operate time is defined as the value from the time the voltage is applied to the relay to the time the armature reaches $x = x_0$. **1971** *Gloss. Electrotechnical, Power Terms (B.S.I.)* I. iii. 15 *Operate current*, minimum current which, when applied in the same direction and immediately following removal of saturation current, will cause the relay to operate. **1985–86** *Hasler Rev.* Winter XVIII. 89/1 The Hasler electronic time measuring unit ELZE . . is specially designed for the measurement and adjustment of relay operate times and release times.

**operatorship** ('ɒpəreitəʃip), *n.* [f. OPERATOR *n.* + -SHIP.] The position or function of an operator; control over an operation, *spec.* (in the *Oil* and *Gas Industries*) the right to operate a well, field, etc.
   **1977** *Offshore Engineer* May 40/3 ETAP . . has the same status as any other working oil company. In fact, it already has operatorship of some offshore leases. **1982** *Financial Times* 3 Dec. (Suppl.) p. i/4

Mobil is also well aware that Statoil, the Norwegian state oil corporation . . is keen to take over the operatorship for itself. **1985** *Times* 21 Mar. 38/2 (Advt.), Two operatorships have already been secured and others are under negotiation. **1987** *Times* 18 June 21/3 British Gas . . had been ordered to sell off . . its operatorship of the Wytch Farm on-shore field, in Dorset, the country's largest on-shore oil project. **1988** *Daily Tel.* 24 Nov. 14/8 The department has a responsibility to help our sector gain operatorship, which will develop the expertise of the independent sector.

**opine** ('əupiːn), *n. Biochem.* [f. OCT)OPINE *n.*: cf. LYSOPINE *n.*] An amino acid whose molecule contains a guanido group.
   **1977** J. TEMPÉ et al. in *Proc. Nat. Acad. Sci.* LXXIV. 2848/2 The Ti plasmid, which is present in all virulent strains of the crown gall bacterium, has been found . . to code for specific amino acids—the opines—of which octopine . . and nopaline . . are examples. **1985** *Nature* 19 Dec. 601/1 Opines have . . been shown to act as specific inducers of the transfer (*tra*) genes carried on *Agrobacterium* tumour-inducing (Ti) plasmids. **1987** *Ann. Rev. Plant Physiol.* XXXVIII. 223 *Asparagus* stem sections were challenged with *Agrobacterium*, and again opine production was evident.

**opinionated**, *ppl. a.* Add: **4.** In weakened use: holding firm views or opinions. *U.S.*
   **1976** *Forbes* (N.Y.) 1 Nov. 127 Bjurman . . has set up shop in Los Angeles with his son . . and four other young, opinionated portfolio managers. **1977** *N.Y. Rev. Bks.* 28 Apr. 42/4 (Advt.), Unattached NYC man, . . sensitive, intellectual, seeks serious, opinionated, literary woman, 26-29, for dinner, theatre, tennis and good conversation. **1986** *Financial World* 15 Apr. 34/3 His eccentric image, humble manner and placid voice notwithstanding, Wal-Mart's CEO is heartily opinionated, possessed of a staunch, personal sense of right and wrong in his business dealings.

**opioid**, *n.* Add: **2.** *Pharm.* and *Physiol.* Any compound resembling opiates in its neurochemical effects, esp. as regards the suppression of pain. Freq. *attrib.*, esp. as *opioid peptide*.
   **1967** W. R. MARTIN in *Pharmacol. Rev.* XIX. 464 We have adopted the term *opioid*, which was proposed by Professor George H. Acheson, to designate those analgesics whose pattern of pharmacological and agonistic effects is similar to that of morphine and have called this pattern of effects the *opioid syndrome. Ibid.* 502 The ubiquitous distribution of the sites of actions of opioids and opioid antagonists in the central nervous system. **1975** *Life Sci.* XVI. 1771 The highly specific interaction of opiates with opiate receptors in the brain . . and the guinea pig ileum . . suggested the existence of endogenous ligands for these receptors. . . The search for such endogenous opioids has been carried out by several groups in addition to our own. **1976** H. W. KOSTERLITZ (*title*), Opiates and endogenous opioid peptides. **1977** *Proc. Nat. Acad. Sci.* LXXIV. 2171/1 The enkephalin antisera we have used display little cross-reactivity with larger opioid peptides, α-endorphin and β-endorphin. **1981** *Brain Res. Bull.* VII. 279 The prototype σ opioid receptor agonist N-allyl-normetazocine . . was injected into the third cerebral ventricle of conscious, unrestrained cats. **1986** *Fortune* 18 Aug. 33/1 Among other things, opioids relieve pain and affect bowel activity. Some opioids found in the hypothalamus . . also appear to stimulate appetite.

**optical**, *a.* and *n.* Add: [A.] [**4.**] **b.** *Computing.* Designating (a part of) a computer requiring infrared, visible, or ultraviolet radiation for its operation, *spec.* as a means of storing or retrieving data, or (usu. in coherent form) as a substitute for electric current in some experimental systems. See also *optical character reader, recognition, optical disc, scanner*, sense 6 below.

**1947** *Ann. Computation Lab. Harvard Univ.* XVI. 147 Optical and photographic storage methods are applicable to the supplementary and permanent storage problems. These methods are called optical in that optical means are used in conjunction with mechanical scanning for switching the data into and out of storage. **1959** *Jrnl. Optical Soc. Amer.* XLIX. 1012 Examples of optical methods of calculation are described, and the construction of an optical analog computer for synthesizing the two-dimensional fourier transform of a function for use in crystal structure determination is described. **1965** *Electronics* 6 Sept. 72/1 Optical analog computers have been in use for several years, but they have really come of age with the laser. An optical computer powered by a laser can multiply a 10,000-element vector by a 10,000 x 10,000 matrix in one millisecond. **1971** *New Scientist* 8 July 80/2 Although most of the big companies can build optical memories in the laboratory, they still say they are a long way from turning out optical computers on the production line. **1980** C. S. FRENCH *Computer Sci.* xxix. 237 Chain printers or optical paper tape reader[s] make transfers of data at rates which correspond to dozens or hundreds of instructions. **1988** *Fortune* 1 Feb. 58/3 The optical computer, using laser beams instead of electrical connections, would work 1,000 times faster than today's electronic variety.

**optimize**, *v.* Add: 'optimized *ppl. a.*
**1862** MRS. J. B. SPEID *Our Last Yrs. in India* ii. 38 Visions of reformed lavatories and optimized bathing apparatus. **1980** *Dædalus* Spring 42 The demands of an optimized whole may require some concessions among parts.

**option**, *n.* Sense 1 b in Dict. becomes 1 c. Add: **[1.] b.** A supplementary item which may be chosen in addition to (or in place of one of) the standard features of a product, esp. a motor vehicle; an optional extra.
**1952** *Southern Automobile Jrnl.* Nov. 83 (*caption*) Wire wheels are an extra-cost option. **1966** *Automobile Topics* Jan. 35/2 From such beginnings the option and accessory business has grown into a huge industry. **1972** *Motoring Which?* Apr. 51/2 Cortina option packs... Carpets, reclining seats, .. adjustable back quarter lights. **1975** *Economist* 5 Apr. 90/3 If the industry makes smaller, standard cars with less options, it will have to raise the profit margin on them, thus making them not so cheap after all. **1987** *Truck* June 97/3 The Gardner engine has been relegated to the position of option just two years after its introduction.

**opto** ('ɒptəʊ), *a.* [Abbrev. of OPTOELECTRONIC *a.*, OPTOELECTRONICS *n. pl.* (used *attrib.*).] Optoelectronic; of or concerned with optoelectronics.
**1981** *Electronics* 30 June 174/2 (*heading*) Few opto engineers in sight. **1983** *Electronic News* 28 Feb. 20/4 The firm's problems with the Optoelectronics division were typical of broad line semiconductor suppliers who must take on the multifarious niches that make up the opto market. **1986** *Times* 1 Apr. 24/6 (*heading*) BT opts for a US opto partner. **1988** *New Scientist* 21 Apr. 51/2 The trigger for these measurements is provided every 5 millimetres by a following wheel fitted with a slotted disk and an 'opto' switch.

**opto-coupler** ('ɒptəʊˌkʌplə(r)), *n. Electronics.* [f. OPTO- + COUPLER *n.*] An electronic component which allows current to pass through it only when a beam of light, etc. within it is unobstructed, and which may be used as an isolator in an electrical circuit.

**1973** *Wireless World* Dec. 596/1 Obviously power gain is required preceding an opto-coupler if a reasonable noise performance is to be obtained. **1975** *Elektor* July-Aug. 728/1 This circuit employs an opto-coupler to give complete isolation from the mains. **1987** *Radio & Electronics World* Feb. 39/2 The 'reflective' opto-coupler .. devices can .. also be used as an external-object detector.
Hence **'opto-coupled** *a.*, of a circuit: closed with an opto-coupler.
**1976** *Pract. Electronics* Feb. 144 (*heading*) Opto-coupled r.p.m. meter. **1988** *Electronics & Wireless World* Oct. 963/2 (*heading*) Two-way opto-coupled link.

**optronic** (ɒp'trɒnɪk), *a.* [Shortened form of OPTOELECTRONIC *a.*] = OPTOELECTRONIC *a.*
**1955** *Proc. IRE* XLIII. 1897/2 The solid state analogs of cathode ray imaging and pick-up tubes .. are only some of the simpler embodiments of possible opto-electronic (optronic) devices. **1986** *Aviation Week* 28 Apr. 115/2 France's Thomson-CSF is developing an optronic surveillance system called Scorpion, which is sized to be used on a Brevel-type RPV or light aircraft.

**orangish** ('ɒrɪndʒɪʃ), *a.* [f. ORANGE *a.* + -ISH.] Somewhat orange in colour; having an orange tinge; orangey. Also *Comb.*, as *orangish-looking*.
**1888** *Bow-Bells Weekly* 29 June 408/1 The other chair had a pretty orangish-looking carpet back and seat. **1977** R. E. HARRINGTON *Quintain* vii. 65 The skin .. tanned to the orangish Southern California badge. **1987** *New Scientist* 2 July 29/1 Epsilon Eridani is an orangish star with a mass about 0.75 times that of the Sun.

**orbit**, *n.* Add: **[2.] f.** *Math.* Each of the subsets of a set which are defined by a given permutation group in the sense that every pair of elements of a particular subset is related by some permutation belonging to the group; also, the single subset thus defined which contains a specified element of the set.
**1959** J. S. LOMONT *Applications of Finite Groups* v. 221 An *orbit* of a normal subgroup *H* of *G* is a maximal set of inequivalent irreducible representations of *H* which are mutually conjugate relative to *G*. **1964** R. BERCOV tr. *Wielandt's Finite Permutation Groups* i. 4 A constituent $G^{\Delta}$ is transitive precisely when $\Delta$ is a minimal fixed block ($\Delta \neq \phi$). In this case $\Delta$ is called an *orbit* or *set of transitivity* of *G*. **1971** POWELL & HIGMAN *Finite Simple Groups* vii. 222 The 12 cosets of *L* which form an orbit under *L*. **1981** *Sci. Amer.* Mar. 24/1 With mesons and baryons, double edge flippers and double edge-pair swappers and double corner-pair swappers you have a full set of tools with which to restore any scrambled cube to Start, as long as it belongs to the same orbit as Start.

**order**, *n.* Senses 10 d (i) and (ii) in Dict. become 10 d (ii) and (iii). Add: **[II.] [10.] [d.] (i)** The dimension of a determinant or square matrix.
**1844** *Trans. Cambr. Philos. Soc.* VIII. 77 Consider the function $U = x\ (\alpha\xi + \beta\eta + ..) + ... x'\ (\alpha'\xi + \beta'\eta + ...) + (n$ lines, and $n$ terms in each line) ... The determinant .. may be expressed as a determinant of the $n^{th}$ order. **1850** [see *MATRIX *n.* 6 a]. **1882** T. MUIR *Treat. Theory of Determinants* i. 6 When the determinant has four, that is 2x2, elements, it is said to be of the second order or degree; [etc.]. **1934** W. L. COWLEY *Adv. Pract. Math.* iv. 68 An example of a fourth order determinant is given in (37). **1966** *Mathematical Rev.* XXXI. 36/1 Matrices *M* of even order behave somewhat differently from those of odd order.

**organ**, *n*. Add: [II.] [5.] **e.** *spec*. The penis; also *male organ*. Freq. in colloq. or euphem. use. Cf. MALE *a*. 1 d, 2 a and MEMBER *n*. 1 b.

**1903** *Eng. Dial. Dict*. IV. 503/1 *Pill*, .. the male organ, the penis. **1922** JOYCE *Ulysses* 266 —Sure, you'd burst the tympanum of her ear, man, .. with an organ like yours ... —Not to mention another membrane. *Ibid*. 299 That part of the human anatomy known as the penis or male organ. **1967** M. CAMPBELL *Lord dismiss Us* (1968) iv. 19 He had the largest organ that anyone had ever seen. It was a truncheon. **1973** L. HELLMAN *Pentimento* 174 Asking myself whether talk about the size of the male organ isn't a homosexual preoccupation. **1987** *Fiction Mag*. June 4/3 Ah, bliss was it .. to have your eager organ, rigid pole, no, your *Excalibur* withdraw and plunge again into another delirious, mutual climax.

**organic**, *a*. and *n*. Add: [A.] [6.] **d.** *Archit*. Designating any of various architectural styles in which the character of the buildings is more or less reminiscent of a natural organism, esp. as regards unity of design; *spec*., in the writings of Frank Lloyd Wright (1869-1959) and subsequently, applied to architecture which attempts to unify a building with its surroundings.

**1908** F. L. WRIGHT in *Archit. Rec*. Mar. 165/2 The work shall grow more truly simple; more expressive with fewer lines, fewer forms; .. more fluent, although more coherent; more organic. **1939** —— *Organic Archit*. p. vii/1 An Organic Architecture means more or less organic society. **1950** E. H. GOMBRICH *Story of Art* xxvi. 404 He [*sc*. Frank Lloyd Wright] believes in what he calls 'Organic Architecture', by which he means that a house must grow out of the needs of the people and the character of the country, like a living organism. **1960** *Times Lit. Suppl*. 4 Mar. 150/3 A well-photographed selection of post-war Italian buildings, with an introduction explaining the so-called 'Resistance', 'Organic' and 'Neo-Liberty' styles. **1978** *Detroit Free Press* 5 Mar. 14/2 Frank Lloyd Wright, the internationally famed architect who preached the gospel of organic architecture. **1986** *Sunday Mail* (Brisbane) 21 Sept. 47/2 They are examples of what architect Christine Valdasz calls her 'organic architecture'.

**e.** Characterized by or designating continuous or 'natural' development in a manner suggestive of the growth of a living being.

**1923** *Psychol. Rev*. XXX. 371 Thinking is not an isolated fact ... It is the final step in an organic learning process. **1940** E. WILSON *To Finland Station* II. xi. 195 It conceives revolutionary progress as an organic development out of the past, for which the reactionary forces have themselves in their way been preparing. **1967** R. SIMPSON *Essence of Bruckner* i. 21 If the slow movement lacks that organic growth and cumulative sense that has become so familiar in the mature Bruckner *adagio*, it also has some lovely things in it. **1970** H. OSBORNE *Oxf. Compan. Art* 796/1 In the language of 20th-c[entury] criticism 'organic' has become current almost always in a commendatory sense though with no clearly defined connotation, suggesting that a work of art is a living and harmonious whole rather than a contrived or unrelated patchwork of elements. **1987** J. UGLOW *George Eliot* ii. 34 Change, she insists, must be gradual, organic, natural and not imposed.

**organically**, *adv*. Add: **4.** Naturally; in the course of unconstrained development.

**1977** *Washington Post* 30 Oct. A14/6 G-P grew organically almost like the trees that were the material basis of its prosperity. **1984** STEWARD & GARRATT *Signed, sealed & Delivered* i. 16/1 In music, an image can develop slowly and organically, changing as the performer changes. **1988** *Boston Globe* 6 Nov. C1/1 Cairo has become a packed, sprawling, organically expanding metropolis of 14 million people.

**organicism**, *n*. Add: **3.** The use or advocacy of organic literary or artistic forms, *i.e.* those in which the parts are interrelated or co-ordinated in the whole. Cf. ORGANIC *a*. 6 a.

**1945** S. C. PEPPER *Basis of Crit. in Arts* iv. 74 Organicism, traditionally known as objective idealism, is the world hypothesis that stresses the internal relatedness or coherence of things. **1956** M. KRIEGER *New Apologists for Poetry* 21 An equally forceful argument against an extreme organicism would point out, via the continuities we find in the history of literary tradition, that poems have common as well as unique properties. **1972** W. K. WIMSATT in G. S. Rousseau *Organic Form* 71 If we had never heard of organic form .. we might well be dedicating this very volume to a struggle to invent and proclaim some doctrine of Romantic organicism. **1986** *Music & Lett*. Oct. 448 A desire for 'symphonic organicism' on traditional lines.

**organized**, *ppl. a*. Add: [2.] **c.** *transf*. Of a person: having one's affairs in order; ready, prepared; freq. in phr. *to get* (oneself) *organized*. Hence, efficient, adept.

**1946** C. FRY *Phoenix too Frequent* (1949) 3 He was certain to have become the most well-organized provost The town has known. **1948** PARTRIDGE *Dict. Forces' Slang* 134 *Organized, get*, pull yourself together, show some efficiency. *To get organized*, to sort out one's ideas or possessions. (Army). **1976** 'B. SHELBY' *Great Pebble Affair* 30 Officially, I had been renting my apartment for three months before I even saw it. That goes to show you how organized Donnely was. **1981** T. MORRISON *Tar Baby* vi. 191 Let the laundry stay there and get yourself organized.

**organizer**, *n*. Add: **3.** That which organizes, or is used in organizing systematically; *spec*. an object (as a purse, folder, or piece of office furniture) with several compartments for filing or storing items separately. Freq. *ellipt*. for *personal organizer* s.v. *PERSONAL a*. 10. Cf. also FILOFAX *n*. orig. *U.S.*

**1966** *Office Appliances* Dec. 64/1 Desk Organizer. .. The 5DO 'Large Form' organizer accommodates legal size files. **1974** *Sears, Roebuck Catal*. Fall & Winter 1251/2 Desk-top or kitchen counter-top Organizer for letters, magazines recipes etc. **1979** *Ibid*. Spring & Summer 114/2 Organizer Bag. Roomy main section has slip-in pocket holding a removable zippered cosmetic case. **1983** *Punch* 27 Apr. 59/3, I see from the mail order catalogues that bags are being called organisers under current sales talk. **1985** *Harrods Mag*. Christmas 74 Travel organiser with document compartments and wallet facility £89. **1988** *Practical Parenting* Apr. 8/3 It has one shelf and two small plastic 'organisers' to hold all your baby's toiletries.

**organo-**, *comb. form*. Add: [2.] [b.] *organochloride*.

**1970** *Biol. Abstr*. LI. 4266/1 Functional state of the liver and stomach in people .. affected by organochloride chemical poisons. **1987** *Woman's Day* (Melbourne) 16 Nov. 57/2 Organochlorides, the chemicals that were detected in Australian meat in the US and Japan, do not cause allergies and their long-term damage, if any, is not known.

**oriental**, *a*. and *n*. [A.] [3.] For 'belonging to south-western Asia, or Asiatic countries generally' read: of, relating to, or characteristic of south-western Asia, or Asiatic countries generally; dealing or connected with the Orient, its culture or affairs (see also *Oriental Jew, languages*, sense 3 d below). (Further examples.)

**1695** EVELYN *Diary* 23 Nov. (1955) V. 224 There dined with us the Bishops of Lichfild, Lincoln, Norwich: Dr. Cowell the greate oriental Traveler & divers others. **1855** E. ACTON *Mod. Cookery* (rev. ed.) xxxii. 613 Turkish or Arabian Pilaw. (From Mr. Lane, the Oriental Traveller.) **1874** GEO. ELIOT *Let.* 10 Dec. (1956) VI. 99 We can resolve to study the Semitic languages and apply to an Oriental scholar to give us daily lessons. **1907** G. B. SHAW *John Bull's Other Island* Pref. p. lviii, Officials who, after years of oriental service, have lost the familiar art of concealing their terrors. **1920** G. BELL *Let.* 17 Oct. (1927) II. xix. 563 So I decided at once to invest myself with the duties of Oriental Secretary, there being no one else in the office who knows Bagdad. **1983** G. PRIESTLAND *At Large* 25 All kinds of Moonies, gurus and oriental meditationists can dance in our streets and hold seminars in our country houses.

**orifacial**, *a.* Restrict *Craniometry* to sense in Dict. Add: **2.** *Anat.* = *OROFACIAL *a.*
**1892** in *Syd. Soc. Lex.*

**original**, *a.* and *n.* Sense 3 e in Dict. becomes 3 f. Add: [B.] [3.] **e.** A person upon whom a character in a literary work is based. Also *transf.* of places.
**1837** J. G. LOCKHART *Mem. Life Scott* I. viii. 265 They staid there for a day or two, in the course of which Scott had his first and only interview with David Ritchie, the original of his Black Dwarf. **1873** J. FORSTER *Life Dickens* II. ii. 30 Mrs. Gamp's original was in reality a person hired by a most distinguished friend of his own . . to take charge of an invalid very dear to her. **1892** GARDINER *Student's Hist. Eng.* 12 Cunobelin, the original of Shakspere's Cymbeline. **1924** A. L. HAYWARD *Dickens Encycl.* 102/1 Maidstone. It is very probable that this old county town was the original of Muggleton. **1952** *Dickensian* XLVIII. 165 George Lear . . remembered a little old lady whom he considered to have been the original of Miss Flite. **1984** A. N. WILSON *Hilaire Belloc* II. xi. 249 Father O'Connor, the 'original' of Father Brown, came down from his Yorkshire parish.

**orofacial** (ɔːrəʊˈfeɪʃəl), *a. Anat.* [irreg. for ORIFACIAL *a.*] Pertaining to the mouth and face; located on or directed at the mouth and that part of the face adjacent to it.
**1960** *Trans. Brit. Soc. Study of Orthodontics 1959* 100/2 It is not possible to cover all the information gained . . in one paper, which is limited . . to that part of the survey dealing with orofacial muscular behaviour. **1967** *Oral Surg., Oral Med., Oral Path.* XXIV. 7 A case has been presented in which closure of an orofacial fistula was achieved with the help of an anticholinergic drug. **1977** *Lancet* 3 Sept. 511/1 Patients with acute orofacial infection often come under surgical care, and the prospects of successful treatment are good because the oral flora are usually sensitive to penicillin. **1988** *Experimental Neurol.* CI. 385 Orofacial conditioning stimulation could produce an increase in antidromic excitability.
Hence oro'facially *adv.*
**1977** *Oral Surg., Oral Med., Oral Path.* XLIV. 830 Periodontal, restorative, prosthetic, and oral surgical services were necessary to rehabilitate this patient orofacially.

**orphan**, *n.* and *a.* [A.] [1.] [a.] Delete small-type note and for def. read: One deprived by death of father or mother, or (more generally) of both parents; sometimes also, one bereft of parental care, *esp.* through abandonment or neglect; a fatherless or motherless child. (Further examples.)
**1852** *Rep. Cases Supreme Court Georgia* X. 71 It will be impossible to conclude that, when the Legislature speaks of an *orphan*, it meant to designate alone a minor whose parents are dead. **1891** T. J.

BARNARDO in *Ann. Rep. Dr Barnardo's Homes 1890* xxv. 5 Six thousand are worse than orphans; they are, as it has been said, 'orphans whose misfortune it is to have a father and mother', for their parents are such as no child could either honour or regret. **1933** H. ALLEN *Anthony Adverse* ix. 126 The method of receiving orphans was simplicity itself. Anyone, without let or hindrance, might leave at the hole in the convent wall provided for that purpose an otherwise unwelcome infant. **1957** *Southern Reporter* LXXXIX. 290/2 It was his opinion that a boy was an orphan when his parent or parents abandoned him. **1988** *Executive Update* June 32/3 For 23 years, the youngster who was abandoned at 18 months kept the desire to end for other orphans the twice-abandoned experience he endured.
**b.** *Orphan's* or *Orphans' Court*, also (now *Hist.*) *Court of Orphans*: in 16th- and 17th-cent. England, and in some States of the U.S., a probate court having jurisdiction over the estates and persons of orphans.
**1568** *Order* 24 July in *Repertory Court of Aldermen* (City of London Corporation Records) XVI. f. 383ᵛ, One of the Aldermen of this cytty . . shall syt every Fryday wekely at eight of the clok in the forenone in the orphanes court of this hall. **1596** in C. Carlton *Court of Orphans* (1974) ii. 31 Court of Orphans holden . . Passion monday last. **1680** *Lex Londinensis* 55 The Orphants Court . . is held before the Major and Aldermen of the City of London, who are Guardians to the Children of all Freemen of London that are or shall be under the Age of 21 years at the time of their Fathers decease. **1784** *Acts 9th Gen. Assembly State of New-Jersey* lxx. 136 The Orphan's Court shall have full power and authority to hear and determine all disputes and controversies . . respecting . . any lands, tenements, goods, chattels or estate, belonging . . to any orphan or person under age. **1828** J. PARKES *Hist. Court of Chancery* xii. 403 There were in some of the North American colonies before the rebellion, and there are . . in several of the United States, courts for the protection of the properties of infants, denominated Orphans' courts. **1909** W. S. HOLDSWORTH *Hist. Eng. Law* III. iv. 397 The London Court of Orphans lasted on till late in the seventeenth century. **1987** *Amer. Bench, 1987–88* (ed. 4) 1088 The Orphans' Courts are courts of special jurisdiction in Maryland. *Ibid.* 1969 [The Supreme Court of Pennsylvania] has exclusive appellate jurisdiction of appeals from the Courts of Common Pleas in cases involving . . decisions of the Orphans' Court Division.

**ortet** (ˈɔːtɛt), *n. Biol.* [f. L. *ort-us* origin + -ET¹.] The original organism (usu. a plant) from which a clone has been produced. Cf. RAMET *n.*
**1929** A. B. STOUT in *Jrnl. N.Y. Bot. Garden* XXX. 33 To indicate the original seedling plant from which the clon [*sic*] is derived the word *ortet* . . may be used. **1966** *Ecology* XLVII. 442/2 The newly established and developing clone may have a relatively simple rooting pattern, i.e., all ramets connected by a single root system initiated by the ortet. **1986** *Forestry* LIX. 161 Cuttings are easier to root the younger (more juvenile) the ortet from which they are taken.

**orthologous** (ɔːˈθɒləgəs), *a. Genetics.* [f. ORTHO- + HOMO)LOGOUS *a.*] Of homologous genes in different species: descended from a single gene in the most recent common ancestor. Of a single gene: descended from the same gene as another specified gene (const. *with*). Also applied to the expressions of such genes. Cf. *PARALOGOUS *a.*
**1970** FITCH & MARGOLIASH in *Evolutionary Biol.* IV. 76 One must compare directly only those sequences whose genes have a lineage that precisely reflects, in a one-to-one fashion, the lineage of the species in which they are found. Such genes may be called *orthologous* (ortho = exact). **1976** *Nature* 29 Jan. 340/2 There is, therefore, no direct evidence that

the β-like chain of the minor haemoglobin of Tarsius is orthologous with either man-ape or New World monkey δ chain. **1986** *Jrnl. Biol. Chem.* CCLXI. 16694/1 The divergence between two orthologous proteins can be used to calculate the unit evolutionary period (UEP). **1988** *Nature* 21 Apr. 685/1 Miyamoto *et al.* apply the sequencing approach to the longest continuous stretch of orthologous DNA yet determined for humans.
Hence **or'thologously** *adv.*
**1970** FITCH & MARGOLIASH in *Evolutionary Biol.* IV. 90 Thus we can establish homology, but whether the two gene groups are orthologously or paralogously related is not determined by this procedure. **1971** *Nature* 29 Jan. 323/1 These criteria are met chiefly by orthologously related proteins with the same function in different species, such as the cytochrome cs or the insulins. **1979** *Systematic Zool.* XXVIII. 135/1 In nature the ancestral splittings of gene lineages . . may coincide with species lineage splittings, in which case the gene lineages are said to be orthologously related.

**orthopædic**, *a.* Add: **ortho'pædically, -ped-,** *adv.*; **ortho'pædics**, *n.* (examples).
**1973** *Rehabilitation Lit.* (Chicago) Oct. 299/1 *(heading)* The efficacy of visual-motor training for orthopedically handicapped children. **1986** *Developmental Med. & Child Neurol.* XXVIII. 360 Preference not to intervene orthopaedically.

**orthopoxvirus** ('ɔːθəʊpɒks,vaɪrəs), *n. Microbiol.* Also **orthopox virus.** [f. ORTHO- + POXVIRUS *n.*] Any poxvirus of the genus *Orthopoxvirus*, including those causing cowpox, monkey pox, and smallpox.
[**1974** *Intervirology* III. 197 It was approved that the following 6 genera be established within the family [Poxviridae]: 3.2.1 *Orthopoxvirus* . . Includes the viruses of vaccinia, variola, alastrim, cowpox, ectromelia, rabbitpox, monkeypox.] **1975** *Jrnl. Hygiene* LXXV. 381 This virus was shown to be a pox virus with many characteristics of members of the Orthopox group. **1979** *Nature* 24 May 297/2 The surveillance of orthopoxvirus infections in animals and man as well as laboratory studies of orthopoxviruses should continue and all necessary steps should be taken to minimise the potential danger of live variola virus stocks. **1980** *Trop. Med. & Hygiene News* Oct. 7 Research on the orthopox viruses. **1988** *Nature* 21 Apr. 755/1 The variola virus may . . have been derived from another animal orthopox virus.

**orthoselection** (,ɔːθəʊsɪ'lɛkʃən), *n. Biol.* [a. G. *Orthoselection* (L. Plate, 1903, in *Über die Bedeutung d. Darwin'schen Selectionsprincips* iv. 187): cf. ORTHO-, SELECTION *n.*] Natural selection occurring in the same direction continuously over a relatively long period, and giving rise to orthogenesis.
**1907** V. L. KELLOGG *Darwinism To-day* x. 276 To attribute orthogenetic results to natural selection is quite right, and some one has proposed the name *orthoselection* to distinguish orthogenetic evolution as produced by selection from such results produced independently, or at least partly independently of selection. **1944** G. G. SIMPSON *Tempo & Mode in Evolution* v. 150 Plate supposed orthevolution to be due to two quite different causes, orthogenesis . . and orthoselection, a term that is self-explanatory and has been rather widely employed, although hardly more respectable etymologically than 'orthevolution'. **1966** G. C. WILLIAMS *Adaptation & Natural Selection* iv. 111 Other examples are apparently real and are attributed by Simpson to continuous genic selection in certain directions, a process he terms 'orthoselection'. **1977** D. M. RAUP in A. Hallam *Patterns of Evolution* iii. 65 Hayami and Ozawa interpreted both examples as showing unidirectional, genetic change resulting from a single cause

(orthoselection). **1986** *Oxf. Surveys in Evol. Biol.* III. 12 The concept of punctuated equilibrium was developed explicitly in contrast to phyletic gradualism equated with orthoselection.

**Osetian** *n.* and *a.*, var. OSSETIAN *n.* and *a.*

**Osmanli**, *a.* and *n.* Add: [B.] b. The language of the Ottoman Turks; Turkish.
**1843** *Penny Cycl.* XXV. 406/1 Osmanli, or Turkish, commonly called so. This dialect . . is spoken by the Turkish conquerors of the Byzantine empire. **1908** T. G. TUCKER *Introd. Nat. Hist. Lang.* 134 *Turkish* (or *Osmanli*, the latter term, however, being properly used of the official and cultivated Turkish, which contains large Persian and Arabic elements). **1959** [see OGHUZ *n.* 2]. **1977** C. F. & F. M. VOEGELIN *Classification & Index World's Lang.* 341 Turkish = Osmanli. Ds. Eastern, Western = Danubian. 24,000,000. Turkey. Also in Bulgaria, Cyprus, Soviet Union (73,000).

**Ossetian**, *n.* and *a.* For 'Also Ossetan' read: Also Osetian; similarly Ossetan. Add: [A.] (Examples of variant spelling.)
**1910** *Encycl. Brit.* X. 392/2 The Scythians . . are believed by many authorities to have been Iranians and to be represented by the Osetians of the Caucasus. **1957** *Whitaker's Almanack 1958* 954/2 Georgians make up about three fifths of the population, the remainder being composed of Armenians, Russians, Azerbaidjani and Osetians. [B.] (Example of variant spelling.)
**1959** E. H. CARR *Socialism in One Country* II. xx. 257 The autonomous Mountaineers' republic was broken up into the North Osetian and Ingush autonomous regions.

**osteichthyan** (,ɒstɪ'ɪkθɪən), *n.* (and *a.*) *Ichthyol.* Also **-ichthyean.** [f. mod.L. *Osteichthy-es,* f. Gr. ὀστέ-ον bone + ἰχθύ-ς fish, + -AN.] Any fish belonging to the class Osteichthyes of bony fish, characterized by a bony endoskeleton. Also as *adj.,* characteristic of the Osteichthyes.
**1955** E. H. COLBERT *Evolution of Vertebrates* iv. 52 The skull showed the basic osteichthyan cranial pattern. **1967** *Jrnl. Linn. Soc. (Zool.)* XLVII. 194 There is no evidence in the osteichthyans of a sclerocoel that divides the sclerotome into cranial and caudal halves. **1974** D. & M. WEBSTER *Compar. Vertebr. Morphol.* viii. 161 Living sarcopterygians, however, have much thinner scales resembling the cycloid scales of most living osteichthyeans. **1982** *Amer. Mus. Novitates* No. 2724. 1/1 The suggestion . . that the intermuscular ribs of Recent sharks are homologous with pleural ('ventral') ribs of osteichthyans.

**osteopetrosis**, *n.* After def. add: Cf. *ALBERS-SCHÖNBERG *n.*, marble bone* s.v. MARBLE *n.* 9.

**ostracize**, *v.* Add: also **ostraci'zation** *n.*, the action of ostracizing, the fact or state of being ostracized, ostracism.
**1898** LD. RUSSELL OF KILLOWEN in R. B. O'Brien *Life Ld. Russell* (1909) xiv. 295 Ostracisation of any persons who have art or part in any such nefarious enterprises. **1946** M. PEAKE *Titus Groan* lx. 359 In his banishment he had felt the isolation of a severed hand . . . As yet . . the horror of his ostracization was too close for him to grasp. **1982** *Observer* 26 Sept. 35/9 Men of a certain social class were assumed to be gentlemen until proved otherwise, and the sanction of their peers was ostracisation.

**otolith**, *n.* Add: c. *Comb.* **otolith organ,** each of the acoustic maculae of the utricle and saccule of the inner ear, which sense the direction of motion of the head and its attitude with respect to the surrounding gravitational field.
**1919** S. S. MAXWELL in *Jrnl. Gen. Physiol.* II. 123 It was suggested that the dynamic function is

performed by the sensory structures of the semicircular canals, the static by the otolith organs of the vestibule. **1934** *Brit. Jrnl. Psychol.* XXV. 45 Changes in the direction or value of *g* set up nerve impulses in the otolith organs. **1961** 'F. O'BRIEN' *Hard Life* vi. 47 The nerves which supply the labyrinth end with a number of cells attired in hair-like projections which, when grouped, form the two otolith organs in the saccule and utricle and the three *cristae* of the semi-circular canals. **1984** J. F. LAMB et al. *Essent. Physiol.* (ed. 2) x. 320 Linear movement in space is detected by the otolith organs of the saccule and utricle.

**oto'lithic** *a.*: also *otolithic membrane*, the flattened gelatinous mass, containing otoliths, which forms that layer of the otolith organ situated next to the lumen of the inner ear; also **oto'litic** *a.* = OTOLITHIC *a.*
  **1932** J. S. FRASER in A. L. Turner *Dis. Nose, Throat & Ear* (ed. 3) xxxi. 277 The stimulation of the macula is the pressure or pull of the otolithic membrane on the hair cells. **1983** *Sci. Amer.* Jan. 46/1 After the saccule is removed from the frog and the otolithic membrane is stripped away the epithelial layer that includes the hair cells is revealed.

‖**ottocento** (ˌɒttoˈtʃɛnto), *n.* (and *a.*) Also Ottocento. [It., lit. 'eight hundred', here short for *mil otto cento* one thousand eight hundred, f. *mil* thousand + *otto* eight + *cento* hundred; cf. CINQUECENTO *n.*, etc.] The nineteenth century, as a period of Italian art, architecture, etc. Also *attrib.* or as *adj.*
  **1928** *Art & Archaeol.* XXVI. 187/2 The collection .. afforded a retrospective survey of portraiture, landscape and figure painting as exemplified by the pioneers of the *Ottocento*, from Appiani, who died in 1817, down to .. the veteran Previati. *Ibid.* 188/2 The Ottocento collection. **1930** *Formes* (Eng. ed.) Jan. 27/1 The 'avant-garde' art group in Italy which took the name Novecento and published it to show that they are at least up to date suddenly discovered the Italian XIXth. century, our Ottocento. **1973** *Times Lit. Suppl.* 14 Sept. 1046/3 Sent music-lovers back to the world of the *ottocento*. **1978** W. M. SPACKMAN *Armful of Warm Girl* 4 His grandfather's marble folly reared its Palladian ruins, studded with busts of ottocento celebrities. **1988** *Financial Times* 23 Aug. 21/1 There is no one living conductor I would rather hear in early Ottocento Italian opera.

‖**ou** (əʊ), *n.*[2] *S. Afr. slang.* Pl. **ouens, ous.** [Afrikaans.] A fellow or chap; a 'bloke'. Cf. *OUTJIE n.
  **1949** B. A. TINDALL *James Rose Innes* i. 7 He was a strict disciplinarian, but always just, and .. we all loved the *'Ou'*. **1961** *Personality* 16 May 27 It's a lekker language, and those overseas ous often sound pretty snaaks themselves. **1963** A. FUGARD *Blood Knot* iv. 87, I stopped at a petrol station and sat up with the night boy in his little room. An elderly ou. **1976** J. McCLURE *Rogue Eagle* v. 92 You better not tell Willie that! He wants to murder the ou! **1979** J. DRUMMOND *I saw him Die* ii. 23, I ought to keep you locked up. The ou that shot Loder .. he's dangerous. **1984** *Frontline* Feb. 24/1 In fact you've never seen such a Harry Casual bunch of ouens in your life.

‖**ou** (əʊ), *a.* *S. Afr. colloq.* Also 9 **oud**; 9– **ou'**. [Afrikaans, f. Du. *oud* old.] Old, elder; freq. used jocularly, or in terms of respect or endearment, as OUBAAS *n.*, **ouboet** 'old brother', OUMA *n.*, **ou maat** 'old pal', OUPA *n.*, etc.
  **1869** [see OUBAAS *n.*]. **1900** B. MITFORD *Aletta* 66 By the time they are found the English will not be here to hang anybody, and we, *ou' maat*—we shall have deserved the thanks of all true patriots for having put out of the way an enemy of our country. **1913** A. B. MARCHAND in C. P. Swart *Africanderisms* (M.A. thesis, Univ. S. Afr., Pretoria, 1934), Hullo, ou maat, cried Edouard coming in with a rush. **1939**

'D. RAME' *Wine of Good Hope* I. vi. 80 'Has Mis' 'Tonia seen the Ou-Missis?' **1953** U. KRIGE *Dream & Desert* i. 10 Kleinboet would call him Ouboet, eldest brother. **1961** D. BEE *Children of Yesterday* 93 'Dolf, ou maat—here's to you.' Perhaps it was the first sign of the drink in him, that 'ou maat'—old friend. **1971** A. FUGARD *Hello & Goodbye* I. 13, I hate them when they're like that—fat and dressed in black .. because somebody's dead, and calling me Ou Sister.

**ouguiya** (uːˈɡiːyə), *n.* Also **ougiya.** [a. Fr., ad. Mauritanian Arab. *ūgiyya* (Arab. *ūqiyya*, ad. Gr. οὐγκία OUNCE *n.*[1]).] The principal monetary unit in Mauritania, consisting of 5 khoums, which replaced the French franc in 1973; also, a note or coin of this value.
  [**1973** *Washington Post* 21 May A24/1 Mauritania .. will change the name of its currency from the franc to the ugiya, the finance minister announced.] **1973** *Ibid.* 30 June A3/1 Novakchott, June 29 —Mauritania's new currency, the ouguiya, went into circulation today. **1973** *Newsweek* 27 Aug. 36/2 In a second slap at France, the republic of Mauritania replaced the French franc with a new currency unit called the *ouguiya*. **1974** *Ann. Reg. 1973* vi. 274 At the end of June, on the same day as a total eclipse of the sun brought hundreds of visitors to Mauritania, the new currency was launched. The denominations were the ougiya (worth 5 CFA francs) and the Khoum (worth one CFA franc). **1979** *Daily Tel.* 12 Apr. 16/5 How it [*sc.* the punt] stands against .. the Zambian kwacha, the Seychelles rupe, the Qatar riyal or the Mauritanian ouguiya is not clear. **1985** *Summary World Broadcasts: IV: Weekly Econ. Rep.* 30 July ME/W1349/A2/4 The amount of the agreement—3m French francs, about 24.8m ouguiyas—is France's contribution in the form of subsidy to our country.

**out**, *adv.* Add: [I.] [1.] i. Of a train, coach, steamer, mail, etc.: going out, departing. Cf. IN *adv.* 6 h.
  **1911** R. BROOKE *Let.* Jan. (1968) 269 Your letter arrived by the last post *in* last night, and I .. didn't get back in time to catch the last post *out*. **1987** R. INGALLS *End of Tragedy* 44, I wanted to be a painter, so I just jumped on the first train out.

[2.] b. *Golf.* [In some cases properly sense 16.] To or at the end of the outward half (usu. the first nine holes) of a golf-course (*in* so many strokes). Cf. HOME *adv.* 3 b.
  **1909** *Daily Chron.* 7 May 8/4 Out in 36, he came home in a good 37, and made certain of a place. **1932** B. DARWIN *Out of Rough* 266 With great bravery he got a nine to the eighteenth, and so finished in 214, 97 out and 117 home. **1969** *Times* 30 May 8/7 Maurice Bembridge .. missed green after green and could only get out in 41. **1982** *Times* 5 Nov. 19/7 Out in 31, Canizares was seven under par at that stage.

[16.] c. Of the tide: having receded from the shore, at its lowest ebb.
  **1673** J. RAY *Observations Journey Low-Countries* 149 Certain Flats .. covered all over with water at full Sea, but about the City when the Tide is out in many places bare. **1719** DEFOE *Crusoe* I. 65 When the Tide was out, I got most of the Pieces of Cable ashore. **1883** L. TROUBRIDGE *Life amongst Troubridges* (1966) 165 Meaning to bathe .. but the tide miles out. **1932** D. L. SAYERS *Have his Carcase* i. 9 The tide was nearly out now, and the wet beach shimmered .. in the lazy moonlight. **1984** T. SOPER *Nat. Trust Guide to Coast* 116 (*caption*) Shore-birds like the turnstone .. will forage over the mud when the tide is out.

d. *Racing.* Short of the finishing-post.
  **1949** *Times* 18 June 6/1 Two furlongs out there was some crowding and bumping, but Richards got through on The Cobbler and dashed to the front in the last furlong. **1960** *Times* 15 June 17/2 Solo Singer fell five furlongs out, bringing down Combwell Beeches when near the front. **1986** *Sporting Life*

*Weekender* 17-19 Apr. 30/3 Peaty Sandy hit the front five from home, was clear two out, and won by a comfortable two lengths.

**[22.] d.** Of a telephone, radio, etc.: out of order, broken down; no longer functioning, inoperative. Cf. DOWN *adv.* 17 c.

**1975** J. HANSEN *Trouble Maker* i. 5 Help's a long way off. Nowhere, if the telephone's out. **1976** *Publishers Weekly* 2 Aug. 108/2 His entire electrical system is out. With no radio and only a limited amount of fuel, it looks like an icy death very soon. **1976** E. P. BENSON *Bulls of Ronda* xxix. 187 He went across to the radio and punched the buttons. There was no sound ... 'The radio's out. I was sure it was in order.'

**[26.] d.** Acknowledged openly as a homosexual (or bisexual); 'out of the closet' (see CLOSET *n.* 3 d). *colloq.*

**1979** *Radio Times* 5-11 May 79/1 If you publish this letter, I would be grateful if you would withhold my full name, because I am not yet fully 'out'. **1983** T. HEALD *Networks* viii. 156 A *Gay News* poll in 1981 found that only forty-three per cent of homosexuals were 'out' at work. **1987** *Venue* 27 Mar. 15/3 Homosexuals find it easier to be 'out' than bisexuals.

**outboard,** *a.*, *adv.* For '*Naut.*, exc. in 3.' read 'orig. and chiefly *Naut.*' and add: **[B.] c.** *transf.* To the outside *of* something; on the far side or away from the centre. *U.S. colloq.*

**1935** PIPPARD & PRITCHARD *Aeroplane Struct.* (ed. 2) xii. 238 A bob weight .. should be placed as far outboard of any wing support as possible. **1966** T. PYNCHON *Crying of Lot 49* v. 110 She found being deftly pinned outboard of one breast this big cerise .. badge. **1973** —— *Gravity's Rainbow* I. 61 The needle slips without pain into the vein just outboard of the hollow in the crook of his elbow. **1986** *N.Y. Post* 9 July 9 The route would follow .. 'outboard' along the West Street roadbed.

**outcome,** *n.* Add: **[2.] b.** *spec.* in *Med.* and *Psychology*, the result or effect of treatment. Freq. used *attrib.*, esp. in *outcome study*, with reference to the assessment of a particular treatment by studying its outcome in a range of cases.

**1926** *Rep. Public Health & Med. Subjects* (Min. of Health) XXXIII. 2 On the average, 'cure' in the sense we associate with the usual outcome of a successful operation for strangulated hernia is not the outcome of the most enlightened treatment of pulmonary consumption. **1941** *Amer. Jrnl. Psychiatry* XCVIII. 438/2 The usual medical criteria regarding outcome of treatment are employed—apparently cured, much improved, improved and unchanged or worse. **1953** SEEMAN & RASKIN in O. H. Mowrer *Psychotherapy Theory & Res.* ix. 228 The outcome studies provide measures of behavioral modification and information about individual differences in such modification. **1959** PARLOFF & RUBINSTEIN *Res. in Psychotherapy* 277/1 The tenor of the discussion strongly suggested that 'outcome' research was generally scorned as being 'applied'. **1967** *Jrnl. Consulting Psychol.* XXXI. 109/2 It is precisely through outcome studies with concurrent measurement or manipulation of variables whose influence is unknown that important variables are likely to be identified. **1981** B. A. FARRELL *Standing of Psychoanal.* ix. 180 Smith and Glass examined a very large number of outcome studies of various types of therapy.

**outcry,** *n.* Add: **[1.] b.** *spec.* A vehement public protest (*against* or *over* something); more rarely, a popular demand *for*.

**1911** G. B. SHAW *Doctor's Dilemma* Pref. p. xlv, A popular outcry for the suppression of a method of research which has an air of being scientific. **1914** —— *Misalliance* Pref. p. lv, There is a continual outcry against the sacrifice of mental

accomplishments to athletics. **1957** W. S. CHURCHILL *Hist. Eng.-Speaking Peoples* III. ix. 296 Andrew Jackson's victory at New Orleans and the success of the peace negotiations produced an outcry against the disloyalty of New England. **1961** J. HELLER *Catch-22* xi. 113 Captain Piltchard and Captain Wren were both too timid to raise any outcry against Captain Black. **1965** A. J. P. TAYLOR *Eng. Hist. 1914-45* i. 26 Northcliffe, greatest of the press lords .. resolved to launch an outcry against the 'shells scandal'. **1988** P. GAY *Freud* iii. 105 There would be an outraged outcry, a veritable 'thunderstorm' over the nonsense, the foolishness, he had produced.

**out-dooring** (aʊt'dɔərɪŋ), *n.* *W. Afr.* [f. OUT-DOOR *a.* (*adv.*) or OUTDOOR(S *adv.* (*n.*) + -ING¹, tr. Ga *kpodziemo* going out.] A traditional ceremony in which a baby is brought outside for the first time to be named.

**[1937** M. J. FIELD *Relig. & Medicine Ga People* 171 On the eighth day, very early in the morning .. two women of the father's family are sent to bring the child from the mother's home .. to its father's house. The friends and relations assemble in the yard outside the house for the *kpodziemo* or 'going out' ceremony.] **1962** B. KAYE *Bringing up Children in Ghana* iv. 58 In the Northern Territories, the child is carried on to a flat roof of the compound to celebrate its out-dooring in some tribes. *Ibid.* 59 In Central Accra .. the naming or out-dooring ceremony, called *kpodziemo*, is performed eight days after birth. **1975** J. WYLLIE *Butterfly Flood* (1977) xxiv. 112 The child's maternal grandmother had taken him from his mother's hut .. eight days after his birth ... The ceremonies continued from the 'outdooring' to the 'namegiving' by the father.

Also **out-'door** *v.* *trans.*, to bring (a baby) out into the open for the first time.

**1962** B. KAYE *Bringing up Children in Ghana* iv. 57 After seven days have elapsed .. it is considered that the child is human, and it is 'out-doored', or brought into the open for the first time.

**outhouse** ('aʊthaʊz), *v.* [f. OUT- + HOUSE *v.*; cf. OUTHOUSE *n.*] *trans.* To store (books, etc.) in a building or area away from the main collection.

**1966** *Times Lit. Suppl.* 10 Mar. 182/3 We are assured .. by the Museum that care has been taken .. to outhouse only books which are thought to be less frequently consulted. **1974** *Daily Tel.* 18 Dec. 10/6 Because of the 'crippling' shortage of space, more than one million books had had to be 'outhoused' at Woolwich Arsenal. **1979** *Ibid.* 27 July 16 Books which could not be stored there should be outhoused in some unspecified place or in a warehouse at Somerstown. **1987** *Financial Times* 24 Oct. (Weekend Suppl.) p. xvii/6 There is talk of outhousing some of the collection.

Hence **'outhousing** *vbl. n.*, the action or process of outhousing books, etc.; (provision for) accommodation or storage away from the main site; also *transf.*

**1967** *Brit. Mus. Rep. Trustees 1966* ii. 53 Further outhousing on a large scale will be necessary before the proposed new library building is completed. **1968** F. J. HILL in R. F. Sewell *Five Years' Work in Librarianship 1961-1965* i. 19 At the Austrian National Library .. storage problems are acute, and co-operative outhousing is considered likely to be the only solution. **1975** *Times Lit. Suppl.* 15 Aug. 920/3 Out-housing is an established practice in university libraries, where it is not impossible to distinguish certain categories of books which will receive considerably less use than others. **1988** *Daily Tel.* 7 June 18/3 The pressure for new homes comes from the out-housing of long-lived pensioners, fissiparous marriages and youngsters leaping prematurely from the parental nest.

‖**outjie** ('əʊki), *n.* *S. Afr. colloq.* [Afrikaans, f. *ou* fellow, chap (*OU n.²*) + *-tjie* dim. suffix.] A child, 'young fellow'; also applied (usu. joc. or contemptuously) to an adult. Freq. in *pl.*

**1960** J. TAYLOR *Ag Pleez Deddy* (*song*), If you wont take us to the zoo then what the heck else can we do But go on out and moera [*sc.* beat up] all the outjies next door. **1963** A. FUGARD *Blood Knot* i. 29 The wind turned and brought the stink from the lake and tears, and a clear memory of two little outjies in khaki broeks. **1978** J. BRANFORD *Dict. S. Afr. Eng.* 175/2 Those outjies up in Johannesburg don't know which side their bread's buttered. **1987** S. ROBERTS *Jacks in Corners* 82 'Listen *outjie*,' I say, 'Shut up .. right away.'

**outlier**, *n.* Add: [**2.**] **d.** *Statistics.* An observation whose value lies outside the set of values considered likely according to some hypothesis (usu. one based on other observations); an isolated point. Also *transf.*

**1907** *Biometrika* V. 312 The 'exceptionals' .. are mostly 'outliers' in the tables of pairs of distributions considered. *Ibid.* XXVIII. 312 (*in figure*) Outliers in samples of 10 & 15. *Ibid.* 317 Even when there are obvious outliers, the process may never get started at all. **1950** *Ann. Math. Statistics* XXI. 38 A natural statistic to use for testing an 'outlier' is the difference between such an extreme observation and the sample mean. **1960** *Technometrics* Feb. 1 At the 1959 meetings of the American Statistical Association held in Washington D.C., Messrs. F.J. Anscombe and C. Daniel presented papers on the detection and rejection of 'outliers', that is, observations thought to be maverick or unusual. **1973** *Computers & Humanities* VII. 136 What .. differentiates 'La Comtesse d'Escarbagnas', at the top of the diagram, from the remaining plays? What is special about an outlier such as 'Dom Garcie'? **1987** K. A. RUBINSON *Chem. Anal.* iv. 132 The validity of outliers can be tested by using statistical methods.

**outper'formance**, *n.* Chiefly *Comm.* [f. OUTPERFORM *v.* + -ANCE, after PERFORMANCE *n.*] The action or process of outperforming, esp. on the stock market; *spec.* performance which is better than the average for a given sector.

**1980** *Amer. Banker* 17 Mar. 6/4 Bank stocks extended to two consecutive weeks their first outperformance of the equity markets this year. **1983** *Sunday Times* 3 Apr. 47 Scottish trusts have outperformed their English counterparts on average over both one and five years. That outperformance has been achieved .. because they have pumped more money into the US. **1988** *Daily Tel.* 9 Dec. 22/4 The shares have been recovering recently ... Gentle outperformance is now likely.

**outplace**, *v.* Senses a, b in Dict. become 1, 2. Add pronunc. '(stress variable)' and for definitions read: **1.** To displace or oust. (Later example.)

**1988** *Computerworld* 6 June 87 Large quantities of these machines are becoming available, with many inquiries about summer delivery of machines being outplaced by corporations upgrading to PS/2 machines. **2.** *spec.* To assist (a redundant employee, usu. an executive) in finding new employment, esp. through an outplacement service; hence (*euphem.*), to discharge through redundancy; = DEHIRE *v.* orig. *U.S.*

**1970** *Time* 14 Sept. 83 Instead of simply bouncing a subordinate, the boss can send him to a firm that specializes in helping unwanted executives to find new jobs. The practitioners have even coined a euphemistic description for the process: 'outplacing' executives who have been 'dehired'. **1973** C. L. BARNHART et al. *Dict. New Eng.* 338/1 Outplace, *U.S.* to place in a new job before actual discharge from a company; help secure new employment. **1981** W. SAFIRE in *N.Y. Times Mag.* 21 June 10/4 If your boss threatens to fire you, put him down with 'You can't

outplace me—I quit!' **1987** *Financial Rev.* (Sydney) 28 Aug. 18/5 Up to 150 staff will be 'outplaced', with the group administrative services unit and the professional services unit (lawyers) being hardest hit.

Hence **outplaced** *ppl. a.*; **outplacer** *n.*, a person or agency that outplaces employees.

**1981** *Forbes* (N.Y.) 19 Jan. 77/1 If you ever do get canned .. you might count yourself lucky to be placed in the hands of the outplacers. **1987** *Amer. Banker* 13 July 13/2 Consulting work has been a popular vocation for retired or outplaced bankers. **1988** *Daily Tel.* 15 Dec. (Appointments Suppl.) p. i/1 Outplacers may be called in to help a small number of senior executives suddenly made redundant.

**outplacement** (stress variable), *n.* orig. *U.S.* [f. OUTPLACE *v.* + -MENT; cf. PLACEMENT *n.*] The provision of assistance to redundant employees (esp. at a senior level) in finding new employment, esp. as a benefit provided by the employer directly or through a specialist service; hence *euphem.*, the discharging of an employee through redundancy; also, the state or condition of being outplaced. Freq. *attrib.*

**1970** *Daily Tel.* 10 July 4/6 Employers with unwanted executives .. resort to 'the dehiring process' or 'executive outplacement'. **1970** *Time* 14 Sept. 83/2 The outplacement firms have their critics. Some industrial psychologists feel that an executive who has been fired needs the determination to reassess his abilities and find a job on his own. **1977** *Time* May 328/1 These half dozen or so organizations, known in the doublespeak world of consulting as 'out-placement' or 'de-hiring' firms. **1983** T. HEALD *Networks* xi. 215 Because nowadays .. the outplacement people are nervous of promising what they can't deliver, they 'help people find jobs for themselves'. **1984** *Times* 5 July 27/1 The concept of outplacement, which comes from the United States, is a euphemism which might straightforwardly be described as severance. **1987** *Sunday Times* 26 July 69/1 Career counselling—or 'outplacement', as the service is called when it is pitched instead at companies that are trying to chop senior executives as mercifully as possible.

**outpsych** (aʊtˈsaɪk), *v. colloq.* (chiefly *U.S.*). Also **outpsyche**, **out-psyche**. [f. OUT- 18 + PSYCH *v.*] *trans.* To win a psychological advantage over (a rival); to defeat through psychological influence or intimidation; = *psych out* s.v. PSYCH *v.* 3.

**1974** H. L. FOSTER *Ribbin'* vi. 251 Billy Jean King eventually outpsyched Riggs and beat him badly. **1976** SMYTHIES & CORBETT *Psychiatry* xii. 228 If one party to a dispute learns that the other party is employing a psychiatrist, they may be motivated to employ one too, to avoid being out-psyched by the opposition. **1980** *Forbes* (N.Y.) 24 Nov. 173/3 Old presidents like Rosenberg are supposed to have the ability to out-psych the vagaries of [the] market. **1984** *Washington Post* 2 June A15/1 Each country tries to psyche out and out-psyche the other. To the best interpreter go the spoils. **1986** *Sunday Express Mag.* 26 Oct. 15/3 It can be difficult to come down after the day-long adrenalin fix of trying to out-psyche the capitalist system.

Hence **out'psyching** *vbl. n.*

**1982** *Sci. Amer.* Aug. 10/1 The lovely thing about the game was how level on level of 'outpsyching' could pile up in our minds. **1987** *N.Y. Times* 25 Oct. v. 13/2 The more ferocious the fight, .. the wearing-down, the out-psyching, the approach to the knockout and the knockout itself, the more spellbinding the event.

**outrage**, *v.*[1] Add: [**2.**] **c.** To cause (a person) to feel profound resentment, anger, or shock; to offend deeply. Also *absol.*

**1921** GALSWORTHY *To Let* II. iii. 152 Jon listened, bewildered, almost outraged by his father's words, behind which he felt a meaning that he could not reach. **1932** W. FAULKNER *Light in August* viii. 177 He had been not hurt or astonished so much as outraged. **1966** *Listener* 6 Oct. 495/2 The latest graduate revue .. does not outrage, but it does not try. **1987** J. UGLOW *George Eliot* 6 Her union with George Henry Lewes had so outraged her brother Isaac .. that he refused to communicate with her.

**outraged**, *ppl. a.* Add: **2.** Profoundly offended or angered; shocked, horrified, appalled; bitterly indignant.
   **1911** G. B. SHAW *Getting Married* 235 The General [*outraged*]: Do you imply that I have been guilty of conduct that would expose me to penal servitude? **1941** E. BOWEN *Look at all those Roses* 130 Throughout tea the outraged Harriet had not suffered in silence: there had been a good deal of mumbling at her end of the table. **1954** W. FAULKNER *Fable* 129 They .. were watching them, the inquisitors, the inspectors, the alarmed and outraged and amazed. **1982** U. BENTLEY *Natural Order* (1983) 24, I felt outraged at having been exposed to such brutality.

**outrate** (aʊt'reɪt), *v.* [f. OUT- 18 + RATE *n.*¹] *trans.* **a.** *Sc.* To outnumber; to outpace. **b.** To outscore in the ratings; to surpass or outdo. orig. *U.S.*
   **1885** 'S. MUCKLEBACKIT' *Rural Rhymes* 27 They doubly can ootrate the 'men'. **1903** in *Eng. Dial. Dict.* IV. 369/1, I was fairly ootrated for he finished an hour afore me. We tried a bicycle run an' I was ootrated by twenty minutes. **1955** *Sun* (Baltimore) (B ed.) 22 Nov. 1/2 (*heading*) American TV outrates pythons in Cambodia. **1975** J. WYLLIE *Butterfly Flood* (1977) xi. 40 A level of noise that outrates the clamour around the bargain counter .. at Macy's. **1988** *High Technol. Business* Apr. 28/3 Glenn's system outrates Japan's Muse and leaves Sarnoff's ACTV in the dust.

**Outremer** ('uːtrəmɛər, ‖utrəmər), *n. Hist.* [a. F. *outre-mer* adv. (as in *pays* or *département d'outre-mer*), f. *outre* beyond + *mer* sea.] The land beyond the sea: applied to the medieval French crusader states.
   **1833** LONGFELLOW *Outre-Mer* 7, I, too, in a certain sense, have been a pilgrim of Outre-Mer; for to my youthful imagination the old world was a kind of Holy Land. **1930** H. LAMB *Crusades* I. xl. 262 Outremer .. consisted of Armenia, the principality of Antioch and the county of Edessa on the north, the long strip of the principality of Tripoli in the centre, and on the south the kingdom of Jerusalem. **1963** *Listener* 14 Mar. 471/1 By the time of the first crusades the cities of Outremer were all rich treasuries for a barbarian rabble to pillage. **1985** J. M. ROBERTS *Triumph of West* iv. 129 By then, the inherent weakness of the Christians of 'Outremer' ('Beyond the sea') had been amply demonstrated.

**outrigger**, *n.* Add: [5.] **c.** A framework extending from the main chassis of some motor vehicles, on to which the body is mounted. Freq. *attrib.*
   **1959** *Motor* 22 Apr. 425/1 To this main backbone, outrigger members are extended to the full width of the centre section of the body. **1959** *Autocar* 24 Apr. 619/1 Fore and aft control of the wheels is by means of a tubular control rod at each side ... At the front these are anchored to the rear outriggers of the frame. **1962** T. P. POSTLETHWAITE *Triumph Herald Cars* xiv. 194 The chassis side members are extended to form out-rigger portions and provide body-mounting points. **1976** *Eastern Even. News* (Norwich) 9 Dec. 17/6 (Advt.), Triumph Herald, 1966, M.O.T.'d, new clutch, starter, sills, outriggers, not rot. **1983** *Truck & Bus Transportation* July 50/3 These chassis will have ZF synchromesh overdrive gearboxes, outriggers will be deleted and .. will be identical with the lower-powered route bus model.

**outro** ('aʊtrəʊ), *n. colloq.* [Irreg. blend of OUT *adv.* and INTRO *n.*, with OUT *adv.* replacing IN-.] A concluding section, *esp.* one which closes a broadcast programme or musical work.
   **1971** *Listener* 23 Dec. 882/2 At the start of the play and during the outro into each cluster of commercials she was discovered lit in limbo. **1980** *Washington Post* 17 May B2/2 This exquisitely edited report .. tells its story without narration (except for Snyder's studio intro and outro). **1984** *Chicago Sun-Times* 23 Apr. 47 It generally takes the veejays less than an hour to tape a five-hour air shift. They move quickly from intro to outro to promo to news. **1985** *Music Week* 2 Feb. 25/3 Dave Goodman .. has added a straight orchestral intro and outro. **1988** *N.Y. Times* 25 Nov. C21/4 We have a strong interest in the intros and outros of our songs.

**outsource** ('aʊtsɔːs), *v. Comm.* (chiefly *U.S.*). [f. OUT- 15 + SOURCE *v.*¹] *trans.* To obtain (goods, etc., esp. component parts) by contract from a source outside an organization or area; to contract (work) out. Also *absol.*
   **1979** *Jrnl. R. Soc. Arts* CXXVII. 141/1 We are so short of professional engineers in the motor industry that we are having to outsource design work to Germany. **1982** *Ward's Auto World* May 37/3 Chrysler in the past few years has closed two of three foundries .., outsourcing some of these requirements. **1983** *Fortune* 7 Mar. 110/2 To a large extent the products out-sourced are low-technology items such as window cranks, seat fabrics, and plastic knobs. **1984** *USA Today* 24 Sept. B2/2 'GM purchased a $1 billion license to automate and outsource as it sees fit,' says MIT labor researcher Harley Shaiker. **1986** *Times* 9 Jan. 29/2 It is now fashionable to outsource everything that is not of strategic consequence to the organisation.
   Hence **'outsourced** *ppl. a.*; **'outsourcing** *vbl. n.*, the obtaining of goods or contracting of work from sources outside a company or area.
   **1981** *Business Week* 31 Aug. 60/3 The .. decline in auto industry jobs .. will make outsourcing a key issue. **1984** *Fortune* 15 Oct. 155/2 The company fought off efforts to curb outsourcing. **1988** *Industry Week* 21 Nov. TM28/2 Outsourced designs and products must be integrated with each other and with in-house designs as the final product moves toward completion.

**outwear** ('aʊtweə(r)), *n.* [f. OUT- 3 + WEAR *n.*] Outer clothing (as opp. to *underwear*); = *outerwear* s.v. OUTER *a.* 3. Freq. *attrib.*
   **1966** *Olney Amsden & Sons Ltd. Price List* 3 Outwear. For Outwear Ranges (Pyjamas, Shorts, Shirts Etc.,) Please ask Traveller for latest list. **1977** *South China Morning Post* (Hong Kong) 22 July 13/2 (Advt.), Babies' outwear from Japan .. $11.00–$56.00. **1980** *Daily Tel.* 9 Apr. 2/1 A Debenhams spokesman said that the week had shown sales up by 30 per cent. with a big rise in outwear clothing. **1988** *Women's Wear Daily* 5 July 10/1 Veteran wool coatmaker Martin Blank is out to make a name for himself in leather outwear.

**over**, *adv.* Add: [II.] [7.] **c.** *over to* (*prep. phr.*): over at. Cf. TO *prep.* 4. *dial.*
   **1897** G. BARTRAM *People of Clopton* 140 I'd had a big job .. over to Noston Wood. **1911** E. WHARTON *Ethan Frome* 193 She .. stayed with Ethan over to the minister's. *a* **1945** A. CHRISTIE *Sleeping Murder* (1976) viii. 71, I was in a job over to Plymouth for a while. **1976** P. G. WINSLOW *Witch Hill Murder* (1977) xv. 202 She just decided to take off home ... Her mom was over to the Brewsters', so there would've been no questions. **1987** 'B. VINE' *Fatal Inversion* xv. 229 He's over to Walnut Tree [geriatric ward] on account of needing a bit of care but he's fit as a fiddle really.

**'overspend**, *n.* [f. the vb.] An amount (of a budget, etc.) overspent; also, the exceeding of projected expenditure, or an instance of this. Cf. UNDERSPEND *n.*

**1976** *Sunday Times* 6 June 62/1 On the housing deficit, a footnote to a table says 'it is most unlikely that a real overspend of as much as half that amount is in prospect.' **1978** *Daily Tel.* 17 June 8/8 The possibility of an overspend in one year in five or ten when adjusting planned spending to accord with cash limits. **1980** *Jrnl. R. Soc. Arts* Feb. 151/1 All these schemes involve..planning on larger and larger projects leading to increased overspend. **1987** *Tree News* Sept. 1/3 The money allotted for landscape is whittled away and used to pay for the inevitable overspend on the buildings.

**overstayer**, *n.* Delete *N.Z. colloq.* and for 'A Polynesian or other immigrant' read 'An immigrant'. (Earlier and later examples.)

**1976** *Times* 17 Sept. 4/6, I think the Home Office could adopt a much more liberal attitude to overstayers, particularly to people from Cyprus or Rhodesia. **1980** LD. DENNING *Due Process of Law* v. ii. 178 Suffice it to say that the amnesty did not apply to these overstayers. If they overstayed before 1973 they were still liable to deportation. **1982** *Times* 19 Aug. 3/2 Mr Darr..is an overstayer, but his supporters are arguing that he and his family should be allowed to stay on compassionate grounds. **1986** *Daily Tel.* 3 Sept. 1/2 When the investigation was launched..the aim was to locate 54 of the 'overstayers'.

**overstitch** ('əʊvəstɪtʃ), *n. Needlework.* (orig. *U.S.*). Also **over-stitch**. [f. OVER- 5 b + STITCH *n.*[1]] A stitch worked over an edge (or over another stitch) in oversewing, usu. to bind, strengthen, or provide a decorative finish.

[**1876** J. S. INGRAM *Centennial Exposition* 380 A 'carpet machine'..intended to sew the breadths of carpets together by the 'over and over' stitch.] **1907** *Sewing Machine Advance* XXIX. 85/2 Weir has perfected a patent on a sewing machine that promises to revolutionize the art of carpet sewing, the device making possible an overstitch, an accomplishment heretofore unknown. **1922** *Sewing Machine Times* Oct. 18/1 Overstitch Mechanism... The combination, in a sewing machine, of a needle actuating mechanism operatively connected with a revolvable shaft located above the throat of the plate. **1923** *Daily Mail* 19 Jan. 15 From the inside of this, at the bottom, is taken a chain-stitch which is caught down with a short over-stitch. **1987** *Washington Post* 12 Nov. B10/1 Threads that appear to be gold are silver foil wrapped around a white silk core and couched (a three-dimensional overstitch) in yellow thread.

Also '**overstitch** *v. trans.*, to sew with an overstitch; '**overstitched** *ppl. a.*; '**overstitching** *vbl. n.*

**1909** WEBSTER, Overstitch v. **1977** *Washington Post* 26 Oct. B3/4 Several quilted jackets..have the overstitching more for decoration than warmth. **1979** *Summary World Broadcasts: Weekly Econ. Rep.: U.S.S.R.* (B.B.C.) 9 Nov. A/19 Synthetic materials.. usually have to be overstitched. **1988** *Chain Store Age Gen. Merch. Trends* May 88/3 Spring/summer items feature overstitched edges and polyester backings.

**overstrike** ('əʊvəstraɪk), *n.* [f. the vb.]

**1.** *Numism.* An overstruck coin.

**1932** *Proc. Brit. Acad.* XVIII. 212 Sextantes, with mint-marks C and MA, of the same class as certain early denarii, are commonly found in Sardinia overstruck on Sardinian bronze. We cannot assign such overstrikes to any date earlier than 237 B.C. **1970** *Ashmolean Mus. Rep. Visitors 1969* 33 Fifth century overstrikes at Rhegium and Messana.

**2.** *Computing.* The action or result of overstriking (OVERSTRIKE *v.* 3 b); = *strike-over*

s.v. STRIKE *v.* 88; a facility which allows or performs this. Freq. *attrib.*

**1977** *Office* Dec. 127/2 Model 2 .. features full-page autopagination, block select, subscripts, superscripts, forms tab, overstrike, [etc.]. **1978** *Computer* Dec. 47/1 This, coupled with the provision of proportional pitch, scrolling, overstrike, underscore, and subscript and superscript capabilities, compounded the speed requirements. **1984** *Austral. Microcomputer Mag.* Jan. 35/3 Underlining, double striking, boldfacing.., ribbon color and various overstrike or strike-out enhancements of the print. **1984** *QL User* Dec. 36 APL statements resemble a mysterious shorthand made up of Greek letters and overstrike characters.

**overstrike**, *v.* Add: 4. *Computing.* To print (a diacritic or other modification of a character) on top of an existing character; to type (two or more characters) in the same position. Also *absol.* Cf. OVER-PRINT *v.* 3 b.

**1981** *Personal Computer World* Aug. 83/3 By using a special character at the beginning and end of the area to be treated, you can underline, boldface, shadow print, slash overstrike (goodness knows why) or dash overstrike (ditto). **1983** I. FLORES *Word Processing Handbk.* iii. 83 A 'not equal' sign is made by overstriking = and / to print ≠. **1987** *Lit. & Linguistic Computing* II. 1. 30/2 One of the essentials is to overstrike the breathings and the accents (and to put the iota subscript where it belongs).

**oxamniquine** (ɒk'sæmnɪkwiːn), *n. Pharm.* [f. OX(Y- + *-amni-* (perh. f. rearrangement of AMIN(O-) + QUIN(OLIN)E *n.*] An anthelmintic drug given orally in the treatment of schistosomiasis caused by *Schistosoma mansoni* infestation; 1,2,3,4-tetrahydro-2-isopropyl-aminomethyl-7-nitro-3-quinolyl-methanol, $C_{14}H_{21}N_3O_3$.

**1972** *Approved Names* (Brit. Pharmacopœia Commission) Suppl. IV. 5 Oxamniquine. **1973** *Trans. R. Soc. Trop. Med. & Hygiene* LXVII. 679 Puerto Rican worms derived from the survivors of treatment of a previous generation with a sub-curative dose of oxamniquine were as susceptible to the drug as were their parents. **1979** *Nature* 14 June 574/3 Oxamniquine will be given to 12 million people (already between 1 and 2 million have been treated) whereas provision of sanitation is planned for only 2.6 million. **1985** *Ann. Rev. Pharmacol. & Toxicol.* XXV. 489 In every case where hycanthone-resistant *S*[*chistosoma*] *mansoni* worms have been isolated from either man or animals, they have been found to be resistant to oxamniquine also.

**oxazine** ('ɒksəziːn), *n. Chem.* [ad. G. *Oxazin* (O. Widman 1888, in *Jrnl. f. Prakt. Chemie* XXXVIII. 197), f. a rearrangement of *Azoxin* (A. Bernthsen 1887, in *Ber. Deut. Chem. Ges.* XX. 942): see OXO-, AZO-, -INE[5].] Any compound containing a ring of one nitrogen, one oxygen, and four carbon atoms in the molecule, such as gallamine blue; *spec.*, any of a class of monocyclic compounds with this structure having the formula $C_4H_5NO$. Originally, any of a class of dyes derived from phenoxazine and containing such a ring.

**1889** *Jrnl. Soc. Chem. Industry* 31 Dec. 1004/2 The colouring matters obtained from the chromogen.. are called oxazines. Widman defines oxazines or azoxines as bodies containing a ring of six atoms: one nitrogen atom, one oxygen atom, and four carbon atoms, which are joined by eight bonds of affinity. This class of bodies is of greater interest, since the author's studies on morphine have rendered it probable that this important base and other alkaloids may be considered as oxazines. **1893** THORPE *Dict. Appl. Chem.* III. 79/1 Oxazine colouring matters. The azines or colouring matters of the saffranine group.. are derivatives of phenazine... The colouring matters of the present group are similarly derived from phenoxazine. **1928** C. E. MULLIN *Acetate Silk & its Dyes* x. 140 The thiazine dyes, such as Methylene Blue, are not usually so satisfactory; but the oxazine dyes, which contain an atom of oxygen in place of the sulfur atom present in the thiazine dyes, are useful. **1955** S. E. KRAHLER in H. A. Lubs *Chem. Synthetic Dyes & Pigments* v. 259 The first oxazine dye was prepared by Meldola in 1879, when he heated an equimolar mixture of 2-naphthol and *N, N*-dimethyl-*p*-nitrosoaniline hydrochloride in acetic acid. **1978** M. SAINSBURY in S. Coffey *Rodd's Chem. Carbon Compounds* (ed. 2) IV. H. xli. 427 Oxazines are six-membered monocyclic structures of the general molecular formula $C_4H_5NO$. Depending upon the relative orientation of the oxygen and nitrogen atoms and the disposition of the double bonds in the heterocycle nine isomeric forms are possible.

**oxer**, *n.* Delete *Fox-hunting slang* and add: [1.] In Fox-hunting, an ox-fence; hence similarly in Horse-racing. *slang.* (Later examples.)
   **1907** C. B. FRY in *Daily Chron.* 12 Nov. 4/4 When a man buys a horse .. if he is after a hunter .. he considers the differences in horses relatively to double-oxers, stone-walls, big banks, and broad ditches. **1958** *Times Lit. Suppl.* 31 Jan. 63/2 Such technicalities of the chase as bullfinches and double oxers. **1963** BLOODGOOD & SANTINI *Horseman's Dict.* 118 [Steeplechasing] *Oxer*, strong cattle fence, railing, hedge and sometimes ditch. On Continent a ditch between two wide hedges.
   **2.** *Show-jumping.* Any of various stylized representations of an ox-fence, used as obstacles; *spec.* a double oxer (DOUBLE *a.* 6). Also *fig.*
   **1929** M. DE LA ROCHE *Whiteoaks* i. 6 Without mishap he jumped the wall, then the first oxer, but as he cleared the bars he kicked the top rail. **1969** C. CAREY *Show-Jumping Summer* i. 8 We cleared the pipe-opening brush fence nicely, and went on over the raised oxer, the double and the high wall. **1976** C. DEXTER *Last seen Wearing* 287 The car, the French, and the spots: .. a triple-oxer over which he would normally have leaped with the blithest assurance, but at which, in this instance, he had so strangely refused. **1986** *New Yorker* 18 Aug. 51/1 There was a big oxer, followed by a tight, trappy turn.

**oxidative**, *a.* Add: **b.** *oxidative phosphorylation Biochem.*, the synthesis of ATP in the mitochondria of eukaryotic cells from ADP and phosphate ions, which utilizes energy liberated in oxidative reactions.
   **1945** *Arch. Biochem.* VI. 440 Previous work on oxidative phosphorylation .. has been carried out using washed minces or concentrated dialyzed cell-free extracts equivalent to several hundred milligrams of tissue in 2 or 3 ml. final volume. **1962**, etc. [see PHOSPHORYLATION *n.*]. **1984** J. F. LAMB et al. *Essent. Physiol.* (ed. 2) i. 8 The mitochondria are the 'power-house' of the cell where ATP is made by a process called oxidative phosphorylation.

**oxide**, *n.* Add: [a.]
   *red oxide*: see RED *a.* 17 e.

**Oxon.** ('ɒksɒn, 'ɒksən), *n.* and *a.* Also Oxon (no point). [Abbrev. of *Oxonia* (see OXONIAN *a.* and *n.*) and *Oxoniensis* adj.] **A.** *n.* **a.** The city, diocese, or university of Oxford. **b.** Now more usually, the county of Oxfordshire.
   [**1248** *Rot. Claus. 33 Hen. III*, m. 15 *dorso* (in Rashdall II. 369 *note*), Presentibus apud Woodstocke tam procuratoribus scolarium universitatis quam Burgensibus Oxon. **1367** (Trinity Term) *Coram Rege Roll* 41 Edw. III. 10. 21 Consuetudo hundredi de Stretford in com. Oxon., talis est [etc.].] **1477** *Rolls of Parlt.* VI. 192/1 The studentes in the Universitees

of Oxon and Cambrigge. **1576** in W. H. TURNER *Select. Rec. Oxford* (1880) 383 The Maior and Burgesses of Oxon do stande so muche .. uppon theire right and royaltie of the Thames. **1645** W. BROWNE *Let. to Wood* 9 Sept. in *Wood's Life* (O.H.S.) I. 122 *note*, Our horse from Oxon.—fell on the enemies quarters at Thame. **1729** S. SWITZER *Hydrost. & Hydraul.* 40 The Rivers Rea and Isis, which break out .. in the county of Oxon .. draw their original from so humble a Plain [etc.]. **1840** [see PECULIAR *a.* 5]. **1881** [see COVER *v.*[1] 17]. **1970** *Kelly's Directory of Oxford* 942 (Advt.), Peter W. Wilson & Co ... Sales of all types of property ... Corn Street, Witney, Oxon. **1986** *Guardian* 21 Aug. 11/8 The Management College, Greenlands, Henley on Thames, Oxon, gives a limited number of scholarships for women to do management courses.
   **B.** *adj.* Of or belonging to the University of Oxford. Usu. succeeding nouns in titles, as *M.A. Oxon.* Cf. CANTAB *a.*
   **1681** (*title*) Materials for union, proposed to publick consideration, with indifferency to all parties. By—M.A. *Pem. Col. Oxon.* **1854** (*title*) Splendours of the future: or, the real Antichrist ... With a notice of certain probable scriptural references to Great Britain. By A.M., Oxon. **1989** *Templeton Coll. Ann. Rev. 1988* 9/2 Roger Undy MA (Oxon) had 13 years of industrial experience .. before studying at Oxford.

**oxygen**, *n.* Add: [3.] [b.] **oxygen fugacity**, the fugacity of oxygen in a particular mineral or rock.
   **1959** *Amer. Jrnl. Sci.* CCLVII. 612 At low total pressures $p_{O_2}$ represents closely the true escaping tendency (fugacity) of oxygen in the system ... The $p_{O_2}$ prevailing at the limiting total pressure above which the gas phase disappeared is a rough measure of the \*oxygen fugacity of the system. **1978** *Sci. Amer.* Aug. 104/2 Dryness, low content of volatile elements and low oxygen fugacity are the three hallmarks of lunar-rock composition. **1987** *Zeitschr. für Anorganische und Allgemeine Chem.* DL. 96 The variation of oxygen fugacity with composition of the zinc ferrite-magnetite solutions that coexist with ZnO (s) is independent of temperature.

**Oz** (ɒz), *n.*[2] and *a. slang* (orig. and chiefly *Austral.*). Also *Aus., Oss.* [Repr. pronunc. of abbrev. of *Australia* and *Australian*: cf. AUSSIE *n.* and *a.*] **A.** *n.* **1.** Australia.
   **1908** *Bulletin* (Sydney) 2 July 15/3 My home is near Kingston, which is in the S.E. of South Oss. **1944** *Barging about: organ of 43rd Austral. Landing Craft Co.* 1 Sept. 6 All the tribes of Oz did gather together. **1970** B. HUMPHRIES in *Private Eye* 13 Feb. 16 (*caption*) If they guess I'm from Oz the shit will really hit the fan. **1988** *Arena* Autumn/Winter 78/1 When you are fronting up for the greatest little country .. —ie Oz—you need to be pretty smart.
   **2.** An Australian.
   **1974** D. O'GRADY *Deschooling Kevin Carew* 38 He enjoyed playing various roles, aesthete, cynic, dinkum Aus., but always with detachment. **1976** *Bulletin* (Sydney) 17 Apr. 5/1 The merest suspicion that Australia could be emerging as a cultural nation is enough to make a red-blooded Oz choke on his meat pie. **1986** *Daily Sun* (Brisbane) 19 Oct. 3/7 Mark's an Oz. Mark Knopfler, singing superstar .., has joined the swelling ranks of overseas stars who have fallen in love with Australia.
   **B.** *adj.* = AUSTRALIAN *a.*
   **1971** *Bulletin* (Sydney) 18 Dec. 30/2 Then I got back to England and found myself facing the 'Oz' educational attitudes. **1978** *TV Week* (Brisbane) 24 June 16/1 There was no mad scramble for cheque books among Oz networks to buy it. **1989** *Sunday Tel.* 26 Feb. 13/1 These Oz intellectuals fell over themselves in a desperate parade of learning heavily-worn.
   **C.** *Comb.*, used in various trivial nonce-wds., as **Ozland** *n.*, **Ozman** *n.*, etc.

**1971** *Frendz* 21 May 9/2 The yippees of America, like the Ozniks of London, are right out of the middle class, Chuck. **1985** *Bulletin* (Sydney) 15 Oct. 10/3 Modern Ozman is the direct descendant of the first white boat people. **1987** *Weekend Australian* (Brisbane) 28 Feb.–1 Mar. 13/7 (Weekend Mag.) (*heading*) Witty response deals a swift blow to the sterile Oz-pop. **1987** *Sunday Mail* (Brisbane) 6 Sept. 18/5 (*heading*) Will Ozcard bring us to this? **1987** *Satellite* (Brisbane) 16 Dec. 9/4 (*heading*) 'Lucy' jumps from volatile Brazil to peaceful Ozland.

**Ozarker** ('əʊzɑːkə(r)), *n.* [f. *Ozark* (see OZARK *n.*), designating a mountainous region of Missouri and Arkansas, + -ER¹.] A native or inhabitant of the Ozark region.

**1927** *Amer. Speech* VI. 283/2, I have never heard a real Ozarker say *waw* when he meant *war*. **1941** O. E. RAYBURN *Ozark Country* i. 23 Old-time Ozarkers manufactured their own bullets in molds. **1980** *Knoxville* (Tennessee) *News-Sentinel* 6 Apr. c4/4 Polite Ozarkers don't use either word in mixed company, for they're bawdy.

**Ozarkian** ('əʊzɑːkɪən -ˈzɑːkɪən), *a.* and *n.* [f. as *OZARKER n.* + -IAN.] **A.** *adj.* Of, pertaining to, or characteristic of the Ozark region or its inhabitants; = OZARK *a.*

**1928** in *Funk's Stand. Dict.* **1930** *Outlook* 10 Sept. 60/3 It is like the hissing of a rattler to the Ozarkian landowner who has controlled this region since our country was organized. **1936** MENCKEN *Amer. Lang.* (ed. 4) vii. 360 Pronunciation of the hillmen . . is identical with Ozarkian usage. **1941** O. E. RAYBURN *Ozark Country* i. 10 This colorful Ozarkian dialect is rapidly passing. **1947** J. H. BROWN *Outdoors*

*Unlimited* 75 I've shot from Texas coastals . . , around through . . Ozarkian woods rims at bevies flushing . . from wintered reed beds. **1971** *Holiday* Apr. 110/3 We got moving in his Renault 17, chatting of things Ozarkian.

**B.** *n.* A native or inhabitant of the Ozark region; = *OZARKER n.*; also, the dialect spoken by these people.

**1928** in *Funk's Stand. Dict.* **1930** *Outlook* 10 Sept. 60/2 The Ozarkians, if such the tribe could be called, have lived lazy, kin marrying, morally clean, but none too God-loving lives. **1949** M. PEI *Story of Lang.* v. 46 This would establish . . Ozarkian and Brooklynese as languages. **1971** J. HARTY *Licklog Holler* v. 43 One Ozarkian . . put it this way: 'I want to be situated all the time so that I can look any damn man in the face and tell him to go to hell.' **1987** *N.Y. Times* 11 Jan. IIA. 2/1 The disarming 'Shepherd of the Hills' . . with John Wayne and Betty Field as Ozarkians.

**Ozzie** ('ɒzɪ), *n.* and *a. slang* (orig. *Austral.*). Also **Ossie**. [Repr. Austral. pronunc. of AUSSIE *n.* and *a.*: see *OZ n.²* and *a.*] = AUSSIE *n.* and *a.* 1.

**1918** *Truth* (Sydney) 28 July 6/5 We consider the term Aussie or Ossie as evolved is a properly picturesque and delightfully descriptive designation of the boys who have gone forth from Australia. **1919** *N.Y. Times* 23 Feb. IV. 12/4 There was nothing an Ozzie liked so much as fighting with a Yankee company. **1973** *Nation Rev.* (Melbourne) 24–30 Aug. 1430/4 (Advt.), Femme, 27, bored by ozzie ockers and oedipal neurotics. **1987** *Daily Tel.* 27 May 13/8 The argument is conducted in robust Ozzie style.

# P

**P.** Add: [II.] **P.C.P.**, *Pneumocystis carinii* pneumonia.

**1975** *Jrnl. Amer. Med. Assoc.* 17 Mar. 1168/2 One of the worst, fastest-moving, and cruelest killers of children is *Pneumocystis carinii* pneumonia (*PCP). **1988** *Amer. Jrnl. Nursing* Aug. 1126/1 Pentamidine isethionate has been used since 1941 to treat trypanosomal diseases . . . But it only became widely available in the United States in 1984, when it was found to be somewhat effective in treating *Pneumocystis carinii* pneumonia (PCP).

**PINC, Pinc, pinc** (also with pronunc. pɪŋk), property income certificate.

**1986** *Estates Gaz.* 28 June 1470/4 Property Income Certificates—*PINCs for short—are a completely new investment vehicle and would require setting up a special market to trade in the units. **1988** *Daily Tel.* 13 Sept. 26/1 Taylor Woodrow's decision to take profits from its St Katharine's Dock development, by offering the World Trade Centre building for unitisation through property income certificates (pincs) has surprised many in the City.

**P.-K., P.K.** (*Med.*), Prausnitz-Küstner; usu. *attrib.* (see *PRAUSNITZ-KÜSTNER *n.*).

**1938** G. C. ANDREWS *Dis. Skin* (ed. 2) ii. 43 The *P.-K. test is not positive by any means in all instances of allergy, nor for all allergens. **1963** *Times* 23 Apr. 15/4 Forty years later modern science has still been unable to find other methods to characterize allergic antibodies. Medical students the world over learn about the Prausnitz-Küstner, or as it is usually abbreviated the PK reaction. **1983** *Allergy* XXXVIII. 171/2 The P-K test results.

[III.] **7. p-code** (*Computing*) = *pseudocode* s.v. PSEUDO- 2; sometimes also explained as 'Pascal code' (see PASCAL *n.* 3).

**1974** *PASCAL Newslet.* Jan., in *SIGPLAN Notices* Mar. 25 The PASCAL-P system is a compiler which generates code (so-called P-code) for a simple, hypothetical stack computer. **1984** *Austral. Personal Computer* Apr. 167 (Advt.), Native machine code (not slow p-code), which runs faster than anything yet seen. **1985** *Personal Computer World* Feb. 161/2 This language, Pascal, became widely known and used, thanks mainly to the portable so-called p-Code (Pascal code) implementations. **1985** *Practical Computing* May 71/3 The programs were first compiled to p-code, and then further compiled to the native code and run.

**pabulum**, *n.* Add: **d.** *fig.* Bland intellectual fare; also, something which constitutes an insipid or undemanding diet (of words, entertainment, etc.); = PAP *n.*[2] 1 c.

This figurative use may have arisen partially through confusion with PABLUM *n.*

**1976** *Economist* 15 May 123/2 This is not pure manufacturers' pabulum . . . Geoffrey Knight's own weary distaste for the staggeringly unprofessional way the project was attacked on both sides of the Channel emerges too strongly for that. **1977** A. CARTER *Passion of New Eve* iii. 39 The radio in the car fed me an aural pabulum of cheapjack heartbreak. **1986** *Newsweek* 17 Nov. 83/2 Older fans, disdaining pop pabulum . . prefer instead the familiar sounds of the past. **1987** *Golf World* Aug. 59/1 His forthright answers are a refreshing change from the evasive, sugarcoated pabulum we are so used to swallowing from our sports heroes.

**PAC** (pæk), *n.*[2] *U.S. Pol.* Also **P.A.C., pac.** [Acronym f. the initial letters of *political action* committee.] **a.** The Political Action Committee of the U.S. Congress of Industrial Organizations (CIO). Now *Hist.*

The CIO was founded in 1938, and in April 1955 merged with the American Federation of Labor. The Congress's PAC, established on 8 July 1943, was still in existence at the time of the merger and later merged with a similar AFL committee to become the AFL-CIO's Committee on Political Education (COPE).

**1944** *Birmingham* (Alabama) *News* 8 Aug. 1/1 He . . asked an enquiry to determine whether some government officials active in PAC work had violated the Hatch 'no politics' act. **1944** *Life* 11 Sept. 91/3 At a C.I.O. executive meeting July 7, 1943 they set up a P.A.C. as a committee to support labor's interest within the established two-party system. **1945** *Britannica Bk. of Year* 236 The complete slate of Democratic candidates endorsed by the P.A.C. . . were elected to the state legislature. **1945** *Sat. Rev. Lit.* (U.S.) 13 Jan. 8/1 From coast to coast there were hysterical cries that the PAC had seized the Democrats' political machinery.

**b.** A committee formed within a corporation or other organization to collect voluntary contributions towards electoral funds, thereby circumventing regulations limiting the size of contributions or prohibiting such organizations from contributing directly to political candidates.

**1975** *Business Week* 2 Dec. 56/1 The ruling that permits business to form political action committees (PACs) presents a tougher problem. Businessmen have long envied labor's right to maintain the Committee for Political Education of the AFL-CIO. **1978** *In Common* Spring 5/2 Corporations, banks and unions are forbidden to contribute directly to candidates for federal office, but they may collect voluntary contributions for their political action committees (PACs), and these in turn may contribute to candidates. **1982** *Times* 3 Nov. 17 It was the Federal Election Reform Act of 1974 which spawned the political phenomena known as pacs . . . With the rise of the pacs has come the creation of a new kind of power-broker on the American scene—the dispenser or controller of pac funds. **1986** *Sci. Amer.* Nov. 54/3, 19 leading SDI contractors, mostly aerospace and electronics companies . . have contributed almost $6 million to various political-action committees (PAC's).

**pace**, *n.*[1] Add: [III.] [7.] **d.** The rate of progression (of speech, writing, etc.); the speed with which the action of a story, etc., unfolds; rhythm, tempo.

**1952** E. O'NEILL *Moon for Misbegotten* I. 63 Before I'm through with you, you'll think you're the King of England at an Irish Wake. (With a quick change of pace to a wheedling tone) Tell me now [etc.]. **1962** K. REISZ *Technique Film Editing* (ed. 9) ii. 132 The submarine is briefly shown surfacing—the shot . . is quickly followed by the explosion itself. With the explosion dying down, the pace suddenly relaxes . . and the calm music takes over. **1976** M. HUNTER *Talent is not Enough* 27, I could give my story the bite and pace it needed. **1982** S. BRETT *Murder Unprompted* vii. 75 The dialogue which ran up to it showed good pace.

**e.** The rate or speed at which life is led; *esp.* in phr. *the pace of life*.

**1953** P. GALLICO *Foolish Immortals* xv. 103 There was a breathlessness to the pace and push of this city

that he found overwhelming. **1977** *Time* 22 Aug. 8/2
Bad Ischl has a leisurely pace, lovely promenades and
open-air concerts. **1982** N. SEDAKA *Laughter in Rain*
(1983) IV. xxiv. 200 The brutal pace drove me to
drink—two vodka martinis and a half bottle of wine
every night. **1987** J. UGLOW *George Eliot* i. 13 The
pace of life had accelerated, the railway had pierced
provincial seclusion.

**pace-maker**, *n.* Add: [3.] [c.] Cf. *PACER *n.* 5.

**pacer**, *n.* Add: **5.** *Med.* = PACE-MAKER *n.* 3 c;
occas. applied to similar devices operating on
other organs.
    **1963** *Amer. Jrnl. Cardiol.* XI. 366/1 Within two to
three days after pacer implantation, the dogs assumed
normal habits of eating and exercise. **1970** *Daily Tel.*
18 May 4/8 Surgeons . . have implanted an electronic
pacer in the neck of a teenager whose breathing
would stop unless he consciously thought about it.
**1978** R. LUDLUM *Holcroft Covenant* xviii. 212 The
'pacer' was shorted in the accident; the man died on
the way to the hospital. **1988** *Lancet* 19 Mar. 638/1
Cardiac pacers are inserted at eight hospitals in
Denmark but at 33 hospitals in Norway, which has
about the same population size.

**pachynema** (pækɪˈniːmə), *n.* *Cytol.* [a. F.
*pachynema* (V. Grégoire 1907, in *La Cellule*
XXIV. 3707: see PACHY-, *-NEMA.] =
PACHYTENE *n.*
    **1909** *Archiv für Zellforschung* III. 437 The
longitudinal pairing of the univalent spireme
segments is completed . . at about the middle of the
synapsis, giving rise to the thick spireme or
pachynema. **1911** *Q. Jrnl. Microsc. Sci.* LVII. 8 In
pachynema the chromatin threads are arranged in the
characteristic bouquet grouping. **1971** *Chromosoma*
XXXV. 21 Of ten buds treated at middle or late
pachynema, three contained normal chiasmatic
chromosomes. **1984** L. W. BROWDER *Developmental
Biol.* (ed. 2) vii. 295 During late pachynema and in
diplonema, miniature nucleoli form in association
with these rings of extrachromosomal DNA.

**pack** *n.*[1] Add: [3.] **f.** *Sport.* In a race: the main
body of competitors following behind the
leader or leaders, esp. when bunched together
as a group; hence, any chasing group of
competitors. Also *fig.* orig. *U.S.*
    **1929** *Sun* (Baltimore) 12 May (Sports Section) 2/1
Paul Bunyan set most of the early pace, with the
winner staying well within the pack. **1935** B.
LYNDON *Grand Prix* iii. 59 In the strung-out pack
which followed, 'Freddie' Dixon began to put his
foot hard down on the throttle-pedal of a Riley. **1946**
*Collier's* Oct. 23/1 According to the patented rules,
the teams shake a man loose from the 'pack' or 'jam'
of five skaters. **1958** *Time* 30 June 68/3 They kept
their 3-liter Ferrari well back in the pack. **1972**
*Village Voice* (N.Y.) 1 June 12/4 When McGovern
was running back in the pack, it was all right to
overlook the dangers of success because the dangers
of defeat were so real. **1988** *National Jrnl.* (U.S.) 19
Mar. 728/3 [He] predicted that a clear front-runner
will emerge from the pack.

**Pac-Man** (ˈpækˌmæn), *n.* orig. *U.S.* Also
PacMan, Pac Man, Pac-man. **a.** A proprietary
name for an electronic computer game in which
a player attempts to guide a voracious, blob-
shaped character through a maze while eluding
attacks from opposing images which it may in
turn devour. Also, the voracious central
character itself.
    **1981** *Ann. Rep. Bally Manufacturing Co. 1980* 7/1
The exciting new *Pac-Man* game appeared in
October 1980. This game utilizes a hide and seek
format with the *Pac-Man* able to evade or destroy the
ghosts while devouring points accumulating energy
dots. **1981** *N.Y. Times* 15 Nov. III. 21/1 For a year

now, the best seller in the $5-billion-a-year video-
game market has been Pac-man. **1982** *London Rev.
Bks.* IV. xxiv. 7/3, I still feel an urge to . . play
PacMan till its microchips wear out. **1982** *Observer*
17 Oct. 21/7 Last year, $1 billion in 25 cent pieces
was retrieved from machines in America playing one
electronic game alone—Pac-Man. **1983** *Official Gaz.
(U.S. Patent Office)* Sept. TM72 Pac-Man . . . For
coin and non-coin operated electronic amusement
apparatus for playing a game on a video output
display . . . First use Oct. 30, 1980. **1984** *InfoWorld* 2
Apr. 33 Avoid arcade games, Dewey said with
conviction. 'We tried games like Pac-Man, but it was
just chaos. Some of the kids would go bananas'. **1986**
*Trade Marks Jrnl.* 13 Aug. 2016/1 Pacman . . .
Amusement apparatus and games. **1989** *Network
World* 6 Feb. 85/5 The user [of the Pac Man virus]
gets to watch as Pac Man eats the file on the screen.
    **b.** Hence *attrib.* with allusion to the game;
*spec.* in *Comm.*, used to describe a situation in
which the object of a takeover bid makes a
counter-bid for the 'predator' or acquiring
company.
    **1982** D. A. DE MOTT in *Wall St. Jrnl.* 31 Aug. 3/1
A budding takeover defense plan that Wall Street
arbitragers and investment bankers alike yesterday
were calling 'the Pac-Man strategy'. 'That's where
my client eats yours before yours eats mine,' a
merger specialist at one major investment banking
firm said. **1982** *Times* 1 Sept. 11/2 The Pac-man
strategy was used by Cities Service to fight off a bid
for the much smaller Mesa Petroleum. Cities bid for
Mesa after Mesa had made an unfriendly offer for
Cities. **1983** *Austral. Microcomputer Mag.* Nov. 96/2
The Boeing 767, 757 and Airbus 300 . . have been
dubbed Pac-Man planes because most of the pilot's
instruments have been replaced with CRTs. **1984**
*Business Week* 2 July 77/1 Wyatt wants shareholder
approval of the charges to assure that no target
company can fight back with a 'Pac-Man defense'.
**1987** *Courier-Mail* (Brisbane) 26 Dec. 16/2 The
board saw the tactic as an ASCAP, an assured
second-strike capability; someone else called it a Pac-
Man defence, after the video gobblers.

**pad**, *n.*[3] Senses 3 b-h in Dict. become 3 c-i.
Add: [3.] **b.** A wad of material (such as cotton
wool or gauze) placed over a wound, etc., as a
dressing. Also, short for *sanitary pad* s.v.
SANITARY *a.* 3.
    **1807-26** [see COMPRESS *n.* 1]. **1881** [see *sanitary
towel* s.v. SANITARY *a.* 3]. **1917** [see *sanitary napkin*
s.v. SANITARY *a.* 3]. **1962** C. ROHAN *Delinquents* 42
You'll need six Modess pads. **1984** J. PHILLIPS
*Machine Dreams* 14, I kept a big bowl of gauze pads
on the table.

**paddock**, *n.*[2] Add: [2.] **c.** Hence *transf.* in
*Motor-racing.* orig. *U.S.*
    **1909** in WEBSTER. **1910** *Indianapolis Star* 22 May
11/7 Two long blasts call cars from paddocks to tape
for next event. **1935** B. LYNDON *Grand Prix* vii. 151
While some cars were being warmed up in the
paddock, Lord Howe unveiled a tablet. **1947** C.
CHAKRABONG *Blue & Yellow* i. 20 As they roared
past the Paddock they were still in a mass. **1969** 'D.
RUTHERFORD' *Gilt-Edged Cockpit* xii. 211 After five
laps they . . drove round to the paddock. **1987**
*Autosport* 28 May 43/4 A meagre field of just 23 cars
occupied the barren paddock for the start of
qualifying.

‖**padma** (ˈpʌdmə), *n.* *India.* [Skr., Hindi *padma*
lotus.] The lotus, *esp.* the flower of the lotus-
plant *Nelumbium speciosum*; hence, an
emblematic representation of the flower (as on
an award or decoration); also used as the first
element in the titles of such distinctions.
    [**1848** J. D. HOOKER *Himalayan Jrnls.* Nov. (1854)
I. x. 229 Low stone dykes, into which were let rows
of stone slabs, inscribed with the sacred 'Om Mani

Padmi om'.—'Hail to him of the Lotus and jewel.']
**1895** *Funk's Stand. Dict., Padma* .. [E. Ind.], the true
lotus. **1939** JOYCE *Finnegans Wake* 598 Padma,
brighter and sweetster, this flower that bells, it is our
hour or risings. Tickle, tickle. Lotus spray. Till
herenext. Adya. **1954** *India News* 21 Aug. 4/2 The
Padma Vibhushan Pahela Varg (first class) has been
awarded to Mr B. G. Kher. **1960** KOESTLER *Lotus &
Robot* I. ii. 98 Each of the chakras (literally, wheels)
has a padma or lotus-flower attached to it. **1971**
*Illustr. Weekly India* 11 Apr. 30/1 The coveted
distinction of the Padma Vibhushan. **1984** R. E.
HAWKINS *Common Indian Words in Eng.* 70 Indian
civil decorations are called the Bharat Ratna, Padma
Vibhushan, Padma Bhushan, and Padma Shri.

‖**padmasana** (ˌpʌd'mɑːsənə), *n.* *Yoga.* [Skr.
*padmāsana*, f. *padma* \*PADMA *n.*, lotus + *āsana*
seat, posture.] In Yogic exercises: the lotus
position, in which the legs are folded and
crossed and the feet turned sole upwards on the
thighs. See LOTUS *n.* 3 c.
**1884** RAM CHANDRA BOSE *Hindu Philos.* vi. 177 It is
called Padmásana (lotus-posture), and is highly
beneficial in overcoming all diseases. **1957** A. W.
WATTS *Way of Zen* I. ii. 54 Most images of the
Buddha show him in the posture of sitting
meditation, in the particular attitude known as
*padmasana*, the posture of the lotus. **1960** J. HEWITT
*Yoga* iii. 61 In Padmasana, your feet crossed on to
your thighs, thrust your hands between knees and
thighs and stand on your hands.

**pædication** ('piːd-, 'pɛdɪˌkeɪʃən), *n.* Also ped-,
and in Lat. form **pædicatio**. [f. mod.L.
*pædicātiōn-em*, n. of action f. *pædicātus*, pa.
pple. of L. *pædicāre* to commit sodomy with.]
Pederasty, sodomy.
**1887** L. C. SMITHERS tr. *F. C. Forberg's Man.
Classical Erotology* ii. 71 But enough of paedication.
**1897** H. ELLIS *Stud. Psychol. Sex* I. v. 118 In
thirteen cases .. *pædicatio*—usually active, not
passive—has been exercised. In all these cases,
however, *pædicatio* is by no means the habitual ..
method of gratification. **1913** Pædicatio [see VOYEUR
*n.* 1]. **1941** G. LEGMAN in J. N. Katz *Gay/Lesbian
Almanac* (1983) 576 Pedication [can be] openly
suggested as a substitute for the desired coitus. **1978**
*Observer* 15 Oct. 34/8 Pedication is subdivided into
Bend Over, Pedication as Insult, [etc.].
Hence (as a back-formation) **pædicate** ('piːd-,
'pɛdɪkeɪt) *v. trans.*, to practise paedication on.
**1941** G. LEGMAN in J. N. Katz *Gay/Lesbian
Almanac* (1983) 580 *One-way man*, a male prostitute
who .. will allow himself to be fellated but not
pedicated. **1983** *Maledicta 1982* VI. 147 Expressions
such as peddle your ass, have a bit of ring (pedicate).

**pædicator** ('piːd-, 'pɛdɪkeɪtə(r)), *n.* Also
pedicator. [a. L. *pædicātor*, agent-n. f. *pædicāre*:
see \*PÆDICATION *n.*] One who commits
paedication; a sodomite.
**1661** O. FELLTHAM *Resolves* (rev. ed.) lxxvi. 352 It
[*sc.* Sodom] was a City of Pædicators and Catamites
[etc.]. **1941** G. LEGMAN in J. N. Katz *Gay/Lesbian
Almanac* (1983) 574 *Bugger*, a pedicator. *Ibid.*, Boys
of this age [*sc.* 15-20] .. fancied by many
homosexuals, both pedicators and fellators.
Also **pædi'catory** *a.*, of or pertaining to
paedication.
**1976** *Times Lit. Suppl.* 17 Dec. 1576/2 The boys
who fell into his hands .. learnt more than the best
pedicatory postures. **1979** *Maledicta* III. 105 This is
a whole pedicatory scenario.

**pædodontics** (piːdəʊ'dɒntɪks), *n. pl.* (const. as
*sing.*) Chiefly *N. Amer.* Usu. pedo-. [f. PAEDO-,
PEDO- + *-dontics* after ORTHODONTIC *a.* and *n.*]
The branch of dentistry dealing with children;
the care of children's teeth.

**1923** DORLAND *Med. Dict.* (ed. 12) 814/2
Pedodontics. **1965** *Jrnl. Dentistry for Children*
XXXII. 209/1 Dr Haney recently told the members
of the American Academy of Pedodontics that [etc.].
**1978** *N.Y. Times* 30 Mar. B18/2 (Advt.), Dentist
experienced for general practice ... Crown & bridge,
periodontic, endodontic, pedodontics. **1988** *Scand.
Jrnl. Dental Res.* XCVI. 457/1 A case group, 101
children aged 3-16 yr, referred for management
problems to clinics of specialized pedodontics.
Hence **pædo'dontic** *a.*; **pædo'dontist** *n.*, a
dentist specializing in paedodontics.
**1923** DORLAND *Med. Dict.* (ed. 12) 814/2
Pedodontist. **1937** W. C. McBRIDE *Juvenile Dentistry*
(ed. 2) ii. 50 The author expresses the opinion ..
from observations in other pedodontic [ed. 1 (1932):
pediadontic] offices that .. there is no more, if as
much, waste time and effort in a child's practice than
in a general practice. *Ibid.*, Most of the fillings done
by pedodontists are presumably inserted momentarily
as the child is in the mood. **1965** *Jrnl. Dentistry for
Children* XXXII. 203/1 The first attempt was .. in
1921, when a few pedodontists attending the ADA
Convention in Milwaukee met at luncheon and
decided to organize. **1981** D. J. FORRESTER *Pediatric
Dental Med.* p. vii/1 When I attempted to plan a
contemporary pedodontic curriculum, I discovered
that a comprehensive presentation of pedodontics
required the use of numerous texts.

**page**, *v.*[2] Add: **4.** *Computing.* To process data
(*esp.* to display text, etc.) on a screen, by
paging: see \*PAGING *vbl. n.*[1] 2 b. Usu. with *adv.*
or *advb. phr.* indicating the direction in which
the text is processed.
**1971** *Proc. AFIPS Conf.* XXXVIII. 542/2
(*heading*) Paging through the data file. **1984** *Which
Micro?* Dec. 33/2 You can page forwards and
backwards through the file.

**paging**, *vbl. n.*[1] Add: [**2.**] **b.** The displaying of
text, etc., on a screen in amounts of one page at
a time.
**1971** *Auerbach on Alphanumeric Displays* xi. 82 In
paging, a new page or screen full of data may be
called in. **1980** *Practical Computing* Oct. 62/3 Paging
is more restful to the eye, and would be ideal but for
the fact that the page mode announces itself via a
small flashing square in the bottom-right-hand corner
which obscures two letters of the text.

**paho** ('pɑːhəʊ), *n. U.S.* Also baho, bahoo. [ad.
Hopi *paáho.*] A wooden stick, decorated with
plumes of feathers and usu. painted, used by
the Hopi Indians as a prayer-stick in various
rituals, esp. in their snake dance; also, a good-
luck charm made in imitation of this.
**1884** J. G. BOURKE *Snake Dance Moquis Arizona*
174 This consecration of the bahos .. was a prayer to
the yellow clouds of the north .. to come quickly and
bring rain. **1893** P. MORAN in *11th Census Moqui
Pueblo Indians* (U.S. Census Office) 70, I tried to buy
a bahoo of one of these attendants, but he declined to
sell it, saying that if he did his stomach would burst
open. **1898** J. W. FEWKES in *Ann. Rep. Board of
Regents Smithsonian Inst. 1896* 535 The priests made
elaborate *pahos* or prayer sticks, some of which were
several feet long, and painted them with .. pigments,
the same as those used by their descendants. **1912** H.
R. VOTH *Papers Field Museum Nat. Hist.* CLVII. 126
Each one, when done, smoked and spurted honey
over his bahos or nakwakosis. **1979** *Arizona
Highways* Apr. 32/2 A *paho* dangles from his rearview
window. **1987** *Resurgence* Nov./Dec. 6/1 On the tree
hung a *paho*, a feather charm, sign that Henry's
garden was under the invisible protection of the
spirits of the land.

**pain**, *v.* Add: [**2.**] **c.** *intr.* Of a limb or joint: to
ache, be painful. *colloq.* and *dial.*

**1934** [see BORROW v.[1] 2 b]. **1967** W. STYRON *Confessions Nat Turner* I. 21 I'd be mighty grateful if you could get them to ease off these chains. My shoulders pain something fierce. **1983** R. K. NARAYAN *Tiger for Malgudi* 107 My knees are paining.

**paintable**, *a.* Add: **painta'bility** *n.*
**1934** WEBSTER *Add.*, Paintability. **1960** *Times* 15 Nov. 16/7 The medieval tradition of Ceylonese art, the paintability of the land, .. are all illustrated in the .. exhibition entitled 'Ceylon, a painter's country'. **1981** *Chemical Week* 13 May 24/1 Cadon resins mold and plate better and offer comparable chemical resistance and paintability, the company claims.

**painter**, *n.*[1] Add: **[1.]** c. *Astron.* (With capital initial.) The constellation Pictor (formerly Equuleus Pictoris) in the southern hemisphere. Formerly called *Painter's Easel* (see sense *4 below).
**1959** SPITZ & GAYNOR *Dict. Astron. & Astronautics* 302 Pictor (the Painter). **1979** in *Macmillan Dict. Astron.*
**4. Painter's Easel** (now *rare*) = sense *1 c above.
**1877** G. F. CHAMBERS *Handbk. Descr. Astron.* (ed. 3) VI. vii. 556 La Caille, in 1752, added—6. Equuleus Pictoris. The Painter's Easel. **1926** *Peck's Southern Hemisphere Constellations* (rev. ed.) 32/2 The Modern Constellations . . . Added by La Caille, A.D. 1752 . . . Pictor (Equuleus Pictoris), the Painter's Easel. **1939** J. G. INGLIS *Easy Guide to Constellations* (Index) p. iv, *Pictor*, Painter's Easel.

**paisan** (paɪ'zɑːn), *n.* *U.S. colloq.* Also **pizon.** [f. PAISANO *n.* or *ad.* It. *paesano* (locally *paesan'*) countryman, compatriot.] A fellow-countryman; a 'buddy'. Freq. used as a form of address, esp. by people of Italian extraction or background. Cf. PAISANO *n.*
**1947** W. MOTLEY *Knock on any Door* xiv. 71 'So long, pizon,' Nick said. Grant laughed. 'So long, pizon.' *Ibid.* xviii. 90 Someday he will be walking on the street and we'll meet and I'll say, 'Hello, pizon.' **1960** 'E. MCBAIN' *Heckler* xiv. 179 I'm Italian, too. A *paisan*, huh? How about that? **1960** —— *Give Boys Great Big Hand* x. 105 'This is Bartholdi . . . What'd you say your name was?' 'Carella.' 'Hello, *paisan.*' **1964** 'E. QUEEN' *Four Men called John* (1976) vii. 83 'You're his brother?' 'Yeah. Couple of North Beach paisans.' **1970** W. WAGER *Sledgehammer* vii. 29 Now that the *paisan* is here the only one to wait for is the little guy. **1980** *N.Y. Times* 25 Oct. 23/5 'Listen, *paisan,*' Pappa said, 'before you marry my daughter, you're gonna have to sleep with me a week.' **1987** *Advertising Age* 23 Nov. 32/3 Just about then they got word from that other great *paisan*, Sinatra.

**pakeha**, *n.* and *a.* Add: *N.Z.* [Maori.] **B.** *adj.* Of, pertaining to, or designating a fair-skinned non-Maori, esp. a New Zealander. *pakeha Maori*, a white man who has adopted a Maori lifestyle (now *rare*).
**1838** J. S. POLACK *New Zealand* II. iii. 102 He [*sc.* the chief] said I was a pákeha maori or native white man. **1845** E. J. WAKEFIELD *Adv. N.Z.* I. 73 We do not want the missionaries from the Bay of Islands, they are pakeha maori, or whites who have become natives. **1859** [see *beach-comber* s.v. BEACH *n.* 4]. **1882** W. D. HAY *Brighter Britain!* II. v. 171 Human nature triumphed over Pakeha morality. **1940** H. BELSHAW in I. L. G. Sutherland *Maori People Today* vi. 224 The .. primary stage . . often represents the first experience of *pakeha* civilization. **1957** *Jrnl. Polynesian Soc.* LXVI. 351 A group of Maori and pakeha students in a District High School east of Rotorua. **1961** D. P. AUSUBEL *Maori Youth* iii. 54 Pakeha pupils lived in a more urban environment. **1985** M. KING (*title*) Being Pakeha. **1985** *National*

*Education* (N.Z.) Nov. 216 We retrace the first Maori and Pakeha contacts.

**Pakkawood** ('pækəwʊd), *n.* Also **pakkawood.** [f. *Pakka-*, of unknown origin + WOOD *n.*[1]; cf. *pakka* var. of PUKKA *a.* (*n.*).] A proprietary name for a hard wooden laminate which is resistant to heat and is used to make handles for cutlery, cooking utensils, etc.
**1955** *Trade Marks Jrnl.* 4 May 459/2 Pakkawood. **1959** *Listener* 15 Jan. 147/2 The handle is made of pakkawood—a new laminated hardboard. **1960** *Guardian* 24 Oct. 6/7 The 'Sky-Line' sandwich knife .. has a handsome pakkawood handle. **1978** *Detroit Free Press* 2 Apr. 9A (Advt.), Ekco six-piece steak knife set. Blades are stainless steel and handles are Pakkawood, finger-carved for an easier, safer grip. **1987** *Los Angeles Times* 6 Aug. VIII. 9/5 The pakkawood handle is heat and water resistant and stays cool.

**pa-kua** (pɑːkwɑː), *n.* Also **ba gua, pa kua,** †**pa-kwa.** [a. Chinese *bāguà* (Wade-Giles *pā-kua*), f. *bā* eight + *guà* divinatory symbols.] **1.** a variety of traditional Chinese symbols or motifs incorporating the eight trigrams of the I Ching; *spec.* an arrangement of these trigrams in a circle round the yin-yang symbol.
**1875** *China Rev.* IV. 73/2 The use of the *Pa-kwa* or 'Eight diagrams' [*sic*]—a collection of strokes arranged in hexagonal form and familiar to the merest tyro in Chinese studies—as a charm to ward off evil influences is universal . . . Go where one will, the inevitable *pa kwa*, carved, painted or written, is almost sure to ornament some portion of the premises. **1913** W. E. SOOTHILL *Three Religions of China* vii. 171 The Yi Ching, one of the five canonical classics .. is founded on a symbol, peculiarly Chinese, known as the pa-kua . . . Confucius became much interested in the pa-kua. **1931** A. U. DILLEY *Oriental Rugs & Carpets* ix. 210 Other primitive motives are .. fortune-telling trigrams called Pa-kua [etc.]. **1962** E. SNOW *Other Side of River* li. 388 Symbols such as the *pa-kua*, or eight trigrams, and the more familiar *yin-yang*. **1971** L. A. BOGER *Dict. World Pott. & Porc.* 102/1 The pa kua or eight trigrams are represented by eight sets of straight lines . . . These eight trigrams are arranged symmetrically around a circular sign which is the symbol of Creation.
**2.** A Chinese system of unarmed combat and physical training, involving boxing, and characterized by continuous walking in a circle.
**1967** R. W. SMITH (*title*) Pa-kua; Chinese boxing for fitness and self-defense. **1972** DA LIU *T'ai Chi Ch'uan & I Ching* (1974) i. 2 Sun is better known for his work in *Sheng I* and *Pa-Kua* (Eight Trigram) boxing. **1979** *Washington Post* 13 Apr. (Weekend Suppl.) 40/1 Staccato commands .. resound, and the orbiting stops. With surprising swiftness, legs pivot around, thighs together, feet pigeon-toed as arms swing out and a kick follows. In a blink the methodical walk resumes in the opposite direction. This is *pa-kua*, an internal system of Chinese boxing for fitness and self-defense. **1986** *Combat* May 50/1 Very shortly I was hooked on these deceptively soft internal styles: Ba Gua with its flowing circles and Xing Yi with its dynamic, explosive straight-line actions.

**palapa** (pə'læpə), *n.* *U.S.* [a. Mexican Sp. *palapa*, orig. a name for the palm *Orbignya cohune*, later also used of its leaves and branches.] A traditional Mexican rustic shelter roofed with palm leaves or branches; also used of any structure built in imitation of this, esp. on a beach. Freq. *attrib.*, esp. in *palapa bar*, a bar built in such a style.
[**1964** *Nat. Geographic* Dec. 872/1 Those roofs over there are covered with *palapa*, coconut leaves.] **1975** *Sunset* Oct. 50/3 Several villages .. offer primitive

bungalows or *palapas* (palm-covered shelters) for a few dollars a night. *Ibid.* 52/3 Popular hangout for Perula locals and visitors is a palapa-style restaurant .. serving octopus, red snapper, pargo—whatever the day's catch. **1980** *Christian Science Monitor* 5 Feb. 15/1 Senor Perez lives next door in a palapa he designed—a conical, open-air Mexican hut. **1986** *N.Y. Times* 20 Apr. VII. 8/2 El Cozumeleno .. has the requisite palapa bar at beachside. **1986** *New Yorker* 4 Aug. 32/2 He will swim for his customary hour, and then rest beneath his palapa.

**Palauan** (pə'lauən), *n.* and *a.* Also **Belauan** (bɪ'lauən). [f. the place-name *Palau* (now *Belau*) + -AN.] **A.** *n.* **a.** A native or inhabitant of the Palau Islands, now the Republic of Belau, in the Caroline Islands of Micronesia. **b.** The Malayo-Polynesian language of the people of these islands. **B.** *adj.* Of or pertaining to these people or their language.
   **1909** WEBSTER, Palauan *n.* **1948** W. KARIG *Fortunate Islands* xiv. 200 All Yaplanders, like their neighbors the Palauans, chew betel. **1953** *Natural Hist.* (N.Y.) LXII. 231 (*caption*) A typical Palauan outrigger. **1961** *Science* 21 Apr. 1203/1 The Palauan words for 'five' and 'hand'. **1975** *Language* LI. 556 Palauan vowel reduction in unstressed syllables is a phonetically motivated process. **1982** *Progressive* May 34/2 The Belauan chain, formerly called Palau from its Japanese pronunciation, has been under the control of various foreign powers for four centuries. *Ibid.* 35/3 In early 1979 the Belauans called a constitutional convention. **1983** *Sea Frontiers* XXIX. 34/1 Babeldaop means 'upper ocean' in Palauan. **1987** *Sanity* Sept. 17/2 By building your understanding of the Belauan people and by learning to love the land and the sea you will know what you are fighting to protect.

**palaver**, *n.* Add: Senses 2 d–f in Dict. become 2 e–g. [2.] **d.** A tiresome or lengthy business (*esp.* one which seems unnecessarily so), a 'rigmarole', a fuss; also, commotion, trouble. *colloq.*
   **1892** J. LUMSDEN *Sheep-Head* 199 Both he and the little boy perished. Much fuss and palaver at the time were made about it in the public prints. **1920** D. H. LAWRENCE *Women in Love* xii. 149 She hated the palaver Hermione made ... She wanted anything but this fuss and business. **1947** H. W. PRYDE *First Bk. McFlannels* v. 50 Inside ma collar's the only place fur the thing [*sc.* a table napkin]. Ach, it's nothin' but a palaver onyewy. **1967** P. BAILEY *At the Jerusalem* III. 154 What a palaver there was before the coach left! Chattering away, rushing around. **1979** J. GRIMOND *Memoirs* iv. 67 We coached him in all the palaver of the court, the standing up and sitting down, the 'Yes m'lud' and 'no, m'lud'. **1987** D. ADAMS *Dirk Gently's Holistic Detective Agency* viii. 53 He went through a palaver similar to his previous one with his coat and hat.

**Paleyan** ('peɪlɪən), *n.* and *a.* Theol. Also 9 **Paleian, Paleyian.** [f. the name of William *Paley* (1743–1805), English theologian + -AN.] **A.** *n.* A follower of Paley or supporter of his theories, esp. of his rationalist, proto-utilitarian, moral philosophy and his view of God as the supreme 'watchmaker' of a universe governed by mechanistic natural laws.
   **1818** S. T. COLERIDGE *Coll. Lett.* (1959) IV. 901 For myself, I cannot agree wholly either with Sir S. Romilly on the one side, or with the Paleyians on the other. **1855** W. BAGEHOT in *National Rev.* I. 284 Let us keep no terms with Paleyans in speculation. **B.** *adj.* Of, pertaining to, or characteristic of Paley or his theology.
   **1825** S. T. COLERIDGE *Coll. Lett.* 23 May (1971) V. 465 The cheerlessness, vulgarity and common-place character of the mechanical philosophy, and Paleyian Expedience. **1862** A. J. MUNBY *Diary* 16 Aug. in D.

Hudson *Munby* (1972) 135 From lips like hers, the Paleian philosophy sounds creditable. **1915** G. B. SHAW in *New Statesman* 8 May 109/2 Darwin's deathblow to the old Paleyan assumption that any organ perfectly adapted to its function must be the work of a designer. **1951** N. ANNAN *Leslie Stephen* iii. 111 So far from being a Paleyan Deity who proves His existence to men by the ingenious mechanism of Nature, the Evangelical God is a God of miracles. **1976** C. E. RUSSETT *Darwin in Amer.* ii. 38 The notion of a higher order beyond the reach of natural selection was as open to Hume's critique as was the Paleyan form of natural theology.

**Paleyology** (ˌpeɪlɪ'ɒlədʒɪ), *n.* nonce-wd. [f. the name of William *Paley* (see *PALEYAN *n.* and *a.*) + -OLOGY.] A dismissive term for the theology of Paley and his followers.
   **1924** R. MACAULAY *Orphan Island* xxv. 320 William has been made Instructor in Science, and twentieth century views of the cosmos have supervened on the dying and despised Paleyology imparted by Miss Smith.

‖**pali** ('pɑːliː), *n.*² Also 9 **parry.** Pl. **pali, palis.** [Hawaiian.] In Hawaii: a steep cliff or precipice, *esp.* on Oahu; also, a pass between the *pali.*
   [**1825** A. BLOXHAM *Diary* 13 May (1925) 40 This pass is called the Parre by the natives, a word signifying a steep cliff or precipice.] **1833** L. SMITH in M. D. Frear *Lowell & Abigail* (1934) 65 Mr Smith .. [invited the mission families to].. see the parry (*pali*) which is seven miles distant. **1862** M. HOPKINS *Hawaii* ii. 12 In some places, streams which have united their waters on their way, rush together over one of these *palis*, or precipices, into the ocean. **1915** W. A. BRYAN *Nat. Hist. Hawaii* x. 113 The Pali is truly Oahu's scenic lion. It is a natural wonder. **1935** L. V. JACKS *Mother Marianne of Molokai* iv. 64 At the base of this peninsula huge mountains called 'pali' fence it across cliffs of more than twenty-five hundred feet sheer fall. **1957** *Encycl. Brit.* XI. 266/1 The most noted panoramic view is that of the windward side, which bursts suddenly on one upon arrival at the Pali (precipice), the only traversable pass. **1989** *Los Angeles Times* 16 Mar. v. 1/1 The lush Nuuanu Valley rises through a pass in the dark green mountains to a precipice called the pali.

**pallet**, *n.*² Sense 1 b in Dict. becomes 1 c. Add: [1.] **b.** A temporary or makeshift bed, usu. consisting of bedclothes spread on the floor. *U.S.* (chiefly *dial.*).
   **1884** 'M. TWAIN' *Huck. Finn* xxvi. 257 Up garret was a little cubby, with a pallet in it. **1925** E. GLASGOW *Barren Ground* II. xiii. 328 She had offered to stay on for the night. 'I can make up a pallet jest as easy as not in yo' Ma's room,' she said. **1930** W. FAULKNER *As I lay Dying* 183 They made a pallet for him with quilts on top of the coffin. **1943** J. STUART *Taps for Private Tussie* xiii. 175 She laid a quilt down on the dirty floor; then she spread a sheet over the quilt and another quilt over the sheet ... Then she took six pillows from the sack Grandpa carried and put two down on each pallet. **1989** *Chicago Tribune* 2 Feb. 13/5 It wasn't unusual for 10 or 15 people to be sleeping on pallets on the floor and on counters.

**palm**, *n.*¹ Add: [2.] **b.** An emblematic representation of this; *spec.* a military decoration in the form of a palm frond, such as that awarded in addition to the French *Croix de Guerre.*
   **1918** *Country Life* Nov. 30 War Cross (Croix de Guerre), instituted 1915; awarded to any one, military or civil, who has been cited in the Order of the Day-citation in Army orders brings the cross with palm ... A palm of silver represents five bronze palms. **1935** J. O'HARA *Appointment in Samarra* i. 10 Lute had the French Croix de Guerre with palm for something he said he did when he was drunk. **1977**

C. HILLIER tr. *Simenon's Maigret & Hotel Majestic* vi. 81 A croix de guerre with three palms and the military medal. **1986** J. B. HILTON *Moondrop to Murder* vii. 64 [She] holds the *Croix de Guerre* with stars and palm.

**palm**, *v.* Add: [2.] c. To steal or filch (something small) by taking and concealing in the palm of the hand.
**1941** J. SMILEY *Hash House Lingo* 42 *Palm*, to steal small articles (gum, candy) by concealing them in the palm of the hand. **1946** S. T. FELSTEAD *Stars who made Halls* xvi. 167 What you really heard, of course, was his heart beating; the watch he had palmed. **1985** G. KENDALL *White Wing* (1986) vii. 83 Joao turned away from the board, and palmed a hypo of nepenthine before heading for a tube to the flight deck.

‖**palmier** (palmje), *n. Cookery.* [Fr., lit. 'palm-tree'.] A small, crisp cake, shaped like a palm-leaf, made from puff-pastry and sugar.
**1929** E. J. KOLLIST *French Pastry, Confectionery & Sweets* iii. 34 *Palmiers*, pigs ears. Ingredients. Puff Paste . . Castor Sugar. *c* **1938** *Fortnum & Mason Price List* 10 Palmiers . . per doz. 4/-. **1956** *Good Housek. Home Encycl.* (ed. 4) 425/2 (*heading*) Cream crisp (palmier). **1970** SIMON & HOWE *Dict. Gastron.* 287/1 *Palmier*, a Parisien speciality of small strips of puff pastry which are rolled in granulated sugar, folded and baked in a moderate oven until the sugar caramelizes. **1980** *Redbook* Oct. 187/2 Palmiers are small, chewy-crisp, heart-shaped puff-pastry cookies that you've probably seen in French-pastry shops.

**pan**, *v.*[1] Add: 8. To hit or strike (a person), to punch; also, to knock (sense) into. *slang.*
**1942** BERREY & VAN DEN BARK *Amer. Thes. Slang* §322/5 *Beat; thrash*, . . pan. **1943** HUNT & PRINGLE *Service Slang* 50 *Pan*, slang for face. Also used instead of 'hit', i.e. to 'pan' a man is to strike him. **1959** I. & P. OPIE *Lore & Lang. Schoolch.* x. 198 If a person does something which doesn't please us we cry 'scrag him', or 'pan him', or 'floor him'. **1963** *New Society* 22 Aug. 5/2 'To pan' is to punch just once. **1977** *Transatlantic Rev.* LX. 149, I start going down the steps to meet them, and maybe pan some sense into their skulls.

**pan-**, *comb. form.* Add: [2.] **pan'lectal** *a.* Linguistics [-LECT], covering all the regional and social varieties (within a language).
**1972** C.-J. N. BAILEY in Stockwell & Macaulay *Linguistic Change* 24 Children constantly revise a single internal grammar of their native language until they arrive at one which will handle the observed variety, asymptotically approaching a *panlectal grammar through the incorporation of a sufficient number of diverse . . types. **1986** *English World-Wide* VII. 187 This emphasis reflects a . . belief that dialects of English share a panlectal identity at this level of structure.

‖**pancetta** (pan'tʃɛtta), *n. Gastron.* [It., dim. *pancio* paunch, belly.] Italian cured belly of pork.
**1954** E. DAVID *Italian Food* 89 Melt some bacon fat and 3 or 4 oz. of bacon or Italian *pancetta* (obtainable in Soho shops). **1984** BARR & LEVY *Official Foodie Handbk.* I. 35 With these ingredients . . like-minded friends can be feasted—and non-Foodies overawed . . pancetta, sliced [etc.]. **1986** *Sunday Express Mag.* 14 Sept. 42/2 Pancetta is the wonderful salted or smoked belly of pork.

**Pancoast** ('pæŋkəʊst), *n. Path.* The name of Henry Khunrath Pancoast (1875-1939), U.S. radiologist, used *attrib.* and in the possessive in **Pancoast('s) syndrome**, the clinical manifestation of a Pancoast tumour, caused by involvement of the brachial plexus and characterized by pain and numbness on the inner surface of the arm, atrophy of the small hand muscles, and Horner's syndrome; **Pancoast('s) tumour**, a carcinoma of the apex of the lung (described by Pancoast in *Jrnl. Amer. Med. Assoc.* (1932) 22 Oct. 1391).
**1941** DORLAND & MILLER *Med. Dict.* (ed. 19) 1556/2 Pancoast's t[umour]. **1951** *Dorland's Med. Dict.* (ed. 22) 1489/2 Pancoast's s[yndrome]. **1956** *Brit. Med. Jrnl.* 15 Sept. 645/1 Pancoast syndrome is a clinical and radiological entity which can be produced by a variety of pathological lesions at the root of the neck. **1960** HARMEL & TAYLOR *Rose & Carless's Man. Surg.* (ed. 19) xi. 204 The so-called Pancoast's tumour of the lung, or a tumour arising from the first rib, may involve the brachial plexus and sympathetic outflow. **1974** J. D. MAYNARD in R. M. Kirk et al. *Surgery* x. 216 Local spread may involve the recurrent laryngeal nerve to produce hoarseness, or infiltrate the brachial plexus to produce a Pancoast syndrome. **1975** RAINS & RITCHIE *Bailey & Love's Short Pract. Surg.* (ed. 16) xxxv. 682 Pancoast 'Tumours'.—These are essentially peripheral lung carcinomas arising at the apex of the lung. **1984** TIGHE & DAVIES *Pathology* (ed. 4) xiv. 128 A tumour arising near the apex of the lung may give rise to Pancoast's syndrome.

**panguingue** (pæŋ'giːŋgiː), *n.* Also -gui. [ad. Tagalog *pangguinggui*.] A card game resembling rummy, played with several packs of cards.
**1909** WEBSTER Panguingue. **1912** *Official Rules Card Games* (U.S. Playing Card Co.) (ed. 16) 15 Panguingui, which in reality, is a fairly simple game. **1926** *Ibid.* (ed. 29) 174 Penalties for foul play in game of panguingue. **1950** E. CULBERTSON *Culbertson's Hoyle* 47 Panguingue, called 'Pan' for short, grew out of Conquian. It is the chief card game in many gambling clubs of the Pacific Coast and the southwestern United States. **1985** *Los Angeles Times* 6 Jan. XI. 2/4 Card games at the casino will be limited to draw poker and panguingue.

**Panhard rod** ('pænɑːd, ‖panar), *n.* [f. *Panhard* (ellipt. f. *Panhard-Levassor*, the name of a French motor company which incorporated the feature on many of its cars).] A torsion bar attached to the rear axle on some motor vehicles.
**1963** *Motor* 16 Oct. 176 Rear suspension: dead axle with torsion bars and Panhard rod. **1979** *Daily Tel.* 11 Apr. 14/6 The live rear axle has trailing arms, coil springs and a Panhard rod. **1983** *Truck & Bus Transportation* Dec. 34/2 The rear tag axle has two 254mm rolling diaphragm air springs with a leading arm panhard rod location.

**paragon**, *n.* (*a.*) Add: [A.] [I.] c. One who (occas. that which) is a model or exemplar *of* (some admired or excellent quality).
**1689** SHADWELL *Bury Fair* II. i, Your ladyship . . has been long held a paragon of perfection. **1756** C. LUCAS *Ess. Waters* I. Ded., The dissolved civil constitution, that paragon of perfect polity. *c* **1874** E. DICKINSON *Poems* (1955) III. 907 We commend ourselves to thee Paragon of Chivalry. **1906** GALSWORTHY *Man of Property* II. i. 3 Having watched a tree grow from its planting—a paragon of tenacity, insulation, and success, amidst the deaths of a hundred other plants less fibrous, sappy, and persistent. **1934** R. GRAVES *I, Claudius* ii. 36 She is a paragon of matronly modesty. **1988** A. N. WILSON *Tolstoy* vi. 132 Tolstoy finds it hard to account for the fact that this paragon of virtue should have died in the arms of a prostitute.

**parallelism**, *n.* Add: 8. *Computing.* The use of parallel processing; the execution of operations concurrently by separate parts of a computer, *esp.* (in later use) by separate microprocessors; also, the capability of a computer to operate in this way.

**1961** J. A. GLASSMAN (*title of M.Sc. thesis, Univ. California*) The effects of digital computer parallelism in solving for the roots of a polynomial. **1978** *Communications Assoc. Computing Machinery* XXI. 67/1 Note that all of the functional units can operate concurrently so that in addition to the benefits of pipelining . . we also have parallelism across the units too. **1984** P. H. WINSTON *Artificial Intelligence* (ed. 2) iv. 139 Of course, action-centered and object-centered systems, as request-centered systems, can have parallelism, so the issue of computational resources . . is a general issue. **1987** *Computer Newslet.* 24 Apr. 11/3 Architectures to support fifth generation languages and software . . almost always involve parallelism to achieve realistic performance.

**paralogous**, (pə'ræləgəs), *a. Biol.* [f. PARA-¹ after HOMOLOGOUS *a.*] Of two or more genes, esp. in different species: descended from a single gene by gene duplication in the course of evolution. Also, characterized or produced by such genes. Cf. *ORTHOLOGOUS *a.*

**1970** FITCH & MARGOLIASH in *Evolutionary Biol.* IV. 76 Following a gene duplication, both genes may evolve different functions while descending side by side in the same phyletic lineage. Such genes may be called paralogous (para = in parallel) and an example might be human myoglobin and α hemoglobin. **1971** *Nature* 29 Jan. 323/2 Sequences suspected to have a paralogous relationship were tested by an empirical method, partly developed by Dayhoff and Eck. **1977** *Ibid.* 28 Apr. 804/1 He states that 'the tRNAs are mostly paralogous', which was news to me, because there are many examples of homologous tRNAs for the same amino acid occurring in related species of organisms. **1987** *Molecular Biol. & Evol.* IV. 81 One may repeat the analysis using the paralogous A and E genes.

Hence **pa'ralogously** *adv.*

**1970** [see *orthologously* adv. (s.v. ORTHOLOGOUS *a.*)]. **1979** *Systematic Zool.* XXVIII. 158/1 As illustrated by the case of hominoid delta chains which are found along with beta chains in adult hominoid red blood cells, there is usually compelling biological evidence to show that such chains are paralogously related to a set of orthologous ones.

**Paralympic** (pærə'lɪmpɪk), *n.* and *a. colloq.* Also **paralympic**. [f. PARA(PLEGIC *n.* + O)LYMPIC *a.* and *n.*: see -ICS.] **A.** *n. pl.* An international athletic competition modelled on the Olympic Games, for paraplegics and other disabled athletes.

**1954** *Bucks Advertiser* 6 Aug. 4/1 (*caption*) The flags of the nations flutter high above Stoke Mandeville Hospital, where paraplegic athletes from all over the world had assembled for the Paralympics. **1964** *N.Y. Times* 8 Nov. v. 2/8, 368 competitors from 21 countries . . will compete . . in the second Paralympics, the new name of the International Stoke Mandeville Games for men and women who, through some misfortune, are unable to walk. **1975** *Oxf. Compan. Sports & Games* 750/1 Paraplegic games. Also popularly known as the 'paralympics' and the 'wheel-chair Olympics', this is an annual sports meeting for semi-paralysed competitors. **1986** *Swimming Times* Sept. 25/2 The England/Wales swimmers have established themselves as the World's best, and the team to beat at the Paralympics in Seoul two years hence. **B.** *adj.* Of or pertaining to the Paralympics, esp. as *Paralympic Games.* Cf. *Paraplegic Games* s.v. *PARAPLEGIC *n.* b.

**1955** *N.Y. Times* 20 July 29/2 Eleven men who work for Pan American World Airways will . . fly to the Fourth International Paralympic Games at Aylesbury in Britain. **1964** *Times* 10 Nov. 8/6 D. Thompson (Britain) won two gold medals in the first full day of the 22-nation 'paralympic' games here today. **1988** *Times* 29 Jan. 34/1 1988 is an Olympic

year. It is also, as fewer people will know, a Paralympic year.

**paralyse**, *v.* Add: [2.] **b.** To bring (a place or its activities) to a standstill. Chiefly *N. Amer.*

**1933** *N.Y. Times* 25 Oct. 31/3 (*heading*) Strike paralyzes trade in Havana. **1959** *Ibid.* 30 Jan. 1/1 The worst fog for many winters . . paralyzed London and most of England and Wales tonight. **1970** A. TOFFLER *Future Shock* (1971) ix. 185 Great cities are paralyzed by strikes, power failures, riots. **1984** *Weekend Australian* 10–11 Nov. 7/1 Half-a-dozen towns and villages have been virtually paralysed since Sunday, when municipal workers went on strike.

'**paralysed** *ppl. a.*: (*b*) intoxicated; incapacitated through drink; cf. PARALYTIC *a.* 3 d (*slang*, chiefly *U.S.*).

**1927** *New Republic* 9 Mar. 72/1 The following is a partial list of words denoting drunkenness now in common use in the United States . . paralyzed. **1945** E. WAUGH *Brideshead Revisited* I. v. 108 The only time I got tight I was paralysed all the next day. **1964** J. WHITE tr. *Leulliette's St. Michael & Dragon* 92 About five o'clock, everyone . . was 'paralysed', completely and utterly drunk.

**paramountcy**, *n.* Add: **b.** *spec.* The supremacy of the British Crown as acknowledged by the Indian Princes during the British raj. *Obs.* exc. *Hist.*

**1820** D. OCHTERLONY *Let.* 21 Mar. in E. Thompson *Making of Indian Princes* (1943) xlv. 283, I hope His Lordship will in Virtue of his Power & Paramountcy forbid all future Invasions of Surhoie & fix himself a Sum which the Rajah *must* take. **1929** *Rep. Indian States Comm.* i. 14 in *Parl. Papers 1928–29* (Cmd. 3302) VI. 1 The paramountcy of the Crown acting through its agents dates from the beginning of the nineteenth century when the British became the *de facto* sole and unquestionable Paramount Power in India. **1947** *Sun* (Baltimore) 9 June 10/1 Simultaneous with the assumption of dominion status by Hindustan and Pakistan, 'paramountcy' will lapse. **1962** P. M. SCOTT *Birds of Paradise* III. i. 153 Independence for British India would mean the end of paramountcy, the end of treaties the British no longer had the means to adhere to. **1985** P. ZIEGLER *Mountbatten* III. xxx. 387 When paramountcy lapsed, he replied, the States could do as they wished, but they could not enter the Commonwealth as Dominions.

**parapatric** (pærə'pætrɪk), *a. Biol.* [f. PARA-¹ 1 + Gr. πάτρα fatherland, after ALLOPATRIC, SYMPATRIC *adjs.*] Of speciation: such that the diverging populations occupy distinct but contiguous areas. Also, occurring in or designating such areas.

**1955** H. M. SMITH in *Turtox News* Feb. 77/1 Recognizable differentiation of parapatric or sympatric populations must of necessity be *preceded* (or accompanied) by the attainment of some sort of reproductive isolation. **1972** J. MURRAY *Genetic Diversity & Nat. Selection* vi. 87 It is . . convenient to distinguish by the term parapatric speciation the special case considered here in which the incipient species are contiguous populations in a continuous cline. **1977** *Nature* 22 Dec. 785/2 Subspecific and even specific differentiation (parapatric speciation) in the absence of barriers to gene-flow is as common and important as divergence with strong barriers. **1983** E. C. MINKOFF *Evolutionary Biol.* xiii. 234/1 These findings are unaffected by subsequent studies showing that the frogs placed by Moore in the species *Rana pipiens* belong in reality to two closely similar species (sibling species) with closely adjacent (parapatric) ranges.

Hence **para'patrically** *adv.*, by means of parapatric speciation; without physical isolation.

**1973** *Nature* 31 Aug. 574/1 The karyotypes coexist parapatrically with little or no interbreeding. **1983** E. C. MINKOFF *Evolutionary Biol.* xiv. 248/2 *Clarkia lingulata*, with tongue-shaped petals and a chromosome number of 2N=18, appears to have formed parapatrically on the periphery of the range of *Clarkia biloba*, a more wide-ranging species with heart-shaped petals and 2N=16.

**paraphyletic** (pærəfaɪˈlɛtɪk), *a*. *Taxon*. [f. PARA-¹ 1 + PHYLETIC *a*.] Of a group of taxa: containing some but not all of the descendants of a common ancestor, esp. when the group has been considered a taxon on the basis of shared primitive characteristics. Cf. POLYPHYLETIC *a*.
**1965** W. HENNIG in *Ann. Rev. Entomol.* X. 104 If one associates species whose agreement rests on symplesiomorphy, then a paraphyletic group is formed. **1972** *Evolutionary Biol.* VI. xi. 344 One will notice .. that the phylogenetic relationships brought out above lead to the suppression of the concept Prosimii, a composite (or better, 'paraphyletic' in Hennig's terminology) assemblage. **1979** *Nature* 6 Sept. 88/1 The Apterygota, Palaeoptera and Exopterygota are regarded as paraphyletic and discarded, although the Entognathan apterygotes are treated as a natural group. **1983** E. C. MINKOFF *Evolutionary Biol.* xxii. 367 Eclectic (Evolutionary) Taxonomy ... Taxa should not be polyphyletic but may be paraphyletic. **1988** *Zool. Jrnl. Linn. Soc.* XCII. 331 These results strongly support the hypothesis that the traditionally defined Capitonidae is paraphyletic.

**paraplegic**, *a*. and *n*. Add: [B.] **b.** Special Combs. **Paraplegic Games**, **Olympics** = *Paralympic Games* s.v. *PARALYMPIC *a*.
**1953** *Bucks Herald* 14 Aug. 7 (*heading*) *Paraplegic games 'starred' wheelchair sportsmen. **1970** *Times* 27 July 2 (*caption*) Mr. Heath with some of the competitors in the third Commonwealth Paraplegic Games which opened in Edinburgh yesterday. **1973** *Maryland State Med. Jrnl.* Nov. 35/1 These games, known also as the International Stoke Mandeville Games, the *Paraplegic Olympics, and the World Games for the Handicapped, have been held every four years. **1988** *Times* 8 July 9/4 (*caption*) Handicapped protesters charging riot police in Seoul .. in an emotional .. demonstration against .. the Paraplegic Olympics to be held in the capital in October.

**parasail** ('pærəseɪl), *n*. Also **para-sail**. [f. the vb.] A parachute designed for parasailing.
**1978** *Aviation Week* 18 Sept. 58/3 All 16 astronaut candidates were given parasail flights to simulate descent in water after ejection from aircraft. **1981** *Courier-Mail* (Brisbane) 18 June 15/2 A para-sail, a specially designed parachute, is attached by rope to a boat. **1986** *Waterski Internat.* June 64/1 The offering includes .. towboats, pontoon boat, .. a huge floating parasail platform and all waterskis and associated equipment.

**parasailing** ('pærəseɪlɪŋ), *vbl. n*. [f. PARA-³ + SAILING *vbl. n*.] The sport of gliding through the air attached to a parachute and towed by a speedboat. Also '**parasail** *v. intr*., to engage in the sport of parasailing; also *trans*., to travel across in this way; **para-sailer**, **-sailor** *n*., one who parasails. Cf. PARASCENDING *vbl. n*.
**1969** *Look* 29 July 32 Some Minnesotans while away many an icy hour parasailing in the snow. **1969** *Ibid.* 33/3 How distant is the para-sailer rising in his diaper-like harness from the infant hurled aloft by his papa? **1975** *Times* 10 May 12/4 For parasailing one takes a boat out .. to a raft and is harnessed to a parachute. A speed boat then takes off and the parachute with it—into the air. The principle is the same as water-skiing .. but one doesn't get wet. **1977** *Times* 2 Apr. 13/3, I did not parasail (that's being

towed behind a speedboat fastened to a parachute). **1978** *Globe & Mail* (Toronto) 17 July 25/1 Para sailing—floating through the air strapped in a special harness under a parachute that plays in the wind as long as a powerful tow boat rides ahead in the foam—is the latest high for thrill seekers in Muskoka. **1981** *Courier-Mail* (Brisbane) 18 June 15/2 The parasailor is clipped into a harness which .. is joined to the para-sail ... The para-sailor and the two people holding the sail run a few steps as the boat speeds up. **1987** *Times* 14 Jan. 10/8 The Indian Prime Minister donned a parachute and took to the skies in a spur-of-the-moment attempt at 'parasailing'. **1987** *Times* 4 Sept. 5 An attempt to para-sail the Channel.

**parasuicide** (ˌpærə's(j)uːɪsaɪd), *n*. [f. PARA-¹ 1 + SUICIDE *n*.²] The action of making an apparent attempt at suicide by deliberately harming oneself, but without actual death as the desired result; an instance of this. Also, a person who has carried out, or is likely to carry out, such an action.
**1969** N. KREITMAN et al. in *Brit. Jrnl. Psychiatry* CXV. 747/1 The 'attempted suicide' patient is not usually addressing himself to the task of self-destruction, and rarely can his behaviour be construed in any simple sense as oriented primarily towards death. To designate this act, which is like suicide yet is something other than suicide, we now propose the term 'parasuicide'. **1971** *Brit. Jrnl. Psychiatry* CXIX. 283/1 A bet on the football pools has, of course, much remoter chances of success than a bet on a horse-race, but parasuicides showed no special preferences for more or less hazardous gambling pursuits. **1977** N. KREITMAN *Parasuicide* v. 88 Parasuicides present a great deal of psychiatric symptomatology of a neurotic or depressive nature .. and the symptomatology is more prevalent immediately after an attempt than at follow-up. **1981** *Brit. Med. Jrnl.* 1 Aug. 337/1 The incidence of parasuicide rises steeply in adolescence. **1984** *Times* 20 Oct. 3/7 The study covers parasuicides—self-injury and drug overdoses—using data collected by the regional poisoning treatment [centre] in Edinburgh, for the years 1968 to 1982.

**parcel**, *n*. Add: [I.] [4.] **d.** *Diamond Trade*. A packet of mixed diamonds offered together for sale.
**1902** G. F. WILLIAMS *Diamond Mines S. Afr.* xvii. 511 The daily productions of diamonds are put away in parcels until there is an accumulation of about 50,000 carats of De Beers and Kimberley diamonds. **1931** G. BEET *Grand Old Days Diamond Fields* 148 Should a digger have a 'parcel' to dispose of without delay, he knew that by going straight to Robinson's office he would receive the immediate and courteous attention of the principal. **1963** H. KEMELMAN *Whistling Tea Kettle* in *Nine Mile Walk* (1968) 124, I knew a diamond merchant who .. carried a fortune in unmounted stones in little folds of paper—parcels he called them. **1976** W. GREATOREX *Crossover* 162 He couldn't let this parcel of first-quality gems slip through his hands.
**e.** *Sci*. A small volume of fluid, forming part of a larger body of the same fluid but either considered as a discrete element of it (in mathematical calculations) or physically extracted from it as a sample.
**1970** F. W. COLE *Introd. Meteorol.* viii. 163 We assumed that the vertical motion of a parcel (or layer) involved no compensating vertical motion in the parcel's surroundings, and that no mixing occurred between the parcel and its environment. **1977** I. M. CAMPBELL *Energy & Atmosphere* viii. 251 Consider a parcel of air near the ground attempting to rise. **1979** *Nature* 20 Sept. 185/2 Studies of SO₂ in polluted air parcels suggest an atmospheric lifetime of about a day. **1982** *Sci. Amer.* Oct. 126/3 Because the magnetic liquid is attracted to regions of higher field intensity a parcel of ferrofluid near the rod must have

work done on it for it to be moved away from the rod. **1989** *Nature* 27 July 269/2 The researchers conclude that parcels of air from the edge of the decaying vortex carried cold, ozone-poor polar air over Australia.

‖**parc fermé** (park fɛrme, ˌpɑːk fɛə'meɪ), *n.* *Motor Sports.* Freq. **parc ferme.** [Fr.] An enclosure or paddock for vehicles, esp. for racing vehicles before or after a race.
**1958** *Times* 21 Oct. 4/7 On arrival at Monte Carlo the competitors will be free to leave the finishing control, after the usual formalities .. before returning their cars to the *parc ferme*. **1960** *Motoring News* 1 Dec. 4/3 The *parc fermé* in Inverness. **1986** *Dirt Bike Rider* July 45/4 Thieves had been able to enter the supposedly guarded parc ferme, select bikes and get clean away. **1988** *Rally Sport* Oct. 28/2 The real test came afterwards, with a road section through rush hour Milan to the overnight *parc ferme* at Monza.

**parch**, *v.* Add: [2.] [a.] Also in *pass.*, to have an extreme thirst (for); to long *for* on account of thirst. (Further examples.)
**1946** E. O'NEILL *Touch of Poet* (1957) II. 66 You must be parched after walking from the road to Simon's cabin. **1980** B. BAINBRIDGE *Winter Garden* vii. 42 'Shall I go after them?' he asked, peering in the direction of the vanished waiters. He was parched for a cup of tea.

**parens** (pə'rɛnz), *n. pl.* Chiefly *Printing.* Freq. with point. [Abbrev. of *parentheses.*] = *parentheses*, pl. of PARENTHESIS *n.* 3 a. Also in *sing.* paren.
**1905** F. H. COLLINS *Author & Printer* 282/2 *Parenthes/is, pl. -es,* abbr. parens., .. the upright curves ( ). **1972** *Scholarly Publishing* Apr. 270 We'll lay you five to one they won't see that comma before a paren. **1975** J. BUTCHER *Copy-Editing* vi. 109 To a printer the word 'brackets' signifies square brackets; round brackets are called 'parentheses' or 'parens.'. **1979** *Amer. Banker* 7 Mar. 5/1 (*table*) Rate of return with rank in parens. **1988** *UNIX Rev.* Sept. 80/2 The definition of ALGOL-60 expressions .. reads: primary: variable Left Paren expression Right Paren.

**parent**, *n.* Add: [4.] c. *Comm. ellipt.* for *parent company* (sense 5 b below).
**1953** E. R. BARLOW *Managem. Foreign Manuf. Subsidiaries* iii. 58 The foreign units will be manufacturing the same products as the parent. **1967** H. B. MAYNARD *Handbk. Business Admin.* x. 9 If the percentage of ownership is 50 percent or more, if the nature of the business is similar to that of the parent, .. the corporation is likely to be consolidated. **1972** *N.Y. Law Jrnl.* 22 Aug. 1/7 The parent .. agreed to sell its subsidiary's business and assets to the trust company for stock of the latter's holding corporation. **1986** *Economist* 11 Jan. 59/2 So heavy were the losses at another, Mostek, that its parent, United Technologies Corporation, sold it to France's Thomson.

**paresis**, *n.* Delete *general paresis*, sense 1 in Dict., and add: [1.] **b.** In full **general paresis.** Chronic inflammation of the brain and meninges, occurring in tertiary syphilis and characterized by progressive dementia and generalized paralysis; = *general paralysis of the insane* s.v. PARALYSIS *n.* 1 b.
**1862** W. D. MOORE tr. E. Salomon in *Jrnl. Mental Sci.* VIII. 365 *General paresis, paresifying mental Disease,* or in Latin *paresis generalis* .. are terms applied to the form of mental disease generally known under the French denomination of *paralysie générale.* [*Note*] 'Paralysie générale' is a singularly inappropriate term; for he who is generally paralysed is certainly dead, and not living. *Ibid.* 366 General paresis occupies a prominent place among affections of the mind. **1874** ROOSA *Dis. Ear* 108 The form of

insanity was general paresis in eight cases. **1883** *Buffalo Med. & Surg. Jrnl.* XXII. 537 (*heading*) Paresis, or general paralysis of the insane. *Ibid.* 539 Paresis is divided into stages, but as it is a progressive disease, these are not always well marked. **1913** *Jrnl. Exper. Med.* XVII. 232 The relationship of paresis to syphilis has, for years, been one of the foremost topics of medical interest ... There are some who contend that paresis is nothing more nor less than a particular form of tertiary syphilis. **1974** V. NABOKOV *Look at Harlequins* (1975) VII. i. 239 During three weeks of general paresis .. I have gained some experience. **1985** L. KENNEDY *Airman & Carpenter* 409 Reilly entered a mental hospital .. suffering from paresis, an untreated syphilitic condition. **1988** *New Scientist* 24 Mar. 59/1 AIDS dementia is very unlike 'general paresis of the insane'.

**Pareto**, *n.* Add: **b.** Special collocation. **Pareto-optimal** *a.*, pertaining to or designating a distribution of wealth, etc., among individuals which is such that any redistribution which is beneficial to one or more individuals is detrimental to one or more others.
**1954** *Économie Appliquée* VII. 211 Unless the conditions, under which the search for Pareto-optimal points is to take place, are explicitly indicated, the definition of a Pareto-optimal region has no sense. **1968** J. M. BUCHANAN *Demand & Supply of Public Goods* vi. 113 Once a point within the Pareto set is attained .. any shift must harm at least one person; no Pareto-optimal moves can be made. **1971** I. J. GOOD in *Public Choice* X. 99 The definition of a Pareto-optimal set is a set such that every point outside it is dominated by at least one point inside it, whereas no point inside it is dominated by any other point in it. **1980** A. J. JONES *Game Theory* v. 239 A two person non-cooperative game with payoffs $P_1$, $P_2$ to player 1 and 2 respectively is a game of pure conflict or an antagonistic game if all outcomes are Pareto optimal. **1986** *Oxf. Econ. Papers* XXXVIII. II. 313 The competitive solution is paretooptimal for given expected paths for demand, supply, and technology.

**parity**, *n.*[1] Sense 7 in Dict. becomes 8. Add:
**7.** *Computing. ellipt.* for *parity bit*, sense 8 below.
**1966** *Communications Assoc. Computing Machinery* IX. 695/2 The overriding consideration affecting the choice of character structure is compatibility with serial-by-bit data communication in order to minimize confusion. An eight bit character structure (7 ASCII bits and parity) satisfies this requirement. **1981** *Your Computer* (Austral.) May–June 100/1 *Parity*, an extra bit on the end of a character or byte for error detection.

**parity**, *n.*[2] Add: **2.** The number of times a particular woman has previously conceived (or *occas.* given birth).
**1921** *Jrnl. Obstetr. & Gynæcol.* XXVIII. 69 The average parity of the multiparæ was 5.7 pregnancies. **1933** J. M. M. KERR *Maternal Mortality & Morbidity* i. 20 The mortalities in mothers of varying parity are presented below, the death-rates being expressed as a percentage of the average rate in all births irrespective of parity. **1964** *Obstetr. & Gynecol.* XXIII. 165/1 The anticipated increase in higher parities was seen in the multiparas, significant numbers of patients with 3 or more prior viable pregnancies being seen. **1987** *Brit. Med. Jrnl.* 8 Aug. 355/1, 64 Women .. were compared with 128 controls individually matched for age, parity, hospital of delivery, and year of delivery.

**parlatic** (pɑːr'lætɪk), *a.* Chiefly *Anglo-Irish.* Also par'latic. [Var. of PARALYTIC *a.*, now dial., of medieval origin: cf. PARALYTIC *a.* 1, quot. 13 .., and *Eng. Dial. Dict.* (1905) IV. 422/1.] Incapable of effective action; intoxicated; also, demented, crazy.

**1907** J. M. Synge *Playboy of Western World* III. 64 Drinking myself silly, and parlatic from the dusk to dawn. **1931** F. O'Connor in *Atlantic Monthly* Jan. 81/1 She was struck too parlatic to speak. **1941** E. Starkie *Lady's Child* II. i. 88 'You will drive me parlatic .. if you don't stop fiddling with that blind!' I used to wonder what she meant by 'parlatic'. **1966** F. Shaw et al. *Lern Yerself Scouse* 76 Half-dreaming, half par'latic on me back.

**parliamentary**, a. (n.) Add: [A.] [1.] [a.] *parliamentary party*, a political party, or its elected Members collectively, in Parliament, as distinguished from the party in the country as a whole. **1906** *Labour Party Q. Circular* Apr. 2 The propaganda work in the constituencies is best assisted by a close pursuance of the Labour policy in the House of Commons by all the members of the Parliamentary Party. **1944** G. B. Shaw *Everybody's Pol. What's What?* xxx. 263 To the people it seemed that the dictators could fulfil their promises if they would, and that the parliamentary parties could not even if they would. **1965** A. J. P. Taylor *Eng. Hist. 1914–1945* i. 28 The Labour party had opposed the war till the last moment. On 5 August it swung round. Ramsay MacDonald resigned as leader of the parliamentary party. **1987** *Sunday Tel.* 28 June 1/2 In the SDP national committee, support for the anti-merger stance of the SDP parliamentary party has hardened.

**parmigiana** (ˌpɑːmɪˈdʒɑːnə), a. *Cookery*. [a. It., = Parmesan *a.*] Designating dishes in which the main ingredient is baked with Parmesan cheese, as *chicken*, *eggplant parmigiana*. (Usu. postpositively.)
   [**1892** M. Gironci *Recipes Ital. Cookery* 15 (*heading*) Soup alla Parmigiana. **1937** 'Countess Morphy' *Good Food from Italy* 57 (*heading*) 'Gnocchi' à la Parmigiana.] **1950** M. Pei in M. La Rosa tr. *Boni's Talisman Ital. Cook Bk.* p. xx, Many vegetables are fried .. ; others are skilfully blended with fresh cheeses and tomato sauce, like the eggplant *parmigiana*. **1969** Ashbery & Schuyler *Nest of Ninnies* xi. 134 'How's the eggplant parmigiana?' 'Delicious,' Alice said. **1976** *Forbes* (N.Y.) 15 Mar. 39/1 Buitoni's frozen eggplant parmigiana, the worst offender, cost 95 cents for a serving. **1984** *Tampa* (Florida) *Tribune* 2 Apr. 1D/4 Rather than have veal parmigiana or a hamburger, I'd have chicken parmigiana or a piece of chicken.

‖**parochet** (paˈroxet), n. *Judaism*. Also **parocheth, paroket, parokhet, parokheth**. [Heb. *pārōket* curtain; cf. Akkadian *parakku* shrine.] A richly decorated curtain which hangs before the Holy Ark in a synagogue.
   [**1890** E. W. Edersheim *Rites & Worship of Jews* I. ii. 28 Within the Sanctuary were two rooms .. the innermost one being the 'Holy of Holies' . . . It was separated from the Holy Place by four pillars . . . A 'Veil' (Hebrew, *parocheth*, separation, parting) hung from the four pillars.] **1902** *Jewish Encycl.* II. 108/2 Before the Ark there is frequently placed a curtain of costly material, called *paroket* after the curtain which in the Tabernacle and Temple screened the Holy of Holies. **1942** *Universal Jewish Encycl.* VIII. 403/2 The use of such curtains probably began in the Middle Ages . . . The favorite color .. is either red or blue; while on the High Holy Days a white Parocheth is sometimes hung in front of the Ark. **1962** *New Jewish Encycl.* 370/2 *Parokhet*, .. Hebrew term for the curtain which in most synagogues hangs in front of the Ark of the Law. **1974** *Jewish Chron.* 19 Apr. 9/1 A parochet (ark curtain) was consecrated .. in memory of the late Rabbi. **1976** Y. L. Bialer *Jewish Life in Art & Tradition* 186 Parochet (plural *parochot*), the beautiful curtain that hangs in front of the *aron ha-kodesh* in both Ashkenazi and Sephardi synagogues. **1987** *N.Y. Times* 26 May B3/2 He gave the synagogue a *parochet*—the curtain that covers the ark holding the Torah scrolls—that was embroidered with the names of his slain family members.

**parry**, v. Add: [2.] c. With direct speech as obj.
**1926** D. H. Lawrence in *Harper's Bazaar* July 122/2 The boy watched the handsome man closely. 'Why, do you think I oughtn't to?' he parried. **1936** W. E. Johns *Biggles & Co.* iv. 99 'Well?' he said abruptly, and Biggles noticed she was a trifle pale. 'That sounds like a question,' he parried awkwardly. **1976** B. Freemantle *November Man* iv. 47 'You've a lot on your mind tonight,' she accused . . . 'Have I?' he parried.

'**parsleyed**, a. *Cookery* (chiefly *N. Amer.*). Also *irreg.* **parslied**. [f. Parsley *n.* + -ed².] Of food: cooked or garnished with parsley.
**1928** *Daily Express* 26 Nov. 5/5 [The fish] rest in parsleyed and lemon-garlanded state on the dinner table. **1956** E. M. Hatt tr. *Countess Savarin's Real French Cooking* 254 *Parsleyed Cucumbers*. Slice coarsely several green cucumbers into a saucepan [etc.]. **1976** R. B. Parker *Promised Land* (1977) xx. 117 We .. had two vodka gimlets each, parslied rack of lamb and blackberry cheesecake. **1977** H. Frank *Single* (1978) i. 29 The eggs were sunny-side up and parsleyed, the toast was hot. **1989** *Chicago Tribune* 19 Jan. VII. 60/3, I have always thought of parslied potatoes as being only one very small step above plain old boiled potatoes.

**partition**, n. Add: [4.] c. *Computing*. (*a*) A self-contained part of a program, or a group of programs within a program library; (*b*) each of a number of (usu. equal) blocks into which some operating systems divide memory in order to facilitate storage and retrieval of information; also, (a part of) a program which may be stored in one such block.
**1968** N. Chapin *360 Programming in Assembly Language* iii. 30 A program library may be divided into groups of programs. These groups are called partitions of the program library. Groups of programs can also be known as phases, but a phase typically includes fewer programs than a partition. **1977** *Gloss. Terms Data Processing* (B.S.I.) VII. 9/1 *Partition*, a self-contained portion of a computer program that may be executed without the entire computer program necessarily being maintained in the internal storage at any one time. **1980** C. S. French *Computer Sci.* xxx. 259 The operating system may organise main storage into blocks of convenient size called partitions. **1985** *Which Computer?* Dec. 48/1 The first thing to do is to decide how many partitions you want and what their respective sizes are going to be. **1986** *Austral. Personal Computer* Sept. 88/3 Pick needs a partition of the hard disk all to itself.

**partner**, n. Add: [3.] [b.] More recently extended (somewhat *euphem.*) to include either of a couple not necessarily joined in marriage.
**1977** *Gay News* 24 Mar. 14/3 It is relatively easy for homosexual partners to back-track from their mistakes in partner selection. **1979** *Washington Post* 28 Oct. H1 Mrs. Watson invited [her] .. to bring her partner .. to Russia next week to help her shove the furniture around. **1985** *Los Angeles Times* 2 Oct. v. 9/3 Staffers .. told teen mothers who sought counseling to bring their partners to future sessions. **1988** *Observer* 22 May 36/5 It's on the train line to Woodmansterne, the little village in Surrey where I live with my partner.

**partocracy** (pɑːˈtɒkrəsɪ), n. *Pol.* [f. Part(y *n.* + -ocracy.] Government or rule by a single political party without opposition; totalitarianism; applied *spec.* to the political organization of the Soviet Union (1917–91);

also, the body of persons forming such a government.

**1966** tr. A. *Avtorkhanov's Communist Party Apparatus* p. v, History has witnessed three main forms of government: autocracy, oligarchy and democracy. The twentieth century has contributed a new form of rule, heretofore unknown: *partocracy*, which is entitled to take its place alongside the classical forms of rule. *Ibid.* p. vi, The term partocracy should be understood to mean not only this form of one-party rule unique in the history of state formations but the science and art of this rule as well. **1969** *Britannica Bk. of Year* (U.S.) 800/3 *Partocracy*, absolute rule by one political party through a government subject to its dictates. **1980** *Sunday Times* 20 July 35/2 The resentment of the workers I talked to was not only directed to what they took as the Partocracy's growing greed. **1983** *Times Lit. Suppl.* 27 May 532/5 The Russian gentry had obvious faults. But on balance it sinned less than the monolithic partocracy which succeeded it after 1917.

**partogram** ('pɑːtəʊɡræm), *n. Obstetr.* [ad. G. *Partogramm*, f. L. *partus* birth: see -O[1], -GRAM.] A graphical record of the progress of a confinement from the onset of contractions.

**1958** *Current List Med. Lit.* (Nat. Lib. Med.) XXXII. R-30/4 The partogramm [*sic*]; aid in practical and scientific obstetrics. **1972** *Proc. R. Soc. Med.* LXV. 700/1 A partogram, which presents in graphical form a low risk course of labour, was recently constructed at Queen Charlotte's Maternity Hospital. **1973** *Brit. Med. Jrnl.* 24 Nov. 451/1 The simple but revolutionary graphic labour records were designed by Philpott in 1971 for application in Central Africa... By the autumn of that year they were in use in Birmingham..and through the platform of the Blair Bell Research Society the partogram was introduced to obstetricians throughout the country. **1984** *Listener* 9 Aug. 3/1 Schwalm in Würzburg was keeping graphs of labour—partograms—to document progress and to detect departures from normal.

‖**partouse** (partuz), *n.* Also **partouze**. *slang.* [Fr., f. *partie* PARTY *n.* + -*ouse* pejorative slang suffix.] **a.** A party at which participants indulge in indiscriminate and collective sexual activity, partner-swapping, and other debauched behaviour; an orgy. **b.** *transf.* A nightclub or similar establishment noted for the wildness or licentiousness of its entertainment.

**1959** E. WILSON *Fifties* 604 In one of Sade's books, when some *partouze* is being arranged,.. the parties are forbidden to laugh. **1974** *Publishers Weekly* 15 Apr. 16/2 (Advt.), When Xaviera and he go to a party .. when she steals the stage at a sex show .. and when they swing with celebrities at a Paris *partouse*. **1981** *Times Lit. Suppl.* 25 Dec. 1502/3 An evening at Plato's Retreat, a New York partouze, costs $25. **1982** *Sunday Times* 31 Jan. 13/1 Loaded invitation to partner-swapping 'partouze' parties. **1982** G. GREENE *J'Accuse* ii. 15 Maître T then pressed her to go with him next day to a '*partouze*'... (A *partouze* is a private sex party at which people swap partners and copulate in public.)

**parvalbumin** (pɑːˈvælbjʊmɪn), *n. Biochem.* [f. L. *parv-us* small + ALBUMIN *n.*] A small calcium-binding muscle protein found in some vertebrates; orig. any of a group of small muscle proteins homologous with this.

**1968** J.-F. PECHÈRE in *Compar. Biochem. & Physiol.* XXIV. 294 Their constancy among the proteins considered is favourable to the presumption that they may have a common genic origin, and suggests that the myogen of lower vertebrates is thus a rich and convenient source of a new class of homologous proteins. The general name of *parvalbumins* is proposed here for these proteins, since it concretely designates one of their main characteristics, viz., their small molecular weight. **1974** *Nature* 20 Dec. 646/1 The only muscle protein whose three-dimensional structure is known is a calcium binding protein from carp (CBP), often called parvalbumin. *Ibid.* 649/1 The presence of parvalbumins in skeletal muscles of higher vertebrates may indicate a calcium binding role directly related to muscle contraction. **1982** *Ibid.* 10 June 504/2 Parvalbumin immunoreactivity in the extensor digitorum longus muscle of newborn rats appears on postnatal days 3 or 4. **1988** *Biochem. & Pharmacol.* XXXVII. 3727/1 CaM, sTnC, cTnC and S100b are also capable of binding to phenyl-Sepharose and to a phenothiazine-affinity column... In contrast, parvalbumin and ICaBP did not bind to these two affinity materials and..they also did not bind to the felodipine-affinity resin.

**parvovirus**, *n.* Add: Also **parvo virus**. Also *spec.* (contextually) = *canine parvovirus* s.v. *CANINE *a.* 3. (Later examples.)

**1977** *Southwestern Veterinarian* XXX. 59 (*heading*) Diarrhea in puppies: parvovirus-like particles demonstrated in their feces. **1985** *Sunday Mail* (Brisbane) 5 Sept. 5/2 'Parvo virus can be deadly,' Dr Campbell Day, a vet at the RSPCA refuge in Fairfield, said. **1986** *Courier-Mail* (Brisbane) 30 Oct. 22/5 A Redbank Plains veterinarian said parvo virus was spread by contact—usually between unvaccinated dogs. **1987** *Greyhound Star* Sept. 9/6 Discussions on racing surfaces, parvovirus and various aspects of nutrition fill up the remainder of the day.

**Pasionaria** (pasjoˈnɑːrjə), *n.* Also **Pasionara**. [Sp., lit. 'passion-flower'.] The nickname of the inspirational Basque Communist leader Dolores (*La Pasionaria*) Ibárruri Gómez (1895-1989), renowned for her emotional oratory and colourful personality, used allusively for a popular leader or figurehead, *esp.* one who is persecuted for supporting a political or other cause.

**1961** *New Statesman* 19 May 806/2 That Pasionaria of English Functionalism, Jane Drew. **1963** *Economist* 30 Nov. 934/2 A classical *Sturm und Drang* figure of the interwar years, a Pasionara of the democratic Left. **1977** *Time* 3 Oct. 90/1 Henry Fonda's little girl who went to Vassar grew up to be not only a gifted actress but the Pasionaria of the antiwar movement. **1986** *New Yorker* 10 Feb. 74/2 'La Pasionaria of middle-class privilege' is what Dennis Healey.. has called Mrs. Thatcher.

‖**paskha** ('pasxə), *n. Cookery.* Also **paska**, (*erron.*) **pashka**. [a. Russ. *paskha* lit. 'Easter', f. Gr. πάσχα PASCH *n.*] A rich Russian cake made with curds, dried fruit, and other ingredients, set in a pierced mould and traditionally eaten at Easter.

**1919** H. S. WALPOLE *Secret City* III. viii. 370 On the table was the *paskha*, a sweet paste made of eggs and cream, curds and sugar. **1930** *Aberdeen Press & Jrnl.* 21 Mar. 7/5 Easter egg ban. Cannot be coloured in Russia... This prohibition includes the sale of 'koolitch' and 'paska' which are special Easter cakes. **1969** R. & D. DE SOLA *Dict. Cooking* 169/1 *Pashka*: (Russian—Easter sweetmeat) Cottage cheese, honey, and ground nuts packed in cone-shaped molds. **1977** *Washington Post* 24 Mar. E4/1 Fresh home-made keilbasa, smoked keilbasa, freshly-made horseradish and Paska (Russian Easter Cheese Cake) will be sold. **1982** L. CHAMBERLAIN *Food & Cooking of Russia* (1983) 263 *Kulich*.. is traditionally eaten with *paskha*, an enriched mixture of curd cheese, spices, nuts, dried fruit and sugar. **1986** *Waterloo* (Ont.) *Chron.* 12 Mar. 30 (Advt.), Coffee cakes .. Easter paskas .. Hot cross buns.

**pass**, *n.*[2] Add: [1.] **e.** *Aeronaut.* A short, sweeping passage made by an aircraft, *esp.* one of a series of such movements, as when diving to fire at a target or to drop a bomb. Also *transf.* of a bird, etc.

**1943** *Sun* (Baltimore) 3 Aug. 4 He followed him into a power dive after two Japanese planes, made one pass without any results and went into a cloud. **1956** W. A. HEFLIN *U.S. Air Force Dict.* 375/2 *Pass,* a short tactical movement, usually in a dive, by a fighter aircraft, calculated to give opportunity for firing at a target. **1959** F. D. ADAMS *Aeronaut. Dict.* 123/2 In 'dragging' a field . . an airplane makes a pass. **1968** M. WOODHOUSE *Rock Baby* xvi. 153, I don't say it was impossible to spot, but . . , short of an overhead pass by a very low-flying helicopter, I thought it would pass muster. **1985** YEAGER & JANOS *Yeager* (1986) 44 The bomber makes a low pass. **1987** *World Mag.* Oct. 26/1 It shows amazing flying skill as it threads through a wood or copse to pursue any prey that escapes the first pass and will also chase and outfly birds in the open.

**passive**, *a.* and *n.* Add: [A.] [7.] **k.** Of, pertaining to, or designating a system in which energy for heating or other purposes is obtained by the absorption of existing radiant energy, usu. sunlight; also applied to a construction designed to make use of solar energy in this way.

**1975** K. L. HAGGARD in *Extended Abstr. Internat. Solar Energy Congr. & Exposition* 443 (*heading*) The architecture of a passive system of diurnal heating and cooling. *Ibid.,* Passive systems of environmental control (min. complex mech[anical] items) contain the potential for a new integral architecture more expressive of our environmental and human conditions. **1978** *Mech. Engin.* Oct. 47/2 The supplementary funds for solar will be 'reprogrammed' . . and allocated as follows: . . passive solar heating and cooling, $5 million [etc.]. **1979** *Farmington* (New Mexico) *Daily Times* 27 May 10C/1 (Advt.), A huge 100% passive solar green house. **1987** *Stock & Land* (Melbourne) 12 Mar. 55/3 (Advt.), Architect designed passive solar home.

**password**, *n.* Add: **2.** *Computing.* A sequence of characters which must be typed in order to gain access (usu. within particular constraints) to a particular computer, telecommunications network, file, etc.

**1965** *Proc. AFIPS Conf.* XXVII. 218/1 The file structure may be essentially closed, with initial access restricted for any user to a particular initial directory (assuming his ability to give a password, for example) and with subsequent access to other directories denied unless specifically permitted. **1969** G. B. DAVIS *Computer Data Processing* xv. 378 A 'lockword' or 'password' which the user must provide in order for file access to be accomplished. **1985** *Which Computer?* Apr. 82/2 A password can be assigned to some functions, but you can't match user names with them. **1986** [see DIAL *v.* 4 c]. **3.** *attrib.* (sense 2) *password protection; password-protected a.*

**1971** *Proc. AFIPS Conf.* XXXIV. 573/2 Conventional print inhibit provisions for password protection are provided by the host system. **1984** *Which Micro?* Dec. 32/2 Each file may be password protected so as to prevent unauthorised access. **1985** *Practical Computing* May 117/2 The best place for a file-disposal facility is on the far side of the password protection.

**pastel**, *n.*² Add: [3.] **b.** *attrib.* (passing into *adj.*). Applied to articles of a pastel shade or colour.

**1932** *Daily Tel.* 25 Apr. 4/4 (*heading*) Pearls on pastel gowns. **1974** *Times-Picayune* (New Orleans) 14 Aug. III. 4/1 Their bouquets were of pastel daisies, miniature carnations, sweetheart roses and baby's breath. **1989** *Oxford Times* (Limited Edition Suppl.) Mar. 13/2 (Advt.), Cane furniture . . . Natural, dark or the very latest rainbow pastel cane.

‖**pasticceria** (pastit∫ɛˈria), *n.* Pl. **-ie.** [It., f. *pasticcio* PASTICCIO *n.* + *-eria* -ERY; cf. PATISSERIE *n.*] An Italian pastry-cook's; a shop which sells pastries.

**1922** J. BAILEY *Let.* 14 Apr. (1935) 216 It is wonderful to sit having one's tea at Giocosa's *pasticceria.* **1980** *Times* 11 Oct. 10/6 A range of puddings . . is generally left to pasticcerie and bars. **1981** *Verbatim* Spring 4/1 Australians are . . now familiar with signs on shops reading *pasticceria.*

**pastoral**, *a.* and *n.* Add: [A.] [II.] [4.] **b.** *Educ.* Of or pertaining to the care or responsibility of a teacher for a pupil's general well-being.

**1954** F. G. PATTON *Good Morning, Miss Dove* 104 Though it was her custom to pay pastoral calls at the residences of her pupils, she had never called upon William's grandmother. **1967** *Counselling in Schools* (Schools Council Working Paper xv) ii. 21 It is possible to underestimate the demanding and time-consuming nature of adequate pastoral care, despite its being commonly accepted in theory as part of the teacher's functions. **1971** *Daily Tel.* 18 Nov. 18 In the last few years, there has been a growing recognition that the school's responsibility for the individual child is pastoral as well as academic. **1989** *Ibid.* 13 Mar. 13/1 Outstanding pastoral system—six housemasters and six heads of year give immediate extra help to anyone struggling with class or homework, freeing class teachers for job of teaching.

**pat** (pæt), *n.*⁴ *U.S. Shooting slang.* [Shortened form of *patridge* PARTRIDGE *n.*] = PARTRIDGE *n.,* used esp. of the ruffed grouse (see PARTRIDGE *n.* B. 1 b). (Recorded chiefly in areas of Michigan.)

**1934** *Field & Stream* Dec. 20/3 The 'r' is often dropped, and colloquial language has it pa'tridge. This is often shortened to 'pat'. **1958** *Ibid.* Dec. 96/3 There are purist pat hunters who swear that a dog is excess baggage in grouse thickets. **1967** *Detroit Free Press* 15 Oct. c8/7 Both dogs froze, noses nearly touching the clump of prickly ash. The pat evidently didn't like the sudden silence, and exploded upward. **1972** *Hunting & Fishing in Michigan* 1/2 Forests and dense bushy areas are home to Ruffed Grouse, or 'Pats'. **1980** *Outdoor Life* (U.S) (Northeast ed.) Oct. 51/2 If you shoot at a flushed pat, you have a responsibility to follow it up.

**patate**, *n.* var. \*PATETE *n.*

**patch**, *n.*¹ Add: [6.] **g.** *Computing.* A small piece of code inserted into a program, to correct a fault (usu. temporarily) or to improve or enhance the functioning of the program.

**1954** *First Gloss. Programming Terminol.* (Assoc. Computing Machinery) 15 *Patch,* a section of coding inserted into a routine (usually by explicitly transferring control from the routine to the patch and back again) to correct a mistake or alter the routine. **1970** O. DOPPING *Computers & Data Processing* xviii. 295 In the final version of the program, however, all the patches should be removed. **1976** A. RALSTON *Encycl. Computer Sci.* 1050/2 The coming of on-line programming has deprived the patch of one of its chief reasons for being. **1983** *Austral. Personal Computer* Aug. 144/3 A neat little patch to WordStar . . stops that program pretending that it is sending display characters down a serial line to a dumb terminal, and makes it print them direct on the screen.

**h.** *Music.* A (usu. preset) configuration of the controls of a synthesizer so as to produce sound of a particular timbre.

**1975** R. S. BRINDLE *New Music* 114 This patch will produce filtered white sound in repeating irregular waves. **1980** B. GRAHAM *Music & Synthesiser* 27 The synthesiser consists of a number of small units, called modules, which can be used in any order that the operator chooses . . . The expression we use for joining the units together is 'setting up a patch'. **1984** *Sounds* 1 Dec. 61/2 And so you go through the split points, programming MIDI channel information, editing sounds (or not) until you have a satisfactory combination of patches. **1986** *Making Music* Apr. 16/1, 70 . . per cent of synths returned to manufacturers are still found to have their factory programs intact. That means less than 30 per cent of the synth-owning public is inventing and storing new patches.

**patch**, *v.* Add: **9.** *Computing.* To correct or improve (a program, routine, etc.) by inserting a patch.
**1962** *Automatic Data Processing Gloss.* (U.S. Bureau of Budget) 38/2 *Patch*, . . (2) to insert corrected coding. **1984** *Austral. Microcomputer Mag.* Jan. 31/3 The version distributed with Kaypro automatically patches the Kaypro operating system with its own cursor control codes.

**patchwork** ('pætʃwɜːk), *v.* [f. the n.] **1.** *trans.* To make a patchwork of; to assemble haphazardly, to cobble together.
**1941** *Punch* 17 Sept. 246/1 It seems that Walt Disney is developing a taste for the simplest method of making a feature-length film: patchworking all the fragments that happen to be about. **1978** A. S. BYATT *Virgin in Garden* xiv. 145 He had no knowledge of other texts from which Simmonds had patchworked his theory of the universe.
**2.** *intr.* To create a patchwork by assembling pieces of fabric. Cf. PATCHWORKER *n.*
**1972** R. GODDEN *Diddakoi* vii. 139 Lots of our mothers patchworked to make the quilts.
**3.** *fig.* To adorn or variegate (a landscape, etc.) *with* areas of contrasting colour or appearance. Usu. in *pass.*
**1973** *Guardian* 19 June 16/2 The fields . . are patchworked with buttercups, pink bistort and purple field geranium. **1988** *Washington Post* 5 Nov. E24/1 Croom is still a bucolic and simple area, patchworked with wooded glens and tobacco fields.
Hence 'patchworked *ppl. a.*, consisting of or decorated with patchwork; *fig.* made up of disparate elements, ramshackle; heterogeneous, motley; 'patchworking *vbl. n.*
**1978** *Washington Post* 1 Oct. H3/2 The patchworking, which is essentially a cut-and-paste job, makes a warm and homey heirloom out of a basic wooden box. **1982** *Computerworld* 8 Mar. 1/3 A five-year, half-billion-dollar plan to modernize its aging, error-prone and patchworked computer systems. **1988** *Washington Post* 11 Dec. (Book World Suppl.) 5/2 The substance of this engrossing though patchworked personal narrative is almost equally divided between these two subjects. **1989** *Chicago Tribune* 19 Feb. (Home Suppl.) 1/4 Evanston matrons are buying embroidered, hand-dyed and patchworked smocks, skirts and drawstring pants.

‖**pate** (pa'te), *n.*[5] *N.Z.* [Maori.] A small evergreen tree of New Zealand, *Schefflera digitata*, of the aralia family, with glossy leaves and soft wood which is sometimes used as tinder. See *PATETE *n.* b.
**1832** *London Med. Gaz.* 22 Sept. 794/1 *Aralia polygama*, . . *Paté* of the natives of New Zealand. *Ibid.* 794/2 This tree is named Paté by the natives of New Zealand, and the wood is used by them for the purpose of procuring fire by friction. **1949** E. C. RICHARDS *Our N.Z. Trees & Flowers* (ed. 2) 45 *Schefflera . . digitata* . . . It was one of the woods used by Maoris to make fire by aid of long continued rubbing with the firestick. . . Seven-Fingered Jack, *pa-te* or *pa-te-te* (creaking). **1978** MOORE & IRWIN *Oxford Bk. N.Z. Plants* 96 *Schefflera digitata*, pate, seven-finger. **1986** B. D. CLARKSON *Vegetation of Egmont National Park* 13 The New Zealand Forest Service (1975) reported that in the lower altitude forests the main species depleted were *Coprosma* spp.,

pate (*Schefflera digitata*), karapapa (*Alseuosmia macrophylla*) . . five-finger (*Pseudopanax arboreus* var. *arboreus*) . . and hen and chicken fern.

**patent**, *n.* Add: [**3.**] [**b.**] esp. patent leather shoes. (Later example.)
**1973** T. PYNCHON *Gravity's Rainbow* I. 64 Red, the shoeshine boy who's slicked up Slothrop's black patents a dozen times.
**c.** = *patent leather* s.v. PATENT *a.* 3 a. Also *attrib.*
**1902** F. Y. GOLDING *Manuf. Boots & Shoes* vi. 228 Patent should be free from flaws. **1930** R. CAMPBELL *Adamastor* 57 O patent soul, asbestos body, And brain of unassembled parts. **1953** H. E. BATES *Nature of Love* 66 A pair of black patent shoes with oval buckles. **1974** *Country Life* 21 Mar. 687/3 Toes are softer . . . Patent is important again.

**patent**, *a.* Add: [**II.**] [**7.**] **b.** *Med.* and *Vet. Sci.* Of a parasitic infection or a period in its development: characterized by the production in the host of reproductive forms of the parasite (orig., ones that could be detected microscopically).
**1926** *Q. Rev. Biol.* I. 399/2 The Patent Period covers the interval during which the parasites can be demonstrated by microscopical technique. **1944** *Jrnl. Infectious Dis.* LXXV. 195/1 Treatment was begun on the third day of the patent parasitemia. **1971** *Jrnl. Parasitol.* LVII. 1151/1 Lambs, reared free of helminths, and 4 months old at the time of inoculation, were used as the source of nematode eggs during different periods of patent infections. **1987** *Ibid.* LXXIII. 931/2 Two additional animals, monkeys SS-68 and SS-61, developed patent parasitemias with prepatent periods of 13 and 18 days following inoculation of 100,000 sporozoites each.

**paternalist**, *a.* and *n.* Add: **B.** *n.* One who embraces the principles and practices of paternalism.
**1934** in WEBSTER. **1962** R. WILLIAMS *Britain in Sixties: Communications* iv. 92 The control claimed as a matter of power by authoritarians, and as a matter of principle by paternalists, is often achieved as a matter of practice in the operation of the commercial system. **1975** *Economist* 25 Oct. (Survey Suppl.) 7/3 A 'progressive intellectual' meant a paternalist, who did not like change very much but was eager to pass on in welfare benefits a larger part of the easy growth in national income which his own anti-growth attitudes now made it slightly more difficult to attain. **1986** E. LONGFORD *Pebbled Shore* ii. 15 By the 1880s 'his workers'—for he was a paternalist—had grown into a . . significant work-force.

**patete** (pa'tete), *n.* *N.Z.* Also patate. [Maori.]
**a.** = KARAMU. **b.** = *PATE *n.*[5]
**1832** *London Med. Gaz.* 22 Sept. 792/2 The Coprosma fetidissima is a shrub indigenous to New Zealand, and is named Karamu, or Patété, by the natives. **1867** J. D. HOOKER *Handbk. N.Z. Flora* II. 767/1 *Patate*, Middle Island, Lyall. *Schefflera digitata. Patete*, Geolog. Surv. *Melicope ternata.* **1882** W. D. HAY *Brighter Britain!* II. vi. 196 The whau-whau-paku (*Panax arborea*) is . . to be noticed for its elegant glossy leaf. The Patate (*Schefflera digitata*) is another small tree remarkable on the same account. **1949** P. H. BUCK *Coming of Maori* II. i. 97 Attracting birds by imitating their notes with a call leaf (*pepe*) from a *patete* or other suitable plant placed on the tongue. **1966** A. H. McLINTOCK *Encycl. N.Z.* III. 482/2 *Schefflera digitata* (patete) is another member of this family [*sc.* Araliaceae] which is widely distributed.

**patha patha** (ˌpatəˈpaːtə), *n.* *S. Afr.* Also pata pata, phata phata. [ad. Xhosa, Zulu *phatha phatha*, lit. 'touch-touch', f. *phatha*, imp. of *ukuphatha* to touch, feel.] **a.** A type of sensuous

Black dance, esp. popular in the townships in the 1960s and 1970s; the music for this.

**1961** *New Statesman* 3 Mar. 358/3 *King Kong's* . . own property . . the Patha Patha (touch-touch) dancing. **1968** *Drum* (Johannesburg) Sept. 5 Performances of pata pata, voodoo and the syncopated clock mambo. **1969** *Post* (S. Afr., Cape ed.) 15 June, Mbaqanga . . came soon after patha-patha (touch-touch) a dance tempo popularised by . . Miriam Makeba. **1976** *Sunday Times* (Johannesburg) 4 Apr. (T.V. Times) 5 London's newest disco craze, brought straight from South Africa . . . They call it the phata phata. **1976** *Time* 28 June 21 Soweto families prefer to visit . . a shebeen . . for stronger drinks and the sensuous local music called pathapatha. **1988** *New Nation* 14–20 Jan. 9 Where are . . the young mingled with the old doing the cassanova, pata-pata or even a bit of fly jazz . . ?

**b.** *transf.* Sexual intercourse. *slang.*

**1977** P. C. VENTER *Soweto* 127 *Phata-phata*, sex. **1979** A. P. BRINK *Dry White Season* 84 'Others looking for phata-phata'—illustrated by pushing his thumb through two fingers in the immemorial sign.

**pathfinder** ('pɑːθfaɪndə(r), 'pæθ-), *n.* (Formerly at PATH *n.*[1] 5.) orig. *U.S.* [f. PATH *n.* + FINDER *n.*] **1. a.** One who discovers a path or way, an explorer; *spec.* one of the frontiersmen or pioneers who settled in and explored the American West. Also *fig.*

**1840** J. F. COOPER (*title*) The pathfinder. **1866** *Harper's Mag.* June 28/1 The great Pathfinder, unfortunately for himself, took the wrong path. **1876** BANCROFT *Hist. U.S.* I. ii. 32 A great forerunner among the pathfinders across the continent. **1932** C. FULLER *Louis Trigardt's Trek* 18 These were the 'pathfinders' of the greater movement that followed in their wake. **1987** *New England Monthly* June 30/2 My daughter needs confidence, a few pathfinder's tips toward adulthood.

**b.** *spec.* in *Scouting* and *Guiding*. The name of a badge awarded for knowledge of local geography (see quot. 1911). Also *occas.* used of a Boy Scout or member of a similar organization.

**1911** *Boy Scout Tests* 244 Pathfinder Badge. It is necessary to know every lane, by-path, and short cut for a distance of at least two miles in every direction around the local Scouts' headquarters . . or for one mile if in a town. **1914** *Girl Guides' Gaz.* Jan. 8 (*in figure*) Girl Guide Proficiency Badges . . . Hospital Nurse . . Pathfinder . . Flyer. **1928** *Observer* 5 Feb. 16/5 Before the war 'Pathfinders' were founded. This was the first German attempt to apply the rules and regulations of Boy Scouts as known in Britain. **1938** 'GILCRAFT' *Outdoor Badges* 47 A wealthy American in 1909 was trying to find a difficult address in London. A boy (who was a Scout) came up to him and asked: 'Can I help you, sir?' The American told him the address he was looking for, and the Scout at once took him there . . . That boy was a Pathfinder . . . He knew his London. That is the stage you have to reach to gain the Pathfinder Badge. **1986** *Scouting* Mar. 6/3 The Pathfinder Award is the worst, being a bright luminous green.

**c.** An aircraft sent ahead of bombing aircraft to locate and mark out the target for attack; also, the pilot of such an aircraft, or any person sent ahead to mark out a site for bombing, for the dropping of troops or supplies, etc.

**1943** *Times* 25 Nov. 4/4 Red tracer bullets were continually fired from the ground at the pathfinders' flares. **1944** [see MARKER *n.* 3 c]. **1944** *R.A.F. Jrnl.* May 168 For the crews of Bomber Command's Pathfinder Force it was all a question of time. **1959** R. COLLIER *City that wouldn't Die* i. 22 As pathfinders their function was to spotlight the target . . with thousands of chandelier flares and incendiary bombs. **1974** C. RYAN *Bridge too Far* III. i. 136 In them were U.S. and British pathfinders—the men who would land first to mark landing and drop zones

for the Market forces. **1977** *Times* 10 June 16/3 A former wartime Pathfinder with DFC and Bar.

**d.** A member of an Anglican organization for children of secondary school age founded in 1952, and subsequently of other similar youth organizations.

**1960** T. L. LIVERMORE in R. E. H. Bowdler *Pathfinder Syllabus Outline Notes—Year 1* 3 Pathfinders is an Anglican attempt to meet the special needs of secondary schoolchildren. The routine and terminology of Sunday School are left behind at 11+ and the developing interests in people and causes are reflected in the syllabus which is planned to cover a four-year course. **1962** *Orbit* Jan. 3/1 It was at Tolworth in Surrey that the Rev. H. C. Taylor, who was then Curate-in-Charge of Emmanuel Church, was led to begin the first Pathfinder Group. *Ibid.* 3/2 Pathfinders regard the Lord Himself as their *real* Pathfinder Leader. **1989** *Church Times* 10 Mar. 20/5 (Advt.), CPAS are wanting to appoint a person of informed evangelical conviction and of proven management ability to be responsible for its CYFA, Pathfinder, Explorer/Climber/Scrambler Sections.

**2.** *fig.* A person who seeks out or promulgates new ideas, etc.; a 'trail-blazer' or trend-setter.

**1898** W. JAMES *Coll. Ess. & Rev.* (1920) 408 Philosophers are after all like poets. They are path-finders. **1973** *Nature* 2 Mar. 67/1 He was an inventor and an innovator, a path-finder and prognosticator. **1984** B. REID *So Much Love* viii. 129 We were path-finders. In the British theatre nobody before had spoken about Lesbianism.

**3.** Special Comb. **pathfinder prospectus** *Comm.*, a prospectus which contains information relating to the proposed flotation of a company but does not state the expected price of shares, and which is issued prior to the official prospectus.

**1984** *Times* 23 Aug. 15/1 As with the Jaguar issue last month, there will be a '*pathfinder' or 'red herring' prospectus, circulated among the institutions, and perhaps more widely in the two to three weeks before the issue. **1986** *Sunday Tel.* 2 Nov. 23/2 British Gas unveiled its pathfinder prospectus last Friday.

**pathogenic** (pæθəʊ'dʒɛnɪk), *a.* (Formerly at PATHOGENESIS *n.*) [f. PATHO- + -GENIC.] **1. a.** *Med.* and *Bot.* Producing, or relating to the production of, physical disease.

**1852** TH. ROSS *Humboldt's Trav.* II. xx. 246 In the torrid zone . . the people multiply pathogenic causes at will. **1896** *Allbutt's Syst. Med.* I. 70 Under ordinary pathogenic conditions suppuration is induced by the growth of micro-organisms within the tissues. **1977** *Whitaker's Almanack 1978* 1030/1 It appears that these proteins . . are possibly involved in the defence mechanism set up by the plant against pathogenic bacteria. **1987** J. DISKI *Rainforest* iii. 36 We will deal with . . the natural history of man's diseases caused by pathogenic organisms.

**b.** *Psychol.* Causing, or tending to cause, mental illness; (potentially) psychologically disturbing.

**1940** HINSIE & SHATZKY *Psychiatric Dict.* 404/2 Pathogenic. **1950** E. H. ERIKSON *Childhood & Society* IV. viii. 268 Mothers who drive on but cannot let go (they are the pathogenic, the 'overprotective' ones). **1953** E. JONES *Life & Work Freud* I. xi. 273 The 'predisposition' necessary for the later traumatic event to become pathogenic. **1977** A. SHERIDAN tr. *J. Lacan's Écrits* iii. 46 It was the experience inaugurated with this hysterical patient that led them to the discovery of the pathogenic event dubbed the traumatic experience. **1985** J. McDOUGALL *Theatres of Mind* (1986) i. 24 Nor did he believe that mental stasis had no effects other than pathogenic ones.

**2.** *fig.* Morally or spiritually unhealthy; having a deleterious effect on society.

**1969** M. HARRIS *Rise Anthropol. Theory* iv. 85 Poor food, disease, and other pathogenic influences could also cause racial differences. **1976** E. FROMM *To have or to Be?* (1979) 17 Our ways of living are pathogenic and eventually produce a sick person and, thus, a sick society. **1979** *London Rev. Bks.* 25 Oct. 21/2 Money, says Attali, is 'pathogenic'. **1987** *N.Y. Times* 8 Mar. VII. 38/1 America .. was more productive, more energetic, more free, largely immune from pathogenic politics and ruinous wars. **1988** *New Republic* 5 Sept. 34/3 He [*sc.* Aleksander Wat] proceeds to define communism as naturally 'pathogenic'.

Hence **patho'genically** *adv.*; **pathogenicity** *n.* (-dʒɪ'nɪsɪtɪ), the state of being pathogenic; the degree to which something is pathogenic.

**1899** A. C. HOUSTON in *Nature* 7 Sept. 434/2 Allowing virulent bacilli .. to develop and display their full power of pathogenicity. **1904** *Brit. Med. Jrnl.* 10 Sept. 559 The cells pathogenically affected by a toxin may not be the cells of origin or antitoxin. **1958** *New Biol.* XXVII. 62 During epidemics there is little doubt regarding the pathogenicity of the yeasts. **1979** *Jrnl. R. Soc. Arts* CXXVII. 647/1 Tests of pathogenicity should be carried out on animals.

**pathological**, *a.* (*n.*) Add: [1.] c. *n.* (*loosely.*) One whose psychological disposition or state is morbid.

**1931** F. R. BARRY *Relevance of Christianity* vii. 189 Plenty of pathologicals who torment themselves .. by worrying over imaginary sins. **1967** *Word* XXIII. 544 The first months were spent in personally filming and recording .. singers, infants, neonates, paranates .. and various pathologicals.

**pathology**, *n.* Add: **3.** *Math.* Any pathological feature or element of a mathematical system, *esp.* grossly abnormal behaviour of a surface or field in the neighbourhood of a particular point.

**1961** *Amer. Jrnl. Math.* LXXXIII. 339 (*heading*) Pathologies of modular algebraic surfaces. **1962** *Proc. Cambr. Philos. Soc.: Math. & Physical Sci.* LVIII. 569 (*heading*) Some plane curve pathologies. **1974** *Nature* 13 Dec. 570/2 Clearly, we should be setting up a self-consistent (Dyson) equation: which means bringing in the contributions of higher loops. (For a similar pathology in calculations of critical temperature see the paper of Dolan and Jackiw.) **1978** *Ibid.* 16 Mar. 213/2 The recent analysis of the general type IX model seems to indicate that the pathologies associated with velocity fields found by Collins and Shikin are probably artefacts of non-generic homogeneous universes. **1988** *Jrnl. Differential Equations* LXXII. 86 In particular, $h = 0$ is a bifurcation point where the set of bounded orbits changes from a single periodic orbit to a 'pathology' of bounded orbits.

**pathotoxin** (,pæθəʊ'tɒksɪn), *n. Biol.* [f. PATHO- + TOXIN *n.*] Any toxin whose presence causes, or contributes towards the causation of, a disease.

**1963** WHEELER & LUKE in *Ann. Rev. Microbiol.* XVII. 225 For those toxins which have been shown to play an important causal role in disease, we propose the term 'pathotoxin'. **1965** *Phytopathol.* LV. 967/1 Victorin .., the 'pathotoxin' .. produced by *Helminthosporium victoriae*. **1973** *Biochem. & Biophys. Res. Communications* LI. 725 Several plant pathogens, including H[*elminthosporium*] *maydis* race T, produce pathotoxins that damage plant cells, producing disease symptoms. **1982** J. B. HARBORNE *Introd. Ecol. Biochem.* (ed. 2) ix. 256 This second pathotoxin is actually toxic to the conidia of the parasite. **1985** *Agric. & Biol. Chem.* XLIX. 559/2 Recently, similar host-specific pathotoxins .. have been isolated from cultures of another unrelated corn pathogen, *Phyllosticta maydis*.

**pathotype** ('pæθəʊtaɪp), *n. Microbiol.* [f. PATHO- + TYPE *n.*: cf. GENOTYPE *n.*², PHENOTYPE *n.*, etc.] Each of several varieties of a particular

micro-organism which differ from one another in their disease-causing behaviour; a pathogenically distinct variety of a micro-organism.

**1961** OKABE & GOTO in *Bull. Faculty Agric. Shizuoka Univ.* No. 11. 42/1 The presence of physiologically specialized strains or pathotypes. **1965** *Ann. Appl. Biol.* LVI. 35 A possible explanation of the apparent inability of resistant S[*olanum*] *nigrum* to select out pathotypes that reproduce freely upon it in the field is that potato crops encourage the multiplication of far too many nematodes incompatible with *S. nigrum.* **1972** *Farmers Weekly* 21 Apr. p. xiii/4 The fear in Britain is that if the frequency of cropping is increased greater selection pressure will result in more of eelworm pathotypes not affected by present resistant varieties. **1973** *Avian Dis.* XVII. 360 Antibodies to Newcastle disease virus of an unknown pathotype have been detected repeatedly in migratory geese and ducks. **1988** *Ann. Inst. Pasteur: Microbiol.* CXXXIX. 198 This work has attempted to evaluate the efficiency of a set of DNA probes for characterizing the various pathotypes of *E. coli* isolated from diarrhoeal stools.

**patina**, *n.* Add: [2.] [b.] An acquired superficial covering or appearance, *esp.* one suggestive of age, a gloss; in later use, any characteristic 'bloom' or aura. (Further examples.)

**1960** C. DAY LEWIS *Buried Day* ii. 28 The box hedges colour the air with a patina of greenish scent. **1977** P. L. FERMOR *Time of Gifts* (1979) iii. 69 The whole place glowed with a universal patina. **1986** J. HUXLEY *Leaves of Tulip Tree* (1987) ii. 54 He had a studio .. where he showed me his work, which intrigued me for its curious patina of colours.

‖**patka** ('pɑːtka), *n.* [ad. Hindi *paṭkā*, f. Skr. *paṭṭikā* turban-cloth.] A kind of light head-covering or puggaree worn by people of the Indian subcontinent, esp. young Sikhs.

**1902** E. D. MACLAGAN *Gazetteer Multan District* (rev. ed.) iii. 86 The ordinary Mahomedan wears a 'patka' or 'pag' or turban on his head, and sometimes a 'kulla' or cap inside. **1979** *Daily Tel.* 5 Sept. 1/4 Bishen Bedi, wearing a pink patka (headdress), white towel and nothing else, picked up [a] glass of champagne. **1986** *Scouting* Mar. (Suppl.) p. 9 i/1 [Sikh] Cub Scouts will wear a patka or 'top knot'—a folded handkerchief on the top of the head in place of the cub cap—while Scouts and Venture Scouts will wear a turban.

**Patmorean** (pæt'mɔərɪən), *a.* Also -ian. [f. the name of the poet Coventry *Patmore* (1823–96): see -AN.] Of, pertaining to, or characteristic of Patmore or his writing. Also (*rare⁻¹*) **Pat'morial** *a.*, in the same sense.

**1855** D. G. ROSSETTI *Let.* 23 Jan. (1965) I. 241, I shall send another batch as soon as possible, being bent on publishing them .. with an *acharnement* almost Patmorian. **1880** G. M. HOPKINS *Lett. to R. Bridges* (1955) 106 *The Brothers* was rather suggested by Wordsworth than Patmore ... I do not myself recognise anything Patmorial in it. **1912** K. BRÉGY *Poets' Chantry* 106 An exquisite piece with what we now know as the Patmorean flavour. **1959** J. C. REID *Francis Thompson* x. 152 The ode is obviously Patmorean. **1981** M. A. WEINIG *Coventry Patmore* iv. 79 There are striking parallels between Patmorean insights and the findings of traditional mystic writers.

**patois**, *n.* (*a.*) Add: [1.] [b.] For '*transf.*' read: *transf.* Esp. jargon, cant; social dialect. (Later examples.)

**1960** I. WALLACH *Absence of Cello* 139 Then, lapsing into the patois of Madison Avenue he murmured, 'We have made great strides deathwise.' **1977** *Rolling Stone* 24 Mar., Why couldn't the ideal interviewer also be a man, so as to avoid more rigorously the pitfalls of current feminist patois.

**patrilineal**, *a.* Add: ˌpatriline'ality *n.* = PATRILINY *n.*

**1968** KWANG-CHIH CHANG *Archaeol. Anc. China* vi. 243 These were possibly segmentary lineages based on patrilineality and primogeniture. **1975** G. A. COLLIER *Fields of Tzotzil* IV. 79 It suggests that patrilineality will be emphasized wherever land is valued for agriculture and can serve as a mechanism, through inheritance, for binding together the affairs of a man and his heirs. **1981** *Nature* 25 June 652/2 A less extreme *p* can fit the paternity hypothesis if more than one generation is considered when contrasting ideal matrilineality against ideal patrilineality (father to son, to son's son, .. etc.).

**patriotic**, *a.* Add: [2.] **c.** *patriotic front*, a nationalist political organization; *spec.* the name of a Black nationalist organization founded by Robert Mugabe and Joshua Nkomo in 1976 to oppose the white Rhodesian government.

**1942** L. B. NAMIER *Conflicts* 40 The depression .. everywhere brought new political forces to the surface, violent and brutal—National Socialists and National Radicals, 'patriotic fronts' and an 'Iron Guard'. **1976** *Times* 11 Oct. 1/4 At a joint press conference in Dar es Salaam yesterday, Mr Nkomo and Mr Mugabe announced that they would send a joint 'Patriotic Front' delegation to the proposed conference in Geneva. **1978** *Detroit Free Press* 5 Mar. A11/1 Friday's agreement excludes the Militant Patriotic Front, whose guerillas have been at war with Rhodesian forces for five years.

**patron**, *n.* Sense 8 in Dict. becomes 8 b. Add: [8.] **a.** (With pronunc. pæ'trɒn.) Also patrón (pa'trɔːn). The owner of a hacienda; in New Mexico, the master or head of a family.

**1863** *Rio Abajo Press* (Albuquerque, N.M.) 7 Apr. 2/2 It had been given him by his 'patron'. **1895** F. REMINGTON *Pony Tracks* 58 You can only go there if Don Gilberto, the *patron* of the hacienda .. will take you in the ranch coach. **1931** M. AUSTIN *Starry Adventure* V. ii. 161 It would be well, while the *Patrón* is away, that Alfredo should not come. **1949** *Pacific Discovery* May-June 13/1 The average *hacendado* or *patrón* .. can make satisfactory profits without modern agricultural implements. **1970** S. L. BARRACLOUGH in I. L. Horowitz *Masses in Lat. Amer.* iv. 125 On some traditional Andean haciendas, peons still kneel to kiss the corner of the 'patron's' poncho to show respect. **1985** I. ALLENDE *House of Spirits* ii. 46 The word went out that there was a new *patrón* at Tres Marías and that we were using mules to clear the land of stones.

**pattern**, *n.* Add: [2.] **c.** *Angling.* A design on which an artificial fly is modelled; hence, a fly of a particular design.

**1886** F. M. HALFORD *Floating Flies* ii. 7 In some instances it has been found necessary to illustrate patterns requiring feathers which are very scarce. **1931** *Hardy's Anglers' Guide* (ed. 53) 63 We have had many successful days using these flies when the ordinary patterns would have been useless. **1961** A. C. WILLIAMS *Dict. Trout Flies* (ed. 3) II. 156 The various patterns designed to imitate it [*sc.* the dark sedge] are all useful suggestions of any of the darker-coloured sedges. **1979** *Angling* July 8/1 My friend tied on a Grey Moth, the only moth pattern we had between us. **1988** *Salmon, Trout & Sea-Trout* June 19/3 These patterns have been extremely successful for me and I have caught sea-trout, brown trout and rainbow trout on them.

[8.] **f.** *Amer. Football.* A pre-arranged play, as one involving a pass by the quarterback to a receiver or a hand-off by the quarterback to a running back; hence, the team formation for such a play. Also *transf.* in other sports. Chiefly *U.S.*

**1954** J. MOORE in *Major Sports Techniques Illustr.* ii. 156/1 A team's offensive patterns are designed to carry the threat of a run, pass or kick. **1957** BATEMAN & GOVERNALL *Football Fundamentals* i. 15 Ideal organization of the bench provides for a team statistician familiar with .. the squad's offensive and defensive patterns. **1966** G. PLIMPTON *Paper Lion* xvii. 169 He was very often the last man back in the huddle, not because he had a longer way to come from running a deep pass pattern [etc.]. **1972** *Even. Telegram* (St. John's, Newfoundland) 23 June 16/1 'He threw all types of patterns extremely well,' Devine said after watching Starr work out at the club's practice field. **1981** J. LEHANE *Basketball Fundamentals* ii. 97 The coach should know his personnel very well as he selects the pattern to be used (for example, two-three, three-two, one-three-one, one-four). **1988** L. WILSON *Amer. Football* v. 78/2 In the pattern shown .. the quarterback's primary target is the flankerback running a 5-out.

**patty**, *n.* Add: **2. a.** A small, flattened cake of chopped or minced food (esp. meat).

**1905** F. M. FARMER *What to have for Dinner* 107 Squash patties .. should be freshly baked and served warm. **1937** *America's Cook Bk.* 222 Season 1 pound lean beef .. and mix thoroughly. Shape into patties. **1973** K. S. NELSON *Eastern European Cookbk.* (1977) 35 With wet hands form mixture into small patties, about 2½ inches round; dust patties lightly in flour. **1989** *Boston Globe* 1 Feb. 52 German immigrants to the US brought recipes for ground beef with them. It is not known exactly when .. the patties first were served on a bun, but there is no doubt hamburgers were a big seller at the 1904 St. Louis World's Fair.

**b.** A thin, circular sweetmeat, freq. peppermint-flavoured. Chiefly *N. Amer.* (orig. *U.S.*).

[**1927** M. DE LA ROCHE *Jalna* ii. 38 Come and have a nice peppermint pâté or a glass of sherry.] **1942** *America's Cook Bk.* (rev. ed.) 766 Maple, coffee and chocolate fondants may also be made into patties. **1965** 'MALCOLM X' *Autobiogr.* (1966) xiii. 300 Appointed Muslim Sisters quickly passed small trays from which everyone took a thin, round patty of peppermint candy. **1978** *Washington Post* 23 Feb. D4/2 A 'chocolaty-covered caramel and peanuts' confection patty-style in a square-shaped, orange-colored wrapper. **1987** *Daily Tel.* 30 May 3/8 He ordered an immediate secret raid which netted nearly 30 items including .. liquorice sticks, gum, Reese's peanut butter cups and peppermint patties.

**c.** *transf.*

**1973** *Reader's Digest* Apr. 206/2 Nurse Allen and Nurse James were now counting patties—small cotton-wool pads that surgeons use to mop up oozing blood and keep the operating area dry. **1978** *Washington Post* 14 May A18/4 They'll mix the dung with straw, form it into patties, and dry it. **1983** G. PRIESTLAND *At Large* 56 Watching the poor of India making cowdung patties for fuel .. you realize that they are people engaged like you in the business of living.

**Pauline**, *a.* and *n.* Add: [A.] **2.** Of or pertaining to Pope Paul VI, esp. with reference to liturgical and other reforms initiated during his pontificate (1963–78) as a result of the Second Vatican Council.

**1965** *Time* 24 Sept. 62/2 The Pauline manner is unmistakable by now. **1971** [see PIAN *a.*]. **1974** *Christendom* Mar. 5 The litany of the Pauline complicities with the Communists is a very long one. **1976** *Times* 9 Aug. 11/2 They [*sc.* the Tridentine party] invest with grave significance the textual and other changes which the new Pauline versions contain in comparison with the mass of Pius V.

**pause**, *n.* Add: [1.] **e.** *ellipt.* for *pause button*, *control* below. The facility for suspending or

interrupting the operation of a tape recorder or similar device; the effect produced by this.
**1965** *Which?* Nov. 324/1 (*table*) 'Pause' can be left locked. *Ibid.*, 'Pause' on microphone. **1985** *Ibid.* Feb. 74/3 Still picture (sometimes called freeze frame or pause) gives you an instant of the programme frozen on the screen. **1986** *Photographer* May 26/1 Play the cassette in the normal way and while listening to it operate the pause on the cassette and video together.
[5.] (In sense 1 e) *pause button.*
**1957** *Tape Recording & Reproduction Mag.* Apr. 12/1 The \*pause button, when depressed, 'cuts out' the tape from the heads, but keeps the machine switched on, with the motors running. **1984** *What Video?* Aug. 27/2 By pressing the Pause button a couple of times it is possible to move the offending noise bar to the top of the TV screen.
*control.*
**1957** *Tape Recording & Reproduction Mag.* Apr. 12/1 An outstanding feature of this deck is a special '\*pause control'. **1965** *Wireless World* July 5 (Advt.), All the standard . . features of 4 tape speeds, frequency correction . . , three Papst outer rotor motors, pause control, [etc.]. **1984** *What Video?* Aug. 20/1 They have auto rewind and both still and pause controls.

**pause**, *v.*[1] Add: [3.] b. *spec.* To stop or suspend the operation of (a device) by using a pause control. Cf. sense \*1 e of the n. *colloq.*
**1981** T. HOGAN *Osborne CP/M User Guide* ii. 49 CP/M can pause the video display screen. *Ibid.*, Pause the screen by typing a Control-S.

**paw**, *n.*[1] Add: [2.] [a.] *paws off*: see OFF *adv.* 9 c. *paws off, Pompey!*: see \*POMPEY *n.* 1.

**payos** ('peɪəs), *n. pl.* Chiefly *N. Amer.* Also **payas, peyas, peyiss,** etc. [a. Yiddish *peyes*, f. Heb. *pē'ōt*, pl. of *pē'āh* corner: see *Lev.* xix. 27.] Uncut ear-locks worn by male Orthodox Jews.
**1898** I. ZANGWILL *Dreamers of Ghetto* iv. 144 Even the *Piyos*, or ear-lock, hung again down the side of the face. **1936** *Menorah Jrnl.* XXIV. 231 Seated around tables . . were some fifty Chassidim, old bearded men with '*peyas and shtreimel*'. **1958** N. LEVINE *Canada made Me* xi. 217 Young boys in skull caps and payasan (long fine strands of hair flapping in front of the ears, like spaniels). **1972** C. POTOK *My Name is Asher Lev* viii. 207 'He is a prodigy, Anna. A prodigy in payos.' 'Payos?' . . 'The hair you are gaping at, the earlocks.' **1973** R. L. SIMON *Big Fix* (1974) v. 39 The streets were crowded with Orthodox Jews in payas. **1976** 'TREVANIAN' *Main* i. 5 An old Chasidic Jew with *peyiss, shtreimel* level on his head, long black coat scrupulously brushed, returns home from work. **1983** *Sunday Times* (Colour Suppl.) 30 Oct. 55/1 His eyes leap back and forth between the salesmen in . . yarmulkas and payess behind the glass showcase.

**pea**, *n.*[1] Add: [III.] [7.] **pea-brain** *slang*, a stupid or empty-headed person; a dunce or fool; also, the supposedly tiny brain of such a person.
**1959** I. & P. OPIE *Lore & Lang. Schoolch.* x. 181 A 'blockhead' is someone who is dense . . . He is—a brainless chump, a brainless gorm, a \*pea-brain, or a putty-brain. **1977** D. RAMSAY *You can't call it Murder* III. 172 Meredith wanted to know if Judith had really 'put the idea of shooting out light bulbs into that pea brain'. **1986** H. JACOBSON *Redback* x. 101 The intellectual pogromists and pea-brains, with their scream-squads of love-mongering mystics who have taken over our educational institutions.
**pea-brained** *a. slang*, having a brain the size of a pea; dull-witted, foolish, stupid.
**1950** W. FAULKNER *Requiem for Nun* II. 99 The \*pea-brained reptilian heads curved the heavy leather-flapped air. **1975** *Time* 7 July 1/1 Vapid, pea-

brained, nonsense-spouting but gorgeous young men of the world. **1987** R. GUY *And I heard Bird Sing* xix. 147 That thickheaded pea-brained two-faced thug.

**peage**, *n.* Restrict †*Obs.* to sense in Dict. and add: **2.** In form ‖**péage** (peaʒ). Toll paid to travel on an *autoroute* in France; also, the gate or barrier at which this is paid.
**1973** A. GREY *Some put their trust in Chariots* xix. 105 If I stopped would the car behind unload a bevy of gunmen who would stick pistols in the faces of the *péage* officials? **1977** *Listener* 12 May 607/2, I came all the way up from Marseilles, took out about 200 francs to pay at the *péage.* **1979** *Country Life* 16 Aug. 488/4 The sign '*Péage*' ('toll') that means you are coming to one . . . How many innocents abroad . . have wondered about this mysterious town Péage. **1980** K. HAGENBACH *Fox Potential* vii. 67 We picked up our tickets at the péage and roared off along . . the autoroute. *Ibid.* xvi. 157 We collected our card from the row of péage booths.

**peal**, *v.*[3] Add: **4.** To cause (bells, etc.) to sound loudly; to ring in peals. *rare.*
**1828** in WEBSTER s.v., *Peal*, . . to cause to ring or sound. **1937** AUDEN *Song for New Year* in *Listener* 17 Feb. 305 Day long and night long the bells I shall peal.

**Peano** (peɪˈɑːnəʊ), *n. Math.* The name of Giuseppe Peano (1858–1932), Italian mathematician, used *attrib.* and in the possessive to designate concepts introduced by him or arising out of his work, as **Peano('s) axioms** *n. pl.*, a set of axioms proposed by him (1891, in *Rivista di Matematica* I. 91) from which may be deduced the properties of the natural numbers; **Peano curve**, any continuous curve, such as the one described by Peano (1890, in *Math. Ann.* XXXVI. 157), which passes through all points of the unit square in two dimensions, esp. when such a curve is the limit of an infinite series of modifications to a simple curve; also used analogously of such a space-filling curve in higher dimensions; **Peano('s) postulates** *n. pl.* = *Peano('s) axioms* above.
[**1897** *Bulletin des Sciences Mathématiques* XXI. 263 Ainsi la courbe de M. Peano est continue.] **1900** *Trans. Amer. Math. Soc.* I. 73 We give below . . a geometric determination of Peano's curve . . . The analytic formulas for the Peano functions given by Cesàro. **1903** B. RUSSELL *Princ. Math.* I. xiv. 125 Peano's primitive propositions are then the following. (1) 0 is a number. (2) If *a* is a number, the successor of *a* is a number [etc.]. **1919** —— *Introd. Math. Philos.* i. 7 Let '0' mean the number one, let 'number' mean the set 1, ½, ¼, ⅛, 1/16, . . . and let 'successor' mean 'half'. Then all Peano's five axioms will be true of this set. **1944** *Annals Math. Stud.* XIII. 117 The consistency of the system obtained from the foregoing by adding also the axiom of infinity (or Peano's postulates in the form given in 5.3 below) is a much more difficult question. **1945** *Duke Math. Jrnl.* XII. 569 Does there exist a Peano curve $x = F(t)$, $y = G(t)$ such that the components $F(t)$, $G(t)$ are respectively the real and the imaginary parts of the values taken by a power series on its circle of convergence? **1955** HALL & SPENCER *Elem. Topol.* iv. 140 The natural numbers or positive integers are given by the so-called Peano axioms. **1976** *Sci. Amer.* Dec. 124/3 Peano curves can be drawn just as easily to fill cubes and hypercubes. **1979** *Ibid.* Feb. 5/1 Yuri Matyasevich showed that there is a Diophantine equation that has no solutions in whole numbers but is such that this fact cannot be proved from the Peano axioms. **1982** W. S. HATCHER *Logical Found. Math.* iii. 88 Mere quantification theory plus the Peano postulates does not suffice for the construction of analysis.

**pearly**, *a.* (*adv., n.*) Add: [A.] [4.] **b.** *pearly whites*, teeth. See sense *C. 2 below. *slang.*

**1935** A. J. POLLOCK *Underworld Speaks* 86/2 *Pearly whites*, the teeth. **1980** *Globe & Mail* (Toronto) 24 Oct. 15/5 Coburn is defeated by his pearly-whites and taut features. **1987** L. HODGKINSON *Smile Therapy* vii. 114 Although crooked teeth may make some people nervous of smiling, there is more to looking happy than displaying a perfect row of pearly whites.

[C.] [2.] *pl. ellipt.* for *pearly whites* above; teeth. *slang.*

**1914** W. L. GEORGE *Making of Englishman* I. iv. 71 Twirl your sunshade, twirl away, tooraloo, and never you mind the words so long as you've the limelight on your pearlies. **1939** JOYCE *Finnegans Wake* 462 My pearlies in their sparkling wisdom are nippling her bubblets. **1973** T. PYNCHON *Gravity's Rainbow* (1975) I. 78 Secretaries .. shiver with the winter cold being inhaled through the madhouses's many crevices, their typewriter keys chattery as their pearlies. **1985** *Sunday Express Mag.* 1 Sept. 5/1 Keanan has long marmalade locks, a silver ring in his right ear and a near-perfect set of pearlies.

**3.** [Perh. *ellipt.* for *pearly whites* = 'frights' (otherwise unrecorded).] *pl.* with *the.* An uncontrollable shaking of the bowing arm sometimes experienced by violinists, etc. before a performance, as a result of nervousness. *Mus. slang.*

**1974** *Guardian* 22 Mar. 14/5 Getting the 'pearlies' is a string player's phrase for tremulousness. **1977** *South China Morning Post* (Hong Kong) 22 July 16/4 Violin players call the shaking hands that accompany pre-performance nerves 'the pearlies' and dread it since they can ruin their bowing technique. **1983** *Brit. Med. Jrnl.* 12 Nov. 1438/1 Tremor—that terrifying disorder (known to professional musicians as The Pearlies) when the bowing arm seems to have a life of its own, its shaking quite out of the control of the patient's conscious mind.

**peck**, *v.*[1] Add: [2.] **d.** *transf.* To type at a typewriter or similar device, esp. with an irregular, tapping sound; freq. const. *at* (a typewriter), *along.* Also *trans.*, to type (something) *out* in this way.

**1901** in *Publ. Circ.* 7 Sept. 227/2 The modern printer merely pecks on a key-board. **1954** *Granta* 6 Nov. 21/1 My boss is disconsolately pecking out a story on King's Road, Chelsea. **1957** WODEHOUSE in *Pick of Punch* 9/1 As I take typewriter in hand and start to peck out these words. **1965** M. BRADBURY *Stepping Westward* i. 40 He sat down at the typewriter which she had bought him as a wedding present and pecked out his note of acceptance. **1976** C. WESTON *Rouse Demon* xxi. 96 Doggedly he kept pecking at the typewriter, scowling at the triplicate form rolled in the platen. **1977** *Askov* (Minnesota) *American* 31 Mar. 8/5 Because of a leg injury .. Ernest Hemingway did a large portion of his writing standing up and pecking away at his typewriter. **1977** A. COOKE *Six Men* iii. 108 There he sat, .. pecking out incomparably saucy sentences on his typewriter. **1985** G. KEILLOR *Lake Wobegon Days* (1986) 253 The pure pleasure of sitting down to the keyboard and tapping letters, the brass matrices clicking into their carriage, then whirring off to take the molten lead as you peck along.

**peckerwood**, *n.* and *a.* Add: **B.** *adj.* Small, insignificant, inferior (often applied to sawmills and to timbering operations). *U.S.* (chiefly *Southern*).

**1866** C. H. SMITH *Bill Arp* 95 If it didn't rain any more and the entire crop was prudently gathered, he might probably make a peck to the acre of peckerwood nubbins. **1941** H. C. NIXON *Possum Trot* 110 Little portable, or 'peckerwood' sawmills which go from timber patch to timber patch. **1946** *Newsweek* 15 Apr. 68/1 Conditions encourage not the

efficient experienced producers but the peckerwood .. operators. **1957** *Time* 23 Sept. 13/1 The answers lie deep within a politician who fought his way out of a peckerwood background. **1963** *Sat. Even. Post* 16 Feb. 70/2 Forestry was a hit-and-run business, with the little peckerwood sawmills stripping the countryside. **1989** *New Yorker* 11 Dec. 136/3 The stern, melodramatic portrait of Earl's older brother Huey as a fantastic demagogue—a Peckerwood Caligula.

**pect** (pɛkt), *n.* N. Amer. *slang.* [Abbrev. of PECTORAL *n.* and *a.*] A pectoral muscle; = PEC *n.* Usu. *pl.*

**1977** *Time* 24 Jan. 37/1 A small group of dedicated people .. have found happiness in the camaraderie of the gyms where they devote themselves to sculpting their lats and pects and stuff to preposterous perfection. **1987** *Los Angeles Times* 26 June III. 1/1 She's a hunk. Body builder. Pects and abs and lats.

**peddle**, *v.* Sense 2 b in Dict. becomes 2 c. Add: [2.] **b.** With illicit merchandise, esp. drugs, as obj. Also *absol.* Cf. PEDLAR *n.* 1 d. *colloq.* (orig. *U.S.*).

**1938** *Amer. Speech* XIII. 190/1 *To push*, to peddle narcotics, especially as a sub-agent or small-time dealer. **1960** 'E. MCBAIN' *Heckler* (1962) v. 44 The alleged pushers who were peddling their lovely little packets of junk . . . Junk is dope. **1978** 'W. HAGGARD' *Poison People* iii. 90 They weren't pushers but higher up the line, the runners to the men that peddled. **1988** *Independent* 16 Sept. 7/1 You need no reminding of the evils which the trade .. brings on those to whom you peddle drugs.

**Penrose** ('pɛnrəʊz), *n. Math.* and *Physics.* [The name of Roger *Penrose* (b. 1931), British mathematical physicist.] **1. Penrose diagram**, a usu. two-dimensional representation of space-time in which infinity is depicted as a boundary to the finite regions (proposed by Penrose 1964, in C. & B. de Witt *Relativity, Groups & Topology* 565).

**1973** HAWKING & ELLIS *Large Scale Structure Space-Time* v. 123 One can also represent the conformal structure of infinity by drawing a diagram of the $(t', r')$ plane ... In fact, the structure of infinity in any spherically symmetric space-time can be represented by a diagram of this sort, which we shall call a *Penrose diagram.* **1979** *Soviet Physics Jrnl.* XXII. 594 A simple method is described for constructing the Penrose diagrams for a given metric. **1982** *Communications Theoret. Physics* I. 229 Some new Penrose diagrams are given. **1986** *Scientia Sinica* (Ser. A) XXIX. 887 The whole spacetime manifold can be expressed in a Penrose diagram.

**2. Penrose process**, a mechanism postulated by Penrose whereby energy can under certain circumstances escape from a black hole (see quot. 1986).

[**1972** *Astrophysical Jrnl.* CLXXVIII. 357 In the Penrose energy-extraction process, a body breaks up into two or more fragments.] **1974** *Internat. Astron. Union Symposium* LXIV. 94 Amplification of electromagnetic and gravitational waves reflected from a rotating black hole .. leads, as well as the Penrose process, to the energy extraction from a Kerr black hole at the expense of its rotational energy and momentum decrease. **1986** *Astrophysical Jrnl.* CCCVII. 38 The Penrose process .. envisages a particle incident from infinity, entering the ergosphere, and splitting into two fragments, one of which follows a negative energy orbit while the other escapes to infinity with a total energy greater than that of the incident particle, thereby extracting energy from the hole.

**3.** Designating: (*a*) (esp. as *Penrose tiling*) any tiling of the plane using tiles of a finite number of shapes according to certain constraints such that no translation of the plane

maps each tile precisely on to another; also applied to the analogous concept in three dimensions; (*b*) (esp. as *Penrose tile*) each of the elements used in such a tiling, lattice, etc.
**1975** R. M. ROBINSON (*title*) Comments on Penrose tiles. **1977** *Sci. Amer.* Jan. 112/2 In 1973 Penrose found a set of six tiles that force nonperiodicity. Soon he found a way to reduce them to four, and in 1974 he lowered them to two... The shapes of a pair of Penrose tiles can vary. *Ibid.* 115/1 To approach the full beauty and mystery of the Penrose tiling one should make at least 100 kites and 50 darts. **1984** *Physical Rev. B* XXXII. 5765/1 The underlying 5 D space-group symmetry of the Penrose lattices has not been revealed before. **1986** *Sci. Amer.* Aug. 39/3 If the Penrose rhombohedrons are to be a good description of a particular shechtmanite alloy, the variations must be small. **1986** *Physica Scripta* T. XIII. 291/1 The projection method, in which cube lattice points in 6-dimensional space contained in a specially selected strip are projected by orthogonal projection into 3-dimensional space. The result is a 3 D Penrose tiling by two different rhombohedra.

**pentapedal** (ˌpɛntəˈpiːdəl), *a. Zool.* [f. PENTA- + PEDAL *a.*[1]: cf. BIPEDAL *a.*] Five-legged; *spec.* designating a method of locomotion, used by kangaroos at slow speeds, in which the hind legs alternate with the fore legs and tail in supporting the body.
**1973** DAWSON & TAYLOR in *Nature* 30 Nov. 313/2 At low speeds the kangaroo does not hop but moves by what can perhaps best be described as a 'pentapedal type' of locomotion, since the animal uses its heavy tail as a fifth leg. **1976** *Ibid.* 29 Jan. 306/2 The pentapedal gait of large kangaroos at slow speeds may reflect a partial answer to this problem, since anatomical specialisations limit the use of quadrupedal locomotion. **1980** *Endeavour* IV. 148/2 Once the animal was hopping, (rather than 'creeping' along the ground using all four limbs and the tail—called pentapedal gait), there was an actual decrease in oxygen consumption with further increases in hopping speed.
So **penta'pedally** *adv.*
**1973** DAWSON & TAYLOR in *Nature* 30 Nov. 313/2 The increase in speed while moving pentapedally was achieved primarily by increasing stride frequency.

**pentatonic**, *a.* (*n.*) Add: **penta'tonicism**, **penta'tonism** *ns.*, the property (of a melody, etc.) of consisting mostly or entirely of notes from a pentatonic scale; the practice (of a composer) of writing pentatonic music.
**1931** M. D. CALVOCORESSI tr. *Bartók's Hungarian Folk Music* 27 Their structure is usually ABCD, and their frank pentatonism evinces their antiquity. **1965** S. ERDELY *Methods & Princ. Hungarian Ethnomusicol.* 119 The melodic descent in bar six corresponds in the spirit of pentatonism. **1966** *New Statesman* 18 Nov. 756/2 The opening allegro's second-subject group, whose pentatonicism is never satisfactorily integrated. **1977** *World of Music* XIX. I–II. 77 Brailoiu.. also pointed out the concept of the 'cycle of fifths', which several other musicologists have also referred to in examining the question of pentatonism. **1986** *Music & Lett.* Oct. 402 True pentatonicism is not necessarily implicit in the theme.

**pepino**, *n.* Sense in Dict. becomes 2. Restrict *Physical Geogr.* to sense in Dict. and add: **1.** A shrub, *Solanum muricatum*, native to south and central America, but widely cultivated elsewhere for its fruit; more usu., the small elongated melon-like fruit of this plant, having a yellow skin with purplish patches and yellow flesh.
**1890** *Garden & Forest* III. 471/2 The Pepo of Peru .. is probably identical with the Pepino of Central America. This Solanum fruit is of the size of a hen's egg or a goose egg; tastes like a melon with a very

fine acid; allays thirst readily [etc.]. **1922** *Bull. Guam Agric. Experimental Station* II. 47 The pepino has many characteristics common to both the cucumber and the musk melon. **1971** J. ROSS *Holiday Cooking Abroad* 118 Pepino, manzana, mayonesa, alcaparras. **1980** *Ann. Appl. Biol.* XCIV. 61 Pepino mosaic virus .. was found in fields of pepino (*Solanum muricatum*) in the Canete valley in coastal Peru. **1988** *Sun* (Brisbane) 13 Apr. 39/4 Pepinos can be eaten straight from the hand and there is no need to peel.

**peppermint**, *n.* Add: [**4.**] **peppermint patty**: see PATTY *n.* 1 b.

**pepperminty** (ˈpɛpəmɪntɪ), *a.* [f. PEPPERMINT *n.* + -Y[1].] Of, pertaining to, or resembling peppermint; that tastes or smells of peppermint; peppermint-coloured.
**1952** *Perfumery & Essent. Oil Rec.* XLIII. 322 Among a random collection of different odorants with rigid molecules, therefore, certain odour names should be very common... By far the most common names are:—Ethereal;.. Musky;.. Pepperminty; [etc.]. **1963** *Nature* 20 Apr. 272/1 The almond odour is considered to be a complex odour, with camphoraceous, floral and pepperminty components. **1981** J. UPDIKE *Rabbit is Rich* i. 39 She is wearing a crisp frock with pepperminty stripes. **1986** *Family Circle* May 70/2 Mint.. comes in some lovely forms.. from the white-and-green of wonderful pineapple to the flat carpeting of the tiny pepperminty leaves of pennyroyal.

**peptidergic** (ˌpɛptaɪˈdɜːdʒɪk), *a. Physiol.* [f. PEPTIDE *n.* + -ergic after ADRENERGIC, CHOLINERGIC *adjs.*] Liberating or stimulated by a neuropeptide; *spec.* designating a neurone which releases one or more particular neuropeptides when stimulated.
**1967** W. BARGMANN et al. in *Zeitschr. f. Zellforschung & Mikroskopische Anat.* LXXVII. 282 It is proposed that in analogy to *cholinergic*, *adrenergic* and *aminergic* neurones those nerve cells which synthesize octapeptide hormones should be termed *peptidergic* [G. *peptidergen*] neurones. It is further suggested to speak of *peptidergic synapses* if the terminals of such neurones are establishing contact with cells of an endocrine organ. **1973** *Nature* 12 Oct. 288/1 During the meeting a pattern of integration of the neurosecretory systems began to emerge, with a growing awareness of the functional association of the aminergic and peptidergic elements of the hypothalamus. **1978** *Lancet* 4 Feb. 272/2, I prefer to maintain an open mind with respect to non-cholinergic, non-adrenergic nerves. Some may indeed be purinergic, others peptidergic, some may release one neurotransmitter, others a combination. **1985** *Brit. Med. Jrnl.* 14 Sept. 738/1 Possibly the pacemaker may consist of an intrapancreatic ganglion with a vasoactive intestinal peptidergic network of neurones. **1987** S. M. STAHL et al. *Cognitive Neurochem.* xii. 210 The bear encounter provokes a massive autonomic hormonal and peptidergic response.

**peptidyl** (ˈpɛptɪdaɪl), *n. Biochem.* [f. PEPTIDE *n.* + -YL b.] Any radical formed from a peptide, esp. by the removal of an $NH_2$ group from an amide group. Usu. *attrib.*
**1966** *Nature* 23 July 383/2 Ribosomes may contain enzyme systems capable of transferring a peptidyl-sRNA from the amino-acid site to the peptide site. **1971** D. J. COVE *Genetics* ix. 131 One site, the peptidyl site will bind a peptidyl-sRNA complex and the other, the amino-acyl site will bind an amino-acyl-sRNA complex. **1977** *Lancet* 19 Mar. 628/2 These may then form cross-links via spontaneous Schiff-base formation with the ε-amino group of a nearby peptidyl lysine or hydroxylysine, or via the aldol condensation of two such aldehydes. **1979** *Nature* 4 Jan. 66/2 Active ribosomes were quantified by allowing the nascent peptidyl chains of active

ribosomes to complete polypeptide synthesis in the presence of the initiation inhibitor, pactamycin. **1988** *EMBO Jrnl.* VII. 3949/1 Antibiotics known to inhibit peptidyl transferase activity had a pronounced effect on photo-crosslinking.

‖**Péquiste** (pekist), *n.* (and *a.*) *Canad. Pol.* Also Pe-. [Canad. Fr., f. the initial letters of *Parti Québécois* + *-iste* -IST.] A member of the Parti Québécois. Also (with lower-case initial) as *adj.*, of or pertaining to the Parti Québécois or its members.
**1970** *Globe & Mail* (Toronto) 27 Apr. 4 In the cities and towns . . the big gainers are the Pequistes. **1976** *Toronto Star* 11 Dec. F5/6 Pequiste Payette, having just watched a small revolution that she helped make, must have had something interesting to say. **1976** *Maclean's Mag.* 27 Dec. 8 Let's suppose that the péquiste government succeeds in its first 18 months in office in delivering the goods. **1977** *Listener* 23 June 808/3 To the dedicated supporter of separatism and René Levesque (they are called 'Péquistes'), such defiance . . smacks of sabotage. **1980** *Gazette* (Montreal) 18 Feb. 1 For the next 15 or 16 weeks, let us try . . to forget that we are Pequistes.

**Percaine** ('pɜːkeɪn), *n. Pharm.* (now *Hist.*). [f. PER- + *-caine* after COCAINE *n.*] A former proprietary name for cinchocaine hydrochloride. Cf. NUPERCAINE *n.*
[**1929** *Klinische Wochenschr.* 2 July 1250/1 Den hier aufgestellten Vorbedingungen entspricht nun ein Präparat, das die 'Ciba' in Basel unter dem Namen Percain zu Versuchen uns zur Verfügung gestellt hat.] **1930** *Chem. Abstr.* XXIV. 917 Percaine, the hydrochloride of 2-butoxy-N(β-diethylaminoethyl)-cinchoninamide, is a white cryst. solid that is easily sol. in water. **1932** T. SOLLMANN *Man. Pharmacol.* (ed. 4) 350 Nupercaine, N.N.R. (introduced as percaine). **1935** *Times* 5 Mar. 4/4 He was satisfied that . . no patient could say with certainty whether he was being sprayed with a cocaine solution or a solution of percaine, which was sometimes used for those purposes. **1941** *Martindale's Extra Pharmacopœia* (ed. 22) I. 439 At the inquest the medical practitioner said that while he had ordered procaine from the chemist he had employed the 2% Percaine solution mistakenly. **1967** *Ibid.* (ed. 25) 1161/2 Cinchocaine hydrochloride . . . [*Note*] This compound was originally marketed under the name Percaine, but accidents occurred owing to the confusion of this name with procaine.

**perception**, *n.* Add: [**8.**] c. An interpretation or impression based upon one's understanding of a situation, etc.; an opinion or awareness.
**1961** *Devel. Program Nat. Forests* (U.S. Dept. Agric. Forest Service Misc. Publ. No. 896) Nov. 14 A cadre of able spokesmen who will help to create a public perception of the university as an institution. **1977** *Washington Post* 8 Jan. E2/5 Judges had a responsibility 'to the total community, whose perception of the judicial branch of the system must remain one that gives the appearance of equal justice'. **1980** *Times* 4 Jan. 10/2 An official added that 'the perception on the street is that the Jews did this to Andy Young'. With very few exceptions, that indeed was the perception of black leaders. **1985** T. DOUGLAS *Compl. Guide Advertising* i. 31 Consumer research showed that the public's perception of Delsey as being soft and strong had fallen back while that of Andrex continued to grow. **1987** *Sunday Tel.* 21 June 11/1 It is the perception of many that contemporary 'art' composers have ceased to write music which ordinary people enjoy listening to. This is not entirely so.

**perfin** ('pɜːfɪn), *n. Philately* (orig. *U.S.*). [f. PERF(ORATED *ppl. a.* + IN(ITIAL *n.*] A postage stamp perforated with the initials or other insignia of an organization, esp. to prevent misuse.
**1952** *S.P.A. Jrnl.* Oct. 65 It concerns the collecting of perfins: stamps which have punched initials or designs. Perfins, by definition, are PERForated INitial stamps. **1955** W. S. BOGGS *Found. Philately* xiii. 184 About 1870 the idea was adopted of punching in a stamp the initials or monogram of a firm . . . Such punched stamps are known as *perfins*. **1957** R. M. CABEEN *Stand. Handbk. Stamp Collecting* xi. 107 Those collecting the syncopated perforations of the Netherlands should keep a sharp watch for 'perfins', or punched stamps, as these were used by about sixty-five firms only. **1968** *Globe & Mail* (Toronto) 13 Jan. 34/1 Perfins . . are postage stamps in which the users have perforated their initials or other insignia as a means of identification and to discourage theft. **1978** V. ILMA *Funk & Wagnalls Guide to Stamp Collecting* 73 You could easily mistake a perfin for a damaged stamp; it is not. **1987** *Daily Tel.* 29 July 17/6 The three certificates . . were found in a two pound bag of mixed perfins—stamps that are perforated with initials.

**perform**, *v.* Add: [**6.**] d. *spec.* To copulate or have sexual intercourse (esp. satisfactorily). *slang.*
**1901** FARMER & HENLEY *Slang* V. 173/2 *Perform*, . . to copulate. **1974** in H. & R. Greenwald *Sex-Life Lett.* 139 My problem is that when I have sex with my wife . . I am potent, strong, and virile; but when I go to bed with any other woman I am quite impotent and unable to perform. **1978** K. AMIS *Jake's Thing* iv. 41 'I . . performed. Not with any distinction, but adequately . . afterwards . . I kept thinking about the trout.' . . 'Hunger is a normal reaction on completion of sexual intercourse.' **1979** J. SCOTT *Clutch of Vipers* i. 10 Frankie had . . [put] her in charge of one of his brothels . . . She did a good job, but never performed herself.

e. *Comm.* Of an investment: to yield a high (low, etc.) return; *esp.* to be profitable.
**1967** *Institutional Investor* Apr. 16/1 The original favorites were sold simply because they ceased to perform. **1968** ROLO & NELSON *Anat. Wall St.* v. 49 'Performance funds' as a group had indeed performed well. **1973** L. RUKEYSER *How to make Money in Wall St.* iv. 25 Make . . each registered representative's compensation a function of how well his accounts have performed. **1984** *Observer* 26 Feb. 27/2 Our shares have underperformed since 1977, this time we have performed. **1987** *Times* 26 Aug. 19/5 We also want our £120 million investment in the company to perform and it is not performing at present.

**performance**, *n.* Add: [**2.**] f. *Comm.* The extent to which an investment is profitable, esp. in relation to other commodities; an instance of this.
**1926** *Forbes* (N.Y.) 1 June 64/3 Until we have had an example of deviation from past performances it is safe to follow precedent. **1931** L. H. SLOAN *Everyman & his Common Stocks* viii. 176 These were among the issues of which the stock market expected the most brilliant future performance. **1947** *Barron's* 29 Sept. 2/3 Disappointing price performance of new bond and preferred stock offerings is . . evoking adverse comment. **1964** *Wall St. Jrnl.* 9 Sept. 8/3 Charts showing the market performance of a single regular investment in a funds share long have been permitted by the SEC. **1989** *Financial Times* 16 Mar. 37/8 Given the shares' strong performance in the first part of this year, some profit taking seems likely in the short term.

**performer**, *n.* Add: **4.** *Comm.* An investment which yields a high (low, etc.) return; *esp.* one which is profitable.
[**1927** J. DURAND *Business of Trading in Stocks* vi. 51 Had he only bought . . a few of those star performers, his profits for the day would have run

into hundreds.] **1939** *Financial World* 11 Jan. 5/3 Store shares have not been spectacular performers. **1955** *Forbes* (N.Y.) 15 July 42/3 The star performers in this very incomplete list are *Fidelity Fund* . . and *Axe Houghton Fund*. **1976** *Economist* 22 May 83/1 Star performers of the 1960s and early 1970s face a less favourable world. **1989** *Bond Buyer* 10 Apr. 3 Financial company bonds were the top performers in the investment grade market.

**Pergonal** (pɜː'gəʊnæl), *n. Med.* [f. PER-¹ + GON(ADOTROPHIN *n.* + -*al* after NEMBUTAL *n.*, VERONAL *n.*, etc.] A proprietary name for various hormonal preparations, *spec.* for a preparation of human menopausal gonadotrophin, containing a mixture of FSH and luteinizing hormone, which is given by injection as a treatment for infertility in women and men deficient in gonadotrophin.
**1963** *Official Gaz.* (U.S. Patent Office) 14 May TM66/1 Pergonal . . . For hormonal preparations used in the treatment of human endocrine conditions. First use on or before Jan. 1, 1962. **1964** *Lancet* 30 May 1197/2 We are indebted to Dr. Hayes, of the Cutter Laboratories, Berkeley, California, for a liberal supply of 'Pergonal'. **1966** *Trade Marks Jrnl.* 30 Dec. 1846/2 Pergonal-500. **1969** *Daily Tel.* 13 Feb. 20/6 Mrs. Maureen Tucker, . . who was treated with the fertility drug Pergonol [*sic*], gave birth to triplets . . yesterday. **1977** *Private Eye* 13 May 14/1 They have found that an extract from the urine of Italian nuns, called Pergonal, allows infertile women to have babies without the risk of multiple births. **1987** *Oxf. Textbk. Med.* (ed. 2) I. x. 15/2 The total dose of Pergonal is increased at monthly intervals till ovulation occurs.

**perilous**, *a.* Add: [**1.**] **b.** Postpositively in allusion to Malory's *Siege Perilous* (see SIEGE *n.* 1 e), *esp.* for emphasis or ironically.
**1931** E. A. ROBERTSON *Four Frightened People* iv. 136 'I suppose . . professionally . . this . . would be described as "The Hazardous Picnic"?' . . '"Perilous", not "hazardous".' . . And invert for emphasis when possible—"The Picnic Perilous". **1983** G. LORD *Tooth & Claw* ii. 11 Others . . regarded her as a challenge; a sort of virgin perilous.

**perinatology** (ˌpɛrɪneɪ'tɒlədʒɪ), *n. Obstetr.* [ad. G. *Perinatologie* (U. Hermann 1969, in *Geburtshilfe & Frauenheilkunde* XXIX. 391); cf. PERINATAL *a.*, -OLOGY.] The branch of obstetrics dealing with the period around childbirth; the study of perinatal care.
**1973** *Jrnl. Perinatal Med.* I. 5/2 The number of unsolved problems in perinatology augments as more attention is devoted to this very important field of medicine. **1975** *Nature* 16 Oct. p.vii, Research workers in clinical obstetrics, perinatology, reproductive biology, immunology, endocrinology and related disciplines presented cogent papers which were followed by informal discussions. **1986** J. W. K. RITCHIE in N. R. C. Roberton *Textbk. Neonatol.* vi. 69/1 Neonatology and fetal medicine . . have evolved as a result of further specialisation within paediatrics and obstetrics and gynaecology . . . Strong links have been forged between the personnel working in both areas, now often collectively referred to as perinatology.
Also ˌperina'tologist *n.*, an obstetrician who specializes in perinatology.
**1971** H. ABRAMSON *Symposium Functional Physiopath. Fetus & Neonate* 3 The responsibility for coordinating the results of these technical methods might well devolve upon the perinatal pathologist working in collaboration with the perinatologist. **1976** *N.Y. Times Mag.* 11 July VI. 21/1 Perinatologists have been concerning themselves with what goes on in the life of the fetus during its nine months of development. **1987** S. PARETSKY *Bitter Medicine* xxviii. 261 The perinatologist is an

obstetrician with a specialty in treating the complications of pregnancy . . . If he'd shown up, then little Victoria Charlotte might have made it long enough to get to the neonatologist.

**perioperative** (ˌpɛrɪ'ɒpərətɪv), *a.* [f. PERI- + OPERATIVE *a.*] Pertaining to or designating the period immediately before and after a surgical operation; occurring in this period.
**1966** *Lancet* 22 Oct. 876/1 The twenty-five cases abstracted below were all sudden deaths after cardiac arrest during the perioperative period. **1977** *Ibid.* 15 Jan. 137/1 To justify an operation with a 3% mortality and a 7% perioperative myocardial-infarction rate, it should be better than the best available medical treatment. **1982** W. J. ALEXANDER in Mathieu & Burke *Infection & Perioperative Period* p. xi, Nosocomial infections can be traced to the perioperative period in more than one of every 20 patients undergoing surgery. **1984** *Brit. Med. Jrnl.* 25 Aug. 497/1 Doctor A would consider . . a single case of perioperative death as harmful as four cases each having a one year prognosis with restricted mobility.
Hence **peri'operatively** *adv.*, during the perioperative period.
**1977** *Circulation* LV. 559 Perioperatively, only one of the 45 patients with Aschoff bodies had clinical or laboratory stigmata compatible with acute rheumatic fever. **1988** *Ann. Surg.* CCVIII. 738/1 All patients were . . monitored perioperatively with serial ECGs, measurements of serum enzymes, filling pressures, and cardiac output.

**peripatetic**, *a.* and *n.* Add: [A.] [2.] **d.** *Educ.* Of a teacher: not attached to a particular school, but going from school to school, etc. in order to give specialist training. Also of, pertaining to, or characterized by this type of teaching.
**1969** *Peripatetic Teachers of Deaf* (Dept. Educ. & Sci.) 17 The duties of peripatetic teachers take them into hospitals, ENT and child health clinics, children's homes, schools and junior training centres. **1977** P. MITTLER *Day Services for Mentally Handicapped Adults* (Nat. Devel. Group for Mentally Handicapped) iv. 26 Some staff might be enabled to develop a peripatetic role. **1983** *Classical Music* Nov. 4/1 (Advt.), Peripatetic music teacher violin/viola. **1990** *Times Educ. Suppl.* 4 May A131 (Advt.), Teacher required . . to provide a peripatetic service for young children . . who have continuing speech and language difficulties.

**peritelevision** (ˌpɛrɪ'tɛlɪvɪʒən), *n.* and *a. Electronics.* [f. PERI- 1 + TELEVISION *n.*] (Designating) equipment and services which are associated peripherally with television, or which may be connected to a television set. Usu. in *peritelevision socket*, a SCART socket.
**1983** *Unesco Courier* May 31/2 The television set . . will become the central core of an array of equipment and services that is becoming known collectively as 'peritelevision'. **1984** Peritelevision socket [see *EUROCONNECTOR *n.*]. **1986** *Times* 11 Nov. 7/2 The Peacock report on financing the BBC . . recommended that peritelevision sockets be fitted to all sets sold after January 1988. **1987** *Political Q.* LVIII. 11 All new television sets should have peritelevision sockets designed to facilitate consumer subscription at low cost.

**permethrin** (pɜː'mɛθrɪn), *n. Chem.* [f. PER-¹ + RES)METHRIN *n.*] A synthetic pyrethroid, $C_{21}H_{20}Cl_2O_3$, employed as an insecticide in the form of a spray.
**1975** *B.S.I. News* Feb. 21/1 Permethrin. **1976** *Jrnl. Hort. Sci.* LI. 111 Permethrin was outstanding both for persistence and high toxicity. **1978** *Daily Tel.* 2 Oct. 3/1 Permethrin, which is used in fly sprays but is not considered harmful to people and pets, is to be added to water supplies in parts of Essex to kill

worms. **1986** *Courier-Mail* (Brisbane) 12 Nov. 1/4 Mr Webster said the permethrin, a chemical already widely used to kill cockroaches, had an immediate effect on household pests.

**permission**, *n.* Add: [**1.**] **b.** (As a count noun.) An authorization to do something; *esp.* a written document confirming that permission has been granted, = PERMIT *n.* 1.
**1718** J. OZELL tr. *Tournefort's Voy.* I. 353 The Caimacan .. gave strangers a permission to defend themselves against these disorderly Rake-shames. **1834** L. RITCHIE *Wand. by Seine* 151 Proceeds of a sale of permissions to eat butter during Lent. **1903** G. B. SHAW *Revolutionist's Handbk.* ii, in *Man & Superman* 188 The Factory Code .. and Trade Union organization .. have .. converted the old unrestricted property of the cotton manufacturer in his will and the cotton spinner in his labor into a mere permission to trade or work on stringent public .. conditions. **1979** *Internat. Jrnl. Sociol. of Law* VII. 349 A man was offered an alternative plot of land with appropriate permissions, onto which he could transfer his small business, a 'kennels'.

**pe'roxide**, *v.* [f. PEROXIDE *n.*] *trans.* To treat or bleach (the hair) with hydrogen peroxide.
**1924** K. WILSON *Successful Hairdresser* vii. 87 After being peroxided nothing can remedy a head of hair. **1963** D. ATHILL *Instead of Letter* iv. 59 Hair which in summer would bleach into golden streaks as though he had peroxided it. **1985** *N.Y. Times* 24 Feb. VII. 7/1 She peroxides her hair and dyes her wings.

**perp** (pɜːp), *n.* *U.S. slang.* [Abbrev. of PERPETRATOR *n.*] The perpetrator of a crime.
**1981** *N.Y. Times* 10 Apr. c6/5 The decoy makes himself available to be robbed or mugged, then the guys in the backup van arrest the perpetrators. They call them 'perps'. **1984** T. N. MURARI *Shooter* vii. 81 Yolande had testified. The perp got twenty-five to life. **1986** F. KELLERMAN *Ritual Bath* (1987) viii. 63 The perp was a foot fetishist.

**persistent**, *a.* Add: [**3.**] **c.** *Ecol.* That remains within an environment for a long period of time: applied esp. to chemically unreactive pollutants, and *occas.* to radioactivity having a long half-life.
**1952** *Oklahoma Agric. Exper. Station Bull.* No. T42. p. 9 Toxaphene was the most persistent of the three insecticides studied, parathion was somewhat less stable, and methoxychlor the least permanent. **1955** *Bull. Atomic Sci.* Jan. 5/1 The long-range genetic danger of exposure .. to low-level, but widespread and persistent radioactivity .. is only beginning to be dimly perceived. **1963** [see RADIOLOGICAL *a.* b]. **1970** [see LINDANE *n.*]. **1987** *Financial Rev.* (Sydney) 21 Aug. 5/1 Before May 25 this year, farmers keen to produce the best potatoes bought chemicals, 'persistent' organochlorines such as heptachlor, to kill bugs.

**personal**, *a.* (*n.*) Add: [A.] [**10.**] *personal organizer*, a portable folder or wallet containing loose-leaf sections for storing personal information (such as appointments and addresses), etc. systematically; hence, a pocket-sized microcomputer or software for a personal computer providing similar functions; cf. FILOFAX *n.*, *ORGANIZER *n.* 3.
**1985** *Los Angeles Times* 20 Aug. IV. 1/2 These busy people all rely on *personal organizers—compact, three-ring binders designed to keep track of various aspects of one's life. **1986** *Observer* (Colour Suppl.) 23 Nov. 61 Now you can buy your oh-so-yuppie 'personal organiser' or designer diary system at your local branch. **1988** *Times* 10 June 27/4 This shop in Bow Lane is the only one in the City to specialize in .. the personal organizer, be it Filofax or one of the other makes.

‖**physis** (fusis, 'faɪsɪs), *n. Philos.* [mod.L., f. Gr. φύσις.] Nature (as denoted by the Greek word φύσις), in various philosophical contexts; *esp.* Nature personified (cf. NATURE *n.* 11 a), or the inherent quality of a being or object (cf. NATURE *n.* 9 a).
**1642** H. MORE *Song of Soul* I. ii. 13 Physis is the great womb From whence all things in th'University Yclad in divers forms do gaily bloom. **1808** J. BARCLAY *Muscular Motions* 262 The ancient Δυναμεις, the ministers of Physis, were classed by Plato under three souls, the rational, animal, and vegetative. **1923** OGDEN & RICHARDS *Meaning of Meaning* ii. 42 The nature of things, their *physis*, was regarded, *e.g.*, by Thales, as supersensible. *Ibid.* 43 Plato has evolved a realm of pure ideality, also described as *physis*, in which these name-souls dwell. **1976** *Times Lit. Suppl.* 10 Sept. 1097/4 In Man, the Word is made flesh: Nous inclines towards sublunary Physis and descends into it.

**pianist**, *n.* Sense c in Dict. becomes d. Add:
**c.** *transf.* A wireless operator. *slang.*
**1955** J. THOMAS *No Banners* xxi. 207 When .. the 'pianist' (wireless operator) arrived .., he would be able to hook up his transmitter and go into action without delay. **1977** J. TARRANT *Rommel Plot* viii. 78 'Still, it wasn't a bad effort for a pianist.' 'Pianist?' 'Wireless Operator.'

**pick**, *n.*³ Senses 5–10 in Dict. become 6–11. Add: [**3.**] **b.** One who is picked or selected as a member of a sports team; also *transf.* N. Amer. *colloq.*
**1976** *Billings* (Montana) *Gaz.* 30 June 2-E/1 The 18-year old Kopsky is an 8th-round pick from St. Louis, Mo. **1976** *National Observer* (U.S.) 13 Nov. 3/6 There is much speculation, and little hard evidence, concerning Carter's likely Cabinet picks. **1985** *Globe & Mail* (Toronto) 10 Oct. c6/5 Bill Derlago will centre Leafs' No. 1 line with Rick Vaive and top rookie pick Wendel Clark on wings. **1988** *Toronto Sun* 13 Apr. 152/3 In the end, the two middle-managers resigned and city personnel committee chairman Ald. Bill Boytchuk rejected the committee's pick.
**c.** *Horse-racing.* A horse fancied as a likely winner; a favourite or tip. Also *transf.* in other sports. Cf. SELECTION *n.* 2 b. *colloq.* (chiefly *N. Amer.*).
**1976** *Washington Post* 19 Apr. D9/1 (*heading*) Graded picks at Pimlico race course. **1977** *N.Z. Herald* 8 Jan. 1-6/6 Punters have often mumbled dire threats about glue factories and knackers' yards when their picks have failed to perform as wished. **1984** *Runner* (U.S.) Oct. 78/2 Zack Barrie and Gidamis Shahanga of Tanzania .. were pre-race picks to upset Cova. **1987** *Golf* June 28/3 Oklahoma State University .. is the pick to take the 1987 team title.
[**4.**] **b.** More generally, a very small portion or amount (*of* something); a particle or jot. Freq. in negative contexts. *Sc.* and *dial.*
**1866** W. GREGOR *Dial. Banffshire* 125 'There hizna a pick o' meal's-corn gehn our's craig this three days.' 'There's nae a pick o' clay on's sheen.' **1916** G. ABEL *Wylins* 31 Nae pick o' hate nor spite. **1929** *Scots Observer* 31 Oct. 14 Scarce a pick o' flesh on his banes. **1958** C. HANLEY *Dancing in Streets* 123 Ah went roon tae Agnes's an' there wisnae a pick on her—he's been drinking the money again an' she was hauf-sterved. **1976** 'W. TREVOR' *Children of Dynmouth* iii. 55, I was saying that to the Reverend Feather and to Dass. They didn't take a pick of notice. **1988** *Times* 13 May 2/1 There is not a pick of evidence that she wilfully encouraged any crime whatever.

**pick**, *v.*¹ Add: [**III.**] [**5.**] [**c.**] Also *pick-your-owner*, a customer or owner of a 'pick-your-own' farm.
**1969** *Farm Jrnl.* (U.S.) Aug. 31/2 Some growers .. let pick-your-owners clean up berries that ripen later.

**1985** *Washington Post* 13 June Md. 13/1 'Darrow was the pioneer pick-your-owner in Washington,' said .. a staunch admirer of the horticulturalist.

**pickney**, *n.* and *a.*, var. PICCANINNY, PICKANINNY *n.* (*a.*)

**pick-up**, *n.* (and *a.*) Add: [A.] [2.] **d.** *Angling.* On a fixed-spool reel: a semi-circular loop of metal which guides the line back on to the spool as it is reeled in.
**1951** A. WANLESS *Fixed Spool Angling* i. 18 Some of the best reels are to be had with a mechanical or finger pick-up, as the angler prefers. **1960** C. WILLOCK *Anglers' Encycl.* 132/1 Practically all pick-ups these days are of the 'full bail' type in which the pick-up is made in one continuous loop of steel. **1987** *Coarse Fishing* Mar. 40/1 After the bait touched bottom I let out a few feet of line then engaged the pick-up.
[3.] **b.** A film which is made by one company and acquired (for distribution, etc.) by another. *U.S. Cinematogr.*
**1978** *N.Y. Times* 26 June c18/2 Both movies are pickups—independently made and financed films that have been picked up for distribution by a major studio. **1983** *Ibid.* 22 May III. 28/3 Fox produced only half a dozen pictures annually, and made up the difference with so-called pickups, films made outside the studio. Despite the deprecatory term, not all of the pickups were undistinguished. **1985** *Standard* 3 Jan. 21/2 The Lean film originated in Britain with our own Thorn-EMI and is what's called in America a 'pick-up'.
[7.] **b.** *transf.* in *Athletics.* The process of increasing speed, esp. at the beginning of a race; hence, the capacity for or rate of such acceleration. (In quot. 1960, a training exercise to develop this.)
**1960** J. K. DOHERTY *Mod. Track & Field* (ed. 2) vi. 222 Wind-sprints or pickups. There are many variations of these. A man repeatedly sprints or 'picks up' until he is winded. **1961** *Times* 22 July 3/2 Radford had the best start in the 100 yards, but his pick-up could not compare with that of Budd. **1988** *Athletics Weekly* 30 Sept. 25/3 First out of the blocks it was again his pick-up which gave him that essential lead.

**picky**, *a.* Add: **'pickily** *adv.*
**1985** *Observer* 8 Dec. 26/8 An American compilation that has the decency to include cricket anecdotes should not be treated pickily.

**picoplankton** ('piːkəʊˌplæŋktən), *n. Biol.* [f. PICO- + PLANKTON *n.*] Plankton consisting of organisms between 0.2 and 2.0 microns in diameter; also used with reference to organisms with a wet weight of the order of $10^{-12}$ g.
**1978** J. McN. SIEBURTH et al. in *Limnol. & Oceanogr.* XXIII. 1261/1 The size fractions occupied by the bacterioplankton (0.2–2.0 μm) and virioplankton (0.02–0.2 μm) have been termed picoplankton and femtoplankton. The basis for this is the fortunate naming of the two larger size fractions in the nanoplankton and microplankton ... This is all the more applicable if the plankton organisms are regarded on the basis of volume (three-dimensional) rather than length (one-dimensional) and are assumed to have a cubic shape and a density of 1 g.cm⁻³. **1980** *Marine Biol.* LVIII. 216/1 Production rates of photosynthetic picoplankton are not known in these (or other) areas but Fay .. has shown that autotrophs smaller than 10 μm may be responsible for more than 60% of the primary production in Antarctic waters. **1983** *Sci. Amer.* June 62/2 The intent was to trap picoplankton: organisms whose wet weight is on the order of a picogram, or $10^{-12}$ gram. **1988** *Jrnl. Phycol.* XXIV. 423/2 The metazooplankton were unable to graze the smaller cells

in the picoplankton which normally are grazed by protozooplankton.
Hence ˌpicoplank'tonic *a.*, of, pertaining to, or designating picoplankton.
**1982** *Marine Biol.* LXVII. 68/1 Our previous assumption .. that a 3 μm filter effectively separated phytoplankton and bacteria was evidently due to our failure to detect the picoplanktonic algal forms. **1988** *Jrnl. Phycol.* XXIV. 416/1 An unprecedented aestival bloom of a picoplanktonic alga that occurred in Narragansett Bay, Rhode Island, during 1985 was accompanied by .. catastrophic mortality of the blue mussel, *Mytilus edulis*. L.

**pictorial**, *a.* (*n.*) Add: [B.] [1.] **b.** A magazine article which consists principally of photographs; a picture-story.
Chiefly with reference to 'pin-up' features in *Playboy* magazine.
**1978** *Washington Post Mag.* 16 July 5 About 25 of the women shot in Washington will eventually be used in a pictorial in the magazine. **1986** *Marketing* 11 Sept. 51/2 By having high profile pictorials the image and tone is set, heightening awareness. **1989** *Washington Post* 27 Feb. B3/4 Three young women .. in the .. April Playboy magazine .. pictorial of 'Girls of the Big East Conference'.

**pidgin**, *n.* Add: Hence **'pidginist** *n.*, a student of pidgin languages.
**1972** J. L. DILLARD *Black English* iii. 112 John Reinecke, in some respects the most remarkable Pidginist of them all. **1987** *English World-Wide* VIII. 100 The existence of KanE was not widely known among pidginists and creolists before Tom Dutton's pioneering work.

**Pidyon Haben** ('pɪdjən ha'bɛn), *n. phr.* Also **Pidyon ha-Ben**, etc. [a. Heb. *pidyōn habēn* redemption of the son.] A Jewish ceremony performed thirty days after the birth of a first-born male child in which the child is redeemed from being given over nominally to the service of the priesthood; = REDEMPTION *n.* 2 b.
The ceremony is based upon Exodus xiii. 2–16 and Numb. xviii. 15, and is not required if either parent is a Cohen or a Levite.
**1879** E. M. MYERS *Jews* II. 59 With the first male issue from its mother, another ceremony is performed. It is called *Pidyan Harben*, redemption of the first born. **1892** I. ZANGWILL *Childr. Ghetto* I. 90 They have invited him for the *Pidyun Haben* to-day. .. Is it not the thirty-first day since the birth? **1929** A. Z. IDELSOHN *Ceremonies of Judaism* III. 50 *Pidyon Habben.* The 'Redemption of the Son' is a ceremony for the first-born, if it be male. **1941** B. M. EDIDIN *Jewish Customs* iv. 53 The special ceremonial obligations of the first-born son do not end with Pidyon Haben. **1982** *N.Y. Times* 24 Oct. II. 32/2 Israel has issued a new silver medal commemorating the traditional ceremony of 'Pidyon Haben', or redemption of the firstborn.

**Piegan** ('piːgən), *a.* and *n.* Also 8 Paegon, 9 Pagon, Peegan; 20 Peigan. [ad. Blackfoot *piikániwa* Piegan.] **A.** *adj.* Of or pertaining to a North American Indian people of the Blackfoot confederacy, inhabiting the Rocky Mountain region of Alberta and Montana. **B.** *n.* (A member of) this people.
*Peigan* is the form preferred by the Indians themselves, and is that used officially by the Canadian government and by others in Canada.
**1790** E. UMFREVILLE *Present State of Hudson's Bay* 200 The Black-foot, Paegan, and Blood Indians. These Indians, though divided into three tribes, are all one nation, speak the same language, and abide by the same laws and customs. *c*1812 D. THOMPSON in A. W. Bowers's *Hidatsa Social & Ceremonial Organiz.* (1965) 301 Another band of these people now dwell in tents near the head of this River .. in alliance with

the Peegans and their allies. **1868** *N.Y. Herald* 29 July 5/2 The Gros-Ventres have agreed .. to keep peace with the whites and all the Indian tribes save the Pagons and Blackfeet. **1871** *Congress. Globe* 41st Congress 3 Sess. App. 68/1 Here, sir .. I find within a convenient distance the Piegan Indians, which, of all the many accessories to the glory of Duluth, I consider by far the most inestimable. **1907** J. W. SCHULTZ *My Life as Indian* i. 8 Several hundred lodges of Piegans. **1910** F. W. HODGE *Handbk. Amer. Indians* II. 246/2 In 1858 the Piegan in the United States were estimated to number 3,700. **1938** M. THOMPSON *High Trails of Glacier Nat. Park* 104 Roes Basin, a corruption of Rose Basin, the name Grinnell bestowed in honor of his hunting companion, Charles Rose, a half-breed Piegan Indian. **1949** *Natural Hist.* May 195/2 The Blackfoot Confederacy includes, beside the Blood, the South and North Piegans and the Northern Blackfoot tribes. **1974** *Encycl. Brit. Micropædia* II. 60 (*caption*) In a Piegan lodge. **1988** *Los Angeles Times* 10 Jan. VII. 6/1 There are five Native tribes still living on the outskirts of Calgary: the Blackfoot, Blood, Peigan, Stoney and Sarcee.

**pier**, *n.*[2] Add: [**2.**] **c.** A long narrow structure projecting from the main body of an airport terminal, containing passenger boarding gates and loading stations. Cf. FINGER *n.* 8 c.
   **1958** *Times* 30 May 7/6 Aircraft can taxi to the .. 900 ft. long glazed pier .. which stretches out from the terminal to provide completely enclosed passenger access. **1968** *New Scientist* 26 Sept. 640/2 There will be .. a moving walkway along the pier to the two terminals [at Heathrow Airport]. **1976** *Times* 27 Jan. 2/8 Concorde Alpha Alpha .. left its pier exactly on time .. but turned back before it reached the take-off runway. **1980** *Guardian Weekly* 21 Sept. 29/4 The latest expansion programme has .. provided .. a third aircraft pier to handle long-haul flights. The three piers can handle .. a total of 32 aircraft.

**Piesporter** ('piːzpɔːtə(r), 'piːs-), *n.* [a. Ger., '(wine) of Piesport', f. *Piesport*, the name of a village near Trier in western Germany, + *-er* adj. suffix.] A white Moselle wine produced in the Piesport region.
   [**1851** C. REDDING *Hist. Mod. Wines* (ed. 3) viii. 230 The best vineyards .. are those of the old Schloss (Castle), the Brauneberger, Pisporter, Graacher, Wehlener, etc.] **1875** H. VIZETELLY *Wines of World* I. iii. 52 For several samples of Piesporter .. Count Kesselstadt had a medal for progress awarded him. **1902** *Hatch, Mansfield Price List* Oct. 21 Piesporter, elegant, with refined flavour. **1935** H. R. RUDD *Hocks & Moselles* xi. 143 When I had got into his cellars I found he had some really good things to show, Piesporter, of all varieties, and well made, too. **1967** R. BERNARD *Death takes Last Train* xvii. 173 The three adults dawdled over their cold meal with the '59 Piesporter. **1986** *Listener* 20 Feb. 13/3 If Piesporter Goldtröpfchen tasted like Brobat it would still command a premium in restaurants; in England, the best-selling German wine is Piesporter Michelsberg.

**pig**, *n.*[2] Sense 1 e in Dict. becomes 1 f. Add:
[**1.**] **e.** An earthenware container filled with hot water and used as a hot-water bottle; also, a stone bed-warmer.
   **1869** R. LEIGHTON *Scotch Words* 7 This nicht is cauld, my leddy, wad ye please, To hae a pig i' the bed to warm yer taes? **1903** *Eng. Dial. Dict.* IV. 496/1 A traveller reported that in Northumberland the people slept with the pigs for warmth. He had been asked if he would have a piggy in his bed. **1924** J. H. BONE *Crystal Set* 31 Ye canna go tae yer bed wantin' yer pig. **1941** J. CARY *House of Children* xxix. 126 'Keep them in the bedroom cupboard till you want them .. like pigs in summer.' A pig was a stone hot-water bottle. **1981** C. MILLER *Childhood in*

*Scotland* 25 The housemaids were .. putting in stone hot-water bottles—known as 'pigs'.

**pig**, *v.* Add: **4.** *intr. to pig out*, to over-indulge or 'make a pig of oneself' by over-eating. Also const. *on* (the food specified) and *transf. slang* (orig. and chiefly *N. Amer.*).
   **1978** T. GIFFORD *Glendower Legacy* (1979) 73 I'm just going to pig out at home. **1981** J. FONDA *Workout Bk.* (1982) 29 Troy and Vanessa .. pig out for days on leftover Halloween candy. **1986** *Courier-Mail* (Brisbane) 11 Oct. (Weekend Suppl.) 9/2 Laura pigs out on junk food and watches late night movies. **1987** *Observer* 15 Nov. 10/2 You may not want to 'pig out', as the brochure pleasantly puts it, on movies and junk food for two days. **1987** *Time* 11 May 29/1 To prevent Americans from pigging out on between-meal snacks, herewith some .. tips.
   **d.** *trans.* To eat or appropriate (food) greedily. Cf. HOG *v.*[1] 5 a, d. *colloq.*
   **1979** G. SWARTHOUT *Skeletons* 96 That finished dinner for her. But not for me. I pigged everything. **1984** A. LURIE *Foreign Affairs* (1985) ix. 217 'There was quite a lot of food.' 'Really? No one offered me any ... Pigging it all for themselves, most likely.'

**pigeon**, *n.* Add: [**3.**] **e.** One who carries a journalist's report from one country to another in order to evade censorship. Cf. sense *2 b of the vb. *Journalists' slang.*
   **1973** *Guardian* 19 May 13/3 A 'pigeon' is someone who carries a journalist's story from one country to another and then sees that it is cabled to the journalist's home office. **1980** *Bulletin* (Sydney) 26 Feb. 84/1 To get their stories out journalists must either make an eight-hour drive through the Khyber Pass into Pakistan .. or they can use 'pigeons', the journalists' trade name for someone who carries news despatches by hand.

**pigeon**, *v.* Add: [**2.**] **b.** *transf.* To smuggle (a news report) out of a country by means of a 'pigeon' (sense *3 e). *Journalists' slang.*
   **1973** *Guardian* 19 May 13/3 Many journalists here [in Cambodia] choose to pigeon all but the most innocuous of stories. **1980** *Bulletin* (Sydney) 26 Feb. 84/1 Overwhelmingly the material from Afghanistan has been 'pigeoned' out of the country.

‖**pikake** ('piːkɑke), *n.* [Hawaiian *pīkake*, lit. 'peacock'.] A Hawaiian name for the Arabian jasmine, *Jasminum sambac.*
   **1933** L. B. ARMSTRONG *Facts & Figures Hawaii* 112 Other Hawaiian *lei* flowers are the *Mauna Loa, Pikaki,* Crown Flowers, [etc.]. **1939** *Good Housekeeping* Aug. 28/3 Our hosts gave us a charming dinner, the table decorated with yards and yards of the pikake flower. **1948** M. C. NEAL *In Gardens of Hawaii* 599 In Hawaii, where they are popular for leis, they were named pikake, meaning 'peacock', because Princess Kaiulani was very fond both of this flower and of peacocks. **1966** J. DIDION *Slouching towards Bethlehem* (1969) 188, I am going to find it difficult to tell you .. what it is in the air that will linger long after I have forgotten the smell of pikake and pineapple.

**pilger** ('pɪldʒə(r)), *v.*[2] *slang* (chiefly *Journalists'*). [The name of John *Pilger*, 20th-cent. Australian-born investigative journalist.] *intr.* Auberon Waugh's word for: to conduct journalism in a manner supposedly characteristic of Pilger, esp. by presenting information sensationally in support of a particular conclusion.
   Hence '**pilgering** *vbl. n.*; also (more or less nonce-wds.) '**pilgerish** *a.*, characteristic of this style of journalism; '**pilgerism** *n.*, a pilgerish statement; '**pilgerist** *n.*, a journalist who pilgers; *adj.* = *pilgerish* adj. above; ‚**pilgeri'zation** *n.*, an instance of pilgering.

**1983** A. Waugh in *Spectator* 5 Nov. 6/2 The last proposition that children go without birthday and Christmas presents .. cannot even be described as a pilgerism, just as a lie. **1984** *Ibid.* 10 Mar. 6/2, I listened to him pilgering on manfully. **1984** F. Johnson in *Spectator* 24 Mar. 12/1 *Le pilgerisme.* From the English verb 'to pilger', this expresses the continuous action of going on the television and suggesting at length .. that war, pestilence, governmental corruption in South-east Asia/Central America/the Lebanon etc. are essentially the fault of the Americans in general and the lack of land reform in particular. **1984** A. Waugh in *Ibid.* 24 Nov. 8/1 It was a brilliant piece of pilgering to claim that he knew of a miner's family in Durham which possessed only one pair of shoes. **1987** *Spectator* 19 Dec. 56/1 The term hypothermia has been hijacked by those that Auberon Waugh has defined for us as pilgerists. *Ibid.* 56/2 The Government was forced to introduce new heating allowance regulations because of the pilgerist media hype. **1988** *Times on Sunday* (Sydney) 28 Feb. 12/2 In the first paragraph of my paper I indicated that the ground was not all that fertile. But why let facts spoil a good 'pilgerisation'? **1989** *Independent* 27 Oct. 19/6 One can excuse a long pilgerish tirade against Thatcher.

**pilot,** *n.* Add: [1.] c. Used in the titles of various books containing navigational information, as the British Admiralty's *Mediterranean Pilot*, etc.; hence *ellipt.* (freq. with cap. initial), any such navigational handbook.
**1693** G. Collins (*title*) Great Britain's coasting-pilot. **1825** S. Cummings (*title*) The western pilot; containing charts of the Ohio River, and of the Mississippi [etc.]. **1895** *Funk's Stand. Dict.* 1341/1 *Pilot,* .. a book of sailing-directions. **1897** M. Kingsley *W. Afr.* xvii. 406 The northern part of the bay I have had no personal experience in navigating but, according to the 'Pilot' it has its drawbacks. **1937** H. Belloc in L. C. Wroth *Way of Ship* ii. 15, I pick up my charts, I read my various 'Pilots' (especially my beloved 'English Channel Pilot I'), and the truth comes out. **1976** 'D. Halliday' *Dolly & Nanny Bird* xiv. 183 The charts for the coast of Yugoslavia were already laid out in the saloon with an open volume of the Med. pilot, and he took me quickly through both. **1984** *Pract. Boat Owner* Feb. 65/1 Every abnormal wave documented in the pilot had occurred between May and October.

**g.** *Motor-cycling. ellipt.* for *pilot jet*, sense 8 a below.
**1939** 'N. I.' *Bk. New Imperial* (ed. 5) 7 It will be necessary to re-check the pilot setting if this has been disturbed. **1987** *Super Bike* June 68/2 All I wanted to do was trickle through the slow corners on the pilot.

[8.] [a.] **pilot jet,** a small jet with a narrow bore in the carburettor of a motor-cycle engine, designed to deliver petrol at a low rate when the engine is idling.
**1929** F. J. Camm *Bk. New Imperial* iii. 41 The *pilot jet. **1960** *Motor Cycling* ('Know the Game' Ser.) 8/2 There is also a 'bleed' from the jet to a point behind the throttle slide through which a small amount of petrol can pass. This is called the pilot jet, and its purpose is to provide for a supply of petrol when the engine is merely idling. **1976** *New Motorcycle Monthly* Oct. 46/1 The pilot jet which is situated just in front of the main jet, should next be removed and checked for blockages.

**pinch-,** *comb. form.* For 'pinch-runner *N. Amer.* (see quot. 1961)' read: **pinch-runner** *Baseball,* one who runs in place of another, esp. at a crucial period of play; hence (as a back-formation) **pinch-run** *v. intr.*, to act as a pinch-runner, freq. const. *for* the player replaced; **pinch-running** *vbl. n.*
**1934** *Newsweek* 13 Oct. 19/2 Manager Frisch .. made the strategical error of using Dizzy Dean as a

**pinch runner. 1940** *Sat. Even. Post* 16 Mar. 39/1 He doesn't stop to consult his lawyer when the manager calls upon him for pinch-hitting or *pinch-running chores. **1942** Berrey & Van den Bark *Amer. Thes. Slang* §678/3 *Pinch-run,* to run for a fellow. **1974** *Spartanburg* (S. Carolina) *Herald* 19 Apr. B5/8 The A's used Allan Lewis, an outfielder with little hitting ability, as a pinch running specialist the last two World Series. **1979** *Tucson* (Arizona) *Citizen* 3 Oct. 2D/1 In '69, he had me pinch run for Frank in the World Series. **1989** *N.Y. Times* 20 Apr. D27/4 If Keith had got on base, I was going to pinch-run for him.

**pincher,** *n.* Add: [1.] b. *spec.* the claw of a crab, scorpion, etc. Usu. in *pl.* Cf. pincers *n. pl.* 2.
**1910** R. W. Hegner *Introd. Zool.* xi. 196 The pinchers or chelipeds. **1940** Blunden *Poems 1930–40* 76 Fixing his pinchers on the snake, Thus spake The crab: 'It's Time for you, mate.' **1986** A. C. Clarke *Songs Distant Earth* IV. xxv. 88 The giant scorpion ignored him completely as it continued to snip away at the seaweed with its formidable pinchers.

**pinching,** *vbl. n.* Senses 5, 6 in Dict. become 6, 7. Add: **5.** *Naut.* Sailing or steering too close to the wind, or closer than is generally advisable. Cf. *luffing* vbl. n. s.v. luff *v.* and pinch *v.* 12 b.
**1958** J. Fisher et al. *Sailing* i. 6 Some people, particularly when racing, are so anxious to press on against the wind that they perpetually luff up too far—a fault which is known as 'pinching'. **1965** E. A. Pearson *Lure of Spring* ii. 55 The jib is generally the first to show signs of pinching; it will flutter at the luff. **1987** *Sci. Amer.* Aug. 27/2 By pinching, or steering closer to the true wind, the yachtsman can shorten the distance through the water.

**pinealocyte** (pɪnɪ'æləʊsaɪt), *n. Anat.* [f. pineal *a.* + -o- + -cyte.] A parenchymal cell, characteristic of the pineal body, which secretes melatonin and other hormones.
**1961** de Robertis & de Iraldi in *Experientia* XVII. 122/2 In a previous paper, it was demonstrated that the main morphological characteristic of the *pinealocyte,* the parenchymal cell of the pineal gland, is represented by club-shaped perivascular expansions connected to the cell edge by thin pedicles. **1967** *Cancer Res.* XXVII. 1306/2 The Syrian hamster is not only a pigmented animal but also contains pigment granules in its pinealocytes. **1976** *Anat. & Embryol.* CXLIX. 299 Bilateral adrenalectomy [in rats] is followed by a relative increase of 24% for the number of pinealocyte terminals adjacent to the pericapillary space. **1987** *Nature* 7 May 69/2 Sugden *et al.* have shown that stimulation of $\alpha_1$-adrenergic receptors in rat pinealocytes potentiates isoprenaline-induced cyclic AMP accumulation in these cells.

**ping,** *v.*[2] Add: [2.] c. *Racing colloq.* Of a horse: to jump (a fence) well; also, to leave (the starting stalls, etc.) swiftly.
**1981** Champion & Powell *Champion's Story* xviii. 193 As we came to the fence Aldaniti stood off far too far away, pinged it, but came down much too steep. **1983** Hughes & Watson *Long live National* 47 Aldaniti .. saw a nice long stride, took off and really pinged it. **1986** *Times* 6 May 35/8 The winner .. was smoothly ridden by George Duffield who reported: 'She did not ping the stalls too well, but ran really well.'

**ping-wing** ('pɪŋwɪŋ), *n. W. Indies* (chiefly *Jamaica*). Also **pingwing.** [Popular alteration of pinguin *n.*] A pinguin plant; also, a fence or thicket of pinguin.
**1933** C. McKay *Banana Bottom* xvii. 179 Around them growing natural fences, hibiscus red and white and pink, six-months, dagger palms, pingwings. **1954**

R. Mais *Brother Man* iv. 148 'Puss run through ping-wing, lef' him tail behind. What's dat?'.. 'Needle an' thread, sewin' cloth,' said Papacita. **1961** F. G. Cassidy *Jamaica Talk* v. 97 *Bush-fence*.. means a live or quick hedge, such as one of pinguin (*pingwing macka*), cactus, or the like. **1971** C. McKay in D. G. Wilson *New Ships* 37 We rooted them out of the ping-wing path To stop the mad bees in the rabbit pen.

**pink**, *n.*⁴ and *a.*¹ Sense A. 11 in Dict. becomes A. 11 b. Add: [A.] [II.] [11.] a. A rosé wine; *vin rosé*, = *pink wine* (b) (sense C. c below). *colloq.*
   **1928** E. I. Robson *Wayfarer in Fr. Vineyards* ii. 28 There are many good pinks or rosés; Tavel (Rhône) is one of them. **1972** *Times* 3 June 28/7 Portuguese pink with a slight sparkle... The great wine from Portugal. **1975** P. V. Price *Taste of Wine* v. 99/2 The wines of Cairanne and Lirac, west of the Rhone, are now becoming better known, and also make good pinks.

**pinkers** ('pɪŋkəz), *n. slang* (chiefly *Naval*). [f. PINK *n.*⁴ and *a.*¹: see -ER⁶.] Pink gin; = *PINK *n.*⁴ 11 b.
   **1961** Partridge *Dict. Slang* Suppl. 1222/2 *Pinkers*, a pink gin: Naval officers': since ca. 1920. By 'The Oxford-*er*'. **1978** D. Clark *Libertines* vii. 133 'It was well known that Middleton was the only one who drank pink gin.'.. 'Rubbish. There were two newcomers... Who knew they didn't drink pinkers?' **1981** *Daily Tel.* 4 May 8/5 The 'snotty' downed the 'pinkers' in one before proceeding to eat his glass.

**'Pinpoint**, *n.*² [f. *PIN* s.v. P II. a + POINT *n.*¹, after *cashpoint*, etc.] A proprietary name for a service whereby customers can use a credit or similar card in conjunction with their PIN number to obtain goods (esp. petrol or train tickets) from an automatic dispenser.
   **1984** *Times* 31 May 3 (*caption*) Alan Whicker getting the first Pinpoint ticket at Euston yesterday. **1987** *Daily Tel.* 24 Feb. 5/2 (Advt.), For motorists.., we're installing Pinpoint machines for buying petrol in Shell garages all over the country. **1987** *Which?* Dec. 565/1 PINPOINT is a..self-service system... There are around 200 PINPOINT terminals in the UK. **1988** *Trade Marks Jrnl.* 30 Nov. 3674/1 (*in figure*) Pinpoint... Automated credit, debit and charge card services, all included in Class 36.

**pin-stripe**, *n.* Add: b. One who wears pin-striped clothing; = *PIN-STRIPER *n.*
   **1983** *N.Y. Times* 11 Jan. A1/1 The Yankee pin stripes belong to New York like Central Park, like the Statue of Liberty, like the Metropolitan Museum of Art, [etc.]. **1986** P. D. James *Taste for Death* VI. ii. 379 He's dredged up a bright young pin-stripe from Maurice and Sheldon.

**'pin-,striper**, *n.* Chiefly *U.S.* [f. PIN-STRIPE *n.* + -ER¹.] One who wears pin-striped clothing; *spec.* (*a*) a player in the New York Yankees baseball team; (*b*) a businessman or -woman, esp. in a large city company. Cf. *PIN-STRIPE *n.* b.
   **1975** *Daily News* (N.Y.) 16 Apr. 77/2 He won't be the only pinstriper getting booed. **1978** *Washington Post* 10 Oct. D1/5 After completing one of the three greatest comebacks in history, the Yankees have made themselves hard to hate. The pinstripers as underdogs? For once, that may be the case. **1979** *Ibid.* 17 Apr. B1/3 A reminder that not all lawyers are corporate pin-stripers, that some of them choose to challenge the system rather than serve it. **1984** *Christian Science Monitor* 21 Aug. 19/3 George Steinbrenner has spent millions upon millions on his New York Yankees. The pin-stripers are three deep in millionaires at every position except the one that counts the most—pitcher. **1988** *Financial Times* 22

June 13/6 Behind him, 23 pin-stripers of either sex were waiting to buy their ticket.

**Pintupi** ('pɪntəpi), *n.* and *a.* Also **Pintubi**. [f. Pintupi *pintupi* impolite expletive (literal meaning unknown), prob. first applied as a nickname to the people by their neighbours the Warlpiri.] **A.** *n.* An Aboriginal people inhabiting the eastern region of the Gibson Desert, Central Australia; also their language. **B.** *attrib.* or as *adj.* Of or pertaining to this people.
   **1933** *Oceania* III. 247 The languages were more or less mixed, the Pintubi particularly making frequent use of the Luritja language. *Ibid.* 'Water no good. It stinks. Dead man in there,' said Lilitjukurpa, a Pintubi native, at the Ilbilla Soak. *Ibid.* 251 Ngalia woman, speaks Pintubi. **1940** *Trans. R. Soc. S. Austral.* LXIV. 187 'Pintubi, 'Pi:ntupi, Loc.: Lake Mackay, Mount Russell, Ehrenberg Range, Kintore Range, Warman Rocks; an unknown distance to west. **1957** *Illustr. London News* 7 Sept. 372/1 The biggest problem faced by the Pintibu [*sic*] tribe in the tough, dry region in which they live is the lack of water. **1964** D. Lockwood *Lizard Eaters* 93 'Ahhhh!' It probably means in Pintubi exactly what it means in English—an expressive sigh of satisfaction. **1982** C. Yallop *Austral. Aboriginal Languages* ii. 43 The *Pitjantjatjara* and *Pintupi* and several other desert peoples of Central and Western Australia actually speak 'dialects' which can be classified as the *Western Desert* language. **1984** *Daily Tel.* 25 Oct. 19/2 Nine nomadic Aborigines who have never had direct contact with white people have been found in Central Australia. Members of the Pintubi tribe, they are a family of three women, two men, two boys, and two girls.

**pin-wheel**, *n.* Add: [2.] b. *transf.* Something shaped or operating like a pin-wheel. Freq. *attrib.*
   **1904** F. M. Farmer *Boston Cooking-School Cook Bk.* (rev. ed.) 71 Fruit rolls (pin wheel biscuit). **1955** *Sci. News Let.* 17 Sept. 186 The gas turbine engine, the powerful 'pinwheel jet' that packs more horse-power per pound, is now being tested in cars by the major automobile manufacturers. **1966** J. S. Cox *Illustr. Dict. Hairdressing* 114/1 *Pinwheel*,.. an arrangement of the hair in which it is coiled around a central point to make a pinwheel bang, pinwheel puff, etc. **1975** *New Yorker* 27 Oct. 39/2 My sons have nothing but love for the grandma who makes them pinwheel cookies. **1984** Roberts & Boothroyd *Fund. Plant Path.* (ed. 2) iv. 54 Some tubular cytoplasmic inclusions.. appear in cross section as pin-wheels.

**piny**, *a.* Add: b. Characterized by the fresh or aromatic smell of pine; pine-scented.
   **1882** Mrs. B. M. Croker *Proper Pride* II. v. 88 She liked their aromatic piny smell. **1931** S. Jameson *Richer Dust* xiv. 421 The water in the bath was faintly brown. The warm piny water soothed her. **1964** J. Masters *Trial at Monomoy* iv. 121 The scent of piny after-shave lotion hung around him. **1975** B. Wood *Killing Gift* II. ii. 52 He smelled of a fresh piny aftershave or cologne.

**pioneer**, *n.* Senses 3 b, c in Dict. become 3 c, d. Add: [3.] b. (Usu. with cap. initial.) In Ireland, a member of the Pioneer Total Abstinence Association; a teetotaller. Also *attrib.*
   **1910** *Membership Card* 31 Oct. in *Golden Jubilee Pioneer Total Abstinence Assoc.* (1981) 3/1 The Pioneer Total Abstinence League of the Sacred Heart. **1912** *Irish Catholic* 3 Feb. 6/5 The Association is divided into two sections—Pioneers and Probationers of two years' trial. **1924** L. McKenna *Life & Work Rev. J. A. Cullen, S.J.* i. xii. 125 The first Meeting of the Brooch League or

'Pioneers' took place on the 16th October, 1901. *Ibid.*, By February, 1904, the whole Total Abstinence League of the Sacred Heart was in fair working order. It consisted of (1) those who took Temporary Pledges, (2) the Pioneers, (3) the Promoters, (4) the Juvenile Branches. **1948** *Pioneer* Jan. 9/1 There are more than 300,000 Pioneers and Probationers in Ireland. **1976** W. MANKOWITZ *Hebrew Lesson* 5 'There's the wine for the Sabbath . . . Take some.' 'Not strong drink. I'm a pioneer.' **1980** J. O'FAOLAIN *No Country for Young Men* iii. 62 Three were on Guinness. The fourth wore a pioneer pin-badge of total abstinence.

**pip**, *n.*³ Add: **3.** Something remarkably good; an excellent person or thing. Freq. *a pip*. Cf. PIPPIN *n.* 3 b. *slang* (orig. and chiefly *U.S.*).
   **1928** HECHT & MACARTHUR *Front Page* II. 76, I got the whole story from Jacobi and I got it exclusive . . . That's right, it's a pip. **1950** *New Yorker* 14 Oct. 120/2 A pip of a shiner. **1972** *Kent Life* July 34/1 It is a pip of a part that stands head and shoulders over the other characters that Pinero thought fit to include in his cast. **1987** *New Yorker* 9 Feb. 92/3 He has written a pip of a meeting between Jerry and the therapist in an empty house.

**pipe**, *n.*¹ Add: [**II.**] [**3.**] [**b.**] (b) *to lay pipe*: of a man, to have sexual intercourse; to copulate, esp. vigorously. *U.S. coarse slang.*
   **1967** E. LIEBOW in T. Kochman *Rappin' & Stylin' Out* (1972) 405 Descriptive phrases such as 'I really laid some pipe last night' tend to replace the more specific, denotative labels for intercourse. **1971** B. MALAMUD *Tenants* 80 That chick . . . I wouldn't mind laying some pipe in her pants. **1971** A. HAILEY *Wheels* xiv. 207 It made him horny just to look at her, and he laid pipe, sometimes three times a night . . when May Lou really went to work.
   [**IV.**] [**11.**] [**b.**] **pipe band**, a band consisting of pipers with drummers and a drum-major.
   **1901** W. L. MANSON *Highland Bagpipe* 137 In the British army there are twenty-two *pipe bands. **1949** 'J. TEY' *Brat Farrar* xxvi. 237 The pipe band . . faded . . into the distance. **1987** *Daily Tel.* 4 Sept. 13/7 The Kachin, who compromised a large part of Orde Wingate's Chindits, have their own pipe band and go into battle against the Burmese playing among other things 'Scotland the Brave'.

**piperoxan** (pɪpəˈrɒksæn), *n. Pharm.* Also -oxane (-ein). [f. PIPER(IDINE *n.* + DI)OXAN *n.*] An experimental antipsychotic drug with alpha-adrenoceptor blocking properties, which has also been used (usu. as the hydrochloride) in the diagnosis and treatment of phaeo-chromocytoma; 2-piperidinomethyl-1,4-benzo-dioxan, $C_{14}H_{19}NO_2$.
   **1950** *Dispensatory U.S.A.* (ed. 24, rev. impr.) II. 2016/2 Piperoxane hydrochloride is an adrenergic-blocking agent of short duration of action which has come into use as a diagnostic test to distinguish between essential hypertension and the hypertension due to an epinephrine-secreting tumor (pheochromocytoma). **1950** *Jrnl. Amer. Med. Assoc.* 4 Nov. 829/2 Piperoxan hydrochloride, is believed by Rosenblueth and Cannon to . . produce the blocking of the passage of epinephrine to its site of action inside the smooth muscle cell. **1955** *Lancet* 17 Sept. 577/1 Bacq and Fredericq (1934) reported on the action of an allied substance, 2(1-piperidylmethyl)-1:4-benzodioxane hydrochloride (933F), . . now known as piperoxan. **1971** *European Jrnl. Pharmacol.* XIV. 98/2 In the present paper, piperoxane, a classical α-adrenergic blocking agent . . was shown to antagonize the inhibitory effect of catapresan on vasomotor centres. **1977** *Lancet* 9 July 96/1 Our laboratory findings suggest an antipsychotic effect for a new class of compounds represented by the alpha-adrenergic antagonist, piperoxane. **1988** *Jrnl. Neurochem.* LI. 1373/1 Activation provoked with

the $\alpha_2$-adrenergic antagonist piperoxane (60 mg/kg), which at the dose used induced a similar activation of noradrenergic metabolism in the LC [*sc.* locus cæruleus] as compared with RU24722 (20 mg/kg), did not induce TH [*sc.* tyrosine hydroxylase] in the LC.

**pipperoo** (pɪpəˈruː), *n. U.S. slang.* [Fanciful expansion of *PIP *n.*³ 3: see -EROO.] Something remarkably good; = *PIP *n.*³ 3.
   **1942** M. GORDON *I've got a Gal in Kalamazoo* (song) 4 Oh, what a gal, a real pipperoo! **1945** *Daily News* (Chicago) 29 Dec. 1/6 A pipperoo movie was thrilling the patrons. **1985** *Washington Post* 10 July B5/3 Of his beloved Nats, Bass recalls 'some real pipperoos'.

‖**pisteur** (pistœr), *n. Skiing.* [Fr., f. *piste* PISTE *n.*² + -*eur* agent suffix.] One employed to prepare the snow on a *piste* for skiers.
   **1963** *Times* 10 Jan. 4/1 Even the *pisteurs* . . remarked that his style surpassed even that of the forerunners. **1984** *Sunday Times* (Colour Suppl.) 4 Nov. 106/1 The run down is very steep indeed and inadequate skiers who attempt it are often admonished by a pisteur positioned near the bottom of the steep section. **1988** *Daily Mail Ski Mag.* Sept. 10/2 The area has masses of wide open pistes kept in impeccable condition by teams of pisteurs and ratracs.

**pistol**, *n.* Add: [**1.**] †e. Someone blustering, eccentric in appearance, or otherwise peculiar. (Usu. *contempt.*) *Obs. north. dial.*
   **1857** J. SULLIVAN *Cumberland & Westmorland* II. iii. 90 'Thou'rt a bonny pistol' is anything but praise. **1894** *Weyver's Awn Comic Olmanac* 18 They've sam pistols o'weyver's to deeal wi'. **1903** *Eng. Dial. Dict.* IV. 524/1 He's a gay pistle wi' a sup o' drink in him. He's a gay pistle is oor laal Jacky.
   **f.** A remarkable person; someone exceptional, esp. for reliability or strength of character. *U.S. slang.*
   **1984** J. DIDION *Democracy* II. x. 153 Your mother's been getting up a party for the Rose Bowl, Harry Victor said. Carol's a real pistol, Dwight Christian said. **1984** J. PHILLIPS *Machine Dreams* 20 What a pistol she was—still working at the dress shop then, hard as nails and took no truck from anyone.

‖**pistou** (pistu), *n. Cookery.* Also pestou. [Prov., = It. *pesto* PESTO *n.*] A sauce or paste made from crushed basil, garlic, cheese, etc., used esp. in Provençal dishes; = PESTO *n.*; also, a vegetable soup made with this sauce.
   **1951** E. DAVID *French Country Cooking* 207 *Pestou* . . is the garlic and basil butter added to soups and used as a sauce for *pasta* and for fish in the Nice district and in Genoa. **1961** S. BECK et al. *Mastering Art French Cooking* 45 The *pistou* itself, like the Italian *pesto*, is a sauce made of garlic, basil, tomato and cheese, and is just as good on spaghetti as . . in this rich vegetable soup. **1979** *Washington Post Mag.* 2 Sept. 27/1 One of the great dishes of southern France is a thick vegetable soup called pistou . . . Properly prepared pistou is not only a treat for the palate, but a feast for the eyes. **1989** *Chicago Tribune* 2 Mar. VII. 2/2 Vegetable soup with basil pistou (a basil, garlic and Parmesan cheese topping), pepper steak with onion sauce [etc.].

**pit**, *n.*¹ Senses 14, 15 in Dict. become 15, 16. Add: [**II.**] **14.** A bed, a bunk. *slang* (orig. *Forces*').
   **1948** PARTRIDGE *Dict. Forces' Slang* 143 Pit; usually *the old pit.* Bed. (Air Force). Where one 'gets down to it'. **1964** J. HALE *Grudge Fight* v. 76 He scrambles into his pit and pulls the blankets over his head. **1982** D. TINKER *Message from Falklands* (1983) iv. 117 In our pits at night we always get rattled around a bit.

**1988** *Climber* June 42/4 The most important item in camping comfort is your pit, after all you spend some 8 hours out of the 24 there.

**pit**, *v.*¹ Add: [**3.**] **b.** To match (one's skill, strength, etc.) *against* an opponent. Freq. in phr. *to pit one's wits against*.
**1898** G. B. SHAW *Candida* I. 106 I'll rescue her from her slavery to them: I'll pit my own ideas against them. **1927** V. WOOLF *To Lighthouse* III. iv. 245 Men..pitting muscle and brain against the waves. **1958** *Argosy* Sept. 12 He was an adventurer pitting his brains against authority, and for once he had lost. **1968** B. ENGLAND *Figures in Landscape* 85 He had immeasurable courage to stand and fight, to pit his strength against mountains and rivers and sun. **1970** T. LUPTON *Managem. & Social Sci.* (ed. 2) iii. 63 Pitting wits against management on piecework rates. **1977** K. M. E. MURRAY *Caught in Web of Words* xvii. 339 The exhilaration of the fell walker, pitting his strength against the wind on a steep slope. **1981** V. GLENDINNING *Edith Sitwell* 4 When she was first pitting her wits and talent against the prevailing Georgianism.

**pit** (pɪt), *v.*² orig. and chiefly *N. Amer.* [f. PIT *n.*²] *trans.* To remove the pit or stone from (a fruit); = STONE *v.* 7.
**1906** A. I. JUDGE *Compl. Course in Canning* 85 Stem the cherries, remove all leaves, pit by any appropriate method. **1937** *Fruit Products Jrnl.* XVI. 232/2 Washed apricots were pitted, steamed, passed through the fine screen of an..extractor. **1954** *Sunset* Oct. 132/1 (*caption*) Pit 30 large dates and stuff them with cooked orange meat. **1979** *Washington Post* 21 June E6/1 Cherries don't have to be pitted. **1979** CUNNINGHAM & LABER *Fannie Farmer Cookbk.* (1988) 425 *Olives.* Green, stuffed, ripe or black Mediterranean. Pit and slice.

**pitch**, *n.*² Add: [**VII.**] [**25.**] **f.** *Typewriting* and *Computing.* The density of characters on a line, usu. expressed as the number of characters per inch.
**1932** CROOKS & DAWSON *Etheridge's Dict. Typewriting* (ed. 3) 225 In an inch of space it is possible to insert varying numbers of letters in a particular type, as *Elite* (*twelve to the inch*) or *Elite* (*ten to the inch*). This spacing is referred to as the 'pitch' of the type. **1954** B. BLIVEN *Wonderful Writing Machine* xii. 209 The correct term for size, in typewriter language, is 'pitch', a measure of letter-space width and a sloppy word because it doesn't tell, definitely, how tall the letters are. *c* **1961** *Imperial Type Faces* (Imperial Typewriter Co.), Elite type..is slightly smaller in size... Its normal 'pitch' is twelve letters per inch. **1974** W. A. BEECHING *Century of Typewriter* ii. 78 Before World War II, most typewriters were equipped with the normal and familiar Pica typewriter type with ten spaces to the inch. The number of spaces to the inch is known as 'the pitch'. **1987** *Graphics World* Nov./Dec. 73 A sheet printed with calibrations in 15-pitch, 12-pitch and 10-pitch measures to speed up character counting of manuscripts.

**pitch**, *v.*¹ Add: [**II.**] [**16.**] **b.** *Comm.* With *for*: to forecast or estimate (a share price, etc.); to aim at (a particular result).
**1983** *Times* 23 Sept. 18/3 Market men expect the sale to go well, with most observers pitching for a striking price of 430p. **1985** A. BLOND *Book Book* iii. 51 He is pitching for a turnover of £6 million. **1988** *Investors Chron.* 8 Jan. 8/2 James Capel suggests between £20m and £21m (£14.4m) with earnings of 34p, while Kleinwort Grieveson pitches for £19.5m.
[**III.**] [**17.**] **e.** *intr.* Of a man: to make sexual advances. Also const. (*up*) *to*. Chiefly *U.S.*
**1903** *Eng. Dial. Dict.* IV. 526/1 *Pitch up to*, to make advances, to make love to. **1930** D. RUNYON *Lily of St. Pierre* in *Collier's* 20 Dec. 32/4, I never think of Lily as anything but a little doll with her hair in

braids, and certainly not a doll such as a guy will start pitching to. **1953** S. BELLOW *Adventures A. March* v. 80, I hugged and pitched on the porches and in the back-yards with girls. **1985** *Amer. Speech* LX. III. 251 She distinguishes *wolves*,..from *pimps*.., from *daddies*.., all three of whom *pitch* but don't *catch*.
**f.** *Comm.* To make a bid or offer *for* business (esp. a client's account). Also without *const.*
**1985** T. DOUGLAS *Compl. Guide Advertising* iv. 110/1 The importance of confidentiality meant that even within the agency no one ever referred to the fact that it was pitching for the Woolworth account. **1985** *Times* 13 Apr. 11/4 (*heading*) Lloyd's pitches for China business. **1986** *Marketing* 11 Sept. 3/2 A corporate campaign for Dee seems certain, but no agencies have yet been asked to pitch. **1988** *Creative Rev.* Jan. 37/2 It's an account which they pitched for and won. **1988** *Times* 29 Oct. 19/7 Repsol, the Spanish oil company, might well pitch.
**g.** *trans.* To discard or throw away (an unwanted object). *N. Amer. colloq.*
**1985** COHEN & SCHLOTZHAUER in D. L. Gold *Comments on Etymol.* XIV. xi. & xii. 10 The pub keeper in full view of the customer broke off a piece of the stem, insuring that the new customer would have a clean area to suck on. When the stem got too short, the thing was pitched. **1987** J. RULE *Memory Board* vii. 108 Patricia had taken such good care of his clothes that he had not had time..to become a disgrace, but Christine did suggest pitching a thing or two.
**h.** To drive (a vehicle) rapidly and somewhat recklessly into a bend or round the track. *colloq.* (chiefly *Motor Racing*).
**1985** *Dirt Bike* Mar. 36/1 If you're flying and you pitch it, it will slide around the turn. **1986** *Road Racer* Aug./Sept. 22/3 The bike steered *too* quickly, feeling as though, once pitched into a turn, it just wanted to carry on falling. **1987** *Motoring News* 3 June 16/2 Where last year Didier didn't look all that fast, this time he did throughout, pitching the white car round in flowing style to snatch the pole from favourite Jean Alesi's Oreca Dallara.
[**VI.**] [**23.**] [**a.**] For def. read: *pitch in*: to set to work vigorously; also, to turn (aside) to a particular objective; to begin. Hence, to add one's contribution to a general effort or fund. *colloq.* (chiefly *N. Amer.*). (Further examples.)
**1924** H. CROY *R.F.D. No. 3* iii. 52 It was a serious thing for a girl on a farm not to pitch in and help with the work. **1943** B. SMITH *Tree grows in Brooklyn* IV. xliv. 283 When her papers were read up, she didn't have to pitch in, as the other readers did, and help the girls who were behind. **1973** J. GARDNER *Nickel Mountain* III. i. 88 Neighbors from here to Athensville and New Carthage had pitched in and helped him lay up the cinder-block house behind the diner. **1985** A. GUINNESS *Blessings in Disguise* vii. 87 The only people who didn't pitch in with something were the Dukhobors, the extreme puritanical sect. **1988** P. AUSTER *In Country of Last Things* 139 Every resident, as we called them, had to agree to certain conditions... No fighting or stealing, for example, and a willingness to pitch in with the chores.

**'pitch-up**, *n. Aeronaut.* [f. PITCH *v.*¹ + UP *adv.*¹] A sudden, uncontrolled, upward pitch of an aircraft, esp. as experienced during a climb or descent; (a tendency towards) deviation of this nature. Cf. PITCH *v.*¹ 19 f.
**1955** *S.A.E. Jrnl.* Apr. 40/2 In pitchup (sometimes referred to as digin, or overshoot) the airplane suddenly pitches up or digs in during a pullup or turn... It is the result of shock-wave formation. **1956** W. A. HEFLIN *U.S. Air Force Dict.* 389/2 *Pitch-up*,..a marked tendency in an aircraft to pitch upward. **1976** *Flight Internat.* 31 Jan. 207/1 The aircraft is believed to have suffered a pitch-up moment on final approach and to have landed in a

flat attitude. **1988** *Pilot* Nov. 41/1 It is a very stable aircraft, laterally, directionally and in pitch, when it will correct a 15 mph pitch-up within the classic one cycle, hands off.

**'pitted**, *ppl. a.*[2] and *a.* orig. *U.S.* [f. PIT *v.*[2] and *n.*[2] + -ED.] Of fruit: having the pit or stone removed; = STONED *ppl. a.* and *a.* 6.
**1903** C. J. BROOKS *Marine Stewards' Guide* 108 Cherry sauce... Add one pint of cherries, pitted, stew about half an hour. **1926** *Daily Colonist* (Victoria, B.C.) 6 Jan. 8/1 (Advt.), Red pitted cherries, 2's, per tin 25¢. **1954** *Fortnum & Mason Christmas Catal.* 3/1, 1 F & M jar pitted olives. **1982** D. SMITH *Compl. Cookery Course* 70 Arrange them in a diamond-shaped pattern .. all over the onion filling, and stud each diamond with a halved, pitted olive.

**pitting** ('pitiŋ), *ppl. a. Path.* [f. PIT *v.*[1]] That pits (sense 5); *spec.* (esp. in *pitting oedema*) designating an oedema in which the swollen area temporarily retains any impression made in it with the fingertips, etc.
**1933** *Endocrinology* XVII. 378 There was slight pitting edema of the ankles and feet. **1948** R. GREENE *Pract. Endocrinol.* x. 3. 22 Textbooks of medicine are strangely silent about the fact that pitting œdema is almost always present in the lower part of the legs of grossly adipose patients. **1961** L. MARTIN *Clin. Endocrinol.* (ed. 3) ix. 245 Frank (1931) first noticed that many women suffered in the days preceding menstruation from great mental tension, often with severe headaches and pitting œdema. **1979** G. BOURNE *Pregnancy* (rev. ed.) xii. 218 The majority of women develop pitting oedema at some stage during their pregnancy. **1987** *Oxf. Textbk. Med.* (ed. 2) I. v. 535/2 Oedema develops, soft and pitting at first, but becoming gradually hard after a year or two.

**'pitting**, *vbl. n.*[2] orig. *U.S.* [f. PIT *v.*[2] + -ING[1].] The removal of the pit or stone from a fruit.
**1916** J. P. ZAVALLA *Canning of Fruits & Vegetables* 12 In California they have a special peach-pitting knife... It is known as 'Carmichael pitting spoon'. **1924** J. H. COLLINS *Story of Canned Foods* viii. 114 Stemming, peeling, slicing, coring, pitting .. are done by machinery. **1957** *Encycl. Brit.* IV. 749/2 Preparatory operations for canning] include .. pitting (cherries), soaking (dry beans, cherries).

**pity**, *n.* Add: [I.] [3.] **c.** Without art. introducing subordinate clause: = 'it is (or was) a pity (that) .. .'. *colloq.*
**1907** G. B. SHAW *Major Barbara* II. 240 Pity you didn't rub some [snow] off with your knees, Bill! That would have done you a lot of good. **1915** H. ROSHER *In R.N.A.S.* (1916) 117 Pity I'm not due for another spot of leave yet. **1922** JOYCE *Ulysses* 315 Still, says Bloom, on account of the poor woman, I mean his wife.—Pity about her, says the citizen. **1956** R. ROBINSON *Landscape with Dead Dons* ix. 79 Pity we got off to a duff start. **1968** E. BOWEN *Eva Trout* (1969) II. iii. 209 Pity it rained when we were on the river, nothing is wetter than a punt. **1976** *Beano* 17 Jan. 12/3 Squirrels can be fierce ... Eek! .. Pity you didn't tell me that earlier, cub!

**pivot**, *n.* Senses 3 e, f in Dict. become 3 f, g. Add: [3.] **e.** *Basketball.* A movement in which the player holding the ball may take one or more paces in any direction with one foot, while keeping the other (the *pivot foot*) in fixed contact with the floor.
**1920** FROST & WARDLAW *Basket Ball & Indoor Baseball for Women* iv. 27 The pivot may be taken on the ball or heel of the foot, but the foot must remain in place. **1929** H. C. CARLSON *Your Basket Ball* v. 88 In the pivot and return pass no. 2 is automatically between no. 1 and his opponent. **1941** J. NAISMITH *Basketball* 66 Closely allied with the dribble is the pivot. **1954** *Basketball* ('Know the Game' Ser.) (rev. ed.) 12/1 The pivot foot may be lifted to pass or

shoot provided the ball is released before the foot touches the ground again. **1982** *N.Y. Times* 5 Apr. c9/4 How many steps is he allowed to take before a pivot foot must be established for the next attempted throw?

**pizotifen** (pɪ'zəʊtɪfɛn), *n. Pharm.* [f. PI(PERIDINE *n.* + BEN)ZO- + -*tifen* altered f. T(H)I(O)PHEN(E *n.*, after TAMOXIFEN *n.*, etc.] A tricyclic drug, $C_{19}H_{21}NS$, with blocking properties at histamine and serotonin receptors, given orally in tablet form as a prophylactic in some cases of migraine.
**1969** *WHO Chron.* XXIII. 439 Pizotifen. **1971** *N.Z. Med. Jrnl.* LXXIII. 5 (*heading*) The treatment of migraine with BC 105 (pizotifen): a double blind trial. **1977** *Lancet* 11 June 1259/2 We have done a small pilot trial of pizotifen combined with maprotiline ('Ludiomil') in patients with depression. **1985** *Brit. Med. Jrnl.* 9 Nov. 1337/1 Appetite may be increased by .. pizotifen. **1988** *Pharmacology* XXXVII. 252/1 In our studies, the 5-HT antagonists cyproheptadine and pizotifen .. inhibited the pressor effect of 5-HT and DHE in a noncompetitive manner.

**placard**, *n.* Add: [I.] [2.] For 'a bill, a poster.' read: a bill, a poster; also, a sign bearing a political or other slogan, carried by a demonstrator, etc., to attract public attention. (Further examples.)
**1864** *Morning Star* 26 May 4 He encounters a sandwich man bearing placards. **1966** D. BAGLEY *Wyatt's Hurricane* iv. 102 If you think I'm going to walk about in the middle of a civil war bearing a placard inscribed 'Prepare To Meet Thy Doom' you're mistaken. **1977** *Washington Post* 17 Nov. A11/3 Police .. ripped some poles from demonstrators' placards.
III. [6.] *placard-carrier; placard-carrying a.*
**1981** *Washington Post* 21 Apr. A2/1 A bagpiper, a juggler and more than a dozen placard-carriers whose signs listed historic events that took place in the tavern. **1987** *Los Angeles Times* 2 Apr. IX. 1/1 In an attempt to rally public interest, about 30 placard-carrying people picketed .. in front of the Safeway store.

**place**, *v.* Add: [3.] **e.** To order or obtain a connection for (a telephone call), esp. through an operator. Chiefly *N. Amer.*
**1943** A. L. ALBERT *Fund. Telephony* viii. 190 This is a very direct method of placing toll calls and gives the telephone user a toll service which compares with local service in speed of completing calls. **1974** U. LE GUIN *Dispossessed* vii. 175 She not only helped him look up the name in the ponderous directory of telephone numbers, but placed the call for him on the shop phone. **1989** *InfoWorld* 3 Apr. 57/3 We had to place several calls before getting through to the technicians.

**placee** (pleɪ'siː), *n. Comm.* (orig. *U.S.*). [f. PLACE *v.* + -EE[1].] An investor to whom shares, etc. are sold by private or private placement.
**1963** *Univ. Chicago Law Rev.* XXX. 216 There was nothing in the record to suggest that private placements were ever made to more than a few placees. **1972** *New York Law Jrnl.* 10 Oct. 3/2 Successive private placements each start a new two-year holding period. The holding of the previous private placee cannot be tacked to the holding of the subsequent placee. **1982** *Financial Times* 23 Nov. 19/6 If the deal goes through Anglo United will be owned as to 53 per cent by ARP, 33 per cent by the private placees and 14 per cent by existing shareholders. **1986** *Times* 9 July 21/1 The shares have been taken up by placees and .. are trading at premium to the placing price.

**place-holder**, *n.* Add: Also placeholder. **2. a.** *Math.* (*a*) A significant zero in the decimal representation of a number. (*b*) In the teaching of mathematics, a symbol (freq. an empty box) used in an expression to denote a missing quantity or operator.

**1950** M. A. POTTER et al. *Math. to Use* iv. 205 Sometimes you have to annex zeros at the right of the product to act as place-holders. **1952** L. J. BRUECKNE et al. *Understanding Numbers* i. 3 The Romans did not have a place holder like our zero. **1966** OGILVY & ANDERSON *Excurs. Number Theory* i. 2 Note the importance of zero as a spacer, or place-holder; 307 is not the same as 37, although $3x^2 + 0 + 7$ *is* the same as $3x^2 + 7$. Here something else is acting as the place-indicator. **1966** MAY & MOSS *New Math for Adults Only* iii. 17/1 The youngster is writing a mathematical sentence with any closed figure, . . as a placeholder for the unknown or unknowns.

**b.** *Linguistics.* An element of a sentence that is required by syntactic constraints but carries little or no semantic information; *spec.* the impersonal pronoun in sentences where the subject clause has been placed after the verb.

**1968** R. W. LANGACKER *Lang. & its Struct.* v. 129 One such rule is Extraposition, which moves the embedded clause to the end of the sentence and leaves behind, as a placeholder in subject position, the semantically empty form *it*. **1984** *Fremdsprachen* XXVIII. 241 English syntax permits 'it', too, as a non-referring subject in certain structures ('It is cold') and as a place-holder in others ('It does not bother me that he is ill'). **1985** *Ibid.* XXIX. 239 Other translations are, of course, possible, e.g. with the German placeholder 'es' or the use of the indefinite pronoun 'man'.

**placeless**, *a.* Add: 'placelessness *n.*

**1973** M. McLUHAN *Let.* 3 Jan. (1987) 459 He challenged the idea of the TV icon and the certification of placelessness. **1986** *Independent* 1 Dec. 23 Agelessness has . . become something of a cliché in any analysis of Grant's enduring appeal. Less often acknowledged . . was his placelessness.

**Placidyl** ('plæsɪdɪl), *n. Pharm.* [f. PLACID *a.* + -YL.] A proprietary name in the U.S. and Canada for ethchlorvynol.

**1955** *Official Gaz.* (U.S. Patent Office) 29 Nov. TM229/2 Placidyl . . for sedative and hypnotic. **1956** *Jrnl. Amer. Med. Assoc.* 5 May 65/2 Preparations for use as stated for the foregoing drug are marketed under the following name: Placidyl. **1974** M. C. GERALD *Pharmacol.* xi. 199 (*table*) Placidyl. **1983** *N.Y. Times* 7 June C1/5 Dr. Farley was impressed with medical journal articles that left him with the impression that Placidyl was 'a fantastic, nonaddicting drug'.

**plagiarize**, *v.* Add: 'plagiarized *ppl. a.*

**1948** P. KAVANAGH *Tarry Flynn* viii. 182 A thrush was singing his plagiarised version of the blackbird's song in one of the poplars behind the house. **1980** *N.Y. Times* 16 Nov. XII. 21/5 When you catch someone with a bought paper, a plagiarized paper, you will give the student the benefit of the doubt.

**plagiogranite** (,pleɪdʒɪəʊ'grænɪt), *n. Petrogr.* [a. Russ. *plagiogranitỹ* (N. Khruschov 1931, in *Trans. Geol. & Prospecting Service U.S.S.R.* XC. 16), shortened f. G. *Plagioklasgranit* (A. G. Högbom 1905, in *Bull. Geol. Inst. Univ. Upsala* VI. 232): see PLAGIOCLASE, *n.*, GRANITE *n.*] Any of a range of granitic rocks which occur esp. in ophiolites and are rich in sodic plagioclase feldspar.

[**1932** A. JOHANNSEN *Descriptive Petrogr. Igneous Rocks* II. 382 'Plagioclase-granite'. Long Bay, Virgin Gorda, West Indies.] **1959** *Bull. Volcanologique* XX. 177 The development of folding processes, accompanied by deep fractures, brought about the formation of a complicated intrusive magmatic complex consisting of gabbro-amphibolites, ultrabasites, plagiogranites, spessartites and acid Na granitoids. **1979** *Nature* 7 June 491/1 A single arcuate (folded?) and fault-bounded block of plagiogranite is present in the much-faulted northern part of the mapped area. **1985** THORPE & BROWN *Field Descr. Igneous Rocks* x. 133/2 The white 'anorthositic' rocks of ophiolites are usually rich in sodium-rich plagioclase feldspar and some of them contain substantial amounts of quartz (up to 30%), so that the term plagiogranite is more appropriate.

**planche** (plɑːntʃ, semi-anglicized plɑːnʃ), *n. Gymnastics.* [a. Fr., lit. 'plank, slab': cf. PLANCH *n.*] A position in which the body is held parallel with the ground, esp. by the arms (as on the parallel bars, rings, etc.).

**1906** *Sandow's Mag.* 24 May 644/2, I can also . . hold the front plache [*sic*] and crucifix on the rings, and several other gymnastic tricks. **1910** *Health & Strength* 16 Apr. 412/2 His long-arm balance, one-arm planches and crucifixes. **1925** *Ibid.* 19 Sept. 271/3, I commenced to practise what is known as a planche, or horizontal. From a hand stand the body is lowered down to this position, and is held there. **1947** *Brit. Amat. Weight-Lifter* Oct. 298/2 We call any movement where the body is held off, and parallel with, the ground a planche. **1968** M. F. MUSKER et al. *Guide to Gymnastics* vii. 135 The two-arm planche can be performed with increased ease by some beginners by doing it on one bar of a set of low parallel bars. **1988** *N.Y. Times* 7 Aug. XXII. 2/3 Mr. Vercroyssen was next on the trapeze with a 'planche'—balancing on the bar on the small of the back, arms and legs extended.

**planesman** ('pleɪnzmən), *n. Naut.* [f. PLANE *n.*[3] + MAN *n.*[1], after *helmsman, steersman,* etc.] One who operates the hydroplanes on a submarine.

**1952** E. YOUNG *One of our Submarines* ii. 32 If the planesman did not keep to the exact periscope depth . . you might find the periscope sticking up several feet out of the water. **1960** H. B. HARRIS-WARREN *Dive!* iv. 37 In a submarine the planesmen correspond to the pilot and co-pilot in the airlines. **1975** A. TREW *Zhukov Briefing* ii. 20 The executive officer's eyes never left the instruments on the panel in front of the planesmen.

**planification** (,plænɪfɪ'keɪʃ(ə)n), *n.* orig. *U.S.* [a. Fr., f. *planifier* to plan: see -FICATION.] Systematic planning or organization; the management of resources according to a plan, esp. of economic or political development; an instance of this.

**1959** *New Yorker* 22 Aug. 72/2 The city . . radiates a sense of 'good government', . . through the planification of its surrounding hills and slopes, marked off by dark cypresses, measured by yellow villas. **1962** *Economist* 8 Dec. 1042/3 M. Robert Marjolin . . finally came out, at a conference in Rome, and used the word *planification.* **1964** *Guardian* 1 Apr. 14/3 France is still a capital importer and closed to foreign issues, and the 'planification' of credits is also an obstacle to a more liberal capital market. **1976** *Maclean's Mag.* 1 Nov. 14/1 His government of technocrats and bureaucrats . . have been frustrated to the screaming point by their planifications. **1976** *Aviation Week* 22 Nov. 70/2 There is an interesting planification in the Soviet Union in order to pursue a vigorous utilization of the space dimension. **1982** *Financial Times* 15 Jan. 19/8 The Fund must . . not emerge as an engine of international planification.

**planigram** ('plænɪgræm), *n. Med.* [f. *PLANI(GRAPHY *n.*: see -GRAM.] An image obtained by planigraphy.

**1936** *Amer. Jrnl. Roentgenol.* XXXVI. 577/1 Vallebona was able to make planigrams of skulls. **1958** *Arch. Ophthalmol.* LX. 266/2 The ultrasonogram represents a horizontal section, or planigram, through a level of the eye. **1968** *Psychiatria, Neurologia, Neurochirurgia* LXXI. 136 The patient..lying in the..lateral decubitus position, planigrams of horizontal planes are made. **1971** *Amer. Jrnl. Roentgenol.* CXIII. 576/1 Since there is a constant difference between the fulcrum setting for the fluoroplanigram and conventional film planigram, the latter can be immediately obtained after the precise plane of interest has been selected from the fluoroscopic presentations.

**planigraphy** (plæ'nɪgrəfɪ), *n. Med.* [a. Du. *planigraphie* (B. G. Ziedses des Plantes 1931, in *Nederlands Tijdschr. voor Geneeskunde* LXXV. 5218); cf. PLANI-, -GRAPHY.] The process of obtaining a visual representation of a plane section through living tissue, by such techniques as tomography, ultrasonography, etc.

**1933** *Year Bk. Radiol.* 428 (*heading*) New method of differentiation in roentgenography (planigraphy). **1938** *Radiology* XXX. 655/1 The authors discuss the various methods of planigraphy and the problem of radioscopy of a plane. **1942** *Amer. Jrnl. Roentgenol.* XLVII. 83 (*heading*) The value of body section roentgenography (planigraphy) for the demonstration of tumors, non-neoplastic disease and foreign bodies in the neck and chest. **1967** *Investigative Radiol.* II. 259/1 Although conventional linear planigraphy does not approach the precision attained with the more elaborate movements afforded by the 'Polytome', 'Mimer' and others, its efficiency can be improved. **1986** B. KEANE in T. F. McAinsh *Physics in Med. & Biol. Encycl.* II. 671/1 Where it is particularly desired to obtain a three-dimensional dissection of some feature, the method of body-section radiography is used. This technique, known variously as tomography, planigraphy, or laminography, is one in which of the three factors x-ray source, patient and film, one is kept stationary during the exposure and the other two move in a related motion.

Hence **plani'graphic** *a.*, of, pertaining to, designating, or produced by planigraphy.

**1936** *Amer. Jrnl. Roentgenol.* XXXVI. 576/1 (*heading*) Planigraphic method. *Ibid.* 579 (*heading*) Ziedses des Plantes' planigraphic apparatus. **1968** *Psychiatria, Neurologia, Neurochirurgia* LXXI. 133 With the exception of the tomographic and planigraphic examinations,..all examinations are carried out stereoscopically. **1978** *Ann. Neurol.* III. 216 Clinical studies which attempt to quantitate ventricular volume should use a computerized or planigraphic measure.

**planktic** ('plæŋktɪk), *a. Biol.* [ad. G. *planktisch* (G. Burckhardt 1920, in *Zeitschr. f. Hydrologie* I. 190), f. *Plankter* PLANKTER *n.*: see -IC I.] Planktonic; used to designate an organism that floats or drifts in water, or a stage in the life of an organism when it does this.

**1962** *Zoologiska Bidrag från Uppsala* XXXV. 311 The cold-water forms of *Synchaeta* belong to those planktic rotifers that are most difficult to determine. **1967** G. E. HUTCHINSON *Treat. Limnol.* II. xix. 236 The adjective planktic would be etymologically sounder than planktonic, but usage unequivocally favors the latter. **1978** *Nature* 26 Jan. 324/2 Shackleton..now believes that because planktic and not benthic foraminifera were analysed for substage 5e in Core V28-238, the isotopic composition may include a temperature effect. **1979** *Ibid.* 5 Apr. 580/2 Some of the described microfossils may have had a planktic phase in their life cycle. **1988** *Biol. Jrnl. Linn. Soc.* XXXV. 6 The larva is not equipped for a planktic life.

**plant**, *v.* Add: [I.] [2.] e. To place (a bomb) in a building, etc., esp. as a terrorist act.

**1916** 'BOYD CABLE' *Action Front* 56 If we can plant a bomb or two in the right spot, it will bottle up any Germans working inside? **1937** R. NARAYAN *Bachelor*

*of Arts* ii. 46 Did you try to plant a bomb..in his house? **1968** L. W. ROBINSON *Assassin* (1969) xvi. 199 He planted another bomb... Bomb squad says it's made of *plastique*. **1981** G. CLARE *Last Waltz in Vienna* (1982) I. 42 They planted bombs in Jewish shops.

[III.] [7.] c. *spec.* to place (a kiss) *on* the lips, cheek, etc., usu. with gusto or deliberation.

**1906** GALSWORTHY *Man of Property* I. ix. 122 Moved by some inexplicable desire to assert his proprietorship, he rose from his chair and planted a kiss on his wife's shoulder. **1937** G. FRANKAU *More of Us* xii. 125 Was this The ruleress of waves, R.N., all-British, Who stooped to plant the Cytherean Kiss? **1942** BERREY & VAN DEN BARK *Amer. Thes. Slang* §355/7 *Kiss,*..Plant a smacker. **1986** *Times* 16 June 5/4 About 100 people applauded and cheered his return and women planted kisses on his cheek.

**plasma**, *n.* Add: [8.] [a.] **plasma diagnostics** (const. as *sing.*), the determination of the physical characteristics of plasmas by experimental methods that do not significantly alter them.

**1961** *IRE Trans. Antennas & Propagation* IX. 317/1 (*heading*) The potential utility of scanning microwave beams in *plasma diagnostics. **1981** *Nature* 1 Oct. 338 Plasma diagnostics using high-resolution X-ray spectroscopy is a field of expanding importance in both fusion reactor research and high-energy astrophysics.

**plasmaneme** ('plæzməniːm), *n. Zool. rare.* [f. PLASMA *n.* + -*neme* after AXONEME *n.*, *MASTIGONEME *n.*, etc.] = *FILOPODIUM *n.*

**1969** VICKERMAN & LUCKINS in *Nature* 13 Dec. 1125/2 The variable antigens of T[*rypanosoma*] *brucei* are located in the surface coat—including that of the trypanosome's filiform appendages, here termed plasmanemes. **1974** *Ciba Symposium* XX. 206 The exoantigen may consist of loosened cell particles covered with surface material, the so-called plasmanemes. **1981** *Jrnl. Protozool.* XXVIII. 313/1 These appendages have been referred to in the past as..plasmanemes.

**plasmatocyte** (plæz'mætəʊsaɪt), *n. Ent.* [f. Gr. πλάσμα, πλασματο- (see PLASMA *n.*) + -CYTE.] Each of the large phagocytic cells, variable in shape but having a large nucleus and basophilic cytoplasm, that make up much of the haemolymph of some insects.

**1941** YEAGER & MUNSON in *Jrnl. Agric. Res.* LXIII. 263 In smears from the later instars, however, especially the fifth and sixth, and from the prepupal and early pupal stages, the blood-cell types, here called plasmatocytes and cystocytes, have been definitely identified among the glycogen-containing cells. **1959** W. ANDREW *Textbk. Compar. Histol.* ix. 366 (*caption*) Types of hemocytes from a butterfly larva, *Laphrygma fragipida*. The large cells are rhegmatocytes..the medium-sized ovoid to spindle-shaped cells, plasmatocytes. **1969** R. F. CHAPMAN *Insects* xxxiii. 676 Plasmatocytes are frequently the most abundant cell type. **1974** *Zeitschr. f. Zellforsch.* CXLVII. 543 In fresh haemolymph preparations plasmatocytes are round, oval, or spindle shaped cells, 10-15 μm in diameter, with a central nucleus occupying approximately 40% of the cell volume. **1987** *Jrnl. Insect Physiol.* XXXIII. 147/2 Plasmatocytes were the only haemocyte type to exhibit locomotory activity over the substratum.

**plasmodiophorid** (plæz,məʊdɪəʊ'fɔːrɪd), *n. Microbiol.* [f. PLASMODI(UM *n.* + -O- + -PHOR(E + -ID.] An endobiotic parasite which produces a plasmodium.

**1975** L. S. OLIVE *Mycetozoans* vi. 193 The plasmodiophorids are a group of obligate, endobiotic parasites that have been variously classified among the fungi, mycetozoans, Proteomyxa, and Rhizopoda.

**1982** *Ohio Jrnl. Sci.* LXXXII. ii. 17 (*heading*) The plasmodiophorid parasitic on *Heteranthera dubia.* **1985** *Canad. Jrnl. Bot.* LXIII. 263 The ultrastructure of plasmodia, sporangia, and cystosori of *Ligniera verrucosa* . . is described and compared with that of other plasmodiophorids.

**plaster**, *n.* Add: [**3.**] **c.** *Med.* = *PLASTER-CAST *n.* 2.
**1905** *Lancet* 28 Oct. 1250/1 Removal of the case may be necessitated by swelling of the limb . . . In [this] case the application of a fresh plaster will probably be required. **1948** E. O. GECKELER *Plaster of Paris Technic* (ed. 2) x. 194 Providing the patient's temperature and symptoms are satisfactory the first plaster should not be removed for at least three weeks. **1976** D. STOREY *Saville* (1978) II. vi. 69 The plasters on his legs had been made in such a way that they could support his weight.

**plaster-cast**, *n.* Add: **2.** *Med.* A casing of plaster of Paris and gauze which provides protection and support for an immobilized limb, etc.; = *PLASTER *n.* 3 c.
**1883** *Med. Age* I. 367/1 The plaster cast with fenestrated openings opposite the site of the wound is a decided improvement over the movable splint. **1907** R. T. TAYLOR *Orthopaedic Surg.* ii. 23 Much has been written and said about the supposed difficult task of cutting off a plaster cast. **1934** KEY & CONWELL *Managem. Fractures, Dislocations & Sprains* i. 37 Plaster casts are frequently bivalved for physiotherapy or inspection of a part and are then strapped on. **1960** E. P. LEONARD *Orthopedic Surg. Dog & Cat* iv. 37 Removal of a plaster cast can be simplified by imbedding a Fetatome wire after the first layer of plaster has been applied. **1987** *Oxf. Textbk. Med.* (ed. 2) I. ix. 89/2 [The patient] should . . walk once the affected part is immobilized by a lightweight plaster cast.

**plastic**, *a.* and *n.*³ Add: [**B.**] [**I.**] [**1.**] **c.** = *plastic money* (sense 9 c of the adj.). *colloq.* (orig. *U.S.*).
**1980** *Time* 29 Sept. 67/2 Visa and MasterCard users will now have to pay more for using plastic. **1985** *Globe & Mail* (Toronto) 10 Oct. B13/2 It [is] easier than ever to spend money without seeing the real thing. 'The acceptance of plastic has reached an all-time high,' John Bennett, senior vice-president of Visa, said. 'Plastic has become a way of life.' **1986** *Sunday Times* 21 Sept. 61/5 (*heading*) Woolies goes for plastic. **1988** *Which?* July 299/2 To use your plastic in a cash machine, you need a personal identification number (PIN).

**play**, *n.* Add: [**II.**] [**10.**] **h.** *Comm.* (esp. *Oil Industry*). An investment or development opportunity; a commercial venture the success of which depends upon speculation. orig. *U.S.*
**1957** *Time* 15 July 83/1 The discovery touched off Canada's biggest oil play since the great Leduc and Pembina oilfields were tapped in 1947 and 1953. **1975** *North Sea Background Notes* (Brit. Petroleum Co.) 4 By 1973 it had been shown that three major 'plays' persist. The first is exemplified by BP's Forties Field, where oil is found in Lower Tertiary sandstones. **1977** R. E. MEGILL *Introd. Risk Analysis* viii. 90 The first well could be a discovery and thus finance the whole play. **1988** *Observer* 15 Jan. 20/1 Charterhall, the investment company . . has sold two of its North Sea 'plays' for £12.25 million.

**play**, *v.* Add: [**V.**] [**28.**] [**c.**] Hence of a gramophone, radio, etc. (esp. one from which music can be heard).
**1930** W. FAULKNER *As I lay Dying* 251 We heard the graphophone playing in the house. **1979** A. BRINK *Dry White Season* III. i. 172 On the sideboard the transistor was playing, turned down very low. **1982** A. BROOKNER *Providence* (1985) vi. 72 A radio was playing very softly.

[**VI.**] [**31.**] [**a.**] For 'Also *intr.*, to be performed' read: Also *intr.*, (of a drama, etc.) to be performed; (of a film) to be shown.
**1919** J. REED *Ten Days that shook World* viii. 195 Even the moving-picture shows . . played to crowded houses. **1947** M. LOWRY *Under Volcano* i. 30 The cinema was dark, as though no picture were playing to-night.

**player**, *n.*¹ Add: [**I.**] [**2.**] **d.** *Comm.* One who speculates or deals; a participant in a particular market or field. Also *transf.* orig. *U.S.*
**1934** J. T. FLYNN *Security Speculation* I. i. 17 The players have no desire to own stocks; no notion of exercising any of the functions of ownership. **1942** BERREY & VAN DEN BARK *Amer. Thes. Slang* §563/1 *Dealer; speculator,* . . player. **1972** D. HALBERSTAM *Best & Brightest* 283 David Bell, who was head of AID and who was not regularly a high-level player, said rather casually that there was no point in talking about cutting off commodity aid, he had already cut it off. **1977** *South China Morning Post* (Hong Kong) 14 Apr. 2/1 Is the speculator any less a 'player' because he sold at less frequent intervals than the few who almost lived in stockbroker's offices and bought and sold each hour of the working day? **1986** *Economist* 14 June 79/1 Other players include the Ford Motor Company, which owns a big thrift and has been talking about selling mortgages through car showrooms.

[**II.**] [**9.**] For def. read: A record-player; hence, any machine for playing back prerecorded discs or cassettes. (Later examples.)
**1977** *Pop. Sci.* Feb. 85/1 They'll . . slip the discs into players wired to their receiver's antenna terminals, and push a button to watch the show. **1982** *New Yorker* 17 May 34/1 'Then how come videodisc isn't an all-out threat?' we asked. 'Money,' Mr. Meckler said . . . 'Who can afford to buy an eight-hundred dollar player? You?' **1988** *Which?* Apr. 186/1 Three players have a multiple disc holder.

**play-list**, *n.* Add: Hence **'playlist** *v. trans.*, to place (a record) on a play-list.
**1979** *Maclean's Mag.* 22 Jan. 5/1 Most of the concerts are sellouts, the album is 'playlisted' on all of the country's FM radio stations. **1988** *Now* (Toronto) 14 Apr. 29/1 Hoarse Opera has . . been playlisted on college and alternative radio stations across Canada.

**play-maker**, *n.* Add: Hence (as a back-formation) **'playmake** *v. intr. Sport* (chiefly *U.S.*), to lead or engage in attacking play; also **'playmaking** *ppl. a.* and *vbl. n.*
**1974** *Anderson* (S. Carolina) *Independent* 23 Apr. 7A/5 Little Ernie DiGregorio, the Buffalo Braves' playmaking guard, and big Ron Behagen, the Kansas City-Omaha Kings' brawny forward, were unanimous choices on the National Basketball Association's All-Rookie team for the 1973–74 season. **1976** *Daily Record* (Glasgow) 23 Nov. 26/1 Danny McGrain is Europe's best full-back and Kenny Dalglish can snatch goals and play-make as no other forward can. **1977** *Washington Post* 14 Jan. D4 Senior guard Skip Brown, whose playmaking had put the Deacons in front. **1984** *N.Y. Times* 7 Oct. v. 11/3 The finesse aspects of the game such as skating, passing and playmaking. **1988** *Boston Globe* 9 Nov. 101/1 If they can't playmake into the offensive end, they'll even resort to more of a dump-and-chase style.

**playmate**, *n.* Add: **2.** *transf.* A companion in amorous (esp. sexual) play, a lover. orig. *U.S.*
**1928** *Publishers' Weekly* 9 June 2393 Gerry Harris was 'a good time girl', who sought men only as playmates. **1942** BERREY & VAN DEN BARK *Amer. Thes. Slang* §443/1 *Lovers,* . . playmates. **1954** *Playboy* Jan. 26 (*caption*) Here's Playboy's playmate for the month of January. A very lovely unpinned

pin-up to help you welcome in the New Year. **1969** *Punch* 22 Jan. p. vii/1, I never caught up with the Playboys and Playmates, but I knew they were out there somewhere. **1977** B. BAINBRIDGE *Injury Time* (1978) xvii. 137 To hell with Marcia, with her flat-mates, her play-mates, her unknown men answering the telephone. **1988** *Star* (Tarrytown, N.Y.) 12 Apr. 16/2 Cecelia is the leader of her half-dozen playmates.

**pleasantry**, *n.* Add: [1.] c. A courteous or polite remark, *esp.* one made in casual conversation. Usu. in *pl.*
**1961** L. P. V. JOHNSON *In Time of Thetans* vii. 58 There were no pleasantries, no shouted greetings, no friendly waves of recognition. **1987** F. WYNDHAM *Other Garden* i. 19 His daughter who, beyond a few muttered pleasantries, hardly spoke at all.

**pledge**, *n.* Add: [5.] d. The promise of a donation to a charity or other cause in response to an appeal for funds; the donation itself. orig. *U.S.*
**1923** *Living Church* 20 Oct. 804/2 We must frankly adopt . . a taxation plan whether it be by pledges, quotas or . . assessments. **1933** *Daily Progress* (Charlottesville, Va.) 25 Jan. 3/6 The 8,000 volunteer canvassers . . have obtained pledges totalling more than $5,000,000. **1968** M. LOUVISH tr. *S. Y. Agnon's Guest for Night* iii. 9 Had they bought the honor with generous donations? Not so. On the contrary, their pledges were scanty. **1986** *Keyboard Player* Apr. 3/2 The money was raised by listeners telephoning pledges for records to be played.

**plenary**, *a.* (*n.*) Add: [A.] [2.] Freq. in *plenary session*.
**1931** *Nature* 10 Oct. 644/2 At the final plenary session of the Congress, this invitation was accepted. **1955** *Bull. Atomic Sci.* June 221/2 Colonialism has never in this century been more unanimously denounced than in the made-over Dutch club where the plenary sessions were held. **1983** A. BULLOCK *Ernest Bevin* i. 25 A plenary session was scheduled for ten o'clock that evening.
b. Of, presented to, or taking place at a plenary session.
**1971** *Nature* 24 Sept. 238/1 A balanced selection of topics over the wide field of acoustics had been chosen for the invited fourteen plenary one-hour lectures. **1976** *Archivum Linguisticum* VII. 154 This phase was turned into a key concept in C. A. Ferguson's plenary paper 'Sociolinguistic research and practical applications' at a recent conference on applied linguistics. **1976** *CRC Jrnl.* July 17/3 In addition to plenary discussion, smaller working groups considered education and youth, self-help, cultural groups, funding and the mechanics of starting a group.
[B.] [2.] For def. read: Short for 'plenary session'; *in plenary*: of an assembly, etc., fully constituted or attended, in plenary session.
**1975** *New Yorker* 26 May 66/3 In his speech to the conference plenary he appeared to be struggling to define the conditions. **1977** *Undercurrents* June-July 5/2 Each group of ten or twenty had elected a 'spokesperson' who met in plenary with other 'spokespeople'.

**plene**, *a.* Substitute for entry: **plene**, (pliːn, 'pliːni:), *adv.*, *a.*, and *n. Heb. Gram.* [ad. L. *plēnē* fully, completely (f. *plēnus* full), tr. late Heb. *mālē* ful(ly); cf. mod.L. *scriptio plena* full writing.] **A.** *adv.* With vowel sounds represented (by means of consonantal letters, the *matres lectionis*); also *transf.* with ref. to other languages. **B.** *adj.* Written *plene*; of or pertaining to this style of notation. **C.** *n.* A vowel or word written *plene*. Contr. with *defective*.

**1828** M. STUART *Gram. Heb. Lang.* (ed. 3) 237/2 (*Index*) Words written *plene* and *defective*. **1867** C. D. GINSBURG tr. *E. Levita's Massoreth Ha-Massoreth* 147 Upon these *plenes* there was no necessity to remark that they are *plene* because they are the most frequent. **1883** *Schaff's Encycl. Relig. Knowl.* II. 1430/2 Rules were laid down concerning . . the plene and defective writings. **1952** I. GELB *Study of Writing* v. 175 We may only speculate as to the reasons which may have led to this reduction of signs, and the best possibility which offers itself is an explanation based on the *plene* writing encountered in many other Oriental systems. **1966** LEVENSTON & SIVAN *Megiddo Mod. Dict.: Eng.–Hebrew* p. vi, We have . . used 'plene' spelling—with full vocalisation in the main entries and partial vocalisation in the sub-entries. **1983** *Trans. Philol. Soc.* 102 The apparently arbitrary changes in preference for certain syllabic signs, or the abandonment of the so-called plene-writing of vowels in some . . words are still of doubtful significance. **1986** ANDERSEN & FORBES *Spelling in Hebrew Bible* iv. 117 The fraction of *defectives* produced by the encoder, times the probability that a *defective* remains *defective*, plus the fraction of *plenes* produced by the encoder, . . equals the estimated fraction of *defectives* in the first copy.

**pleomorphic**, *a.* Add: (*c*) *Path.*, (consisting) of or designating a (usu. benign) tumour, esp. an adenoma of the salivary glands, which contains a mixture of several cell types and different kinds of neoplastic tissue.
**1948** R. A. WILLIS *Path. Tumours* xvii. 321 (*heading*) Pleomorphic salivary adenomas and adenocarcinomas (so-called 'mixed tumours'). *Ibid.* 322 Some workers . . have retained the term 'mixed' as appropriately denoting the variety of structure in the growths . . . I prefer to discard it in favour of the purely descriptive adjective 'pleomorphic'. **1954** S. DUKE-ELDER *Parsons' Dis. Eye* (ed. 12) xxxiii. 545 Tumours of the lacrimal gland show a very marked resemblance to those of the parotid. Much the commonest is a pleomorphic adenocarcinoma, frequently characterized histologically by myxomatous material (the so-called 'mixed tumour'). **1987** *Oxf. Textbk. Med.* (ed. 2) I. VI. 159/2 Epithelial tumours of the lung have been most frequent but anaplastic and pleomorphic growths have also been seen.

**plerion** ('plɛrɪɒn), *n. Astron.* [Irreg. f. Gr. πλήρ-ης full + -ιον neut. noun ending.] A supernova remnant of a relatively short-lived type, characterized by a flat radio spectrum and by radio emission which is not confined to an outer shell but originates in all parts of the remnant's volume.
**1978** K. W. WEILER in *Memorie Societa Astronomica Italiana* XLIX. 546 Because it is cumbersome and somewhat of a misnomer to refer to this class of supernova remnants as Crab-like or filled-center, we would like to suggest the new name of *plerion* to identify the group. **1979** *Astron. & Astrophysics* LXXV. 310/1 The close similarity of these properties to those of plerions (i.e. Crab-like SNR's) suggest that GRS's and plerions represent different manifestations and/or products of one and the same physical phenomenon. **1984** *Astrophysical Jrnl.* CCLXXXII. 161/1 A smaller number of SNRs are filled-center remnants, or Crab Nebula-like remnants after the best known member of the category (also called 'plerions' or 'plethoric' remnants). **1988** *Nature* 31 Mar. 419/1 The properties of a 'pulsar bubble' or plerion have been investigated in the past by computing the evolution from the early phases until the formation of a fully developed Crab-like supernova remnant.
Hence **pleri'onic** *a.*, designating such a remnant.
**1979** D. CLARK *Superstars* iv. 54 The number of these 'plerionic' remnants—so-called from the Greek

word meaning 'filled centre'—is difficult to estimate, since they tend to mimic ionized hydrogen regions in some of their properties. **1987** *Nature* 3 Dec. 457/1 This is .. about an order of magnitude less than that of Crab Nebula-like 'plerionic' remnants.

**plessite** ('plɛsaɪt), *n.* *Min.* [ad. G. *Plessit* (Reichenbach 1861, in *Ann. Phys.* CXIV. 269), erron. f. Gr. 'πλέω, πλέσσω voll machen, füllen' (cf. πλήσσειν to strike, πλήθειν to become full): see -ITE[1].] An inhomogeneous mixture of kamacite and taenite found in some iron meteorites.

**1891** *Amer. Jrnl. Sci.* XLII. 66 These physical and chemical correspondences justify, I think, the conclusion that in the Welland siderolite there are but two distinct nickel-iron alloys, viz: kamacite and taenite; and that the so-called plessite is merely thin alternating lamellæ of kamacite and taenite. **1926** *Proc. R. Soc.* A. CXII. 633 A comparison photograph in which the kamacitic-taenitic specimen was mounted on the crystal holder below the plessitic specimen established the complete identity of the lines from the plessite with those from kamacite and taenite separately. **1940** *Phil. Mag.* XXIX. 561 The $a_2$-material will be the granular structureless form of plessite as distinguished from the form of plessite which contains fine crystals of kamacite and taenite in octahedral arrangement. **1976** *Nature* 23 Sept. 302/2 The size and shape of the $\epsilon$-kamacite, taenite and plessite components are consistent with membership of chemical group IVA in the classification scheme of iron meteorites.

**plethodontid** (ˌplɛθəʊ'dɒntɪd), *a.* and *n.* *Zool.* [f. mod.L. family name *Plethodontidæ*, f. *Plethodon* type genus (f. Gr. πλήθ-ος great number, mass + ὀδοντ-, ὀδούς tooth): see -ID[3].] **A.** *adj.* Belonging to or characteristic of the family Plethodontidae or lungless salamanders. **B.** *n.* A plethodontid salamander.

**1930** *Copeia* II. 52 We have studied the courtship of a series of plethodontid salamanders. *Ibid.* 53 Although many records were made of the courtship of the plethodontids, in no case were spermatophores actually seen to be deposited. **1949** *Bull. Zool. Soc. Amer.* LX. 1367/2 While salamanders are an archaic group, the plethodontids or lungless salamanders are highly specialized and relatively advanced. **1977** *Herpetologica* XXXIII. 364/2 Detailed analyses of adult morphology are available for all genera of hemidactyliine plethodontids. **1985** *Jrnl. Compar. Neurol.* CCXLI. 99/1 The projectile tongue of plethodontids contains a skeleton and several muscles. **1988** *New Scientist* 7 Apr. 43/2 Most plethodontid salamanders mate on land, in damp conditions such as the margins of streams.

**-plex** (plɛks), *suffix*[1]. [The L. suffix *-plex* (related to *plicāre* to fold).] A terminal element equivalent to Eng. *-FOLD*, attached chiefly to cardinal numbers (and adjs. meaning 'many') to form adjs., as *simplex, duplex, triplex, multiplex,* etc.; occurring in Eng. adjs. deriving directly from these (the earliest of which are recorded in the late 16th cent.). The use of *duplex* and related words in *Telegr.* led to the occasional development of further terms on L. analogies, as *contraplex, diplex,* in the late 19th cent. From the early 20th cent. the sequence *duplex, triplex,* etc. has been used for nouns designating 'a building or dwelling divided into two (three, etc.) floors, residences, or the like', and has given rise to analogous formations, as *fourplex, eightplex,* etc., esp. in the U.S. (illustrated below).

**1974** R. J. BOND *Calif. Real Estate Pract.* i. 4/2 The duplex, triplex, and quadruplex (or fourplex) are forms of housing where the owner .. can live in one unit while renting the others. **1976** *Billings*

(Montana) *Gaz.* 16 June 11-C/5 (Advt.), Year old 8 plex [etc.] ... Pocket the income from our well located four plex. **1986** *Toronto Star* 28 May D1/4 (Advt.), Large Victorian triplex. Potential for legal 6 plex. Lane, private drive.

**-plex** (plɛks), *suffix*[2]. [A clipped form of COMPLEX *n.*] A terminal element in several blends designating integrated industrial facilities or other organizations characterized by (the expanded form of) the initial element, as *METROPLEX *n.*, NUPLEX *n.*, *wasteplex.*

**1975** *Nature* 17 Jan. 149/1 A project .. which is intended to estimate how much of the raw materials needs of such a typical area could be met by a wasteplex, a single, central, all-purpose recycling centre.

**plinker** ('plɪŋkə(r)), *n.* *colloq.* [f. PLINK *v.* + -ER[1].] **a.** An airgun or other cheap, low-calibre firearm.

**1982** R. DE SOLA *Crime Dict.* 115/2 Saturday-night specials are also known as plinkers. **1985** *Survival Weaponry* Dec. 35 (Advt.), Lightweight back garden 'plinker'. **1988** *Guns & Weapons* Autumn 56/1 If there were more established courses of fire for the modern pocket auto or revolver, it would lift these guns out of the plinker/fun gun category that they have been placed in by many competitive shooters.

**b.** One who shoots with such a gun, esp. casually.

**1985** *Los Angeles Times* 9 Sept. I. 16/4 Smaller guns are useful for 'plinkers', or casual shooters. **1987** *N.Y. Times* 12 Oct. A14/1 Gloria Lind calls herself a 'plinker', someone who shoots .22-caliber pistols at paper targets.

**plod**, *n.*[1] Add: **2.** Also **P.C. Plod.** [In allusion to Mr Plod the Policeman in Enid Blyton's *Noddy* stories for children: see *NODDY *n.*[5]] A policeman, a police officer; also, the police. (*joc.* or mildly *derog.*)

**1977** *It* June 6/1 Two irradiated plods sweat and struggle beneath an undeserved karmic penalty. **1978** P. O'DONNELL *Dragon's Claw* viii. 147 They could be on their way home before P.C. Plod has got his notebook out. **1981** *New Society* 16 July 93/3 'It's the plods, chucking bricks,' said a soul-boy, giggling in disbelief. **1984** J. MALCOLM *Godwin Sideboard* xvi. 126 'Now see here, PC Plod, you keep your bloody—' 'Stop it!' **1986** 'J. GASH' *Moonspender* v. 44 The good old days spent .. bribing the Plod in London's East End. **1987** *Private Eye* 29 May 8/3 The poor plod in the Metro who has the task of patrolling what is now one of the worst areas in North London for crimes against property.

**plonker**, *n.* Add: [**2.**] For def. read: A foolish or inept person. (Later examples.)

**1982** *N.Y. Times* 12 Feb. 2D/1 'If you want to influence the general liquidity situation ...,' the economic plonker begins, pretending to expect a reply. **1987** *Match Fishing* Feb./Mar. 52/1 To say that I was a plonker at the game was an understatement, but I wanted to learn. **1988** *Smash Hits* 19 Oct. 9/3, I look at a dress and think because it's fashionable it'll look good and then I go out with it on and realise what a plonker I look.

**plore** (plɔː(r)), *n.* [Irreg. f. EX)PLORE *v.*] Professor R. Gregory's term for an exhibit in a science museum which the visitor is encouraged to handle or otherwise explore; a hands-on exhibit. Cf. *EXPLORATORY *n.* 2.

**1986** R. GREGORY *Hands-On Sci.* i. 11 As the usual museum terms .. are too passive .. we have coined the word 'plore', meaning a model, an experiment, or a problem to *explore.* **1986** *Daily Tel.* 17 Nov. 12/4 His [*sc.* Professor Gregory's] 'plores' .. are experiments through which visitors 'discover' phenomena themselves. **1987** *Nature* 16 July 213/1

The talk is of 'plores', 'experiments' and 'games', as brigades of enthusiasts pull levers, press buttons, prod and bully exhibits into life. **1989** *New Scientist* 23-30 Dec. 79/2 The slogan 'Science you can handle' says it all. The 'plores', as the experiments are called, spread over two floors.

**plotter**, *n*. Add: [4.] [b.] Hence, any device capable of drawing with a pen under the control of a computer.
**1970** *Computers & Humanities* IV. 315 The SC4020 can be used in a high speed plotter mode, with the normal character set available on a line printer. **1985** *Personal Computer World* Feb. 177/3 The serious application with the highest number of potential uses for a low-cost plotter is the production of business graphics from the spreadsheet models.
6. Comb. (sense 4 b) *plotter-printer*.
**1981** *Electronics* 28 July 6E/2 Epson MX-82 bit-image *plotter-printer prints 80 characters/s[econd] bidirectionally.
**plotter pen**, a pen designed or intended for use with a plotter.
**1981** *Electronics* 17 Nov. 140 The line sensor is mounted within a special housing machined to the same dimensions as a standard *plotter pen. **1985** *Globe & Mail* (Toronto) 9 Oct. B18/1 (Advt.), Free—with purchase of each plotter—plotter pens and transparencies. **1989** *InfoWorld* 20 Mar. 54/1 Even though most plotter pens are capped, using old pens on an important plot probably won't produce the best plot possible.

**plough**, *n*.[1] Add: [B.] [4.] **b.** In *Yoga*, a position assumed by lying on one's back, and swinging one's legs over one's head until the feet approach or touch the floor.
**1925** *Yoga-Mīmānsā* July 228 Halāsana or the Plough Pose ... The pose is called Halāsana because in its practice the body is made to imitate the Indian plough. **1966** R. C. HITTLEMAN *Yoga for Physical Fitness* I. 48 In the Plough the vertebrae are bent outward, beginning with the base of the spine and progressing upward. **1987** P. WESTCOTT *Alternative Health Care for Women* III. 120 Yoga poses such as the Fish, Plough and Shoulder Stand can all benefit piles.

**plough**, *v*. Add: **ploughed** *ppl. a.*: also, drunk (*slang*, chiefly *U.S.*).
**1890** BARRÈRE & LELAND *Dict. Slang* II. 138/2 *Ploughed* (common), drunk. **1963** *Amer. Speech* XXXVIII. 174 One who is in the more extreme states of drunkenness is referred to as: *plowed*. **1985** G. V. HIGGINS *Penance for Jerry Kennedy* xxvi. 208, I did not get drunk ... You and Frank did. You got absolutely plowed.

**plough-in** ('plaʊɪn), *n. Naut*. [f. PLOUGH *v*. + IN *adv*.; cf. PLOUGH *v*. 4 c, 6 c.] The uncontrolled downward pitching of a hovercraft caused by part of the leading edge of the skirt touching the water when the craft is moving at speed, often resulting in a capsize; an instance of this.
**1965** *Engineering* 26 Nov. 680/1 Two Westland SR-N5 hovercraft overturned earlier this year, due to a phenomenon known as 'plough-in'. **1968** ELSLEY & DEVEREUX *Hovercraft Design & Construction* viii. 74 A plough-in occurs when the bowskirt contacts the water because the craft is operating at an excessive nose-down angle of trim. **1982** CLAYTON & BISHOP *Mech. Marine Vehicles* vi. 317 The skirt construction must be robust and flexible to prevent capsizing ('plough-in') during manoeuvres.

**plucked**, *ppl. a*. Add: [1.] **c.** *Mus*. Of a stringed instrument: designed to be played by plucking.
**1930** tr. C. Sachs in O. Andersson *Bowed-Harp* i. 30 Towards the west come the late mediæval plucked

lyres of the Norwegians. **1961** A. C. BAINES *Mus. Instruments* i. 45 They are subdivided into two groups, plucked lutes, and bowed lutes and fiddles. **1984** *New Grove Dict. Mus. Instruments* II. 642/2 'Plucked drums' have a string knotted below the centre of the membrane.

**plug**, *n*. Add: [2.] **n.** *Hort*. A small piece of turf or pre-planted soil used esp. for filling or seeding lawns. orig. and chiefly *U.S.*
**1947** *Puerto Rico Federal Exper. Station Circular No. 26*. 15 Holes are dug in the existing sod about 12 inches apart both ways, and the Manila grass plugs are set at their previous depth. **1954** ROCKWELL & GRAYSON *Compl. Bk. Lawns* ix. 94 While most lawns in the U.S. are grown from seed, some grasses .. are established .. by inserting 2-4 inch square 'plugs', spaced 12 to 18 inches apart each way, in the prepared soil. **1961** L. N. WISE *Lawn Bk*. iii. 99 The plugs or sod pieces are .. dropped into corresponding size holes that have been laid out in some definite pattern. **1976** *National Observer* (U.S.) 31 Jan. 2/6 (Advt.), Every plug guaranteed to grow in any soil in your area. **1984** *Gainesville* (Florida) *Sun* 3 Apr. 2A/5, I ordered some zoysia grass plugs from Lakeland Nurseries .. and charged it to my MasterCard credit card.
**o.** *Med*. Any of the small patches of scalp with strong hair-growth which are grafted on to a balding area in hair transplantation.
**1973** *Cutis* XI. 90/1 Three days later, 30 plugs were transplanted two inches behind the suture line previously described, on the left frontoparietal area. **1979** P. KINGSLEY *Compl. Hair Bk*. (1980) 77 About a year after he first saw me, the count went to a plastic surgeon in London and had a thousand transplanted plugs put in his scalp. **1983** *Which?* Sept. 392/1 Punch grafting—plugs of between 12 and 15 hair follicles are taken from the back and sides of the head (where the hair is still growing thickly) and reimplanted in the balding areas. **1987** *Muscle & Fitness* Oct. 33/2 I've got a friend who had a hair transplant a few years ago and I could tell where the plugs of hair that were used in the transplant came from.
[11.] **plug-compatible** *a*. *Computing*, pertaining to or designating computing equipment which is operationally compatible with a given device or system to which it may be plugged in; also as *n*., a plug-compatible device.
[**1971** *Wall St. Jrnl*. 4 Feb. 30/2 Some users opt for the guaranteed service, performance and higher price tag that IBM offers, rather than the uncertain glories or the disasters which might result from plug-to-plug compatible independent hardware.] **1971** *Electronic News* 8 Nov. 23/3 D. James Guzy, executive vice-president of the Santa Clara, Calif. *plug-compatible peripheral equipment manufacturer. **1978** *Times* 15 Sept. 21/5 The 'plug-compatible' suppliers (who sell peripheral units, add-on memories and most recently central processors which can easily replace IBM equipment). **1979** *Financial Times* 19 Feb. 26/5 It seems that the plug compatibles have found the ideal market. **1985** *Which Computer?* Dec. 117/1 The 'plug-compatible' market is big business and savings can be in the order of 10 to 30 per cent.
hence **plug-compatibility** *n*.
**1981** *Economist* 8 Aug. 67/1 Burroughs .. fears that talk of *plug-compatibility might be misinterpreted by customers as a sign that the company will be abandoning its own computer architecture to copy IBM's.

**plug**, *v*. Add: [6.] **b.** *Golf. pass*. and *intr*. Of a golf ball: to become stuck or embedded where it lands. Also *transf*., of the player.
**1937** P. LAWLESS *Golfer's Compan*. 373 Plugged! .. My ball disappeared in the mud and could not be found. **1959** *Times* 29 May 5/1 Sewell got a brave half .. after being plugged in the bunker. **1987** *Golf*

*World* Aug. 42/2 After a hooked drive on the fifth hole, which apparently plugged in the rough, Stadler . . awarded himself a free drop.

**plugged**, *ppl. a.* Sense 3 in Dict. becomes 4. Add: **3.** *Golf.* Of a ball: stuck or embedded where it lands.
**1954** *Pop. Golf* July 34 (*caption*) The 1954 Amateur Championship will be remembered for the Joe Carr, Peter Toogood Incident of the plugged ball in the mud patch. **1987** *Golfer's Compan.* June 11/1 When the Colonel arrived the player asked whether he wasn't entitled to a drop from a plugged ball in a hazard.

**plum**, *n.* Add: [2.] **b.** The wood of the plum-tree.
**1902** G. S. BOULGER *Wood* 296 Woods of Commerce . . . *Plum, Sour* (*Owénia vénosa* . . ). Queensland. Known as 'Tulip-wood' . . . Highly coloured. **1920** A. L. HOWARD *Man. Timbers of World* 228 Plum . . is a very handsome wood . . reddish-brown, with darker and lighter streaks of the same colour. **1948** F. H. TITMUSS *Conc. Encycl. World Timbers* 110 Another timber known as 'Plum' is the Sapodilla Plum. This hardwood timber is not of the same botanical family as that producing the true Plum. **1980** *Early Music* Jan. 100 (Advt.), Sets of lute ribs available in figured and plain sycamore, cherry, yew and plum.

**plumbago**, *n.* Add: [2.] **b.** Used *attrib.* of drawings, esp. miniatures, made with a plumbago or 'lead' pencil. Chiefly *Hist.*
**1904** G. C. WILLIAMSON *Hist. Portrait Miniatures* I. vi. 61 It is a very dainty piece of plumbago work. **1963** D. FOSKETT *Brit. Portrait Miniatures* i. 38 Plumbago miniatures were in vogue from about 1660-1720. **1976** *Times* 30 Mar. 19/4 A fine plumbago miniature of Charles II by Robert White, dated 1678.

**plummy**, *a.*[2] Add: [2.] **c.** *transf.* Of a person: having a 'plummy' voice; hence, aristocratic, upper-class. Also of places, etc. associated with such persons. *colloq.*
**1976** *New Yorker* 26 Jan. 101/1 The atmosphere of Albany remained more elusive than the plummy Victorian coziness of Baker Street. **1977** *Time Out* 17-23 June 61/1 When translated—the rather plummy waitresses 'deliver' the translation to every table—the result is a good range of imaginative bistro food. **1981** *Washington Post* 3 May C2/2 A posh place in London—the Kensington Gore, no less, plummy as its name. *Ibid.* 14 May D15/4 He's not one of those plummy Etonians whose first brush with the stage came when their nanny took them. **1983** *Listener* 24 Nov. 38/2 He was both prissy and plummy. He wore a monocle.

**plunge**, *v.* Add: [5.] **d.** *fig.* Of currency, prices, etc.: to drop sharply in value or amount.
[**1901** *Wall St. Jrnl.* 20 July 1/2 The market is not like a balloon plunging hither and thither in the wind.] **1946** *N.Y. Times* 31 Oct. 35/6 The stock market . . , after prices had plunged to new lows for the year, suddenly reversed the trend and rallied substantially. **1964** *N.Y. Times Index 1963* 741/1 Stocks and bonds plunge to lowest level since May '62 break. **1977** *Time* 15 Aug. 12/3 Inflation was raging (at 22%), the lira was plunging, and the country was sustained at the brink only by massive loans from abroad. **1989** *Daily Tel.* 10 Oct. 1/1 The pound plunged against the Deutschemark yesterday.

**plush**, *n.* and *a.* Add: Hence **'plushness** *n.*
**1977** *Washington Post* 28 Oct. B7/1 The 'plushness' of the agency's quarters. **1988** *Christian Science Monitor* 19 May 21 One could appreciate the vigor and tonal plushness of the Dvorak.

**plutography** (pluː'tɒgrəfɪ), *n.* [f. Gr. πλοῦτο-ς wealth + -GRAPHY.] Tom Wolfe's term for the graphic depiction of the lives of the rich, esp. as a genre of popular literature and journalism.
**1985** *Money* Aug. 40/1 Social observer Tom Wolfe . . calls the '80s the age of plutography, when a reverence for riches prevails. **1986** T. WOLFE in *N.Y. Times* 15 June VII. 30/3 We live in the epochal moment of plutography, which is the great new American vice of the 1980's. **1987** *Fortune* 6 July 19/3 Magazines that author Tom Wolfe lumps together as *plutography*, the graphic depiction of the acts of the rich.
Hence **pluto'graphic** *a.*, characteristic of plutography.
**1986** *N.Y. Times* 31 Mar. C17/1 Curiosity has grown more shameless and more feverish—more plutographic, in fact.

**pluviculture** ('pluːvɪkʌltjʊə(r), -tʃə(r)), *n. joc.* [f. L. *pluvi-a* rain + CULTURE *n.*, after *agriculture*, etc.] The art or science of rain-making; the production and implementation of schemes for inducing rain.
**1925** D. S. JORDAN in *Science* 24 July 81/2 The modern diversions of pluviculture, chiropractics and hormonism are everywhere treated with respect. Of these none can be more scientific than is pluviculture. **1926** W. J. HUMPHREYS *Rain Making* p. vii, What Dr. David Starr Jordan has happily tagged 'pluviculture'—the growing and marketing of rain-making schemes, a never-failing drought crop. **1980** C. C. SPENCE (*title*) The rainmakers: American 'pluviculture' to World War II. **1981** *Nature* 23 Apr. 654/3 Interest in pluviculture is revived whenever a drought occurs.
Hence **pluvi'culturist** *n.*, one who claims to be able to induce rain by scientific means.
**1925** *Science* 24 July 82/1 The pluviculturist has next to build a modest shack or to set up a tent for his chemical operations. **1981** *Nature* 23 Apr. 654/2 The pluviculturists depended on occasional coincidences with the occurrence of natural precipitation to demonstrate the viability of their rainmaking operations.

**ply**, *n.* Senses 4, 5 in Dict. become 5, 6. Add: [I.] **4.** *Computing.* The number of half-moves ahead investigated by a game-playing program in planning the next move (esp. in chess); also, a half-move investigated in such a calculation.
**1959** A. L. SAMUEL in *IBM Jrnl. Res. & Devel.* III. 214/1 [Draughts] Playing-time considerations make it necessary to limit the look-ahead distance to some fairly small value. This distance is defined as the *ply* (a ply of 2 consisting of one proposed move by the machine and the anticipated reply by the opponent). **1975** M. NEWBORN *Computer Chess* ii. 11 By looking ahead one move, or one *ply.* **1976** *Sci. Amer.* July 66/2 Usually the computer search goes to a depth of only four or five plies (half-moves). **1983** *New Scientist* 1 Dec. 673/3 Such is the nature of the game [of chess] that a 20-ply search is not yet realistic.

**pneumaturia** (njuːmə'tjuːrɪə), *n. Path.* [ad. F. *pneumaturie* (F. P. Guiard 1883, in *La France Médicale* I. 195), altered form of *pneumo-urie* (Raciborski 1860, in *Gaz. des Hôpitaux* XXXIII. 263): cf. PNEUMATO-, PNEUMO-, -URIA.] The passage of gas through the urethra during urination.
**1883** *Lancet* 3 Mar. 375/2 Dr. Guiard proposes the term 'diabetic pneumaturia', to denominate a condition which he has observed in four cases of urinary infection in the male, complicated with glycosuria. **1898** *Jrnl. Amer. Med. Assoc.* XXXI. 375/1 The cases of pneumaturia may be roughly divided into three groups. **1952** *Radiology* LIX. 63/1 Primary pneumaturia is rare and is due to fermentation of urine in the bladder through the

agency of some fermenting organism. **1989** *Dis. Colon & Rectum* XXXII. 67/2 Four weeks postoperatively right testicular pain, urinary frequency, and pneumaturia developed.

**pneumocystis** (njuːməʊ'sɪstɪs), *n. Path.* [a. mod.L. generic name *Pneumocystis* (M. & Mme. P. Delanoë 1912, in *Comptes Rendus* CLV. 660): see PNEUMO- and CYSTIS *n.*] The protozoan *Pneumocystis carinii*, which inhabits the lungs and is a common infective agent in immunocompromised individuals. *pneumocystis (carinii) pneumonia, pneumonitis* (also *PCP* (see \*P II.) and occas. *ellipt.*), a severe and often fatal form of pneumonia caused by infection with this organism, and characterized by the proliferation of cysts within the lung cavity, leading to tachypnoea.
[**1953** *Ann. Pædiatrici* CLXXX. 1 The etiology of this pneumonia was solved by the discovery of the parasite *Pneumocystis carinii* . . . We therefore propose to call this pneumonia *parasitic* or *pneumocystic*. **1954** *Zentralblatt f. Allgemeine Path. und Pathologische Anat.* XCII. 424 (*heading*) Zur Morphologie der *Pneumocystis carinii* und zur Pathogenese der Pneumocystis-Pneumonie.] **1955** *Jrnl. Clin. Path.* VIII. 23/1 Bachmann (1953) found pneumocystis in all of the 14 cases of plasmacellular pneumonia which he examined. **1956** *Amer. Jrnl. Path.* XXXII. 1 Knowledge of pneumocystis pneumonitis has developed far more rapidly in Europe than in the United States or elsewhere in the world. **1956** *Jrnl. Path. & Bacteriol.* LXXII. 457 It is tempting to speculate whether the rare cases of pulmonary microlithiasis alveolaris may not possibly be explained as the ultimate outcome of a pneumocystis pneumonia in an adult. **1957** *Lancet* 12 Jan. 59/2 (*heading*) 'Pneumocystis carinii' pneumonia. **1958** *Pediatrics* XXI. 349/2 It seems unlikely at this time that this case could be included under the diagnostic heading of Pneumocystis carinii pneumonia. **1960** *Arch. Dis. Childhood* XXXV. 495/1 *Pneumocystis carinii* pneumonia has been found associated with congenital agammaglobulinaemia, [etc.]. **1970** *Cancer* XXV. 696/2 Early diagnosis of pneumocystis carinii pneumonitis is imperative since it has been shown that pentamidine or hydroxystilbamidine are therapeutic agents of significant efficacy. **1984** *Ann. Internal Med.* C. 62/1 The 71-year-old wife of a 74-year-old hemophiliac who had received factor VIII concentrate and subsequently died due to *Pneumocystis carinii* pneumonia. **1987** *Oxf. Textbk. Med.* (ed. 2) II. xv. 9/1 Transbronchial biopsy should be suitable if the diagnosis is likely to be . . diffuse infection (e.g. disseminated tuberculosis or pneumocystis). **1988** *Brit. Med. Jrnl.* 6 Aug. 382/2 In all 19 patients positive for pneumocystis, it was the first episode of pneumocystis pneumonia.

**poché** ('pɒʃeɪ, ‖pɔʃe), *n. Archit.* [a. Fr., pa. pple. of *pocher* to sketch, stencil.] The method or result of representing the solid part of a building (as a wall, etc.) by a darkened area on an architectural plan; (*rare*), a pen for doing this. Also *transf.*
**1927** J. HARBESON *Study Archit. Design* xix. 135 Part of this desired effect is to give an idea of the third dimension as well as the floor area, for instance making thicker the points of poché that support big rooms, as we shall see later. **1946** T. BUSS *Simplified Archit. Drawing* 27 This method, called *poché*, is also used for filling in walls and partitions in a display plan of a building. *Ibid.* 31 For fine work, use a ruling pen filled with diluted poster color, or a water-color brush or poché for filling in the spaces. **1979** *Jrnl. R. Soc. Arts* Nov. 765/2 Basically we have a mixed urban type here: a more or less solid *poché* of infill space, warehouses and offices which is carved out by the discs-screens and, to one side, by a pie-segment of brick and granite.

Also '*poché v. trans.*, to darken or fill *in* with shading on a plan.
**1968** E. R. WEIDHAAS *Archit. Drafting & Design* 303/2 Poché, to darken in a wall section with freehand shading. **1980** N. SILVER in Michaels & Ricks *State of Lang.* 327 In American schools of architecture prior to the mid-seventies, 'please poché in the walls' meant, simply, 'go darken the area between the parallel lines representing walls on the plan'.

**pock**, *v.* Add: Hence '**pocking** *vbl. n.* and *ppl. a.*
**1931** E. LINKLATER *Juan in Amer.* i. 24 All had so far escaped the pocking which was their due, and Dr Jenner was not too well pleased. **1958** 'W. HENRY' *Seven Men at Mimbres Springs* xv. 181 There was the same split-second pause between the acrid blast of the black powder and the pocking spatter of the shot getting home fifteen yards out. **1982** *Sci. Amer.* Jan. 81/3 The prevalence of small craters suggests the pocking of a landscape by the ejecta from the impacts of larger projectiles.

**pocket-book**, *n.* Sense 3 in Dict. becomes 4. Add: 3. The female pudenda. *U.S. slang.*
**1942** Z. N. HURSTON in *Amer. Mercury* July 92 'Trying to snatch my pocketbook, eh?' she blazed. **1969** M. ANGELOU *I know why Caged Bird Sings* xi. 71 Momma had drilled into my head: 'Keep your legs closed, and don't let nobody see your pocketbook.' **1983** *Maledicta 1982* VI. 124 Almost half the women . . said they had no name for their genitals until the age of 15, and used many odd euphemisms ( . . pocketbook for vagina, . . etc.).

**pod**, *n.*[2] Add: [7.] **b.** *transf.* Any more or less enclosed unit containing components associated with a particular function (as control, etc.), forming a usu. detachable or separate part of a larger system. Freq. with qualifying word. Cf. MODULE *n.* 4 d.
**1972** L. M. HARRIS *Introd. Deepwater Floating Drilling Operations* xi. 121 The control pod serves as a lower terminal for the hose bundle and houses the critical moving parts of the subsea hydraulic-control system. **1977** *Sci. Amer.* July 106/2 (Advt.), The HP 3820 costs $17,750 including rechargeable battery pod, leveling base, and carrying case. **1987** *Electronics & Wireless World* Jan. 86/4 Plug-in pods for the emulation of 68000/68010 and 68008 processors are available for the Position SDT (symbolic debugging tool).

**podgy**, *a.* Add: '**podginess** *n.*, the quality or condition of being podgy.
**1924** *Glasgow Herald* 3 Jan. 6 The average Briton of to-day retains the lithe carriage . . of youth at an age when his Early-Victorian ancestor had long subsided into whiskered podginess. **1979** R. COX *Auction* x. 253 [His] well-cut suit failed to disguise the podginess of his figure.

**podiform** ('pɒdɪfɔːm), *a.* [f. POD *n.*[2] + -I- + -FORM.] Having the form of a pod; *spec.* designating a thick pod-shaped deposit of a mineral, esp. chromite. Cf. POD *n.*[2] 6.
**1961** T. P. THAYER in *Symposium Chrome Ore 1960* 203 In most podiform deposits . . the chromite shows an obscure to well-developed pattern of subparallel olivine- or serpentine-filled fractures superposed on the original textures. **1978** *Nature* 12 Oct. 539/2 Massive sulphide deposits (Cu, Ni) occur on Karmoy and the neighbouring small islands, though as yet no podiform chromites have been observed in the serpentinised peridotites. **1983** *Econ. Geol.* LXXVIII. 293/1 Podiform chromite deposits are the only economic concentrations of chromite that occur in ophiolite peridotites, i.e., alpine-type peridotites. **1988** *Ann. Rev. Earth & Planetary Sci.* XVI. 167 Phanerozoic orogenic belts can practically be outlined by igneous-related ores . . that may have formed at

midocean ridges, such as podiform chromite and perhaps some Cyprus-type massive sulfides.

**podocyte** ('pɒdəʊsaɪt), *n. Anat.* [f. PODO- + -CYTE.] Each of the epithelial cells whose irregular pinnate processes envelop the capillaries of the glomerular capsules of the kidney, interlocking with those of other such cells to form the outermost layer of the barrier through which substances are filtered out of the blood.

**1954** B. V. HALL in *Proc. 5th Ann. Conf. Nephrotic Syndrome* i. 9 This figure shows the characteristic irregularities of the nuclear membrane of the so-called epithelial cells, which we have termed podocytes. **1960** *Jrnl. Urol.* LXXXIII. 791/1 The podocytes (foot cells) sit upon the glomerular basement membranes with thousands of little 'pedicels' (Hall) or foot processes. **1978** *Nephron* XXII. 439/2 It has been suggested that aminonucleoside induces proteinuria by a toxic action on podocytes. **1988** *Acta Anat.* CXXXIII. 303/2 In this model of polycystosis, glomerular cysts develop, whose presumptive parietal layer is exclusively formed by podocytes.

Hence **podo'cytic** *a.*, pertaining to, consisting of, or designating a podocyte or podocytes.

**1955** B. V. HALL in *Proc. 6th Ann. Conf. Nephrotic Syndrome* i. 2 These large processes were called trabeculae; incompletely pictured here in section on the left of the micrograph and to the right of the podocytic nucleus. **1957** *Amer. Heart Jrnl.* LIV. 5 The endothelial ultrafiltration slit-pore may be confined to the folded borders of the endothelial cells, so that its total area is probably very much less than that of the podocytic slit-pore. **1979** *Nature* 29 Feb. 655/2 They form junctional complexes with the parietal epithelium of Bowman's capsule on one side and visceral podocytic epithelium on the other. **1988** *Laboratory Investigation* LIX. 677/2 The podocytic microfilament system may actively modify the width of the slit pores and thus may be able to regulate the solute efflux across the glomerular wall.

**podomere** ('pɒdəʊmɪə(r)), *n. Zool.* [f. PODO- + -MERE.] Each of the sections of a segmented leg or other appendage of an animal, esp. an arthropod.

**1909** in *Cent. Dict. Suppl.* **1935** R. E. SNODGRASS *Princ. Insect Morphol.* v. 85 A clearly defined limb segment, definitely correlated with muscle attachments, is termed a podomere, or podite. **1979** *Nature* 29 Mar. 490/3 The nicest device she [*sc.* Dr. Sidnie Manton] discovered was surely the rock of the arthropod coxae, lining-up the dorsal hinge joints to translate the depression of proximal podomeres into effective rotation of the legs. **1987** *Jrnl. Paleontol.* LXI. 225/1 An explanation for the capability for the high limb-swing angles in *Cruziana reticulata* may lie in the evolution in some trilobite lineages of specialized coxa-body and inter-podomere articulations.

**pogamoggan** (‚pɒgə'mɒgən), *n. N. Amer. Obs. exc. Hist.* Also 9 pocomagan, pogamagan, pukamoggan; 20 pogamogan. [a. Ojibwa *pakama:kan* club, lit. '(something) used for striking'.] A kind of club, usu. consisting of a piece of stone or iron attached to a wooden handle, formerly used by some North American Indians.

**1801** A. MACKENZIE *Voy. from Montreal* 37 The pogamagan is made of the horn of the rein-deer, the branches being all cut off except that which forms the extremity. c**1804** P. GRANT in L. F. R. Masson *Les Bourgeois* (1890) II. 332 In war, they use the *pocomagan* . . ; it consists of a piece of wood, a foot and a half long, curved at one end, with a big heavy knob, in which is fixed a piece of long sharp iron. c**1840** D. THOMPSON *Narr. Explorations W. Amer. 1784-1812* (1916) I. xxii. 330 They dashed at the

Peeagans, and with their stone Pukamoggan knocked them on the head. **1893** *Outing* Oct. 10/1 Originally, no doubt, each action meant something, as the stealthy approach . . the hurling of the tomahawk or pogamoggan, and so on. **1925** R. FROST *Let.* 21 July in *Sel. Lett.* (1964) vi. 315, I should have had a gun with me, but I hadn't. I hadn't even a pogamogan.

**Poincaré** ('pwæ̃kare), *n. Math.* and *Phys.* The name of Jules-Henri *Poincaré* (1854-1912), French mathematician and physicist, used *attrib.* and in the possessive to designate various concepts introduced by him or arising out of his work, as **Poincaré('s) conjecture**, the hypothesis that any simply connected compact 3-dimensional manifold is topologically equivalent to a 3-dimensional sphere; **Poincaré cycle**, (a single circuit of) a simple closed curve in the phase space of a system, representing one possible solution of the governing differential equations; **Poincaré sphere**, a sphere on which the polarization of a beam of light can be represented by a particular point, and which is also used in other optical calculations.

[**1928** *Communications Physical Lab. Univ. Leiden* No. 191c. 29 The representation [of polarization] on a sphere given by Poincaré.] **1943** *Rev. Mod. Physics* XV. 85 (*heading*) Boltzmann's estimate of the period of a Poincaré cycle. **1951** *Proc. Indian Acad. Sci.* A. XXXIII. 201 To represent the Poincaré sphere in two dimensions the stereographic projection is used in this paper. **1976** *Encycl. Brit. Macropædia* XVIII. 514/1 Poincaré conjecture. **1986** *New Scientist* 4 Sept. 43/1 Poincaré's Conjecture concerns just how close these family resemblances are and, in particular, how closely the 3-sphere resembles the 2-sphere. **1988** *Physics Lett.* A. CXXVI. 311 Tube-like standing waves subject to a 'final' condition may resemble unparametrised orbits of the universe, with 'quantum Poincaré cycles' coinciding with its durations. **1988** *Optik* LXXIX. 185/2 Let us see fig. 4 presenting a Poincaré sphere with two points representing different birefringent media, located on the opposite ends of a diameter.

**point**, *n.*[1] Add: [A.] [III.] [15.] c. A percentage share in the profits of a business or other venture. Chiefly in *pl.*

**1977** G. V. HIGGINS *Dreamland* x. 123 Sometimes they allowed established lawyers to buy into the [law] firm, selling points, as they are now known, at prices which varied with the times. **1978** *TV Week* (Austral.) 26 Aug. 13, I have points (a share of profits) in Capricorn One. **1978** M. PUZO *Fools Die* xxxii. 368 When we go over budget, you start losing your points in the picture. **1986** EPSTEIN & LIEBMAN *Biz Speak* 172 *Points* (media/publishing), percent of profits in a movie or TV deal.

[D.] [19.] **point spread** *N. Amer. Sport*, (a forecast of) the number of points or the margin by which the stronger team is expected to defeat its weaker opponent, used for betting purposes (see *SPREAD *n.*[1] 2 j).

**1951** *N.Y. Times* 18 Jan. 1/1 Poppe is also alleged to have confessed that he and Byrnes agreed for a fee to do all they could to exceed the *point spread in their team's victories. **1969** Z. HOLLANDER *Mod. Encycl. Basketball* 51 Early in 1951 the rumors of wrongdoing turned into fact. Junius Kellogg, a 6-8 star at Manhattan College, reported that he had been offered $1,000 to control the point spread of a game. **1990** *Washington Times* 26 Mar. c6/2 Out of 32 first-round games, with three rated even by most betting lines, the underdog covered the point spread 14 times.

**pointable**, *a.* Restrict *rare*[-1] to sense a in Dict. and add: **b.** Capable of being pointed or aimed; *spec.* of a telescope, gun, etc.: that can be pointed at an object; easy to point, rotatable.

**1890** in *Cent. Dict.* **1979** *Aviation Week* 26 Mar. 48/3 The spacecraft could contain two pointable optical sensors, one .. for mapping .. and one .. for quick look data. **1980** *Sci. Amer.* Apr. 64/3 A pointable telescope with an aperture of 2.5 centimeters (one inch) that uses the spin motion of the spacecraft to scan an object. **1987** *Shooting Life* Spring 90/3 These pheasants were high .. calling for the combination of a competent shot, a very pointable gun and some heavyweight ammunition.

**point-blank**, *a.*, *n.*, and *adv.* Add: [A.] [1.] b. *point-blank range: loosely,* a distance so short that the shot cannot miss the mark; also *transf.*, esp. in *Sport.*
   **1942** W. FAULKNER *Go down, Moses* 193 Dogs mangled and slain and shotgun and even rifle shots delivered at point-blank range. **1977** *Washington Post* 10 Jan. D2/4 Chicago goalie .. stopped Peter McNab from point-blank range. **1979** A. BRINK *Dry White Season* III. xi. 266 Knock on the door. When he opened they fired five shots at point-blank range. **1989** *Newsday* (Nassau ed.) 13 May 18 Dalers goalie .. made several saves from point blank range.
   [C.] [1.] b. *loosely,* from so close as to be bound to hit the target.
   **1975** *Economist* 13 Sept. 68/3 It was not clear whether Miss Fromme even knew how to fire the gun she aimed at the president point-blank. **1985** L. McMURTRY *Lonesome Dove* i. 20 They kept bumping into Indians in the smoke and having to shoot point-blank.

**pointelle** (pɔɪn'tɛl), *n. U.S.* [Cf. POINT *n.*³ and Fr. dim. suffix *-elle.*] a. With capital initial. A proprietary name for a range of knitted sweaters incorporating eyelet-holes to give a lacy effect. b. A similar pattern or stitch worked on other garments or for trimming; a garment knitted in this style. Freq. *attrib.*
   **1956** *Official Gaz.* (U.S. Patent Office) 10 Apr. TM78/2 Pointelle. For sweaters. Use since March 1953. **1973** *Mademoiselle* Feb. 151 A rib-banded camisole pricked with peepsy pointelle. **1974** *Sunday* (Charleston, S. Carolina) 28 Apr. 3-c/3 (Advt.), Perky prints, knit pointelles,.. T-shirts [etc.]. **1978** *Detroit Free Press* 2 Apr. 13A (Advt.), Machine washable polyester group includes varied sleeve styles, necklines, skirts and pointelle trimmed jackets. **1980** P. R. HARSTE *Knitting Bk.* vii. 101 It is sometimes difficult to gauge a pattern properly in Pointelle patterns because of the yarnovers. **1984** *New Yorker* 2 Apr. 82/1 (Advt.), The linen/cotton sweater with an all-over delicate pointelle stitch. **1987** *N.Y. Times* 4 June A2/1 (Advt.), Our .. cotton sweater has a pointelle collar.

**pointer**, *n.* Add: [3.] h. *Computing.* A numerical representation of the address in memory of a piece of data, esp. as part of a composite data type.
   **1963** P. M. SHERMAN *Programming & coding Digital Computers* viii. 152 These index registers point to the locations in memory; hence they are called pointers when so used. **1973** C. W. GEAR *Introd. Computer Sci.* vii. 278 It is assumed that the first word can be used to store .. a pointer if the doublet is used for an access table entry. **1980** C. S. FRENCH *Computer Sci.* x. 53 We regard each word in our sentence as a data-item or datum which is linked to the next datum by a pointer. **1987** *Electronics & Wireless World* Jan. 56/1 When the allocated section of memory is full, the data starts overwriting the same section so that using a pointer allows the most recent six seconds of speech to be retained.

**'pointing**, *n. Horse-racing.* [Shortened f. *point-to-pointing* s.v. POINT *n.*¹ D. 11: cf. -ING¹.] Point-to-point or cross-country racing; steeplechasing.

**1976** *Horse & Hound* 10 Dec. 71/4 (Advt.), Proved to be a good bold hunter with great potential for pointing/eventing. **1986** *Sporting Life Weekender* 17-19 Apr. 50/2 The Heythrop is regarded by many to be the show-case of pointing. **1987** *Horse Internat.* Mar. 26/3 Several top horses started 'between the flags', not to say jockeys, and pointing now provides a lucrative market.

**poison**, *n.* Add: [5.] [a.] poison pill, (*a*) a pill containing poison; *spec.* one taken in extreme circumstances (by secret agents, etc.) to commit suicide; (*b*) *transf.*, any of a number of ploys (such as a conditional rights issue) adopted by the victim of an unwelcome take-over bid to make itself unattractive to the bidder (orig. *U.S.*).
   **1946** P. BOTTOME *Lifeline* xxxv. 269 With his hands tied securely behind him Mark could not reach the poison pill he had been given for such emergencies. **1975** *Times* 29 Aug. 6/8 There are many organizations working against Mrs Gandhi ... Ours is serious ... We all carry poison pills in our pockets. **1983** *N.Y. Times* 19 June III. 14/4 Lenox played hard to get .. and implemented a novel anti-takeover devise to discourage Brown-Forman Distillers takeover bid. The move is called the 'Poison Pill defense'. **1985** *N.Y. Times Mag.* 27 Jan. 10/3 My favorite repellent is the poison pill ... To make stock less attractive to sharks, a new class of stock may be issued: this is 'a preferred stock or warrant .. that becomes valuable only if another company acquires control. Because it becomes valuable to the target, it becomes costly to the buyer; when the buyer takes the bite, to follow the metaphor, he has to swallow the poison pill'. **1985** *Sunday Times* 20 Oct. 59/1 A poison pill granted to Merrill gave it the right to buy SCM's two major businesses.

**poke**, *v.*¹ Add: [1.] i. *Shooting.* To aim (one's gun) at a moving target, rather than swinging and firing. (*Poking* is typically considered a fault.) Now freq. *absol.* or *intr.*
   **1898** *Encycl. Sport* II. 329/2 Do not allow him to poke his gun about and *seek* for his aim, or he will acquire the 'following' trick. **1924** E. PARKER *Elem. Shooting* vii. 184 It is not difficult if you take the bird far enough out; you throw your gun up on what looks almost like a stationary mark, you pull the gun the same instant (if you poke or dwell on the bird you are done), and he drops into the heather. **1946** J. W. DAY *Harvest Adventure* iv. 54 His performances at elk and boar were no better, and he was, I believe, a 'poking' shot at driven birds. **1987** *Shooting Mag.* Mar. 43/2 If you are a quick and instinctive shot, a short-barrelled gun may be best ... But it's also easier to stop your swing and 'poke'.
   [7.] [b.] *intr.* For 'to stick out' read: 'protrude; to stick *out*, *up*, etc.' (Earlier and later examples.)
   **1611** [see HULCH *n.*]. **1905** [see *wig-tail* s.v. WIG *n.*³ 5]. **1915** V. WOOLF *Voyage Out* iv. 58 He was a Skye terrier, one of those long chaps, with little feet poking out from their hair. **1922** JOYCE *Ulysses* 355 Canon O'Hanlon stood up with his cope poking up at his neck. **1951** E. BOWEN *Shelbourne* vi. 158 Upon his flank rebel rifles came poking out through the railings of the Green. **1965** M. BRADBURY *Stepping Westward* vii. 318 His English socks poked out beneath the too-short trouser cuffs of his American seersucker suit. **1980** B. BAINBRIDGE *Winter Garden* i. 10 His awareness of flowers was .. poor... The things either poked up out of the ground or lolled in vases.

**pole**, *n.*¹ Add: [2.] f. *Angling.* (*a*) A rudimentary fishing-rod, esp. one used without fittings other than a line connected to the tip of the rod (chiefly *N. Amer.*); (*b*) *ellipt.* for *roach-pole* s.v. ROACH *n.*¹ 2 b.
   **1688** [see SNAPPER *n.*¹ 6 a]. **1830** *New Hampsh. Hist. Soc. Coll.* (1832) III. 84 They [*sc.* pickerel] are taken

three ways: 1st. A pole of from 12 to 20 feet, with a line about the same length is provided with a hook [etc.]. **1897** F. MATHER *Men I have fished With* 30 You h'ist 'em out too quick with a pole, throw that away . . and when you get a fish haul him in hand under hand. **1903** J. A. HENSHALL *Bass, Pike, Perch & Others* 103 Very often hand lines or stiff cane poles are used in estuary fishing. **1917** S. LEACOCK *Frenzied Fiction* (1918) xiii. 169 As for the railroad man . . you can tell him because he carries a pole that he cut in the bush himself, with a ten-cent line wrapped round the end of it. **1934** E. MARSHALL-HARDY *Angling Ways* x. 74 The lightest roach pole is a heavy and cumbersome affair . . . The only portion of these poles in which there is any action is the top foot or eighteen inches. **1962** K. KESEY *One flew over Cuckoo's Nest* iii. 235, I sat down and held the pole and watched the line swoop out into the wake. **1982** D. CARR *Success with Pole* 9 Twenty years ago, around 2% of match anglers would have carried poles; now 99% have them.

**g.** *Athletics.* The long, slender rod of wood, fibre-glass, etc., used by a competitor in pole-vaulting.

**1888**, etc. [see *pole-vaulter, -vault* (sense 5 c below)]. **1955** *Track & Field Athletics* (Achilles Club) 228 The new tapered metal poles are as springy as the heavier bamboo ones. **1973** J. BRONOWSKI *Ascent of Man* (1976) i. 36 In the act of vaulting, the athlete grasps his pole, for example, with an exact grip that no ape can quite match. **1986** *N.Y. Times* 17 Feb. III.1/4 Dial failed to clear a height . . because his poles did not arrive in time and he was forced to use borrowed ones.

**h.** *Skiing. ellipt.* for *ski-pole* s.v. SKI *n.* 2 b. orig. *U.S.*

**1920** *Lit. Digest* 14 Feb. 115, I need not describe these poles to you, as any dealer will know what you mean by ski-poles. **1938** *Ski Bull.* 9 Dec. 7/2 (Advt.), Complete ski stock available,—skis, boots, bindings, poles. **1963** S. PLATH *Bell Jar* viii. 101 There was a skier in front of me and a skier behind me, and I'd have been knocked over and stuck full of skis and poles the minute I let go. **1986** *Skiing Today* Winter 44/3 Positively reaching out down the mountain the pole is planted, the skier rises upward and forward, pressure is taken off the edges, and weight is transferred to the uphill ski.

**[5.] [c.] pole fishing**, the action, practice, or art of fishing with a (roach) pole.

**1982** D. CARR *Success with Pole* 9 'Modern' pole fishing started with the introduction by Continental match anglers, some 15 to 20 years ago, of fibre glass poles, which were much lighter and had a better action than the old cane poles. **1988** *Coarse Fishing Handbk.* June/July 6/3 Pole fishing is . . a means of taking big bags of fish at high speed—ideal for those early season attacks on roach with hemp and tares.

**police**, *n.* Add: [**6.**] **policeperson** [see PERSON *n.* 2 f], a gender-neutral term for a policeman or policewoman (not standard).

**1978** R. HILL *Pinch of Snuff* ix. 94 'For a *policeperson*,' she said, 'you are not too idiotic.' **1981** J. K. GALBRAITH *Life in our Times* xxx. 485 Chairperson, Congressperson, Policeperson.

**policeman**, *n.* Senses 1 d, e in Dict. become 1 e, f. Add: [**1.**] **d.** *fig.* A person or entity that acts like a policeman; used *esp.* of a country, with reference to its international peace-keeping role or similar function.

**1887** RIDER HAGGARD *Allan Quarterm.* 20 The stern policeman Fate moves us and them on. **1907** G. B. SHAW *John Bull's Other Island* Pref. p. xxxii, In Ireland England is nothing but the Pope's policeman. **1979** *Time* 8 Jan. 25/3 [Iran] is the 'policeman' of the crucial Persian Gulf sea-lanes through which 40% of the non-Communist world's oil is shipped. **1979** *Guardian* 15 Mar. 3/4 The underlying US strategy

will be to persuade Egypt to join with Israel in acting as the policeman of a Middle East peace.

**‖pollo** ('poʎo, 'pollo), *n. Gastron.* [Sp. and It., chicken.] In the names of various chicken dishes, esp. of Italian or (Mexican-) Spanish origin, as *pollo con arroz*, chicken with rice, *al Diavolo*, devilled chicken, etc.

**1846** R. FORD *Gatherings from Spain* xi. 131 The pollo *con arroz*, or the chicken and rice . . is eaten in perfection in Valencia, and therefore is often called *Pollo Valenciano*. **1920** G. SAINTSBURY *Notes on Cellar-Bk.* 221, I should like to draw attention to the 'Pollo con Arroz', an excellent Spanish dish. **1955** R. L. SORCE *La Cucina* vi. 98 Devilled chicken (*Pollo al Diavolo*). **1974** E. BRAWLEY *Rap* II. xxvii. 3/3 They loved it, and ordered beer after beer, . . and after that tacos and pollo mole and enchiladas. **1984** W. GARNER *Rats' Alley* ix. 172 Claas, poking viciously at his *pollo con gambas* . . in the airport restaurant.

**poll-tax**, *n.* Add: Also **poll tax. b.** *spec.* = *community charge* s.v. *COMMUNITY n.* 11. *colloq.*

**1985** *Times* 20 May 12/6 It is the dreaded poll tax that I am referring to. **1986** *Independent* 17 Nov. 6 Scottish opposition parties concentrated on the assumed unfairness of the poll tax, which takes no account of an individual's ability to pay. **1988** *Ann. Reg. 1987* 29 Particular emphasis was placed on the poll tax as a way of forcing local councils to become fully 'accountable' to all their electors.

**Polonian** (pə'ləʊnɪən), *a.*[2] [f. the name *Poloni-us* (see below) + -AN.] Characteristic of or resembling Polonius, an elderly and sententious courtier in Shakespeare's *Hamlet*.

**1956** C. P. SNOW *Homecomings* xxxv. 171 'No, Lewis, I want you to listen to them. Listening never did any of us any harm, and talking usually does,' said Bevill, in one of his Polonian asides. **1968** *Listener* 4 July 18/2 Your Polonian television critic, Mr Francis King . . , feeling tetchily about the arras for Hamlet, is showing his age at last. **1971** *New Statesman* 16 Apr. 532/3 Compared with the Polonian but still unfathomable Burghley, his short life of 33 years is an open book.

**polyocracy** (pɒlɪ'ɒkrəsɪ), *n.* [f. POLY-, freq. taken as shortened f. POLYTECHNIC *n.*, + -OCRACY.] A section of the establishment collectively considered to represent a progressive, esp. left-wing, political alignment, esp. on social issues. With *the*.

**1975** K. WATERHOUSE in *Daily Mirror* 23 Oct. 12/5 The Polyocracy . . . *Education*: . . more likely polytechnic or similar. *Job*: Teacher, social worker, writer, artist. *Ibid.* 27 Oct. 12/2 What Colonel Blimp is to the middle class and Alf Garnett to the working class, so the militant Marxist Squatter, drop-out or demonstrator is to the Polyocracy. **1979** *Observer* 7 Oct. 9/6 There is another, though connected, explanation. It lies in what can be termed the Rise of the Polyocracy . . . Today the expansion of higher education, together with the consequent rise of the supposedly 'caring' professions . . has produced a new race of activists. **1984** *Spectator* 1 Sept. 13/2 The newspaper relies for much of its readership . . on what has been called the polyocracy, the new establishment of teachers, social workers, race relations and equal opportunity officials and almost everyone in the bureaucracies of local government. **1989** *Boardroom* July 62/2 Neither should settlers be concerned about what the Polyocracy will do to Islington schools when the time comes.

**polyversity** (pɒlɪ'vɜːsɪtɪ), *n.* [A blend of POLYTECHNIC *n.* and UNIVERSITY *n.*] An educational institution which combines features of a university and a polytechnic.

**1970** *Daily Tel.* 7 Jan. 2 An amalgamation of universities, polytechnics and colleges of education into vast new 'polyversities' was proposed last night by Jack Straw, president of the National Union of Students. **1970** *Guardian* 26 Jan. 10/3 Locally, institutions should be merged to form new, comprehensive centres of higher education —'polyversities'. **1984** *Economist* 21 Jan. 26/3 A polyversity would have to be financed from both the government-funded university grants committee (UGC) and the politically versatile Ilea. **1986** *Times Higher Educ. Suppl.* 13 June 4/1 Namibia's only 'polyversity', which is just five years old, is finally beginning to look and feel like the thing that it is supposed to represent. **1988** *Times* 15 June 12/1 Some polytechnics want to change their names if not to universities, at least to 'polyversities'.

**Pompey,** *n.* Senses 1, 2 in Dict. become 2, 3. Add: **1.** Colloq. phr. *paws off, Pompey!* = *hands off* s.v. HAND *n.* 54. Now *rare.*

Orig. an anti-Napoleonic catch-phr. app. meaning '(keep your) hands off (i.e. away from) Pompey', where *Pompey* was possibly a nickname for Nelson or Portsmouth; however, the later use of a comma suggests that *Pompey* came to be perceived as the person addressed, with *off* becoming an adverb. Later still *Pompey* was dropped: see OFF *adv.* 9 c.

**1803** *Cartoon* 16 Apr. in M. D. George *Catal. Pol. & Personal Satires Dept. Prints & Drawings Brit. Mus.* (1978) VIII. 138, I ax pardon Master Boney, but as we says *Paws off Pompey*, we keep this little Spot to Ourselves. **1834** MARRYAT *Jacob Faithful* I. xii. 212 Although she liked to be noticed so far by the other chaps, yet Ben was the only one she ever wished to be handled by—it was 'Paws off, Pompey', with all the rest. **1839** THACKERAY *Catherine* in *Fraser's Mag.* Nov. 542/1 Paws off, Pompey; you young hang dog, you. **1932** S. GIBBONS *Cold Comfort Farm* xx. 276 He was just reaching out in a dreamy, absent kind of way . . when Mrs Beetle gave a sharp dab at his hand, exclaiming: 'Paws off, Pompey!'

**pom-pom,** *n.* Add: [**1.**] **b.** *transf.* Something that resembles a pom-pom in shape and texture.

**1936** I. JONES *China Boy* 25 He thought it one of the fluffy pom-poms that had been blown thither from the garden where the old lady had planted a clump of Holy Thistles. **1968** H. HARMAR *Chihuahua Guide* 242 *Pompon*, a rounded tuft of hair on the tail (Poodle). Sometimes miscalled Pom-Pom. **1983** *Jinty Ann. 1984* 21/1 A sniffy, haughty sort of dog, with . . a little pom-pom of hair stuck on his head like a wig.

**pooey** ('puːɪ), *int.* and *a. slang.* [f. *poo*, var. of POOH *int.* (*n.*) + *-ey* -Y[1].] **A.** *int.* An expression of violent distaste, revulsion, derision, or contempt: esp. used by (or in imitation of) children. Cf. POOH *int.*, PHOOEY *int.* **B.** *adj.* Of, contaminated by, or resembling excrement; nasty, unpleasant, distasteful.

**1951** W. SANSOM *Face of Innocence* xv. 222 Ah-ha to you back. And pooey on you too. **1967** PARTRIDGE *Dict. Slang* Suppl. 1303/2 *Poohy, . . pooey*, lit. or fig., faecal; hence disgusting . . since ca. 1935 . . . Hence *poohy!* or *pooey!*, rubbish. Perhaps slightly influenced by U.S. *phooey!* **1982** *N.Y. Times* 23 Sept. C17/1 A hungry crocodile, who opens wide, takes one taste of her and cries, 'Yecht, pooey'. **1986** *Los Angeles Times* 21 Sept. (Calendar section) 61/1 'Who cares if she looks wrong as long as she sounds right?' 'I'm afraid I care.' 'Pooey,' said Leopold. **1988** *Sun* (Brisbane) 12 Oct. (Comics section) 43 Do you know how to tell the difference between a raisin cookie and a chocolate chip cookie? . . Pooey!

**pooh,** *int.* (*v.*, *n.*) Add: **pooh** *v.*: (*b*) *intr.*, to defecate (*slang*, orig. *children's*).

**1980** *Times* 7 May 19/5 The yellow spots found on local cars . . were pollen stains, caused by that darling of the conservationists, the bee, numbers of which

had been pooing on the cars. **1982** C. JAMES *Flying Visits* (1984) 163 The citizens of Munich are . . dog-crazy . . but have somehow trained their pets not to poo.

**pooh pooh,** *int.* (*n.*, *a.*) Add: [**B.**] **2.** Freq. as **poo-poo.** Faeces, excrement (also in *pl.*). Phr. *to do* (*go, make,* etc.) *poo-poo*(*s*), to defecate. *colloq.* (chiefly *children's*).

**1960** WENTWORTH & FLEXNER *Dict. Amer. Slang* 401/2 *Poo-poo*, feces. **1976** M. KARAPANOU *Kassandra & Wolf* xvi. 26 Peter serves. Roast beef and carrots sauté. For me it's spinach, to go poopoo. **1981** *Times Lit. Suppl.* 15 May 541/4 Friends of mine used the word 'aka' in the toilet training of their child, under the . . impression that this is the term used by Amerindians of the Navajo persuasion to denote pooh-poohs. **1983** *Washington Post* 1 Apr. D8/1, I gotta make poo poo. **1988** *Mother & Baby* Apr. 63/3 Show her the nappy and tell her that she can do her wee-wee and poo-poo (or whatever your family words are!) in the potty instead of the nappy now that she is a big girl.

**poorly,** *adv.* and *a.* **B.** For '(Always *predicative.*)' read: (Always *predicative* of persons, animals, etc.) and add: Also *euphem.,* seriously ill, in a serious condition (esp. in hospital). (Later examples.)

**1979** *Guardian* 31 Jan. 4/4 Last night Adrian was said to be 'poorly' in the burns unit of a hospital. **1988** *Times* 8 Jan. 4/7 Yesterday he was on oxygen and I was up with him all night. He hasn't needed oxygen today but he is still quite poorly. *Ibid.* 15 Nov. 3/6 Nine children were . . still receiving hospital treatment . . . Two were in a 'poorly condition'.

**Pooter** ('puːtə(r)), *n.*[3] The family name of Charles *Pooter* (see POOTERISH *a.*), used of a type of person characterized by parochial self-importance, over-fastidiousness, or lack of imagination.

**1961** *Listener* 16 Nov. 833/3 We need its rocket to launch us beyond the world of the Pooters. **1962** *Times* 14 June 15/3 There is an element of Pooter in many of us. **1971** [see KEEP *v.* 57 j]. **1977** *Economist* 5 Nov. 131/1 It also proves that a Crossman is as prone to mishap as a Pooter. **1983** *Guardian Weekly* 13 Nov. 9/1 There is a dull chronicling of food, flats, and girl friends which suggests a Pooter armed but doggedly recording the long littleness of life on the run.

**pootle** ('puːt(ə)l), *v. colloq.* [Blend of POODLE *v.* and TOOTLE *v.*] *intr.* To move or travel (*around, along,* etc.) in a leisurely manner; = POODLE *v.* 2; TOOTLE *v.* 3. Also *fig.*

**1977** D. E. WESTLAKE *Nobody's Perfect* II. iii. 108 Kelp pootled around a while longer, found a parking place. **1986** *Marketing Week* 29 Aug. 22/1 The core business—the W H Smith chain—continues to pootle along quite successfully. **1987** *Which?* Oct. 495/1 Not a lot of noise . . . When just pootling about, quieter than average. **1988** *Bicycle* Midsummer 57/1 Pootling through Nottingham recently, I came across a branch of a shop called Concept Man.

**pooty** ('puːtɪ), *n.*[1] *dial.* [orig. unknown: first recorded in the writings of the poet John Clare, the son of a Northamptonshire labourer.] (The shell of) the grove snail, *Cepaea nemoralis.* Freq. *attrib.,* as *pooty shell.*

**1821** J. CLARE *Village Minstrel* I. 10 Searching the pooty from the rushy dyke. *Ibid.* II. 16 The painted pooty-shell. **1825** —— *Let.* 7 Feb. in J. W. & A. Tibble *Prose of John Clare* (1951) 183, I have been seriously and busily employed this last 3 weeks hunting Pooty shells. **1937** [see PADGE *n.*]. **1973** *Country Life* 5 Apr. 907/1 There are also a few pooties, John Clare's name for grove snails (*Cepaea nemoralis*) that are both banded and black. **1980** G.

NELSON *Charity's Child* iii. 45 Do 'e remember .. the pooty shells I collected?

**pop**, *n.*[1] Add: **8.** The ability of a horse to jump fences, esp. with spirit. Usu. with qualifying word, as *good pop*. *colloq.*

**1977** *Horse & Hound* 25 Mar. 66/1 Genuine little pony with a good 'pop' and excellent mouth and manners. **1982** BARR & YORK *Official Sloane Ranger Handbk.* 159/1 Must have a good pop in him to pop over the fences. **1987** *Field* Nov. 66/2 This chestnut had the 'pop' of a showjumper, which he is, and was also extremely fast.

**pop.** (pɒp), *n.*[9] Also without point. [Shortened f. POPULATION *n.*] Abbreviated form of POPULATION *n.*, esp. in statistical contexts.

**1818** J. E. WORCESTER *Gazetteer of U.S.* 237/2 *Perquimans*, co. E. part of N.C. Pop. 6,052. Slaves 2,017. Chief town, Hertford. **1866** *Chambers's Encycl.* VIII. 711/1 Siena, a city of Central Italy, 60 miles south of Florence by railway. Pop. 22,624. **1880** W. WHITMAN *Daybks. & Notebks.* (1978) III. 616 Pop of Sarnia 5000. **1910** *Encycl. Brit.* XI. 549/1 Geelong, a seaport .. situated on an extensive land-locked arm of Port Phillip known as Corio Bay . . . Pop. of the city proper (1901) 12, 399. **1939** *Florida* (Federal Writers' Project) II. 184 Jacksonville (25 alt., 129,459 pop.), the State's largest city. **1961** WODEHOUSE *Ice in Bedroom* iii. 25 The town's Pop, as the guide book curtly terms it, is four thousand nine hundred and sixteen. **1988** *Times* 15 June 25/3 In the US .. licences [to sell a product] are priced on the basis of the number of potential customers. These 'pop' values—the per person of population the licences cover—are regarded in America as a useful way of assessing anticipated cash flow.

**pop** (pɒp) *n.*[10] *U.S. colloq.* [Abbrev.] = POPSICLE *n.*

**1960** WENTWORTH & FLEXNER *Dict. Amer. Slang* s.v., *Pop*, . . the common written and spoken abbr. for a popsicle, any ice or ice cream frozen on a stick and sold by street vendors or refreshment stands. **1974** H. L. FOSTER *Ribbin'* iv. 124 Usually the New York City folks call ice cream on a stick a pop while to the Buffalonians it is the soda that is called pop. **1983** *N.Y. Times Mag.* 28 Aug. 16/2 A sultry summer Sunday is a time for people to drive somewhere with the kids and when they arrive to buy them a pop. A what? You know, a pop—short for Popsicle—ice on a stick.

**pop**, *v.*[1] Add: [**2.**] **c.** Of the ears: to make a small popping sound within the head as pressure is equalized between different parts of the auditory canal, esp. during a change of altitude.

**1962** *Underwater Swimming* ('Know the Game' Ser.) 15 It is often possible to assist ears that are difficult to clear by pinching the nose and blowing gently, when the ears will be felt to 'pop' as the pressures equalise. **1977** D. BAGLEY *Enemy* xxxvi. 300 My ears popped as the pressure changed. **1984** R. FRAME *Winter Journey* (1986) ii. 134 We started to come down at last—through another cloud like grey steam—and I felt my ears pop. **1989** *Chicago Tribune* (Sunday Mag.) 30 Apr. 18/2 The ride takes 90 seconds, your eyes widen, your ears pop about four times.

[**3.**] **b.** To open (a can of beer, etc.) with a pop by pulling the tab. Often *to pop open*. *colloq.* (chiefly *N. Amer.*).

**1976** *National Observer* (U.S.) 10 Apr. 18/2 Settled now on a sofa in the youth center, popping cans of Busch Bavarian. **1976** T. O'BRIEN *Northern Lights* I. 76 He .. popped open two cans of beer. **1978** M. KENYON *Deep Pocket* vi. 67 Carter popped a [beer] can. **1985** A. LURIE *Foreign Affairs* viii. 186 Electricians and carpenters .. pop open cans of soda. **1987** *New Yorker* 24 Aug. 26/2 Steve popped another beer.

**11.** *trans. Computing.* To retrieve (a piece of data, etc.) from the 'top' of a stack; also (const. *up*), to remove the top element of (a stack); = *PULL *v.* 1 g. Also *absol.* Opp. *PUSH *v.* 1 o.

**1962** R. S. LEDLEY *Programming & Utilizing Digital Computers* v. 178 The push-down list can be conceived as a non-branched threaded list made up by placing each new element 'on top' of the list in the same memory location . . . When an element is removed from the list, it is always taken off the top by removing it from this same memory location and the remaining elements are then made to 'pop up'. **1963** [see *PUSH *v.* 1 o]. **1964** *Proc. AFIPS Conf.* XXVI. 47 Termination of a subexecution results in the LIFO list being popped up and the cell returned to the SCL (also returning the SCB space). **1976** M. M. MANO *Computer Sys. Archit.* vii. 267 A return to the running program is effected by first popping the contents of registers out of the stack and then popping the return address and placing it into *PC*. **1983** *Your Computer* Aug. 64/1 The resume command .. simply restores the registers by popping them in reverse order. **1985** *Austral. Personal Computer* Oct. 181/3 In Forth, we use the operator . (dot) to pop the stack.

**popper**, *n.* Add: **8. a.** One who takes pills (esp. of stimulant drugs) freely; a 'pill-popper'. Also, any drug-taker. Orig. as the final element in Combs. *colloq.* (orig. *U.S.*).

**1936**, etc. [see *joy-popper* s.v. JOY *n.* 10]. **1953** [see *skin-popper* s.v. SKIN *n.* 16]. **1967** *Evening Echo* (Bournemouth) 28 Aug. 9/3, I suppose that the natural contempt that a sophisticated man feels towards 'Flower-boys', 'Beatnicks' and Poppers has somehow to be explained away. **1985** *Marketing Mag.* (N.Z.) July 13/1 Most New Zealanders, twenty or even ten years ago, would have dismissed vitamin poppers, joggers or vegetarians as 'nuts'.

**b.** A capsule of amyl or (iso)butyl nitrite, taken by drug-users for its stimulant effect; a bottle or other container of the drug. Freq. in *pl. slang* (orig. *U.S.*).

The capsule is typically crushed or 'popped', and the drug taken by inhalation.

**1967** J. DIDION *Slouching towards Bethlehem* (1968) I. 80 Las Vegas .. a place the tone of which is set by mobsters and call girls and ladies' room attendants with amyl nitrite poppers in their uniform pockets. **1969** E. M. BRECHER *Sex Researchers* (1970) 320 Among the many drugs which came into use during the 1960's .. was the 'popper'—a capsule containing a volatile chemical previously used by victims of heart disease. **1979** S. WILSON *Glad Hand* I. i. 9 *Bill* . . . Give him a popper . . . *Carson* (*breaking popper under Clement's nose*) Personally, I never touch the stuff until five seconds after orgasm. Bad for the heart. **1982** *New Scientist* 16 Dec. 715/1 Poppers are commonly bought through sex shops, and if the bottles are labelled at all, their chemical contents are rarely listed. **1985** R. SILVERBERG *Tom O'Bedlam* (1986) VI. i. 208 She closed the door behind him and looked about for something to offer him, a drink, a popper, anything to calm him. **1988** *Times Lit. Suppl.* 29 May 597/3 Maybe immune-system failure was due to 'poppers'—for then the condition would be self-inflicted, and thus self-limiting.

**poppy** ('pɒpɪ), *a.*[2] *colloq.* [f. POP *a.* (*n.*[8]) + -Y[1].] Characterized by a popular, light style; popular, 'upbeat'; *spec.* of a group, music, etc.: having a sound characteristic of mainstream pop music.

**1970** *Guardian* 25 July 6/1 He is a barrister, a playwright, and a poppy newspaper columnist on the side. **1981** *New Musical Express* 7 Mar. 11/1 We're not poppy in the same way as someone like the Moondogs are poppy. **1986** *Southern Star* (Brisbane) 21 Oct. 26/3 They describe their music now as psychedelic, less poppy, more menacing. **1987** *Q* Oct. 99/3 Too gloomy to seem any more a proper pop group, .. too poppy to fit comfortably into the gothic underground, Depeche Mode survive with a firm following that seems to have grown with them. **1988** *Tower Records' Top* Feb. 7/3 The Subway Organisation were riding high with poppy 12" EP's by the Flatmates.

**pornbroker** ('pɔːn,brəʊkə(r)), *n.* [f. PORN *n.* + BROKER *n.*, punningly after PAWNBROKER *n.*] One who buys, sells, or deals in pornography.
   **1967** *Times Lit. Suppl.* 19 Jan. 45/2 (*heading*) The pornbrokers. **1976** *New Society* 12 Aug. 338/2 Sir Robert Mark's spring clean of London bookshops forced hard pornbrokers to work out of a suitcase. **1981** *Observer* 4 Jan. 3/1 It was Bernard Brook-Partridge, Chairman of the Greater London Council, who said of Soho's pornbrokers: 'We are out to gun these buggers down.' **1984** *Times* 28 Aug. 11/6 A fragile but ever-strengthening bridge is being built over the murky waters of the pornbrokers in the square mile.

**port**, *n.*[1] Add: [I.] [2.] e. Hence, any point (other than a sea-port) at which passengers embark or disembark, or at which goods are loaded or unloaded, esp. on arrival in a country; *spec.* as *inland port.* Freq. *ellipt.* for AIRPORT *n.*
   **1934** *Jrnl. R. Aeronaut. Soc.* XXXVIII. 816 For carrying out the landing, the aeroplane is first of all communicated with at a sufficient height by wireless by the ground stations and is conducted to the port. **1956** W. A. HEFLIN *U.S. Air Force Dict.* 394/2 Port, .. short for 'air-port'. **1975** *Economist* 29 Mar. 96/1 It [*sc.* the scheme] could apply to any inland port, any barge wharf, almost any container depot. **1987** *Wantage & Grove Herald* 29 Jan. 8/2 The port is used by importers and exporters who want to clear customs formalities but avoid delays at ports and airports. **1989** *Financial Times* 14 Apr. 16/5 One of the biggest industrial schemes planned for Leeds is at the inland port of Stourton.

**pose**, *n.*[5] Add: [1.] b. *Dancing.* A position adopted by a dancer in which the body is held static, as in an arabesque, etc.
   **1922** BEAUMONT & IDZIKOWSKI *Man. Classical Theatr. Dancing* Pl. XIII (*caption*) Pose from first exercise on *port de bras.* **1957** G. B. L. WILSON *Dict. Ballet* 220 *Pose*, a static position as against the dancer in movement. **1967** CHUJOY & MANCHESTER *Dance Encycl.* 740/1 Poses in ballet include attitude, arabesque, etc. **1980** M. FONTEYN *Magic of Dance* 198 He will end a ballet with the dancers in a uniform pose, all kneeling.

**posh**, *a.* Add: Also pejoratively, (affecting to be) superior, upper-class, or genteel; 'snooty'. (Earlier and further examples.)
   **1915** *Blackwood's Mag.* CXCVIII. 255/2 Posh may be defined, very roughly, as a useless striving after gentlemanly culture. **1958** A. SILLITOE *Saturday Night & Sunday Morning* vii. 95, I suppose you're too stuck up now you've got such a posh job. **1979** *London Rev. Bks.* 25 Oct. 1/4 He gets a menial job at a posh private school. **1987** N. HINTON *Buddy's Song* xiii. 73 The people were obviously very rich and they talked in an extremely posh way.

**post-**, *prefix.* Add: [B.] [1.] [b.] *post-feminist.*
   **1981** *N.Y. Times* 15 Feb. II. 24/6 Some theatergoers, accustomed to the outspoken quality of *post-feminist playwrights, might say that the play could only have been written by a woman. **1983** *N.Y. Times* 20 Jan. C17/4 (*heading*) British stage feminists and U.S. post-feminists. **1986** *Washington Post* 8 Apr. A19/1 An intra-gender battle .. between feminists and post-feminists.
   **post-Bang**, occurring after, and esp. as a result of, the 'Big Bang' (see BIG *a.* B. 2) on the London Stock Exchange in October 1986.

**1986** *Sunday Times* 1 June 59/2 The Bank of England is worried that dealing in stocks and shares could become too dispersed after the Big Bang ... There is a particular danger of this with the new *post-bang gilts market. **1989** *Financial Times* 14 Jan. (Weekend Suppl.) p. xvi/1 The Big Bang has become a firing spree as financial houses face up to the post-Bang competition.
   [c.] *post-feminism.*
   **1983** *Time* 10 Jan. 60 (*heading*) *Postfeminism: .. from novels to humor, women are moving beyond doctrine. **1986** *New Statesman* 9 May 12/2 The new romanticism is also the world of 'post-feminism' where feminism's angry euphoria has dissipated in a sea of uncertainty.

**Poussiniste** (puːsæ'niːst), *n.* Also in anglicized form Poussinist (-ist). [a. Fr. *Poussiniste*, f. the name of Nicolas *Poussin* (see POUSSINESQUE *a.*).] An admirer or imitator of Poussin, *spec.* one of a group of late 17th c. French artists and critics who (in opposition to the Rubénistes) considered mastery of design, as epitomized in the work of Poussin, more important than the exuberant and expressive use of colour, as exemplified by that of Rubens. Cf. *RUBÉNISTE *n.*
   **1938** *Burlington Mag.* Jan. 4/1 It has been possible to show *Rubénistes* and *Poussinistes* together: to set against the loose exuberance of Rubens the ordered wildness of Poussin's *Triumph of Pan.* **1938** *Times* 1 Jan. 13/6 There was still a survival of classical mannerism, based on Michelangelo and Raphael, which became active in France and gave rise to the battle between the Rubénistes and the Poussinistes. **1970** *Oxf. Compan. Art* 906/2 In the later 17th c. Poussin's name was used in the Académie to give support to those who believed in the superior importance of design in painting (Poussinistes) in opposition to that of Rubens, who stood for the importance of colouring. **1987** *N.Y. Rev. Bks.* 26 Feb. 22/4 It makes the opposition between academic and modernist style essentially different from earlier warring camps, like the Poussinists against Rubenists, or Venetian against Florentine.

**Prague**, *n.* Add: **3. Prague Spring**, a name applied to the brief period of liberalization in Czechoslovakia in 1968 (ended by Soviet intervention in August of that year) during which the Communist Party Secretary Alexander Dubček (1921–92) introduced a programme of political and other reforms; cf. *SPRING *n.*[1] 6 i.
   [**1968** *Sat Rev.* (U.S.) 13 Apr. 8/1 Spring blooms in Prague ... Spring in Eastern Europe this year is forcing new shoots of freedom out from still-frozen ideological soil.] **1969** *Foreign Affairs* XLVII. 266 The eight-month 'Prague spring', the Soviet invasion of August 20 and its grim consequences have stirred strong emotions. **1972** *Times* 6 May 5/3 About 40 people are believed to be still detained. These include a number of prominent liberals of the 'Prague spring' of 1968. **1981** *Christian Order* XXII. 272 The first 'Polish Spring' of 1956, the Hungarian uprising of the same year, and the 'Prague Spring' in 1968 were all started by prominent dissenters within the ruling Communist parties. **1988** *Plays Internat.* Aug. 50/3 We appeared on .. television ... It was the time of the Prague 'spring'.

**‖prakriti** ('prakriti), *n. Hindu Philos.* Also 20 prakrti. [Skr. *prakṛti* nature.] Primordial nature or first principle; matter as opposed to spirit; *spec.* in Sankhya philosophy, the potentially productive principle (freq. personified as female) which, with the animating principle (*PURUSHA *n.*), gives rise to the material, sentient universe.

**1785** C. WILKINS *Bhăgvăt-Gēētā* 142 God is represented under the figure of Măhă-Pŏŏrŏŏsh, the great man or prime progenitor; in conjunction with Prăkrĕĕtĕĕ, nature or first principle, under the emblem of a female engendering the world with his . . supernatural power. **1832** *Asiatic Researches* XVII. 212 Nature, Prakr̥iti . . is defined to be of eternal existence and independent origin, distinct from the supreme spirit . . the plastic origin of all things. **1913** J. N. FARQUHAR *Crown of Hinduism* vi. 237 [Sāṅkhya] . . teaches the existence of prakr̥iti, an eternal fundamental substance from which all phenomenal nature arises. **1953** F. VREEDE *Living Hindu Philos.* iv. 27 The opposition of purusha to prakriti represents the complementarity of two universal aspects of reality: 'essence' and 'substance'. **1964** B. HEIMANN *Facets Indian Thought* iv. 59 All effects . . are potentially contained in the great reservoir of primary Matter before, and after, their actual manifestation. Prakr̥ti is their common efficient and material cause. **1986** J. LIPNER *Face of Truth* 41 It is the non-conscious, primal, causal, 'material' principle of the world (namely . . Prakr̥ti).

**Prausnitz–Küstner** ('praʊznɪts 'kʏstnə(r)), *n. Immunol.* The names of Carl Willy *Prausnitz* (1876–1963), German bacteriologist, and Heinz *Küstner* (b. 1897), German gynaecologist, used *attrib.* (esp. in *Prausnitz-Küstner reaction*) with reference to the injection of serum from an allergic subject into the skin of another individual, followed after 1-2 days by injection of the allergen, which produces a weal if a reagin (also known as a *Prausnitz-Küstner antibody*) is present. More commonly abbreviated as *P(-)K* (see \*P II.).

An injection of this type was carried out by Prausnitz, using Küstner as his subject, and reported in *Centralblatt f. Bakteriol., Parasitenkunde und Infektionskrankheiten: Erste Abteilung* (1921) LXXXVI. 160.

**1929** *Arch. Dermatol. & Syphilol.* XIX. 193 All those forms of idiosyncrasy in which a clear and certain Prausnitz-Küstner reaction is obtained . . belong to one special group. **1937** R. W. FAIRBROTHER *Text-bk. Med. Bacteriol.* x. 130 The production of passive hypersensitiveness can be readily demonstrated by means of the Prausnitz-Küstner test. **1951** WHITBY & HYNES *Med. Bacteriol.* (ed. 5) vii. 97 The Prausnitz-Küstner Reaction. The presence of antibodies (or reagins) in the serum of hypersensitive patients can be demonstrated by the P-K reaction. **1973** R. G. KRUEGER et al. *Introd. Microbiol.* xxv. 606/2 It is now believed to be the distinct class of immunoglobulins that is responsible for reagenic activity (that is, the so-called Prausnitz-Kustner antibody . . ). **1976** *Clin. & Exper. Immunol.* XXV. 159 The highly purified allergen fragment inhibits . . Prausnitz- Küstner reactions in non-allergic volunteers sensitized with the sera of patients sensitive to green peas. **1983** *Allergy* XXXVIII. 168/2 In the Prausnitz-Küstner serum transfer test HBsAg-negative serum from one birch pollen allergic donor was used.

**preclear** (priː'klɪə(r)), *n.* Also pre-clear. [f. PRE-B. 2 + CLEAR *n.*] In Scientology, a person who has begun a course of dianetic therapy but is not yet a 'clear' (see \*CLEAR *n.* 6).

**1950** L. R. HUBBARD *Dianetics* III. iii. 176 The terms *pre-release* and *pre-clear* are used to designate an individual entered into and undergoing dianetic therapy. The term *pre-clear* is used most commonly. **1968** *Economist* 3 Aug. 40/2 In this state he is known as a 'preclear'. **1987** *Sydney Morning Herald* 21 Nov. 83/7 They could make 'real money', he noted, if each clinic could count on 10 or 15 pre-clears . . a week, each paying $500 for 24 hours of auditing.

**priceable** ('praɪsəb(ə)l), *a. U.S.* [f. PRICE *v.* + -ABLE.] Capable of being priced or costed;

having a calculable value. Also **'priceableness** *n.*

**1797** COLERIDGE in *Sotheby's Catal. Bks. & MSS.* 30 Nov. (1891) 58 So much for the priceableness of the volume—not for the saleability. **1934** in WEBSTER. **1981** *Amer. Banker* 12 June 4/2 Theory suggests that interest-rate risk presents thrifts with a priceable opportunity. **1987** *N.Y. Times Mag.* 5 Apr. 29/1 For many of us, reputation is our most valuable, if least 'priceable', asset.

**pricey**, *a.* Add: Hence **'pricily** *adv.*, expensively; also **'priciness** *n.*

**1981** *Washington Post* 11 Dec. (Weekend section) 48/1 Gifts for the aspiring ascending have to combine practicality and priceyness. **1982** *Ibid.* 14 Mar. H1/2 The entire meal costs about $3.50 per person, despite the comparative priciness of the ingredients for the first course. **1986** *Nation* (N.Y.) 15 Oct. 419/2 He lets his aging face . . do most of his work for him, and his trim body (pricily dressed) does the rest. **1987** *Financial Times* 1 June 22/8 Priciness, however, is but the latest in a list of complaints Israel's hotels have grown accustomed to hearing over the years. **1987** *Washington Post* 23 Oct. (Weekend section) 23/4 Plans, says Circle spokesman Freeman Fisher, include: . . Pricily overhaul the Circle Uptown.

**pricing** ('praɪsɪŋ), *vbl. n.* [f. PRICE *v.* + -ING[1].] The act or process of establishing a price for goods or services; the overall level of prices so fixed. Freq. *attrib.*

Often as the second element in Combs., e.g. ROAD-*pricing*, SHADOW-*pricing*, TRANSFER-*pricing*, etc.

**1865** *Morning Star* 1 June 2/3 The layers of the odds complaining that nothing but the favourites were backed, notwithstanding their tempting 'pricing' of the outsiders. **1881** F. J. CROWEST *Phases Mus. Eng.* v. 146 One of the forms in which we find the Art seriously hampered presents itself to us in the music publishing interest—in the pricing of Songs and of Sheet-music generally. **1920** P. H. NYSTROM *Econ. of Retailing* xiv. 231 The net results of each pricing system can be . . understood by a table. **1932** W. L. CHURCHILL *Pricing for Profit* 20 Faulty pricing works against the producer whether he overprices or underprices. **1969** D. C. HAGUE *Managerial Econ.* iv. 92 The kinked demand curve is derived from the . . curves we have already been using in our analysis of trade association pricing. **1976** P. R. WHITE *Planning for Public Transport* vii. 153 Limited-stop surveys, pricing policy and developments in Devon. **1982** *Times* 15 Sept. 18/6 Coupons on United Kingdom municipal authority fixed interest bonds rose by up to one quarter point at par pricing. **1989** *Computerworld* 1 May 72/1 Pricing ranges from $7,500 to $11,600, depending on testing environment. The unit is slated for shipment in June.

**pricker**, *n.* Add: **6.** A thorn, spine, or prickle of a plant. *dial.* and *U.S. colloq.*

*a* **1876** E. LEIGH *Gloss. Words Dial. Cheshire* (1877) 160 The prickers on a brimble. **1887** T. DARLINGTON *Folk-Speech S. Cheshire* 300, I say, wench, cost tha tay me a pricker aït o' my fom? **1907** *Dialect Notes* III. 196 Boys get prickers in their feet when they go barefoot. **1939** C. MORLEY *Kitty Foyle* x. 95 She'd [*sc.* the catbird] come flying through the whole mess of prickers in one clean swoop. **1969** C. BURKE *God is Beautiful, Man* (1970) 122 That's a very pretty rose. . . It's got prickers on it. **1981** T. MORRISON *Tar Baby* v. 137 There in the moonlight was a basket of pineapples, one of which he rammed into his shirt mindless of its prickers.

**pricking**, *vbl. n.* Add: [6.] c. In *Lace-making*, the transferring of a design by means of pricks from a pattern to an underlying card or other surface, which is then used as a guide or template; the pattern copied or guide produced in this way.

*c* **1890** tr. *T. de Dillmont's Encycl. Needlework* 480 The pricking of the pattern beforehand is particularly important in the case of the common torchon lace, where the real beauty of the design consists in its regularity. **1930** *Ibid.* (new ed.) 710 The pattern or 'pricking'.. consists of a design transferred to a card, certain parts of which are pricked out. **1953** M. POWYS *Lace & Lace-Making* iv. 26 Straight lace, all the threads being hung on the lace pillow at the top of a straight pricking. **1976** P. NOTTINGHAM *Technique of Bobbin Lace* i. 14 To copy a pricking from a book. Fasten the tracing paper firmly over the pattern and mark in each dot using a sharp pencil. **1979** E. LUXTON *Technique of Honiton Lace* ii. 20 The prickings in this book are the actual size for working. .. Great care should be taken that the holes are pricked accurately, as the finished appearance of the lace depends largely on a good pricking. **1988** *Lace* July 10/2 This cape is very large indeed and the pricking itself is divided into 2 halves.

**prickle,** *n.*[1] **[2.]** Delete †*Obs.* and add:
App. obsolete by early 14th. cent.; the mod. use appears to represent a separate development (orig. *dial.* and *U.S. colloq.*).
**1895** in *Funk's Stand. Dict.* **1898** N. MUNRO *John Splendid* xxiii. 223 A prickle's at my skin that tells me here is dool. **1942** BERREY & VAN DEN BARK *Amer. Thes. Slang* §134/1 *The prickles,* a pricking sensation. **1975** M. DUFFY *Capital* i. 48, I shall feel the prickle of heat and grass. **1985** J. WINTERSON *Oranges are not the Only Fruit* 109, I felt a prickle at the back of my neck.

**[7.] b.** *pl.* A tendency or capacity to react argumentatively; defensiveness, prickliness, touchiness. Cf. *PRICKLE *v.* 3 b, PRICKLY *a.* 1 b.
**1975** L. GILLEN *Return to Deepwater* ii. 38 'You've got the McCourt prickles, anyway,' he told her tactlessly. **1975** D. FRANCIS *High Stakes* iii. 49 Before I collected you, I expected honesty, directness and prickles.

**prickle,** *v.* Add: **[3.] b.** *fig.* To react defensively or angrily to others' behaviour, a situation, etc.; to bristle. Const. *with* (an emotion), *at* (a source of provocation). Cf. *PRICKLE *n.*[1] 7 b, PRICKLY *a.* 1 b.
**1983** S. COOPER *Seaward* iii. 17 The field was still, prickling with tension ... Faintly from the nearest group of golden soldiers a shout rose: 'Charge!' **1983** G. HARRIS *Seventh Gate* ii. 29 You're easy to tease and I like to watch you prickle, like a marsh kitten refusing to be stroked. **1989** *Los Angeles Times* 23 July (Book Rev. section) 10/1 Lawyers will prickle at the simplistic approach he takes to explaining the common law.

**primal** ('praɪməl), *v. Psychol. colloq.* [f. the adj.] *intr.* To participate in primal therapy; to release emotion, tension, etc. in primal screaming. Also *trans.,* to subject (a person) to primal therapy.
**1971** J. LENNON in *Rolling Stone* 10 Jan. 34/4 It's a process that is going on. We primal almost daily. **1977** *Undercurrents* June–July 26/3 Everyone is permitted to primal when they wish. **1977** *Rolling Stone* 5 May 74/2 Check out the singing on 'Taxman, Mr. Thief', and tell me anyone has been more pissed off since John Lennon was primaled. **1978** *Listener* 19 Oct. 501/1 Much of the emotion that gushes out from people 'primalling' or in psychodrama, concerns real or imagined parental neglect and even desertion.

**primase** ('praɪmeɪz), *n. Biochem.* [f. PRIM(ER *n.*[2] + -ASE.] Any enzyme which catalyses the synthesis of primers, esp. of primer DNA or RNA.
**1977** R. MCMACKEN et al. in *Proc. Nat. Acad. Sci.* LXXIV. 4190/1 Among the single-stranded .. phage DNAs thus far tested in replication systems *in vitro,* the ϕX174 class is unique in being converted first to a multiprotein intermediate .. to enable the synthesis of a primer by *dnaG* protein (primase). **1978** ROWEN & KORNBERG in *Jrnl. Biol. Chem.* CCLIII. 758/2 Based on its role in priming DNA replication rather than in transcribing DNA regions for synthesis of messenger or other defined RNAs, [etc.].. we propose that the *dnaG* protein be designated primase. **1982** T. M. DEVLIN *Textbk. Biochem.* xvii. 855 In other systems, including phage ϕ, initiation is achieved by the action of a primase. **1986** *Ann. Rev. Biochem.* LV. 760 Primase synthesizes 5′-terminal oligoribonucleotides of discrete length, about 10 nucleotides, and of random sequence.

**prime,** *a.* (*adv.*) Add: **[4.] c.** In trivial or ironic use: excellent, splendid; wonderful. (Usu. *predic.* or as exclamation.) *colloq.*
*a* **1637** B. JONSON *Sad Shepherd* (1783) I. vi. 22 Had you good sport i' your chace to-day? ... O prime! **1837** DICKENS *Pickw.* xxix. 310 'Capital!' said Mr. Benjamin Allen. 'Prime!' ejaculated Mr. Bob Sawyer. **1842** BARHAM *Black Mousquetaire* in *Ingol. Leg.* 2nd. Ser. 2 Your thorough French Courtier .. Thinks it prime fun to astonish a citizen. **1899** E. NESBIT *Story of Treasure Seekers* xii. 244 We had a feast—like a picnic—all sitting anywhere, and eating with our fingers. It was prime. **1941** M. E. CHASE *Windswept* 58 It's mighty prime of you to trust a plain country carpenter like me to do your job for you. **1981** W. RUSSELL *Educating Rita* I. iii. 17 Oh that's prime, isn't it? That's justice for y'. I get failed just cos I'm more well read than the friggin' examiner!

**prime,** *v.*[1] **[3.] [a.]** For def. read: To charge or furnish (a person) fully *with* information; to prepare, make ready, or train fully *for* a particular purpose or *to* carry out a specific task. (Later examples.)
**1863** J. H. SPEKE *Jrnl. Discovery Source of Nile* xiv. 441, I primed him well to plead for the road. **1938** S. BECKETT *Murphy* ix. 165 Bom, primed by Bim, expected nothing from Murphy. **1951** W. C. WILLIAMS *Autobiogr.* ix. 40 We went two or three times a week and saw men being primed for duels. **1984** S. BELLOW *Him with his Foot in his Mouth* 288, I considered whether Sable was priming me to make her a proposal.

**primigravid** ('praɪmɪˌgrævɪd), *a.* (*n.*) *Obstetr.* and *Zool.* [f. PRIMIGRAVID(A *n.*] Pregnant for the first time. Occas. as *n.* = PRIMIGRAVIDA *n.*
**1949** *Amer. Jrnl. Obstetr. & Gynecol.* LVII. 1210 Among primigravid women the problem of age and aging in relation to pregnancy and parturition is as old as the practice of obstetrics. **1955** *Obstetr. & Gynecol.* VI. 568/2 He studied a series of 622 consecutive primigravid parturients at term. **1966** *Jrnl. Obstetr. & Gynaecol.* LXXIII. 670/1 Two hundred primigravid patients having spontaneous vaginal vertex deliveries were studied. **1977** *Lancet* 18 June 1273/1, 15–20% of primigravid and 5–10% of multiparous women develop pregnancy-associated hypertension. **1981** *Trop. & Geogr. Med.* XXXIII. 61 (*heading*) Calcium metabolism in African primigravids. **1988** *Amer. Jrnl. Vet. Res.* XLIX. 2068/1 Primigravid swine were vaccinated orally with a live enterotoxigenic *Escherichia coli* (ETEC) strain that produces pilus antigen K99.

**primitive,** *a.* and *n.* Add: **[B.] 10.** *Computing.* A simple operation or procedure, *esp.* one of a limited set from which more complex operations or procedures may be constructed; also *spec.* in computer graphics, a simple geometric shape which may be generated by such a subroutine. Cf. senses A. 5 a and e above.
**1958** *Communications Assoc. Computing Machinery* Feb. 1 By 'primitive' is meant a self-sufficient routine; a second-generation routine is one which calls on one or more primitives. **1968** *Pattern*

*Recognition* I. 170 Any one of the halfplanes determined by the sides of the polygon will actually be a parallel translation of the halfplanes *Hi* determined by the chosen directions. These halfplanes play the role of primitives or signs. **1971** N. CHAPIN *Computers* xiv. 381 An operation may be a macro in one programing language and a primitive in another. **1985** *Practical Computing* Sept. 83/2 Graphic primitives—arcs, lines, etc.—are generated on an internal CRT, with automatic exposure control as standard.

**primo**, *a.* and *n.* Add: [A.] **2.** First-class, first-rate; of top quality. *slang* (orig. and chiefly *U.S.*).
    **1975** *High Times* Dec. 105/1 (Advt.), A creamy cheesecake made fresh daily in New York, using only 'primo' natural ingredients. **1986** *Amer. Film* June 4/1 The Taylor murder had all the elements of a primo Hollywood thriller. **1987** *Performance* Sept./Oct. 8/1 Anna Thew (once, I'm told, a go-go dancer but now a primo avant-garde film maker).

‖**Principe** ('print∫ipe), *n.*² Also with lower-case initial. Pl. Principi, (anglicized) Principes. [It., f. L. *princeps, princip-* chief, prince.] An Italian prince.
    **1930** E. POUND *XXX Cantos* 133 And when the Prince Oltrepassimo died . . a cat sat there licking himself And then stepped over the Principe. **1971** P. A. ALLUM *Politics & Society in Post-War Naples* (1973) ii. 47 The nobility has fallen into desuetude and the *principi* and *marchesi* who survive are *rentiers* for the most part. **1979** N. SLATER *Falcon* iii. 59 The Principes and Contes of Roman society. **1986** J. MONEY *Capri* iv. 75 The family . . branded Gordon-Lennox as a rich, harsh English aristocrat who had wronged the poor, helpless Principe.

**principled**, *ppl. a.* Add: Hence 'principledness *n.*, the quality of being principled; uprightness.
    **1969** E. GOFFMAN *Where Action Is* 162 The sudden high cost of correct behaviour may serve only to confirm his principledness. **1984** *Daily Tel.* 13 Feb. 5/2 Every publication, every article should fascinate and convince the readers by its grasp of life and principledness, keen thought and vivid style.

**print**, *n.* [B.] [I.] [6.] For def. read: A printed (usu. cotton) fabric or piece of cloth (freq. *attrib.*); also, a garment or other article made of printed fabric; the pattern printed on the cloth. (Later examples.)
    **1946** B. MACDONALD *Egg & I* v. xxii. 216 Mrs. Hicks had on a blue flowered print, a touch of orange lipstick, . . and lots of bright pink 'rooje' scrubbed into her cheeks. **1967** P. BAILEY *At Jerusalem* III. 156 Nurse Barrow took the orange print from its hanger.

**print**, *v.* Add: [I.] [3.] **d.** *Shooting. intr.* Of a bullet: to make an impression on or hit the target; also of a gun: to cause bullets to strike the target (too high, low, etc.). orig. *U.S.*
    **1970** R. A. STEINDLER *Firearms Dict.* 105/2 Flyer or *flier*, bullet that for known or unknown reasons prints or hits outside of the rest of the group fired with the same gun. **1987** *Combat Handguns* Aug. 10/2 While this second pistol seems to print a little low, its accuracy is comparable to our first P85. **1988** *Guns & Weapons* Autumn 62/1 The first shot, which was fired double action, printed just under 50mm (2″) from the bull.

**prion** ('pri:ɒn), *n.*² *Microbiol.* [f. by rearrangement of the initial letters of '*pr*oteinaceous *i*nfectious particle': cf. VIRION *n.*] A hypothetical infectious particle consisting only of protein, and thought to be the cause of some diseases.
    **1982** *Daily Tel.* 22 Feb. 15/7 Dr Prusiner . . believes the prion may be the cause of illnesses formerly blamed on 'slow viruses' . . . Diseases in this category . . include Parkinson's disease, diabetes melitus and rheumatoid arthritis. **1982** S. B. PRUSINER in *Science* 9 Apr. 141/3 Because the dominant characteristics of the scrapie agent resemble those of a protein, an acronym is introduced to emphasize this feature. In place of such terms as 'unconventional virus' or 'unusual slow virus-like agent', the term 'prion' (pronounced *pree-on*) is suggested. **1985** *Sci. Amer.* July 50/1 If the protein alone is found to transmit scrapie, the workers will have determined what a prion is by making one. **1987** C. A. CLARKE *Human Genetics & Med.* (ed. 3) xii. 99 Scrapie . . is caused by an organism containing neither DNA nor RNA and called a prion.

**prior**, *a.* (*adv.*) Add: [A.] **e.** *ellipt.* as *n.* A prior conviction. Chiefly in *pl.* Cf. PREVIOUS *a.* 2 e. *U.S. slang.*
    **1978** J. WAMBAUGH *Black Marble* ix. 161 Burglary . . rarely drew a state prison term, unless you had lots of priors. **1985** E. LEONARD *Glitz* i. 13 The guy he killed was running on speed and trailing a life-time of priors, destined . . to crash and burn or die in jail.

**prioress**, *n.* For pronunciation read: ('praɪərɪs, praɪə'rɛs) and add: Hence **prioresship, prioress-ship** *ns.*, the (period of) office of a prioress.
    **1914** P. GUILDAY *Eng. Catholic Refugees on Continent* xi. 380 They were able to continue during the prioress-ship of Mother Margaret Clement in peace and amity. **1938** SR. MARY EMMANUEL *Life Sr. Marie de S. Pierre* iv. 40 Under the Prioresship of Mother Marguerite of the Blessed Sacrament . . the church was consecrated.

**prismane** ('prɪzmeɪn), *n. Chem.* [f. PRISM *n.* + -ANE.] Any saturated hydrocarbon whose molecule contains six carbon atoms linked together in the shape of a triangular prism; *spec.* the isomer of benzene, $C_6H_6$, which has this structure.
    **1964** *Tetrahedron Lett.* May 1418 Prismane or 'Ladenburg benzene' ($C_6H_6$), which has local $C_s$ symmetry, should have a $J_{C-H}$ of about 180 c.p.s. **1967** *New Scientist* 26 Jan. 220/1 The first pure and properly characterized derivative of 'prismane', as it is called, has been synthesized. **1972** DEPUY & CHAPMAN *Molec. Reactions & Photochem.* iv. 64 In this system a photostationary state . . is established which involves a benzvalene derivative, a prismane derivative, and a Dewar benzene derivative, as well as the two tri-*t*-butylbenzenes. **1983** McQUILLIN & BAIRD *Alicyclic Chem.* (ed. 2) viii. 191 It is therefore easy to understand the thermal stability of prismanes.

**prismatic**, *a.* Add: [2.] **b.** Of a measuring instrument: incorporating or making use of a prism or prisms. *prismatic binocular(s)* = *prism-binocular(s)* s.v. PRISM *n.* 7; *prismatic compass*, a surveying compass so arranged that by means of a prism the bearing of the object sighted can be read at the same time as the object itself is seen.
    **1859** F. A. GRIFFITHS *Artil. Man.* (1862) 371 The traversing may be performed . . with the Prismatic compass. **1865** *Reader* 7 Oct. 409/2 A useful little instrument, called by the inventor a 'Topograph' . . combines a plane table, prismatic compass, level, and cinometer. **1960** J. GLENDINNING *Princ. & Use Surveying Instruments* (ed. 2) II. xiii. 278 The prismatic astrolabe is designed specially for the determination of latitude and longitude. **1974** R. PEARSALL *Collecting & Restoring Sci. Instruments* iv. 99 True field glasses had to await 1859 for the Frenchman A. A. Boulanger to introduce prismatic binoculars.

**prison**, *n.* Add: [3.] [d.] **prison sentence**, a judicial sentence committing an offender to prison; the period of time served.
[**1904** *Northwestern Reporter* C. 5/1 The court.. may, in its discretion, impose a State's Prison sentence upon this class.] **1912** *Ibid.* CXXXV. 243/2 Defendant was persistent in saving his wife from a prison sentence. **1931** L. LE MESURIER *Boys in Trouble* xv. 162 If the Magistrate.. decides.. to.. give a short prison sentence.. what will happen during the actual period of the sentence? **1978** F. MACLEAN *Take Nine Spies* iv. 148 Kawai was simply given a short prison sentence.

**privateer**, *n.* Sense 5 in Dict. becomes 6. Add: **5.** *Motor Racing* (orig. and chiefly *U.S.*). A competitor who races at his own expense as a private individual, rather than as a member of a works team.
**1979** *Arizona Daily Star* 22 July C10/1 As a privateer, Serrano drove himself to the races and for the last half of the series even served as his own mechanic. **1985** *Dirt Bike* Mar. 45/1 (Advt.), 'Gold Superpro' is outrageously overdesigned and intended for working pros or serious privateers only. **1987** *Rally Sport* Jan. 67/3 Glyn Jones finished 14th, a fine effort for a privateer, in his Opel Manta 400.

**privatize**, *v.* Add: '**privatizer** *n.*
**1980** *Economist* 7 June 68/1 Treasury ministers, privatisers by instinct, are not worried about forgoing BNOC's potential oil profits. **1986** *Sun* (Melbourne) 10 Jan. 8/3 Last year, Mr Carlton described the Premier as the best privatiser in the business.

**privilege**, *n.* Add: [2.] **f.** An entitlement enjoyed by all the inmates of a penal or psychiatric institution as part of the normal regime, but which the authorities may withdraw as a punishment.
**1902** *Encycl. Brit.* XXXII. 7/2 The privilege of correspondence with friends outside and of receiving visits has been enlarged. **1954** STANTON & SCHWARTZ *Mental Hosp.* xii. 250 A mental hospital is a place where ordinary civil liberties are called 'privileges'. **1966** T. CAPOTE *In Cold Blood* IV. 265 The privileges granted ordinary prisoners were denied them; no radios or card games, not even an exercise period. **1969** W. S. BURROUGHS *Wild Boys* 27 Converted patients are allowed a quarter grain of morphine every night before lights out, a privilege which is withdrawn for any trespass. **1989** *Observer* 20 Aug. 30/2 The governor had told the women that to go to the toilet was not a right but a privilege and he withdrew that privilege.

**priviligentsia** (ˌprɪvɪlɪˈdʒɛntsɪə), *n. Pol.* Also **privilegentsia**. [Blend of PRIVILEGE *n.* and INTELLIGENTSIA *n.*] In Communist states, a class of intellectuals and party bureaucrats enjoying certain social and economic privileges over ordinary citizens (see *NOMENKLATURA *n.*); hence more widely, a class of any society regarded as enjoying or promoting privileged status.
**1960** *Guardian* 1 Apr. 8/3 That group of people whom Professor Shapiro very aptly called the Communist priviligentsia. *Ibid.* 8/5 The sudden rebellion of the Hungarian priviligentsia at the end of 1954. **1981** *Times Lit. Suppl.* 6 Mar. 258/2 Diverse, often contradictory, interests represented, subsidized and intimidated by the priviligentsia of federal bureaucracy. **1985** *Daily Tel.* 28 Jan. 16/1 An unholy alliance of Labour 'egalitarians' and the Tory 'priviligentsia'. **1987** *Economist* 30 May 72/2 These bureaucrats get their jobs under the nomenklatura or priviligentsia system, whereby Communist party members nominate their friends in return for kickbacks and privileged access to rationed goods. **1987** *Sunday Tel.* 9 Aug. 20/1 When technology is expanding as fast as it.. is now, freer markets bring

gains to everybody except the conservative privilegentsia.

**privity**, *n.* Add: [5.] **b.** *Maritime Law.* Responsibility for bringing about loss or damage, which may be treated as grounds for extending normally limited liability to the person(s) concerned.
[**1734** *Act* 7 Geo. II c. 15 §1 For ascertaining and settling how far Owners of Ships and Vessels shall be answerable for any Gold, [etc.].. which shall be made away with by the Masters or Mariners, without the Privity of the Owners thereof.] **1867** *Law Rep.: Admiralty & Ecclesiastical* (Council of Law Reporting) I. 106 The next question is, whether there is any privity. Perhaps there is some difficulty in that word; but, without laying down any precise rule.. the question is, whether there was any fault here to which it might be said the master was privy, according to the terms of the statute. **1965** *Mod. Law Rev.* XXVIII. v. 584 Section 503 [of the Merchant Shipping Act 1894].. provides that the owner of a ship shall not be liable to damages above a certain amount where, without his actual fault or privity, certain types of loss or damage are caused. **1979** *Fortune* 23 Apr. 22/3 In a number of cases, judges have discovered some fault or 'privity' on the part of the shipowner in causing the accident. Such privity—the appointment of an incompetent master, for example—may defeat limitation of liability.
[**6.**] **b.** *privity of contract*, the limitation of the contractual relationship to the two parties making a contract, which prevents any action at law by an interested third party such as a beneficiary.
**1650** T. IRELAND tr. *Abridgment of Coke's Reports* 59 Notwithstanding the assignement, and the privity of estate removed by the act of the Lessee himselfe the privity of contract remains. **1861** HURLSTONE & NORMAN *Exchequer Reports* V. 706 There are many cases in which the action will lie although there is no privity of contract. **1959** A. G. GUEST *Anson's Law of Contract* (ed. 21) iii. 86 It is a general rule of English law that a contract cannot confer any rights on one who is not a party to the contract, even though the very object of the contract may have been to benefit him... He is unable to sue because there is no privity of contract between him and the promisor. **1972** *Mod. Law Rev.* XXXV. I. 71 As an illustration of statute ignoring the malevolence of privity of contract the new Article iv bis provides a fine example.

**pro**, *prep.* and *a.* Add: [A.] [2.] **b.** pro 'bono *attrib. phr.* (*Law*, orig. and chiefly *U.S.*), of legal work: undertaken without charge, for the public good; also designating a lawyer who specializes in such work.
**1969** *New Republic* 11 Oct. 22/1 The big [legal] firms began to promise [young graduates] more free time to engage in *pro bono* work—the phrase used to describe work in the public interest such as representing indigents. **1970** *N.Y. Times* 23 Aug. 38/4 Until recently pro bono practitioners confined themselves to the representation of individual indigent clients in criminal and civil law. **1971** *Federal Suppl.* (U.S.) CCCXXIV. 1191/1 The resources of the bar for *pro bono* work are limited. **1979** B. MALAMUD *Dubin's Lives* ix. 359 I'd.. like to represent poor people in court. I like that pro bono stuff. **1982** 'E. LATHEN' *Green grow Dollars* xiii. 105 You don't learn much about patents doing pro bono work... I'm talking about damages. And you learn plenty about them in pro bono work. **1984** *Gainsville* (Florida) *Sun* 28 Mar. 2B/1 Davis had been a long-time pro bono volunteer attorney... Davis has handled more pro bono cases than any other attorney in the.. circuit.

**pro-**, *prefix*[1]. Add: [II.] [5.] [a.] **pro-'choice** *a.* and *n.* (orig. *U.S.*), in favour of upholding a woman's legal right to choose whether to have an abortion; also as *n.*, a pro-choice policy.

**1975** *Ms* Sept. 103/1 The legal battles .. have virtually all been decided in favor of pro-choice. **1976** W. W. WATTERS *Compulsory Parenthood* xiv. 241 The commonly used phrase 'pro-abortion', rather than the more accurate term 'pro-choice', is an example of this distortion. **1986** *Parl. Affairs* XXXIX. III. 363 'Pro-life' senators opposing those allied with the 'pro-choice' movement.

**pro-'family** *a.* (orig. and chiefly *U.S.*), promoting stable family life; *spec.* opposed to the legalizing of abortion.

**1977** *Washington Post* 13 July A4/1 Carter's 'pro-family' reform of a 'viciously anti-family' child welfare system. **1984** B. FRISHMAN *Amer. Families* i. 15 Some 'pro-family' activists .. noisily pressed their antiabortion and 'morality' platform.

**prob** (prɒb), *n.* [Shortened f. PROBLEM *n.*]
**1.** (With point.) Written abbrev. of PROBLEM *n.*, esp. in sense 5.
[**1795** C. HUTTON *Math. Dict.* II. 603/2 Newton Princip. lib. 1 prob. 22 proposes to describe a Trajectory that shall pass through five given points.] **1864** in WEBSTER. **1905** F. H. COLLINS *Author & Printer* 301/1 *Prob.*, probable, -ly, problem.
**2.** *colloq.* (Now usu. without point.) A problem or difficulty; *no prob*(*s*) = *no problem* s.v. PROBLEM *n.* 3 d.
**1934** WODEHOUSE *Thank you, Jeeves* xi. 146 Quite a prob., I mean to say, and I was still brooding on it when the garden gate clicked and I perceived Jeeves walking up the path. **1979** *Washington Post Mag.* 11 Feb. 13/1 'We are resp.,' he continued. 'We have ex. refs., we make 30,000 p., we have neither pets nor kids, we are avail. immed. What's our prob.?' **1983** McGOWAN & HANDS *Don't cry for me, Sergeant Major* iv. 77 'No probs,' said the Para's commanding officer ... 'He'll burn himself out in a couple of laps.'

**prob.** (prɒb), *adv.* Occas. (*colloq.*) without point. [Shortened f. PROBABLY *adv.*] Probably (*esp.* as a written abbrev.).
**1730** BAILEY *Dict. Britannicum* s.v. *Poach*, .. prob. of *pocher*, F to beat one's Eyes black and blue. **1887** D. DONALDSON Jamieson, Suppl., *Cup*, a term in golfing applied to a small cavity or hole in the course, prob. made by the stroke of a previous player. **1937** PARTRIDGE *Dict. Slang* 600/2 *Paddy's lantern*, the moon: nautical ... Prob. after parish-lantern. **1977** N. ADAM *Triplehip Cracksman* iv. 47 He was prob waiting for someone to come up.

**problematique** (ˌprɒbləmə'tiːk, ‖prɒblematik), *n.* [a. F. *problématique* (also used).] The complex of issues associated with a topic, considered collectively; *spec.* the totality of environmental and other problems affecting the world. Cf. PROBLEMATIC *n.*
**1972** *Washington Post* 2 Mar. A18/3 East and West will be working toward a unified version of what the Club of Rome calls the planet-wide *problematique*—all of mankind's worst problems rolled into one. **1974** A. KING in W. L. Oltmans *On Growth* xvi. 102 The environmental problems .. receive the most attention. Perhaps partly because they are the easiest part of this complex which we call the *problématique*. **1979** *Summary World Broadcasts: Eastern Europe* (B.B.C.) 29 Mar. A1 Much attention in these studies is attached to the problematique of deformation of socialism. **1981** *N.Y. Times Bk. Rev.* 4 Jan. 10/1 Mr. Muller expresses his central diagnosis of the 'world problematique', as the futurologists call it. **1985** *Christian Science Monitor* 6 Feb. 15/2 Soviet scholars responded with interest to reports issued by the Club of Rome on the 'world problématique'.

**problematize**, *v.* Restrict †*Obs. rare*⁻¹ to sense 1. Add: **2.** *trans.* To render problematic;

to view or interpret (an issue, etc.) as a problem requiring a solution.
**1910** G. SAINTSBURY in *Cambr. Hist. Eng. Lit.* V. 200 Hamlet himself is capable of being problematised to the *n*th. **1977** *Dædalus* Fall 66 Instead, the very setting up of such institutional arrangements was transposed from a given into a problem to be explained, or was 'problematized'. **1988** *Paragraph* XI. 239 It problematizes the notion of place; when we read the index we do not know whether or not the entries which it gives are themselves detached, displaced fragments.
Hence ˌproblemati'zation *n.*
**1983** *Social Sci. Citation Index 1976–1980* XVIII. 51210 (*title*) Governability—studies on its problematization. **1985** R. HURLEY tr. *Foucault's Hist. Sexuality* II. 10 How, why, and in what forms was sexuality constituted as a moral domain? Why this ethical concern that was so persistent despite its varying forms and intensity? Why this 'problematization'? **1988** *Paragraph* XI. 238 Barthes's continual problematization of his own actuality is strategic, then, and affirmative.

**procercoid** (prəʊ'sɜːkɔɪd), *n.* (and *a.*) *Zool.* [ad. F. *procercoïde* (F. Rosen 1918, in *Bull. Soc. Neuchateloise des Sci. Nat.* XLII. 43), f. Gr. κέρκος tail: see PRO-² 1, -OID.] The earliest parasitic form of the larval stage of certain tapeworms, in which the body is solid and has begun to develop a scolex but retains the posterior hooks found in the preceding embryonic stage. Also *attrib.* or as *adj.*
**1918** *Jrnl. Amer. Vet. Med. Assoc.* LIII. 359 The procercoid loses its hooks and the caudal appendix, if these have not already been lost in the copepod. **1927** *Jrnl. Parasitol.* XIV. 108 This larva resembled very closely the procercoid of D[*iphyllobothrium*] *latum* as figured by Janicki and Rosen. **1935** BORRADAILE & POTTS *Invertebrata* (ed. 2) vi. 229 The larva [in Tetrarhynchidea] which may be of either the procercoid or cysticercoid type occurs in marine invertebrates of many kinds, fish and occasionally reptiles. **1942** D. L. BELDING *Textbk. Clin. Parasitol.* xxv. 407 When the injected copepod is ingested by a suitable species of fresh-water fish, the procercoid larva penetrates the intestinal wall in a few days and enters the muscles, viscera and connective tissues. **1962, 1973** [see PLEROCERCOID *n.*]. **1987** *Oxf. Textbk. Med.* (ed. 2) I. v. 570/2 The procercoid larva or sparganum ingested by a human actively penetrates the intestinal wall to reach the peritoneal cavity, whence it begins to migrate systemically.

**prochloraz** (prəʊ'klɔːræz), *n. Chem.* and *Agric.* [f. PRO-¹ + CHLOR(O- + IMID)AZ(OLE *n.*] An imidazole derivative applied to a wide variety of plants as a systemic fungicide, esp. against eyespot disease.
**1977** *B.S.I. News* Nov. 23/1 Prochloraz. **1979** *Pesticide Sci.* X. 239 A comparison is made of the effects on B[*otrytis*] *cinerea* of vinclozolin, procymidone, iprodione and the related experimental fungicide *N*-propyl-*N*-[2-(2,4,6-trichlorophenoxy)-ethyl]-imidaole-1-carboxamide (prochloraz ..), which is also effective against this organism. **1984** *Ann. Appl. Biol.* CIV. Suppl. 44 The most effective fungicide, regarding the ability to decrease lesion spread, lesion number and sporulation was prochloraz. **1986** C. A. HEATON *Chem. Industry* v. 251 Prochloraz .. is a protectant and eradicant fungicide which is effective against a wide range of diseases affecting field crops, fruit and vegetables.

**prodd** (prɒd), *n.* Also 20 prod. [A mistranscription by Grose of *rodd* bow assembly of crossbow, in *Office MS 1 Ed. VI* (Soc. Antiquaries: reprinted in *Archæologia* (1800) XIII. 400).] **a.** A lightweight crossbow designed to shoot stones or bullets rather than bolts; cf. ARBALEST *n.* and STONE-BOW *n. Obs. exc. Hist.* **b.** The bow or bow assembly of a modern crossbow.

The MS should prob. be interpreted as reading '[components of] Crosbows called Rodds', in which case the first sense is not based on historical evidence. **1786** GROSE *Armour & Weapons* 59 There were two sorts of English cross bows, one called Latches, the other Prodds. **1824** MEYRICK *Ant. Armour* III. 48 The prodd was found as suitable for casting bullets as the barreled cross-bow. **1960** H. HAYWARD *Antique Coll.* 88/2 A light version of the cross-bow fitted with a sling to fire bullets or stones, and known as a prodd or stone-bow, was much used from medieval times onwards for shooting small game. **1965** F. BILSON *Bowmanship* vii. 117 By far the most efficient prods (or bows) used in the modern cross-bow are of composite construction. **1988** *Guns & Weapons* Autumn 92/1 In common with the majority of 'tracked' crossbows, the Prod assembly on the Spirit is set below centre.

**prodrug** ('prəʊdrʌg), *n. Biochem.* and *Physiol.* [f. PRO-² 1 + DRUG *n.*¹] Any (usu. biologically inactive) compound which may be metabolized *in vivo* to produce a drug; a compound from which a given drug is metabolized.
**1968** *Jrnl. Pharmaceutical Sci.* LVII. 779/2 Carbonate and carboxylate esters prepared as potential prodrugs of acetaminophen were shown to have a variety of physicochemical properties, particularly lipid and water solubilities. **1978** *Nature* 23 Nov. 405/1 As lipid-soluble drugs rapidly pass the blood-brain barrier, we synthesised a 'prodrug' from ADTN. **1985** *Jrnl. Med. Chem.* XXVIII. 108/1 Results with brain tissue in vitro and in vivo suggest that the compound behaves as a 'prodrug' which releases its GABA activity in the CNS following hydrolysis. **1989** *European Jrnl. Pharmacol.* CLIX. 257 (*heading*) Antiinflammatory action of salicylates: aspirin is not a prodrug for salicylate against rat carrageenin pleurisy.

**production**, *n.* Senses 3-7 in Dict. become 4-8. Add: [I.] **3.** *Linguistics.* In transformational grammar, a rewrite rule for the generation of expressions. Hence *transf.* in *Computing* and *Artificial Intelligence* = *production rule*, sense 8 c below.
**1960** Y. BAR-HILLEL et al. in *Bull. Research Council Israel* IX. F. 5 A simple phrase structure system .. is an ordered couple $\mathfrak{P} = (V, P)$, where .. *P* is a finite set of *productions* of the form $X \to x$ ($o \neq x \neq X$) (read: rewrite the symbol *X* by the nonempty string *x*.) **1980** C. S. FRENCH *Computer Sci.* xxviii. 233 Parsing is the process of defining the productions which when applied by recursion result in the given legal sentence or expression. **1984** P. H. WINSTON *Artificial Intelligence* (ed. 2) vi. 201 A production can mark an item in short-term memory. **1988** P. N. JOHNSON-LAIRD *Computer & Mind* xviii. 333 John Anderson has developed a semantic network that similarly does not decompose meanings but instead uses productions—the computational equivalent of meaning postulates .. —to make inferences.
[V.] [8.] [c.] **production rule** *Computing* and *Artificial Intelligence*, any rule which associates a particular condition with an action to be taken when the condition is satisfied.
**1971** B. BRAINERD *Introd. Math. of Language Study* iv. 155 Intuitively speaking, a production grammar is a finite set of rules, the production rules, which can be applied to certain strings in order to generate other strings. **1985** V. D. HUNT *Smart Robots* ii. 43 Because of their modular representation of knowledge and their easy expansion and modifiability, *production rules are now probably the most popular artificial intelligence knowledge representation, being chosen for most expert systems. **1988** P. N. JOHNSON-LAIRD *Computer & Mind* ix. 162 A grammar .. cannot do anything. It needs a

program to make use of it. Production rules similarly must rely on a program before they can do anything.

**productive**, *a.* (*n.*) Sense 1 c in Dict. becomes 1 d. Add: [A.] [1.] **c.** *Philol.* Of an affix or word element: readily or frequently used in the formation of new words.
**1902** *N.E.D.* s.v. *-lent* suffix, *-lentus* was a productive suffix. **1939** L. H. GRAY *Foundations of Lang.* vi. 161 If one of the components of a compound possesses so general a meaning that it readily admits of combination with a considerable number of words, it may become productive, i.e., it may become a regular formative element. **1968** B. FOSTER *Changing Eng. Lang.* iv. 188 Another productive ending which has been created quite unexpectedly .. is '*-burger*'. **1973** A. H. SOMMERSTEIN *Sound Pattern Anc. Greek* ii. 9 There is a productive suffix—τηριο—which forms adjectives from verb stems. **1980** *Amer. Speech* LV. 37 All three terms are semantically accessible and productive in the speech of the areas where they occur.

**profilin** (prəʊ'filın), *n. Biochem.* [f. PRO-¹ + FIL(AMENTOUS *a.* + ACT)IN *n.*] A protein which inhibits the polymerization of actin by binding to the monomer.
[**1976** L. G. TILNEY in *Jrnl. Cell Biol.* LXIX. 55/1 We will refer to the periacrosomal material subsequently as profilamentous actin or 'profil. actin'.] **1977** L. CARLSSON et al. in *Jrnl. Molecular Biol.* CXV. 466 We .. suggest that profilactin (qualified, if necessary, by the name of the source) is used as a general term for this non-filamentous form of actin in cells. From this nomenclature we derive the name profilin for the 16,000 molecular weight auxiliary protein (more specifically, spleen profilin for the protein in spleen extracts). **1984** HOLTZMAN & NOVIKOFF *Cells & Organelles* (ed. 3) II. xi. 285 Some of the proteins, like 'profilin', which is widely present, bind to G-actin and inhibit polymerization. **1989** *Jrnl. Biol. Chem.* CCLXIV. 4830/2 Addition of either gelsolin or profilin to PIP [*sc.* phosphatidylinositol 4-phosphate] vesicles does not cause their aggregation.

**progenote** (prəʊ'dʒiːnəʊt), *n. Microbiol.* [f. PRO-² + GEN(E *n.* + -ote after PROKARYOTE *n.*] The hypothetical ancestor of all prokaryotes and higher organisms, being supposedly either a single cell, a simpler biochemical entity, or one of a small number of either of these.
**1977** WOESE & FOX in *Jrnl. Molecular Evol.* X. 3 Such organisms would necessarily be on a level of complexity far simpler than the procaryotic. Organism[s] of this type, in the throes of evolving genotype-phenotype relationship, are properly designated *progenotes*. **1986** M. KOGUT tr. *Schlegel's Gen. Microbiol.* iii. 84 It is thought that the archaebacteria and the eubacteria both developed from primordial cells called progenotes. **1988** *Nature* 14 Jan. 111/3 The metabolic properties of the original cell (the progenote) are not specified in this method.

**project**, *v.* Add: [II.] [11.] **c.** To calculate or forecast on the basis of present trends. Cf. PROJECTION *n.* 7 d. Chiefly *Econ.*
**1961** *Ethical Outlook* XLVII. 93/2 Genuine human leadership .. can project long-term goals for itself. **1964** R. K. SRIVASTAVA *Projecting Manpower Demand* ii. 8 If manpower considerations are accepted as one of the criteria that ought to influence long-term economic planning, it becomes necessary to 'project' manpower demands for given future periods. **1977** *Sci. Amer.* Jan. 43/2 If 11 million 1977-model automobiles are sold in the U.S., as is projected [etc.]. **1986** *Times* 23 Dec. 17/7 Contrary to developments in past cyclical upturns, inflation is projected to remain relatively subdued.

**projectable** (prəʊ'dʒɛktəb(ə)l), *a.* [f. PROJECT *v.*
+ -ABLE.] That may be projected; capable of
being projected.
  **1909** in WEBSTER. **1973** T. PYNCHON *Gravity's
Rainbow* I. 126 He'd seen himself a point on a
moving wavefront, propagating through sterile
history—a known past, a projectable future. **1989**
*Advertising Age* 29 May 12/5 Asking a nationally
projectable sample to name the first advertising that
comes to mind.

**prolegomenon**, *n.* Add: c. *fig.* Something that
forms an introduction (*to* a subject, event, etc.);
a preliminary.
  **1964** I. L. HOROWITZ in I. L. Horowitz *New Sociol.*
43 Exhaustion of all relevant statistical .. knowledge
was a necessary prologemena [*sic*] to set forth key
classifications. **1973** *Times Lit. Suppl.* 6 Apr. 401/5
'The War of 1812', remembered, if at all, as a
prolegomenon of the launching, as a national hero, of
General Andrew Jackson. **1974** R. QUIRK *Linguist &
Eng. Lang.* iv. 70 The often unexciting data which
must constitute a prolegomenon to full critical
appraisal. **1984** A. CARTER *Nights at Circus* I. v. 89
The clock coughed up the prolegomena to its chime.
  ¶ **d.** The *pl.* form *prolegomena* used as the
*sing.*
  **1964** [see sense c above]. **1972** L. S. HEARNSHAW in
Cox & Dyson *20th-Cent. Mind* I. vii. 232 His book
was a prolegomena to .. social psychology. **1981** LD.
ANNAN *Politics of Broadcasting Enquiry* 3 This
prolegomena is not, I hope, the product of old age
and garrulous egotism.

**prolific**, *a.* Add: [2.] c. Of a creative artist:
producing much work.
  **1931** H. READ *Meaning of Art* II. 121 Delacroix was
one of the most prolific of painters. **1969** J. GROSS
*Rise & Fall Man of Letters* v. 132 An astonishingly
prolific writer, in his own time Lang enjoyed a dozen
different reputations: the collections of fairy tales and
the translations of Homer which keep his name
current represent only a fraction of his output. **1980**
'M. FONTEYN' *Magic of Dance* 271 The most
successful, and undoubtedly most prolific, house
composer was an Italian, Cesare Pugni, with three
hundred and twelve ballets to his credit. **1985** B.
GUEST *Herself Defined* iii. 29 May Sinclair was a
prolific novelist whose books sold well.

**PROLOG** ('prəʊlɒg), *n.* *Computing.* Also
Prolog. [f. PRO(GRAMMING *vbl. n.* + LOG(IC *n.*]
A high-level programming language derived
from Lisp and devised for use in artificial
intelligence.
  [**1975** P. ROUSSEL in *SIGPLAN Notices &
SIGART Newslet.* (1977) Aug. 115/2 (*title*) Prolog:
manuel de référence et d'utilisation.] **1977** *Ibid.* 109/1
Prolog is a very simple, but surprisingly powerful,
programming language developed at the University
of Marseille .. , as a practical tool for 'logic
programming'. **1978** *Computing Rev.* Mar. 126/2
This paper describes the structure and operation of
an interactive program system for statistical purposes,
PROLOG. **1984** *Listener* 1 Nov. 38/2 Dr Robert
Kowalski of Imperial College, London, a leading
expert in computer logic .. helped to develop
PROLOG, the computer language which the
Japanese have taken as their prototype for ICOT
research. **1985** *Times* 21 Mar. 36/4 (Advt.),
Experience in computer modelling, a knowledge of
LISP, PROLOG, POPLOG plus a good honours
degree in Maths, Physics or Computer Science.

‖**prominenti** (promi'nɛnti), *n.* *pl.* [It.
'prominent ones', pl. of n. f. the adj. *prominente*
prominent.] Prominent or eminent persons;
leading personages. Cf. PROMINENT *n.* 1 b.
  **1948** P. J. GRIGG *Prejudice & Judgment* ii. 52 A not
very successful effort was made to institute an annual
Civil Service dinner, .. attended by the professional
heads of the other services and *prominenti* from the

outside world. **1963** *Times* 24 Jan. 11/2 A person ..
under whom the various *prominenti* of the party will
be content to serve. **1978** 'J. HIGGINS' *Day of
Judgement* v. 69 It was an army group headquarters
for most of the war, then a prison for *prominenti*.
**1988** *Observer* 9 Oct. 17/4 Others among the
*prominenti* [in the Conservative Central Office] will
remain.

**promotable**, *a.* Add: Hence **promota'bility** *n.*,
suitability for promotion.
  **1961** in WEBSTER. **1976** *National Observer* (U.S.) 7
Aug. 11/3 Gibbs graduates are known for their
promotability. **1987** *Independent* 15 Jan. 6/6 All civil
service recruits are assessed early in their careers as
to their ultimate promotability to the very top jobs.

**pronate**, *v.* Add: **b.** *intr.* Of a limb, esp. the
forearm or (in running) the foot: to undergo
pronation. Of a person: to pronate a foot (while
running, etc.).
  **1912** A. H. TUBBY *Deformities* (ed. 2) I. III. xiv. 674
The readiness to pronate and the degree of pronation
is a measure of the weakness of a feeble foot. **1950**
MOREHOUSE & COOPER *Kinesiology* iv. 99 Exceptional
instances in which feet do not pronate have been
reported. **1984** *Which?* June 274/1 It's perfectly
possible to pronate on one foot and supinate on the
other! **1986** *Sci. Amer.* Mar. 94/3 Soft materials
allow the foot to shift and to pronate excessively.
This kind of movement is thought to be the cause of
some knee injuries.
  Hence 'pronating *vbl. n.* and *ppl. a.*
  **1890** W. JAMES *Princ. Psychol.* II. xx. 161 Pronating
movements .. are frequently indulged in when the
back of the fore-arm feels an object against it. **1978**
G. A. SHEEHAN *Running & Being* xi. 158 The
pronating or flattening foot sets up stresses and
torques.

**pronethalol** (prəʊ'nɛθəlɒl), *n.* *Pharm.* Also
**pronetalol** (-'nɛt-). [f. PRO(PYL *n.* + N(APHTHYL
*n.* + ETHA(NOL *n.* + *-O)LOL] A beta-
adrenoceptor blocking drug, 2-isopropyl-
amino-1-(2-naphthyl)ethanol, $C_{15}H_{19}NO$,
formerly used in the treatment of angina
and cardiac dysrhythmias. Superseded by its
structural derivative, propranolol.
  **1963** *Brit. Jrnl. Pharmacol.* XXI. 63 The
β-blocking agent pronethalol .. significantly reduced
the combined toxicity of yohimbine and imipramine.
**1964** *WHO Chron.* XVIII. 439 Pronetalol. **1972**
*Materials & Technol.* V. xxi. 810 Beta receptor
blocking drugs such as propranolol and pronethalol
find their application in the treatment of certain
cardiac conditions. **1987** *Molecular Pharmacol.*
XXXI. 101/2 Drugs with higher lipophilicity, such as
exaprolol, Kö-1124, alprenolol, propranolol,
metipranolol, doberol, and pronethalol, had a
severalfold higher perturbation effect at the
hydrocarbon membrane core than at the region close
to the polar lipid part.

**prong**, *n.*² Add: [2.] d. The penis. *coarse slang.*
  **1969** P. ROTH *Portnoy's Complaint* 133 What I am
standing there making with her hand on my prong is
in all probability my future! **1974** G. F. NEWMAN
*Price* v. 170 Feeling via his prong stimulated his
central nervous system, precipitating orgasm. **1984**
M. AMIS *Money* 22 This old prong has been sutured
and stitched together in a state-of-the-art cosmetics
lab.

**pronounceable**, *a.* Add: Hence
**pronouncea'bility** *n.*
  **1967** *Amer. Jrnl. Psychol.* LXXX. 416 In this
study, the effect of pronounceability on interference
is investigated. **1988** *English Today* July 38/2 Their
pronounceability makes them more like words than
other initialisms.

**pro-nuncio** (ˌprəʊ'nʌnʃɪəʊ, -sɪəʊ), *n.* R. C. Ch.
Also with capital initials and occas. as one

word. [ad. It. *pro-nunzio*: see PRO-¹ 4 and NUNCIO *n.*] A papal ambassador to a country which does not accord the Pope's ambassador automatic precedence over all other ambassadors.

**1965** *Tablet* 6 Nov. 1252/1 A new diplomatic post has been created by the Holy See—that of pro-nuncio. .. The new office of a pro-nuncio will allow the Holy See to send a diplomatic mission of ambassadorial rank to countries that do not accept the [1815] Congress of Vienna ruling. **1966** *Times* 18 Feb. 10/3 The Pro-Nuncio was devised in October of last year specifically for the cases of Zambia and Kenya, which would not have wanted full Nuncios. **1971** *Month* Mar. 67/1 Dr Simonis is rung up at his apartment .. by the Pronuncio. **1982** *Sunday Times* 17 Jan. 9/4 Our man at the Vatican, Sir Mark Heath, will become an ambassador; and the Vatican's man in London, Archbishop Bruno Heim, will be a pro-nuncio. **1986** *Tablet* 21 June 663/2 In welcoming the pro-nuncio, the president .. mentioned Jewish concern about the Carmelite convent at Auschwitz.

**property**, *n.* Add: [8.] [a.] **property income certificate** *Stock Market* (*temporary*), an investment unit entitling the holder to a share in the rental income of a property development; abbrev. *PINC* s.v. *P II. a.

**1986** *Estates Gaz.* 3 May 278/2 The unit to be held by investors and traded in the new market will be known as a *Property Income Certificate. **1986** *Daily Tel.* 6 Aug. 19/7 The taxman has given his scheme, called property income certificates .. at least half a nod of approval, by confirming its 'tax transparency'. **1989** *Financial Times* 15 July 4/3 The Pinc, the property income certificate, killed by the fact that the equity market does not value property as highly as the property industry.

**proposition**, *n.* Add: [6.] **c.** *euphem.* A proposal or invitation to engage in sexual intercourse; a sexual advance or 'pass'. Cf. PROPOSITION *v.* 2. orig. *U.S.*

**1942** BERREY & VAN DEN BARK *Amer. Thes. Slang* §354/2 *Proposition*, a proposal for an illicit love affair. **1958** I. BROWN *Words in Our Time* 88 There is thus a nice distinction between a proposal, which implies marriage, and a proposition, which does not. **1976** J. MASTERS *Himalayan Concerto* xiii. 161, I didn't take her up on a proposition she made me .. a bodily proposition. **1982** *Chicago Sun-Times* 25 Nov. 7/1 Some weeks ago I wrote about Karen Downs, an attractive woman who was sick of the catcalls and propositions she received every time she set foot outside her house.

‖**proprio motu** ('prɒprɪəʊ 'məʊt(j)uː), *adv. phr.* [late L., 'by his (its, etc.) own motion'.] = *EX PROPRIO MOTU *adv. phr.*

**1681** VISCT. STAIR *Modus Litigandi* 43 The Lords *proprio motu* will reject the Testimony. **1891** *Athenæum* 3 Jan. 20/1 For the time the question must be considered shelved, but the change must soon come, and will probably now be adopted by the universities *proprio motu*. **1894** G. N. CURZON *Probl. Far East* vii. 214 Realising that the foreigner, having once been allowed to meddle with Korea *proprio motu*, could not be permanently excluded from closer relations. **1932** *Scots Law Times Rep.* 25/1 The Commissioners .. have no power *proprio motu* to award a greater sum than £50. **1989** *All Eng. Law Rep.* 21 July 772 The volume of trade in PL(PI) products had become considerable because pharmacists were supplying them proprio motu.

**Protean**, *a.* Add: '**proteanism** *n.*, capacity for change; changeableness, variability.

**1951** R. HARGREAVES *This Happy Breed* vii. 77 The proteanism of his endless duties knows no limitation. **1982** *Times Lit. Suppl.* 9 Apr. 404/2 Some writers sport their proteanism like a badge of their power.

**pro'tectable**, *a.* [f. PROTECT *v.* + -ABLE.] Capable of being protected (esp. by legislation); = PROTECTIBLE *a.* Also, arousing protective feelings.

**1946** *Rep. Cases Supreme Court Indiana* CCXXIII. 484 The beer dealer's complaint shows clearly that no protectable property right is alleged. **1962** A. E. TURNER *Law Trade Secrets* III. i. 120 The distinction between protectable secret subject-matter, and 'personal' skill, knowledge and experience which the courts will not protect from use or disclosure. **1977** *Washington Post* 6 Nov. F3/5 She becomes flirtatious, girlish, sexy, infinitely protectable and appealing. **1986** *Christian Science Monitor* 21 Aug. 23/2 The right to change one's mind is probably as protectable as the public's right to know.

**proto-**, *comb. form.* Add: [2.] [b.] '**protostome** *Zool.*, an invertebrate animal whose mouth develops from the protostoma or opening to the blastopore.

**1959** L. H. HYMAN *Invertebrates* V. xxi. 605 The differing fate of the blastopore, becoming the anus in deuterostomes, the mouth in lophophorates and other *protostomes. **1989** *Development* CV. 244/2 Both in their appearance and timing, these cytoplasmic lobes resemble the meiotic polar lobes formed in protostomes such as the gastropod *Ilyanassa obsoleta*.

'**protovirus** *Microbiol.*, a body of genetic material which cannot reproduce but from which a virus may subsequently develop; *protovirus hypothesis*, a theory of oncogenesis (now discarded) involving such entities.

**1970** H. M. TEMIN in *Perspectives in Biol. & Med.* XIV. 22 This oncogene theory differs from the *protovirus theory proposed here ... The protovirus theory .. suggests that leukemia viruses do not preexist but arise from other elements, protoviruses, by genetic change. **1973** *Amer. Jrnl. Clin. Path.* LX. 19/2 The protovirus hypothesis states that a DNA polymerase-RNA complex (protovirus) is present in normal cells, that this complex has a special role in normal cell development, and that RNA tumor viruses evolved from this normal cellular protovirus. **1985** *Med. Hypotheses* XVIII. 154 The protovirus hypothesis .. which states that the information for cancer is apparently vertically transmitted also implies that cancer is endogenous to mankind.

**protocol**, *n.* Add: [5.] **d.** *Computing* and *Telecommunications.* A (usu. standardized) set of rules governing the exchange of data between given devices, or its transmission via a given communications channel.

**1966** MARILL & ROBERTS in *Proc. AFIPS Conf.* XXIX. 428/1 The establishment of a message protocol, by which we mean a uniform agreed-upon manner of exchanging messages between two computers in the network. **1972** *Proc. IEEE* LX. 1402/2 Sites with mass storage will generally wish to be accessible from other computers in the net, which generally requires the implementation of a full set of standard and specialized network protocols. **1980** *Sci. Amer.* Sept. 126 (Advt.), Other interface protocols are also available, including RS-232C, GP-Io (parallel), and BCD. **1986** *TeleLink* Sept./Oct. 9/3 The modem .. has set the standard for mobile modem communications using its own widely-accepted protocols.

**protruberance** *n.*, erron. var. *PROTUBERANCE *n.* (sense 3).

**protuberance**, *n.* Add: ¶3. With spelling *protruberance*, prob. influenced by *protrude*.

**1978** *Jrnl. S. Afr. Vet. Assoc.* XLIX. 62/2 Specimens of the .. internal occipital protruberance were taken for histopathological examination. **1985** *Canad. Jrnl. Microbiol.* XXXI. 698/2 Close inspection of many cells revealed that protruberances and germ tubes emanated from all aspects of the cell surface . . . Protruberances were extensions of the cytoplasm.

**provider**, n. Add: **b.** spec. One who provides the means to support a family, a bread-winner. Freq. as *good provider*.

1862 C. F. BROWNE *A. Ward his Book* 226 Then I axed him was Lewis a good provider? 1885 I. M. RITTENHOUSE *Jrnl.* 25 Sept. in *Maud* (1939) xi. 358 He knew Elmer to be reliable and steady, one who would be always a good 'provider' and take care of me. 1914 in H. Wentworth *Amer. Dial. Dict.* (1944) 480/1 A generous husband. A good purveder. 1969 P. ROTH *Portnoy's Complaint* 149 Just think of the years to come—her two babies without a father, herself without a husband and provider. 1986 R. FRAME *Long Weekend* (1988) 28 His wife became the provider, living on her wits, and he became the dependent.

**Provie** ('prɒvɪ), n. (and a.) *colloq.* Also Provvie. [Abbrev. of PROVISIONAL *a.* (*n.*)] A member of the Provisional I.R.A.; = PROVO *n.*[3] Freq. in *pl.* Also *attrib.* or as *adj.*

1972 *Guardian* 8 May 1/2 The 'Provvies' (Provisional IRA). 1975 G. SEYMOUR *Harry's Game* iv. 55 Those Provie rats who could murder a man in front of his bairns. 1977 J. JOHNSTON *Shadows on our Skin* (1979) 36 She thinks, you know, you'll get mixed up with the Provies. 1983 *Observer* 13 Nov. 7/2, I was surprised when he became a Provie.

**provisional**, a. and n. Add: [A.] [1.] **c.** Of a postage stamp: put into circulation temporarily, usu. owing to the unavailability of the definitive issue.

1911 *Dict. Philatelic Terms & Phrases* 143 'Provisional stamps' are those intended to meet a temporary need, usually due to failure of supply, sometimes owing to stamps being required urgently and there being no time to prepare a design, and such stamps may be bisected . . or surcharged. 1929 K. B. STILES *Stamps* i. 7 'Tentative' is exactly the word to describe provisional stamps. It implies that they are to be in postal use for *a short while only.* 1979 R. CABEEN *Stand. Handbk. Stamp Collecting* 435 Unless the reason for the provisional issue disappears within a short time, the stamp or stamps are replaced by definitive issues.

[B.] [1.] For def. read: Something that is provisional, *esp.* a provisional stamp. (Earlier and later examples.)

1885 E. B. EVANS *Philatelic Handbk.* 93 *Ecquador* . . Provisionals. *Black* surcharge; value in words in two lines. 1912 *Gloss.* (Philatelic Congress Gt. Brit.) 21 *Provisionals,* stamps temporarily put into circulation, usually when the supply of a certain value has been exhausted. 1929 K. B. STILES *Stamps* i. 7 A striking illustration of definitives and provisionals is to be found in the postal history of Portugal. 1975 B. GUNSTON *Philatelist's Compan.* 246 Provisionals may be crude local productions, reprinted issues from another country, or an issue overprinted by a successful revolutionary administration.

**prowess**, n. Restrict 'Now chiefly *literary*' to sense 1 a and add: [1.] **c.** Exceptional ability or talent (in a particular field or undertaking); skill, expertise.

1916 JOYCE *Portrait of Artist* (1969) 181 Side by side with his memory of the deeds of prowess of his uncle Mat Davin, the athlete, the young peasant worshipped the sorrowful legend of Ireland. 1928 E. O'NEILL *Strange Interlude* I. 20 The boy, for all his good looks and prowess in sport and his courses, really came of common people and had no money of his own. 1940 W. FAULKNER *Hamlet* II. ii. 126 His reputation as a gambler . . got him the obedience of the negro field hands even more than . . his proved prowess with a pistol. 1965 'MALCOLM X' *Autobiogr.*

ii. 31, I didn't yet appreciate how most whites accord to the Negro this reputation for prodigious sexual prowess. 1974 'J. HERRIOT' *Vet in Harness* (1975) xii. 89 Siegfried's prowess as an animal doctor was highly regarded. 1987 N. F. DIXON *Our Own Worst Enemy* (1988) xi. 171 We continue to assess mental prowess by such ridiculous contests as *Mastermind.*

**proximal**, a. (*n.*) Add: [A.] [2.] **d.** Geol. Designating or characteristic of an area close to a sedimentation zone, volcanic vent, or other region of geological activity.

1949 F. J. PETTIJOHN *Sedimentary Rocks* xiv. 444 The terms 'proximal', 'axial', or 'distal' also may be applied to the deposits according to their position in the trough of deposition. The proximal sediments are those coarse clastics nearest the source area. 1978 *Nature* 20 July 242/1 The dominant rock in the psammitic formations is a very proximal thick-bedded lithic greywacke with thin silty or shaly partings. 1985 THORPE & BROWN *Field Descr. Igneous Rocks* v. 55 The proximal zone (*ca.* 5–15 km from the central vent) has a higher proportion of lava flows, with a variety of pyroclastic flow deposits.

**Prufrockian** (pruːˈfrɒkɪən), a. [f. the name of J. Alfred *Prufrock,* the central character of T. S. Eliot's poem *The Love Song of J. Alfred Prufrock* (1917), + -IAN.] Resembling or characteristic of the timid, passive Prufrock or his world of middle-class conformity and unfulfilled aspirations.

1977 L. GORDON *Eliot's Early Years* iii. 62 It is a logical, if extreme, answer to the Prufrockian world of ridiculous conformity. 1979 S. WEINTRAUB *London Yankees* x. 357 A middle-aged man . . confesses his understanding . . in Prufrockian terms. 1981 N. POLK in W. Faulkner *Sanctuary* (Afterword) 297 Horace Benbow . . is an effete, timorous, Prufrockian figure who wallows in a fashionable and literary sort of nihilism. 1989 *Sunday Times* 25 June G3/3 He is not really Prufrockian. After Oxford he got a lectureship at Uppsala, where emancipated Swedish women 'sorted him out' sexually with a directness that would have horrified Prufrock.

‖**prunelle** (prynɛl), n. [Fr., = sloe, f. *prune* plum + dim. suffix *-elle*; cf. PRUNELLO *n.*] A French sloe brandy.

[1899 *Wine Trade Rev.* 15 Jan. 71/1 (Advt.), Crême de Menthe, Prunelle de Bourgogne, & Crême de Cassis: Simon Aîné, Chalons s/Saône. Agents: R. R. Mège & Co.] 1917 *Harrods Catal.* 1292/1 Prunelle—Cusenier's . . Simon Aîné, stone bottles. 1946 A. L. SIMON *Conc. Encycl. Gastron.* VIII. 134/2 *Prunelle,* a French liqueur, the informing flavour of which is that of fresh sloes. 1973 M. A. SINCLAIR tr. *Simenon's Maigret & M. Charles* vi. 132 He . . poured himself a small glass of *prunelle.*

**pseudo-**, *comb. form.* Add: [2.] [a.] 'pseudo-,cleft *a.* Linguistics, applied to a two-clause sentence derived by transformation from a single clause, resembling a *cleft sentence* (see CLEFT *ppl. a.* d) but conveying emphasis typically through the use of a relative *wh*-nominal clause (as 'what we want is *x*' from 'we want *x*'); similarly *pseudo-cleft transformation,* etc.; also *absol.* as *n.*

1967 P. S. ROSENBAUM in *Jrnl. Linguistics* III. 114 The grammaticality of the corresponding passive sentence (66a) and the pseudo-cleft (66b) is evidence that the string that she drinks beer is a noun phrase complement sentence. 1967 —— *Gram. Eng. Predicate Complement Constructions* iv. 75 The pronominal head of this construction no longer exists in a form to which the pseudocleft sentence transformations can apply. 1976 *Archivum Linguisticum* VII. 122 Pseudo-cleft sentences, as well as cleft sentences, may be regarded as the result of the topicalization of . . simple declarative sentences.

**1977** *Language* LIII. 338 While a pseudo-cleft transformation can apply to sentences whose matrix verb is *hate*.., it cannot apply to sentences with *endeavor*. **1979** *Trans. Philol. Soc.* 34 Pseudo-cleft variants such as:.. What I am waiting *for* is *for* Mary to leave where both occurrences of *for* (italicized) appear overtly. **1985** *Word* XXXVI. I. 3 These two examples illustrate what is probably the most general and widespread function of pseudo-clefts in discourse: the highlighting of theme.

also **'pseudo-clefting**, the process of transforming a sentence into a pseudo-cleft sentence.
**1975** *Language* LI. 40 In Spanish.. \*pseudo-clefting applies to all kinds of NP's alike. **1978** *Amer. Speech* LIII. 24 In the following transforms, for example, clefting and pseudoclefting move *you* into a position of prominence and cause it to lose a possible impersonal interpretation.

**'pseudoprime** *Math.*, any integer *p* which is such that $a^p - a$ is a multiple of *p* for a given positive integer (or base) *a*, or (in full *absolute pseudoprime*) for all positive integers *a*; also occas. as *adj.*
**1971** G. E. ANDREWS *Number Theory* 258/1 (Index), \*Pseudo-primes. **1978** *Amer. Math. Monthly* LXXXV. 293, 561 (= 3 x 11 x 17) is an 'absolute pseudoprime', i.e. it divides $a^{561}$ - a for every a. **1980** *Math. of Computation* XXXV. 1003 We investigate the properties of three special types of pseudoprimes: Euler pseudoprimes, strong pseudoprimes, and Carmichael numbers. **1988** H. E. ROSE *Course in Number Theory* i. 12 Extremely efficient methods exist for checking whether or not an integer is pseudoprime with respect to some fixed integer *n*.

**psychographic**, *a.* and *n.* Add: [A.] **2.** Of or pertaining to psychographics. orig. *U.S.*
**1975** *Chemical Week* 6 Aug. 21/2 Other types of marketers concentrate on sophisticated demographic and psychographic analyses of customers' attitudes toward products. **1986** *Times* 5 Aug. 2/1 A series of standard questions which classify people into one of nine groups.. known in the jargon of the market research trade as a 'psychographic' system. **1989** *Precision Marketing* 29 May 1/1 The flexible scoring system enables the building society to examine the transaction details and psychographic characteristics of its customers.
**B.** *n. pl.* The study and classification of members of a community according to their attitudes, aspirations, etc., esp. in market research. Cf. DEMOGRAPHIC *n.* orig. *U.S.*
**1968** *N.Y. Times* 4 Jan. 61/3 He lists these magazines in an ad Holiday will soon be running that will announce its entry into the wonderful world of 'psychographics'. **1976** *Business Week* 13 Dec. 47/2 Data on demographics, psychographics (measurement of attitudes) and life-style are being fed into retailers' computers. **1983** *Maclean's* 19 Sept. 19/3 De Jong cited the Tories' use of 'psychographics'—a neo-conservative tactic that groups people by attitudes rather than the traditional demographics of age, employment or income. **1987** *Times* 13 June 28/4 Central to the Y & R findings were the concerns of a central group of voters—comprising about 40 per cent of the population and known in psychographics as 'mainstreamers' or 'belongers'.

**pteranodon** (tə'rænəʊdɒn, -nədən), *n. Palæont.* [f. mod.L. *Pteranodon* (O. C. Marsh 1876, in *Amer. Jrnl. Sci. & Arts* XI. 507): see PTERANODONT *n.*] = PTERANODONT *n.*
**1881** *Amer Jrnl. Sci.* XXI. 343 In the same geological horizon with the gigantic forms (Pteranodon beds), the remains of a small Pterodactyl have been found. **1885** C. F. HOLDER *Marvels Anim. Life* 202 The great bat-like creature.. was at one time very common on this continent [America], and was a flying reptile known as the Pteranodon. It differed from the European Pterodactyles in being

toothless. **1924** C. SCHUCHERT *Text-bk. Geol.* (ed. 2) II. xxxvi. 526 The pteranodons were the organic aëroplanes of Cretaceous time. **1958** W. H. JOHNSTON tr. *Fochler-Hauke's Our World & its Beginnings* viii. 230 The saurians gradually evolved into veritable giants. So far as is known the record is held by the pteranodon (i.e. the toothless flyer) which inhabited North America in the Cretaceous period. **1975** G. EWART *Be my Guest!* I. 14 You had no family Winging pteranodons. **1989** *New Scientist* 26 Aug. 59/1 A static model.. of a pteranodon hanging from the roof.

**pterodactyloid** (tɛrəʊ'dæktɪlɔɪd), *a.* and *n. Palæont.* [f. PTERODACTYL *n.* + -OID.] **A.** *adj.* Having the form or character of a pterodactyl; *spec.* belonging to the extinct suborder Pterodactyloidea of pterosaurs of the late Jurassic and Cretaceous, characterized by a long neck and a small or vestigial tail. **B.** *n.* A pterodactyloid pterosaur.
**1895** *Funk's Stand. Dict.*, Pterodactyloid, a. & n. **1933** A. S. ROMER *Vertebr. Paleont.* viii. 177 In the Jurassic there appeared a second, derived group, the pterodactyloids. **1954** W. E. SWINTON *Fossil Amphibians & Reptiles* xiii. 95 The Pterodactyloid and Rhamphorhynchoid reptiles are all of Jurassic age. **1977** A. HALLAM *Planet Earth* 273 An unusual recent find was the partial skeleton of an enormous pterodactyloid, *Quetzalcoatlus*. **1985** D. NORMAN *Illustr. Encycl. Dinosaurs* 171/1 (*caption*) Here we see a typical medium to large-sized 'rhamphorhynchoid' with 6·6ft (2m) wing-span.. and a large 'pterodactyloid' with 39ft (12m) wing-span.

**pub** (pʌb), *n.*[2] Chiefly *colloq.* Also with point. [Shortened from PUBLICATION *n.*; cf. \*PUB *v.*[2]] = PUBLICATION *n.* 2; also in titles = publications. Freq. as *pub date.*
**1904** RICHARDSON & MORSE *Writings on Amer. Hist.*, *1902* p. xvi, Colonial Society of Massachusetts Publications. Boston. Pub Col Soc of Mass. **1929** G. G. GRIFFIN *Ann. Rep. Amer. Hist. Assoc.*, *1925* p. xv, Am. Jew. hist. soc. pub. American Jewish historical society, publications, N.Y. **1973** *Publishers Weekly* 13 Aug. 30/2 Mark Twain.. decided to publish 'Huckleberry Finn' by subscription in advance of publication. After pub date, Twain received an unexpected publicity break. **1987** *Boxing News* 21 Aug. 3/3 Your *Boxing News* has all of the USA boxing pubs.. beat by a mile.

**pub** (pʌb), *v.*[2] Also with point. [Shortened from *publish(ed)*: see PUBLISH *v.*; cf. \*PUB *n.*[2]] **a.** *pa. pple.* Of a book, etc.: published. (Chiefly as a written abbreviation.) **b.** *trans.* = PUBLISH *v.* 4 a. Chiefly *colloq.*
**1877** W. WHITMAN *Daybks. & Notebks.* (1978) I. 70 Williams's copper plate Map of US, Canada, Central Am, West Indies pub by Brenner & Atwood 402 Locust st Phil. **1888** *Ibid.* II. 451 Pieces pub'd in Herald. **1959** *Official Gaz.* (U.S. Patent Office) 19 Nov. TM64/1 Representation of gladiator on a shield .. Pub. 8-25-59. **1977** in *Amer. Speech* (1982) LVII. 28 Boowatt is pubbed by Garth Danielson. **1978** PURDY & MILLGATE *Coll. Lett. T. Hardy* I. 102 Tauchnitz paid £60 to pub. *A Laodicean* later in 1882.

**published**, *ppl. a.* Add: [1.] **b.** Of a writer: that has appeared in print; having had works published.
**1864** J. A. SYMONDS *Let.* 6 July (1967) I. 488 If you come with Green & me you will have all the published Dramatists, tutti quanti, to read at pleasure. **1976** *Economist* 1 May 124/1 She was a published poet while still at university. **1989** *Chicago Tribune* 13 Aug. VI. 5/4 What more could happen to a person (or a person's gray-haired, size 14 mother) after 50? Even one who had been a published writer?

**Puebloan** (puːˈɛblʊən, ˈpwɛblʊən), a. Also with lower-case initial. [f. PUEBLO n. + -AN.] Of, pertaining to, or characteristic of Pueblo Indians or their culture. Also **Pueblan** a.

**1895** Funk's Stand. Dict. II. 1444/2 Pueblan architecture, the style of American aboriginal architecture exhibited in buildings and remains in Mexico, New Mexico and Arizona. **1931** Discovery Dec. 374/2 Investigations . . on behalf of the Bureau of American Ethnology, have thrown valuable light on the stage of development reached in the late Basket Maker and early Puebloan phases. **1937** Southwestern Lore Sept. 30 A few dish-like vessels . . were also found, which are definitely not Puebloan but are Hohokam. **1987** Amer. Anthropologist LXXXIX. 999/1 Fieldwork on this puebloan ruin situated under a rock overhang in the canyon wall continued from 1970 through 1973.

**puerilism** (ˈpjuːərɪlɪz(ə)m), n. Psychol. and Psychiatry. [prob. ad. F. puérilisme childishness: see PUERILE a. and -ISM.] The state or condition of behaving like a child; childish behaviour; spec. (a) (in an adult) a reversion to infantile behaviour, usu. as a symptom of mental disorder; (b) (in a child) that stage of normal development which follows infantilism and precedes puberty.

**1934** H. C. WARREN Dict. Psychol. 218/2 Puerilism, a condition of mental non-development or degeneration, in which the patient's mental processes and behavior seem to return to the immature type characteristic of childhood or early adolescence. **1936** J. HUIZINGA In Shadow of Tomorrow xvi. 150 This quality I have ventured to call by the name of Puerilism, as being the most appropriate appellation for that blend of adolescence and barbarity which has been rampant all over the world for the last two or three decades. **1940** L. HINSIE Psychiatric Dict. 451/2 From the standpoint of psychiatry puerilism is childishness; it is the stage following infantilism or infantility and is followed by the stage of puberism or puberty. **1979** C. LASCH Culture of Narcissism V. 103 They play with the 'blend of adolescence and barbarity' that Huizinga calls puerilism. **1987** New Scientist 5 Mar. 58/4 Guy Troughton's illustrations are particularly frustrating, however, ranging from the enchanting and accurate to examples of puerilism.

**puff**, n. Sense 2 d in Dict. becomes 2 e. Add: [**2.**] **d.** A lightweight bed-covering filled with cotton, down, or some other material; a quilted coverlet or duvet. Chiefly N. Amer.

**1907** Dialect Notes III. 248 Puff, a bed covering filled with cotton. Recent. **1939** L. M. MONTGOMERY Anne of Ingleside viii. 52 Mrs Parker considerately left a candle with him and a warm puff, for the July night was unreasonably cold. **1976** New Yorker 3 May 40/1 'I'll say one thing about that old puff,' she says. 'I spent many a night of our marriage sewing the panels where they were ripped.' **1986** R. B. PARKER Taming Sea-Horse (1987) x. 63 An unfolded sofa bed unmade with . . silk sheets and a pale gray puff comforter.

**puff-ball**, n. Add: **4.** Fashion. A short full skirt which is gathered in round the hemline to produce a soft, puffy, billowing form. Usu. attrib., as puffball dress, skirt, etc.

[**1960** Times 27 Jan. 12/5 The important silhouette for dresses for after five o'clock is best described as a slender but loosely fitting sheath . . with puff-ball drapery.] **1968** J. IRONSIDE Fashion Alphabet 46 Puffball: See Balloon. **1986** Artseen Dec. 14 (Advt.), Astrakhan Puffball skirt £145. **1987** Times 9 June 25/1 Christian Lacroix, the Paris designer, . . is credited with introducing the pouffe, otherwise known as the puffball, into the grandest parties. **1988** Sunday Mail (Brisbane) 16 Oct. 17/2 She has abandoned skintight leathers and puffball minis, platinum rinses and bootlace ties.

**puffinosis** (pʌfɪˈnəʊsɪs), n. Ornith. [f. mod.L. Puffin-us + -OSIS.] An epizootic viral disease of sea-birds, originally observed in the Manx shearwater, Puffinus puffinus.

**1948** MILES & STOKER in Nature 26 June 1017/1 We suggest that the name 'puffinosis' is suitable for this epizootic disease of Puffinus puffinus puffinus. **1953** Jrnl. Animal Ecol. XXII. 131 Though our evidence is scanty we suggest, tentatively, that puffinosis may be primarily a disease of gulls of several species and exist over a wide area. **1965** Brit. Birds LVIII. 432 In 1965 some young Oystercatchers Haematopus ostralegus were found dying with blistered and swollen legs and feet; these were all in areas where puffinosis occurs and it is possible that they were suffering from the disease. **1977** S. CRAMP et al. Birds W. Palearctic I. 148/2 Colonial nesting [amongst Manx shearwaters] may be advantageous in reducing predation, though disadvantageous in facilitating interference between pairs (causing egg losses) and spread of epizootics of puffinosis. **1982** Arch. Virol. LXXIII. 1 The most common clinical sign of puffinosis is blisters on the webs of the feet . . , although conjunctivitis and locking of the ankle joint of the legs . . have also been observed.

**Puginian** (pjuːˈdʒɪnɪən), a. [f. the name of A. W. N. Pugin (see PUGINESQUE a.) + -IAN.] Of or relating to Pugin or his style and philosophy of architecture; = PUGINESQUE a.

**1976** Connoisseur CXCI. 10/3 The impressive buffet stacked with Puginian plate. **1977** D. WATKIN Morality & Archit. II. ii. 40 Here we have a clearly stated Puginian view of architecture as essentially a socially manipulative force. **1978** Archit. Design XLVIII. 318/1 A Puginian fear of symmetry. **1986** Country Life 18 Dec. 1962/1 At the House of Lords . . Puginian principles of honest construction might have been thought to apply.

**pull**, n.² Add: [**I.**] Sense I. 6 in Dict. becomes I. 7; senses II. 7-10 become II. 8-10 and III. 11. For introductory text read: The act, action, faculty, or result of pulling. [**5.**] **b.** A drawing-in or inhalation of smoke from a cigarette, pipe, etc.; = DRAW n. 1 e.

**1889** P. H. EMERSON Eng. Idyls 46 ''Bout-four-an'-a-half-mile,' jerked out Ben, between strong pulls at his pipe. **1903** T. P.'s Weekly 6 Nov. 724/2 After a dozen meditative pulls of his pipe, Harry proceeded. **1953** J. WAIN Hurry on Down 99 Bunder's eyes narrowed a little, and he took a pull at his cigarette. **1965** R. P. JHABVALA Backward Place iv. 233 She took a long pull from her cigarette and filled her lungs with smoke. **1983** G. LORD Tooth & Claw ix. 66 'Jeez,' he continued after a long pull on his smoke.

**6.** A pulled muscle or tendon (esp. in Sport); = STRAIN n.² 4. colloq.

**1938** A. THORNDIKE Athletic Injuries vii. 62 Injuries to muscles and tendons produced by muscular contraction are of great interest. Masquerading under the term 'pull', these injuries often constitute a serious and painful lesion. **1961** K. RAWLINSON Mod. Athletic Training x. 99 If the pull is in the tendon . . we strap in as in figure 34. **1978** G. A. SHEEHAN Running & Being xi. 157 Hamstring pulls . . were thought to be due to the enormous number of footstrikes occurring per hour.

**pull**, v. Sense 6 a in Dict. becomes 6; sense 6 b is deleted. Add: [**I.**] [**1.**] **g.** Computing. To retrieve (a piece of data, etc.) from the 'top' of a stack (STACK n. 1 f). Also const. up and absol. Opp. *PUSH v. 1 o. Cf. *POP v.¹ 11.

**1967** Proc. AFIPS Conf. XXX. 495/1 The cycle time is 1 μsec for either write and push down one step or read and pull up one step. **1980** Redbook Oct. 4/2 I've learned recently how to collapse data, how to pull tables and how to scan the banners. **1985** Austral. Personal Computer Oct. 181/3 The inverse operation, taking a number from the stack, is called 'pulling' the number, or 'popping' it from the stack.

[III.] [17.] c. *N. Amer. Sport.* To withdraw (a player) from the game; *to pull the goalie* (*Ice Hockey*), to replace the goalkeeper during the course of a game with an additional attacking player. Also, to disqualify (a competitor).

**1942** BERREY & VAN DEN BARK *Amer. Thes. Slang* §645/2 Retire a player . . .*pull.* **1968** *Globe & Mail* (Toronto) 5 Feb. 18/7 Marlboros pulled goalie Gerry McNamara and Obie O'Brien fired the puck into an empty net. **1976** *Washington Post* 19 Apr. D3/2 With . . Quebec goalie Richard Brodeur pulled in favor of a sixth attacker, McLeod stopped a blistering shot from Serge Bernier. **1980** *Running* Sept. 40/3 We saw . . the sensational disqualification of joint leaders Bautista and . . home favourite, Anatoly Solomin. In fact, four of the leading eight at 5 km were later 'pulled', along with three others from the pack.

**d.** *intr. Amer. Football.* Of a lineman (esp. a guard): to withdraw from and cross behind the line of scrimmage to block opposing players and clear the way for a runner.

**1942** J. DA GROSA *Functional Football* (ed. 2) vi. 144 The defensive man can pull to either direction. **1956** A. DANZIG *Hist. Amer. Football* III. 19/1 We started doing this in 1934 and found that a center could snap the ball and pull in one movement. **1969** BENGTSON & HUNT *Packer Dynasty* II. 16 A former guard, he knew well who it is who opens holes . . 'pulls' suddenly from his usual position to complete special assignments. **1991** *Don Heinrich's Pro Preview* 96/2 Surprisingly, he does his best work running and pulling. He plays too high to be a consistent in-line drive blocker.

**e.** *trans.* To take back into one's possession or control; to recall or rescind (a document); hence, to withdraw from publication, circulation, or use; *spec.* to cancel or revoke (a business deal, esp. a share issue). Also *absol. colloq.* (orig. *U.S.*).

**1967** S. FAESSLER in *Atlantic Monthly* Apr. 107/1 One day a month was given over to repossessing merchandise from deadbeats. 'Today I am pulling,' he would say grimly. **1972** H. KEMELMAN *Monday the Rabbi took Off* xlv. 263 'They [*sc.* the police] pulled his passport, didn't they?' 'No . . . Officially they had just mislaid it.' **1973** R. HAYES *Hungarian Game* lii. 312 He had moved easily in dip circles until the . . State pulled his visa. **1978** G. BORDMAN *Amer. Musical Theatre* ii. 96 Previous commitments forced it to be pulled when its initial booking ended. **1986** *Times* 11 Oct. 21/5 Some dealers were convinced the deal had been pulled at the last minute after a disagreement over the price. **1987** *Economist* 24 Oct. 29/2 Many in the City thought the chancellor . . would lose his nerve and pull the issue.

**pulling,** *ppl. a.* Add: **b.** *pulling guard* (*Amer. Football*), an offensive guard who withdraws or pulls back from the line of scrimmage to block for a runner: see *PULL v.* 17 d. Also *pulling lineman,* etc.

**1958** J. HOLGATE *Fundamental Football* iv. 27 Notice in Figure 4-7e how the pulling lineman points his toes as he steps off to his right. **1964** *Sports Illustr.* 5 Oct. 73/1 His best play is a sprintout run-pass option when he fakes to the fullback and follows both pulling guards. **1977** *Washington Post* 18 Sept. (Mag. section) 19/3 Paul Zimmerman . . moonlighted as a pulling guard for the Paterson (New Jersey) Pioneers. **1988** *Gridiron* Nov. 54/1 It's a very simple play in which . . you bring a pulling guard to the left side of the field while everybody else blocks down.

**pumpkin,** *n.* Add: [2.] **c.** As an endearment, esp. for children. (Also with hypocoristic suffix -s². ) *U.S. colloq.*

**1942** BERREY & VAN DEN BARK *Amer. Thes. Slang* §185/2 *Terms of endearment,* . . pumpkins. **1980**

*Verbatim* Summer 18/1 Edible terms as endearments. . . Punkin. **1987** J. WILCOX *Miss Undine's Living Room* ii. 23 Listen, pumpkin, I thought you ought to know.

**punctuated,** *ppl. a.* Add: **3.** *punctuated equilibrium* (*Biol.*), a view of evolution as proceeding by isolated outbursts of rapid speciation between long periods of little or no change; evolutionary development of this kind.

**1972** ELDREDGE & GOULD in T. J. M. Schopf *Models in Paleobiol.* 109 We have . . named our alternate picture . . punctuated equilibria. **1978** *Evolutionary Biol.* XI. 596 (*caption*) In the actual example of punctuated equilibrium reported on . . the change between two species of the same genus . . was actually observed. **1981** *Nature* 9 July 116/1 Recent sophisticated geochronological studies have provided sufficiently precise dates for existing fossil material to test the hypothesis of punctuated equilibrium. **1985** S. J. GOULD in *Times Lit. Suppl.* 18 Jan. 70/1, I have always wanted to learn more (as an originator of punctuated equilibrium) about Huxley's commitment to saltationism.

**punctuation,** *n.* Sense 6 in Dict. becomes 7. Add: **6.** *Biol.* Rapid or sudden speciation, as suggested by the theory of punctuated equilibrium; an instance of this.

**1976** *Amer. Jrnl. Sci.* CCLXXVI. 24 Both the punctuations and the equilibrium were imposed on the data by interpretation. **1981** *Nature* 9 July 120/1 The geologically sudden appearance of robust australopithecines in South and East Africa between 2.1 and 2.0 Myr seems to represent an obvious example of punctuation.

**punctu'ationist** *n.,* (*b*) *Biol.* = PUNCTUATIONALIST *n.;* also *attrib.* or as *adj.;* **punctu'ationism** *n.* = *PUNCTUATIONALISM n.*

**1981** *Nature* 1/8 Jan. 13/1 One study known to me which does support the punctuationist view is that of Williamson on 21 species of fresh-water molluscs in the lake Turkana region of Africa. **1983** *Times Lit. Suppl.* 18 Feb. 152/5 An introductory outline of the case for punctuationism is followed by a review of the fossil evidence relating to human evolution. **1986** *Observer* 5 Oct. 25/3 'Punctuationists'—who argue that evolution characteristically occurs in short 'bursts' of tens of thousands of years, followed and preceded by long periods of 'stasis'—are really only sophisticated gradualists.

**punctuational** (pʌŋktjuˈeɪʃənəl), *a.* [f. PUNCTUATION *n.* + -AL¹.] **1.** Pertaining to or consisting of punctuation.

**1909** in WEBSTER. **1963** D. B. THOMAS in Brown & Foote *Early Eng. & Norse Stud.* 195 There is little correlation between contemporary preceptive punctuational practice and the phonetics of any Western European language. **1985** *N. & Q.* Sept. 419/1 What has it come to, one may wonder, when teachers of literature have to handle the term with these punctuational tongs?

**2.** *Biol.* Of, pertaining to, or in accordance with punctuationalism; (of evolution or an evolutionary change) taking place rapidly, esp. in a single generation or a series of steps occurring relatively close together.

**1977** *Paleobiol.* III. 115 A punctuational view of change may have wide validity at all levels of evolutionary processes. **1981** *Nature* 1 Jan. 13/2 The deduction that species selection is the sole cause of trends rests . . on the . . assumption that punctuational changes are as likely to occur in a direction opposite to that of the trend as parallel to it. **1983** *Man* XVIII. II. 407/2 Palaeontologist Steven Stanley . . argues that . . evolution is punctuational not gradual. **1987** *Nature* 10 Dec. 516/1 If punctuational changes are random, then the main features of evolution are not the summed consequences of changes caused by selection within populations.

Hence **punctu'ationalism** *n.*, (belief in or advocacy of) the theory of punctuated equilibrium; **punctu'ationalist** *n.*, one who believes in or advocates the theory of punctuationalism; also *attrib.* or as *adj.*
**1978** *Science* 6 Jan. 58/3 A convinced punctuationalist, he contrasts bivalves and mammals to support . . the hypothesis that rate of evolution is determined by rate of speciation. **1978** *Guardian Weekly* 26 Nov. 1/3 The alternative theory is called . . 'punctuationalism'. **1983** E. C. MINKOFF *Evolutionary Biol.* xxi. 352/2 A number of invertebrate paleontologists have been won over to the punctuationalist viewpoint. **1985** D. HULL in D. Kohn *Darwinian Heritage* xxvi. 774 Disagreements between the punctuationalists and gradualists are a 'debate within the Darwinian framework'.

**punishing**, *ppl. a.* Add: Hence **'punishingly** *adv.*
*a* **1948** D. WELCH *Voice through Cloud* (1950) vi. 55 The face of the Irish nurse stiffened. She seemed to bristle . . . She quickly threw the towel across and started to scrub me punishingly. **1973** *Times* 31 Dec. 13/8 It [*sc.* a role] was punishingly difficult to learn. **1984** A. BROOKNER *Hotel du Lac* iii. 37 His hair was punishingly short. **1987** P. LOMAS *Limits of Interpretation* vi. 67 Freud . . had a huge capacity for punishingly hard work.

**Punjabi**, *n.* and *a.* Add: [A.] c. (Usu. with lower-case initial.) A kind of loose shirt or tunic worn by Bengalis, esp. on formal occasions; a kurta.
**1937** H. HOUSE *I spy with my Little Eye* 3 Four rows of men sitting in white punjabis. **1981** *Statesman* 15 June (Note Bk.) 16/3 Special sweets are made for 'Jamai Sasthi', there are special advertisements for Santipuri dhoti and punjabis made of 'garad'. **1985** D. LAPIERRE *City of Joy* III. lxx. 403 The presents for the groom's family . . were made up of two *dhotis*, as many vests, and a punjabi, the long tunic that buttons up to the neck and goes down to the knees.

**punker** ('pʌŋkə(r)), *n.*² *colloq.* (chiefly *N. Amer.*). [f. PUNK *n.*³ + -ER¹, perh. as a shorter form of PUNK-ROCKER *n.*; *punk* alone, the short form in the U.K., has other well-established senses in N. America.] A punk-rocker.
**1977** *Rolling Stone* 19 May 37/4 She didn't like the punkers one bit. **1982** M. ATWOOD *Bodily Harm* I. 12 He had a massive head, with the hair clipped short like a punker's. **1988** P. MONETTE *Borrowed Time* vi. 141 We threaded our way down the jammed sidewalks . . with punkers and beer drinkers, queens and commoners.

**punkette** (pʌŋ'kɛt), *n.* [f. PUNK *n.*³ + -ETTE.] A female punk-rocker.
**1984** STEWARD & GARRATT *Signed, Sealed & Delivered* v. 98/1 There are still quite a few dyed-in-the-wool punkettes, like the Gymslips, who preserve that original style. **1986** *Daily Mirror* 23 Aug. 6/5 Punkette style. Belts, buckles, straps. **1988** *Independent* 6 Sept. 16/8 Not all teenage daughters are rebellious punkettes with dyed hair.

**punkish** ('pʌŋkɪʃ), *a.* [f. PUNK *n.*³ + -ISH.] Characteristic of or resembling a punk-rocker.
**1977** *Sounds* 9 July 42/2 The punk siren grabbed hold of a passing leather-jacketed delinquent . . and proceeded to kiss him with punkish passion. **1984** E. FAIRWEATHER et al. *Only Rivers run Free* iii. 139 Her short, punkish hairstyle. **1988** *Sun* (Brisbane) 30 Mar. 29/6 Although the . . character is supposed to be punkish, the song . . is not overtly punk.

**pup**, *v.*¹ Add: **b.** *transf.* and *fig.*
**1890** *Dialect Notes* I. 75 *Pup*, to calve (used seriously). 'So-and-so's cow has *pupped*'. **1941** *Wine & Food* Summer 54 *Wine* has kept the same name

since it was first pupped. *a* **1966** 'M. NA GOPALEEN' *Best of Myles* (1968) 319 The daddy of every other Man ever pupped by scholarly dirt-shovellers. **1987** *Washington Post* 18 Oct. G2/1 These [plants] have also pupped and a number of them live in 6-inch pots.

**pupilage**, *n.*¹ Add: [2.] **b.** *spec.* in *English Law*. Apprenticeship to a member of the Bar that qualifies a barrister to practise independently.
**1852** E. W. COX *Advocate* I. xx. 207 The very purpose of the pupilage in Chambers is to witness the practice of the law which the Student has learned or is learning from. his books. **1912** J. J. G. SLATER *Should I Go to Bar?* III. i. 47 During pupilage [it is] customary to attend the various courts to see the work begun in chambers carried to a conclusion. **1977** *Prof. Careers Bull.* Autumn 1/2 Pupilages are difficult to find. **1978** R. HAZELL *Bar on Trial* iv. 83 In 1959 the Inns made pupillage compulsory, by amending the Call declaration to include an undertaking not to practise at the English Bar without doing twelve months' pupillage. **1981** R. SCRUTON *Fortnight's Anger* iii. 66 'I . . am just preparing Bar finals.' 'Pupillage fixed? Want any help? Can I speak to . . ?' **1982** E. USHER *Careers in Law* iii. 42 You still have to do pupillage before you can start to develop your own practice . . . Some barristers never undergo pupillage because, for instance, for jobs in industry there is no requirement for them to do so.

**purée**, *v.* Add: **'puréeing** *vbl. n.*
**1952** *House & Garden* Oct. 194/1 Those most onerous kitchen jobs: chopping, beating and puréeing. **1984** BARR & LEVY *Official Foodie Handbk.* I. 30/1 Nouvelle cuisine requires a lot of old-fashioned puréeing, whisking and mincing.

‖**purusha** ('puruʃə), *n. Hindu Philos.* Also 8 Pŏŏrŏŏsh, 9- purusa. [Skr. *puruṣa*, lit. 'man': in Hindu mythology, a being sacrificed by the gods in order to create the universe.] The universal spirit or soul; *spec.* in the Sankhya philosophy, the animating principle which, with cosmic matter (*PRAKRITI *n.*), gives rise to the material, sentient universe.
**1785** C. WILKINS *Bhăgvăt-Gēētā* 142 Pooroosh . . is a term in theology used to express the vital soul, or portion of the universal spirit of Brăhm inhabiting a body. **1827** H. T. COLEBROOKE in *Trans. R. Asiatic Soc.* I. 31 The theistical Sánc'hya recognises . . by Purusha, not individual soul alone, but likewise GOD . . the ruler of the world. **1877** M. WILLIAMS *Hinduism* 200 The aim of the Yoga is . . fusion or blending of the individual spirit . . with Purusha, 'the universal spirit'. **1923** S. RADHAKRISHNAN *Indian Philos.* I. I. iv. 259 The Sāṁkhya philosophy establishes a dualism between puruṣa and prakrti. **1925** D. H. LAWRENCE *Reflections on Death of Porcupine* 127 They've all decided that the beginning of all things is the life-stream itself, energy, ether, libido, not to mention the Sanskrit joys of Purusha, Pradhana, Kala. **1953** [see *PRAKRITI *n.*]. **1972** D. BLOODWORTH *Any Number can Play* xxi. 20 Purusha, the One, is like a great actor, and we are all the different roles he has split himself into. **1987** V. P. KANITKAR *We are Hindus* xi. 127 Purusha is the animating principle of nature, which interacts with Prakriti, resulting in material and physical creation and . . mental awareness.

**push**, *v.* Add: [1.] o. *Computing*. To prepare (a stack) to receive a piece of data, etc. on the 'top' (usu. const. *down*); also, to transfer (data, etc.) to the 'top' of a stack. Opp. *PULL *v.* 1 g, (*occas.*) *POP *v.*¹ 11. Cf. PUSH-DOWN *a.* 1.
**1962** [see *POP *v.*¹ 11]. **1963** B. F. GREEN *Digital Computers in Res.* v. 95 The initial set up pushes down lists for storing the input symbol, the replacement symbol, and the name of the list and also pushes down a temporary storage cell that will hold

the current location on the list as the routine progresses. The final cleanup pops up these four push-down lists, leaving them exactly as they were when the routine was entered. **1967** H. HELLERMAN *Digital Computer Syst. Princ.* viii. 342 Operations implicitly reference the operand(s) at the top of the list, and the result operand replaces the operand(s) at the top of the list. The structure thus behaves as if an entered item 'pushes down' the other items. **1976** M. M. MANO *Computer Syst. Archit.* vii. 267 The interrupt cycle automatically pushes the return address into the stack. **1983** *Your Computer* Aug. 63/1 Next, we push the remaining registers on the stack.

[**6.**] **b.** To exert muscular pressure internally, esp. during the second stage of labour; to bear down.

**1956** L. R. CELESTIN tr. *F. Lamaze's Painless Childbirth* III. iv. 140 When the head .. presents itself .., the woman should push more steadily. **1959** D. G. WILSON CLYNE *Conc. Textbk. Midwives* III. xxxii. 124 Many patients push voluntarily before full dilatation, and so deceive the inexperienced. **1962** S. KITZINGER *Experience of Childbirth* x. 137 Occasionally the urge to push comes very suddenly and more or less overwhelmingly. **1971** H. & M. BRANT *Dict. Pregnancy* 136 While pushing down you should feel as though the breath is down in the abdomen and not held high in your chest. **1983** *Brit. Med. Jrnl.* 30 July 309/2 Full cervical dilatation alone does not endanger the fetus, and if it is diagnosed at routine vaginal examination the mother should not be encouraged to push until she feels the urge to do so.

[**10.**] **d.** *Photogr.* = *push-process* vb. s.v. PUSH-. Freq. const. *to*.

**1970** *Light & Film* iv. 130/1 When a photographer intentionally underexposes a picture, he 'pushes' the film; he simply assumes that it is more sensitive than it really is and arbitrarily assigns it an ASA number higher than the standard one specified. **1977** J. HEDGECOE *Photographer's Handbk.* 67 (*caption*) Most color reversal films can be 'pushed' in speed and then given carefully controlled additional first development time. **1979** *Amat. Photographer* 10 Jan. 90/1 A black and white negative film such as Tri-X or HP5 can be pushed quite easily to 1600 or 3200ASA. **1987** *Camera Weekly* 25 July 38/1 Push processing .. can also affect colour balance with a pronounced shift towards blue the more stops you try and push the film.

**pushable** ('puʃəb(ə)l), *a.* [f. PUSH *v.* + -ABLE.] That can be pushed, in various senses of the vb.

**1979** *SLR Camera* Mar. 9/2 The new film is pushable. **1982** *Washington Post* 12 Nov. 56/1 Pokes all the pushable buttons and ultimately one spits out a farecard. **1988** *Newsday* 13 Nov. 2/5 When we were recording the album it was a really good sound, .. it was a really good tape, we'd say 'Yeah, that's pushable.'

Hence **pusha'bility** *n.*

**1979** *SLR Camera* Jan. 61/1 But perhaps the biggest advantage that the new Ektachrome 400 has is its pushability.

**pussums** ('pusəmz), *n. colloq.* [f. PUSS *n.*[1] + *-ums*, after *diddums*; cf. also PUSSENS *n.*] A term of endearment for a cat; *transf.* applied to a sweetheart.

**1924** H. DE SÉLINCOURT *Cricket Match* iii. 54 You know Pussums mustn't be on the table. **1942** BERREY & VAN DEN BARK *Amer. Thes. Slang* §185/2 *Terms of endearment*, .. pussums. **1950** C. S. LEWIS *Lion, Witch & Wardrobe* xiv. 141 Would you like a saucer of milk, Pussums? **1980** 'D. SHANNON' *Felony File* vi. 147 Poems to my dear Kitty pussums. **1983** *Listener* 6 Jan. 15/3 Jealous husbands, wives or pussums may disfigure you.

**pussy**, *n.* Add: [**7.**] [**b.**] **pussy('s)-toes** *U.S.*, any of various woolly plants of the genus *Antennaria*; *spec.* the mouse-ear (MOUSE-EAR *n.* 4 c) or ladies'-tobacco, *A. plantaginifolia*.

**1892** F. D. BERGEN in *Jrnl. Amer. Folk-Lore* V. XVII. 98 *Antennaria plantaginifolia* ... pussy's toes. **1949** *Chicago Tribune* 9 Jan. VI. 5/7 In early summer, one may see blue, white and yellow violets, .. pussytoes, salt and pepper, poppies .. and wild columbine. **1975** *New Yorker* 7 Apr. 44/1 They harvest the old flower heads at random. Boneset, Saint-John's-wort, common everlasting, pussytoes. **1985** R. M. STERN *Wildfire* I. i. 5 White pussy-toes and yellow meadow cinque-foil clung to rock and what soil there was.

**pustulan** ('pʌstjʊlæn), *n. Biochem.* [f. *PUSTUL(IN *n.* + -AN I. 2.] A glucan, originally isolated from the lichen *Umbilicaria pustulata*, and present in various other lichens.

**1953** WHISTLER & SMART *Polysaccharide Chem.* xviii. 338 Pustulan, a polysaccharide isolated from the large lichen *Umbilicaria*, differs from lichenan in that it possesses β-1,6′ linkages and a specific optical rotation of -44°. **1965** *Jrnl. Bacteriol.* XC. 1019 Changes in activity of β-1,3-glucanase (with laminarin as substrate) and β-1,6-glucanase (with pustulan as substrate) have been measured during the conjugation process, in addition to changes in the activity of several control enzymes which would not be expected to be related to the conjugation process. **1977** *Jrnl. Microscopy* CXI. 145 The diffraction data obtained for crystals of pustulan with the 'frozen hydrated' electron diffraction technique are the first crystallographic data obtained for this polysaccharide. **1985** *Jrnl. Immunol.* CXXXIV. 2593/1 Despite their different linkages and chain structures, β-glucans from yeast (present in yeast mannan), barley, algae (laminarin), and two different fungi (pachyman and pustulan) inhibited monocyte ingestion of E[r] [*sc.* rabbit erythrocytes] and/or zymosan particles.

**pustulin** ('pʌstjʊlɪn), *n. Biochem.* [a. Ger. *Pustulin* (B. Drake 1943, in *Biochem. Zeitschr.* CCCXIII. 389), f. mod.L. *pustulāta* (see def. of *PUSTULAN *n.*) + *-in* -IN[1], after LICHENIN *n.*] = *PUSTULAN *n.*

**1943** *Chem. Abstr.* XXXVII. 5711 Lichenin is found in the lichen *Cetraria*; pustulin in *Umbilicaria*. **1954** *Acta Chemica Scandinavica* VIII. 985 Drake called the polysaccharide pustulin, but following the suggestion of Whistler and Smart, the name pustulan is adopted.

# Q

**qinghaosu** (tʃiŋhaʊ'suː), *n.* *Med.* and *Pharm.*
[a. Chinese *qīnghāosù*, f. *qinghao* the name of
the plant *Artemisia annua*.] A naturally-
occurring sesquiterpenoid compound, extracted
from the Chinese plant *Artemisia annua*, which
has been used to treat malaria; = \*ARTEMISININ
*n.*

**1977** *Chem. Abstr.* LXXXVII. 98788g The new
sesquiterpene lactone Qing Hau Sau [*sic*].. was
isolated from *Artemisia annua*. **1979** *Chinese Med.*
*Jrnl.* XCII. 811/1 An effective antimalaria constituent
was extracted from a traditional Chinese medicinal
herb—Qinghao.. in 1972. It was named Qinghaosu.
**1989** *Sci. Amer.* June 91/1 From the first to the 18th
century, Chinese scholars extolled the virtues of the
*qing-hao* plant (*Artemisia annua*) in the treatment of
malaria. The efficacy of decoctions of this species was
reconfirmed in 1971, and the active principle was
identified the next year: it is an unusual
sesquiterpene lactone peroxide named qinghaosu.

**quad** (kwɒd), *n.*[8] *slang* (orig. *N. Amer.*).
[Shortened form.] = *quadriceps* (s.v. QUADRI-
II). Usu. in *pl.*

**1958** *Muscle Power* Feb. 40/2 *Quads*, those
troublesome curves that cause muscleheads to walk
with bent knee. **1981** J. FONDA *Workout Bk.* (1982)
120 (*heading*) Quad stretch stretches quadriceps.
**1984** *Running* Sept. 17/3 The lack of shock
absorption should have murdered my quads, but the
need to land gently neutralised this. **1986** *Ibid.* Apr.
6/4 The date of the Waterloo XV, a 'quad-sapping'
15 km combination of road, field, trail, sand dunes
and seashore, takes place on Monday.

**quaff**, *v.* Add: Hence **'quaffable** *a.*, (of a wine)
that can be drunk copiously.

**1982** *Washington Post* 1 Dec. E1/2 It is an
intensively fruity, soft-bodied wine,.. charming and
eminently quaffable. **1987** *Wine Soc. Ann. Rev.*
*1986-87* 21 Apr. 12 Were it not for 'a little local
difficulty' we would here in Britain already be able to
drink the very quaffable wines of Argentina.

**quagma** ('kwægmə), *n.* *Particle Physics*. [f.
QUA(RK *n.*[2] + G(LUON *n.* + PLAS)MA *n.*: cf.
MAGMA *n.*] A hypothetical state of matter
consisting of free quarks and gluons; a body of
matter in this state.

**1985** GREINER & STÖCKER in *Sci. Amer.* Jan. 66/1
The matter in such a nucleus consists of quarks and
the particles that bind them together, the gluons; it is
a quark-gluon plasma, or quagma. **1986** *Physics Lett.*
B. CLXVI. 45 We show that if the density of grand
unified monopoles at $T \approx 200$ MeV is of the order of
or greater than $4.4 \times 10^{21}\text{cm}^{-3}$ they annihilate all of
the strange matter produced in the quagma-hadron
phase transition which the universe undergoes at this
temperature. **1988** *New Scientist* 3 Mar. 45/1 Theory
suggests that when the density of energy in nuclear
matter is high enough, the quarks and gluons will no
longer remain confined but will form a quagma.

**qualification**, *n.* Add: [1.] **b.** *spec.* in
*Accounting*. A modifying statement in an
auditor's report that indicates any account
items which have been excluded from the
examination or about which there is doubt or
disagreement; the action of recording such a
statement.

**1916** *Incorporated Accountants' Jrnl.* XXVII. 133/2
Qualifications often represent an honest difference of
opinion between directors and auditors. **1924**
KOHLER & PETTENGILL *Princ. Auditing* (1925) xiv.
161 Insertions in the certificate indicating a limited
scope in the examination are called 'qualifications'.
**1954** E. L. KOHLER *Auditing* (ed. 2) xvi. 587
Following are examples of recent additions to short-
form reports that express qualifications or disclosures
believed necessary for the information of the reader
or for the protection of the accountant. **1976**
*Economist* 14 Feb. 79/2 The auditors would not
regard a qualification of the accounts as necessary.
**1982** *Sunday Times* 10 Jan. 51/7 Press speculation
over possible audit qualifications in the Polly Peck
accounts. **1988** *Financial Times* 12 Feb. 9/8 The
recent qualification of the ECGD's accounts for last
year by the National Audit Office.

**qualified**, *ppl. a.* (and *n.*) Add: [II.] [5.] [a.]
*qualified certificate*.

**1916** *Incorporated Accountants' Jrnl.* XXVII. 135/1
An auditor cannot compel his client to be
conservative under penalty of receiving only a
qualified certificate.

**qualify**, *v.* Add: [7.] **b.** *spec.* in *Accounting*. To
enter a qualification (sense \*1 b) in (an
auditor's report on company accounts).

**1924** KOHLER & PETTENGILL *Princ. Auditing* (1925)
xiv. 162 The importance of when and how to qualify
a certificate is something that only years of
experience can teach the auditor. **1968** *Times* 10 Feb.
11/3 Binder, Hamlyn, chartered accountants, have
qualified the latest accounts from Gorringes
department stores. **1975** *Economist* 8 Nov. 116/2 Its
1974-75 accounts were heavily qualified by its
auditors. **1985** T. LUNDBERG *Starting in Business* iv.
54 If the auditor is not convinced that the accounts
reflect the true state of the company's affairs, then he
will 'qualify' the auditor's report accordingly.

**quark** (kvaːk), *n.*[1] [Ger., = curd(s), cottage or
curd cheese.] A low-fat soft cheese of German
origin.

**1931** E. SACKVILLE-WEST *Simpson* III. 249 Simpson
had begun.. to taste a spoonful of the bubbly white
*Quark*. **1985** *Los Angeles Times* 25 Apr. 39/1 A
wonderful selection of fresh produce,.. kibble wheat
and a low-fat cheese called quark. **1987** *N.Y. Times*
18 Feb. c6/6 Dr. Lund pointed to carbonated milk
beverages under development, cream liqueurs,
fermented milk products such as kefir and quark, and
specialty cheeses.

**quarkonium** (kwaː'kəʊniəm), *n.* *Particle*
*Physics*. Pl. -ia. [f. QUARK *n.*[2] + -ONIUM 2.] A
meson consisting of a quark bound to the
corresponding antiquark; matter, or a system,
consisting of such a particle or particles.

**1977** QUIGG & ROSNER in *Physics Lett.* B. LXXI.
153/1 In this note we describe some features of the
logarithmic potential as applied to quarkonium
families. **1979** *Nature* 12 July 107/3 They [*sc.* gluons]
do play a pivotal part in the decay of heavy
quark-antiquark bound states ('quarkonia') produced
by electron-positron annihilation at high energies.
**1982** *Sci. Amer.* May 42/1 Quarkonium is closely
analogous in structure to positronium. In
quarkonium the bound quark and the antiquark are..
identical in size and mass, and the allowed modes of
motion in quarkonium are similar to those in
positronium. **1986** B. G. DUFF *Fund. Particles* iv. 49

Again, in direct analogy, the bḃ system has also been studied and a number of states observed .. which are referred to as 'beautyonium'. In general, such qq̄ systems are called 'quarkonia'.

**quarter**, *n*. Add: [V.] [**31.**] **quarter-pounder**, something that weighs a quarter of a pound; *spec.* a hamburger of this weight.
**1946** R. A. KNOX *Retreat for Priests* viii. 82 Trying his luck as he crossed the lake, and bringing in his two *quarter-pounders. **1972** *N.Y. Times* 3 Nov. 42/1 The four-cent rise in the price of McDonald's 'quarter-pounder' cheeseburger was not an 'increase', but an adjustment. *Ibid.*, McDonald's .. said its new 'quarter-pounder' burgers were four ounces of meat. **1977** C. McFADDEN *Serial* (1978) xxxviii. 82/2 She .. ducked into McDonald's for a Quarter Pounder. **1986** *Daily Tel.* 11 June 15/1 'You'll have to wait for the quarter-pounder', they announce; meanwhile, your fries sit shivering on the tray.

**quasicrystal** ('kweɪzaɪ‚krɪstəl), *n. Physics.* [f. QUASI- 2 + CRYSTAL *n*.] A regular aggregation of molecules of a particular compound in a structure which has some of the properties of a crystal lattice, such as the ability to diffract radiation as a crystal does, but whose spatial periodicity is incommensurable. Cf. *quasicrystalline* adj. s.v. QUASI- 2 b.
**1984** LEVINE & STEINHARDT in *Physical Rev. Lett.* LIII. 2477/2 We began a long, systematic investigation of the properties of the Penrose lattice to see if other such lattices might exist in 2D and 3D. We find that the Penrose lattice is just one of an infinite set of 2D and 3D lattices that exhibit the BOO and self-similarity properties of a crystal, but have quasiperiodic (QP), rather than periodic, translational order. We term such lattices 'quasicrystals'. **1985** NELSON & HALPERIN in *Science* 19 July 235/2 Structures containing several incommensurate spatial periodicities, which are not simply periodic but nevertheless have a diffraction pattern with δ-function Bragg peaks, might be called 'quasicrystals', by analogy with the term 'quasi-periodic motion' that is used for simple dynamic systems having two incommensurate periods. **1986** *Physica Scripta* T. XIII. 295 Well-facetted external shapes of domains of the quasicrystal material were .. observed in the specimen. **1988** [see *PENROSE *n*.].

**quasquicentennial** (‚kwæskwɪsɛn'tɛnɪəl), *n.* and *a. U.S. rare.* [Irreg. f. L. *quadrans* quarter, after SESQUICENTENNIAL *a.* and *n.* For the coinage, see quot. 1962[1].] **A.** *n.* A one-hundred-and-twenty-fifth anniversary. **B.** *adj.* Pertaining to a one-hundred-and-twenty-fifth anniversary.
**1962** *N.Y. Times Bk. Rev.* 18 Mar. 8/3 Delavan, Tazwell County, Ill., decided to hold a celebration in honor of the 125th anniversary of its founding ... [Delavan] went to the Funk & Wagnalls dictionary people. From there it received the suggestion of 'Quasquicentennial', meaning a hundred plus a fourth ... F.& W. warned it wouldn't appear in a single one of its dictionaries until it establishes itself. **1962** *Pantagraph* (Bloomington, Illinois) 30 Aug. 23/1 The Delavan Quasquicentennial Celebration doesn't officially begin until noon today. **1986** *Christian Cent.* 15 Jan. 55 Last September 24 I was the Quasquicentennial Lecturer in Religion at Simpson College in Indianola, Iowa. **1988** *Washington Post* 24 June (Weekend section) 6/1 As we work our way through the four-year Civil War Quasquicentennial, there are reenactments and demonstrations scheduled from here to Christmas.

**Queenslander**, *n.* Add: **b.** *transf.* A colonial-style house typical of Queensland.
**1986** *Cairns* (Queensland) *Post* 24 Feb. 13/4 (Advt.), Huge beautifully restored Queenslander ... For a large family who need room & enjoy early Qld.

architecture. **1988** *Townsville* (Queensland) *Bull.* 26 Mar. 29/6 The best features of an old Queenslander (huge rooms, high ceilings, lots of breezes).

**Quetelet** ('kɛtəleɪ), *n.* The name of Lambert Adolphe Jacques *Quételet* (1796–1874), Belgian statistician, used *attrib.* and in the possessive to designate various concepts introduced by him or arising out of his work, as **Quetelet's curve** *Statistics* (now *rare*), the normal probability curve; **Quetelet('s) index** *Med.* and *Anthropol.*, the mass of an individual in kilograms divided by the square (formerly the cube) of his height in metres.
**1909** in *Cent. Dict.* Suppl., Quételet's curve. **1958** *Chambers's Techn. Dict.* Add. 1007/1 *Quetelet's index*, weight of human body divided by cube of height; obsolescent. **1977** *Lancet* 29 Jan. 214/2 The results of multiple regression analysis of blood-pressure .. on renal mobility .., allowing for age, parity, and height-adjusted weight (Quetelet index defined as weight/height[2]..), showed that renal mobility and Quetelet index were significantly associated with mean blood-pressure. **1984** ABRAHAM & LLEWELLYN-JONES *Eating Disorders* ix. 110 Obesity is defined in several ways, one being when the Quetelet Index is 30 or more.

**queue**, *n.* Add: [**3.**] **b.** *Computing.* A list of data items, commands, etc. stored in such a way that the most recently stored item cannot be, or by software convention is not, retrieved before all of the previously stored items have been retrieved. (Also formerly, = STACK *n.* 1 f.)
**1963** BROOKS & IVERSON *Automatic Data Processing* vi. 310 If a pool is organized as a backward-chained stack, then the component next taken from the pool is the component last added to it. The queue of components in the pool therefore obeys a so-called last-in-first-out, or LIFO discipline. **1970** H. A. RODGERS *Dict. Data Processing Terms* 86/2 *Queue*, .. an ordered sequence of items waiting to be serviced according to their order. **1983** *Austral. Personal Computer* Aug. 98/3 To use an array 'Q' to represent a queue is almost as simple. All you need is a pointer 'S' to the start of the queue and a pointer 'E' to the end of the queue.

**quiet**, *a.* Sense 2 d in Dict. becomes 2 e. Add:
[**2.**] **d.** *Stock Exchange.* Of a commodity: displaying little fluctuation in price.
**1932** *Daily Tel.* 8 Oct. 4/2 Oats quiet of sale ... Miller's wheatfeed quiet. **1985** *Times* 6 Aug. 20/6 Softs were quiet, except for coffee, which weakened again.

**Quincy** (kɛ̃si), *n.* [Fr., the name of a wine-producing region in the upper Loire valley.] A dry white wine produced in the Quincy region of France.
**1935** A. L. SIMON *Wines & Liqueurs* 41 *Quincy fumé*, a notable white wine of Berry (France). **1960** P. M. SHAND *Bk. French Wines* 341 'Quincy' is a dry, pale-yellow wine best drunk while still young. **1969** V. ROWE *Loire* 28 Sancerre and Quincy, Chinon and Bourgueil are very good wines. **1976** *Times* 25 Sept. 8/5 Yapp's list includes the fairly unusual Reuilly, Quincy and Menetou Salon. **1987** *N.Y. Times* 29 Mar. x. 10/6 Lunch usually includes soups .. and cheese, pate, crackers and wine .. ; one house wine is a Delaunay Quincy 1984.

**quinestrol** (kwɪ'niːstrɒl), *n. Pharm.* [f. QUIN(IC *a.* + *estr*(ogen ŒSTR(OGEN *n.* + -OL.] A synthetic oestrogen, $C_{25}H_{32}O_2$ (a derivative of ethinyl-oestradiol), which is included in some oral contraceptives.
**1966** *Fertility & Sterility* XVII. 531 Quinestrol, ethinylestradiol-3-cyclopentyl ether, is a new orally active synthetic estrogen. **1974** *Amer. Jrnl. Obstetr. & Gynecol.* CXVIII. 45/1 Quinestrol is an estrogen

with prolonged activity due to its storage in and slow release from fat in both animals and women. **1981** H. M. BOLT in R. R. Chaudhury *Pharmacol. of Estrogens* iii. 35 Metabolites of quinestrol are largely secreted into human bile as glucuronidates.., and possibly re-absorbed after hydrolysis of the conjugates by bacterial enzymes.

**quinquina**, *n.* Restrict *Med.* to senses in Dict. and add: **2.** Any of several (fortified) French wines containing quinine.
**1905** *Army & Navy Co-op. Soc. Rules & Price List* 15 Mar. 496/3 Quinquina, Bordeaux. *Ibid.* St. Raphael Quinquina. **1917** *Harrods Gen. Catal.* 1292/2 Quinquina Dubonnet. **1942** [see PASTIS *n.*]. **1953** R. M. LOCKLEY *Trav. with Tent* i. 41 A glass of *quinquina.* **1965** O. A. MENDELSOHN *Dict. Drink* 275 *Quinine wine,* sweet fortified wine to which is added a little quinine and perhaps other 'botanicals' to give a bitter taste. Their brands are legion, e.g., Quinquina (French).

**quint** (kwɪnt), *n.*[4] *N. Amer.* [Shortened f. QUINTUPLET *n.*] = QUIN *n.*[2]
**1934** *Newsweek* 18 Aug. 21/1 Fed at three-hour intervals, the Dionne 'quints' since their birth have consumed about a beer barrel of mother's milk shipped in from Toronto and Montreal. **1972** C. BUCHANAN *Maiden* xxii. 185 The five Dionne girls were hopping out of a canoe... The quints' long, long Pettijohn legs in short shorts—what legs! **1979** *Internat. Herald Tribune* 29 May 24/7 Cecile's easy, outgoing manner.. suggested she had overcome the traumas.. and the sorrows that plagued the quints in younger years. **1984** *Miami Herald* 6 Apr. 6A/1 Three days later, two separate funds.. were established to help Peggy Jo Kienast care for the quints, now 14.

**Quiteño** (kiːˈtɛnjəʊ, ‖ kiˈteɲo), *a.* and *n.* [Amer. Sp., f. *Quito* (see below).] **A.** *adj.* Of, pertaining to, or characteristic of Quito, the capital city of Ecuador. **B.** *n.* A native or inhabitant of Quito.
**1935** S. F. PAYNTER in *Old Cornwall* Summer 19 The more respectable members of Quiteño society often make up parties and visit their friends' houses. **1939** *House Beautiful* Feb. 30/1 We Quiteños, when we die, we hope to go to heaven. **1958** A. TOYNBEE *East to West* ii. 4 The high point of Quiteño art and architecture is the church and cloister of San Francisco. **1967** J. L. PHELAN *Kingdom of Quito in 17th Cent.* viii. 179 Side-by-side with licentious living, the Quiteños produced some of the most perfect examples of baroque architecture.. and baroque sculpture in the Spanish-speaking world. **1974** *Encycl. Brit. Micropædia* VIII. 360/3 Among the most admired of Quiteño churches and convents are La Compañia,.. San Francisco, [etc.]. **1978** *Financial Times* 12 Dec. 3/6 Newly-opened by-pass tunnels.. have been packed with Quitenos enjoying an afternoon drive.

**quiteron** (ˈkwɪtərɒn), *n. Electronics.* [f. initial letters of *qu*asiparticle *i*njection *t*unnelling *e*ffect (the phenomenon on which the device depends for its operation) + -T)RON.] A superconducting device with switching and amplifying

characteristics similar to those of a transistor, but capable of operating at lower power levels.
**1982** *U.S. Patent 4,334,158* 8 June, The operation of the present device is based on QUasi-particle Injection Tunneling, and hence is called the QUITERON. It relies on heavy injection of excess quasi-particles in order to cause a superconducting gap to drastically change, and generally to vanish. **1983** *New Scientist* 10 Feb. 369/3 The quiteron is not the first superconducting device that engineers have considered for chips. **1983** *Your Computer* (Austral.) Apr. 18/3 The patented device is called the quiteron by its IBM inventor, Sadeq M Faris. **1987** *Appl. Physics Lett.* L. 295/2 The gain of the quiteron depends upon gap suppression of the central film and is strongly dependent upon injection level.

**quoad**, *Lat. prep.* Add: **d. quoad hanc (hunc)**, 'as far as this woman (man) is concerned' used with reference to the nullity of marriage or to sexual impotence. Also (*rare*) **quoad illam**, 'as far as that woman is concerned'.
**1719** BARON & FEME *Treat. Husbands & Wives* (ed. 2) xxxii. 376 In Berry's Case, the first judgment was given upon a libel, which was that he was *frigidus*..; but no mention whether *maleficiatus*, or not, *quoad hanc* only, or *frigidus a natura*. **1853** J. E. P. ROBERTSON *Rep. Cases Eccl. Courts* II. 630 The only case in the books, and that was collusive, in which a sentence of nullity quoad hanc has been pronounced, is that of *The Countess of Essex.* **1922** *Times* 11 Oct. 11/5 This ancient judgment.. throws great difficulty in the way of a woman who.. finds it difficult to.. obtain evidence of adultery; *quoad hanc*, in one case before me, she almost failed. **1960** *Times* 12 July 3/7 The husband's incapacity—not a general impotence, but incapacity *quoad hanc.* **1974** *Rayden's Pract. & Law Divorce* (ed. 12) I. vi. 162 The averment of impotency *quoad hunc* or *quoad hanc* is sufficient to support a decree.

**quota**, *n.* [3.] For def. read: The maximum number (of immigrants or imports) allowed to enter a country within a set period; hence, more generally, a maximum number or quantity (produced, caught, enrolled, etc.) that is permitted at one time. Also, a regulation that imposes such a restriction. (Further examples.)
**1954** 'W. MARCH' *Bad Seed* ii. 29 Our enrolment is limited, as you probably know; and already we have our quota for next term. **1974** [see PELAGIC *a.* b]. **1984** A. C. & A. DUXBURY *Introd. World's Oceans* xiv. 458 The world quota of incidental porpoise kill for 1980 was set at no more than 31,000. **1984** N. BARBER *Woman of Cairo* I. xii. 145, I am a member, though. One of the Egyptian quota. **1986** *Farmers Weekly* 3 Jan. 6/4 The Milk Marketing Board is now urging farmers to defy their quotas but, if this leads to the national quota being exceeded, it will be the farmer.. who will pay the fine.

**quotidian**, *a.* and *n.* Add: [A.] [3.] **b.** *absol.*
**1965** *Listener* 28 Jan. 155/3 He treats the bizarre with the same tortured care that many nineteenth-century European writers devoted to the quotidian. **1984** A. BROOKNER *Hotel du Lac* iii. 37 The here and now, the quotidian, was beginning to acquire substance.

# R

**rab** *n.*, var. *RAV *n.*

**rabbit**, *n.*[1] Sense 1 d in Dict. becomes 1 e. Add: [1.] **d.** Rabbit's fur.
**1906** KIPLING *Puck of Pook's Hill* 116 Our Lord of Pevensey.. being clothed in his second fur gown reversed with rabbit. **1951** N. MITFORD *Blessing* I. xii. 123 'What a seasonable hat.' 'I love my little bit of rabbit.' **1956** N. MARSH *Off with his Head* (1957) iii. 45 He dropped his rabbit cap. **1981** E. LONGFORD *Queen Mother* iv. 64 Queen Alexandra had had hers lined with rabbit instead of ermine to save expense.

**race**, *v.*[1] Add: [2.] **d.** Of the heart or pulse: to beat fast.
**1948** WODEHOUSE *Uncle Dynamite* II. v. 68 As Lady Bostock made her way to the study, her heart was racing painfully. **1955** D. EDEN *Darling Clementine* xvi. 156 There was a taut look of excitement that she had never seen before in his face. Her own pulses began to race. **1988** M. FORSTER *Elizabeth Barrett Browning* iv. 64 Delight as well as dread made her heart race. **1989** *Daily Tel.* (Colour Suppl.) 26 Aug. 51/1 In her [*sc.* Jane Austen's] writing we can still hear the pulse-beats of Awful Lydia and Silly Kitty racing at the prospects of beaux and conquests.

**racing**, *vbl. n.*[1] Add: [2.] **racing form** *U. S.* = form sheet s.v. *FORM *n.* 22.
**1910** S. P. WILSON *Chicago by Gas Light* 43 It is no uncommon sight to see the place crowded with men and women waiting for the '*racing form' to appear hot from the printing press. **1930** F. I. ANDERSON *Bk. Murder* III. 66 A handsome fire laddie.. lifted the basement blinds and sat down in Number 56 to study his morning racing forms. **1988** *Washington Post* 14 Aug. B6/1 The National Weather Service provides the meteorological equivalent of the racing form.

**rack-rent**, *n.* For def. read: A very high, excessive, or extortionate rent; a rent equal (or nearly equal) to the annual value of the land; now *spec.* in English law, a rent of at least two thirds of the annual value of the property. (Further examples.)
**1875** *Public Health Act* 38 & 39 Vict. c.55 s.4 'Rackrent' means rent which is not less than two thirds of the full net annual value of the property out of which the rent arises; and the full net annual value shall be taken to be the rent at which the property might reasonably be expected to let from year to year. **1950** *Times* 25 May 11/4 The expression 'rack rent' was stated in the definition in section 17 to have the same meaning as in section 343 of the Public Health Act, 1936. **1976** S. R. SIMPSON *Land Law & Registration* iii. 32 The consideration for it is normally a 'rack-rent', which is rent fixed by reference to the full annual value of the site and the premises on it; it no longer means an excessive or 'stretched' rent, which is how it originally got its name. **1980** *Daily Tel.* 22 Apr. 25/3 The site, which has been empty for years, had been put out to tender by the city authorities and I understand that Norwich Union's offer is 30 p.c. of rack rent to the city.

**racy** ('reɪsɪ), *a.*[2] [f. RACE *v.*[1] or *n.*[1] + -Y[1].] Designed or suitable for racing.
**1951** [see FLOOZIE *n.*]. **1955** *Times* 28 June 5/6 The Westminster, although a good looking car, is by no means racy in appearance. **1976** *Southern Even. Echo* (Southampton) 3 Nov. (Advt.), Halogen headlights, sports wheels,.. racy steering wheel, [etc.]. **1984** *Practical Boat Owner* Feb. 60/2 Helming this racy vessel.. was cruel work. **1987** *India Today* 15 Jan. 98/2 (Advt.), The toughest, raciest, safest motorcycle of them all.

**rad** (ræd), *a.*[3] *N. Amer. slang.* [Perh. a shortening of RADICAL *a.*: cf. sense *3 g.] Used as a term of approval: = COOL *a.* 4 e; calmly detached; admirably up to date; outstandingly enjoyable, 'fantastic'.
**1982** *Maclean's* 6 Sept. 48 Kim Robb.. sat down with a group of Prairie teenagers to discuss things that were 'cool'... 'The word now,' says Robb,.. 'is rad.' **1985** *New Yorker* 25 Mar. 41/1, I jam on the taboos, but my sister was rad. **1987** *BMX Plus!* Sept. 10/1 This was just the start of the raddest one-week vacation a freestyler has ever had. **1988** *Sunday Mail Mag.* (Brisbane) 16 Oct. 25 (*caption*) Your son thinks he's so rad!

**raddie** ('rædɪ), *n. local slang* (now somewhat derog.). [Perh. shortening of RADICAL *n.*, with reference to the political views of Italian exiles in the 19th cent.] A Londoner of Italian descent.
**1938** F. D. SHARPE *Sharpe of Flying Squad* xix. 209 Then one asked: 'Are there any 'Raddies' here?' (Raddies means Italians.) They forced their way into a clubroom where they found an unfortunate 'Raddie'. **1981** P. INCHBALD *Tondo for Short* iv. 46 Don't kid yourself, Franco; you're not Florentine, you're a bleeding raddie. Nine-tenths cockney. *Ibid.* viii. 90 'What's raddie?' asked little Gracie... 'People like us, pussycat. London Italians, Italian Londoners... It's rude. Like coon or wog.' **1982** —— *Sweet Short Grass* xii. 98 A middle-aged raddie copper. **1985** *Daily Tel.* 30 May 18/3 Many thousands of Italian refugees came to settle in England (mostly in Holborn), where their descendants are still known as the 'raddis', for 'radicals'.

**radial**, *a.* and *n.* Senses B. 6-7 in Dict. become 7-8. Add: [B.] **6.** *Radio.* Each of a number of wires attached radially (freq. in a horizontal plane) to the base of a vertical antenna, which partially reproduce the reception and transmission characteristics of a horizontal sheet of conducting material attached at this point.
**1939** *A.R.R.L. Antenna Bk.* xii. 93/1 Better results can be expected as the length of the radial wires is increased... As many radials as possible should be used. **1952** *QST* May 12/1 The antenna at W5CSU is operated with a ground system of 16 radials varying between 25 and 40 feet in length. **1961** *Amat. Radio Handbk.* (ed. 3) xiii. 365/1 The inner conductor.. is connected to the vertical rod or wire and a set of four or more quarter-wave radials is connected to the sheath. **1976** *CB Mag.* June 7/1 (Advt.), Electrical design of the long, .64 wavelength vertical radiating element plus full size radials guarantee unequalled performance. **1981** P. CHIPPINDALE *Brit. CB Bk.* ix. 133 Instead of your car the normal home-base aerial.. has radials at the bottom which take its place.

**radical**, *a.* and *n.* Add: [A.] [3.] **g.** *slang* (orig. *Surfers'*). At or exceeding the limits of control and safety; hence, as an evaluative term:

remarkable, outstanding; amazing, 'far out', 'cool'.

**1968** W. WARWICK *Surfriding in N.Z.* p. iv, *Radical*, extreme. **1971** *Times* 9 Aug. 5/1 The surfbums have a language all their own; they talk about . . radical turns, [and] boogalooing. **1983** W. Safire in *N.Y. Times Mag.* 8 May 10 What is a current expression of approval? '*Bold rave, radical* and *dual* are in,' reports Miller. **1985** *Dirt Bike* Mar. 56/3 Oh sure, I pulled holeshots just about every moto, but the power was just too radical for me to handle, what with my bad shoulder and all. **1985** E. LOCHHEAD *True Confessions* 6 The Young Mothers' Meeting we had there was Really Radical. **1987** *Boards* Mar. 6/1 Conditions were described as 'radical' by the 30 or so other sailors who were out, and it was obviously fairly cold. **1988** *Independent* (Mag.) 24 Dec. 10/3 'Radical' . . no longer has rebellious or left-wing connotations but means . . wonderful or remarkable.

**radicand** ('rædɪkænd), *n. Math.* [f. L. *rādīcand-um* gerundive of *rādīcāre*: see RADICATE *v.*] The number or expression from which a root is to be extracted.

**1889** G. CHRYSTAL *Algebra* (ed. 2) I. x. 182 We shall restrict the radicand, *k*, to be positive. **1937** MICHELL & BELZ *Elem. Math. Analysis* II. x. 626 Denoting the quadratic radicand by $X$, so that $X = ax^2 + bx + c$, . . the function to be integrated may be denoted by $R(x, \sqrt{X})$. **1984** *Mathematical Rev.* LXXXIV. 1743/1 For an odd radicand $\gamma$ in the extension $F(\sqrt{\gamma})$ ($\gamma$ in the ring of integers $R$) the 2-factor in the discriminant depends on the residue ring $R/4R$.

**radicchio** (ræ'diːkɪəʊ, ‖ra'dikkjo), *n.* [a. It. *radicchio* chicory.] A variety of chicory, originally from Italy, having reddish-purple white-veined leaves.

[**1978** *Garden* (R. Hort. Soc.) CIII. 68/1 The popular local way of cooking red chicory—*radicchio arrosto*.] **1981** *Times* 12 Dec. 12/7, 6 leaves radicchio, red endive. **1984** BARR & LEVY *Official Foodie Handbk.* 6/1 Foodies are the ones talking about food in any gathering—salivating over restaurants, recipes, radicchio. **1986** *St. Louis* (Missouri) *Post-Dispatch* 28 May 1D/3 The big public market specializes in . . sophisticated imports from rice to radicchio. **1987** *Daily Tel.* 16 Oct. 19/8 Smoked salmon dressed with radicchio.

**Raffaelle ware** (ræfaɪ'ɛlɪ ˌwɛə(r)), *n. Ceramics.* Also 8–9 **Raphael's ware** and varr. [f. the name of the Italian painter, *Raffaello* Santi (Raphael; 1483–1520) + WARE *n.*³] A type of sixteenth-century Italian majolica whose pictorial designs were heavily influenced by (and once attributed to) Raphael; also, a modern imitation of this.

**1773** in A. V. B. Norman *Wallace Collection: Catal. Ceramics* (1976) I. 25 Very fine old Raphael's ware bottle curiously painted. **1774** *Descr. Villa of H. Walpole* 107 A salver of Raphael fayence; story of the prodigal son. **1842** *Valuable Contents of Strawberry Hill* xii. 127 A magnificent specimen of the rare old faenza or Raphael's ware, the design most masterly. **1872** W. CHAFFERS *Keramic Gallery* I. 27 In England it was in the last century called *Raffaelle ware*, on account of the impression which existed, that the great Raffaelle himself condescended to paint on some of this ware. **1905** F. LITCHFIELD *Pott. & Porc.* (new ed.) ii. 18 The fallacy that Raffaelle actually decorated the majolica known as Raffaelle ware, has been exploded. **1960** R. G. HAGGAR *Conc. Encycl. Continental Pott. & Porc.* 376/2 [Raphael's] influence was such, that although he never painted maiolica, it was formerly . . thought that he did so. In consequence maiolica with such decorations was referred to as 'Raphael fayence' or 'Raffaelle ware'. **1981** 'J. GASH' *Vatican Rip* x. 83 Knowing I was there, she wisely glossed over a piece of so-called Rafaello

ware . . and instead sold a little harlequin table of about 1790.

**raffish**, *a.* Add: **b.** Careless of conventional morals or manners; attractively disreputable in appearance or behaviour; rakish.

**1937** *Harper's Mag.* June 101/1 The raffish, free-for-all girl finds a devoted husband. **1958** *Spectator* 27 June 831/2 [He] displayed a certain raffish elegance in his long, dark jacket and dog-tooth trousers. **1962** I. MURDOCH *Unofficial Rose* xxxvi. 343 Her soft peppery hair . . was cut short in a neat yet raffish style about her beaming countenance. **1977** P. L. FERMOR *Time of Gifts* 11, I moved . . into older circles which were simultaneously more worldly, more bohemian and more raffish. **1985** *N.Y. Times* 17 Mar. 11. 4/2 Burgess (played by Alan Bates) is saucy, witty, a bit raffish of course, but above all still an Englishman. **1989** *Observer* (Colour Suppl.) 3 Sept. 24/1 Sag Harbor has a more raffish, agreeable, even faintly Bohemian air.

**Rafi** (ra'fi), *n.* [Heb., f. acronym of *Rěšīmat Pōʿālē Yiśrāʾēl* Israel Workers List.] In Israel, a left-wing political party formed as a breakaway group in 1965 by Ben-Gurion (1886–1973), and now part of the Labour alignment in the Knesset.

**1965** *New Statesman* 12 Nov. 726/1 Ben Gurion's group, Rafi, which polled almost 9 per cent, suffered from the fact that it was . . less a group capable of winning power for itself than aiming at undermining that of another party. **1978** *Washington Post* 25 July A12/1 Begin accused the Labor Party of branding as neo fascists Labor members who broke away from Ben-Gurion's faction and founded the Rafi party. **1981** *N.Y. Times* 9 Jan. A9/2 This position may be designed as a threat by Mr. Begin to prevent the resignation of two Cabinet members—Education Minister Zevulun Hammer . . and Finance Minister Yigael Hurwitz of the Rafi faction.

**rag**, *n.*¹ Add: [**9.**] **rag-out** [cf. *to get one's rag out*, sense 3 c above], in the British coal industry, a sudden, short, unofficial strike; = *wildcat strike* s.v. WILD CAT *n.* 4 c.

**1955** *Times* 9 May 4/4 '*Rag-outs*' or short, impulsive strikes were common. About seven weeks ago there was a 'rag-out' of packers at Markham Main. **1987** *Daily Tel.* 31 Jan. 2/8 These stoppages, which are heat of the moment walkouts—or what they call in the industry the 'rag-out'—had affected almost all Britain's 125 mines apart from 15.

‖**Ragamala** (rɑːɡəˈmɑːlɑː), *n. Indian Art.* Also **Raga-mala, Rag(-)mala.** [a. Skr. *rāgamālā*, used in Indian music to denote a series of (usu. 36) ragas, each of which expresses a specific mood or sentiment, f. *rāga* RAGA *n.* + *mālā* necklace, garland.] A series of miniature paintings based on situations and vernacular poems inspired by the ragas.

*a* **1794** W. JONES *Works* (1799) I. 431 Similar images [of the personifications of the Rāgas] . . are . . represented by delicate pencils in the *Rāgmālàs*. **1834** N. A. WILLARD *Treat. Music of Hindoostan* 63 Very little resemblance remained between the pictures of the Ragmala and that which should have been represented. The generality of amateurs are more solicitous of possessing a copy of the drawings denominated Ragmala than of ascertaining its accuracy. **1920** E. B. HAVELL *Handbk. Indian Art* III. 211 Specially characteristic of the Hindu artist's spiritual outlook are the pictures representing the Rāg-mālas, or melody-pictures, in which Indian music is translated into pictorial terms. **1948** B. GRAY *Rajput Painting* 5 There is . . a general Mogulization of *Ragmala* paintings after 1725. **1973** K. EBELING *Ragamala Painting* 13 Ragamala paintings are visual interpretations of Indian musical modes previously envisioned in divine or human

form by musicians and poets. **1984** *Art & Artists*
Mar. 23/2 Ragamala paintings, a particular type of
miniature which endeavours to illustrate a poem
describing the mood created by music. There are
thirty-six moods in a Ragamala, a garland of melody.

**rage**, *n.* Add: [7.] **c.** The action or an instance
of raging (*RAGE *v.* 4 f); a party; a good time.
*Austral.* and *N.Z. colloq.*
    **1980** *N.Z. Listener* 6 Dec. 56 The notice-board told
me that the last rage of the year would take place that
night and later in the evening the sound of the rage
filled the campus. **1985** *Skyline* (Austral.) 15 Nov. 8
(Advt.), Have a rage at our Castaway BBQ where the
order of dress is strictly Castaway style! **1986**
*Courier-Mail* (Brisbane) 26 June (Suppl.) 8/1 The
Roxy churns out an endless stream of disco, dancing,
and drinking, tailor-made for young working people
who .. are looking for 'a rage'.

**rage**, *v.* Add: [4.] **f.** Of a person: to revel, to
have a good time, to 'party'. Cf. *RAGER *n.* c.
*Austral.* and *N.Z. colloq.*
    **1979** *Sunday Sun* (Brisbane) 18 Nov. 67/3 *Rage*,
have a good time, go out on the town. **1982** *Sydney
Morning Herald* 18 Sept. 1/2 Teenagers still rage at
weekends, check out spunks of both sexes and try to
avoid hassles with the olds. **1985** *Courier-Mail*
(Brisbane) 4 Nov. 31 (Advt.), Quick. Get ready to
rage. **1986** *Sun* (Sydney) 9 Dec. 26/2 'Over
Christmas, I'll probably be drinking too much and
raging too much,' said the .. breakfast Bimbo. **1987**
*TV Week* (Melbourne) 28 Mar. 4/1 'I still go out and
rage occasionally,' says the former sidekick to Greg
Evans .. , 'but I can't do it like I used to, not five
nights a week.'

**rager**, *n.* Add: **c.** A person who enjoys having a
good time; a dedicated party-goer. Cf. *RAGE *v.*
4 f. *Austral.* and *N.Z. colloq.*
    **1972** J. S. GUNN in G. W. Turner *Good Austral.
Eng.* iii. 55 Copies of pop magazines like Go-set
yielded expressions like .. *lick, mover, rager*, [etc.].
**1987** *TV Week* (Melbourne) 28 Mar. 4/1 'Look, I've
always been a rager,' she says, shrieking. **1988**
*Courier-Mail* (Brisbane) 6 July 21/2 Ragers eat at any
time .. but .. usually between midnight and 5 am,
just after the party has finished and before the disco
starts. **1988** *Sunday Mail* (Brisbane) 21 Feb. 36/5
Downstairs on the boom-boom floor, the pretty
ragers purred and boogied their youth into another
dawn.

**ragged**, *a.*[1] Add: [2.] [**d.**] *spec.* in *Typogr.*, of a
right-hand margin: uneven; = UNJUSTIFIED *ppl.
a.* 3 b; hence **ragged right**, an unjustified right-
hand margin or a piece of text set with this;
also as *advb. phr.*, (set) in this style.
    **1949** MELCHER & LARRICK *Printing & Promotion
Handbk.* 131/1 The lines of this paragraph have been
deliberately left unjustified .. presenting a ragged
appearance at the right-hand edge. **1961** WEBSTER
1875/1 *Ragged*, .. uneven—used of the ends of lines
of text in printing. **1966** *Gloss. Automated Typesetting
& Related Computer Terms* (Composition
Information Services, Los Angeles) (ed. 2) 102
Unjustified type: usually denotes any typeset matter
which is characterized by an uneven or ragged right-
hand margin. **1969** *Chicago Man. Style* (ed. 12) xix.
441 The left edge is even—that is, each line begins
directly under the line above—but the right edge
runs *ragged* (*ragged right*, the designer calls it). **1979**
G. A. GLAISTER *Gloss. Bk.* (ed. 2) 409/1 Ragged
setting may be more troublesome than straight
setting since it has its own rules, such as the
avoidance of hyphenated line endings. **1980** C.
BURKE *Printing Poetry* iii. 32 Some .. of the problems
in a prose setting can be obviated by setting it
'ragged right', that is by leaving the right-hand
margin unjustified.

**raggedy**, *a.* Add: [2.] **c.** *fig.* As a general term
of disparagement: miserable, unpleasant; very
inferior; meagre. *colloq.* (chiefly *U.S.*).
    **1970** R. D. ABRAHAMS *Positively Black* v. 122
There were the Dalton Brothers, four of a kind.
They shot a motherfucker for a raggedy dime. **1976**
*Woman's Day* (U.S.) Nov. 2/3 Since Friday night has
always been a raggedy time for our family, .. I
decided to label that night on the menu calendar ..
Every Man for Himself. **1978** *Washington Post* 4 Feb.
E4/1 In the ensuing 25 years, most of them spent in
raggedy third place, ABC did more than either CBS
or NBC to move television away from New York. **1986**
M. HOWARD *Expensive Habits* 133 Life is rough,
raggedy.

**ragtail** ('rægteɪl), *a.* orig. and chiefly *U.S.* Also
**rag-tail**. [f. RAG *n.*[1] + TAIL *n.*[1]; perh. influenced
by phr. *rag, tag, and bobtail*: see BOBTAIL *n.* C.
4.] Of people, things, and their appearance:
oddly assorted, disorganized or disorderly;
untidy, shabby, scraggly.
    **1972** J. MOSEDALE *Football v.* 79 He coached two
tumultuous years for the New York Titans, a ragtail
predecessor of the Jets in the American Football
League. **1977** *Washington Post* 27 Oct. C11/2 A
'ragtail group' led by a white minister came to his
office several years ago, 'talking management and
rehabilitation'. **1983** *Listener* 3 Feb. 37/4 Big Joe .. is
persuaded by a ragtail posse to show off his legendary
skills with a sixgun. **1983** *Christian Science Monitor*
27 June 21/1, I see you in the garden and think once
more, for each there is a place where, when it is
found, the ragtail odds and ends of amorphous
dreams, unfinished thoughts may fuse and come
together. **1986** *Look Now* Oct. 15/3 Image-wise, the
tough, brazen bitch is tamed. Gone is the rag-tail
hair, the net skirts.

**rail**, *v.*[2] Add: **8.** *trans.* and *intr.* In windsurfing,
to sail the board on its edge or 'rail' (RAIL *n.*[2] 2
g), so that it is at a sharp angle to the surface of
the water.
    **1986** *Boards* May 46/2 If you're sailing over waves
you need to be constantly powering and depowering
the rig so that the board is always railed at the right
angle for maximum speed and lift to windward. **1987**
*On Board* Mar. 47/2 It took the board very close to
the wind and made it easy to rail. **1987** B. OAKLEY
*Windsurfing* (1988) 96 (*caption*) The more you pull
down on the boom, the more you rail. **1988** *Boards*
June 59/4 With so little dagger to push against it is
almost impossible to rail.

**rainbow**, *n.* Add: [2.] **d.** A very wide variety or
range *of* related things.
    **1839** P. J. BAILEY *Festus* 247 A rainbow of sweet
sounds, Just quavering the soothed sense. *a*1861 E. O.
HAUSER in *Webster*, s.v., A catchall large enough to
hold a rainbow of opinions. **1977** *New Yorker* 20
June 93/1 The switching of instruments becomes
almost ritualistic, and although it results in a rainbow
of timbres and tones, it adds a hyperactive note. **1985**
*Sydney Morning Herald* 27 July 41/2 At Woodstock
you had the war, rebellion .., bad acid—a rainbow of
things. **1989** *Business Week* 20 Mar. 134/3 The
challenge for companies is to provide flexibility and a
rainbow of options so both men and women can raise
their families as they see fit and still contribute.

**raise**, *n.*[1] Restrict *Obs.* to sense 2 a and add:
    [2.] **b.** *Weightlifting.* An act of lifting or raising
a part of the body while holding a weight. Usu.
with defining word.
    **1925** *Health & Strength* 14 Feb. 104/3 The
'Abdominal Raise' .. is performed by, first of all,
adopting the prone position. **1936** W. A. PULLUM
*Weight-Lifting Made Easy* (rev. ed.) iv. 48 (*heading*)
Lateral Raise—Lying. **1956** *Muscle Power* June 42/2
He then .. performs the side lateral raise, lifting the
weights off to the sides instead of to the front. **1985**

*Bodypower* June 5 At the top of each rep Gladys contracted the calf muscle fully, just as she did for the standing raises. **1987** *Muscle & Fitness* Oct. 57/1 For bent-over raises, I do six sets of six to eight reps with 60-pound dumbbells.

**raise**, *v.*[1] Add: [9.] **c.** *Immunol.* To stimulate production of (an antiserum, antibody, or other biologically active substance). Freq. const. *against* or *to* the appropriate target cell or substance.

**1971** I. M. ROITT *Essent. Immunol.* i. 7 In one experiment, antibodies raised to *m*-aminobenzene sulphonate were tested for their ability to combine with *ortho*, *meta* and *para* isomers of the hapten and related molecules. *Ibid.* 12 Each antiserum raised by immunisation against a given antigen.. tends to contain a variety of different antibodies. **1978** *Nature* 23 Mar. 355/1 Rabbit antiserum was raised against human plasma fibronectin and was also reactive against murine cell surface fibronectin. **1983** *Oxf. Textbk. Med.* I. v. 392/1 Specific antisera can be raised in rabbits. **1987** *Ibid.* (ed. 2) I. IV. 53/1 A number of B cell differentiation antigens have been found using murine monoclonal antibodies raised against human lymphocytes.

**raita** ('raɪtə), *n. Indian Cookery.* Also raitha. [a. Hindi *rāytā*.] A side dish of yogurt flavoured with vegetables, herbs, fruit, or other ingredients.

**1954** S. CHOWDHARY *Indian Cooking* (1966) 136 (heading) Rāita alu: potatoes in curd. *Ibid.* 137 Rāita is always served cold. *Ibid.* 138 (heading) Sweet rāitas. **1978** *Chicago* June 216/2 Table d'hote dinners.. [include] saffron rice with almonds.. raitha, a cooling yogurt concoction, etc. **1985** N. SAHGAL *Rich like Us* i. 18 'That? Oh it's just a piece of cucumber,' said Nishi, 'in yogurt—*raita*.' **1986** *Sunday Express Mag.* 1 June 52/2 She loved the saffron pillau, the green lentil dal,.. and the tomato mint raita.

‖**rajkumar** ('rɑːdʒkʊmɑː(r)), *n.* Fem. -kumari. [Hindi, ad. Skr. *rājākumāra* (fem. *-kumārī*), f. *rājan* king + *kumāra* young boy.] An Indian prince (or princess).

**1912** *Thacker's Indian Directory* 77 (*in table*) Khaira (Monghyr)... Raj Kumar Guru Prasad Singh of. **1934** *Minutes of Evidence Joint Comm. Indian Constitutional Reforms* 2296/1 in *Parl. Papers 1932–33* VIII. 1, I fully endorse what the Rajkumari has said in all particulars. **1948** *Statesman's Year Bk.* 106 Portfolios held by the Ministers (15 August, 1947)... *Health.*—Rajkumari Amrit Kaur. **1955** EARL WINTERTON *Fifty Tumultuous Years* 57 Our party being accommodated in what was normally the house of the Raj-Kumar, the son and heir of the Maharana. **1971** *Illustr. Weekly India* 4 Apr. 10/1 They once sold diamonds of Golconda to sultanas and rajkumaris. **1978** 'M. M. KAYE' *Far Pavilions* xiv. 223 The Rajkumaries and their ladies. *Ibid.* xxiii. 333 That first attempt to kill the little Rajkumar.

**raking**, *ppl. a.*[1] Add: **b.** *raking light* (*Art* and *Photogr.*), bright light, usu. beamed obliquely, revealing texture, detail, technique, etc.

**1961** in WEBSTER. **1966** R. E. MATES *Photographing Art* i. 18 Raking light is particularly useful in recording the condition of a painting; however, the contrast it creates is too great for a normal photographic rendition. **1972** *Times Lit. Suppl.* 28 Apr. 496/2 It is clear in a raking light that there is a buried picture underlying 'Praxitella'. **1981** *N.Y. Times* 17 May (Long Island Weekly section) 20/1 Ken Otsuka's 'Moment of Eternity', a study of pebbles seen under raking light. **1988** *Pop. Photography* Sept. 65 Strong, raking light creates a multitude of shadows that emphasize surface texture.

**ral** (ræl), *n. Newfoundland dial.* Now *rare.* Also Ral, Rall. [Of uncertain origin; prob. f. Ir.

Gael. *raille* trickster, profligate.] A rogue or ruffian; a trouble-maker; *spec.* in allusive phr. *winter of the Rals* (see quot. 1846).

**1846** P. TOCQUE *Wandering Thoughts* 137 Numbers of the inhabitants [of St. John's], rendered desperate by want, began to break open the stores... This winter [1817] is universally designated by the old inhabitants of Conception Bay as the 'Winter of the Rals'. **1858** R. LOWELL *New Priest in Conception Bay* I. 123 The schoolmaster, who had been in the island for a good many years, said that the [tumultuous] scene 'reminded him of the 'Ralls' they had years ago'. **1895** D. W. PROWSE *Hist. Newfoundland* 406 Many more incidents could be related about the winter of the 'Rals', or 'Rowdies'. **1924** G. A. ENGLAND *Vikings of Ice* 236 'Ah, gi' lang, ye ral!' another retorted. **1955** L. E. F. ENGLISH *Historic Newfoundland* 34 Ral [means] a disorderly fellow. **1969** in Halpert & Story *Christmas Mumming in Newfoundland* 28 The word 'ral' (an Irishism) entered the Newfoundland vocabulary to distinguish a volatile element of the populace which, for several generations to come, was to play its part in history.

‖**Rallié** (ralje), *n.* (*a.*) Also rallié. *French Hist.* [Fr., pa. pple of *rallier*: see RALLY *v.*[1]] **a.** *pl.* In the French Third Republic, (a political grouping of) monarchists and imperialists who, deferring to a Papal encyclical of 1892, 'rallied' in support of the Republic. **b.** In extended use, a group (or a member of a group) of adherents or ralliers to a cause, esp. one on the political right. Also *attrib.* or as *adj.*

[**1893** *Times* 22 Aug. 3/1 The 'Rallied'.. have failed to convince the electors of their sincerity.] **1898** J. E. C. BODLEY *France* II. IV. iv. 388 The word 'Rallié'.. is one of those pregnant terms which express a whole chapter of national history. *Ibid.* 389 The great majority of Frenchmen who were of age in 1870, and who have since supported the Republic, were 'Ralliés'. **1906** *Social-Democrat* 15 Feb. 99 The Left would include all the Republicans, while the Right would be Royalists and Imperialists, but some of the latter would claim to be Republicans. This section calls itself the 'Ralliés', those who have accepted the Republic. **1920** E. M. SAIT *Govt. & Politics of France* x. 340 The A.L.P... is descended in direct line from the Rallies of 1893. **1961** *Encounter* Jan. 9/1 Auxiliaries (*harkis*).. include many *ralliés*—ex FLN soldiers who have come over, voluntarily or after capture. **1970** W. JOHNSON *Cameroon Federation* x. 244 The exiled UPC.. declared the *ralliés*.. to be 'agents of Franco-American imperialism'... The *rallié* elements of the UPC emerged from the April elections strengthened by the success of their candidates.

**ralph** (rælf), *v. slang* (orig. and chiefly *U.S.*). Also Ralph. [Of uncertain origin: app. use of the masc. forename, but perh. echoic.] *intr.* To vomit or gag (freq. with *up*). Also *trans.*

**1967** in *Current Slang* I. iv. **1974** *Village Voice* (N.Y.) 11 July 19/3 He ralphs up the downers and the quarts of beer. **1975** *Verbatim* Sept. 16/2 From the mean streets come some of the best: *to ralph up* 'to vomit'. **1980** L. BIRNBACH et al. *Official Preppy Handbk.* 113/2, 20 verbal expressions for vomiting... 14. *Ralph.*

**ram** (ræm), *n.*[5] *slang* (orig. and chiefly *Austral.*). [Of uncertain origin; perh. a transf. sense of RAM *n.*[1] See AMPSTER *n.*] An accomplice in petty crime; the henchman of a swindler or trickster; a confederate, a decoy.

**1941** BAKER *Dict. Austral. Slang* 59 *Ram*, a trickster's confederate. **1944** *Amer. Speech* XIX. 188 [Australian] rhyming slang does not always appear as such, as.. in the case of *amster* or *ampster*, a crook's confederate, also known as a *ram*; a rhyme was made (*amsterdam*, a *ram*), but shortly the phrase was cut back to *amster*, and the origin.. is obscured. **1960**

WENTWORTH & FLEXNER *Dict. Amer. Slang* 418/2 *Ram*, .. an accomplice of a crook. *More common in Austral. than in U.S.* **1966** BAKER *Austral. Lang.* (ed. 2) xi. 246 The ram would say, 'Give the old boy a fair go; he's nearly too old to spin them!'

Hence **ram** *v.*[3] *intr.*, to act as a 'ram'.

**1952** *Coast to Coast 1951-2* 199 Siddy might have been ramming for you, but what you didn't know, my lad, was that he was helping me to hook you. You were a goner from the start. **1964** H. P. TRITTON *Time means Tucker* (rev. ed.) 33 A gentleman with an umbrella, three thimbles and a pea was demonstrating how 'the quickness of the hand deceives the eye' and was raking in the money at a great rate. When business slackened, another gentleman would pick the pea with surprising regularity... No one seemed to wake up to the fact that the second gentleman was 'ramming' for the first gentleman.

**Rambouillet** ('ræmbəlei, ‖rãbujε), *n.* [The name of a town in northern France, which provided the location for a sheep farm founded in 1783 by Louis XVI.] †**1.** = RUMBULLION *n.*[2] 1. *Obs.*

**1802, 1824** [see RUMBULLION *n.*[2] 1].

**2.** Used *attrib.* and *absol.* to designate a breed of large, hardy sheep, developed from the Spanish merino at Rambouillet but bred elsewhere (esp. in Austral. and N.Z.) for its meat and its heavy fleece of fine wool; also, a sheep of this breed.

[**1809** R. R. LIVINGSTON *Ess. Sheep* iii. 129 Dr. Parry, who has lately written a treatise on the merino sheep in England, acknowledges that the wool of the Rambouillet flock is finer than that imported from Spain.] **1847** *Monthly Jrnl. Agric.* Oct. 171 Somewhat inclined to *throatiness*, but not so much so as the Rambouillets .. wool whiter within than the Rambouillet. **1868** W. LATHAM *States of River Plate* (ed. 2) I. ii. 78 The distinctive characteristics of the 'Rambouillet' variety of the Merino are those of considerably larger carcase, longer wool, weightier fleece, fewer skin folds, and better fatting qualities than the German varieties admit of. **1891** R. WALLACE *Rural Econ. Austral. & N.Z.* xxvi. 358 The Rambouillet or French Merino ... Several of the best flocks in New South Wales belong to this variety. **1963** G. S. MAXWELL *Navajo Rugs* i. 7 In 1903 the French Merino, called Rambouillet, were brought in. **1966** *Jrnl. Reproduction & Fertility* XI. 277 Seven black-faced, crossbred Rambouillet ewes in anoestrus were hysterectomized between 1st June and 20th July. **1973** *Materials & Technol.* VI. iii. 240 Selective breeding there produced a big-framed type of sheep carrying a heavy fleece of fine fibres; this was known as the 'Rambouillet' breed.

**ramen** ('rɑːmen), *n.* [Jap., prob. f. Chinese *lā* pull, stretch, lengthen + *miàn* noodle.] In Japanese cookery: quick-cooking Chinese noodles, usu. served in a broth with strips of meat and pieces of vegetables. Occas. const. as *pl.*

**1972** NAGASAWA & CONDON *Eating Cheap in Japan* (1977) 32 Chinese noodles in pork broth seasoned with soy sauce ... Thinly sliced pork and ham strips, a bit of spinach and sliced leeks are usually on top ... Rāmen is the most popular and cheapest Japanese style Chinese food. **1978** *Washington Post* 30 Nov. EI/3 The Japanese eat a lot of rice, but they love noodles, including the quick-cooking flavored *ramen* noodles first introduced in that country in the 1950's. **1980** E. ANDOH *At Home with Japanese Cooking* 96 Sapporo (the largest city of Hokkaidō island) is famous for its Chinese-style soup noodles, known as *ramen*. *Ibid.* 223 *Ramen* .. are sold as fresh, fresh-dried and instant noodles at almost every Oriental grocery in the U.S. **1986** V. SETH *Golden Gate* xii. 269 For John and Jan a bowl of ramen Capped with a raw egg serves for brunch. **1989** *Los Angeles Times*

9 July (Book Rev.) 15/4 That crazy, singsong, nonsensical English that one used to see on packages of ramen and in instruction manuals for rice cookers and radios.

**ramp**, *v.*[2] Add: **3.** *Comm.* [Prob. after RAMP *n.*[5] a.] To drive up the price of (a company's shares) in order to gain a financial advantage; hence, to increase rapidly the level, value, etc., of. Freq. with *up*.

**1977** *Economist* 12 Feb. 77/1 Without section 54, companies might, for example, ramp up their shares before making a paper bid in order to acquire a company on the cheap. **1979** REESE & FLINT *Trick 13* 73 You know that one of Mosey's sidelines is ramping shares?.. Ramping—you know, boosting. You buy shares in a company, then plug it for all you're worth, pretending you have inside knowledge. **1984** *Daily Tel.* 23 Oct. 17/1 Almost for amusement the price was ramped up to 438p at one point before support was withdrawn. **1985** *Investors Chron.* 8 Nov. 48/2 A move into profits .. depends on how quickly Jaguar (and other motor manufacturers) ramp up pre-launch production of the new cars. **1989** *Sunday Times* 19 Feb. D7/1 The Fed is under pressure from Wall Street to ramp up interest rates and thus slow down the American economy.

**ramrod**, *n.* [2.] [c.] For def. read: With sexual connotations; sometimes *spec.* the erect penis (*coarse slang*). (Earlier and later examples.)

The first quot. is ostensibly taken from Capt. C. Morris's *Plenipotentiary* (c 1790), but in all editions available for consultation 'fine parts' appears in place of 'ramrod'.

**1902** FARMER & HENLEY *Slang* V. 370/1 The Nymphs of the Stage did his ramrod engage. **1942** BERREY & VAN DEN BARK *Amer. Thes. Slang* §121/39 *Male pudendum*, .. ramrod. **1979** A. SILLITOE *Storyteller* I. iv. 58 I'd undone my belt and zip on our way across, and fell onto her with my ramrod already out.

**‖Ramsch** (rɑːmʃ), *n. Cards.* Also ramsch. [Ger., lit. 'junk, jumble, bankrupt or soiled goods'. Cf. ROUNCE *n.*[2]] A round of skat in which knaves are trumps, and the object is to avoid gaining the most points.

**1868** W. B. DICK *Mod. Pocket Hoyle* 196 The game of Rounce, as played in the United States, is derived from the German game of *Ramsch*, and in its principal features resembles Division Loo. **1887** E. E. LEMCKE *Illustr. Gram. Skat* (ed. 2) II. 47 In Ramsch everyone plays for his own account and he who scores the highest number of points pays ten chips to the others. **1911** *Encycl. Brit.* XXV. 166/2 The usual games in skat are the following ... In Ramsch, which takes place when none of the players will risk a game, each player takes (as in whist) all the tricks he makes—but only knaves are trumps—and the loser is he who makes most points. **1949** A. A. OSTROW *Compl. Card Player* 628 A ramsch is scored as follows: The player who takes the least points in counting cards scores 10 points. **1976** *National Skat & Sheepshead Q.* Mar. 20 As Skatmeister, would you advise the proper procedure to follow in the play of a Ramsch which we encountered recently. **1989** *Encycl. Brit.* X. 859/3 *Ramsch* is played if all three players pass, the object being to win fewest points in tricks, with knaves trumps.

**‖rancio** ('rɑːnθiəu, ‖'ranθio), *a.* (*n.*) Also Rancio. [Sp., lit. 'rancid, mature', f. L. *rancidus*.]

**A.** *adj.* Of wines: having the distinctive bouquet, nutty flavour, or tawny colouring characteristic of certain well-matured, fortified, or dessert wines. **B.** *ellipt.* as *n.* A wine of this kind.

**1851** C. REDDING *Hist. Mod. Wines* (ed. 3) vi. 151 Good Grenache wine is .. ten or twelve years attaining full perfection. It then takes the designation of *rancio*, or rusty, or, as some call it, tawny. **1939** B.

COLLIER *Catalan France* viii. 200 With dessert we drank an excellent Rancio from the neighborhood of Barcelona. *Ibid.* xii. 273 A Rancio is not necessarily a wine of the Roussillon; it may be Spanish; but in any case it is pretty certain to be Catalan. **1965** A. SICHEL *Penguin Bk. Wines* III. 172 Used in connexion with these four wines [*sc.* Maury, Côtes d'Agly, Rivesaltes and Banyuls], the word 'Rancio' is roughly equivalent to our 'Tawny' when applied to port. As a description of other wines in the southern area it takes on only its basic meaning of 'old developed'—it does not in those cases mean that the wine has been matured in wood. **1986** *Daily Sun* (Brisbane) 30 Nov. 9/1 Rancio wines are made from over-ripe grapes and are covered by the French-controlled appellation regulations.

**rangoli** (ræŋ'gəʊlɪ), *n.* [a. Gujarati and Rajasthani *raṅgolī*.] A Hindu geometric design or painting made from coloured powder, rice flour, etc.
**1960** *Guardian* 24 Oct. 10/4 Womenfolk decorate their doorsteps to the intricate geometrical designs of rangolis—patterns of coloured chalk dabbed between thumb and forefinger. **1969** E. BHAVNANI *Decorative Designs & Craftsmanship of India* iii. 36 Known as Rangoli . . these hand-made patterns are generally done in white with multi-coloured insets. **1985** K. SPINK tr. *D. Lapierre's City of Joy* (1986) xliv. 243 Expressions of popular joy on occasions of celebration and great solemnity, *rangolis* are marvellous geometric compositions outlined in rice flour and coloured powders and are designed to bring good fortune. **1988** *Newsday* 14 Oct. III. 21/2 Rangoli or floor painting, intricate designs done in softstone or powder, will also be shown.

**ranitidine** (ræ'nɪtɪdiːn, -'naɪ-), *n. Pharm.* [f. *ranit-*, blend of FU)RAN *n.* and NIT(RO-, + -IDINE.] A substituted furan, $C_{13}H_{22}N_4O_3S$, with histamine $H_2$-receptor blocking properties, given (usu. in tablet form) as the hydrochloride to inhibit the secretion of gastric acid in the treatment of peptic ulcers and related conditions.
**1979** *Lancet* 10 Feb. 320/2 Ranitidine may have even fewer non-specific adverse side-effects than those reported occasionally for cimetidine. **1981** *Gut* XXII. s4/1 The degree of acid inhibition comparable with that produced during treatment with four daily doses of cimetidine was . . produced by a twice daily dose of ranitidine. **1985** *Investors Chron.* 8 Nov. 61/1 (Advt.), Sales of ranitidine by Glaxo subsidiaries during the year increased by over £180 million. **1989** *Encycl. Brit.* XVII. 516/2 The $H_2$-receptor antagonist drugs, such as cimetidine and ranitidine, rapidly established a place in the treatment of conditions involving the hypersecretion of gastric acid.

**rant**, *v.* Add: [1.] c. To speak or discourse vehemently, intemperately, or wildly; freq. with *on* (implying duration) or const. *at* (a person), *about* (a subject), to 'go on' (at one about something). Also in phr. *to rant and rave*.
**1898** S. MACMANUS *Bend of Road* 203 The mother, sure enough, raived an' ranted all over the house about it. **1959** F. ASTAIRE *Steps in Time* (1960) viii. 64 J. C. Huffman, the stage director, was a very capable man for this type of show and he really screamed and ranted to get his points across. **1961** S. CHAPLIN *Day of Sardine* viii. 164, I know a lot of people that rant on about their religion and it doesn't do any good. **1974** J. GARDNER *Nickel Mountain* I. x. 44 Callie's hand was reaching once more toward Henry Soames' wrist, but he ranted on, trying to tell the story to Willard Freund. **1983** N. BAWDEN *Ice House* II. iv. 73 All the same, I shouldn't have ranted on at you. **1984** D. LEAVITT *Family Dancing* (1985) 113 It's easy for you to just stand there and rant and rave.

**ranunculin** (ræ'nʌŋkjʊlɪn), *n. Biochem.* [f. RANUNCUL(US *n.* + -IN[1].] A glycoside, produced by various species of buttercup, esp. *Ranunculus bulbosus*, which if eaten may be metabolized to give the toxic vesicant protoanemonin.
**1951** HILL & VAN HEYNINGEN in *Biochem. Jrnl.* XLIX. 332/2 When the tissues are crushed the protoanemonin is liberated enzymically from a glucosidic precursor in the plant. The glucoside itself . . is stable both as a solid and in aqueous solution. This substance . . we propose to call ranunculin, as it has been obtained from several species of *Ranunculus*. **1953** *Proc. Brit. Weed Control Conf.* I. 256 All three species [*Ranunculus bulbosus, R. acris* and *R. repens*] contain a glycoside, ranunculin. **1971** *Science* 26 Feb. 763/1 The innocuous glycoside ranunculin, found in buttercups, . . breaks down to release the aglycone protoanemonin.

**rap**, *n.*[1] Add: [5.] c. A style of popular music (developed by New York Blacks in the 1970s) in which words (usu. improvised) are spoken rhythmically and often in rhyming sentences over an instrumental backing; a song or piece in this style. Cf. *RAP *v.*[1] 3 e. orig. *U.S.*
**1979** *Village Voice* (N.Y.) 3 Dec. 86/2 This meeting of the bullshitters is more groove than rap. **1982** *Face* May 57/2 There is even a Rap single of 'Mama' available. **1983** *N.Y. Times* 18 May C19/5 Rap, the streetwise, intensely rhythmic pop sound that has come roaring out of Harlem, Brooklyn and the South Bronx . . is entering a second critical phase in its evolution. **1987** *Sounds* 30 May 14/3 Later, while attending New York University, Rubin moved closer to the rap scene. At hangouts like Negril and the Roxy, he met all the right people in the rap movement. **1988** *Tower Records' Top* Feb. 7/5 Cartel distributors, Revolver, have great hopes for the . . hip-hop EP . . consisting of 'Anyone', 'The Dark' and 2 raps.
[7.] **rap group**, (*b*) a group which plays rap music.
**1980** *Washington Post* 31 Aug. G2/5 That's the kind of popularity that got [Kurtis] Blow booked into the Capital Centre last night, along with another rap group, the Sugarhill Gang. **1987** *New Musical Express* 9 May 30/3 But when he realised that black classmates were listening to a different rap group each week he decided that rap was much more progressive than rock 'n' roll.
**rap music** = sense *5 c above.
**1982** N. H. & S. K. MAGER *Morrow Bk. New Words* 218/2 *Rap music*, . . personal lyrics sung with no melody in a syncopated beat. **1987** *Times* 13 Nov. 21/6 Rap music is said to have come from the black ghettos of New York.

**rap**, *v.*[1] Add: [3.] e. To perform rap music; to talk or sing in the style of rap. Cf. *RAP *n.*[1] 5 c. orig. *U.S.*
**1980** *Washington Post* 31 Aug. G2/5 'We threw down most violently on it,' Jackson says, meaning that they rapped over the music. **1983** *N.Y. Times* 14 Aug. XXII. 2/6 Thomas Fidos is not with Sound Masters but, as a member of another group, he raps under the name of Mr. T. **1984** *Wall St. Jrnl.* 4 Dec. 16 (*heading*) If folks are clappin' and things Start to happen, the man is rappin'. **1987** *Daily Tel.* 6 Aug. 10/7 'I don't rap in an American accent.' . . He raps in Cockney or Caribbean English.

**rapper**, *n.* Add: [1.] f. A person who performs or is involved in rap music. Cf. *RAP *n.*[1] 5 c. orig. *U.S.*
**1979** *Billboard* 3 Nov. 64/3 The Philadelphia-based rapper, Kurtis Blow, will soon record a 'Christmas Rapping' 12-inch record 'with holiday appeal'. **1982** *Washington Post* 31 Dec. D7/4 All the rappers really talked about was themselves. **1984** *Wall St. Jrnl.* 4 Dec. 16/1 Many raps still brag about the rapper's

financial success and superior cool but others talk about such topics as friends and basketball. **1986** *Sunday Express Mag.* 28 Dec. 27/3 The best records were by oldies Paul Simon and Peter Gabriel, with young black New York rappers Run DMC. **1988** *Sunday Sun* (Brisbane) 3 July (Suppl.) 12/3 Then the inevitable happened. Like flared jeans and yo yos, rappers became an endangered species.

**rapping**, *vbl. n.*[1] Add: [**2.**] **d.** Rhythmical speaking (often improvised and in rhyming sentences) to the accompaniment of a (prerecorded) sound track; a style of popular music characterized by this; = *RAP *n.*[1] 5 c. orig. *U.S.*

**1979** *Village Voice* (N.Y.) 31 Dec. 57/1 That collaboration would result in royal rapping as well as elegantly intimate harmonies. **1981** *N.Y. Times* 15 July c19/1 Miss Harry and Mr. Stein,.. who have long been involved in funk rhythms, rapping and other.. black music trends. **1984** STEWARD & GARRATT *Signed, Sealed & Delivered* v. 100/2 In the USA, rapping, a sung-spoken style, is deep-rooted in black music. **1987** *Daily Tel.* 6 Aug. 10/7 Rapping is chanting in verse to a heavy beat with more than a touch of agit-prop. **1989** D. CLARKE *Penguin Encycl. Popular Mus.* 959/1 When MCs added rapping over the music.. it became rap, also called hip-hop.

**rapture**, *n.* Add: [**4.**] **b.** *the Rapture (of the Church, of the Saints)*: the taking up of believers to heaven at the Second Coming of Christ, according to some Millenarian teaching (after *1 Thess.* iv. 16–17, *Luke* xvii. 34–36).

**1848** J. N. DARBY *Exam. Statements Apocalypse by B. W. Newton* 20 The immensely important fact of the rapture of the Church... Nor can this rapture take place till after He has left the throne. **1849** tr. *Darby's Notes on Apocalypse* vii. 22 The Scripture.. not only applies that expression [sc. 'the coming of Jesus'] to the day of the Lord, but also to.. the rapture of the Church, which goes to meet the Lord in the air. **1849** *Retrospect of Events that have taken place amongst Brethren* 7 Mr. Newton earnestly denied the 'secret rapture of the Saints', as it was technically termed. **1903** W. KELLY *Rapture of Saints* 3, I am not aware that there was any definite teaching.. that there would be a *secret* rapture of the saints at a secret coming. **1937** A. REESE *Approaching Advent Christ* xv. 227 This 'any-moment' view of Christ's Return only originated about 1830, when Darby gave forth.. the mistaken theory of the Secret Coming and Rapture. **1970** *Redemption Tidings* 23 Apr. 8/1 It would seem that, as the date of the Rapture draws near, humanity is becoming.. exceedingly space-conscious. **1988** *Times Lit. Suppl.* 29 Jan. 120/3 Pre-millenialist bumper-stickers include the legend: 'WARNING: In case of Rapture driver will disappear'.

**rapture**, *v.* Add: **2.** *trans.* To take up (believers) to heaven at the Second Coming of Christ. Usu. in *pass.* Cf. *RAPTURE *n.* 4 b.

**1962** J. B. PAYNE *Imminent Appearing of Christ* i. 32 For soon after 1830 a woman.. announced the 'revelation' that the true church would be caught up (raptured) to heaven before the tribulation and before Christ's return to earth. **1984** *Time* 5 Nov. 73/3 Falwell's followers believe Christians will be swept or 'raptured' into heaven before the great Tribulation. **1987** *Times* 20 Apr. 20/2 People will be raptured out of automobiles as they are driving along.

**Ras** (ræs), *n.*[2] and *a.* Also **ras.** [Shortened form of RASTAFARI *n.* or RASTAFARIAN(ISM) *n.*] **A.** *n.* **a.** = RASTAFARIAN *n.* **b.** = RASTAFARIANISM *n.* **B.** *adj.* = RASTAFARIAN *a.*

**1961** *Daily Gleaner* (Kingston, Jamaica) 8 June 1/9 'Bongo Man', the witness explained, was the name Rases used for calling one another. **1969** D. SCOTT in Ramchand & Gray *West Indian Poetry* (1972) 77 One

of his sons made it,.. Enough to bury the Old Ras With respect. **1973** N. FARKI *Countryman Karl Black* i. 11 The Ras did not have to say that as Karl knew .. that the locksmen who worshipped Rastafari were mostly peaceful people. **1973** 'TREVANIAN' *Loo Sanction* (1974) 167 'They ain't going to get nothin.' She said this last in a low-down Ras accent. **1979** *Guardian* 7 Sept. 10/7 Surprising how quickly the.. white ear can pick up the language of Ras.

**rascal**, *n.* Add: [**3.**] **d.** In Papua New Guinea: a member of a criminal gang; a thief or hooligan.

**1985** *Telegraph* (Brisbane) 20 June 17/1 (*heading*) Armed 'Rascal' gangs terrorise PNG's capital. **1985** *Courier-Mail* (Brisbane) 24 June 3/3 Seven 'rascals'—the PNG term for the gangsters who infest the national capital and caused the PNG Government to declare a state of emergency and a nightly curfew 10 days ago—took part in the attack. **1986** *New Yorker* 12 May 59/1 The Port Moresby police refer to robbers and burglars as 'rascals'. **1988** *Courier-Mail* (Brisbane) 27 Sept. 8/7 The attackers were what in Papua New Guinea are described as 'rascals', criminal gangs who operate in urban areas and whose services can be hired.

‖**rassolnik** (ras'soljnik), *n.* Also **rasolnik, rassolnick, razsolnik.** [Russ. *rassol'nik*, f. *rassol* brine + *-nik* -NIK.] A hot Russian soup of salted cucumbers, meat (rarely fish), potatoes, etc.

**1924** A. GAGARINE *Russ. Cook Bk.* II. 26 Razsolnik. .. This is a very popular soup in Russia but few foreigners like it. **1935** M. MORPHY *Recipes of All Nations* 433 Rassolnick (Salt cucumber soup). **1979** 'D. GRANT' *Moscow 5000* i. 35 His mother was.. drinking thick *rasolnik*—pickled vegetable soup. **1982** L. CHAMBERLAIN *Food & Cooking of Russia* (1983) 55 The classics, *shchi, ukha, borshch, rassol'nik* .. all held their own on the aristocratic, francophile tables of nineteenth-century Russia.

**ratchet**, *v.* [**b.**] For def. read: To move (something) with, or as with, a ratchet. Freq. const. *up.* (Earlier and later examples.)

**1973** T. PYNCHON *Gravity's Rainbow* II. 193 But the clock over the bar only clicks once, then presently again, ratcheting time minutewise into their past. **1981** *Times* 18 Apr. 11/1 The spring detent, a small spring which ratchets the teeth of a wheel. **1988** *New Scientist* 17 Mar. 29/1 He said: Maybe we are ratcheting ourselves to a new warmer climate.

**rating**, *vbl. n.*[1] Senses 4 a, b in Dict. become 4 b, c. Add: [**4.**] **a.** An assessment according to an established scale of the value or performance of something offered commercially; *spec.* in *Comm.*, of the profitability of a company's shares.

**1909** J. MOODY *Moody's Anal. Railroad Investments* I. Pref. 15 A table of bond records and ratings, in which the position of each bond issue is shown in the average results worked out in the tables. The issues are all then given a rating, indicating their general security and strength as shown by the record. **1924** *N.Y. Times* 13 June 29/1 Moody's Industrial Rating Book for 1924 is now ready. **1935** F. W. JONES in A. L. Bernheim *Security Markets* xvi. 613 The investment value of stocks, particularly common stocks, is.. subject to such rapid and wide changes, that rating becomes much less significant than in the case of bonds. The bond ratings are, on the other hand, of real value. **1936** *Consumers Union Rep.* May 8/1 The ratings of the stockings are based on the results of both laboratory tests and tests of wear in actual service. **1960** *Which?* May 103/1 With such a complicated product as a TV set, it is difficult for manufacturers to produce an absolutely standard product. *Minor* differences in ratings between brands should not, therefore, be taken as too significant. **1973** *Ibid.* Feb. 36/1 The laboratory tested the records to see how 'hi-fi' they were. The Table gives ratings, under *technical quality*. **1976** *Fortune* Apr. 132/2 The ratings are not the sole determinants of a bond's price. **1984** *Which? Car Suppl.* Oct. 21/3 Our ratings are estimates based on the trade value of a two year old car as a proportion of the current price of a new car. **1989** *Banker* Feb. 35/3 Ratings.. give comfort to the investor ... You need more than price to determine whether or not to buy.

**rationalism**, *n.* Add: **6.** *Archit.* The application of rationalist principles to architecture, characterized by the rejection of ornament and adoption of geometrical simplicity and functionalism.
   **1956** N. PEVSNER *Englishness of Eng. Art* ii. 31 When Europe decided to abandon the Rococo, English rationalism was a welcome discovery. **1964** J. SUMMERSON *Classical Lang. Archit.* v. 38/1 If the rationalism of Laugier pulled in one direction, the wildly irrational inventions of .. Giambattista Piranesi .. pulled in another. **1977** *Progressive Archit.* May 82/1 The theory of rationalism is a reductionist one. It searches for essences—of building types, or urban spaces, even of the alienation produced by the city which both horrifies and fascinates. **1988** *Ibid.* Mar. 122/1 The abstract compositional laws were given material form through the former's [*sc.* Perret's] faith in structural rationalism.

**rationalist**, *n.* and *a.* Add: **4.** *Archit.* **a.** An adherent of rationalism (*RATIONALISM *n.* 6).
   **1975** *Archit. Design* XLV. 365/3 To some extent the work of the Rationalists can only be understood in the Italian context. **1979** *Archit. Rev.* July 3/3 There are architects around who actually call themselves Rationalists again ... They have that same obsession with pure geometric forms and they even quote such eighteenth-century theorists as Laugier, Quatremere and so on. **1984** tr. *Le Monde* in *Guardian Weekly* 10 June 13/2 The great rationalist [*sc.* Le Corbusier] abandoned the precision of the slide rule and plunged .. into the murky mystique of .. *inexpressible space.*
   **b.** As *adj.* Adhering to or characterized by rationalism.
   **1975** *Archit. Design* XLV. 368/4 All these schemes .. are concerned with the city .. as a continuous fabric, whereas the modern movement looked upon the city as an organisation of individual building types ... But the members of the Rationalist Group interpret this common aim in two basically different ways. **1979** *Jrnl. R. Soc. Arts* Nov. 770/2 Their scheme, for student housing, 1976, is reduced to Rationalist fundamentals: street, arcade, balcony and window. **1983** *N.Y. Times* 4 Dec. II. 40/4 Housing that is unusually inviting, even gracious—far more so than the rationalist housing produced in Germany by the architects of the International Style.

**Ratrac** ('rætræk), *n.* A proprietary name for a tracked vehicle used for impacting the surface of a skiing *piste.*
   [**1969** *Schweizerisches Patent-, Muster- und Marken-Blatt: Fabrik- und Handelsmarken* 28 Nov. 654/1 Hinterlegungsdatum : 15. Juli 1969, 18 Uhr Dr. K. Schleuniger & Co., Universitätsstrasse 87, Zürich 6.—Fabrikation und Handel. Raupenfahrzeug. (Int. Kl. 12) RATRAC.] **1971** *Country Life* 14 Oct. 964/2 In bad weather the marked [ski] runs are patrolled .. and the *pistes* themselves are maintained in safe condition with Ratrac machines. **1974** H. EVANS et al. *We learned to Ski* 16 Cold well-beaten snow is what happens to powder snow when lots of people have skied over it, or it has been packed by a machine. (These 'Ratracs', as they are known, are crosses between caterpillar tractors, rollers and lawn mowers.) **1986** *Official Gaz.* (U.S. Patent Office) 22 Apr. TM58/2 Logan Manufacturing Company, Logan, Ut ... RATRAC For crawler-type tractors for use principally upon snow ... First use .. 1973. **1988** *Daily Tel.* 29 Oct. (Weekend Suppl.) p. iii/6 A

half-day off-piste run across glaciers to La Grave, which starts with a Ratrac ride at 3,500 metres.

**ratty**, *a.* Add: 'rattiness *n.*
   **1979** *Washington Post* 2 Mar. (Weekend section) 21/4 His rattiness is supposed to come off as generosity. **1985** *Los Angeles Times* (San Diego County ed.) 26 Aug. 8/2 Bleach-eaten holes added yet another dimension to the rattiness of these jeans.

**rav**, *n.* Sense in Dict. becomes 2. Delete existing variant list and etym., and add: *Judaism.* Also (in sense 1) **rab**, (in sense 2) **rov**. [ad. Heb. and Aramaic *rab* great (one), master (cf. RABBI *n.*[1]); in sense 2 partly through Yiddish.] **1.** *Hist.* A title given to some of the Babylonian rabbis of the second to the fifth centuries.
   **1706** I. ABENDANA *Discourses Eccl. & Civil Polity of Jews* v. 167 Rab Chasda was Rector of the School of Sora after the Decease of Rab Huna. **1819** L. ALEXANDER *Hebrew Ritual* III. 288 Rab is the same person that is called Rav Abo .. that is, our Holy Doctor. **1876** H. POLANO tr. *Selections from Talmud* 28 Death of Rab Ashi. **1930** M. WAXMAN *Hist. Jewish Lit.* I. v. 126 Abba Areka .. or, as he was later known, Rab, i.e. the master, .. himself a Babylonian. **1971** *Encycl. Judaica* II. 866 Rav Ashi: head of the Academy of Sura.

‖**ravalement** (ravalmã), *n. Mus.* [Fr., orig. in the phr. *à ravalement* (A. Bemetzrieder 1771, in *Leçons de clavecins* I. 13), f. *ravaler* to bring down, restore.] The action or an instance of altering and extending the range of a keyboard instrument by rebuilding; hence, an instrument which has been altered in this way.
   [**1940** C. SACHS *Hist. Mus. Instruments* xvi. 376 When musicians after 1700 had no more use for this obsolete transposition, the two keyboards were shifted and completed to coincide. The instrument became what the French call *à ravalement* or 'let down'.] **1959** R. RUSSELL *Harpsichord & Clavichord* iii. 48 *Ravalement* was applied to virginals as to harpsichords. **1961** A. BAINES *Mus. Instruments Through the Ages* iv. 82 Reconstructions usually involved the lengthening and widening of the instruments, .. an operation known in France as *ravalement.* **1974** *Early Music* Jan. 41/1 Many of the instruments thought to have been made by the famous 17th century Flemish makers are in fact not even 'ravalements', but complete 18th-century fakes. **1986** *Ibid.* Aug. 450/1 Gilbert, playing on an 18th-century French ravalement of a 1671 Couchet, is more measured.

**rave**, *v.*[1] Add: [**3.**] [**a.**] *to rant and rave*: see *RANT *v.* 1 c.

**ravishing**, *ppl. a.* Add: **4.** In trivial use: very attractive, delightful.
   **1926** A. HUXLEY *Let.* 10 Aug. (1969) 271, I had a very pleasant evening .. with Anita Loos, who is ravishing. **1927** H. T. LOWE-PORTER tr. *Mann's Magic Mountain* I. v. 346 Frau Stöhr had read it early, and pronounced it simply ravishing. **1958** P. GIBBS *Curtains of Yesterday* xiv. 130 'How do you think I look, Father?' she cried gaily. 'Ravishing!' he said, good-humouredly. 'And very expensive!' **1978** [see POACHED *ppl. a.*[1] c]. **1989** C. HARKNESS *Time of Grace* (1990) v. 79 Although one could hardly have called her suntanned, she was very slightly golden ... She looked ravishing.

**raw**, *a.* (*n.*[2]) Add: [**A.**] [**6.**] [**b.**] Freq. *fig.* or in fig. context.
   **1933** G. GREENE in *Spectator* 8 Dec. 854 A raw sensibility, a bundle of shrieking nerves which barred the possessor hopelessly from any easy comfort. **1962** [see FETISHIZED *a.*]. **1984** *Weekend Australian* 10/11 Nov. 6/5 None [of the banners] has been disturbed, .. perhaps because public sensitivies are too raw.

**1987** J. SMITH *Masculine Ending* vi. 84 'Wild goose chase,' he said grumpily. It appeared she had touched a raw nerve.

**re**, *n.*[3] Substitute for def.: [Graphic abbrev.] Abbreviation of RUPEE *n.*

**Re** (riː), *n.*[4] [Abbrev.] A colloquial abbreviation of REINSURANCE *n.*, used esp. in the names of reinsurance companies.
**1952** *Spectator Insurance Year Bk.* 187/1 The majority of capital stock is held by George O. Tiffany, [*et al.*] . . as trustees under a voting trust agreement with the Swiss Re–North American Corp. **1967** *National Underwriter* (U.S.) 10 Feb. 14/3 The case is that of Emily M. Baron vs General Re of London. **1983** *Re Report* May, If reinsurance is your business, the Re report is your newsletter. **1984** *Sunday Times* 5 Feb. 54/2 A second major shareholder is Ocean Re.

**re-**, *prefix.* Add: [5.] [c.] *re-keyboard v.*
**1967** KARCH & BUBER *Offset Processes* iv. 79 A key is then punched, which makes the carriage move to the left, and the entire line is *re-keyboarded. **1984** *Dictionaries* VI. 162 Rather than type copy on typewriters, which must be rekeyboarded to transcribe it into machine-readable form, these editors now keyboard directly onto floppy disks.

**reach**, *n.*[1] Add: [II.] [11.] b. *Broadcasting.* The number of people who listen to or watch a programme or channel at any time during a specified period.
**1951** E. F. SEEHAFER *Successful Television & Radio Advertising* (ed. 2) iv. 104 *Reach*, or *cumulative audience*, may be defined as the number of different homes tuned to a specific program over a given period of time. **1961** *Sponsor* (N.Y.) 11 Sept. 11. 117/1 On two similar schedules, Station 'A' has the greater reach. **1974** C. WEINBERG et al. *Advertising Managem.* IV. 115 *Reach* is the number of people who see the advertising campaign at least once. **1975** *Independent Broadcasting* Aug. 19/2 The cumulative weekly audience figures, now usually called the 'weekly reach', represents all those people who listened to a station at some time during a measured week. **1984** *Listener* 26 Jan. 25/2 The channel's 'reach' figure, for the proportion of the total population watching it at any point of the week, was 51.2 per cent. **1989** *Sunday Tel.* 24 Sept. 45/3 Audience reach grew steadily, with three-quarters of us tuning in [to Channel Four] sometime during a given week.

**reach**, *v.*[1] Add: [I.] [8.] [b.] For def. read: With personal object, in various applications. Now *esp.*, of a communication: to come to, be received by; of a person: to communicate with (a person, an audience, or the public). (Further examples.)
**1938** C. CONNOLLY *Enemies of Promise* I. i. 17 A writer has no greater pleasure than to reach people, nobody enjoys isolation less than an artist. **1959** *Broadcasting* 5 Oct. 35/1 The report presents a profile on how many people are reached. **1959** J. W. KRUTCH *Human Nature & Human Condition* vii. 133 Educators and publicists must study 'mass communication' so they can reach the common man. **1966** H. MOORE *On Sculpture* 218 Certainly the shelter drawings did seem to get through to a much larger public than I'd ever reached before. **1988** L. GORDON *Eliot's New Life* ii. 63 Eliot wanted to reach a popular audience, but looked down on it.

**read**, *v.* Add: [I.] [5.] j. *Biol.* To interpret or translate (genetic information); *spec.* to extract genetic information from (a particular sequence of nucleic acids), or to extract from a given sequence the genetic information necessary to synthesize (a particular substance).

[**1957** F. H. C. CRICK et al. in *Proc. Nat. Acad. Sci.* XLIII. 418 We further assume that all possible sequences of the amino acids may occur (that is, can be coded) and that at every point in the string of letters one can only read 'sense' in the correct way.] **1961** *Nature* 30 Dec. 1227/1 The sequence of the bases is read from a fixed starting point. This determines how the long sequences of bases are to be correctly read off as triplets. **1965** [see TRANSCRIPTASE *n.*]. **1977** *Time* 14 Nov. 48/1 They broke down and then analyzed the RNA in the archaebacteria's ribosomes, the structures that 'read' the message of the master molecule DNA and produce the protein necessary for life. **1989** *Nature* 14 Sept. 166/2 According to the wobble rule, not only CUG but also CUA may be read to specify serine in C[*andida*] *cylindracea.*

[9.] [a.] Add to def.: Hence, to substitute or understand *for* (what is said or written).
**1868** M. E. G. DUFF *Pol. Survey* 16 For monasteries, we should read convents, mission-houses, and seminaries. **1966** 'A. HALL' *9th Directive* xxi. 193 For snatch read abduction. For swop read exchange. Never a bloody spade. **1967** *Listener* 4 May 593/2 Links between the cultures of 'Indonesia' (read southeast Asia) and west and central Africa.

**readathon** ('riːdəθɒn), *n.* orig. *U.S.* [f. READ *v.* + -ATHON.] A protracted session of reading, esp. aloud and by a group, usu. for charitable purposes.
**1936** *Detroit Free Press* 5 Jan. 1/6 The Tabernacle Baptist Church Bible 'Readathon' came to a breathless close tonight with M. E. Powell . . guessing within an hour and 39 minutes of when the reading would end. **1968** *Telegraph* (Brisbane) 26 Aug. 5/1 The chairman of the British and Foreign Bible Society . . will start a 70-hour Bible readathon at 8 o'clock tonight. **1979** *Forbes* (N.Y.) 5 Feb. 45 There's a veritable *thon*-ic boom in fundraising these days—readathons, . . dancethons, and so on. **1981** *Tuscaloosa* (Alabama) *News* 26 Mar. 11 A month-long read-a-thon . . in which each child obtained sponsors and pledges for each book he or she read. **1984** *Sunday Tel.* 27 May 10/4 The first 'readathon' is being launched by Mencap and Books for Students. **1989** *Bookseller* 23 June 2135/2 (Advt.), Readathon 1989—the national sponsored reading event in aid of The Malcolm Sargent Cancer Fund for Children.

**readerly** ('riːdəlɪ), *a.* [f. READER *n.* + -LY[1]; cf. WRITERLY *a.*] 1. *Lit. Theory.* [tr. F. *lisible* (R. Barthes *S/Z* (1970) I. p. x.).] Immediately accessible to a reader; simply readable, without commentary or interpretation.
**1975** R. MILLER tr. *Barthes's S/Z* 4 Opposite the writerly text, then, is its countervalue, its negative, reactive value: what can be read, but not written: the readerly. We call any readerly text a classic text. **1985** *N. & Q.* Mar. 97/2 The aim of a critical edition is to ascertain as far as possible what the author wrote. This must surely be worthy of attention even in this age of readerly texts. **1986** JEFFERSON & ROBEY *Mod. Lit. Theory* (ed. 2) iv. 108 The readerly text is the one that as readers we passively consume, whereas the writerly text demands the reader's active cooperation.
2. Of or pertaining to a reader.
**1979** *Washington Post* 27 May G3/1 He may also offer readerly advice: 'Rusanov [in *Cancer Ward*] is quietly drawn [etc.].'. **1985** *New Yorker* 26 Aug. 21/1 Heartfelt readerly thanks. **1986** *Year's Work Eng. Stud.* 1983 239 Brady suggests that his 'judicious intimidation' of the reader . . results in readerly insecurity and self-judgement. **1989** *Los Angeles Times* 25 June 3/2 'My blood ran cold' is an understandable readerly response to Gerard's cold-blooded descriptions of 'lovers' past and present.

**reading**, *vbl. n.* Sense 1 e in Dict. becomes 1 f. Add: [1.] e. The action or an instance of inspecting and interpreting signs for the purpose of divination.

**1867** [see *palm-reading* s.v. PALM *n.* 9]. **1877** G. STEWART *Fireside Tales* 75 Although 'reading out of the fire'.. as well as cup-reading, was not new to the hermit, yet he knew little of these arts. **1960** [see *hand-reading* s.v. HAND *n.* 65]. **1963** G. J. McCALL in A. Dundes *Mother Wit* (1973) 420/2 Hoodoo doctors—after careful spiritual 'reading' of the client—prescribe courses of action. **1975** I. McEWAN *First Love, Last Rites* (1976) 28 She had been doing a reading that afternoon and the cards were still spread about the floor. **1979** V. S. NAIPAUL *Bend in River* ii. 28 He had given me a reading and had seen great things in my hand.

**ready**, *a.*, *adv.* and *n.* Add: [**A.**] [**I.**] [**1.**] [**d.**] (*b*) As part of an instruction to competitors at the start of a race, esp. in phr. *ready, steady, go!*

**1960** G. W. TARGET *Teachers* 8 'Come on, I'll race you.'.. 'Come on an' try.' 'Right—ready, steady, GO!' **1972** M. KENYON *Shooting of Dan McGrew* xiii. 104 'Let's run for it,' Henry said. 'Ready, steady, go,' Kate said. **1978** 'F. PARRISH' *Sting of Honeybee* i. 5 'Readeeeee—steadeeeee—go!' called Dan Mallett. Two of the children kicked their ponies into a canter. **1985** C. MARSH (*title*) Ready, steady, go! Running to win in the Christian life.

**Reaganism**, *n.* Add: Hence **'Reaganaut** *n.* [prob. after ARGONAUT *n.*] = *Reaganite* below; **Reaga'nesque** *a.*, of or resembling Ronald Reagan or his policies; **'Reaganite** *n.*, a supporter of Reagan or his policies; also *attrib.* or as *adj.*

**1970** *National Observer* (U.S.) 19 Oct. 11/2 Reaganites scoff at Jess Unruh's guerrilla theater. **1976** *Dun's Rev.* Feb. 41/2 Senator Henry Jackson.. has combined a Reaganesque anti-Soviet stance with a hard anti-oil company position. **1980** *N.Y. Times* 29 Sept. A19/1 *Attorney General*: Caspar Weinberger, longtime Reaganaut.. is talked about for this post. **1987** *Observer* 22 Nov. 10/2 The old Reaganauts fear that the President's weakness could be more damaging to their interests than an active liberal Democrat could be. **1989** *Sunday Times* 19 Feb. (Business Section) 10/1 These conditions sprang not merely from a Reaganesque ideological belief in market mechanisms.

**Reaganomics** (reɪgəˈnɒmɪks), *n. pl. U.S.* [Blend of *Reagan* (see REAGANISM *n.*) and *econ*)*omics* (ECONOMIC *n.* 2 c).] The economic policies of President Reagan, *esp.* those of promoting the unrestricted action of free-market forces in commerce and reducing the taxation of earnings from investment.

**1980** *Washington Post* 5 Oct. 61 Carternomics and Reaganomics, as they bend easily in the political wind, sometimes defy definition. **1984** *Christian Science Monitor* 2 Mar. 32/3 The whole purpose of Reaganomics was to return the country to a pre-Roosevelt period, a laissez faire, dog-eat-dog society. **1985** *Times* 11 July 5/1 The deep federal spending cuts and tax decreases which became known as Reaganomics. **1989** *Sunday Tel.* 31 Dec. 44/1 Ignored Vietnam veterans brushed aside by the platitudes of Reaganomics.

**realize**, *v.*[2] Add: [**1.**] e. *refl.* (Cf. SELF-REALIZATION *n.*)

**1876** F. H. BRADLEY *Ethical Stud.* ii. 61 If what we meant by self-realization was, that I should have in my head the idea of any future external event, then I should realize myself practically when I see the engine is going to run off the line, and it does so. **1937** C. CAUDWELL *Illusion & Reality* v. 97 If only *they* could realise themselves.. this would of itself ensure the freedom of all. **1957** L. P. HARTLEY *Hireling* xv. 118 She seems to have realized herself,

become a person in her own right. **1983** S. NAIPAUL *Hot Country* ix. 125 He had left her free to follow her own inclinations, to be whatever she wanted to be; or, as he had put it, to 'realise' herself.

f. *trans. Linguistics.* To manifest (a linguistic unit, structure, or set of features) phonetically, phonologically, graphically, or syntactically.

**1945–9** *Acta Linguistica* V. 88 The phonemes of a given language are realized in concrete sounds and sound-attributes. **1968** J. LYONS *Introd. Theoret. Linguistics* iii. 131 By virtue of their occurrence in words of one prosodic class rather than another, they are realized phonetically in different ways. **1980** BROWN & MILLER *Syntax: Ling. Introd. Sentence Struct.* xii. 182 In the form *walk-ed*, *walk* realizes the lexeme WALK and *-ed* realizes the grammatical morpheme {past}.

**really**, *adv.*[2] Add: [**2.**] c. *iron.* Expressing disbelief.

**1915** CHESTERTON *Antichrist* in *Poems* 88 Do they read it all in Hansard With a crib to read it with—'Welsh Tithes: Dr. Clifford Answered.' Really, Smith? **1979** *Washington Post* 29 May B1/2 Really... Like somebody says 'War is hell,' or 'You can't fight city hall,' and you say 'really'. Very flat, fatalistic, passive. Really.

**ream**, *v.*[3] Sense 5 in Dict. becomes 5 b. Add: [**I.**] [**2.**] c. *U.S.* To extract juice from (a fruit) with a reamer (\*REAMER *n.* 2); to extract (juice) by reaming.

**1933** *Fruit Products Jrnl.* July 325/1 Juice was prepared by reaming the cut halves of the fruit on a fast revolving burr. **1979** *Sunset* Apr. 152/3 With a sharp knife, cut 10 to 12 oranges neatly in half. Ream the juice from each orange half.

[**II.**] For '*fig.*' read: *transf.* and *fig.* [**5.**] a. To commit sodomy with. (Cf. RIM *v.*[3] 1 b.) *U.S. coarse slang.*

**1942** BERREY & VAN DEN BARK *Amer. Thes. Slang* §508/7 Commit sodomy,.. *ream.* **1976** 'TREVANIAN' *Main* (1977) x. 205, I warn him, but he don't listen. And you.. tell me he's got himself reamed. **1979** T. WOLFE *Right Stuff* (1981) iv. 75 The man reams him so hard the pain brings him to his knees.

[**b.**] (Earlier related example.)

[**1946** *Jrnl. Amer. Sociol.* Mar. 421 The expressions 'to have one's ass chewed' or 'to have one's ass reamed', referring to reprimands by superiors.]

**reamer**, *n.* Add: **2.** *U.S.* A device or utensil for the extraction of juice from citrus fruit, having a central ridged dome on which a half fruit is pressed and twisted.

**1926** *Montgomery Ward Catal. 1926–27* 553/1 Large reamer for oranges and lemons. **1931** E. D. WANGNER *Amer. Home Bk. Kitchens* ii. 26 Does she have an orange or lemon reamer that screws firmly to the table? **1963** C. ADAMS *1001 Questions answered about Cooking* i. 19 A reamer is really needed for cooking, as well as for making fresh fruit juice. **1979** *Washington Post* 29 Nov. E1/2 The lemon reamer and a pair of shears went.. to join a collection of seldom used cookware and gadgets. **1984** *Which?* June 272/1 The reamer is pushed into a citrus fruit with the top cut off and either the reamer or the fruit is twisted to make the juice come out.

**reaming**, *vbl. n.* Add: [**1.**] b. *U.S.* The twisting of a fruit on a reamer in order to extract its juice.

**1948** M. INGRAM *Viscosity of Orange Juice* 13 One may distinguish between two extremes in method of extraction: on the one hand the juice is extracted by reaming (as in the usual hand operation). **1954** TRESSLER & JOSLYN *Chem. & Technol. Fruit & Fruit Products* xii. 427 In the early days of orange juice canning, juice was extracted by hand reaming.

**re-arrange**, v. Add: **re-a'rranged** ppl. a.
  **1873** [see TORRENTIAL a. 1]. **1976** Daily Record (Glasgow) 22 Nov. 27/5 The re-arranged game at Pittodrie on Wednesday. **1988** A. BROOKNER Latecomers i. 13 Fibich, as gaunt as ever, but with expensively rearranged teeth.

**re'base**, v. [RE- 5 a.] trans. To set on a new base; spec. in financial contexts, to establish a new base level for (a price index, etc.).
  **1976** Economist 21 Feb. 70/4 The chancellor has given a consistent series back to 1970 rebased on the conventional national-income accounts basis. **1979** Daily Tel. 29 June 1/2 The Government has been examining .. the question of whether there is a case for re-basing the price index. **1983** National Jrnl. (U.S.) 10 Sept. 1843/1 The Fed .. 'rebased' M-1 on the average level of the second quarter and set the target for the second half of 1983 at a slightly higher 5 to 9 per cent. **1986** Your Business Mar. 13/2 (caption) USM index (against FT share/rebased). **1989** What Investment Jan. 87/2 Under normal circumstances, Mr Houseman would have paid Capital Gains Tax on the sale of his second house but since it was acquired well before 31 March 1982, it will be 'rebased' at that date.
  So **re'basing** vbl. n.
  **1962** (title) Wholesale price index rebasing factors (U.S. Bureau of Labor Statistics). **1985** Financial Times 1 July 15/4 In an index in which many of the prices have moved very little, the difference, as a result of the rebasing, will be slight.

**re'birthing**, vbl. n. [Prob. f. RE- 5 a + BIRTHING vbl. n., influenced by REBIRTH n.] A therapeutic technique of controlled breathing simulating the trauma of birth.
  **1976** San Francisco Chron. 20 Dec. 1/2 Rebirthing .. is supposed to make a client .. relive his own birth and clear him of negative images that he has carried unconsciously into adulthood. **1977** ORR & RAY Rebirthing in New Age ii. 41 What we were then [August 1974] naming a 'baptism' and later changed to 'rebirthing'. It was timely that Frederick Le Boyer's first article in this country on 'Birth Without Violence' had come out. **1977** Washington Post 14 Oct. (Weekend section) 24/2 Waterfarm also offers rebirthing, special intensive workshops and something called a 'delight intensive'. **1988** Fitness May 19/1 As well as many written and verbal processes the conscious breathing technique commonly referred to as Rebirthing is used to help get beyond the complex, and often restrictive, mind games we play with ourselves.
  Also **re'birth** v. trans., to treat (someone) by the process of rebirthing; **re'birther** n., one who practises rebirthing.
  **1976** San Francisco Chron. 20 Dec. 4/1 Since April, 1974, more than 10,000 people have been rebirthed by Orr and his followers at Theta Seminars. Ibid., The loving feeling that comes from a rebirther's coaching and his touch. **1977** ORR & RAY Rebirthing in New Age iv. 77 People who are destructive usually don't get rebirthed. Ibid. 79 After rebirthing over ten thousand people, we have evolved a new theory of hyperventilation. Ibid. 80 Relaxing in the presence of the rebirther produces the syndrome. **1985** Observer (Colour Suppl.) 21 Apr. 7/1, I had tried to explain to her over breakfast that Ms Artemis was coming to rebirth me.

**reboot** (riː'buːt), n. Computing. [f. *REBOOT v.] An act or instance of rebooting a computer or an operating system.
  **1981** 80 Microcomputing Aug. 44/1 The reboots happen for no reason at all. **1982** Computerworld 26 Apr. 65/1 The IM [sc. Internal Memory] boards are said to be designed to avoid reboots and data losses and to run at high speeds. **1984** Practical Computing Jan. 86/1 The next reboot will take you across to Concurrent CP/M. **1988** Dr. Dobb's Jrnl. Software Tools Nov. 64/3 After installing itself it .. does a

warm reboot, which reinitializes the computer without doing a memory check.

**reboot** (riː'buːt), v. Computing. [f. RE- 5 a + BOOT v.⁴] trans. To boot (a computer, etc.) again, esp. after a power failure or other breakdown. Also absol.
  **1978** Bell System Technical Jrnl. LVII. 2185 A fairly large fraction of these users .. are capable of 're-booting' the operating system. **1980** Christian Science Monitor 28 Nov. 24/3 It is a command to stop in our tracks and relinquish everything we have written to the maw of the computer until it can be rebooted, whatever that means. **1982** Byte May 330/2 Even if you don't add these detection routines to your system, knowing what the computer is doing will help you avoid rebooting unnecessarily. **1985** Practical Computing May 96/3 The user simply unplugs the failed peripheral, then reboots the system. **1988** PC Mag. Oct. 62/2 You can reboot and start up the system with the adjusted parameters.

**rebuffal** (rɪ'bʌfəl), n. [f. REBUFF v. + -AL¹; perh. infl. by REBUTTAL n.] An act or instance of rebuffing; a rebuff, a repulse or rejection.
  **1967** Economist 15 July 246/2 The community's rebuffal of the Spanish advances since 1964 has made the liberals' position harder. **1981** Times 15 Dec. 5/3 The dialectical logjam of argument and rebuffal might be shifted in the next 10 years or so. **1984** Financial Times 8 May 18/4 Hanson lifted its offer to $23 a share the following day. But USI and Kelso held out, with repeated rebuffals. **1989** Summary World Broadcasts: Far East (B.B.C.) 25 Feb. III. C. 1/1 Several ulema and clergymen .. described the enforcement of the state of emergency as timely for reliably defending the country and the rebuffal of aggression from abroad.

**rebuildable** (riː'bɪldəb(ə)l), a. [f. REBUILD v. + -ABLE.] Capable of being rebuilt.
  **1978** Detroit Free Press 2 Apr. 16F/5 (Advt.), Wanted: Rebuildable & used refrigs, freezers, stoves, clean late models. **1980** Dirt Bike Oct. 13 (Advt.), They're here right now—the new 'F' series motocross shock .. and they're rebuildable so you really save. **1988** N.Y. Times 12 Sept. A14/6 'I said, "houses are rebuildable,"' said Ms. Costantino. 'But he wouldn't listen.'

**recall**, v.¹ Add: [1.] d. Computing. To transfer or call (a program, data, etc.) again to a location in local memory where it can be processed, displayed on screen, etc. rapidly.
  **1966** Proc. AFIPS Conf. XXIX. 150/1 An alphanumeric or special character macro identification code used in recalling the macro is keyed next. **1976** Chemical Week 3 Mar. 31/2 It has put quality-related data on a time-sharing computer where it's easily recalled. **1984** Mail on Sunday 2 Dec. (Colour Suppl.) 6/2 (Advt.), You can keep 16 preset programmes in the memory ... Each one can be recalled at the touch of a button. **1988** Which? Nov. 524/3 Hard disk drives are much faster at storing and recalling programs .. than floppy disk ones.

**receiver**, n.¹ Add: [5.] g. That part of a firearm which houses the action and to which the barrel and other components are attached.
  **1872** C. NORTON Amer. Breech-Loading Small Arms ii. 80 Unscrew the barrel from the receiver. **1895** Montgomery Ward Catal. Spring & Summer 466/2 Receiver, complete with Guard. **1959** W. FAULKNER Mansion i. 38 He took from its corner behind the door the tremendous ten-gauge double-barrelled shotgun which had belonged to his grandfather, the twin hammers standing above the receiver almost as tall as the ears of a rabbit. **1974** Encycl. Brit. Macropædia XVI. 897/2 In all early bolt actions one or more projections, frequently called lugs, revolved from open space into recesses in the receiver, the rear

portion of the weapon. **1985** *Survival Weaponry* Dec. 6/1 If the recoil spring could be put into the receiver, it would be possible to dispense with the butt.

**recessed** (rɪ'sɛst), *a.* [f. RECESS(ION *n.*[1] + -ED[1].] Characterized by or suffering economic recession.

**1956** *Atlantic Monthly* 198/6 Very few workers, even in Coventry, the capital of recessed cardom, had yet been forced to sell house and home. **1981** *Christian Science Monitor* 11 Feb. 6/2 Its latest nudge to money rates—at a time when the recessed domestic economy might be better served by lower interest rates—shows its concern. **1987** *N.Y. Times Mag.* 9 Aug. 8/4 In a recessed economy, the offer made to Mr. Gedman would put him among the top income-earners in Houston.

**re'charger**, *n.* [f. RECHARGE *v.* + -ER[1].] A device for recharging batteries or battery-powered equipment.

**1959** *Electronics World* Sept. 104/2 A built-in recharger, permitting insertion in any a.c. outlet for renewal, uses a miniature stepdown transformer and rectifier. **1963** *Pop. Mechanics* Sept. 192 Once the radio has been modified, the recharger plugs into what used to be its earphone jack. **1979** D. FRANCIS *Whip Hand* i. 9, I took the battery out of my arm and fed it into the re-charger. **1989** *Byte* Aug. 99/2 The main emergency light sources are Black & Decker Spotlighters connected to wall recharger units.

**recon.** ('riːkɒn), *a. colloq.* Also without point. [Written abbrev., in advertisements.] Of engines: = *reconditioned* ppl. a. (s.v. RECONDITION *v.*).

**1976** *Milton Keynes Express* 16 July 34/3 (Advt.), 1970 Austin Maxi 1500. In brown, recon engine has done approx. 6,000 miles. **1977** *Custom Car* Nov. 84/1 (Advt.), Custom Mini, recon. balanced 1000cc engine. **1977** *Horse and Hound* 10 June 42/4 (Advt.), 1971 Bedford TK 330 diesel, recon. engine.

‖**reconcentrado** (ˌriːkɒnsən'trɑːdəʊ), *n. Obs. exc. Hist.* [Sp., pa. pple. of *reconcentrar* to bring together, to concentrate.] In the Cuban war of independence (1895–8), any of the rural Cubans concentrated in garrisoned towns or detention camps by the Spanish military authorities.

**1898** R. DAVEY *Cuba* 108 The miserable *reconcentrados* .. who, between the two camps, have been systematically starved to death. **1902** 'MARK TWAIN' in *N. Amer. Rev.* May 624 It was Funston's example that made us copy Weyler's *reconcentrado* horror. **1910** *Encycl. Brit.* VII. 604/2 'Reconcentracion' of non-combatants .. produced extreme suffering and much starvation (as the reconcentrados were largely thrown upon the charity of the beggared communities in which they were huddled). **1927** C. CHAPMAN *Hist. Cuban Republic* iv. 81 The keynote of his methods was his so-called reconcentrado (reconcentration) policy. All Cubans (men, women, and children) were ordered to move into garrisoned Spanish towns or concentration camps, and no civilian was to go into the rural districts without a passport.

**recon'figure**, *v.* (Formerly at RE- 5 a.) [RE- 5 a.] *trans.* To configure again or differently; *spec.* in *Computing*, to adapt (a system) to a new task by altering its configuration. Also *intr.* for *refl.*

**1964** M. McLUHAN *Understanding Media* II. xxxi. 313 The viewer of the TV mosaic, with technical control of the image, unconsciously re-configures the dots into an abstract work of art. **1968** *Sci. News* 15 June 570/2 The air traffic control and navigation complex .. is essentially a hodgepodge of war surplus systems which have been reconfigured using modern components. **1974** *Sci. Amer.* Aug. 15/2 (Advt.), And

when you've finished the task, you can re-configure the system for a different task, or return the instrument and the calculator to normal bench use. **1984** *Sunday Times* 4 Nov. 80/4 If an element fails, the device switches itself off and then on again, automatically reconfiguring to eliminate the bad part. **1985** *Personal Computer World* Feb. 17 (Advt.), Crestmatt packages may be reconfigured to suit individual business needs.

Hence ˌreconfigu'ration *n.*

**1969** *Word Study* Apr. 5/2 A nonengineer might be satisfied with 'Change the base drawing', but since the engineer knows that the drawing is a configuration, any modification to it is naturally a reconfiguration. **1983** *Mini-Micro Syst.* Feb. 106/2 One trend is to have increasingly sophisticated reconfiguration within the network control and management domain.

**reconstruction**, *n.* Add: [1.] **d.** The reorganization of a public company, whereby it is wound up and immediately re-formed as a new company under similar ownership, for the purposes of redistribution of capital, etc.; an instance of this.

**1871** *Law Rep. Equity Cases* (Incorporated Council of Law Reporting) XII. 504 Sanctioning a scheme for the reconstruction of a company under liquidation, by a transfer of its assets to a new company to be formed for the purpose. **1930** A. PALMER *Company Secretarial Pract.* xx. 269 The term reconstruction is applied to many schemes put forward by companies for the purpose of writing off capital which has been lost or has ceased to be represented by available assets. **1943** *Univ. Toronto Law Jrnl.* V. 280 'Reconstruction' .. is normally used to refer to the transfer of the undertaking of a company to a new company with substantially the same shareholders as the old with the intention that the undertaking shall be continued. **1969** in J. B. Saunders *Words & Phrases legally Defined* (ed. 2) IV. 275/1 Where an undertaking is being carried on by a company, and is in substance transferred, not to an outsider, but to another company, consisting substantially of the same shareholders, .. there is a reconstruction. **1986** *Times* 20 May 34/1 (Advt.), The successful candidate will ideally .. have around two years post qualification experience in corporate and commercial law, including acquisitions, mergers and reconstructions and most types of commercial agreements. **1987** *Financial Times* 19 May 9/7 PW, Mr Homan says, wishes to shift the emphasis away from simply the orderly disposal of assets towards reconstruction.

**recumbent**, *a.* (and *n.*) Add: [A.] [2.] **b.** Designating a type of bicycle ridden in a recumbent position. orig. and chiefly *N. Amer.*

**1980** *Christian Science Monitor* 20 Aug. 18/1 Recumbent bicycles are not totally new. Some designs attracted comment around the turn of the century. **1983** *Sci. Amer.* Dec. 126/2 In the same year the French inventor Charles Mochet built a supine recumbent bicycle (with the rider pedaling while lying on his back) that he later streamlined. **1985** *City Cyclist* (Toronto) Summer 7/2 On a recumbent bike, you sit lower or lie flat. **1988** *New Scientist* 7 Jan. 63/1 The recumbent bicycle is not a new idea. The first patent for a recumbent design, the 'Normal Bicyclette', was taken out in the early 1890s.

[B.] Restrict † to sense in Dict. **2.** Short for 'recumbent bicycle': see sense 2 b of the adj.

**1982** *Bicycling* May 53 (*caption*) The first serious production enclosed recumbent (50 will be built this year; 500 next year) is being offered for $3,800 by Cyclodynamics. **1983** *Sci. Amer.* 133/1 A problem is that a recumbent is hard to see on a road and so is perhaps more vulnerable to automobiles. **1986** *Pop. Mechanics* Nov. 12/4 In return for the money and effort expended on the record chase, the Easy Racers

Shop owners hope to see an increase in the popularity of recumbents.

**redeem**, v. Add: [2.] **d.** To exchange (trading stamps, coupons, etc.) *for* goods, discount, or money. *Occas. absol. orig. U.S.*
**1904** *Laws State of N.Y.* II. dclvii. 1652 Persons who sell or issue trading stamps shall redeem them in money or goods at face value. **1915** *Lit. Digest* 5 June 1363/1 Last year there were over $100,000,000 worth of coupons, trading-stamps, and similar premium-giving devices sold. On this vast amount there were only ten to twelve million dollars' worth redeemed. **1932** *Business Week* 10 Feb. 12/2 Its stamps are purchased and issued to consumers by retailers, redeemed by the S & H premium stores. **1957** *Jrnl. Retailing* Winter 165/2 Some of them .. redeemed stamps for merchandise rather infrequently. **1976** *Sunday Mail* (Glasgow) 21 Nov. 8 (Advt.), Player's No. 10 ... If you decide to make the switch from coupons you will be able to redeem your existing coupons or exchange them for cash. **1989** *Guardian* 23 June 25/4 Public confidence in the stamp empires was growing, reflected in a tendency to redeem later for that more valuable item (2.5 to 3 books) rather than trade in quick.

**'redial**, n. [RE- 5 a.] The facility on a telephone by which (in the event of a number being engaged, etc.) the number just dialled may be automatically redialled by pressing a single button. Also *last number redial*.
**1982** *Byte* Aug. 459/3 Touch-Tone transmitter allows outward dialing in PABX .. applications, including automatic redial and speed dialing. **1982** *Computerworld* 29 Mar. 29/1 It has last-number-redial capability in case the user encounters a busy signal. **1984** *HFD* 9 Jan. 93/3 Two line and hold, for example, are becoming commonplace on basic phones, while memory and redial permeate the lines at the high end. **1987** *Sunday Express Mag.* 31 May 71/1 There's a last number redial button, for those constantly engaged numbers.

**redistri'butionist**, n. (and a.) [RE- 5 a.] One who advocates the redistribution of wealth. Cf. *welfare-statist* n. s.v. WELFARE STATE n. Also *attrib.* or as *adj.*
**1966** T. PYNCHON *Crying of Lot 49* vi. 181 They'd call her names, proclaim her .. as a redistributionist and pinko. **1976** *Economist* 27 Mar. (Survey Suppl.) 13/3 Mr Cameron is a left-winger of the good old straightforward redistributionist sort, and he came to office with the conviction that it was time to give the workers a bigger share of the cake. **1978** W. F. BUCKLEY *Stained Glass* 229 Sometimes in a redistributionist excess he would think of it as his and Meister Gerard's chapel. **1981** *Industry Week* 4 May 9 It will be there that we will see just how far the newfound conservatism will allow tempering the fanatic rush that redistributionists have been in to meet new social goals. **1986** *Nat. Westminster Bank Q. Rev.* Nov. 3 Redistributionists also discovered that in a welfare state redistribution takes place as a result of direct income transfers through the expenditure side of the budget.

**red-'light**, v. Also red light, redlight. [f. the n.]
**1. trans.** To force (a thief, tramp, etc.) out of a moving train (see quot. 1931). Hence *fig.*, to discharge or expel; to dispose of, kill. *U.S. slang* (orig. *Circus*).
**1919** *Billboard* 20 Dec. 87/3 The roughnecks found out that I had some money, and that night I was redlighted off the show. **1927** J. TULLY *Circus Parade* xvi. 254 The light still gleamed in the open door of the car from which we had been red-lighted. **1931** G. IRWIN *Amer. Tramp & Underworld Slang* 156 *Red light*, to do away with. The term originated with the .. custom of disposing of an undesirable member of a circus or carnival crew by taking him out on a train platform after dark and hurling him off the train ...

A red light is a danger signal in any case, and on a railroad indicates a full stop. **1932** D. HAMMETT in *Amer. Mag.* Oct. 96/1 What's the circus and carnival slang term for kicking a guy off a train while it's going? Red-lighting. Sure, that's it—red lights. Who'd you red-light, Ferris? **1941** J. SMILEY *Hash House Lingo* 46 *Redlight*, to discharge from a position. **1960** WENTWORTH & FLEXNER *Dict. Amer. Slang* 424/1 *Red-light*, .. *1.* To push a person off or out of a moving railroad train ... *2.* To stop one's automobile and eject a passenger so that he has to walk home under inconvenient or embarrassing circumstances. **1984** *Verbatim* X. III. 22/1 The circus's jargon is rich and colourful ... *Redlight*, to toss a cheat, thief, or other bad character off a moving train.
**2.** To signal, warn, or stop by means of a red light. Hence *fig.*, to alarm, alert, or deter. *colloq.*
**1969** in P. Adam-Smith *Folklore Austral. Railwaymen* 187 Just before we got to the New Town siding, I red-lighted Mick the driver to pull up. **1975** J. GORES *Hammett* (1976) xiii. 92 I really red-lighted Shuman, and this must have been his idea of a smart way to get back at me.
Hence **red-'lighting** vbl. n.
**1927** J. TULLY *Circus Parade* xv. 229 Red-lighting was an ancient and dishonourable custom indulged in by many a circus twenty years ago. **1932** [see sense 1 above].

**red line**, n. Add: **2.** A red mark (on a gauge or dial) indicating a safety limit or critical point; *spec.* in *Aeronaut.* and *Motoring*, the line on a tachometer which denotes the maximum safe speed, r.p.m., etc. Hence, a maximum speed or safety limit. Also *transf.* and *fig.* Chiefly *U.S.*
**1956** W. A. HEFLIN *U.S. Air Force Dict.* 431/1 *Redline*, .. a red mark or line on the airspeed indicator in certain airplanes, indicating the safe maximum speed of the airplane; also a line on other indicators to indicate a danger point. **1973** *Sci. Amer.* Apr. 11/1 Coming down the mountain I kept the engine constantly at red-line in first, second and third gears. **1975** *High Time* Dec. 119/2 You can bet the pilot's pucker factor is almost at redline. **1980** D. CAMERON *Ballooning Handbk.* iii. 44 For lesser flights it is enough to .. keep an eye on the temperature gauge, being ready to slow or stop the climb as it approaches the 'red line'. **1982** J. A. ANGELO *Dict. Space Technol.* 238/2 *Redline*, .. term denoting a critical value for a parameter or a condition that, if exceeded, threatens the integrity of a system, performance of a vehicle, or success of a mission. **1987** *Super Bike* June 68/1 Presuming that they know by now which gearing to pull .., I reckon the true redline is more like 8000 rpm.

**red-line**, v. Add: **b.** *Aeronaut.* and *Motoring.* *trans.* and *intr.* To set the maximum safe speed of (an aircraft, car, motorcycle, etc.); to drive at maximum speed, to push (the speed, etc.) to the limit. *colloq.* (chiefly *U.S.*).
**1956** W. A. HEFLIN *U.S. Air Force Dict.* 431/2 *Redline*, .. to set a recommended limit on the airspeed of an airplane. Usually in passive, as in 'the C-47 is redlined at 150 knots'. **1966** *Publ. Amer. Dial. Soc.* 1964 XLII. 8 *Redline*, .. to drive at top rpm, i.e., speed at which tachometer indicator reaches warning mark, usually red. **1980** *Verbatim* Autumn 11/2 Of course, in an emergency there were no rules ... 'I drove the son-of-a-bitch 'til the wings were ready to come off. I red-lined everything—air speed, rpm, manifold pressure.' **1987** *Super Bike* June 56/2 As stock, it redlines through six gears yet there's a spare 2500 rpm to lure the tuner.

**redoubtable**, a. (and n.) Add: **re'doubtably** adv.
**1895** *Funk's Stand. Dict.*, Redoubtably. **1979** *Washington Post* 29 Apr. A3/4 A .. redoubtably

powerful woman who is a member of the state Executive Council.

**reducible**, *a.* Add: [4.] **c.** *spec.* in *Math.* Of a polynomial: capable of being factorized into two or more polynomials of lower degree. Of a group: expressible as the direct product of two of its subgroups.
**1674** [see sense 4 b above]. **1885** A. CAYLEY *Coll. Math. Papers* XII. 251 A seminvariant which is not reducible is said to be irreducible, or otherwise to be a perpetuant. **1934** WEBSTER s.v. *Algebra*, A reducible algebra is an algebra, *A*, expressible as the sum of two proper subalgebras, *B* and *C*, such that the products *BC*, *CB* and the intersection of *B* and *C* are the zero element. **1965** PATTERSON & RUTHERFORD *Elem. Abstr. Algebra* iv. 126 If *F* is the field of real numbers, then the polynomial $2-x^2$ over *F* is reducible, since $\sqrt{2}-x$ and $\sqrt{2}+x$ are factors. **1971** POWELL & HIGMAN *Finite Simple Groups* iii. 149 *V* is completely reducible, i.e., a direct sum of irreducible modules.

**reductive**, *a.* and *n.* Add: Hence **re'ductiveness** *n.*, the quality of being reductive.
**1980** *Times Lit. Suppl.* 22 Aug. 928/2 [Robert] Lowell's great originality .. only a great poet could be so reductive, with a reductiveness—and of an American kind—that leaves Yeats standing. **1989** *Chicago Tribune* 3 Mar. v. 3/5 The reductiveness of these books is the price of bringing clarity to a subject too often treated as a kind of noble tragedy.

**Reeperbahn** ('riːpəbɑːn), *n.* [a. Ger., lit. 'rope-walk', f. *Reeper* rope-maker + *Bahn* way, path.] The name of a street in the red-light district of Hamburg, used allusively of similar districts elsewhere.
**1976** P. O'DONNELL *Last Day in Limbo* x. 151 Cast no slurs on Tring... They regard us as the Reeperbahn of Hertfordshire. **1980** *Times* 22 Oct. 13/7 Helping to rescue the theatre .. by wooing the seaside-postcard buyer and Reeperbahn user. **1984** J. MORRIS *Journeys* 12 The Reeperbahn or 42nd Street of Sydney is King's Cross.

**refer**, *v.* Add: [I.] [6.] **d.** Phr. *refer to drawer*: on a cheque, a bank's instruction to the payee to send back to the drawer a cheque that cannot be honoured. Abbrev. *R.D.* s.v. *R* II. 2 a.
**1881** *Jrnl. Inst. Bankers* II. 367 Returning a cheque unpaid, marked with one of the usual answers—'Not provided for', 'Refer to drawer' &c. **1911** W. THOMSON *Dict. Banking* 440/2 'Refer to drawer', is a milder form of answer than 'N/S', 'not sufficient'. **1971** *Reader's Digest Family Guide to Law* 316/2 A 'bounced' cheque is one that is returned to the person who paid it in with the words 'refer to drawer' or R/D on it. **1987** *Daily Tel.* 31 Jan. 33/1 Banks return cheques marked either 'refer to drawer', or 'refer to drawer, please represent'... The first implies 'There is no way we are going to pay.'

**reference**, *n.* Add: [7.] **b.** A book or work of reference; a reference book. *U.S.*
**1972** *Publishers Weekly* 10 Apr. 20 (Advt.), *Webster's Intermediate Dictionary* is the newest—and brightest—member of the Merriam-Webster family of dictionaries and references. **1973** *Sci. Amer.* Jan. 108/2 *The Guide to Simulation Games for Education and Training*... This valuable reference is available from Information Resources, Inc. **1977** *Verbatim* May 8/1 (Advt.), This one-of-a-kind reference tells you everything you've always wanted to know about your favorite fictional sleuths and their creators.

**referentiality** (refərɛnʃɪ'ælɪtɪ), *n.* [f. REFERENTIAL *a.* + -ITY.] The fact or quality of being referential or of having a referent, esp. (in Literary Theory) of having the external

world, rather than the text, language, etc., as referent.
**1976** J. CULLER in *Mod. Lang. Notes* XCI. 1383 Whenever a work seems to be referring to the world one can .. postpone the referentiality of the fiction to another moment or another level. **1977** N. ROJAS (*title*) Referentiality in Spanish noun phrases. **1985** *Canad. Jrnl. Linguistics* XXX. 343 Were this claim to be true, then syntactic research would be limited .. to .. making superficial observations about .. pronouns and agreement, definiteness and referentiality. **1986** JEFFERSON & ROBEY *Mod. Lit. Theory* (ed. 2) i. 33 In poetic language referentiality is irrelevant and the emphasis is on the means of expression itself. **1988** *Times Lit. Suppl.* 24 June 705/1 The customary oppositions of truth and error, referentiality and non-referentiality .. and of fact and fiction have been constantly 'called into question' .. in his own writings.

**refill**, *v.* Add: Hence **re'filled** *ppl. a.*, that has been filled again.
**1958** P. SCOTT *Mark of Warrior* I. 38 Ramsay took the refilled glass. **1979** J. GERSON *Omega Factor* i. 40 Julia came into the room carrying the refilled teapot.

**re'finish**, *v.* [RE- 5 a.] *trans.* To apply a new finish to (a surface). Also *absol.* Hence **re'finished** *ppl. a.*, **re'finishing** *vbl. n.*
**1904** F. T. HODGSON *Up-to-Date Hardwood Finisher* 191 (*heading*) Refinishing oak doors. **1934** *Amer. Home* XI. 273/1 (*heading*) Floor refinishing is no afternoon tea. It's hard work. *Ibid.*, Ready to be refinished, the first operation is to remove the old, original surface. **1950** R. P. KINNEY *Compl. Bk. Furnit. Repairing & Refinishing* xiii. 219 To refinish, if rusted, clean with coarse steel wool. **1962** G. GROTZ *Furnit. Doctor* viii. 143 Sandpaper is never used in refinishing because of the danger of it cutting through the finish. **1976** *Laurel* (Montana) *Outlook* 23 June 19/5 (Advt.), Refinished walnut dining table. **1983** *Which?* Oct. 447/3 Timber frames (and any sub-frames) will still need repainting or refinishing regularly.

**re'flag**, *v.* [RE- 5 c.] *trans.* To fit or supply with a new flag; *spec.* to register (a ship) under a new national flag or flag of convenience, esp. enabling it to qualify for protection through disputed waters.
**1934** in WEBSTER. **1983** *Travel Weekly* 12 May 1/4 (*heading*) Congressmen launch bill to reflag vessels. **1987** *Daily Tel.* 22 July 1/2 The two [Kuwaiti] tankers, the first of 11 to be reflagged under American colours. **1989** *Christian Science Monitor* 6 Apr. 19/4 The Soviet offer to lease and reflag ships to Kuwait.
Hence **re'flagged** *ppl. a.*, **re'flagging** *vbl. n.*
**1977** *Business Week* 4 July 22/2 'We do not like reflagging'—bringing foreign-built ships under the American flag. **1987** *Daily Tel.* 22 July 1/2 Two reflagged Kuwaiti tankers hoisted the Stars and Stripes. **1987** *Times* 22 July 4/6 Would she confirm that she would not .. permit the reflagging of ships which are not British ships with the British ensign? **1987** *Jordan Times* 21 Oct. 1 The convoy consists of two reflagged Kuwaiti ships.

**re'fluffable**, *a. U.S.* [RE- 5 a.] Of a pillow, etc.: that may be fluffed or plumped up again. (Trade jargon.)
**1976** *Honolulu Star-Bull.* 21 Dec. B-5 (Advt.), Polyester filled refluffable billow pillows. **1978** *Detroit Free Press* 5 Mar. A19/4 (Advt.), Down and feather pillows ... All are naturally refluffable. **1984** *Sears Catal. 1985* Spring-Summer 1274 Polyester fill Pillow has 20 ounces of fill in standard size and provides refluffable medium support.

**reformat** (riː'fɔːmæt), *v.* (Formerly at RE- 5 a.) Chiefly *Computing*. [f. RE- 5 a + FORMAT *v.*] *trans.* To make (data, etc.) conform again to a particular format; to revise or represent in another format (occas. const. *into*, *to*).

**1967** Cox & Grose *Organization Bibliogr. Rec. by Computer* IV. 88 The user may initially employ his own Preprocessor to edit and reformat his data prior to entering it into the system. **1973** *Computers & Humanities* VII. 214 The cards were built onto a disk file by a program that reformatted the material into fixed-length records. **1982** *Papers Dict. Soc. N. Amer.* **1979** 139 Computer-stored dictionaries can be updated and reprinted, or extracted and reformatted. **1985** *Personal Computer World* Feb. 173/3 As text is entered, inserted and deleted, WordStar 2000 automatically reformats text to the current margins.

Hence **re'formatting** *vbl. n.*

**1967** Cox & Grose *Organiz. Bibliogr. Rec. by Computer* v. 114 An experimental vehicle .. for on-line computer-aided editing and reformatting of MARC records. **1983** *Austral. Personal Computer* Aug. 40/3 The combination of the mouse and keyboard allows fast selection, editing and reformatting of text.

**refresher**, *n.* Add: [2.] **b.** A short course of instruction or study designed to bring one up to date with developments, esp. in an academic or professional field; = *refresher course.* orig. *U.S.*

**1941** A. Hooper (*title*) Mathematical refresher. **1943** 'Cleo et Anthony' *Sex Refresher* p. ix, The very nature of a 'refresher' prohibits a comprehensive .. coverage of the subject. **1954** J. D. Constance (*title*) Hydraulics refresher for professional license. **1976** Ld. Home *Way Wind Blows* vii. 104 As a result of my years at the Scottish Office, when Mr Heath asked me in 1969 to examine the question of devolution .., I needed but a short refresher. **1984** A. Hailey *Strong Medicine* I. viii. 69 Others already employed were brought to headquarters in small groups for a ten-day refresher.

**refusenik**, *n.* Add: **2.** *transf.* One who refuses to obey orders, esp. as a protest. *colloq.*

**1983** *Sunday Times* (Colour Suppl.) 30 Oct. 39/4 Army regulations appear to have been altered to permit convicted 'refusniks' to be served with new call-up orders the moment they leave prison. **1986** *City Limits* 10 Apr. 7 The 30 'refuseniks' who would not go to Wapping have been joined by 50 people. **1987** *Courier-Mail* (Brisbane) 8 Dec. 19/1 (*heading*) 'Refuseniks' of Voyager lobby Hawke.

**reggae**, *n.* Add: Hence **'reggaefied** *a.*, influenced by or arranged as reggae music.

**1976** *New Musical Express* 31 July 39/5 He crooned Sam Cooke's 'Bring It On Home To Me', .. and his own reggaefied 'Baby Lay Your Head (Down On My Bed)'. **1986** *City Limits* 15 Jan. 41 The limp reggaefied pop/soul .. fails to prepare you for the live show.

**reggo** *n.*, var. *REGO *n.

**regiospecific** (ˌriːdʒɪəʊspəˈsɪfɪk), *a. Chem.* [f. L. *regio* REGION *n.* + SPECIFIC *a.*] Regionally specific; *spec.* designating or characterized by reactions and processes which take place preferentially at some locations (esp. sites on a single molecule) rather than at others owing to local factors (such as the geometry of the molecule).

**1968** Hassner & Boerwinkle in *Jrnl. Amer. Chem. Soc.* XC. 217/1 In nitromethane–methylene chloride ionic addition of BrN₃ to styrene proceeds in a regiospecific manner. **1972** Buchanan & Sable in B. S. Thyagarajan *Selective Org. Transformations* II. 10 Ion-pair intermediates involving a benzylic cation have also been proposed to account for regiospecificity and predominantly *cis* addition of deuterium bromide to *cis*- and *trans*-1-phenylpropene. **1977** *Jrnl. Organometallic Chem.* CXLI. c30 The organic

skeleton in this complex thus derives from the formal reductive coupling of two pyrylium moieties in a regiospecific, yet unsymmetrical fashion. **1988** *Nature* 10 Mar. 121/1 The preorganization of extracellular macromolecular substrates for regiospecific nucleation and the subsequent development of biominerals with controlled micro-architecture can be clearly demonstrated in many systems.

Hence ˌ**regiospeci'ficity** *n.*, the state of being regiospecific; the extent to which a particular reaction is regiospecific.

**1968** A. Hassner in *Jrnl. Organic Chem.* XXXIII. 2684/2 We have proposed that the course of such reactions be referred to as regiospecific, the term being derived from the latin ward [*sic*] *regio* denoting direction. Regiospecificity then refers to the directional preference of bond formation. **1977** *Jrnl. Organometallic Chem.* CXLI. c31 Clearly the regiospecificity encountered here is determined by the coordinating presence of an iron carbonyl fragment. **1978** *Further Perspectives Organic Chem.* (CIBA Symp.) 73 The regiospecificity of the formylation (90%) at the 6-position.

**rego** ('rɛdʒəʊ), *n. Austral. slang.* Also **reggo.** [f. REG(ISTRATION *n.* + -O².] Motor-vehicle registration. Freq. *attrib.*

**1967** J. Wynnum *I'm Jack, all Right* 39 Everything is sweet except for the bloody silly reggo sticker. **1973** H. Williams *My Love* 12 There's a bit of bull and form-filling about reggo and comprehensive insurance and number plates. **1975** *Sydney Morning Herald* 15 Nov. 67 (Advt.), Austin 1800, 8 mths rego. Gd tyres, radio. **1982** R. Hall *Just Relations* 130 If the cops catch us they'll have us cold: no rego, one headlamp, baldy tyres. **1987** *Telegraph* (Brisbane) 25 Feb. 18/4 Without the cool $1 million boost, .. your MRD rego bill could have been noticeably higher.

**regular**, *a.*, *adv.*, and *n.* Add: [A.] [4.] [c.] Also *transf.* of a person: having bowel movements or menstruation occurring at the proper intervals.

**1880** *Lancet* 14 Feb. 244/1 Patients, when asked if they have a motion of the bowels every day, .. may insist that they are quite regular in that respect. **1934** in J. E. Barker *New Lives for Old* (1935) x. 153, I am now 10 stone 10 lbs. 9 ozs., I am very regular and there are no signs of any of the old troubles. **1962** H. Lourie *Question of Abortion* i. 9 When did you start having periods? .. So you've been absolutely regular for fourteen years? **1975** P. Dickinson *Living Dead* xxviii. 192 'Does that mean you've started your baby?' .. 'I hope so. I've missed a period and I'm pretty regular usually.' **1982** N. Rees *Slogans* 162 Keep 'Regular' with Ex-Lax. Ex-Lax chocolate laxative; US, current 1934.

**reheat**, *v.* Add: **b.** *intr.* for *pass.* Of food: to undergo reheating (well or badly).

**1974** *Times* 23 Nov. 13/2 The following recipe reheats very well and can be made in advance. *Ibid.* 21 Dec. 9/5 Red cabbage .. reheats well. **1980** *Washington Post* 27 Mar. E1/2 Kedgeree also reheats well, so .. last night's supper can become next morning's good breakfast. **1989** *Chicago Tribune* 7 May xx. 7/3 Lachman advises against taking home onion rings and french fries. They won't reheat well, she said.

**re'home**, *v.* [RE- 5 a.] *trans.* To find a new home for (a pet or domestic animal). Hence **re'homing** *vbl. n.*

**1974** *Country Life* 11 Apr. 892/1 It costs the Trust £10 to rescue, kennel and eventually re-home an abandoned dog. **1982** *Daily Tel.* 25 Aug. 3/2 The horses could be re-homed. **1989** *Ibid.* (Weekend Suppl.) 21 Jan. p. viii/5 We think it's like prison to leave a dog in kennels [after its owner has died] ... Direct rehoming is the best answer. **1990** *Today* 12 Mar. 12 We took near enough 400 dogs there last year .. principally because they were unable to be rehomed.

**Reich**, *n.* First sense in Dict. becomes 1; combinations become sense 2. Add: [2.] **'Reichschancellor**, partial anglicization of *Reichskanzler* below; also *Reich chancellor*.
**1933** *N.Y. Times* 31 Jan. VI. 3/4 (*heading*) Hitler is named Reich Chancellor. **1954** K. S. PINSON *Mod. Germany* viii. 160 There was no cabinet in the German Reich. There was one minister, the Reich chancellor. **1977** E. DAVIDSON *Making of Adolf Hitler* ix. 363 By naming Hitler as Reichschancellor, you have delivered up our holy Fatherland to one of the greatest demagogues of all time. **1981** 'E. TREVOR' *Damocles Sword* ii. 9 Outside the Reichschancellory the massed crimson banners hung... The Reichschancellor was among his guests.
hence **'Reichschancellery**, the building or premises occupied by the office of the Reichschancellor.
**1975** tr. *Melchior's Sleeper Agent* vii. 153 It seemed to him as if all the *Bonzen*—all the big shots—in Germany were hurrying through the bunker corridor deep under the Reichschancellery. **1980** D. GRANT *Emerald Decision* i. 10 Menschler spoke of the last days, when his Germany had gone up in flames with two bodies in the grounds of the Reichschancellery.
**'Reichsführer (SS)** [Ger., 'the Reich's leader (of the SS)': see FÜHRER *n.* and *S.S.* (= Schutzstaffel) s.v. S 4 a], a title bestowed on Heinrich Himmler (1900-45) in 1929 as commander of the S.S. (see also quot. 1934, applied *loosely* to Hitler).
**1934** *Times* 3 Aug. 12/1 Herr Hitler becomes in effect Reichsführer—Leader of the Reich— with more power over 66,000,000 Germans than the Hohenzollern Emperors. **1953** W. FRISCHAUER *Himmler* ii. 29 On 6 January 1929, he [*sc.* Hitler] issued an order which appointed Heinrich Himmler Reichsfuehrer (Reich leader) of the S.S. Black Guards. **1979** J. GARDNER *Nostradamus Traitor* v. 15 An official notification .. was signed by Himmler as Reichsführer of the SS.
**'Reichskanzler** [G. *Kanzler* CHANCELLOR *n.*], Prime Minister or Chancellor of the Reich, a title conferred on Hitler in 1933.
**1934** in *Statesman's Year-bk.* (1971) 939 The working constitution of Germany provides for a *Reichskanzler* who is the 'Leader' in all political activities in Germany. **1980** R. BUTLER *Blood-Red Sun at Noon* (1981) II. i. 128 Adolf Hitler had become *Reichskanzler* of Germany.
**'Reichsminister**, a minister of the (Third) Reich; also *Reich minister*.
**1934** *Times* 1 May 16/2 It is announced to-night that Dr. Frick, the Reich Minister of the Interior, is to take over from to-morrow the Prussian Ministry of the Interior. **1971** K. R. STADLER *Austria* vi. 187 Not until a year later was Seyss made Reich Minister. **1979** J. GARDNER *Nostradamus Traitor* v. 15 'Who told you all this?' .. 'Fräulein Hildebrandt, the Reichsminister's secretary.' **1987** *Washington Post* 20 Dec. (Bk. World) 3/4 A working-class childhood friend of the brothers is .. a Nazi stormtrooper and ultimately a Reichsminister.

‖**Reichsthaler** ('raıçstalə(r)), *n.* Now *Hist.* Also **Reichstaler**, etc. [Ger., f. *Reichs* gen. of *Reich* empire, kingdom, state + *Thaler* (mod. *Taler*) dollar; cf. REICH *n.* and THALER *n.*] = RIX-DOLLAR *n.*[1]
**1819** REES *Cycl.* XXIX. s.v., *Reichsthaber* [sic], in Commerce. See *Rix-dollar*. **1829** C. BRADFORD *Jrnl.* 11 Sept. in Londonderry & Hyde *More Lett. from Martha Wilmot* (1935) 333 A Reich's Thaler, piece of money, which they have here, was named so because it was first coined in the Joachims Thal in Bohemia. **1957** *Chambers's Encycl.* IV. 584/1 The Imperial dollar was known as the Reichstaler. **1962** R. A. G.

CARSON *Coins* 355 The thaler which had been proscribed was again permitted to be issued in 1566 at a value of 68 kreuzer and this denomination, known as the reichsthaler, soon ousted the silver gulden. **1980** *Early Music* Jan. 58/1 The theorbist Francesco Arigoni and the archlutenist Gottfried Bentley are listed in the Hofkapelle rosters for 1711 and 1717 (on the latter date at salaries of 400 *Reichsthaler* each).

**rein**, *n.*[1] Add: [1.] c. *pl.* A harness with straps or a 'leash' attached, put on to a young child to prevent it from straying.
**1922** C. BARNETT *Common Sense in Nursery* iv. 76 A safety chain is essential, especially if there is a toddler about who may be tempted to 'push Baby along'; .. the kind made like a child's reins is the most effective. **1948** A. CUTHBERT *Housewife Baby Bk.* x. 100/1 A pair of reins is useful when a toddler is being taken for a town walk and is likely to dash out into a dangerous road. **1954** MRS. S. FRANKENBURG *Common Sense in Nursery* (ed. 4) ix. 115 When he is walking in the street, reins are essential: he will like 'being a horse'. **1966** *Olney Amsden & Sons Ltd. Price List* 3 *Baby harness* .. Kiddie Kare Reins 20/-Doz. **1977** P. LEACH *Baby & Child* v. 331 You will both be far more comfortable if you use reins.

**reindustriali'zation**, *n.* Also **re-industrialization**. [RE- 5 a.] The process or policy of economic revitalization in which the industry (of a particular country or region) is modernized or developed.
**1968** *Punch* 17 Apr. 553/2 The ideal site .. would be the Midlands—within reach of the regions now undergoing reindustrialisation, Scotland, the North-East, the North-West, and, of course, of London. **1979** *Washington Post* 9 Sept. B7/4 What we are ultimately addressing is the reindustrialization of America, and a new industrial revolution won't happen by itself. **1981** *Omni* Mar. 122/3 If the reindustrialization of America is to be more than an empty slogan, .. government and industry must form joint study groups to examine macroengineering projects. **1986** *Word 1985* XXXVI. 1. 5 The article .. devotes considerable space to showing that 'reindustrialization' is a wrong solution to the U.S. economic problems. **1989** *Amer. Banker* 31 July 7/1 According to Mr. Howell, 1992 also will mean the reindustrialization of Europe.

**rein'dustrialize**, *v.* [RE- 5 a.] *trans.* and *intr.* To industrialize again; to revitalize the industry of (a country or region).
**1980** *Fortune* 24 Mar. 152/2 The isolationism of today is an unwillingness to recognize that there is a fundamental need to reindustrialize America. **1980** *National Jrnl.* (U.S.) 7 June 944/2 Either the United States must 'reindustrialize' .. or government must pick tomorrow's industrial 'winners' and shove them in the right direction. **1981** *N.Y. Times* 11 Jan. XII. 66/1 This is not a welcome development, especially if you want to reindustrialize America. **1983** *Business Week* 29 Aug. 37/1 The 'third way' [is] an attempt to reindustrialize without the disruptions of the free-market policies of .. Reagan or the inflationary expansionism of .. Mitterand.
Hence **rein'dustrializer** *n.*
**1985** *Inc* Apr. 36/1 There were lots of people out there with axes to grind—the small-business camp, the big-business camp, the deindustrializers and the reindustrializers.

**reinforcement**, *n.* [5.] For def. read: That which reinforces or strengthens; *spec.* (*a*) the strengthening structure or material employed in reinforced concrete or plastic; (*b*) a small adhesive ring of paper or plastic placed over a punched hole (in filing paper) and designed to prevent the paper from tearing. (Further examples.)

**1948** C. E. Chapel *Aircraft Basic Sci.* ii. 84/2 The true monocoque has as its only reinforcement vertical bulkheads formed of structural members. **1963** E. H. Edwards *Saddlery* xiv. 96 The head and gullet are strengthened with steel plates and there is also a steel reinforcement laid on to the underside of the tree. **1963** R. L. Collison *Mod. Business Filing & Archives* v. 84 For precision work lever punches, with sliding guides for correct positioning, and self-adhesive linen reinforcements, are necessary. **1967** P. Roth *Portnoy's Complaint* (1971) 14 Patiently fastens reinforcements to a term's worth of three-ringed paper, lined and unlined both.

**‚reintermedi'ation**, *n. Finance.* [RE- 5 a.] The transfer or bringing back of borrowing and investments from an outside credit business into the banking system. Cf. \*DISINTER-MEDIATION *n.*

**1978** *Business Week* 28 Aug. 27 Under current law, ..businessmen tend to sell out for stock to avoid taxes, 'and the natural reintermediation of funds isn't occurring'. **1980** *Daily Tel.* 6 Aug. 1/3 More than half [the commercial bill business] has been run down and replaced by direct bank lending..as part of a process known as 'reintermediation' in banking circles. **1987** *Amer. Banker* 26 Oct. 12/2 Everyone who's liquidating positions is sitting on a pile of cash. It's a tremendous opportunity for 'reintermediation', and the banks ought to be going after it. **1988** *Financial Times* 10 Nov. IV. p. iii/1 After the years of 'disintermediation',..there seems now to be some measure of reintermediation.

Hence ‚reinter'mediate *v. intr.* and *trans.*

**1979** *Daily Tel.* 13 Aug. 14 Controlling the monetary base alone would simply mean that the banks disintermediated or reintermediated as necessary to meet their ratios. **1981** *Financial Mail* 28 Aug. 986/3 These non-bank loans have flowed back to the banks (they are being re-intermediated).

**re'jigger**, *v. U.S. colloq.* [RE- 5 c; cf. REJIG *v.*] *trans.* To alter or rearrange, to shift around; to manipulate or present (information, etc.) in a new way.

*a*1961 in Webster s.v., Executives rejigger their organization charts. **1977** *Time* 3 Jan. 70/1 Amis has rejiggered the present according to a formula beloved by armchair historians and sore losers: What would have happened if? **1979** *Time* 8 Oct. 89/1 Rejiggering assignments because of pregnancy is a fact of life these days in the armed forces. **1986** *Fortune* 4 Aug. 8/1 Corporations might get some relief from an average 52% tax rate, and personal tax laws could be rejiggered to encourage spending rather than savings.

Hence **re'jiggering** *vbl. n.*

**1976** *Business Week* 8 Nov. 46/3 Rogers & Wells.. has come up with a rejiggering of the terminology.. of the agreements. **1981** *N.Y. Times* 18 Jan. IV. 4/2 But Friday is now Monday, the hitch not another rejiggering of the plan but rather the diversion of Mr. Miller's attention to the Iranian hostage banking negotiations.

**rekey** (riː'kiː), *v.* Chiefly *Computing.* [f. RE- 5 a + KEY *v.*] *trans.* To enter (a key-stroke or data, esp. text) again at a keyboard.

**1966** *Proc. AFIPS Conf.* XXVIII. 266/1 This is done by backspacing over incorrect keystrokes and re-keying the correct strokes. **1982** *Computers in Bk. Production* (Oxf. Univ. Press typescript) 509 The Divisions need to be able to accept material from authors which is already in machine readable form, without having the text rekeyed. **1986** *Your Computer* (Austral.) May 16/3, I rekeyed some material, realised I could re-create more, and told her. **1988** A. C. Amos in Butler & Stoneman *Editing, Publishing & Computer Technol.* 52 The fact that, with one of the largest data entry jobs ever, the Oxford English Dictionary chose to rekey the text rather than scanning it is indicative of some of the potential complications in using a Kurzweil.

Hence **re'keying** *vbl. n.*

**1971** *Computers & Humanities* VI. 40 If no re-keying of the text is necessary, making changes does not create new errors. **1986** *Daily Tel.* 21 Nov. 16/8 If you could feed printed words into a computer without rekeying, it would be wonderful.

‖**relais** (rəlɛ), *n.* Pl. **relais.** [Fr., lit. 'relay', stage, coaching-inn'.] In France, a restaurant or café (sometimes also providing overnight accommodation); *relais routier* [cf. ROUTIER *n.*[2] 2], one of an association of roadside restaurants orig. designed for lorry drivers and now well known for high-quality food at reasonable prices.

**1965** *New Statesman* 5 Nov. 713/1 These diners are roughly equivalent to our pull-ups and the French *relais routiers* before they were turned into haunts of gastronomic fashion. **1972** W. P. McGivern *Caprifoil* (1973) ii. 44 We'll use Billy's Relais as a mail-and-phone drop. **1974** *Times* 10 Oct. 16/3 The swallows which normally fly south..are in the habit of pausing to take a bite at..a *relais routiers*. **1979** A. Scholefield *Point of Honour* 56 The Relais deserved its one rosette in the Guide. **1980** *Guardian* 3 May 13/2 Walkers and cyclists can benefit from the quiet routes and *relais*... Overnight *relais*..may be grand châteaux or big farmhouses.

‖**relance** (rəlɑ̃s), *n. Pol.* [Fr.] A revival or relaunching (of a policy, etc.); reorientation.

**1974** *Financial Times* 8 July 12/2 If to-day's Schmidt-Giscard talks in Bonn should lead to a political *relance* of the Community, the Labour Government could be somewhat embarrassed. **1979** *Dædalus* Winter 2 No sooner was the battle..ended by his [*sc.* de Gaulle's] retirement, than a new setback hit the champions of *relance*: the *relance* of Messina after the debacle of EDC, the *relance* of the Hague after de Gaulle, and now..renewed monetary cooperation. **1984** *Foreign Affairs* Winter 645 Many factors have contributed to the desire for a European *relance*.

**related**, *ppl. a.* Add: [**2.**] **c.** In *Comb.* with preceding noun.

**1951** *Jrnl. Abnormal Psychol.* XLVI. 557/1 Needs could act as sensitizers, lowering the recognition thresholds for need-related stimuli. **1963** *Punch* 20 Mar. 398/2 There must be a wage-related contributory insurance system. **1970** *Jrnl. Health, Physical Educ. & Recreation* Mar. 46/1 Team handball..is often confused with a popular squash-related sport also dubbed handball. **1975** *Petroleum Economist* Aug. 288/1 The Department of Energy.. expects that oil-related employment will increase as more companies enter the offshore market. **1986** *N.Y. Rev. Bks.* 16 Jan. 43/1 It was also held to be the cause of the milder form of the illness known as AIDS-related complex.

**relation**, *n.* Add: [**6.**] **d.** *pl. euphem.* Sexual intercourse (*ellipt.* for *sexual relations* s.v. SEXUAL *a.* 2 a).

**1927** *Weekly Dispatch* 26 June 1 A group within the Church in America..sanctions an 'open mind' on the subject of relations between the sexes without marriage. **1963** M. McCarthy *The Group* i. 23 She and Mother had talked it over and agreed that if you were in love and engaged to a nice young man you perhaps ought to have relations once to make sure of a happy adjustment. **1966** B. Malamud *Fixer* (1969) III. ii. 85 He undressed himself and his intentions were to have relations with a Russian woman. **1981** G. Swift *Shuttlecock* xi. 76 Did you always have good, healthy relations with your wife? **1981** H. Rawson *Dict. Euphemisms* (1983) 234 *Relations.* Uncles? Aunts? Cousins? Uh-uh. As with intercourse, it is the prefatory 'sexual' that is here delicately omitted, e.g. 'They smoked some grass and then they had relations'.

**relativize**, *v*. Add: '**relati,vizer** *n*., one who or that which relativizes; *spec*. in *Linguistics*, a relative word or form; '**relati,vizing** *vbl. n*. and *ppl. a*.

**1969** P. L. BERGER *Rumor of Angels* ii. 35 (*heading*) The perspective of Sociology: Relativizing the Relativizers. **1975** *Foundations of Lang*. XIII. 297 One of the three relativizing morphemes of the language. **1976** *Language & Lang. Behavior Abstr*. X. 671/2 Conditions of use of the relativizer morphemes. **1978** R. E. TERWILLIGER in P. Moore *Man, Woman, & Priesthood* x. 140 This relativizing of Jesus sometimes became quite radical. **1986** *National Rev*. 14 Feb. 34/1 Ecumenism has been viewed by many traditionalists as a liberalizing and relativizing enterprise. **1987** *English World-Wide* VIII. 246 Most are similar to English constructions in which the noun relativizer *that* or *who* is deleted. **1988** *N.Y. Times* 21 June A16/4 Her argument is.. that the Holocaust revisionists.. could become part of what she calls the 'relativizing' of the Nazis' actions.

**release**, *v*.[1] Sense 6 c in Dict. becomes 6 d. [II.] [6.] [b.] For def. read: To free (something) from physical restraint or confinement, to allow to move freely, drop, or escape. Phr. *to release one's hold, grip (on)*. Also *absol.*, and *intr*. for *pass*. (Later examples.)

**1852** C. BARTER *Dorp & Veld* viii. 116 As soon as he has seized the bait.., he tightens the string, releases the trigger, and.. receives the bullet in his head. *a*1864 A. GESNER *Coal, Petroleum* (1865) 28 The downward stroke of the walking-beam releases the Auger Stem and Bit for an instant as the Jars slide together. **1875** J. HEATH *Croquet Player* 23 The player has only to release his hold, and the clip, closing, fastens itself on the hoop. **1907** *Westm. Gaz.* 21 Nov. 4/2 The adjustment of which is easily affected by releasing a lock-nut. **1912** CONRAD '*Twixt Land and Sea* v. 60, I felt a slight shudder under my hand and released my grip. **1920** F. SCOTT FITZGERALD in *Smart Set* July 29/1 The bouncer.. released his hold on Peter, who.. rushed immediately around to the other table. **1930** D. VERRILL *Aircraft Bk. for Boys* xi. 189 Pulling the rip-cord and releasing the parachute. **1940** [see SCHRADER *n*.]. **1945** *Tee Emm* (Air Ministry) V. 35 When the tug started its take off run the glider decided it was best to release. **1946** H. REED *Map of Verona* 22 This is the safety-catch, which is always released With an easy flick of the thumb. **1950** J. O. HIRSCHFELDER et al. *Effects of Atomic Weapons* i. 14 To release the energy equivalent to twenty kilotons of TNT. **1955** [see SPANSULE *n*.]. **1969** W. GASS *Icicles* i. 122 Fender's fork poked through the crust of his pie, releasing steam. **1978** *Amateur Photographer* 29 Nov. 88/4 If the dark slide is left in the camera body the shutter won't release until it's moved. **1986** 'W. TREVOR' *News from Ireland* 228 No blind had yet been released, no curtain or shutter opened. **1988** J. G. BALLARD *Running Wild* 36 Payne leaned over the bath-taps and released the water from the tub.

**c**. *transf.* orig. *Psychol*. To ease or relieve (a tension); to free, give rein to (an emotional or instinctual drive).

**1933** W. S. TAYLOR *Critique of Sublimation in Males* ix. 89 This young man's total tension of balked dispositions will be eased considerably if in his new environment he can find.. situations which can release those response patterns that he had ready. **1936** P. T. YOUNG *Motivation of Behavior* v. 247 Tension and release occur constantly in the trivial events of daily life. The phone rings; a tension is built up and instantly released by answering the call. **1946** P. M. SYMONDS *Dynamics of Human Adjustment* v. 126 The mother whose own love life is not satisfied and whose sexual needs are not met may release her tensions by sharp, frequent scoldings and punishment of her children. **1961** C. & W. M. S. RUSSELL *Human Behaviour* vi. 283 Exploration for a mate with whom the individual can enjoy himself is now replaced by appetitive behaviour for situations which will release the masturbatory mechanisms. **1967** M. ARGYLE *Psychol. Interpersonal Behaviour* x. 195 The method.. releases extremely powerful emotional forces. **1987** P. AUSTER *Country of Last Things* (1988) 116, I enjoyed throwing those books into the flames. Perhaps it released some secret anger in me.

**releaser**, *n*. Add: **d**. *Psychol*. Any external stimulus which produces a specific but non-reflex act of behaviour.

**1969** L. TIGER *Men in Groups* iv. 85 The defenders and policemen must be males. Females will not suffice... This is because females cannot act as 'releasers' for the behaviours appropriate to managing interferences to social order. **1970** *Nebraska Symposium on Motivation* XVII. 285 The car must provide some 'releaser' stimuli to call attention to itself, such as lack of license plates, hood or trunk open, or a tire removed. **1975** BROWN & HERRNSTEIN *Psychology* v. 304/2 Do not have the anonymity of citizens of New York; for that reason, they may require a stronger 'releaser' to signify that a car is truly nobody's property. Zimbardo and two graduate students created the releaser by enthusiastically applying a sledge hammer to the car. **1981** B. A. FARRELL *Standing of Psychoanalysis* v. 71 If an interpretation *p* served as a releaser, then.. this may not be 'due to' the fact that it states the truth about the patient.

**relevé**, *n*. Add: **3**. *Ecol*. [First used in Fr. in this sense in 1922 Braun-Blanquet & Pavillard *Vocab. de Sociol. Végétale* 1.] A detailed description of the floristic or phytosociological characteristics of a small area within a stand of vegetation, considered as a sample; also, an area used as the basis for such a description, or the vegetation found there.

**1930** F. R. BHARUCHA tr. *Braun-Blanquet & Pavillard's Vocab. Plant Sociol.* 6 The Sociological 'Relevé'.. is a floristic enumeration accompanied by coefficients or numbers corresponding with analytical or synthetic characters mentioned below. It may relate to any plant population or to a particular example of a definite association. **1962** *Jrnl. Ecol. L.* 765 It must now be shown how one decides that a group of relevés forms an association. **1983** *Watsonia* XIV. 251 Relevés were made of *Schoenus ferrugineus* stands to illustrate the range of vegetation types in which the plant occurs. *Ibid*., At site B the intricate mosaic of vegetation-types demanded its sampling as a composite, single unit (relevés 5–7).

**relief**, *n*.[2] Add: [3.] [a.] Also with preceding defining word, as *drought relief, famine relief*, etc.

**1876**, etc. [see *famine relief* s.v. FAMINE *n*. 5 a]. **1977** *Time* 30 May 25/2 Carter gestured toward the normally fertile valley and promised farmers that he would speed the flow of $2.2 billion in drought relief. **1987** M. HOCKING *Irrelevant Woman* vi. 70 The doctor's young wife.. had called at the vicarage to sell flags for cancer relief. **1989** *Newsday* 21 Aug. 1. 31/3 Some have lobbied for federal disaster relief for the states hardest hit by the epidemic.

[5.] **d**. *Baseball*. *in relief*, in the position or role of relief pitcher.

**1976** *Billings* (Montana) *Gaz*. 27 June 7-F/5 At Omaha, he pitched in relief only once in three years and even in his short stays with the Royals he was used as a starter most of the time. **1979** *Arizona Daily Star* 1 Apr. C1/5 After Johnson walked Brad Mills to load the bases again, Steve Conroy entered the game in relief. **1984** *N.Y. Times* 8 Apr. 1/3 Righetti has pitched for the first time in relief and has pitched well.

[9.] [b.] **relief pitcher** *Baseball* = RELIEVER *n*. 1 d, *esp*. a player who regularly fulfils this role.

**1914** *Harper's Weekly* 23 May 25/1 Ayers performed the trick while acting in the rôle of *relief pitcher. There is perhaps no more trying situation in baseball than that of rescue twirler. **1976** *Billings* (Montana) *Gaz.* 16 June 1-c/4 Fingers . . compiled a 1.35 earned run average in 16 World series appearances and was generally recognized as the American League's No. 1 relief pitcher.

**relieve**, *v.* Add: [3.] [a.] Add to def.: In *pa. pple.*, eased or freed from anxiety. (Further examples.)
**1861** T. HUGHES *Tom Brown at Oxford* I. v. 83 Tom felt greatly relieved, as he was beginning to find himself in rather deep water. **1874** HARDY *Far from Madding Crowd* II. xx. 243 Nevertheless, he was relieved when it [*sc.* the performance] was got through. **1920** *Chambers's Jrnl.* Dec. 849/2 The Prince . . was considerably relieved to find that he was not on the visitor's executionary list. **1949** 'J. TEY' *Brat Farrar* x. 81 They wouldn't bother to look for him. They would be too relieved to have him out of their hair. **1960** C. DAY LEWIS *Buried Day* ii. 39, I was relieved to find that the great singer had met something of the same difficulty in this apparently simple song. **1984** A. CROSS *Sweet Death* ix. 94, I must know. I'd be relieved, grateful, if you could find out.
[5.] **e.** *intr.* Baseball. To act as relief pitcher.
**1954** *Post-Herald* (Birmingham, Alabama) 7 June 7/2 Winning pitcher was Dave Benedict, who relieved in the first inning and scattered four hits the rest of the way. **1976** *Billings* (Montana) *Gaz.* 27 June 2-F/4 Jerry Koosman chalked up his seventh win in 13 decisions, but his first victory since May 27 after losing five straight starts. Bob Apocada relieved for the Mets in the seventh. **1979** *Boston Globe* 10 Oct. 27/2 If the Series goes seven games, Kent Tekulve of the Pirates will relieve in seven games.

‖ **relleno** (re'ʎeno), *n.* [Sp., lit. 'stuffed'.] A *chile relleno* or Mexican stuffed green pepper: see *CHILLI *n.* 2. Chiefly *pl.*
**1906** M. SOUTHWORTH *101 Mexican Dishes* 36 Rellenos. Grind fine a pound of well-cooked veal and add to it a Spanish sausage (chorizo), a half-cupful, each, of seedless raisins and blanched almonds . . . Broil sweet Mexican green peppers . . . Serve with tomato sauce. **1974** C. LARSON *Matthew's Hand* i. 10 He would try to teach her how to cook a decent relleno. **1987** *San Diego Union* 26 Mar. II. 2/5 An alternate way to make these rellenos is to stuff the meat mixture into whole green chiles.

**remineralization** (ˌriːmɪnərəlaɪ'zeɪʃən), *n.* *Med.* and *Dent.* [f. RE- 5 a + MINERALIZATION *n.*] The natural process of restoring the depleted mineral content of bones or of filling in dental cavities from a supply of calcium and phosphate ions.
**1934** in WEBSTER. **1968** MCLEAN & URIST *Bone* (ed. 3) xv. 236 Demineralization or removal of bone minerals without alteration in the underlying organic matrix does not occur in the living animal, and as a descriptive term it serves no useful purpose. The same objections can be raised to the term remineralization. **1979** WILLIAMS & ELLIOTT *Dental Biochem.* xv. 254 Remineralisation can be detected in arrested lesions in dentine. **1985** *Which?* Jan. 19/2 Once decay is well advanced, remineralisation can't restore the broken enamel surface of the tooth.
So **re'mineralize** *v. trans.*, to repair or restore (bones, teeth, etc.) in this way; also *intr.*
**1934** in WEBSTER. **1958** W. F. & M. W. NEUMAN *Chem. Dynamics Bone Mineral* vii. 184 These demineralized sections . . remineralize spontaneously in vitro. **1976** E. P. LAZZARI *Dental Biochem.* xiv. 288 *In vitro* studies indicate that saliva has the capacity to remineralize slightly decalcified enamel surfaces. **1983** *Washington Post* 9 Jan. M15/2 Women are often

given estrogen in the first years after menopause to see whether that will help remineralize the bones.

**remote**, *a.* (*n.*) and *adv.* Add: [A.] [3.] [f.] **remote sensing**, the automatic acquisition of information about the surface of the earth or another planet from a (great) distance, as carried out from satellites and high-flying aircraft (cf. SENSING *vbl. n.* 2 b); freq. *attrib.* See also *REMOTE CONTROL *n.* (Further examples.)
**1962** *Proc. 1st Symposium Remote Sensing Environment* 130 We will then have a series of remote sensing records made over this volcano up until the time she erupts and after she erupts. **1986** *Sci. Amer.* Jan. 28/1 Remote sensing includes not only ordinary photoreconnaissance, . . but also the imaging of the earth's surface.
[4.] **e.** Of a person: seemingly set apart or distant from others in manner; withdrawn, reserved; aloof.
**1894** H. JAMES *Death of Lion* in *Yellow Bk.* I. 19 Paraday, still absent, remote, made as if he had not heard the question. **1929** J. B. PRIESTLEY *Good Companions* III. ii. 487 Miss Trant seemed so dreamy and remote these days that she was considered unapproachable for the time being. **1952** R. C. HUTCHINSON *Recoll. Journey* ii. 16, I had feared but scarcely disliked him: he was too remote to be disliked. **1988** E. YOUNG-BRUEHL *Anna Freud* ii. 92 Max was remote and depressed after his wife's death.
[B.] **2.** *ellipt.* for *REMOTE CONTROL *n.* (now usu. in sense 2).
**1966** M. WOODHOUSE *Tree Frog* xxv. 181 Dr Chapman worked out a gadget which drip-feeds pentothal automatically . . . We switched it off by remote five minutes ago. **1977** *Weekly Times* (Melbourne) 19 Jan. 54/4 (Advt.), John Deere 420 Crawler, 40 h.p. Remotes, PTO, tracks in good condition. Motor sound. **1984** *Sears Catal. 1985* Spring–Summer 940 Record-A-Call 675 has a remote with toll saver that doesn't just retrieve messages but changes outgoing announcements, even erases or accumulates messages. **1987** *Q* Oct. 85/2 You can do other selection tricks, programming up to 32 tracks from six discs yourself, choosing tracks from the remote and having your choice confirmed in its readout.

**re,mote con'trol**, *n.* (Formerly at REMOTE *a.* 3 f.) [f. REMOTE *a.* + CONTROL *n.*] Also hyphened in attrib. use. **1.** Control of apparatus, etc., at a distance. Freq. used *attrib.* to designate a device through which such control is exercised or (occas.) a remote-controlled device.
**1904** L. ANDREWS *Electricity Control* i. 8 It is probable . . that for installations of a few thousand horse-power only, some simple method of mechanical remote control will be generally preferred. **1920** *Wireless World* 7 Aug. 356/1 Pilot's and mechanic's cockpits are not very roomy compartments and therefore it has become standard practice to employ 'remote control', that is to say the main portion of the wireless apparatus . . are [*sic*] fitted in one or two boxes which can be suspended in any convenient part of the main fuselage of the machine; these circuits being controlled by a small unit . . which may be fitted on the dashboard of the machine. **1933** *Times* 16 May 9/2 A remote control device for the selection of several alternative wireless programmes will soon be made available to the public. **1933** *Bureau of Standards Jrnl. Res.* (U.S.) XI. 482 Remote-control junction boxes . . provide direct 2-way communication with the landing aircraft. **1957** *Economist* 9 Nov. 525/2 Because of their radioactivity, none of the materials can be handled normally. All operations are carried out painstakingly by remote control. **1974** *Harrods Christmas Catal.* 69/1 Remote-control Gantry Crane, battery operated . . . 28″ high. £8.50. **1981** *Oxford Jrnl.* 15 May (Advt.), 14″ Colour Portable TV with infra-red remote control hand unit.

**2.** With ellipsis of *unit*, etc.: a (usu. hand-held) remote-control device, *esp.* one for operating a television set or other domestic audio or video appliance.

**1921** *Wireless World* 15 Oct. 439/1 The instrument is assembled from a Mk III ebonite top, .. the parts of an aeroplane 'remote control', etc. **1950** G. MARX *Let.* 6 Dec. (1967) 168, I have solved the television problem by having a remote control installed on the ugly box. **1979** R. JAFFE *Class Reunion* (1980) II. vii. 254 Ken snapped off the TV with his remote control. **1983** J. WILCOX *Mod. Baptists* (1984) iii. 18 'I can't get the remote control to work,' he said, holding up the brown box.

Hence **re͵mote-con'trol** *v. trans.* (and *absol.*), to operate by remote control; so **re͵mote-con'trolled** *ppl. a.*

**1943** *Gloss. Terms Electr. Engin.* (*B.S.I.*) 84 *Remote-controlled substation*, a substation the operation of which is controlled at a distance. **1966** P. O'DONNELL *Sabre-Tooth* xv. 203 Two transmitters .. were remote-controlled from the H.Q. section. **1970** 'B. MATHER' *Break in Line* xv. 187, I wondered if he were still in Calcutta or was remote-controlling from London. **1988** J. G. BALLARD *Running Wild* 8 The avenues and drives were swept by remote-controlled TV cameras.

**removal,** *n.* Add: [**3.**] **c.** *Anglo-Irish.* In full, *removal of remains.* The formal taking of a body to the church for the funeral service. Cf. LIFT *n.*[2] 1 c.

**1890** *Pall Mall Gaz.* 24 Nov. 4/2 (*heading*) The late Lady Rosebery. Removal of the remains to-day. **1939** JOYCE *Finnegans Wake* 544 Private chapel occupies return landing, removal every other quarter day. **1949** *Irish Times* 15 Oct. 12/1 The family .. wish to return their sincere thanks to .. all who attended removal of remains, Mass and funeral. **1967** *Irish Press* 30 Dec. 2/5 The wife and family .. wish to thank most sincerely all those .. who sent Mass cards, floral tributes, telegrams, letters of sympathy, attended removal, Requiem Mass and funeral. **1979** *Southern Star* (Eire) 29 Sept. 4/1 His fellow employees as well as members of Kilmac G.A.A. formed guards of honour at the removal and funeral. **1986** *Evening Press* (Eire) 21 May 2/1 Removal to Holy Family Home Chapel at 6 o'clock this (Wednesday) evening.

**renewal,** *n.* Senses a, b, and c in Dict. become 1 a, b, and 2. Add: [**1.**] **c.** The state or process of being renewed by the Holy Spirit; *spec.* = CHARISMATIC *renewal* or the charismatic renewal movement. Cf. RENOVATION *n.* 2 a.

**1890** H. C. G. MOULE *Veni Creator* x. 208 Such asking and finding led at once to a repentant renewal of surrender and of faith, and so back to the rest, and to the readiness, which are for us, by the Holy Ghost, in Jesus Christ our Life. **1894** A. J. GORDON *Ministry of Spirit* v. 84 As the words 'regeneration' and 'renewal' used in Scripture mark respectively the impartation of the divine life as a perpetual possession and its increase by repeated communications, so in our sealing there is a reception of the Spirit once for all, which reception may be followed by repeated fillings. **1935** D. A. VONIER *Spirit & Bride* xii. 136 Those renewals are truly something from the outside because the Spirit came and did work which He had not done before .... After His coming (= Holy Ghost) He abides, and it is this abiding presence that is the constant renewal of life; not a fresh advent like the one of the first Pentecost. **1972** S. TUGWELL *Did you receive Spirit?* v. 40 'Baptism in the spirit' .. still is the hallmark of all Pentecostal-inspired renewal in all the churches, including now the Roman Catholic. **1983** RICHARDSON & BOWDEN *New Dict. Christian Theol.* 438/1 Renewal is based on belief in the Holy Spirit as a real gift imparted by the glorified Lord Jesus to his disciples. **1987** *Church Times* 18 Sept. 7/2 The convergence of their viewpoints shows how little the Renewal Movement is the respecter of denominations.

Hence **re'newalism** *n.*, the beliefs and practices characteristic of the movement for charismatic renewal; also **re'newalist** *n.* and *a.*

**1975** *Daily Tel.* 9 Dec. 14 A letter to your newspaper is not the ideal vehicle for a full treatment of the machinations of the renewalists. **1983** *Current Digest Soviet Press* 28 Sept. 14/1 The 'renewalist' tendencies in the preaching of a number of denominations. **1985** *Times* 22 Apr. 12/6 Ironically, the most balanced and sensitive criticisms of Restorationism and Renewalism, come from the classical Pentecostals. **1988** HIGTON & KIRBY *Challenge of Housechurches* 10 The renewalists .. look for changes within the framework of their own denomination.

**renovationist** (rɛnəˈveɪʃənɪst), *a.* and *n.* [f. RENOVATION *n.* + -IST.] **A.** *adj.* Characterized by or favouring renovation; of or pertaining to (esp. political) renewal or reform.

**1934** A. WERTH *France in Ferment* xiii. 264 These 'Renovationist' theories become anti-parliamentary, anti-democratic, and begin to verge on Fascism and Totalitarianism. **1948** J. TOWSTER *Political Power in U.S.S.R.* 346 These renovationist practices will continue in the future. **1981** *Time* 24 Aug. 44/2 He was a founder of the potent renovationist Greater Baltimore Committee in 1955.

**B.** *n.* An advocate of renovation or renewal; *spec.* a member of a political party favouring reform.

**1983** *Financial Times* 6 Apr. 4/5 The so-called 'renovationists', comprising, in Tokyo and Fukuoka, an alliance between the Socialist and Communist parties. **1986** *New Yorker* 21 July 82/3 Leaders of the allegedly most moderate, sensible, democratic faction of the Peronist party, the so-called Renovationists, had issued a statement sneering at the Radicals' 'mediocrity'. **1989** *Chicago Tribune* 16 May (North ed.) 4/2 Menem beat the Renovationists in internal party primaries .. to become the presidential candidate.

**renter,** *n.*[1] Add: **8.** Something that is rented or hired out, *esp.* a rental car or videocassette. *colloq.* (chiefly *U.S.*).

**1979** 'L. EGAN' *Hunters & Hunted* x. 176 'New car?' .. 'No, I'll have to get one. This is a renter'. **1986** *Video Today* Apr. 49/2 There is also a best of category selection and a chart of the year's best renters. **1986** R. FORD *Sportswriter* v. 129 We would end up .. driving out in my renter to some little suburban foot-lit lanai apartment.

**reo'ffend,** *v.* [RE- 5 a.] *intr.* Of a previously convicted offender: to offend again; to commit a subsequent offence.

**1934** in WEBSTER *Add.* **1977** *Times* 21 June 3/2 Of 500 children passing through their intermediate treatment programmes .. 87 per cent had not reoffended. **1978** *Sentences of Imprisonment* (Rep. Adv. Council Penal Syst.) xiii. 123 Many offenders sent to prison for the first time do not subsequently re-offend. **1986** *Psychol. Today* Mar. 64/1 We believe that sex offenders are less likely to reoffend if they can develop more satisfactory sexual relationships with appropriate partners.

Hence **reo'ffending** *vbl. n.*

**1975** *Economist* 8 Feb. 92/1 Professor Morris's new system does not remove the need to treat criminals so as to prevent their reoffending. **1989** *Daily Tel.* 6 July 3/7 It is hardly surprising the rate of reoffending is so high. Sex offences are a form of addiction.

**reopen,** *v.* Add: **reopening** *ppl. a.*: *spec.* as *reopening clause Industr. Rel.* (orig. *U.S.*) = *REOPENER *n.*

**1945** *Guide to Labor Contracts* (Soc. of Plastics Industry) 28 The .. reopening clause partially commits the company to a forty-eight .. hour week. **1979** *Daily Tel.* 26 May 2/5 An important feature of the deal is a 're-opening' clause, which enables the union to go back to the Post Office and ask for more if other postal unions settle higher claims. **1988** *Monthly Labor Rev.* Jan. 10/2 In State and local government .. contracts often have reopening clauses.

**re'opener**, *n.* *Industr. Rel.* (orig. *U.S.*). [f. REOPEN *v.* + -ER¹.] More fully, *reopener clause*: a clause in a contract between union and management which allows for the reopening of negotiations within the term of the contract; = REOPENING *clause*.

**1960** *Monthly Labor Rev.* May 516/2 Both increases, negotiated under wage reopeners of contracts signed .. were expected to set the wage pattern for other woolen .. workers. **1975** *Business Week* 8 Sept. 25/2 Recently, it won a 28% wage increase over three years .. and a 1976 wage reopener. **1979** *Times* 24 Nov. 1/7 The management resisted union demands for .. a reopener clause entitling the unions to apply for more money before the expiry of the 12-month agreement. **1989** *Oil & Gas Jrnl.* 10 July 19/1 Many of the new, longer term contracts also contain reopeners, which are clauses that allow periodic renegotiation of the contract if certain aspects become unrealistic.

**rep**, *n.*⁴ For def. read: [Abbrev. of REPETITION *n.*¹] **1.** = REPETITION *n.*¹ 2 b. *School slang.* **2.** = *REPETITION *n.*¹ 4 e (esp. in *Body-building*). Usu. in *pl.*

**1953** *Tomorrow's Man* (Chicago) Mar. 43/2, I followed the exercise religiously .. regarding reps, sets, rhythm, and so forth. **1969** F. RYAN *Weight Training* 57 As you become stronger, you are going to find that doing the three sets of eight reps is easier. Keep the same amount of weight but increase the reps to nine. **1979** COE & SUMMER *Getting Strong* iii. 34 Use a light-to-moderately-heavyweight on the barbell until you can do 6-8 reps. **1985** *Marathon & Distance Runner* Dec. 41/3 You have not only got to become more mentally tuned to do a lot more longer reps but you have got to start thinking like a 5000 metre runner too.

**rep** (rɛp), *v.*¹ [Abbrev. of REPEAT *v.*] *trans.* To repeat (stitches or part of a design): as a direction on knitting patterns, etc. Also *absol.*

**1951** D. M. BECKETT *Knitted Garments for Family* 6 With No. 12 needles and double wool cast on 121 stitches. Continuing in single wool, rib as follows:- p.1, *k.1, p.1, rep. from * to end. **1957** NORBURY & AGUTTER *Odhams Encycl. Knitting* 35/1 Rep. rows 1 to 4 inclusive to form the pattern. **1970** M. HAMILTON-HUNT *Knitting Dict.* 127 Rep the last row inserting the hook the first time into the same ch sp as last st. **1986** *Knit & Stitch* June 16/2 Rep for Front.

**rep** (rɛp), *v.*² *colloq.* (orig. *U.S.*). [f. REP *n.*⁵] *intr.* and *trans.* To act as a representative for (a company, product, etc.).

*a* **1961** E. YATES in *Webster* s.v., Inquired what brand we were repping for. **1975** *Broadcast* 14 July 10/2 Capital, Clyde and City have decided to raise their [advertising] rates ... BMS .. reps all three stations. **1976** *Bookseller* 19 June 2752/2 (Advt.), Sales manager for hire ... 2 seasons successful repping 40 UK & US pubs. list.
Hence **'repping** *vbl. n.* and *ppl. a.*
**1961** WEBSTER, *Repping* n. **1976** *Bookseller* 19 June 2752/2 (Advt.), Sales manager .. with repping company operating throughout Middle East. **1979** *Yale Alumni Mag.* Apr. (Suppl.) cn22/2 Jack managed to work in some business-manufacturers' repping. **1988** *Rugby News* Nov. 48/2 After the stint at repping I started working for ICAN.

**re'package** (riː-), *v.* [RE- 5 a.] *trans.* To package again; *spec.* to redesign the packaging of (a product) to make it more attractive to the public; to present for sale in a different form. Also *fig.*

**1918** THOM & FISK *Bk. Cheese* vi. 84 Cheese of any group may be run through mixing and molding machines and re-packaged in very different form from that characteristic of the variety. **1938** *Printers' Ink Monthly* May 12 (*heading*) Wholesale line re-packaged. **1958** *Mod. Packaging* Dec. 96/2 A package-design firm was called in to repackage the two sluggish items. **1966** *Electronics* 31 Oct. 42 Smallest model of IBM's new 4 Pi computer family, configured for a tactical missile. For other applications, the same basic design can be repackaged. **1975** *Business Week* 18 Aug. 98/3 MCA plans to repackage the thousands of films in its library for Disco-Vision. **1983** *Listener* 20 Oct. 5/1 The same set of ideas can be repackaged just so often. **1989** *Institutional Investor* Jan. 90 Why not repackage the state's GOs to make them attractive to parents financing a child's education?
Hence **re'packaged** *ppl. a.*; **re'packager** *n.*; **re'packaging** *vbl. n.*
**1958** *Mod. Packaging* Dec. 96/1 If bold repackaging of two slow sellers can change inventories into back orders, why not apply the same strategy to the whole line? **1975** *Chem. Week* 5 Feb. 26/3 J. C. Penney and Sears .. are repackagers. **1975** *Aviation Week & Space Technol.* 10 Mar. 24/1 The production avionics includes a repackaged radar in place of the brassboard version on the SID airplane. **1989** *Tulsa World* 25 July B6/3 Brainerd is a licensed pharmaceutical repackager.

**repetition**, *n.*¹ Add: [I.] [4.] e. *Sport.* A training exercise or activity which is repeated; (*a*) in *Athletics*, any of the circuits run during *repetition training*; (*b*) in *Weight-training*, etc.: the exercise of raising and lowering a weight. Usu. in *pl.*, as part of a series or 'set'.

(*a*) **1955** F. STAMPFL *On Running* ii. 48 A miler .. engaged on five three-quarter-mile repetitions will have no option but to run more slowly than at racing pace. *Ibid.*, The six-miler should dispense with time trials altogether, sticking, rather, to three repetitions of two miles at racing speed. **1984** *Runner* (U.S.) Oct. 63/2 Coe ran a set of 20 200-meter repetitions, averaging 27 seconds, resting only 25-45 seconds between each. **1986** *Runner* Mar. 36/2 She loves repetitions on the track and runs them as fast as anyone.
(*b*) **1956** *Strength & Health* Nov. 49/2 They [*sc.* the exercises] need not include excessive repetitions. **1962** J. CYRIAX *Bench Weight Training* II. 25 The partner may change his position or exercise after the first or second set of repetitions. **1974** G. HOOKS *Weight Training in Athletics* iv. 53 It is a good idea to lower the number of repetitions in each set so that heavier weights can be handled. **1988** *Muscular Devel.* Nov. 27/2 One must train at the highest level of intensity, performing each repetition properly and safely.
[6.] **repetition running** *Athletics*, a form of INTERVAL *running* in which the athlete races fast, but rests between circuits instead of keeping on the move.
**1955** F. STAMPFL *On Running* ii. 48 When *repetition-running reaches racing speed, the individual runs should never extend to more than a half of the actual racing-distance. **1964** J. K. DOHERTY *Mod. Training for Running* v. 114 Repetition running over distances between 220 yards to 880 yards. **1985** H. WILSON in H. Payne *Athletes in Action* 41, I would suggest that repetition running becomes more useful than interval running as the competition season approaches.
**repetition training** *Athletics*, training by repetition running.

**1966** R. CLARKE *Unforgiving Minute* vii. 64 We.. pressed on with \*repetition training, running one-quarter repetitions between the furlong posts. **1978** F. S. PYKE et al. in *Focus on Running* vi. 137 The ability to sustain a sprinting effort depends on the quality of the lactic acid energy system which is taxed by repetition training.

**repetitive,** *a.* Add: **re'petitively** *adv.*
**1934** WEBSTER, Repetitively. **1961** *Travel Topics* June 91 A type of border display which is repetitively used whenever advertising the facilities. **1987** M. BERGMANN *Anat. of Loving* xx. 269 They.. experience the feeling that something repetitively goes wrong in their love relationships.

**replicar** ('rɛplɪkɑː(r)), *n.* orig. *U.S.* [Blend of REPLICA *n.* and CAR *n.*[1]] A motor-car which is a full-sized, functional replica of a vintage or classic model, *esp.* one custom-built from a kit.
**1977** *Business Week* 22 Aug. 78/3 'Replicars', like reproductions of fine antique furniture, are being sold widely, with prices far below original car prices. **1979** *N.Y. Times* 28 Jan. XII. 14/1 Most of the replicar companies are small, the result of individuals' efforts to meet a very present demand for the past. **1979** C. JAMES *Flying Visits* (1984) 86 This is custom-car headquarters of the universe... Where the original has been lost, a 'replicar' replaces it. **1985** *Forbes* (N.Y.) 28 Oct. 378/1 Chandler.. warns novice buyers to beware of socalled replicars—modern fiberglass copies of classics, often on Volkswagen chassis. **1987** *Modern Motor* (Sydney) Apr. 114/2 The 8o's have seen a revolution in America in kit cars, now called replicars.

**repo** ('riːpəʊ), *n.*[1] *colloq.* (orig. and chiefly *U.S.*). [Shortening; see -o².] = *repurchase agreement* s.v. \*REPURCHASE *n.* b.
**1962** R. BLAHUT *A to Z of Finance* s.v., When the charges on dealers' loans secured by Government securities is substantially more than their market yields, then the dealers resort to 'buy-back' or 'Repo' (Repurchase option) deals. **1963** [see *repurchase agreement* s.v. REPURCHASE *n.* b]. **1972** *Banking Law Jrnl.* LXXXIX. 1109/2 One popular method used by banks to pass the benefits of the interest exclusion among themselves or to acquire them from dealers was a 'repurchase agreement' or 'repo'. **1984** *Times* 20 Mar. 20/7 With £2.2 billion of bills already tied up in 'repos' with the Bank of England, there were clearly going to be problems in finding sufficient fresh paper. **1989** *Reuters Gloss.: Internat. Econ. & Financial Terms* 79 In West Germany, repos usually run for about one month and are the central bank's main instrument for steering the money market.

**repo** ('riːpəʊ), *n.*² *U.S. slang.* [Shortened f. REPOSSESSION *n.*, REPOSSESSED *ppl. a.*, etc.: see -o².] **1. repo man** = \*REPOSSESSOR *n.*
**1970** *Wall St. Jrnl.* 21 July 1/1 Mr. Civerolo and his helper are auto repossessors, or 'repo men'. **1985** *Business First* 2 Dec. 1. 1 (*heading*) The repo man reclaims what isn't possessed. **1986** *Semper Floreat* (Brisbane) 7 Oct. 22/1 Repo Men are to capitalism what hit-men are to organised crime—the hired help. **1988** *Runner's World* July 51/3 Mark's been living hand-to-mouth. For the last year, he's been one step ahead of the Repo Man.
**2.** Something (*esp.* a motor car) which has been repossessed.
**1972** J. GORES *Dead Skip* i. 8 I've got a repo for you... Seventy-two Mercury Montego hardtop. **1989** *Austin* (Texas) *Amer.-Statesman* 29 Apr. c28/2 (Advt.), '85 Maxima.. Bank repo.. Good condition.
Hence **'repo** *v. trans.*, to repossess when a purchaser defaults on payments.
**1972** J. GORES *Dead Skip* i. 8 Mercury Montego hardtop... Repo'd at Seventh Avenue and Cabrillo. **1987** S. PARETSKY *Bitter Medicine* vii. 70 She's from the collection agency, come to repo the car.

**repoint,** *v.* Add: Hence **re'pointing** *vbl. n.*
**1955** *Practical Householder* Nov. 118/1 Re-pointing is the reconditioning of the mortar courses in brickwork with a new binding mixture. **1968** M. WOODHOUSE *Rock Baby* viii. 85 There were deep cracks in the wall where it needed repointing. **1988** *Which?* Apr. 163/2 Replacing damaged mortar is known as repointing.

**reportorial,** *a.* For def. read: Consisting of, pertaining to, or characteristic of, reporters; also, written in the style of a (newspaper) report. (Further examples.)
*a*1961 C. P. AIKEN in *Webster* s.v., It is too topical, too transitory, too reportorial. **1977** *Fortune* Dec. 72/1 The book is.. reportorial: a final section describes the efforts of communications officers at the Bank of America to overthrow the old ways. **1989** *Boston Globe* 15 Aug. 60/2 Many of the stories are strictly reportorial, saving us from tedious, older-but-wiser morals.

**repo'ssessor** (riː-), *n.* Chiefly *U.S.* [f. REPOSSESS *v.* + -OR.] One who repossesses goods; *spec.* a person hired by a credit company to repossess an item when the purchaser defaults on payments.
**1934** in WEBSTER. **1956** *Calif. Appellate Rep.* 2nd Ser. CXLI. 694 [He] was a 'car repossessor' for a finance company. **1969** *Stanford Law Rev.* XXII. 33 If deficiency judgments were eliminated, the defaulting purchaser would be spared his own and the repossessor's court costs. **1976** *Billings* (Montana) *Gaz.* 4 July 5-c/3 A television repossessor, knowing that an 11-year-old girl was home alone, demanded angrily that she unlock the door. **1988** *Philadelphia Inquirer* 20 Nov. B1 Because I'm a repossessor there's a stigma attached to me.

**repudiation,** *n.* [2.] [b.] For def. read: *Law.* The action or stated intention of refusing or failing to comply with the terms of a contract, esp. of debt repayment; a denial of contract. Cf. REPUDIATE *v.* 3 b. (Further examples.)
**1904** D. B. W. SLADEN *Playing the Game* II. iii. 184 The Japanese traders who dealt with them were, many of them, welshers who looked to repudiations for their profits. **1921** F. POLLOCK *Princ. Contract* (ed. 9) 292 A contract may be broken or discharged by repudiation, that is, by conduct manifestly repugnant to the due fulfilment of the terms. **1988** *Times* 1 Dec. 41/3 It was urged that while the authority's dismissal of him amounted to a repudiatory breach of contract, Dr Guirguis had never accepted.. such repudiation.

**repudiatory,** *a.* Delete *rare* and for def. read: Of, pertaining to, or favouring repudiation (of a debt or other obligation). (Further examples.)
**1936** *Pennsylvania State Rep.* CCCXXIII. 512 It was the practice of the states, at that time of grave economic distress, of enacting repudiatory legislation. **1972** *Mod. Law Rev.* XXXV. 1. 44 It also seems to exclude the possibility of recovery on repudiatory breach generally. **1981** *Times* 25 Feb. 26/1 The common law rule that a contract is determined by the acceptance of repudiatory conduct and not by the repudiatory conduct itself applies to contracts of employment.

**repurchase,** *n.* Add: **b.** Special Comb. **repurchase agreement** (orig. *U.S.*), a contract in which the vendor of (esp. government) securities agrees to repurchase them from the buyer, usu. on a specified date; cf. \*REPO *n.*[1]
**1924** G. G. MUNN *Encycl. Banking & Finance* 495/2 *Repurchase Agreement.* This term has two applications: (1) Bonds are sometimes sold by one bank or investment house to another with the privilege of repurchase... (2) Member banks may borrow from a Federal Reserve bank through the

instrumentality of a repurchase agreement, which, to all intents and purposes, is a collateral advance. **1938** R. B. WESTERFIELD *Money, Credit & Banking* xxxi. 629 An exception to this reserve bank initiation in the purchase . . and sale of government securities is found in the so-called 'sales contract' or 'repurchase agreement'. **1963** *Wall St. Jrnl.* 5 Nov. 18/3 Securities dealers look to repurchase agreements, or 'repos', as a way to obtain short-term financing and the device long has been used in connection with Government securities. **1987** M. BRETT *How to read Financial Pages* xiv. 163 [The Bank of England] may have entered into arrangements to buy securities and sell them back later (repurchase agreements or repos) which act as a short term loan.

**re'sealable**, *a*. [f. RESEAL *v*. + -ABLE.] Capable of being resealed or of resealing (esp. of a container for food or drink, or that which seals it).
    **1947** *Mod. Packaging* Apr. 99/1 First to adopt an entirely new type of can with a resealable closure is American Home Foods, Inc., for G. Washington instant soluble coffee. **1968** *Mod. Metals* Jan. 84 (*heading*) New aluminium cap is tamperproof, resealable. **1989** *Los Angeles Times* (Orange County ed.) 2 Mar. IV. 2/3 We are hoping to offer people small plastic, resealable kegs.

**resectable** (riː'sɛktəb(ə)l), *a. Surg.* [f. RESECT *v*. + -ABLE.] That may be resected.
    **1948** *Cancer* I. 234/2 The inoperable group was found to have had symptoms over a somewhat shorter period of time than had the group with resectable lesions. **1985** *Brit. Med. Jrnl.* 1 June 1643/2 It is our policy to assess all [other] potentially resectable focal solid liver lesions by direct visualisation at either laparoscopy or laparotomy.
    Hence re,secta'bility *n*., the condition of being resectable.
    **1962** *New England Jrnl. Med.* CCLXVII. 235/2 The results paralleled the results of azygography in predicting probable inoperability in 1 case and suggesting resectability in the other 3. **1980** *Recent Adv. Surgery* X. 6 The potential resectability of large tumours.

**resident**, *a*. and *n*.[1] Add: [A.] [2.] c. *Computing.* Of a program, file, etc.: occupying a permanent place in memory, esp. in main memory or the memory built into a particular device, and hence rapidly accessible during processing. Also designating the active module of a larger program, the rest of which is stored outside main memory.
    **1966** C. J. SIPPL *Computer Dict.* 160/1 The term resident is used to denote a part of the executive which resides in core memory at all times. Examples of resident routines are the dispatcher, the real-time clock routine, and the internal-error processing routines. **1967** *IBM Systems Jrnl.* VI. 13 The System Loader (also called Program Fetch) is part of the resident Supervisor. **1971** N. CHAPIN *Computers* xiv. 393 The overlay and segmentation feature permits a program to be broken into sections with some of the sections always to be resident (present) in internal storage. **1979** *Sci. Amer.* Jan. 105/1 (Advt.), With as many as 16 resident character sets—any two of which may be used on any line. **1984** *QL User* Dec. 24 With the programs permanently resident in ROM the transfer of information is virtually simultaneous. **1986** *Practical Computing* Oct. 23/2 One advantage . . is that MS-DOS function 27H can be used to allow a program to terminate but stay resident.

**residual**, *a*. Add: Hence **re'sidually** *adv*., to a residual extent; in a residual degree.
    **1957** *Proc. London Math. Soc.* VII. 29 Mal'cev . . proved an even more general result, giving sufficient conditions, and also necessary ones, for a free product of residually nilpotent groups to be itself

residually nilpotent. **1963** *Proc. Cambr. Philos. Soc.* LIX. 555 The theorem of Gruenberg that a free product of residually finite groups is itself residually finite. **1980** *Christian Science Monitor* 24 Jan. 7/2 The council's powers and responsibilities would fall into three categories: those exercised unilaterally, those 'shared' with Israel, and those to remain 'residually' with Israel. **1987** A. S. BYATT *Sugar* 114 Their country, the guide book said, was Confucian, Buddhist, Catholic, residually shamanistic.

**resistentialism**            (rɛzɪ'stɛnʃəlɪz(ə)m),        *n*. [Humorous blend of L. *rēs* thing(s) and F. *résister* RESIST *v*. with EXISTENTIALISM *n*.] P. Jennings's mock philosophy which maintains that inanimate objects are hostile to humans.
    **1948** P. JENNINGS in *Spectator* 23 Apr. 491/1 Resistentialism is a philosophy of tragic grandeur . . . Resistentialism derives its name from its central thesis that Things (*res*) resist (*résister*) men . . . Resistentialism is the philosophy of what Things think about *us*. **1950** —— *Oddly Enough* 147 'Things are against us.' This is the nearest English translation I can find for the basic concept of Resistentialism. **1977** *Fontana Dict. Mod. Thought* 540/1 The absence of any physical basis for resistentialism is more than counterbalanced by its appeal as a psychological theory. **1978** *Verbatim* May 11/1 It forms the basis of Clark-Thrimble's classic experiment in resistentialism. **1986** *Times* 2 July 16/6 More and more people come to recognize the basic truth of Resistentialism (basically, that it is not men who control things, but things which increasingly control men). **1988** *Newsday* 21 June (Discovery) 5/4 The technical   term   for . . mechanical   insolence   is 'resistentialism'.
    Hence **resi'stentialist** *n*., an adherent of resistentialism; also as *adj*.
    **1948** P. JENNINGS in *Spectator* 23 Apr. 491/2 To the resistentialist man is no-Thing . . . Things are the only reality, possessing a power of action to which *we* can never aspire. *Ibid*. In the musical field there is already a school of resistentialist composers among the younger men. **1989** *New Republic* 29 May 26/3 Irwin is . . a 'resistentialist'—malfunctioning things are always conspiring against him.

**re'skill** (riː-), *v*. [RE- 5 a.] *trans*. To teach or equip with new skills; *spec*. to retrain (workers) in the skills required by a modern business. Also *transf*. Cf. RETRAIN *v*.
    **1985** *Financial Times* 9 Apr. 25/3 We recognise the need to . . reskill the workforce. **1985** *Times* 12 Dec. 31/1 We have heard a great deal about the importance of training or re-skilling the workforce to revitalize British industry. **1986** *Daily Tel.* 20 May 2/5 We must reskill the workforce, from top management to shop floor. **1989** *Guardian Weekly* 22 Jan. 28/2 The ginger-group . . which recently made radical proposals for reskilling and reinvigorating the government machine. **1989** *N.Y. Times* 16 Apr. III. 31/2 We are caught up in a treadmill of retraining, reskilling, retooling the current work force for job descriptions that are as narrow and as shortsighted as the ones they have just come from.
    So **re'skilling** *vbl. n.*
    **1983** *N.Y. Times* 12 June IV. 19/1 A safer method of managing chronic unemployment is 'reskilling'. **1988** *Times* 25 May 13/1 The decision due to be made today by the Trades Union Congress exemplifies one of those wider purposes—the 'reskilling' of the unemployed at a moment of economic regeneration.

**re'skin** (riː-), *v*. [RE- 5 a.] † **1.** *refl*. To re-cover (oneself) in skin. *nonce-use*.
    **1820** COLERIDGE *Let.* 25 May (1971) V. 48 A Suicide . . sinking below the organizing power [may] be employed fruitlessly in a horrid appetite of re-skinning himself, after he had succeeded in fleaing his Life.

**2.** *trans.* To replace or repair the skin of (an aircraft or motor vehicle). See SKIN *n.* 9 c.
**1976** *Business Week* 12 Apr. 67/3 They will replace worn out structures, 'reskin' corroded surfaces, and retire their early jets after 18 years or 20 years. **1977** *Aviation Week & Space Technol.* 13 June 60/3 A 3,000-lb. payload could be carried if the wing were reskinned. **1982** *Business Week* 4 Oct. 76/2 'Reskinning' a car with new sheet metal over the same old engine, transmission, and suspension can cost $200 million. **1989** *Aviation Week & Space Technol.* 24 July 67/2 It's a matter of doing the right maintenance and control... You can always reskin the airplane.
Hence **re'skinned** *ppl. a.*; **re'skinning** *vbl. n.*
**1975** *Internat. Antique Airplane News* (1976) IV. 30/2 While the wing was in the process of re-skinning we started on the engine mount. **1978** *Times* 6 Jan. 17/2 A larger version will mean a complete 'reskinning job'. **1979** *Economist* 3 Feb. 76/2 New cars cost at least three times as much, even for simple 'reskinned' replacements. **1983** *Truck & Bus Transportation* July 78/1 This mounting design.. allows the bodies to easily be lifted off for refitting and reskinning at the end of their service life.

**resolvase** (rɪ'zɒlveɪz), *n. Biochem.* [f. RESOLVE *v.* + -ASE.] An enzyme which promotes the resolution of two transposons contained in a cointegrate.
**1981** R. R. REED in *Cell* XXV. 713/2 These results have led to the suggestion that the regulatory role of the *tnpR* product upon expression of the divergently transcribed *tnpA* and *tnpR* genes and its recombinational activity may both result from specific binding to a single site... To emphasize this major function, the *tnpR* protein has been renamed 'resolvase'. **1983** J. R. S. FINCHAM *Genetics* x. 270 Reciprocal recombination, specifically catalysed in the recombination sequence of the transposon by the *tpnR* product ('recombinase' or 'resolvase'), resolves the cointegrate into two separate plasmids. **1988** *Nature* 28 Apr. 862/1 Resolvase catalysed substantial relaxation of the mutant substrate into topoisomers of reduced negative superhelicity.

**restorationism**, *n.* Add: **2.** A House Church movement which seeks to restore the beliefs and practices of the early Christian church; the doctrine and principles of this movement.
**1985** A. WALKER *Restoring Kingdom* i. 22 The term 'Restorationism' denotes a qualitative understanding of (so members believe) the work of the Holy Spirit. **1985** *Church Times* 27 Dec. 7/1 Mr. Walker sees the emergence of Restorationism as one of the most significant and hopeful events of recent times.

**restorationist**, *n.* and *a.* Add: [A.] [1.] For 'restorationism' read 'restorationism (sense 1)'.
**3.** One who seeks to restore practices or institutions which have been abolished or have fallen into disuse; *spec.* a person favouring the restoration of capital punishment.
**1975** *Economist* 6 Dec. 10/1 Few restorationists admit openly that what they want is simply institutionalised vengeance. **1988** *Daily Tel.* 27 Sept. 9/1 The motion selected for debate, while not containing any reference to the death penalty, will nevertheless give restorationists ample opportunity to press their case. **1989** *New Republic* 13 Mar. 38/1 Sklar terms the populists 'restorationists' who wanted to restore the older competitive capitalism by curbing the giant corporations.
**4.** An adherent of restorationism (esp. sense 2); one who seeks to restore the beliefs and practices of the early Christian church.
**1985** A. WALKER *Restoring Kingdom* i. 22 Restorationists wish to restore or return to the New Testament pattern (as they see it) of the Early Church. **1985** *Church Times* 27 Dec. 7/2, I do not like the sound of the Restorationists, but I've got a

feeling that someone is trying to tell us something. **1988** *Independent* 28 Nov. 9/1 The restorationists are proudly supernaturalist.
**B.** *adj.* Of, pertaining to, or favouring restorationism (esp. sense 2) or the ideals of restorationists.
**1979** *Summary World Broadcasts: Far East: Internal Affairs: China* (B.B.C.) 3 Mar. BII/3 The 'restorationist' group which emerged after the defeat of the revolution in 1905.. came from the Left to oppose Lenin's correct line. **1985** A. WALKER *Restoring Kingdom* ii. 40 Wallis's vision was Restorationist but without the discipleship doctrines that were to become such a hallmark of the mature movement. **1988** *Independent* 28 Nov. 9 (*heading*), South Coast apostle leads a 'restorationist' crusade. **1989** *Church Times* 17 Feb. 6/3 Both the Charismatic Movement and the Restorationist house churches have been socially superior to Pentecostalism.

**restrained**, *ppl. a.* Add: **b.** Of a person: held in place by a seat-belt or safety restraint.
**1984** *Which?* Aug. 347/3 Steering wheel offers little protection to the head or face of a restrained driver. **1985** *Brit. Med. Jrnl.* 1 June 1621/1 Data on 2520 occupants of cars involved in accidents were analysed .. to investigate the effect of rear seat passengers on injury to restrained and unrestrained front seat occupants and vice versa. **1989** *Derbyshire Times* 8 Sept. 11/1 A child does not have to be restrained.. if the seats are being occupied by restrained adults.

**result**, *n.* Senses 3 d, e in Dict. become 3 e, f. Add: [3.] **d.** *pl.* The outcome of trading over a given period, expressed as a statement of profit or loss announced by a business, esp. annually.
**1877** R. W. RAYMOND *Statistics Mines & Mining* 185 The final results of several mining and reducing enterprises.. are very discouraging. **1899** *Westm. Gaz.* 4 Jan. 6/3 The year-end stocktaking results. **1930** *Economist* 3 May 1008/2 A preliminary statement issued by this progressive company of bazaar proprietors reports excellent results for the year ended March 31, 1930. **1960** R. KENNEDY *Introductory Accounting* viii. 124 The Revenue and Expense Summary account also facilitates the transfer of the operating results (net income or net loss) to the proprietor's capital account. **1977** (*title*) Financial results of the oil majors, 1976 (Shell Internat. Petroleum Co.). **1980** *Times* 5 Aug. 17/7 Only then will it emerge whether there are any writebacks to profits arising from the results of the first six months of this year.

**reticulospinal** (rɪ,tɪkjʊləʊ'spaɪnəl), *a. Anat.* [f. RETICULO- + SPINAL *a.*] Designating or relating to a tract of nerves in the spinal cord that originate in the reticular formation of the brain stem.
**1956** *Jrnl. Neurophysiol.* XIX. 524 Two descending tracts are involved, viz. the vestibulo-spinal and the reticulo-spinal tract. **1960** *Ibid.* XXIII. 286 Vestibular responses at lumbosacral levels reflect activity mediated predominantly via reticulospinal pathways or their functional continuations as propriospinal intersegmental relays. **1972, 1974** [see RUBRO-]. **1979** *Sci. Amer.* Sept. 92/3 All three of these fiber systems descending into the spinal cord (reticulospinal, tectospinal, and rubrospinal tracts by name) must be seen as bearing information.. that may have antecedents in wide regions of the brain.

**retinal**, *a.* Add: **b.** *retinal detachment Path.*, a condition in which the surface of the retina becomes detached from the underlying layer of epithelium, producing a scotoma. Cf. *detached retina s.v.* *DETACHED ppl. a.* 2.
**1882** W. A. BRAILEY in *Trans. Ophthalm. Soc.* II. 91, I originally called it 'a case of retinal detachment' which was wrongly attributed to the presence of a choroidal sarcoma. **1965** *Amer. Jrnl. Ophthalm.* LX.

191/1 The introduction of scleral buckling procedures opened new avenues of approach in the treatment of retinal detachments previously considered of unfavorable prognosis. **1987** *Investigative Ophthalm. & Visual Sci.* XXVIII. 2038/1 Little is known of the effects of retinal detachment upon the physiology and metabolism of the neural retina.

‖ **retiré** (rətire), *n.*[2] *Ballet.* [Fr., pa. pple. of *retirer* to pull or draw back.] A movement in which one leg (bent and fully turned outwards) is raised until the toe(s) touch the knee of the other leg.

**1941** C. W. BEAUMONT *Third Primer Class. Ballet* c. 43 Facing corner 2, . . do 4 *retirés* travelling diagonally backwards to corner 4. **1957** G. B. L. WILSON *Dict. Ballet* 228 *Retiré*, . . the raising, from the fifth position, of the fully turned out thigh until it is at right angles to the body with the toe in line with the knee-cap of the supporting leg and closing front or back, in the fifth position. **1975** 'M. FONTEYN' *Autobiogr.* I. i. 21 Had my mother not drawn attention to the way in which Pavlova was performing her *retirés* I might have no memory at all of that genius of the dance. **1984** *Dance Theatre Jrnl.* Feb. 43/2 The hair's breadth stop, the retiré suspended in time, eternal.

‖ **retornado** (rɛtɔːˈnɑːdəʊ), *n.* [Pg., f. pa. pple. of *retornar* RETURN *v.*[1]] A Portuguese subject who returns to settle in Portugal instead of remaining in a former Portuguese colony after independence.

**1976** *Economist* 5 June 45/2 Nobody knows for sure exactly how many *retornados* there are now in Portugal. **1978** *Guardian Weekly* 7 May 13/2 He is a retornado—he came back from 'over there'. A colonist? Come, he hadn't been 20 years in Angola when the dream came to an abrupt end outside the mob-besieged gates of Luanda's airport. **1984** *Times* 25 Apr. 17/3 Portugal . . has, against many predictions, absorbed its *retornados*. **1987** *Financial Times* 30 Oct. p. vi/4 The country had . . to make room for 700,000 'retornados' from overseas—with a further influx still expected from Macao.

**retort** *n.*[2] Sense 5 in Dict. becomes 6. Add:
**5.** A vessel in which canned or packaged foodstuff is sterilized by heating directly or under pressure. Cf. AUTOCLAVE *n.* 2, DIGESTER *n.* 4 a.

**1897** PRESCOTT & UNDERWOOD in *Technol. Q.* X. 185 The introduction of digesters or 'retorts', about 1870, was the next . . step in the development of sterilizing apparatus. **1912** A. W. BITTING *Canning of Foods* 23 The cans are collected in large iron baskets, which usually hold 270 No. 2 or 180 No. 3 cans, and three baskets fill a retort. **1937** O. & T. W. JONES *Canning Pract. & Control* iii. 41 When the contents of the can at the centre have been heated to the same degree as the retort, then the whole of the contents will be at that temperature. **1951** M. B. JACOBS *Chem. & Technol. Food* III. 1874 The position of the can in the retort during a still cook has been found to be significant. **1969** J. G. BRENNAN et al. *Food Engin. Operations* x. 208 Non-agitating batch retorts are used extensively. **1988** *Vegetarian* Mar.-Apr. 29/1 The cans are . . automatically filled, the remaining end sealed into place and then they are heated in a huge pressure cooker, called a retort, at up to 250°F for a half to one hour.
**6. retort pouch**, a type of flexible packaging in which food is sterilized by heating in a retort (sense 5).

**1972** *Food Technol.* Aug. 65/1 There has been a need for a commercially sterile, flexible package in which undesirable microorganisms can be eliminated or deactivated. This has been accomplished with Continental Can Company's flexible *retort pouch. **1984** *Financial Times* 10 Feb. 12/7 The use of polyester film is expected to more than double between 1982 and 1995 because of its expanded application in frozen food packaging and retort pouches.

**retrench** *v.*[1] Add: [5.] **d.** *euphem.* To make (an employee) redundant; to sack.

**1975** *Sunday Tel.* (Brisbane) 16 Mar. 5/4 The best workers were kept on while others were retrenched. **1978** D. BLOODWORTH *Crosstalk* xix. 153 Not now. Not with Denis Healey cutting government spending by a billion pounds . . . He was being forced to retrench Hilliard and four senior men as it was. **1987** *India Today* 15 Jan. 119/2 The plan to shut down the textile mill in Delhi, retrench 5,000 workers and sell the mill's real estate . . has run into trouble.

**retri'butionist**, *n.* [f. RETRIBUTION *n.* + -IST.] = RETRIBUTIVIST *n.*

**1939** *Mind* XLVIII. 153 Even Bradley, the fiercest retributionist of modern times, says 'Having once the right to punish we may modify the punishment'. **1986** *Daily Tel.* 10 Mar. 14/2 By the same token, of course, the retributionist holds that those who, in a deliberate manner, inflict death should themselves die.

**re'tributivism**, *n.* [f. RETRIBUTIVE *a.* + -ISM.] The policy or theory of retributive justice.

**1969** N. WALKER *Sentencing in Rational Soc.* i. 5 Its unsophisticated form penal retributivism asserts . . that the penal system should be designed to ensure that offenders atone by suffering for their offences. **1987** *Columbia Law Rev.* Apr. 510 Much of the philosophical discussion of retributivism centers around the question whether it is morally desirable that persons get their just deserts.

**retrievable**, *a.* Add: Hence re,trieva'bility *n.*

**1895** in *Funk's Stand. Dict.* **1976** *Linguistics* CLXXVII. 53 The complete retrievability of particular characteristics from the questionnaires allows us to make *qualitative* comparisons by cross-sectionalizing. **1985** *Library Assoc. Rec.* Apr. 136/2 (Advt.), Abstractors, well used to meeting the demands of brevity, readability and retrievability that enquirers need.

**retrieve**, *n.* Add: [3.] **e.** *Angling.* The act, method, or process of reeling or drawing in a line.

**1972** *Field & Stream* May 168/2, I began catching fish in 2 to 6 feet of water . . . I also changed my retrieve. **1977** *Chicago Tribune* 2 Oct. III. 10/2 One of the best ways to handle loose line for distance casting when wading is to form extra large coils of line on the retrieve. **1986** *Trout Fisherman* July 31/2 Avoid jerking the line at all costs, and try to keep the retrieve as smooth as possible.

**retrieve**, *v.* Add: [II.] **9.** *Angling.* To reel or bring in a fishing-line.

**1961** in WEBSTER. **1966** K. T. LILLIECRONA *Salt-Water Fish & Fishing in S. Afr.* i. 21 All one has to do is cast in this multi-hook trace among the fish, count twenty slowly and then retrieve to find every hook with a pinky on it. **1987** *Trout Fisherman* Mar. 64/2 Always retrieve right up to the boat, as they'll often follow right in, even on a sunken line. **1988** *Sea Angling Q.* Summer 44/3 When he reaches the breakers, with you retrieving furiously, he'll probably change course and make off downtide.

**retro** ('rɛtrəʊ), *n.*[2] and *a.* [a. F. *rétro* n. and adj. (1973), abbrev. of *rétrograde* adj.] **A.** *n.* Something that imitates or harks back to a former style; *esp.* a style or fashion (of dress, music, etc.) that is nostalgically retrospective.

**1974** *Guardian Weekly* 18 May 14/1 The icy charms of the Group TSE's productions, beginning as far back as 1969's 'Eva Peron', have been in the vanguard of the French vogue for 'retro'. **1983** *Daily Tel.* 18 Mar. 17/4 No retro from this designer, . . but just gorgeous colour. **1985** *Times* 19 Mar. 13/2 At Hyper Hyper the young innovators mixed 1960s and 1970s retro with dandyish frock coats. **1986** *Q* Oct. 69/3 Carmel have set up camp on that sacred turf the Americans now delight in calling 'retro'. A throwback. Something you missed the first time round but wouldn't mind a small portion reheated because you always wondered what it tasted like. **1987** *Daily Tel.* 12 Aug. 11/7 'Retro'..is the latest 'in' word in California's ever-surprising lexicon and may be applied in a laudatory sense to anything from the past that is being brought back into fashion.

**B.** *attrib.* and as *adj.* Of, pertaining to, or characterized by this style; that looks back to or is a revival of something in the past.

**1977** *Times Lit. Suppl.* 14 Jan. 25/2 She will be eighty-five this year, so her Georgianism is real, not retro. **1979** *N.Y. Times* 24 Jan. c8/4 We thought that if we closed our eyes, retro fashion would go away. No such luck. **1982** *Face* May 38/2 It managed..to reconstruct Art Deco as a complete period fantasy, dutifully retro but also fantastically modern. **1984** E. JONG *Parachutes & Kisses* ix. 157 She..slipped a scrawled card into his breast pocket... Kevin was delighted... (Any guy who wore a 'retro' tux would *have* to be.) **1985** *Village Voice* (N.Y.) 8 Jan. 55/3 The rhythmically retro little track, for instance, exposes the not-necessarily-endearing frailty of her voice. **1986** *Times* 1 July 11 Black patent Grace Kelly handbags, long black gloves and high-heeled slingbacks are retro accessories to the elegant look.

**retro-**, *prefix.* Add: [3.] **d.** *Org. Chem.* Prefixed to the names of reaction types in order to designate the equivalent processes taking place in reverse, esp. in **retro-ene reaction**, the reverse of an ene reaction.

**1969** H. M. R. HOFFMANN in *Angewandte Chem.* (Internat. ed.) VIII. 556/1 Retro-ene reactions, *e.g.*, the decarboxylation of β-ketoacids and the formation of olefins by ester pyrolysis. **1972** DEPUY & CHAPMAN *Molec. Reactions & Photochem.* vii. 140 Retro-Diels-Alder reactions may be carried out in the vapor phase in the absence of all solvents and catalysts. **1974** GILL & WILLIS *Pericyclic Reactions* vi. 205 Retro-ene type reactions..are very much more common when one or more of the six atomic participants is a heteroatom, and notably oxygen. **1989** tr. *Elschenbroich & Salzer's Organometallics* viii. 108 The retrodiene cleavage of a silabicyclo [2.2.2] octadiene is exploited.

**retroposon** (ˌrɛtrəʊˈpəʊzɒn), *n. Genetics.* [f. RETRO(VIRUS *n.* + -*poson* after TRANSPOSON *n.*] A sequence of genetic material capable of undergoing transposition via an RNA intermediate.

**1983** J. ROGERS in *Nature* 10 Feb. 460/3 Several classes of dispersed repeated sequences in mammalian DNA share common properties which imply that they are derived from RNA... A new name seems to be required for the RNA-derived type of sequence, and I suggest 'retroposons', to denote their RNA origin and their dispersed positions. **1987** *Nature* 6 Aug. 557/2 The presence of endogenous viral retroposons encoding reverse transcriptase. **1988** E. PAYS in A. J. Kingsman et al. *Transposition* 332 TRS-1 harbours distinctive features of retroposons, such as a poly(A) tail and a gene for reverse transcriptase.

**retrotransposon** (ˌrɛtrəʊtrænsˈpəʊzɒn, -trɑːns-), *n. Genetics.* [f. RETRO(VIRUS *n.* + TRANSPOSON *n.*] = *RETROPOSON *n.*

**1985** J. D. BOEKE et al. in *Cell* XL. 496/1 Our data suggest that reverse transcription of Ty, like that of retroviruses, regenerates the 3'U5 from the 5' end of the message and the 5'U3 from the 3' end. We therefore propose the term *retrotransposon* for Ty and related elements. **1986** *Heredity* LVII. 279/1 The overall structure of this integrated DNA parallels that

of the 'retrotransposon' class of eukaryotic transposable elements such as the Ty elements of yeast and the *copia* family of *Drosophila*. **1987** *Nature* 6 Aug. 557/2 Retrotransposons have been described in wheat and maize.

**return**, *n.* Add: [III.] [13.] **c.** = *return key*, sense *16 c below.

**1981** DUNN & MORGAN *PET Personal Computer for Beginners* i. 4 Try typing in other words and pressing *Return* when you have finished, to see what happens. **1984** *Which Micro?* Dec. 83/2 The keys are simple enough, with..return for jump. **1986** *Sci. Amer.* Aug. 10/3 The simplest misdirection is based on the carriage-return key (called variously 'return' or 'enter').

[IV.] [16.] [c.] **return key** *Computing*, a key pressed to simulate a carriage return (esp. in a word-processing program) or to transfer data from an input buffer to a program or computer; a carriage-return key.

**1978** *Getting Started with your PET* (Total Info. Services Workbk. 1) i. 5 The 'Return' key must be pressed at the end of each line. **1985** *Practical Computing* July 59/1 However, all the keys are sensibly placed, and my only real criticism is that the Return key is far too small.

**return**, *v.*[1] Add: [III.] [16.] **e.** *Racing.* To report or announce (a starting price); also, to set (a horse, etc.) *at* a given price. Freq. in *pass.*

**1951** E. RICKMAN *Come Racing with Me* xvii. 174 At all the principal meetings, the same two experts 'return' the starting prices which accompany every racing result. **1986** *Greyhound Star* Aug. 16/1 Paddy Hancox's charge, returned at 5-2, broke first and soon opened up a lead.

[IV.] [21.] **d.** *Amer. Football.* To collect the ball from (a kick or fumble by the opposing team) and carry it upfield; to intercept (a pass) and run with the ball. Also with ball as obj.

**1955** R. K. PARKER *We play to Win* xiv. 128 It isn't often you play it perfectly and return a kick off for a touchdown. **1963** A. SHERMAN *Bk. Football* vii. 151 (*heading*) How to return the kickoff. **1972** J. MOSEDALE *Football* x. 143 Eight times he returned punts for touchdowns—a record. **1988** *Touchdown* Nov. 21/1 On the ensuing kickoff..Woodson displayed his immense athletic talents as he returned the ball 92 yards for a touchdown. **1991** *Sports Illustr.* 21 Jan. 25/2 Cornerback Mark Collins picked it off and returned it 11 yards to set up a Giants field goal.

**returner**, *n.* Add: [1.] **b.** *spec.* One who returns to employment after a long interval, *esp.* a woman who resumes work after leaving it to raise children. Freq. as *woman returner*.

**1963** *Guardian* 21 Jan. 4/1 We are allowed to take 'off-ration' part time teachers, married women returners..and a few other special categories. **1981** *Daily Tel.* 14 Dec. 7/5 The newcomers, the young graduates with non-vocational degrees, or women returners who..lack recent experience. **1984** *Times* 16 Aug. 23/3 What of the qualified returner whose skills are rusty? **1989** *Your Business* Feb. 55/1 Other sources of labour will have to be found... The most likely one is married women 'returners', who will often work part-time.

[2.] **b.** *Amer. Football.* A player who collects the ball from a kick downfield, etc. and carries it back towards the opposing team.

**1963** R. SMITH *Pro Football* x. 117 He was the most feared kickoff returner in the game. **1972** D. KOWET *Golden Toes* xvi. 114 The returner will bring it back for more yardage against the kicking team. **1988** L. WILSON *Amer. Football* v. 82/1 When the center snaps the ball, the two wide players sprint down-field heading straight for the returner.

**re-use**, *v.* Add: Hence **re-'used** *ppl. a.*
   **1877** J. C. Cox *Notes Churches Derbyshire* III. 241 A remarkable . . example of the palimpsest or re-used brass. **1979** P. LEVI *Head in Soup* i. 20 Decoration made of the reused coloured marbles of the old imperial buildings.

**Revere** (rə'vɪə(r)), *n.* Chiefly *U.S.* Also **Paul Revere**. The name of Paul *Revere* (1735-1818), American silversmith renowned for his midnight ride in April 1775 to warn the American colonial forces of the approach of the British, used *attrib.* and *absol.* to designate silverware made by Revere, or in a similar Colonial style by his contemporaries or as modern reproductions. (Proprietary as a name for jewellery and copper-bottomed cooking pots.)
   *Revere* is used in preference to *Paul Revere* to designate silver actually made by Revere.
   *c* **1901** in *Outl. Life & Wks. P. Revere* (Towle Manuf. Co.) 17 It is reserved for the 'Paul Revere' to exemplify the elegant simplicity which . . distinguishes the taste of our forefathers. *a* **1908** in *Hist. Publ. Towle Manuf. Co.* 36 The Paul Revere ware here illustrated exemplifies these qualities to a marked degree and was prepared as much to supplement the Paul Revere pattern of flat-ware . . as to create in the spirit of this famous colonial craftsman an artistically meritorious design. **1929** *National Republic* Nov. 32/1 In an exhibition held in Boston in 1906, sixty-five Revere pieces were exhibited. **1950** *House Beautiful* July 56 (*caption*) The classic Paul Revere bowl symbolizes the typically American faculty for simplification. Today Lunt's reproduction (above) captures this same purity of design. **1974** *North Myrtle Beach* (S. Carolina) *Times* 17 Apr. 3/6 (Advt.), 9-in. silver Revere bowl. **1976** G. McDONALD *Confess, Fletch* vii. 39 A Revere coffee service awaited them on a butler's table. **1986** *Christian Science Monitor* 5 May 38/2 The couple received a silver Paul Revere bowl from the society.

**reverse**, *n.* Add: **13.** *Amer. Football.* A play in which a player passes the ball to a team-mate moving in the opposite direction, thereby reversing the direction of attack.
   **1937** B. W. BIERMAN *Winning Football* xiv. 176 The shift is right and the play a reverse to the left, good for 4 yards. **1952** L. R. MENGER *Spread Formation Football* xii. 133 The halfback reverses can be used to strike the flanks. **1961** J. SALAK *Dict. Amer. Sports* 361 On a double reverse, the direction of the ball changes twice. **1974** R. T. BARAN *Coaching Football's Polypotent Offense* viii. 147 The specials include both passes and reverses and really make the offense polypotent. **1988** *Touchdown* Nov. 16/1 Gentry's touchdown . . came after he had scampered 58 yards on a reverse with quarterback Jim McMahon.

**reverse**, *a.* and *adv.* Add: **[5.]** **[a.]** *reverse takeover* (*Comm.*), a takeover in which a small, usu. private company assumes control over a larger, public one.
   [**1959** *Business Week* 21 Feb. 43/1 About 150 ex-IBM salesmen are checking into Gardner, Mass., this week to help put the finishing touches on a merger with a reverse twist . . . It was the smaller outfit that swallowed the larger.] **1967** *Business* Jan. 43/1 He wrote to the sole surviving director . . outlining his plans for a reverse take-over. **1973** *Times* 2 Oct. 21/3 This is a reverse takeover with GB capitalized at £12.9m against BSG's £8.8m. **1986** *Business Rev. Weekly* 19 Sept. 34/3 The main thrust of the long days of talks was a scheme for Holmes a Court to sell out of BHP. The proposal involved a reverse takeover of BHP.

**review**, *n.* Add: **[II.]** **9.** A facility for playing a video or audio recording during a fast rewind, so that it can be stopped when a desired point is reached.
   Occurs almost invariably in association with CUE *n.*[2] 1 d, the term for the analogous forward function.
   **1978**, etc. [see CUE *n.*[2] 1 d].

**revision**, *n.* Add: **[1.]** **c.** *Med.* Surgery to make good any deterioration in a patient's condition which has occurred as a result of a previous surgical operation, *esp.* the repair or replacement of an artificial joint or other prosthetic appliance; an instance of this.
   **1947** *Jrnl. Bone & Joint Surg.* XXIX. 48 Fifteen months later, a blow on the hip resulted in formation of a small sinus, and revision may be necessary if osteitis under the mold and sinus formation persist. **1969** *Ibid.* A. Ll. 1476 The remaining revisions were made necessary by inadequate tissue repair under the cup. **1973** R. G. TRONZO *Surg. Hip Joint* xxii. 731/1 Many surgeons today would convert the arthroplasty to a total hip replacement rather than attempt a cup revision. **1987** *Brit. Med. Jrnl.* 29 Aug. 514/2 A new epidemic of patients requiring joint revision is starting to make inroads into operating lists: in Oxford one in five operations to replace hips are now revisions.

**rhamphorhynchoid** (ræmfəʊ'rɪŋkɔɪd), *a.* and *n. Palæont.* [ad. mod.L. *Rhamphorhynchoidea*, f. *Rhamphorhynchus* (the type genus), f. Gr. ῥάμφος beak + ῥύγχος snout: see -OID.] **A.** *adj.* Belonging to the extinct suborder Rhamphorhynchoidea of pterosaurs of the late Triassic and early Jurassic, characterized by a short neck and a long bony tail. **B.** *n.* A rhamphorhynchoid pterosaur.
   **1895** *Funk's Stand. Dict.* s.v., Rhamphorhynchoid, *a.* **1945** A. S. ROMER *Vertebr. Paleont.* (ed. 2) xxviii. 543 Pterosaur remains are rare except in the Niobrara Chalk of the Upper Cretaceous. The rhamphorhynchoid type is extinct, and by the Upper Cretaceous we find surviving only short-tailed pterodactyloids. **1981** *Sci. Amer.* Feb. 100/1 In 1956 Erich von Holst . . constructed a model of a rhamphorhynchoid from rice paper, balsa wood and aluminum. **1987** *Nature* 6 Aug. 481/2 The rhamphorhynchoid's long, rudder-tipped tail acted as an auxiliary control surface.

**rhapis** ('reɪpɪs), *n. Bot.* [mod.L., f. Gr. ῥαπίς rod.] Any of various south-east Asian dwarf palms of the genus *Rhapis* (family Palmæ), having a slender stem, leaves deeply divided into narrow, ribbed segments, and yellowish flowers; *spec.* the ground-rattan, *R. excelsa*, which is much cultivated, esp. in Japan, for its variegated foliage.
   **1910** [see GEONOMA *n.*]. **1987** *Sunday Sun* (Brisbane) 1 Mar. 91/6 The Rhapis palm is called the lady palm because it is slender and elegant.

‖**rhathymia** (rə'θaɪmɪə), *n. Psychol.* [ad. Gr. ῥᾳθυμία light-heartedness, easiness of temper, f. ῥᾳθυμεῖν to take a holiday, be idle.] In the factorial analysis of personality: a factor which predisposes a person towards light-heartedness and freedom from worry; hence, the state or condition of being cheerful and carefree; optimism.
   **1936** J. P. & R. B. GUILFORD in *Jrnl. Psychol.* II. 122 A new factor analysis will soon be made in the hope of describing factor IV more explicitly. We have tentatively identified this variable as factor *R*, the letter *R* standing for a word coined from the Greek 'rhathymia' which means freedom from care. **1948** *Brit. Jrnl. Psychol.* June 188 The probable connexion of the liability to joy emotions . . with certain 'types' or 'factors'—'extraversia', 'rhathymia', 'surgency'. **1959** J. P. GUILFORD *Personality* xvi. 413 Eysenck . . has proposed the hypothesis that restraint

vs. rhathymia is equivalent to introversion-extraversion. **1969** *Brit. Jrnl. Social & Clinical Psychol.* VIII. 275 Rhathymia in otherwise introversive individuals facilitates the already existing tendency towards use of isolation relative to repression while restraint inhibits it. **1972** *Encycl. Psychol.* III. 155/1 Rhathymia manifests itself in an unconcerned, carefree, merry attitude. **1981** *Personality & Individual Differences* II. 94 Most of the normal Egyptian groups had higher mean scores than British samples on Rhathymia.

**rheo-** *comb. form.* Add: ˌrheoigˈnimbrite *Petrogr.* [ad. It. *reoignimbrite* (A. Rittmann 1958, in *Bollettino d. Sedute d. Accad. Gioenia in Catania* IV. 524)], an ignimbrite whose character has been altered after formation by partial melting and flow.
    **1958** *Bollettino d. Sedute d. Accad. Gioenia in Catania* IV. 533 A. Rittmann..defines ignimbrites...He discusses..their occurrence, structure and texture, comparing and contrasting them with flows of acid lavas and with secondary flows of ignimbrites, for which he proposes the term '*rheoignimbrite*'. **1966** *Earth-Sci. Rev.* I. 165 If the entire depositional unit became mobilized, it may be exceedingly difficult to distinguish a rheoignimbrite from a lava flow. **1976** A. & L. RITTMANN *Volcanoes* (1978) 49 Rheo-ignimbrites..look like fairly flat, thick lava-flows lying in the middle of the ignimbrite sheet from which they came... The lower part..looks more homogeneous, and its glassy splinters are no longer so clearly defined as in ordinary ignimbrites.

**rhinal**, *a.* Add: **2.** *Neurol.* Pertaining to or designating the regions of the brain concerned with the sense of smell; *spec.* designating the sulcus which separates the anterior region of the parahippocampal gyrus from the medial occipitotemporal gyrus.
    **1890** W. TURNER in *Jrnl. Anat. & Physiol.* XXV. 106 The demarcation..is due to the presence of a fissure, more or less distinctly defined in different animals, which has been named the *rhinal* or *ectorhinal* fissure. **1958** *Gray's Anat.* (ed. 32) 1031 The parahippocampal gyrus..is..bounded on its lateral side by the collateral and rhinal Sulci. **1975** *Brain Res.* XCV. 1 All ventral temporal neocortical areas contribute some afferents to the transitional zones of periallocortex..forming the walls of the rhinal sulcus. **1987** S. M. STAHL et al. *Cognitive Neurochem.* vi. 77 Does this imply that the memory function previously attributed to the hippocampus should correctly be attributed to the rhinal cortex?

**rhodanese** (ˈrəʊdəniːz), *n. Biochem.* Also **rhodanase** (-eiz). [a. G. *Rhodanese* (K. Lang 1933, in *Biochem. Zeitschr.* CCLIX. 246), f. *Rhodan* thiocyanogen: cf. -ASE.] A naturally occurring enzyme, also called thiosulphate sulphurtransferase, which catalyses the formation of thiocyanate and sulphite from thiosulphate and cyanide radicals.
    **1933** *Chem. Abstr.* XXVII. 5349 There is present in the organism an enzyme rhodanese which brings about the union of S with HCN. **1945** *Arch. Biochem.* VII. 459 The Schütz rule does not apply to the reaction catalyzed by rhodanese, since the ml. of rhodanate formed divided by the square root of the ml. of rhodanase solution used do not give a constant value. **1968** A. WHITE et al. *Princ. Biochem.* (ed. 4) XXVI. 598 Liver contains rhodanese, a sulfhydryl-containing enzyme which promotes formation of thiocyanate from $CN^-$ and $S_2O_3^=$. **1978** *Nature* 11 May 124/1 Rhodanese..is..widely distributed in nature and especially abundant in mammalian liver and kidney. **1987** *Oxf. Textbk. Med.* (ed. 2) I. vi. 56/2 The principal route of detoxification of cyanide in the body is by conversion to thiocyanate by rhodanase, an enzyme present in liver and muscle.

**rhodo-** *comb. form.* Add: ˈrhodolite *Min.* [see -LITE], a pale rose or purple-coloured garnet intermediate in composition between pyrope and almandite.
    **1898** HIDDEN & PRATT in *Amer. Jrnl. Sci.* V. 296 The analysis proves that this garnet is not almandine nor wholly pyrope and is distinctive enough in color alone to merit a varietal name. We, therefore, propose the name of *Rhodolite*, from the two Greek words ῥόδον, *a rose*, λίθος, *a stone*. **1931** *Amer. Mineralogist* XVI. 563 Excellent samples of rock which contain much gedrite are still to be found on the dump which, however, has been so carefully picked over for rhodolite that good samples are rare. **1977** V. GISSING tr. *Kouřimský's Illustr. Encycl. Minerals & Rocks* 237 The light rose-red to faintly violet mixtures of pyrope and almandine are called rhodolites and they occur in California.

**rhotic** (ˈrəʊtɪk), *a. Phonetics.* [f. *rhot-*, as in RHOTACISM *n.*, + -IC.] Of or pertaining to a variety or dialect of English in which *r* is pronounced not only in pre-vocalic position but also before a consonant or word-finally; characterized by r-pronouncing.
    **1968** J. C. WELLS in *Progress Rep. Phonetics Lab. Univ. Coll. London* (unpublished) June 56 It was possible to divide respondents into three categories: A. (*non-rhotic*) Those who had nonprevocalic r-colouring neither for *-er* nor for *-a*; B. (*rhotic*) Those who had nonprevocalic r-colouring for *-er* but not for *-a*; C. (*hyperrhotic*). **1970** —— in *Jrnl. Linguistics* VI. 240 The local accents of the West of England, though..are rhotic. **1982** TRUDGILL & HANNAH *Internat. Eng.* ii. 13 Rhotic accents are those which actually pronounce /r/, corresponding to orthographic *r*, in words like *far* and *farm*. **1983** *Trans. Yorks. Dial. Soc.* LXXXIII. 28 Benjamin Disraeli..who from his social background could be expected to have been a 'non-rhotic' speaker was in fact 'rhotic'. **1988** *English World-Wide* IX. 57 Bansal ..recommends a rhotic accent for Indian speakers for better international intelligibility.
    Hence **rhoˈticity** *n.*, the quality or character of being rhotic; **ˈrhoticizing** *ppl. a.* [see -IZE], that renders or tends to make rhotic.
    **1973** J. C. WELLS *Jamaican Pronunc. in London* i. 29 The other two characteristics [of an American accent] have been mentioned already. One is the full rhoticity of most kinds of American English. *Ibid.* v. 99 Adolescents have not been subject to so much rhoticizing pressure. **1983** *Trans. Yorks. Dial. Soc.* LXXXIII. 28 An r would normally be sounded before a consonant or at the end of a word as well as..before a vowel. This area of 'rhoticity' is greater than the comparable one for the non-dialect forms of speech.

**rhythmic**, *a. and n.* Add: [A.] **4.** Special collocation: **rhythmic gymnastics** *n. pl.* (usu. const. as *sing.*), gymnastics performed in a rhythmical manner, esp. incorporating dance-like routines and performed with ribbons, hoops, or other accessories (often as a competitive sport); cf. EURHYTHMIC *n.*
    **1912** *Standard* 27 Nov. 9/5 Eurythmics [*sic*] is a word which Professor Jacques-Dalcroze has invented to describe his 'rhythmic gymnastics'. *a* **1975** in K. Kjeldsen *Women's Gymnastics* (ed. 2) 92 (*record title*) Music for teaching rhythmic gymnastics. **1989** *Daily Tel.* 4 Nov. 36/4 (*caption*) Bianca Panova.., the Bulgarian champion, practising..for the Rhythmic Gymnastics International at Wembley Conference Centre tomorrow.

**rib**, *n.*[1] Add: [I.] [2.] **b.** *Pottery.* An implement (made orig. of bone) for shaping or smoothing the surface of the piece being made.
    **1825, 1832** [see PROFILE *n.* 6]. **1880** C. A. JANVIER *Pract. Keramics* v. 55 He presses the bottom of the plate with an instrument called a profile, or rib, which..gives the exact profile of the outside of the

plate. **1940** B. LEACH *Potter's Bk.* iv. 72 The fingers of the left hand press outwards and upwards on the inside of the . . pot and are supported on the outside . . by a wooden rib if a smooth surface is required. **1964** H. HODGES *Artifacts* i. 27 This may be done by hand, but more commonly a curved piece of wood or bone, called a rib, is used. **1977** R. FOURNIER *Illustr. Dict. Pract. Pottery* (rev. ed.) 192/1 Ribs often have one flat and one curved edge and are made of a flat sheet of a rigid material.

**'ribber**, *n.*³ *Knitting.* [f. RIB *n.*¹ or *v.*¹ + -ER¹; cf. RIBBED *ppl. a.* 2 b and RIBBING *vbl. n.* 2.] (An attachment to) a knitting-machine for producing rib stitch.
**1891** *Textile World* May 8/1 (Advt.), Brinton, Denney & Co... Manufacturers of plain or automatic ribbers. **1934** TAYLOR & DASH *Knitting Equipment of Seamless Hosiery Industry* vii. 74 The Hosiery Code limited the use of knitting equipment, including ribbers, to two shifts totaling 80 hours per week. **1955** *Mod. Textiles* June 69/2 Fidelity Machine Co. showed their latest automatic ribber for half hose. **1976** *Evening Post* (Nottingham) 13 Dec. 14/8 (Advt.), All models, ribbers and accessories available. **1986** *Knit & Stitch* June 21/1 Garment may be knitted on any double bed machine with ribber.

**ribbit** ('rɪbɪt), *n.* (and *int.*) Also ribit. orig. and chiefly *N. Amer.* [Echoic.] The characteristic sound made by a frog. Also as *int.*
David Carroll, the Smothers Brothers programme manager, notes: 'I do not believe that the use of the word was a 'first', as I am some seventy-two years old, and I recollect hearing the expression as a child when imitating a frog sound' (*private let. to Ed.*, 8 Mar. 1986).
*c*1968 in *Smothers Brothers Comedy Hour* (annotated T.V. script for rebroadcast programme) No. 8. 62 That's right. Ribit! I am. I am a frog. **1978** M. THALER *Yellow Brick Toad* 25 If an ordinary frog says 'Ribbit' . . what does a steelworker frog say? Rivet. **1981** D. CLEVELAND *Frog on Robert's Head* 26 He never walked anywhere. Instead, he hopped. He never spoke, except to say 'Rrrrrrrribet'! He wore swim fins to school. **1985** *Washington Post* 5 July A17/1 The frog in the pond croaks 'ribbit'. **1989** *Sunday Sun* (Brisbane) 1 Oct. 75 (*in comic strip*) [Frogs] Ribit . . worp . . needeep . . ribit.

**ribophorin** (raɪbəʊ'fɔərɪn), *n. Biochem.* [f. RIBO(SOME *n.* + -PHOR(E + -IN¹.] Any of a number of membrane proteins involved in binding ribosomes to the rough endoplasmic reticulum during protein synthesis.
**1978** G. KREIBICH in *Jrnl. Cell Biol.* LXXVII. 465/2 These proteins, which were designated *ribophorins*, were isolated together with the bound polysomes. **1980** *Nature* 31 Jan. 436/1 Two additional membrane proteins have been observed in the ribosome-bearing fraction of the endoplasmic reticulum in animal cells and have been termed 'ribophorins'. **1984** HOLTZMAN & NOVIKOFF *Cells & Organelles* (ed. 3) ii. iv. 146 According to one hypothesis, two of the proteins ('ribophorins') serve as receptor sites that help to bind the ribosomes.

**ribozyme** ('raɪbəʊzaɪm), *n. Biochem.* [f. RIBO(NUCLEIC *a.* + EN)ZYME *n.*] Any RNA molecule capable of acting as an enzyme.
**1982** K. KRUGER et al. in *Cell* XXXI. 154/2 Because the IVS [*sc.* intervening sequence] RNA is not an enzyme but has some enzyme-like characteristics, we call it a ribozyme. **1983** *Jrnl. Molecular Biol.* CLXVII. 602 The secondary structure model developed for fungal mitochondrial introns . . provides a clear rationalization for the structures that make up the active site of the 'ribozyme'. **1987** *Nature* 19 Feb. 677/2 First, snRNPs [*sc.* small nuclear ribonucleoprotein particles] may be 'ribozymes', by analogy with RNase P where the RNA component of a ribonucleoprotein

complex is able to cleave transfer RNA precursors at a specific site. **1988** *Daily Tel.* 20 Aug. 4/1 Ribozymes enable scientists to chop up RNA in a predictable way, a trick which could be used to destroy viruses such as polio or Aids.

**Ricardian** (rɪ'kɑːdɪən), *a.*² and *n.*² [f. med.L. *Ricard-us* Richard + -IAN.] **A.** *adj.* **a.** Of or pertaining to the time of Richard I, II, or III of England; belonging to or characteristic of this period; supporting King Richard or his policies.
**1941** A. STEEL *Richard II* iv. 116 The mildly Ricardian Monk of Westminster and the extremely hostile Walsingham. **1977** *Times Lit. Suppl.* 25 Feb. 224/4 English writings after the Black Death, especially the great Ricardian poets. **1984** C. HAMMOND (*title*) Ricardian Britain: A guide to places connected with Richard III.
**b.** *spec.* Of, pertaining to, or advocating the view that Richard III was a just king misrepresented historically on the basis of antagonistic Tudor propaganda.
**1963** *Ricardian* May 1 May we take this opportunity of asking all members to send their Ricardian theories, entries, articles . . donations and malmsey butts to Miss C. M. Cook. **1977** G. AWDRY *Richard III Society* f. 14ᵛ, Academics' wary or hostile attitude to the Ricardian propositions. **1978** *Sunday Times* (Colour Suppl.) 15 Jan. 20/3 On behalf of the Richard III Society, Potter has conducted a correspondence in *The Times* with anti-Ricardian historian, A. L. Rowse. **1983** J. POTTER *Good King Richard?* xxvi. 263 The correspondence columns of *The Times* provide a regular battleground for Ricardian skirmishing.
**B.** *n.* One who adheres to the view that Richard III was a just king (see sense b above); a historian sympathetic to Richard III; also, a member of the Richard III Society.
*The Ricardian: the Journal of the Richard III Society* was first published in 1961.
**1977** G. AWDRY *Richard III Society* f. 24, The Hon. Donald F. Lybarger . . had evidently been an unattached, unfound individual Ricardian for some time. **1983** *Financial Times* 10 Sept. 1. 12/3 Ricardians do not accept that their king was responsible for the death of the princes held in the Tower of London. **1983** J. POTTER *Good King Richard?* xxvi. 255 In 1956 this . . body was re-constituted . . under the title of the Richard III Society, and revisionists began to call themselves Ricardians. **1985** *Smithsonian* Mar. 84/2 Ricardians have made considerable strides in recent years, and the patron of the Richard III Society in London is now a member of . . [the] Royal Family.

**Riccadonna** (rɪkə'dɒnə, ‖rikka'donna), *n.* [a. It., lit. 'rich lady'.] A proprietary name for a type of Italian vermouth.
**1906** *Trade Marks Jrnl.* 10 Oct. 1443 Riccadonna . . Fermented liquors and spirits. **1968** 'E. PETERS' *Grass Widow's Tale* xiv. 186 He says no Cognac, but there's a bottle of Riccadonna Bianca. **1973** P. EVANS *Bodyguard Man* v. 41, I ordered a Riccadonna at the bar. **1978** *Times* 8 July 8/6 Anyone travelling . . in Italy, [can] compare the styles of Cora, Riccadonna and many others including the new rosé.

**richie** ('rɪtʃɪ), *n. slang* (orig. and chiefly *U.S.*). Also richy. [f. RICH *a.* + -IE.] A wealthy person, esp. one who is young. (Usu. *contemptuous.*)
**1966** W. HAGGARD *Power House* ii. 14 So this was the modern richie, the left-leaning millionaire. **1978** *Detroit Free Press* 2 Apr. (Detroit Suppl.) 9/2 'I don't disguise myself,' Smith says, 'but I never show the same face twice, I play any role from bum to richy-type.' **1979** *Globe & Mail* (Toronto) 29 Sept. 11/6 The thrust for the bylaw came from 'summer people, richies and university profs'. **1986** *Shetland Times* 14 Nov. 19 She and her non-conformist friends despise

the wealthy students, or 'richies', as they call them. **1986** *Cambridge* (Mass.) *Chron.* 6 Mar. 3A/3 Her only chance of going to the prom is her budding relationship with Blaine .. , a 'richie'.

**riddling**, *vbl. n.²* Add: [1.] **b.** *Wine-making.* In *méthode champenoise*, the action or process of turning a wine bottle periodically to move sediment towards the cork; = REMUAGE *n.*
    **1946** *Encycl. Brit.* V. 216/1 The repeated action, called 'riddling', shifts the sediment along the glass until it comes to rest on the cork. **1961** *Times* 23 Dec. 7/6 What is riddling? .. The gentle but regular twisting and turning of bottles of champagne to encourage the unwanted sediment created during fermentation to settle on the cork. **1976** *National Observer* (U.S.) 4 Dec. 8/4 French experts like Maudière and Lucien Dambron .. came out of retirement to teach the American workers the art of riddling, or turning bottles to maneuver sediment onto the corks. **1987** N. RANKIN *Dead Man's Chest* 175 Their Schramsberg Winery .. revolutionized California sparkling wines, using .. *méthode champenoise* with all its arts of terrage, riddling and disgorging.

‖**rien ne va plus** (rjɛ̃ nə va ply), *int. phr.* Also rien n'va plus. [Fr.] No more bets: in roulette, the call made by the croupier while the wheel is spinning. Also *fig.* Cf. *les jeux sont faits* (the stakes are set) s.v. JEU *n.* 2
    **1871** *Catal. Exhib. R. Acad. Arts* CIII. 12 The Salon d'Or, Homburg .. W. P. Frith, R.A. 'Le jeu est fait—rien ne va plus.' **1904** A. BENNETT *Great Man* xxv. 278 The croupier was saying sternly, 'Rien ne va plus'. **1922** JOYCE *Ulysses* 496 Sieurs et dames, faites vos jeux! ( .. Tiny roulette planets fly from his hands.) Les jeux sont faits! (The planets rush together, uttering crepitant cracks.) Rien n'va plus. **1932** *New Yorker* 5 Mar. 36/2 There was that breathless spinning moment, then the fateful 'Rien ne va plus.' .. Then the decision. 'Noir.' **1964** J. A. WYKES *Gambling* ix. 217 Players continue to place their bets while the ball is in motion until the croupier calls *rien ne va plus* (no more bets). **1972** *Times* 10 Feb. 15 (*heading*) Rien ne va plus pour Mintoff. **1982** *Economist* 25 Dec. 82/3 Successive French governments have made it plain that Japan can always have 3% of the domestic market. After that, rien ne va plus—and to hell with Gatt and all that nonsense about free trade.

**rifle**, *n.³* Add: [2.] **c.** A marksman (*esp.* a hunter) armed with a rifle. Cf. GUN *n.* 5 a.
    **1933** 'H. WADE' *Policeman's Lot* 266 At last there were the two figures—stalker and 'rifle'—making their way slowly towards the glen where the stag still waited. **1977** D. SEAMAN *Committee* 9 He was aware that some famous rifles had missed completely at half that distance. **1988** *Shooting Life* June 63/1 Early season may find the rifle stalking his stag under a hot July sun, or on a still August day when he is eaten alive by midges.

**rigger**, *n.¹* Add: [1.] **c.** A person who erects and maintains scaffolding, lifting tackle, or similar equipment.
    **1915** *Census Eng. & Wales 1911* (Cd. 7660) X. 309/2 Rigger (Copper Rolling Mills) .. Rigger (Iron Blast Furnaces) .. Rigger (Engineering), [etc.]. **1942** R. L. HAIG-BROWN *Timber* X. 130 A hooker or a rigger getting his seven or eight bucks won't get very het up because a section man only gets forty cents an hour. **1962** *Testing & Licensing Construction Equipment Operators* (U.S. Dept. Navy) p. A-1a, Under what conditions is it permissible for a rigger or signalman to ride on the hook or load? **1977** *Sci. Amer.* Feb. 128/1 A lone rigger coolly turns a crank, while a few others shoulder heavy rollers into place. **1981** R. AIRTH *Once a Spy* ix. 91 He'd started life in a circus, but not as a performer ... Angelo had worked as a rigger and handyman. **1986** *Sunday*

*Express Mag.* 7 Dec. 34/2 Hogan was working as a rigger on Sydney Harbour bridge, earning $120 a week.

**right**, *a.* Add: [III.] [17.] [c.] (*b*) Of a work of art, esp. a painting: having a correct attribution. Opp. WRONG *a.* 5 d.
    **1969** C. IRVING *Fake!* (1970) xiv. 173 The thing I dislike most is being called in to tell if a painting is right or wrong. **1986** *Sunday Times* 7 Sept. 1/4 If a painting is not great, but 'right', it could cost £700,000 to £1m. If it is 'wrong', it could be just £70,000 to £100,000. **1987** *Observer* 26 Apr. 40/2 Many are obviously 'not right' so far as serious collectors or dealers are concerned.

**rigid**, *a.* and *n.* Add: [B.] [2.] **b.** A lorry or truck which is not articulated. Cf. ARTICULATED *ppl. a.* 2 b.
    **1970** *Commercial Motor* 25 Sept. 114 The future of the tipper .. lies with maximum-load four-, six-, and eight-wheeled rigids rather than articulated vehicles. **1981** *Times* 18 June 20/3 This would enable Cummins to lift its own share of the diesel market for rigids from 7 per cent to 18 per cent in four years. **1985** *Sunday Times* 24 Feb. 7/3 (Advt.), A new area of business led Harry Rawlings to look beyond his fleet of 140 heavy rigids. **1988** *Truck & Driver* Oct. 7/1, I always check to see which way the drag is going before I alter the direction of the rigid.

**Rigmel** ('rɪgmɛl), *n. Textiles.* [f. RIG(ID *a.* + -MEL (of unknown origin).] A proprietary name for a process for preshrinking cotton or cotton-based fabrics. Freq. used *attrib.*, esp. in *Rigmel process*, or to designate fabrics made by this process. Cf. SANFORIZED *a.*
    **1931** *Trade Marks Jrnl.* 17 June 844 Rigmel. **1952** *Official Gaz.* (U.S. Patent Office) 17 June 652/1 Rigmel. **1957** *Times* 14 Jan. 11/3 Rigmel, shrink-resist finish for cottons only. **1969** A. J. HALL *Stand. Handbk. Textiles* (ed. 7) v. 316 In the 'Rigmel' process the fabric is drawn around a roller or similar curved surface whilst pressed against the upper surface of a thick blanket covering the roller. Just as it commences to travel on a straight path it is flattened by downward pressure of a kind of hot ironing plate or shoe.

**Rilkean** ('rɪlkɪən), *a.* [f. the name of Rainer Maria *Rilke* (1875-1926), German poet and writer + -AN.] Of, pertaining to, or characteristic of Rilke or his work.
    **1948** K. VAUGHAN in *Penguin New Writing* XXXIV. 120 The penetrating, Rilkean sense of delight that transfixes the smallest objects in his pictures, extends to the actual materials with which he worked. **1953** S. SPENDER *Creative Element* iii. 58 The actual is inaccessible to him unless it flows into his own Rilkean thought-stream. **1964** *Mod. Lang. Rev.* LIX. 240 All the other motifs are very much in the Rilkean manner. **1970** E. LUCIE-SMITH *Brit. Poetry since 1945* 240 Hill seems to be a kind of Rilkean symbolist. **1984** P. DE MAN *Rhetoric of Romanticism* 287 A very Rilkean synthesis of rising and falling.

**rimu**, *n.* Add: **2.** The straight-grained wood of the rimu tree, which is reddish-brown when first cut but subsequently fades to a light brown figured with light and dark streaks, and which is used for furniture and interior fittings. Also *attrib.*, made of this wood. Chiefly *N.Z.*
    **1851** *Illustr. Catal. Gt. Exhib.* IV. 1001/2 Specimens of New Zealand furniture woods: .. Rimu (*Dacrydium cupressinum*). **1875** T. LASLETT *Timber & Timber Trees* xxxviii. 308 The specific gravity of the Rimu, when seasoned, is about 678. **1934** *Archit. Rev.* LXXVI. 70/2 Birch and hard maple from North America, rimu and matai from New Zealand .. are all good flooring timbers and offer a very wide choice of

colour and texture. **1970** B. J. RENDLE *World Timbers*
III. 166 Being generally available in New Zealand in
a wide range of sizes and usually free of defects, rimu
is the most popular timber for building construction.
**1977** *N.Z. Herald* 8 Jan. 4 6/3 (Advt.), Licensed
restaurant with attractive rimu panelling. **1984** *Metro*
(Auckland) Mar. 39/3 We walk . . into the main
chapel where 120 can be comfortably seated on rimu
chairs.

**ringette** (rɪ'ŋɛt), *n. Canad.* [f. RING *n.*[1] +
-ETTE.] A form of ice hockey played (usu. by
women or girls) with a straight stick and a
rubber ring, and in which no intentional body
contact is allowed.
    **1974** *Citizen* (Ottawa) 11 Dec. 26/3 Following are
the results of games played in the Gloucester
Ringette Association. **1975** R. WILSON *For Love of
Sport* 188 Ringette, unlike hockey, was uniquely
designed for girls, is being developed for girls and is
played mainly by girls. **1979** *Globe & Mail* (Toronto)
12 Feb. S16/2 Mrs. Keast knows of one woman who,
at 55, is an avid ringette player. **1986** *Waterloo*
(Ontario) *Chron.* 12 Mar. 27/2 Waterloo ringette
teams are preparing for the provincials. **1989**
*Waterloo* (Ontario) *Rec.* 7 Dec. E11/1 The deb
qualifying tournament may be the best ringette
played this season.

‖ **Rinzai** (rɪn'zaɪ), *n.* [Jap., ad. Chinese *Lin-chi*,
the name of the place (now in Hebei province)
at which the Zen master Yi-xuan (d. 867) lived.
His teachings reached Japan in the 12th cent.]
One of the three principal branches of Zen
Buddhism. Cf. SOTO *n.*, *OBAKU *n.*
    **1833** *Chinese Repository* Nov. (1834) II. 323 There
are now in Japan the following sects . . 1. Zen; of
which there are three subdivisions, viz. Rinzai,
Syootoo, and Oobate, named after Chinese monks.
**1894** *Trans. Asiatic Soc. Japan* XXII. 430 The Zen
sects . . are divided . . into three divisions. The *Rinzai*
. . from 1168 A.D., the *Sōtō* from 1223 A.D. and the
*Obaku* from 1650 A.D. **1917** A. K. REISCHAUER *Stud.
Japanese Buddhism* iii. 117 The chief difference
between the Soto and the Rinzai branches of the Zen
sect is that the former puts more weight upon book
learning as a subsidiary aid to silent meditation. **1949**
[see SOTO *n.*]. **1978** C. HUMPHREYS *Both Sides of
Circle* v. 57 From 1900 until his death in 1966 he
worked unceasingly . . to teach as much as can be
taught in words of the purpose and remarkable
technique of Rinzai Zen Buddhism.

**rip**, *v.*[2] Add: [I.] [1.] **e.** To attack verbally; to
criticize severely. *N. Amer. colloq.*
    **1984** *Miami Herald* 6 Apr. 7F/3 He's the guy who
ripped ABC for its big-name, bad-fight
extravaganzas. **1985** *Globe & Mail* (Toronto) 10 Oct.
c2/6 Quisenberry might have been inclined to
complain about his teammates' goofs, but he said: 'I
won't rip my teammates.' **1986** *Daily News* (N.Y.) 23
May 7/2 Tenants rip sentences in 'reign of terror' . .
as a Manhattan judge imposed light jail terms on two
landlords.
    [II.] [9.] **d.** *intr.* With *into*: to unleash a verbal
attack at; to criticize sharply, castigate. *colloq.*
    **1940** *Cobbers* (Brisbane) 20 Dec. 1 Many . . watched
Sgt. Gordon Owens . . drilling the two culprits and
ripping into them. **1958** *N.Z. Listener* 16 May 21/3
He came down and ripped into them: 'Who do you
think you're going to play—a kindergarten?' **1970** D.
WILLIAMSON *Coming of Stork* (1974) 5 They've been
ripping into me about punctuality. **1989** G. DALY
*Pre-Raphaelites in Love* vi. 279 At his first exhibition
the press ripped into him.

**Risc** (rɪsk), *n. Computing.* Also RISC, risc.
[Acronym f. the initial letters of *r*educed
*i*nstruction *s*et *c*omputer (or, in later use,
*c*omputing).] A type of microprocessor
designed to be capable of a limited set of

operations, which consequently has relatively
simple circuitry and performs basic computing
tasks quickly; microprocessing in such an
environment. Chiefly *attrib.*
    **1980** PATTERSON & DITZEL in *Computer Archit.
News* 15 Oct. 25 We shall examine the case for a
Reduced Instruction Set Computer (RISC) being as
cost-effective as a Complex Instruction Set Computer
(CISC). **1983** *Electronics* 11 Aug. 149/1 The first
commercial computer designed with the high-
performance reduced-instruction-set-computer RISC
architecture that can outspeed conventional
computers by as much as 2:1 has been introduced by
Pyramid Technology Corp. **1986** *Fortune* 17 Mar.
8/4 Spectrum is Hewlett-Packard's plunge into
reduced instruction set computing, or risc. **1986**
*Practical Computing* Oct. 92/1 The Risc chip has
32-bit architecture with a 32-bit external data bus
and a 26-bit address bus which gives a 64 Mbyte
uniform address space. **1988** *Computer Weekly* 19
May 13/1 The revolt . . comes in direct response to
AT&T's own efforts to unify Unix around Sun's new
Sparc Risc (reduced instruction set) chip design.

**riser**, *n.* Add: [II.] [7.] **c.** *Theatr., Cinematogr.*,
etc. A low platform on a stage or in an
auditorium or studio, used to give greater
prominence to a speaker, performer, etc.; any
of a group of similar platforms arranged in
steplike fashion.
    **1959** W. S. SHARPS *Dict. Cinematogr.* 126/1 Riser,
a small platform or block used to raise a prop or
performer above ground or floor level. **1961** A.
BERKMAN *Singers' Gloss. Show Business Jargon* 75
Risers, platforms made of wood or metal, used on
stages or in recording studios for the purpose of
raising certain sections of the orchestra. **1977** *Chicago
Tribune* 2 Oct. VI. 8/2 Many older halls . . have
seating behind the orchestra. Mainly, they are
intended, like the risers in Chicago's Orchestra Hall,
to hold a chorus. **1984** *Guardian* 29 Oct. 28/7 The
positioning of the riser is a work of art. It is normally
arranged to show the President at the best angles and
in the most flattering light. **1987** *New Yorker* Dec.
35/3 The audience assembled at the theatre . . and
carefully climbed the risers and took their seats.

**rishitin** (rɪ'ʃiːtɪn), *n. Biochem.* [f. Jap. *Rishi-ri*
the name of a variety of potato + *-t-* + *-IN*[1].] A
terpenoid phytoalexin and anti-fungal
compound found in the tubers of some varieties
of white potato.
    **1968** K. TOMIYAMA et al. in *Phytopathology* LVIII.
115/2 The yield was 30-40mg/kg of tuber tissue. We
propose to designate this compound as *rishitin*,
because it was originally isolated from the potato
variety Rishiri. **1976** *Nature* 1 Jan. 64/1 A large
quantity of rishitin has been reported on the tubers
of susceptible cultivars treated with the DNA
fraction from the resistant hybrid. **1982** J. B.
HARBORNE *Introd. Ecol. Biochem.* (ed. 2) ix. 240
Several substances, among them the sesquiterpenoid
rishitin, were characterized in the potato-blight
interaction originally investigated by Müller and
Börger.

**rising**, *pr. pple.* Add: [2.] **c.** *rising fives n. pl.*,
children approaching the age of five, *esp.* those
thus qualified to start school; occas. in *sing.*
    **1975** *Language for Life* (Dept. Educ. & Sci.) xx.
293 One of the most profitable achievements was to
build up a pre-reception class for rising-5s. **1976**
*Milton Keynes Express* 18 June 4/4, I would like this
opportunity to . . make absolutely clear the teachers'
position concerning the 'rising fives'. **1986** *Ideal
Home* Sept. 103/4 In many areas, rising-fives are
freely admitted to the local infant school. **1987** *News
Let. Friends of Girls' Public Day School Trust* 19 The
Junior Department thrives. There is a waiting list for
our new rising five class. **1989** *Church Times* 27 Jan.

12/4 Has he been 'into' plainsong since he was a 'rising five'?

‖**risposta** (ris'posta), *n. Mus.* [It. = reply.] In a fugue: = RESPONSE *n.* 4. Cf. ANSWER *n.* 8.

**1876** STAINER & BARRETT *Dict. Mus. Terms* 379/2 *Risposta*, . . a reply or answer to a fugue-subject. **1946** E. BLOM *Everyman's Dict. Mus.* s.v., *Risposta*, another term for the 2nd statement of a fugue subject, which is rather like an answer to a question and is, in fact, technically called the Answer. **1986** *Early Music* Aug. 361/1 The three-part *risposta* sung by virtuoso soloists.

**ritard** (rɪ'tɑːd, 'riː-), *a.* (or *adv.*) and *n. Mus.* [Abbrev.] **A.** *adj.* (or *adv.*) With point : = RITARDANDO *a.* (or *adv.*). Cf. RIT *n.*[4]

**1890** *Cent. Dict.* s.v. *Ritardando*, a.
**B.** *n.* = RITARDANDO *n.* Also *transf.*
**1976** *Washington Post* 19 Apr. c5/4 Hill uses a placid tempo and styles too much of the time, and the questionable ritards became sadly predictable. **1983** T. J. O'GRADY *Beatles* iii. 29 The result . . is a psychological ritard and a clear signal to the listener that something exceptional is about to happen. **1985** *New Yorker* 3 June 34/1 There are some tricky ritards and repeats in this music.

‖**Ritterkreuz** ('ritər,krɔits), *n.* [Ger., f. *Ritter* knight + *Kreuz* cross; cf. RITTER *n.*] The Knight's Cross of the Iron Cross, a German decoration instituted by Hitler and awarded for distinguished service in war. Cf. *iron cross* s.v. IRON *a.* 4 c.

**1941** *Newsweek* 6 Oct. 6/2 As for the Knight's Cross of the Iron Cross, the term Ritterkreuz (Knight's Cross) is used to designate generically a certain grade of any order given in several grades. **1978** 'D. KYLE' *Black Camelot* i. 7 [The] uniform bore the insignia of a captain in the Waffen SS . . . The man . . held Oak Leaves to the Ritterkreuz—the Knight's Cross of the Iron Cross. **1981** S. DUNMORE *Ace* II. ix. 217 They asked his advice on how they too might become Experten wearing the cherished Ritterkreuz, the ultimate badge of heroism. **1986** M. ROSS *Lohengrin* xiii. 127 He . . lifted the ribbon supporting the *Ritterkreuz* over his head and handed it to Kurt.

**roach**, *n.*[4] Add: [2.] b. As a term of contempt: an unpleasant or despicable person, esp. a woman considered unattractive or licentious. *U.S.*

**1930** G. LONDON *Deux Mois avec les Bandits de Chicago* 258/2 *Roach* (diminutif de cockroach): Prostituée de bas étage. **1942** BERREY & VAN DEN BARK *Amer. Thes. Slang* §397 *Contemptible person*, . . roach. **1959** *Amer. Speech* XXXIV. 154 Unpopular girls (and on rare occasion unpopular men), with no reference whatsoever to looks, are *roaches*, *beasts*, and *pigs*. **1974** T. MORRISON *Sula* 113 They watched her far more closely than they watched any other roach or bitch in the town.

**roaster**, *n.* Senses 2 a–c in Dict. become 2 b–d. Add: [1.] b. *spec.* A manufacturer of coffee products; an industrial processor of raw coffee beans. Cf. *coffee-roaster* (a) s.v. COFFEE *n.* 5 b.

**1894** J. M. WALSH *Coffee* vi. 191 An experienced roaster can readily discern when the coffee is properly roasted, by the light bluish vapor. **1910** *Tea & Coffee Trade Jrnl.* Jan. 27/1 The roaster . . who had previously depended upon San Francisco, began purchasing coffee in Eastern cities. **1957** *Encycl. Brit.* V. 946/2 Most roasters operating over larger areas . . pack coffee by the vacuum process either in metal cans or in glass jars. **1973** *Times* 18 Oct. (Brazil Suppl.) p. v/1 For six successive seasons new supplies have been below roasters' requirements. **1986** *Times* 26 Aug. 16/2 Any sign of panic buying by

one roaster could quickly spread through the industry.
[2.] a. A pan or dish in which meat, etc. may be roasted; a roasting-tin. Also *roaster pan.* orig. and chiefly *N. Amer.*

**1658** in *Southold* (N.Y.) *Town Rec.* (1882) I. 449 An Inventorie of the personall estate whereof Elizabeth Payne widdow dyed possest [includes] . . a brush, a roster, [etc.]. **1841** *Southern Lit. Messenger* VII. 662/1 There too lies a mutilated coffee-pot, a crownless hat and a lidless tin-roaster. **1942** A. F. HARLOW *Weep no more, My Lady* xvi. 285, I have a huge covered roaster for these big ones [*sc.* hams]. **1974** *Trafford Catal.* Spring/Summer 795/2 Non-stick roaster with extra deep cover. **1987** *New Yorker* 6 July 48/3 A Cookin' Good chicken baking . . in a roaster pan.

**rob**, *v.* [1.] [a.] For def. read: *trans.* To deprive (a person) of something by unlawful force or the exercise of superior power; to despoil by violence. Also *fig.*, esp. recently in sense 'to overcharge (a customer)', and *refl.* (Further examples.)

**1934** G. B. SHAW *On Rocks* II. 236 Out of those wages the laborer has to pay half or quarter as rent to the landlord. The laborer is ignorant: he thinks he is robbed by the landlord; but the robbed victim is me. **1976** *Church Times* 30 July 7/2 She may have been fleeced in Florence, robbed in Ravenna, grossly overcharged in Ostia . . ; but *Baedeker* at least has not tried to put one over on her. **1987** *Sunday Express Mag.* 1 Feb. 14/3 Bob still thinks my Chanel suit cost 70 quid, and even then he thinks I was robbed.
[3.] [a.] For def. read: To plunder, pillage, rifle (a place, house, etc.). Also *transf.*, esp. in recent use in *Archæol.* (freq. with *out*). (Further *transf.* examples.)

**1977** [implied in *ROBBED ppl. a.* 1 b]. **1982** *Rescue News* No. 26. 4/4 The grave was partially cut into a wall trench which had already been robbed out. **1987** *Bull. Glasgow Archaeol. Soc.* Mar. 18 On top of the mound there were stone buildings, which were continually robbed over the centuries.
[5.] [a.] For def. read: To carry off as plunder; to steal. Also *transf.* in *Archæol.*, to remove (stones, etc.) from a structure for use as building material. (Further example.)

**1981** *Glasgow Archaeol. Jrnl.* VIII. 52/1 Almost everything above the Roman floor levels had been destroyed or robbed away.

**robbed**, *ppl. a.* Add: [1.] b. *Archæol.* Freq. *robbed-out.* From which stones, etc. have been removed for use elsewhere. Cf. *ROB v. 3 a.

**1977** *Rescue News* No. 13. 2/3 This site was chosen because of its proximity to the Roman theatre, the largest yet known in Britain, and, as expected, the robbed out corner was found. **1979** *Country Life* 6 Dec. 2143/2 An outer and inner courtyard which are marked by traces of robbed walls. **1982** *Rescue News* No. 26. 6 (*caption*) In the foreground is the robbed-out apse.

**robust**, *a.* Add: [3.] d. Of wine, food, etc.: full-bodied, rich; strong in taste or smell.

**1961** *Woman's Jrnl.* Sept. 31/2 There are also Spanish and Portuguese wines that go well with strongly flavoured foods. The robust Spanish Chablis, the Rioja Burgundy, and the Portuguese Vila Real are examples. **1975** P. V. PRICE *Taste of Wine* v. 64/2 The steeply-terraced vineyards alongside the swiftly-flowing Rhône could not make wines other than robust and moderately full-bodied in style. **1986** A. TAYLOR *Old School Tie* vi. 59 *Calèche* . . Elizabeth Taylor's favourite perfume . . I prefer it to the more robust *Je Reviens*.

**rock**, *n.*[3] Add: [2.] c. **rockfest** *U.S. colloq.* [FEST *n.*], a festival having performances by rock musicians as a central feature.

**1969** *Milwaukee Jrnl.* 30 Aug. A3/2 Another three day rock fest opened Saturday. **1973** *National Rev.* (U.S.) 31 Aug. 922/3 N.Y. Public Health Department says Watkins Glen rockfest's 600,000 attendance made it '[the] largest public gathering ever recorded in the history of the U.S.' **1989** *Chicago Tribune* 28 May III. 2/3 Saturday's $516,900 Grade II Illinois Derby was an acid rockfest.

**rock**, *v.*[1] Add: [6.] **ġ**. To sway *with* (mirth etc.).
**1921** *Glasgow Herald* 22 Dec. 7 For nearly half an hour he kept the Dail rocking with laughter. **1922** JOYCE *Ulysses* 304 They both laughed heartily, all the spectators, including the venerable pastor, joining in the general merriment. That monster audience simply rocked with delight. **1979** *Washington Post* 1 July D4/1 Tell that story to Peterson .. and he rocks with laughter. **1988** J. HELLER *Picture This* v. 44 Socrates would have rocked with mirth at Aristotle's long face and ludicrous dress.

**'rockish**, *a.*[2] orig. *U.S.* [f. ROCK *n.*[3] + -ISH.] Characteristic or reminiscent of rock music.
**1977** *Detroit Free Press* 11 Dec. C22/4 What he does do, and do well, is put his rockish ballad voice to baby songs such as 'Baby, You're the One'. **1978** *Country Life* 21 Dec. 2136/1 Can a rockish idiom be fitted to a dramatic purpose? **1980** *Washington Post* 11 Nov. B3/2 She frolicked through vaguely rockish numbers, a straight middle-of-the-road ballad or two, a bit of '30s musical nostalgia and a song by Johnny Cash. **1989** *Boston Globe* 21 July 26/4 Frisell showed he hasn't lost any of his subtlety and humour, and he has added a hard, rockish edge.

**rockster** ('rɒkstə(r)), *n.*[2] [f. ROCK *n.*[3] + -STER.] One who performs rock music. Cf. ROCKER *n.*[1] 1 d.
**1960** *Punch* 9 Mar. 345/1 The top teenage rocksters .. play to packed theatres. **1977** *Times Lit. Suppl.* 3 June 682/2 Jerry, ropeful Notting Hill rockster. **1989** *Newsday* 15 June 11. 3/1 Last night, rockster David Bowie was allegedly, apparently, reportedly entertaining a gaggle of pals in the new hip zone.

**rock-stone**, *n.* Add: Now chiefly *W. Indies.* (In quot. 1847, a small stone or pebble.) (Further examples.)
**1847** P. H. GOSSE *Birds of Jamaica* 274 The youth picked up a 'rock-stone', as pebbles are called in Jamaica, and delivered the missile with so skilful an aim, that the bird dropped to the ground. **1863** H. M. WADDELL *29 Yrs. W. Indies & Cent. Afr.* ix. 182 The poor horses were plunging every step among rock stones, tree roots, and mud holes. **1943** in Cassidy & Le Page *Dict. Jamaican Eng.* (1967) 384/1 Racca Tone, Rack tone; .. rokka-tone. **1987** M. COLLINS *Angel* ii. 21 The man .. held a huge rock-stone in each hand.

**rockumentary** (ˌrɒkjʊ'mɛntərɪ), *n.* (and *a.*) *colloq.* (orig. *U.S.*). Also **rock-umentary**. [f. ROCK *n.*[3], after DOCUMENTARY *n.*] A documentary (usu. a film) on the subject of rock music or rock musicians. Also *attrib.* or as *adj.*
**1977** *Boston Globe* May 3 16/3 The four young men in *Beatlemania* .. helped mitigate ennui with the aid of the most engrossing scenics ever to counterpoint a rockumentary. **1985** *TV Guide* 2 Mar. (N.Y. Metro ed.) A107/2, 1984's *This Is Spinal Tap*, Rob Reiner's affectionate, sophisticated and very funny 'rockumentary' about a fictitious British heavy-metal group, is the ultimate sendup movie. **1986** *Flicks* Summer 15/1 Rockumentary concert movie with the charismatic Sting. **1988** *Courier-Mail* (Brisbane) 15 Nov. 28/6 SBS at 7.30 has what it is billing a 'rockumentary'—an account of Australian singer Jeannie Lewis' last trip to Mexico.

**rocky**, *a.*[2] Add: Hence **'rockily** *adv.*[2]
**1977** C. McCULLOUGH *Thorn Birds* vi. 109 Jims

standing obediently but a little rockily waiting for his turn. **1984** *N.Y. Times* 5 Aug. (Connecticut Weekly section) 20/4 While the course of true love runs rockily onstage during August, the people behind the scenes at Connecticut Stage will be actively planning a smooth future.

**rod**, *n.*[1] Add: [III.] [6.] **c.** *Carpentry.* A narrow length of wood on which the dimensions of a joinery assembly are marked, usu. in horizontal and vertical section, as an aid to construction.
**1890** *Cent. Dict.* s.v. *Rod, Setting-out rod*, a rod or gage [*sic*] used in making window frames, doors, etc. **1898** B. & H. P. FLETCHER *Carpentry & Joinery* xxv. 275 Commence by drawing a floor line AB on the rod. **1907** P. N. HASLUCK *Cassell's Carpentry & Joinery* 289/1 A rod stands in the same relation to a craftsman as a scaled drawing does to a designer. **1950** M. T. TELLING *Carpentry & Joinery* I. 38 A joiner's working drawing usually consists of a horizontal and vertical section of the job set out on a board 9 in. or so in width, and from this drawing or rod the timber is marked directly. **1979** A. B. EMARY *Woodworking* viii. 38 Figure 8.2 illustrates how to make a rod for the door and shows that two drawings are required, a full-size vertical section and a full-size horizontal section through the work.

**Rodney** ('rɒdnɪ), *n.*[2] The name of George Brydges, Lord *Rodney* (1718-92), English Admiral, used *attrib.* and *absol.* of a type of decanter designed with a wide base for use on shipboard.
**1943** *Apollo* XXXVIII. 140/1 There was the barrel-shaped 'Rodney' decanter with ringed neck from 1788 to 1795. **1970** G. SAVAGE *Dict. Antiques* 358/2 Rodney decantors are, in general, the more profusely ornamented. **1986** 'J. GASH' *Moonspender* xxii. 175 He served brandy from a Rodney decanter. .. The name is Admiral Rodney's . . . True Rodneys are post 1782, the year of his great victory. **1988** R. FEILD *Which? Guide to Buying Antiques* (rev. ed.) 60/1 Ships' decanters ('Rodneys' for example) from 1780 with wide flattened bases and bodies.

‖**rogan josh** ('rəugən dʒɒʃ), *n.* Also **roghan josh**, (*erron.*) **rog(h)an gosht**, etc. [Urdu *rogan josh, raugan-josh* (preparation of mutton) stewed in ghee, f. Urdu *rogan*, Urdu, Pers. *raugan* oil, ghee + Urdu, Pers. *-josh* stew. The element *josh* is obsolete as an independent word in Urdu, and is sometimes mistakenly replaced by *gosht* (Urdu, meat).] A north Indian dish of curried meat (usu. lamb) cooked in a rich sauce.
**1934** S. N. M. KHAN *Finest Indian Muslim Cooking* 48 (*heading*) Rogan-gosh curry. **1966** S. ABDULLAH *House of India Cookbk.* ix. 89 Roghan-josh curry. 2 lbs. stewing beef. 2 lbs. butter. 2 cups buttermilk. 2 tsp. garlic powder. [Etc.] **1969** M. ATWOOD *Taste of India* 239 Rogan josh—a popular North Indian lamb curry. **1971** R. RUSSELL tr. *Ahmad's Shore & Wave* vii. 78 The night before all of them had gone to a restaurant at Kulhri Bazaar, where you could get the best *roghan josh* in India. **1974** K. AZIZ *Step by Step Guide to Indian Cooking* 8 The prowess of a north Indian cook is often judged by her ability to prepare roghan gosht. **1975** FROUD & LO *Internat. Curry Dishes* 76 Roghan Josh. The spicy, creamy sauce in which the lamb is cooked is characteristic of Kashmiri cooking. **1985** N. SAHGAL *Rich like Us* xxi. 222 The blazing truths she tactlessly tumbled out with, .. [that] had to be swallowed with the *roganjosh* at dinner. **1988** *Prima* Aug. 125/1 Tesco's have introduced .. Lamb Rogan Gosht with Pilau Rice.

**Rogernomics** (ˌrɒdʒə'nɒmɪks), *n. pl.* [f. the name of *Roger* Douglas (see below) + *-nomics*, after *Nixonomics* and *Reaganomics*.] The economic policies of the Hon. Roger Douglas

(b. 1937), N.Z. Minister of Finance from 1984-8.

**1985** *Marketing Mag.* (N.Z.) July 7/1 If present trends continue the government may end the year some $8 million poorer than in 1984. Some people may be confused at this subtlety of Rogernomics. **1987** *Daily Tel.* 8 Apr. 13/1 New Zealanders have coined their own word to describe his policies: 'Rogernomics'. **1989** *Guardian* 16 Aug. 9/1 Mr. Lange, after ousting the architect of Rogernomics, Labour's reforming Finance Minister Mr Roger Douglas, was faced with a caucus vote which put him back in the Cabinet.

**roily**, *a.* For first def. read: Muddy, turbid; turbulent; also *fig.* (Further examples.)

**1928** V. L. PARRINGTON in N. Foerster *Reinterpretation Amer. Lit.* vii. 156 The movement of naturalism .. was cut across .. by a sporadic outburst of romanticism that .. yielded a roily flood of historical fiction. **1976** *Globe & Mail* (Toronto) 21 Apr. s8/4 Normally it is time for heavy, layered clothing when streams are high and roily and bait fishing comes into its own. **1978** *N.Y. Times* 9 Jan. D6/1 The company .. has weathered a procession of roily events—suits, scandals, fires, financial headaches, floods, [etc.]. **1985** R. CARVER *Fires* 86 The Mississippi—High roily under a broiling sun.

**roll**, *v.*[2] Add: [I.] [5.] **j.** *Cinematogr.* and *Television.* To display (opening or closing credits, etc.) moving up the screen on or as on a roller. Also occas. with *up.*

**1967** *Listener* 6 Apr. 471/2 Roll your credits. **1972** A. DRAPER *Death Penalty* i. 5 The television screen was rolling the football results. **1977** K. O'HARA *Ghost of T. Penry* xvi. 165 She stood up, imagining the closing shots ... Joe said 'Roll up credits'. **1989** *Daily Tel.* 8 Nov. 19/8 The videotape flickers to a close. Roll the credits: doctor's name, patient's name and file number, hospital, expected delivery date, and so on.

[II.] [12.] **i.** *Cinematogr.* and *Television.* Of credits: to appear on the screen, moving upwards on or as on a roller.

**1967** *Listener* 29 June 863/1 There's a certain measure of wit in *The Frost Report*, and so there should be, considering the number of writing credits that roll at the end. **1976** *Broadcast* Dec. 20/1 How few viewers can remember his name after the credits have rolled upwards to the greater glory of stars, director and producer? **1988** R. RAYNER *Los Angeles without Map* 47 The last thing the camera shows is fear on her face, and the end credits roll.

**rollable**, *a.* Add: Hence **rolla'bility** *n.*, capacity to roll, ease of rolling.

**1971** W. A. PRYOR in R. E. Carver *Procedures Sedimentary Petrol.* vii. 143 Pivotability or rollability is a measure of the motion response of a grain to a set of standard physical conditions in a gravity-driven system. **1983** *Mod. Railroads* XXXVIII. iii. 95/1 As each car rolls into its proper classification track, its rollability and speed is measured by radar and entered into the computer. **1986** *Bicycle* July 46/1 You should be convinced that the recent advances made in weight, resilience and rollability make these new tyres worth a second look.

**roller**, *n.*[1] Add: [I.] [4.] **e.** The platen of a typewriter (see PLATEN *n.* 3 b); orig., any of the cylinders (including the platen) which served to hold and move the paper.

**1880** *U.S. Pat. 224, 183* 3 Feb. 1/1 The construction of the key-levers of the rollers for holding the paper. **1888** J. HARRISON *Man. Remington Standard Typewriter* 18 On top of the typewriter are two rollers. The larger one is covered with hardened india-rubber, the smaller is of wood. **1920** H. ETHERIDGE *Dict. Typewriting* 181 The platen (or cylinder) of a typewriter is the large roller in the centre of the carriage. **1959** *Sears, Roebuck Catal.*

Spring & Summer 837/2 You can't buy a better portable [typewriter] ... Removable roller for easy, thorough cleaning. **1980** J. THOMSON *Alibi in Time* vi. 72 On the front stood a typewriter, a half-completed page still in the roller.

**'Roller**, *n.*[4] *slang.* [f. ROLL(S-ROYCE *n.* + -ER[6], prob. influenced by ROLLER *n.*[1]] A Rolls-Royce motor car.

**1977** I. DURY *Songbk.* (1979) 62 Lat-er on he drove a Rol-ler chauf-fer-in' for foreign men. **1982** *New Society* 4 Nov. 205/2 Their appetite for double vodkas and fat cigars and gold watches and 'Rollers' (Rolls-Royces). **1985** L. GRIFFITHS *Arthur Daley's Guide to doing it Right* 111 Now I think only good people get Jaguars and Rollers—those who deserve them. **1989** *Observer* 15 Jan. v. 3/1 In the new series .. Jools meets a Martian .. and takes him on a guided tour of Britain in the Roller.

**roll-in roll-out** ('rəʊlɪn 'rəʊlaʊt), *n. Computing.* Also roll out/roll in, etc. [f. *to roll in, to roll out*: see ROLL *v.*[2] 1 f.] The process of switching (usu. large) bodies of data, instructions, etc. between the main and auxiliary memories of a computer system in order to process several tasks simultaneously.

[**1970** O. DOPPING *Computers & Data Processing* ix. 123 Roll-in and roll-out together are often called core swapping.] **1973** H. KATZAN *Operating Syst.* vi. 152 If the ROLL parameter is used and a job step requires more main storage than was requested in the REGION parameter, the roll out/roll in routines attempt to assign additional main storage from the dynamic area. **1974** TSICHRITZIS & BERNSTEIN *Operating Syst.* iv. 79 One solution to the foregoing difficulties is to permit the system to move entire jobs in and out of core after their initial loading. This strategy, called swapping or roll-in-roll-out, can be implemented by using a relocation register. **1976** W. Y. ARMS et al. *Computing* xi. 263 Roll in roll out is simple and effective in many circumstances, but is not suitable for large time sharing systems because the computer can easily find that it spends all its time dumping and retrieving the user area. **1983** PETERSON & SILBERSCHATZ *Operating Syst. Concepts* v. 149 When the higher-priority job finishes, the lower-priority job can be swapped back in and continued. This variant of swapping is sometimes called roll-out/roll-in. **1990** *Dict. Computing* (ed. 3) 397/1 *Roll-in roll-out*, a method of handling memory in a system dealing with a number of simultaneously active processes.

**roll-up**, *n.* and *a.* Add: [B.] **2.** *Comm.* **roll-up fund**, a form of investment fund in world currencies on which no dividend is paid and the income is taxed as a capital gain instead of as income. Also *absol.* and *roll-up share*, etc.

**1983** *Financial Times* 18 Jan. 7/4 A government consultative document on proposals to clamp down on international tax avoidance failed to mention offshore roll-up funds. **1983** *Times* 2 July 14/7 (*heading*) Schroder offers roll-up to smaller investors. *Ibid.*, 'Roll-up' funds .. are based in Bermuda and managed out of Jersey. **1983** *Observer* 3 July 21/4 Offshore currency funds offering 'roll up' shares have recently been attracting tax-conscious savers. **1986** *What Investment* July 14/2 (Advt.), There are monthly feature articles delving deep into relevant topics, such as offshore funds, technology for the unit trust industry, roll ups, .. [etc.]. **1989** *European Investor* Feb. 42/3 SICAVS are barred from offering roll-up funds to investors, because the Government insists that dividends must be paid to investors on the nail, so that they can be taxed.

‖**Romagna** (ro'maɲa), *n. Agric.* [It.: see ROMAGNOL *n.* and *a.*] = *ROMAGNOLA *n.*

**1934** *Animal Breeding Abstr. 1933* I. 241 A pedigree bull was used on Romagna cows ... The crossbred calves at birth weigh less than the

Romagna. **1966** M. H. FRENCH *European Breeds of Cattle* II. ii. 172 The Romagna Improved (*gentile*) breed..is larger and more precocious than the Romagna Mountain (*di montagna*) breed.

**Romagnola** (rəʊməˈnjəʊlə, ‖romaˈɲola), *n. Agric.* [a. It. *Romagnola*: see ROMAGNOL *n.* and *a.*] A large Italian breed of cattle, orig. developed from Podolian cattle as a draught animal but now raised primarily for beef, characterized by a silver-grey hide with a white dorsal stripe; an animal of this breed.
[**1912** R. LYDEKKER *Ox & its Kindred* vi. 124 A very different type is presented by the cattle of the Roman Campagna, which are large, silver-grey animals, with a white dorsal stripe, usually a pale ring round the eye, and a straight profile. **1925** *Nat. Geographic Mag.* XLVIII. 641/2 In Italy, especially in the district about Rome, one will see large, silver-gray cattle, with great horns, muscular and lean of flesh, commonly used for draft purposes. These are known as Roman or Campagna cattle.] **1937** *Animal Breeding Abstr.* V. 391 The Romagnola and Tuscany breeds, originating probably from Lombard and Ostrogoth herds, show Podolian ancestry. **1970** J. E. ROUSE *World Cattle* I. 1. 192 The Romagnola was developed as a draft animal in the lower Po valley.. but..the breed is now raised primarily for beef. **1976** *Burnham-on-Sea Gaz.* 20 Apr. (Advt.), The Quarkhill herds of Charolais, Chianina, Romagnola and Marchegiana cattle. **1980** H. M. & D. M. BRIGGS *Mod. Breeds Livestock* (ed. 4) ix. 190 In contrast to the Chianina..the Romagnola are much shorter in leg.

**romance**, *v.* Add: [**5.**] **b.** To seek to persuade (esp. a rival or client), often by means of attentiveness or flattery; to court the favour of; to pursue. orig. *U.S.*
**1961** in WEBSTER. **1962** *Washington Daily News* 3 July 27/1 It was their seventh success in the last 10 tries and they're playing as if they mean to continue romancing the Yankees who are only a few percentage points in front of them. **1985** *New Yorker* 22 Apr. 94/3 There were oilies who could not be bombed out of the downtown banks, it was said, and Patterson, at Jennings' bidding, was prepared to romance them. **1988** *Daily Tel.* 25 Nov. 11/1 Will putative investors be similarly wary when they are romanced with all the glitz and glamour that attend privatisation campaigns?

**Romanist**, *n.* Add: **5.** *Art.* Any of several 16th-cent. Dutch and Flemish painters influenced by the techniques of Italian Renaissance artists.
**1885** MRS. H. ROSSEL tr. *Wauters's Flemish School of Painting* x. 130 The brotherhood of the Romanists were composed of people who had journeyed to Rome. **1910** M. INNES *Schools of Painting* xvi. 148 After Massys and Mabuse comes a period of rapid deterioration in Flemish art. The sixteenth century painters of Antwerp were in all essentials mere copyists of the Italians; they are known as the 'Romanists'. **1914** M. ROOSES *Art in Flanders* iii. 163 The plagiarists of the Italian style lost more and more the Flemish qualities which were still admired in the first Romanist painters, Gossaert and Van Orley. **1959** P. & L. MURRAY *Dict. Art & Artists* 279 Romanists were the Northern artists who went to Italy and returned filled with the idea of rivalling Raphael and/or Michelangelo. **1984** E. LUCIE-SMITH *Dict. Art Terms* 163/1 *Romanists*, Northern European artists of the 16th c. who were heavily influenced by Italian Renaissance art (in particular, the work of Raphael and Michelangelo). They included Mabuse, Van Orly and Maerten van Heemskerck.

**Romney** (ˈrɒmnɪ, ˈrʌmnɪ), *n.* The name of George *Romney* (1734–1802), English portrait

painter, used *attrib.* to designate fashions resembling those in portraits of women painted by Romney. Also *absol.*, (the subject of) a portrait by Romney.
**1905** in C. W. Cunnington *Eng. Women's Clothing* (1952) ii. 67 The rage for the picture-frock for evening, of the Greuze or Romney style. **1909** MRS. H. WARD *Daphne* i. 16 A white muslin dress, *à la* Romney, with..a black-and-white Romney hat deeply shading the face beneath. *Ibid.* iii. 49 This room..bore witness to Miss Floyd's simplicity—like the Romney dress. **1909** W. J. LOCKE *Septimus* iv. 58 Zora came down coated and veiled, her face radiant as a Romney in its frame of gauze. **1937** M. SHARP *Nutmeg Tree* iv. 50 It makes you look like a Romney.

**romp**, *n.* Add: [**2.**] **c.** Chiefly in *Sport.* A victory by a substantial margin; an easily-won game. *colloq.* (orig. *U.S.*).
**1961** in WEBSTER. **1974** *State* (Columbia, S. Carolina) 3 Mar. 1-D/7 USC scored 104 points enroute to a 104-55 romp over DePauw back in December. **1976** *Ilkeston Advertiser* 10 Dec. 18/2 This match was not the romp for Borough that the score-line suggests. **1985** *Los Angeles Times* 20 Feb. (Home ed.) III. 4/1 Oilers, who trailed, 2-0, early in the second period, scored six consecutive goals to turn the game into a romp. **1988** *Rugby World & Post* Nov. 37/1 Ten tries..were scored against the Royal Navy at Penzance in a 44-3 romp.

**romp**, *v.* Add: [**2.**] **c.** *to romp it*, to win a contest, esp. an election, easily.
**1967** *Economist* 28 Jan. (Survey Suppl.) p. x/1 There are the makings of trouble here for the future of good federal government in Australia. The Liberals, quietly led by Mr Holt, romped it. It was not an election of very positive thinking. **1981** *Guardian Weekly* 12 Apr. 22/3 If a widening grin is the test of a novel's entertainment value in retrospect, A Good Man In Africa romps it. **1984** *Sun* 7 Nov. 1 (*headline*) Reagan romps it.

**roofless**, *a.* Add: Hence ˈrooflessness *n.*
**1850** *Househ. Words* 14 Dec. 267/1 In all conditions, from neat snug finish, to cheerless rooflessness. **1988** *Daily Tel.* 24 Dec. 4/8 A major review of the working of the 1977 Homeless Persons Act is being carried out... One option is to change the present definition of homelessness to rooflessness.

**root**, *n.*[1] [**II.**] [**11.**] [**d.**] Add to def: *spec.* with reference to West Indian culture and society (cf. sense *23 b).
**1978** *Sunday Times* 29 Jan. 43/2 She is, she says, 'roots', and roots is 'just our culture; the social standings that affect us as Jamaicans living in Jamaica'. **1986** *City Limits* 16 Oct. 41 For the DJ, crossing over is more than simply a move from roots to respectability or even from black to white audiences.
[**IV.**] [**23.**] **b.** *pl.* used *attrib.* (quasi-*adj.*). Expressive of a distinctive (sometimes specified) ethnic origin or cultural identity; freq. in *roots music*; so, traditional, authentic; *spec.* of black or W. Indian culture or society; *roots reggae* (formerly at sense 23 a), a style of reggae music considered as an expression of the black Jamaicans' cultural identity.
**1977** MCKNIGHT & TOBLER *Bob Marley* x. 127 What reaches our ears is no longer roots reggae. **1978** *Oxford Times* (City ed.) 24 Feb. 15 This is a good example of roots reggae complete with chunky rhythm and 'dub' echoes. **1979** *Trinidad Guardian* 17 Dec. 7/2 What Ellsworth has described as 'roots music'. **1983** *N.Y. Times* 13 Feb. 11. 28/3 Mr. Davis's romantic sensibility, Mr. Wadud's interest in mysticism and ritual, and Mr. Newton's fondness for black roots music like blues and gospel interact throughout the written and improvised portions of each piece. **1984** *Southern Rag* No. 22. 7/2 Closing

our borders and ears to foreign roots music is the quickest way to guarantee the stagnation of our own traditions. **1986** *City Limits* 29 May 77 The ability to laugh at oppression, to bridge the gap between roots culture and mainstream pop. **1987** *Times* 14 Aug. 16/5 'Roots' music in 1987 can be . . practically anything, in fact, other than the dreaded post-Sixties, Anglo-American trinity of rock, pop and disco. **1988** *Compact Disc & Video Insight* (W. H. Smith) No. 4. 40/3 Skaggs has rekindled his enthusiasm and roots sensibilities.

**root**, *v.*[2] Add: [**2.**] c. To cheer or spur (someone) *on*. Chiefly *N. Amer.* (orig. *U.S.*).
   **1942** BERREY & VAN DEN BARK *Amer. Thes. Slang* §223/9 *Urge*; *incite* . . *root on*. **1961** C. W. NEW *Life H. Brougham to 1830* 202 There were competitions between classes . . . Their respective monitors rooted them on. **1984** J. HELLER *God Knows* IX. 231 You were in command. I know what you were doing. You were probably rooting him on all the time, weren't you? **1988** *Boxing* Nov. 22/3 Sugar Ray's mother, who rooted him on enthusiastically from ringside, had shadow-boxed a better fight than her son's.

**rootsy** ('ruːtsɪ), *a.* [f. *ROOT *n.*[1] (see sense 23 b) + -Y[1].] Of music: of a rudimentary, uncommercialized kind; full-blooded; authentic; so, in generalized use, traditional, ethnic, homespun.
   **1976** *Sounds* 11 Dec., The flip is 'Love Is The Drug' . . Jacob's anti-drug song, a rootsier sound with Horsemouth's militant drumming going snap-crackle-pop-snap. **1977** *Westindian World* 3–9 June 13/3 Although this album is much more rootsy than the last, it is still very much in the ebb and flow of the 'international reggae' stream. **1982** *Face* May 11/2 Alison places an ad in the local paper for a 'rootsy blues band'. **1986** *Los Angeles Times* 21 May VI. 2/5 I'm not here to put any new innovations on you . . . I'm still using things that are already there: the basic American rootsy sound with country and blues and so forth. **1986** *Sunday Express Mag.* 14 Sept. 54/1 Yoakam . . is . . a musician with a mission. His object? To bring the rootsy heartland sounds of Appalachian song back into the mainstream. **1988** *Skateboard!* July 6/2 We want ten o'clock to seven o'clock drops, full tuck eleven o'clock roll-backs, and all that rootsy pipeyness not shown in Wheels of Fire.

**'rope-a-dope**, *n.* *U.S. Boxing slang.* [f. ROPE *n.*[1] (sense 2 c), perh. infl. by ROPE *v.*[1] (sense 4), + A *a.*[2] + DOPE *n.*] A tactic whereby a boxer rests against the ropes and protects himself with his arms and gloves, so goading an opponent to throw tiring, ineffective punches. Freq. *attrib.*
   The strategy is particularly associated with Muhammad Ali (b. 1942), world heavyweight champion three times between 1964 and 1978, who is said to have coined the phrase.
   **1975** *Sports Illustr.* 26 May 74/1 Rope-a-dope had worked against George Foreman in Zaire; it is doubtful that the technique will ever work again against an Ali opponent. **1976** *Newsweek* 4 July 93/1 (*heading*) Rope-a-Dopes . . . Each time Mohammed escaped by scrambling to the ropes. **1979** *Arizona Daily Star* 22 July C4/2 Pedroza worked his version of the Muhammad Ali rope-a-dope early on, laying on the ropes while Olivares flailed away at the champion's body. **1980** *N.Y. Times Mag.* 2 Mar. 42/2 As age caught up with him [sc. Ali], he started counter-punching, and he developed the rope-a-dope style, where he would let the other guy punch himself out and then come back and put him away.

‖**roquette** (rɔkɛt), *n.* [Fr.: see ROCKET *n.*[2]] A herb with bitter-tasting leaves; = ROCKET *n.*[2] 1.
   **1902** M. G. KAINS in L. H. Bailey *Cycl. Amer. Hort.* IV. 1546/2 Roquette or Rocket-Salad (*Erica Sativa* . . ), a low-growing hardy annual from southern Europe . . . In America it is but little grown. **1930** L. H. BAILEY *Hortus* 534/1 Roquette; *Erica sativa*. **1953** D. C. HOGNER *Herbs* vi. 137 Native to Southern Europe, roquette is found wild today in some parts of the United States. **1989** *Encycl. Brit.* X. 177/3 Roquette grows to about 70 centimetres (2½ feet) tall. Four-petalled, white, purple-veined flowers top its flower stalks.

**Rossby** ('rɒsbɪ), *n.* The name of Carl-Gustaf *Rossby* (1898–1957), Swedish meteorologist, used *attrib.* with reference to his work on fluid flow, as **Rossby number** *Meteorol.*, the ratio of the inertial force to the Coriolis force for a particular fluid flow; **Rossby wave** *Physics* and *Meteorol.*, a long wavelength fluctuation of a current in a fluid system having no divergence and subject to Coriolis force; *esp.* a lateral fluctuation of a jet stream, with wavelength comparable with the radius of the earth.
   **1951** D. FULTZ in *Jrnl. Meteorol.* VIII. 262 A number expressing the influence of rotation, which it is proposed to name the '*Rossby number'. **1985** *Deep-Sea Res.* XXXII A. 557 With increasing Rossby number the anticyclonic circulations in the subtropical Atlantic and Indian Ocean parts of the two-ocean domain become more and more isolated from each other. [**1951** *Jrnl. Meteorol.* VIII. 264/2 The velocity . . of Rossby long waves relative to a basic current.] **1963** *Deep-Sea Res.* X. 735 Damped, stationary *Rossby waves can occur in the ocean superimposed on a steady west to east flow. **1974** *Earth-Sci. Rev.* X. 203 Planetary or Rossby waves, though probably unimportant in the fluid interior of the Earth, are of interest to earth scientists in general, because of their pervasive role in the general circulation of oceans and atmospheres. **1974** *Nature* 5 Apr. 539/1 The intense Kuroshio current may generate a series of Rossby waves, which can propagate across the entire Pacific Basin. **1974** *Encycl. Brit. Macropædia* X. 163/1 If floor conditions are neither divergent nor convergent . . , the absolute vorticity should not change with time . . . This explains the reason for the formation of long planetary waves, the so-called Rossby waves, in the upper-tropospheric flow patterns.

**rotation**, *n.* Add: [**2.**] e. *Baseball.* The (usual) order in which pitchers start successive games during a season; also, a team's regular starting pitchers. Freq. in *starting rotation*.
   **1963** E. RICHTER *Making of Big-League Pitcher* x. 107 He is expected to instruct, to advise the manager on rotation plans. **1970** R. HOOPES *What Baseball Manager Does* 45 For a starting rotation, he wants at least three . . solid starters. **1978** *Detroit Free Press* 2 Apr. 6E/3 The Pirates have Bert Blyleven in the same starting rotation with John Candelaria. **1988** *First Base* Autumn 31/3 Mets pitcher David Cone, who replaced injured Rick Aguilera in the starting rotation. **1989** P. DICKSON *Baseball Dict.* 329/2 A modern manager likes to leave spring training with his rotation set for, at least, the early weeks of the season.

‖**rôtisseur** (rotisœr), *n.* [Fr., f. as ROTISSERIE *n.*] One who cooks roast meats for sale or who sells these; *esp.* a chef specializing in roasting.
   **1766** SMOLLETT *Trav.* I. v. 68 Above twenty dishes, extremely well dressed by the *rotisseur*, who is the best cook I ever knew, in France, or elsewhere. **1841** C'TESS BLESSINGTON *Idler in France* II. i. 10 An English *rôtisseur* and an Italian confiseur. **1971** *Guardian* 8 Jan. 9/1 He was chef de cuisine at the Empress Restaurant in Mayfair . . . He started . . as chef rôtisseur, for roasting is a craft which even French cooks are prepared to delegate to an Englishman. **1986** M. BOND *M. Pamplemousse on Spot* ii. 27 Edouard became the *rôtisseur*.

**roto-tom** ('rəʊtəʊtɒm), *n.* Also roto tom, rototom. [f. ROTO- + TOM-)TOM *n.*] A shell-less drum, tuneable (by rotation) within a range of an octave or more; usu. one of a set.
**1968** W. J. SCHINSTINE *Roto-Tom Solos for Melodic Drummer* (TRY Publishing Co.), The Roto-Tom is a unique pitched drum concept... Designed by Mr. Al Payson of the Chicago Symphony Orchestra, the Roto-Tom has been developed by Remo for both professional and school use. **1969** PEINKOFER & TANNIGEL *Handbk. Percussion Instruments* 115 *Roto Toms*... The number of drums in such sets has so far ranged from 6 to 13 small-sized instruments. **1972** E. RICHARDS *World of Percussion* 45 (*caption*) Roto Toms. These plastic-headed drums can be tuned quickly by turning the whole drum while putting tension on the head. **1978** J. HOLLAND *Percussion* iv. 111 Rototoms are now in vogue with percussionists in all spheres—from schools to rock groups, marching bands to symphony orchestras. Their portability, size and relatively low cost make them valuable in many ways. **1986** *Melody Maker* 19 Apr. 49/8 (Advt.), Drum kit,.. cymbals, plus hard cases and roto toms.

**round**, *n.*[1] Add: [III.] [15.] b. *Austral.* The routine covering of news stories in a specific field by a journalist. Usu. in *pl.*
**1934** *Newspaper News* (Sydney) 1 Oct. 11/1 He.. left there to do Trades and Labour rounds, Police rounds and special writing for *The Evening News.* **1946** H. BAXTER *Reporter's Experiences* (ed. 2) 147 A Shire Council meeting, writing paragraphs, following enquiries on rounds, with hospital, morgue, fire brigade, police stations [etc.]. **1961** C. McKAY *This is the Life* 25 At night, about half past seven, I started on police rounds.

**round**, *a.* Add: [II.] [9.] d. Of a wine: having a good balance between taste, smell, and alcoholic strength; full and mellow. Also of spirits.
**1975** P. V. PRICE *Taste of Wine* v. 78/3 Is the wine moderately supple and round or does it seem slightly harsh or thin? **1984** *Sunday Tel.* (Colour Suppl.) 16 Sept. 18/3 It [*sc.* whisky] was smooth, round ('we never say sweet, or people think of sugar') and hit the spot with a slow, warm embrace.

**round**, *v.*[1] Add: [III.] 15. *round out Aeronaut.* = FLARE *v.* 4 d.
**1949** *Jrnl. R. Aeronaut. Soc.* LIII. 957/1 The cabin floor angle in the steeper types, such as Dakotas and Lancastrians, is changed as slowly as possible by slow rounding out and by landing with the tail just off the ground. **1956** W. A. HEFLIN *U.S. Air Force Dict.* 448/1 *To round out*, to flare out.

**round-house**, *n.* Add: [3.] c. *Archæol.* A circular structure believed to have been a house, known esp. in Britain from remains of Bronze or Iron Age date.
**1948** *Proc. Prehistoric Soc.* XIV. 69 This roundhouse is situated on the steep eastern coast of South Uist. **1987** *London Archaeologist* Winter 349/2 Of particular importance for the prehistoric period was the discovery of evidence for numerous round-houses.

**'round-out**, *n. Aeronaut.* [f. vbl. phr. *to round out*: see *ROUND *v.*[1] 15.] The smooth, curving descent of an aircraft levelling out to land; = FLARE-OUT *n.* 2.
**1956** W. A. HEFLIN *U.S. Air Force Dict.* 448/1 *Roundout*, a flareout. **1978** *Aviation Week & Space Technol.* 30 Oct. 57/3 After recovering from the high round-out, the aircraft was so far down the runway that this editor suggested a go-around. **1987** *R.A.F. Yearbk.* 22/1 Touchdown after round-out at about 70 knots.. gives a landing run of under 400 yards.

**roundsman**, *n.* Add: 4. *Austral.* A journalist who specializes in a particular field. Cf. *ROUND *n.*[1] 15 b.
**1938** *Newspaper News* (Sydney) 1 Oct. 1/5 He has been successively a.. casual football reporter, police roundsman, general reporter, departmental roundsman, Parliamentary reporter, [etc.]. **1972** J. BELFRAGE in G. W. Turner *Good Austral. Eng.* vi. 107 It is the style of the political roundsman, and it reflects the tradition of 'boots and. all' in-fighting which grew out of the turbulent nineteenth century politics. **1984** *Inst. Public Affairs Rev.* (Austral.) Autumn 56/1 Mr Hawke.. will tell you how badly the Canberra Press gallery compares with the Melbourne industrial roundsmen of his day. **1988** R. McKIE *We have no Dreaming* 47 A colleague, the regular parliamentary roundsman for the *Telegraph*, one of the most erratic and gifted political journalists I have ever known.

**rubber**, *n.*[1] [III.] [11.] c. For def. read: A rubber tyre for a wheel; *collect.*, the tyres of a vehicle. Also, by extension, a car. Occas. used in colloq. phrases expressing speed or acceleration. Chiefly *U.S.* (Further examples.)
**1945** L. SHELLY *Jive Talk Dict.* 16/2 *Rubber*,.. an automobile. **1965** 'MALCOLM X' *Autobiogr.* iv. 69 At sixteen, I didn't have the money to buy a Cadillac, but she had her own fine 'rubber', as we called a car in those days. **1970** C. MAJOR *Dict. Afro-Amer. Slang* 98 *Rubber*, car. **1989** *Austin Amer.-Statesman* 29 Apr. c22/1 (Advt.), Good shape, great running car, good rubber.

**Rubéniste** (‖rybeniːst, 'ruːbənɪst), *n.* Also Rubeniste, Rubensiste, and anglicized Rubenist. [a. F. *Rubéniste*, f. the name of *Rubens* (see RUBENS *n.*).] An admirer or imitator of Rubens, *esp.* one of a group of late 17th c. French artists who followed Rubens: see *POUSSINISTE *n.*
**1938** *Burlington Mag.* Jan. 4/1 It has been possible to show *Rubénistes* and *Poussinistes* together: to set against the loose exuberance of Rubens the ordered wildness of Poussin's *Triumph of Pan.* **1938** *Times* 1 Jan. 13/6 There was still a survival of classical mannerism, based on Michelangelo and Raphael, which became active in France and gave rise to the battle between the Rubénistes and the Poussinistes. **1970** *Oxf. Compan. Art* 1023/1 The battle of the Poussinistes and the Rubensistes.. in which De Piles played the part of Rubens's advocate, illustrates the breadth of his influence; the work of Watteau, Fragonard, and Delacroix, its depth. **1978** *Jrnl. R. Soc. Arts* CXXVI. 701/1 The unfortunate tendency to denigrate fellow *Rubénistes* in the footnotes. **1986** *Oxf. Art Jrnl.* Jan. 68/1 The success of the *Rubénistes* .. had the effect of permitting .. eclecticism.

**rubeosis** (ruːbɪ'əʊsɪs), *n. Path.* [ad. G. *Rubeose* (C. von Noorden *Die Zuckerkrankheit und ihre Behandlung* (ed. 7, 1917) v. 262), f. L. *rubens* reddish: see -OSIS.]
Originally used to denote a reddening of the facial skin in diabetics: the meaning borrowed into Eng. was suggested by R. Salus 1928, in *Med. Klinik* 17 Feb. 258/1.]
In full, *rubeosis iridis (diabetica).* A serious eye condition in which proliferation of blood-vessels in the iris leads to ischmaemic neovascular glaucoma and blindness.
[**1917** C. VON NOORDEN *Die Zuckerkrankheit und ihre Behandlung* (ed. 7) 633 (Index), Rubeosis.] **1934** *Arch. Ophthalm.* XII. 420 The name 'rubeosis' which Salus bestowed on his cases was first used by von Noorden. *Ibid.*, The eye affected by glaucoma showed a typical rubeosis iridis. **1940** S. DUKE-ELDER *Text-bk. Ophthalm.* III. xxxv. 2385 Rubeosis of the iris.. is a rare condition characterized by a peculiar non-inflammatory vascular proliferation affecting particularly the iris in diabetics, and usually associated with glaucoma. The condition was first described by Salus (1928). **1945** *Amer. Jrnl.*

*Ophthalm.* XXVIII. 125/1 Rubeosis does not depend entirely upon the severity of the diabetes. **1976** *Brit. Jrnl. Ophthalm.* LX. 818/2 There were no cases of rubeosis or neovascular glaucoma in the treated group. **1983** *Byte* Oct. 447/1 Suzanne.. lost her sight from a combination of neurovascular rubeosis and retinopathy.

**rub-off**, *n.* Restrict *slang* to sense 1 in Dict. and add: **2.** Whatever 'rubs off' or has influence on a person or thing through close contact, association, or familiarity; influence (usu. beneficial); (as a count noun) an influence; a side-effect, a secondary consequence. orig. *U.S.*

**1974** S. MARCUS *Minding Store* x. 222 All of our stores get a ruboff value from the Fortnights, though our downtown Dallas store reaps the major benefits. **1979** M. MCCARTHY *Cannibals & Missionaries* 362 'Rub-off' from constant exposure to beauty can develop taste. **1983** *Truck & Bus Transportation* Aug. 17/2 Income [from storage] would more than cover the cost of setting up and maintaining proper warehouse facilities and, of course, the rub-off is that storage generates local moves in and out of the warehouse. **1985** *National Educ.* (N.Z.) Nov. 199/1 But already, the sole charge principal, Mrs. Rae Hooper, can see a beneficial rub-off. **1987** *Motor Sport* June 563/2 There must be some rub-off on the fellow or girl who has, say, a Renault 5 in the car park, and sees a turbocharged Renault come home victorious in a Grand Prix.

**ruck** (rʌk), *v.*⁷ [f. RUCK *n.*¹ 3 c; cf. RUCKING *vbl. n.*³] *intr.* **a.** *Rugby Union.* To struggle for possession of the ball at a loose scrummage. **b.** *Australian National Football.* To play as one of the three members of a ruck (see RUCK *n.*¹ 3 c (b)).

**1938** *Dominion* (Wellington, N.Z.) 20 June 13/1 All through the spell they used their weight and rucked with determination. **1954** *Ibid.* 17 May 10/4 They rucked and tackled well and it was not surprising that they wilted in the dying stages. **1963** *Footy Fan* (Melbourne) I. VII. 21 When he rucked with Bill Morris, he always feared he might spoil Morris' leaps for the ball and more or less played the role of understudy. **1968** *Sunday Times* 25 Feb. 23/2 Yet he rucks with the best, and one's memory will long cherish the sight of him defying three Harlequin forwards who were trying to wrest the ball from him. **1982** B. BEAUMONT *Thanks to Rugby* iii. 35 Someone who.. relished tackling, falling on the ball, rucking and mauling and all the other chores of a rugby forward. **1986** *N.Z. Herald* 5 Feb. IV. 3 They are pretty good players. They ruck better than Fijians. Not all of their football, though, would pass A1 at Twickers.

**rude**, *a.* and *adv.* Add: [A.] [I.] [4.] **c.** *spec.* Considered offensive through reference to or representation of sexual or excretory organs or functions; indecent, dirty, smutty.

**1961** H. S. TURNER *Something Extraordinary* ii. 27 Rude verses, under the counter pin-ups and obscene novelties. **1963** 'J. LE CARRÉ' *Spy who came in from Cold* (1964) iv. 30 Miss Crail looked up sharply from her card index, as if she had heard a rude word. **1979** A. CARTER *Bloody Chamber* 107 He made salads of the dandelion that he calls rude names, 'bum-pipes' or 'piss-the-beds'. **1981** H. JOLLY *Bk. Child Care* (new ed.) xxxiii. 312 Knowing what naked people look like.. should be something that happens naturally. A child is then far less likely to become obsessed with 'rude' pictures.

**rumbling**, *vbl. n.* Restrict †*Obs.*⁻⁰ to sense 3 a in Dict. Add: [3.] **b.** *pl.* Early indications that some significant change is imminent or likely to occur; also, murmurs or grumblings of discontent. Occas. in *sing.*

**1959** F. ASTAIRE *Steps in Time* ii. 14, I remember being aware of rumblings around our house—conversations about New York—a railroad trip being discussed. **1964** *Observer* 12 Jan. 10/7 The Negro's protest today is but the first rumbling of the 'underclass'. **1975** *Economist* 11 Jan. 34/1 Mr Sadat used the same slogan to lull the rumblings of social discontent. **1989** *N.Y. Times* 18 June 22/1 The first rumblings of momentous change in the Adirondack Park were heard in 1985.

**rump**, *n.*¹ Add: [3.] **d.** (Not pejoratively.) That which is left; the rest or the remainder.

**1969** D. ACHESON *Present at Creation* (1970) xviii. 161 The rump of the organization would be renamed the Office of Intelligence Coordination and Liaison. **1977** *Modern Railways* Dec. 474/1 The old Boulby site is served by a new connection to the rump of the Scarborough-Whitby coastal line, closed to through traffic in 1958, at Skinningrove. **1981** *Times* 9 July 24/5 The lightning collapse left practically no time for investors to save themselves. It is the liquidation of this rump of gold, bought at the inflated prices of that time, which had depressed the gold price over the past 18 months. **1983** *Times* 10 Aug. 15/6 The US houses could well match buyers and sellers outside and put the 'rump' of the shares they could not clear each day through the market via a small broker.

**runability** (rʌnə'bɪlɪtɪ), *n.* Also **runnability**. [f. RUN *v.* + -ABILITY; in some cases perh. f. RUNNABLE *a.* and -ITY, though the adj. is not recorded in these technical uses.] The capacity for running or for being run; *spec.* in *Paper-making* and *Printing*, the degree of ease with which paper passes through a machine.

**1935** *Bull. Virginia Polytechnic Inst.* Sept. 5 The ability of a molten metal to flow under the influence of a given pressure is one of the properties of the metal... For lack of a better term this property will be referred to as 'runability'. **1965** WEINER & ROTH in *Inst. Paper Chem.* (U.S.) *Bibl. Ser.* No. 215. p. iv, The behavior of paper in printing can be described in two broad categories, viz., printability and runnability... Runnability covers all of the characteristics of the paper which contribute to the ease, efficiency, and convenience of using the paper in the printing process. **1978** *Rugby World* Apr. 21 It would seem reasonable to think also that the 'runability' and stamina development demanded of the top-class player today would preclude most former internationals from participating in the same match without similar preparation. **1980** *Forest Products News* (N.Z.) XVII. 1. 4/2 Testers examine.. the coefficient of friction which determines runability. **1982** *Equity Life* No. 48. 33/1 These [orienteering] maps show 'runability' of the terrain ranging from the 'fast run' of open forest to 'fight' of a thicket. **1988** *Graphic Arts Monthly* Aug. 140/2 Trade-off of properties essential to printability and runnability will be necessary if.. weight is further reduced.

**runnable**, *a.* Add: Also (*erron.*) runable. **2. a.** Capable of being run, in various senses; manageable, operable, negotiable; *spec.* of rivers, waterways, etc.: sufficiently deep to be navigable, esp. by small boats.

**1977** *Washington Post* 28 July IV. 10 (*caption*) Area whitewater enthusiasts have been bunching up at the few runnable rapids left by the drought in the Potomac River Basin. **1983** *Ibid.* 8 Apr. (Weekend Suppl.) 49/1 But plenty of other little creeks were runnable that weekend, still high enough from earlier rains to make passage possible by canoe or kayak. **1985** *New Yorker* 26 Aug. 28/3 Yes, darling. I've found a much more runnable house, in Battersea. **1985** *Ward's Auto World* Aug. 55/1 We have people here fully capable of doing a fully runable prototype vehicle.

b. *Computing.* Of a program or instructions: that can be executed, esp. without further compilation or linking; capable of being carried out.

**1982** *Byte* Mar. 332/2 Pascal/Z . . requires three separate CP/M commands to transform a source file into a runnable program. **1989** *UNIX Rev.* Feb. 79/1 Having written the code, one usually wishes to actually *run* the program. The intermediate step, that of translating your code into runable binaries, is what this column is about.

**runner,** *n.* Sense 20 in Dict. becomes 21. Add: [I.] [1.] h. *Amer. Football.* A player who runs in possession of the ball on an attacking play; a ball-carrier. Cf. RUSHER *n.*[2] 3.

**1890** *Outing* Feb. 386/2 It was left to Princeton and Yale to . . generalize it into the principle that has made rushers and backs, runners and rushers alike in the rushing game of the last four years. **1894** STAGG & WILLIAMS *Amer. Football* 43 The end-rusher has to meet the runner under most trying circumstances. **1922** *Outing* May 65/2 Hunt counted the yards by fives . . till the runner hurled himself across the line. **1957** *Encycl. Brit.* IX. 473/2 Massed defenders could be either crushed down or split asunder to give the runner free passage toward the enemy goal. **1986** *Touchdown* Apr. 20/4 The runner has known from high school that you shouldn't run backwards, you shouldn't give up yardage.

i. Colloq. phr. *to do a runner*: to escape by running away (esp. of a thief or police suspect), to abscond; hence *gen.*, to depart hastily and unceremoniously. Cf. DO *v.* 11 d.

**1981** B. ASHLEY *Dodgem* viii. 162 Kids disappeared on their own, parents frantic or couldn't care less, grown-ups done a runner. **1985** *Venue* 20 Apr. 47/3, I dropped the video and did a runner across the roof, but I was stuck and couldn't get down! **1986** *Times* 21 June 3/8 He had been put into police cells and given a kicking after he 'tried to do a runner'. **1986** J. MILNE *Dead Birds* Pref. p. 4 The passenger jumped out and did a runner.

[5.] h. *Shooting.* A wounded game bird which runs along the ground but cannot fly. Also *fig.*

**1900** TUDWAY & HALL in A. E. T. Watson *Young Sportsman* 389 There should be under-men with retrievers in attendance, whose business it is to collect runners and birds that are not immediately recovered. **1949** C. E. HARE *Lang. Field Sports* (rev. ed.) vi. 78 *Runner*, a bird, usually a wounded one, that travels fast without flying. **1950** 'H. GREEN' *Nothing* 100 'They have to learn to fly some time. I know Mary will be all right but Jane doesn't want Philip a runner . . . Wounded bird, broken wing Jane,' Mr Abbot explained. **1966** R. JEFFRIES *Death in Coverts* viii. 93 Toby, Miss Harmsworth's dog, flashed past him with a runner in his mouth. **1988** *Shooting Life* June 45/3 He . . persevered despite his own hunger to account for that strong runner you told him about and which he had already marked even as it fell.

[II.] 20. *Austral. colloq.* A lightweight, soft-soled, canvas shoe, worn for sport or as casual wear; a sand-shoe or tennis shoe. Usu. *pl.*

**1970** J. S. GUNN in W. S. Ramson *Eng. Transported* iv. 64 We should investigate the areas of use of such duplications as . . sandshoes/sneakers/tennis shoes/runners. **1972** *Sunday Mail* (Brisbane) 13 Feb. 2/2 Readers . . claim Queenslanders have a wide range of words that aren't used anywhere else. Mrs G. E. Hanson (Toowoomba) offers 'runners' as a Queensland word for tennis shoes. **1979** *Verbatim* Summer 7/2 What are sandshoes in South Australia may be called runners in Victoria. **1983** *Austral. Women's Weekly* Aug. 21/1 In Victoria you exercise in runners, in NSW in sandshoes or tennis shoes, although the word 'runner' is catching on across the country.

‖**ryu** (rɪ'uː), *n.* Also 9 riu. Pl. ryu. [Jap. *-ryū* stream, current, (hence) school, style.] A Japanese style or school of art, esp. martial arts, music, flower arrangement, etc. Freq. as final element in Combs. Also ryugi [*gi* rule, norm] in same sense.

**1879** *Trans. Asiatic Soc. Japan* VII. 346 Takanobu was a pupil of the Yamato riu. **1892** *Trans. & Proc. Japan Soc.* I. 6 It is not in my power to enumerate all the different schools (*Riu*) of *Ju-jitsu* . . . Next comes a school called the *Kito-Riu*. **1913** E. J. HARRISON *Fighting Spirit Japan* iii. 44 Eventually many distinct *ryugi*, sects, or schools, came into existence . . . I was first introduced to the Tenshin Shinyo-ryu, which is an amalgamation of the Yoshin-ryu and the Shinnoshindo ryu. **1973** *Times Lit. Suppl.* 3 Aug. 899/2 Mme Harich-Schneider is, however, careful not to let the biases of her own ryū (schools) run away with her. **1977** *Early Music* July 418/1 (Advt.), Shakuhachi. Hand-crafted in the traditional manner. Kinko-ryu or Tozan-ryu models. **1987** *Karate* Feb./Mar. 17/1 The historical Togakure ryu continues to pass down its teachings and traditions under the guidance of the ryu's 34th Grandmaster.

**Ryukyu** (rɪ'uːkjuː), *a.* and *n.* Also 9 Riu-kiu. Pl. Ryukyus. [a. Jap. *Ryūkyū*: see *RYUKYUAN *n.* and *a.* The forms *Li-kyu* and *Liukiu* (also *Loo-Choo*) represent the Chinese pronunciation.] = *RYUKYUAN *n.* and *a.*

**1808** J. LEYDEN in *Asiatick Researches* X. 264 The Korean, Formosan, *Li-kyu*, or rather *Riu-kiu* languages. **1934** WEBSTER s.v. *agglutinative languages*, Other agglutinative tongues include: Ainu; Japanese and Korean, with Ryukyu, or Liukiu. **1950** *Columbia Encycl.* (ed. 2) 1725/3 In 1879 the Ryukyus were incorporated into the Japanese empire. **1958** *Japan* (Japanese Nat. Commission) xxv. 782/1 The . . *kansen-odori* [dance] . . was performed at the coronation of the Ryūkyū ruler. **1963** *Columbia Encycl.* (ed. 3) 1856/3 Although the Ryukyus were incorporated into the Japanese empire in 1879, the Chinese never formally gave up their claims and as late as 1945 still asserted their rights over them. **1973** *Guardian* 13 Mar. 3/5 Many intellectuals suspect that Expo '75 is an opportunity to complete the Japanisation of the Ryukyus, begun when Japan seized the islands in the late nineteenth century. **1978** *Language* LIV. 207 Martin . . sketches the parallel structure in Ryukyu.

**Ryukyuan** (rɪuː'kjuːən), *n.* and *a.* [f. Jap. *Ryūkyū*, the name of a group of islands several hundred miles south of mainland Japan, the largest of which is Okinawa, + *-AN*: see *RYUKYU *a.* and *n.*] A. *n.* A native or inhabitant of the Ryukyu islands; also, (any of) the group of Japanese dialects spoken there. Cf. OKINAWAN *n.* and *a.* B. *adj.* Of or pertaining to the Ryukyu islands, their people, or their language.

**1958** tr. K. Kōta in *Japan* (Japanese Nat. Commission) i. 76/1 In 1871 . . 66 Ryūkyūans drifted to Taiwan or Formosa. **1963** S. SAKAMAKI (title) Ryukyu. A bibliographical guide to Okinawan Studies surveying important primary sources and writings in Ryukyuan, Japanese, Chinese, and Korean. **1967** *Economist* 10 June 1122/2 But there are other steps which America could take to pacify disgruntled Ryukyuans. For instance, more could be done to help the economy. **1977** C. F. & F. M. VOEGELIN *Classification & Index World's Lang.* 190 In every classification, Ryukyuan represents maximum diversity in the small Japanese family. **1986** *N.Y. Times* 7 Sept. II. 39/6 Its season will also feature Sato Takako's Ryukyuan Dance Company from Okinawa, Nov. 21-22.

# S

**S.** Add: [I.] [4.] [a.] **SEAQ** ('si:æk), Stock Exchange Automated Quotation system, a computer system for the display of share prices and transactions on the London Stock Exchange.
**1984** *Financial Times* 18 July 40/5 The SE also plans to develop a monitoring system for share dealing—the Stock Exchange Automated Quotation System (*SEAQ)—on which prices will be disclosed. **1986** *Daily Tel.* 28 Oct. 21 Institutions deal in larger quantities than the SEAQ minima set by market makers... The small deals rate shown on the SEAQ screen.

**SETI** ('sɛtɪ) (*U.S.*), search for extraterrestrial intelligence (any of a number of NASA projects investigating the possibility of intelligent life in outer space).
**1976** *N.Y. Times Mag.* 12 Sept. 64/5 Drake was deeply involved in the search for extraterrestrial intelligence, which astronomers refer to as *SETI. **1977** P. MORRISON et al. *Search for Extraterrestrial Intelligence* (1979) i. 19 It seems clear to us that the SETI effort should be cast as a cooperative international endeavor. **1988** *Sunday Mail* (Brisbane) 20 Nov. 4/1 Success of the SETI program depends heavily on the radio telescope at NASA's Tippinbilla complex.

**SL** = *SENDERO LUMINOSO *n.*
**1986** *Ann. Reg. 1985* 80 An attack by the *SL on APRA headquarters on 7 October.. was followed by a new state of emergency in six Departments and the first reported defections from the movement.

**STEP**, sixth term entrance paper (for sixth-form pupils seeking entrance to the University of Cambridge).
**1985** *Times Higher Educ. Suppl.* 22 Mar. 8/4 Candidates will take the *STEP exams in May in a maximum of two subjects. **1991** *Sunday Tel.* 3 Feb. 6/2 [The candidate] had been asked for two As and a B, instead of the usual three As and a grade 1 in a 'step' paper.

**sab** (sæb), *n.*² *slang.* [Abbrev. of SABOTEUR *n.*] A hunt saboteur; *hunt sab*: see *HUNT *n.*² 6. Also **sab** *v. trans.*, to disrupt as a hunt saboteur; **'sabbing** *vbl. n.*
The word arose amongst saboteurs as a name for themselves.
**1978** *Times* 12 Apr. 14/9 Sabs have been horsewhipped, ridden down, struck. **1983** *Sunday Times* 6 Mar. 11/2 The battle between the hunters and the 'sabs' is now an integral part of the hunting scene. He is a veteran of countless sabbing missions. **1986** *Peace News* 19 Sept. 9/1 For two seasons I went and 'sabbed' my local hunt. **1988** *Green Line* Oct. 9/1 The hunting season is upon us once again, and the sabs take to the 'killing fields' with their usual courage and expertise.

‖**Sabora** (sa'bo:ra), *n.* Freq. in pl. **Saboraim**. Also **savora**; 8 **Sebura**. [Aram. *sābōrā*, f. *sḫar* to think, have an opinion.] Any of a group of Jewish scholars of the 6th century C.E. who contributed explanations and revisions to the Babylonian Talmud.
**1797** *Encycl. Brit.* XVII. 224/1 *Seburai, Seburæi*, a name which the Jews give to such of their rabbins or doctors as lived and taught some time after the finishing of the Talmud. **1888** *Ibid.* XXIII. 37/1 As regards the Babylonian Talmud, the *Amoraim* were succeeded by a new order of men called *Saboraim*..

who ventured only occasionally to revise and authenticate the sayings of their predecessors. **1905** *Jewish Encycl.* X. 610 *Sabora* (plural *Saboraim*), title applied to the principals and scholars of the Babylonian academies in the period following that of the Amoraim. **1989** *Encycl. Brit.* XXII. 430/2 According to the tradition of the *geonim*.. the Babylonian Talmud was completed by the 6th century *savoraim* ('expositors'). But the extent of their contribution is not precisely known.
Hence **Sabo'raic** *a.*, of or pertaining to the Saboraim.
**1961** in WEBSTER. **1986** *Jrnl. Theol. Stud.* XXXVII. I. 157 The Saboraic editors.. merely make final additions to it [*sc.* the Talmud].

**sac** (sæk), *n.*⁴ *Chess colloq.* [Abbrev. of SACRIFICE *n.*] = SACRIFICE *n.* 5 c.
**1965** *Chess Life* Nov. 249/1 A careful study of the position after the 'sac' shows that White will win the opponent's Queen in return. **1977** *Guardian Weekly* 4 Dec. 23/4 A positional pawn sac to take the initiative. *Ibid.* 23/5 The queen sac is not hard to find. **1986** *Christian Science Monitor* 5 Feb. 30/3, I had been preparing this sac for the past couple of moves.

**sacralize**, *v.* Add: Hence **'sacralized** *ppl. a.*
**1979** J. HALIFAX *Shamanic Voices* (1980) i. 21 Matsúwa,.. fiercely beckoning individuals.. to the sacralized ground before him. **1986** P. B. CLARKE *Black Paradise* vi. 81 Rastafarians also present themselves.. as a chosen race, along the same lines as the Jews; this, some may argue, is simply a sacralized form of racism.

**saddle**, *n.* Add: [II.] [5.] m. *Mus.* On stringed instruments: (*a*) [lit. tr. G. *Sattel*] = NUT *n.*¹ 14 a (*rare*); (*b*) the slight ridge at the base of an instrument, preventing wear on the belly, over which the gut securing the tail-piece to the end-pin passes; (*c*) an adjustable ridge on the bridge of a guitar which determines the length of the strings or their height above the fingerboard.
[**1908** R. DUNSTAN *Cycl. Dict. Mus.* 355/1 *Sattel* (G.), 'a saddle'. The 'nut' (of a violin, &c.).] **1941** H. PANUM *Stringed Instruments Middle Ages* 187 On their way from the tailpiece to the pegs, the strings on bowed instruments.. just before they reach the pegbox.. cross a narrow strip of hard wood—the *saddle* or *nut*—found on all fingerboard instruments. **1964** S. MARCUSE *Mus. Instruments* 573/1 A low saddle assists the tailpiece in keeping clear of the belly. **1979** C. FORD *Making Mus. Instruments* iii. 87 The purpose of the tail-gut saddle is to carry the tail gut over the edge of the belly. **1984** *New Grove Dict. Mus. Instruments* II. 101/1 The modern bridge, with the strings passing over the saddle to be tied to a rectangular block.. is also attributable to Torres, and has become standard since his time. **1986** *Making Music* Apr. 29/2 If the note is sharper than the harmonic move the bridge saddle back... If the note is flat move the saddle forwards. **1989** *Guitar Player* Mar. 19/1 The line of the fretboard should be.. right where the saddle starts coming out.

**safari**, *n.* Add: 4. *attrib.* or as *adj.* Sandy brown or beige; of the colour of clothes worn on safari.
**1976** *Milton Keynes Express* 18 June (Advt.), 43/1 Ford Capri 3.0 Ghia, safari beige. **1981** *Woman's Jrnl.* Mar. 6 (Advt.), Gold for getaway people; safari

is the colour, superb is the cut, fine poplin flying suit with hat. **1981** *Times* 23 June 12/6 The safari and copper colours of clothing.

**safety** ('seıftı), *v.* orig. and chiefly *U.S.* [f. SAFETY *n.*] *trans.* **a.** *Aeronaut.* To secure (an aircraft component, esp. a nut) against loosening due to vibration. **b.** *Weaponry.* To apply the safety-bolt or safety-catch of (a weapon, esp. a firearm) (cf. SAFETY *n.* 8). **c.** *gen.* To make safe; to secure against failure, hazard, or damage.

**1927** C. LINDBERGH *We* vi. 104, I removed the rubber band safetying the belt. **1956** W. A. HEFLIN *U.S. Air Force Dict.* 452/1 *Safety*, . . to secure an aircraft *part* against loosening from vibration; *specif.*, to secure a *nut* by a wire or cotter pin. **1976** *Lebende Sprachen* XXI. 150/2 In order to meet the exceptionally high equipment requirements, the manufacturer should consider safetying the thumbscrews with CRES lockwire. **1978** B. SHARE *Emergency* 105 Gun button safetied. **1980** BENT & McKINLEY *Aircraft Maintenance & Repair* (ed. 4) xv. 502/1 When a cotter pin is installed to safety a castle nut, the pin is placed through the grooves in the castellated portion of the nut and through the drilled hole in the shank of the bolt. **1984** *Back Stage* 23 Nov. 10B/1 When you're shooting in a public area with limited space, accidents are always a possibility. Cables must be secured, lights must be triple-safetied, and gear must be constantly checked for vibration damage.

Hence **'safetied** *ppl. a.*; **'safetying** *vbl. n.* (in quot. 1977, 'acting as safety man' (*U.S. Football*)).

**1956** W. A. HEFLIN *U.S. Air Force Dict.* 452/1 Safetied, *a.* **1977** *Washington Post* 24 May IV. 6/4 Ken Houston . . has made himself at home here with his solid citizenship and all-pro safetying. **1980** BENT & McKINLEY *Aircraft Maintenance & Repair* (ed. 4) xv. 502/2 The double-twist method of safetying should normally be used. *Ibid.*, Thus, the safety wire should be applied so it will tend to tighten the item safetied. **1989** *Brantford* (Ontario) *Expositor* 14 Mar. D3/5 Extended warranty, new tires, safetied.

**saggy**, *a.*[2] Add: Hence **'sagginess** *n.*

**1946** K. TENNANT *Lost Haven* (1947) xxi. 355 Jamaica complained of the 'sagginess' of the weather. **1986** *New Yorker* 24 Mar. 40/3 Flab and a general sagginess had set in.

‖ **sai** (saı), *n.*[3] Pl. unchanged. [Jap., a. Okinawa dial.] A type of dagger of Okinawan origin characterized by two sharp prongs curving outward from the hilt and often used as one of a pair.

**1973** *Express* (Trinidad & Tobago) 27 Apr. 31/3 The experts will give exhibitions in Kobudo (weaponry) displaying their martial skill with the sai. **1981** *Best of Karate '81* Spring 59/3 However, other weapons, chain and sickle, long pole, short staff, nunchaku, sai, dagger, spear, bow and arrow, etc., are included in the arsenal of Seong Leong Kwan. **1989** P. CROMPTON *Compl. Martial Arts* 65 A pair of gleaming sai, wielded by an expert, thrills any audience at a martial arts demonstration.

**sail**, *v.*[1] Add: [II.] **12.** Causatively: to send (an object) 'sailing' through the air; to throw or project.

**1934** in WEBSTER. **1936** J. G. COZZENS *Men & Brethren* i. 12 Ernest thumbed loose his clerical collar and detached the black linen stock, sailing them onto the top of the bureau. **1961** *Washington Post* 25 Jan. A23/4 He sailed his racquet into the stands, with no serious casualties resulting. **1986** T. McGUANE *To skin Cat* (1989) 49, I pitched the paper, sailing it past their expressionless faces.

**sailor**, *n.* Add: [4.] **b.** Short for BOARDSAILOR *n.*

**1984** *USA Today* 6 Apr. 2C/3 The Olympic boardsailing trials are June 12–22 . . . Two weeks earlier, Hall will conduct an elite session . . for six sailors, and then he will step back and watch his sailors compete against each other. **1988** *Guardian Weekly* 22 May 26/1 These park manoeuvres seem to go on for ever. There are three wind-surfing sailors in Bermuda shorts and bellhop tops who roll in on wheeled surfboards and hand out a picnic to the nannies.

**saint**, *a.* and *n.* Add: [A.] [4.] [d.] **St. Louis** (lwi), used *attrib.* to designate a kind of crystal glass manufactured at the St. Louis glass-house in the Munzthal, Lorraine, from the mid-eighteenth century; also *absol.*, an article (esp. a paperweight) manufactured there.

**1969** P. O'DONNELL *Taste for Death* ii. 29 His eye fell on the glass paperweights . . 'That's a St. Louis . . . The other two are Baccarat and Clichy-la-Garenne.' **1973** *Times* 17 Apr. 18/4 A St Louis green overlay relief lizard weight made £4,800. There was also a very rare St Louis aventurine ground weight at £2,400. **1979** N. & I. LYONS *Champagne Blues* 11 The crystal pendants on the Saint-Louis chandelier.

**St(e).-Maure** (sētmɔr), a cylindrically-shaped cheese made from goat's milk, named after the village in the Touraine where it is chiefly produced.

**1951** *Good Housek. Home Encycl.* 489/1 [Goats' milk] is widely used for making cheeses, for example, Saint Maure. **1961** *List of French Cheeses* (Harrods) Sept., *Sainte-Maure*, the most widely produced goat's milk cheese of the Touraine. It has quite a mild flavour, and, when the rind is blueish in colour, it indicates that the cheese is of the highest quality. **1982** D. SMITH *Compl. Cookery Course* 462 *Saint-Maure* . . is cylindrical, firm to the touch and full-flavoured.

[B.] [5.] **c.** *ellipt.* for *ST. HELENIAN *n.*

**1983** *Times* 19 Mar. 8/6 To the traveller, St Helena presents an idyllic prospect . . but this lonely little colony of 5,500 souls faces a bleak future. . . The Saints, though not a resentful people, compare their lot with that of the Falkland Islanders. **1985** *Observer* 16 June 17/1 'I'm a Saint,' he said. 'Not, I mean, that I'm saintly, of course.' He laughed. 'But from St Helena Island. That's what people from there are called.'

**salami**, *n.* Sense 2 in Dict. becomes 3. Add: **2.** Ellipt. for *salami technique* in sense *3 below.

**1979** *Amer. Banker* 11 Apr. 10/2 Salami is a truly automated crime. It's taking small slices over a period of time. It's taking very small amounts of money from very large numbers of accounts, say in a bank savings system, and transferring them automatically into a favored account. **1984** *Sunday Tel.* (Colour Suppl.) 10 June 49/1 *Salami*, one of the most common fraud techniques. **1985** *Today's Computers* July 105/3 The tried and tested salami (decimal cents) type of fraud would flourish, but at a much higher level. **1989** *Independent* 9 Mar. 1/4 Many of the people detected nothing of the 'salami' . . or 'Logic Bomb', the tools of hackers intent on crime.

[3.] **salami technique**, a way of carrying out a plan by means of a series of small or imperceptible steps; *spec.* (orig. *U.S.*) a type of computer fraud in which small amounts of money are transferred from numerous customer accounts into an account held under a false name.

**1975** *Economist* 5 Apr. 64/2 The German government used a '*salami technique' of reflation throughout last year. It authorised a bit more public spending here, a slightly bigger subsidy there. The first reflationary slices were small and tentative. The next were more substantial. **1981** P. SOMERVILLE-LARGE *Living Dog* ii. 27 Michael's way of embezzling involved what is known in America as the salami or thin-slice-at-a-time technique. It relied on stealing tiny sums of money from other people's accounts. **1984** *Financial Rev.* (Austral.) 7 May 30/2 A favourite play of the computer criminal is the 'salami' technique which involves the alteration of instructions which can be used to change interest payments to accounts. **1989** *N.Y. Times* 19 Aug. 1. 22/5 The 'salami technique' of publishing, in which one good idea is sliced into smaller publishable parts.

**sambo** ('sæmbəʊ), *n.*² [Russ., acronym f. *samozashchita* (more commonly *samoborona*) *bez oruzhiya*, lit. 'self-defence without arms'.] A type of judo wrestling which originated in the Soviet Union. Freq. *attrib.*, in *sambo wrestling*.
  **1964** *Maclean's Mag.* 21 Mar. 63/1 The Russians have, for generations, been practising something called sambo wrestling which is so close to judo that .. a team of sambo wrestlers .. held the best of the Tokyo University men to a draw. **1973** *Tehran Jrnl.* 15 Sept. 8/7 The first-ever world championship for Sambo wrestling wound up here tonight with the Russians making an almost unchallenged sweep of the gold medal tally. **1975** *Bangladesh Times* 21 July 6/3 The first international sambo competition was held in Teheran in 1973. **1983** P. BILLS *Wrestling* 14 These names are merely the equivalent of styles in other parts of the world such as 'Sumo' in Japan and 'Sambo' in Russia. **1985** *Times* 20 July 11/3 A couple of years ago, interested in sambo, he found it had become extinct in Britain.

**sammie** ('sæmɪ), *n.* slang (chiefly *Austral.* and *N.Z.*). Also **sammo**. [f. *sam-* (the sound of the first syllable of *sandwich* as actually pronounced) + -IE (or in variant, -O²).] A sandwich.
  **1978** E. MALPASS *Wind brings up Rain* xv. 152 I've cut some ham sammies. **1980** *Herald* (Melbourne) (City Ed.) 20 Mar. 2/6 The six-point sammo in plastic covering. **1988** *Courier-Mail* (Brisbane) 6 Apr. 35/3 Speciality shops selling exotic sammies full of prawns and avocado.

‖**samn** (sam), *n.* Also **samna**. [Arab. *samn*, Egyptian Arab. (colloq.) *samna*.] In the Middle East: a type of clarified butter, similar to ghee, from which the water has been extracted by boiling.
  **1888** C. M. DOUGHTY *Trav. Arabia Deserta* I. ii. 35 The *samn* or clarified Beduin butter of this droughty highland is esteemed above other, in Syria. **1910** *Encycl. Brit.* II. 261/1 A large proportion of the milk is made into *samn*, clarified butter. **1929** F. STARK *Let.* 8 Oct. in *Lett. from Syria* (1942) 190 He went to Shahba with a load of samn. **1974** *Encycl. Brit. Micropædia* II. 408/2 *Samna* is the name for butterfat in Egypt.

‖**samogon** (səmɑ'gɒn, anglicized 'sæməgɒn), *n.* [Russ., f. *samo-* self + *gon-* stem of *gnat'* to distill.] In Russia, illegally distilled spirit, similar to vodka.
  **1928** *Observer* in *Lit. Digest* (N. Y.) 22 Dec. 14/2 After the adoption of the New Economic Policy .. a flourishing trade in samogon, an illegal substitute for vodka distilled from grain, grew up. **1932** *Ann. Amer. Acad. Pol. & Social Sci.* CLXIII. 227/2 The peasants turned to samogon, vodka distilled at home. **1974** T. P. WHITNEY tr. *Solzhenitsyn's Gulag Archipel.* I. i. ii. 87 One could easily recognize that neither burglary, nor murder, nor samogon distilling, nor rape ever seemed to occur at random intervals or in random places throughout the country. **1987** *Times* 21 Mar. 5/3 *Sovietskaya Rossiya* disclosed that the anti-alcohol campaign was being 'seriously undermined' by an upsurge in the brewing of samogon, a home-made spirit with a fiery taste and potentially lethal after-effects.

**Samos** ('seɪmɒs), *n.* [ad. Gr. Σάμος (see SAMIAN *a.* and *n.*).] Any of several types of fortified dessert wine (including Muscat) produced in Samos.
  **1865** R. DRUITT *Rep. Cheap Wines* viii. 83 *Samos* and *Patras* are new rich wines of full body and peculiar flavour. **1926** P. M. SHAND *Bk. Wine* x. 258 When I was about sixteen I tasted some soi-disant Samos clandestinely in France. **1957** L. W. MARRISON *Wines & Spirits* viii. 168 Especially in the islands, several richer and more alcoholic wines are made for export . . . The most well known of these are *Mavrodaphne*, and *Samos* wine. **1975** P. V. PRICE *Taste of Wine* v. 74/2 Today a dry Samos is also made; both must by law be 100 per cent Muscat.

**sampaguita** (sæmpə'giːtə), *n.* [a. Filipino Sp. *sampaguita*, dim. of Tagalog *sampaga* Arabian jasmine.] A local name in the Philippines for the Arabian jasmine, *Jasminum sambac*; the flowers of this tree.
  **1902** *Encycl. Brit.* XXXI. 667/1 Valuable essential oils are obtained from the flowers of the ilangilang, sampaguita, and champaca. **1966** MRS. L. B. JOHNSON *White House Diary* 25 Oct. (1970) 434 There were more 'Blue Ladies'—Mrs. Marcos' hostess committee—with fragrant leis of sampaguita for each of the First Ladies. **1980** *N.Y. Times* 7 Sept. x. 7/1 In busy commercial districts where brightly painted minibuses called jeepneys ply, sampaguita leis are hawked by young vendors.

**sanction**, *n.* Add: [6.] c. *spec.* In military intelligence, the permission to kill a particular individual. Also, a killing due to this.
  **1980** KEENE & HAYNES *Spyship* xv. 170 You'd like the Sanction, I take it? . . Reestablish contact when Sanction is completed. **1983** P. NIESEWAND *Scimitar* xiv. 378 His apartment was on the third floor, so the agents knew they would have to use another method of sanction . . . It was clear that Ross alone would kill that night while Lyle watched. **1988** 'R. DEACON' *Spyclopaedia* 411 *Sanction*, intelligence agency approval for a killing.

**sand**, *n.*² Add: [10.] [a.] **sand-barite** *Min.* [BARITE *n.*] = ROCK-ROSE *n.* 5.
  **1906** H. W. NICHOLS in *Publ. Field Columbian Museum Geol. Ser.* III. 31 (*heading*) *Sand-barite crystals from Oklahoma. **1923** *Proc. Oklahoma Acad. Sci.* III. 102 Barite and especially the form known as 'sand barite rosettes', has long attracted attention as one of the most widely disseminated of Oklahoma minerals. **1947** *Rocks & Minerals* XXII. 706 Farther north in the Baharia Oasis sand barite crystals are found in the Nubian Sandstone. **1962** *Amer. Mineralogist* XLVII. 1189 Sand-barite analogs of sand-calcite single crystals were discovered recently by Mr. Everett Hill on land adjoining his ranch . . south of Hot Springs, South Dakota. **1983** S. I. TOMKEIEFF et al. *Dict. Petrol.* 494/2 *Rock rose*, . . a local Oklahoma term for sand barites.

**sandbag**, *v.* Add: [3.] b. *transf.* To underperform in a race or competition in order to gain an unfair handicap or other advantage. *slang*.
  **1985** *Los Angeles Times* 7 Oct. III. 13/2 If the Rams had crunched the Vikings by three or four touchdowns, Robinson would have had to admit he was sandbagging, that he really might be sitting on . . a truly hot team. **1986** *Telegraph* (Brisbane) 11 Nov. 40/1 Did Australia III 'sandbag' on the last leg of her America's Cup Defender Trials match yesterday to allow stablemate Australia IV to win and gain two vital points? **1988** *Daily Tel.* 7 Sept. 17/6 I've actually seen them sandbagging—setting up the boat to sail slow.
  Hence **'sandbagging** *vbl. n.*
  **1940** O. JACOBY *On Poker* v. 35 Sandbagging occurs when a player who has a good hand .. decides

to pass in the hope that someone else will open. **1965** *Richmond* (Va.) *Times-Dispatch* 19 Dec. c-7 Ten Detroit bowlers lost $21,000 of $30,000 in prizes .. when they were judged guilty .. of 'sandbagging'—gaining an unfair advantage in handicap and classified tournaments by using .. established league averages which did not reflect their true abilities. **1983** *Age* (Melbourne) 10 Sept. 5/6 Sandbagging around several lowlying homes continued yesterday as the floodwaters rose. **1986** *Telegraph* (Brisbane) 11 Nov. 40/3 My colleagues .. said they were astounded at the result, which produced loud jeers and cries of 'sandbagging' from yachting journalists.

**sandbagger**, *n.* Add: [3.] **b.** *transf.* In sport, a person who deliberately underperforms in order to gain an unfair handicap or other advantage. Cf. *SANDBAG v. 3 b. slang.

**1965** *Richmond* (Va.) *Times-Dispatch* 19 Dec. c-7 (*heading*) Managers look out for 'sandbaggers'. **1984** *Toronto Star* 28 Mar. b10/3 At most pro-ams, you hear the word 'cheat' throughout the tournament because of sandbaggers. That wasn't the case .. last year ... The system is .. self-adjusting and that eliminates people who came in with inflated handicaps. **1987** *Dirt Bike* June 53/2 A great choice for big kids, experts and the local 16-year-old sandbagger trying to get through another season of cherry picking in the mini class.

**Sandinist** (sændɪ'niːst, 'sændɪnɪst), *a.* and *n.* [ad. Sp. *Sandinista* SANDINISTA *n.* (*a.*): see -IST.] = SANDINISTA *n.* (*a.*)

**1969** *Tricontinental* July 43/1 The Sandinist Front has rejected the terms 'villains', 'highwaymen', and 'bandits' that the Nicaraguan and Costa Rica press are using to describe the Nicaraguan patriots. **1977** *Washington Post* 14 Oct. a21/6 Many of the Sandinists are believed living in exile in Costa Rica. **1978** *N.Y. Times* 29 Jan. iv. 4/1 Perhaps more than any other guerilla group in Latin America, Nicaragua's Sandinist National Liberation Front .. has won the support or sympathy of broad sectors of the population. **1987** J. R. THACKRAH *Encycl. Terrorism & Pol. Violence* 220 The year before their deaths, the Sandinists split into three factions, the smallest of which was the Marxist - Leninist GPP.

**'sandpaper**, *v.* Add: **b.** *fig.* To bring to perfection, to refine.

**1890** in *Cent. Dict.* **1927** *Daily Tel.* 21 June 13/7 Borotra was wisely sand-papering his ground strokes; there was much rust on them. **1947** P. LARKIN *Girl in Winter* ii. i. 91 And therefore this reserve, this sandpapering of every word and gesture until it exactly fitted its place in the conversation .. —this was not natural. **1956** O. WELLES *Mr. Arkadin* ii. i. 96, I started on a series of interviews which I conducted conscientiously, and which, sandpapered by an impoverished young writer, were published with some success.

**‖Sangam** ('saŋgam), *n.*¹ [Tamil *caṅkam*, *śaṅgam*, ad. Skr. *saṅgha* association.] Any one of three important Tamil literary academies in southern India which flourished until the 4th century A.D. Also used *attrib.* to designate the (period of) literature associated with these academies, esp. the third.

**1856** R. CALDWELL *Compar. Gram. Dravidian Lang.* Introd. 86, It is the concurrent voice of various traditions that Tiruvalluvar lived before the dissolution of the Madura *Sangam*; i.e., the college of literati, or board of literary examiners, at Madura. **1897** M. S. SASTRI *Ess. Tamil Lit.* i. 40 We should therefore think that the Saṅgams contained only poets who eulogized their patrons by their poetical compositions and were supported by them, and that they were not like the Sanskrit colleges of the northern countries. **1955** K. A. N. SASTRI *Hist. S. India* xiv. 348 The literature of the Saṅgam Age, the

oldest body of works now known in the Tamil language. **1966** N. SUBRAHMANIAN *Saṅgam Polity* i. 3 The Tamil *Saṅgam* was a body of Tamil scholars or poets, a literary academy, which was established by the Pāndyan kings; and it flourished at Madurai. **1975** K. KRIPALANI in A. L. Basham *Cultural Hist. India* xxi. 303 The extant Sangam poetry .. was written in the second and third centuries A.D., if not earlier. **1984** *Unesco Courier* Mar. 5 Some of the kings of these dynasties are mentioned in Sangam literature .. and the age between the 3rd century BC and the 2nd century AD is called the Sangam Age.

**‖sangam** ('saŋgam), *n.*² Also 9 sungum. [Hindi, f. Skr. *saṃgama*.] In India, a river confluence.

**1857** LADY FALKLAND *Chow-chow* I. xiii. 265 On reaching the Sungum .. the landscape from the bridge is perfectly enchanting. Sungum means junction of rivers. Here the Moota and Moola join their waters. **1968** *New Yorker* 1 June 39/3 Among the four Khumba *melas*, the one at Prayaga is preëminent, because it takes place by the *sangam* .. —the spot where the right bank of the Ganga meets the left bank of the Yamuna. **1973** *Sunday Standard* (Delhi) 7 Jan. 9/3 The holy Sangam—confluence of the Ganga, Yamuna and invisible Saraswati at Allahabad. **1989** *Adventurers* Sept. 37/3 Through the mist waves of Naga Babas .. run joyously down to the *sangam*—the point where the Ganges and the Jumna join the mythical Sarasvati River.

**sangoma** (sæŋ'gəʊmə, ‖saŋ'gɔːma), *n.* Also isangoma, (*erron.*) sangome. [a. Zulu *isangoma*; cf. Swazi *sangoma*.] In Southern Africa, a witchdoctor, usu. a woman, claiming supernatural powers of divination and healing.

[**1870** H. CALLAWAY *Relig. Syst. Amazulu* III. 281 The doctor is called Isanusi, or Ibuda, or Inyanga of divination, or Umungoma.] **1893** I. FORSYTH *Gold Concession* 72 Slinking leopards, stately lions, and ravening wolves waited continually to do the bidding of the great sangome (prophetess, or witch). **1905** R. PLANT *Zulus* 21 An Isanusi or Isangoma, that is a diviner, would be called in to discover the cause of this persistent illness. **1930** R. E. PHILLIPS *Bantu are Coming* i. 16 They have been smelled out by the *isangoma* (witch-doctor) and punished. **1967** *Drum* 27 Aug. 12 I'm tough, tough, mighty tough. And its thanks to Soweto's so-sexy sangoma, Sarah Mashele, who gave me her full rejuvenating treatment the other day. **1979** J. DRUMMOND *Patriots* xvi. 83 A sangoma is a witch doctor; not a dispenser of medicines, but a diagnostician, often a woman, who interprets dreams, casts fortunes. **1988** *Personality* (Durban) 4 July 79/3 You sing about your mother who was a healer, a sangoma.

**sanitary**, *a.* Add: [3.] **sanitary protection**, a collective term for the products (as tampons, sanitary towels, etc.) used by women during menstruation.

**1939** *Woman* 14 Oct. 42/1 *Sanitary protection is now worn internally. **1979** *Guardian* 27 Mar. 9/5 A campaign for free sanitary protection through the NHS started in 1973 when the Government imposed VAT on towels and tampons. **1985** [see *SANPRO *n.*].

**sanitize**, *v.* Add: ‚saniti'zation *n.*; 'sanitizing *vbl. n.* and *ppl. a.*

**1940** *Amer. Jrnl. Public Health* XXX. 346/2 The tumblers were placed in the sanitizing solution immediately after being subjected to the usual barkeepers' rinse. *Ibid.* 347/1 The chemical is very stable over long periods of time and under heavy usage, another favorable characteristic for the practical sanitization of eating and drinking utensils. **1947** *Canad. Jrnl. Res.* XXV. F. 89 The organisms are present in a partially dried film of skim-milk, thus simulating conditions encountered in the sanitizing of food handling utensils and equipment. **1977** *Times Lit. Suppl.* 20 May 611/1 America's entrance into the Second World War did not tempt him to reconsider his decision. He found nothing morally or intellectually sanitizing about it. **1986** *Daily Tel.* 21 May 16/6 The sanitisation of music is well under way. For years now, Dvorak's String Quartet No 12 in F has been called .. the 'American Quartet'. **1986** *Year's Work Eng. Stud. 1983* 416 For the Joyce of *Ulysses* it is now an expansive mode after its 'sanitizing' effect in *Dubliners* and *A Portrait*.

**sanpro** ('sænprəʊ), *n. Advertising jargon.* [Shortened f. *sanitary protection.*] = *sanitary protection* s.v. *SANITARY a.* 3.
**1985** *Observer* 14 Apr. 43/3 'Sanpro' is advertisese for sanitary protection (the euphemisms start from the top in this industry). **1987** *Cosmopolitan* Sept. 154 Recently the IBA authorised a trial re-introduction of TV advertisements for Sanitary Protection, or sanpro as it is termed in the neatly packaged world of PR. **1988** *Grocery Update* June 3/2 Haircare, sanpro, dental, cosmetics, baby and OTC medication come under the spotlight in each issue. **1989** *Marketing* 25 May 9/2 Delaney feels that reticence about advertising sanpro and condoms is often the result of 'hypocrisy and squeamishness'.

**Sanskritize**, *v.* Add: '**Sanskritized** *ppl. a.*
**1934** *Times Educ. Suppl.* 14 Apr. 113/4 Attempts to replace these Persian words with highly Sanscritized forms had .. proved a failure. **1986** *English Today* Apr. 33/2 Raja Rao .. has innovated vernacularized and Sanskritized ('high') styles.

‖ **Sant** (sant), *n.* [Hindi, Punjabi *sant,* f. Skr. *sát* pious, venerable.] An Indian holy man; (a title of) a devotee or ascetic, esp. in north and east India.
**1909** M. A. MACAULIFFE *Sikh Religion* IV. 298 The Guru said, 'a son shall be born in his house whom you shall call Sant Das.' **1934** 'H. MACDIARMID' *Stony Limits* 131 It is world-wide, ageless. It is the Sufi *Nida* and *Sant.* **1968** W. H. McLEOD *Gurū Nānak & Sikh Religion* v. 153 The first of the great Sants was Nāmder (A.D. 1270-1350). **1972** *Times* 31 Oct. 17/7 The Sant, meaning holy man, was at the centre of the struggle in the first half of the 1960s for a Sikh-dominated Punjabi-speaking state. **1984** *Listener* 17 May 13/3 The Sant sits cross-legged on his bed and courteously answers my questions in Punjabi.

**Saperavi** (sæpə'rɑːvɪ), *n.* Also **Sapperavi**. [a. Russ., f. Georgian *sap'eravi* (adj.) of or pertaining to paint or dye, (n.) type of grape or wine made from this, f. *p'eri* colour, painting, dyeing.] A red wine from the Republic of Georgia.
**1926** P. M. SHAND *Bk. Wine* ix. 249 The principal Crimean wines are .. Sapperavi, Soudak, Kakour. **1961** *New Statesman* 15 Dec. 921 (Advt.), Saperavi No. 5: dry red (full bodied). **1968** A. H. GOLD *Wines & Spirits of World* 467 Mukuzani and *Saperavi* are two dark strong red wines of 14° alcoholic strength from the eastern side of Georgia in the Tiflis region. **1987** *N.Y. Times* 20 Apr. D10/5 Saperavi, akhasheni and napareuli, the best-known reds.

**sapple** ('sæp(ə)l), *n. Sc.* [f. the vb.] *pl.* Soap suds, soap bubbles. Also *transf.*
**1821** J. GALT *Ayrshire Legatees* x. 265 Rubbin' the clothes to juggons between their hands, above the sapples. **1880** J. NICHOLSON *Poems* 87 Sapples o' the sea-bree Stickin' in her hair. **1931** *Scots Mag.* Sept. 425 She straightened as she saw him, and rubbed the sapples off her hands and arms. **1953** *Kirriemuir Free Press* 3 Sept., On washin'-days 'twas reamin' ower Wi' rowth o' sapples.

**sapple** ('sæp(ə)l), *v. Sc.* [Frequentative of *sap,* Sc. var. of SOP *v.*: cf. SAPPY *a.* 5 a.] *trans.* To saturate in water, to rinse, wash out; *spec.* to soak (clothes) in soapy water. Also *intr.* (esp. for *refl.*) and '**sappling** *vbl. n.*

**1836** A. CUNNINGHAM *Ld. Roldan* I. ix. 255 His Sunday finery will have got a sappling! **1850** R. STEWART *Musings of Stray Hours* 60 She had nae other wish, than in whiskey to sapple. **1897** A. J. ARMSTRONG *Robbie Rankine* 18 His claes were gey weel sappled wi' the wat grass. **1985** E. LOCHHEAD *True Confessions* 102, I sappled through my nylons and kept myself nice.

**Sarakatsan** (særəkæt'sæn), *n.* (and *a.*) Pl. -s; also **Sarakatsani**. [ad. mod. Gr. Σαρακατσάνοι the Sarakatsans.] (A member of) a nomadic pastoral people of northern Greece. Also *attrib.* or as *adj.*
**1868** *Trans. Ethnol. Soc.* VI. 316 The Bomœi or Bovians .. have passed from Grecian into Turkish territory, and under the name of Sarakatsani have established themselves in Agrapha. **1961** R. JENKINS *Dilessi Murders* 114 The Arvanitákis brothers were .. very probably of that Greek family of nomad shepherds called Sarakatsans. **1964** J. K. CAMPBELL *Honour, Family & Patronage* i. 5 Mme Chatzimichalis also emphasizes the unity of Sarakatsan art forms. **1978** *Antiquaries Jrnl.* LVIII. 178 The Vlahs (Aromuni) and Sarakatsani are classed as 'Nomadic'. **1978** *Times* 16 Aug. (N. Greece Suppl.) p. iv/7 The traditional costumes of the Sarakatsan, a Greek community of nomadic shepherds.

**sardony** ('sɑːdənɪ), *n.* [Back-formation f. SARDONIC *a.,* perh. after *irony.*] = SARDONICISM *n.*
**1935** S. DESMOND *Afr. Log* xxii. 107 He seemed to get both its sardony and its humour. **1978** *Times Lit. Suppl.* 24 Nov. 1359/2 An ingenious story about story-telling that relies for its effect on sardony rather than pathos. **1984** *Sunday Times* 23 Sept. 42/4 Waugh's sardony rose to the occasion.

**satnav** ('sætnæv), *n.* Chiefly *Naut.* Also **sat-nav**. [Acronym f. *satellite navigation.*] Navigation assisted by continuous positional information obtained from communications satellites; a navigation system capable of receiving this information.
**1975** *Petroleum Rev.* XXIX. 103/1 This company will show integrated sat-nav system, autro-nav transponder system, [etc.] **1981** *New Scientist* 5 Feb. 340/1 It may well be the spectre of Japan that has hastened the downward movement of the prices of satellite navigation systems—satnavs—to the sailor. **1987** *Yachting World* Apr. 62/1 Sailing up the Red Sea using satnav, I was regularly obtaining from one of the satellites a fix that was over 20 miles from my calculated position.

**saturnine**, *a.* and *n.* Add: [A.] [1.] c. Of appearance or mien: dark, grim, louring.
**1776** E. TOPHAM *Lett. Edin.* 83 The men are large and disproportioned with unfavourable, long, and saturnine countenances. **1891** O. WILDE *Pict. Dorian Gray* xi. 214 How evil he looked! The face was saturnine and swarthy, and the sensual lips seemed to be twisted with disdain. **1955** R. CHURCH *Over Bridge* (1956) iv. 45 A woman still handsome in a saturnine way, with hair jet-black. **1989** *Independent* 19 Oct. 13 With the saturnine appearance of an opera Machiavelli, he at least looks more interesting than his mentor.

**Saudiization** (ˌsaʊdiaɪ'zeɪʃən), *n.* Also **Saudization**. [f. SAUDI *n.* and *a.* + -IZATION.] The process or result of rendering (more) Saudi Arabian in character, esp. by the transfer of posts in industry from foreigners to Saudi nationals.
**1980** *Oil & Gas Jrnl.* 6 Oct. 6 Saudi Arabian joint ventures are aiming at more 'Saudization', i.e., more Saudi nationals employed. **1982** *Sci. Amer.* Jan. s8 (Advt.), Throughout the economy emphasis is being

placed on 'Saudiization'. **1986** *Times* 19 Feb. 11/1 No mention was made about the Saudi-isation of jobs and accommodation. **1989** *Media Internat.* May 39/2 Saudi TV.. programming is a very sensitive issue, given the zealous protectionism of a 'pure' Islamic state culture, combined with intense pressure towards Saudiisation.

**-saur** (sɔː(r)), *suffix*. [ad. mod.L. *-saur-us* or directly f. Gr. σαῦρ-ος lizard (as in SAURO-, SAURIAN *a.* and *n.*).] Used in the names of dinosaurian reptiles and other extinct reptile groups, usu. as an anglicization of mod.L. forms, as in ICHTHYOSAUR *n.*, PTEROSAUR *n.*, etc.

**sausage**, *n.* Add: [**2.**] i. *Naut.* A length of moulded plastic or other yielding material suspended horizontally in a quayside or boat, and serving as a fender against collision or buffeting. Cf. FENDER *n.* 2 b.
**1968** *Guardian* 29 Feb. 5/5 The first step .. would be to create a breakwater of plastic sausages to absorb the energy of waves. **1988** *Motorboats Monthly* Oct. 121/2 The alongside berths are notorious for their giant fenders. Known as sausages, they keep vessels off at the water line.
[**4.**] [**c.**] *sausage-like a.*
**1852** H. MARTINEAU in *Househ. Words* 27 Mar. 33/2 She is making it [*sc.* clay] into *sausage-like rolls. **1986** *N.Y. Times* 4 May XI. 33/3 Steak Portuguesa had a sausage-like flavor.

**sausagey** ('sɒsɪdʒɪ), *a.* [f. SAUSAGE *n.* + -Y¹.] Resembling a sausage, esp. in appearance or shape; sausage-like.
**1921** D. H. LAWRENCE *Sea & Sardinia* III. 106 Now it [*sc.* Cagliari Cathedral] has .. oozed out baroque and sausagey, a bit like the horrible baldachins in St. Peter's at Rome. **1984** J. UPDIKE *Witches of Eastwick* i. 19 She .. wore pants suits .. so tight the flesh below her belt was bunched in sausagey rolls.

**sauté**, *a.* and *n.* Add: **sautéed** *ppl. a.*
**1896** F. M. FARMER *Boston Cooking-School Cook Bk.* xx. 285 Sautéd potatoes. **1941** A. L. SIMON *Conc. Encycl. Gastron.* III. 90/2 Sautéed potatoes. **1980** J. KRANTZ *Princess Daisy* xxiv. 421 Roast wild boar with sautéed apples and lingonberries.

**save**, *n.²* Add: [**2.**] b. *Baseball.* The credit given to a relief pitcher for maintaining the team's lead through a threatening situation in a game won by the pitcher's team; also, the act of preserving the lead in this way. (Chiefly as a statistical measure.)
**1962** *Washington Daily News* 3 July 27/2 They had two on base when Wagner came up with his save. **1963** *Official Baseball Guide* 223 Only one save could be given in a game, and a reliever who received the victory was not eligible for a save. **1977** *Washington Post* 5 June D8/2 A junior All-Metropolitan selection who .. was credited with a save in yesterday's triumph. **1985** *Globe & Mail* (Toronto) 9 Oct. c3/1 Pitchers are given two points for each save and relief win. **1987** *First Base* Summer 13/1 A reliever is credited with a save if he comes into the game with his team ahead and keeps them there.
**4.** *Computing.* An act of saving a file: see *SAVE v.* 8 g.
**1982** *380z Disc System User Guide* App. B. 7 *Save*, the transfer of a program or data from immediate (and usually volatile) memory to a backing store of non-volatile memory (usually disc or tape). **1984** S. CURRAN *Word Processing for Beginners* ix. 116 When the disc looks to be around three-quarters full, it is actually getting full to bursting, and will be liable to reject further saves.

**save**, *v.* Add: [**I.**] [**8.**] g. *Computing.* To preserve the contents of (the whole or part of main memory) by transferring a copy to non-volatile storage, usu. tape or disk, from which it can subsequently be retrieved when required. In later use freq. with *adv.* or advb. phr. denoting the location where the copy is to be stored.
**1961** *Proc. National Symposium on Machine Translation* (U.S.) 328 The information cell of the matching text form is saved. **1964** *Proc. AFIPS Conf.* XXVI. 354/1 Since both data and subroutines change from day to day, a working procedure was developed which consists of writing a disk save tape(s) daily. These areas are the only disk areas saved. **1979** *Personal Computer World* Nov. 49/1 To save programs they must first be moved out of the way of the DOS, control switched back to the 6502, 65DOS booted in and finally the program saved. **1984** *Acorn User* Nov. 99/1 An interrupt-driven program saver that automatically saves a copy of the current program in memory .. to disc every four minutes or so. **1987** *Desktop Publishing Today* Nov. 33/1 You could take a sheet of Letraset, scan the complete alphabet, modify characters and then save it to the system as a font.

**saver**, *n.* Add: [**4.**] b. *Marketing.* A fare or tariff promoted as one that saves the consumer money; a concessionary ticket, esp. for rail travel. Freq. *attrib.*
**1977** *Times* 17 Mar. 2/4 British Rail is to halve the present £30.00 second-class return fare between London and Glasgow for an experimental period on selected trains... The ticket.. is being called the 'Big City Saver'. **1986** *Rail Enthusiast* May 39/1 A card that .. could enable us both .. to travel at half fare on Standard Returns and a third off Savers. **1988** *Holiday Which?* Mar. 88/1 Offpeak weekend savers from £99. **1988** *Financial Times* 9 Apr. (Weekend FT) 1/4 He spends .. £37 on the British Rail saver ticket to York.

**Savi** ('sævɪ), *n. Ornith.* [The name of Paolo Savi (1798-1871), Italian zoologist and geologist, who described the bird (1824, in *Nuovo Giornale de Letterati* VII. 341).] **Savi's warbler**, a warbler, *Locustella luscinioides*, found in marshland and reed-beds of central and eastern Europe, similar in appearance to the reed-warbler but with a song more like that of the grasshopper warbler.
**1843** W. YARRELL *Hist. Brit. Birds* I. p. vi, Savi's Warbler: *Salicaria luscinoides* [sic]. **1911** *Encycl. Brit.* XXVIII. 317/1 Savi's warbler, *Locustella luscinioides*, .. was only recognized as a constant inhabitant of the Fen district of England a few years before its haunts were destroyed by drainage. **1956** *Brit. Birds* XLIX. 326 The rufous brown colour of the back and lack of streaking .. together with such short bursts of reeling indicated a Savi's Warbler (*L. luscinioides*). **1985** E. SIMMS *Brit. Warblers* xiii. 146 Since the year 1960, Savi's Warblers have occurred with increasing frequency in Britain.

**Savora** *n.*, var. *SABORA n.*

‖**scala mobile** ('skala 'mobile), *n. Econ.* [It., lit. 'moving stair, escalator'.] In Italy, a system of wage indexation introduced in 1945 whereby earnings are linked by a sliding scale to rises in the retail price index.
[**1948** *Economist* 1 May 717/2 The sliding scale which is now in force for adjustment of wages to rising (but not to falling) prices.] **1965** G. H. HILDEBRAND *Growth & Struct. Econ. Mod. Italy* viii. 202 Criticism of the existing *scala mobile* involved several issues. **1976** *Business Week* (Industr. ed.) 21 June 42/2 He says the scala mobile, under which Italy's huge public payroll is adjusted regularly for inflation, should be modified as part of a new social contract with the unions similar to Britain's. **1989** *Financial Times* 30 June 1. 2/7 A dangerous

deterioration in Italian industrial relations was narrowly avoided yesterday when employers agreed to retain the scala mobile system of wage indexation for another year in return for a vague trade union commitment to help contain rising labour costs.

‖**scala naturae** ('skeɪlə næ'tjʊəriː, 'skɑːlə næ'tjʊərɑɪ), n. [mod.L., lit. 'ladder of nature'.] = scale of nature s.v. SCALE n.[3] 5 a; the chain of being (CHAIN n. 4 a).
[**1859** DARWIN Origin of Species v. 149 Beings low in the scale of nature are more variable than those which are higher.] **1888** Encycl. Brit. XXIV. 806/1 Lamarck represents most completely . . the highwater mark of the popular but fallacious conception of a scala naturae. **1972** Science 2 June 986/3 The concept of evolution, at that period, still evoked in most naturalists the image of the scala naturae, the ladder of perfection. **1983** E. C. MINKOFF Evolutionary Biol. iii. 50/2 Buffon's criticisms of Linnaeus were several. He objected especially to any arbitrary subdivision of nature, for he believed that the scala naturae was a continuum.

**scale**, v.[3] Add: [I.] [2.] b. To send (a flat object, esp. a stone) sliding or skimming across a surface or through the air. Also transf. U.S.
c**1870** in Dict. Amer. Eng. IV. 2029/2 To scale, to go, or make go, sideling . . to skip, ricochet, or cause to do so. **1877** BARTLETT Dict. Amer. (ed. 4) 644 Scaling stones (upon the water) was a common New England expression for what English boys call 'making ducks and drakes'. **1928** in Funk's Stand. Dict. **1959** F. ASTAIRE Steps in Time (1960) xi. 101, I yanked that wig off my head and scaled it across the entire length of the stage. **1982** J. MAY Many-Coloured Land II. xiii. 226 The knight picked a blood-smeared golden hoop from the mess and scaled it far out over the lake, where it sank without a trace.
8. To arrange on a scale; to graduate.
**1934** in WEBSTER. **1964** C. CHAPLIN My Autobiogr. xi. 185 The Essanay Company . . was scaling its terms according to the seating capacity of a theatre. **1977** South China Morning Post (Hong Kong) 13 Apr. 11/3 Triad membership fees are scaled on the basis of how much the recruit is prepared to pay or can be made to pay.

**scalie** ('skeɪlɪ), n. Austral. slang. [f. SCALE n.[1] + -IE.] An official who checks that the load of a road transport vehicle is not above the permitted weight.
**1976** Truckin' Life I. III. 47 His parting words to Harry left no doubt that the scalies would be waiting for him at the end of the tough road. **1979** Truck & Bus Transportation Sept. 90/2 Axle load limits, very much a talking point in Australia—are quoted in Imperial tons, 32 is the permissable gross, but axle weights are measured in kgs by road 'scalies'. **1984** Bulletin (Sydney) 7 Aug. 68/1 Detours through the back roads to avoid the 'scalies' who man the highway truck-weight checking stations. **1986** Truckin' Life Aug. 18/3 There's a scalie around the N.S.W. north coast who can tell how heavy you are by the temperature of your tyres.

**scallop**, n. Add: [2.] d. An escalope.
**1723** J. NOTT Cook's & Confectioner's Dict. sig. D7, Take . . Scollops of Veal or Mutton larded with Bacon. **1845** E. ACTON Mod. Cookery ix. 218 Slice very thin the white part of some cold veal, divide and trim it into scallops not larger than a shilling. **1986** B. FUSSELL Eating In vi. 67 For traditional veal scalloppine, instead of breading the scallops, dust them with seasoned flour and sauté.

**scammer** ('skæmə(r)), n. slang (orig. U.S.). Also skammer. [f. SCAM v. + -ER[1], perh. after SCHEMER n.] A criminal, esp. a petty crook or swindler; one who lives outside the law by his or her wits.

**1972** J. WAMBAUGH Blue Knight (1973) v. 69 You been a friggin' scammer all your life, fracturing every friggin' law you had nuts enough to crack. **1974** Rolling Stone 26 Sept. 91/1 Trader Red was a dope smuggler, or skammer as he preferred to be called. **1980** L. SANDERS Tenth Commandment (1981) III. vii. 373 'You're good,' he said, 'but not that good. Never try to scam a scammer.' **1982** TV Times Mag. 19 June 9/1 There's a word for Stan [Ogden] . . and you won't find it in a dictionary. The word is scammer. For the uninitiated, it means someone who practises the art and craft of the workshy . . , ensuring oneself of a living wage without, heaven forbid, working. **1984** N.Y. Times 25 Nov. (Long Island Weekly section) 29/2, I roll cigarettes, talk to mysterious strangers over the phone and try to outscam the scammers. **1989** Internat. Business Week 6 Mar. 20/1 Costa Rica's growing popularity among scammers was scaring off legitimate investment.

**scammered** ('skæməd), a. slang. ?Obs. [Of uncertain origin:
Partridge links the word with the dial. scammed 'injured, bruised', or Somerset dial. scammish 'rough, awkward, untidy' (Eng. Dial. Dict.); cf. also north dial. scam 'a stain, stigma', scam v., scamy adj. (Northumb. Words 1893).]
Intoxicated, drunk.
**1859** HOTTEN Dict. Slang 86 Scammered, drunk. **1891** 'F. W. CAREW' No. 747 xxxvii. 435 He'll think he was scammered overnight. **1940** M. SADLEIR Fanny by Gaslight II. 385 He's badly scammered, and out for women.

**Scamperdale** ('skæmpədeɪl), n. Saddlery. [Prob. f. the name of Lord Scamperdale in R. S. Surtees's Mr. Sponge's Sporting Tour (1853).] A type of Pelham bit (see PELHAM n.) in which the mouthpiece is angled back to prevent chafing.
**1934** W. FAWCETT Riding & Horsemanship iv. 51 Here is a bit which has been invented by a friend of mine. It is called the 'Scamperdale' and is the best bit I know. **1938** S. MARSH Hunting, Showing & 'Chasing iii. 59 My experience of the pelham has been that it is so liable to pinch the lips and jaw-bone, a drawback which I have overcome with a straight-barred bit in introducing the 'Scamperdale' bit with movable mouth and inverted ends. **1952** R. S. SUMMERHAYS Encycl. for Horsemen 243/1 Scamperdale Pelham Bit. An angle mouth, straight bar bit made popular by Sam Marsh. **1965** C. E. G. HOPE Riding v. 63 Other varieties of Pelham are: . . Scamperdale . . . It was introduced by Mr Sam Marsh. **1981** E. HARTLEY-EDWARDS Country Life Bk. Saddlery & Equipment 128/3 The Scamperdale has the mouthpiece turned back.

**scapegoat**, n. Add: Hence **'scapegoatism** n. = SCAPEGOATING n.
**1961** in WEBSTER. **1969** Worship XLIII. 630 The dedicated anti-Communist [is] . . an apostle of scapegoatism. **1983** Times 7 July 1/7 The American action, he said, was 'a prime example of scapegoatism'.

**scarf**, n.[1] Add: [3.] [a.] Also, a square piece of material worn tied (usu. folded) round the head; = SQUARE n. 10 e.
**1917** Harrods Gen. Catal. 1420 (caption) Chiffon Motor Scarf, wide hem-stitched border . . in all the latest shades. 4/6. **1959** Encounter Oct. 32/2 A voile scarf tied babushka-style. **1978** J. MORRIS Oxford II. ii. 15 Despondent women look in with Paisley scarves on their heads, on their way to scrub floors or clean office desks. **1988** N. LOWNDES Chekago iv. 184 Marina looks silly in that pill-box hat . . . Why couldn't she have worn a scarf?

**SCART** (skɑːt), n.[4] Electronics. Also Scart, scart. [a. Fr., acronym f. the initial letters of Syndicat des Constructeurs des Appareils Radiorécepteurs et Téléviseurs, the committee which designed the connector.] Used *attrib.* with reference to a 21-pin socket used to connect video equipment. Cf. *EUROCONNECTOR n.*, *PERITELEVISION n.*

**1983** *Television* Dec. 73/2 Fidelity's Model CM14 14in. colour monitor will accept RGB, RGBY or a composite video input, plus audio, via a 21-pin scart socket. **1984** [see *EUROCONNECTOR n.*]. **1986** *Video World* Dec. 55/3 You need to use a SCART plug even for the relatively routine task of copying to and from other video, or feeding a video monitor. **1988** *What Video?* July 46/3 All audio/video connections are routed via the now seemingly ubiquitous Scart socket. *Ibid.* Nov. 87/2 It's worth noting..that Philips actually give a pin-out diagram of the Scart connections in the owner's manual.

**scattergraph** ('skætəgrɑːf, -græf), *n.* Statistics. Also as two words. [f. SCATTER *n.* + GRAPH *n.*] = SCATTERGRAM *n.*

**1935** KURTZ & EDGERTON *Dict. Statistical Terms & Symbols* s2 *Scattergraph*, same as scatter diagram. **1968** *Economist* 10 Aug. 68/3 Our 'scattergraph' shows the five-year record of the trusts measured against their market value. **1986** *Eng. World-Wide* VII. 37 The scatter graph..plots the Rounding scores against the Fronting scores.

**scavenge** ('skævɪndʒ), *n.* (Formerly at SCAVENGE *v.*) [f. SCAVENGE *v.*] **1.** = SCAVENGING *vbl. n.* 2 a. Freq. *attrib.*

**1912** A. P. CHALKLEY *Diesel Engines* vi. 156 On the up stroke the scavenge ports..are closed before the exhaust ports. **1925** *Glasgow Herald* 1 Apr. 11/2 This new type of engine, with its straight through scavenge and absence of air and exhaust valves. **1930** *Engineering* 21 Nov. 645/3 The scavenge pumps for the Junkers engine are mounted on the locomotive frame. **1949** T. D. WALSHAW *Diesel Engine Design* xviii. 338 Typical figures for an engine supercharged to give 50 per cent. increase in available B.H.P. are: 30 per cent. through scavenge (i.e. a volume of air equal to 30 per cent. of the cylinder volume is swept through the exhaust valve), and the amount of overlap would be about 135°. **1955** *Know your Tractor* (Shell) i. 11 The air for combustion assists removal of the exhaust gases; it is therefore known as 'scavenge' air, and its admission to the engine as 'scavenging'. **1957** [see LUBE *n.* and *v.*]. **1975** A. J. WHARTON *Diesel Engines: Questions & Answers* 19 Even in slow running engines, this allows only a very short period of time for scavenge to be completed.

**2.** An act of scavenging, in senses 2 b and 3 b of the vb.

Webster (1934) gives '*Scavenge, n.*, act or process of scavenging' but it is not clear whether this reflects anything other than sense 1.

**1978** *Guardian Weekly* 17 Sept. 24/3 Wales's twice-annual scavenge for Arms Park international tickets. **1982** P. FITZGERALD *At Freddie's* iii. 24 The others ran, like little half-tame animals on the scavenge, through the alleys of the great market.

**scenographer**, *n.* Add: **2.** A designer of theatrical scenery.

**1928** *Art Bull.* X. 243 The neoclassic period had great scenographers like the Venetian Pietro Gonzaga. **1938** *New Statesman* 23 July 152/2, I think he made a vital mistake in his scenographer, that very gifted artist Christian Bérard, who was occasionally so successful in the *Symphonie Fantastique.* **1966** *Romanian Rev.* XX. iv. 100 The architect who has abandoned his..field to serve the theatre, as scenographer, may wonder whether he has not preferred a minor branch of the profession. **1973** *Cosmopolitan* July 27/1 Scenographer Derek Jarmon has transformed a City of London loft with low tables, mattresses and cushions, and an enormous string hammock slung from wall to wall. **1989** *Chicago Tribune* 7 May XIII. 28/1 The young scenographer's introduction to architecture came in

the middle 1970s, when he was helping design a production of 'As You Like It'.

**scenography**, *n.* Add: **3.** The design of theatrical scenery; scenic design.

**1928** *Art Bull.* X. 248 The schools of scenography were closed because a few specialized artists were sufficient to meet the demand of the managers. **1938** *New Statesman* 23 July 152/2 Here the element of decor or scenography has a chance to show its importance in the art of ballet. **1965** *World Theatre* XIV. 303/2 It has the reputation of being the only Institute of its kind..where a systematic study is undertaken of scenography. **1971** J. BURIAN *Scenogr. J. Svoboda* I. 9 He taught a course on scenography for directors. **1983** *Daily Tel.* 19 Sept. 12/8, I don't like that improvisation, it doesn't go with the concept of the show, which is all tied into one knot—mise-en-scène, music, balletic moves, the 'scenography' of the whole. **1988** *Renaissance Stud.* II. 235 More likely, however, was simply the greater degree of importance attached to the functional meaning and historic associations of the *entrata.* The erudition of the processional scenography hid from no one's view the quintessential affirmation of power.

**schafskopf** ('ʃɑːfskɔpf), *n.* Cards. Also schaffskopf, schafkopf. [a. Ger., f. *Schaf* sheep + *Kopf* head.] = SHEEP'S HEAD *n.* 2 b.

**1886** E. E. LEMCKE *Skat* 4 Skat..bears a great resemblance to the Wendish game of '*Schafskopf*' (Sheepshead). **1913**, **1951** [see SHEEP'S HEAD *n.* 2 b.]. **1960** *Economist* 12 Mar. 989/1 Presidential candidates beat their way..to shake hands with *schafskopf* players in the back rooms of taverns, and to greet factory workers at 5 o'clock in the morning. **1978** *Fortune* 22 May 45/1 Cards are on hand for those who like to play *Schafskopf*—Sheep's Head, a traditional Milwaukee-German game—after lunch in one of the half-dozen ornate booths.

**schedular** ('ʃedjʊlə(r), U.S. 'skɛdjʊlə(r)), *a.* [f. SCHEDULE *n.* + -AR¹, after F. *cédulaire* (1796).] Of or pertaining to a schedule; (esp. of a system of taxation) organized according to a schedule.

**1928** *Daily Tel.* 30 Oct. 10 A bi-lateral convention for countries which do not discriminate between 'schedular' and 'global' taxes. **1949** M. B. CARROLL in A. G. Buehler et al. *Income Tax Administration* (Tax Inst. Inc.) xliii. 391 Many of the European states have a so-called schedular tax on dividends in addition to the tax on profits payable by the company. **1955** N. DENNIS *Cards of Identity* II. 137 Information on all matters must..be..given *in advance* to all committees so as to avoid schedular confusion. **1964** ECKSTEIN & TANZI in *Role Direct & Indirect Taxes in Fed. Revenue Syst.* (Conf. Rep. Nat. Bureau Econ. Res. & Brookings Inst.) 223 Italy has a schedular income tax in addition to a global tax. **1978** KAY & KING *Brit. Tax Syst.* vi. 96 The schedular system—by which the year of assessment and date of payment do not necessarily correspond and differ for different kinds of income. **1988** *Financial Times* 2 Sept. 9/2 The administrative difficulties resulting from the UK's complex schedular taxation system.

**Scheiner** ('ʃaɪnə(r)), *n.*¹ The name of Christoph Scheiner (*c*1575-1650), German astronomer and experimenter, used in the possessive and (formerly) with *of* to designate various concepts introduced by him, as **Scheiner's experiment** (also †**experiment of Scheiner**) *Ophthalm.*, an experiment to demonstrate accommodation and the focusing ability of the eye in which when two objects are viewed in line through a pair of pinholes made close together in a card held near one eye, the object not in focus appears as a double image (now *rare*); **Scheiner's halo** *Astron.*, a faintly luminous halo occasionally observed around the sun or moon at an angle of

23°–32°, due to refraction of light by pyramidal ice crystals in the upper atmosphere.

**1870** *Amer. Jrnl. Med. Sci.* LX. 414 In the number of this Journal for January, 1870, will be found a description of a test for ametropia, based on the experiment of *Scheiner. **1886** C. M. CULVER tr. *Landolt's Refraction & Accomm. of Eye* iii. 243 When one looks at a small object placed at a distance for which the eye is not adapted, through minute openings, the distance between which is less than the diameter of the pupil, the object appears multiple . . . This is known as Scheiner's experiment. [**1905** *Compt. Rend.* CXL. 1368 Qu'il me soit permis encore d'expliquer la tache irisée, semblable au sommet du halo ordinaire et distante du Soleil de 28°, qu'a vue et mesurée M. Besson. Elle était, sans doute, un fragment du halo de Scheiner.] **1983** *Jrnl. Physical Chem.* LXXXVII. 4177/1 The second sighting of *Scheiner's halo was made in 1677. **1987** *Sci. Amer.* May 51/2 Diamond-shaped ice gives rise to a rarely detected atmospheric phenomenon called Scheiner's halo.

**scheming**, *ppl. a.* Add: Hence 'schemingly *adv.*

**1895** *Funk's Stand. Dict.*, Schemingly, adv., in a scheming manner; like a schemer. **1979** *Summary of World Broadcasts* (B.B.C.) 15 June (Far East) III. A3/1 They schemingly proposed changing the venue of and delaying the sixth session of the non-aligned conference.

**schiffli** ('ʃɪflɪ), *n.* [Swiss Ger., = G. *Schiffchen* shuttle.] Used *attrib.* to designate (*a*) a type of embroidery machine with diagonal shuttles which work on fabric stretched on a movable frame; (*b*) a style of fine embroidery done on such a machine. Also occas. *absol.* and *adverbially*, as *schiffli embroidered.*

**1892** G. S. COLE *Compl. Dict. Dry Goods* (rev. ed.) 123 In 1875 a machine, called the 'Schiffli', was invented and worked by steam . . . The embroideries made by this machine are usually known as 'Schiffli goods'. **1923** E. DYER *Textile Fabrics* x. 164 Plauen, *Schiffli*, and *burnt* laces all refer to laces made on the Schiffli machine. **1946** BENDURE & PFEIFFER *America's Fabrics* xiii. 404 A *schiffli machine* is not a lace machine but an embroidery machine. *Ibid.* 407 The schiffli can make many lace patterns. **1960** *Textile Terms & Definitions* (Textile Inst.) (ed. 4) 125 *Schiffli Embroidery Machine*, an embroidery machine consisting of a multiplicity of lockstitch sewing elements working on a basic net or fabric which is attached to a frame which is movable vertically and horizontally according to the requirements of the pattern. **1984** *Sears Catal.* 1985 Spring/Summer 1288 Ensemble features authentic schiffli embroidery on the entire top of the bedspread. **1986** *Meredith* (New Hampsh.) *News* 9 July 19/2 The maid of honor . . wore a gown of maize matte taffeta with scalloped schiffli embroidered bodice.

**schlong** (ʃlɒŋ), *n. U.S. slang.* Also shlong. [ad. Yiddish *shlang*, f. MHG *slange* (G. *Schlange*) serpent.] The penis. Also applied contemptuously to a person.

**1969** P. ROTH *Portnoy's Complaint* 50 His *shlong* brings to mind the fire hoses coiled along the corridors at school. **1978** J. KRANTZ *Scruples* i. 6 'You,' she said . . , 'are a putz, a schmekel, a schmuck, a schlong . . .' **1985** E. LEONARD *Glitz* xii. 106 Witness saw him cut the guy's schlong off. **1985** T. BOYLE *Only Dead know Brooklyn* xxv. 218 He's stark naked and he's got about the longest schlong I ever seen on a white man.

**schlump** (ʃlʊmp), *n. slang* (chiefly *U.S.*). Also schloomp, shlump. [App. a Yiddish formation; cf. Yiddish *shlumperdik* dowdy, cogn. w. G. *Schlumpe* slattern.] A dull-witted, slow, or

slovenly person; a slob; a fool. Freq. used as a term of affectionate abuse.

**1948** *Life* 15 Mar. 23/2 Schlump is a friendlier, more sympathetic term than 'schmo', which has completely replaced 'jerk'. **1968** L. ROSTEN *Joys of Yiddish* 350 That *shlump* can depress anyone. **1979** J. HELLER *Good as Gold* viii. 350 Kissinger would not be recalled in history as a Bismarck . . but as an odious *shlump* who made war gladly. **1980** *Washington Post* 20 Nov. F1/1 She was the All-American schlump, the 'she's so pretty, too bad she can't lose some weight' working girl, the patron saint of imperfect. **1986** *Daily News* (N.Y.) 23 May (Suppl.) 10/1, I laughed at a poor schlump being gobbled up by a giant Venus flytrap. **1987** S. BELLOW *More die of Heartbreak* 39 To Dad, Benn was a schlump, an incompetent.

**schmeer**, *n.* Substitute for etymology: [f. *SCHMEER v.*]

**schmeer** (ʃmɪə(r)), *v. N. Amer. colloq.* Also schmear, schmere, shmear, shmeer, shmir. [ad. Yiddish *shmirn* to smear, grease, flatter.] *trans.* To flatter; to bribe. Also *absol.*

**1930** *Amer. Speech* VI. 126 Schmeer . . , meaning 'smear', is used figuratively in the sense of complimenting a customer, praising her appearance or her taste, and thereby encouraging a sale. **1945** A. KOBER *Parm Me* 154 With one hend they gung to give you the money and with the odder hend they sticking out to collect yet a tip . . . Sooo . . you *shmere* here, you *shmere* there, and when you finndished *shmereing* hommuch is left by you in pockit? **1964** W. MARKFIELD *To Early Grave* (1965) iv. 66 Nickie the elevator man . . the more you *shmeer* him the more he hates your guts. **1968** L. ROSTEN *Joys of Yiddish* 353 Do the officials expect to be *shmeered* there? **1986** S. STEINMETZ *Yiddish & English* v. 67 Shmir . . . In Yiddish slang it also means 'a bribe' (and as a verb, *shmirn* 'to bribe').

**school**, *n.*[1] Add: [I.] [3.] e. *U.S.* A course of training given by an organization to its staff.

**1935** E. W. WILLIAMS *Fire Fighting* i. 7 Good energetic men . . know that competition for higher positions is keen and that the instruction received in the school will better enable them to hold such positions. **1974** *News & Press* (Darlington, S. Carolina) 25 Apr. 1/5 Members of the Darlington, Hartsville, Timmonsville and Lamar police departments during an in-service school held last week at Lake Darpo. Also present for the school were members of the Darlington County Sheriff's Department.

**schoolie** ('skuːlɪ), *n.*[2] *Angling colloq.* [f. SCHOOL *n.*[2] + -IE; cf. the rare earlier SCHOOLY *n.* with a more specialized sense.] Any small fish that is normally found in a school or shoal.

**1980** *Outdoor Life* (U.S.) (Northeast ed.) Oct. 122/2, I asked Mann about using the worm on schoolies and learned that indeed he had fished plastic crawlers behind a cork quite a bit larger than the Skimmer Head. **1986** *Sea Angling Handbk.* Summer 41/2, I was amazed at . . the fight this schoolie put up. **1987** *Courier-Mail* (Brisbane) 3 July (Great Outdoors Suppl.) 5/5 The smaller 'schoolies' are particularly fond of beach worms but will accept most surf baits.

**schooly** ('skuːlɪ), *a. colloq.* [f. SCHOOL *n.*[1] + -Y[1].] Suitable for school; having the typical or traditional characteristics of a school.

**1963** C. GLYN *Don't knock Corners Off* x. 84 'Well, I'll think of something schooly', she said. **1971** *Petticoat* 24 July 3/4 The perfect accessories are long schooly sox. **1981** E. NORTH *Dames* vi. 97 It was not . . an ordinary school. It must not be a schooly school. **1982** BARR & YORK *Official Sloane Ranger Handbk.* 80/1 Girls' boarding schools are on the whole far more trad and schooly than boys' boarding schools.

**Schotten–Baumann** ('ʃɒtən 'baʊmən), n. Organic Chem. The names of Carl Ludwig Schotten (1853-1910) and Eugen Baumann (1846-96), German chemists, used attrib. (esp. as Schotten-Baumann method, reaction) and occas. in the possessive with reference to a type of reaction in which a primary or secondary amine reacts with an acid halide in basic aqueous solution to form an amide; also used with reference to analogous reactions involving primary and secondary alcohols.
**1895** Jrnl. Chem. Soc. LXVIII. I. 139 A convenient modification of the Schotten-Baumann method is also suggested. **1902** J. B. COHEN Theoret. Org. Chem. xxxiv. 468 A simple and rapid method for preparing small quantities of esters .. is that known as Schotten-Baumann's reaction. **1920** A. K. MACBETH Org. Chem. xxv. 214 The operation is carried out by shaking the substance with benzoyl chloride and dilute alkali ... The is known as the Schotten-Baumann reaction. **1935** P. H. GROGGINS Unit Processes in Org. Synthesis x. 514 As the esters formed by the Schotten-Baumann method are insoluble in the aqueous alkali, they are readily separated. **1958** PACKER & VAUGHAN Mod. Approach to Org. Chem. xxiv. 788 An improvement on the original Schotten-Baumann method is the use of pyridine in place of aqueous alkali. **1964** N. G. CLARK Mod. Org. Chem. xxiii. 485 'Benzoylation' is .. often used for characterizing amines, and may also be performed by a Schotten-Baumann technique. **1981** J. W. BUTTLE et al. Chemistry (ed. 4) xxi. 461 The more usual derivative for amines, however, is the benzenecarboxamide, prepared from benzoyl chloride (the Schotten-Baumann reaction).

‖**schwerpunkt** ('ʃveːrpʊŋkt), n. [G. Schwerpunkt centre of gravity, focal point, f. schwer heavy, weighty + Punkt point.] Focus, emphasis; strong point; esp. Mil., the point of main effort.
**1952** C. WILMOT Struggle for Europe i. 19 He [sc. Hitler] had insisted on placing the Schwerpunkt of the offensive in the Ardennes. **1961** J. H. PLUMB Sir Robert Walpole II. ii. 51 Hanover would be the diplomatic schwerpunkt of Europe, where Southern as well as Northern problems would have to be solved. **1970** J. MARSHALL-CORNWALL Grant as Mil. Commander xvi. 125 During the day Bragg realized that the Schwerpunkt of Grant's attack was directed on the right flank at Tunnel Hill. **1988** Foreign Affairs Spring 738 Once a suitable gap [in NATO's defences] has been found, it becomes the schwerpunkt .. through which the Soviets pour available operational maneuver groups and reinforcements.

‖**Schwundstufe** ('ʃvʊnt͜ʃtuːfə), n. Philol. [Ger., f. Schwund diminution, loss + Stufe step, grade.] = zero grade s.v. ZERO n. 7 d.
**1897** Jrnl. Germanic Philol. I. 295 ī the 'schwundstufe' of eị (o). **1900** H. H. CHADWICK in Indogerman. Forsch. XI. 153 According to this, -ē- represents an older -ēi-, the regular schwundstufe thereto being shown by -ī- which appears in other .. forms. **1900** Amer. Jrnl. Philol. XXI. 181 It is also possible that the base tu̯ī- 'dwindle, waste away' may be the schwundstufe of tāu-io-. **1933** PMLA XLVIII. 1039 Verbs of motion are .. likely to have a Schwundstufe present in Germanic.

‖**Schwung** (ʃvʊŋ), n. [Ger., = swing, energy, vitality.] Energy; verve; panache.
**1930** Times Lit. Suppl. 30 Oct. 893/1 That crisp tailored little figure with her dash of chic, of Schwung and pep. **1974** Times 8 Mar. 12/6 The more Maazel conducts the orchestra these days, the more one regrets that he is no longer its chief. Their

accompanying of the Rachmaninov C minor concerto had just the Schwung lacking in the soloist's contribution. **1979** Nature 5 July 48/1 Superimposed on this general trend, Suess drew with 'cosmic schwung', medium-term variations through his data.

**sciapod** ('saɪəpɒd), n. Also skiapod ('skiːəpɒd). [Either a back-formation from SCIAPODES n. pl. or a new formation on its Latin or Gr. base.] A monster of medieval iconography having the form of a man with a single large foot; one of the Sciapodes.
**1915** G. C. DRUCE in Archaeol. Jrnl. CCLXXXVI. 141 Below the giant is the sciapod, a very interesting prodigy. **1945** H. H. HENSON Jrnl. 16 Dec. in Retrospect (1950) III. vi. 309 He showed us the most interesting features of the church, the carved pews, the bench-ends including the Skiapod. **1955** M. D. ANDERSON Imagery Brit. Churches III. xiii. 182 On a bench-end at Dennington (Suffolk) the sciapod is shown lying under the shade of his feet (the carver has incorrectly given him two). **1973** P. WHITE Eye of Storm v. 200 She became spellbound by the artist's image of what he called a skiapod .. this half-fish half-woman. **1983** W. WEAVER tr. Eco's Name of Rose 337 Sciopods [sic], who run swiftly on their single leg and when they want to take shelter from the sun stretch out and hold up their great foot like an umbrella.

**scientific**, a. and n. Add: [A.] [3.] b. Site of Special Scientific Interest, an area of land designated (and thereby protected) by the Nature Conservancy Council as of special scientific interest in terms of flora, fauna, or geology; = S.S.S.I. s.v. S 4.
[**1949** National Parks & Access to Countryside Act 12, 13 & 14 Geo. VI c. 97 §23 (side-note) Duty of Conservancy to inform local planning authorities of areas of special scientific interest.] **1953** Rep. Nature Conservancy to 30th Sept. 1952 i. 8 (heading) Sites of special scientific interest. **1962** (title) Notifications under the National Parks .. Act, 1949 in East Riding, Yorkshire. Sites of Special Scientific Interest (S.S.S.I.) notified under Section 23. **1979** Jrnl. R. Soc. Arts CXXVII. 405/2 The whole of the harbour and its shorelines have been defined as a Site of Special Scientific Interest. **1986** Oban Times 22 May 2 It was declared a site of special scientific interest in 1974 and is an important area for all year round mountain recreation.

**scientifical**, a. Add: Hence **scientifi'cality** n., the property or quality of being scientifical; = SCIENTIFICITY n.
Orig. as a translation of Nietzsche's Wissenschaftlichkeit.
**1909** J. M. KENNEDY tr. Nietzsche's Wks. III. 84 Whither shall the poor fellows fly .. —where but to the most obtuse, sterile scientificality .. ? **1978** World Marxist Rev. Oct. 13 World realities, manifested in infinitely different forms .. furnish clear proof of the scientificality of Marxism.

**scientometrics** (,saɪəntəʊ'mɛtrɪks), n. pl. (const. as sing.). Information Sci. [Prob. tr. Russ. naukometriya (Nalimov & Mul'chenko Naukometriya (1969)), f. naúka science: cf. scient- (in L. scientia knowledge) and *BIBLIOMETRICS n. pl.] The branch of information science concerned with the application of bibliometrics to the study of the spread of scientific ideas; the bibliometric analysis of science.
[**1963** D. J. DE S. PRICE Little Sci., Big Sci. ii. 55, I think we have now laid the theoretical basis for this study of science. It is remarkably similar to the study of econometrics.] **1976** Survey Spring 70 There are two major sources of science statistics in the USSR: publications of the Central Statistical Directorate .. and research literature devoted to scientometrics.

**1984** *Nature* 16 Aug. 608/1 The reliance on citations was part of the 'science of science' movement led by Bernal's disciple D. J. Price, and now carried on as 'scientometrics'.

So **sciento'metric** *a.*, **sciento'metrical** *a.*, of or pertaining to scientometrics.

**1976** *Survey* Spring 72 Whatever shortcomings the Soviet scientometrical literature may have, it does represent an important source of science indicators. **1977** *Eurim II* (Aslib) 57/2 The theme of a conference organized by the institute led by the author was the intensification of scientometric activities. **1988** *Scientometrics* XIV. 467 (*heading*) Conclusions and scientometric consequences.

**scissors**, *n. pl.* Add: [2.] **g.** *Angling.* The fleshy area on the side of the jaw of a game fish.

**1951** C. RICHARDS *Informative Fishing* ix. 159 Some are hooked back in the throat, I will admit, others in the gills, but many can be—and are—hooked as cleanly as in any other form of bait fishing. I have had them caught in the lip and in the scissors. **1987** *Trout & Salmon* Mar. 82/4 But fishing something just subsurface in a twisting, boisterous stream . . also results in a trout taking and becoming hooked in the scissors before the angler is conscious of any such interception.

**scolecodont** ('skəʊlɪkəʊ,dɒnt), *n. Palæont.* [f. Gr. σκωληκ(ο)-, σκώληξ worm + ὀδοντ-, ὀδούς tooth.] The jaw of an annelid worm, found as a microfossil in some rocks.

**1933** CRONEIS & SCOTT in *Bull. Geol. Soc. Amer.* XLIV. 207 Recent investigations have shown that annelid worm jaws . . are actually common paleontologic objects. Because of their probable importance in future micropaleontologic investigations, we are, for convenience, here proposing for these fossils the designation *Scolecodonts.* **1961** J. CHALLINOR *Dict. Geol.* 176/1 Scolecodonts are found fossil [*sic*] from the Ordovician onwards. They are composed of silica and chitin, the latter becoming carbonized to a jet black appearance in the process of fossilization. **1989** *Nature* 5 Jan. 28/2 Among the objects of interest are acritarchs, . . chitinozoans, scolecodonts, . . and pteridophyte spores.

**scombrotoxic** (skɒmbrəʊ'tɒksɪk), *a. Path.* [f. Gr. σκόμβρο-ς (see SCOMBER *n.*) + TOXIC *a.*] Involving or designating a kind of poisoning caused by eating the decomposed flesh of scombroid fish, which may contain high levels of histamine and other toxins, or by eating similarly contaminated canned fish, and having symptoms similar to those of allergic reactions to histamine; also applied to the toxins causing this reaction and to fish which may contain them.

**1967** B. W. HALSTEAD *Poisonous & Venomous Marine Animals of World* II. vi. 640 (*heading*) List of fishes reported as scombrotoxic. *Ibid.* 646 With the increasing amount of evidence that bacteria had a direct bearing on histamine production it was important to identify the strains of bacteria responsible for this activity, and to determine whether histamine was indeed the scombrotoxic agent. **1980** *Brit. Med. Jrnl.* 5 July 71/1 Fifty incidents of scombrotoxic fish poisoning affecting nearly 200 people have been reported in Britain, the majority in 1979. **1981** *Ibid.* 14 Feb. 572/1 Scombrotoxic fish poisoning as seen in Britain is usually due to mackerel which has been stored too long unrefrigerated.

**scope** *v.*[2] Restrict '†*Obs. rare*' to senses in Dict. and add: **3.** *to scope out*, to investigate or assess (a person or a state of affairs); to examine; to check out. *U.S. slang.*

**1977** *Amer. Speech 1975* L. 65 *Scope out vt*, investigate. 'Let's scope out the situation.' **1984** J.

McINERNY *Bright Lights* 33 You have scoped out and fixed a number of colossal blunders. **1986** R. B. PARKER *Taming Sea-Horse* (1987) xv. 91, I . . leaned against the front wall . . and scoped things out. **1988** *Analog* Feb. 74/2 They'd scoped-out their market and created a product that customers wanted to buy at a price they were willing to pay.

**Scorpius** ('skɔːpɪəs), *n. Astron.* [a. L. *scorpius*: see SCORPION *n.*]
Occurring only as an occasional variant of *Scorpio* until it was readopted, orig. in the US, in the 20th c.]
= SCORPIO *n.* 1.

*c*1000 in *Leechd. Early Eng.* (1866) III. 246 An þæra tacna ýs ʒehaten aries. Þ is ramm . . . Seofoða libra. Þæt is pund oððe pæʒe. Eahtoðe scorpius. Þ is þropend. *a*1450 in F. N. Robinson *Chaucer's Wks.* (1957) 551/1 Tho lokid I doun upon myn est orisounte, and fond there 10 degrees of Scorpius ascendyng, whom I tok for myn ascendent. **1589** [see CLUTCH *n.*[1] 1 g]. **1926** G. FORBES *Wonder & Glory of Stars* i. 22 Names of Constellations, with three-letter abbreviations officially adopted: And = Andromeda . . Scl = Sculptor . . Sco = Scorpius (the Scorpion). **1955** *Sci. News Let.* 25 June 407/1 To the left, we see the fine summer constellation of Scorpius, the scorpion, in which red Antares is prominent. **1964** [see COSMIC *a.* 3 b]. **1987** P. MOORE *Astron. Encycl.* 374/1 Scorpius (the Scorpion—often less correctly, called Scorpio).

**scotch** *n.*[4], var. *SCUTCH *n.*[4]

**scotch** *v.*[3], var. *SCUTCH *v.*[3]

**scotching** *vbl. n.*, var. *scutching* vbl. n. s.v. *SCUTCH *v.*[3]

**scotoma**, *n.* Add: Hence **sco'tomatous** *a.*, pertaining to, characterized by, or affected by a scotoma or scotomata.

**1900** in DORLAND *Med. Dict.* **1970** O. SACKS *Migraine* iii. 73 Cardinal characteristics of migraine aura, in its visual (scotomatous), tactile (paraesthetic), and aphasic forms. **1973** *Nature* 1 June 295/1 The patient seems to be unable to distinguish between the presence and absence of visually presented targets whenever they are presented in the scotomatous area.

**scotophor** ('skəʊtəʊfɔː(r)), *n. Electronics.* [f. SCOTO-[2] + -*phor* after PHOSPHOR *n.*] Any substance which darkens when bombarded with electrons, and which may therefore be used as a coating for the screens of cathode-ray tubes in order to provide the reverse of the imaging behaviour of phosphor coatings.

**1946** [see TENEBRESCENCE *n.*]. **1955** *Electronics* Feb. 170/1 Potassium chloride (KCL) has been found to be the most suitable scotophor, or screen material, for practical dark-trace tubes. **1968** *U.S. Pat.* *3,413,505* 1 This disclosure deals with a dark trace cathode-ray tube including a scotophor screen and improved means for erasing an image from the screen. **1983** K. NASSAU *Physics & Chem. Color* ix. 199 Suitably doped KCl has been used as a scotophore [*sic*] 'dark-bearer', providing a slowly bleaching phosphor in a radar display-type cathode ray tube.

**Scotticize**, *v.* Add: Hence ,Scottici'zation *n.*, the action or process of making Scottish.

**1968-9** *Ethnologia Europaea* II.-III. 118 The land names suggest changes due largely to scotticisation of language and forms of land holding and land use. **1986** W. KAY *Scots* (1988) 62 His text has a similar degree of anglicisation of style or scotticisation of English as his predecessor's.

**Scottish**, *a.* and *n.* Add: Hence **'Scottishly** *adv.*

**1814** Byron *Let.* 3 May (1975) IV. 113 The Camesa or Kilt (to speak Scottishly). **1976** *Times* 8 July 16/2 He smiled Scottishly.

**scout**, *v.*[1] Add: **5.** *intr.* and *trans.* To observe and report on the performance of a team or club against which one is due to play. *Sport* (orig. and chiefly *U.S.*).

**1908** [implied in SCOUTING *vbl. n.*[1] 1 c]. **1941** *Sun* (Baltimore) 8 Oct. 13/4 Coaches Charlie Erickson and Dick Jamerson who scouted Fordham in its 16–10 win over Southern Methodist. **1961** [see SCOUTING *vbl. n.*[1] 1 c]. **1980** Hoy & Carter *Tackle Basketball* vii. 106 Firstly, well-prepared opponents may gain advance knowledge of their opposition's system by scouting and hearing the call, and so be in a position to thwart it. **1987** *First Base* Summer 12/1 He will have scouted the batters he is to face thoroughly.. will know who hits well and badly on the type of surface and time of day for that day's game.

**6.** orig. *N. Amer.* **a.** *trans.* To observe (a team, a company, etc.) with a view to recruiting suitably talented persons to one's organization (esp. a sports club); to assess (an individual) with this purpose.

**1936** *Esquire* Sept. 159/2 'Jesse Laskey's Broadway Booneing' means that the vet producer is scouting plays and talent in N.Y. **1972** *Hockey News* (Montreal) 6 Oct. 11/2, I remember the late Stafford Smythe telling me to scout the bush-league teams.. very carefully because the kids there were trying harder. **1977** *Rolling Stone* 5 May 45/4 Still, no one seems to have scouted him; he was offered no athletic scholarships. **1981** *N.Y. Times* 26 Oct. C2/2 Most of the pro teams have scouted him this season. Most of them look at him and say he's too small.

**b.** *intr.* To look for suitably talented persons with a view to recruiting them to one's organization; to act as a (talent) scout (see SCOUT *n.*[4] 2 e).

**1950** *Sport* 7–11 Apr. 14/1 He was scouting for Birmingham City at the time of his appointment to manage his old club. **1971** H. Seymour *Baseball: Golden Age* II. p. vi, I.. scouted unofficially.. for two major-league clubs. **1981** *Christian Science Monitor* 22 Oct. 14/3 After retiring as a player in 1960 Lasorda scouted for the Dodgers for five years, managed in the minor league system for seven, and spent four seasons as a coach. **1989** *Washington Post* 14 Sept. B6/1 All had either coached or scouted for Denver after their playing days.

**scow**, *n.*[2] Add: [1.] **d.** Used as a term of disparagement for an old, usu. clumsy boat. Also *transf. colloq.* (orig. and chiefly *N. Amer.*).

**1891** 'Mark Twain' *Lett.* (1917) II. xxxi. 557 We were allowed to go through the wrong arch, which brought us into a tourbillon below which tried to make this old scow stand on its head. **1922** E. O'Neill *Anna Christie* (1923) II. 50 What is a fine handsome woman like you doing on this scow? **1946** R. E. Higginbotham *Wine for my Brothers* vi. 149 The only pleasant thought in him the idea of getting off this scow when she reached port. **1958** E. A. McCourt *Revolt in West* ix. 76 The Police slipped out of the Fort.. and boarded an old scow on the Saskatchewan River. **1982** I. Asimov *Foundation's Edge* (1983) vi. 84 I've been looking for that hyper-relay as though I were on my old scow of a training ship, studying every part of the ship by eye. **1985** *Los Angeles Times* 4 Sept. III. 3/3 The old scow was quickly replaced by a new, sleeker craft and a highly competent crew.

**scow** (skaʊ), *n.*[3] [Perh. two words: in sense a, prob. a transf. use of SCOW *n.*[1]; sense b may represent a transf. use of SCOW *n.*[2] I.] **a.** *Orkney* and *Shetland.* 'A big gaunt woman' (G. Lamb, *Orkney Wordbk.* (1988) s.v.). **b.** *slang* (chiefly *U.S.*). A disparaging term for a woman.

**1866** T. Edmondston *Etym. Gloss. Shetland & Orkney Dial.* 99 'A great scow of a woman'—a tall, thin, bony woman. **1927** *Peace's Orkney Almanac* 135 Me hert's sair ower peerie Johnnie sweein' trou siccan a twa-faced scow. **1960** Wentworth & Flexner *Dict. Amer. Slang* 449/2 *Scow*,.. a large, ugly, and/or unpleasant woman. **1970** R. Lowell *Notebk.* 143 Often the Dutch were sacks, their women a sack, Obstinate, undefeated hull of the old scow. **1970** G. Greer *Female Eunuch* 265 More familiar terms in current usage refer to women as receptacles for refuse.. as.. scow.

**Scrabble**, *n.*[2] Add: Hence **'Scrabbler** *n.*, one who plays Scrabble.

**1954** Orleans & Jacobson *More Fun with Scrabble* i. 7 This book is designed to give the Scrabbler more opportunities to enjoy his Scrabble board and tiles. **1978** *Times Lit. Suppl.* 1 Dec. 1384/2 This innovative, intelligent and enjoyable dictionary will not serve for reading *Hamlet* or Burns..; scrabblers and crossword-puzzlers will find it uncooperative. **1989** *Los Angeles Times* 20 May v. 13/5 Higher-rated Scrabblers—like poker's master bluffers—frequently commit parricide with impunity.

**scrag**, *v.* Add: [1.] **e.** [Perh. back-formation on SCRAGGY *a.*[1], with ref. to the resultant appearance.] To scrape or drag (one's hair) *back* or *up.* Also *transf. rare.*

**1937** N. Coward *Present Indicative* I. 63 Stoj's appearance at night with her hair scragged back in Hinde's curlers. **1958** L. Durrell *Mountolive* xv. 291 Their little faces were heavily painted, their hair scragged up in ribbons and plaits. **1981** B. Ashley *Dodgem* vi. 132 The net curtain was scragged aside and she was over the sill.

**scrambler**, *n.* Add: **4.** A motor-cycle designed for use over rough terrain, esp. in moto-cross riding; = *trail-bike* s.v. TRAIL *n.*[1] 17. Also appositively, in *scrambler-bike.*

**1969** *Time* 2 May 31/1 The foursome would prefer tough scramblers, 'with big drive sprockets, knobby wheels—and more vroom'. **1977** *Belfast Tel.* 22 Feb. 26/9 (Advt.), Schoolboy Scrambler, excellent condition, £485 o.n.o. **1986** *N.Y. Times* 16 Nov. x. 16/3 Semver. rents bicycles at $8, mopeds at $10, scooters from $15 to $18 and cross-country scrambler bikes from $20 to $30. **1988** *Washington Post* 8 May (Book World) 15/2 Ralph is a modern shepherd, complete with scrambler-bike and a scrappy education.

**scrape**, *n.*[1] Add: [II.] [8.] **b.** *U.S. colloq.* A hand-to-hand fight, a skirmish; a brawl. Now *rare.*

**1812** *Massachusetts Spy* 19 Aug. 3/1 A scouting party of about 100 men went down towards Malden; when they arrived near the river Canau, they got into a scrape with about the same number of Indians. **1839** W. McNally *Evils & Abuses Naval & Merchant Service* 66 American and French seamen have never met on shore.. without a row and fight... Every American officer and seaman.. deplored the fatal termination of one of those scrapes, in which a young French lieutenant was killed. **1919** Mencken *Amer. Lang.* 81 Scrape (for fight or difficulty). [*Note*] Of late the word has lost its final *e* and shortened its vowel, becoming *scrap.* **1954** L. Armstrong *Satchmo* i. 8 There was a great big shooting scrape in the Alley.

**scraper**, *n.* Sense 11 in Dict. becomes 12. Add: [III.] **11.** *ellipt.* for SKY-SCRAPER *n.* 4.

**1928** *Melody Maker* Feb. 228/1 The 'Radiac' [theatre] was built somewhat squat in order to strike a note of originality amongst the 500 feet 'scrapers' which surrounded it. **1942** Berrey & Van den Bark *Amer. Thes. Slang* §83/11 Skyscraper,.. scraper. **1983** *Observer* 11 Dec. 25/1 Just over the crest stood the abandoned University of Chicago building, a charred,

SCRAPPY

black-stoned old scraper. **1988** *Courier-Mail* (Brisbane) 27 June 3/1 (*heading*) Premier queries scraper.

**scrappy**, *a.*¹ Add: **2.** Lean; scrawny; meagre. orig. and chiefly *U.S.*
 **1941** B. SCHULBERG *What makes Sammy Run?* v. 83 All the instinct for self-preservation of a scrappy kitten. **1985** N. SAHGAL *Rich like Us* xiii. 151, I couldn't hear his grumbling comment because lusty cheers and more Long Lives rose when Ravi announced loans at scrappy interest rates for Delhi's taxi drivers. **1987** T. WOLFE *Bonfire of Vanities* (1988) ix. 205 In his palmy days he had been pudgy, too, but he had looked 'scrappy' as the Yanks liked to say. **1988** *Coarse Fishing Handbk.* June/July 56/4 There are some scrappy sized pike living in the deeper areas, and you'll need the maggots to catch a dace, gudgeon or minnow for bait.

**scratch**, *n.*¹ Sense 5 c in Dict. becomes 5 d. Add: [I.] [5.] **c.** *Golf.* A handicap of zero; also, the number of strokes in which a player with a handicap of scratch might be expected to complete a course (cf. *scratch player*, sense 12 a below).
 **1897** *Country Life* 23 Jan. 82/2 Mr Glover, playing from scratch, was round in 86. **1905** H. VARDON *Compl. Golfer* xxii. 251 A player whose handicap was several strokes removed from scratch. **1941** R. R. MARETT *Jerseyman at Oxford* ix. 138, I was never really worth more than bare 'scratch', and clean outside the 'tiger' class. **1955** R. BROWNING *Hist. Golf* 126 Some outstanding player was rated at scratch, and others handicapped from him. **1982** S. B. FLEXNER *Listening to Amer.* 265 Each hole was assigned a *score, ground score*, or *scratch*, all meaning the number of strokes a moderately good player would be expected to take and which each player tried to equal or better. **1988** *Today's Golfer* July 144/3 By limiting overseas entrants to those with handicaps of scratch or better?
 [6.] **c.** A technique, freq. used in rap music, in which a record is briefly interrupted during play and manually rotated backwards and forwards to produce a rhythmic scratching effect; also, the style of music characterized by this.
 **1982** *Melody Maker* 4 Dec. 12/3 The New York Scratch 'n' Rap Revue. **1987** *New Musical Express* 14 Feb. 27/4 The 12″ dance record is an inevitable liaison with the hi-technology of synthesisers and the rough treatment of rap and scratch.
 **d.** *ellipt.* for *scratch video* (sense 12 b below).
 **1985** *Honey* June 18/2 Scratch is a playful reaction to the endless offerings and noise of 'the media'. It interrupts the normal passive flow of TV, bends it a bit. **1985** M. WILCOX et al. *Subverting Television* (pamphlet) 3/1 Just playing with the TV remote-control console, quickly switching stations at random, is a basic scratch. **1985** *Listener* 12 Dec. 20/2 Scratch is completely on the outskirts. **1986** *Photographer* May 26/1 A simple scratch can be built up by recording the chosen music/sound onto the audio channel of the video recorder then switch[ing] between channels as the vision is being recorded.
 [V.] [12.] [a.] For 'attributive uses of sense 5 b' read 'attributive uses, as (sense 5 b)', and add: (senses 6 c, d) *scratch band, -music, -record, -tape, technique*, etc.
 **1984** *N.Y. Times* 15 July VI. 45/1 Brahms wrote just what he wanted. He didn't have to think, 'Will a *scratch band in Duluth be able to play this?' **1987** *Blues & Soul* 3–16 Feb. 9/1 Faze One have fixed it for a 14 year old London rap fan who wrote to the popular show Jim'll Fix It asking to appear with a rap and scratch band. **1983** *N.Y. Times* 25 Dec. I. 47/1 On Tuesday, Mr. Hancock and a band that included the '*scratch' disk jockey Grand Mixer D. Street appeared at the Ritz. **1983** *Women's Wear Daily* 17 June 4/2 At the clubs for younger people,

like the 321 .., where KROQ DJs play frenetic pop and *scratch music. **1982** *N.Y. Rocker* Jan. 27/2 He created terms for the various sound effects he could achieve: violin phase, punch phase, fake phase, *scratch phase. **1988** *Listener* 31 Mar. 38/1 *Peace on Earth* had all the hallmarks of a technical exercise .. reminiscent of a disc jockey's '*scratch' recordings in the way it manipulated actuality to the detriment of 'meaning'. **1984** *Washington Post* 27 Apr. (Weekend section) 37/3 Brad Shapiro .. produces her outrageous records and stage show, backed by a fine funk outfit, flavored with horns and the latest *scratch and synth sounds. **1988** *Art* Feb. 31/1 Malcolm invited me to programme some *scratch tapes at the NFT. *Ibid.* 32/2 *In the Name of the Gun* used *scratch staccato techniques.
 [b.] **scratch-mix** *a.*, of or pertaining to a style of music in which several records are intercut with each other, using the scratch technique, to create a 'collage' of rhythmic sound.
 **1987** *New Musical Express* 14 Feb. 27/4 Pete Shelley's move from The Buzzcocks to a 12″ gay classic 'Homo-Sapiens' and John Lydon's rearranged public image, appearing with *scratch-mix pioneer Africa Bambaattaa, the self-proclamied Zulu warrior of the hip hop scene, compounded the drift. **1987** *Daily Tel.* 6 Aug. 10/7 He mentioned graffiti artists, breakdancers, body poppers, rappers and scratch mix DJs.
 so **scratch-mix** *v.*; **scratch-mixing** *vbl. n.*
 **1985** *Los Angeles Times* 16 July VI. 6/1 All the groups performed without bands, as deejays provided the backing by *scratch-mixing records on turntables. **1987** *New Musical Express* 14 Feb. 26/1, I say, I say, I say, did you hear the one about the dermatologist, he thought *scratch-mixing was a form of eczema. **1987** *Daily Tel.* 6 Aug. 10/7 Scratch mixing is messing about with other people's music on records.
 **scratch video**, a technique or genre of video-making, in which a number of short, sharp images are cut and mixed into a single film and fitted to a synchronized, usu. rap music, soundtrack; such a video.
 **1985** *Listener* 12 Dec. 20/2 *Scratch video, an innovative method of pilfering pictures to create often controversial video collages. **1987** *Ibid.* 12 Nov. 27/1 Scratch video is one of the more invigorating genres to emerge from the video revolution.

**scratch**, *v.* Add: [7.] **e.** To cancel, abandon, 'scrap' (an undertaking or project).
 **1923** WODEHOUSE *Inimitable Jeeves* vii. 71 Thinks I'm not a good bet? Wants to scratch the fixture? Well, perhaps he's right. **1966** *Electronics* 17 Oct. 104 In the air, these indications tell the crew whether all subsystems are operating properly. If they aren't, the crew can decide whether to scratch the mission or formulate a new plan of attack. **1973** D. RAMSAY *Deadly Discretion* 103 Scratch that. I'm not out to make enemies. **1987** *Newsweek* 18 May 9 These aides .. succeeded in scratching another Broadhurst party scheduled for mid-May. **1989** *Institutional Investor* (Internat. ed.) May 181/1 A growing number of big players [*sc.* banks, etc.] seem prepared to scratch stabilization charges—even if this might mean bearing the entire cost of stabilization.
 [9.] **d.** *intr.* To play music using the 'scratch' technique (see *SCRATCH *n.*¹ 6 c); to act as a 'scratch' disc jockey.
 **1982** *Melody Maker* 4 Dec. 12/2 There are guest deejays cutting, scratching and whomping. **1984** *New Yorker* 5 Mar. 42/3 The d.j.s take the basic tapes, overdub them, drop out some instruments,.. and scratch—which means rotate the record backward to the beat with your finger. **1987** *New Musical Express* 14 Feb. 51/2 Never able to resist a joke, Eddie raps, scratches and twists the pillar with all the deftness of Grandmaster Flash.
 **e.** *trans.* To manipulate (a record) using the 'scratch' technique.

**1984** *N.Y. Times* 17 June 11. 28/6 The Rockit Band includes Grandmixer D. ST., whose instrument is a turntable and who makes sounds by 'scratching' records back and forth. **1988** *Jackie* 2 Apr. 2 Hasn't stopped moving .. since he scratched his first disc.

**scratcher**, *n.* Add: [**1.**] **f.** (*a*) A person, *esp.* a disc jockey, who employs 'scratch' techniques (see *SCRATCH *n.*[1] 6 c); (*b*) a maker of scratch videos (s.v. *SCRATCH *n.*[1] 12 b).

**1982** *Melody Maker* 4 Dec. 12/3 Last week's invasion of our capital by a 19-strong squad of New York breakers, scratchers, rappers, skippers and grafitti artists. **1985** *Times* 5 Jan. 17/8 McLaren .. now does for Puccini and Bizet what he did for the Bronx scratchers and breakers. **1985** M. WILCOX et al. *Subverting Television* (pamphlet) 1/2 Taking the opposite approach of the scratchers who cut fast and furious to convey their message, Young instead presents us with the power of slow, even mundane, human activity. **1989** *Face* Jan. 23 MCs Kelz and Krissy Kriss, along with scratcher Lynx, provide the harder edge of the Smith and Mighty sound.

**scratching**, *vbl. n.* Add: [**a.**] (Examples in senses 9 d and 12 of the vb.)

**1982** *N.Y. Times* 8 Dec. C30/3 The Supreme Team includes a disk jockey who's adept at 'scratching', manipulating a record on a turntable in order to get a scratchy, percussive rhythm. **1985** M. WILCOX et al. *Subverting Television* (pamphlet) 2/1 The fluid scratching of Welsh and the Goldbacher/Flitcroft team .. exploits all the sensual effects of video processing. **1987** *Blues & Soul* 3–16 Feb. 30/2 At the same time in the US of A, deejay Jazzy Jeff has made it to the American finals by winning the Philadelphia heat with his transformer-style scratching.

**scratchy**, *a.* Add: [**4.**] **d.** Demanding relief by or as if by scratching, itchy.

**1943** A. RANSOME *Picts & Martyrs* xiii. 120, I .. saw him uncurl his proboscis and shove it in and start sucking blood up out of the back of my hand ... It was scratchy afterwards. **1970** A. TYLER *Slipping-Down Life* viii. 112 My eyelids feel scratchy.

**screen**, *v.* Add: [**7.**] **b.** *intr.* for *pass.* Of a film, television programme, etc.: to be shown or screened.

**1986** *Auckland Star* 7 Feb. A1 The series will screen between 5.30 pm and 7 pm. **1986** *Los Angeles Times* 24 Feb. VI. 2/1 'Scandal' (1950), the most rarely seen of all Kurosawa films, screens Thursday only at the Nuart as part of its Kurosawa Festival.

**script**, *n.*[1] Add: [**5.**] **d.** *Artificial Intelligence.* A formalized description of a commonly occurring situation, consisting of facts or events which are usually interdependent, which is intended to assist comprehension (usu. by a machine) of esp. textual descriptions of such a situation in which not all the details are made explicit.

**1975** R. C. SCHANK in Bobrow & Collins *Representation & Understanding* ix. 264 Some of the episodes which occur in memory serve to organize and make sense of new inputs. These episodic sequences we call *scripts*. **1977** SCHANK & ABELSON *Scripts, Plans, Goals & Understandings* iii. 38 The first special mechanism must be able to recognize that a script—a standard event sequence—has been mentioned. **1983** BROWN & YULE *Discourse Analysis* vii. 245 Some empirical research has shown that treating scripts as 'action stereotypes' .. for people's knowledge of routine activities can produce experimental results to support the views of Schank and his collaborators. **1987** *Austral. Personal Computer* Dec. 131/3 The script also contains other information, such as what kinds of people or things are found in the restaurant, and what types of actions these people or things are allowed to do.

**scroll**, *v.* Add: **5.** *Computing.* **a.** *trans.* Originally, to move (text displayed on a screen) *up* or *down* as if it were on a scroll stretched vertically across the screen, in order to view other parts of the text; to effect such movement in (a screen, or part of it, which displays such text); also, in later use, to move (text or other displayed material) to the left, right, etc. (also without const.) in a similar manner. Cf. *PAGE *v.*[2] 4.

**1971** *Auerbach on Alphanumeric Displays* xi. 82 The data on the screen can be scrolled up or down to bring in new data, line by line, at the bottom or at the top of the screen. **1974** *Proc. AFIPS Conf.* XLIII. 251/1 Sequential windows behave like typewriter simulations (text is scrolled through them). **1978** *Sci. Amer.* Dec. 148/2 (Advt.), These windows can even be scrolled individually, both vertically and horizontally, to a width of 160 columns and a length of several thousand lines. **1980** *Practical Computing* Sept. 60/1 The semicolon prompt accepts a command, holds it on screen during execution, and scrolls it up a line on completion. **1983** *Your Computer* Sept. 129/2 This is a programme to scroll part of the screen one byte at a time, laterally.

**b.** *intr.* Of displayed text, etc.: to move in this way (usu. *up* or in a specified direction). Of a display: to move displayed material upwards by scrolling.

**1977** *Broadcast* 10 Oct. 12/2 Transmission is started by pressing the 'Send' key. The text will then scroll up to the end of the entered text. **1980** *Practical Computing* June 64/3 If an address is outside the currently-displayed fields, the window scrolls to portray that region of the table in which the address resides. **1983** R. HASKELL *Atari BASIC* xiv. 129/2 The data value in location 53279 will keep being displayed and will scroll off the screen. **1985** J. FULLER *Mass* vii. 197 Ruffalino was leaning over the shoulder of a rewriteman, watching the story scroll out on the screen.

**c.** To move through text on a screen by scrolling, esp. vertically or horizontally.

**1979** *Computer Peripherals* Feb. 9/5 The devices then permit the operator to .. scroll through the memory a line at a time. **1981** *Practical Computing* Mar. 71/2 You can scroll in either direction, rolling text through the screen to reach the start or finish of the document. **1984** M. GRIMES *Dirty Duck* iii. 25 There's that sonnet that looks like a suicide threat—want me to scroll up to that? **1989** A. DILLARD *Writing Life* vi. 90, I have been doing some scrolling, here and elsewhere, scrolling up and down beaches and blank monitor screens.

**d.** The infin. used *attrib.* with the sense 'scrolling'.

**1982** *What's New in Computing* Nov. 20/4 The scroll rate can be varied between 60 and 1.9 line feeds per second. **1985** *Practical Computing* Aug. 72/2 The vertical and horizontal scroll bars are used to move to different parts of the keyboard or grid. **1986** V. G. CERF in T. C. Bartee *Digital Communications* iv. 165 Most services today use screen or scroll mode command user interfaces.

**scrollable** ('skrəʊləb(ə)l), *a. Computing.* [f. SCROLL *v.* + -ABLE.] Of text, etc. on a screen: capable of scrolling. Of a screen or window: that permits scrolling.

**1982** *What's New in Computing* Nov. 50/4 The model 'AD' adds a built in 16 character scrollable display to the above spec. **1988** *Byte* Fall 114/2 The Open Look is purported to be .. similar to the Mac environment in its use of icons, scrollable windows, and pull-down/pop-up menus.

**scrolling** ('skrəʊlɪŋ), *vbl. n.* (Formerly at SCROLL *v.*) [f. SCROLL *v.* + -ING[1].] **1.** Decoration with scrolls; scroll-work.

**1731** T. Boston *Gen. Acct. My Life* (1908) 332 With some difficulty I carried the scrolling of my letter some length. **1989** *Which?* July 344/1 Letterboxes, worktops, intricate scrolling, slicing floorboards, and curved cuts of any kind—these are the staple diet of a jigsaw.
 **2.** *Computing.* The process of scrolling text, etc. on a screen.
 **1971** *Auerbach on Alphanumeric Displays* v. 17 The normal version of scrolling is to eliminate the top line of displayed data, move all lines of data up the screen one line, and insert a new line at the bottom. **1974** *Proc. AFIPS Conf.* XLIII. 251/1 The text on the upper portion of the screen is unaffected by the scrolling .. which takes place during typewriter simulation on the lower portion. **1980** *Practical Computing* June 66/1 Cursor movement and scrolling in each side of the display are independent of the other half. **1985** *Computing Equipment* Sept. 31/3 The 15in non-flicker screen displays up to 31 lines of 80 characters at a time though, by means of scrolling, this can be increased to 94 lines long of 250 characters wide.

**scrounge** (skraʊndʒ), *n.* (Formerly at SCROUNGE *v.*[1]) *colloq.* [f. the vb.] **1.** The action of scrounging; freq. in phr. *on the scrounge.*
 **1927** *Daily Express* 17 Aug. 3 (*heading*) Suffolks on the scrounge. Village trek for recruits. **1950** *Landfall* Mar. 127, I drained my fifth warm bottle-full ages ago and have been on the scrounge ever since. **1956** L. Godfrey in *Pick of Today's Short Stories* vii. 94 'Besides,' added Trouncer .. 'it's a good scrounge.' **1981** 'J. Gash' *Vatican Rip* i. 7 I'm an antique dealer. .. I was on the scrounge and feeling very sorry for myself.
 **2.** One who scrounges; a scrounger.
 **1937** Partridge *Dict. Slang* 739/1 *Scrounge,* .. a 'scrounger'. **1960** Wentworth & Flexner *Dict. Amer. Slang* 453/2 *Scrounge,* 1 a habitual borrower; .. 2 one who asks for small items that others are about to throw away or sell. **1980** *Quilt World* Sept./Oct. 4/1 When you're a scrounge, a consistent scrounge, a garage sale sign is a call to adventure.

**scroungy** ('skraʊndʒɪ), *a. colloq.* (orig. and chiefly *U.S.*). [f. SCROUNGE *v.*[1] + -Y[1].] Shabby or dirty in appearance; sordid, disreputable; more generally, of poor quality, inferior.
 **1949** (heard by Prof. A. L. Hench, Univ. of Virginia, and glossed as 'disreputable': 22 Oct.) **1959** 'E. McBain' *'Til Death* (1961) xiii. 153 I'll continue commuting to a scroungy squadroom in perhaps the world's worst neighborhood. **1960** Wentworth & Flexner *Dict. Amer. Slang* 453/2 *Scroungy,* .. bad; inferior; terrible; usu. as a result of being very cheap. **1973** T. Pynchon *Gravity's Rainbow* (1975) i. 35 One sunburned, scroungy unit of force preserving the Sheik and the oil money against any threat from east of the English Channel. **1977** *Zigzag* Mar. 4/2 They all walk around together, the three of them, real grubby, kind of scroungy guys. **1981** G. Winokur *Depression* p. v, I was fascinated with the scroungy, low life diseases .. in that clinic.

**scrow**, *n.* Add: **5.** [Perh. a different word.] A state of confusion or agitation; a commotion or fuss. *Sc.* and *north. dial.*
 **1808** J. Mayne *Siller Gun* iii. 73 To bell the cat wi' sic a scrow, Some swankies ettled; But oh! they got a fearfu' cow, Ere a' was settled! **1861** E. Waugh *Rambles in Lake Country* 184 Then, there was a girt cry—'Eh, Mr. Wilson's i' t' watter!' .. and there was sek a scrowe as nivver. **1936** A. Ransome *Pigeon Post* xvi. 172 You'd no call to bring her chasing up the valley for nothing, and her in a scrow with her papering and painting. **1984** *Jrnl. Lakeland Dial. Soc.* No. 46. 19 Henry Becky wazn't ower suited, an did nowt but twine aboot scrow Annie waz mekin.

**scrub**, *v.*[1] Add: **[3.] f.** Of tyres: to slide or scrape across the road surface, esp. when cornering. Also *trans.* with *off*, to lose or cause the loss of (speed) by 'scrubbing'. Cf. SCRUB *n.*[2] 1 b.
 **1976** *Autocar* 26 June 7/2 It's about 10 yards from the mouth of the side street to the alley, and I have to scrub off about 20 mph in that distance. **1980** Ellinger & Hathaway *Automotive Suspension, Steering, & Brakes* xv. 228/1 The tire scrubs on the road surface as the wheel direction is changed. **1980** *Dirt Bike* Oct. 46/1 You scrub off some speed with the killer brakes and catch a gear or two down. **1983** *Times* 11 Apr. 8/4 Managed to spin it about three times to scrub off some of the speed, but hit the bank head-on, still going fast. **1989** *Aviation Week* 27 Nov. 84/2 Harold Marthinsen .. said the nose-gear tires 'were scrubbing' as the aircraft moved down the runway.

**scrubbed**, *a.* Restrict †*Obs.* to senses in Dict. and add: **3.** Covered or overgrown with scrub. With qualifying advb., as *densely-* or *heavily-scrubbed.* *Austral.* and *N.Z.* exc. as *scrubbed over.*
 **1870** R. P. Whitworth *Martin's Bay Settlement* 13/1 The land was densely scrubbed with undergrowth. **1899** *North-Western Advocate* (West Devonport, Tasmania) 10 Mar. 3/2 The country .. was a succession of undulating, heavily-scrubbed land. **1910** *Huon Times* (Franklin, Tasmania) 5 Nov. 2/5 It was necessary for a gate to be erected owing to the property being densely scrubbed and heavily timbered. **1981** *Ann. Rep. Berks., Bucks. & Oxfordshire Naturalists' Trust* 3/2 The site which has a good display of chalk grassland flowers was heavily scrubbed over, to such an extent that its botanical interest was at stake.

**scrum**, *v.* For entry substitute:
**scrum** (skrʌm), *v.* [f. the n.] **1.** *intr. Rugby Football.* With *down*: to form or engage in a scrummage. Also *transf.*
 **1922** E. Raymond *Tell England* i. ii. 41 Three of us placed our shoulders against the lower end, while the rest scrummed down, Rugby fashion, in row upon row behind one another. **1982** *Financial Times* 18 Dec. 13/3 Well, he seems all right, but would you like to scrum down with him? **1989** *Ibid.* 24 Apr. 24/4 Long before their new partnership was even dreamt of, the two men scrummed down together for University College, Dublin, later competing on opposite teams in senior club rugby.
 **2.** Without const. **a.** *Rugby Football.* To scrummage.
 **1937** Partridge *Dict. Slang* 740/1 *Scrum,* to scrimmage: C. 20: Rugby Football coll. **1949** *Rugby League Gaz.* Nov. 5/2 The referee .. ordered the nonplussed players to scrum opposite the linesman while that worthy continued to flag 'ball-back'. **1981** *N.Y. Times* 23 Sept. A1/1 While the players scrummed and kicked in the mud, the shouts of 1,000 demonstrators confined to a knoll 100 yards away reached the field. **1987** *Rugby World & Post* Mar. 16/2 (Advt.), We have been unable to scrum the way we want to scrum because people have been injured.
 **b.** *transf.* To jostle, crowd.
 **1925** A. S. M. Hutchinson *One Increasing Purpose* i. xxv. 153 The trouble with me is .. feeding and frivoling at night and weekends where the masters live and where we scrum at shows. **1938** P. Lawlor *House of Templemore* ix. 98 Young calves 'scrumming' to dip their heads in the long troughs of milk. **1939** G. Greene *Confidential Agent* i. i. 3 A rugger team was returning home and they scrummed boisterously for their glasses. **1948** C. Day Lewis *Otterbury Incident* iv. 49 Everyone was scrumming around behind him.

**scrunch**, *v.* Add: **[2.] d.** *trans. Hairdressing.* To style (hair) by squeezing or crushing with the hands to give a crinkled or tousled look.

**1983** *Hairdressers' Jrnl. Internat.* 26 Aug. 20 Hair was given a firm perm, then cut into layered bob, left to dry naturally, then gently scrunched with gel. **1987** *Pract. Hairstyling & Beauty* June/July 15 The fringe is scrunched with fingers for a fuller, more solid effect. **1987** *Hairdo Ideas* July 58 To style, he used mousse and his hands to scrunch her hair into a beautiful halo of curls.
  4. Special Comb. **scrunch-dry** v. *trans.* and *absol. Hairdressing,* to blow-dry (hair) while squeezing or crushing it with the hands, to give a crinkled or tousled look; also **scrunch dry** *n.*, and **scrunch-drying** *vbl. n.*
  **1985** *Hair* Summer 15 (*caption*) She can \*scrunch-dry her hair. **1986** *Good Housekeeping* May 43/2 Rod just used mousse and a scrunch-drying technique to give it more body and to make it .. more modern. **1986** *City Limits* 12 June 78 After .. a careful considered cut and a 'scrunch' dry, I emerged with a rejuvenated head. **1986** *Hair Flair* Sept. 11/1 You can scrunch dry with a soft hold mousse for casual day-time waves. **1990** *Essentials* Sept. 146/3 For a little extra fullness and bounce, Melanie then scrunch-dried Karen's hair using Valence 3 Natural Hold Mousse.

**scrungy** ('skrʌndʒɪ), *a. slang* (chiefly *U.S.*). [Prob. related to \*SCROUNGY *a.* and SCUNGY *a.*; cf. also GRUNGY *a.*] Dirty, grimy; sleazy, shabby, or tatty.
  **1974** *Sunday Mail* (Brisbane) 28 Apr. 17/6 John and Lyn Daley are also having trouble trying to get workmen, and say they're sick and tired of the house looking 'so scrungy'. **1977** *Rolling Stone* 16 June 43/3 As the scrungy taxi passenger, he has driver De Niro stop the cab and look at his wife's lurid silhouette up against a window. **1980** *Washington Post* 11 May K8/6 Far better to get a scrungy, spontaneous, misspelled I-love-you card from your children any other day of the year than Mother's Day. **1988** *Los Angeles Times* 18 July v. 1/1 Their clothing is either scrungy or flamboyant; mostly they look as if they had dressed to work in the garage. It isn't Ascot.

**scuddy**, *a.*[2] Add: Hence **'scuddiness** *n.* (esp. in *Wine-Making*).
  **1831** J. BUSBY *Let.* in *Jrnl. Rec. Visit Princ. Vineyards* (1834) 59, I thought it was easy to account for the scuddiness which so generally attacks Sherry Wines ... The grapes were by no means in reality decayed. This shook my faith in scuddiness being the result of the employment of decayed grapes. **1972** *Bottlers' Year Bk. 1972-73* 395 Scuddiness.

**scuff**, *v.* Add: **[2.]** c. To mark or damage the surface of (shoes, furniture, etc.) by scraping or rubbing; to make shabby by wear and tear.
  **1909** WEBSTER, *Scuff*, v.t. .. to injure or make shabby by wear. **1940** R. CHANDLER *Farewell, my Lovely* xxxvii. 280 The speedboat scuffed the *Montecito*'s ancient sides. **1973** F. KING *Flights* ix. 133 She kicked at the pavement, scuffing her sandal with ochre dust. **1988** N. LOWNDES *Chekago* iv. 173 Boris's eldest son was sitting on a low nursery chair outside his parents' room scuffing the heels of his new school shoes.
  d. To shuffle, drag, or push (one's feet) *in(to)* or *through* something.
  **1909** WEBSTER, *Scuff*, v.t. .. to drag while moving; to shuffle; as, to scuff the feet. **1936** M. MITCHELL *Gone with Wind* xxxi. 519 She paused to .. scuff her feet deeper into the strip of old quilting wrapped about them. **1938** M. K. RAWLINGS *Yearling* ix. 78 The lavender petals of the chinaberry blooms were falling. Jody scuffed his bare toes through them. **1980** W. GOLDING *Rites of Passage* (1982) 137, I threw on my greatcoat, scuffed my feet into slippers and felt my way out on deck. **1986** P. BARKER *Century's Daughter* iv. 44 Liza scuffed her feet in the dust.

‖**scugnizzo** (sku'ɲittso), *n.* Pl. scugnizzi. [It. (Neapolitan) dial.] In Naples, a street urchin. Usu. in *pl.*
  **1957** M. WEST *Children of Sun* i. 26 Peppino laid a hand on my arm and drew me away. '*Scugnizzi*, Mauro. The urchins of Naples. Let's go!' I fumbled in my pocket and found a thousand lire note which I thrust into the hand of the weeping crone. **1961** 'W. HAGGARD' *Arena* xi. 91 There was more in Naples than *scugnizzi*. **1978** *Times Lit. Suppl.* 3 Mar. 250/2 British soldiers .. chopping off the fingers of *scugnizzi* who tried to climb into the backs of lorries. **1980** T. HOLME *Neapolitan Streak* 121 When we were children, my sister and I were *scugnizzi*—the gutter kids of Naples.

**scupper**, *v.* Senses a, b in Dict. become 1, 2. For etym. read: [f. SCUPPER *n.* The connection is perh. explained by Fraser & Gibbons *Soldier & Sailor Words* (1925) s.v. *Scuppered*: A man killed in action or falling in heavy weather would naturally roll into the scuppers.] Add:
  3. To sink (a vessel) deliberately; = SCUTTLE *v.*[2] 1 a (with which it is sometimes confused).
  **1976** *Oxf. Compan. Ships & Sea* 763/2 *Scupper*, .. deliberately to sink a ship by opening the seacocks in her hull or by blowing a hole in her side below the waterline. It has, presumably, the same general origin as scuttle. **1982** *Summary World Broadcasts:* Soviet Union 31 Mar. A1/10 'Explosives!' one of the sailors guessed. 'They are going to scupper the ship. But why?' **1988** *Daily Tel.* 24 Dec. 9/1 Hitler's 89ft custom-built yacht, Ostwind, is to be scuppered by .. a marine company chief on whose property .. the battered relic of the Third Reich was abandoned.

**'scurrier**, *n.*[2] [f. SCURRY *v.* + -ER[1].] One who or that which scurries.
  **1890** in WEBSTER. **1949** E. HYAMS *Not in our Stars* xx. 266 They scurried or loafed about and both scurriers and loafers looked as helpless and purposeless as ants. **1986** T. BARLING *Smoke* iii. 75 'A regular scurrier is our Vic.' 'Any problems?' 'No. They made for the underground carpark like you said, Chas.'

**scurry**, *n.* Add: [2.] For def. read: *Sporting*. A short, quick run or race on horseback; in Show-jumping and Carriage-driving, a race 'against the clock', in which faults are counted as additional time penalties. Freq. *attrib.* (Later examples.)
  **1946** M. C. SELF *Horseman's Encycl.* 197 *Scurry jumpers*, this class is judged on time with one second added for each fault instead of the usual scoring. **1953** *Show Jumping* ('Know the Game' Ser.) 15 A result is always obtained after one round. (Such competitions are:- 'Fault and Out', 'Relay', 'Take Your Own Line' and 'Scurry'.) **1973** *Country Life* 18 Oct. 1136/2 The Eldonian Double Harness Scurry was the scene of a potentially dangerous accident when Gill Greig .. was run over by the cart. **1986** *Horse Internat.* May 31/2 The native breeds .. have been very successful in every form of driving competition from cross country to scurry driving to concours d'elegance.

‖**scusi** ('skuzi), *v. imp. colloq.* [It., ellipt. for *mi scusi* 'excuse me', f. *scusare* to excuse.] 'I beg your pardon', 'Excuse me'.
  **1919** W. H. DOWNING *Digger Dial.* 56 [Italy] *Scusi!*, excuse me! **1975** 'D. JORDAN' *Black Account* vii. 44, I think I said '*Scusi*' or something stupid and he .. closed the door. **1986** W. GARNER *Zones of Silence* xvi. 141 'Oops!' she said, high-pitched and clarion with just a trace of a slur. '*Scusi*, everyone, better safe than whatsit.'

**scutch** (skʌtʃ), *n.*[4] *Building.* Also 20 scotch. [f. \*SCUTCH *v.*[3]] A cutting tool resembling a two-ended adze or pick, used for roughly dressing the cut surface of a brick or stone, and also for cutting bricks.

**1885** R. HOLLAND *Gloss. Words County of Chester* 304 *Scutch*,.. a bricklayer's hammer with two faces for cutting bricks. **1910** *Encycl. Brit.* IV. 521/2 After the bolster and club hammer have removed the portion of the brick, the scutch, really a small axe, is used to hack off the rough parts. **1936** *Archit. Rev.* LXXIX. 240/4 (*caption*) The brick-saw with its entwined strands of wire, used for cutting the soffit lines to allow the scutch or brick-axe.. to enter without splitting the brick. **1975** C. M. HARRIS *Dict. Archit.* 430/1 *Scutch, scotch,* a bricklayer's tool, with a cutting edge on each side, for cutting, trimming, and dressing brick or stone.

**scutch** (skʌtʃ), *v.*³ *dial.* and *techn.* Also 9-scotch. [App. Sc. var. of SCOTCH *v.*¹ (*Sc. Nat. Dict.*), but cf. SCUTCH *v.*¹,².] *trans.* In various dial. uses (orig. *Sc.:* now also *U.S.*): to smooth or trim the surface of (a stone, hedge, log, etc.) with a slashing or slicing motion; *spec.* in *Building,* to dress (stone, or the cut surface of a brick) with a scutch (\*SCUTCH *n.*⁴).

**1848** A. SOMERVILLE *Autobiogr. Working Man* xii. 144 Each hewer had a labourer allotted to him to do the rougher work upon the stone with a short pick, technically to 'scutch' it. **1895** *Funk's Stand. Dict., Scotch,* .. specifically to dress, as stone, with a pick or picking-tool. **1907** W. M. COCKRUM *Pioneer Hist. Indiana* viii. 186 The first thing to do was to cut three large logs the length of the building was wanted and scutch one side and lay them so they were level, on a range with each other.

Hence **scutched** *ppl. a.;* **'scutching** *vbl. n.*

**1861** *N. & Q.* XI. 116 The bark of these trees [*sc.* hollies] was exactly the 'raw material' of his.. manufacture. Forthwith he removed to Sawry.. where.. I found the.. neighbours ready to point out 'the old scutching-house', as they called it. **1866** *Trans. Highland & Agric. Soc. Scotl.* I. 23 For several years past more attention has been paid to the regular and proper scutching of the hedges. **1890** *Cent. Dict., Scotching,* in masonry, a method of dressing stone either with a pick or with pick-shaped chisels inserted into a socket formed in the head of a hammer. Also *scutching.* **1893** J. P. ALLEN *Pract. Building Construction* v. 70 Scutched work is similar to the last [*sc.* hammer-dressed work], but more finely executed. **1975** C. M. HARRIS *Dict. Archit.* 430/1 *Scutching,* a method of finely dressing stone with a hammer, the head of which is composed of a bundle of steel points.

**scutter** ('skʌtə(r)), *n.*² *U.S. dial.* [Of uncertain origin: perh. f. SCUTTER *v.*² (see also *Sc. Nat. Dict.*).] One who or that which is remarkable or extraordinary; (often familiarly) a great rascal or scamp, a 'devil'.

**1940** *Sat. Even. Post* 6 Jan. 15/1 He's a pure D scutter, ain't he, papa? **1958** H. BABCOCK *I don't want to shoot Elephant* 164 He'll lick the stuffing out of any interloper who tries to bring me a bird ... 'Right humorsome old scutter,' I commented. **1960** V. WILLIAMS *Walk Egypt* I. vi. 50, I swear, .. every time I think of the way that little scutter done—and me only trying to be neighborly. **1978** J. CARROLL *Mortal Friends* I. i. 6 The scutter, Brady thought. Serves me right. The ingrates.

**scutter** *v.*² Add: **'scuttering** *ppl. a.*

**1929** W. FAULKNER *Sound & Fury* 96 Spoade was in the middle of them like a terrapin in a street full of scuttering dead leaves. **1983** *Listener* 20 Jan. 36/2 The more dramatic start of the First—still subdued, but with scuttering strings underneath—is tense and dramatic.

**scutum,** *n.* Add: **4.** *Astron.* (With capital initial.) A small constellation of the southern hemisphere, lying between Aquila and Serpens.

Originally named *Scutum Sobiescianum* by J. Hevelius (*a* 1687, in *Prodromus Astronomiæ* (1690) viii. 115), after John III *Sobieski* (1629-96), king of Poland; this was later changed to *Scutum Sobieski(i)*.

[*a* **1719** J. FLAMSTEED *Historia Coelestis Britannica* (1725) III. 58 In Constellatione Aquilæ.. quæ est J. Hevel. Scuti 2ª.] **1773** *Encycl. Brit.* I. 487/2 (*table*) Scutum Sobieski. **1875** *Ibid.* II. 817/1 (*table*) Scutum Sobieskii. **1890** G. F. CHAMBERS *Handbk. Astron.* (ed. 4) III. XIV. viii. 221 This constellation is sometimes called Clypeus Sobieskii, but Scutum simply is now its more usual designation. **1930** C. H. PAYNE *Stars of High Luminosity* vii. 89 The discontinuity noted by Krieger in the direction of the Scutum cloud would, if substantiated, strengthen the case for separate groups materially. **1961** *Listener* 7 Dec. 977/1 Systems such as the Sword-Handle in Perseus and the aptly named 'Wild Duck' cluster in Scutum.

**scuzz** (skʌz), *n. colloq.* (orig. and chiefly *N. Amer.*). Also **scuz**. [Prob. abbrev. of DISGUSTING *ppl. a.,* though perh. a blend of SCUM *n.* and FUZZ *n.*¹] **1.** (Formerly at SCUZZY *a.*) One who or that which is disgusting or unpleasant.

**1968** *Sunday Sun* (Baltimore) 3 Nov. D1/5, I.. did 'Midnight Cowboy' where I'm *Ratso Rizzo,* a complete scuzz. **1972** J. WAMBAUGH *Blue Knight* vi. 78 One white, bearded scuz in a dirty buckskin vest and yellow headband. **1984** *Time* 10 Dec. 92/1 Axel .. hails from Detroit, where the fuzz's lot is mostly scuzz. **1984** *Sounds* 29 Dec. 23/2 More wild.. rock'n'roll .. as with the other three volumes of this scuzz. **1988** M. ATWOOD *Cat's Eye* (1989) xl. 230 In the larger picture, we're just a little green scuzz on the surface.

**2.** Special Comb. **scuzzbag** (also **scuzzball,** **-bucket**), a contemptible or despicable person; also as a general term of abuse; cf. SCUMBAG *n.* 2.

**1983** *Time* 11 July 72/2 He calls a minister a '\*scuzzbag'. **1986** *Los Angeles Times* 5 Jan. (Comic Suppl.) 3/3 What kind of scuz-bag would turn in his own. **1986** *InfoWorld* 13 Jan. 58/1 Each and every magazine and newspaper has long known the lineup of products (Mac Plus with its \*scuzzball hard disk port, [etc.]). **1989** *Newsday* 17 Sept. (TV Plus) 85/4 Her cheating husband, Ernie, a crotch-grabber who brings new meaning to the word '\*scuzzbucket'.

**scuzzy,** *a.* For label and etym. read: *slang* (orig. and chiefly *N. Amer.*). [f. SCUZZ *n.* + -Y¹.] Substitute for def.: Disgusting in appearance, behaviour, etc.; dirty, grimy, murky; (esp. of a person) despicable, disreputable, 'sleazy'. (Later examples.)

**1983** *Fortune* 16 May 129/1 'If a scuzzy steel mill came in here and offered me $200 a ton off, I'd throw him out,' says the senior steel buyer. **1985** *Listener* 24 Oct. 42/1 A local plumber's kid perfectly at home among his scuzzy pals. **1987** *New Musical Express* 25 Feb. 24 Zeppelin were really dumb: visibly hanging out.. with the scuzziest groupies in town. **1990** *Raw* 21 Feb.-6 Mar. 3/2 It looks like *Raw*'s going to be locked in combat with the noisiest, scuzziest hombres till dawn.

Hence **'scuzziness** *n.*

**1980** 'E. McBAIN' *Ghosts* iv. 65 He was accustomed to the scuzziness of the Eight-Seven, where.. the carpeting.. was.. tattered and frayed.

**scyphate** ('saɪfeɪt), *a. Numism.* [ad. med.L. (*nummus*) *scyphatus,* traditionally interpreted as 'cup-shaped (coin)', f. L. *scyphus* cup: see SCYPHUS *n.* However, the term is said to predate the development of concave Byzantine coinage (P. Grierson 1971, in *Numism. Chron.* 7th Ser. XI. 253-60), and ulterior derivation from colloq. Arab. *shiffī* having a lip, rimmed + L. *-atus* has been proposed.] Of a coin (esp. from the late Byzantine Empire): having the shape of a shallow bowl; concave, cup-shaped.

**1899** G. F. HILL *Handbk. Greek & Roman Coins* vi. 155 There are a few instances of a slight concavity although never attaining to the peculiar *scyphate* fabric of the late Byzantine coins. **1908** W. WROTH *Catal. Imperial Byzantine Coins Brit. Mus.* I. p. lv, The old (flat) nomisma was thus reduced in weight, but the new (scyphate) nomisma retains the original weight . . of the old solidus. **1957** *Numismatist* Aug. 940 Occasionally a scyphate bronze, usually of Alexius III, will be found in bulk lots. **1962** R. A. G. CARSON *Coins* 216 [The Empress Theodora] was represented on . . scyphate nomismata as a standing figure holding a labarum. **1971** *Ashmolean Mus. Rep. Visitors 1970* 44 The major accession was a selection of 75 scyphate copper coins from a thirteenth-century hoard.

**scyphi-**, *comb. form.* Add: **scyphistoma**: hence **scyphi'stomal** *a.*, pertaining to or consisting of a scyphistoma.

**1959** W. ANDREW *Textbk. Compar. Histol.* xii. 463 Cassiopeia constricts off ciliated buds from the *scyphistomal stalk. **1977** J. COHEN *Reproduction* x. 188 Most coelenterate medusae have a polyp stage (or a scyphistomal equivalent) on the sea-bed.

**seajack** ('si:dʒæk), *v.* [f. SEA *n.* + HI)JACK *v.*; cf. SKYJACK *v.*] *trans.* To hijack (a ship) at sea. Also with the crew or passengers as obj.

**1975** *Courier-Mail* (Brisbane) 6 Sept. 15/11 Five girls who embark on a Mediterranean yachting holiday are sea-jacked and held as hostages. **1985** *Daily News* (N.Y.) 10 Oct. 3/1 His uncle . . was reported murdered . . yesterday by Palestinians who seajacked the Italian cruise liner Achille Lauro. **1987** *Amer. Speech* LXII. 181 The female tenth grader . . remarked: 'I'm afraid to go the Bahamas; I don't want to get seajacked.' **1989** *Economist* 5 Aug. 15 A jet carrying away the man responsible for seajacking the *Achille Lauro* in 1985.

Hence **'seajack** *n.*, a hijacking at sea; **'seajacker** *n.*, one who hijacks a ship; also **'seajacking** *vbl. n.*

**1985** *Daily News* (N.Y.) 9 Oct. 1 (*heading*) Warships tail seajackers. *Ibid.* 11 Oct. 40/5 The Achille Lauro, the object of the seajack . . steamed into Port Said, Egypt early yesterday. **1985** *Economist* 19 Oct. 13/2 Abu Abbas's bit of the Palestinian Liberation Organization has now admitted responsibility for the seajacking. **1986** *Christian Science Monitor* 17 Nov. 29/1 Such incidents as . . the seajacking of the Achille Lauro. **1987** *Time* 20 July 29/3 They vividly remember him . . sipping a glass of red wine while directing the interception by Navy jets of the Egyptian airliner carrying the seajackers.

**section**, *n.* Add: [1.] e. A Caesarean section; = CÆSAREAN *n.* 2. *colloq.*

**1960** G. W. TARGET *Teachers* 211 Well, you see, I was small—though I've broadened out since then—and they said my babies would always be too big, I'd always have to have a section. **1978** S. KITZINGER *Experience of Childbirth* (ed. 4) 315 During labour the obstetrician may decide that a section is necessary if there is evidence of foetal distress. **1986** *Daily Tel.* 5 Feb. 19/1 Delays in ordering sections . . contributed, it is alleged, to the death of two children.

**sector**, *n.* Senses 2 h and i in Dict. become 2 i and j. Add: [I.] [2.] h. *Aeronaut.* A route or journey flown non-stop by a commercial airline, often as part of a longer flight schedule.

**1950** STROUD & MEARLES in James & Stroud *World's Airways* ii. 56/1 It was for the operation of the Singapore-Brisbane sector that the D.H.86 was designed. **1961** *Observer* 12 Feb. 1/5 The pilots claim that the four 'sectors' a day allotted to Comet pilots under the summer schedules are 'too much'. A 'sector' is the journey between a take-off and a

landing. **1976** *Aviation Week* 16 Feb. 22/3 For Europe in 1990, the predicted total of 435 billion seat miles offered is expected to be broken down to 250 billion seat miles for long-range routes and 185 billion seat miles on short/medium-range sectors. **1986** *Aircraft Illustr.* July 374/2 The series 3A-RA and 3B-RA had a range . . of 1,770 statute miles, permitting . . an unrefuelled sector from London to Istanbul.

**secure**, *n.* Add: **2.** *Naut.* A signal sounded on board a ship, instructing seamen to cease activities.

[**1881** *Naval Encycl.* 730/1 Secure!, a command in exercising or working heavy guns, meaning to so arrange the breeching and tackles that the gun shall be in no danger of breaking loose in a sea-way.] **1909** [see *SECURE *v.* 5 c]. **1921** *Jrnl. R. Naval Med. Service* VII. 142 When the captain deems the ship outside the range of further action and the 'secure' has been sounded. **1923** *Man. Seamanship* (Admiralty) II. 45 After dinner similar instructional work is carried out until the 'secure' is sounded at 15.40.

**secure**, *a.* Add: [3.] g. Whose loyalty can be relied on; not a risk to security.

**1969** *Listener* 12 June 814/1 This village, Xuan Dong, is reckoned 'secure', meaning not under the influence of the Vietcong. **1978** R. V. JONES *Most Secret War* xlviii. 480 The Americans had reversed their agreement to the documents coming to London—on the advice of Perrin and Walsh who had told them that my officers and I were not secure enough. **1979** A. PRICE *Tomorrow's Ghost* i. 10 'They don't take just anyone in R and D. You have to have a security clearance, for a start.' . . 'No problem, dearie. I'm absolutely secure.'

[4.] b. Designed to be difficult to escape from. (Chiefly applied to penal and psychiatric institutions or areas within them.)

**1960** V. DURAND *Disturbances Carlton Approved School* 53 in *Parl. Papers 1959-60* (Cmnd. 937) IX. 625 It is possible . . that many of the schools which train boys of senior age might find it advantageous to have one or two secure rooms . . ready for the separation of boys who suddenly become difficult to handle in what appears to be only a transient phase of conduct. **1962** 'J. BELL' *Crime in our Time* VI. ii. 220 More prisons both of the 'open' and the 'secure' types. **1975** in *Hall & Morrison's Law relating to Children & Young Persons* (1977) (ed. 9) V. 1197 A secure unit may be defined as a room, or an area . . in which special features have been incorporated for the express purpose of presenting a physical barrier to any attempt on the part of a child accommodated in such room or area to leave it without permission. **1976** *Economist* 11 Sept. 22 So far there has been no opposition from the local community . . to the secure ward. **1987** *Openmind* Feb.-Mar. 5/1 Sectioned by her husband, she was then confined in a secure unit.

**secure**, *v.* Add: [5.] c. *U.S. Navy.* (a) *trans.* To restore (equipment, engines, a vessel) to a normal state of readiness after action or drill. (b) *intr.* To be released *from* drill or duty; to go off duty; also occas. *causatively*, to release (a crew member) *from* drill or duty.

**1909** T. BEYER *Life in Navy* 42 After Secure has sounded everything is re-stowed, magazines are locked and the keys returned to the captain. The keys of the magazines can be secured only with the special permission of the captain. **1918** L. E. RUGGLES *Navy Explained* 131 Secure, to stop drilling, to knock off a certain task. To secure from drill such as general quarters, abandon ship, collision, or fire drill. **1927** G. BRADFORD *Gloss. Sea Terms* 153/2 A signal . . to signify that the engines are needed no longer, and may be secured. **1945** J. BRYAN *Diary* 8 Apr. in *Aircraft Carrier* (1954) 152 When a ship is secured from general quarters, the doors and hatches and scuttles are not closed, made secure—they're opened.

I don't get it. **1946** T. HEGGEN *Mister Roberts* 94 The engine room called the bridge for permission to secure the main engines. **1956** *Amer. Speech* XXXI. 190 An hour or more of drilling, and the boots are ready to *secure* (turn in for the night). **1957** M. SHULMAN *Rally round Flag, Boys!* (1958) xx. 235 It was a routine training exercise... The launchers were all in firing position... Walker secured the troops from alert. **1978** H. WOUK *War & Remembrance* v. 44 You're securing from this duty. **1988** NOEL & BEACH *Naval Terms Dict.* (ed. 5) 248 Secure from fire drill.

**securitize**   (sɪˈkjʊərɪˌtaɪz),   *v.*   *Comm.*   [f. SECURIT(Y *n.* + -IZE] *trans.* To convert (assets, esp. loans) into securities, usu. for the purpose of raising capital by selling them to other investors.

**1981** *Amer. Banker* 26 Oct. 27/1 Those mortgages that tend to be securitized through the secondary mortgage market pipeline and sold to a still reluctant group of institutional investors. **1983** *Estates Gaz.* 6 July 24/3 (*title*) The multi-faceted revolution in securitising residential mortgages. **1985** *Times* 7 Mar. 15/6 A move to 'securitise' corporate debt, that is permit the creation and merchandising of new negotiable loan instruments, should help it reduce the volume of advances. **1989** *Banker* Feb. 3/2 DKB's assets will be growing more slowly than in the past as the bank securitises more of its loans.

Hence **se͵curiti'zation** *n.*, the action or process of securitizing assets; **se'curitized** *ppl. a.*

**1982** *Amer. Banker* 13 Oct. 11/3 Closer integration of mortgage and bond markets has been accomplished by a process known as 'securitization'. **1983** *U.S. Banker* Jan. 22/1 The mortgage market is becoming securitized. **1987** *Daily Tel.* 26 Aug. 15 Securitisation is the trick that these lenders use (and which building socities ultimately will) to keep on lending even when their own balance sheets do not have the capital to permit it. **1988** *What Mortgage* May 80/4 Though securitised loan sizes in the issue range from £16,000 to £425,000, the average loan is a safe sounding £40,110.

**secy.**, *n.* Chiefly *U.S.* Also without point. [Graphic shortening.] A written abbreviation of SECRETARY *n.*

**1801** J. TAYLOR *Let.* 10 June in J. Steele *Papers* (1924) I. 218 The present Secy. altho' *a full blooded Yankee*, .. knows the importance of this place. *c*1895 E. LOVEKIN in J. Burnett *Useful Toil* (1974) III. 291, I .. was Selected Secy to a local Club. **1926** *Who's Who in Amer. Jewry* 447/1 Member: Amer. Soc. Mechanical Engnrs. (former secy. New Orleans section). **1943** S. LEWIS *G. Planish* xiv. 130, I even took the virtuous Bunny Nimrock, the secy, out to lunch. **1989** *Aerospace Amer.* July 13/2 Defense Secy. Richard Cheney's revised Pentagon budget.

**sedimenter** (ˈsɛdɪˌmɛntə(r)), *n.* [f. SEDIMENT *n.* + -ER¹.] A device for removing sediment and other extraneous material from diesel fuel.

**1962** *Engineering* 12 Jan. 43/1 The sedimenter has little resistance to flow and is not subject to choking. **1986** C. CULPIN *Farm Machinery* (ed. 11) ii. 30/1 (*caption*) Primary fuel sedimenter for removal of water and relatively large particles of rust, metal or grit. *Ibid.* 30/2 Most sedimenters, once full of water, provide no further protection.

**seed**, *n.* Sense 8 in Dict. becomes 9. Add:
   **8.** *Math.* A number taken as the initial value for a series of applications of a given algorithm, usu. in order to generate a sequence of pseudo-random numbers.

**1971** *Jrnl. Statistical Computation & Simulation* I. 41 *Seed*, .. that randomly selected number, $0 \leqslant U_0 \leqslant 1$, from which all succeeding random numbers derive by means of an algorithmic, pseudo-random, number

generator. **1972** G. A. MIHRAM *Simulation* ii. 48 A fundamental requirement for the use of the technique was an initial, user-supplied, number .. from which the first random number could be generated. This initial number .. is termed the random number seed, or seed. **1984** *Which Micro?* Dec. 36/3 Here we have .. a 32 bit number which can act as a seed or a number. **1988** J. GLEICK *Chaos* 63 Repeat the process, using the new population as the seed, and you get ·*1353.*

**seeder**, *n.* Sense 3 in Dict. becomes 5. Add:
   **4.** [f. SEED *v.* 10.] A device for extracting seeds from fruit. orig. *U.S.*

**1895** in *Funk's Stand. Dict.* **1897** *Sears, Roebuck Catal.* 102/1 The Crown Raisin Seeder. Patented October 26, 1896... Seeds one pound of raisins in five minutes with less waste than any machine made. **1977** *Washington Post* 1 Sept. (Maryland Weekly) 3/2 Over at the Old Timer's Show exhibits haven't changed for years. Spinning wheels, crock churns, grape seeders, wood pumps, oil lamps, antique engines and smoothing irons are some of the 500 items that have been standard displays. **1989** *Grocer* 29 Apr. 27/1 (Advt.), When production demands seeded products, a section of the standard belt is wheeled out and replaced by the seeder unit.
   **5.** With defining word: a plant that produces seeds (in a particular way or under particular conditions).

**1927** *Daily Express* 11 Aug. 3/1 The 'Daily Express' £5 prize competition for the tallest hollyhock by a certain date... 'Longfellow' is a Watford entry. 'Please hurry up, because he is going to seed,' is the urgent request accompanying the entry. Early seeders must take their chance... Hollyhocks become broody at their own risk. **1977** J. L. HARPER *Population Biol. of Plants* xxii. 701 It may be the last dying burst of reproduction that is critical for the multiplication of a particular genotype and the precocious seeder will be at no advantage. **1987** *Vegetatio* LXX. 17/2 Populations of the obligate-seeder, B[*anksia*] *ericifolia*, were even-aged. **1989** *Oecologia* LXXX. 304/1 We hypothesized that tissues of seedlings of the obligate seeder, C[*eanothus*] *megacarpus*, would have greater drought tolerant characteristics than tissues of seedlings of either R[*hus*] *laurina* or *C. spinosus.*

**seeker**, *n.* Add: [**2.**] c. *Mil.* (A device in) a missile which locates its target by detecting emissions of heat, light, radio waves, etc. Cf. *heat-seeker* s.v. HEAT *n.* 14 d.

**1949** *Gloss. Guided Missile Terms* (U.S. Dept. Defense Res. & Devel. Board) (rev. ed.) 93 *Seeker*, *target*, a homing guidance device. **1956** W. A. HEFLIN *U.S. Air Force Dict.* 461/2 *Seeker*, .. esp. a missile that finds its target by means of the light, heat, or the like emitted by the target. **1959** *Space/Aeronautics* Aug. 131/1 The seeker determines the target-missile relationship, solves the equations of relative motion, and generates the steering commands for the autopilot. Among the many types of seekers, infrared units have proved simplest and most accurate. **1977** *Aviation Week* 25 July 16/3 A missile with a monopulse seeker with tail controls on an AIM-7E-size airframe. **1984** *Ibid.* 19 Mar. 79/2 The seeker would permit detection of tanks through trees and reduce the effects from camouflage. **1987** *Internat. Combat Arms* Sept. 51/1 Marconi Defense Systems claims that the advanced seeker on the Sea Eagle can respond to current ECM efforts.

**seekingly** (ˈsiːkɪŋlɪ), *adv. rare.* [f. SEEKING *ppl. a.* + -LY².] In an enquiring manner; searchingly.

**1925** T. DREISER *Amer. Tragedy* I. II. xxvi. 333 He looked at her seekingly. **1988** E. WELTY in D. & J. Abse *Music Lover's Lit. Compan.* 176 Powerhouse looks at him seekingly.

**segment**, *n.* Sense 4 d in Dict. becomes 4 e. Add: [4.] **d.** *Broadcasting.* A division of time within which a discrete item may be broadcast; hence, a separate broadcast item, usu. one of a number which make up a programme. orig. *U.S.*

**1946** R. J. LANDRY *This Fascinating Radio Business* iv. 79 A radio program . . is usually fifteen minutes, thirty minutes or sixty minutes in length although odd-length segments occur now and then. **1947** H. BETTINGER *Television Techniques* ii. 13 There are limitations imposed by the length of time that can be allotted to a given program segment. **1950** H. J. SKORNIA et al. *Creative Broadcasting* ii. 8 The radio day is divided into time segments, determined by the audience available, and what the audience is doing. **1962** A. NISBETT *Technique Sound Studio* 273 A 'talk' is a programme or programme segment which consists of one person talking at the microphone. **1976** *New Yorker* 19 May 133/1 The 'Today Show' and ABC's 'Good Morning America' also ran segments on Carter. **1982** 'E. MCBAIN' *Beauty & Beast* viii. 127 The television people . . probably want to . . tape you in Tampa for the eleven o'clock segment there. **1984** *N.Y. Times* 1 Sept. 1. 41/6 ABC, CBS and NBC shared the award for outstanding investigative journalism, for segments of news programs.

**f.** *Marketing.* One of a number of sections of a market each of which is distinguished by a different set of requirements.

**1956** *Jrnl. Marketing* XXI. 5/2 Recent introduction of a refrigerator with no storage compartment for frozen foods was in response to the distinguishable preferences of the segment of the refrigerator market made up of home freezer owners whose frozen food storage needs had already been met. **1964** *Harvard Business Rev.* Mar. 83/1 Sound marketing objectives depend on knowledge of how segments which produce the most customers for a company's brands differ in requirements and susceptibilities from the segments which produce the largest number of customers for competitive brands. **1975** *Forbes* (N.Y.) 15 Feb. 38/3 Arcata is well positioned in the growth segments of the market. **1980** *Chemical Week* 23 July 29 A downturn in demand for polyvinyl chloride (PVC) plastics, the most dynamic segment of the chlorine market, is a major factor in the slide in chlorine demand.

**segment**, *v.* [3.] For 'Cf. senses 4 c, d of the sb.' read: Cf. senses 4 c, e, f of the n. (Further examples.)

**1964** *Harvard Business Rev.* Mar. 83/1 Once you discover the most useful ways of segmenting a market, you have produced the beginnings of a sound market strategy. **1981** *Times* 18 Aug. 17/5 It segmented the market, dividing beer drinkers into categories and providing a beer and a price for each. **1988** *Media Week* 2 Sept. 9/1 Dear suggested that it might be possible in future economically to publish titles aimed at local markets segmented not by geography but by interest groups.

**segmentation**, *n.* Add: 3. *Marketing.* The division of a market into segments (sense *4 f).

**1956** *Jrnl. Marketing* July 5/1 *Segmentation* is based upon developments on the demand side of the market and represents a rational and more precise adjustment of product and marketing effort to consumer or user requirements. **1964** *Harvard Business Rev.* Mar. 83/1 Segmentation analysis . . is based on the proposition that once you discover the most useful ways of segmenting a market, you have produced the beginnings of a sound marketing strategy. **1976** *National Observer* (U.S.) 21 Feb. 20/3 Segmentation is no answer for the typical daily newspaper, whose profits depend on its ability to bring an advertiser's message into the overwhelming majority of homes in his marketing area. **1986** *Marketing Week* 29 Aug. 24/2 Horizon's marketing

strategy, which is founded upon segmentation and winning back travel agent support.

**segregationalist** (sɛgrɪ'geɪʃənəlɪst), *a.* and *n.* [f. SEGREGATIONAL *a.* + -IST.] **A.** *adj.* = SEGREGATIONIST *a.*

**1965** *Economist* 1 May 525/2 The United States Supreme Court continues hard on segregationalist heels. **1969** *Year Bk.* 10/1 Political rally for segregationalist presidential candidate, George Wallace. **1983** *N.Y. Times* 17 Oct. A20/4 A Sunday amendment will fortify the segregationalist walls that continue to fragment our society. **1989** *Daily Tel.* 23 Oct. 10/4 Virginia is one of the old Confederate Southern states that clung to its segregationalist traditions until recent years.

**B.** *n.* = SEGREGATIONIST *n.*

**1987** *Financial Times* 13 May 15/3 No mob of hard-core segregationalists materialised and President Eisenhower sent in federal troops to enforce compliance with the courts.

‖**seiza** ('seɪza), *n.* [Jap., f. *sei* straight, right, just + *za* seat, sitting.] An upright kneeling posture adopted in meditation and as a means of concentrating oneself, often serving as part of the preparation for combat in martial arts.

**1956** K. TOMIKI *Judo* i. 13 In the Orient, to keep the upper part of the body upright so that the center of gravity may lie in the abdominal region was from olden times regarded as a first step to the culture of the mind, and was practised in the *Seiza* (a form of meditation cure). **1965** *Judo* Oct. 21/2 After the exercise period the Master faces the class, . . the senior grade in the class calls '*Seiza*' and on this command the class and Master assume a kneeling position sitting on their heels with straight backs, in readiness for the next instruction, which is *Sensei ni Rei* (a bow to the Master). **1986** *Fighters* May 51/1 Mokuso is meditation done in the kneeling 'seiza' position with the student attempting to attain mushin (empty mind state).

**seize** (siːz), *n. Mech. rare.* [f. SEIZE *v.*] An instance of seizing (sense 11); cf. SEIZING *vbl. n.* 1.

**1912** F. A. TALBOT *Motor-Cars* 35 The heat causes the cylinder and the piston rings to expand until at last they become jammed irremovably together, precipitating what is known in motoring parlance as a 'seize'. **1986** *Kart & Superkart* Aug. 12/1 Reg Gange completed the weekend with a seize coming out of Mansfield corner on the last but one lap. **1987** *Ibid.* Oct. 26/3 Goff had suffered a seize, the reason seemed inexplicable, the piston was wet enough.

**select**, *v.* Add: 3. The infin. used *attrib.* or in *Comb.* to designate that part of a device which is employed in selecting one of its modes of operation.

**1974** P. CAVE *Mama* (new ed.) viii. 64 Mama strolled over to the juke-box, gave it a vicious kick and smiled with satisfaction as the green 'select' light snapped on. **1976** *Aviation Week* 31 May 43/1 Activation of the weapon-select button also automatically cues the onboard computer to provide the proper firing solutions for the particular weapon selected. **1984** *Mag. of Bank Admin.* Apr. 134/3 A new concept in HELP . . allows the user to select the desired operation or data file simply by hitting the 'select' key. **1987** *Internat. Combat Arms* Sept. 80/2 It is a select-fire weapon equipped like the rest of the H & K line with either a solid or retractable butt stock and is extremely accurate at ranges to 200 meters.

**selectron** (sɪ'lɛktrɒn), *n.*[2] *Particle Physics.* [f. S(UPER- + ELECTRON *n.*] The supersymmetric counterpart of the electron, with spin 0 instead of ½.

**1982** *Physics Lett.* B. CXVI. 280/1 The selectron decays very rapidly to an electron and a photino. **1984** *Times* 16 Feb. 10/5 In the case of the electron, the supersymmetric version, the 'selectron' would have the same electromagnetic properties, but unlike the electron would have zero spin. **1985** *Nature* 3 Jan. 9/1 Superelectrons (selectrons) would have Bose statistics, while superphotons (photinos) would be fermions. **1986** *New Scientist* 2 Jan. 26/1 The theory of supersymmetry predicts that the electron should have a partner called the selectron, but the theory does not give the selectron's mass.

**self**, *pron.*, *a.*, and *n.* Add: [C.] [I.] [4.] c. *Immunol.* Matter which is regarded by an individual's immune system as a normal constituent of that individual and is therefore not subject to attack by it.
[**1948** BURNET & FENNER in *Heredity* II. 318 There are enzymic groups adapted genetically to 'fit' a sufficient number of marker constituents to allow differentiation of 'self' from 'foreign'.. organic material.] **1965** *Ann. N.Y. Acad. Sci.* CXXIV. 10 The reaction is against self-antigen which is not recognized as 'self'. **1967** [see *immunologic* adj. s.v. IMMUNOLOGY *n.*]. **1983** *Oxf. Textbk. Med.* I. IV. 42/1 The marked biological diversity of self-antigens, together with the complexity of the cellular organization of the immune system, and the damaging potential of immune reactivity towards self. **1987** *Sci. Amer.* May 70/3 If a foreign peptide matches the sequence at the crucial sites.. the *T* cell sees the sequence as 'self' and does not respond.

**self-**, *prefix.* Add: [3.] [a.] (Examples of *self-dual*.)
**1910** VEBLEN & YOUNG *Projective Geom.* I. i. 28 The point and plane are said to be *dual* elements; the line is *self-dual*. **1955** W. PAULI *Niels Bohr* 47 The self-dual tensor with $(n,m) = (2,0)$ or $(0,2)$, and the symmetric tensor with trace zero $(2,2)$ remains invariant like the scalar $(0,0)$. **1986** P. C. WEST *Introd. Supersymmetry & Supergravity* xii. 73 $A_{ij}$ and $B_{ij}$.. are real antisymmetric self-dual tensors of rank two.

**self-antigen** (ˌsɛlf'æntɪdʒən), *n. Immunol.* Also as two words. [f. *SELF *n.* 4 c + ANTIGEN *n.*] Any substance (usu. a protein) produced by an individual which can be treated under certain conditions as an antigen by that individual's immune system.
**1965** *Ann. N.Y. Acad. Sci.* CXXIV. 10 The reaction is against self-antigen which is not recognized as 'self' and is another example of immunocytes doing what they 'know how to do', even at the expense of a harmful reaction to the body. **1969** LANDY & BRAUN *Immunol. Tolerance* 189 The scheme shown.. could easily explain the development of natural non-responsiveness to self antigens. **1971** W. BRAUN in *McGraw-Hill Yearbk. Sci. & Technol.* 105/1 The normal process of development of nonresponsiveness (tolerance) to self-antigens might be associated with an early maturation of lymphocytic cells. **1979** *Nature* 25 Jan. 330/2 The clonal selection theory put forward by Burnet in 1959 .. proposed that all lymphocytes potentially able to make antibodies against self antigens were eliminated if they met them during foetal life. **1984** TIGHE & DAVIES *Pathology* (ed. 4) iv. 32 The term 'autoimmunity' is used to describe the situation in which the specific immune response is directed at a self-antigen.

**self-assurance**, *n.* Add: **self-a'ssuredness** *n.*
**1961** in WEBSTER. **1977** R. V. ALLEN in *Q. Jrnl. Libr. of Congress* July 220/1 An.. amusing contrast was evidenced between his grandiose but ultimately fruitful projects and the self-assuredness of the duke, who did exactly as he bloody well pleased. **1989** *Boston Globe* 14 Sept. 25/2 These people.. recall vividly Dukakis' clipped phrases and self-assuredness in meetings.

**self-deprecatory** (ˌsɛlf'dɛprəkətərɪ, -keɪtərɪ, -dɛprə'keɪtərɪ), *a.* [SELF- 1 e.] = *SELF-DEPRECIATORY *a.*
Of the two combinations *self-depreciatory* and *self-deprecatory* the former is, strictly speaking, the better-formed, since it reflects the long-established use of the verb *depreciate* in the sense 'disparage, belittle'. The latter combination, however, which reflects the relatively recent use of *deprecate* in this sense (see *DEPRECATE *v.* 3 b), appears from the evidence to be now somewhat the commoner of the two.
**1939** *Burlington Mag.* Oct. 168/2 Bacon's answer.. was too self-deprecatory. **1939** A. HUXLEY *After Many a Summer* i. 3 Jeremy.. half extended his arms in the gesture of a self-deprecatory mannequin. **1961** P. JENNINGS *I said oddly, diddle I?* 144 This last always seems to me like a self-deprecatory clearing of the throat. **1989** *Chicago Tribune* 6 Apr. v. 13/2 Eisenhower has an easy-going, self-deprecatory manner that.. masks a strong temper and strong convictions.

**self-de'preciatory**, *a.* [SELF- 1 e.] Tending to depreciate or disparage oneself.
**1862** 'GEO. ELIOT' *Romola* vi, in *Cornh. Mag.* Aug. 153 Romola did not make this self-depreciatory statement in a tone of anxious humility. **1966** N. NICOLSON in H. Nicolson *Diaries & Lett.* (1966) 27 That self-depreciatory humour that he reserved for us. **1981** G. WINOKUR *Depression* xii. 113 These changes are coloured by the patient's guilt and self-depreciatory symptoms.

**self-flage'llation**, *n.* (Formerly at SELF- 1 a.) [SELF- 1 a.] **1.** The action or practice of whipping or scourging oneself, esp. as a form of religious discipline; an instance of this.
**1845** R. H. BARHAM *Brothers of Birchington* (*Ingol. Leg.*) in *New Monthly Mag.* June 146 Oh, such a Knout. For his self flagellations! **1909** *Encycl. Relig. & Ethics* II. 77/2 Thus arose the practice of self-flagellation, first introduced in certain religious houses of Central Italy. **1967** *Spectator* 1 Dec. 683/1 The law, if not the Scout Code, permits.. self-flagellation. **1983** *Lit. Rev.* Jan. 11/2 That he [*sc.* Gladstone] also occasionally whipped himself made a small sensation when it was first revealed... It is easy to forget how common self-flagellation used to be among the devout.
**2.** *fig.* Excessive self-criticism.
**1925** T. DREISER *Amer. Trag.* (1926) I. i. ix. 61 Instead of the vulgar and secretive mission producing a kind of solemnity and mental or moral self-examination and self-flagellation, they laughed and talked. **1959** *Encounter* July 65/2 His self-flagellation, his dislike of his earlier self. **1987** *N.Y. Times* 24 Aug. A16/5 If the.. speech.. had been given seven months earlier, Mr. Haig declared, Congress would not have held the hearings that he called 'an orgy of self-flagellation that has made America a laughing stock around the world'.

**self-indulgence**, *n.* Add: **self-in'dulgently** *adv.*
**1891** *N.E.D.* s.v. *Easily* adv., Without pain, discomfort, or anxiety, luxuriously, self-indulgently. **1975** *Times Lit. Suppl.* 28 Nov. 1404/3 The danger.. of self-indulgently allowing enthusiasm for the women's cause today to obstruct sensitive understanding of women's situation yesterday.

**self-'loader**, *n.* orig. and chiefly *U.S.* [SELF- 4.] **a.** A semi-automatic firearm. **b.** A mechanism for the automatic loading of freight; hence, a vehicle or vessel equipped with such a mechanism.
**1956** W. A. HEFLIN *U.S. Air Force Dict.* 462/1 *Self-loader*, .. a self-loading firearm or gun. **1986**

*Railway Age* Mar. 86/2 United States Systems, Inc., is offering a new Vac Tank package for converting dry bulk pneumatic trailers into self-loaders. **1986** *N.Y. Times* 12 Mar. C18/4 He traveled on a variety of tramp ships and self-loaders, taking pictures of ships and port facilities all over the world. **1988** *Air Transport World* Oct. 80/3 The DC-10 freighters are equipped with a fold-away 'self-loader' at the cargo door that enables them to serve remote airports that lack cargo lifters. **1989** *Los Angeles Times* 5 Apr. II. 6/3 The only practical difference between the modern military style self-loader and its commercial cousin is magazine capacity.

**self-reliance**, *n.* Add: **self-re'liantly** *adv.*
**1934** in WEBSTER. **1980** *Summary World Broadcasts: Eastern Europe* (B.B.C.) 29 Jan. A1/5 A lasting guarantee for the maintenance of general peace and security, for the ensurance [*sic*] of each people's right to develop freely and self-reliantly.

**self-satisfied**, *ppl. a.* Add: Hence **self-'satisfiedly** *adv.*
**1984** *Washington Post* 13 Oct. F4/5 'It's like with kids. If they see panic in their parents' eyes, they'll start to go crazy.' Gossage smiled self-satisfiedly. 'There's no panic here.' **1985** *Industry Week* 7 Jan. 34/2 Nissan is 'self-satisfiedly anti-union' at its Smyrna, Tenn., truck plant, alleges Mr. Anderson.

**self-seeking**, *ppl. a.* Add: **self-'seekingness** *n.*
a**1902** S. BUTLER *Way of All Flesh* (1903) l. 231 He saw it and unconsciously recognised the unrest and self-seekingness of the man. **1983** *Rev. Eng. Stud.* XXXIV. 498 What comes across in performance, especially in the second half of the play, is not self-seekingness but loyalty to the King.

**self-sufficient**, *a.* Add: **self-su'fficiently** *adv.*
**1906** SOMERVILLE & 'ROSS' *Some Irish Yesterdays* 81 There was a time, not long ago, when every self-respecting evening paper and most of the magazines had something sufficiently—or self-sufficiently —illuminating to say about Karma or the Mahatma. **1989** *Newsday* 5 May (Weekend Suppl.) 23/1 Bob Benner and his family are homesteading on the 14-acre farm, living self-sufficiently by growing their own vegetables and fruits and raising their own animals.

**sell**, *n.*² Add: **6. sell-in.** *Marketing.* The sale of goods to retail traders, esp. at wholesale prices, prior to public retailing; wholesale selling. orig. *U.S.*
**1961** W. SANSOM *Last Hours of Sandra Lee* vi. 125 It's a good product and a good campaign .. but we seem to have jimmied the sell-in somehow. **1972** *Times* 8 May (Japan Suppl.) p. v/4 Britain achieved a sell-in in the shape of a 30 per cent increase in exports to Japan. **1979** P. CAREY *War Crimes* in *Fat Man in Hist.* (1980) 170 They had had a highly successful sell-in of our existing lines of frozen meals. **1985** *Chain Store Age: Gen. Merchandise Trends* LXI. 123/3 The product must be available for sell-in and shipment prior to the movie's release. Retailers often take a wait-and-see attitude on movie product.

**sell**, *v.* Add: [**B.**] [**I.**] [**3.**] k. *transf.* Of a publication or recording: to attain sales of (a specified number of copies).
**1860** THACKERAY *Roundabout Papers* vi, in *Cornh. Mag.* Aug. 256 The Cornhill Magazine .. having sold nearly a hundred thousand copies. **1938** E. WAUGH *Scoop* I. i. 3 His novels sold fifteen thousand copies in their first year. **1948** *Illustrated* 6 Mar. 4/1 American magazines sell millions of copies because of their 'cheesecake' pictures. **1958** *Listener* 2 Oct. 498/1 Today a novel needs to sell 5,000 copies for a publisher to break even. **1966** *Melody Maker* 15 Oct. 1 Interest in the new Stones single is much less than in previous records by the group even though it is claimed to have sold more than 250,000. **1980** *Daily*

*Tel.* 21 Aug. 14 The book has sold 10,000 copies since May. It is now reprinting.

**sellathon** ('sɛləθɒn), *n. colloq.* (orig. *U.S.*). Also **sell-a-thon.** [f. SELL *v.* + -ATHON.] Any concentrated sales effort; a sales marathon.
**1976** *S9* (N.Y.) May/June 121 (Advt.), Everyone wins in the big new S9 Super Sellathon. **1978** *Broadcast* 29 May 20/2 Anyone else embarking on such a sellathon, should run a few VTR screen tests before making their final choice of presenter. **1987** *Los Angeles Times* 23 Dec. VI. 3/5 The Baghdad fest to take its place alongside the world's other big TV/cable sellathons. **1989** *Institutional Distribution* XXV. 48/1 [The] marketing program for 1989 was outlined to Nugget Distributors members at the group's January Sellathon in Honolulu.

**semantic**, *a.* and *n.* Add: **se'manticism** *n.*
**1949** R. K. MERTON *Social Theory* viii. 219 Not only ideological analysis .. but also .. Marxism, semanticism, propaganda analysis, Paretanism and .. functional analysis have .. a similar outlook on the role of ideas. **1951** *Theology* LIV. 272 To exclude all mention of Logical Positivism and Semanticism on the Continent and in the United States. **1979** *Jrnl. R. Soc. Arts* Nov. 782/2 There was a semanticism about the very best examples of the nineteenth century.

**semaphore**, *n.* Add: **'semaphoring** *ppl. a.*
**1907** *Outlook* 17 Aug. 204/2 Some years ago a French inspector came over to study our management of traffic. 'I found nothing,' he said, 'save semaphoring *gendarmes.*' **1981** J. BARNETT *Firing Squad* iii. 18 Smith raised an open palm in reply to the semaphoring arm.

**semelparity** (sɛməl'pærɪtɪ), *n. Biol.* [f. L. *semel* once + PARITY *n.*²] The state or condition of being semelparous.
**1954** L. C. COLE in *Q. Rev. Biol.* XXIX. 118/1 The writer proposes to employ the term semelparity to describe the condition of multiplying only once in a lifetime, whether such multiplication involves fission, sporulation, or the production of live young. **1975** E. O. WILSON *Sociobiology* xvi. 338/2 Iteroparity is the optimum strategy if the cost in fitness due to reproduction gradually increases with age, or if the benefit gradually decreases, or both. If neither condition holds, the best pattern is semelparity—reproduction in one large, usually suicidal burst. **1979** MANN & MILLS in P. J. Miller *Fish Phenology* (Symposia Zool. Soc.) vii. 162 It is claimed that increased fluctuations in environmental conditions do not always cause selection for increased reproductive effort and a trend towards a single reproduction in an organism's lifetime (semelparity).

**semelparous** ('sɛməlpərəs), *a. Biol.* [f. L. *semel* once + -PAROUS.] Of or designating a species or organism which reproduces only once during its lifetime. Cf. *ITEROPAROUS *a.*
**1954** L. C. COLE in *Q. Rev. Biol.* XXIX. 118/1 Nearly all annual plants and animals, as well as many protozoa, bacteria, insects, and some perennial forms such as century plants and the Pacific salmon, are semelparous species. **1966** G. C. WILLIAMS *Adaptation & Nat. Selection* vi. 175 The origin of semelparous life cycles is one aspect of the evolution of aging. **1970** *Amer. Naturalist* CIV. 8 Among the perennial organisms the two strikingly different kinds of life-history strategies are the repeated reproducers, or iteroparous organisms, and the big-bang reproducers, or semelparous organisms. **1984** *Nature* 26 July 271/2 These plants [*sc.* some purported biennials] are more properly described as semelparous (single-reproducing) perennials.

**semic** ('siːmɪk), *a.* [f. SEME *n.* + -IC, after Fr. *sémique* (*c*1960, according to Robert *Suppl.* (1970); *Funk's Stand. Dict.* (1895) II. 1626/1 has '*semic*, .. of or pertaining to semeion',

which appears to be an unconnected formation.] Of or relating to semes.
**1973** D. OSMOND-SMITH tr. *Bettetini's Lang. & Technique of Film* i. 4 Denotation is the generic and primitive function of the sign, whose capacity for connotation..derives from its history and development, its context, its expressive richness.. and everything that can contribute to those of its semic components that transcend the basic level of signification. **1973** [see SEME *n.*]. **1975** L. ZAWADOWSKI *Inductive Semantics & Syntax* I. iii. 55 This is due to a set of simple and definable grammatical relations, viz. semic relations, that occur in the texts of this system. **1986** JEFFERSON & ROBEY *Mod. Lit. Theory* (ed. 2) iv. 109 Barthes identifies.. the semic code which determines themes.

**semi-detached**, *a.* (and *n.*) Add: Hence ˌsemi-de'tachment *n.*, the state or condition of being partially detached. Also *transf.* and *fig.* (in quot. 1859, punningly). *rare.*
**1859** E. EDEN *Semi-Detached House* i. 1, I should hate my semi-detachment, or whatever the occupants of the other half of the house may call themselves. **1963** *Punch* 16 Jan. 92/2 An alternative to murder or divorce is the well-known English semi-detachment.

**semiochemical** (siːmɪəʊˈkɛmɪkəl), *n. Biol.* [f. Gr. σημεῖο-ν sign + CHEMICAL *n.*] Any chemical that conveys a biological message from one organism to another, esp. in such a way as to modify the behaviour of the recipient organism.
**1971** LAW & REGNIER in *Ann. Rev. Biochem.* XL. 533 The blatant nasal affront provided by the skunk, the hound with his nose to the ground in pursuit of his prey, and the female cat advertising her sexual availability..are familiar examples of chemical communication between animals. For the chemical substances that deliver these messages, we propose the name *semiochemicals*. **1980** *Trop. Med. & Hygiene News* Aug. 5 Insect semiochemicals—pheromones, kairomones, oviposition deterrents, and other behavior modifiers. **1981** W. J. LEWIS in D. A. Norlund et al. *Semiochemicals* i. 7 Programs utilizing semiochemicals, as well as other biological methods, do not lend themselves as readily to development, adoption, and implementation by our agribusiness systems as do conventional pesticides. **1984** *Brit. Med. Jrnl.* 24 Nov. 1459/1 A review in the 'British Journal of Dermatology'..suggests that kissing promotes the exchange of semiochemicals or pheromones, the hormone like substances that promote sexual bonding. **1988** *Nature* 24 Mar. 355/2 In addition to recognition of the queen, the five mandibular gland semiochemicals may also be involved in worker orientation during swarming, suppression of worker ovary development and egg laying, [etc.].

**semiotic**, *a.* (and *n.*) Add: **semi'oticist** *n.*
**1973** D. OSMOND-SMITH tr. *Bettetini's Lang. & Technique of Film* i. 9 The difficulty that has most obstructed the semioticist's work would seem to have been that of searching out and formulating a metalanguage. **1984** *Amer. N. & Q.* Sept./Oct. 22/1 How many allusions of this kind has this Joyce scholar and semioticist hidden openly in his narrative?

**Semliki Forest** (sɛmˈliːkɪ ˈfɒrɪst), *n. Biol.* and *Med.* [The name of a forest near the *Semliki* River in east Central Africa (see quot. 1944).] Used *attrib.* in **Semliki Forest virus**, an insect-borne togavirus used extensively as an experimental organism in genetic research.
**1944** SMITHBURN & HADDOW in *Jrnl. Immunol.* XLIX. 141 The agent was isolated from wild-caught mosquitoes... The mosquitoes from which it came were caught in the Semliki Forest in western Uganda; hence the name Semliki Forest virus. **1954** *Jrnl. Exper. Med.* XCIX. 430 A number of arthropod-borne viruses can be classified into two

sharply different groups, designated A and B. Group A consists of Eastern equine encephalitis.., Semliki Forest, Sindbis, Venezuelan equine encephalitis.., and WEE viruses. **1967** *Virology* XXXII. 141/1 The precise sites of synthesis of Semliki Forest virus precursor materials and of their assembly into virus nucleoids are not known. **1979** *Nature* 4 Jan. 14/3 Semliki Forest Virus binds preferentially to MHC products on the cell surface. **1988** J. C. BELL et al. *Zoonoses* 189 The causative agent is the Semliki Forest virus (Togaviridae). There is no vaccine.

**semp** (sɛmp), *n.* [Origin uncertain; perh. repr. shortened pronunc. of an alternative name *Louis d'or simple*.] A name in Trinidad for a variety of tanager, *Euphonia* (formerly *Tanagra*) *violacea*, which is sometimes kept as a songbird.
**1937** *Ibis* I. 532 *Tanagra violacea lichtensteini*.. Semp. Common in Trinidad, and observed..in Tobago on one occasion only... The male is a good singer, and on that account favoured by the natives as a cage-bird. **1961** G. A. C. HERKLOTS *Birds Trinidad & Tobago* 253 Semp or Louis d'Or simple *Tanagra violacea rodwayi*. **1966** K. S. LA FORTUNÉ in J. Figueroa *Caribbean Voices* I. 1. 18 And heard Soul-stirring melodies From the semp's throat. **1968** —— *Legend of T-Marie* viii. 32 Semps, Acravats and Taraudeas sang as they flew over him. **1990** *Guardian* 24 May 22/6 Like the semp that flew up from the carpet of quailed fruit.

**Semtex** ('sɛmtɛks), *n.* [Commercial name given by manufacturer, prob. f. the name of *Semtín*, a village in E. Bohemia, Czech Republic, where it is made, + -*ex*, perh. repr. the initial syllable of *explosive* or *export*.] A malleable, more or less odourless plastic explosive, manufactured in several grades and known largely through its use by terrorists.
**1985** *N.Y. Times* 9 Dec. A7/1 Police officials told Agence France-Presse that the explosive might have been Semtex, which they called the 'signature' explosive of Middle Eastern terrorist groups. **1987** *Los Angeles Times* 15 May 1. 13/6 Manufactured in Czechoslovakia and known commercially as Semtex, the explosives were also used in several letter bombs sent recently to senior British civil servants in London. **1988** *Daily Tel.* 27 Aug. 1/7 The Czechs were replying to a Foreign Office request for help in fighting terrorism and in tracing the growing consignments of Semtex reaching the IRA from Col Gaddafi of Libya. **1989** *Japan Times* 20 May 6/3 The sweet, fudge-like confectionery was found to contain Semtex plastic explosive.

**Senderista** (ˌsɛndeɪˈriːstɑː, ˌsɛndɛˈriːstə), *n.* and *a.* Pl. **Senderistas**. [Sp., f. *SENDER(O LUMINOSO *n.* + -*ista* -IST.] **A.** *n.* A member of the revolutionary Peruvian guerrilla organization *Sendero Luminoso* or *Shining Path*. **B.** *attrib.* passing into *adj.* Of or pertaining to this organization or its members.
**1982** *Business Week* 27 Sept. 7/2 The Senderistas appear to have deep roots in the cultural and nationalist movement; on the other hand, they may be a front for the Communist hegemony or become its pawn. **1983** *N.Y. Times Mag.* 31 July 20/4 Shouting Senderista slogans and songs, the peasants escorted the group to the community meeting hall. *Ibid.*, Only one badly wounded Senderista managed to escape. **1985** *Maclean's* 25 Feb. 44/1 Deriving their communist ideology from the teaching of Mao Tse-tung, the Senderistas are led by Abimael Guzman (nom de guerre, Col. Gonzalo), a hermit-like former professor of philosophy at the University of Ayacucho. **1988** *New Yorker* 4 Jan. 42/3 Whenever a bus or truck left the city, Senderista guards stopped it and took the name of everyone aboard. The passengers were warned that if the police or soldiers came while they were away their families would be killed. **1990** *Sunday Correspondent*

1 Apr. 37/3 The Senderistas, moreover, are now said to be receiving substantial sums in protection money from the cocaine lords of the Peruvian Amazon.

**Sendero Luminoso** (sɛn'dɛərəʊ luːmɪ'nəʊsəʊ, ‖sɛn'dɛro lumi'noso), *n.* [Sp., lit. 'shining path' (see quot. 1983).] The name of a neo-Maoist Peruvian revolutionary movement, founded in 1970 as the Communist Party of Peru, but subsequently becoming a clandestine guerrilla organization, which engaged in terrorist activities throughout the 1980s. Occas. *ellipt.* as *Sendero.* Cf. *SHINING *path.*
  **1981** *Washington Post* 1 Sept. A14/1 No one immediately claimed responsibility for the attacks on the U.S. buildings, but police suggested a leftist group called Sendero Luminoso (Lighted Path) was responsible. **1982** *Ann. Reg. 1981* 85 In January 130 people were arrested at Ayacucho on suspicion of complicity with the maoist terrorist organization Sendero Luminoso. **1983** *N.Y. Times Mag.* 31 July 22/2 In 1970, he [*sc.* Abimael Guzmán] and his followers .. founded the Communist Party of Peru, the organization that would become known as Sendero Luminoso. The term is taken from an earlier Peruvian ideologist, José Carlos Mariátegui: 'Marxism-Leninism will open the shining path to revolution.' **1988** *New Yorker* 4 Jan. 35/3 Unlike other revolutionary movements .. Sendero hasn't opened itself to journalists: there have been no clandestine interviews with leaders, no conducted tours of areas under Sendero control. **1990** *Observer* 1 Apr. 17/3 The treasury is so empty that the government .. certainly cannot pay all the soldiers needed to protect candidates around the country from the fanatical Sendero Luminoso guerrillas.

**sengi** ('sɛŋgiː), *n.* Also **senghi**. Pl. unchanged. [a. Kikongo *sengi, senki,* f. F. *cinq* five (i.e. sous).] In Zaire, a monetary unit introduced in 1967, equal to 100 makuta (see LIKUTA *n.*).
  **1967** *Times* 26 June 17/6 The Congo devalued its currency by about two-thirds yesterday and introduced a new system of zaires, makuta and senghi. **1987** A. ROOM *Dict. Coin Names* 192 *Sengi,* the smallest main monetary unit of Zaire ... The name is a native one, that of the Senga (Nsenga) people who originated from what is now Zaire, but who today have settled in the Zambezi River area of eastern Zambia. The unit was introduced in 1967 and there is now only a 10-sengi coin as the lowest denomination.

**‖señorito** (seɲo'rito), *n.* [Sp., dim. of SEÑOR *n.* Cf. SEÑORITA *n.*] In Spain, (a title of respect for) a young gentleman; freq. used *derog.,* to denote one who affects wealth but leads a frivolous existence.
  **1843** BORROW *Bible in Spain* II. xii. 271 This is a young Señorito, lately arrived from Madrid. **1921** J. B. TREND *Picture Mod. Spain* 67 Your hero isn't really a man of the people; he's falsified. Like you, he can't be anything but a *señorito.* **1950** G. BRENAN *Face of Spain* vii. 164 In Andalusia .. the peasant does not exist. The land there produces a lighter, more mobile sort of man, who, as soon as he has a little money, shines his shoes and dresses up as a señorito. **1953** S. BEDFORD *Sudden View* I. xi. 103 Please call back the Señorito. The Señorito took fright. He did not understand. Tell the Señorito it is the dentist. **1970** R. A. H. ROBINSON *Origins of Franco's Spain* i. 35 *La Conquista del Estado* did not take sides .. in the elections, which it termed a farce for *señoritos.* **1978** J. AIKEN *Go saddle the Sea* i. 12 Senorito Felix may .. bid you goodbye. **1988** *Washington Post* 7 Aug. C14/4 Garcia worked there for a while .. loading guns and dressing game for the 'senoritos', as he disparagingly calls the wealthy members.

**sensational,** *a.* Add: [**3.**] **c.** Of a person, an action, a product, etc.: giving rise to great public excitement and interest. Hence, in trivial use: remarkable, exciting, striking.
  **1898** G. B. SHAW *Plays Pleasant & Unpleasant* I. p. xix, It is quite possible for a piece to enjoy the most sensational success on the basis of a complete misunderstanding of its philosophy. **1918** *Rose Annual* 148 The most sensational Rose among Climbers of the year was undoubtedly that fine Hybrid, Mermaid. **1927** *Melody Maker* Aug. 800 (Advt.), The sensational hit. Sweeping the country like a cyclone. **1953** K. TENNANT *Joyful Condemned* xvi. 136 The staff-room was split over the sensational row between Miss Page and the Head. **1969** *Daily Tel.* 12 Apr. 13 Musicologically sensational and musically highly enjoyable was Alan Hacker's performance on the basset clarinet. **1979** J. HANSEN *Skinflick* x. 77 How about a sports car? .. Let it roll off a cliff and catch fire. Just like TV. Sensational. **1984** *Financial Times* 28 Apr. 19/2 Americans seem to be fond of salads as a first course, which can be a sensational start to a dinner if as good as this one.

**sensationalize,** *v.* Add: **sen'sationalized** *ppl. a.*
  **1963** *Ann. Reg. 1962* 440 A sensationalized story set largely in the U.S. Senate and the White House. **1982** *Daily Tel.* 9 Nov. 6/3 The clamour for legislation .. was often simply the reaction of well-meaning people to sensationalised and abbreviated accounts of particular cases.

**'sentencing,** *vbl. n.* [f. SENTENCE *v.* + -ING[1].] The action or process of passing sentence. Freq. *attrib.*
  **1933** *Jrnl. Criminal Law* Jan. 812 Some judges have the reputation of being severe and others of being lenient in their sentencing tendencies. **1948** L. PAGE *Sentence of Court* x. 166 Sentencing—or, as I have preferred to call it, the treatment—of an offender is a skilled business which calls for certain qualities of mind in the judge and .. for certain specialized knowledge on his part. **1958** *Law & Contemporary Probl.* XXIII. 496 The emphasis here will be upon the relation between the sentencing decision and the criminal justice system. **1973** *N.Y. Law Jrnl.* 31 Aug. 1/3 New crimes and felony categories are created, sentencing ranges are altered. **1980** *Oxf. Compan. Law* 1131/1 In the United Kingdom, sentencing is a matter entirely for the court, not for the jury.

**‖seoi nage** (seoi nage), *n. Judo.* Also **seoi-nage, seoinage.** [Jap., f. *seoi* to bear on one's back (f. *se* back + *oi* to bear) + *nage* throw.] = *shoulder throw* s.v. SHOULDER *n.* 9 c.
  **1932** E. J. HARRISON *Art of Ju-Jitsu* iv. 37 The *seoinage* is not an ideal form of attack for a tall man to adopt against a shorter adversary. **1941** M. FELDENKRAIS *Judo* vi. 115 A very tall man cannot become expert in *Seoie-Nage* [sic]. **1954** E. DOMINY *Teach Yourself Judo* 191 *Seoi nage,* shoulder throw. **1966** *Judo* Oct. 11/2 Peters, failing to make any sort of defence in time, hurtled over his back a Tsurikomi-goshi or possibly Seoi-nage for waza-ari. **1988** *Black Belt Internat.* I. v. 83/3 Ajala of London [produced] .. one of the most spectacular throws of the day, a text book ippon seoi nage .. which had to be seen to be believed.

**‖separatum** (sɛpə'rɑːtəm), *n.* Pl. **separata.** [L., neut. sing. of *sēparāt-us,* pa. pple. of *sēparāre:* see SEPARATE *v.*] A copy or reprint of an article published as part of a larger work, issued for separate distribution; an offprint, = SEPARATE *n.* 3.
  **1892** C. A. M. FENNELL *Stanford Dict.* 716/2 *Separatum,* pl. *separata,* sb., a separate copy of a scientific or literary paper which is published in a volume or part of a volume with other matter. **1956** F. C. AVIS *Bookman's Conc. Dict.* 268/2 *Separatum,* a

separate copy, especially a reprint, of a series of papers, etc.; plural = Separata. **1961** *Facilities for Adv. Study & Res.* (Univ. Oxford) 36 There is a good departmental library, including many British and foreign periodicals, and a wide range of books and separata.

**Sepharose** ('sɛfərəʊz), *n. Chem.* A proprietary name for any of several preparations of agarose used in chromatography or electrophoresis. Cf. SEPHADEX *n.*

   **1965** *Trade Marks Jrnl.* 10 Nov. 1482/2 *Sepharose* .. polymers being chemical compounds for industrial use in the purification of chemical substances. Aktiebolaget Pharmacia .. Sweden .. 24th July, 1965. **1975** WILLIAMS & WILSON *Biologist's Guide Princ. & Techniques Pract. Biochem.* iii. 82 (*table*) Characteristics of some Sepharose gels. **1979** *Experientia* XXXV. 161/1 A column of 1.5 × 30 cm packed with the lectin-sepharose was equilibrated in phosphate buffered saline, pH 7.2. **1986** R. F. DOOLITTLE *Of Urfs & Orfs* v. 64 Usually it is possible to obtain very pure antibodies by passing the antiserum over an affinity column in which the synthetic peptide has been attached to Sepharose (or a comparable support).

**septage** ('sɛptɪdʒ), *n. N. Amer.* [f. SEPT(IC *a.* + -AGE, after SEWAGE *n.*] Waste matter or sewage contained in a septic tank. Freq. *attrib.*

   **1977** *Victoria* (B.C.) *Times* 13 Sept. 17/1 A new example of bureaucratic mangling of the English language didn't sneak past Oak Bay council this week. The word is 'septage' ... The Capital Regional District .. was proposing approval for it to take on the function of 'septage disposal'. **1981** *N.Y. Times* 15 Mar. (Connecticut Weekly section) 24/6 The major sources of ground water .. contamination are solid-waste disposal; septage disposal; oil spills; industrial development [etc.]. **1986** *Jrnl. Water Pollution Control Federation* LVIII. 969/2 A pumper truck is usually used to remove and transport the septage slurry. **1989** *Whole Earth Rev.* Spring 38/3 Ocean Arks staff built a prototype aquatic ecosystem for the town of Harwich on Cape Cod to treat cesspool or septage wastes.

**septenar** ('sɛptɪnɑː(r)), *n. Pros.* [ad. L. *septēnārius*; cf. F. *septénaire* and -AR².] = SEPTENARY *n.* 5, SEPTENARIUS *n.*

   **1911** R. W. BOND *Early Plays from Italian* 82 These septenars, or fourteeners, popularized by Phaer .. form in the contemporary drama the transition from the irregular dancing doggerel to the rhymed decasyllabic ... In the *Marriage of Wit and Science* regular septenars alternate with rhymed decasyllabics. **1945** E. K. CHAMBERS *Eng. Lit. at Close of Middle Ages* iii. 131 From this period [*sc.* the latter part of the 15th cent.] we have some of the tales [of Robin Hood] themselves. They are written in septenars. **1962** R. W. BURCHFIELD in Davis & Wrenn *Eng. & Medieval Stud.* 100 As .. the word occurs in the final position in the septenar, the stem vowel must be long.

**sequencer**, *n.²* Add: **3.** *Mus.* A programmable electronic device capable of storing a sequence of musical notes, chords, or other signals which can then be reproduced when required.

   **1975** J. E. ROGERS in Appleton & Perera *Devel. & Pract. Electronic Mus.* v. 190 Sequencers and keyboards have at most a few hundred memory positions. **1984** D. CROMBIE *Synthesizer & Electronic Keyboard Handbk.* 72/3 There are three basic types of sequencer: analog, digital and hybrid-computer sequencers. **1985** *Listener* 24 Oct. 43/4 The Synclavier also has a 'sequencer', which is like a word processor for music: you can use it to program the machine to play 'Chopsticks' for you. **1989** *Rhythm* Mar. 30/2 Musicians create their rhythm patterns in the sequencer rather than on the drum machine.

‖**Serenissima** (sere'nissima), *n.* [It., fem. of *serenissimo* most serene.] With *the*: 'the most serene city', a historic title for Venice or the former Venetian republic. Also *la Serenissima.*

   **1909** H. A. DOUGLAS *Venice & her Treasures* i. 6 This intercourse with Constantinople was an important factor for centuries in the history of 'Serenissima'. **1956** D. VARÈ *Ghosts of Rialto* ii. 10 Though continually at war with some other power, the Venetian Republic was known as *la Serenissima*, 'the most Serene'. **1965** R. SHECKLEY *Game of X* (1966) vii. 52 He was a true Venetian. Like many other subjects of the Serenissima, he believed in style over content, art over life. **1977** *Times* 3 Nov. 12/5 To write a definitive English history of the Serenissima is a worthy ambition for any Venetian *aficionado.* **1989** *Encycl. Brit.* XXIX. 498/2 The uncommon harmonies of Venetian stone, air, water, and time are fully orchestrated in St. Mark's Square .., for centuries the social and political centre of *La serenissima.*

**serging** ('sɜːdʒɪŋ), *n. Needlework.* [f. SERGE *n.* + -ING¹.] The method of close-stitching or overcasting used to prevent material fraying at the edge; stitching of this kind.

   **1908** W. H. BAKER *Dict. Men's Wear* 218 *Serging,* an overcasted stitch employed to hold ravelling edges of seams. **1933** J. E. LIBERTY *Pract. Tailoring* iii. 23 *Serging.* This is an overstitch used in conjunction with loose edges which are apt to fray. The needle is placed over the edge at each stitch at the slant (as in felling) and forms a row of stitching on and over the edge of the material. **1956** A. WAISMAN *Mod. Custom Tailoring for Men* I. 7 *Overcasting or serging stitch.* This stitch is used to preserve the unfinished .. edges of garment seams. **1962** D. J. DUFFIN *Essent. Mod. Carpet Installation* (ed. 2) iv. 55 Serging does not wear as well as binding and is not recommended where there is heavy traffic. **1988** *Toronto Sun* 13 Apr. 48 (Advt.), With the new 1988 machine you just set the color-coded dial and see magic happen. Straight sewing, zig-zag, buttonholes, .. professional serging stitch .. all this and more without the need of old-fashioned cams or programmers.

**Seri** ('sɛrɪ, 'sɛərɪ), *n.* and *a.* Also 9 Ceris; pl. 9 Ceres, Ceris, Seris, 20 Seri. [a. Sp., f. Opata (Uto-Aztecan); cf. Papago *se:l.*] **A.** *n.* **a.** (A member of) an American Indian people inhabiting western Sonora state, Mexico, and Tiburón Island in the Gulf of California. **b.** The Hokan language of this people.

   **1829** R. W. H. HARDY *Trav. Mexico* xii. 300 The Céres, like the Malay pirates of India, neither gave nor received quarter. **1854** J. R. BARTLETT *Pers. Narr. Explor. Texas* I. xx. 464 He was a full-blooded Ceris, and came originally from the island of Tiburon. **1891** D. G. BRINTON *Amer. Race* I. ii. 110 The Seris or Ceris are described as thieves and vagrants. **1898** *17th Ann. Rep. U.S. Bureau Amer. Ethnol. 1895-96* I. 259* The warfare of the Seri is largely sortilegic. **1929** E. SAPIR in *Encycl. Brit.* V. 140/2 Hokan proper, which includes Seri (coast of Sonora), Yuman (in Lower California) and Tequistlateco or Chontal (coast of Oaxaca). **1948** A. L. KROEBER *Anthropol.* (rev. ed.) vii. 280 The Seri, so far back as we know them, have also been outrightly parasitic on other groups, so far as they could, by force, cajolery, or suffrance, much like Gypsies. **1965** *Language* XLI. 305 Seri and Tequistlatec, both separate branches of Hokan. **1989** *Encycl. Brit.* X. 650/2 The 300 to 400 surviving Seri in the late 20th century constituted a single community composed of the remnants of several groups.

   **B.** *adj.* Of or pertaining to the Seri or their language.

   **1829** R. W. H. HARDY *Trav. Mexico* xii. 298 It is believed that the Céres Indians have discovered a method of poisoning their arrows. **1854** J. R. BARTLETT *Pers. Narr. Explor. Texas* I. xx. 463, I requested . . an Indian of the *Ceris* tribe from whom I could obtain a vocabulary of his language. **1898** *17th Ann. Rep. U.S. Bureau Amer. Ethnol. 1895-96* I. 169* The Seri face-painting would seem to be essentially zoosematic, or symbolic of zoic tutelaries. **1948** A. L. KROEBER *Anthropol.* (rev. ed.) vii. 279 At the extreme edge of this concept we have peoples like the Seri Indians or the Negritos, whose attitudes are in part like those of Gypsies. **1979** *Tucson Mag.* Apr. 64/1 (Advt.), Seri Indian carvings.

Also **'Serian** *n.*, the language family comprising the Seri language alone.
**1915** A. L. KROEBER in *Univ. Calif. Publ. Amer. Archaeol. & Ethnol.* IX. 279 (*title*) Serian, Tequistlatecan, and Hokan.

**serial**, *a.* and *n.* Add: [**B.**] **c.** A military unit or group of units organized under a single commander for troop movements or for drill; hence more generally, any squad, esp. of police officers, formed for a special purpose. orig. *U.S.*
**1942** GARBER & BOND *Mod. Mil. Dict.* (ed. 2), *Serial*, one or more march units, preferably with the same march characteristics, placed under a single commander for march purposes. **1974** C. RYAN *Bridge too Far* III. i. 137 A special serial of 38 gliders carrying General Browning's Corps Headquarters, bound for Nijmegen, travelled with them. **1976** *Daily Mail* 8 Nov. 14/5 What a dreadful example of management it is to send serials (squads) of 20 constables containing two, three and sometimes more women to potentially violent demonstrations. **1987** *Daily Tel.* 29 Jan. 3/2 Pc Alan Tappy recalled seeing a number of youths running off to get reinforcements as the police serial and firemen reached the Tangmere block where rioters had set fire to the supermarket.

**'serializable**, *a.* [f. SERIALIZE *v.* + -ABLE.] Capable of being arranged in a series; suitable for publishing or broadcasting in serial form.
**1988** *Communications ACM* Mar. 303/1 Actions have precisely the properties that are needed to solve the concurrency and failure problems. First, they are serializable: the effect of running a group of actions is the same as if they were run sequentially in some order. **1989** N. SHERRY *Life Graham Greene* I. xxxi. 456 It is, roughly speaking, a panoramic novel of London . . and I should think would be serialisable. **1989** *Byte* XIV. 262/3 The database server must execute interleaved transactions so that the result of their execution is serializable.

**series**, *n.* Add: [**II.**] [**8.**] **b.** A set or class of aircraft, motor vehicles, etc. developed over a period and sharing many features of design or assembly.
**1935** C. G. BURGE *Compl. Bk. Aviation* 550/2 '*Series*' *aircraft and engine*, every complete aircraft or every engine, the various essential parts of which are constructed in accordance with the 'type' design. **1953** W. A. SHRADER *Fifty Years of Flight* 124/2 Spratt Aircraft Co. . . test-flies another in a series of tilt-wing flying boats designed by George Spratt. **1968** MILLER & SAWERS *Technical Devel. Mod. Aviation* v. 130 Douglas matched this series with the DC-7 in 1953, also using the turbo-compound engine and 2 feet 3 inches longer than the 6B. **1970** K. BALL *Fiat 600, 600D Autobook* i. 9/2 Early models of the 600D series incorporated a centrifugal oil filter alone. **1988** *Flight Internat.* 17 Dec. 13/1 Hazelton Airlines of New South Wales, Australia, has ordered its first Shorts 360, a .300 series aircraft.

**seriously**, *adv.*² Add: [**2.**] **b.** As an intensifier: very, really; substantially. Esp. as *seriously rich.* *colloq.* (orig. *U.S.*).
**1981** *Washington Post* 7 June K8/6 He became seriously rich, but in 1977 experienced a mid-wealth crisis. **1987** *Observer* 22 Feb. 53/7 The *World of*

*Interiors*, where an antique curtain tassel could cost a couple of hundred. Seriously rich. Seriously cool. **1990** *New Musical Express* 28 July 48/6 (Advt.), Seriously attractive young lady (24) seeks interesting friends all ages.

**sero-**, *comb. form.* Add: **sero'prevalence**, the prevalence of a given pathogen in a population as measured serologically.
**1980** *Amer. Jrnl. Vet. Res.* XLI. 784/1 Secular *seroprevalence studies indicated the emergence of CPV infection in the United States dog population-at-large in 1978. **1988** *Science* 15 Jan. 253/2 In 88 studies in 52 cities, CDC discovered that seroprevalence among drug addicts depends on where they are found.

**'serovar** *Microbiol.* [after CULTIVAR *n.*] = SEROTYPE *n.*
**1973** S. P. LAPAGE et al. in *Internat. Jrnl. Systematic Bacteriol.* XXIII. 106/1 An infrasubspecific term is used to refer to the kinds of taxa below subspecies. Examples: *serovar, chemovar, forma specialis.* **1975** *Acta Microbiologica Acad. Sci. Hung.* XXII. 179 Serologically, the two species appear strongly related if not identical, but they are different from all L[*isteria*] *monocytogenes* serovars. **1984** R. W. WHEAT in W. K. Joklik et al. *Zinsser's Microbiol.* (ed. 18) ii. 10/2 Subspecies designations, such as serotypes (serovars) or phage types (phagevars), are used to indicate the mode of variation.

**serpentarium** (sɜːpənˈtɛərɪəm), *n.* orig. and chiefly *U.S.* [f. SERPENT *n.* + -ARIUM.] A building or enclosure in which snakes (and other reptiles) are confined, as for public display or observation; a snake-house or reptiliary. Cf. OPHIDIARIUM *n.*
**1895** in *Funk's Stand. Dict.* **1955** *Amer. Jrnl. Trop. Med. & Hygiene* IV. 1135 This is the case of one of us (W. E. H.), a white male, age 43, who is the director of a serpentarium in Miami, Florida. **1965** T. HELM *World of Snakes* viii. 101 With the establishment of his Serpentarium in 1948, Haarst's career has made him a worldwide medical wonder. By successfully self-immunizing himself with cobra venom his blood has become a valuable serum. **1977** *Daily Tel.* 5 Sept. 3/6 Desperate attempts by a father to force open the jaws of a 2,000 lb. crocodile failed as his six-year-old son was dragged under water at the Miami Serpentarium on Saturday. **1989** *Summary World Broadcasts Weekly Econ. Rep.: U.S.S.R.* (B.B.C.) 6 Oct. A16/1 There are some 1,000 adders in Belorussia's first serpentarium which has opened in Vitebsk Oblast's Sennenskiy Rayon.

**serpentine**, *n.* Senses 10 a, b in Dict. become 10 b, c. Add: [**10.**] **a.** *Equestr.* A riding exercise consisting of a series of half-turns to right and left alternately, testing the rider's control and the horse's suppleness. Cf. CARACOL *n.* 3.
[**1711** *Milit. & Sea Dict.* (ed. 4), *Caracol*, as *Wheel by Caracol*; used only among the Horse, and is a Serpentine or Rounding Motion of Wheeling.] **1861** T. MARTIN *Bk. of Aids* ii. 25 *Serpentine*, . . the leading file inclines to the right across the school, . . and makes a zigzag course down the school. **1946** M. C. SELF *Horseman's Encycl.* 364 The serpentine may be done at all gaits, the faster the gait the larger in diameter the turns. **1976** R. L. V. FFRENCH BLAKE *Elementary Dressage* 72 In the Intermediate test . . there is a six-loop serpentine the full width of the arena with flying changes. **1986** *Your Horse* Sept. 34/3 The rider should . . be capable of riding basic school movements—turns, circles, serpentines and loops.

**serve**, *n.*² Sense 3 in Dict. becomes 4. Add: **3.** A serving or helping of food. *colloq.*
**1920** A. ASHFORD *True Hist. Leslie Woodcock* in *Daisy Ashford: her Bk.* ix. 38 'Where is that child'

said Mr. Earlsdown after having 3 serves of the bacon. **1986** *Sun* (Melbourne) (Travel Suppl.) 10 Jan. 2/4 The Time Out editors advise that many of the recommended restaurants offer free seconds if you can scoff all the generous first serves.

**sesh** (sɛʃ), *n. colloq.* (orig. *Services'*). [Repr. pronunc. of abbrev. of SESSION *n.* 7; cf. SECESH *n.* and *a.*] A session or bout, esp. of drinking.
   **1943** *Airflow* (Ceylon) Christmas 368/1 An Orderly Sergeant, roused from a convivial 'sesh' on Boxing Night. **1944** G. NETHERWOOD *Desert Squadron* 119 Empty lager bottles . . signified that Hans and Fritz also knew the joys of a desert 'sesh'. **1985** M. MUNRO *Patter* 61 A session . . is a spell of drinking . . . Sometimes shortened to *sesh*: 'That was a rare wee sesh last Friday.' **1987** *Financial Times* 18 July 1. 6 'We're not going to win a prize for graphics,' said Syd Silverman in a sesh this week.

**sessile**, *a.* Add: Hence **se'ssility** *n.*
   **1903** *Amer. Geologist* XXXI. 204 Such cases as these make cameration appear as a result of vertical sessility and therefore allow us to infer from such cameration, this sessile mode of life. **1940** *Nature* 30 Mar. 484/2 Altenburg . . notes that hermaphroditism is related to sluggishness and sessility. **1982** *Acta Biol. et Med. Germanica* XLI. 145 The loss of this glycoprotein might thus be associated with a loss of sessility of bovine lymphoid cells.

**session**, *n.* Add: [**7.**] **d.** A period devoted to heavy drinking; a drinking-bout. *colloq.* (chiefly *Austral.*).
   **1943** [implied in *SESH *n.*]. **1949** L. GLASSOP *Lucky Palmer* 215 I'll join you in a beer later, but I don't want to get into a session. **1955** D. NILAND *Shiralee* 51, I don't want to make a session of it . . . I'd just like a drink to pick me up. **1962** K. SIMONS *Not with Kiss* 26 'What's the drum on the party tomorrow night?' 'Oh, just a bit of a session for the boys.' **1981** C. WILLIAMS *Open Cut* 148 She has to go longer hours . . . Bloke'll shoot off for a session. She has to make up her own entertainment. **1985** M. MUNRO *Patter* 61 A session or bevvy-session is a spell of drinking, a booze-up.

**set**, *n.*[2] Add: [**II.**] [**9.**] **e.** *Body-building.* A fixed number of repetitions of a particular exercise, performed as a unit.
   **1956** *Muscle Power* June 41/2 Which brings us up to his routine . . . The exercises, the weights, the sets and the repetitions will now be listed here. **1961** *Ibid.* Nov. 27/1 Going in for high sets of high reps he soon trimmed that 'smoothness' away. **1985** *Bodypower* June 5/1 Gladys began to grimace during the 8th rep but managed to perform two more for her first set.
   **f.** A group of waves of similar height and force. *Surfing slang.*
   **1963** *Surfing Yearbk.* 43/1 Set, a group of waves. **1977** *Fortune* Aug. 75/2 Prone on his board, Hastings paddles out beyond the line of breakers, and then watches for a set of waves to roll in. **1986** *Wavelength Surfing* II. 11. 68/2 The surf was a constant 2–3ft with the occasional 4–5ft set, and the scoring average for the six scoring waves was around 6.0–7.5 per heat.

**set**, *v.*[1] Add: [**B.**] [**III.**] [**17.**] **c.** *transf.* To place the action of (a fictional or imaginative work) *in* a particular setting. Usu. in *pass.* Cf. LAY *v.*[1] 20 b.
   [**1888** H. MORLEY *Shakespeare's Merry Wives of Windsor* 12 Shakespeare sets Falstaff in the close air of a tavern; and he has set his healthy women among fields by the riverside.] **1900** *Daily News* 15 Aug. 6/4 The story, which is set in a middle-class milieu, succeeds in being homely. **1951** G. GREENE *Lost Childhood* 108 The novels were now set in Cumberland; the farms, the village shops, the stone walls, the green slope of Catbells became the background of her pictures and her prose. **1989** M.

LANE *Literary Daughters* ii. 66 *Belinda*, set in polite London society, . . established Maria's range.

∥**set** (sɛt), *a. Philol.* [Skr., f. *sa- + it* 'i'.] In Sanskrit, designating a root after which the vowel *i* appears before certain suffixes and endings (such roots being now widely explained as reflecting a type earlier having a laryngeal suffix). Also *transf.* of reconstructed Indo-European roots and formations based on them in various languages.
   **1897** S. C. VASU *Ashtádhyáyi of Pánini* II. VII. ii. 1366 A root which is *optionally* Set before other affixes, is *invariably* aniṭ before Nishṭhâ. **1939** E. PROKOSCH *Compar. Germanic Gram.* 129 Sanskrit grammar . . distinguishes between *sēṭ*-bases and *aniṭ*-bases, i.e., bases with or without *i < ə* (*sa-* 'with', *an-* 'without'). **1952** W. P. LEHMANN *Proto-Indo-European Phonol.* iii. 28 The laryngeal theory demands a change of analysis of some of the most important IE form classes, such as the set-roots. **1962** C. WATKINS *Indo-European Origins of Celtic Verb* 1. 186 In Indo-European, seṭ roots formed only a limited number of kinds of presents . . . The Celtic verbs continue Indo-European athematic seṭ presents. **1970** G. NAGY *Gr. Dial.* i. 45 For the extension of complex *-is-* from seṭ-roots as replacement of simplex *-s-* and for the morphophonemic conditioning, cf. Kurylowicz, *Apophonie*, 252–257.

**seven**, *a.* and *n.* Add: [**A.**] [**2.**] [**f.**] (*e*) the group of countries (Austria, Denmark, Norway, Portugal, Sweden, Switzerland, and the U.K.) which were the original members of the European Free Trade Association from 1959; cf. SIX *a.* 2 j.
   **1959** *Daily Tel.* 20 Nov. 1/1 The creation of the 'Six' and the 'Seven' should under no circumstances lead to a trade war in Europe. **1978** *Internat. Relations Dict.* (U.S. Dept. State Library) 13/1 The original members . . were referred to as 'The Seven' . . as a counterpart to 'The Six' original members of the Common Market.

**seven** ('sɛv(ə)n), *v. U.S. slang.* [f. SEVEN *n.* (see sense 3).] *intr.* Const. *out.* In the game of craps: to throw a seven, and hence to lose one's bet; occas. with dice as subj. Also *transf.* Cf. *to crap out* s.v. CRAP *v.* 3.
   **1934** *Sun* (Baltimore) 29 Jan. 14/3 The rattle of dice across the floor accompanied by deep-throated entreaties of 'come on, Little Joe' . . 'Seven out, dice.' **1942** BERREY & VAN DEN BARK *Amer. Thes. Slang* §750/5 Seven-out, to turn up a seven instead of one's point, a losing throw. **1957** *Encycl. Brit.* VII. 328/2 He continues to throw the dice until his point appears again, in which case he wins, or until a seven appears, in which case he is said to 'seven out' or 'crap out'—when he loses the dice and loses the dice. **1975** S. BELLOW *Humboldt's Gift* (1976) 70 'Why do you push it, Charlie?' he said. 'At our age one short game is plenty . . . One of these days you could seven out.'

**sevener**, *n.* Senses in Dict. become 2 a, b. Add: **1.** *Islam.* With capital initial. A member of the smaller of the two Shiah sects (the 'Seveners' and the 'Twelvers'), acknowledging only seven Imams; = ISMAELIAN *n.* Usu. in *pl.* Cf. TWELVER *n.*[2]
   **1845** *Encycl. Metrop.* XXIV. 441/2 The *Imámís* appear to have derived from the Ghulát the doctrine of a present but invisible Imám, the successor of the seventh or the twelfth of the visible Imáms. From these numbers their two principal branches are denominated Seb'ís (Seveners) or Ithná'asharís (Twelvers). **1957** *Encycl. Brit.* XII. 710/2 The Isma'ilis or Seveners are the followers of Isma'il, whom they regard as the 7th imam, rather than his younger brother, Musa (797), who is accepted by the Twelvers. **1979** *Sunday Tel.* (Colour Suppl.) 27 May

25/3 'Khomeini is an *Ayatullah*,' said the Aga Khan. 'He is not Imam of the Twelve Shias, whereas I am Imam of the Ismaili Seveners.'

**Severan** (sɛ'vɛərən, 'sɛvərən), *a.* [f. the L. cognomen *Sevĕr-us* (see below) + -AN.] Of, pertaining to, or characteristic of the Roman Emperor (Lucius) Septimius Severus (reigned A.D. 193-211) and, more generally, of the period of rule of the dynasty established by him (A.D. 193-235).
   **1918** M. PLATNAUER *Life & Reign Emperor Lucius Septimius Severus* vi. 110 The simplest solution seems to be to see in Spartian the embodiment of a 'Severan' source—possibly the emperor's own speech mentioned in xi. 4. **1966** J. M. KELLY tr. *Kunkel's Introd. Roman Legal & Constitutional Hist.* ix. 127 The period of internal peace which had lasted . . from Augustus up to the time of the Severan emperors, had not in fact resulted in a lasting strengthening of the Empire. **1972** A. PRICE *Col. Butler's Wolf* xvi. 187 The First Lusitanians were stationed here during the Severan reconstruction. **1988** *Classical Rev.* XXXVIII. 362 They begin in the Severan period and continue into the fourth century with the majority apparently coming in the mid-third century.

‖**seviche** (se'vitʃe), *n.* Also **ceviche**. [S. Amer. Sp. *seviche, cebiche*.] A Spanish-American dish of raw fish or seafood marinaded in lime or lemon juice, usu. garnished and served as a starter.
   **1951** C. H. BAKER *S. Amer. Gentleman's Compan.* I. ii. 33 Any fresh white-meated fish does well, except the oily mackerel tribe; and we prefer *Seviche* made either of fish or shrimps alone, not mixed. **1966** P. BENTON tr. *N. Lyon's Fish for All Occasions* (1967) 195 In Peru ceviche is made with *aji*, a hot red pepper which is freshly pounded for each dish in which it appears. **1977** *Time* 19 Dec. 56/2 Back in style are New England boiled dinners, Kentucky burgees, Florida conch seviche. **1986** *Times* 26 Feb. 13/1 Raw fish . . from Japanese *sushi* . . to South American *seviche* 'cooked' without heat in lime juice.

**Sevin** ('sɛvin), *n.* Also **sevin**. A proprietary name for a preparation of 1-naphthyl N-methylcarbamate, used as an insecticide of low toxicity to animals.
   **1958** *Trade Marks Jrnl.* 9 Apr. 368/2 *Sevin* . . Insecticides. Union Carbide Corporation . . United States . . 21st January, 1958. **1962** *Times* 9 Mar. 17/1 One of the more recent insecticides, sevin, has aroused interest because it is chemically of a new type. **1977** *Arab Times* 13 Nov. 4/5 Although banned in this country five years ago . ., DDT use was permitted for airplane spraying in combination with another chemical, Sevin. **1985** *Listener* 3 Jan. 3/3 Union Carbide in Bhopal was making a particularly powerful pesticide, called Sevin Carbaryl.

**sewable** ('səʊəb(ə)l), *a.*[2] [f. SEW *v.*[1] + -ABLE.] Capable of being stitched or sewn, or made by sewing; suitable for sewing. So **sewa'bility** *n.*
   **1960** *Clothing Machine Engineer* Winter 47 The sewability of threads. **1970** *Cabinet Maker & Retail Furnisher* 23 Oct. 174/2 Doubts were expressed about the sewability and the possibility of upholstering such features as piping and buttons with such a bulky fabric. **1972** *Where?* Feb. 34/2 The only limitation in this competition is that the flag should be somehow sewable. **1988** *N.Y. Times* 18 Dec. (New Jersey Weekly section) 29/2 The rules seem to be that whatever is sewable, goes.

‖**sewamono** ('sewamono), *n.* Pl. unchanged. [Jap., f. *sewa* everyday life + *mono* piece, play.] In Japanese kabuki and bunraku theatre: a domestic drama or melodrama.
   **1911** *Encycl. Brit.* XV. 170/1 Gradually the Kabuki developed the features of a genuine theatre; the actor and the playwright were discriminated, and, the performances taking the form of domestic drama (*Wagoto* and *Sewamono*) or historical drama (*Aragoto* or *Jidaimono*), actors of perpetual fame sprang up. **1957** *Oxf. Compan. Theatre* (ed. 2) 412/2 The Japanese theatre recognizes three main classes, the *jidaimono* or histories . .; the *sewamono* or melodramas; and the *shosagoto* or dances. **1975** J. R. BRANDON *Kabuki* 5 In the late seventeenth century, three major divisions of kabuki drama were recognized: *sewamono* . . *jidaimono*; and dance pieces, called *shosagoto*. **1980** R. ILLING *Art of Jap. Prints* i. 13 The plays were broadly categorised into *jidaimono*, . . and *sewamono*, plays about everyday contemporary life.

**sexer** ('sɛksə(r)), *n.* Also **sexor**. [f. SEX *v.* + -ER[1].] One who determines the sex of a chicken, by anatomical examination. Freq. as *chicken sexer*.
   **1933** *Poultry Rec.* Dec. 178/1 It was fortunate that the progressive Chick Sexing Propagate Association donated as a prize to the Grand Champion chick sexer of Japan a free trip to America. **1940** *Poultry Sci.* XIX. 237/2 Many sexors fairly efficient in sexing White Leghorns are not as accurate when working on the heavy breeds. **1955** FUNK & IRWIN *Hatchery Operation & Managem.* viii. 129 A good sexor can easily sex 700 to 800 chicks per hour, and the faster sexors can sex 1,000 or more chicks per hour. **1971** *Observer* 7 Nov. 19/4 (*caption*) A Japanese chicken sexer at work in deepest Dorset. He can get through 1,000 in an hour. **1986** *Daily Tel.* 20 June 11/8 A chicken sexing firm at Occold, Suffolk, is recruiting a sexer from South Korea, because it cannot find one in this country.

**sexercise** ('sɛksəsaɪz), *n.* orig. *U.S.* [Blend of SEX *n.* and EXERCISE *n.*] **a.** Sexual activity regarded as exercise. **b.** (An) exercise designed to enhance sexual attractiveness or to improve sexual performance.
   **1942** BERREY & VAN DEN BARK *Amer. Thes. Slang* §355/1 *Caressing*, . . sexercise (*sex exercise*), sexperiment (*sex experiment*), sexploration (*sex exploration*), [etc.]. **1967** E. O' RELLY *Sexercises: Isometric & Isotonic* iii. 19 For best results you are advised to space your sexercise periods allowing . . one day's rest between sessions. **1973** I. ROBINSON *Survival of English* v. 173 A sort of sexual acrobatics of which the elementary stages are presumably the 'sexercises for a happier love life' promised by an article in the October 1972 *She*. **1976** *Lancet* 13 Nov. 1078/2 Sexercise-induced asthma. **1979** J. HOFER (*title*) Sexercise: how to exercise your way to sexual fitness. **1985** *Los Angeles Times* 8 Dec. I. 2/5 A judge has rejected pleas by two Playboy centerfolds to halt distribution of a 'Sexercise' videotape they said they performed in unknowingly.

**sexploitation**, *n.* Add: **sex'ploiter** *n.*, one who or that which exploits sexually, *esp.* a sexually exploitative film.
   **1942** BERREY & VAN DEN BARK *Amer. Thes. Slang* §438/4 *Sexploiter*, a sex exploiter. **1970** *World Bk. Year Bk.* 426 The line between the sexploiters and the ordinary Hollywood film was beginning to disappear. **1981** *Times* 29 Jan. 4/4 It is the sexploiters who have been intolerant.

**Sézary** ('sɛzərɪ, ‖sezari), *n. Path.* [The name of Albert *Sézary* (1880–1956), French dermatologist, who described the condition in 1938 (*Bull. Soc. Fr. Derm. Syph.* XLV. 254).] Used *attrib.* or in the possessive, esp. as *Sézary('s) syndrome*, to designate a type of cutaneous lymphoma with symptoms including exfoliative dermatitis, intense pruritus, and the presence in the blood of atypical T lymphocytes with convoluted nuclei (sometimes called *Sézary cells*). (The syndrome is thought

to be caused by human T cell leukaemia virus type 1, HTLV-1.)
**1953** *Brit. Med. Jrnl.* 16 May 1087/1 *(heading)* Sézary's reticulosis with exfoliative dermatitis. **1955** *Ibid.* 29 Jan. 258/1 Sézary cells in air-dried Romanovski films . . are approximately twice the size of normal polymorphs. *Ibid.* 258/2 The features of Sézary's syndrome are intense pruritus, generalized erythrodermia, pigmentation, and superficial lymphadenopathy, associated with the presence of unusual monocytoid cells in the blood. **1961** *Jrnl. Amer. Med. Assoc.* 19 Aug. 471/1 In our experience, erythrodermic mycosis fungoides is the condition most frequently confused with the Sézary syndrome. **1968** *Blood* XXXI. 722 The nucleus of the lymphocyte has a round contour or a single deep notch and can be easily distinguished from the Sézary cell. **1978** M. BURNET *Endurance of Life* x. 145 A type of lymphocytic leukaemia, spoken of as Sezary's disease.

**Shabak** (ʃæ'bæk), *n.* [a. mod.Heb., acronym f. the initial letters of *šērūt bittāḥōn kĕlālī* general security service; cf. SHIN BET *n.*] The division of the Israeli security service concerned with counter-espionage and internal security (properly a department of *Shin Bet*).
**1972** F. FORSYTH *Odessa File* v. 106 To the left sits the chief of the Shabak, sometimes wrongly referred to as the Shin Beth. **1980** *Times* 13 Aug. 1/3 The head of Shabak, the Israeli general security service . . the Shabak chief. **1983** *N.Y. Times* 29 Dec. A2/5 Many Arabs say they feel themselves under close surveillance by the Shin Beth, also known as the Shabak, the Israeli secret police. **1987** *Polit. Dict. State of Israel* 270/2 The founder of the *Shabak* in 1948 and its Head until 1954 was Isar Harel. The name of the current Head of *Shabak* is never revealed for security reasons. **1988** 'R. DEACON' *Spyclopaedia* 37 The purely counter-espionage section of Shin Beth is *Sheruth Bitakhon Klali*, more usually known as Shabak.

**shacky** ('ʃækɪ), *a.*[2] *colloq.* [f. SHACK *n.*[3] + -Y[1].] Of buildings, etc.: resembling or suggestive of a shack; dilapidated or ramshackle; run-down.
**1921** S. KAYE-SMITH *Joanna Godden* III. 194 She had wanted Great Ansdore [farm] very much, though . . it was shacky and mouldy. **1979** N. MAILER *Executioner's Song* I. ii. 531 Shacky ranch houses stretched as far as the smog would allow the eye to see. **1982** J. HANSEN *Gravedigger* vii. 76 Haven't you made this place attractive? Really rustic instead of just shacky. **1987** *Motor Sport* June 572/1 The once very 'shacky' town of Bracknell in Berkshire is now a brash New Town.

**shade**, *v.*[1] Add: [9.] **e.** To surpass (a particular age or weight) by a narrow margin; to eclipse or merit by a shade. *colloq.* (orig. *U.S.*).
**1934** in WEBSTER. **1941** B. SCHULBERG *What makes Sammy Run?* iv. 70 Pancake couldn't have been over five foot five and looked as if he shaded two hundred pounds. **1947** C. AMORY *Proper Bostonians* vi. 123 During the Civil War, then a lady shading sixty, she still had enough of her buoyant charm to sell kisses for charity. **1957** D. NILAND *Call me when Cross turns Over* vii. 172 She's pretty, sure—but I don't know, I think I can hold my own with her . . . Her figure's no better than mine; in fact, I'd shade her a bit, I'd say. **1976** *New Motorcycle Monthly* Oct. 10/3 The CB400F just shaded a five-star rating, so we must class the CB550F as [four stars]. **1986** *New Yorker* 2 June 20/3 All the women who got into what they thought were the glamorous occupations and find themselves shading thirty-five or forty and alone.

**shadow**, *v.* Add: [12.] **d.** To accompany (a person) at work, esp. for a short period, either for training purposes or to gain understanding of the profession in question. orig. *U.S.*

**1975** *Research & Devel. Project in Career Educ.* 31 July 29 Would you recommend the person shadowed for others interested in this career? **1976** E. ANDREWS *Exploring Arts & Humanities Careers in Community* 16 A class of 30 students interested in crafts wished to shadow 30 different craftspeople. **1980** M. WATSON *Operation Shadow* 1 They then 'shadow' their parent or assigned adult host by spending a half or full day at the work site. **1988** D. LODGE *Nice Work* I. iii. 54 A working party was set up last July . . and one of its recommendations . . is that each Faculty should nominate a member of staff to 'shadow' some person employed at senior management level in local manufacturing industry. **1991** W. SELF *Quantity Theory of Insanity* 24 If you shadow me this morning, you can get to know some of the patients informally this afternoon.

**shaft**, *n.*[2] [4.] [h.] After 'pipe' add: the pole of a paddle, to which the blade is attached (cf. LOOM *n.*[1] 5).
**1893** J. D. HAYWARD *Canoeing* iii. 27 The paddle generally used with the paddling . . canoe, is that known as the double blade; it consists of a shaft with a blade at each end. **1986** *Practical Woodworking* 349/1 It is normal for the paddle blades to be fixed at right angles to each other on the shaft so the upper blade passes through the air in a 'feathered' mode.

**shahtoosh** (ʃɑːˈtuːʃ), *n.* Also shah tus(h. [a. Punjabi *šātúš*, ult. f. Pers. *šāh* king + Punjabi *tūš*, Kashmiri *tósa* fine shawl-stuff.] Wool of high quality from the neck-hair of the Himalayan ibex; a material woven from this.
*a*1868 F. H. COOPER in B. H. Powell *Handbk. Econ. Products Punjab* I. II. 180/2 Plain shawls, or sadha safed chádurs of shah túsh, are known to have been purchased . . from 80 to . . 200 rupees. **1954** *Kashmir* Jan. 5/1 The weaving of a single shahtoosh shawl or blanket extends over a few months. **1970** *Sunday Mail Mag.* (Brisbane) 19 July 11/4 The rare Ibex goat starts to moult and rubs its neck against the rocks leaving tufts of hair which natives collect and weave into a cloth—shahtoosh. **1974** S. MARCUS *Minding Store* (1975) xi. 231 One year we featured . . robes made of shahtoosh, the rarest and most costly fabric in the world, which I had come across on my first trip to India. **1986** F. AMES *Kashmir Shawl* iii. 61 Among wealthy Indians a pashmina or shah tus (pronounced tooch) shawl is still considered a symbol of opulence.

**shake**, *v.* Add: [III.] [20.] **f.** *trans.* To dismiss or remove by means of a shake-out; *esp.* to get rid of (redundant staff) through reorganization.
**1905** *Westm. Gaz.* 8 July 1/2 Fence-sitters and faint-hearts are to be shaken out, so that . . those who thwart us at the commencement shall not come back after victory as nominal supporters. **1947** *Sun* (Baltimore) 18 Jan. 1/2 The Communist Finance Minister . . said he would not insist upon his plan to call in Italian currency to 'shake out' gains of black marketeers and war profiteers. **1966** *Guardian* 7 Dec. 8/4 The men shaken out of BMC are predominantly unskilled. **1972** *Oxford Econ. Papers* XXIV. 89 Surplus labour should be 'shaken-out' from overmanned industries. **1989** *Times* 8 July 17/2 A few people who were temperamentally inclined to take cash were shaken out.

**shake-down**, *n.* Add: [2.] **d.** A period or process of adjustment or change.
**1946** D. C. PEATTIE *Road of Naturalist* i. 10 The four-hundred-year shake-down of the Graeco-Roman civilization. **1960** *New Left Rev.* Nov.-Dec. 3/2 The mixed economy will emerge naturally in the process of shake-down. **1976** *National Observer* (U.S.) 13 Mar. 8/6 'We had to expect some problems,' explains an executive of a bank in Montgomery County, Maryland, that is in the midst of its shakedown period. **1986** *U.S.A. Today* 11-13 July A9/1 There's probably going to be a shakedown in some of these

organizations in cities that haven't been successful for a prolonged period.
**e.** A trial run; = *shakedown test* below. orig. *U.S.*
   **1958** *Sci. Amer.* Jan. 28/3 The experience with the first two Soviet satellites provided a valuable shakedown for the Minitrack system. **1975** *Aviation Week & Space Technol.* 27 Oct. 73/1 All phases of testing, including shipyard testing, demonstration and shakedown. **1985** *Truck & Driver* June 21/1 As an introduction to the season it's been a good shakedown. **1987** *Rally Car* Apr. 102/1 They were using this event as a shake down before the Skip Brown, unfortunately .. the cambelt failed on Warren 1.

**shambly** ('ʃæmblɪ), *a. colloq.* [f. SHAMBLE *n.*[1] and *v.*[2] + -Y[1].] That shambles, shambling; awkward, ungainly; disorganized, ramshackle, rickety.
   *a* **1937** W. E. LLEWELLYN in Partridge *Dict. Slang* 750/1 Their hands were in a grab half-hook, always, and their shoulders shambly. **1958** L. WHISHAW *As far as you'll take Me* xii. 193 There are a few little shacks .. and a shambly village hall. **1973** J. BURROWS *Like an Evening Gone* i. 16 Arnold came in first, very limp .. and shambly. **1973** T. MORRISON *Sula* (1974) II. 106 It was small .. and so shambly, and .. it would have been better if I had gotten the dust out from under the bed. **1985** L. KENNEDY *Airman & Carpenter* (1986) I. i. 29 The banker Dwight Morrow, a small rather shambly man.

‖ **shang** (ʃæŋ), *n.*[2] [Chinese *shǎng*.] A unit of land measurement in China, equivalent to approximately 15 *mu* in most areas of the northeast, and 3 or 5 *mu* in the northwest (1 *mu* = 0.0667 hectares).
   **1887** *Chinese Times* 1 Oct. 786/3 The summer crops on over 40 *shang* of ground give no promise of harvest. **1966** F. SCHURMANN *Ideology & Organization in Communist China* vii. 421 One laborer can plow and sow fifteen *shang* of land each year.

**shanghai**, *v.* Add: **shang'haied** *ppl. a.*; **shang'haiing** *vbl. n.*
   **1872** J. D. McCABE *Lights & Shadows N.Y. Life* 784 The various methods of forcing a sailor to sea are called 'Shanghaiing'. **1901** HALL & OSBORNE *Sunshine & Surf* iv. 41 Instead of being off the shores of South America, the shanghaied cargo was lying in the harbour at Papeete. **1937** E. POUND *Let.* 30 Oct. (1971) 297 Thank heaven I have what is probably a Shanghai'd (pirated) edtn. of Kung and Mantse. **1985** J. A. MICHENER *Texas* v. 276 Even children witnessed murders and shanghaiings .. and endless brawls.

‖ **shanti** ('ʃɑːntɪ), *int.* and *n. Hinduism.* Also **shantih.** [a. Skr. *śānti(h)* peace, tranquillity.] Peace: repeated three times at the end of an Upanishad as a prayer for the peace of the soul.
   **1896** MEAD & CHATTOPÂDHYÂYA *Upanishads* I. 12 Oṁ shântiḥ shântih shântih ... Oṁ Peace, Peace, Peace! **1923** T. S. ELIOT *Waste Land* v. 25 Datta. Dayadhvam. Damyata. Shantih shantih shantih ... [*Note*] Shantih. Repeated as here, a formal ending to an Upanishad. 'The Peace which passeth understanding' is a feeble translation of the content of this word. **1962** A. HUXLEY *Island* iv. 32 Such an extraordinary sense of peace. *Shanti, shanti, shanti.* **1976** B. GRIFFITHS *Return to Centre* xvii. 120 All desires are here fulfilled, the soul has entered into its rest, it attains to peace—*shanti*—the peace that passes understanding. **1984** D. DABYDEEN *Slave Song* 25 O Shanti! Shanti! Shanti! So me spirit call, so e halla foh yu.

‖ **sharashka** (ʃæ'ræʃkə), *n.* Now *Hist.* [Russ., perh. shortened f. *sharashkina kontora* 'a

bureaucratic or questionable organization', but poss. ironic (cf. Ushakov 1940, in *Tolkovyĭ Slovar' Russkogo Yazȳka*: *sharashka*, a hard object or stick for beating).] In the U.S.S.R.: a prison camp in which scientists and other specialists were held in conditions thought comfortable or luxurious by others in the prison system. (Soviet prisoners' slang.)
   **1968** T. P. WHITNEY tr. *Solzhenitsyn's First Circle* p. x, All the zeks at the Mavrino sharashka belonged .. to the realm of GULAG. **1974** —— tr. *Solzhenitsyn's Gulag Archipel.* I. II. iv. 590 And so it was that I got to those paradise islands myself (in convict lingo they are called 'sharashkas') and spent half my sentence on them. **1977** *Guardian Weekly* 26 June 22/2 Didn't his author work gratefully too in the same *sharashka*, or Island of Paradise, as the zeks called these 'soft' research camps? **1985** *Listener* 28 Feb. 24/1 Solzhenitsyn's Gulag time was in fact much mitigated by the long spells he spent in a *sharashka*. These were special camps, filled with scientists and experts of all kinds, which were run more or less like factory estates.

**share**, *n.*[3] Add: [6.] **share economy**, a system of economic organization in which employees receive a share of their company's profits as a regular element of their pay; contr. with *wage economy* s.v. *WAGE n.* 4.
   **1983** M. L. WEITZMAN in *Econ. Jrnl.* XLIII. 779 There is .. a tendency for a *share economy to pay out a higher total real income to labour than a wage economy after a recessionary shock. **1986** *Economist* 29 Mar. 44/1 Professor Martin Weitzman .. argues that a 'share economy' .. would have two big advantages over a 'wage economy'.

**share**, *v.*[2] Add: [4.] [a.] Also *absol.*
   **1932** W. FAULKNER *Light in August* i. 25 'I'd take it kind for you to share.' 'I wouldn't care to. You go ahead and eat.' **1981** 'M. UNDERWOOD' *Double Jeopardy* xiv. 115 Rosa .. glanced round the room. 'It reminds me of the days when I used to share,' she said. 'Except there were five of us.'
   [8.] **shareware** *Computing* (orig. *U.S.*), software, often distributed informally, which is available free of charge for evaluation, after which a fee is usually requested for continued use.
   **1983** *InfoWorld* 15 Aug. 64/1 It certainly was a different bag of mail I received in response to the last *shareware installment. Usually .. the ratio of downloaders requesting programs to the uploaders donating them is about 20 to 1. **1989** *Daily Tel.* 19 Jan. 27/5 As some of the best value software .. is available to anybody who can dial the right telephone number, the field of shareware and public domain software is a seam worth mining.
   also **'sharedness** *n.*, the quality or fact of being shared.
   **1947** L. MacNEICE *Dark Tower* 13 That feeling of *sharedness* .. given to a play by every fresh production. **1977** DOUGLAS & JOHNSON *Existential Sociol.* p. xiv, We have tried to show that any such ideas of sharedness (or patterns) must be seen in the context of the pluralistic, conflictual, and necessarily problematic nature of our lives. **1986** *Word* XXXVII. 50 If we are to regard cultural representations as conceptually real to members of the culture, their sharedness cannot merely be assumed.

**sharp-witted**, *a.* Add: **sharp-'wittedly** *adv.*
   **1934** WEBSTER, Sharp-wittedly. **1988** *New Leader* 28 Nov. 22/2 Dean's Night sharp-wittedly cornered all that is reductive in classical technique.

**shay-shay** *n.*, var. *SHEY-SHEY n.*

**she**, *pers. pron.* Add: [I.] [4.] c. *Black English* (chiefly *W. Indies*). Used for *her* in the possessive case.

c**1875** M. McTURK *Ess. & Fables in Vernacular* (1949) 11 De Paason hab a li'le Daag an 'Kankah' was she name. **1973** *Word 1970* XXVI. 82 This dog is she own. **1982** *Dict. Bahamian Eng.* 181/2 *She*, .. her (object, possessive; rare except on the Out Islands). **1984** D. DABYDEEN *Slave Song* 19 Yesterday she womb bin live an stirrin wid clean, bright Blood. **1986** B. GILROY *Frangipani House* iii. 11 He like Token when he see she photo.

[**13.**] **she-male**, (*b*) *slang*, a passive male homosexual or transvestite.

**1983** L. R. N. ASHLEY in *Maledicta 1982* VI. 144 Gays use shemale for faggot. **1984** *Sunday Times* (S. Afr.) *Mag.* 11 Nov. 14/3 And the cause of Marilyn's misery? Well it appears he has been finally ditched by George in favour of another shemale called Gemma.

**sheared**, *ppl. a.* Add: [1.] b. Of dressed fur, fabric having a pile, etc.: trimmed to a close and even finish.

**1939** M. B. PICKEN *Lang. Fashion* 61/2 Sheared beaver has been .. recently introduced. *Ibid.* 63/2 *Sheared beaver*, beaver with some thick underfur sheared away, removing the tendency to curl in moist weather . . Sometimes called *shaved beaver*. **1951** R. T. WILCOX *Mode in Furs* vii. 157 As we write .. natural sheared raccoon is coming to the fore. The pelt is .. sheared to reveal a deep piled fur. **1976** *Billings* (Montana) *Gaz.* 27 June 9-A (Advt.), Bath towels . . . Regular terry and sheared terry.

**shed**, *v.*[1] Add: [**10.**] i. Of an employer, etc.: to divest oneself or dispose of (excess workers or jobs), esp. by sacking or redundancy. *colloq.* (freq. *euphem.*).

**1975** *Economist* 8 Mar. 85 In the year to last September, the industry shed about 100,000 of its workforce. **1979** *Times* 6 Dec. 21/3 (*heading*) British Shipbuilders to shed 1,400 workers. **1982** *Economist* 28 Aug. 22/1 The environment secretary .. is fond of using his own department's record in shedding jobs as a stick to wave at local government. **1987** *R.A.F. Yearbk.* 35/1 Each year, the Arrows shed three pilots and take on an equal number.

**sheeting**, *ppl. a.* Add: **2.** Of rain, etc.: falling in a sheet or sheets, torrential. Cf. SHEETED *ppl. a.* 2.

**1940** 'M. INNES' *Secret Vanguard* xiii. 138 It had been quenched by a downpour of rain. She was standing .. in sheeting torrents of water. **1981** M. HATFIELD *Spy Fever* 10 He .. stumbled through the sheeting rain.

‖**shegetz** ('ʃeigɪts), *n.* orig. and chiefly *U.S.* Also **shagetz**, **shagitz**, **sheigetz**, etc. Pl. **shkotsim** ('ʃkɔːtsɪm) and varr. [Yiddish *sheygets*, *sheykets*, ad. Heb. *šeqeṣ* thing detested (because uncircumcised): see SHIKSA *n.*] In Jewish speech: a gentile boy; also, a Jewish boy who does not conform to Jewish practices. (*derog.*)

**1901** M. WOLFENSTEIN *Idyls of Gass* iv. 76 *Shah-Shegetz!* Thou hast but to try it, and thou wouldst soon find out! **1928** *Menorah Jrnl.* XV. 520 The women fought with the girls ... While they were struggling, a half-naked *sheigetz* came over and slyly untied the string on a girl's petticoat ... The young *shkotsim* formed a circle and began dancing around her. **1937** M. LEVIN *Old Bunch* ii. 320 Listen, those *shkotsim* are after only one thing. **1947** *Commentary* Oct. 371/1 When I went home with a cut lip my mother couldn't give me the 'fighting with *shkutzim*' slap. **1956** G. GREEN *Last Angry Man* 35 The last nice young *shagitz* I let talk to me sold me twenty dollars' worth of expensive fertilizers. **1969** P. ROTH *Portnoy's Complaint* 8 How he hated their guts .. the whole pack of them up there in Massachusetts,

*shkotzim* fox-hunting! playing polo! **1973** E. JONG *Fear of Flying* vi. 107 They all seemed to have hollow cheekbones and lank blond hair. She was hung up on the midwestern *shagetz* the way certain Jewish guys are hung up on *shikses*.

**shell**, *n.* Add: [III.] [23.] f. *Mus.* The cylindrical or hemispherical frame of a drum which supports the skin or head.

**1879** GROVE *Dict. Mus.* I. 463/2 [A kettledrum] consists of a metallic kettle or shell, more or less hemispherical. **1891** O. LANGEY *Celebr. Tutors: Side Drum, Xylophone* 12 The modern drum .. should be of moderate depth, about nine inches in the shell. **1928** F. E. DODGE *Dodge Drum School* 27 The street drum should be made with solid wooden shell. **1964** S. MARCUSE *Mus. Instruments* 156/1 The body of tubular and vessel drums is also called *shell*, which acts as a resonator. **1989** *Rhythm* Apr. 13/2 The shells are only four plies thick, the same as Ludwig's Super Classic drums.

g. The more or less rigid (freq. plastic) outer casing of any manufactured object.

**1972** *Guardian* 31 Oct. 11/4 Ski boots are now injection-moulded plastic shells lined with foam padding. **1983** *Your Computer* Sept. 21/2 The only problem with the .. port is that the case cut-out around it is not big enough for most DB-25 plug shells. I got around that temporarily by removing the connector shell. **1988** *Arena* Autumn/Winter 105 (Advt.), TDK's new chrome position tapes . . . With new wrapping, new shells, improved construction.

**shell**, *v.* Add: [6.] b. *Baseball.* To score heavily against (an opposing pitcher or team). Freq. in *pass.* Cf. SHELLAC *v.* 2.

**1942** BERREY & VAN DEN BARK *Amer. Thes. Slang* §677/30 *Make many hits*, .. pump out hits, shell, unleash a barrage. *Spec.* hammer *or* pound out a win, *to win by scoring many hits.* **1976** *Billings* (Montana) *Gaz.* 26 June 1-B/1 Not that Billings starter and loser Bill Dawley or reliever Rick Lear were shelled. Each gave up four hits. *Ibid.* 6 July 2-C/7 Each singled twice and drove in three runs to support Gary Ross' five-hit pitching Monday night as the California Angels shelled the Cleveland Indians 8-1. **1987** *First Base* Summer 21/3 Gooden .. was shelled twice by Boston in the World Series, finishing 0-3 in the postseason.

**shelter**, *n.* Add: [1.] h. = *tax shelter* s.v. TAX *n.*[1] 7 b.

**1976** *Billings* (Montana) *Gaz.* 17 June 3-C/4 A shelter, in general, is an investment which allows someone with idle money to claim a large tax deduction in one year, while the investment does not produce taxable income until later years. **1978** *Time* 4 Dec. 74/1 Shelters enable people to generate paper losses to write off against their regular income, thus shielding their cash from the full bite of the IRS.

**shelver**, *n.*[2] Restrict *rare* to sense in Dict. and add: **2.** One who shelves books, esp. in a library. orig. *U.S.*

**1952** W. H. JESSE *Shelf Work in Libraries* vii. 64 The inexperienced shelver is not sure that where he thinks a book belongs is its proper location. **1966** *Occupations in Field of Library Sci.* (U.S. Employment Service) 33 Library page; runner; shelver; shelving clerk; stack clerk. **1979** E. F. BROWN *Cutting Library Costs* viii. 146 There may be time only for putting all the 500's together, .. leaving the final sub-arrangement to the shelvers before they begin to shelve. **1983** *Amer. Libraries* Apr. 174/1 One of the staffers, a 19-year-old shelver, found a youth in the stacks and told him he would have to leave.

**shey-shey** ('ʃeiʃei), *n. Jamaica.* Also **shay-shay**. [Prob. f. F. *chassé*: cf. SASHAY *n.* and *v.*] A rhythmical, shuffling dance usu. danced by women to jazz music and song.

c**1920** in Cassidy & Le Page *Dict. Jamaican Eng.*

(1967) 404/2 *Song* Me wi' dance de shay-shay. **1929** M. W. BECKWITH *Black Roadways* 214 The shay-shay, that erotic dance to jazz music . . . The shay-shay is danced with a single partner and always to song. **1933** C. McKAY *Banana Bottom* vi. 71 He was engaged in writing down their songs, jammas, shey-sheys and breakdowns. **1959** A. SALKEY *Quality of Violence* iv. 62 The three women were spinning and screaming . . . They untied their turbans and improvized a 'shey-shey' reel. **1971** —— in *One Love* 7 We have been quick to recognise the excellence and the appeal in the musical alternative of the *Shey-Shey*.

**shibboleth,** *n.* Add: [3.] [a.] Hence, a moral formula held tenaciously and unreflectingly, esp. a prohibitive one; a taboo.
**1930** N. COWARD *Private Lives* II. 54 All the futile moralists . . . Laugh at them . . . Laugh at everything, all their sacred shibboleths. **1940** W. FAULKNER *Hamlet* III. i. 169 Eating . . things which the weary long record of shibboleth and superstition had taught his upright kind to call filth. **1963** J. MOYNAHAN *Deed of Life* III. i. 98 Lilly remains an annoying little man, . . who may be refreshingly free from the duller middle-class shibboleths, but . . is also unpleasantly self-conscious and humorless. **1977** C. McCULLOUGH *Thorn Birds* xvii. 412 She was untroubled by shibboleths like hitting below the belt. **1988** F. SPALDING *Stevie Smith* ii. 36 From the Anglo-Catholic point of view, the 1914-18 war helped break down a number of shibboleths.

**shield,** *n.* Add: [I.] [3.] **b.** *Astron.* (With capital initial.) The constellation Scutum. Formerly in full *SOBIESKI'S SHIELD *n.*
[**1928** *Funk's Stand. Dict.,* Shield of Sobieski.] **1960** P. MOORE *Guide to Stars* v. 51 Adjoining it [*sc.* Aquila] is one of the modern groups—Scutum, the Shield, which contains a magnificent star-cluster known popularly as the Wild Duck. **1979** R. KERROD *Stars & Planets* 38/2 Scutum, the Shield, is another tiny constellation, and because it straddles the Milky Way it has rich star fields and is a fine region to sweep with binoculars.

**shift,** *n.* Add: [IV.] [11.] **b.** A field or piece of land used in crop rotation. Chiefly *Sc.*
**1838** W. SEWALL *Diary* (1930) 197 Shucked out 5 rows of the 14 acre shift. **1796** C. MACDONALD *Echoes of Glen* 91 The 'shift' was as little as one acre. **1969** *Huntly Express* 19 Sept. 2 He noticed something amiss near his tattie shift. **1980** D. K. CAMERON *Willie Gavin* vi. 55 His rotation of crops in his humble *shifts* (the crofter's name for his small fields) adhered to the old order.
[V.] [14.] [d.] Hence applied also to changes of grammatical function. Cf. RANKSHIFT *n.*
**1929** I. A. RICHARDS *Pract. Crit.* III. i. 185 In conversation, perhaps, we get the clearest examples of these shifts of function, the normal verbal apparatus of one function being taken over by another. **1972** M. L. SAMUELS *Linguistic Evol.* iv. 67 Is it the prior shift of the old form to a new meaning . . which creates the *need* for a new form? **1978** *Language* LIV. 119 This is evidenced in some syntactic rules, such as Dative Shift and Heavy-NP Shift.
[h.] *Amer. Football.* A change of position made immediately before a snap by two or more players of the team in possession of the ball.
**1901** W. CAMP in *Outing* XXXIX. 219/2 The wing-shift had its novelty but it was fatal to the Indians in New Haven last season. **1910** *Minneapolis Tribune* 30 Oct. (Sporting section) 1/5 The Minnesota offense with the shift plays and the fake forward passes proved confusing to the Chicago defense. **1925** K. K. ROCKNE *Coaching* viii. 76 If they did not come to a distinct pause and started their charge all over again, I believe the line shift lost most of its value, as there is not much deception in a line shift. **1957** *Encycl. Brit.* IX. 478/2 In the first few

years after World War I Notre Dame relied a good deal on the line shift, but Rockne dropped this when the rule makers removed all advantage from the shift by requiring a full halt between the final jump and the snap of the ball, robbing the play of its momentum. **1987** *Touchdown* Feb. 16/1 But the play was called back for one of pro football's less-frequent infringements, an illegal shift.

**shift,** *v.* Add: [III.] [12.] **g.** *colloq.* To sell. Cf. MOVE *v.* 1 f.
**1976** *New Musical Express* 12 Feb. 25/3 Fleetwood Mac . . finally cracked the America market in a Big Way last year, shifting over three million copies of their album. **1986** *Marketing* 11 Sept. 6/1 He hopes to shift 5,000 holidays in the coming year by exploiting a market not yet covered by most major short break operators. **1990** *Church Times* 19 Jan. 9/2 He was also hopeful that some £40,000-worth of unsold books would eventually be shifted.

**shifter,** *n.* Add: 7. *Linguistics.* A word whose referent can only be understood from its context.
**1922** O. JESPERSEN *Language* vi. 123 A class of words which presents grave difficulty to children are those whose meaning differs according to the situation [e.g. father, home] . . . Such words may be called shifters. **1962** U. WEINREICH in Householder & Saporta *Probl. in Lexicogr.* 38 Another dichotomy is that between symbols and indexes (deictic elements, 'shifters', 'egocentric particulars'). **1977** A. SHERIDAN tr. *J. Lacan's Écrits* vi. 182 The *I*, as subject of the sentence in direct style, left in suspense, in accordance with its function as a 'shifter', as it is called in linguistics, . . itself remained in a state of oscillation. **1980** D. DONOGHUE in Michaels & Ricks *State of Language* 548 Linguists since Jesperson call such words *shifters*, words understood only in their contexts; such words as *I, you, now, here, tomorrow.*

‖**Shihan** ('ʃihan), *n.* [Jap., f. *shi* master, teacher + *han* exemplary.] An honorific title in Judo.
**1954** E. DOMINY *Teach Yourself Judo* App. 190 *Shihan,* a teacher. **1968** K. SMITH *Judo Dict.* 181 *Shihan,* a title conferred on a Judoka who has been promoted to Twelfth Dan . . . The meaning of Shihan is Doctor or Pastmaster. **1988** *Martial Arts Illustr.* I. 1. 25/1 A year later he returned to Tokyo for further study and obtained a rank of Godan (5th degree black belt) and with it the title of 'Shihan' (Master).

**shill,** *n.* Add: **b.** *transf.* One who poses as a disinterested advocate of another but is actually of the latter's party; a mouthpiece, a stooge.
**1976** *Dun's Rev.* Apr. 43/3 AEI was always suspect on Capitol Hill and in academic circles as being a shill for the corporate viewpoint. **1976** *U.S. News & World Rep.* 5 July 12/3 The former California Governor had to be prodded to run for President and 'has no desire to be a shill for Ford'. **1980** *Washington Post* 7 Dec. (Business section) 3/2 They take pains to avoid seeming to be shills for their individual industries. **1983** *Chicago Sun-Times* 12 July 7 Observer? Baloney. Will was no observer. Breslin calls Will a 'shill' for the president and he is exactly right.

**shim** (ʃim), *n.*[3] [Blend of SHE *pers. pron.* and HIM *pers. pron.*] A transvestite or transsexual. Also, an effeminate or passive homosexual man.
**1975** *Variety* (U.S.) 19 Feb. 4/2 Divine has let it be known that the term to use is not transvestite, not transsexual, not he, she or it . . but 'shim'. **1980** J. WAINWRIGHT *Kill of Small Consequence* xl. 89 He looked a gay type, a typical shim. **1986** *Sunday Mail* (Brisbane) 19 Oct. 72/4 Police at Fortitude Valley in Brisbane have coined a new name for the so-called ladies of the night working in the world's oldest profession. They're called Shims—think about it.

**'shimmering**, *ppl. a.* Add: Hence **'shimmeringly** *adv.*
**1934** in WEBSTER. **1979** *Washington Post* 15 June c3/1 The weather was shimmeringly perfect. **1988** *Los Angeles Times* 23 Mar. VI. 5/1 'Starfish', the group's new album—propelled by the shimmeringly psychedelic single, 'Under the Milky Way'—is looking like the breakthrough for the band.

**shining**, *ppl. a.* Add: [2.] **d.** *Shining Path* [tr. Sp. *Sendero Luminoso*] = *SENDERO LUMINOSO n.*
[**1981** *Washington Post* 21 Sept. A17/4 The only political group to have been singled out in the assaults is an apparently tiny Maoist organization called Sendero Luminoso, which means 'shining path'.] **1982** *N.Y. Times* 9 Sept. A2/3 Shining Path has almost no support nationally, being roundly condemned even by Peru's many Communist parties. **1984** *Guardian Weekly* 11 Mar. 11, 11 Peruvian regions..where a state of emergency had been declared because of the revolutionary activities of the (Maoist) Shining Path (Sendero Luminoso) movement. **1986** *Independent* 7 Oct. 9/2 The curfew is..to prevent sabotage..by the increasingly active Maoist 'Shining Path'. **1988** *New Yorker* 4 Jan. 31/1 It was there [*sc.* in Ayacucho] that Sendero Luminoso, the Shining Path, which is one of the most ruthless and secretive movements in Latin-American history, came into being.

**Shinkansen** ('ʃinkɑnsen), *n.* Pl. unchanged. [Jap., f. *shin* new + *kansen* (f. *kan* trunk + *sen* line).] In Japan, a railway system carrying high-speed passenger trains, orig. between Tokyo and Osaka; a train which travels on this. Also *transf.* (usu. with lower-case initial) a similar train or system elsewhere (cf. *bullet train* s.v. *BULLET n.¹* 8).
**1968** *Japanese Nat. Railways News Lett.* May 5 A plan is in progress to improve the design of the Shin Kansen type electric railcars to be used on the New San-yo Line which is an extension of the New Tokaido Line. **1973** *Times Lit. Suppl.* 13 Apr. 410/1 Its seclusion is invaded only by noise-pollution, the clatter of the neighbouring Shinkansen bullet trains. **1978** C. JAMES *Flying Visits* (1984) 53 Nowadays you travel up and down the Tokaido on the *Shinkansen*, known to the world as the Bullet Train. (Shinkansen really just means New Line, but the world wants romance.) **1983** *Hamlyn Encycl. Transport* 94/2 No other train is allowed to use the *Shinkansen* line and the entire line is controlled from one central control-point in Tokyo. **1984** *Railway Gaz. Internat.* Feb. 104/2 With the [Seoul-Pusan] shinkansen postponed, Mr Choi's attention is now focused on developing a diesel train which can run on the existing track.

**Shinola** (ʃaɪ'nəʊlə), *n. U.S.* [f. SHINE *n.* or *v.* + -OLA.] A proprietary name for a brand of boot polish, used esp. in the colloq. phr. *not to know shit from Shinola* (and varr.), denoting ignorance or innocence; also in *neither shit nor Shinola*, neither one thing nor the other; also occas. euphemistically for 'shit'.
**1903** *Official Gaz.* (U.S. Patent Office) 8 Sept. 537/1 Shinola. The word 'Shinola'. Used since January 1, 1900. *c*1930-40 Rhyme (remembered by R. I. McDavid) in *Amer. Speech* (1985) LX. 156 There was a young man from Arcola Who didn't know shit from Shinola. **1975** J. GOULET *Human Ape* (1977) xxv. 146 You're neither shit nor Shinola, as they say... You're not a gorilla and you aren't human. **1978** *Washington Post* 29 Dec. A17/3 Outside of gloves, and maybe cameras, I don't know shinola about garments or any of that technical stuff. **1981** *Ibid.* 4 Oct. L5/5 It will be what Bette Midler calls 'the same old Shinola' on public television. **1987** *Fortune* 13 Apr. 87/1 We'll package them together for people who don't know s— from Shinola. **1987** *Christian Science Monitor* 14 Aug. 21/3 A squib of

Vaseline from the visor, a smear of Shinola from a shoe can put demons into a well-thrown baseball. **1989** *Boston Globe* 5 Oct. 49/1 Pinhead Ivy League professors who impress the Shinola out of the brightest little boy from Brookline High.

**Shipibo** (ʃɪ'piːbəʊ), *n.* and *adj.* Also Sipibo. [Panoan, said to mean 'little monkey people'.]
**A.** *n.* **a.** (A member of) a South American Indian people inhabiting the upper Ucayali River region in the Andes Mountains of Peru.
**1805** J. SKINNER *Present State Peru* 446 In the year 1651, Friar Alonzo Caballero proceeded from the Payansos to the Callisecas and Setebos, inhabiting the banks of the Ucayali... These establishments were shortly afterwards attacked by the Sipibos, whose cruelty led them to put all the ecclesiastics to death. **1875** P. MARCOY *Trav. S. Amer.* II. 51 Except for the occur[r]ence which I have just related, nothing remarkable marked our entrance on the territory of the Sipibos, where we found excellent tobacco, which the Indians amused themselves with smoking in the shape of great cigars, ten inches long and very clumsily made. **1922** W. C. FARABEE *Indian Tribes E. Peru* 104 The Sipibo worship the moon as mother of all men. **1927** K. G. GRUBB *Lowland Indians of Amazonia* vi. 84 The *Shipibo*, *Shetebo* and *Konibo* are often grouped together under the name of Chama. **1948** A. L. KROEBER *Anthropol.* (rev. ed.) xviii. 836 Curiously, a series of primitive forest tribes, such as the Sipibo, in or near lowland interior Peru, still paint their pottery with designs that..are reminiscent of them [*sc.* Marajó ceramics designs]. **1989** *Encycl. Brit.* X. 747/2 When Spanish missionaries, soldiers, and explorers first contacted the Shipibo in the mid-16th century, they met with hostile and often deadly resistance.
**b.** The Panoan language of this people.
**1948** *Internat. Jrnl. Amer. Linguistics* XIV. 22/1 In Shipibo there are a number of morphemes that are lexically meaningless. **1964** E. A. NIDA *Toward Sci. Transl.* ix. 214 In Shipibo, a language of Peru, one must use the phrase 'she left the fever'..rather than 'the fever left her'. **1988** *Canad. Jrnl. Linguistics* XXXIII. 33 Total reduplication is involved..in Shipibo and Akan.
**B.** *adj.* Of or pertaining to the Shipibo, their culture, or their language.
**1875** P. MARCOY *Trav. S. Amer.* II. 57 This stream, rising from a detached arm of the central cordillera, and about thirty yards broad at its confluence with the Ucayali, counts on both banks about a dozen residences of Sipibo Indians. **1948** J. H. STEWARD *Handbk. S. Amer. Indians* III. 562 In 1925, Tessmann reported..that many Shipibo workers had withdrawn from plantations to live scattered between Contamana and the mouth of the Utoquinea River. **1983** *Washington Post Mag.* 26 June 35/1 Geometric-painted cloths from the Shipibo Indians of Peru. **1986** *Hi-Fi Answers* Nov. 81/1 The melody of a Shipibo indian mother singing a lullaby was modulated by the rhythm of a Spanish dance.

‖**shippo** (ʃip'po), *n.* Also shipo. [Jap., = 'seven precious things', f. Chinese *qī* (Wade-Giles *ts'ih*) seven + *bǎo* (*pao*) treasure.] Japanese cloisonné-enamel ware. Also *attrib.*
**1875** C. PFOUNDES *Fu-So Mimi Bukuro* 179 Temples and pagodas built of *Shipo*—seven precious jewels. **1880** *Trans. Asiatic Soc. Japan* VIII. 270 The various ingredients used in the preparation of the colour..are..the same as are used for the production of cloisonné enamel (*shippô yaki*). **1889** tr. *Rein's Industries of Japan* III. 430 The metal decorations of the Japanese by means of enamel (Shippô), i.e. opaque coloured glassy flux. **1962** H. GARNER *Chinese & Japanese Cloisonné Enamels* x. 100 The term *shippō*, used in Japan to describe enamels, literally means 'seven precious things'. It was used originally to describe a group of materials including gold, silver, and various jewels whose identity is a little uncertain. **1964** H. B. BOGER *Traditional Arts of*

Japan xxiii. 311 It was not until the closing years of the sixteenth century that the art of working with enamels was actually introduced into Japan from China, and because it resembled the seven precious things mentioned in Buddhist sutras, it was called *shippo*, literally meaning seven-treasures. **1987** *Los Angeles Times* 5 Feb. v. 5/1 Seventy-one Japanese enamels from the 14th through the 20th centuries will be on view at Los Angeles County Museum of Art in 'Shippo: the Art of Enameling in Japan' starting today.

**Shirburnian** (ʃɜː'bɜːnɪən), *n.* (and *a.*) [f. pseudo-L. *Shirburnia*, based on the medieval forms (e.g. *Scireburne*) of *Sherborne*, the name of a town in Dorset and of a public school situated there + -AN.] A pupil or former pupil of Sherborne school. Also *attrib.* or as *adj.*
**1859** (*title*) The Shirburnian. **1883** *Sherborne School List* 5 Old Shirburnian Scholarships. **1900** T. C. ROGERSON *Sherborne Register 1823-1900* xl, No Shirburnian .. will dispute the value of such a heritage. **1960** C. DAY LEWIS *Buried Day* vi. 113 [Alec] Waugh's name was struck off the roll of old Shirburnians. **1978** A. WAUGH *Best Wine Last* xvii. 225, I went down to Sherborne for the Old Shirburnian golf society meeting.

**Shirley Temple** (ˌʃɜːlɪ 'tɛmp(ə)l), *n.* [f. the name of *Shirley Temple* (b. 1928), American child film star.] A non-alcoholic drink, usu. consisting of ginger ale and grenadine, served so as to resemble a cocktail.
**1966** B. ROLLIN *Non-Drinker's Drink Bk.* 21 *Shirley Temple Sardi.* Served to children at Sardi's Restaurant in New York in lieu of a champagne cocktail . . . Dash grenadine . . . Crushed ice . . . Ginger ale . . . Maraschino cherry. **1973** T. PYNCHON *Gravity's Rainbow* (1975) II. 246 He stops at last in front of Slothrop, who's putting together a Shirley Temple for himself. **1977** U. CURTISS *In Cold Pursuit* (1978) xiii. 160 Jenny looks as though a Shirley Temple would set her on her ear. **1988** *Advertising Age* 12 Sept. 103/1 Shirley T, a cherry-flavor soft drink modeled after the familiar 'Shirley Temple' kiddie cocktail.

**shisha** ('ʃiːʃə), *n.* [Hindi and Urdu, ad. Pers. *shīsha* glass, mirror.] Used *attrib.* in *shisha embroidery*, *stitch*, *work*, etc. to designate mirror work (see MIRROR *n.* 17 c) and items connected with it.
[**1957** *Encycl. Brit.* XXII. 12/2 Exquisite work in chain stitch is characteristic of the Punjab, Rajputana and Cutch. In one type, known as *shishadar* . . , small pieces of mirror glass are introduced into the design and bound down by stitching round them.] **1967** E. SHORT *Embroidery & Fabric Collage* 15 (*caption*) Indian 'shisha' or mirror embroidery. **1973** E. WILSON *Embroidery Bk.* (1975) vii. 349 Any crewel stitches could be combined with shisha work, but traditionally the stitches used were limited to herringbone, chain, cretan, and French knots. **1981** *Good Housek. Embroidery* 84 Shisha stitch . . . Materials. Shisha glass or large sequins. **1987** *Workbox* Spring/Summer 42/2 (Advt.), Lots of small beads, shisha mirrors, snake skins.

**shit**, *n.* Add: [2.] c. (As a count-noun.) An act of defecation.
**1928** in A. W. Read *Lexical Evidence from Folk Epigraphy in Western N. Amer.* (1935) 75 Roses are red Violets are blue I took a shit & so did you. **1961** PARTRIDGE *Dict. Slang* Suppl. 1113/2 Gone for a shit. **1978** K. AMIS *Jake's Thing* v. 52 She monitored his shits, managing to be on reconnaissance patrol past the lavatory door or standing patrol in sight of it whenever he went in and out. **1986** *Guardian* 29 Mar. 21/7 If all those millions of people in Glasgow would just come out here at the weekend and each of them would pick up a stone and put it in his pocket

and each of them would have a shit, I should have the best farm in the whole of Scotland.

**shitake**, *n.* var. SHIITAKE *n.*

**shitty**, *a.* Add: Hence 'shittiness *n.*
**1976** *Listener* 10 June 746/2 Fielding Gray, that 'treacherous, shallow boy' turned into a 'plain shit'. . . The undergraduates of Lancaster College, the Cambridge centre of so much of the action and the key to Fielding Gray's abundant shittiness. **1985** *Maledicta* VIII. 101 Shittiness is also associated with nervous disorders.

**shivery**, *a.*[2] Add: 4. Special collocation: **shivery grass** *Austral.* and *N.Z.*, the little quaking-grass, *Briza minor*. Cf. *shivering grass* s.v. SHIVERING *ppl. a.*[2] 2 c.
**1926** F. W. HILGENDORF *Weeds N.Z.* 249/1 (Index), *Shivery grass. **1930** A. J. EWART *Flora Victoria* 158 B[riza] Minor L., Shivery Grass. **1936** F. CLUNE *Roaming round Darling* xiii. 114 He has a marvellous collection of native grasses, nardoo, Mitchell, neverfail, and a dozen others, including shivery. **1967** M. MORRIS in *Coast to Coast 1965-66* 126 She sat .. watching the wind take shape in the patch of shivery-grass. **1986** *Sunday Mail Mag.* (Brisbane) 22 June 15/1 Shivery grass can be grown among annuals and is a pleasant addition to a mixed bed.

**Shiv Sena** (ʃɪv 'seɪnɑ), *n.* [Hindi, etc., f. *Shiv* SIVA *n.* + *senā* army.] In India, the name of a Hindu nationalist organization centred in Maharashtra.
**1967** *Times of India* (Delhi) 9 Feb. 5/3 'Victory to Shiv Sena' is the slogan painted on a roadside wall at Jacob Circle [Bombay]. **1969** *Capital* (Calcutta) 27 Feb. 358/1 In Bombay, the Shiv Sena, in its attempt to drive out all the non-Maharashtrians from the city, committed atrocities on them. **1979** *Times of India* 17 Aug. 3/4 The Shiv Sena chief, Mr. Bal Thackeray, was seen in an entirely different light in a T.V. programme last week. **1987** *Blitz* (Bombay) 3 Jan. 5/2 Also absent in the march .. were the BJP, Shiv Sena and the Muslim League.

**shkotzim**, *n. pl.*: see *SHEGETZ *n.*

‖**Shoah** (ʃɒˈɑː, also anglicized 'ʃəʊə), *n.* [mod. Heb. *šōˈāh*, lit. catastrophe.] *the Shoah*: the Holocaust (see HOLOCAUST *n.* 2 d).
**1967** *Judaism* XVI. 267 We speak of it as 'the Holocaust'. But there have been other holocausts, and they were nothing like this. In such a linguistic perplexity Jews .. turn to Hebrew . . . Thus we try the word *sho'ah*. **1971** *Encycl. Judaica* VIII. 831 The 'Holocaust' (also known as the Catastrophe, the *Sho'ah* .., the *Ḥurban*) .. is the most tragic period of Jewish Diaspora history. **1986** *Times* 5 Mar. 14/5 Cardinal Hume said .. he personally regarded the Nazi Holocaust—the Shoah—as the most shameful episode in human history. **1988** *Times* 9 July 11/1 A gathering of distinguished Jewish and Christian theologians, historians, and other experts on the Shoah—as the holocaust is more properly called. **1988** J. BOWDEN *Jesus* xi. 166 The experience of the Holocaust, the Shoah, and Christian failure to react more firmly .. to Hitler's persecution of the Jews still casts its dark shadow.

**shoat** (ʃəʊt), *n.*[3] orig. *Austral.* [f. SH(EEP *n.* + G)OAT *n.*] The offspring of a sheep and a goat.
**1969** D. F. ELDER *Let. to Editor* 17 Sept., Although it has not appeared in print, the radio and television news programmes have also been using the word 'shoats'. **1971** *New Scientist* 8 July 66/1 Hundreds of people have claimed success in breeding shoats or geep. **1985** *Daily Tel.* 12 Aug. 7/1 The shoat began as a normally conceived lamb by one set of sheep and a normally conceived kid by two goats. **1987** *Sydney Morning Herald* 28 Nov. 2/8 Chimeras of goats and sheep have been made—the 'shoat'—and in one case

the embryos of four breeds of mice were successfully combined and grown.

**shocker**, n.¹ Add: [1.] **b.** Any device designed to deliver an electric shock, esp. as an aid to catching fish.

**1953** ROUNSEFELL & EVERHART *Fishery Sci.* xv. 259 (*heading*) Electric shocker. **1958** *Canad. Fish Culturist* XXIII. 37 The shocker has worked quite well in the streams fished so far where depths ranged from 6 inches to 3 feet. **1973** *Black Panther* 7 July 12/1 When she asked one officer the purpose of a strange device he was carrying, she was informed that it was an electric shocker. **1985** R. SILVERBERG *Tom O'Bedlam* I. iii. 32 She touched her fingertip to his arm and he felt a little sting, as though she had . . tapped him with a shocker. **1987** *Sports Illustr.* 20 Apr. 10 Biggest one I saw must have been 75 pounds. Couldn't get her in the net . . . I had to switch the shocker off and let her go.

‖**shodan** ('ʃɒdæn), *n. Judo* and *Karate.* [Japanese, f. *sho* primary + *dan* grade.] A degree of proficiency equivalent to first Dan or first degree Black Belt; also, a holder of this degree.

**1913** E. J. HARRISON *Fighting Spirit of Japan* iv. 59 From *shodan* upwards a black belt is worn. **1917** *National Police Gaz.* (U.S.) 4 Aug. 3/1 He is known in Japanese as a shodan, or one who is now qualified to teach the art of judo. **1946** *Judo* (The Budokwai 1954) I. 39 On my attainment of the *shodan* grade at this school, Hagiwara personally presented me with two manuscript text-books on his *ryugi's* system of *atemi* and methods of resuscitation known to the initiated as *kwappo*. **1981** *Best of Karate* Spring 29/3 At the time of his discharge and consequent return to the States Craig had not yet become a shodan. **1987** *Fighting Arts Internat.* No. 41. 36/1 The highest graded competitor was to be *shodan* (1st degree black belt).

**shonda** ('ʃɒndə), *n. Jewish colloq.* (chiefly *U.S.*). Also **shanda**, **shondah**. [ad. Yiddish *shande:—* MHG. *schande* (cf. SHOND *n.*¹).] A disgrace. Also occas. in phr. ‖*a shande un a kharpe*, a shame and a scandal.

**1962** *Amer. Speech* XXXVII. 205 The popular tendency toward bilingual diminutives . . transforms the exclamation *a shande un a charpe* 'a shame and a scandal' to *a shandie and a harpie*—which many second-generation American-Jews use without thinking. **1969** H. GOLDEN *Right Time* ix. 111 We were interrupted . . by the arrival of several friends, nameless now but drunk then . . . 'They can't be Jewish friends?' . . 'They can be and are.' . . 'It's a *shanda* . . to them.' **1972** *N.Y. Times Mag.* 3 Dec. 146/5, I was appointed groundskeeper and sexton of the prison church (the Jewish inmates . . were aghast; '*A shondah und a charpah!*'). **1979** J. HELLER *Good as Gold* vii. 269 Greenspan answered coldly, 'You're a *shonda* to your race.' 'You're a credit to yours.' **1983** E. PIZZEY *Watershed* xxiv. 204 Do you remember when your Uncle Max was infatuated with that lean and hungry hyena called Lydia? I remember Julia screaming at him down the 'phone: 'the disgrace . . a shonda . .'. **1987** *Washington Post* 4 Jan. 14/2 A Chicago rabbi . . [was] transported into near apoplexy by the sight of the novel [sc. *Portnoy's Complaint*], which he was convinced represented a shonda.

**shonk** (ʃɒŋk), *n.*² *Austral. slang.* [Back-formation from SHONKY *a.*²] One engaged in irregular or illegal business activities; a 'shark'.

**1981** *Truckin' Life Mag.* Aug. 29/3 The governments could control the numbers of middle men and stop any 'shonks' from operating. **1984** *National Road Freight Industry Inquiry* (Austral.) vii. 170 In the industry these temporary operators are commonly termed 'shonks'. **1988** *Daily Mirror* (Sydney) 9 Sept. 71/4 (*heading*) 'Shonks' cause building blues.

**shoot**, v. Add: [I.] [4.] [a.] (*e*) to drive past (a traffic signal indicating that one should stop or slow down). Cf. JUMP *v.* 10 b, RUN *v.* 40 d.

**1937** PARTRIDGE *Dict. Slang* 761/1 *Shoot the amber*, (of a motorist) to increase speed when the amber light is showing, in order to pass before the red ('stop') light comes on. **1958** *Sunday Times* 6 July 10/4 The mind races at 60 m.p.h. in a built-up area, so to speak, and shoots all the traffic-lights. **1972** *Police Rev.* 10 Nov. 1463/1 The letter of the law required that such emergency vehicles should not 'shoot the red lights'. **1986** M. HOWARD *Expensive Habits* 112 Automotive fantasy he calls it at school, listening to his friends' tales of shooting stoplights, cruising down Columbus Avenue.

**shooter**, *n.* Senses 10, 11 in Dict. become 11, 12. Add: **10.** A marble which is used for 'shooting' (see SHOOT *v.* 26 a); a taw. orig. and chiefly *U.S.*

**1892** S. CULIN in *Proc. Numism. & Antiq. Soc. Philadelphia 1890–1* 123 The boys regard certain shooters as lucky, and value them highly in consequence. **1927** *88 Successful Play Activities* (Playground & Recreation Assoc. Amer.) 26 Players shall provide their own shooters, which may be of any material except metal. **1971** *Readers' Digest Bk. 1000 Family Games* vi. 164 The boy or girl whose shooter comes to rest closest to the lag line will take the first shot, the player whose shooter is the next closest is the second to play, and so on. **1983** U. CURTISS *Death of Crow* xii. 130 Big clear shooter in the centre cup, five marbles each in the surrounding ones . . a vivid mixture.

**shoot-out**, *n.* [1.] [a.] Delete 'Also *fig.*, a dispute or competition.' **b.** *fig.* An intense and decisive contest.

**1975** *Business Week* 27 Oct. 94 F He would like congress to fund a 'shoot-out' contest between two prototype platforms. **1976** *Washington Post* 19 Apr. A4/1 Church's strategy is to have the decisive shoot-out on the Senate floor in a major public debate. **1978** *Fortune* 31 Dec. 59 In the quick-draw tradition of the Old Wild West stagecoach, the two major lines have responded to adversity . . by taking on one another in a fierce and profitless shootout over passenger fares. **1985** *Dirt Bike* Mar. 24/1 In our year-end shootout the Kawasaki finally came out on top by virtue of sheer horsepower. **1987** *Darts World* Mar. 24/3 He reduced the arrears to 3–1 with a 21-dart shootout. **1988** *Squash World* May/June 19/4 Cardwell and Irving set off at a furious pace and a memorable shoot-out looked in prospect as they shared the opening two games in just 20 minutes.

**shop**, *n.* Add: [3.] **f.** [Prob. inferred from such expressions as *closed shop*, *open shop*, where the sense is essentially 3 a.] A group of trade union members within a particular place of employment.

**1956** *Cine Technician* May 75/2 The Associated Rediffusion Shop at Wembley was now very well organised. Mr. A. Shine is their Shop Steward and the first lot of subscriptions have been received in the office. We have in this shop approximately 80 per cent membership. **1958** *ACTT Ann. Rep. 1957–58* in P. Seglow *Trade Unionism in Television* (1978) v. 101, 12 highly organised union shops. **1977** *Film & Television Technician* Mar. 9/1 (*caption*) Well to the fore in the massive demonstration for a new Hospital in Hemel Hempstead, were local ACTT members from the Kodak Shop. **1984** *Broadcast* 7 Dec. 5/1 The 180 members of the shop met on Wednesday morning to discuss the station's 5% pay offer.

**shopaholic** (ˌʃɒpə'hɒlɪk), *n. colloq.* [f. SHOP *n.* or *v.* + -AHOLIC.] A compulsive shopper.

**1984** *Washington Post* 11 Sept. C3/4 [The rumour] that Diana is a 'shopaholic' . . was described as 'absolute rubbish'. **1985** *Times* 21 Oct. 3/3 The Princess is not a shopaholic, nor is she a determined and domineering woman. **1986** *N.Y. Times* 16 June C11/6 Miss Damon..is forming Shopaholics Limited, a self-help group for overspenders in Brooklyn. **1990** *Social Work Today* 18 Jan. 14/4 In a post festive article on 'Shopaholics' the Mirror quoted Dr. Max Glatt..who runs a clinic to help those who don't know how to stop themselves spending.

**shopper**, *n.* Add: [1.] **d.** A small-wheeled bicycle with a basket, suitable for use while shopping.
**1973** *Exchange & Mart* 15 Nov. 36/1 (Advt.), Wanted: Moulton or Raleigh Shopper plus boys sports cycle. **1978** WATSON & GRAY *Penguin Bk. Bicycle* iii. 79 The small-wheel 'shopper'. **1987** *Bicycle Action* Aug. 7/2 The saddle..was bright, bright red and..looked like the sort of thing you see on a shopper which may explain why it had such a clumsy appearance on a touring bike.

‖ **Shorin ryu** ('ʃorin 'rjuː), *n.* [Jap., f. *Shorin(-ji)* = Chinese *Shǎolínsì*, name of a temple at which the Zen founder Bodhidharma came to teach (527 A.D.) + *ryū* style: cf. *\*RYU n.*] One of the two main styles of Okinawan karate (also known as *Shuri-te*).
**1974** D. F. DRAEGER *Mod. Bujutsu* vii. 135 Hayashi also studied under the supervision of Nagamine Shojin of the Shorin Ryu, and Higa Seko of the Okinawa Gojo Ryu. **1980** *N.Y. Times* 5 July 1. 6/3 Harvey Lee..won four times before falling to Terry Garrett, a practitioner of what he calls Shorin-Ryu Karate—and a proficient kick fighter. c**1985** SCOTT & PAPPAS *Fighting Arts* 69 The roots of all Shorin Ryu groups can be traced back to a group of important nineteenth-century teachers. **1988** *Fighting Arts Internat.* IX. II. 24/2 Shorin-ryu has natural stances and breathing and basic techniques which are easily assimilable and lend themselves to the development of *kumite* (sparring).

**short**, *a.*, *n.*, and *adv.* Add: [C.] [6.] **c.** *to go, walk,* etc. *short*: (of a horse) to take short strides, esp. as a symptom of lameness.
**1753** CHAMBERS *Cycl.* Suppl. s.v. *Beat*, A horse.. beats upon a walk, when he walks too short, and thus rids but little ground. **1850** 'HARRY HIGHOVER' *Horsemanship* viii. 147 His [*sc.* a horse's] stepping short does not arise from his feet being actually bruised, but to insure his safety on an unequal and unsteady surface. **1938** F. C. HITCHCOCK *To Horse!* i. 39 Watch carefully for any signs of going short or lameness. **1955** D. M. GOODALL *Know Your Pony* iv. 60 Lameness may be suspected if the pony is going short on any leg, particularly at the trot. **1963** *Horseman's Dict.* 179 *Short* (*to go*), for a horse to walk, trot or gallop with a shortened stride indicative of some unsoundness not definable as actual lameness. **1976** M. MAGUIRE *Scratchproof* x. 145 He dredged up the old one [*sc.* story] about the horse going short on him—you know, not striding out. His action went scratchy.

**short**, *v.*[1] Add: [4.] **b.** To give short measure to; to cheat (a person) out of something. Also *fig. U.S. colloq.*
**1942** BERREY & VAN DEN BARK *Amer. Thes. Slang* §491/6 *Short, short one for his end,*.. to withold more than one's share. *Ibid.* §491/7 '*Shortchange*',.. short. a**1961** *Time* in WEBSTER s.v., Shorted him on his favorite hog jowl and turnip greens. **1973** W. HARRINGTON *Mr Target* (1974) I. 11 He counted the thousand Myron had given him. He didn't trust the detective not to short him. **1978** *Business Week* 22 May 118/3 In a general inflation, even the winner may wind up getting shorted. **1985** *Sports Illustr.* 21 Oct. 14/2 Sometimes we were shorted and didn't get five cards.

**8.** *Comm.* To sell (a commodity, stock, etc.) short (see SHORT *adv.* 11). Also *absol.* orig. *U.S.*
**1959** *Barron's* 28 Dec. 9/1 Often during a bull market an outside news event..will cause a great many people to short the market. **1965** R. E. DAVIS *Profit & Probability* ix. 185/2 Never short a very thin issue with only 750,000 shares. **1975** *Business Week* 24 Mar. 128/1 For the past five years, there was a great deal of money to be made shorting... But relative to the risk now, short selling in most cases doesn't make sense. **1988** *Times* 1 July 26/3 Big Wall Street houses.. had shorted bonds on the expectation that the long bond would be yielding 10 per cent by now.

**shorten**, *v.* Add: **8.** *intr. Horsemanship.* Ellipt. for *to shorten (one's) stride* s.v. STRIDE *n.* 1 c. Usu. said of the horse; occas. metonymically of the rider. Also with *up.*
**1981** *Washington Post* 27 Oct. E4/5 His strategy was to 'keep the flow of the horse's stride steady and not shorten up around the corners'. **1986** *Horse & Rider* Sept. 16/1 He is fairly short backed and so he can shorten and bounce as required. **1987** *Carriage Driving* Spring 11/1 My first duty after the initial inspection was to observe each of the novice singles at the walk and trot to ascertain soundness..and..I felt that two of the ponies were shortening behind.

**shorthold** ('ʃɔːthəʊld), *n.* [f. SHORT *a.* + HOLD *n.*, after FREEHOLD *n.*, etc.] A type of lease or system of tenure in which the tenant agrees to rent a property for a fixed short term and the landlord retains the right to recover property at the end of the term (also as *protected shorthold*). Freq. *attrib.*, as *shorthold lease, tenancy,* etc.
**1976** *Housing (Shorthold Tenancies) Bill. Explanatory Memorandum.* The object of the Bill is to create a new standard form of tenure of dwellings which will allow the owners of vacant property and people seeking rented accommodation to enter into simple but secure arrangements for short tenancies of fixed term. The Bill suggests that this new form of tenure should be known as 'shorthold'. A shorthold lease may cover any period between a minimum of one year and a maximum of three years. **1979** *Hansard Lords* 25 Oct. 202 The Government will be introducing a new form of shorthold letting in the Housing Bill this Session. **1980** *Jrnl. R. Soc. Arts* Mar. 208/1 The proposed 'Shorthold tenancy' will be an interesting experiment but it hardly touches the nub of the problem of existing tenancies. **1987** *Independent* 30 Sept. 2/3 Shorthold guarantees that the landlord can recover his property after a minimum six months; in return the tenant can seek registration of the rent.
Hence **'short,holder** *n. rare,* a tenant who rents a property under a shorthold lease.
**1976** *Housing (Shorthold Tenancies) Bill* 1 The lessor of a shorthold shall be known as the landlord and the lessee shall be known as the shortholder.

**short-term**, *a.* Add: Hence **,short-'termer** *n.,* one who is engaged in some activity for a short time only; *spec.* = SHORT-TIMER *n.* 3.
**1961** WEBSTER *Short-termer,* a person serving a short prison sentence. **1977** *New Yorker* 24 Oct. 120/3 Short-termers are in and out of Green Haven before the administration can get to know them. **1989** *Spectator* 14 Jan. 29 He believes that civil servants.. ought to be refreshed by.. the incursion of irregulars and short-termers.

**,short-'termism**, *n. U.K.* [f. SHORT-TERM *a.* + -ISM.] Concentration on short-term investments, projects, etc. for immediate profit, at the expense of long-term security or development.

**1986** ASHDOWN & HOLME (*title*) Investing in our future: tackling short-termism in the British economy. *Ibid.* ii. 13 The harmful effects of short-termism can be seen throughout the British economy, starving the future. **1986** *Independent* 12 Nov. 18 The growing friction between industry and the City over the alleged 'short termism' of financial institutions' investment attitudes. **1989** *Investors Chron.* 17-23 Mar. 13/1 That the Chancellor has abolished the rule that investments in PEPs must be held for one calendar year could perhaps be seen to encourage short-termism.

Hence ,short-'termist *n.* and *a.*

**1987** *Financial Times* 19 Jan. 1. 18/2 One [camp] is confident that . . things are shaping up nicely for the Government in election year. This camp should perhaps be dubbed the 'short-termists'. **1987** *Daily Tel.* 30 Jan. 20/2 This dramatic contrast between short-termist Britain and long-term-minded Europe and America seems to need a little modifying. *Ibid.* 20/5 Short-termists ask brutal questions like: 'How much does it cost in cash terms now?' **1990** *Observer* 25 Nov. 26/3 There has been talk of BTR floating off its US interests . . . This appears short-termist and fraught with tax and US legislative hurdles.

‖**shosha** ('ʃəʊʃə), *n.* Pl. unchanged. [Jap., f. *shō* mercantile + *sha* society, company.] = *SOGO SHOSHA n.*

**1976** *Newsweek* 23 Feb. 44/1 Foreign firms doing business in Japan have long considered an arrangement with a local *shosha*, or trading house. **1989** *Business Tokyo* Summer 19/2 Many of Japan's *shosha*, or general trading firms, conduct trade in Vietnam through front companies and little known subsidiaries.

**shot**, *n.*[1] Add: [I.] [9.] e. *colloq.* (orig. *U.S.*). A single occasion of doing or obtaining something; a turn, a 'go'; usu. in phr. (so many) *dollars* (*cents*) *a shot*.

**1939** *Time* 27 Nov. 56/2 The 'juke-box', which retails recorded music at 5¢ a shot. **1979** W. KENNEDY *Ironweed* ii. 40 When Francis turned up in Albany only weeks back to register for the Democrats at five dollars a shot, he met Pee Wee again. **1986** *N.Y. Times* 13 Nov. D25/2, 50,000 [copies] to newsstands for sale at $3.95 a shot.

**shotcrete** ('ʃɒtkriːt), *n.* *Building.* [f. SHOT *ppl. a.* + CON)CRETE *a.* and *n.*] = GUNITE *n.*

**1950** *Building Sci. Abstr.* XXIII. 358 This report . . briefly reviews the advantages and disadvantages of the process and establishes recommended practices for placing and mixing 'shotcrete'. **1951** W. L. CHADWICK et al. in *Proc. Amer. Concrete Inst.* XLVII. 186 To avoid the cumbersome term 'pneumatically-placed mortar' the word 'shotcrete' is used to refer to this material. **1962** J. J. WADDELL *Pract. Quality Control for Concrete* xiii. 276 When cement mortar is sprayed on a surface, the product is variously known as pneumatically applied mortar, shotcrete or 'Gunite'. **1971** *Daily Colonist* (Victoria, B.C.) 28 Feb. 7/4 On the sides and roof [of a tunnel] a substance called shotcrete is sprayed from a nozzle to form a coating some six inches thick. **1979** *Internat. Railway Jrnl.* Feb. 25/1 Immediately following excavation the tunnel walls are normally stabilized with a shotcrete lining. **1983** P. FERRIS *Distant Country* xv. 179 The Sub-Agent was at the damaged shaft. They were spraying the walls with shotcrete.

**shotgun** ('ʃɒtgʌn), *v.* *colloq.* (orig. and chiefly *U.S.*). [f. SHOT-GUN *n.*] **1.** *trans.* To shoot with a shotgun. (In quot. *a* 1880 with cognate obj. *to shotgun one's way.*)

*a* **1880** in G. A. Sala *Amer. Revisited* I. vi. 87 Our people sabred and shot-gunned their way to liberty. *a* **1961** in WEBSTER s.v., An enemy who shotgunned him from ambush. **1977** *Washington Post* 30 Oct. F6/2, I didn't have to worry about some beer-sodden

cowboy shotgunning me right through my sleeping bag. **1978** S. BRILL *Teamsters* i. 23 One of the star prosecution witnesses had been shotgunned to death. **1981** J. WAINWRIGHT *All on Summer's Day* 143 He's the murderer. He shotgunned his wife and her fancy man. **1988** *Modern Painters* Autumn 64/2 The . . cheesecake . . is . . the perfect antithesis to a backdrop of plywood canvases shotgunned and spraycanned out in the heart of the country.

**2.** To force as if with a shotgun; to bring about forcibly.

*a* **1961** A. ROTH in WEBSTER s.v., Shotgunned western Europe into federal unity. **1978** *Nat. Westm. Bank Q. Rev.* Nov. 10 No matter how dubious their case, domestic forces can affect trade policy, at least at the margin, by 'shotgunning' their import complaints through the expanding number of statutory procedures now available to them. **1982** *Fortune* 22 Mar. 121/1, I shotgunned a marriage of the two firms to design the project. It lasted about two months. They lacked rapport.

Hence 'shot,gunned *ppl. a.*; 'shot,gunner *n.*; 'shot,gunning *vbl. n.*

**1975** *Victorian* (Victoria, B.C.) 24 Sept. 16/1 Shotgunners after wildfowl are unaffected by the ban. **1978** *Business Week* 5 June 116F/2 To avoid lawsuits and government fines . . they [*sc.* chemical producers] . . are trying to forestall safety and environmental hazards. *Legal shotgunning.* The threat of litigation alone is ample incentive. **1981** *Washington Post* 2 July B13/1 Members of a motorcycle gang weighted a shotgunned body with cinderblocks and tossed it into the quarry. **1988** *Oxf. Mail* 11 Nov. 1/2 PC Shaw said he was selected as the shotgunner who was to fire if Davies made a threatening move.

**Shotokan** (ʃəʊ'təʊkæn), *n.* Also **Shoto-kan.** [Jap., f. *shō-* right, true + *to* way + *kan* mansion.] One of the five main styles of karate. Usu. *attrib.*

Founded by Funakoshi Gichin (1870-1957), the originator of karate, and now the most widely practised style in the U.K. and a number of other countries.

**1963** E. PARKER *Secrets of Chinese Karate* iii. 33 Karate has taken on many styles in Japan—*Waddoryu, Shoto-kan, Shudo-kan,* etc. **1966** *Karate Mag.* Dec. 32 Demonstrating the Shotokan style of Gedan Barai, a block to an attack on the lower part of the body. **1974** *Exchange & Mart* 24 Oct. 106/4 (Advt.), Shotokan hold-alls £2.75 plus 20p p&p. **1977** *Spare Rib* June 34/2 (Advt.), Karate Shotokan style tonight by woman Black Belt. **1984** *Business Week* 12 Nov. 153/2 Learning shotokan karate calls for you to defeat an opponent with kicks and punches while blocking the ones headed your way. **1988** *Black Belt Internat.* I. v. 46/1 The style of karate taught at the club is Shotokan.

**shotting** ('ʃɒtɪŋ), *vbl. n.* [f. SHOT *v.* + -ING[1].] The action of weighting with shot; *esp.* in *Angling,* the weighting of the line with shot.

**1881** MRS. P. O'DONOGHUE *Ladies on Horseback* III. vi. 83 If a hunting-habit be properly cut it will require no shotting. **1979** *Angling* July 17/3 The curious types of float and even more curious shotting methods I see used and recommended. **1986** *Angling Times* 25 June 15/1 Most of us ended up fishing wagglers and maggot for roach and skimmer bream, with very light shotting.

**Showa** ('ʃəʊwə), *n.* [Jap., f. *shō* clear, bright + *wa* harmony, concord.] The traditionally auspicious name or reign-title given to the period of rule of the Japanese emperor Hirohito (1926-89).

**1927** *Ann. Reg. 1926* II. 271 The Taisho era thus ended and the new era, to be named 'Shōwa' (enlightened peace), began. **1957** *Encycl. Brit.* XII. 926/2 Emperor Taisho died on Christmas day, 1926, and was succeeded by his son . . , who adopted

Showa as the title of his reign. *Ibid.*, In November and December 1928 the new emperor . . made several pronouncements declaring the policy of the Showa era. **1978** C. JAMES in *Observer* 4 June 25/6 Looking at the shrines, temples and palaces you feel that the continuity between the ancient Heian Period and the current Showa Era remains largely unbroken. **1989** *Economist* 14 Jan. 51/1 With the passing of Showa, or 'enlightened peace', as Hirohito's reign was known (and as he himself will now be formally called), Japan has cut its last link to the second world war.

**show-boat**, *n.* Add: **2.** One who seeks to attract public attention; a 'show-off'. *slang* (chiefly *U.S.*).
   **1953** BERREY & VAN DEN BARK *Amer. Thes. Slang* (1954) §402/2 *Pretentious person*, . . show-off, show boat. **1969** *Time* 28 Feb. 22 National chairmen rarely serve as showbosses. **1978** *Chicago* June 118/2 The Attorney General's regulations urge that 'observations about a defendant's character' be avoided. Neither Thompson nor Skinner was an *incorrigible* showbout, however. **1981** R. AIRTH *Once a Spy* vi. 70 'What do you make of *him*?' 'Either a nutter or a showboat.'

**'showboat**, *v. U.S. slang.* [f. *SHOW-BOAT *n.* 2.] *intr.* To perform or behave ostentatiously; to show off. Also *trans.* and *refl.*
   **1951** in Wentworth & Flexner *Dict. Amer. Slang* (1960) 474/1 *Showboat*, to show off. **1969** *Time* 31 Jan. 75/2 The 98-year-old ballet is traditionally noted for . . the opportunity it affords a ballerina to showboat her versatility. **1981** J. D. MACDONALD *Free Fall in Crimson* x. 111 He was a good officer. He didn't showboat and draw fire. **1984** *N.Y. Post* 7 Feb. 482 Opal Alone always prefers to 'showboat' herself. **1987** R. BUSBY *Snow Man* iv. 45 The Europeans are enough of a handful without DEA prima donnas showboating all over the place.

**shred**, *v.* Add: **[4.]** **c.** *fig.* To defeat overwhelmingly; to trounce. *slang* (orig. *U.S.*).
   **1966** *N.Y. Times* (Internat. ed.) 22 Apr. 12/5 The Celtics shredded the Los Angeles Lakers . . with a third-quarter explosion and scored a 120–106 victory. **1980** *Newsweek* 17 Nov. 7/1 His counter-revolution shredded the old Democratic victory coalition. **1987** *Speedway Star* 26 Sept. 16/3 Despite losing Mel Taylor in a Heat 4 accident at West Row, Fen Tigers shredded Eagles.
   **d.** *Surfing.* To cut or plough rapidly through (the water, etc.) on a surfboard; also *transf.*, to travel along (a track, etc.) at speed. Also *intr.*
   **1977** G. F. R. FILOSA *Surfer's Almanac* 194 *Shred*, to rip, to perform alaia style in superb fashion. **1985** *Surfer* Sept. 86/3, I love the way they . . just shred everything in sight—carving, slashing aerials and snapbacks. *Ibid.* 104/3 When the surf is flat Zamba can be found in a number of places. She might be shredding up a trail on her dirtbike. **1987** *Dirt Wheels Mag.* Aug. 31/1 A Warrior showed up during practice but didn't sign up after seeing the *Dirt Wheels* Mojave shred the track! **1988** P. & S. HILL *Skate Hard* 75/1 Chances are if you want to shred vertical you need a ramp.

‖ **shrikhand** (ˈʃrɪkand), *n.* Also **shrikand**. [Gujarati, f. Skr. *śrī-khand* sandalwood.] An Indian sweet dish consisting of curd cheese mixed with sugar, almonds, saffron, and cardamom.
   **1950** V. CHITALE *In Transit* ii. 32 Saffron for the *shrikhand*. **1977** *Times* 10 Dec. 9/6 The mouth-tingling sweet called shrikhand, in which the dominant impressions are cardamom and good curd cheese. **1979** J. SANTA MARIA *Indian Sweet Cookery* 123 Shrikand is made all over India with local variations in ingredients. **1986** *Los Angeles Times* 28 Sept. 103/3 *Ras malai*, pistachio-laden cheese balls soaked in saffron-sweetened milk, and *shrikhand*,

saffron spiced yogurt with cardamom, nuts, and candied fruits.

**shrinker**, *n.* Add: **3.** A psychiatrist, = *head-shrinker* (b) s.v. HEAD *n.*[1] 74; hence extended to other specialists working in related disciplines. Cf. SHRINK *n.* 2. *slang.*
   **1967** M. M. GLATT et al. *Drug Scene* 117 (Gloss.), *Shrinker*, . . psychiatrist. **1975** S. BELLOW *Humboldt's Gift* 161 Lawsuits and psychoanalysis were real. As for the lawyers and the shrinkers, they were delighted with him. **1980** J. B. HILTON *Anathema Stone* x. 102 It had to be the clinic for her. Maybe they'd left it too late; or maybe she was too clever for the shrinkers. **1983** *People* 14 Feb. 123/1 It took me a couple of years with a shrinker to develop a protective covering.

‖ **shtreimel** (ˈʃtreɪm(ə)l), *n.* Also **shtreiml, streimal.** Pl. **-lach,** (anglicized) **streimls,** etc. [Yiddish, f. MHG. *streimel* stripe, strip.] A round, broad-brimmed hat edged with fur worn by some Chasidic Jews.
   **1905** S. HIRDANSKY tr. *Zunser's Jewish Bard* 27 Hats were . . known by distinctive names. There were 'ear-hats' shtreimlach . . and many others. . . A scholar always wore a shtreimel. **1924** *New Palestine* 15 Aug. 114/1 Sephardim in fezes and Ashkenazim in fur streimlach. **1936** *Menorah Jrnl.* XXIV. 231 Seated around tables . . were some fifty Chassidim, old bearded men with '*peyas and shtreimel*'. **1966** L. DAVIDSON *Long Way to Shiloh* viii. 116 He came back in with a *shtreiml*, the big round fur hat of the ultra-pious. **1972** H. KEMELMAN *Monday the Rabbi took Off* xv. 103 They saw a Chassid, brave in his Sabbath finery, the broad-brimmed black felt replaced by a fur streimal. **1988** *Jerusalem Post* ('In Jerusalem' Suppl.) 7 Oct. 2/4 At one point [he] knocked off the *streimls* of a few onlookers who were not heeding his orders.

**shunter**, *n.* Add: **[1.]** **b.** A locomotive used for shunting.
   **1949** D. M. DAVIN *Roads from Home* II. vii. 175 Geordie Smith on his shunter had just given a rake of meat waggons a bit of a nudge. **1962** D. ABSE *Poems: Golders Green* 20 The shunters slave on silver parallels . . . Only posh expresses sport proper names. **1979** *Railway Gaz. Internat.* Mar. 219/2 Designed by Hunslet, the shunters are of 0-8-0 wheel arrangement and wheelbase is 3750 mm. **1984** 'TIRESIAS' *Notes from Overground* 34 A seemingly innocuous message —'Will a shunter go to the Bristol end of Platform 1' can spell trouble.

‖ **shunto** (ˈʃuntəʊ), *n.* [Jap., f. *shun* spring + *tō* fighting.] The annual round of wage-bargaining which takes place every spring in Japan; the 'labour offensive'.
   **1967** *Japan Labor Bull.* May 1/1 With the approach of April, Shunto (the spring wage offensive) is exhibiting aspects of a full-fledged confrontation. **1976** *Newsweek* 3 May 22/3 Among Japan's rites of spring, as predictable as the cherry blossoms in the parks, is the '*shunto*', the annual round of wage bargaining. **1989** *Economist* 25 Mar. 94/3 In the ritual *shunto* (spring labour offensive), which reaches a peak over the next two weeks, the unions will demand a 6–8% pay rise.

**shura** (ˈʃuːrə), *n.* [a. Arab. (also Urdu and Pers.) *šūrā* consultation. Cf. Turk. *şûrà* council.] **a.** The Islamic principle of (rule by) consultation. **b.** Hence, an Islamic consultative council or similar advisory body; loosely, a council or parliament.
   **1960** *Encycl. Islam* (rev. ed.) I. 84/2 On 'Umar's death, as one of the *Shūrā* or council of six who had to choose a new caliph, he played a leading part in the appointment of 'Uthmān. **1962** A. HOURANI *Arabic Thought in Liberal Age* vi. 144 *Maslaha* gradually turns into utility, *shura* into parliamentary democracy. **1974** *Encycl. Brit. Macropædia* IX. 921/2

Whereas early Islām had confirmed the pre-Islāmic democratic Arab principle of rule by consultation (shūrā).., those practices soon gave way to dynastic rule with the advent of the Umayyads. The *shūrā* was not developed into any institutionalized form and was .. soon discarded. **1981** *Times* 3 Mar. 12/4 Under the Islamic tradition of Shura, information about the needs of Saudi society does percolate upwards. **1982** *Christian Science Monitor* 23 Mar. 13/2 Mr. Tilmessani refused a seat to the advisory Shura Assembly created by Mr. Sadat 1½ years ago. **1989** *Independent* 23 Jan. 9/1 The Afghan mujahedin guerillas have fallen out again, shortly before they were to have held a *shura*, or consultative council.

‖**shuriken** (ʃuri'ken), *n.* [a. Jap. *shuri-ken*, lit. 'dagger in the hand', f. *shu* hand + *ri* inside + *ken* sword, blade. The traditional Japanese meaning is 'a small dagger thrown with its blade pointing forwards as it flies through the air'.] In the martial arts (esp. ninjutsu): a weapon in the form of a small star with a number of projecting blades or points, thrown with a spinning motion at the target.
**1978** RIBNER & CHIN *Martial Arts* vii. 178 The ninja.. stuffed their pockets with *shuriken*, sharp-pointed weapons shaped like stars or crosses that could be thrown like darts at people. **1980** *Washington Post* 30 Sept. B11/5 'I came because I expected some of my team to be here,' he says, while hurling shurikens.. into a sheet of plywood. **1985** *N.Y. Times* 4 Oct. A30/1 Shurikens—palm-sized throwing stars with razor points—spin through the air like little buzz saws. **1989** P. CROMPTON *Compl. Martial Arts* 77/1 Because a few hooligans have used these stars in public, there has been an outcry in the West, demanding that the shuriken should be banned from sale.

**shush**, *v.* Add: **3.** To make a soft, shushing sound; to move with the sound of a rush of air.
**1975** 'L. GILLEN' *Return to Deepwater* iii. 47 They.. were just turning the last corner in the curved carriageway, the trees shushing softly overhead in the morning breeze. **1983** L. NIVEN *Integral Trees* xx. 206 Now close the outer line... Open the inner. Air shushed into the airlock. **1986** D. POTTER *Ticket to Ride* (1987) xxii. 170 The automatic door into the next carriage shushed open.

**shut** (ʃʌt), *n.*² *Shropsh. dial.* Also †shut(t)e. [ME. *shute*, f. OE. *scyte*: see SHUTE *n.*¹ For earlier references to the word in surnames and place-names outside Shropshire, see *M.E.D.* s.v. *shute n.* (e).] A narrow alley-way or passage, often serving as a short cut between two streets.
**1300** in T. F. Dukes *Antiq. Shropsh.* (1844) App. p. xvii, Et sic per quandam viam usque le mersiche justa Andolph Shute. *a***1500** in *Trans. Shropsh. Archæol. Soc.* (1882) 106 Per Watling strete usque la Wodewardes Shutte. **1700** in *Shropsh. Parish Reg.: Diocese of Lichfield* XV. 590, Oct. 27. John, s. of John & Mary Roe, in baret's shut.. borne. *c***1817** in G. F. Jackson *Shropsh. Word-Bk.* (1879–81) 379 A *shut* in Shrewsbury language denotes, not, as might be imagined, a *cul-de-sac*, or alley shut at one end, but, on the contrary, one open at both extremities. **1882** J. RANDALL *Severn Valley* ix. 185 They lean and nod and sometimes touch, forming dark arcades, locally known as 'shuts'. **1922** S. WEYMAN *Ovington's Bank* iii. 35 The alleys—dubbed in Aldersbury 'shuts'.

‖**shuto** ('ʃuːtəʊ), *n. Karate.* [Jap., f. *shu* hand + *tō* sword.] A sharp, chopping blow delivered with the forward edge of the hand; = *karate chop* s.v. KARATE *n.*
**1959** E. J. HARRISON *Man. Karate* ii. 17 *Tegatana*, sometimes called *shuto* (*handsword*)... In this method the thumb is bent. **1972** *Austin Morris Express* (Oxford) July 8/3 Dave Smith in action with

the Shuto blow, that devastating blow with the forward edge of the hand. **1981** *Best of Karate* Spring 9/3 President Marcos put his karate training to good use by using a well-aimed kick and a shuto to stop the attack, thus saving the Pope's life and narrowly averting a world-wide tragedy. **1988** *Black Belt Internat.* I. v. 51/1 The second technique is a composite technique which combines shuto or knife hand strikes with a reverse heel kick to the kidneys and an O-soto-gari to take your partner down to the floor.

**shutter**, *n.* Senses 2 a–j in Dict. become 2 b–k. Add: Also 7 shuter. [**2.**] **a.** *Theatr.* Either of a pair of movable flats or back-scenes run in from opposite wings to meet in the middle of the stage. Also †*side shutter*. Now chiefly *Hist.*
**1634** in R. Southern *Changeable Scenery* (1952) i. 36 Not to draw ye upper shuters but ye masqu[er]s form ye under being draw[n]e. *c***1640** *Lansdowne MS. 1171* in *Portfolio* (1889) 92/1 Came down from yᵉ roof before yᵉ upper part of yᵉ syde shutters, whereby yᵉ grooves above were hidden, and also yᵉ house behind them. **1889** *Portfolio* 91/2 Inigo Jones.. worked his changes by means of slips or, as he calls them, 'shutters', with a large painted scene on a frame at the back. There are several sets of designs for these shutters at Chatsworth. **1921** [see RUN *v.* 50 d]. **1985** *Observer* 16 June 19/1 'Figaro' is simply 'The Marriage of Figaro' itself, reduced for six solo singers and a piano quartet, given in what looks like a budget touring production, wittily designed on shutters.
**l.** *Building.* = FORM *n.* 18 b. Cf. SHUTTERING *vbl. n.* 2 b.
**1965** G. P. MANNING *Wynn's Design & Construction of Formwork* (ed. 5) i. 3 If necessary shutters should be given a further coat of mould oil before re-use. **1973** J. S. FOSTER *Structure & Fabric* I. ii. 27/2 Steel formwork units combining wall and floor shutters. **1989** *Construction News* 8 June 29/1 Soon after blasting, the roof was stabilised with steel fibre reinforced shotcrete and rockbolting, followed by concreting within an elaborate hydraulically positioned shutter.

**shuttler**, *n.* Delete '(sense 3)' in etym. and restrict *rare* to sense in Dict. Add: **2.** One who habitually travels back and forth between destinations, a commuter; *esp.* one who uses shuttle flights.
**1962** *Punch* 11 Apr. 577/1 We might try to displace 'commuter', a word that all despise and everybody uses. '*Shuttler*' might attract—or '*in-and-outer*'. **1963** *New Yorker* 15 June 113/2 Benny Profane is the hero. .. Most of his time is spent traveling uselessly back and forth... Herbert Stencil.., too, is a ceaseless shuttler. **1980** *Washington Post* 9 Mar. H1/1 Each creator.. is an extremely successful product of the Broadway theater, an accomplished shuttler between New York and Hollywood. **1986** *Sunday Tel.* (Colour Suppl.) 24 Aug. 22/1 With the coming of air travel after the Second World War, Lichine was one of the first persistent shuttlers.

**shyster**, *n.* Add: 'shysterism *n.*
**1926** *Spectator* 12 June 980/2 He is an uncompromising enemy of sham and shysterism in politics. **1981** J. WAINWRIGHT *Urge for Justice* iii. 168 I'd accepted the brief, knowing that I'd be defending a guilty man. That, of itself, smacked of shysterism.

**siblicide** ('sɪblɪsaɪd), *n. Ornith.* [f. SIBL(ING *n.* + -*icide*: see -CIDE 2.] The action by a young bird of killing a sibling or fellow nestling.
**1982** *Natural Hist.* Jan. 18/2 Evolutionary biologists.. tend to discuss such phenomena as the siblicide of boobies in the language of adaptation. **1984** *Sunday Times* 16 Sept. 80/7 Young egrets had a habit of killing off their nest-mates—'siblicide' was the apparent cause of death in many brood reductions. **1985** *Behavioral Ecol. & Sociobiol.* XVIII. 416 Siblicide may be an evolutionary response on the

part of the dominant chick to 'anticipated' food shortages that might occur later in development. **1988** *Birder's World* July/Aug. 19/1 If both hatch, the first (and larger) nestling evicts the smaller in a form of 'siblicide', leaving a single chick.

‖ **sic et non** (sɪk ɛt nɒn, older siːk ɛt nəʊn), *n. phr.* [L., lit. 'yes and no', the title of a work by Peter Abelard, 12th-c. French theologian and philosopher.] A method of theological argument used by Abelard and later Scholastics, in which contradictory passages of scripture are presented without commentary, in order to stimulate readers to resolve the contradictions themselves. Freq. *attrib.* Also *transf.*
   **1917** E. F. ROGERS *Peter Lombard* vi. 64 Lombard was more dependent on the model of Abelard's 'sic et non': the gathering of 'authorities' in a systematic, methodical way, for and against a doctrine. **1969** T. F. TORRANCE *Theol. Sci.* i. 7 The scientific methods developed in scholastic theology.., which derived from the *sic et non* procedure of Abelard. **1974** *Speculum* XLIX. 649 [In Muslim religious law] the *sic-et-non* method was part and parcel of the Islamic orthodox process for determining orthodoxy. **1983** W. WEAVER tr. *Eco's Name of Rose* III. 185 The abbey ..was not corrupted by disputation, by the quodlibetical conceit that would subject every mystery..to the scrutiny of the sic et non. **1989** *Encycl. Brit.* I. 26/1 When he [*sc.* Abelard] returned to Saint-Denis he applied his *Sic et non* methods to the subject of the abbey's patron saint.

**side-bar**, *n.* Add: [6.] **b.** *transf.* Something which is secondary or additional; a supplementary piece of information, a side issue. Freq. *attrib.* orig. and chiefly *U.S.*
   **1952** *N.Y. World Telegram* 25 June 25/2 Now he has a side bar job, whether it is hustling beer or sports equipment. **1977** *Washington Post* 8 Nov. A8/2 Strauss and other high officials have indicated they hope to resolve the steel issue in so-called 'sectoral' or sidebar talks. **1979** *Ibid.* 10 Aug. D10/2 I'll tell you an interesting sidebar about one book. **1980** *Amer. Banker* 8 Jan. 14/3, I believe that to most of these, high asset banking is a sidebar ... To this bank it's in the mainstream. **1983** *Daily Tel.* 1 Nov. 18/2 An interesting sidebar to the Grenada crisis is the fact that the island is the only country in the world where more girls than boys are born almost every year.

**sidero-**, *comb. form*[1]. Add: [2.] **,siderodromo'phobia** *joc.* and *rare* [Gr. δρόμος course, way + -PHOBIA], fear of rail travel.
   **1897** tr. *T. Ribot's Psychol. of Emotions* II. ii. 213 Every morbid manifestation of fear is immediately fitted with a Greek designation..and we have aïcmophobia, belenophobia..even \*siderodromophobia (fear of railways). **1981** *N.Y. Times* 11 Feb. C2/1 Four phobias that are likely to make life difficult Climacophobia (fear of stairs); Iophobia (fear of rust); Siderodromophobia (fear of railroad trains), and Triskaidekaphobia (fear of 13 people at table).

**'siderophore** *Biochem.* [-PHORE], any of various chelate ligands involved in the transport of ferric iron in micro-organisms.
   **1973** C. E. LANKFORD in *CRC Crit. Rev. Microbiol.* II. 290/2 In consideration of possible existence of functional ferrous-iron chelating compounds in the microbial world [etc.],.. the term siderochrome could become nondescriptive of functionally related compounds of microbial origin. A term such as \*siderophore might be more appropriate. **1979** *Nature* 3 May 15/3 Enteric and other bacteria have been known for some time to synthesise low molecular weight siderophore molecules of high iron affinity. **1986** M. KOGUT tr. *Schlegel's Gen. Microbiol.* vii. 263 Microorganisms generally excrete siderophores only when the supply of iron is growth limiting.

**sideways**, *adv.* and *a.* Sense 3 d in *Dict.* becomes 3 e. Add: [3.] **d.** As an intensifier: thoroughly, to the limit of one's tolerance. *colloq.*
   **1956** B. HOLIDAY *Lady sings Blues* (1973) x. 97 There was nothing anybody in California could show me, anything there was doing out there I'd seen before and sideways. **1974** *Times* 9 Feb. 11 Broadstairs bored him sideways, and he taught me to press on. **1985** A. BLEASDALE *Are you Lonesome Tonight?* 55 *Older Presley:* .. Listen, man,.. there's just one thing you could do for me. *Duke:* Yeah? *Older Presley:* Yeah. Go screw yourself. Sideways.
   [7.] **b.** *fig.* That treats a subject from a different or unconventional angle; indirect, 'off-beat'.
   **1982** *Christian Science Monitor* 1 Apr. 19/1 A real experimenter, Benning takes a sideways approach to storytelling: He splits his plot into bits and pieces, and interrupts these with digressions into the realm of pure film. **1987** *Sun* 21 Feb. 14/2 Jasper Carrott takes his final sideways look at recent events. **1988** *New Scientist* 29 Oct. 67/2 Although *Dealing with Dirt* is ostensibly aimed at a fairly young audience.. many an adult might enjoy this sideways look at the application of science to problems of everyday life.

**Sig.** (sɪg), *v.*[2] *imp. Med.* [Abbrev. of L. *signā* imp. sing., or *signētur* 3rd pers. sing. pres. subj. pass., of *signāre* to sign, mark, etc.] An instruction ('label it..' or 'let it be labelled..') used on medical prescriptions and indicating to the pharmacist the directions for taking the medicine which should be marked on its container. Cf. SIGNATURE *n.* 8.
   **1896** C. S. WEEKS-SHAW *Nursing* vii. 91/1 *S.* or *Sig.*, *signa*, write. **1913** C. EGGLESTON *Essentials Prescription Writing* 15 The signatura gives the necessary direction to the patient for his use of the preparation... The signatura is usually indicated by either of the following abbreviations of the Latin word *signa*: S., Sig.,—of these, the latter is to be preferred. **1964** *Australasian Post* 21 May 13 *Sig.* means 'let it be labelled'. **1988** *Prescription issued at Georgetown Univ. Hospital, Washington, D.C.* 26 Feb., Chloroquine Phosphate 250mg .. Sig.: take 2 tab p.o. each week.

**sign**, *n.* Add: [I.] [1.] **d.** *spec.* Any of the gestures used as a means of communication with or between the deaf and dumb in a system of sign language.
   **1644** BULWER *Chirol.* 5 Men that are borne deafe and dumbe; who can argue.. rhetorically by signes, and with a kinde of mute and logistique eloquence overcome their amaz'd opponents. *a* **1706** EVELYN *Diary* an. 1677 (1955) IV. 113 There din'd this day at my Lords, one Sir Jo: *Gaudy* a very handsome person, but quite *dumb*: yet very intelligent by signes. **1865** TYLOR *Early Hist. Mankind* ii. 17 The mother-tongue of the deaf and dumb, is the language of signs. **1880** *Daily News* 11 Nov. 6/2 The oralists say that under the French system signs only are taught. **1965** W. C. STOKOE et al. *Dict. Amer. Sign Lang.* 293 Some 'signs' for numbers in ASL are simply configurations shown as letters are. **1990** *New Scientist* 27 Oct. 32/1 Just as words consist of a range of vowels and consonants, combined in specific ways within each language, signs consist of arrangements of handshape, as well as the hands' location, orientation and movement.

**silly**, *a.*, *n.*, and *adv.* Add: [A.] [6.] In predicative use. **b.** *to drink* (oneself) *silly*: i.e. to intoxication (cf. DRINK *v.*[1] 12 a). Similarly, *to bore*, *scare*, etc. (oneself or another) *silly*: i.e. thoroughly, to an excessive degree. *colloq.*
   **1907** J. M. SYNGE *Playboy of Western World* III. 64 Drinking myself silly, and parlatic from the dusk to dawn. **1934** G. B. SHAW *Too True to be Good* Pref. 5 We are all amazed.. when we hear of the

multimillionaire passing the public house without going in and drinking himself silly. **1965** J. BETJEMAN in *London Mag.* 3 June 57 Where we can warm and hug each other silly. **1975** *Country Life* 25 Dec. 1798/1 Many ornamental trees and shrubs..had flowered themselves silly in 1974. **1989** *Marketing* 25 May 16/2 He says owners can now stuff dogs silly without ruining their digestions.

**Simon** ('saɪmən), *n.²* orig. *U.S.* [The male personal name.] **Simon Says**: a children's game in which players must obey the leader's instructions if (and only if) they are prefaced with the words 'Simon says..'; also, the command itself. Cf. WIGGLE-WAGGLE *n.* a.
  [**1853** 'P. PAXTON' *Stray Yankee in Texas* xx. 205 After playing 'Simon', 'What is my Thought Like', and a dozen similar games, one of the company arose.] **1856** 'G. FORREST' *Every Boy's Bk.* 13 Simon Says.. No player is to obey his commands unless prefaced with the words, 'Simon says'. **1938** WOOD & GODDARD *Compl. Bk. Games* x. 581 If he omits the 'Simon says—' the order must be ignored. **1979** *Business Week* 7 May 95/1 As one former executive of the company puts it: 'It's like a game of "Simon Says". You have to wait for the word from the headquarters Simon before you make any capital appropriation.' **1982** *N.Y. Rocker* Jan. 27/1 Cowboy would say stuff like 'Throw your hands up in the air' .. or a Simon-Says type thing.

**simuliid** (sɪ'mjuːliːɪd), *n.* and *a.* *Ent.* [f. mod.L. family name *Simuliidæ*, f. SIMULIUM *n.*: see -ID³.] **A.** *n.* Any fly of the family Simuliidae, comprising small blood-sucking gnats which spread parasitic disease; = *buffalo gnat* s.v. BUFFALO *n.* 5.
  **1895** in *Funk's Stand. Dict.* **1913** *Canad. Entomologist* XLV. 406 The commonest Simuliid around Boston, in Spring, is *Simulium hirtipes.* **1963** *Canad. Jrnl. Zool.* XLI. 947 An understanding of the role of simuliids in the transmission of parasites necessitates accurate identification of the flies. **1978** *Nature* 22 June 626/1 The vectors, simuliids or 'blackflies' prefer rapid running water as their habitat.
  **B.** *adj.* Of or pertaining to the family Simuliidae; consisting of members of this family.
  **1895** in *Funk's Stand. Dict.* **1913** *Canad. Entomologist* XLV. 407 The parasitised Simuliid larvæ are unable to pupate and are finally killed by the worm. **1961** *Ann. Entomol. Soc. Amer.* LIV. 716/1 The simuliid fauna of Wisconsin is comprised of 27 described species. **1976** *Lancet* 18 Dec. 1366/2 Drugs for killing the parasitic worm itself..are too dangerous for mass medication and the only practicable alternative is an attack on the vector, the simuliid blackfly.

**Sindbis** ('sɪndbɪs), *n.* *Biol.* and *Med.* [The name of the village of *Sindbis* in Egypt (see quot. 1955).] **Sindbis virus**, an insect-borne togavirus, related to Semliki Forest virus and also used extensively in genetic research. Also *absol.*
  **1953** R. M. TAYLOR in *Atti del VI Congresso Internazionale di Microbiol.* III. 239 If further investigation substantiates that this is a hitherto undescribed virus, it is suggested that it be provisionally designated as the Sindbis virus. **1955** *Amer. Jrnl. Trop. Med. & Hygiene* IV. 844 Subsequent studies indicated that Ar-339 was a hitherto undescribed virus; it was therefore provisionally designated as 'Sindbis' virus, the name of the Egyptian village where the mosquitoes from which the virus was first isolated were captured. **1963** *Virology* XX. 443/2 The base ratios of Sindbis virus RNA are quite different from those of two other major groups of RNA viruses represented by poliovirus..and influenza virus. **1980** R. W.

CHAMBERLAIN in R. W. Schlesinger *Togaviruses* vi. 192 Whataroa virus..is apparently an offshoot of Sindbis that came about because of geographic isolation.

**sinker**, *n.¹* Add: [III.] [8.] [c.] Also *sinker ball.*
  **1960** J. BROSNAN *Long Season* 77 It helps to have a good sinker ball, or some other special pitch that is consistently hit into the ground. **1985** *New Yorker* 5 Aug. 36/1 The Mets' win had been against the Cubs' experienced left-handed sinker-ball pitcher Steve Trout.
  **9.** *Windsurfing.* A very short board designed only for sailing in strong winds (as it will otherwise not support the rider's weight).
  **1986** *Courier-Mail* (Brisbane) 8 Aug. 32/5 Unless you have tremendous natural talent, there is no way you can learn on the type of 'sinker' you will be wanting once you get the hang of things. **1987** *Boards* Mar. 28/1 He..returned home the proud possessor of a locally custom made sinker. **1989** C. BODEN *Successful Windsurfing* 11 There is no point in buying a sinker unless you regularly sail in winds of force 5 and over.

**sinopis** (sɪ'nəʊpɪs), *n.* [a. L. *sinōpis*: see SINOPLE *n.*] = SINOPER *n.* 2 a.
  **1857** BOSTOCK & RILEY tr. *Pliny's Nat. Hist.* VI. xxxv. xii. 236 There are three kinds of sinopis, the red, the pale red, and the intermediate... Used medicinally, sinopis is of a soothing nature and is employed as an ingredient in plasters and emollient poultices. **1934** H. HILER *Notes Technique of Painting* ii. 134 We are told that Apelles and Micomachus created masterpieces with a palette of four colours: White, Melos earth... Yellow, Attic ochre... Red, Sinopis earth [etc.]. **1969** R. MAYER *Dict. Art Terms & Techniques* 363/1 *Sinopia*, .. an obsolete name for native red iron oxide pigment. Known also as sinope, sinoper, and sinopis.

‖**sinseh** (sin'se), *n.* [ad. Malay *sinse*, variant of *singse*, *sengse*, *sengsai* Chinese physician, prob. ad. Chinese dial. (Changchew) *sin-seⁿ* (Chinese *xiānsheng*), Amoy *sien-siⁿ* teacher, mister, sir, doctor.] In Malaysia, Singapore, and Indonesia: a traditional Chinese physician or herbalist.
  **1972** *Sunday Times* (Kuala Lumpur) 30 Apr. 5/8 Mr. Fong Tiang Luen and his wife, both sinsehs,.. operate two drug stores in town. **1977** *Grimsby Even. Tel.* 27 May 7/8 The leaders were 'Sin-sehs' or 'Incense-Pot Masters', the third-highest ranking members in the triad hierarchy. **1981** *Sunday Mail* (Brisbane) 2 Aug. 15/2 Government researchers have found that many of Singapore's 1000 Chinese physicians are secretly mixing modern drugs with traditional herbal medicines... The traditional physicians, known as sinsehs, deny the charges.

**sinsign** ('sɪnsaɪn), *n.* *Philos.* and *Ling.* [f. SIN(GLE *a.* or L. *sin(gulum* one + SIGN *n.*] A term used by C. S. Peirce (1839–1914) to designate a sign which is a thing (e.g. a diagram or weathercock) or an event (e.g. a cry). Later, taken to be a symbol that is an individual instance or 'token', rather than a universal or 'type'. Cf. *LEGISIGN *n.*
  *a***1914** C. S. PEIRCE *Coll. Papers* (1932) II. II. ii. 142 A *Sinsign*.. is an actual existent thing or event which is a sign. It can only be so through its qualities; so that it involves a qualisign. *Ibid.* 148 Each Replica of it will be a Dicent Sinsign of a peculiar kind. **1934** *Mind* XLIII. 496 Peirce's distinction between his sinsign or token and his legisign or type is a distinction depending purely upon the nature of the sign itself. **1966** [see QUALISIGN *n.*]. **1972** T. TODOROV in *Screen* (1973) Spring/Summer 22 The total number of words in a text equals the number of tokens or sinsigns; the amount of different words give us the number of types or legisigns.

**siphonous** ('saɪfənəs), *a. Bot.* [f. SIPHON *n.* + -OUS; cf. SIPHONEOUS *a.*] = SIPHONACEOUS *a.*

**1960** *Nature* 2 July 82/1 Comparatively little is known at present about the chemical nature of the cell wall constituents of siphonous green algae, especially that of the non-septate groups. **1969** *Jrnl. Phycol.* V. 284/1 The highly specific distribution of siphonaxanthin and siphonein . . may serve as an additional aid in the classification of the siphonous green algae. **1975** *Nature* 6 Nov. 32/2 The siphonous line (that is the coenocytic condition) is seen as an evolutionary *cul-de-sac*. **1978** *Bio Systems* X. 76/1 The close association of the desmids and coccoid green algae with the flagellated, filamentous and siphonous green forms has long been recognised.

**sirenin** ('saɪrənɪn), *n. Biochem.* [f. SIREN *n.* + -IN[1].] A hormone, secreted by the female gametes of fungi belonging to the genus *Allomyces*, which attracts male gametes of the same group.

**1958** L. MACHLIS in *Nature* 28 June 1790/2 Sirenin (I am indebted to Dr. A. Vegis for suggesting, what seems to me, this aptly descriptive name) is the name, used here for the first time, for the chemotactic sexual hormone from the water-mould *Allomyces* which attracts the male gametes and is produced by the female gametes. **1976** *Ann. Rev. Microbiol.* XXX. 231 Sirenin activity is very specific, and the hormone does not attract either female gametes and asexual spores of *Allomyces* . . or male hyphae of *Achlya*. **1982** J. B. HARBORNE *Introd. Ecol. Biochem.* (ed. 2) vii. 178 Sirenin, which acts as a sex pheromone in the water mould *Allomyces*.

**sister**, *n.* Add: [2.] c. Used by homosexual men to denote a fellow homosexual, esp. one who is a friend rather than a lover; a male homosexual. *slang* (orig. *U.S.*).

**1941** G. LEGMAN *Lang. of Homosexuality* in G. W. Henry *Sex Variants* II. App. VII. 1176 *Sister in distress*, a homosexual male in trouble, usually with the police. **1972** B. RODGERS *Queens' Vernacular* 181 A sister is sexually neutral with his comrades; he is a chum, not a lover. Sisters are in the same business, but only as competition. **1977** *Gay News* 24 Mar. 33/3 A lot of your letters mention views about sister-gays. **1986** PENROSE & FREEMAN *Conspiracy of Silence* (1987) 51 Most of their mutual gay friends assumed that they had begun as lovers and then, in the parlance of the homosexual world, become sisters.

**sit**, *v.* Add: [II.] [13.] f. Without compl. or adv.: to remain untouched or unused.

**1987** *N.Y. Times* 2 July C10/2, I had two choices: Let the place sit, or fix it up like a Hollywood home. **1989** *Classic & Sportscar* Feb. 16/1 It had been sitting for 20 years, so is . . ripe for restoration.

**six**, *a.* and *n.* Add: [B.] 8. Familiar shortening of *M.I.6* (s.v. M III. 6 a).

**1969** W. GARNER *Us or Them War* ii. 24 He thought he might strike a better bargain with us than with Five or Six. [*Note*] M.I.5 and M.I.6. **1975** J. GRADY *Shadow of Condor* iii. 65, I think the Special Branch . . . No sense letting Five and Six directly involve themselves. **1982** G. LYALL *Conduct of Major Maxim* iv. 35 When you agreed to meet comrade Blagg you didn't know anything about . . the involvement of Six.

**sixsome**, *n.* Add: [1.] c. A company or party of six persons.

**1934** WEBSTER, *Sixsome*, a group of six persons or things; now esp., a group of six persons playing together. **1967** P. M. HUBBARD *Country of Again* vi. 74 I'll make it a sixsome, with two non-bridge-players. **1981** *Daily Mail* 30 Nov. 17/6 In fact their meetings have been in foursomes and sixsomes. **1987** *Daily Express* 28 Mar. 20 The Waltons' saucy sixsome, Britain's first surviving sextuplets, are three-and-a-half years old.

**sixteen**, *a.* and *n.* Add: [C.] [1.] 1662 [from the year of its publication], the revised edition of the Book of Common Prayer published in 1662, the use of which was mandatory in the Church of England until the introduction of a series of alternative services in the 1960s and the subsequent publication of the Alternative Service Book in 1980.

**1976** *Oxf. Diocesan Mag.* July 18/2 Of course the old congregation do not altogether approve of 'all these children', and sigh for 1662 and the Te Deum. But the grumblers have reduced their numbers to a half-dozen. **1981** D. BREWER in Martin & Mullen *No Alternative* xxii. 195 Those who say that 'Cranmer' or '1662' is now incomprehensible. *Ibid.* 196 Canon Brett asked his Mothers' Union . . whether they preferred 1662 or Series 3.

**size**, *n.*[1] Add: [II.] [10.] g. Bodily weight; muscular bulk or power. *colloq.* (orig. *U.S.*).

**1985** E. LEONARD *Glitz* xii. 102 He was a big strong Italian fella and I see you're going to have size on you. **1985** *Bodypower* Oct. 17/2 Please can you advise me as to which method builds size, using squats and bench press as an example. **1987** E. LEONARD *Bandits* ii. 28, I felt Maureen was gonna put on size.

**sizeable**, *a.* Add: 'sizeably *adv.*

**1911** in WEBSTER. **1975** *Forbes* (N.Y.) 1 Feb. 9/1 Sizably upping the price of gas and oil by heavy additional federal taxes. **1988** *WorldPaper* 11 Dec. 12/4 The first batch of graduates have obtained jobs with salaries ranging from $300 to $670 monthly, sizeably higher than those of graduates from other programs.

**sizzler**, *n.* Add: [2.] c. A lively, exciting time or event, esp. in Sport. orig. and chiefly *U.S.*

**1942** BERREY & VAN DEN BARK *Amer. Thes. Slang* §642/3 *Fast game*, fast fight, sizzler, whirlwind mix, whizbang. **1976** *Business Week* 19 Jan. 19/1 For U.S. chemical companies, 1976 is starting off as a real sizzler. Sales of organic chemicals could be up as much as 25% or 30% over the first half of 1976. **1986** *Sunday Mail* (Brisbane) 25 May 55/5 (*heading*) Balu scores in a sizzler. **1987** *Times* 28 Oct. 48/1 The clash will be a sizzler but the competitive aggression must be controlled.

**skat**, *n.* Add: b. *collect.* The two cards dealt to the table in a game of skat. Cf. WIDOW *n.*[1] 3 b.

*c*1868 W. B. DICK *Mod. Pocket Hoyle* (ed. 4) 145 After the cards have been cut, and before dealing, the dealer lays aside the two top cards, face downwards. These two cards are called the 'Scat'. **1911** *Encycl. Brit.* XXV. 166/1 After the cards have been shuffled and cut, the dealer first deals three cards to each player, then four and again three, laying aside two cards (the skat). **1957** *Encycl. Brit.* XX. 727/2 Solo grand is played without use of the skat. **1974** *National Skat & Sheepshead Q.* Mar./Apr. 9, I found the Club 8 and Spade 7 in the skat.

**skatathon** ('skeɪtəθɒn), *n.* orig. *Canad.* Also skate-a-thon, skate-athon. [f. SKATE *v.* + -ATHON.] A prolonged period of skating, organized in order to raise money for a charity or cause.

**1970** *Toronto Daily Star* 24 Sept. 17/5 Teams of minor hockey players and figure skaters will take part in a day-long skatathon at Doublerink Arena, Highway 7. **1973** *Kingston* (Ontario) *Whig-Standard* 20 Feb. 9/7 A total of 292 skaters from 39 teams completed 100 laps in a skate-a-thon for the Picton District Minor Hockey League Saturday. **1980** *Washington Post* 15 Feb. (Weekend section) 3/1 Skaters, ice or roller, can test their endurance for a good cause this Monday, because rinks all around Washington are sponsoring Skate-A-Thons. **1986** *Auckland Metro* Feb. 64/2 We . . had a card from pupils at Remuera Intermediate who held a skate-athon to raise money for us.

**skedaddle**, v. Add: **ske'daddling** vbl. n.
**1863** C. H. SMITH in Southern Confederacy (Atlanta, Georgia) 13 May 2/1 But ther wer no panik, no skeedadlin. **1979** A. SILLITOE Storyteller I. ii. 26 He was even more ashamed of his panicky skedaddling than of having read his poetry.

**skeletal**, a. Sense d in Dict. becomes e. Add: **d.** Suggestive of a skeleton owing to extreme thinness; emaciated, skinny.
**1952** W. PLOMER Museum Pieces xxii. 182 She now put out a long, thin forearm, almost skeletal in its refinement. **1962** O. MANNING Spoilt City I. iii. 34 He was tall, skeletal, narrow-shouldered and stooped like a consumptive. **1980** J. WAINWRIGHT Dominoes i. 9 The skeletal impression extended to his hands; long-fingered, knuckle-boned and almost flesh-less. **1988** P. SAYER Comforts of Madness xxii. 120 If it were possible to stretch me out they would see how much I had shrunk. My legs are now very thin, skeletal, drawn up and outwards.

**skeleton**, n. Add: [1.] [b.] Hence used ellipt., without mention of a closet or cupboard.
**1936** G. B. SHAW Simpleton II. 67 When you mention . . the Day of Judgment . . the pious ones—think we have come to dig up all the skeletons and put them through all of their shocking criminal trials. **1965** 'P. QUENTIN' (title) Family skeletons. **1976** A. PRICE War Game (1979) I. i. 34 If he'd been fair . . , they might have felt a tiny bit inhibited about putting his skeletons on display so prominently. **1984** N.Y. Times 5 Mar. B8/3 Fraser and Califano and I know where all the skeletons are buried... We created the problem in the first place.

**skelf** (skɛlf), n.² Sc. Also 7 skelv(e, 9 skelve. [Prob. ad. obs. Du. schelf scale, flake, or splinter of wood, and ult. cognate with SKELF n.¹] **1.** A sliver or splinter, usu. of wood, esp. one lodged in the skin.
c**1610** J. MELVILLE Mem. (1827) 24 They wer hurt . . with skelves of stanes be the force of our battery. Ibid. 84 The King Hendre 2 being hurt in the head with the skelv of a spair. **1808** JAMIESON, Skelve, . . a thin slice, lamina. **1884** 'CRUCK-A-LEAGHAN' & 'SLIEVE GALLION' Lays & Legends N. of Ireland 88 Nor a skelf av thir hides, nor a tuft av their hair. **1895** J. NICHOLSON Kilwuddie (ed. 4) 197 'What's the maitter wi' yer finger, guidman?' 'I think I hae gotten a skelf . . intill't.' **1914** N. MUNRO New Road xxx. 308 He . . cut a skelf from the boarding of one hole. **1926** Contemp. Rev. July 125 He shows the wounds he has received from a dragoon in O'Connell Street, and a skelf from a bobby's bâton at a Labour meeting in Phoenix Park. **1947** H. W. PRYDE First Bk. McFlannels ii. 22 He had a skelf in his finger. **1959** Bulletin (Glasgow) 8 May 11/4 Don't neglect the pricks from rose thorns, rusty (or even clean) wires, a skelf of wood—anything like that should be treated at once, with respect and hot fomentations. **1979** L. DERWENT Border Bairn i. 11 Extracting a skelf from a sore thumb. **2.** A small or slight person; one who is a nuisance. colloq.
**1927** Scots Mag. June 172 Pit doon that fryin'-pan, ye wee skelf. **1951** N. B. MORRISON Hidden Fairing 97 A wee skelf of a man put in his head. **1975** W. McILVANNEY Docherty II. x. 181 'Away, ya skelf,' the man went on. 'You young yins think ye inventit men an' women.' **1985** M. MUNRO Patter 63 The weight's fell aff her—she's nuthin but a skelf.

**skell** (skɛl), n.² U.S. slang. [Of uncertain origin; perh. shortening of skeleton.] In New York, a homeless person or derelict, esp. one who sleeps in the subway system.
**1982** N.Y. Times Mag. 31 Jan. 21/3 Other New Yorkers live there [sc. the subway] . . eating yesterday's bagels and sleeping on benches. The police in New York call such people 'skells'. Ibid., These 'skells' are not merely down and out. Many

are insane, chucked out of New York hospitals. **1988** Newsday (N.Y.) 22 Feb. 6 The delirious, crazy people whom cops call 'skells', the down-and-outs, the grungy and hopeless, garbage-heads who use any foreign substance known to man to alter reality.

**skelp**, n.² Add: [1.] **b.** Without article: iron or steel in the form of long narrow strips or sheets, used in the manufacture of pipes, gun barrels, etc.
**1835** W. GREENER Gun viii. 39 (heading) Twopenny, or Wednesbury skelp. **1852** C. TOMLINSON Cycl. Useful Arts I. 818/1 These [pieces of scrap-iron] are sorted and used in preparing iron of various qualities, known as wire-twist, . . twopenny, or Wednesbury-skelp, sham-damn-skelp. **1948** Beaver Dec. 4 The iron barrels were forged of what was termed 'sham damn skelp'. **1968** Globe & Mail (Toronto) 13 Feb. B8/5 Canadian Phoenix . . has to purchase skelp and plate from other sources. **1984** E. P. DeGARMO et al. Materials & Processes in Manuf. (ed. 6) xiv. 364 Both of these processes . . utilize steel in the form of skelp—long, narrow strips of the desired thickness.

**skene** ('ski:nɪ), n.³ Theatr. [a. Gr. σκηνή hut, tent: see SCENE n.] In ancient Greek theatre, a three-dimensional structure or building forming part of the scene (SCENE n. 1), which provided a background to the performance and could be decorated according to the theme of the play; a stage-building.
**1899** P. GARDNER in Jrnl. Hellenic Stud. XIX. 257 Agatharchus . . could paint the front of the skênê to look like a palace with pillars and cornices. **1929** D. S. ROBERTSON Handbk. Greek & Roman Archit. xvi. 271 The Greek theatre, consisted . . of two quite separate parts, a high auditorium . . and a much lower stage-building, or skene. **1939** M. BIEBER Hist. Greek & Roman Theater v. 123 The northern wall . . of the hall . . was used as early as the beginning of the fifth century as the back of the wooden skene, and as early as the end of the same century as the back of the stone skene. **1962** P. D. ARNOTT Greek Scenic Conventions 5th Cent. B.C. i. 5 A skene of some sort would have been needed by the actors, to serve as a changing room and provide a focal point for entrances. **1986** Hesperia (U.S.) LV. IV. 423 The 4th-century skene . . consisted of a long central building with projecting paraskenia and lateral wings at either end.

**skewgee** (skju:'dʒi:), a. colloq. (chiefly N. Amer.). [f. SKEW a. + -gee, prob. as in AGEE adv. (also AJEE adv. and cf. on the jee s.v. JEE n.); cf. SKEW-WHIFF a. and adv.] Askew, awry, crooked; in a mixed-up, confused state.
**1890** Cent. Dict., Skew-gee, a., crooked; skew; squint. Also used as a noun: as, on the skew-gee. (Colloq.) **1897** E. BRODHEAD Bound in Shallows viii. 165 When folks gets all skew-gee brooding on things, why, it seems only right to straighten 'em out. **1905** Dialect Notes III. 64 Your tie is on all skewgee. **1958** E. BIRNEY Turvey viii. 88, I have to roll down a flock of skewgee old blackout blinds at night. **1985** C. MacLEOD Plain Old Man xix. 175 Let me straighten out your curls. You're all skewgee.

**-ski** (ski), suffix. colloq. (orig. U.S.). Also -sky. [ad. Russ. -skiĭ adj. suffix, jocularly taken in English as an essential characteristic of Russian words (prob. after RUSSKI a. and n.), esp. attached to nouns.] A suffix appended to a word or phrase in humorous imitation of Russian. Cf. BUTTINSKY n.
**1902**, etc. [see BUTTINSKY n.] **1916** Dialect Notes IV. 304 In this [cartoon] one old Russian asks another, who is represented as fishing, 'Got a bitesky?' The fisher answers 'Not yetsky!' **1922** WODEHOUSE Clicking of Cuthbert i. 30 The niblicksky is what I use most. Goot-a-bye, Mrs. Smet-thirst.

**1933** S. JAMESON *Women against Men* 260, I shall want a letter or something—Mrs. Thingski recommends—sober, honest, good cook, reliable. **1936** MENCKEN *Amer. Lang.* (ed. 4) 222 At the time of the Russian-Japanese War (1904-5) the suffix *-ski* or *-sky* had a popular vogue, and produced many words, e.g., *dunski, darnfoolski, smartski, devilinsky, allrightsky* and *buttinski*. **1973** *Guardian* 1 Feb. 1 Concordski will go ahead... The Soviet airline Aeroflot will press ahead with plans to introduce its own supersonic airliner, the Tu 144, whatever happens to Concorde. **1979** W. H. CANAWAY *Solid Gold Buddha* i. 16 Now pissoffski. Can't you see when you're not wanted? **1988** *Sun* 14 Oct. 3 We bet the comrades will be thrilled to bitski!

**skim**, *n.* Add: [1.] **e.** A thin coating (*of* a substance); a film. orig. *N. Amer.*
**1951** W. FAULKNER *Requiem for Nun* 227 That same white tide sweeping them in: that tender skim covering the winter's brown earth, burgeoning through spring and summer into September's white surf. **1962** M. E. MURIE *Two in Far North* II. viii. 178 There was only a light skim of snow as yet. **1966** D. BAGLEY *Wyatt's Hurricane* ix. 259 Then, a few miles further on, they ran into water on the road, just a skim at first, but deepening to over six inches. **1979** M. MCMULLEN *But Nellie was so Nice* I. i. 12 She put on a light skim of makeup.. and left the apartment gratefully. **1989** *Independent* 10 Aug. 6/5 The trick of adding a skim of asphalt—bitumen and stone—to provide a running surface was not invented until 1901.
[4.] **c.** The action or process of skimming a profit from gambling receipts; the money taken in this way. Cf. SKIM *v.* 2 d. Chiefly *U.S.*
**1972** T. P. MCMAHON *Issue of Bishop's Blood* xiii. 152 The take in Las Vegas is on the order of eight and a half millions a week. A good chunk of that dough, the skim, goes through Gentilli's hands. **1982** *Washington Post* 12 Oct. A8/2 One method of obtaining this money is.. to buy casinos in Nevada using front men and then insert their own personnel to effect a skim. **1984** *N.Y. Times* 28 Jan. 1. 9/4 Cash equivalent to the spurious 'fill' slips was removed from the casino cashier's cage, the books were balanced and the skim was complete. **1986** T. BARLING *Smoke* xvii. 396 OK. But we get the whole skim from the London casinos.
[5.] **skim coat** *Plastering* = *setting coat* s.v. SETTING *vbl. n.* 14.
**1895** in *Funk's Stand. Dict.* II. 1680/1 *Skim coat*, .. A thin finishing coat of plaster. **1898** *Internat. Corresp. Schools Instruction Paper: Masonry* II. 137 The first layer applied is called the *scratch* coat; the second, the *brown* or *finishing* coat; and the third, the *skim, white*, or *finishing* coat. **1990** *Do it Yourself* Apr. 8/2 The beading.. is not seen after the skim coat of plaster has been applied.

**skimmer**, *n.* Add: [7.] **e.** *Angling.* A small bream.
**1971** K. SEAMAN *Canal Fishing* xi. 108 Bob Ivey.. says he knows of a stretch of canal.. which contains bream of a size that would astonish those anglers who think it holds only 'skimmers'. Skimmers, which are very small bream, exist in quantity in many canals and are not difficult to catch once they have been located and encouraged to feed. **1987** *Match Fishing* Feb./Mar. 18/3 The best feeding pattern when fishing for skimmers on the float was little and often.

**skin**, *n.* Senses 11-16 in Dict. become 12-17. Add: [II.] [8.] **j.** *slang* (orig. *U.S.*). A condom.
In quots. 1975, 1990 with reference to the use of *skin* (or *sukin*) in Japanese as a katakana word or transliteration equivalent of the English.
**1960** WENTWORTH & FLEXNER *Dict. Amer. Slang* 482/1 *Skin*, .. any thin rubber or animal membrane contraceptive; a condom; a rubber. **1971** B. THORNBERRY tr. *Hansen & Jensen's Little Red School-Bk.* (ed. 2) 98 Boys use sheaths, sometimes

called durex, skins, or French letters. **1975** *Forbes* (N.Y.) 15 Oct. 68/3 More than 100 Japanese companies employ so-called 'skin' saleswomen to sell condoms door-to-door to the lady of the house. **1976** T. SHARPE *Wilt* xvi. 160 'You got those rubbers you use?' he asked suddenly... 'I want those skins.' **1990** *Sunday Correspondent* 4 Feb. 42/5 She's one of Japan's Skin Ladies—her job is to sell condoms door-to-door.
**k.** *slang* (orig. *U.S.*). A paper for rolling cigarettes (esp. in smoking marijuana).
**1969** FABIAN & BYRNE *Groupie* xxx. 202 Passed the chick a plastic bag with skins and hash inside. **1969** *Gandalf's Garden* VI. 11/2 *Skins*, cigarette papers. **1980** S. MCCONVILLE in Michaels & Ricks *State of Lang.* 525 It [*sc.* tobacco].. is smoked in a *roll-up* or *spliff*, the paper of which is called a *skin*.
**11.** A sub-division of a tribe; = MOIETY *n.* 4. Now only *Austral.*
**1876** W. G. PALGRAVE *Dutch Guiana* v. 165 Besides the 'Grand Man' of their own 'skin', in negro phrase, each tribe enjoys or endures the presence of a European official. **1927** *V & P* (W. Austral.) I. III. 83 The hurt, or the injury that I might do to one A, a native, is a hurt done not primarily to him, but done to the.. group or skin, as they call it, of which he is a member. **1944** W. E. HARNEY *Taboo* (ed. 3) 153 Old Toop-Toop was a Jimara native, that is, of the Jimara sub-section, or as the natives call it, 'skin' of the Mudbura tribe. **1958** R. STOW *To Islands* ii. 48 It was their custom to address one another as brother-in-law, since Justin had given Gunn a skin name, a classification in the tribe, which put them in this relationship. **1978** B. SCOTT *Boori* (1979) 148 Aboriginal tribes were divided into either four or eight 'skins'. Each 'skin' was associated with an animal, bird or insect, as a totemic division. **1986** *Canberra Times* 2 Apr. 7/2 The 'skin' name was the way of identifying an Aboriginal as part of a group.

**skin**, *v.* Add: [I.] [1.] **d.** *transf.* To cover (a surface) with a (thin) layer, esp. as in veneering; to coat or finish. Usu. in *pass.*
**1946** E. DIEHL *Bookbinding* II. iv. 51 Then immediately the pasted sheet is 'skinned' by placing over it a piece of unprinted newspaper large enough to cover the sheet.. for a bare second and is then pulled off. **1987** *Yachting World* Apr. 102/3 The seats are comfortable and both seat tops and cockpit sole are skinned with laid teak. **1989** *Aviation News* 3-16 Feb. 862/4 The Cirrus Major 3 in this airframe caused heavy tail surface vibrations made acceptable only by skinning the tailplanes to stiffen the assembly.

**skinny**, *a.* and *n.* Add: [B.] [1.] **c.** A thin example of its type. *colloq.*
**1961** *John o'London's* 30 Nov. 603/1 Among the Skinnies is a delicious giggler, *Uncle Shelby's ABZ Book.* **1978** *N.Y. Times* 30 Mar. A16 (Advt.), You can trade an even 12.50 for an exclusive YSL skinny [*sc.* tie]. **1987** *Hot Rod* Aug. 57/1 Rolling stock consists of highly polished Weld wheels fore and aft fitted with Michelin.. skinnies up front and Pro Trac .. balloons out back.

**skip**, *n.*[1] Add: [1.] **c.** An act or instance of absconding; a flit. *colloq.* (orig. *N. Amer.*).
**1942** BERREY & VAN DEN BARK *Amer. Thes. Slang* §58/2 *Hasty or unceremonious departure*, .. skidaddle, skip, slope. **1978** R. LUDLUM *Holcroft Covenant* xxviii. 331 It was a very professional skip. **1981** 'A. HALL' *Pekin Target* xi. 95 I'd left my things in Room 29 as.. routine procedure for a skip, to let them assume I was simply out for the evening. **1987** *Age* (Melbourne) 7 Nov. (Weekend Suppl.) 6/5 'Sometimes, our clients sit down in front of us and cry,' says Mrs Roberts. Some contemplate suicide or 'doing a skip'.

**skipper**, *n.*[2] Add: **6.** *Scouting.* **a.** From 1912, a title for the (adult) leader of a troop of Sea

Scouts (after 1949, Sea Explorers in the U.S.).
**b.** An adult leader of Girl Scout Mariners (in U.S., 1934 to 1980) or Sea Rangers (in U.K.).
**c.** In extended use, a colloq. name for a scoutmaster, or troop leader.

**1912** W. BADEN-POWELL *Sea Scouting & Seamanship for Boys* ii. 28 Officer spoke English to our skipper, but gave boat's crews orders in German. **1929** *Handbk. for Scoutmasters* xx. 450 The success of the Sea Scout Program is dependent upon the Skipper. **1938** *Sea Sense* i. 6 The idea of being a ship's crew can be carried out by the Skipper. **1977** *Guider* July 331/2 She was a Guider in this Company, a Brown Owl of the first Teignmouth Pack, a Sea Ranger Skipper and a District Commissioner. **1985** S. JACOBSON *Brit. & Amer. Scouting & Guiding Terminol.* ii. 31 In 1934 the Girl Scout Mariner program had been launched... The names for the Troop Leader and her Assistant/s/ were usually 'Skipper' and 'Mate/s/'. **1986** *Scouting* Mar. 15/1 He'd asked my 'Skipper' whether someone could write an article for *The Scout* on our Troop's camp.

**skipper**, *v.*[2] Add: Hence **'skippering** *vbl. n.*

**1968** *Observer* (Colour Suppl.) 22 Dec. 21/1 He has lived in hostels or skippered—lived without visible means of support. 'My skippering was organized,' he said. **1983** *Daily Tel.* 31 Oct. 14/6 No decent woman can get a bed in this town under £7 a night. And the 'skippering' allowance paid to vagrants is £2.95 a day. **1987** *Economist* 26 Dec. 61/3 Most of the advisory services try to persuade young people to get out of central London... They sleep on friends' floors, or resort to 'skippering'—taking over a deserted house or flat with no furniture and often no lavatories.

**skirted**, *ppl. a.* Add: [1.] **d.** Of a mobile home: fitted with skirting (see *SKIRTING *vbl. n.* 6). N. Amer.

**1972** *Fairbanks* (Alaska) *Daily News-Miner* 3 Nov. 21/6 (Advt.), 14 x 60 mobile home, skirted for winter with entrance way. **1976** *Billings* (Montana) *Gaz.* 2 July (Advt.), 3 bdrm Detroit Vanguard, already skirted & set up on lg. lot w/low rent! Can commute to Blgs or move trailer. **1989** *Austin Amer.-Statesman* 29 Apr. c40/6 (Advt.), 3 choice repo's—Set up, skirted. As low as $350 monthly.

**skirting**, *vbl. n.* Add: **6.** A border or screen enclosing the space beneath a mobile home and concealing the wheels, plumbing, etc. N. Amer.

**1961** *Mobile Home Jrnl.* 24 May (*caption*) Skirting is of the same siding material [aluminium]. **1972** R. H. NULSEN *Mobile Home Man.* (rev. ed.) 1. viii. 340 (*caption*) Skirting is a requirement in modern mobile home parks. **1979** *Arizona Daily Star* 5 Aug. 12/4 (Advt.), Home includes 1 year warranty, skirting and awning.

**Skokomish** (skəʊˈkəʊmɪʃ), *n.* (and *a.*) [ad. Twana *sqʷuqʷóʔbəš*, f. *sqʷuqʷóʔ* river + *-bəš* (earlier *-məš*) people.] **a.** A Salishan people, now few in number, inhabiting the Puget Sound in N.W. Washington State. **b.** The Salishan language of this people. Also *attrib.* passing into *adj.* Cf. TWANA *n.*

**1844** C. WILKES *U.S. Exploring Exped.* IV. xii. 437 After passing further down the canal, they found the Scocomish tribe who inhabit its Southern end. **1854** H. R. SCHOOLCRAFT *Indian Tribes U.S.* IV. 598 Indians of Puget Sound. Skoskomish .. Head of Hood's Canal. *Ibid.* 600 The Tuanooch and Skoskomish tribes speak the same language. **1855** *Ibid.* VII. 701 The Tuanok and Skokomish tribes reside along the shores of Hood's canal. **1874** H. H. BANCROFT *Natural Races Pacific States N. Amer.* I. 301 The *Skokomish* live at the upper end of Hood Canal. **1909** A. L. KROEBER in *Jrnl. R. Anthrop. Inst.* XXXIX. 81 Chinook and Skokomish, both of the

North Pacific Coast, are alike in indicating the condition of the connecting relative. **1911** *Encycl. Brit.* XXIV. 80/1 *Salishan*, the name of a linguistic family of North American Indian tribes, the more important of which [include] the Salish .., Skokomish, Spokan and Tulalip. **1928** *41st Ann. Rep. U.S. Bureau Amer. Ethnol.* *1919-24* 376 Plates 63-75 give some other Klikitat baskets and also work of the Salishan, Skokomish and Chimakuan Quilente. **1960** W. W. ELMENDORF *Struct. Twana Culture* v. 259 In nearly all respects the Skokomish acted as a village unit in their economic and social life. *Ibid.*, The ethnic name of the Skokomish is of course an extended-area term .., not derived from a single-site name. **1977** C. F. & F. M. VOEGELIN *Classification & Index World's Lang.* 301 *Salish* .. 23. Twana = Toanhuch = Toanhooch = Tuadhu = Skokomish. Fewer than 10 [speakers]. Washington.

**skosh** (skəʊʃ), *n.* *U.S. slang* (orig. *Forces*'). [ad. Jap. *sukoshi* a little, somewhat.] A little, a small amount; freq. used *advb.* in the expression *a skosh*, slightly, somewhat.

[**1955** *Amer. Speech* XXX. 44 Along with .. everyday greetings, Bamboo English employs *sukoshi* 'few, some' and its antonym *takusan* 'plenty', both of which are forthwith made into two-syllable words, dispensing with the voiceless Japanese *u*.] **1959** (recorded by Prof. A. L. Hench, Univ. of Virginia) 10 May, 'Just a skosh,' he said. When I asked him what he meant he said he had picked the word up in Korea. It means 'a little bit'. 'Just a little bit left' was his meaning. **1977** *Detroit Free Press* 19 Dec. 4-c/1 In the ad, a slightly out-of-breath jogger laments middle-age body bulge and tells how glad he is that a new line of Levis for men is constructed with 'a skosh more room where I need it'. **1988** *Cycle World* Sept. 37/1 The GSX-R's seat is more comfortable than the Yamaha's thinly padded perch, and its bars are a skosh higher.

**skull**, *n.*[1] Add: [1.] [c.] For def. read: *slang.* Orig., the head of an Oxford College or Hall (*obs.*). Subsequently *gen.*, one who is in charge, a chief or head; also, an expert. Cf. GOLGOTHA *n.* 2. (Further examples.)

App. obsolescent in the U.K. by mid-19th cent., but soon afterwards recorded in the U.S. and subsequently Austral.

**1880** *Slang Dict.* 32/1 *Skull*, the head of the house; the President of the United States; the Governor; the head man. **1944** D. BURLEY *Orig. Handbk. Harlem Jive* 104 Now, this skull was in there, Jack, he was frantic. **1948** G. H. JOHNSTON *Death takes Small Bites* v. 107 'Who does he fix the deal with?' 'God knows! D'ye think the skulls tell us that?' **1964** —— *My Brother Jack* 325 You knowing all the brass-hats and the skulls down at the Barracks... I don't suppose you could pull some strings for me? **1978** R. BEILBY *Gunner* 135 The little man nodded towards Whiteside and the captain... 'Them skulls with you?'

**slab**, *n.*[1] Senses 1 c-e in Dict. become 1 d-f. Add: [1.] **c.** *Mountaineering.* A large, smooth body of rock lying at a (usu. sharp) angle to the horizontal.

**1904** J. N. COLLIE in *Alpine Jrnl.* XXII. 10 [The ridge] was impossible, being made up entirely of bare slabs and perpendicular pitches. **1955** S. STYLES *Introd. Mountaineering* xi. 127 The term *thank-god hold*, which has become part of British climbing jargon, originated on the third ascent of the slab on Route II, Lliwedd East Buttress. **1965** A. BLACKSHAW *Mountaineering* vi. 173 As well as slabs providing Moderate or Difficult climbing (e.g. Idwal Slabs) there are some slabs providing very hard and serious climbing. **1986** *Climber* May 19/2 Climb directly up iced slabs to below corner.

**g.** *transf.* in *Statistics.* Any of the bands in a system of fiscal or other stratification. Freq. *attrib.*

**1963** *Times* 22 Feb. 5/3 When estate duty is reduced it should be done by graduating the rates on a 'slab' basis as in surtax. By this method the top rate of duty applicable to an estate would be levied only on its top 'slab' and the lower rates . . on the lower 'slabs'. **1988** *Hindu* 25 Feb. 7/1 The increase per ticket in second class mail express is proposed to be Rs. 2 at the lowest slab, progressively rising to a maximum, for distances beyond 750 km of Rs. 15.00.

**slab** (slæb), *n.*⁴ *Angling* (orig. *N.Z.*). [Of uncertain origin; cf. SLAB *a.*² and SLAT *n.*⁴] A weak or spent game fish, *esp.* a diseased trout; a kelt.

**1952** A. G. MITCHELL in *Chambers's Shorter Eng. Dict.* (Austral. ed.) Suppl., *Slab*, a poorly conditioned trout. **1968** *Times* 22 Oct. 3/2 Brown trout fishermen in the South Island of New Zealand are familiar with individual fish which show very little fight once they have been hooked. It now turns out that these fish, known locally as slabs, are suffering from a heart disease. **1986** *Coarse Fishing* June 12/3 Despite a couple of big slabs priming right in front of us we could not get a touch.

**slam**, *v.*¹ Add: [2.] **e.** *Sport.* To score (a goal, etc.) with a powerful kick or strike; to accumulate (a large total) in this way. *colloq.*

**1959** *Punch* 6 May 611/1 The players are naturally pleased when one of their team gets, 'hits', or 'slams' a goal. **1986** *Philadelphia Inquirer* 11 July C2/5 George Foster slammed a three-run double and Bob Ojeda scattered seven hits as host New York snapped a three-game losing streak by beating Atlanta. **1987** *Wisden Cricket Monthly* Aug. 39/2 Instead of bowlers rampaging at the start Hardie and Gooch slammed 202 for the first wicket on the way to a total of 280 for 2.

[5.] **[b.]** For def. read: To criticize severely. Also, in later use, to repudiate or contradict (an allegation, etc.). *colloq.* (orig. *U.S.*). (Further examples.)

**1973** C. MULLARD *Black Britain* II. vi. 68 By . . producing the facts about immigration which slam his own exaggerations, they are, like it or not, playing into Powell's hands. **1985** *Courier-Mail* (Brisbane) 10 Dec. 3 (*heading*) Card artists slam claims of deception. **1989** *Construction News* 8 June 4/4 Criticisms that the Government sees road building as the only solution to the capital's congestion problems were slammed as a myth by Mr Bottomley.

[6.] **b.** *Naut.* Of a boat: to crash into the trough of a wave, or into the wave itself; to plunge or pitch.

**1958** J. L. KENT *Ships in Rough Water* ix. 120 Ships occasionally 'slam' when driven through rough seas. **1976** M. MACHLIN *Pipeline* lvi. 566 The lifeboat was now slamming through the choppy two and three foot high waves at over twenty knots. **1986** *Practical Boat Owner* July 57/1 Of course, she's more likely to slam if wave-hopping. **1988** *Motor Boat & Yachting* Oct. 98/4 It gave an exciting ride, slamming and skittering in the chop and returning its crew safely with broad grins on their faces.

**slant**, *n.*¹ Add: [2.] **b.** *Amer. Football.* (*a*) An attacking play in which the ball-carrier moves into the line of scrimmage at an oblique angle. (*b*) In full, *slant-in.* A pass pattern in which a receiver runs diagonally towards the goal-line from the line of scrimmage.

[**1927** G. S. WARNER *Football for Coaches & Players* 143 (*caption*) 10 precedes 11, the ball carrier, in a driving, slanting tandem, hitting between E and F. For a sure gain of a few yards this is a better play than A-3.] **1947** D. X. BIBLE *Championship Football* iv. 33 Straight-ahead plunges and slants are direct plays. **1953** C. C. CALDWELL *Mod. Football for*

*Spectator* vii. 142 Slant charge. In this type of charge, the defensive lineman moves obliquely across the line of scrimmage. **1957** *Encycl. Brit.* IX. 478/2 Reverses . . are even more important in the double wing formation than they are in the single wing, but slants and plunges also are effective. **1982** S. B. FLEXNER *Listening to Amer.* 243 Stanford during his own long career, refined the single wing at Pitt and combined it with his own *unbalanced line* and *slant plays.* **1988** L. WILSON *Amer. Football* ii. 29/1 If you are running a slant-in, look for the ball over your inside shoulder.

**slant**, *adv.* and *a.* Add: Hence 'slanty *a.* = SLANTING *ppl. a. a.*

**1928** *Daily Express* 22 Dec. 8/3 With bright slanty eyes like a mouse, and the pretty animation of a tit in a spring hedgerow. **1983** *New Scientist* 10 Feb. 387/2 RND, STEP and NOT share keys with obscure wiggly brackets, slanty lines and arrows pointing every which way.

**slap**, *n.*¹ [1.] [a.] After 'an impact of this nature' read: Also, the sound of this.

**1940** W. VAN T. CLARK *Ox-Bow Incident* iii. 195 Even in the wind you could hear the horses snort about it, and the slap of leather and the jangle of jerked bits. **1969** E. BRATHWAITE in Ramchand & Gray *West Indian Poetry* (1972) 78 Slap of the leather reins Along the horse's back and he'd be off. **1985** M. GEE *Light Years* vi. 72 Davey shut up his *Time Out* with a slap.

**g.** *Jazz slang* (orig. *U.S.*). The percussive sound made when the strings of a double-bass strike the fingerboard in slap-bass playing; the technique itself, *ellipt.* for *slap-bass s.v.* SLAP *v.*¹ 11. Cf. SLAP *v.* 1 e.

**1934** R. P. DODGE in *Hound & Horn* VII. 600 The remaining instruments, bass, fiddle, guitar, banjo and tuba . . have contributed . . a few individual elements such as the 'slap' of the bass. **1984** *Sounds* 29 Dec. 37 (Advt.), Bass course series . . Slap and Funk.

**3.** [Prob. f. SLAP *v.*¹ 3.] Theatrical make-up, as rouge, grease-paint, etc.; also *transf.* more generally: any cosmetic make-up, esp. applied thickly or carelessly. *slang* (orig. *Theatr.*).

**1860** HOTTEN *Dict. Slang* (ed. 2) 217 *Slap*, paint for the face, rouge. **1885** 'CORIN' *Truth about Stage* iv. 101 Have you got a bit of slap (colour) to give me? *a***1890** *Sporting Times* in Barrère & Leland *Dict. Slang* (1890) II. 253/1 She nullified the virtues of her toilet preparations; Or in other words, she doctored Maudie's slap. **1904** W. S. MAUGHAM *Merry-go-Round* 273 'I surmised that you were in some trouble,' murmured Miss Ley, 'for I think you've rather overdone the—slap. Isn't that the technical expression?' **1956** A. WILSON *Anglo-Saxon Att.* II. iii. 387 Many of Vin's guests came in costume with plenty of slap. **1960** J. R. ACKERLEY *We think the World of You* 110 She was all dolled up, her face thick with slap. **1972** B. RODGERS *Queen's Vernacular* 183 *Slap* (Brit gay sl, *fr* dated cant) face makeup 'Are you forty under all that slap?' **1989** *Daily Tel.* (Weekend Suppl.) 6 May p. iii/1 'Do you mind if I put my slap on while we talk?' she says, proceeding to do so with an efficiency that speaks of years in crowded dressing rooms. **1990** *Q* Mar. 28/3 Lloyd Cole is having his slap applied. 'In a perfect world,' he muses, eyes shut, 'I'd have a make-up artist and a dresser sort me out every morning.'

**slap**, *v.*¹ Sense 1 d in Dict. becomes 1 e. Add: [1.] **d.** To strike (the ball or puck) with a sharp slap; also, to score (a run, etc.) by hitting in this way. Cf. SLAP SHOT *n. N. Amer. Sport.*

**1912** *N.Y. Tribune* 12 Oct. 10/5 Cady, after fouling off three balls, slapped a single through the box. **1935** J. T. FARRELL *Judgment Day* viii. 183 Studs watched the infield practice, the grounders slapped hard, cutting over the dirt, the ball snapped around from player to player. **1964** F. MAHOVLICH *Ice*

*Hockey* ix. 54 Get a friend to feed you passes which you can slap at the goalmouth.

[3.] **d.** To apply or daub (a substance, esp. paint or make-up), usu. thickly or carelessly. Cf. *SLAP n.*[1] 3. *colloq.*

**1903** FARMER & HENLEY *Slang* VI. 243/1 *Slap*, . . (theatrical). Make-up. Also as *verb*. **1918** 'TAFFRAIL' *Little Ship* ii. 26 The dockyard-maties had slapped on the service gray paint over coal-dust and dirt alike. **1944** M. LASKI *Love on Supertax* iii. 36 She slapped the Orange Skin Food on to her face. **1960** *News Chron.* 16 Feb. 6/6 Barbara goes into the dressing-room to slap on the old goo. **1970** *Sunday Times* 3 May 28/6 Women take hours getting themselves done up to attract men, slapping on pancake, painting their eyes. **1983** I. WATSON *Bk. of River* (1984) II. 55, I soon found that painting isn't a matter of slapping on a fresh coat, then sitting back to admire it.

**slasher**, *n.* Add: **5.** *attrib.* Designating cinematographic films which depict the activities of a vicious attacker whose victims are slashed with a blade, as **slasher film, movie**. In early use, designating 'snuff movies' (see SNUFF *n.*[1] 7).

**1975** *Whig-Standard* (Kingston, Ontario) 2 Oct. 3/6 New York City police detective Joseph Horman said . . that the 8-millimetre, eight-reel films called 'snuff' or 'slasher' movies had been in tightly controlled distribution. **1975** *Globe & Mail* (Toronto) 20 Nov. 7/4 Police in New York are investigating the circulation of eight such snuff or slasher films. **1982** *Forbes* (N.Y.) 27 Sept. 176/2 Paramount's low-budget slasher film Friday the 13th Part 3 in 'super 3-D' was roundly thrashed by critics ('Trash', said Newsweek). **1989** *Empire* Sept. 97/4 A silly psychic slasher movie with photographer . . haunted by visions of the murders committed.

**sleaze**, *n.* Add: **3.** *Comb.* **sleazebag** orig. *U.S.*, a sordid, despicable person, *esp.* one considered morally reprehensible; also *attrib.* or as *adj.*

**1981** *Time* 9 Nov. 112/1 Guy Caballero, a *sleazebag in a modified Panama and a white three-piece blend, appears frequently on-camera to . . fawn before his audience. **1985** *National Times* (Austral.) 22 Nov. 7/1 We are not giving away any principles, because we do have a few on this side of the House, unlike the sleazebags over there. **1986** *Legal Times* 16 June 8/1 'This was no sleazebag lawyer.' In more stately language, the committee says the same thing.

**sleazeball** *U.S.* = *sleazebag*; also *attrib.* or as *adj.*

**1983** *Atlantic Monthly* July 44/2 'What kind of a *sleazeball are we dealing with here?' Tsongas put that question in a form that made the TV news. **1986** R. FORD *Sportswriter* i. 13 It was stated in court by X's sleaze-ball lawyer. **1990** *Sounds* 12/1 Boss Hog are the sweat-stained, mutoid metal noise product of the festering minds of those gun-slinging, sleazeball lovers, Jon Spencer and Christina.

**sleaze factor**, the sleazy or sordid aspect of a situation; *spec.* (*U.S. Pol.*) applied to scandals and alleged corruption involving officials of an administration.

**1983** L. BARRETT *Gambling with Hist.* xxvii (*chapter-title*) The *sleaze factor. **1984** *Sunday Times* 26 Aug. 17/8 Lurking round the campaign trail now will always be the shadow of her husband and his own sleaze factor. **1988** *Courier-Mail* (Brisbane) 7 July 6/5 Mr Meese . . had become the outstanding symbol of the so-called 'sleaze factor' which has bedevilled the Reagan administration.

**sleeper**, *n.* Add: [I.] [5.] **c.** A sofa, chair, or other form of seating which can be converted into a bed; a chair-bed or sofa-bed. orig. *U.S.*

**1973** *Washington Post* 13 Jan. A19/5 (Advt.), Kroehler Full Size sleeper. **1974** *State* (Columbia, S. Carolina) 15 Feb. 11-B/2 (Advt.), Sleeper sofa with mattress, used, $25. **1989** *Austin Amer. Statesman* 29

Apr. A7/2 (Advt.), With a queen-size sleeper on one side and a relaxing incliner on the other, this sectional is massive yet beautifully styled. **1991** *Oxford Star* 11 July 3 (Advt.), Examples of sofa-bed bargains . . permanent sleeper . . £429.

**sleep-out**, *n.* and *a.* Add: [A.] **2.** The act or instance of sleeping out of doors, esp. as a form of collective protest on behalf of the homeless. Cf. SLEEP-IN *n.* 1.

**1961** WEBSTER 2140/3 *Sleep-out*, . . an outing on which the participants sleep outdoors. **1967** V. W. MUSSELMAN *Making Children's Parties Click* x. 126 The sleep-out and the slumber party can be planned for either boys or girls. **1984** *N.Y. Times* 3 Dec. B7/5 To those who occasionally accompanied the officials on such hamlet sleepouts, the experience could be mentally and physically harrowing. **1987** *Daily Tel.* 4 Mar. 8/8 The streets of Washington were littered with celebrities last night as actor Martin Sheen led a 'sleep-out' to spotlight the plight of the homeless.

**sleeve**, *v.* Add: [4.] **b.** With *down*. To reduce in size the bore of (a firearm or engine), by fitting metal shafts, etc. within the barrel or cylinder. Also with the barrel, etc. as obj.

**1976** 'J. CHARLTON' *Remington Set* iv. 26 If they sleeve them down they can get ammo for them under British jurisdiction. **1986** *Dirt Bike Rider* July 19/1 KTM have utilised some left over 500 bottom-ends and sleeved down a 500 barrel to come up with a 345 cc engine. **1987** *Classic Racer* Summer 53/3 The engine was sleeved down to 122 cc, fixed up with alloy flywheels in the place of bob-weights, and the barrel was turned round front-to-back.

**5.** To provide with or enclose in a protective cover. Cf. SLEEVE *n.* 7 e.

**1980** *Musicians Only* 26 Apr. 14/6 Samea will look at each disc before it is sleeved and will play both sides of random samples. **1986** *Camera Weekly* 110 (Advt.), Hand negative cutting and sleeved in sixes. **1988** D. MACCARTHY *Prodfact 1988* (Brit. Farm Produce Council) 98 Celery will keep best if sleeved and stored in a refrigerator.

**slepton** ('slɛptɒn), *n. Particle Physics.* [f. S(UPER- + LEPTON *n.*] The supersymmetric counterpart of a lepton, with spin 0 instead of ½.

**1982** ELLIS & NANOPOULOS in *Physics Lett.* B. CX. 44/2 Suppression depends on the differences $\Delta m_{sl}^2$ in (mass)[2] between spin-zero superpartners (squarks and sleptons) of the quarks and leptons in different generations. **1986** *Nature* 16 Oct. 597/1 It is not clear how the scale of supersymmetry breaking is determined nor how this is related to the masses of the physical 'observable' sparticles—squarks ($\tilde{q}$), sleptons ($\tilde{l}$), gluinos ($\tilde{g}$), photinos ($\tilde{\gamma}$), and so on. **1989** P. D. B. COLLINS et al. *Particle Physics & Cosmol.* x. 243 Gauge bosons are partnered by spin-½ gauginos, and these cannot be identified with any of the quarks and leptons. So the latter have to be partnered by new spin-0 squarks and sleptons.

**slide**, *n.* Add: [III.] [11.] **c.** *U.S.* A kind of open-backed shoe or slipper. Usu. in *pl.*

[**1931** 'D. STIFF' *Milk & Honey Route* 209 *Kicks*, shoes. Also called *slides*.] **1975** *Footwear News* 21 July 6 The slide is emerging as a top fashion theme. **1979** *Arizona Daily Star* 8 Apr. B7/4 (Advt.), Our sexy 'Ursula' slides are your ticket to a sensational summer! Natural, khaki, white, rust or wine leather vamps on poly bottoms.

**slidy** ('slaɪdɪ), *a.* [f. SLIDE *v.* + -Y[1].] That slides or causes to slide; slippery, slithery.

**1880** W. T. DENNISON *Orcadian Sketch-Bk.* 4 The rock grew sae slidy, that his taes could help him neen. **1907** KIPLING *Let.* 10 Dec. (1983) 56 A slippery slidy red leather box—like a huge Tiffany jewel case. **1971** T. BOULANGER *Indian Remembers* 70 We also was making a huge flat sleigh with tamarack. After it was fixed it was very slidy. **1983** *Christian Science Monitor* 18 Oct. 42/1 This 18th-century

Edinburgh clergyman, by the grace of water-gone-solid-with-cold and the inspiration of shoes-gone-slidy-with-steel, has attained that .. indescribable ideal of nonchalant balance.

**slifting** ('slɪftɪŋ), *n. Linguistics.* [f. s(ENTENCE *n.* + LIFTING *vbl. n.*] In transformational grammar, a rule or transformation which promotes material from an embedded sentence following a cognitive verb to a main sentence.
    **1973** J. R. ROSS in M. Gross et al. *Formal Anal. Nat. Lang.* 134 Such structures .. are converted by a rule which I will refer to as *Slifting* (= sentence lifting). **1976** *Language* LII. 396 Slifting, a rule which fronts the complements of verbs of saying and thinking .., has created the appropriate environment. **1977** *Canad. Jrnl. Linguistics 1976* XXI. 153 Sentences like the following are basically the same in meaning .. (1) I believe Ralph came. (2) Ralph came, I believe. These have been described .. as related by a transformational rule of Sentence-Lifting or Complement Preposing (to be abbreviated here as 'Slifting'). **1980** *Studies in Lang.* IV. 121 Possibly the path of derivation involves *Extraposition and Slifting* .. followed by a rule which can .. convert a parenthetical clause to a surface adverb.

**slim**, *n.* Add: 3. Usu. with cap. initial. [After the severe weight loss associated with the disease.] In Central Africa: = AIDS *n.* More fully, *Slim disease.*
    **1985** *Lancet* 19 Oct. 849/1 A new disease has recently been recognised in rural Uganda. Because the major symptoms are weight loss and diarrhoea, it is known locally as slim disease. **1986** *Listener* 5 June 10/1 Museveni's government has now been forced at least to recognise the AIDS problem (called 'Slim' in East Africa). **1987** *Oxf. Textbk. Med.* (ed. 2) I. v. 154/2 Enteropathic AIDS and severe weight loss (frequently due to Cryptosporidiosis) is characteristic in Africa, known in some localities as 'slim' disease. **1990** *Independent on Sunday* 1 Apr. (Sunday Rev.) 10/4 Because it is the skilled élite .. who have most money to spend on womanising, it is this group which is suffering the worst ravages of Slim.

**slim**, *a.* Add: [1.] **g.** Of commodities, etc.: low in price or value; economical. *colloq.*
    **1970** *Which?* Sept. 272/2 Pricewise they want it slim. When you get there they're standing over you wanting a Rolls-Royce job. **1981** *Times* 31 July 20/3 Aeronautical & General tumbled a further 18p to 340p, .. now 60p slimmer than a week ago.
    **h.** Of an organization: trimmed down to an efficient or economical level, in terms of staffing, business, etc.
    **1976** *Birmingham Post* 16 Dec. 6/4 A slimmer public service was inevitable. **1989** *Forbes* (N.Y.) 20 Mar. 129/1 Unum has become slimmer and more focused since .. he .. cut $25 million out of annual expenses.

**sling**, *n.*² Sense 3 d becomes 3 e. [3.] **d.** Hence, a similar device used for carrying a baby or small child.
    **1856** DICKENS *Dorrit* (1857) II. i. 323 The child carried in a sling by the laden peasant woman .. was quieted with picked-up grapes. **1966** C. W. HAMILTON *Oil Tales of Mexico* ii. 15 Her infant is carried on her back in a sling made from a rebosa. At feeding time, the rebosa is hitched to the side and the baby is nursed. **1975** H. JOLLY *Bk. Child Care* viii. 124 In developed countries, carrying a baby in a 'papoose' sling or attached to a frame on the back is becoming more popular as an occasional substitute for pushing him in a pram. **1983** P. LEACH *Parents' A to Z* (1985) 581 Pushchairs tend to put their occupants at exactly the level of vehicle exhaust pipes. She may be better off if you carry her in a sling. **1988** *Mother* Apr. 45/1 A Mothercare sling .. was marvellous and even with my bad back I found it was invaluable.

**slip**, *n.*³ Add: [II.] [4.] **g.** More fully, *gun slip.* A case or holder for carrying a gun.
    **1977** *Tackle & Guns* Dec. 3/1 (Advt.), Ranger economy gun slip. **1981** *Sporting Gun* Aug. 30/1 Features of the slip are a full length heavy duty nylon zip, sturdy carrying handle and snap-on shoulder strap. **1986** *Air Gunner* Sept. 37/2 The fleece-lined gun slip has a shoulder strap and two carrying handles. **1987** M. PAULET *Shooting from Scratch* iv. 83 Don't put a wet gun into a dry slip. Wipe it over first.

**slip**, *v.*¹ Add: [I.] [8.] **f.** With advb. phrase: to drop or fall in value, etc. by the amount stated. Chiefly of share prices.
    **1961** *U.S. News & World Rep.* 22 May 109/1 Prices of those bonds have slipped a bit since then. **1971** *Daily Tel.* 28 Oct. 1/4 The Dow Jones industrial average slipped 8.98 points to 836.38, its lowest closing level in more than nine months. **1979** *Ibid.* 15 Aug. 18/4 Glaxo shed 6 to 428p and ICI and Beechams at 340p and 141p both slipped 2p. **1989** *European Investor* Feb. 70/2 The following day the shares slipped 2 per cent to 1357p.
    [II.] [22.] **e.** *Boxing.* To avoid (a punch) by moving quickly to one side. Also *intr.* or *absol.*
    [**1889** E. B. MICHELL in H. Pollock et al. *Fencing, Boxing, Wrestling* 170 Another mode of shifting ground, more properly called 'slipping' is shown in Fig. VII.] **1897** R. G. ALLANSON-WINN *Boxing* iv. 29 Vary your defence as much as possible, so as to leave your antagonist in doubt as to whether you are going to guard, duck, or slip, in order to avoid his blow. **1901** G. B. SHAW *Admirable Bashville* II. i. 304 Cashel was clearly groggy as he slipped the sailor. **1952** *Amat. Boxing* ('Know the Game' Ser.) 24/2 *(caption)* Slipping a straight left and countering with right. **1986** *World Boxing* Sept. 37/1 He's learned how to slip a jab, and even though Green's jab is good, it isn't as good as a Pinklon Thomas jab.

**Slipperette** (slɪpə'rɛt), *n.* In *U.K.* s-. [f. SLIPPER *n.* + -ETTE.] A proprietary name for a type of slipper or slipper-shaped foot-covering made of soft fabric (*U.S.*); also, a disposable slipper, esp. of a kind distributed to airline passengers.
    **1931** *Official Gaz.* (U.S. Patent Office) 29 Dec. 1125/2 Slipperette. For footwear—namely, rectangular bags of knitted or crotcheted fabric adapted to be worn on the feet as low socks. **1957** *New Yorker* 2 Nov. 140/3 Slipperette stretch slippers. For home or travel. Nylon with lamé trim for ladies. **1980** *Daily Mail* 14 Mar. 8 (Advt.), [British Airways] Free eye-shades and slipperettes.

**slippery**, *a.* Add: [1.] **d.** Of a vehicle or its shape: creating only low air resistance; streamlined. *colloq.*
    **1981** *Pop. Hot Rodding* Feb. 88/1 The reason for the tremendous gain in speed is the Monza's very slippery shape and small frontal area. **1982** *Observer* 31 Jan. 44/6 The new shape is obviously very slippery—the makers give a drag coefficient of 0.34. **1985** *Austral. Business* 4 Sept. 82/1 The company now has the world's three most aerodynamically efficient cars. The Audi, the Renault 25 and now the Vortex are the 'slipperiest' cars around. **1986** H. I. ANDREWS *Railway Traction* iv. 78 This difference is well known to drivers, who are accustomed to describe one type of locomotive as more slippery than another.

**slit**, *v.* Add: 4. To narrow (the eyes) into slits, esp. for protection against the wind, rain, etc., as a sign of distrust, or in order to concentrate one's gaze; to half-close.
    *a***1961** J. R. ULLMAN in WEBSTER, Morning sunlight flooded in upon him, and he slitted his eyes against the glare. **1964** O. E. MIDDLETON in C. K. Stead *N.Z. Short Stories* (1966) 203 With a half-smile he

slits his eyes against the smoke. **1975** M. Duffy *Capital* iii. 132 Meepers began to chip away at the hard earth, slitting his eyes against the flying fragments. **1989** *Washington Post* 8 Mar. D3/2 Slitting his eyes as if sensing a trick question, the secretary said, 'It's just a very worthwhile institution.'

**Sloanie** ('sləʊnɪ), *n.* (and *a.*) *slang.* [f. Sloane (Ranger *n.* + -ie.] A Sloane Ranger. Also *attrib.* or as *adj.*

**1982** Barr & York *Official Sloane Ranger Handbk.* 153/1 'A Sloanie has a pony' is . . ingrained in the Sloane mind. **1985** *Observer* 22 Sept. 2/5 Another batch of Sloanies cashed in. **1986** *Listener* 5 June 35/4 She has to be literally beaten by her mother into marrying Cary Elwes—Guilford—who resembles a low-grade Sloanie with a taste for whores and bad liquor. **1989** *Independent* 3 July 3/5 Jeremy Taylor, one-time organiser of the Gatecrashers' Ball—a Sloanie teenage rave—was behind the party.

**slobbish** ('slɒbɪʃ), *a. colloq.* [f. slob *n.*[1] + -ish[1].] Of, like, or characteristic of a slob (sense 3); loutish, slovenly, inveterately uncouth and lazy.

**1980** *N.Y. Times* 25 July C8/5 In addition to Mr. Murray, who plays the country club's slobbish, possibly retarded, assistant greenskeeper, the cast includes Michael O'Keefe. **1984** *Observer* 7 Oct. 21/6 Her slobbish cousin Willie . . has been living off his wits as a cardsharp in New York since leaving Hungary 10 years before. **1986** *Sight & Sound* Q. Winter 4/3 It's not science fiction, more a good-naturedly slobbish, kitchen sink comedy for the video age. **1988** *Daily Tel.* 30 Nov. 16/2 Miss Kingsley is sound on the Street; I share her plaudits for the 'repulsively real' Fred Gee and her plaudits for Jean Alexander as Hilda mourning for the slobbish Stan.

**slomo** ('sləʊ 'məʊ, 'sləʊməʊ), *n. Cinematogr. colloq.* (chiefly *U.S.*). Also slo-mo. [Abbrev. of *slow motion* s.v. slow *a.* 14 *a.*] Slow motion; slow-motion replay or a facility for producing this. Freq. *attrib.*

**1978** *Washington Post* 10 Feb. E5/4, I realize that a videotape slo-mo replay is to our advantage. **1979** *Ibid.* 16 Sept. M4 The NFL Films . . had it in slo-mo, and in overheads. **1980** *Broadcast* 7 July 10/2 Producer to slomo operator: 'Go back to where you were before I told you to go where I told you to go.' **1987** *Which Video?* Jan. 4/3 Apart from the Hi-Fi facility there's a 14-day, six-event timer, advanced trick frame with five-speed slomo (1/36, 1/24, 1/15, 1/10 or 1/6), [etc.].

**sloshing** ('slɒʃɪŋ), *ppl. a.* [f. slosh *v.*[1] + -ing.] Splashing or slopping; containing a liquid which sloshes about.

**1924** *Chambers's Jrnl.* Sept. 578/1 At the third cast there was a queer sloshing rise. **1958** 'W. Henry' *Seven Men at Mimbres Springs* ix. 94 A sloshing mannequin made of their lone water barrel topped by the sack of flour. **1977** *Washington Post* 21 Mar. A5/5 Subject to the sloshing ebb and flow of the ocean's tides, it will never run dry. **1984** *Time* (Overseas ed.) 6 Feb. 52/3 In one dreamlike scene, Russian soldiers are shown marching in slow motion, each carrying a rifle and a sloshing goldfish bowl.

**slot,** *n.*[2] Add: [2.] h. *Motor Rallying.* A turning or other opening, *esp.* one marked for the driver to take. *slang.*

**1963** P. Drackett *Motor Rallying* iii. 35 *Slot,* entrance to a road. *Wrong-slot,* quite simply—taking the wrong road. **1987** *Rally Sport* Jan. 87/3 [They] missed a slot in the village of Tegryn and were close to PC9 before realising their mistake.

i. *Ice Hockey.* An unmarked area in front of the goal affording the best position for an attacking player to make a successful shot at goal.

**1967** *Maple Leaf Gardens Mag.* 15 Mar. 59/1 Note the centreman is in the white section in this diagram. In hockey this area is termed the 'slot'. More goals are scored from here than anywhere else. **1968** *Globe & Mail* (Toronto) 17 Feb. 41/3 The Marlie forwards sped into the slot on the least excuse to take a swipe at the puck that Hawk defenders left in front of their netminder. **1980** *N.Y. Times* 27 Nov. B9/1 Lying on his side, he poked the puck to Cashman in the slot. **1986** *New Yorker* 31 Mar. 21/2 Our goalie was subjected to . . slap shot after slap shot raining in from the blue line, the slot.

j. *Computing.* Any elongated, more or less rectangular socket; *spec.* = *expansion slot* s.v. \*expansion *n.* 8.

**1978** *Practical Computing* July-Aug. 4 The chassis . . has three additional slots for expansion boards. **1982** F. J. Galland *Dict. Computing* 30 *Cage,* a group of slots with electrical connectors used to hold replaceable printed circuit boards in a functional unit. **1983** *Practical Computing* 97 (*caption*) Softward ROMs up to 16K can be plugged into a slot above the keyboard. **1988** *Which?* Nov. 527/1 Computers with more slots are more versatile.

**slot,** *v.*[2] Add: [2.] c. To kill or injure (a person) by shooting. *Army slang.*

**1987** *New Breed* Sept. 58/3 During the Rhodesian conflict . . 'troopies' on external raids into Frelimo territory (Mozambique) regularly sought (and found) bayonets on the bodies of those they 'slotted'. **1989** *Times* 27 July 3/5 If you can't get a good conviction then you get someone slotted (slang for shot).

**sludge,** *n.* Sense 4 in Dict. becomes 5. Add:
4. *fig.* An amorphous or undifferentiated mass.

**1906** Joyce *Let.* 3 Dec. (1966) II. 200 This he learned I suppose from the stolidly one-languaged Sludge [of teachers]. **1971** *Oz* No. 36. 46/3 The Underground can no longer go on evading the issue, with the aid of . . the whole reactionary super-groupy sludge. **1982** *Times* 16 Nov. 11/1 The pungent character of each instrument is reduced to a sludge of pentatonically tinted Mantovani.

**sludgy,** *a.* Add: 4. *fig.* Sluggish, tedious; confused and undefined, 'muddy'.

**1901** C. J. C. Hyne *Master of Fortune* xii. 296, I shall get a sludgy paragraph in the papers for the *Grosser Carl,* headed 'Gallant rescue', with all the facts put upside down. **1921** G. B. Shaw *Back to Methuselah* Pref. 72 There is no question of a new religion, but rather of redistilling the eternal spirit of religion and thus extricating it from the sludgy residue of temporalities and legends that are making belief impossible. **1984** J. Updike *Hugging Shore* (1985) 160 Hemingway . . would have hated this overlong, sludgy and frequently humiliating book.

**slug,** *n.*[2] Senses 6-7 in Dict. become 7-8. Add:
6. *gen.* A thick piece or lump *of* some material; also, a portion or amount, *esp.* a large one.

**1867** *2nd Ann. Rep. Missouri State Board Agric.* *1866* 16 They suffer severely with inward fever . . . Our remedy is to drench them with lard, or slugs of fat bacon. **1929** *Amer. Speech* V. 75 A large amount is a 'slew' or 'slug'. **1977** *Economist* 21 May 116/2 They might be liable either to another slug of capital gains tax or more likely . . income tax. **1983** G. Benford *Against Infinity* I. iii. 24 Old Matt shrugged, his face wrinkling into a fine-threaded map as he chewed on a hemp slug.

**slug,** *v.*[2] Sense 3 in Dict. becomes 4. Add:
3. To drink deep draughts or slugs (of); to swig. *slang.* a. *intr.* Also const. *up. rare.*

**1856** Porter's *Spirit of Times* 6 Sept. 7/1 Let's slug up and prepare for business. **1973** M. Amis *Rachel Papers* 30 Dozy afternoons slugging on opiate cough mixtures.

b. *trans.* Also const. *down.* Chiefly *N. Amer.*

**1979** *Washington Post* 31 Aug. D3/1 At change games, players wearily slumped into their chairs and slugged water, soft drinks or Gatorade as if trying to extinguish fires in their bellies. **1980** in S. Terkel *Amer. Dreams* 237, I used to give him shaves, a couple, three times a week. And slug beer with him. **1986** *Glaswegian* Dec. 5/3 We slugged 'ginger' and maybe Tizer in a cup. **1989** *Chicago Tribune* 20 Apr. 7/3 In the car, slugging down beer and raucously celebrating their graduation night .. are two terminally troubled teenagers.

**sluggardly,** *a.* Add: Hence **'sluggardliness** *n.* = SLUGGARDNESS *n.*

**1977** *Economist* 30 Apr. 90/1 The trade cycle has changed from seesaw to sluggardliness.

**slump,** *n.²* Sense 4 in Dict. becomes 5. Add: 4. A dessert consisting of stewed fruit with a biscuit or dough topping; a fruit cobbler. *U.S.* (chiefly *New England*).

**1831,** etc. [see *apple slump* s.v. APPLE *n.* 3 c]. **1905** *Dialect Notes* III. 19 *Slump,* .. a dish of dough and fruit, as 'apple slump'. **1939** I. WOLCOTT *Yankee Cook Bk.* 365 Slump. What State-of-Mainers call cooked fruit topped with dumplings or biscuit dough. **1947** BOWLES & TOWLE *Secrets New England Cooking* xi. 178 Both the grunts and the slumps were transition desserts, halfway between the boiled and baked puddings but simpler to make. **1965** *National Observer* (U.S.) 29 Nov. 20/4 But even the failures tasted good, so I told her to put on a brave face and call it a prized old New England recipe for blueberry 'slump'. **1986** B. FUSSELL *I hear Amer. Cooking* IV. xvii. 313 In America, the English pudding pies made of custard and fruit .. were named 'slumps', 'crunches', and 'grunts'.

**slurp,** *v.* Add: **'slurper** *n.,* one who slurps while eating or drinking.

**1974** *N.Y. Sunday News Mag.* 3 Feb. 14/1 The spaghetti slurpers were respectfully silent. **1986** *Los Angeles Times* 13 Mar. IV. 1/2 Urged by mothers tired of cleaning up behind ham-fisted slurpers, the maker of the two-stick Popsicle has decided to phase out their product.

**slushy,** *a.* Add: Hence **'slushily** *adv.*

**1961** in WEBSTER. **1972** *Guardian* 18 Mar. 13/3 The Anglo-Chinese thaw gets slushily under way. **1984** S. TOWNSEND *Growing Pains A. Mole* 26 'Don't upset yourself, Mrs Mole,' the woman said slushily. 'We are here to help, you know.'

**smart,** *a.* Add: [II.] [15.] **smart card** (also **smartcard**) orig. *U.S.* [cf. INTELLIGENT *a.* 5], a plastic bank card or similar device with an embedded microprocessor, used in conjunction with an electronic card-reader to authorize or provide particular services, esp. the automatic transfer of funds between bank accounts.

**1980** *N.Y. Times* 14 Dec. III. 4/3 They preferred to write checks, knowing these would not clear until the next pay check had arrived. '*Smart card' holders could react the same way. **1983** *Electronics* 10 Mar. 52 The Army started to explore the smart card in January 1982 as a complete records-keeping vehicle. **1984** *New Scientist* 8 Mar. 25/2 The most recent, and most adventurous approach to credit cards is the 'smartcard', with built in microchip. **1988** *Times* 23 Feb. 30/7 The beauty of the algorithm .. is that it can be built into hardware that will fit even on 'smart cards', and enables the identity of end-users to be checked in less than a second.

**Smarties** ('smɑːtɪz), *n. pl.* Also s-. A proprietary name for candy-covered milk chocolate buttons in a variety of colours.

**1939** *Trade Marks Jrnl.* 8 Nov. 1496/1 *Smarties* .. chocolate confectionery. **1954** G. GREENE in *Twenty-One Stories* 221 'I got some chocolates,' Mr Thomas said ... He handed over three packets of Smarties.

**1962** *Times* 29 Jan. 13/5 The children insisted on a dolls' tea party ... Yes, I did have it with food .. teensy weensy plates of currants, chopped up smarties and sugar lumps. **1965** *Official Gaz.* (U.S. Patent Office) 26 Jan. TM157/1 *Smarties* .. for Candy. First use Apr. 17, 1950. **1978** R. WESTALL *Devil on Road* x. 62 She'd even knocked the tin of vitamin-pills over one night and started scoffing them like Smarties. **1988** *Times on Sunday* (Austral.) (Suppl.) 6 Mar. 25/1 He approached words like a child approaching an overturned truck that had spilled its load of Smarties.

**smash,** *n.¹* Add: 7. A party, *esp.* one that is noisy or unrestrained. Cf. BASH *n.* 2 (ii) and THRASH *n.¹* 3. *N. Amer. slang.*

**1963** *Amer. Speech* XXXVIII. 171 [Kansas Univ. slang] A particularly rough and noisy party: .. *smash.* **1968** *Globe & Mail* (Toronto) 3 Feb. 3/7 The Liberals are still planning a big party, but now they are thinking in more modest terms ... There are two difficulties in the sort of all-out smash originally contemplated. **1977** *New Yorker* 26 Sept. 38/3 Every spring the Thrales gave a party ... They called this decorous event 'our smash'.

**Smell-O-Vision** ('smɛlə‚vɪʒən), *n.* Also Smellovision, etc. [f. SMELL *n.* or *v.* + -*o*- + VISION *n.,* modelled on the names of other proprietary production techniques, as *VistaVision,* etc.; cf. also TELEVISION *n.*] A style or technique of cinematographic presentation in which pictures on the screen are accompanied not only by sound but also by appropriate smells released into the auditorium. (The process has not been widely used.) Cf. SMELLIE *n.*

A proprietary name in the U.S. for a similar special-effects technique involving 'scent-emitting stickers' with televised film (*Official Gaz.* (U.S. Patent Office), 1986, 16 Dec. TM126/1).

**1958** *Listener* 30 Oct. 706/1 Mr. Mike Todd, junior, .. has discovered and will shortly introduce a new thing in the film industry: Smello-vision. **1976** *Oxf. Compan. Film* 34/1 Mike Todd backed a system called Glorious Smell-O-Vision with a thriller, *The Scent of Mystery.* **1983** *Christian Science Monitor* 31 Mar. B4/2 Inside, the McCormick Building is a different world. It is a quaint, period world, rather like a sepia movie in 'smellovision'. A rich, strong scent perfumes the air. **1987** *Guardian* 23 Mar. 15/8 Whatever happened to Smellovision?

**smiley,** *a.* Add: [1.] c. *smiley face,* a round cartoon-style representation of a smiling face (usu. black on yellow), freq. used as a symbol of hope, peace, solidarity, etc. in youth culture. Also *absol.* as *n.*

**1972** *Times* 1 Dec. 20/3 China—new from France with the Smiley face in black on yellow. In packs of four: cups and saucers, £2.55; tea plates £2.45. **1981** *Aviation Week & Space Technol.* 19 Oct. 11/1 The Pacific Southwest smiley face black line under the nose had been erased. **1986** D. LEAVITT *Lost Lang. Cranes* (1987) 198 Brad's eye roved the room, which had recently taken on a second identity as an art gallery and was filled with murals depicting the deconstruction of the smiley face. **1989** *Face* Dec. 63/1 In the crowd you may also spot the odd man in navy Top Man tracksuit, immaculate new trainers and strange accessories such as bandanas or Smiley badges—these are plain-clothes policemen or tabloid journalists.

**smiling,** *vbl. n.* Add: [1.] b. In electrophoresis, the curving of bands of material on a gel as a result of differing rates of migration of material at its centre and edges.

**1982** R. W. DAVIES in Rickwood & Hames *Gel Electrophoresis Nucleic Acids* iv. 144 When polyacrylamide gels are electrophoresed, differential heating in the centre of the gel compared to the edges causes oligonucleotides at the centre to run faster than those at the edge ... This effect has been called 'smiling' because of the form of the dye-front. **1986** *Electrophoresis* VII. 54/2 'Smiling'.. makes the nucleic acid sequence difficult to interpret. **1988** *Nature* 2 June 477/3 The system virtually eliminates 'smiling' and the related sample mobility artefacts which commonly occur in sequencing gels.

**smith**, *n.* Add: [1.] **b.** *fig.* As the second element in Combs. One who employs or makes with skill that denoted by the first element, as *finger-smith*, *tunesmith*, *wordsmith*, etc. and other more or less nonce-formations: see at first element or as main entries.

**Smithsonian** (smɪθ'səʊnɪən), *a.* (and *n.*) [f. the name of James L. M. *Smithson* (1765-1829), British chemist and mineralogist, who endowed the Institution, + -IAN.] **1. a.** Of or pertaining to Smithson. Freq. in **Smithsonian Institution** (incorrectly *Institute*), an educational and research centre which nowadays administers numerous museums, galleries, etc., founded in 1846 in Washington, D.C. Hence, of or pertaining to the Institution.

**1826** J. SMITHSON *Will* 23 Oct. in *Smithsonian Misc. Coll.* (1901) XLII. 6, I then bequeath the whole of my property, subject to the Annuity.. to the United States of America, to found at Washington, under the name of the Smithsonian Institution, an Establishment for the increase and diffusion of knowledge among men. **1840** *Niles' Reg.* 7 Mar. 11/3 Mr. Adams rose.. to make a report from the select committee on the Smithsonian bequest. **1892** J. C. DUVAL *Young Explorers* xiii. 180, I believe he sent them subsequently to the Smithsonian Institute. **1946** *Nature* 7 Sept. 329/1 Study of precise solar-terrestrial relationships has been a major Smithsonian activity for many years. **1984** *Jrnl. Field Archaeol.* XI. 341/1 A repository.. has been established at the Conservation Analytical Laboratory of the Smithsonian Institution.
**b.** *absol.* as *n.* **the Smithsonian**, the Smithsonian Institution.
**1879** W. J. RHEES *Smithsonian Inst.* p. viii, The Smithsonian is not a Government Institution. *a***1936** KIPLING *Something of Myself* (1937) v. 123 The Smithsonian, specially on the ethnological side, was a pleasant place to browse in. **1983** L. TAYLOR *Mourning Dress* vi. 132 The Smithsonian's second example is a shoulder cape of deepest mourning.
**2.** Designating an agreement concerning the restoration of fixed parities between the major world currencies concluded in December 1971 between the members of the International Monetary Fund, at the Smithsonian; also, of or pertaining to this. *Econ. Hist.*
**1972** *Economist* 1 July 14/2 Our opening comment on the Smithsonian agreement of December 18th last was that.. we doubted if it would last for six months. **1978** *N.Y. Times* 30 Mar. D1/6 The yen.. was repegged at the Smithsonian rate of 308 to the dollar in December 1971. **1986** *Times* 3 Jan. 16/1 Sterling had started the year by.. recovering to just over 78 on the Smithsonian index. **1989** *Encycl. Brit.* XXI. 852/1 The Smithsonian Agreement proved to be only a temporary solution to the international currency crisis.

**Smith Square** ('smɪθ 'skwɛə(r)), *n.* *U.K. Pol.* [The name of a square in Westminster, the location since 1958 of the headquarters of the British Conservative Party. The square also contained the headquarters of the Labour Party (Transport House, q.v.) between 1928 and 1980.] By metonymy, the leadership of the Conservative Party; occas. the leadership of both the Conservative and Labour parties.

**1968** R. COLLIN *Locust on Wind* xiv. 127 'He's not uncomplicated enough to make the top in politics,.. they feel they can't trust him.' 'But this Anglo-German Amity business.'.. 'Another thing that scares his Smith Square chums off.' **1976** *Times* 8 Mar. 13/3 Unless.. we are eventually to finish up with the outrage of a party list system, whereby Smith Square would bureaucratically decide Buggins's turn. **1980** *Economist* 8 Mar. 67/1 Nobody, Labour or Tory, is prepared to make real cuts in staffing. An honest message from Smith Square to the 30% of the electorate who will bother to vote is that domestic rates are a much less onerous tax than people think. **1987** *Independent* 27 Sept. 19/4 According to ministers there is almost as much dead wood in Smith Square as in Kew Gardens.

**smithy**, *n.* Add: [1.] **c.** [Said to have arisen through a misreading of Longfellow's line (quot. 1839 below).] A blacksmith. *U.S.*
[**1839** LONGFELLOW *Poems* (1848) 73 Under a spreading chestnut tree The village smithy stands.] **1847** *Graham's Mag.* Apr. 262/1 Was he some Smithy, grim and old, Whose anvil iron changed to gold. **1900** *Everybody's Mag.* Jan. 36/2 The smithy and his mate opened their 'establishment' within a few hours of their arrival, and did a 'roaring trade'. **1940** *Miami Herald* in *Amer. Speech* (1941) XVI. 152/2 Miami Smithy: Olin M. Berry doesn't stand under a spreading chestnut tree, as did Longfellow's village blacksmith, but he is an old hand at the rapidly disappearing trade of horse-shoeing. **1982** *N.Y. Times* 21 Nov. XI. 12/5 The main concern of a smithy is to make sure that his shoeing keeps a horse healthy.

**smoke**, *v.* Restrict †*Obs.*⁻¹ to sense 7 in Dict. and add: [7.] **b.** To cause (a tyre) to smoulder as a result of friction with the road surface, when accelerating or driving fast around corners, etc. *colloq.*
**1977** *Chicago Tribune* 21 Nov. VI. 8/8 He moved out to try and over-take Bonnett on the outside, smoking his tyres badly as he fought for traction. **1985** *Sports Illustr.* 9 Sept. 14/3 [He] charged into the lead in his dark green Monte Carlo, driving so hard he was smoking his tires in the turns. **1988** *Autosport* 29 Sept. 71/1 Boswell behind him was putting everything into the chase, smoking the inside rear tyre every time he came onto the pit straight out of Goddard Corner.

**smoker**, *n.* Add: [2.] **f.** *Oceanogr.* A submarine hydrothermal vent from which water and mineral particles issue; *spec.* = *black smoker* s.v. *BLACK a.* 19 a. Also, a chimney or other structure created at such a vent by the deposition of minerals.
**1980** *Science* 28 Mar. 1425/1 Edifices atop the mounds are classed as either black or white, and those venting particulates are dubbed smokers. **1981** *Nature* 22 Jan. 219/2 Another difficulty is that similarly dense populations of large animals have been found in the proximity of 'smokers'—hot-water vents where the dominant, conspicuous flow emerges at temperatures up to 350°C. **1983** *Sci. Amer.* Apr. 83/1 The formation of a massive sulfide deposit such as the deposits in ophiolites, which contain millions of tons of ore, would seem to require a forest of smokers. **1984** *Listener* 12 Jan. 35/1 Volcanic 'smokers', nearly two miles deep on the floor of the Pacific, produce clouds of black sulphides.

**smokestack**, *n.* Add: **3.** Special Comb. **smokestack industry** orig. *U.S.*, any of the heavy manufacturing industries, typically coal-powered and associated with high levels of pollution and outmoded technology (usu. in *pl.*); also *absol.* used *attrib.*, of, pertaining to, or characterized by the smokestack industries, as *smokestack city*, *economy*, etc.

**1979** *Business Week* 31 Dec. 118/2 The mostly bedrock, *smokestack industry stocks that make up the Dow held little fascination for investors. **1980** *N.Y. Times* 24 Aug. 1. 38/1 Now, with fewer resources to spend .. the odds are to go with the winners . . . 'The smokestack cities' face the most problems, Mr. Sternlieb said. **1982** in *Amer. Speech* (1983) LVIII. 179 This is not a smokestack economy as it was 10 years ago. **1983** *Chicago Sun-Times* 21 May 13 The new cliches about the decline of 'smokestack industries' have dramatic power when you drive past the miles of cold, quiet stacks along Lake Erie. **1985** *Sunday Times* 4 Aug. 51 Those lorries with gas cylinders, associated with the bygone days of smokestack industries, are also less important. **1988** *Business Rev. Weekly* 8 Apr. 6/2 For the past 10 years or so smokestack industries have been unpopular because they have been seen as pollutors of the environment.

**smoothie**, *n.* and *a.* Add: [A.] **2.** A smooth, thick drink consisting of fresh fruit, esp. banana, puréed with milk, yoghurt, or ice cream. Chiefly *U.S.* and *Austral.*
**1977** *Washington Post* 2 June F12/3 There are some definite winners among the selections: Freshly made onion rings, a yogurt and fruit drink called a 'smoothie', [etc.]. **1986** *Auckland Metro* Feb. 29/3 Buttermilk is an ideal replacement for yoghurt in the breakfast smoothie or for milk in a standard milkshake. **1987** *Sunday Tel.* (Colour Suppl.) 7 June 30/2 In New York now, there are entire bars which cater for trendy non-drinkers. They serve nothing but a selection of mineral waters, soft drinks and non-alcoholic cocktails (called 'smoothies'). **1989** *Sunday Mail* (Brisbane) 1 Jan. 34/1 It's worth noting that the shop underneath makes ripper soymilk smoothies. Buy yourself a strawberry job with frozen yoghurt.

**smudge**, *n.*[1] Sense 4 in Dict. becomes 5. Add: **4. a.** A photograph, *esp.* one taken by a street or press photographer; (see also quot. *a* 1931). **b.** = *smudger *n.* b. *slang.*
*a* **1931** W. KERNÔT *Unpubl. Gloss. Amer. Cant* in Partridge *Dict. Underworld* (1949) 647/1 Smudge [Photograph of a fingerprint]. **1934** P. ALLINGHAM *Cheapjack* iv. 40 It was not until I'd taken over twenty smudges that the driver thought it time to tell me that the whole bunch of 'em was a lot of barmies. **1968** J. LOCK *Lady Policeman* viii. 65 The 'smudge's' normal procedure is to step in front of people and 'click' his camera. **1986** *Melody Maker* 19 Apr. 6/1 Madonna Ciccone-Penn took time out from her full-time hobby of punching out publicists and running over smudges. **1990** *Q* Mar. 28/3 Cole is on his way to a photo session with acclaimed French smudge Claude Gassian.

**smudger**, *n.* Add: **b.** A photographer, *esp.* a street or press photographer. Cf. *smudge *n.*[1] 4.
**1961** PARTRIDGE *Dict. Slang* Suppl. 1282/1 *Smudger*, an inferior street photographer. **1979** *Daily Mail* 8 Sept. 17/4 *Smudger*, secret service photographer. **1988** *National Trust Mag.* Summer 5/1 (Advt.), Ian is .. a 'smudger'. His assignments, or shoots, take him all over the world.

**smush** (smʌʃ), *v. colloq.* and *dial.* (now chiefly *U.S.*). [Alteration of MUSH *v.*[2]: cf. SMASH *v.*[1] and SMUSH *n.*] *trans.* To mash or crush.
**1825** JAMIESON Suppl., *Smush*, .. to bruise; to reduce to small particles; to grind to powder, Roxb. **1887** T. DARLINGTON *Folk-Speech S. Cheshire* 353 'Smushin' the crud' (curd) is a regular operation of cheese-making, and by many dairy-maids is done by squeezing it through the fingers. **1914** *Dialect Notes* IV. 156 [Cape Cod] *Smush* v., mash . . . Used only in a figurative sense or when the product is wet. 'He smushed the clam.' **1987** J. WILCOX *Miss Undine's*

*Living Room* iv. 46 He sank onto the foot of the bed, smushing a box of Cap'n Crunch.

**snack**, *v.* Add: [3.] **b.** Const. *on.*
**1972** T. McHUGH *Time of Buffalo* viii. 85 Most of the participants snacked on raw morsels taken still warm from the slain buffalo. **1979** P. DRISCOLL *Pangolin* ix. 77 The stalls were tiny places .. crowded with Chinese snacking on noodles. **1985** *Sunday Times* 24 Feb. 36/6 They stood in the clubhouse snacking on Mars Bars and Nut 17 muesli bars with raisins. **1989** M. ATWOOD *Cat's Eye* xi. 330, I can eat haphazardly now, snack on junk food and take-outs.

**snazzy**, *a.* Add: Hence 'snazzily *adv.*; 'snazziness *n.*
**1961** WEBSTER, *Snazziness*, the quality or state of being snazzy. **1980** *Christian Science Monitor* 24 July 19/1 Even if the movie bombs, a fortune can be made from the lavishly produced and snazzily packaged disc. **1981** *N.Y. Times* 7 June 1. 51/1 David Amram's brief 'Fanfare' captured a sort of modernist snazziness. **1985** *Time* 1 Apr. 34/3 Iacocca's salesmanship—his hucksterism, even—accounted for much of his personal success in the mid-'60s, when carmakers were discovering the youth market. For snazziness and corporate profligacy, Detroit has not equaled itself since. **1989** *Washington Post* 31 Dec. (Book World section) 10/1 [He] was not a popular figure with his employees. 'A snazzily dressed Gila monster in a Panama hat' is how Jones describes him.

**sneak**, *n.* Add: [1.] **c.** *colloq.* A tell-tale, an informer.
**1886** H. BAUMANN *Londinismen* p. v, Are smashers and divers And noble contrivers Not sold to the beaks By the coppers an' sneaks? **1915** W. S. MAUGHAM *Of Human Bondage* xxi. 86 'It would serve you right if I told him,' said Mr. Carey. 'If you like to be a perfect sneak you can.' **1934** LD. BERNERS *First Childhood* iii. 33 She was a spoil-sport and a sneak. **1959** I. & P. OPIE *Lore & Lang. Schoolch.* x. 189 One who blabs to a teacher or to a senior is a .. 'rotten sneak'. **1989** *Independent* (Mag.) 11 Feb. 22/1 It started with a tip-off . . . *The Sun* was told by one of its regular sneaks, paid on a story-by-story basis that [etc.].
**[2.]** Restrict *Cant* to sense a. **[b.]** Substitute for def: A stealthy movement; a sneaking departure or expedition. *quarterback sneak*: see QUARTERBACK *n.* 3. *slang* (chiefly *U.S.*). (Later examples.)
**1904** 'O. HENRY' *Cabbages & Kings* xvii. 303 Well, we three made a sneak around the edge of town so as not to be seen. **1930** *Liberty* 11 Oct. 30/3 Rube copped a sneak on the joint to find out if it was ready. In twenty minutes he gives the O.K. **1936** WODEHOUSE *Laughing Gas* iv. 51 She had said something about her chances of doing a quiet sneak to bed at a fairly early hour.

**sniff**, *v.* Add: [4.] **d.** orig. *U.S. slang.* To inhale (a powdered narcotic substance or the narcotic fumes of glue, etc.).
**1934** C. DE LENOIR *100th Man* i. 13 Sniffing heroin or cocaine is 'sleigh-riding'. **1951** *N.Y. Times* 13 June 24/3 Then one day we met another fellow and he offered us some heroin. I sniffed this too. We called it 'horse' and 'H'. **1965** 'MALCOLM X' *Autobiogr.* vii. 110 As the pros did, I too would key myself to pull these jobs by my first use of hard dope. I began with .. sniffing cocaine. **1970** *New Scientist* 12 Nov. 314/1 Young people who turn on by sniffing the vapour of airplane glue .. sometimes .. drop dead. **1974** [see SNORT *v.*[1] 7]. **1986** P. BARKER *Century's Daughter* i. 7 Some of the houses were used by drunks, others by teenage gangs sniffing glue.

**sniggery** ('snɪgərɪ), *a. colloq.* [f. SNIGGER *v.* + -Y[1].] Characterized by sniggering; prone to or liable to cause sniggering; hence, immature, prurient.

**1960** *Times* 4 Mar. 4/7 The erotic verse is smutty and sniggery. **1972** J. BELFRAGE in G. W. Turner *Good Austral. Eng.* vi. 110 The juxtaposition of three concepts thought by many Australians to be sniggery and low—females, beards and beer—complete a picture which is just sufficiently 'off' in taste to render it mildly obscene. **1984** *Guardian* 10 Nov. 18/2 Suddenly all hushed and sniggery conversation was drowned by a sound of awesome power. **1988** *Los Angeles Times* 2 May VI. 5/5 There's a smarmy, sniggery quality to its fusion of boys' adventure serial with soft-core bawdiness.

**snippy**, *a*. Add: Hence **'snippily** *adv*.; **'snippiness** *n*.
**1935** E. CARR *Jrnl.* 24 Jan. (1966) 169, I suppose first we must climb to the rise above the trivial snippiness, quit bickering and open our eyes wider and get stiller—quit fussing. **1977** D. E. WESTLAKE *Nobody's Perfect* (1978) ii. 26 It was an English-accented female voice that answered, snippily, saying, 'Hold on for *Mister* Stonewiler, please.' **1985** *N.Y. Times* 21 Apr. II. 22/3 The novelist Kingsley Amis recently wrote to The Times of London snippily opining that subsidized artists were less interested in pleasing the public than in impressing 'critics, colleagues, friends, experts, bureaucrats'. **1987** *Los Angeles Times* (San Diego County ed.) 13 Oct. VI. 3/1 Vanda Eggington is a natural comedienne, at one point playing a self-righteous church lady with Gilda Radner snippiness.

**snitty** ('snɪtɪ), *a*. *slang* (orig. and chiefly *U.S.*). [f. SNIT *n.²*] Ill-tempered, sulky.
**1978** *Washington Post* 17 Sept. H1/4 In 1977.. snitty bickering between the Hollywood and New York factions of the TV Academy reached a new pitch of schismatic feverishness. **1981** T. BARLING *Bikini Red North* ii. 58 Don't make me laugh when I want to be snitty. **1986** *City Limits* 29 May 59 Before we get a snitty letter from Sir Peter we would like to recall the last time the NT staged 'Othello'. **1987** *People* 4 May 7/3 A sixteen-year-old orphan, the child of an affair, who lives with her half brother.. and his snooty, snitty wife.

**snobby**, *a*. Add: Hence **'snobbily** *adv*.
**1856** D. G. ROSSETTI *Let.* 18 Dec. (1965) I. 310 They have treated you snobbily enough there. **1987** *Times Lit. Suppl.* 7 Aug. 846/1 The *dolce vita* set from Rome went on vacation there, drifting snobbily south to primitive Sicily.

**snooker**, *n.²* Add: **2**. In this game, the placement of the balls in such a way that the object ball is blocked by another and cannot be struck directly by the cue ball; a shot which achieves this placement.
**1924** W. SMITH *How to play Snooker* vi. 67 If you *can* contrive to leave a snooker, so much the better. **1936** J. DAVIS *Improve Your Snooker* xi. 57 If a snooker will pay you better than attempting to pot a ball, then by all means snooker your opponent. **1965** *Billiards & Snooker* ('Know the Game' Ser.) (ed. 5) 28/2 If no snooker is possible.., the mere fact of having placed the cue ball far away from the ball 'on' handicaps the opponent. **1986** *Snooker Scene* July 19/2 Leading 10-8, Harris was well placed to go three in front again with Grennan needing a snooker on the green.

**snoot**, *n*. Add: **4**. [Prob. a back-formation from SNOOTY *a*.] One who is snooty; a snob. Also occas., snootiness. *colloq*.
**1941** BAKER *Dict. Austral. Slang* 68 *Snoot*, a disagreeable person. **1942** BERREY & VAN DEN BARK *Amer. Thes. Slang* §402/3 *Snob*, .. snoot. **1971** D. O'CONNOR *Eye of Eagle* iv. 26 He was no snoot, yet he had kept me at a distance. **1977** S. L. ELLIOTT *Water under Bridge* 15 Those Melbourne snoots.. look down their noses at us Sydneyites. **1984** *Washington Post* 4 Apr. B4/1 The emphasis is on

fashion and manners; the sensibility part British snoot, part Gothamite chicquer-than-thou. **1989** *Sunday Times* 14 May G5/1 Val.., tumbling hair and champagne glass in hand, mingles with these snoots at publishers' parties.

**snubby** ('snʌbɪ), *n*. *U.S. slang*. Also snubbie. [Prob. abbrev. of *SNUB NOSE *n*. 2 or SNUB-NOSED *a*., rather than directly f. the adj.] A small, cheap, short-barrelled handgun; a snub-nosed revolver.
**1981** *Washington Post* 22 Nov. C1/3 (*heading*) Ban 'snubbies' and solve the great handgun debate. **1983** E. LEONARD *LaBrava* (1985) xv. 158 You want a snubbie. This one, .38 Special, two-inch barrel. **1984** *New Yorker* 12 Nov. 133/1 That arsenal is made up chiefly of snub-nosed handguns—or snubbies, as they're called. The snubbies are more dangerous than bigger handguns for the obvious reason that they are so easily concealable. **1986** *Target Gun* Aug. 17/1 They are hardly concealable—an essential element of the snubby concept—and they carry adjustable sights.

**snub nose**, *n*. Add: **2**. *slang* (chiefly *U.S.*). A snub-nosed handgun; = *SNUBBY *n*.
**1979** *Washington Post* 8 Nov. F1/5 A .38-caliber snub nose, department issue, rests on his hip, beneath his jacket. **1982** B. FANTONI *Stickman* xxii. 151, I pulled out my gun... Flicking the safety catch off my snub nose, I tensed my trigger finger. **1988** *Guns & Weapons* Winter 76/2 The .38 snubnose or .45 automatic that many people think of when they hear the word 'handgun'.

**soap** (səup), *n.²* *slang*. [Respelling, after SOAP *n.¹*, of *sope* f. *so(dium)* *Pe(ntothal)* s.v. PENTOTHAL *n*.] Sodium pentothal, or a mixture of this and an amphetamine, used as a truth drug.
**1975** *Observer* (Colour Suppl.) 23 Nov. 25/4 *Soap*, .. the principal ingredient in truth serum. **1980** J. GARDNER *Garden of Weapons* III. xiv. 372 Soap—as the Service called it—would sometimes produce spectacular results: the so-called first truth drug. *In pentathol veritas.* **1983** M. HARTLAND *Down among Dead Men* xv. 128 Dr. Berry.. gave me a soap injection... It makes you semi-conscious and you talk without any inhibitions—you know, 'the truth drug'. **1988** 'R. DEACON' *Spyclopaedia* 412 *Soap*, nickname for the truth drug, specially treated sodium pentathol.

**soapy**, *a*. Add: [6.] **b**. [After SOAP *n.¹* 1 h.] Characteristic or redolent of a soap opera. *colloq*. (orig. *U.S.*).
**1961** in WEBSTER. **1980** *Chicago Tribune* 2 July III. 10/3 (*heading*) Soapy clones, 'real' people tales follow the leaders in prime time. *Ibid.*, If that's not soapy enough for you, 'Midland Heights' also has a J.R. Ewing-type villain. **1985** *Mail on Sunday* 6 Jan. 35/4 Anna of the Five Towns.. is the sort of gloriously photographed evocation of a classic novel where British television scores over its soapy American counterparts. **1989** *Newsday* 13 Jan. III. 2/3 Though the script remains sentimental and a little soapy, the writing is witty and smart.

**sober**, *v*. Add: **'soberingly** *adv*.
**1923** *Glasgow Herald* 22 Oct. 10 The Government has to steer its way amid the external obstacles of which Labour, if it were in power, would become soberingly aware by actual contact. **1989** *Time* 20 Mar. 26/1 NSA has figures that make the insider threat look soberingly real. An agency log of cases involving computer crime or computer espionage showed that up to 90% of known security breaches are the work of corporate or Government insiders.

**Sobieski's Shield** (sɒbɪ'ɛskɪz), *n*. *Astron*. (now *rare*). [tr. mod.L. *Scutum Sobieskii*: see *SCUTUM *n*. 4.] The constellation Scutum.

**1773** *Encycl. Brit.* I. 487/2 (*table*) Sobieski's Shield. **1797** *Phil. Trans.* LXXXVII. 133 The constellation of Sobieski's Shield consists of a very few stars. **1893** J. E. GORE *Visible Universe* 129 This branch includes several spots of superior brilliancy, of which the most remarkable are:.. one covering 'Sobieski's Shield' (Scutum), [etc.].

**soca** ('səʊkə), *n.* Also **sokah**. [f. a blend of SO(UL *n.* + CA(LYPSO *n.*] A variety of calypso, originating in Trinidad during the early 1970s, which incorporates elements of other regional music traditions, esp. Afro-Caribbean soul, Indo-Trinidadian, Hispano-Trinidadian, and French Caribbean music. Freq. *attrib.*

[**1973** (*song-title*) Soul calypso music.] **1977** (*song-title*) Sokah, soul of calypso. **1978** *Washington Post* 23 Aug. IV. 2/5 Because the studio is not fully soundproof, the fan sometimes interferes with the soca, the latest music from Trinidad. **1980** *Trinidad Guardian* 11 Feb. 1/6 The banned 'Soca Baptist' by Blue Boy.. brought out the real Carnival spirit from southerners. **1981** *Listener* 2 July 14/1 The programme.. was about 'black music' in Britain.. arguing for the importance of calypso and 'soca' (soul-calypso). **1982** K. Q. WARNER *Trinidad Calypso* i. 21 In an attempt to introduce more variety and variation in his compositions, Lord Shorty, by his claim, sought to find the 'soul of calypso' and thus coined the term 'soca'... The new beat, masterly arranged by Ed Watson.. was an instant hit.. and the controversy raged: is Soca Calypso? **1984** STEWARD & GARRATT *Signed, Sealed & Delivered* 12/1 Few people would guess that some soca, reggae, lovers'-rock and, particularly, soul and dance music sometimes outsell 'chart' records. **1989** *Penguin Encycl. Pop. Mus.* 1093/2 Soca lyrics initially treated the same sort of topics as calypso, but there is a tendency towards blandness aimed at crossover success.

**Socceroo** (sɒkəˈruː), *n. Austral. colloq.* [Blend of SOCCER *n.* and 'ROO *n.*², on analogy with *KANGAROO *n.* 3 i.] In *pl.* (With capital initial.) The name of the Australian international soccer team. Occas. *sing.* in *attrib.* use.

**1973** *Sydney Morning Herald* 15 Nov. 1/10 Now that the Australian Soccer team is basking in honour and glory after its World Cup victory over South Korea it can surely do without the name 'Socceroos' which is being increasingly applied to it. **1979** L. SCHWAB *Socceroos & their Opponents* 4 Australia's national team, which was dubbed 'the Socceroos' during the 1973-74 World Cup mission, has comprised many extraordinary players. **1983** *Advertiser* (Adelaide) 12 Dec. 33/6 Socceroos through to semi-finals. **1986** *Telegraph* (Brisbane) 31 Oct. 43 (*heading*) National coach Frank Arok will be closely watching his Socceroo squad over the next three days to find a replacement mid-field.

**social**, *a.* and *n.* Add: [12.] **social dialect** *Linguistics*, a dialect spoken by a particular social group or class.

**1949** H. KURATH *Word Geogr. Eastern U.S.* 7 This leveling of social differences inevitably entailed a leveling of *social dialects. **1971** ALLEN & UNDERWOOD *Readings in Amer. Dialectol.* 355 Social dialects include not only the dialects of various social classes but also the special argots and cants of certain sub-cultures existing within and yet outside our society. **1975** F. WEST *Way of Lang.* 50 Social dialects may reflect different levels of education, wealth, social position, job or profession, or even the speaker's home location. **1986** C. E. BILLIARD in Montgomery & Bailey *Lang. Variety in South* 365 (*title*) Correlates among social dialects, language development, and reading achievement of urban children.

**socialist**, *n.* Add: [1.] [a.] Also, a member of a Socialist political party. (Further examples.)

**1871** *Observer* 9 Apr. 6/4 Most of the decrees are the work of illiterate members of the *Internationale*; they consist of candid attacks on the rights of property,.. such as you may expect from vulgar Socialists. **1886** *Pall Mall Gaz.* 19 July 3/2 If the police, as the Socialists declare, discriminate against them on account of their opinions, let evidence be brought to prove it, and the Socialists will have everybody's sympathy. **1898** J. E. C. BODLEY *France* II. IV. vii. 427 Significant also is the attitude of the Socialists, who now compose the radical left-wing. **1917** *19th Cent.* July 141 The Mensheviki or Minimalists (Moderate Socialists)... The Bolsheviki (Extreme Socialists). **1927** *Daily Tel.* 15 Mar. 9/2 The Labour-Socialists.. are in favour of the proposals for the abolition of blind booking and restrictions on advance booking. **1947** *News Chron.* 8 Apr. 2/5 He is an extreme Left-Wing Socialist... In the Commons he is, of course, dubbed a 'fellow-traveller' and a 'crypto-Communist'. **1974** J. WHITE tr. *Poulantzas's Fascism & Dictatorship* III. iii. 132 Mussolini.. decided.. to sign a peace pact with the socialists, whom the representatives of medium capital were still counting on to pursue their policy of class collaboration.

‖ **société anonyme** (sɔsjete anɔnim), *n. Comm.* [Fr.] In French civil law: a limited company. See *limited* LIABILITY. Abbrev. *S.A.* s.v. S 4 a.

**1869** *Bradshaw's Railway Manual* XXI. 346 Belgian Eastern Junction... The amended statutes.. constituting it a *Société Anonyme*. **1907** J. H. CLAPHAM in *Cambr. Mod. Hist.* X. xxiii. 747 The law subjected the *société anonyme* to a troublesome supervision. **1949** *Trade Marks Jrnl.* 6 Apr. 304 Taittinger.. Champagne. Etablissements Taittinger Mailly & Cie (a Societe Anonyme organised under the laws of France). **1977** 'J. LE CARRÉ' *Hon. Schoolboy* I. iv. 81 The *société anonyme* was registered in Paris.

**sock**, *n.*¹ Sense 6 in Dict. becomes 7. Add: **6.** *Aeronaut.* Shortening of *wind-sock* s.v. WIND *n.*¹ 32. orig. *U.S.*

**1933** *Sun* (Baltimore) 20 Sept. 7/8 The Department of Commerce aeronautical officials have chosen the Frederick airport as the scene of experiments with a new type wind cone which may replace the conventional 'sock' that has guided landing airplanes for years. **1939** *Florida* (Federal Writers' Project) III. 461 Red and white boundary stripes and a yellow 'sock' bellying in the wind mark the Holopaw Emergency Landing Field. **1954** W. A. HEFLIN *U. S. Air Force Dict.* 477/1 *Sock*, *n.*, short for 'windsock'. **1958** 'N. SHUTE' *Rainbow & Rose* viii. 297, I took my attention from the runway and looked at the sock properly.

**sod** (sɒd), *n.*⁴ *Sc. dial.* [Origin unknown.] The rock-dove, *Columba livia*.

**1885** C. SWAINSON *Provincial Names & Folklore Brit. Birds* 168 Sod (Forfar). **1913** H. K. SWANN *Dict. Eng. & Folk-Names Brit. Birds* 220 *Sod*, a Forfar name for the rock-dove. **1973** *Times* 17 Feb. 14/8 How has the rock dove gained the title of 'sod'?

**sod**, *v.*³ Senses 1, 2 in Dict. become 2, 3. Add: **1.** *trans.* (and *absol.*) = SODOMIZE *v.*

**1879** *Pearl* I. 156 My arse he can't sod Because I am troubled with Fistula. **1976** A. POWELL *Infants of Spring* 79 It's a cold day for sodding.

**sodide** ('səʊdaɪd), *n. Chem.* [f. SOD(IUM *n.* + -IDE 1.] An alkalide in which the anion is sodium.

**1977** J. L. DYE in *Sci. Amer.* July 104/2 One can imagine.. a hypothetical analogue of a simple salt such as sodium chloride, but with sodium as both positive and negative ion. Perhaps the salt would be called sodium sodide. **1982** *Inorg. Chem.* XXI. 1966/2 We.. report the first synthesis of two sodide salts which contain the crown ether 18-crown-6. **1984** GREENWOOD & EARNSHAW *Chem. of Elements*

(1986) iv. 110 Na reacts with crypt in the presence of EtNH₂ to give the first example of a sodide salt of Na⁻.

**softnomics** (sɒft'nɒmıks), *n. pl.* [f. SOFT *a.* (as in *software*) + ECO)NOMIC *n.* 2.] A term coined in Japan for the study of the shift in the economy of developed countries from the basis of manufacturing industry to that of service industry, esp. information technology.

**1983** *Sci. Amer.* Nov. J23/2 Whatever one may think of the aesthetics of the term 'softnomics', it does convey a sense of where the Japanese see their technology and economy moving. The shift is from sheer quantity toward quality, from hardware toward software. **1986** D. HOWELL *Blind Victory* v. 36 The ugly word 'softnomics' has been dreamed up by Japanese thinkers to describe the study and behaviour of the soft, dispersed sort of economy which is replacing the old industrial structure in advanced countries. **1987** *Times* 25 Feb. 12/2 Its work, still in progress, has led to the establishment of a new discipline known as 'softnomics'—the study of long-term changes in advanced industrial society. **1989** *Economist* 7 Oct. 97/2 Some researchers, including Mr Tsunemasa Oda of the Softnomics Research Institute, think this high savings by woopies is a passing fashion.

‖**sogo shosha** (ˌsəʊgəʊ 'ʃəʊʃə), *n.* Pl. unchanged or (occas.) **-s.** [Jap., = 'integrated trading company'.] In Japan, a very large company that engages in the international buying and selling of a wide range of goods and services. Cf. *SHOSHA *n.*

**1967** L. HOLLERMAN *Japan's Dependence on World Econ.* xiv. 239 Among the factors that condition the impact of liberalization is Japan's 'unique institution', the trading company (sōgō shōsha). **1972** *Guardian* 16 Oct. 11/1 Japan's giant sogo shosha, or all-round trading companies, are a strictly Japanese phenomenon, unknown in any other country. They are independent firms which buy and sell not just specific goods but almost everything. **1974** *Columbia Jrnl. World Business* Spring 78/2 In 1973 the *Sogo shoshas* had over 800 offices worldwide. **1985** *Euromoney* Jan. 134/3 Any bank would be making a mistake trying to emulate massive traders like Philipp Brothers or a Japanese *sogo shosha.*

‖**Sohyo** ('soːhjoː), *n.* [Japanese *Sōhyō,* shortened form of Nihon Rōdō Kumiai Sōhyōgikai.] In Japan, the left-wing trade union federation.

**1953** *Far Eastern Econ. Rev.* 22 Oct. 534/1 Prior to the organization of Sohyo, that is, from 1946 to 1949, Japan's labor movement was divided into two major labor bodies—the National Congress of Industrial Unions (Sambetsu) and the General Federation of Trade Union[s] (Sodomei). **1954** *Economist* 24 July 270/2 More than half the six million organised workers now belong to Sohyo. **1958** *Economist* 1 Nov. 421/1 Mr Kishi's statement earlier this year that a 'showdown' with the powerful trades union federation Sohyo was pending. **1963** *Times* 16 Feb. 7/7 This year the left-wing Sohyo (general council of Japanese trade unions) with a membership of four million is demanding an average overall increase of 5,000 yen (about £5) a head. **1977** J. WATANUKI *Politics in Postwar Jap. Society* i. 29 Sōhyō supports the Socialists and *Dōmei* supports the Democratic Socialists.

‖**soigneur** (swaɲœr), *n.* [Fr., f. *soigner* to take care of.] In cycling, a person who gives training, first aid, massage, and other assistance to a team.

**1972** F. ALDERSON *Bicycling* ix. 181 The individual's main prop is the 'soigneur'—trainer, attendant, masseur, adviser and nursemaid. **1977** G. NICHOLSON *Great Bike Race* (1978) viii. 93 The team-manager, Alec Taylor, and the two *soigneurs,* Auguste Naessens (Belgian) and Rudy Van der Weide (Dutch) .. were rigorously questioned into the night. **1988** *Cycling Weekly* 30 June 38/2 Room for the mechanics to spread over the grass and a plentiful and easily attainable supply of water for washing bikes, large rooms for the *soigneurs* and their massage tables, and private dining areas for the riders to gorge in peace.

‖**sokaiya** ('soːkaija), *n.* Pl. unchanged. [Jap., f. *sōkai* general meeting + -*ya* dealer.] Usu. in *pl.* 'A person who holds a small number of shares of stock in a number of companies and attempts to extort money from them by threatening to cause trouble at the general meeting of the stockholders' (*Kenkyusha's New Japanese-English Dict.* (1974)).

**1971** *Newsweek* 14 June 49/1 The only blemish on the smooth proceedings has been the irritating presence of parasitic *sokaiya,* professional hecklers and blackmailers whose threats to disrupt meetings or to reveal embarrassing bits of information have forced management to part with millions of dollars every year in payoffs. **1980** *Times* 19 May 23/6 The *Sokaiya*—Japan's unique group of strong-arm gangsters who can be hired to control or disrupt shareholders' meetings. **1983** *Internat. Managem.* Sept. 30/2 The first Sokaiya—the name translates as shareholder's meeting man—concentrated on simple blackmail. **1984** *Fortune* 5 Mar. 8/1 This year *sokaiya* switched sides and attacked management because Sony, obeying a year-old government reform outlawing the practice, didn't pay them a fee to cooperate.

**Solas** ('səʊlæs), *n.* Also SOLAS. [Acronym f. the initial letters of *Safety of Life at Sea.*] Used *attrib.* to designate (any of the provisions of) an international convention governing maritime safety adopted in 1960, or that of 1974 by which it was superseded.

The 1974 convention was adopted in 1980.

**1965** *Daily Tel.* 31 Dec. 13/6 Let me reassure him: they do carry them [*sc.* life-rafts] now. The International 1960 Solas .. Regulations were ratified last year and came into force in May this year. **1971** *Engineering* Apr. 19/2 Today many merchant ships in international trade operating under SOLAS safety requirements maintain liferafts which can carry from six to 25 people. **1980** *Jrnl. R. Soc. Arts* July 518/1 The two conventions having the major impact on the tanker industry at the present time are: the 1974 SOLAS (Safety of Life at Sea) Convention, and, the 1973 MARPOL (Marine Pollution) Convention. **1988** *Daily Tel.* 25 Oct. 7/6 The rules, known as the 1974 Solas (safety of life at sea) regulations, set standards for sub-dividing a ship so that if water gets into one section it does not spread to the rest.

**solicitor,** *n.* Add: Hence **solici'torial** *a.*

**1940** G. FRANKAU *Self-Portrait* xix. 105 Yet pressed I was, with a solicitorial document addressed to the office, demanding '£120 plus 6s. 8d. being the cost of this letter' under threat of an immediate writ. **1988** *Times* 4 July 25/1 An undertaking, given in the context of an underlying transaction of a solicitorial nature, to provide security for a loan could be within the ordinary course of a solicitor's business.

**solidly,** *adv.* Add: **7.** Continuously; without interruption. (Cf. SOLID *a.* 21 d.)

**1937** W. H. SAUMAREZ SMITH *Let.* 20 Sept. in *Young Man's Country* (1977) ii. 91, I was on tour solidly from the 12th till the 16th. **1943** D. WELCH *Maiden Voyage* xvii. 142 Mr Butler talked solidly to the Consul and did not think of leaving until after tea. **1967** A. S. BYATT *Game* xi. 165 She spent the next few weeks solidly working, closed away in the library. **1987** M. IGNATIEFF *Russian Album* v. 90 He cried solidly for six weeks.

**solo,** *n.* and *a.* Restrict *Obs.* to sense 5 a. Add: [A.] [II.] [5.] **b.** A motorcycle without a side-car attached; also, a bicycle designed for one rider.

**1924** T. E. LAWRENCE *Home Lett.* (1954) 359 A solo isn't as secure on a wet road as a side-car outfit. **1935** *Motor Cycle* 22 Aug. 247/2, I wonder if we shall see a revival .. of those two-seater solos? **1985** *Tandem Club Jrnl.* Apr. 11 The run that we thought might be a non-event .. saw a total of 13 tandems and 3 solos gather for lunch. **1987** *Back St. Heroes* June 22/2 It was common-place for enthusiasts of the day to ride a solo to work and attach a sidecar for weekend jaunts.

**somato-,** *comb. form.* Add: **,somato,mammo'trophin** *Physiol.* (also **-tropin**), any of several hormones having both growth-promoting and lactogenic properties; **human chorionic somatomammotrophin,** a hormone of this kind which is produced by the human placenta during pregnancy.

**1968** C. H. LI et al. in *Experientia* XXIV. 1288/1 In order to eliminate confusion by the use of different terms for the same hormone, we wish to propose that henceforth the hormone be called human chorionic *somato-mammotropin . . .* It has both growth hormone (somatotropin) and lactogenic hormone (mammotropin) activities. **1970** *Jrnl. Obstetr. & Gynæcol.* LXXVII. 747/1 The raised plasma levels of growth hormone (HGH) in radioimmunoassay are probably due to the presence in the blood of pregnant women of chorionic somato-mammotrophin. **1970** *Ital. Jrnl. Biochem.* XIX. 111 Human chorionic somatomammotrophin (H.C.S.), a protein synthesized in the placenta from early pregnancy, shares some interesting features with human growth hormone. **1984** J. F. LAMB et al. *Essent. Physiol.* (ed. 2) xii. 392 These hormones are known as human chorionic gonadotrophin (HCG) and human chorionic somatomammotrophin (HCS, also known as human placental lactogen). **1987** K. MURRAY in Bu'lock & Kristiansen *Basic Biotechnol.* xix. 505 Insulin and chorionic somatomammotropin, a polypeptide hormone resembling B-gonadotropin, have also been produced in *E. coli.*

**somebody,** *n.* Add: **4.** *W. Indies.* Also **s'mady, s'mody.** A person; a human being.

**1826** C. WILLIAMS *Tour through Island of Jamaica* xxvi. 195 You wicked somebody. **1873** C. RAMPINI *Lett. from Jamaica* 175 Bragging ribber nebber drown somebody. **1910** ANDERSON & CUNDALL *Jamaica Negro Proverbs & Sayings* 28 John Crow say him a dandy man, but him put on bald head fe mek fas' s'mody fine fault wid him. **1918** E. C. PARSONS *Folk-Tales of Andros Island, Bahamas* (Mem. Amer. Folklore Soc.) 61 Dey set two sheet, an' fix it under bed like it was two somebody layin' down. **1961** F. G. CASSIDY *Jamaica Talk* viii. 168 In 1955 I heard the remark about a fruit: 'S'mady can eat it'—that is, it is edible by human beings.

**somn-,** *comb. form.* Add: **somnambulant** *a.*: hence **som'nambulantly** *adv.*

**1920** E. SITWELL *Children's Tales* 12 The puppets move somnambulantly through the dark of our hearts. **1983** *Financial Times* 5 Apr. 15/6 The ENO had a chorus involved in its work, not somnambulantly detached therefrom. **1987** I. McEWAN *Child in Time* i. 8 She walked slowly, somnambulantly.

**Somocist** (sɒ'məʊsɪst), *n.* and *a.* Also Somozist. [ad. Sp. *Somocista* \*SOMOCISTA *n.* and *a.*] = \*SOMOCISTA *n.* and *a.* B.

**1978** E. RANDALL tr. D. Tijerino's *Inside Nicaraguan Revolution* 170, 1966 . . July . . Burning of Somocists' vehicles to protest proclamation of presidential candidacy of Anastasio Somoza Debayle. *Ibid.* 173 Massive national protest in all cities of country against Somocist repression of Sandinist militants. **1981** P. CAMILLER tr. H. Weber's *Nicaragua* iii. 50

Where the Somozists still controlled a town, .. committees carried out the task of preparing an insurrection and giving logistic support. **1987** J. R. THACKRAH *Encycl. Terrorism & Pol. Violence* 220 There has been a threat from armed 'Somocist' groups (i.e. those identified with the former Somoza regime).

**Somocista** (,sɒməʊ'siːstə), *n.* and *a.* Also Somozista. [Sp., f. the name of Anastasio *Somoza* Portocarrero (1896-1956) and his sons Luis and Anastasio Somoza Debayle, who between them held the presidency of Nicaragua almost continuously from 1937 to 1979 + *-ista* -IST.] **A.** *n.* A follower of the Somoza family; a member or supporter of its regime (cf. SANDINISTA *n.* and *a.*). **B.** *adj.* Of or belonging to the Somozas or their followers.

**1978** *Washington Post* 25 Sept. A18/6 In travelling through Nicaragua's battle-torn cities .. I found only one Nicaraguan who admitted being a 'Somocista'. **1979** *Foreign Affairs* LVIII. 46 The trial of Somocista officials. **1981** *N.Y. Times* 16 Nov. C4/3 'It happens many times that one brother is a Somozista and one is a Sandinista,' says Mr Cordero. **1984** *Ibid.* 9 July A19/2 Many of Mr. Reagan's Nicaraguan contras come straight out of the old Somozista regime, a terrorist dictatorship if ever there was one. **1990** *Daily Tel.* 23 Feb. 17/5 Her husband's brother .. is critical of Mrs Chamorro's political bedfellows, claiming some are 'Somocistas' responsible for her husband's assassination.

‖**somon** ('sɒmɒn), *n.* Also **sumon, sumun.** Pl. unchanged or **-s.** [Mongolian, lit. 'arrow'.] In Mongolia: an administrative division subordinate to the \*AIMAK *n.*

**1902** *Encycl. Brit.* XXX. 811/1 Each of these again was divided into *sumons* or squadrons, each containing 150 families. **1934** H. HASLUND *Tents in Mongolia* 338 Mongolia is divided into *aimaks* (tribes); these again into *hosyun* (banners, standards) which in their turn are divided into *sumon* (arrows). **1956** I. MONTAGU *Land of Blue Sky* ix. 96 The somon centre you will come upon on the grasslands as an apparently fair-sized settlement of from twenty to thirty buildings . . . Mongolians speak of these centres (= the bag centres) casually as if they were themselves somons and bags, though properly these designations belong to the territorial divisions of which they are headquarters. **1964** *Whitaker's Almanack 1965* 891/1 The country [sc. Mongolia] . . is today divided into 18 *aimaks* (provinces) and beneath these into more than 300 *somons* (counties). **1980** *Summary World Broadcasts: Far East: Weekly Econ. Rep.* (B.B.C.) 13 Aug. A21 Drug stores now operate in every agricultural association, somon and State farm in the country.

**son,** *n.*[1] Sense 9 in Dict. becomes 10. Add: **9.** *Computing.* An updated file, usu. on a removable magnetic medium, which has been created from a corresponding father (\*FATHER *n.* 11).

**1962,** etc. [see \*GRANDFATHER *n.* 1 c]. **1970** O. DOPPING *Computers & Data Processing* xvi. 265 The new master tape ('son') is retained till the next updating run in which it serves as the old master tape ('father'). **1985** *English Today* July-Sept. 13/3 There is also an increasing number of attractive even humorous terms in computing . . . A grandfather file, father file, and son file are a series of updated files.

**sooey** ('suːɪ), *int.* *U.S. dial.* [Origin obscure; perh. alt. f. sow *n.*[1] or echoic. Cf. SHOO *int.*[1]] An exclamation used to call or drive pigs. Also (*rare*) as *v. intr.*

**1892** *Dialect Notes* I. 266 For driving pigs away, common words are: *s·u-i, s·u-boi,* [etc.]. **1893** H. A. SHANDS *Some Peculiarities of Speech in Mississippi* 58 *Sooey,* .. the sound used to drive hogs out of one's way. **1941** W. FAULKNER *Men Working* I. 21 'Sooey out of here,' he said. The shoat gave a grunt of startled surprise. **1949** H. HORNSBY *Lonesome Valley* 107 Hiey there! Sooey! Whoopee! Start moving, you son of a bitch! **1982** *Washington Post* 11 Feb. E3/2 'I guarantee you, you'll hear me call the hogs.'.. He offers a quiet 'woo, pig, sooey!' as a foretaste. **1989** *Newsday* 27 Aug. (Sports) 8/2 Ken Hatfield's defense gave Hog-hat wearers plenty of reasons to shout 'sooey' as opposing offenses averaged under 100 yards rushing per game.

**sook** (suːk, sʊk), *n.* and *int. Sc.* and *U.S. dial.* Also **suck, suke**. [Prob. f. SUCK *v.*: see *Eng. Dial. Dict.*] **A.** *n.* A familiar name for a cow (in Scotland *rare*, a calf). **B.** *int.* A call used to summon or drive cattle (in Scotland, generally calves); freq. in phr. *sook cow*.
**1850** L. H. GARRARD *Wah-to-Yah* xii. 178 The.. cows looked quite different from the patient, chewing 'Suke' of the American farmer. **1867** G. W. HARRIS *Sut Lovingood* 24 Yu mout jis' es well say.. Suke cow tu a gal. **1880** W. H. PATTERSON *Gloss. Words Antrim & Down* 101 Suck! Suck! a call to a calf. **1893** H. A. SHANDS *Some Peculiarities of Speech in Mississippi* 76 *Suke* (sûk), the commonly used word for calling cows. The word *cow* is sometimes added to it, so as to make *sukow* (sûkau), the *u* being long drawn out in the pronunciation. **1897** *Amer. Anthropologist* X. 98 In Virginia and Alabama it [*sc.* the call to a cow] becomes *sookow, sookow*. **1906** H. PITTMAN *Belle of Bluegrass Country* xii. 176 'Sook Cow, Sook Cow,' called the milker. **1961** *Amer. Speech* XXXVI. 266 [The expression] *sook boss*.. is an obvious combination of Midland *sook!* and Northern *boss!*, both calls to cows in pasture. **1978** A. FENTON *Northern Isles* liii. 438 Orkney call words to calves were *peed*.., and 'sook! sook!' or 'sucko! sucko!' (from 'suck').
Similarly '**sookie** *n.* (**sucky, sukey**, etc.) in same senses.
**1838** B. DRAKE *Tales & Sk.* 154 With a bellicose bellow, forwards and downwards went the old sukey. **1844** R. HUDDLESTONE *Poems* 67 Here's the merchant for the ca'ves... Sucky's tae the fox gane. **1892** *Dialect Notes* I. 237 *Suke*. Cows are often called by the word *sûk* or *sûki* (Kansas City). **1922** J. SILLARS *McBrides* iii. 36 The lassies laughed and cried 'suckie, suckie', and put on their boots. **1930** F. NIVEN *Three Marys* ix. 56 Mary's cry of 'Sookie, sookie, sookie!' sounded at the ordained times. **1940** J. STUART *Trees of Heaven* 82 Anse calls, 'Swookie, swookie, cows!'

**sooty** ('sʊtɪ), *n. slang* (orig. *U.S.*). [f. SOOTY *a.*] An offensive name for a Black person.
**1838** *Hesperian* Dec. 117/1 The night was enlivened by the music of a cracked fiddle, in the hands of a negro lad, while two or three small sooties kicked up a dust about them. **1986** *Sunday Express Mag.* 28 Dec. 18/4, I am not racialist, but I can't bear to watch the sooties any more—it's like Uncle Tom's Cabin. **1986** G. F. NEWMAN *Set Thief* iv. 48 Pick your fucking feet up, sooty.

‖**sopaipilla** (sopaɪ'piʎa), *n.* [Amer. Sp., dim. of Sp. *sopaipa* a kind of sweet fritter.] In South and Central America and neighbouring parts of the U.S., a small (usu. square) piece of wheat dough deep-fried and eaten with honey or sugar, or occasionally as a bread.
**1934** E. FERGUSSON *Mexican Cookbk.* 90 Cut into small squares, they make *Sopaipillas*. Cut large and round.., they make *Bunuelos*. **1949** F. C. DE BACA GILBERT *Good Life* 76 As the *sopaipillas* are fried and drained and still hot, roll in the sugar and cinnamon mixture. **1958** E. E. ZELAYETA *Elenya's Secrets of Mexican Cooking* 198 The *sopaipillas* will puff up like little pillows. Serve hot as a bread. **1979** G. SWARTHOUT *Skeletons* 95 She ordered dinner —gargantuan Guaymas shrimp and *bollas*.. and *sopapilla* [*sic*] and coffee. **1987** *San Diego Union*

(Food Suppl.) 26 Mar. 2/3 You will need to experiment to find the right temperature—too cool and the sopaipillas won't puff up.

‖**sorbetière** (sɔrbətjɛr, anglicized sɔːbətɪ'ɛə(r)), *n.* [Fr., f. *sorbet* sorbet.] A domestic ice-cream making machine, originally hand-cranked and now usually electric, in which the ice-cream mixture is stirred as it is being frozen.
**1965** E. DAVID *French Provincial Cooking* (ed. 2) 446 The old hand-cranked ice tub or sorbetière can still be bought at big department stores. **1979** *Times* 15 Nov. 20/2 It is.. dismaying.. to find Vergé and Conran agreeing that a sorbetiere is essential for making smooth ices. **1986** *House & Garden* July 123/2 The ice-cream is best made in a *sorbetière* or ice-cream maker. **1988** *Times* 5 Sept. 11/7 Do we really need to throw away our whisks and sorbetières?

**sorry**, *a.* Add: [1.] **d.** *ellipt.* for *I am sorry. colloq.* (*a*) Expressing apology or regret.
**1914** G. B. SHAW *Fanny's First Play* 167 Sorry. Never heard of him. **1923** *Radio Times* 28 Sept. 19/2 No! sorry, I thought you were Cardiff. **1938** E. WAUGH *Scoop* II. ii. 157, I will say you're a quick worker. Sorry to barge in on the tender scene. **1954** W. FAULKNER *Fable* 76 He said, 'All right. Sorry. I didn't know you had a wife.' **1982** W. J. BURLEY *Wycliffe's Wild-Goose Chase* i. 17 'Sorry to bother you on a Sunday morning...' 'Think nothing of it'.
(*b*) Interrogatively, requesting an interlocutor to repeat words that the speaker failed to catch or to understand.
**1972** T. STOPPARD *Jumpers* II. 62 Miss Moore, is there anything you wish to say at this stage? *Dotty* (*in the sense of 'Pardon?'*): Sorry? *Bones*: My dear, we are all *sorry*—. **1978** P. HOWARD *Weasel Words* vii. 46 For its part 'sorry' is coming to mean: 'Please say that again; I did not hear you.'

‖**sosaku hanga** ('sɔːsaku 'haŋga), *n.* Also **Sosaku Hanga**. [Jap., lit. 'creative print'.] A Japanese art form consisting of wood-block prints which are created by one artist, who combines the functions of designer, cutter, and printer; a print made in this way.
[**1949** S. FUJIKAKE *Jap. Wood-Block Prints* (ed. 2) 126 The Nippon Sōsaku Hanga Kyōkai [= Society] .. was formed in June, 1918, by a coterie of artists.] **1956** O. STATLER *Mod. Jap. Prints* Pref. p. xxi, *Torinoko*, a paper which is very popular among the *sosaku hanga* artists. **1965** ZIGROSSER & GAEHDE *Guide to Collecting Orig. Prints* iii. 28 Even in Japan there is a new kind of original print, *Sōsaku Hanga*, following the example of the West in uniting the functions of the designer, cutter, and printer. **1968** J. A. MICHENER *Mod. Jap. Print* 11 The newer print artists preached that the artist himself must do the designing, carving, and printing. A new term was devised to describe such a print—*sosaku hanga*, meaning 'creative print'. **1980** R. ILLING *Art Jap. Prints* xi. 164 From about 1914 some Japanese artists .. began to both carve and print their own prints. Calling their prints *sosaku hanga*, 'creative prints',.. they were finally accepted in Japan and began to receive international acclaim.

‖**sottoportico** (ˌsotto'pɔrtiko), *n. Arch.* Also as two words, and as It. dial. **sottoportego**. [It., f. *sotto* under + *portico* PORTICO *n.*] The covered passage running behind an arcade or colonnade and freq. beneath the projecting first floor of a building.
**1909** WEBSTER, *Sotto portico*,.. an arcade; a street passageway under the overhanging story of a building. **1927** C. MACKENZIE *Vestal Fire* I. vi. 95 It was a large villa... One reached it by a *sotto portici* [*sic*]. **1981** B. HEALEY *Last Ferry* ii. 30 The sottoportico at the bottom end of St. Mark's Square. **1983** E. WEBSTER *Venetian Spy-Glass* viii. 75, I followed Renzo.. through the maze of *calliselle* and

*sottoporteghi.* **1984** 'J. GASH' *Gondola Scam* xiii. 105 A *sottoportego,* a little alley going under a building.

**soubresaut,** *n.* Add: **2.** *Ballet.* A jump made with straight legs and well-pointed toes, with the feet remaining in fifth position.
   **1916** *Dancing Times* Sept. 327 [Espinosa's] 'Syllabus of Dancing' . . . Steps of Elevation. —Changements, soubresauts [etc.]. **1947** N. NICOLAEVA-LEGAT *Ballet Educ.* IV. 112 *Soubresaut* can be executed jumping up and down on the same spot, or upward and forward, upward and backward, to the side, in *effacé,* or in *croisé*; but the legs must always be straight, and perpendicular to the floor. **1948** A. VAGANOVA *Basic Princ. Classical Ballet* vii. 87 Soubresaut is a jump from both feet on both feet. . . The arms in soubresaut are free.

**soucouyant** (suku'jã), *n.* *W. Indies.* Also **soucriant, sukuyâ, sukunyah.** [Creole, prob. related to Fula *sukunyadyo,* Sininke *sukunya* sorcerer, witch.] In the folklore of the Eastern Caribbean, a malignant witch believed to shed her skin by night and suck the blood of her victims.
   **1934** 'J. RHYS' *Voyage in Dark* III. iv. 192 Lying in the dark . . frightened of soucriants that fly in through the window and suck your blood— . . you know them in the day-time—they look like people but their eyes are red and staring and they're soucriants at night. **1955** *Caribbean Q.* IV. II. 103 The shrine is said to have originally been the gift of one Ma Monrose in thanksgiving for the saving of her child from a sukuyâ who had carried him off. **1968** K. S. LA FORTUNE *Legend of T-Marie* xxxv. 128 The Sangre Grande Court House was packed. The streets were lined with people who came to get a glimpse of the 'Soucouyant'. **1973** S. SELVON *Ways of Sunlight* I. 14 He heard of soucouyants which sucked your blood while you slept. **1982** D. SUTCLIFFE *Brit. Black Eng.* ii. 36 Her tale of the sukunyah (or soucouyen), the skin-changing vampire. **1988** P. A. ROBERTS *W. Indians & their Lang.* vi. 153 The tales contain . . familiar and unfamiliar beings, animals and places, e.g. men and soucouyants, dogs and tigers, backyards and kingdoms.

**soulie** ('saʊlɪ), *n.* *slang.* [f. SOUL *n.* + -IE.] A fan of soul music.
   **1978** *Daily Tel.* 1 Nov. 19/6 Two gangs of rival pop music fans, known as the 'Soulies' and the 'Freaks'. **1986** *City Limits* 16 Oct. 41/1 There's a basic rhythm to all Cameo's music. A heartbeat. It's the heart of suburban soulies, of urban would-be sophisticates.

**sound,** *n.*[3] Add: [8.] [b.] **sound bite** orig. *U.S.,* a brief extract from a recorded interview, statement, etc., usu. edited into a news report on account of its aphoristic or provocative quality; *transf.,* a phrase or sentence intended by its speaker to be quoted in this way.
   **1980** *Washington Post* 22 June L2/5 Remember that any editor watching needs a concise, 30-second sound bite. Anything more than that, you're losing them. **1983** *Time* 6 June 55 TV's formula these days is perhaps 100 words from the reporter, and a 'sound bite' of 15 or 20 words from the speaker. **1988** *Independent* 24 Sept. 10 This has been the election of the 'sound-bite' . . . Through a crafty choice of venues and irresistible one-liners, George Bush has been relentlessly associated on the television news with simple, feel-good themes. **1989** *Daily Tel.* 23 Nov. 48/8, I prepared my speech to include a number of sound bites.

**soupy,** *a.* Add: **'soupily** *adv.*
   **1979** *Washington Post* 26 Oct. (Weekend section) 31/1 Richard Gere and Lisa Eichhorn as the soupily romantic Anglo-American couple of films of the period, but with such additional troubles as impotence and doubt. **1985** *Financial Times* 28 Nov. I. 15 Lights go down, storms gather and break

outside and Miss York pops some soupily orchestrated Satie, Mahler or an interminable passage of the Korngold Violin Concerto on her expensive hi-fi.

**sousaphone,** *n.* Add: Hence **sou'saphonist** *n.,* a performer on the sousaphone.
   **1934** in WEBSTER. **1949** *Instrumentalist* Nov.-Dec. 22/1 (Advt.), The sousaphone chair-stand . . . A must for beginner or girl sousaphonist. **1989** *Washington Post* 19 Mar. G11/1 All exceptional musicians, but the standouts are saxophonist Roger Lewis, band-leader/trumpeter Gregory Davis and sousa-phonist Kirk Joseph.

‖**sous vide** (suː 'viːd, ‖su vid), *adv. phr., a., n.* [Fr., f. *sous* under + *vide* vacuum.] (According to, designating, or following) a method of preserving esp. partially cooked food by vacuum-sealing in a package and then chilling.
   **1986** *N.Y. Times* 19 Jan. x. 28/5 Everything is prepared by traditional methods but then preserved sous vide, in vacuum-packed bags. **1987** *Listener* 29 Jan. 12/2 It was Albert Roux who prepared the *sous vide* lunch. **1987** *Restaurant Business* 20 Nov. 64/2 Used in Europe already for some time, *sous vide* is becoming more and more popular in this country. **1988** *Popular Foodservice* Oct. 34/2 A few hot dishes, made using the sous vide method, are included. **1989** *Times* 23 Jan. 3/2 *Sous vide* involves pasteurizing food, putting it in a vacuum and keeping it chilled.

**South 'Asian,** *a.* [f. *South Asia,* the name given to the part of Asia (including Afghanistan, Pakistan and the Indian sub-continent) which is bounded in the east by Burma, in the west by Iran, and in the north by the Central Asian republics and China.] Of or relating to South Asia or its inhabitants.
   An isolated example of the collocation in the sense 'Australian' occurs in the title of a short-lived quarterly, the *South Asian Register,* published in Australia in 1827.
   [**1951** *Internat. Social Sci. Bull.* III. 783 (*title*) The impact of modern technology on the social structures of South Asia. *Ibid.,* The countries dealt with in this paper are India, including the country now known as Pakistan, Burma, Siam, Malaya, Indonesia, Indochina and Ceylon.] **1962** R. D. LAMBERT (*title*) Resources for South Asian area studies in the United States. **1971** R. RUSSELL in *Aziz Ahmad's Shore & Wave* 7 The novel in Urdu, as in all the modern languages of the South Asian sub-continent, is of very recent growth. **1976** C. P. MASICA *Defining Ling. Area: S. Asia* p. xi, The specific problem . . is that of the territorial delineation of the South Asian, or 'Indian', [*sic*] linguistic area. **1979** *Summary World Broadcasts: Far East* (B.B.C.) 12 Apr. AI/3 A multilateral declaration by all South Asian countries that they would not acquire nuclear weapons. **1986** *Ann. Reg. 1985* 272 The new regional grouping of seven countries—India, Pakistan, Bangladesh, Nepal, Sri Lanka, Bhutan and the Maldives—the South Asian Association for Regional Cooperation (SAARC).
   Hence **South 'Asianist** *n.,* a student of or expert on South Asia and its affairs.
   **1978** *Pacific Affairs* LI. 528 This is a sensitive in-depth study of structural change which should be read by South Asianists. **1984** *Jrnl. R. Asiatic Soc.* 172 The book is well produced, and its forthright discussion of the predicament of Indian tribal groups contains much of interest both for South Asianists and for those more generally concerned with social change and development among tribes.

**southern,** *a.* Add: [4.] **d. Southern Oscillation** *Meteorol.,* an approximately cyclic variation in the position and intensity of the principal anticyclones and depressions of the southern hemisphere.

**1923** G. T. WALKER in *Mem. Indian Meteorol. Dept.* XXIV. 285 In summer it [*sc.* Vienna] is a weak adherent of the second group in the 'southern' oscillation, having negative associations with Samoa and Peninsula rain. *Ibid.* 323 By the southern oscillation is implied the tendency of pressure at stations in the Pacific .. and of rainfall in India and Java .. to increase, while pressure in the region of the Indian Ocean .. decreases. **1976** *Nature* 13 May 94/1 The Southern Oscillation is not .. some local or even hemispheric phenomenon, but rather a .. manifestation of the general tendency of the atmosphere/ocean system to vary on this kind of timescale. **1990** J. GRIBBIN *Hothouse Earth* vii. 162 When the temperature pattern over the oceans reverses, the winds also reverse, a phenomenon known to meteorologists as the Southern Oscillation.

**southing**, *vbl. n.* Add: **3.** *Cartogr.* and *Surveying.* Distance south of a point of origin or line of latitude.

**1767** R. GIBSON *Treat. Pract. Surveying* (ed. 2) v. 219 The Difference of Latitude, or the Northing or Southing of any Stationary Line, is the Distance that one End of the Line is North or South from the other End. *Ibid.* 221 If the Sum of the Northings be equal to that of the Southings, and the sum of the Eastings be equal to that of the Westings, the Field-Work is truly taken, otherwise not. **1804** T. FENWICK *Treat. Subterraneous Surveying* II. 199 In whatever denomination the bearing length is, in the same denomination must the integral part of the northing or southing and easting or westing be. **1846** J. GUMMERE *Treat. Surveying* (ed. 14) i. 84 The Difference of Latitude, or the Northing or Southing of a line, is the distance that one end is further north or south than the other end. **1902** [see *NORTHING vbl. n.* 3]. **1950** J. CLENDINNING *Princ. Surveying* v. 57 Latitudes and departures are also sometimes called *northings* or *southings* and *eastings* or *westings*, according to the direction in which they run. **1972** W. SCHOFIELD *Engin. Surveying* I. iii. 102 The vertical axis is the *North-South axis* ... Distances measured along the N-S axis are called *latitudes*; .. those south of the origin are *Southings* and negative.

**space**, *n.* Sense 10 d in Dict. becomes 10 e. Add: **[10.] d.** Any one of a limited number of places in which a person or thing may be accommodated.

**1907** *N.E.D.* s.v. *Place n.* 13 a, A space at table. **1918** A. P. HERBERT *Bomber Gipsy* 21 We who must mourn those spaces in the Mess. **1958** M. L. KING *Stride toward Freedom* v. 86 By the time the meeting started, virtually every space was taken, and hundreds often overflowed into the streets. **1968** R. V. BESTE *Repeat Instructions* xiii. 140 He put the car in the garage ... He chose a space at street level. **1985** D. JOHNSON *Fiskadoro* iii. 78 There were no spaces on the flights.

**spale**, *n.²* Add: **[1.] c.** *Basket-making.* A thin strip of wood woven to form the cross-slat of a wooden basket; such strips collectively. Also *ellipt.* for *spale basket.*

The ellipt. use is noted in *S.N.D.* as having been recorded from Ayrshire in 1928.

**1959** D. WRIGHT *Baskets & Basketry* vi. 136 Spale: thin strips of wood such as oak or chestnut woven into a basket; sometimes used as stakes or sticks with other materials as weaving. *Ibid.* iii. 79 The Italians in particular are alive to the possibilities of using traditional spale and willow shapes in new ways. **1964** H. HODGES *Artifacts* x. 146 Cleft larger timbers were also used for basket-making .. clefts (spelks, spales, swills, laths) .. have been split radially from the timber. **1966** *Third Statistical Acct. Scotl.* XVIII. ii. xvi. 145 The broader and thicker strips of oak that went from side to side of the basket were called

'spales'. **1972** *Daily Tel.* 5 Aug. 9/4 In the small workshop alongside his cottage he showed me how the spales (baskets) are made.

**spalt**, *v.* Restrict *dial.* to sense 1. Delete 'Hence **spalting** *vbl. n.*' and add: **2.** *intr.* To become spalted.

**1977** *Fine Woodworking* Summer 51/1 Apple spalts, but oh boy does it crack!

Hence **spalting** *vbl. n.*

**1733, 1854** [see sense 1 above]. **1977** *Fine Woodworking* Summer 50/1 Spalting is caused by water and fungus. **1980** R. B. HOADLEY *Understanding Wood* ii. 35 (*caption*) As certain white rots develop, dark zone lines form, as on this piece of sugar maple, above. This type of decay is called spalting. **1990** *Woodworker* July 723/2 Beech .. is excellent for carving on top of an already turned piece, as the spalting weakens the fibres in the wood.

**spalted** ('spɔːltɪd), *ppl. a.* [f. SPALT *v.* + -ED²: cf. SPALT *a.*] Of timber: having a distinctive lined grain caused by bacterial decay and valued for its decorativeness.

**1977** M. LINDQUIST in *Fine Woodworking* Summer 50/1 There is no official documentation of spalted wood that I have been able to find. Apparently nobody was crazy enough to consider using 'rotten' wood in the past ... One important reason it wasn't used was the lack of the kind of abrasives that are available today. Any turning done with spalted wood requires extensive sanding. *Ibid.* 50/2 Finding spalted wood at just the right point is crucial. **1982** L. KALLEN *No Lady in House* vii. 67 The unusual grain of the wood that swirled around the bottom and up the sides of the bowl as though it were alive and moving ... That's spalted maple, that is. **1986** *Practical Woodworking* July 344/1 As spalted throughout and there was enough for 25 lamps. *Ibid.*, If you want spalted timber, buy it in the round, store in damp conditions and allow the decay to proceed. **1989** *Chicago Tribune* 1 Dec. VII. 52/2 Karpowicz has been using maple that is spalted—an early form of decay in which bacteria creates [*sic*] dark lines in the wood like ink drawing.

**span**, *n.²* Add: **[3.] b.** A team or gang, esp. of workers; a work party.

**1913** M. CLEAVER *Young S. African* 75, I suppose the old span in the Specials [i.e. police] is getting less and less as they are drafted off to the front. **1949** H. C. BOSMAN *Cold Stone Jug* 107, I said .. that we were greatly privileged to have Jimmy Gair in our span. He reflected very great honour on the stone-yard. **1956** A. SAMPSON *Drum* xiv. 190 After breakfast we were divided into many work 'spans' (parties). I spent my first day with a span cutting grass. **1969** A. PATON *Kontakion* 87 The group with which each boy paraded was called his *span*, which is the Afrikaans word for 'team' or 'gang'. **1976** *Darling* 3 Mar. 67, I have six labourers ... I try to lead by example ... I can do this with a small span of six, but when there are more their negative attitudes are too strong for me. **1986** M. DINGAKE in N. Mandela *Struggle is my Life* (1988) III. ii. 222 There was a possible glimpse of some communal section span .. hidden in the wood along the road to give us a clear passage.

**Spanish**, *a.* (*adv.*) and *n.¹* Add: **[B.] [2.] e.** Spanish wine.

**1977** F. BRANSTON *Up & Coming Man* xv. 172 We .. broke open a fine crusted bottle of Sainsbury's Spanish which we had been hoarding against the day when we could afford to cook in wine again. **1982** J. N. CHANCE *Hunting of Mr Exe* iii. 45 'I have a Spanish, highly thought of by those wanting a lot for the money,' Seth said, and .. came back with .. a large bottle of Spanish Burgundy. **1983** N. FREELING *Back of North Wind* 158 Now do you want to drink Spanish, or will you all stick to Monsieur Taittinger?

**Sparine** ('spɛəriːn), *n. Pharm.* [f. *spar-* (of unknown origin) + -INE⁵.] A proprietary name for promazine hydrochloride.

**1956** *Official Gaz.* (U.S. Patent Office) 2 Oct. TM12/1 *Sparine* ... For tranquillizing agent. First use Dec. 21, 1955. **1956** *Trade Marks Jrnl.* 12 Dec. 1239/1 *Sparine* ... Pharmaceutical products for use as anti-convulsants and as sedatives ... 30th August, 1956. **1971** D. FRANCIS *Bonecrack* viii. 111 Some brand of promazine. Sparine, probably. **1981** M. C. GERALD *Pharmacol.* (ed. 2) xvi. 331 Among the phenothiazines lacking antipsychotic activity that are used for their antiemetic effects are promazine (Sparine), promethazine (Phenergan), and thiethylperazine (Torecan).

**sparrow**, *n.* Add: [1.] e. *pl.* (Usu. with capital initial.) In the Philippines, the members of a sparrow unit (see sense *4 a below); a sparrow squad.

**1983** *Christian Science Monitor* (New England ed.) 17 May 12/3 They [*sc.* the NPA] have small units called 'sparrows' which concentrate on seizing guns from soldiers. 'They're called that because sparrows blend into their surroundings so well.' **1986** *Los Angeles Times* 18 Aug. I. 7/2 As she tells it, her 26-year-old husband .. was an assassin, a member of an elite rebel liquidation squad known as the Sparrows. **1987** *Sunday Mail* (Brisbane) 15 Nov. 27/1 The operations are in response to the killing of 16 people in and around Manila in the past fortnight, all of them thought to be the victims of 'Sparrows'. **1988** *Facts on File* 22 Apr. 292/1 Kintanar was believed to be the chief organizer of the guerrilla assassination squads known as 'Sparrows'.

[4.] [a.] **sparrow squad** = *sparrow unit* below. **1987** *U.S. News & World Rep.* 16 Mar. 42/1 Every day, newspapers carry accounts of three or four violent incidents somewhere in the country—local officials ambushed by NPA 'Sparrow Squad' assassins, or guerrillas killed by military patrols. **1988** *Weekend Australian* (Brisbane) 30 Jan. 1/4 The two spokesmen .. represented the NPA's Alex Boncayao Brigade (ABB), an urban warfare unit established in Manila in 1984 to carry out assassinations through the operation of small armed units called sparrow squads.

**sparrow unit** *colloq.* [after their fast in-and-out tactics], in the Philippines, any of a number of small guerrilla squads representing the militant sector of the Communist Party, which conduct attacks on policemen, government officials, etc.

**1984** *Summary World Broadcasts: Far East* (B.B.C.) 30 June B3 Police operations revealed that members of the so-called sparrow unit were involved in kidnap-for-ransom and other extortion activities to raise funds for their armed struggle against the government. **1989** *Christian Science Monitor* 28 Apr. 19/3 Urban assassination teams, or 'sparrow' units, have killed several Philippine police officers, soldiers, and officials.

**spartakiad** (spɑːˈtækɪæd), *n.* Also -iade and with cap. initial. [ad. Czech, Russ. *spartakiáda*: see SPARTACIST *n.*; cf. OLYMPIAD *n.*]

Said to have been coined in Czech by J. F. Chaloupecký in 1921: see *Malá Československá Encyklopedie* (1987) V. 789/2.]

In the Soviet Union and other Eastern European countries: a popular sporting event characterized by the participation of large numbers of people in a wide range of sports.

**1928** *Internat. Press Corr.* (Vienna) 24 May 532/2 The bourgeoisie of Czechoslovakia .. having witnessed .. the brilliant course of the first Spartakiade in 1921 .. and having constantly persecuted the Red Sport League, dissolved this group today. **1958** *Praha Guidebk.* 98 We shall not readily forget the first National Spartakiad of 1955 .. in which almost half a million gymnasts took part. **1964** V. & J. LOUIS *Sport*

*in Soviet Union* IV. 11 The *Spartakiad* had begun with eliminating competitions in towns and villages, followed by inter-regional rounds. **1977** J. RIORDAN *Sport in Soviet Society* xi. 382 The third summer *spartakiad* was held in Czechoslovakia in 1973, and the fourth winter games in Bulgaria in late 1973. **1987** *Boxing News* 21 Aug. 23/3 Kaden took up boxing at 10, and was runner-up in a national spartakiad in East Berlin at 12. **1989** *Times* 5 Apr. 46/2 The Soviet leadership has always maintained in public that a third of the population takes part in the spartakiads.

**spathodea** (speɪˈθəʊdɪə), *n.* [a. mod.L. genus name *Spathodea* (A. M. F. J. Palisot de Beauvois *Flore d'Oware et de Benin* (1804) I. 46): see SPATHA *n.*, -ODE¹.] The African tulip tree, *Spathodea campanulata*, one of the evergreen family Bignoniaceae, grown as an ornamental throughout the tropics for its clusters of tulip-shaped orange and scarlet flowers.

**1873** C. J. G. RAMPINI *Lett. from Jamaica* 64 Beside the court-house stood a splendid Spathodea in full blossom. **1930** F. B. YOUNG *Jim Redlake* IV. vi. 633 They must be nearing some river, it seemed, for the trees grew taller. In front of them stood one, a huge spathodea Jim thought, with a cold, gleaming trunk that shot straight upward .. like a pillar of silver. **1973** J. C. WELLS *Jamaican Pronunc. in London* i. 15 /tSini/ 'Spathodea tree'. **1983** D. CAUTE *The K-Factor* i. 13 She showed him her imported trees, her spathodia [*sic*], her Australian blackwood, her monkey puzzle.

**spatiography** (speɪʃɪˈɒgrəfɪ), *n. rare.* [f. *spatio-*, taken as comb. form of L. *spatium* SPACE *n.*¹ + -GRAPHY.] The scientific description of the features of (outer) space; the topography of space.

**1958** H. STRUGHOLD in Alperin & Stern *Vistas in Astronautics* I. VI. 283 We need a topographical description of space, something that—in analogy to geography—we might perhaps call 'spatiography'. **1961** in WEBSTER. **1962** M. V. GLENNY tr. *Gartmann's Space Trav.* 40 To find his way man will need to employ a kind of space geography, or 'spatiography', as it is called.

**spear**, *v.*³ Add: 3. *trans.* (and *absol.*) a. *Ice Hockey, Lacrosse*, etc.: to jab (an opponent) illegally with the point or end of the stick. *N. Amer.*

**1963** *Globe & Mail* (Toronto) 14 Mar. 7/5 Spearing .. is sometimes done in self-defense ... 'I spear any forward who runs interference and sticks too close.' **1977** *Washington Post* 3 Jan. D2/1 The Blues' Garry Unger was observed shoving the butt end of his stick at Marson, then Gassoff speared Patey. **1988** *Ibid.* 10 Apr. C11/2, I like hard-nosed hockey. But the use of the stick tonight was atrocious. .. Rick Tocchet spears Dale Hunter above and below the eye, he spears Scott Stevens.

b. *Amer. Football.* To ram or butt (an opponent) illegally with the helmet.

**1964** *Jrnl. Amer. Med. Assoc.* 4 May 419/1 Over 60% of the players receiving head injuries were coached to 'spear', or use their helmet-protected heads against the bodies of the opponents. **1971** C. OLSON *Prevention Football Injuries* v. 45 About 60% of head injuries and 44% of neck injuries occurred in players who were coached to 'spear'. **1980** *N.Y. Times* 28 Oct. A37/5 From film study, it looked as if Hartenstine had speared Jaworski with his helmet and at the least should have been penalized 15 yards.

**spearing**, *vbl. n.* Add: 2. *N. Amer.* a. *Ice Hockey, Lacrosse*, etc. The illegal action of jabbing a member of an opposing team with the point or end of the stick.

**1957** PATRICK & MONAHAN *Let's play Hockey* 36, I think spearing is a deliberate attempt to injure an opponent, and for this reason I believe it should be a major, five-minute penalty. **1963** *Albertan* (Calgary) (Sports section) 10 Dec. 11/2 'Spearing is dangerous, too, but there's more high-sticking' Thompson said. **1970** M. BRAITHWAITE *Never sleep Three in Bed* x. 126 Fist fights were frequent, and butt ends, spearing, and all the other neat little tricks were as common then as now. **1983** *Washington Post* 7 Mar. D8/1 Holt has taken some foolish sentences for spearing, unsportsmanlike conduct and unnecessary stick fouls.

**b.** *Amer. Football.* The illegal action of ramming or butting a member of an opposing team with the helmet.

**1964** *Jrnl. Amer. Med. Assoc.* 4 May 421/1 The practice of head-blocking and head-tackling known as 'spearing' must be examined carefully... One must question the place of spearing in high school football. **1973** R. C. SCHNEIDER *Head & Neck Injuries in Football* vi. 116 The mechanism for such injury whether due to 'stick-blocking' or 'spearing', may involve impairment of the vascular supply to the brain stem. **1979** *Facts on File* 9 Mar. 176/1 The committee added an automatic first down to the established 15-yard penalties for spearing (ramming or butting with the helmet), kicking an opponent,.. and striking the ball carrier. **1987** *QuarterBack* Mar. 14/1 Spearing, that flagrant abuse of the rules, has been banned for 10 years and paralysing neck injuries have dropped.

**specialist**, *n.* Senses 2b-c in Dict. become 2c-2d. Add: [**2.**] **b.** *U.S. Stock Exchange.* A member of a stock exchange who buys and sells only a single stock or a narrow range of stocks, typically having or sharing responsibility for maintaining a stable market in this sector.

**1900** S. A. NELSON *ABC of Wall St.* xxxv. 159 Specialists. Brokers who deal in one or two stocks only. **1907** —— *Consolidated Stock Exchange N.Y.* xiii. 69 The successful specialist if trading in an active stock must be a robust man, have a strong voice, be quick-witted, and always willing to trade. **1919** H. S. MARTIN *N.Y. Stock Exchange* xxi. 254 If, however, the broker is busy at a post other than Steel, and cannot leave that post to fill the order to buy Steel, he can send the order to another broker, or may give it to a Specialist. **1934** *Sun* (Baltimore) 3 Mar. 15/8 New York Stock Exchange 'specialists' today objected emphatically to provisions of the pending securities market control bill which would require them to abandon the practice of trading on their own account. **1963** B. E. SHULTZ *Securities Market* (ed. 2) xvi. 302 A 'floor give-up' in which specialists and two-dollar brokers give up the names of the firms for which they are acting. **1988** *Times* 12 Feb. 24/5 The specialist in New York assumes an obligation to act to prevent volatile price movements in the shares for which he has the sole obligation to make a market.

**speciation**, *n.* Add: Hence **speci'ational** *a.*, pertaining to or resulting from speciation (esp. in phr. *speciational evolution*).

**1944** G. G. SIMPSON *Tempo & Mode in Evolution* vii. 203 The pertinent data of paleontology fall into patterns of the phyletic mode. It has naturally resulted that paleontologists have overemphasized this mode..just as most experimentalists have overemphasized and overgeneralized from the speciational mode. **1983** W. C. KIMLER in M. Grene *Dimensions of Darwinism* v. 125 The creaking of the synthesis at present around its adaptationist and speciational ideas is perhaps to be expected as the result of a fresh ecological input. **1988** E. MAYR *Toward New Philos. of Biol.* xxvi. 483 It has been shown that 'speciational evolution' (perhaps a better term than punctuationism) is fully consistent with Darwinism. **1989** *Cladistics* V. 58 Speciational evolution, via punctuational change, is at least a viable explanation for the distribution of allozyme character change found among species of lizards in the genus *Sceloporus*.

**specificity**, *n.* Add: [**1.**] **d.** *Med.* The extent to which a diagnostic test is specific for a particular condition, trait, etc., calculated as the proportion of tests on individuals who do not have the condition, etc., that give negative results.

**1954** A. B. KURLANDER et al. in *Diabetes* III. 216/1 *Specificity* may be defined as the ability of the test to classify as negative those who do not have the condition being screened for and is calculated as the percentage screening negative of those determined not to have diabetes. *Ibid.* 218/2 The specificity ratings of blood sugar tests by the Somogyi-Nelson and Wilkerson-Heftmann methods were satisfactory—98·0 and 96·8 per cent respectively. **1955** *Sci. Amer.* Mar. 68/2 The three procedures represent an ascending scale of sensitivity and a descending scale of specificity. **1977** I. M. ROITT *Essent. Immunol.* v. 131 As with most immunological techniques as sensitivity is increased, specificity becomes progressively reduced. **1987** *Oxf. Textbk. Med.* (ed. 2) I. v. 442/2 This test has a sensitivity of up to 96 per cent and a specificity of 99 per cent.

**specifier**, *n.* Senses a, b in Dict. become 1 a, 2. For def. read: **1.** One who specifies. **a.** The writer or drawer-up of a patent specification. **b.** *Comm.* and *Industry.* One who draws up specifications for the materials, dimensions, etc. of a product or project (see SPECIFICATION *n.* 4 d). (Examples in sense 1 b.)

[**1949** (*title*) The construction specifier..published quarterly by the Construction Specifications Institute, Inc.] **1964** *Builder* 17 Apr. 804/1 Some specifiers always used the same suppliers (including wholesalers) or the same brands on quite different kinds of jobs. **1971** *Cabinet Maker & Retail Furnisher* 1 Oct. 11/1 Lloyd Duncan are continuing to handle sales to direct specifiers, including the furniture industry. **1976** *Liverpool Echo* 23 Nov. 11/1 (Advt.), National building company seeks experienced specifier representatives. **1986** *Independent* 18 Nov. 6/2 £5,000m is wasted because of bad design and wrong specifications... If the industry, and that includes architects, specifiers and builders, got its act together..all this money would be invested in building new homes or repairing existing..houses.

**spectator**, *n.* Add: [**2.**] **c.** More fully *spectator pump*, *shoe.* A woman's dress shoe, usu. with a white body and contrasting darker toe and heel; occas. a similar shoe worn by a man. *N. Amer.* (orig. *U.S.*).

**1941** M. KETTUNEN *Fund. Dress* xiv. 431 Other sport models, commonly known as 'spectator' sport shoes, come in more standard styles. **1946** *Glamour* Sept. 74 (Advt.), Eileen spectators! Smart young moderns wear these..spectators. **1963** M. McCARTHY *Group* ii. 42 Wearing her white sharkskin sports dress and brown-and-white spectator pumps. **1969** *Sears Catal.* Spring/Summer 422/2 Strut into spring sporting a high-powered spectator pump. Hand-rubbed leather upper set off by contrasting perforations and bold stitching. **1970** A. TYLER *Slipping-Down Life* xi. 154 Mr. Casey was in a blue suit and white spectator shoes. **1975** *Daily Mirror* 21 Mar. 24/7, I lived in Canada from 1946 to 56 and every summer the ladies wore court shoes which they called 'spectators'... The toe caps and heels were either brown or navy blue, the rest white. And very smart, too.

**spec'tatorish** *a.*, characteristic of a spectator or observer.

**1977** *Oxf. Diocesan Mag.* Nov. 17/2 There is something spectator-ish in treating knowledge as purely or even largely an intellectual affair. **1982** *Times Lit. Suppl.* 26 Mar. 334/2 His republicanism.. strikes one as of a similarly spectatorish kind, as of one who cannot countenance anything of which he is not himself a part.

**spectrograph**, *n.* Add: **spectro'graphical** *a.* = *spectrographic* adj.
**1968** *Nuclear Instruments & Methods* LXV. 253 It has been emphasized that the spectrometer is also suited for spectrographical use with multi-detectors. **1982** *Acta Physiol. Scand.* CXVI. 67 Spectrographical scanning of LMW-Zn preparations obtained by gel chromatography .. gave identical absorption curves with those obtained by scanning of a zinc-citrate solution.

**specular**, *a.* Add: [I.] [3.] **d.** [F. *spéculaire* (J. Lacan 1949, 'Le stade du miroir' in *Revue Française de Psychanalyse* XIII. 450: paper orig. presented in 1936).] In psychoanalytic theory: of, pertaining to or characteristic of the 'mirror stage' of infant development, or to any response associated with this.
**1968** A. WILDEN tr. J. Lacan in *Language of Self* (1974) 135 The joyful assumption of his specular image by a being still unable to control his motor functions and still dependent on his mother to nurse him. **1973** MATIAS & WILLEMEN tr. M. Cegarra in *Screen* Spring/Summer 137 According to Metz, there is no discontinuity (dynamic tension), but continuity as a specular relation. **1977** A. SHERIDAN tr. *Lacan's Écrits* i. 5 Paranoic alienation .. dates from the deflection of the specular *I* into the social *I*. **1985** T. MOI *Sexual/Textual Politics* vii. 135 Caught in the specular logic of patriarchy, woman can choose either to remain silent, .. or to *enact* the specular representation of herself as a lesser male. **1990** C. NORRIS in Boyne & Rattansi *Postmodernism & Society* v. 124 They are thus caught up in a specular relation or a pattern of unwitting dialectical reprise that ends up by confirming every last theorem of the 'false' sciences that Marx set out to controvert.

**Speewah** ('spiːwɑː), *n. Austral.* Also **Speewa**, etc. [The name of a remote locality reputedly north-west of Swan Hill in Victoria, and of a legendary sheep station supposedly situated there.] An imaginary place used as the setting for unlikely and tall stories of the Australian outback. Also, a story of this kind.
**1890** *Truth* (Sydney) 16 Nov. 1/4 Dear Mr *Truth*—I have just returned from 'the Spewah country', where we have to crawl on our hands and knees to get under the clouds. **1911** *Bulletin* (Sydney) 17 Aug. 14/3 If any snagger boasted of having shorn 32 sheep in the breakfast 'run', there was always someone present to mention that 'Crooked Mick', at Speewah, had done 33 in the same time. **1944** A. MARSHALL *These are My People* 154, I had heard of Speewa, that mythical station used as a setting for all the lies put over on new-chums ... It's a big place. When I was there they had to get two Chinese to mix the mustard with long-handled shovels. **1962** *Australasian Post* 25 Oct. 38 The Speewah lies way out west o' sunset where the crows fly backwards to see where they're coming from. **1965** B. WANNAN *Fair Go, Spinner* ii. 64, I had a relation on Speewah station. He told me what he'd seen there; I won't deny it sounds a lie But then I've never been there. **1979** *Courier-Mail* (Brisbane) 12 May 1/2 Each must tell a speerwah, or bush yarn, for more than four minutes.

**spelk**, *n.* Add: [2.] **b.** A type of woven basket made of narrow strips of wood or 'spelks'.
[**1926** FITZRANDOLPH & HAY *Rural Industries Eng. & Wales* I. vii. 97 The tools used and the methods of making oak-spelk baskets are nearly the same in all districts.] **1949** K. S. WOODS *Rural Crafts Eng.* viii. 142 The baskets have various names in different districts—scuttles or sculls, spelks, skips, or whiskets. **1953** A. JOBSON *Househ. & Country Crafts* xviii. 171 Besides besoms, wiskets (swills, spelks, slops or skips elsewhere, to which might be added Sussex trugs), are made in this Wyre Hill yard. **1968** J. ARNOLD *Shell Bk. Country Crafts* 260 The Furness 'spelk' is

made with rent oak strips or bands, rendered pliable by a period of boiling.

**speller**, *n.*[2] Add: **4.** *Comput.* = *spelling checker* s.v. *SPELLING vbl. n.*[2] 3.
**1980** *Communications Assoc. Computing Machinery* XXIII. 682/1 A similar approach is including common misspellings in the dictionary with the correct spelling ... This approach has not been included in any current spellers. **1986** *Australian* (Brisbane) 14 Oct. 48/2 Like most programs these days, it includes a speller. **1988** *PC Mag.* May 34/2 The best stand-alone spellers and word processors use much faster look-up routines.

**spelling**, *vbl. n.*[2] Add: [3.] **spelling checker** *Computing*, a program which checks the spelling of words in files of text, usu. by comparing them with a stored list of acceptable spellings.
**1980** *Communications Assoc. Computing Machinery* XXIII. 676/3 There are two types of spelling programs: *spelling checkers and spelling correctors. **1983** *Trans. Philol. Soc.* 37 A spelling-checker of the future .. might recognize not merely non-English words, but words occurring in non-English positions.

**spermatophyte**, *n.* Add: Hence **spermato'phytic** *a.*, belonging to or characteristic of the phylum Spermatophyta; = SPERMOPHYTIC *a.*
**1905** B. D. JACKSON *Gloss. Bot. Terms* (ed. 2) 356/2 *Spermatophytic*, relating to seed-bearing plants. **1964** *Acta Botanica Neerlandica* XIII. 97 (*title*) The bitegmic spermatophytic ovule and the cupule—a reappraisal of the so-called pseudo-monomerous ovule. **1973** *Phytopath. Zeitschr.* LXXVII. 251 Associations of parasitic fungi can be highly independent of spermatophytic vegetation. **1983** *Feddes Repertorium* XCIV. 683 The list contains 61 species of 10 rust genera growing on 74 different host species of 26 spermatophytic families.

**spherand** ('sfɛrænd, 'sfɪərænd), *n. Chem.* [f. SPHERE *n.* + -AND[2], after LIGAND *n.*] Any of a class of organic ligands with molecules in the form of a hollow sphere, which bind selectively cations of alkali metals and are more stable than cryptands.
**1979** D. J. CRAM et al. in *Jrnl. Amer. Chem. Soc.* CI. 6753/1 We suggest the class name 'spherands' for such ligand systems, and the class name 'metallospherium' salts for their complexes with metal salts. **1987** *Sci. Amer.* Dec. 23/3 Another type of host, called a spherand, .. is still stabler. **1988** P. D. BEER in T. E. Edmonds *Chem. Sensors* ii. 42 Whereas the crown ethers and, .. the cryptands, the spherands and the host parts of their complexes are conformationally the same. **1988** *Nature* 7 July 10/1 Lehn's cryptands, Cram's spherands and their derivatives, all organic 'host' compounds that bind to smaller 'guests', exemplify this field of designer chemistry.

**spiceless** ('spaɪslɪs), *a.* [f. SPICE *n.* + -LESS.] Without spice or spices (*lit.* and *fig.*); lacking pungency, insipid.
**1942** E. PAUL *Narrow St.* xxii. 181, I open Racine and mumble the metre of that spiceless abracadabra. **1980** *Washington Post* 10 Jan. DC5/2 The [salad] dressing was watery and spiceless. **1988** *Newsday* 1 Aug. 95/2 The Pirates .. were unable to put any flavor in a spiceless series with their running game.

**spiffy**, *a.* Add: Hence **'spiffily** *adv.*; **'spiffiness** *n.*
**1977** *Washington Post* 26 Apr. B5/4 They were a very spiffily dressed bunch. **1981** *N.Y. Times* 30 Oct. C34/4 Mr. Marash is the bearded correspondent who seldom wears a tie, thereby offering an alternative to the sartorial spiffiness of Jim Jensen and Roland

Smith. **1985** R. WHELAN *Robert Capa* ii. 29 He is spiffily dressed in a suit jacket, tie, and sweater: a radical in bourgeois clothing.

**spika** ('spıkə, 'spiːkə), *v.* Also **speaka**, **spik(ka)**, etc. [Repr. broken English pronunc. of *speak*: see SPEAK *v.* and cf. SPIC *n.*, SPIGGOTY *n.*] = 'speak': a representation or imitation (usu. jocular or patronizing) of its pronunciation by one whose first language is not English. Chiefly in negative contexts.

**1889** KIPLING *From Sea to Sea* (1899) II. xx. 404 One small [Japanese] boy..said suddenly: 'I spik Englees,' and collapsed. **1901** G. B. SHAW *Capt. Brassbound's Conversion* I. 235 That rascal (*indicating Marzo*) would cut a throat for a dollar if he had courage enough. *Marzo.* I not understand. I no spik Englis. **1950** 'D. DIVINE' *King of Fassarai* xviii. 143, I been in hospitals... I spika da language. **1959** 'M. M. KAYE' *House of Shade* iii. 29 'Did you take my passport?.. When you were ragging my room?' 'Rag—? Sorry; I no speaka-da English.' **1976** C. WESTON *Rouse Demon* xii. 54 No spikka, I suppose. What the hell do they teach these kids in school? **1977** A. SCHOLEFIELD *Venom* I. 41 Remember our agreement? You no spikada French and I no spikada Pakistani. **1983** P. L. BROWN *Fjord of Silent Men* vi. 35, I work with a magazine called *Norske Kvinner*—'Norwegian Women' if you donta speaka da lingo.

**spike**, *n.*[2] Sense 2 i (b) in Dict. becomes 2 i (c). Add: [2.] [i.] (b) Any sharp narrow peak on a graph representing the sudden rapid increase of some parameter to a high level immediately followed by a rapid decrease; also used of an event, brief period of activity, etc., such as might be so represented.

**1961** in WEBSTER. **1970** O. SACKS *Migraine* (1981) x. 205 It has been impossible to define any EEG abnormality which bears a *specific* relation to migraine, as wave-and-spike patterns do to epilepsy. **1978** *Nature* 11 May 141/1 A series of brief episodes of relatively heavy influx of tree pollen ('spikes'), separated by longer intervals with little or no pollen. **1988** *New Yorker* 26 Oct. 70/2 The five-minute spike of greatest downpour occurred at about one-thirty.

(*d*) *Comm.* A sudden rapid increase, esp. of prices.

**1982** *Times* 6 Sept. 13/7 Technology issues were joined by the big oil companies in the upward spike of prices. **1983** W. SAFIRE in *N.Y. Times Mag.* 10 Apr. 16 As a noun, *spike* now figures prominently in the lingo of economists. It has replaced *peak* in discussions of lofty upthrusts on charts. **1988** *Sunday Times* 10 Apr. D1/2 Many analysts believe that an upward 'spike' into the range of DM3.15 to DM3.20 is quite possible.

**k.** *Volleyball.* An act or instance of spiking the ball. See *SPIKE *v.*[1] 7 a.

[**1933** R. E. LAVEAGA *Volley Ball* vi. 97 The second method or the running spike attack is essential.] **1934** *Official Volleyball Rules* 69 Three men on the Texas team would jump in a group to block the spike. **1953** C. M. EMERY *Mod. Volleyball* iii. 29 The spike should be made as the body reaches to maximum height. **1964** *Volleyball* ('Know the Game' Ser.) (ed. 2) 20/1 The counter to the 'smash' or 'spike' is the 'block'. **1978** G. WRIGHT *Illustr. Handbk. Sporting Terms* 67/3 Because of the net's height, the player making the spike is invariably in mid-air. **1989** *Times* 24 Nov. 44/3 Only those in the front box may 'block' at the net an opponent's 'spike' with hands raised above the net.

**l.** A segment of hair shaped artificially into an upright point on the head, as part of a distinctive hairstyle (usu. in *pl.*); a hairstyle characterized by these.

**1981** *Washington Post* 22 Jan. DC1/4 (*caption*) The punk look includes leather jackets and hair combed into spikes. **1983** *Times* 5 July 8/8 Gels can be used on damp or dry hair for slicked-back styles, sleek bobs and spikes. **1983** *Harpers & Queen* Aug. 70/3 The Inn Place... Packed with quiffs, spikes and non-stop dancers. **1987** *Sunday Sun* (Brisbane) 1 Mar. (TV Suppl.) 9/1 Johnson..sported a new haircut when he returned—a sort of spike.

**spike**, *v.*[1] Sense 7 in Dict. becomes 8. Add: [5.] **g.** To plant a concealed microphone in (a place); to bug, esp. with a spike microphone. Also in extended use. *slang.*

**1974** 'J. LE CARRÉ' *Tinker, Tailor* xvii. 145 Clear a foreign letter box, prime a safe house, watch someone's back, spike an embassy... You might think he was acting on instructions from the fifth floor. *Ibid.* xxi. 172 A one-time operation to spike a pair of Belgian arms dealers. **1982** *Verbatim* Spring 2/2 *Spike*, to tap a telephone, open mail, plant a microphone. **1983** D. GETHIN *Wyatt* vi. 38 Quittenden's plumbers..were the crack team who could spike a high security building in under an hour. **1984** *Christian Science Monitor* 27 Apr. 32/1 Police..spiked the walls of the besieged building with microphones.

**7. a.** *Volleyball.* To strike (the ball) sharply downward into the opposing court, at a speed and angle which makes return difficult. Also *intr.*

**1922** *Official Volley Ball Rules* 18 A player may not 'spike' or 'kill' the ball when he is playing a back position. **1964** *Volleyball* ('Know the Game' Ser.) (ed. 2) 29 'Rotation' drills are very useful in volleyball... A sets the ball up, B spikes, C retrieves, then sets, A spikes, B retrieves, and so on. **1989** *Times* 24 Nov. 44/1 Noel Despaigne..strikes the ball downwards—or spikes it in the parlance of the game—from a height of about 11 feet at something approaching 100mph.

**b.** *Amer. Football.* To throw (the ball) down hard on its end, causing it to bounce up spectacularly, esp. in triumph after scoring a touchdown.

**1976** *Webster's Sports Dict.* 411/2 *Spike*,.. to throw the ball down hard especially in the end zone after scoring a touchdown. **1977** *Washington Post* 20 Sept. D5/4 Bryant was given his touchdown too—and a penalty against the Ducks..for spiking the ball in anger when he thought at first he had been denied. **1985** *Los Angeles Times* 26 Nov. III. 5/2 Denver tight end Clarence Kay caught a touchdown pass and started to spike the ball, but Rod Martin tipped it out of his hands. **1989** *Boston Globe* 10 Sept. 77/5 We haven't had a delay-of-game call other than when Ray Alexander spiked the ball.

**spiker**, *n.*[2] Add: **3.** *Volleyball.* A player who spikes the ball, *esp.* one skilled at this. See *SPIKE *v.*[1] 7 a.

**1934** *Official Volleyball Rules* 31 One of these men is called a 'set-up' man and the other the 'attack' or the 'spiker'. **1942** R. E. LAVEAGA *Volleyball* v. 47 In studying the movement of the attack the spiker leaves the floor as soon as.. the set up is made. **1953** *Mod. Volleyball* iii. 31 The spiker should land facing the net. **1965** B. J. TROTTER *Volleyball for Girls & Women* iv. 83 The Key-Set.. reverse sets the ball to the right forward spiker. **1989** *Times* 24 Nov. 44/3 The setter is often the key figure, always playing the ball from just in front of and below the level of the net.. and adroitly placing it.. for a spiker.

**spiker** ('spaɪkə(r)), *n.*[3] *N.Z. colloq.* [f. SPIKE *n.*[2] + -ER[1].] = *spike-buck* s.v. SPIKE *n.*[2] 6.

**1924** J. FORBES *N.Z. Deer Heads* p. xvi, The same day.. we saw the first bull—a spiker. **1972** P. NEWTON *Sheep Thief* ix. 72 Jim was just able to pick up the dark shape of a single deer... It was a well-grown spiker. **1981-2** *Deer Farmer* (N.Z.) Summer

10/2 This does not simply apply to mature bucks; in fact spikers are the worst.

**spill**, v. Add: [II.] [10.] **d.** *Sport.* To drop (the ball); esp. in *Cricket*, to put down (a catch). *colloq.*

**1975** *Sunday Times* 22 June 24/4 Seven catches were put down... Edwards.. spilt Lloyd at mid-wicket off Lillee. **1976** J. SNOW *Cricket Rebel* 114 Some poor fielding on our part which saw four chances spilled in the slips. **1990** *Sunday Times* 11 Feb. B6/5 He was formidable in the tackle and never spilled or gave up the ball when he took the French midfield head on.

**spin**, n.¹ Add: [2.] **g.** *fig.* A bias or slant on information, intended to create a favourable impression when it is presented to the public; an interpretation or viewpoint. Freq. in phr. *to put a positive* (*negative,* etc.) *spin on. colloq.* (chiefly *U.S. Pol.*).

**1978** *Guardian Weekly* 22 Jan. 18/1 The CIA can be an excellent source [of information], though, like every other, its offerings must be weighed for factuality and spin. **1979** *Washington Post* 15 Mar. A17/2 American spokesman Jody Powell gave a press briefing and put a negative spin on the talks. **1980** *N.Y. Times* 7 Sept. I. 35/1 President Carter's chief economist.. tried to put a positive spin on what has generally been perceived as a dismal economic picture. **1984** *USA Today* 6 Apr. 3D/1 *New England Monthly* is resolutely Yankee in its subject matter, with a spin that suggests it is for and by that generation we've been hearing so much about lately. **1989** *Independent* 1 June 9 None of the 'collies' believes Mr Baker. In the American political vernacular, he is trying to put a 'spin' on the Bush triumph.

[9.] **spin doctor** *Pol. colloq.* (orig. *U.S.*), a political press agent or publicist employed to promote a favourable interpretation of events to journalists.

**1984** *N.Y. Times* 21 Oct. IV. 22/1 They won't be just press agents trying to impart a favorable spin to a routine release. They'll be the \*Spin Doctors, senior advisers to the candidates. **1988** *Globe & Mail* (Toronto) 24 Oct. A1/3 Some of the spin doctors (whose nickname is believed to come from baseball, where pitchers put spin on a ball to control its direction) will be using cellular phones to call in policy specialists. **1990** *Maclean's Mag.* 2 Apr. 11/3 We were treated to the insights of Elliott Abrams,.. the administration's most versatile spin doctor on Nicaraguan affairs.

hence **spin-doctoring** n.

**1986** *Washington Post* 7 Aug. A1/2 Today the competing camps engaged in a game of persuasion and perception: '\*spin doctoring', as the craft of explaining to reporters what really happened is known in political circles. **1990** *Sunday Tel.* 17 June 21/8 For the first time in living memory, Tory Central Office handled an election campaign successfully, and it was not all spin-doctoring.

**spin**, v. Add: [II.] [13.] **c.** *trans.* Of a veterinary surgeon: to reject or disqualify (a horse), esp. from a competition. Freq. in *pass.*

**1974** T. FITZGEORGE-PARKER *Vincent O'Brien* i. 12 He was twice sold to big English owners, but each deal broke down because the vets 'spun' him for his wind. **1985** *Eventing* Oct. 29/2 A further two were spun by the inspection committee,.. which put paid to the Italian team's chances. **1987** *Carriage Driving* Spring 12/1 Unsuitable mounts, poor tack, worn shoes and unfit riders.. resulted in competitors being 'spun' well before the completion of the ride.

**spinal**, a. (and n.) Add: [7.] **c.** *absol.* as n. Short for *spinal anæsthetic* (or *anæsthesia*); also, = EPIDURAL n. *U.S. Med. colloq.*

**1938** H. K. BEECHER *Physiol. Anesthesia* i. 72 The reduced blood volume must be restored at once, for 'spinal' subjects tolerate blood loss poorly. **1947** S. M. SHANE *Out of this World* viii. 72 You wish you could understand how this miraculous thing called a spinal works. **1960** J. UPDIKE *Rabbit, Run* 203, I have no legs,.. it's the funniest feeling... They gave me a spinal. **1977** M. FRENCH *Women's Room* (1978) i. 68 'It's time for the spinal,' the woman wailed... 'Tell the doctor to come.' **1988** *Acta Anaesthesiol. Belgica* XXXIX. 181/1 The results of these procedures are germane to my opposition to the provision of a spinal for Caesarean section.

**spindle**, n. Add: [II.] [6.] **b.** The vertical rod at the centre of the turntable of a record-player, which keeps the record in place during play; freq. one on which records are stacked for automatic record-changing.

**1940** *Gramophone* Dec. 163/2 This changer is fitted with a spring loaded spindle to minimise the chances of record slip. **1955** D. KEENE *Who was Wilma Lathrop?* ii. 19 Wilma stacked the spindle with records. **1961** E. N. BRADLEY *Records & Gramophone Equipment* i. 22 The most likely cause of wow is a *swinger*—a record whose spindle hole is not exactly central and so turns eccentrically as a result. **1976** *Gramophone* Oct. 695/1 [The record changer's] overarm can be removed and a stub spindle can be substituted for single record use. **1983** J. FULLER *Convergence* xxix. 296 The Beethoven quartets were still on the turntable... He lifted them on the spindle and switched the machine on.

**spinner**, n. Add: [II.] [7.] **g.** A device or machine consisting of a rotating drum which acts as a centrifuge, esp. to remove excess liquid from its contents; *spec.* = SPIN-DRIER n.

**1961** *Guardian* 22 Mar. 8/3 A built-in spin-rinse percolating downwards through the clothes to give an effective rinse, hitherto lacking in the conventional spinner. **1963** A. J. HALL *Textile Sci.* vi. 282 Detergent liquor.. has to be removed in successive stages of mangling (or by hydro-extraction using a 'spinner' or centrifuge). **1971** *Which?* Mar. 81/1 We also bought the Hoover Twosome—a single tub washer with a spinner which can be bought separately and clipped on. **1981** CLARK & SWAINE *Home Managem.* x. 242 Some physical action is still required.. in lifting the washing from the wash tub into the spinner. **1985** *Chicago Tribune* 19 Sept. VII. 6/2 Bloomstrand suggests using a salad spinner for washing and drying lettuce.

‖**spinto** ('spinto), a. (and n.) *Mus.* [It., pa. pple. of *spingere* to push.] Designating a lyrical voice [It. *lirico spinto*] of powerful, dramatic quality; hence (of music, etc.), characterized by this. Also *absol.* as n., one who sings in a *spinto* style.

**1955** *Saturday Rev.* (U.S.) 26 Feb. 62/3 There is plenty of work for both of us. We have different voices. I am a lyric soprano (*Spinto*), not a coloratura. **1961** *Times* 13 May 5/2 Miss Rae Woodland has a strong *spinto* lyric soprano. **1972** *Times* 24 May 15/4 Tannhäuser, Lohengrin, Siegfried and Walther are German *spinto* parts. **1981** LD. HAREWOOD *Tongs & Bones* ii. 42 A fine *spinto* tenor who sang everything. **1987** *Sunday Times* (Colour Suppl.) 14 June 48/4 The operatic landscape is littered with burnt-out *spintos* who sang too much too soon.

**spiraculate** (spɪˈrækjʊleɪt), a. *Zool.* [f. SPIRACUL(UM n. + -ATE² 2.] Possessing a spiracle or spiracles.

**1920** I. F. & W. D. HENDERSON *Dict. Sci. Terms* 299/1 *Spiraculate*.., having spiracles. **1961** *Paleont. Contrib.: Echinodermata* (Univ. Kansas) §3. 19/1 A primitive spiraculate form is judged to be one having paired spiracles (five), four anal deltoids, conical shape of theca, lancet covered by side plates, [etc.]. **1988** *Proc. Kon. Nederlandse Akad. van Wetensch.* B. XCI. 168 Further study of the anatomy of the spiraculate blastoids will further contribute to this problem.

**spitzer** ('spɪtsə(r)), *n.* Also with capital initial. [f. G. *spitz* sharp, pointed, the initial element of *Spitzgeschoss* pointed bullet + -ER[1].] Used *attrib.* to designate a type of cone-shaped bullet with a sharp-pointed end, orig. produced for the German infantry.

**1905** *Field* 2 Dec. 973/2 (*heading*) A .303 Spitzer cartridge. **1916** *United Service Mag.* LIII. 87 The newer type of spitzer ammunition will chamber in the old M. 1888 rifle. **1987** *Guns Rev.* July 499/1 The design emphasis was switching to spitzer bullets both for the military and for the match shooter.

**splatter**, *n.*[2] Restrict labels '*Sc.* and *U.S.*' to sense 1. [2.] For def. read: A spot or patch of colour, etc. splattered on to a surface, a spatter; = SPLASH *n.* 5 a. Also *fig.* (Later examples.)

**1969** *Daily Tel.* 21 Apr. 12/6 Other leather is speckly and *ombre* with tiny splatters of black on grey. **1979** A. BOYLE *Climate of Treason* ii. 43 The British Empire was held to be a solid and impressive entity, a splatter of red across the earth's surface, at least in the school atlases. **1986** P. D. JAMES *Taste for Death* I. xi. 86 The splatter of grease marks above the ancient gas stove,.. the general air of discomfort, uncaring, negligence, dirt.

**spliceosome** ('splaɪsəʊ,səʊm), *n. Cytol.* [f. SPLICE *v.* + -O[1] + -SOME[4].] A large ribonucleoprotein complex involved in splicing mRNA.

**1985** BRODY & ABELSON in *Science* 24 May 967/2 The complex is stable enough to be only slightly modified at 400 m*M* KCl.., and we think that this stability reflects the importance of this structure. We propose that this particle be called a 'spliceosome'. **1985** P. J. GRABOWSKI et al. in *Cell* XLII. 352/1 Since the 60S complex described here may be a cellular entity essential for splicing, we suggest the term spliceosome (splicing body). **1986** *Science* 19 Sept. 1294/2 The structure of the spliceosome is probably the final determinant in the specificity of splicing. **1987** *Nature* 8 Oct. 489/3 The third zone.. binds RNA and has some similarities to the proteins of 'spliceosomes'. **1988** *Sci. Amer.* June 41/1 It turns out that snRNP's [*sc.* small nuclear ribonucleoproteins] and their pre-mRNA substrate probably account for no more than a third to half of the mass of a spliceosome.

**split**, *n.*[1] Sense 4 d in Dict. becomes 4 e. Add: [4.] **d.** *Weight-lifting.* The action or technique of thrusting simultaneously one foot forward and the other backward to support the weight during a lift; the posture or attitude so assumed.

[**1922** W. A. PULLUM *Weight-Lifting made Easy* v. 70 In 'splitting' the feet, distribute the weight principally over the forward foot.] **1955** J. MURRAY *Weight Lifting* iii. 63 There are two basic styles of snatching... The first is the 'split'. **1959** *Muscle Power* May 46/2 Turn the hands under the weight as you lunge past it into the split. **1964** B. WATSON *Tackle Weightlifting this Way* viii. 74 You will find your progress quickens if you make a special point of leaning back slightly.. when you go down in the split. **1975** *Oxf. Compan. Sports & Games* 1095/1 The two main techniques used are the split and squat as in the two hands snatch. **1984** *Weight Lifting* ('Know the Game' Ser.) (ed. 2) 6/3 The lifter may recover in his own time, either from a split or a squat.

**f.** *Sport.* The time taken to complete a portion of a race, esp. recorded by a split-second watch and used as a comparative measure of performance. Cf. *split time* s.v. *SPLIT ppl. a.* 3 a.

**1958** *Track & Field News* Mar. 11/1 For the record, the splits on Delany were 60.9, 2:03.2, and 3:05.3. **1962** *Swimming World* Nov. 4 The pool-side walking coach and the shouted time split can now be replaced by large, easy to read clocks at each end of the pool for intermittent pace references. **1988** *Road Racing & Training* 6/2 It's my guess that we're bang on target—that is 5½-minute-mile pace which should give us a 10 km split of 34:11.

**split**, *ppl. a.* Add: [3.] [a.] *split time Sport* = *SPLIT n.*[1] 4 f.

**1964** J. K. DOHERTY *Mod. Training for Running* 189 This was 1.2 seconds slower than his best time of :22.0 for the 220 and gave him *split times* of :23.2 and :24.2 for the 440, reasonably close to an even pace. **1989** *Los Angeles Times* (Orange County ed.) 14 May III. 16/4 Hundeby.. recorded his best split time ever, 46.8 seconds.

[5.] **c.** Special collocation. **split-finger(ed** *a.* *Baseball*, designating a pitch thrown with the motion of a fastball, but with the index and middle fingers spread wide apart along the seams, so that it has little backspin and dips sharply and deceptively as it approaches the plate; freq. as *split-finger(ed) fastball*; cf. *forkball* s.v. *FORK n.* 16 a.

**1980** *Boston Globe* 1 May 57/3, I was just a fireballer until last spring when the late Freddie Martin who taught Sutter the *split-fingered fastball* .. taught me the change. **1986** *New Yorker* 1 Sept. 86/1 Two pitches.. bounced by Bob Brenly for passed balls in the three-run second (both split-finger specials, by the look of them). **1991** *Baseball Illustr.* XXVII. 110/1 Charlton, a lefthander with a mean split-fingered fastball, started last summer as part of a bullpen troika that called itself The Nasty Boys because of their effect on NL hitters.

**split**, *v.* Sense 4 f in Dict. becomes 4 g. Add: [I.] [4.] **f.** *Cards.* In Pontoon, Poker, etc.: to divide (a pair dealt as the opening cards of a hand) to form two new hands. Also *absol.* orig. *U.S.*

**1866** W. B. DICK *Amer. Hoyle* (rev. ed.) 516 A (the dealer) drew two eights, splitting and drew to both. **1889** *N. Y. Clipper* 26 Oct. 554/1 You had a perfect right to split your openers and draw for a flush. **1930** B. DALTON *Round Games with Cards* 63 Should any player receive a pair.. he may 'split', and bet on each card. **1963** G. F. HERVEY *Handbk. Card Games* 285 If a punter holds a pair.., he may announce his intention to split... The banker, if he holds a pair, may also split. **1981** G. BRANDRETH *Everyman's Indoor Games* 106 An additional rule sometimes encountered is that when a punter is dealt a pair as his first two cards (e.g. two queens) he may 'split' the hand to form two separate hands.

**h.** *Comm.* To divide (a stock) into two or more stocks of the same total value; also const. *up*. Cf. *split-up* s.v. SPLIT-. Chiefly *U.S.*

**1927** *N.Y. Times* 13 July 32/2 Two plans are said to be under consideration. One is to split the stock on a two-for-one basis, and the other contemplates a three-for-one split-up. **1932** B. F. WINKELMAN *Ten Yrs. Wall St.* xviii. 172 Denial was forthcoming in reference to the rumor that the stock would be split up. **1957** G. L. LEFFLER *Stock Market* (ed. 2) xxxi. 511 One of the most certain stimulants to the market price of a stock is an announcement that the directors intend to split the stock. **1966** R. P. KENT *Corporate Financial Managem.* xx. 483 The decision of a corporation whose common stock is selling at $150 to split it up 5 or 1 would appear to be fully in harmony with prevailing thinking. **1982** *Financial Times* 2 July II. 16/1 The directors.. are proposing.. a cash capital repayment of 15p per share..; splitting the existing 25p ordinary shares into new shares of 10p; and the introduction of employee share option schemes.

[II.] [11.] **d.** *Comm.* Of stocks: to be divided into two or more stocks of the same total value. *U.S.*

**1967** *N.Y. Times* (Internat. Ed.) 11 Feb. 9/6 When a stock splits, the number of shares held could double or triple and, in some instances, though not all the price advances after such a split. **1978** J. HYAMS *Pool* xii. 196 The stock had split three times. **1987** *Fortune* 17 Aug. 104/2 The weaker dollar and stronger copper prices boosted MIM Holdings, and the Australian mining company. Both his Hong Kong stocks split.

**spoiler**, *n.* Add: [2.] **d.** *Sound Recording.* An electronic device incorporated into a piece of recording equipment in order to prevent unauthorized recording, esp. of a compact disc by a digital audio tape deck; also (in full *spoiler signal*), an electronic signal, inaudible during normal listening, which ruins the recording of any record or soundtrack into which it is incorporated.

**1979** *New Scientist* 17 May 522/2 The BPI's chimera is a spoiler signal, buried in the original recording ... Spoilers can be made to perform under laboratory conditions, but in practice they are a dead duck. They can, for instance, easily be defeated by a simple anti-spoiler circuit. **1981** *Ibid.* 5 Nov. 359/2 As spoilers and levies are contradictory (one prevents taping while the other taxes it), the government is unlikely to change its mind on a levy while such confusion exists. **1986** *Times* 3 Sept. 23/3 The .. music industry .. wants legislation requiring all dat machines to carry an anti-copying device called a spoiler so that dat cannot pirate copyright material. **1988** *Which?* July 345/3 CBS recently tried to introduce a 'spoiler' system called Copycode. This, it was claimed, would prevent any CD/DAT recording.

**sponge**, *n.*[1] Add: [I.] [1.] **d.** A piece of sponge or similar material (esp. one impregnated with spermicide) inserted into the vagina as a form of barrier contraceptive.

**1823** *To Married of Both Sexes of Working People* (handbill) 3 If the sponge be large enough, that is; as large as a green walnut, or a small apple, it will prevent conception. **1902** F. HOLLICK *Origin of Life* (new ed.) xxxviii. 428 No certain dependence can be placed upon introducing any object into the vagina before association, as a sponge, for instance, which, on being withdrawn, may bring the semen with it. **1933** C. I. B. VOGE *Chem. & Physics of Contraceptives* v. 196 The sponge itself acts as a barrier and the action of coitus forces the spermicide out of the sponge into the vaginal cavity. **1983** *N.Y. Times* 13 Mar. 25/3 Physicians said the sponge proved to be about as effective as the diaphragm in tests on 2,000 women in several countries, including the United States.

[IV.] [13.] [b.] **sponge-fly** = *spongilla fly* s.v. *SPONGILLA n.*

**1901** J. G. NEEDHAM in *Bull N.Y. State Mus.* No. 47. 560, I would suggest that as a common name for the insects of these two genera, spongilla flies, or *sponge flies, would not be inappropriate. **1968** *Oxf. Bk. Insects* 36/1 *Sponge-fly (Sisyra fuscata).* A small, semi-aquatic Lacewing which flies from May to September.

**spongilla** (spʌn'dʒɪlə), *n. Ent.* Also Spongilla. [mod.L. *Spongilla* the name of a genus of freshwater sponges, f. L. *spongia* SPONGE *n.*[1] + mod.L. dim. *-illa.*] *spongilla fly,* any neuropteran insect of the family Sisyridae, whose larvae are parasitic on freshwater sponges; a sponge-fly.

**1901** [see *sponge-fly* s.v. SPONGE *n.*[1] 13 b]. **1942** S. W. FROST *Gen. Entomol.* xiv. 282 The larvae of the Neuroptera are almost entirely predacious. The spongilla flies (Sisyridae) and the mantispids (Mantispidae) alone are parasitic. **1952** J. CLEGG *Freshwater Life* vi. 108 In particular the larvae of

Spongilla flies (*Sisyra*) .. live on the surface of, or embedded in, the sponges. **1956** H. P. CHANDLER in R. L. Usinger *Aquatic Insects Calif.* ix. 235/2 Spongilla-flies are likely to occur wherever the proper species of sponge is to be found. **1972** SWAN & PAPP *Common Insects N. Amer.* xvi. 181 The larvae .. of the Planipennia are terrestrial, excepting the spongillaflies (Sisyridae). **1989** D. J. BORROR et al. *Introd. Study Insects* (ed. 6) xxvii. 366/2 There are six species of spongillaflies in North America.

**spongiocyte** ('spɒndʒɪəusaɪt), *n. Histol.* (now *rare*). [f. SPONGIO- + -CYTE.] **a.** Any cell of the neuroglia.

**1894** P. A. FISH in *Jrnl. Compar. Neurol.* IV. 175 As a convenient correlative *spongiocyte* may used for the glia or neuroglia cell.

**b.** Any cell of a type found in the zona fasciculata of the adrenal cortex, whose cytoplasm contains droplets of lipid which when removed give the cell a spongy appearance.

[**1902** *Comptes Rendus Soc. de Biologie* LIV. 1310 La zone externe de la couche fasciculée des capsules surrénales est constituée, chez le cobaye, par l'agglomération de cellules irrégulières, volumineuses, .. décrites par Guiyesse (Thèse de Doctorat, Paris, 1901). Selon ce dernier, ces cellules dites *Spongiocytes,* ont un corps protoplasmique trabéculaire.] **1930** MAXIMOW & BLOOM *Text-bk. Histol.* xxxiv. 705 The cell appears to be made up of a spongy vacuolated cytoplasm ... Because of this appearance these cells are sometimes called 'spongiocytes'. **1961** *Lancet* 19 Aug. 416/1 Noticeable enlargement of the fasciculata which is made up of spongiocytes full of lipoid. **1985** C. R. LEESON et al. *Textbk. Histol.* (ed. 5) xiv. 452/2 Since lipids are removed by the usual technical procedures, the cells here appear vacuolated and have a spongy appearance; hence sometimes they are called spongiocytes.

**spongo-**, *comb. form.* Add: '**spongocoel** (-siːl) *Biol.* [Gr. κοιλία a hollow, cavity], the central cavity in the body of a sponge.

**1940** L. H. HYMAN *Invertebrates* I. vi. 288 A radially symmetrical vase-like body consisting of a thin wall enclosing a large central cavity, the *spongocoel, opening at the summit by the narrowed osculum. **1988** *Zool. Jrnl. Linn. Soc.* XCIV. 230 Such an arrangement is not conspicuous in other sponge associates, living in the host spongocoel.

**spontaneism** (spɒntə'niːɪz(ə)m, -'neɪɪz(ə)m), *n. Pol.* [ad. F. *spontanéisme* (1968); cf. SPONTANEITY *n.* and -ISM.] In Marxist theory, direct revolutionary action represented by the spontaneous uprising of the proletariat.

**1970** B. BREWSTER tr. *Althusser & Balibar's Reading Capital* (1975) II. v. 141 Kautsky's and Lenin's thesis that Marxist theory is produced by a specific theoretical practice .. and that Marxist theory must be '*imported*' into the proletariat, was absolutely rejected—and all the themes of spontaneism rushed into Marxism through this open breach. **1971** —— tr. *Althusser's Lenin & Philos.* 53 Politically, Lenin is famous for his critique of 'spontaneism', which .. is .. directed against .. a political ideology which, screened by an exaltation of the spontaneity of the masses, exploits it in order to divert it into an incorrect politics. **1974** J. WHITE tr. *Poulantzas's Fascism & Dictatorship* IV. i. 145 *Spontaneism*, i.e. contempt for organization, and the abstract cult of direct and 'spontaneous' action, no matter where or how.

Hence **sponta'neist** *n.* [cf. F. *spontanéiste*], one who advocates spontaneism; also *attrib.* or as *adj.*

**1971** R. GOMBIN in Apter & Joll *Anarchism Today* 19 The end result of this criticism led the 'spontaneists' to some extremely unorthodox conclusions. **1974** J. WHITE tr. *Poulantzas's Fascism & Dictatorship* IV. i. 147 We should .. recognize the quite striking .. collusion between the 'spontaneist' elements, anarcho-syndicalists etc., .. and the fascist parties, which they often joined openly, forming their 'left' wing. **1976** *Guardian Weekly* 19 Sept. 11/1 A variety of Maoist movements is active in France ... Their members, apart from those who for a time espoused the cause of 'spontaneist Maoism' (the so-called 'Spontex-Maos'), have on the whole .. adopted the term Marxist-Leninist. **1977** N. YOUNG *Infantile Disorder?* xi. 216 The radical Spontaneists called the Russian revolution a 'counter revolution'; and the critique of bureaucracy was extended even to Cuba and China.

**spoom** (spuːm), *n.* [Prob. ad. It. *spuma* foam, fizzy soft drink.] A type of sorbet containing fruit juice or wine, whipped egg white, and syrup.
**1907** G. A. ESCOFFIER *Guide Mod. Cookery* (1959) 758 Spoom is a kind of sherbet prepared from a syrup at 20°. **1929** E. J. KOLLIST *French Pastry, Confectionery, & Sweets* xii. 202 *Spoom*, the ingredients and preparation are the same as Sorbet. **1961** N. FROUDE et al. *Montagné's Larousse Gastronomique* 536/1 Spooms are made from fruit juices or wines ... They are served in glasses, like sherbets. **1982** *N.Y. Times* 24 Mar. C15/3 A menu from the Elysée Palace in honor of the King and Queen of Spain in 1905 continued for 29 courses, including something called 'spoom of cherry brandy', which was like a sorbet.

**sport**, *n.*[1] Add: [III.] [11.] [b.] **sportsdrome** [-DROME], a sports complex.
**1964** *Punch* 6 May 655/2, I wouldn't mind a whoppin' \*Sportsdrome. Ice skatin', greyhound racin', the lot. **1980** R. MABEY *Common Ground* II. iii. 161 The conversion of a derelict market garden to a swimming pool or a sportsdrome represents a conversion of countryside into 'occupied' land.

**sporty**, *a.* Sense 2 in Dict. becomes 2 b. Add: [2.] a. Of clothes, etc.: suitable for outdoor sports or for informal wear; designed in a casual sporting style; hence, sportingly fashionable or stylish. orig. *U.S.*
**1913** *Dialect Notes* IV. 22 *Sporty*, attractive, stylish. Usage general in Nebraska. 'I think my shoes are real sporty.' 'What a sporty dress!' **1946** E. O'NEILL *Iceman Cometh* I. 5 Joe Mott is a Negro, about fifty years old, brown-skinned, stocky, wearing a light suit that had once been flashily sporty but is now about to fall apart. **1965** P. O'DONNELL *Modesty Blaise* vi. 67 The dress here was casual and sporty, the people mostly young to middle-aged. **1984** *Footwear News* 4 June 35/2 Domestic resources also said they would focus on casual, sporty, flat and low-heeled shoes.

**spot**, *n.*[1] Add: [III.] [7.] f. In greyhound racing: one hundredth of a second. Usu. in *pl.*
**1977** *Daily Mirror* 16 Mar. 29/3 His time of 29.47s. was thirteen spots faster than that recorded by Gaily Noble two races later. **1986** *Greyhound Mag.* Sept. 14/1 The proof wasn't long in coming, an eight length victory in 29.44, twenty two spots faster than any other heat winner. **1988** *Greyhound Star* June 8/3 He had improved 50 spots in his three qualifying trials and ran second in his first race after coming from fifth place.

**spot**, *v.* Add: [III.] **11.** *Sport.* Const. with dative of person. To give or concede (an advantage or lead) to an opponent. *U.S. colloq.*
**1934** J. T. FARRELL *Young Manhood* x. 163 We'll play fifty straight pool, and I'll spot you ten. **1939** *Sun* (Baltimore) 21 June 14/2 No fighter can spot Mr. Joe Louis his entire offensive program and hope to wrest the world's championship from him. **1972** *Newsweek* 31 July 42/3 After arrogantly spotting Spassky a two-game lead, Fischer had proceeded to

catch up to his opponent. **1985** *Los Angeles Times* 14 July III. 6/2 The Dodgers, .. could have spotted the Cubs an extra out for nine innings, and it wouldn't have mattered.

**spotter**, *n.* Sense 2 d in Dict. becomes 2 e. Add: [2.] d. In gymnastics, trampolining, etc.: a person stationed to prevent possible accident or otherwise to provide safety assistance to the performer.
**1937** *Jrnl. Health & Physical Educ.* Mar. 151/2 For a straddle vault over the long horse the left hand of the spotter holds the arm of the performer while the right hand pushes hard on the buttocks. **1964** *Simple Gymnastics* ('Know the Game' Ser.) (ed. 3) 40/2 The spotter stations himself near the performer so that if anything untoward happens he can quickly move in to prevent a nasty fall. **1974** *Rules of Game* ii. 41 Spotters are compulsory at each side and end of the trampoline to ensure the safety of competitors. They are forbidden to speak to competitors. **1987** *Bodybuilding* Oct. 73/1 Always have an adult spotter around to retrieve the weights.

‖**Sprachbund** ('ʃpraːxbʊnt), *n.* Linguistics. [Ger., f. *Sprache* speech, language + *Bund* union, tr. Russ. *yazykovýĭ soyúz* (N. S. Trubetzkoy, in *Evraziĭskiĭ Vremennik* (1923) III. 116), f. *yazýk* language + *soyúz* union.] A linguistic community containing members of different language families which have developed some common characteristics through geographical proximity; the process of linguistic change producing this.
**1943** H. V. VELLEN in *Pacific Northwest Q.* XXXIV. III. 271 From a synchronic point of view, Salish and Sahaptin belong to one *linguistic area*—if I may thus translate Prince Trubetzkoy's term *Sprachbund*. **1975** P. FRIEDRICH *Proto-Indo-European Syntax* 39 The pertinent portion of this Eurasian syntactic *Sprachbund* is dominated by Caucasian, Altaic, and Dravidian languages. **1980** *Amer. Speech* 1976 LI. 254 An author writing a book dealing with diachronic linguistics in the 1970s ought to include a discussion of contact phenomena such as bilingualism, *Sprachbund*, and pidgin and creole languages. **1984** *English World-Wide* V. 203 The processes, context and content operating at the time had led to an enormous variety of language forms in the Sprachbund, including features which have since died out, continued, or changed in form or function.

**spread**, *n.*[1] Add: [I.] [2.] j. *N. Amer. Sport.* The difference between the number of points (goals, etc.) scored by competing teams in a match, *esp.* a winning margin; *spec.* in *Betting*, = *point spread* s.v. \*POINT *n.*[1] D. 19; also, = *goal difference* s.v. GOAL *n.* 6.
**1945** *Newsweek* 12 Feb. 78/2 A point system was established in hoop betting, and bookmakers protected themselves with a two-point 'spread'. **1951** *Chicago Daily News* 17 Jan. 34/3 The former player said he would not know until before the game what the final betting 'spread'—the difference in the point score—would be. **1968** *Globe & Mail* (Toronto) 17 Feb. 39/7 If Canada ties Russians, Swedes beat Czechs—Russia wins gold on goal spread, Canada takes silver ... Russia has the best spread—33. **1980** *Washington Star* 20 Nov. C7 Eagles and Falcons (both 9-2), continue to share the NFL's best record at beating the spreads. **1988** *Ice Hockey News Rev.* 19 Nov. (Suppl.) 3/1 The brilliant Czech did it again .. with a marker which opened up a 2 goal spread in Flyers favour.

**spreadsheet**, *n.* Add: Hence **'spreadsheeting** *n.*, the provision or use of a spreadsheet program.
**1983** *Philadelphia Inquirer* 17 Apr. P9/2 Enough software for either word processing or electronic spreadsheeting. **1986** W. SAFIRE in *N.Y. Times Mag.*

1 June 14/5 Some of the knowledge for achievement—arithmetic, spreadsheeting, grammar —can be delegated to machines.

**spring**, n.¹ Add: [II.] [6.] i. *transf*. The initial stages of a period of political liberalization, esp. in a Communist state; the first steps in a programme of political and economic reform. Freq. with qualifying word, esp. *Prague Spring* s.v. *PRAGUE *n*. 3.
[**1905** G. GAPON *Story of My Life* x. 133 That temporary change in the attitude of the Government and the educated class toward each other which has been called the political spring-time of Russia, and which began [in 1904] with the succession of Prince Sviatopolk Mirski to the old post of Plehve.] **1917** M. J. OLGIN *Soul of Russian Revolution* ix. 98 The second half of 1904, known as 'Spring', was .. marked by a strong Liberal movement. *Ibid.* 101 December 12th .. was the end of the 'Spring' ... The semi-official *Moscow Courier* hailed the end of the 'notorious Spring'. **1956** *Summary World Broadcasts* (B.B.C.) 25 Oct. II A. 15 The great rehabilitation of truth, the break with political lies—this is the first essential characteristic of the Polish spring in October. **1968**, etc. [see *Prague Spring* s.v. *PRAGUE *n*. 3]. **1968** *Problems of Communism* Nov.-Dec. 1 Czechoslovakia. The brief spring of 1968. **1982** *Time* 11 Jan. 25/2 The church has no illusions about restoring the 'Polish Spring' of Solidarity, but it is seeking to make life under martial law as bearable as possible for the Polish people. **1988** *Lit. Rev.* Aug. 61/3 In 1979, President Chung-hee was assassinated and the short-lived 'Seoul Spring' erupted.

**sprint**, v. Add: [2.] c. With adv. accusative of distance.
**1901** G. B. SHAW *Admirable Bashville* II. 305 But many felt that Byron shewed bad taste In .. Sprinting a hundred yards to show the crowd The perfect pink of his condition. **1982** *Time* 18 Oct. 64/3 When I trained, I wasn't used to sprinting the last two miles.

**sprinter**, n. Add: 2. A vehicle designed to travel rapidly over short distances; *spec*. a type of passenger train making short, frequent journeys at speed.
**1984** *Practical Boat Owner* Feb. 44/1 The boat herself is a light displacement sprinter. **1984** *Times* 20 Nov. 4/5 The new 'Sprinter' train is said to be fast, quiet and comfortable. **1986** *Scotsman* 31 July 5/4 The introduction of sprinter-class diesels .. showed that their intention would be to make the most of the line. **1989** *Brit. Business* 14 Apr. 15/2 The Sprinters will be used on the busy tourist routes .. [and will] be capable of running at 120 kilometres per hour.

**spruce-up** ('spruːsʌp), n. colloq. (orig. *U.S.*). [f. vbl. phr. *to spruce up*: see SPRUCE *v.*¹ 1 b.] The action or process of sprucing up; a cleaning- or tidying-up, refurbishment, renovation. Also *fig.*
**1946** E. O'NEILL *Iceman Cometh* I. 50, I must have my shoes soled and heeled and shined ... A general spruce-up. **1974** *News & Reporter* (Chester, S. Carolina) 22 Apr. 6-A/5 (Advt.), Is it time for a spruce-up loan? .. Is it time to start saving for a new chair, room or house? **1978** *Detroit Free Press* 16 Apr. F8/3 (Advt.), Spring spruce up sale. We do small and large paint jobs. **1986** *N.Z. Listener* 15 Feb. 31/2 Sports, too, could do with a bit of a spruce-up.

**spudgel** ('spʌdʒəl), n. dial. (chiefly *Newfoundland*). [Of uncertain origin, but perh. related to SPUD *n*., SPUDDLE *v*.]
First recorded in Newfoundland sources, though the Eng. dial. uses doubtless predate this.]
A small bowl or bucket with a long handle used for scooping water (esp. when bailing out a boat) and for similar purposes.

**1775** G. CARTWRIGHT *Jrnl*. 4 June (1911) 159 The boat proved so leaky, that the spudgel was scarce ever out of hand. **1891** G. SWEETMAN *Gloss. Words Wincanton* 13 *Spudgel*, .. a bowl with hood and handle. **1937** *Beaver* June 23/1 The engine .. pumped the water out of the boat, which with the help of a spudgel kept the level sufficiently low. **1975** V. BUTLER *Little Nord Easter* 38, I had two big long-handled spudgels aboard. I said 'Jack, here, take one of those and .. if you ever worked in your life, work now, if you don't want to drown.' **1988** J. LAVERS *Dict. Isle of Wight Dial*. 85 *Spudgel*, a bucket with a long handle used for baling out water or liquid manure.

**spunk**, n. Add: [5.] d. *Austral. slang*. A sexually attractive person; freq. as *young spunk*.
**1978** J. ROWE *Warlords* 205, I can always round up a boatload of horny looking young spunks, but there's no guarantees for old gits like us from the amateurs. **1982** *Sydney Morning Herald* 18 Sept. 1/2 Teenagers still rage at weekends, check out spunks of both sexes and try to avoid hassles with the olds. **1985** *Truckin'* *Life* Apr. 113/2 Just as we're pullin' through the outskirts of town, there it is; a right spunk, a nubile nymph lookin' for somewhere to go and no-one to take her there. **1986** *Sunday Mail* (Brisbane) 25 Oct. 80/5 No matter how skittish she might feel, old girls of 59 mustn't even flutter an eyelash at a young spunk.

**spurion** ('spjʊəriən), n. Particle Physics. [a. G. *Spurion* (Dürr & Heisenberg 1961, in *Zeitschr. f. Naturforsch*. A. XVI. 726): see SPURIOUS *a.*, -ON¹ 1 a.] Any hypothetical subatomic particle introduced to facilitate mathematical calculations but having no physical reality (orig. one with isospin ½ and hypercharge ±1).
**1961** *Zeitschr. für Naturforsch*. A. XVI. 726 The results of the calculations may be interpreted by describing the strange particles as composed of ordinary particles and a 'spurion' taken from the groundstate 'vacuum'. **1963** *Nuovo Cimento* XXVIII. 133 These 'bosons' do not have any Lorentz properties, *i.e.* mass and spin ... They are called 'spurions' because of their similarity to the particle introduced by Wentzel, D'Espagnat and Prentki in connection with weak interactions. **1983** *Nucl. Physics* B. CCXXII. 280 We must deal with diagrams which involve spurions of more than one type. **1986** P. C. WEST *Introd. Supersymmetry & Supergravity* xviii. 194 We will .. use the spurion technique to investigate the divergence induced by soft terms.

**squad**, n.¹ Add: [4.] d. *ellipt*. for *squad car*. Police slang.
**1974** *Amer. Speech* 1971 XLVI. 78 Police sedan, police car, squad car, squad, prowl car. **1980** 'A. BLAISDELL' *Consequence of Crime* (1981) x. 170 When he passed the last window he broke into a run, and dived for the squad on the passenger side. **1984** 'D. SHANNON' *Destiny of Death* (1985) vii. 148 Bill Moss, riding a squad on night watch, .. picked up a man lying against the curb in the street.

**Squarial** ('skwɛəriəl), n. temporary. Also squarial and (in early use) squaerial. [Blend of SQUARE *a*. and AERIAL *n*.] A proprietary name for a type of diamond-shaped dish aerial for receiving satellite television broadcasts.
The company that produced the aerials, British Satellite Broadcasting, merged with Sky Television in Dec. 1990, and production of the aerial ceased.
**1988** *Daily Tel*. 3 Aug. 4/4 British Satellite Broadcasting .. has exclusive rights to the 'squaerial'. .. Flat and diamond-shaped, the 12-inch aerial can be fixed to the wall of a house. **1988** *Broadcast* 2 Sept. 12/3 The fanfare which surrounded BSB's launch of the 'squarial' last month has been dulled by

allegations . . that the square receiving dish may never appear as a working product. **1989** *Times* 16 Feb. 3/1 More than a million British homes will have dishes or 'squarials' by the end of 1989. **1989** *Independent* 20 July 1 British Satellite Broadcasting admitted that the 'squarial' satellite TV receiver featured in its advertising may never see the light of day. **1990** *Daily Tel.* 15 Oct. 19/4 [He] has secreted his BSB squarial on a rear chimney.

**squark** (skwɔːk, skwɑːk), *n.*[2] *Particle Physics*. [f. S(UPER- + QUARK *n.*[1]] The supersymmetric counterpart of a quark, with spin 0 instead of ½.
   **1982** *Physics Lett.* B. CXIV. 235 A non-vanishing baryon asymmetry can be generated by the decay of coloured Higgs bosons and Higgs fermions into quarks and squarks. **1984** *New Scientist* 17 May 16/2 Supersymmetric theorists . . have had to make up lots of new names for the unseen 'sparticles', such as the spin-0 supersymmetric quarks and leptons ('squarks' and 'sleptons'). **1986** *Nature* 14 Aug. 592/3 The Tevatron should see squarks, the superpartners of quarks, if their masses are less than 200-300 GeV.

**squash**, *n.*[1] Add: Hence **'squasher** *n.*[2] *U.S.*, one who plays squash rackets, a squash player.
   **1977** *Dun's Rev.* Sept. 73/3 A squasher can belong to his Broad Street Club for $50 a year plus $8 per prime-time half hour. **1987** *Christian Science Monitor* 16 Nov. 18/4 Veteran squashers, however, teach more than how to win trophies.

**squat**, *n.*[1] Add: **9.** Special Comb. **squat thrust**, a physical exercise in which the legs are thrust backwards to their full extent from a squat position; also, = *BURPEE *n.*
   **1950** K. F. WELLS *Kinesiology* xxiii. 415 The *squat-thrust, both with and without the dip is commonly included among conditioning exercises. **1988** *Physiques Internat.* Nov. 55/1, I still hold World Records in two events, the arm dips which I managed 100 reps in one minute, and the squat thrusts which still stands at 118 reps in the same time.

**squat**, *v.* Add: [II.] [6.] **e.** In Weight-lifting, to perform a squatting exercise while holding a specified weight. Usu. const. *with* (the weight) or with adv. accusative indicating the weight or the number of times the exercise is repeated.
   **1956** *Muscle Power* Mar. 21 Anyone who . . squats 10 reps with 770 lbs . . is liable to accomplish the incredible. **1958** *Ibid.* Feb. 7/2 We also thought . . that he could not possibly do much more when he was squatting with a mere (to himself) 800 lbs. **1978** *Globe & Mail* (Toronto) 2 Feb. 48/1 Wighton . . can squat more than 400 pounds after working out much of the summer in a universal gym. **1985** *Bodypower* Oct. 26/2 The new professional sensation Rich Gaspari squats with 700 lbs for reps! **1986** *Flex* Feb. 83/2 Tina Woodley . . squatted 325 pounds for 6 reps the day after her show!

**squawk**, *n.* Add: **3.** An identification signal given out by an aircraft: see sense *3 of the vb. *slang* (orig. *U.S.*).
   **1975** *Aviation Week* 12 May 55/1 There was no reply from, or further contact with, N6876P and the squawk of N6876P disappeared from the radarscope. **1982** J. GARDNER *For Special Services* i. 12 Ninety-five seconds after the first 'squawk', the three red zeros disappeared from the screen. **1987** *Pilot* Apr. 11/2 We were given a squawk and identified and told to expect radar vectors to Runway 03R. **1987** *Independent* 30 May 3/6 Equipment cannot automatically decode an airliner's identity signal—or 'squawk'—into its call sign and height.

**squawk**, *v.* Add: **3.** *trans.* Of an aircraft, etc.: to transmit or emit (an identification signal), enabling the plane's position to be plotted on a

radar screen. Cf. SQUAWK BOX *n.* b. *slang* (orig. *U.S.*).
   **1956** W. A. HEFLIN *U.S. Air Force Dict.* 485/1 *Squawk*, . . of an airborne IFF set: to emit a signal. *Slang.* **1963** *Amer. Speech* XXXVIII. 120 *Squawk*, . . to transmit signals by using a parrot. 'Roger, we are now squawking mode 3, code 30 on our parrot.' **1967** R. J. SERLING *President's Plane is Missing* iii. 55 'Washington Center, Air Force One Squawk ident.' 'Roger, identing.' **1982** J. GARDNER *For Special Services* i. 11 His eyes remained on the huge radarscope . . . The indicator numbers 12 —'squawked' by the Boeing's transponder—flicked off and changed. **1988** *Pilots Internat.* Nov. 39/1 Usual transmission is 4321, until requested to squawk a particular code.

**squeal**, *v.* Add: [4.] **b.** To cause (something, esp. the tyres of a motor vehicle) to make a squealing noise.
   **1965** J. A. MICHENER *Source* 5 As the two friends talked a jeep squealed its brakes outside the customs area. **1970** *Current Slang* (Univ. S. Dakota) IV. 19 *Hot dog*, one who shows off by squealing his tires and gunning his motor as he drives around among his friends. **1975** M. DUFFY *Capital* iii. 119 A lone car squealed its tyres through his gate. **1982** J. D. MACDONALD *Cinnamon Skin* xx. 218 The plane squealed its tires on the runway.

**squeeze**, *n.* Add: [2.] **c.** A close friend, esp. a girlfriend or lover; a sweetheart. Cf. *main squeeze* s.v. MAIN *a.* 11. *slang* (chiefly *N. Amer.*).
   **1980** E. A. FOLB *Runnin' down some Lines* 255 *Squeeze*, close friend; favorite male or female lover or companion. **1985** *Age* (Victoria) 19 Sept. 2/3 The 'Vice' squad speaks in a verbose and near unintelligible jargon: 'the boss's new squeeze' [etc.]. **1986** R. FORD *Sportswriter* ix. 241, I would love to grill him about his little seminary squeeze, but he would be indignant.

**squid**, *n.*[1] Sense 5 in Dict. becomes 6. Add: **5.** A lead disc used as a puck in the game of octopush.
   **1969** *Triton* Apr. 58/1 Octopush—the Rules 1. The squid must never be handled whilst a match is in play. **1971** *Observer* 23 May 19/2 (*caption*) Octopush . . the name of the game for skindivers. Players try to push a lead puck (called a squid) through the other team's goal (gulley). **1985** *Daily Tel.* 24 June 20/4 (*caption*) Players use masks, fins and snorkels as they move a lead weight (the squid) about on the bottom of the pool with wooden or plastic pushers. **1988** *Observer* 3 Apr. 17/1 Two teams of eight swimmers armed with wooden pushers attempt to propel a 3lb lead disc, or squid, along the bottom of a swimming pool and into their opponents' goal.

**squillion** ('skwɪljən), *n.* (and *a.*) *colloq.* [Arbitrary alteration of *million*, *billion*, etc.; cf. ZILLION *n.*] **a.** Hyperbolically: a very large number of millions; an enormous number. Freq. as *adj.*
   **1943** Z. N. HURSTON in *Amer. Mercury* LVII. 456/2 The deep blue sea . . was a pearly blue, like ten squillion big pearl jewels dissolved in running gold. **1982** *Computerworld* 23 Aug. 48/3 (*caption*) Huh! It doesn't even go up to a zillion squillion. **1986** *Independent* 16 Dec. 14/3 The Prime Minister intends to fill the gap between the Queen's Christmas broadcast and the Boxing Day walk by reading Sir Frank Layfield's squillion-word report on Sizewell. **1988** *Smash Hits* 19 Oct. 79/1 Squillions of francs . . were spent.
   **b.** *ellipt.* for 'a squillion dollars (pounds, etc.)'; a very large amount of money.
   **1986** *Weekend Australian* 26 Apr. 15/1 There's a quantum leap between making squillions out of exporting things where no particular care is required

to exporting manufactured goods. **1987** *Financial Rev.* (Sydney) 18 Aug. 24 (*heading*) Goward chases his first squillion with Westmex.

Hence **squillio'naire** *n.*, one who is extraordinarily wealthy; a multimillionaire.

**1979** *United States 1980/81* (Penguin Travel Guides) 547 Objects are exhibited alongside Rembrandts, Titian's 'The Rape of Europa', and other pieces collected with the advice of Bernard Berenson, the art scholar who coined the term 'squillionaire'. **1989** *Private Eye* 1 Sept. 8/1 Several of the squillionaires at the back start shouting abusive remarks about the morality of queue-barging.

**squinch**, *v.* Add: Hence **'squinched** *ppl. a.* (also with *up*).

**1899** B. W. GREEN *Word-bk. Virginia Folk-Speech* 359 *Squinched-up*, to have a squinched-up look, to be thin and shrivelled; a lean and shrunken look. **1941** AGEE & EVANS *Let Us now praise Famous Men* III. 399 Annie Mae is all squinched up on the bed like the devil was after her. **1954** J. STEINBECK *Sweet Thursday* 42 There are squinched up mean walks and blustering walks, shy creeping walks, but this was a gay walk. **1955** F. O'CONNOR *Wise Blood* xi. 185 She brushed it back .. looking down into his squinched face. **1988** A. TYLER *Breathing Lessons* (1989) I. ii. 54 She caught sight of the squinched blue chicory flower lolling above one ear.

**squinny**, *v.*[1] Add: Hence **'squinnying** *ppl. a.*

**1973** G. M. BROWN *Magnus* iv. 75 Creak of parchment. Old crafty squinnying eyes. Old parchment mouth moving. **1984** *Listener* 9 Aug. 19/2, I noticed, through my squinnying gaze, a pink bulky man in an electric-blue suit.

**squish**, *n.* Add: 4. *Linguistics.* A continuum or linear progression held to exist between categories (esp. parts of speech) normally considered discrete.

**1972** J. R. Ross in *Proc. 8th Regional Meeting Chicago Linguistic Soc.* 317 To show that a squish exists, I will cite a number of grammatical processes which work most for verbs, less for adjectives, and least for nouns. **1976** *Language* LII. 392 We have a gradience or squish depending on two hierarchies. **1988** *Amer. Speech* LXIII. 342 Some hitherto common count nouns will move into the title category, or at least further towards the titleness end of the squish.

**squishy**, *a.* Add: Hence **'squishiness** *n.*

**1929** R. O. PROWSE *Prophet's Wife* I. i. 9 The track was fairly dry, for no rain had lately fallen: but in places it betrayed her to a squishiness of puddles and soft black mud. **1979** *London Rev. Bks.* 25 Oct. 1/4 The novel has joined the ranks of those .. novels whose pride and purpose seems to consist in establishing the dullness of experience, its inherent squishiness.

**squit**, *n.*[3] *dial.* and *colloq.* [f. SQUIT *v.*; perh. related to SQUIT *n.*[1]] Diarrhoea. Now only in pl. *the squits.* See SQUITTER *n.* 1.

**1841** C. H. HARTSHORNE *Salopia Antiqua* 576 *Squitt, squitters*, looseness of the body. **1976** M. MAGUIRE *Scratchproof* xi. 170, I thought you had me in the car ... You fair gave me the squits. **1988** D. LODGE *Nice Work* IV. iii. 166 'Olive oil doesn't agree with me.' 'Gives you the squits, does it?'

‖ **Staatsoper** ('ʃtɑːtsoːpər), *n.* [Ger., lit. 'state opera'.] The principal opera house in Vienna, which is partially subsidized by the Austrian government; *transf.*, its resident company. Cf. *Volksoper* s.v. VOLK *n.* 3 b.

**1928** J. A. MAHAN *Vienna of Yesterday & Today* ix. 210 Two opera houses, the Staatsoper .. and the Volksoper . . are in use every day of the season. **1931** J. D. NEWTH *Austria* ix. 167 The Opera—to be exact the Staatsoper—for with the Burgtheater it has always been a state undertaking—is open all the year round except for six weeks in the summer. **1964** ROSENTHAL & WARRACK *Conc. Oxf. Dict. Opera* 423/2 In 1918 the Hofoper became the Staatsoper, and the music and artistic director was Franz Schalk, who held the position until 1929. **1968** *Vogue* 15 Apr. 23/1 Theoretically, the difference between the Wells and the Garden is that between *Volksoper* and *Staatsoper* in Vienna. **1989** *Encycl. Brit.* XIV. 489/2 The Vienna Staatsoper.., which was completely rebuilt after World War II, ranks today with La Scala in Milan and the Hamburg and Munich operas.

**Stabex** ('steɪbɛks), *n. Comm.* Also **stabex.** [Shortened f. *stabilization of export prices.*] A scheme operated by the European Community guaranteeing developing countries in Africa, the Caribbean, and the Pacific a minimum price for staple commodities in the event of a shortfall in their export earnings.

**1975** *Church Times* 21 Feb. 12/5 To be formally ratified in Togo on February 28, the agreement contains major concessions—including the entirely new 'stabex' .. scheme .. to protect peasant famers and others against the hardships of weather failure and adverse price variation. **1978** J. PAXTON *Dict. Europ. Econ. Community* (rev. ed.) 148 A.C.P. bananas were to enjoy duty-free access and were also to be included in the Stabex scheme. **1983** *Financial Times* 4 Oct. 16/1 It offers some protection against declining prices for a range of ACP commodities through the Stabex mechanism. **1988** D. LEONARD *Pocket Guide Europ. Community* III. xxii. 161 A particular feature of the second and third Lomé Conventions has been the inclusion of a stabilisation fund (known as Stabex) ... Altogether 48 basic commodities are included, and in 1986 some 25 payments were made from the fund, totalling just under Ecu150 mn.

**stabilator** ('steɪbɪleɪtə(r)), *n. Aeronaut.* [f. STABIL(IZER *n.* + ELEV)ATOR *n.*] A control surface on the tail of an aircraft, which combines the functions of a horizontal stabilizer and an elevator.

**1954** *Aeroplane* 24 Dec. 919/2 The control system [of the F-84F] .. includes .. a one-piece slab-type tailplane, which Republic call a 'Stabilator'. **1956** W. A. HEFLIN *U.S. Air Force Dict.* 485/2 *Stabilator*, a one-piece stabilizer mounted on the top of the vertical stabilizer. **1978** D. B. THURSTON *Design for Flying* xii. 185 On some aircraft the stabilizer and elevator are combined into one surface, referred to as an all-moving horizontal tail or stabilator. **1987** *Flight Internat.* 10 Oct. 27/1 By selecting the stabilator (the adjustable elevator at the tail of the Apache) to 20°, the attitude could be altered sufficiently to give me increased forward visibility as we settled among the trees.

**stabilism** ('steɪbɪlɪz(ə)m), *n. Geol.* [f. L. *stābil-is* stable + -ISM, after *MOBILISM *n.*] The hypothesis that the continents are not capable of lateral movement (opposed to the theory of continental drift). So **'stabilist** *n.*, one who believes in stabilism or in its application in a particular case; also as *adj.*

**1973** A. HALLAM *Revolution in Earth Sci.* iii. 26 Leading Dutch geologists working in the East Indies found that Wegener's ideas made more sense than those of the 'stabilists' in accounting for the complexities of structure. *Ibid.* viii. 108 About the only common element that one can extract from such a hotchpotch of views is a belief in a 'stabilist' rather than a 'mobilist' Earth. **1976** *Nature* 2 Sept. 83/2 The stabilists believe that the Caribbean Sea is an ancient oceanic structure. *Ibid.* 83/3 Such surveys .. may resolve many of the problems of the stabilism-mobilism controversy.

**Stableford** ('steɪb(ə)lfəd), *n. Golf.* Also **stableford**. [The name of Dr. Frank B. G. Stableford (*c*1870-1959), medical practitioner, who devised this method of scoring.] Used *attrib.* and *absol.* with reference to a kind of stroke-play competition in which points are awarded according to the number of strokes taken to complete each hole.

**1937** H. LONGHURST *Golf* ii. ix. 273 The Stableford system gains yearly in popularity, as more and more people come to understand its working and to realize . . that it is not so complicated as it seems. **1951** *Rules of Golf* (ed. 16) 93 Play under the Stableford system is really a form of Bogey Competition. **1979** *Golf Illustr.* 15 Feb. 5/3 They came up with six sub-par net scores in a heart-warming round that totalled 41 Stableford points which earned them first place in the 18-hole fourball competition. **1987** *Golf World* Aug. 29/3 He is also the instigator of the Terry Wallace Charity Shield golf challenge, a nine-hole stableford open to visually handicapped players.

**stack,** *n.* Add: [**1.**] **g.** A vertical arrangement of public-address or hi-fi equipment.

**1971** *Melody Maker* 9 Oct. 30/6 Semi-pro bands cannot expect to be accepted immediately . . . If you have something to offer someone will eventually take notice. Then . . is the time to buy your Les Paul and 200 watt stack. **1984** *Sounds* 29 Dec. 4/5 First prize of a Marshall 3210 compact stack. **1986** *Video Today* Apr. 4/1 (Advt.), It'll fill any cassette deck's gap in a midi Hi-Fi stack.

[**5.**] [**b.**] Before 'also' read: *a vertical overhead exhaust-pipe on a diesel-powered truck or similar vehicle* (*slang,* orig. *U.S.*).

**1961** *Amer. Speech* XXXVI. 273 Northwest Truck Drivers' Language . . . *Broom stack; dirty stack,* a stack that is flaming or smoking. **1971** M. TAK *Truck Talk* 154 *Stack,* a vertical exhaust pipe on a diesel rig. **1987** *Truck & Driver* July 27/1 Stacks carry the exhaust gases away from the driver so he will not be choked when operating the external controls of the crane.

**stacked,** *ppl. a.* Senses 6, 7 in Dict. become 7, 8. Add: **6.** *Computing.* Of a task: placed in a queue for subsequent processing. Of (a stream of) data, etc.: consisting of or stored in a stack.

**1958** *Communications Assoc. Computing Machinery* Oct. 19 A sizeable subgroup is writing a common monitor system which . . will run stacked jobs of all kinds in three distinct phases. **1969** P. B. JORDAIN *Condensed Computer Encycl.* 483 An operating system that allows for stacked jobs has provision for recognizing and acting on end-of-job/start-of-next-job indications in the input. **1981** *Computing Surveys* XIII. 359/1 Means must be provided to recognize whether a stacked quantity is a pointer. **1989** *Rhythm* Apr. 54/3 The *Impulse* is a . . trigger to MIDI interface . . featuring . . stacked MIDI note numbers.

**staff,** *v.* Add: **staffed** *ppl. a.,* provided or peopled with staff, manned.

**1888** MRS. H. WARD *R. Elsmere* III. xxxiii. 54 A powerful church of the new type, staffed by friends and pupils of Pusey, rose in the centre of R—. **1976** P. R. WHITE *Planning for Public Transport* iv. 83 Service times per passenger, either from staffed office or machine, are thus reduced.

**stage,** *n.* Add: [**9.**] **d.** *Sport.* Any of the sections into which a long-distance race or rally is divided. In quot. 1943, a racing competition for a particular category of contestants (*U.S.*).

**1943** *Sun* (Baltimore) 13 Aug. 14/5 The stage for three-year-old trotters was won by Camay. **1958** *Health & Strength* 19 June 8/1 There was an impressive crowd to watch the stage winner. **1967** *Guardian* 14 July 1/2 Tommy Simpson, the British cyclist, died early this evening after collapsing during a mountain stage of the Tour de France. **1977** G.

NICHOLSON *Great Bike Race* (1978) viii. 91 He had risen to seventh overall, and this was still his position on the morning of July 13 when the Tour set out on the thirteenth stage from Marseille to Carpentras. **1986** *Grand Prix Internat.* July 10/3 The equally notorious Ouninpohja stage will be shortened and the faster sections will be by-passed.

**stagflationary** (stæg'fleɪʃən(ə)rɪ), *a. Econ.* [f. STAGFLATION *n.* + -ARY[1], after *inflationary.*] Of, pertaining to, characterized by, or involving stagflation.

**1971** *Sunday Times* 27 June 54/6 The antitrust movement could play a part in curing the stagflationary disease—the combination of rising prices and rising unemployment. **1980** *Economist* 25 Oct. 98/3 How France achieved that . . is one of the unsung puzzles of the stagflationary 1970s. **1989** *Times* 22 Apr. 20/4 Robert Fleming, the broker, says sell the shares because of what it describes as the 'stagflationary' outlook for the British economy.

**stagger,** *n.*[1] Add: [**1.**] **c.** A preliminary, unpolished rehearsal or run-through of a play, television programme, etc. Also *stagger through. Theatr.* and *Broadcasting slang.*

**1964** *Sound & Vision Broadcasting* Summer 31/2 The voice of the producer . . requesting opening shots for a 'stagger through'. **1972** R. TYRRELL *Work of Televison Journalist* vii. 124 The first run-through of a programme is often referred to—advisedly—as a 'stagger' . . . After the first stagger, there is a coffee break for the studio crew and an opportunity for the director to follow up some of his notes. **1975** *Time Out* 7 Feb. 48/3 John McGrath's 'The Fish in the Sea' . . has qualities which even a stagger through twelve days before opening night in an upstairs pub room with half the cast going down with flu . . can't obscure.

**staircase** ('stɛəkeɪs), *v.* [f. the *n.*] *intr.* Of a tenant: to purchase a freehold incrementally through a shared ownership scheme.

**1988** *Times* 20 Sept. 13/3 An increasing number of rural landowners are prepared to give, or sell at well below market value, sites to housing associations for the provision of affordable homes for village people. Some of them, however, are deterred from doing so because of the right of the first occupant to 'staircase'. **1989** *Guardian* 6 May (Weekend Suppl.) 27/3 When buyers 'staircase', they will take on more of the home at the prevailing market price rather than the original amount, so the housing association reaps the benefit of increasing values. **1990** *Sunday Correspondent* 6 May 43/4 Career progression means they can usually afford to staircase to outright ownership.

**staircasing** ('stɛəkeɪsɪŋ), *vbl. n.* (Formerly at STAIRCASE *n.*) [f. STAIRCASE *n.* and *v.* + -ING[1].] **a.** The supplying or providing with a staircase or staircases. **b.** *transf.* and *fig.* Structural organization characterized by staged rises in elevation (also in sense of the vb.).

**1729** in Willis & Clark *Cambridge* (1886) I. xii. 563 At a Congregation . . agreed to proceed in Covering flooring sashing staircasing of the new Building. **1911** *Chambers's Jrnl.* Apr. 212/2 The hills are huge fellows, and the Douro's gorges are thrilling; but the latter come before and after the miles of too regular staircasing east and west of Peso da Regoa. **1988** *Daily Tel.* 15 Aug. 2/1 The countryside groups condemn the Government's refusal to act against 'staircasing' which they say is leading to a shortage of homes to rent in rural areas.

**stalish** ('steɪlɪʃ), *a.* [f. STALE *a.*[1] + -ISH.] Somewhat stale.

**1743** W. ELLIS *Mod. Husbandman* Aug. ii. 5 Having ready his March strong stalish Beer. *a***1889** BROWNING *New Poems* (1914) 71 Hang your kickshaws and your made-dishes Give me bread and cheese and radishes—Even stalish bread and baddish cheese. **1983** R. FULLER in *Listener* 22 Sept. 19/1 Partridge has a good few stale or stalish or forgotten Martian comparisons.

**stalk**, *n.*[1] Add: **[5.] f.** In a motor vehicle: a flexible arm holding the mounting by which a seat-belt latch is secured.
**1974** *Motoring Which?* Oct. 133/2 [The] safety belts didn't fit very well. The centre stalk was too long—it could rest at the side of your stomach. **1988** *Daily Tel.* 14 Oct. 3/2 When he examined a Datsun car, .. he unscrewed the console between the two stalks for the seat belts and several driving licences fell out.

**stalky**, *a.* Add: **2.** Of wine: retaining a marked tannic, unripe taste from excessive contact with the grape-stalks during production.
**1967** A. LICHINE *Encycl. Wines* 508/2 *Stalky.* Hardness in wine from the tannin in the stalks. **1975** P. V. PRICE *Taste of Wine* x. 183/3 A markedly stalky wine tends to be a little unbalanced, sometimes unripe, the inner toughness unlikely to develop into a harmonious wine. **1983** *Daily Tel.* 21 Feb. 14/5 It's a bit 'stalky' but quite drinkable. **1989** *Financial Times* 7 Oct. p. xv/5 Ratcliffe and Daniel told the Chileans to forget about their beloved old oak vats and rely on stainless steel; hence the fresh, slightly stalky but fruity taste of their 1987 Campo dei Fiori.
Hence **'stalkiness** *n.*
**1972** *Bottlers' Year Bk. 1972-73* 402 *Stalkiness* (*Wines*), a peculiar harshness due to the employment of too much pressure during squeezing, stalks and pips being thereby crushed. **1975** P. V. PRICE *Taste of Wine* x. 183/3 In very young wines .. , stalkiness can be attractive.

**stamp**, *n.*[3] Add: **[IV.] [20.] stamp hinge** = HINGE *n.* 1 d.
**1905** *Gibbons Stamp Weekly* 8 Apr. (Advt. section) 5 We have just prepared a new *stamp hinge, size as above, put up in air-tight tin boxes. **1989** *Los Angeles Times* 7 Dec. E34/2 Many collectors and investors will not even look at a mint stamp if the gum has been disturbed by a stamp hinge.

**standardize**, *v.* Add: **[1.] c.** *intr.* Esp. const. *on*: to adopt as one's standard.
**1916** H. G. WELLS *Mr. Britling* I. i. 16 They had standardized and machined wholesale, while the British were still making the things one by one. **1946** DU BOIS & PRIBBLE *Plastics Mold Engin.* 353 It is common practice to standardize on the size and design of the transfer chamber and plunger used with hand molds. **1958** *Listener* 21 Aug. 259/2 The next big stumbling block is to get all the airlines to agree to standardise on this navigation system. **1970** *Daily Tel.* 24 Oct. 13 Their airlines are trying to standardise on American-engined planes. **1989** *Nature* 11 May 82/2 That the Ministry of Education should have decided to standardize on computers with TRON architecture is easily understood.

**stand-off**, *a.* and *n.* Add: **stand-'offishly** *adv.*
**1961** in WEBSTER. **1987** *N.Y. Times* May A25/3 In modern media politics, a network television appearance that shows him coming out of the White House to be standoffishly supportive of Mr. Reagan is equivalent to lengthy whistle-stopping.

**star**, *n.*[1] Add: **[I.] [12.] j.** Telecommunications. = *star network*, sense 20 below.
**1973** DAVIES & BARBER *Communication Networks for Computers* iv. 104 To connect a given number of devices in a simple ring needs no more lines than to connect them as a star, and each extra line enhances the whole network to some degree. **1983** *Personal Computer World* Mar. 144/1 The previous article .. concluded by considering one of the simplest of networks, a 'star' of lines all connected to just one central switch or node. **1984** L. UHR *Algorithm-Structured Computer Arrays & Networks* iv. 85

Finkel and Solomon .. defined stars as having *p* computers interconnected via a bus, with each computer linked to two buses. **1986** I. JACOBS in T. C. Bartee *Digital Communications* i. 40 Fiber is much better suited for a star architecture.

**[II.] [22.] [a.] star-fruit**, (*b*) = CARAMBOLA *n.*
**1965** B. M. ALLEN *Malayan Fruits* 131 Bĕlimbing Manis: Carambola. *Averrhoa carambola* Linn . . Other names: Bĕlimbing Batu . . Kambola, Caramba, Star-fruit (but do not confuse with Star Apple). **1988** J. BACON *Exotic Fruits* 20 Carambola, .. barbadine, granadilla (West Indies), star fruit. This distinctive tropical fruit . . has a brilliant-yellow translucent skin, and when cut in cross-section it resembles a star.

**starch**, *v.* Add: **4.** In *Boxing*, to defeat by knockout; to floor. *slang* (*N. Amer.*).
**1975** *Globe & Mail* (Toronto) 5 Apr. 47/1 Foreman, it says here, wouldn't even need the skilled collusion of such hamdonnies to starch the five of them in succession. **1984** *Toronto Star* 28 Mar. B1/6 Prior to that he had starched Ray Seales at Boston on Feb. 2, 1979. **1990** *Los Angeles Times* 4 Feb. C9/1 A promotional video cassette sent out to the boxing media showing scenes of Pazienza starching inferior opponents.

**starter**, *n.* Sense 9 in Dict. becomes 10. Add:
**[II.] [7.] c.** *Railways.* = *starting signal* s.v. STARTING *vbl. n.* 2 a.
**1963** E. F. CARTER *Railway Encycl.* 288 The advanced starting signal has the same uses as a 'starter'. **1967** G. F. FIENNES *I tried to run a Railway* iv. 45 Romford's advanced starter .. must have been at danger. **1983** A. VAUGHAN *Signalman's Twilight* (1984) v. 240 In the three minutes it'll take the down fast to clear Uffington the goods can be pulling on down to the starter. **1987** *Railway World* Nov. 674/1, I closed the regulator as we ran alongside the platform and braked gently to a stand at the Bingley Junction starter.
**9.** *Naut.* A cane or knotted rope's end used for beating slackers (see START *v.* 27). Now *Hist.*
**1905** J. MASEFIELD *Sea Life in Nelson's Time* vi. 167 The officer would .. say: 'Start that man'. The boatswain's mate at once produced a hard knotted cord, called a starter, with which he beat the man unmercifully about the head and shoulders, till the officer bade him to desist. **1938** C. S. FORESTER *Ship of Line* i. 21 'You've been free with that starter of yours, Thompson' he said. **1962** —— *Hornblower & 'Hotspur'* xx. 248 Mayne had swung his 'starter', his length of knotted line that petty officers used on every necessary occasion—too frequently, in Hornblower's judgement. **1981** D. POPE *Life in Nelson's Navy* vi. 85 Bosun's mates carried—until an Admiralty order banned them halfway through the war—another which was hated and feared by the seamen, a rattan cane known as a 'starter'. **1987** W. GOLDING *Close Quarters* v. 56 The petty officers .. were using their 'starters' in earnest.

**starting**, *vbl. n.* Add: **[2.] [b.] starting rotation**: see *ROTATION *n.* 2 e.

**start-up**, *ppl. a.* and *n.*[2] Add: **[B.] [2.] b.** A business enterprise that is in the process of starting up. Freq. *attrib.*, as *start-up company.* orig. *U.S.*
**1976** *Forbes* (N.Y.) 15 Aug. 6/2 The .. unfashionable business of investing in startups in the electronic data processing field. **1977** *Ibid.* 1 Jan. 101/2 Various companies—some of them cash cows, some of them 'adolescent' companies, some of them young startups. **1977** *Business Week* (Industrial Ed.) 5 Sept. 77/1 An incubator for startup companies, especially in the fast-growth, high-technology fields. **1984** *Australian* 6 Nov. 22/5 An innovative Texas-based start-up company is unveiling a new computer. **1985** *Times* 13 Dec. 24/3, 75,000 sq ft of accommodation for young start-up technology

companies. **1986** *Your Business* Mar. 11/3 There are the small businesses; the heroic little start-ups in their garages and garden sheds.

**stash** (ʃtæʃ), *n.*² *U.S. colloq.* [Abbrev.; cf. TASH *n.*] = MOUSTACHE *n.* 1 a.
**1940** D. W. MAURER *Big Con* 123 He had a little red stash, and he pulled it all out a few hairs at a time. **1955** *Publ. Amer. Dial. Soc.* XXIV. 147 The pickpocket will try to find out if the officer will *cop*. 'That big fink with the stash will always cop'. **1966** J. S. COX *Illustr. Dict. Hairdressing* 143/1 *Stash* moustache. Slang. **1971** *Time* 5 July 55/1 Sandy is a superannuated swinger, complete with stash, burns and a 17-year-old hippie on his arm.

**Stasi** ('ʃtaːzi, 'staːzi), *n.* Now *Hist.* [Ger., acronym f. *Staatssicherheit(sdienst)* 'state security (service)'.] The internal security force of the German Democratic Republic (East Germany), abolished in 1990.
[**1953** N. MUHLEN *Return of Germany* ii. 30 The Gestapo had ceased to exist, but .. its employees had now joined a new fraternity called the *Staatssicherheitsdienst* (State Security Service).] **1964** L. DEIGHTON *Funeral in Berlin* xxv. 141, I knew that STASI knew where the girl was. **1979** R. COX *Auction* ii. 33 An officer in the Staatssicherheit, known colloquially as the Stasi. **1985** S. STEVENS *Anvil Chorus* xi. 154 For his SCE keep Bock agreed to spill what he knew of East German security; he also promised to deliver an important Stasi agent who wanted to defect. **1990** *Independent* 13 Apr. 1/5 Allegations that up to 10 per cent of its [*sc.* the Volkskammer's] 400 members worked as informers for the now-disbanded internal security service, the Stasi.

**stasigenesis** (stæsɪ'dʒɛnɪsɪs), *n. Biol.* [f. Gr. στάσις STASIS *n.* + GENESIS *n.*: cf. ANAGENESIS, CATAGENESIS, CLADOGENESIS *ns.*] A stable phase of evolution, characterized by a lack of significant change over a long period of time.
**1957** J. S. HUXLEY in *Nature* 7 Sept. 454/1, I therefore propose the term *stasigenesis* to cover all processes leading to stabilization and persistence of types and of patterns of organization, from species up to phyla. **1958** *Nature* 25 Jan. 289/2 This new formation of families started in the Pliocene, the period that represented the climax of fissipede evolution, after which it started on its stable phase of 'stasigenesis'. **1965** *Evolution* XIX. 255/1 It is not demonstrated or probable that anagenesis outweighs cladogenesis just in the Miocene to early Pliocene. The *data* do not really indicate that stasigenesis set in from Pliocene to Recent. **1980** *Current Topics in Cellular Regulation* XVI. 147 Stasigenesis appears to impose on life evolutionary homeostasis, or stability in confining variation within limits of general patterns. **1989** *Canad. Jrnl. Bot.* LXVII. 2937 The fossil record suggests stasigenesis in the evolutionary history of some members of the genus *Equisetum* since the beginning of the Tertiary, and perhaps longer.
Hence ₁stasige'netic *a.*, characterized by stasigenesis.
**1965** *Evolution* XIX. 255/1 The slope both for 'basal families' and for the whole suborder is slightly *steeper* in the phase considered stasigenetic than in the phase considered cladogenetic.

**'statementing**, *vbl. n.* [f. STATEMENT *n.* + -ING¹.] **1.** *U.S. Banking.* The issuing of bank statements.
**1981** *Amer. Banker* 2 June 24/1 Applications [of electronic banking services] might include periodic and dynamic statementing, balance and status enquiries, and transaction histories. **1987** *U.S. Banker* Oct. 128/3 FDR will collect information from credit cardholders and do the statementing and storing of information for us.

**2.** *U.K. Educ.* The stating of the special educational needs of a child or children.
[**1981** *Education Act* c. 60 s. 7(1) The local education authority who are responsible for the child shall, if they are of the opinion that they should determine the special educational provision that should be made for him, make a statement of his special educational needs.] **1985** *Times* 12 Apr. 2/7 At the heart of the problem is the new system of notifying local authorities and the education department of children with handicaps, known as 'statementing'. **1990** *ACE Bull.* Mar.-Apr. 3/1 An information pack explaining the 1981 Act and the statementing process.
Hence '**statement** *v. trans.*, (*a*) to make a statement of the special educational needs of (a child); (*b*) to enter on a bank statement (*rare*); '**statemented** *ppl. a.*
**1983** *Times Educ. Suppl.* 1 Apr. 17/3 Government-funded projects will look at the wider special needs group as well as the 'statemented' minority. **1984** *Ibid.* 30 Mar. 25/3 Whereas l.e.a.s argue against 'statementing' children with moderate learning difficulties .. parents .. assess the risk of 'buying' integration. **1985** W. SAFIRE in *N.Y. Times Mag.* 6 Oct. 12/5 A statement .. announcing 'Service charges will be *statemented* the 22 of each month'. **1990** *Times Educ. Suppl.* 18 May A4/1 Almost one in 10 of the l.e.a.s is delegating the funding for statemented pupils to schools.

**statesperson** ('steɪts,pɜːsən), *n.* [f. *state's* genitive of STATE *n.* + PERSON *n.*, after STATESMAN, STATESWOMAN *ns.*] A statesman or stateswoman (used as a common gender form).
**1976** *National Rev.* (U.S.) 23 Jan. 18/1 Much of the credit for last year's record goes to Indian statesperson Indira Gandhi, who wearied of democracy and is now dabbling in dictatorship. **1981** *Economist* 25 Apr. 13/1 As twentieth-century summits go, the talks between the prime ministers of Britain and India were unremarkable. The two statespersons exchanged courtesies and aired disagreements. **1986** *New Yorker* 10 Feb. 99/1 The place they give her will be a large one—larger than any granted to date to any British statesperson of the century except Churchill. **1989** *Ibid.* 23 Oct. 104/2 Genscher has become Europe's senior statesperson.

**static**, *a.* and *n.* Delete *Machinery* at sense A. 6. Add: [A.] [6.] **d.** Fixed or held in place, on the ground, etc., freq. in contrast to something that can move; stationary, not mobile.
**1958** *Observer* 9 Feb. 11/4 The American Polaris .. will free still further the Western nuclear deterrent from dependence on large static bases. **1960** *Library Assoc. Rec.* Aug. 261/2 A library centre is a static service-point. **1966** J. S. COX *Illustr. Dict. Hairdressing* 143/1 *Static blade*, the lower blade in a pair of hand clippers .. over and against which the upper mobile blade moves. **1976** *Star* (Sheffield) 20 Nov. 11/1 (Advt.), Gailey offer a bigger range of Tourers and static Holiday Caravans than ever. **1986** *Times* 28 May 38/6 Velodrome and internal arena: .. Static seating for 6,000 spectators. **1988** *Economist* 30 Apr. 20/2 Sites for static caravans are hideous.
**B. 6.** A caravan permanently located on a site.
**1989** *Caravan, Motorcaravan & Camping* July 101/2 With 135 pitches and no statics, Mrs Allcock books in visitors, Derek personally takes them to their pitch. **1989** *Practical Caravan* Sept. 81/2 Our park is fairly limited in terms of availability of pitches—six tourers and 15 statics—and we find many people coming back year after year.
Hence '**staticness** *n.*
**1944** C. L. WRENN in *Trans. Philol. Soc. 1943* 37 The very staticness of our spelling often leads to an increased and exaggerated sensitiveness on the part of the philologist to every kind of vagary of orthography. **1987** *Performance* Sept./Oct. 20/2 Its

anguished staticness contains a strange kind of collective pain.

**staticky** ('stætɪkɪ), *a.* *U.S.* *colloq.* [f. STATIC *n.* + -Y².] Subject to or characterized by static; made faint or shrill with static; resembling static.

**1960** H. WAUGH *Road Block* i. 12 'Roger, wilco, and out,' the staticky voice sang. **1979** C. KILIAN *Icequake* viii. 102 'It's so good to hear you! Is everyone safe?' There was a staticky pause. 'I don't know.' **1984** *New Yorker* 13 Aug. 26/1 In Chicago, where we lived, all the incompatible states of Europe were pressed together down at the staticky right end of the dial. **1985** D. DeLILLO *White Noise* i. iii. 11 That little staticky sound of rustling nylon. **1988** A. TYLER *Breathing Lessons* (1989) III. i. 191 And on such a staticky, inadequate radio.

**statie** ('steɪtɪ), *n.* *U.S.* *slang.* [f. *state(trooper* s.v. TROOPER *n.* 3 b + -IE.] A state trooper.

**1934** J. O'HARA *Appointment in Samarra* 186 Ride out to the state police barracks and watch the staties drill and shoot. **1989** R. BANKS *Affliction* xxi. 299 Study at the trooper academy down in Concord and become a statie.

**station**, *n.* Sense 9 e in Dict. becomes 9 f. Add: [II.] [9.] e. *Bot.* A location at which a particular plant species (often an uncommon one) is growing.

**1805** TURNER & DILLWYN *Botanist's Guide Eng. & Wales* I. p. xv, It has been suggested that the *Botanist's Guide*, by pointing out the Stations of plants, may possibly lead to the extirpation of some which are least common. **1818** T. WALFORD *Sci. Tourist Eng., Wales & Scotl.* I. *Herefordshire*, There are many rare plants in Herefordshire; but their stations not being particularized in the County History, I can only add the few following. **1912** J. W. WHITE *Flora of Bristol* 269 This bramble is extremely rare in the county as a whole, for but one station is given by Mr. Murray in *Fl. Som.* **1937** A. H. WOLLEY-DOD *Flora of Sussex* p. liii, *Cicuta virosa* has two or three Sussex stations, all more or less doubtful. **1980** *Watsonia* XIII. 170 There are four main stations of *Fritillaria meleagris* L. in E. Suffolk, .. three of which are managed by the Suffolk Trust for Nature Conservation.

**stationer**, *n.*² Restrict *rare*⁻¹ to sense a in Dict. Add: **b.** *Newfoundland dial.* A migratory fisherman, living in a temporary on-shore community during the summer fishing season. Cf. STATION *n.* 13 a.

**1905** W. T. GRENFELL *Harvest of Sea* 113 The men that have remained are called 'stationers'; the others are green-fish catchers. **1924** G. A. ENGLAND *Vikings of Ice* 261 Thousands of outport men migrate almost as regularly as the seals themselves... If they pick some berth and settle down, they're called 'stationers', 'squatters', or 'roomers'. **1942** *Little Bay Islands* 14 Many stationers went to the French Shore each summer. **1969** in Halpert & Story *Christmas Mumming in Newfoundland* 23 From the same communities the Labrador 'stationers' also 'went down north'. **1979** A. ANDERSON *Salt Water, Fresh Water* 319, I had a crew of five men and I had twenty-five stationers.. and I was bringing them home on the vessel, and we got caught in a gale of south-east wind off St Anthony.

**stative**, *a.* and *n.* Add: 'statively *adv.*
**1976** J. S. GRUBER *Lexical Struct. Syntax & Semantics* I. vi. 162 *John remains in the room in order to see who arrives*. In the .. sentence above we have *remain* being used statively, treating John as an inanimate object. **1988** PLATT & HO in *English World-Wide* IX. 72 Is it possible that .. Singaporean Chinese are more inclined not to mark past tense on verbs used statively or non-punctually, at least in their spoken English?

**stealth**, *n.* [4.] **a.** Delete †*Obs.* (Later examples.)

Outside the phrase *by stealth* (sense 5 below) this sense appears to have been very rare during the 19th c.

*a*1886 E. DICKINSON *Poems* (1955) III. 1129 Each one of us has tasted With ecstasies of stealth The very food debated To our specific strength. **1938** L. HUGHES *New Song* 11 The rape and rot of graft, and stealth, and lies. **1943** [see UNLIVED *ppl. a.*² b]. **1964** I. FLEMING *You only live Twice* x. 126 *Ninjutsu* .. the art of stealth or invisibility. **1969** *Maclean's Mag.* Aug. 1/3 The qualities that make business click—qualities such as moxie and timing and stealth. **1987** G. TINDALL *To City* i. 2 He had begun keeping his Notebook .. in stealth and anxiety as if it represented some private, slightly shameful vice.

**b.** Ellipt. for *stealth technology, stealth bomber*, etc.: see sense *6 b below.

**1979** *Aviation Week & Space Technol.* 29 Jan. 121/2 Stealth cannot be overemphasized... Those technologies are really not here today. **1988** *Sun* (Brisbane) 21 Apr. 9/2 The Stealth, known as the B-2 bomber.

[6.] **b.** *attrib.* Designating or connected with a branch of technology concerned with rendering aircraft hard to detect by radar, or an aircraft designed in accordance with this.

[**1975** *Aviation Week & Space Technol.* 23 June 9/2 Advanced Research Projects Agency has funded studies on high-stealth aircraft through USAF Aeronautical Systems Div.] **1979** *Ibid.* 29 Jan. 121/2 Key technologies that have been identified are the following: Stealth technology. Engines and fuels. Avionics. **1981** *New Scientist* 8 Oct. 86/3 In the air the US will go ahead with the B1 bomber and will develop the 'Stealth' bomber, an aircraft that will employ as yet unperfected technology to make itself invisible to enemy radar. **1987** *Internat. Combat Arms* Sept. 30/1 What Stealth designers seek to do is lower an aircraft's RCS, or radar cross section—that is, the measure of its visibility to radar. **1989** *New Scientist* 20 May 34/2 One possible application for the cloth, says Kuhn, is for 'Stealth' aircraft.

**steam**, *v.* Add: [I.] [7.] **d.** *to steam in*, to start or join a fight. *slang.*

**1961** *New Statesman* 14 Apr. 576/2 As the underworld put it, 'he steamed in like a slag and roughed them up as he topped them'. **1976** *Scotsman* 24 Dec. 15/1 As an amateur, Hope used to come to the gym and spar with Charles. He used to steam in and, if only for self protection, Charles was obliged to spank him sometimes. **1987** *Daily Mail* 2 Sept. 6/3 The term [steaming] was coined .. from the Cockney slang 'to steam in', used when a group of youths pile in for a fight.

**e.** *colloq.* To perform the action of *STEAMING *vbl. n.* 6.

**1987** *Daily Mail* 2 Sept. 6/5 Usually unemployed and young, .. they steam en masse into shops or on to buses, seize what they want from their victims and then break up. **1988** *Daily Tel.* 13 Feb. 3/1 A gang of 25 knife-wielding black youths .. 'steamed' through a late-night suburban British Rail train. **1989** *Times* 14 July 3/6 Several members of a mob of young robbers who 'steamed' through crowds at the Notting Hill Carnival in 1987 were jailed yesterday.

[II.] 13. *colloq.* To subject (a place or those in it) to, make (one's) way by, steaming (see *STEAMING *vbl. n.* 6). *rare.*

**1987** *Daily Tel.* 2 Sept. 11/7 Crowds of youths 'from nowhere', never seen at Notting Hill before, could be seen from the stall, 'steaming' and pillaging their way through crowds of revellers. **1987** *Times* 13 Nov. 21/6 Late-night passengers on the Underground found themselves being steamed. A gang of about 20 youths went from carriage to carriage, threatening and robbing passengers.

**steamer**, *n.* Add: **12.** *colloq.* A wetsuit.
**1982** *Surf Scene* No. 7. 21/2 Boots, steamer, hood and even gloves become a necessity. **1986** *Boards* May 18/1 (Advt.), Probably the best .. double lined steamer... This is the suit for warmth and durability. **1987** B. OAKLEY *Windsurfing* (1978) Gloss. 117/2 A true steamer should use a waterproof 'blind stitch' on the seams to prevent water penetration.
**13.** *colloq.* A member of a gang engaged in steaming (see \*STEAMING *vbl. n.* 6).
**1987** *Daily Tel.* 2 Sept. 3/1 Many of the assaults and robberies were committed by gangs of 'steamers'—groups of up to 50 men who ran down the streets in close formation, attacking and robbing anyone in their path. **1988** *Sunday Times* 21 Feb. A18/8 Last November, steamers .. hit crowds outside a rock concert at Hammersmith Odeon. **1990** *Times* 1 Jan. 1/7 Police earlier arrested a team of 20 suspected 'steamers' who had gathered in a .. food bar and were believed to be planning .. pick-pocketing.

**steaming**, *vbl. n.* Add: **6.** *colloq.* The action, by a gang, of passing rapidly through a public place (or train, etc.) robbing bystanders (or passengers) by force of numbers.
Evidence to substantiate the U.S. origin of the term alleged in quot. 1987[1] is not forthcoming.
**1987** *Hackney Gaz.* 24 Apr. 48/1 'Steaming' gangs will return—police. Hackney's steaming mobs laid low at the weekend—but a senior policeman has warned that the giant gangs of muggers will return. .. The gangs call their terrifying form of robbery 'steaming', a term first coined in America's violent inner city ghettos. **1987** *Daily Tel.* 2 Sept. 11/5 This was the first time I had seen 'steaming', the name given to open stealing in numbers. A gang of marauding youths, acting quickly and then dispersing on a pre-arranged plan, are hard to resist. **1988** *Times* 8 July 4/1 Four youths were acquitted yesterday .. of conspiring to commit robbery during the 'steaming' of a London Underground train.

**steen** (stiːn), *a.* *U.S. slang.* Also *'steen.* [Aphetic form of *sixteen.*] An indefinite, (fairly) large number of; 'umpteen'.
**1886** *Tid-Bits* IV. 37/2 And so I've lost a year of wooing, And more than 'steen years will repay. **1900** K. U. CLARK in *Independent* 2573/2 Endless repetitions are not unfitly designated as occurring 'steen' times. **1915** S. FORD *Torchy, Private Sec.* xiii. 225 It's no trick at all to go into the average Rube village, 'steen miles from a railroad. **1934** S. LEWIS *Work of Art* xxv. 338 'I've told you lots of times about building a really first-class inn,' said Myron... 'Yes, sure, steen thousand times,' said Effie. **1944** *Kansas City Star* 10 Dec. D8/7 If 'steen thousand women would give up their share. **1951** *Amer. Speech* XXVI. 65/2 *Steen.* One would judge this word to be abstracted from *sixteen.* It has, I think, been familiar to me for many, many years, often in hyperbolical combinations; e.g., 'I have steen million things to do'.

**steenth** (stiːnθ), *a.* and *n.* *U.S. slang.* Also *'steenth.* [Aphetic form of *sixteenth.*] **A.** *adj.* **a.** Sixteenth. **b.** Latest in an indefinitely long series; 'umpteenth'. **B.** *n.* A sixteenth part.
**1895** KIPLING in *Idler* Apr. 392 My name is Emory—Julian B. Emory—193, 'Steenth Street, corner of Madison. **1899** S. WATERLOO *Launching of Man* iv. 36 What do I care .. about the 'steenth 'power' of anything? **1915** S. FORD *Torchy, Private Sec.* xvi. 289 Letter writin' ain't your long suit... 'Yours of the steenth just received' .. may do for vice-presidents and general managers; but it's raw style to spring on your best girl. **1927** B. REYNOLDS *Cocktail Continentale* iv. 60 For the steenth time, you ride in a Chandler car. **1935** G. & S. LORIMER *Heart Specialist* 263. **1981** *N.Y. Times* 9 July D10/3 On Friday, June 19, the option closed at 1/16. In Wall Street language, that's known phonetically as 'a

steenth'... Every day that same week .. Conoco's July 70 call had closed at 'a steenth', which is as low in price as an option can get.

‖**stelline** (‖stelˈliːne, steˈliːnɪ), *n. pl.* Also **stellini**. [It., f. *stellina, stellino* little star, starlet (dim. *stella* star).] Small, star-shaped pasta pieces.
**1958** *Catal. County Stores, Taunton* June 17 *Naples Macaroni .. Small—Stelline, Tubettini—a lb. 1/4.* **1974** *Times* 14 Sept. 4/4 Every form of pasta, from the tiny *stelline*, which go into clear soups to the handkerchief-sized *lasagne* must be made with hard grain flour. **1984** *N.Y. Times* 8 Feb. c4/5 Small pastas, those tiny shapes that could stand in for rice or potatoes or give any sauce a new lease on life: tubetti, tubettini, orzo, stelline, acini pepe, seme mellone. **1984** BARR & LEVY *Official Foodie Handbk.* I. 35 Packets of Arborio rice, dried farfalle, stellini, penne, rigatoni... Tagliatelle in the freezer. **1989** *Reader's Digest Compl. Guide Cookery* III. 328/2 Italian pasta names ... *Stellini* (stars).

**stem**, *n.*[1] Add: **[4.] l.** [By metonymy from sense 4 c.] A pipe used for smoking opium or crack. *U.S. slang.*
**1925** *Flynn's* 18 Apr. 116/1 *Stem*, an opium pipe. **1948** H. L. MENCKEN *Amer. Lang.* Suppl. II. 681 In English the pipe is a *stem, saxophone, gong, gonger, dream-stick, joy-stick* or *bamboo.* **1990** *Village Voice* (N.Y.) 30 Jan. 37/1 Now the johns drive up, they don't even say hello. They just go, 'Hey, you got a stem [a crack pipe] on you?'

**stemmed**, *ppl. a.* Add: **b.** Of small fruit: having had the stem removed.
**1961** in WEBSTER s.v., Stemmed berries. **1979** CUNNINGHAM & LABER *Fannie Farmer Cookbook* 658 *Uses* [for currants]: *Raw*, stemmed and generously sugared... *Cooked,* .. in jellies. **1984** J. DIDION *Democracy* I. vii. 35 People who all knew exactly what Inez Victor did with the stemmed strawberries she picked up at Gristede's.

**stenotope** (ˈstɛnəʊtəʊp), *n. Ecol.* [ad. G. *stenotop* adj. (F. Dahl 1896, in *Sitzungsber. d. k. Preuss. Akad. d. Wissensch.* 28), f. Gr. στενό-ς narrow + τόπ-ος place.] A stenotopic organism.
[**1896**: see EURYTOPE *n.*] **1938** J. R. CARPENTER *Ecol. Gloss.* 256 *Stenotope,* .. of/ organisms restricted to a single habitat. **1959** *Ann. N.Y. Acad. Sci.* LXXVIII. 373 Referring to the closed and artificially limited environment used in germfree studies, a better term for this kind of environment would be stenotope. **1981** S. J. GOULD in R. M. May *Theoret. Ecol.* (ed. 2) xiii. 299 The greater geological longevity of stressed eurytopes does not imply that evolutionary trends towards their domination should exist within clades—for stenotopes may, on average, persist for shorter times, yet speciate at such a markedly greater rate that they increase steadily in relative frequency for species within clades.

**stenotopic** (stɛnəʊˈtɒpɪk), *a. Ecol.* (Formerly at STENO- in Dict.) [f. STENOTOP(E *n.* + -IC 1.] Of an organism: tolerant of only a restricted range of habitats or ecological conditions. Opp. \*EURYTOPIC *a.*
**1937** ALLEE & SCHMIDT *Hesse's Ecol. Animal Geogr.* viii. 121 A subspecies, species, genus, family, etc., that inhabits a small range may be referred to as stenotopic, one with a wide range as eurytopic. **1949** J. H. KENNETH *Henderson's Dict. Sci. Terms* (ed. 4), *Stenotopic,* having a restricted range of geographical distribution. **1967** *Oceanogr. & Marine Biol.* V. 546 This species is also stenotopic; it needs exposed rocky shores, but where the wave-action is not too strong. **1976** *Nature* 24 June 695/1 A major terminal extinction event .. will tend selectively to eliminate the larger, more specialised, more stenotopic species.

**stepper**, *n.* Sense 4 in Dict. becomes 5. Add: 4. *colloq.* (orig. *U.S.*). A person who steps, *esp.* a dancer.
**1934** WEBSTER, *Stepper*,.. a dancer, esp. a step dancer. **1954** L. ARMSTRONG *Satchmo* viii. 127 Papa Gar .. was the proudest stepper in the whole parade. **1981** *Westindian World* 25 Sept. 6/7 It's a great steppers tune with a good, hard rhythm all the way through it.

**sterile**, *a.* Add: [7.] **b.** *fig.* Screened or cleared by security forces; *spec.* of a telephone line, not tapped. orig. *U.S.*
**1973** *Newsweek* 7 May 88/3 The so-called sterile concourse—the long airport corridor that only ticketed, searched travelers may enter—means that a passenger must be searched each time he changes planes and concourses. **1973** *Harper's Mag.* Oct. 79/1 A 'sterile' telephone in Washington (permitting them to operate without being bugged or observed by rival spies from other government agencies). **1977** R. LUDLUM *Chancellor MS.* xix. 203 Except for our taps his phones are sterile; there is no surveillance on him but our own. **1984** *Observer* 10 June 3/7 The economic summit .. had left large chunks of central London 'sterile' these last few days. That is police jargon for any security area out of bounds to the general public. 'You can't go in there, guv, it's all a sterile area'.

**stethoscope**, *n.* Add: **'stethoscoped** *a.*, equipped with a stethoscope.
**1972** *Guardian* 23 Oct. 11/1, I can .. think of few things more autocratic than the power of a gynaecologist to exercise his right of decision over whether or not a woman shall continue to carry a child she does not wish to bear ... White-overall'd stethoscoped Napoleons. **1984** *Canad. Business* July 186/3 As the founder of the Bathtub Doctor, with its catchy advertising image of a stethoscoped doctor rushing off to revive expiring tubs, he popularized home refinishing of bathtubs.

**St. Helenian** (sənt həˈliːnɪən), *n.* and *a.* [f. the name of *St. Helena* (see below): see -IAN.] **A.** *n.* A native or inhabitant of the island of St. Helena in the South Atlantic, a British territory since 1834 (previously controlled by the East India Company). **B.** *adj.* Of or pertaining to St. Helena.
[**1697** W. DAMPIER *New Voy. round World* xx. 547, I found the *Santa Hellena* Manatee to be, by their Shapes .. those Creatures called Sea-Lyons.] **1938** P. GOSSE *St. Helena 1502–1938* xiv. 373 These are some of the blessings which the St. Helenians enjoy. **1957** O. BLAKESTON *Isle of St. Helena* III. x. 131 The pretty St. Helenian girls must .. have made very much the same impression. **1963** *Guardian* 7 Jan. 7/2 St. Helenian children are 2 inches shorter than English children of the same age. **1969** M. S. TAYLOR *St. Helena—Ocean Roadhouse* x. 138 To the St. Helenian, a wedding is the most important of family festivals. **1981** *Observer* 18 Jan. 6/8 St Helena has an unemployment problem ... Many St Helenians are on social security ... The plan to send a small number of St Helenian families to the Falklands .. is likely to go ahead.

**stick**, *n.*¹ Add: [II.] [14.] **c.** A small group of soldiers assigned to a particular duty.
**1953** *Mars & Minerva* Aug. 17/2 Climbing 'Stick'. .. Twelve Section, which was formed as a climbing section at the end of last year .. has recently had some very good week-ends on the Cornish cliffs and in N. Wales. The 'Stick' was formed with the object of having a section in the Regiment which could be trained to lead on rock, snow and ice. **1985** *Times* 3 July 12/2 A Toyota Land Cruiser with a stick of heavily armed guards. **1988** *Times of India* 23 Feb. 1. 4/3 The modified 7.62 bore rifles carried by the 'stick' (the complement of eight infantrymen aboard

the ICV [Infantry Combat Vehicle]) can fire 40 rounds a minute and can hit up to a distance of 300 metres.

**stick**, *n.*⁴ Add: **6.** *Stock Exchange.* A large quantity of unsold stock; *spec.* the proportion of shares which must be taken up by underwriters after an unsuccessful issue. (Freq. as *underwriting stick*). See STICKY *a.*² 3 a.
**1982** *Observer* 21 Nov. 17/3 The underwriters .. now have to take up over £400 million worth of shares—the biggest 'stick' in Stock Exchange history. **1988** *Sunday Times* 15 May D5/1 It .. was left with 'the stick'—City terminology for a tranche of unwanted stock.

**stick**, *v.*¹ Add: [III.] [23.] **f.** *slang.* to stick one (or *it*) on (someone): to hit.
**1960** *Times* 21 Sept. 3/7 We could hear his footsteps... As he got near Lutt 'stuck it on him'. He only hit him once. The chap went down and I grabbed him as he fell. **1967** *Guardian* 6 June 5/3 If that doesn't stop, I'm going to stick one on that bastard. **1986** *Making Music* Apr. 24/3, I could have fallen through the floor—I thought he was there to stick one on me.

**sticky**, *a.*² Add: [1.] **f.** Damp with sweat.
**1961** M. G. EBERHART *Cup, Blade, or Gun* xi. 127 She felt cold and hot, sticky and chilly at the same time. **1968** J. LOCK *Lady Policeman* viii. 60 My serge skirt feels heavy, my feet feel hot and sticky. **1978** *Washington Post* 8 Aug. B7/1 The air has become almost saturated with moisture. As a result, the perspiration lies on your skin and you feel hot and sticky. **1988** P. P. READ *Season in West* vii. 94 Feeling sticky after a day in a dirty city .. Birek decided to take a bath.

**stiff**, *a., n.,* and *adv.* [B.] [3.] [b.] For def. read: A poor competitor, a sure loser; *spec.* a racehorse or boxer that is unlikely to win, occas. one which is not intended to win. Cf. STIFF *a.* 2 b. *slang* (orig. *U.S.*). (Further examples.)
**1912** J. SANDILANDS *Western Canad. Dict., Stiff*, a corpse, or about as valueless as a corpse. Frequently used in reference to players who are of no use in the game. **1918** *Chrons. N.Z. Expeditionary Force* 7 June 205/1 Remarks are heard on the 'tinny' luck or otherwise of the players, while the 'stiffs' [unlucky players] bemoan their luck. **1989** *Times Lit. Suppl.* 13 Jan. 27/2 He behaved a lot like a manager of prize-fighters who has a stable of stiffs, one of whom he might send out against the opposition at selected times.
**c.** A commercial venture, esp. in the entertainment business, which merits or meets with public indifference; a flop. *colloq.* (orig. *U.S.*).
**1937** *Sunday Jrnl. & Star* (Lincoln, Nebraska) 26 Sept. C-D. 12/3 *Stiff*, the only negative term in the list, describes a bust, a flop, a complete failure. **1949** *Amer. Weekly in N.Y. Jrnl.-American* 30 Oct. 21/2 Juggy listened to the tune and was disheartened. 'It's a stiff,' he said—meaning that it was no good. **1981** A. NIGHTINGALE *Chase Fade* 91/2 A 'stiff' in record company parlance means a flop. **1987** *Hi-Fi News* Jan. 57/2 When you think about it, these are likely to be the most popular products in our market, as receivers are total stiffs as far as the UK is concerned (it seems that only the Yanks buy them in great numbers).
**5.** *slang.* An erection (of the penis).
**1980** 'T. HINDE' *Sir Henry & Sons* x. 77 What Selby does each night for our entertainment is the Wolves dormitory, getting an enormous pink stiff on his .. cock. **1983** AMAN & SARDO in *Maledicta 1982* VI. 23 *Erection (males)*, .. stiff, stiffer, etc.

**stiffy**, *n.* Restrict '*U.S. slang*' to senses 1 and 2. Add: **3.** *U.K. slang.* A formal invitation card (made of thick cardboard).
**1980** *Sunday Times* 20 July 32/2 'Here are your Stiffies,' said the organiser, giving me a wad of party invitations thicker than six chapters of The Rainbow. **1987** *Daily Tel.* 27 Oct. 40/7 Nigel [Lawson] had in hand a gilt-edged stiffy for a banquet at the Stock Exchange.

**stimulating**, *ppl. a.* Add:     Hence **'stimulatingly** *adv.*
**1927** *Observer* 13 Nov. 9 They are stimulatingly dealt with here, and Mr. Mumford is not less successful with Henry James. **1987** C. LLOYD *Year at Gt. Dixter* 47 New hydrangea leaves and shoots have a stimulatingly sharp smell.

**stinger**, *n.*[1] Add: **[2.] b.** *U.S.* = STING *n.*[2] 2.
**1895** in *Funk's Stand. Dict.* **1926** J. K. STRECKER in J. F. Dobie *Rainbow in Morning* (1965) 77 In an article referred to above, I mention the stinging snake and its so-called stinger. **1957** J. KEROUAC *On Road* IV. iv. 168 Suddenly a bug flew into his arm and embedded a long stinger in it that made him howl. **1972** *Sci. Amer.* Apr. 93/2 Even in the winter bees too cold to fly can protrude their stingers; a mass of cold clustered bees with protruded stingers reminds one of a porcupine.
**5.** *Mil.* With capital initial. The name of a type of lightweight, shoulder-launched anti-aircraft missile with infrared homing, manufactured in the U.S.
**1975** *Aviation Week & Space Technol.* 17 Mar. 42/2 The Stinger missile system has experienced problems in technical development that have caused the program to be extended about 14 months in development. **1982** *Daily Tel.* 5 Aug. 5/1 Mr Pattie refers to adverse Press comment comparing the performance of Blowpipe unfavourably with the American heat-seeking missile, Stinger. **1987** tr. *Gorbachev's Perestroika: New Thinking* II. v. 177 The transfer of the Stingers to the counter-revolutionary bands .. is simply immoral and totally unjustifiable. **1990** *Combat & Survival* July 19/3 The Stinger missile is a battle-proven way to take out helicopters, which is more than can be said of British shoulder-launched systems.

**stock**, *n.*[1] Senses A. 39–64 in Dict. become A. 40–65. Add: **[A.] [IV.] 39.** On a set of bagpipes, any of the wooden sockets, fixed in holes in the bag, into which the pipes and chanter fit. orig. *Sc.*
**1876** D. MACPHEE *Compl. Tutor for Highland Bagpipe* in *Bagpipe Wks.* (1978) p. iv, In doing this it is necessary to take off the cover and cork the Stocks securely. **1906** 'H. FOULIS' *Vital Spark* xiv. 102 There's nothing will put a pipe bag in trum but some treacle poured in by the stock. **1925** W. A. COCKS *Tutor for Northumberland Half-Long Bagpipes* 7 A few spoonfuls are warmed and poured into the bag after removing the drones and chanter and corking up the stocks. **1966** F. COLLINSON *Trad. Mus. Scotl.* 169 The small-pipes, both Lowland and Highland, are alike in other respects, and all have drones in one stock. **1984** *New Grove Dict. Mus. Instruments* I. 99/1 The chanter, drones and blowpipes are attached to the bag by being inserted into tubular wooden stocks which are tied into apertures in the leather.

**stocker**, *n.* Add: **8.** *U.S. colloq.* A 'stock' component or vehicle (i.e. as regularly manufactured and held in stock, not customized).
**1971** *Choppers Mag.* Nov. 27 (*heading*) Chops are safer than stockers. **1974** *Motorcross Action Mag.* June 40/3 That solution doesn't do the owner of a stocker any good, since adding gears is not exactly known as privateer technology. **1980** *Dirt Bike* Oct. 36/3 Rex Staten put the gearbox failures in the proper light when he told us that he raced his

practice stocker for most of the year without problems. **1988** *Super MotoCross* Sept./Oct. 53/1 The carburetor is a stocker modified to incorporate a true choke circuit.

**stockpile**, *v.* Add: **3.** *intr.* To form a stockpile; to accumulate. orig. *U.S.*
**1961** in WEBSTER. **1962** M. MCLUHAN *Gutenberg Galaxy* 174 As de Chardin explains in his *Phenomenon of Man*, new invention is the interiorization in man of the structures of earlier technology; and therefore it stockpiles, as it were. **1985** *Times* 14 Aug. 10/2 Meanwhile grain is stockpiling in other regions.

**stoichiometry**, *n.* Add: **stoichio'metrically** *adv.*
**1934** WEBSTER, *Stoichiometrically* adv. **1969** *Proc. 6th Cellulose Conf.* 69 The evidence is in favor of right-handed helices with stoichiometrically bound water. There is a novel inter-chain hydrogen bond system at the center of the structure. **1983** *New Scientist* 28 Apr. 206/1 Industry needs about 1.5 million tonnes of pure ethanol, free from water, each year. To remove water from fermented alcohol on this scale would require quite uneconomic amounts of energy. So it's usually made by stoichiometrically adding water to ethylene over an acid catalyst.

**stone**, *n.* Add: **[5.] k.** A round piece or counter, orig. made of stone, used in various board games, esp. the Japanese game of go (see GO *n.*[2], and sense 13 below).
**1890** B. H. CHAMBERLAIN *Things Japanese* 137 Nineteen straight lines crossing each other at right angles make three hundred and sixty-one *me*, or crosses ... These may be occupied by a hundred and eighty white and a hundred and eighty-one black stones (*ishi* . .). **1975** *Way to Play* 22/1 Each player [in backgammon] has 15 pieces ... The pieces are variously known as 'counters', 'stones', or 'men'. **1989** *New Yorker* 6 Feb. 26/3 Go .. is played with round black and white pieces, called 'stones', on a grid.

**stop**, *v.* Senses 15 e, f in Dict. become 15 f, g. Add: **[15.] e.** *Boxing.* To defeat (an opponent) by a knockout. orig. *U.S.*
**1895** in *Funk's Stand. Dict.* **1921** H. C. WITWER in *Collier's* 19 Feb. 22/4 He packed a wicked right and had stopped a lot of good men before Kid Roberts cut him short with a one-round knockout. **1939** *Ring* May 14/2 Corbett won the Championship by stopping John L. Sullivan in the twenty-first round. **1949** P. CUMMINGS *Dict. Sports* 433/2 A boxer 'stops' his opponent in the third round. **1976** *Liverpool Echo* 6 Dec. 16/6 A capacity crowd saw Harry Orr (Salisbury) take the top junior trophy for stopping Steve Crighton (Birch Green, Skelmersdale) in two rounds. **1986** *World Boxing* Sept. 6/2 Hilton completely dominated the entire fight before finally stopping Benitez in the ninth.
**h.** *Racing.* To check (a horse) in order to stay out of the running; = PULL *v.* 17 a. Also *transf.*
**1954** R. DAHL *Someone like You* 232 Wouldn't it be safer if we use Jackie all the time and simply stop him the first half dozen races so he come last? **1960** C. SMIRKE *Finishing Post* iv. 38 To 'stop' a horse without being detected requires greater skill and jockeyship than to win. **1962** D. FRANCIS *Dead Cert* iv. 34 There had been rumours .. that Sandy had 'stopped' a few horses and had been rewarded handsomely by bookmakers. **1982** T. BIDDLECOMBE *Winner's Disclosure* iii. 43 What I absolutely abhor is the truly unscrupulous individual who will persuade a jockey to stop a horse or deliberately not win a race, for financial reward.

**Stoppardian** (stɒ'pɑːdɪən), *a.* [f. the name of Tom *Stoppard*, British dramatist (b. 1937 in Czechoslovakia) + -IAN.] Of, pertaining to, or characteristic of the plays of Tom Stoppard.

**1978** *Listener* 7 Dec. 761/4 He opened .. with an examination of Tom Stoppard's plays. This consisted of an extremely mannered interview with the playwright ... The interview had a particularly Stoppardian air. **1979** *N. & Q.* June 282/1 It is an interpretation and, in Stoppardian fashion, we may observe that often truth is only an interpretation. **1981** *Event* 16 Oct. 49/5 The decisive Stoppardian touches are also present. **1989** *N.Y. Times* 26 Dec. C15/3 There is only one characteristically Stoppardian problem. It is not often clear which side of the fence he is standing on.

**stopper**, *n.* Sense 10 in Dict. becomes 11. Add: [1.] h. *Baseball slang.* A pitching ace, *spec.* (*a*) a starting pitcher depended on to win a game or reverse a losing streak; (*b*) a relief pitcher who prevents the opposing team from scoring highly.
**1948** *San Francisco Examiner* 10 Mar. 20/4, I had been known as the 'stopper' for the Sox for a long time and I really had to be on September 13, 1946, in Cleveland, the day we clinched the American League championship. **1954** *Collier's* 9 July 45/1 The 'stoppers', usually the most dependable on the staff, are apt to get the nod most any time. **1979** *Washington Post* 21 Aug. D2/5 Flanagan .. has replaced the injured Jim Palmer as the Oriole stopper and is baseball's hottest pitcher, winning seven of his last eight games. **1985** *Los Angeles Times* 8 July III. 6/1 In the old days, before relief pitchers became such a factor in baseball, a 'stopper' was a starting pitcher. **1985** *New Yorker* 5 Aug. 33/3 Any self-respecting team should have at least one ace, or stopper.
**10.** *colloq.* A stopping train. (See STOPPING *ppl. a.* 2.)
**1969** *Guardian* 11 Jan. 12/3 There was no boat train to Tilbury, only a drab, scheduled service stopper, taking tired Christmas shoppers from London to all stations east. **1976** *Railway Mag.* Aug. 409/1 We had to follow a d.m.u. 'stopper' and suffered a succession of signal checks. **1981** A. VAUGHAN *Signalman's Morning* xiv. 162 There was the stopper, waiting patiently at the home signal.

**storable**, *a.* Add: Hence **stora'bility** *n.*
**1975** *Chemical Week* 19 Nov. 19/1 The convenience and storability of dry material has made it the choice of small users despite prices that are about 50% higher than tabs on liquid. **1977** *Jrnl. R. Soc. Arts* CXXV. 564/2 Apples with good storability. **1984** *Washington Post* 30 Sept. B1 The tree will be identical to its source. So all the advantageous genetic qualities—such as size, disease resistance, appearance, taste, storability and productivity—will be bred in.

**stormer**, *n.* Add: **3.** *U.K. slang.* Something of surpassing size, vigour, or excellence.
**1978** *Hot Car* July 89/3 A sleeper is any car that looks harmless, but is in fact a real stormer—jus' right for scaring the locals. **1984** *Sporting Life* 1 Nov. 13/1 Redwood Lass ran a stormer. **1988** *Autosport* 29 Sept. 80/3 Baird made an absolute stormer of a start to get away in the lead from the green. **1988** *Times* 29 Aug. 3/2 We had a lot of complaints .. about big parties going on into the early hours, not just ordinary parties but real stormers.

**storming**, *ppl. a.* Add: **3.** *slang* (chiefly in *Sport*). Displaying outstanding vigour, speed, or skill.
**1961** *Boxing News* 20 Oct. 11/2 The Filipino tried hard to put in a storming finish. **1972** *Times* 13 Sept. 9/6 To score by a neck from Day Two, who came with a storming run in the last 100yds. **1987** *Kart & Superkart* Oct. 8/3 From pole position he failed to get away at the change of lights but then proceeded to give a storming display to take the lead .. on lap six.

**straddle**, *n.* Add: [I.] [1.] c. *Athletics, Gymnastics*, etc. A movement in which the legs are held wide apart, esp. in vaulting or dismounting from apparatus; *spec.* in *Athletics*, a style of high jump in which the jumper clears the bar horizontally and face down, with the legs straddled either side. Freq. *attrib.*
The straddle jump was popularized by David Albritton at the U.S. Olympic trials in 1936.
**1905** *Gymnastic Nomencl. Y.M.C.A. N. Amer.* 35 *Straddle*, the thighs are abducted while passing over the apparatus and may be: a) Forward or Front b) Backward or Back. **1937** *Athletic Jrnl.* May 10/2 This is a typical take-off for Albritton when using either the roll or straddle style of jump. **1942** W. WEST *Gymnast's Man.* 95 In the straddle dismount the performer passes over the apparatus with the legs in the spread or straddle position. **1949** *Dict. Sports* 434 *Straddle vault*, Gymnastics, a vault over a buck in which the performer straddles its ends, the legs passing on the outside of the arms. **1951** F. A. M. WEBSTER *Indoor Athletics & Winter Training* viii. 96 The Straddle jump is .. merely the ordinary Scissors jump turned upside down. **1952** D. CANHAM *Field Techniques Illustr.* iv. 29 In the Straddle, however, the take-off leg trails and is not tucked under as it is in the Western Roll. **1964** G. C. KUNZLE *Parallel Bars* ii. 41 These elementary straddles are useful movements in their own right, and the single leg straddle into support is a useful start to an exercise. **1986** *Gymnastics* ('Know the Game' Ser.) (ed. 4) 23/2 This vault is a natural progression from the straddle vault over buck or box broadways. **1990** G. CARR *Fund. Track & Field* 85 In recent years the Fosbury Flop technique of high jumping has superseded the straddle and the world records for both males and females are held by flop jumpers.

**streaming**, *ppl. a.* Add: **7.** *Computing.* Pertaining to, designating, or making use of a form of tape transport, used mainly to provide backup storage, in which data may be transferred in large quantities without interruption while the tape is still in motion.
**1979** *Electronics* 24 May 208/3 In its high-speed 'streaming' mode, the unit's half-inch tape races along at 100 in./s, taking data on the fly in large blocks of up to a full disk at a time. **1980** *Ibid.* 23 Oct. 240/2 There does not seem to be a consensus as to which way the industry will go—to floppies, tape cartridges, or streaming tapes. **1986** *Which Computer?* Oct. 24/3 (Advt.), A single Minstrel 4 holds up to 160 MBytes formatted-disk capacity, with onboard streaming back-up of up to 60 MBytes. **1988** *Times* 13 Apr. 31 The M240 .. offers three disk drive slots (with the option of integral streaming tape units for rapid disk back-up).

# T

**tape**, *n.*[1] Add: [4.] **tape streamer** *Computing*, a streaming tape drive (see *STREAMING *ppl. a.* 7*).

**1981** *Electronics* 17 Nov. 188/1 *(caption)* 125-in./s *tape streamer has capstan and tensioner for 45-in./s start-stop operation. **1985** *Which Computer?* Apr. 66/1 Connections can be made to .. an external tapestreamer.

# U

**Unix** ('juːnɪks), *n. Computing.* Also **UNIX.** [f. as a play on the earlier \*MULTICS *n.*, with *uni-* one for *multi-* many (after the relative compactness of the newer system) and with phonetic respelling of *-ics* as *-ix.*] A proprietary name for a multi-user operating system orig. designed for use with minicomputers.

**1973** *Bell Lab. Rec.* LI. 200 Some of the concepts, especially for file-handling, appeared in a time-shared operating system called UNIX, which was designed and implemented at Bell Labs. **1978** *Bell Syst. Techn. Jrnl.* LVII. 1991 C..is sufficiently expressive and efficient to have completely displaced assembly language programming on UNIX. **1983** *Austral. Personal Computer* Aug. 66/2 Xenix, the Microsoft implementation of Unix disk operating systems for microcomputers. **1985** *Official Gaz.* (U.S. Patent Office) 29 Oct. TM63/1 *UNIX*...For computer programs... First use 12-14-1972. **1986** *Trade Marks Jrnl.* 5 Mar. 522/2 *Unix*..Computer programmes, computing apparatus; [etc.] **1989** *N.Y. Times* 25 Oct. D1/4 A wider industry agreement on a single Unix standard would also increase the possibility that Unix will be widely adopted in the business computer market.

# V

**virus**, *n*. Add: [2.] **d.** *Computing*. Any sequence of code (*esp.* one capable of being inserted in other programs) which when executed causes itself to be copied into other locations, and which is therefore capable of propagating itself within the memory of a computer or across a network, usually with deleterious results. See also *computer virus* s.v. *COMPUTER *n*. 3.

**1972** D. GERROLD *When Harlie was One* 175 You know what a virus is, don't you? ... The VIRUS program does the same thing. **1975** J. BRUNNER *Shockwave Rider* II. 176 I'd have written the worm as an explosive scrambler, probably about half a million bits long, with a backup virus facility and a last-ditch infinitely replicating tail. **1984** F. COHEN in Finch & Dougall *Computer Security* 144 We define a computer 'virus' as a program that can 'infect' other programs by modifying them to include a possibly evolved copy of itself ... Every program that gets infected may also act as a virus and thus the infection grows. *Ibid.* 146 On November 3, 1983, the first virus was conceived of as an experiment to be presented at a weekly seminar on computer security. The concept was first introduced in this seminar by the author, and the name 'virus' was thought of by Len Adleman. **1985** *Time* 4 Nov. 94/3 A few years ago, Richard Skrenta Jr. ... wrote a virus program called Cloner. Every 30th time a disk containing the program is used, the virus harmlessly flashes a few verses across the screen; then the interrupted task resumes where it left off. **1989** *Accountancy* June 148/4 The .. Centre will also diagnose any disks sent in by users for any viruses.

# W

**wage**, *n*. Add: [**4.**] **wage economy**, a system of economic organization (or section of the economy) that is based on the payment of a regular, fixed wage in return for labour; contr. with *share economy* s.v. *SHARE *n.*³ 6.

**1971** *Cahiers d'Études Africaines* XI. 314 Out of 4 million people in Malawi only 130,000 are in the *wage economy. **1983** *N.Y. Times* 24 Apr. VII. 14/4 The rise of the national marketplace and of a wage economy strained the old informalities.

**white**, *a*. Add: [**11.**] [**e.**] **white smoker** *Oceanogr.*, a sea-bed vent (see *SMOKER *n.* 2 f) which ejects water rich in white particles.

**1980** *Earth & Planetary Sci. Lett.* XLVIII. 2/2 The '*white smokers' have plumes of hydrothermal fluids issuing from distinct chimneys at rates of tens of centimeters per second and temperatures of 100–350°C. **1982** *Proc. Biol. Soc. Washington* XCV. 781 During ALVIN Dive 1214 to the East Pacific Rise geothermal vent area at 21°N in the Pacific Ocean off western Mexico four specimens of a large eunicid polychaete were collected at the base of a white smoker.